PRESS GANG

Also by Roy Greenslade

Goodbye to the Working Class

Maxwell's Fall

ROY GREENSLADE

PRESS GANG

HOW NEWSPAPERS MAKE PROFITS FROM PROPAGANDA

MACMILLAN

First published 2003 by Macmillan
an imprint of Pan Macmillan Ltd
Pan Macmillan, 20 New Wharf Road, London N1 9RR
Basingstoke and Oxford
Associated companies throughout the world
www.panmacmillan.com

ISBN 0 333 78311 5

1 3 5 7 9 8 6 4 2

A CIP catalogue record for this book is available from the British Library.

Typeset by SX Composing DTP, Rayleigh, Essex
Printed and bound in Great Britain by
Mackays of Chatham plc, Chatham, Kent

For Theodore Gabriel Kelly

CONTENTS

Acknowledgements

Over the course of more than three years, many people helped in my researches for this book. I would like to thank the following, whose assistance, whether great or small, proved invaluable: Guy Black, Arthur Brown, Judith Burns, Ernie Burrington, Eddie Campbell, David Chipp, Hugh and Jodi Cudlipp, Nick Davies, Tony Delano, John Diamond, Elizabeth Dobson, Bob Edwards, Robin Esser, Harold Evans, Stephen Fay, Charles Garside, Geoffrey Goodman, Philip Graf, Felicity Green, Trevor Grove, Bill Hagerty, Bert Hardy, Georgina Henry, Alan Hobday, Anthony Holden, Ian Jack, Simon Jenkins, Bryn Jones, Ian Katz, Neil Kinnock, Louis Kirby, Richard Lambert, Val and Lynn Lewis, Nicholas Lloyd, Tim Minogue, Mike Molloy, Aldo Nicoletti, David Norris, Julian Petley, Edward Pickering, Laurie Pignon, Beryl Pinnington, Amanda Platell, Peter Preston, Alan Rusbridger, Christine Ruth, Anthony Sampson, Bernard Shrimsley, Tom Smith, Polly Toynbee, Percy Trumble, Steve Turner, David Walker. I owe a special debt of gratitude to Brian MacArthur, who has always been more of a friend than a rival, and remains the nicest guy ever to become a Fleet Street editor.

I must also thank the *Guardian*'s media editor, Janine Gibson, for her patience and tolerance during certain stressful periods of research and writing. Thanks also to the *Guardian*'s research department, led by the now-retired Helen Martin and Maryvonne Grellier; to the staff of the British Newspaper Library at Colindale, especially Christopher Skelton-Foord, Ed King and Jill Allbrooke; and to the staff at the London Library, particularly Christopher Phipps, and several fellow writers who inhabit the reading room and make working there a joy. Commuting from Brighton to London was made tolerable by the fun and friendship offered by the 6.08 'train gang'.

Thanks are due to my agent, Charles Walker, who had faith in the project from the start, and to my commissioning editor, Jeremy Trevathan, who showed great understanding after discovering that here was a journalist who didn't write to deadline, and to Peter James, who did such sterling work editing the manuscript.

Finally, I want to thank my family: Damon, Natascha and especially Noreen, my beautiful wife, who began to think the book would never end, but didn't allow that to assuage her enthusiastic support. Love conquers all.

Of course, none of these people is reponsible for any mistakes. If we accept that newspapers are the first rough draft of history, then this book should be seen as the first rough draft of newspaper history, and therefore mistakes are inevitable. It was the *Guardian* that was the first newspaper to introduce a readers' editor in order to correct errors, great and small. So, in keeping with the spirit of that superb initiative, I want to hear from anyone who believes there are factual inaccuracies, and in future editions I will do my best to put matters right.

Co. Donegal, Ireland, April 2003

Illustrations

PART ONE: 1945–1950

1. PRINTING FOR VICTORY

> Amidst the euphoria of victory in 1945, the nation offered not a triumph of the will but a suspicion of change and the paralysis of doubt'[1]

On 1 January 1945 the *Daily Express* front-page splash headline proclaimed, 'HITLER: NO PEACE IN 1945', while its main feature inside was entitled: 'What will peace be like?' The newspaper and its readers were not fooled by the braggadocio of Hitler's New Year message as his retreating troops fought in vain to ward off the Allied forces. More British blood would be spilled on the relentless drive through Germany, but every Briton now believed that victory was only a matter of time. After almost six years of war the people, the politicians and the press were looking tentatively towards the coming peace. News coverage over the next five months was, naturally enough, dominated by the Allied progress towards Berlin. Along the way there were odd lapses of taste. The *Daily Mirror*, which regularly referred to Germans as Huns, published a front-page picture of a dead German soldier, his arm raised in *rigor mortis* to the sky, under the headline 'Heil Hitler!'[2] Doubtless, readers liked the black humour.

The *Mirror* was certainly regarded as having been particularly effective during the war. 'It provided the daily talk and perhaps the daily thinking of millions who had never read a daily paper before.'[3] It was the forces' favourite at a time when the forces were everyone's favourite. Apart from the front-line news, the features and leading articles in most newspapers were already beginning to reflect a peacetime agenda. They clearly expressed people's deep-seated weariness with war. Their other central aspiration was altogether more vaguely conveyed: the desire for peace was tempered by a growing insistence that it must be a different kind of peace from the one which had existed in the 1930s. But different in what way? How was change to be achieved? And by whom? If the people knew, the papers didn't.

Newspapers themselves were not neutral spectators. They not only had an interest in how things might work out; they had a view about how they would prefer them to do so. Most, but not all, decided to pass on those views to their readers. Unlike the people, largely victims of war seeking a better future, many newspapers had found the war a godsend. Sales and profits rose while competition, if not entirely suspended, was muted. By government dictat, newsprint was rationed and all papers, from national dailies to local weeklies, were restricted to publishing a set number of pages, usually four an issue by late 1942. Similarly, the available advertising was spread evenly across the range of titles, a saviour to many of the weaker papers. Circulations were supposedly stabilised at approximate pre-war ratios, though owners managed to raise them substantially by agreeing to reduce paginations. Despite censorship, there was plenty of reader interest, with people often buying two or three titles a day.

The first release of the harshest restrictions came in September 1943, after the coalition government was persuaded that extra papers should be published to satisfy demand from members of the armed forces. The cabinet relented again in June 1944 to allow another small increase following D-Day, though the size of each issue was still pegged. So the papers in the early months of 1945 tended to look very strange indeed compared to the previous decade. The broadsheet *Daily Express*, which published twenty-four pages before the war, managed with just four, while the *Daily Mirror* and *Daily Sketch*, both tabloids, had eight. The recognised 'paper of record', the *Times*, was allowed ten.

In their different ways, they used every bit of available space, cramming in words, making it tough for the eye to follow, with minimal use of pictures. Even the *Daily Mirror*, pioneer of the picture-paper phenomenon, usually did without a photo on its front page. In an obvious attempt to modernise, there was a spate of changes to the mastheads, mostly restyled by the typographical maestro Stanley Morison. He was responsible for the more classical and readable Roman titles of the *Times*, *Daily Herald*, *Daily Mail*, *Financial Times*, *Reynolds News* and the *Daily Worker*.

Almost every paper had been produced without the help of many of their journalistic stars, who had joined the forces. Soon these servicemen who had fought side by side against a common enemy would be fighting each other. Some were aware of their destiny. None more so than the immensely self-confident Lieutenant-Colonel Hugh Cudlipp, commanding officer of the British Army Newspaper Unit, who had already edited a national paper and would eventually set popular paper records as *éminence grise* at the *Daily Mirror*. Colonel David Astor, son of a wealthy newspaper owner, winner of the Croix de Guerre for his bravery with the Royal Marines in France, knew he was about to edit the *Observer*. Lieutenant-Colonel Michael Berry, the shy second son of the press tycoon Viscount Camrose, twice mentioned in dispatches and awarded the MBE for his part in planning the invasion of Europe, expected his elder brother to inherit their father's *Daily Telegraph*, but he knew he would play some part in his family's sprawling press empire.

Others about to be demobbed had no idea of their fate. Major Alastair Hetherington, of the Royal Armoured Corps was yet to start a career that would see him edit the *Guardian* for nineteen years. Major William Deedes of the Queen's Westminsters, winner of the Military Cross, could not have envisaged his editorship of the *Daily Telegraph*. Nor could Major 'Tiny' Lear of the Royal Berkshire Regiment have foreseen becoming editor of the *News of the World*. John Junor, a pilot with the Fleet Air Arm, ended the war as editor of its magazine *Flight Deck*, but had no clue he would go on to edit the *Sunday Express* for a record-breaking thirty-two years.

As these men either returned to their papers or set out on 'civvy street' careers that would lead them to Fleet Street, the press gradually became embroiled in a series of incidents and controversies which have been repeated at regular intervals ever since. Almost every dispute involving the press in the following half-century was uncannily prefigured in the events of the 1945–50 period. Government attacked press; press attacked government. Heated claims of political bias and supposed proprietorial interference in editorial affairs were commonplace. Concerns about the increasing concentration of ownership and the growing commercialisation of the press were aired by both politicians and journalists. The debate about public service ethic versus the rights of private owners was centre stage. There were examples of intrusion into privacy, racism, rows over MPs taking money for leaking information to papers and the misuse of the libel laws. An editor needlessly committed a contempt of court. Though the phrase was not used, anxieties began to surface about 'dumbing down' in order to maximise sales.

Before exploring some of these issues, let's briefly consider the papers produced in these years. They emerged from the war flush with profits and, in most cases, with steeply rising circulations.[4] The dailies sold 10.4 million before the war. By May 1946, the figure was up to 13.4 million. Sunday sales went from about 16 million to approximately 25 million. These London-based papers were recognised as the world's highest sellers, mainly because Britain's geography and well-developed communications meant they could be distributed to every corner of the country overnight. That situation was enhanced as more papers, following the lead of the *Express*, also published simultaneously in Manchester and Glasgow.

In 1945 the *Daily Express* enjoyed a circulation of 3.3 million copies a day, rising week by week. It also had the advantage of having Fleet Street's most experienced proprietor in Lord Beaverbrook and editor in Arthur Christiansen. A million behind, but coming up fast, was the *Daily Mirror* under Harry Guy Bartholomew. The *Daily Herald* sold more than 2 million, with the *Daily Mail* not far behind and rising. The *News Chronicle* was selling 1.5 million, and the *Daily Sketch* probably sold almost 900,000.[5] The communist *Daily Worker*, banned for a period during the war, claimed more than 100,000 buyers. There were just two national broadsheets, the *Times* and the *Daily Telegraph*, which together sold just over 1 million in 1945.[6] The *Manchester Guardian*, not yet regarded as a national paper but enjoying an international reputation, sold about 100,000, while the *Financial Times* managed fewer than 50,000.

On Sundays, the *News of the World* had a huge sale, almost 7.5 million, followed by the *Sunday People* with 4.6 million, the *Sunday Pictorial* with

3.4 million, and the *Sunday Express* with 2.3 million. The *Sunday Dispatch* recorded a sale of about 1.6 million, while the *Sunday Chronicle* managed 1.1 million, *Reynolds News* held on to 700,000, and the Manchester-based *Empire News* probably sold some 2 million.[7] It was the *Sunday Dispatch* which recorded the era's most sensational sales rise. In what he was later to describe as 'a complete fluke', editor Charles Eade started to publish extracts from the Kathleen Winsor novel *Forever Amber*, expecting to do fairly well from his planned seven-week serialisation. After the first week, when demand exceeded supply, he shrewdly decided to extend the serial to forty weeks. 'I had no idea it would be such a hit', he said with a modesty rare among editors.[8]

London also had three competing evenings. The *Evening News* was selling 1.5 million, followed by the *Star* with about 1 million, and the *Evening Standard* with 650,000. It was said that the *Standard* sold in the West End, the *Star* in the East End, and the *News* managed both ends and the middle. Most other cities had competing morning and evening titles. The British loved their newspapers. City-centre streets reverberated to the incomprehensible shouts of paper-sellers, usually old men in shabby macs. Factory workers boarding their morning buses inevitably had a paper tucked under their arms. Office staff on trains had their heads buried in papers. According to a Unesco report, 570 daily papers were being sold for every thousand of the UK population, a far higher penetration than in the United States (357 per thousand).[9]

Some titles boasted key components that would endure for decades to come. In the *Express* was the William Hickey column, Rupert the bear, cartoons by Giles and Osbert Lancaster and Beachcomber's whimsical By the Way column. In the *Mirror*, the Old Codgers conducted Live Letters next to cartoon strips such as Jane and Garth, the Useless Eustace pocket cartoon, Patience Strong's homespun homilies, and features by Noel Whitcomb, a snobbish man who came to hate the hand that fed him.[10]

In the *Daily Telegraph* was Peterborough's column, an island of gossipy froth amid a sea of news. In the *Times*, letters from the great and the good ran next to leading articles which demanded attention from their elite readership. But there was little that lasted in the lacklustre *Daily Mail* of that year, nor in the *Daily Herald* and *Daily Sketch*.

Statistics aside, the men who owned and edited these papers were an extraordinary bunch. By far the most important proprietor of the period was Lord Beaverbrook, followed by Lords Rothermere and Kemsley. In 1948, the three owned 43 per cent of the total general newspaper market.[11] Of the popular paper editors, the irascible Bartholomew and the legendary Christiansen stand out from the crowd, though there must be a special mention for the flamboyant Frank Owen, short-lived editor of the *Daily Mail* and long-lived drinker, womaniser and raconteur. Among the serious papers, the workaholic *Times* editor Robin Barrington-Ward was a thorn in the

Tories' side, while the *Daily Telegraph*'s Arthur Watson was their faithful supporter. At the *Manchester Guardian*, A. P. Wadsworth was enhancing his paper's reputation as a liberal and well-informed voice. And here I must note the first history lesson: editors can be brilliant under any proprietor but they cannot achieve greatness unless they have either a brilliant owner or, better still, no owner at all.

Beaverbrook: failed politician and victorious journalist

Beaverbrook bestrides the early part of this history, even though he was sixty-six in 1945 and his form of press barony was, by then, an anachronism. In some ways he was aware of the world having changed. Never an orthodox Tory, he had 'no sympathy with the prevailing policies' of either party.[12] Nothing had come of his bizarre political hopes during the inter-war years and they were obliterated in a 'post-war world order [which] might have been designed to frustrate and annoy Beaverbrook'.[13] He could not face up to the dominance of the United States and continued to place his faith in Britain's empire, which gradually elided into Commonwealth 'despite Kiplingesque lamentations in the Beaverbrook press'.[14]

Nor did Beaverbrook betray any understanding of the economic developments, and the consequent changes in society and politics, which were to render his form of ownership obsolete. Around him still were Fleet Street's nobility, so it seemed that things were no different from the 1930s. The idiosyncratic, iconoclastic Beaverbrook, inheritor of the Northcliffe mantle, carried on after the war as he had before, running his papers as organs of personal propaganda, poking his nose into the businesses of his rivals, making political mischief, courting publicity and revelling in his notoriety.

The importance of Beaverbrook was the way in which he came to personify a form of newspaper ownership, however outdated, which had profound effects on the public perception of the press. It also affected the views of journalists and politicians. The insistent calls from 1945 for restrictions on the power of proprietors and a brake on the growth of media monopolies were largely traceable to hostility to Beaverbrook. He was the lightning rod for every complaint about press misbehaviour. Yet his empire was far from the biggest and, in later years, would deteriorate due to its relative smallness. No matter. Beaverbrook was seen as Britain's own Citizen Kane, a role he appeared to enjoy.

It wasn't simply that his *Daily Express* was the highest-selling morning paper and his London *Evening Standard* the best of its kind. For fifty years he virtually ruled the fortunes of Fleet Street, holding sway over other owners, mixing and meddling in their activities. Similarly, in his ubiquitous roles as political fixer, adviser to prime ministers and confidant of the business and political elite, he exercised enormous influence behind the scenes. Or, to be more precise, he seemed to do so. With Beaverbrook it was difficult to tell the difference between appearance and reality. Even his private messages may not be what they seem. He once wrote to his trusted manager, E. J. Robertson: 'I don't care whether you make money or not. All I want to see Mr Robertson is a great newspaper, strong in reserves and so completely and absolutely set up in finance that no other newspaper can ever challenge us. Even after you and I have laid down our task Mr Robertson.'[15] This quote should be coupled with his famous statement to the Royal Commission about owning his papers purely to make propaganda. Beaverbrook understood the essential link between profits and propaganda. The pair marched hand in hand.

But Beaverbrook rarely meant what he said. He flattered his enemies. He wrapped praise inside criticism. He ruthlessly exploited people he called his friends. He indulged in random acts of kindness to people he hardly knew. He professed to loathe the socialism yet surrounded himself with left-wingers, such as Tom Driberg, Michael Foot and the cartoonist David Low. No wonder Beaverbrook's many biographers have found his maverick behaviour hard to analyse.

Everyone who worked for or met Beaverbrook, known variously as the 'Principal Reader' and the 'Lord' (but rarely the 'Beaver'), had a view about him. There is perhaps no better short description of him than a single sentence by Bob Edwards, twice editor of the *Daily Express*: 'He was kind, brutal, considerate, selfish, honest, eccentric and a bit mad, but utterly sane in his judgement of newspapers.'[16] A 1949 *Observer* piece to mark his seventieth birthday described him as 'a golliwog itching with vitality' and his *Express* leaders as 'political baby talk'.[17] The historian A. J. P. Taylor thought him the reincarnation of Richard Cobden.[18] The politician Michael Foot regarded him as 'bewitching' with a radicalism that was 'deep and abiding'.[19] Columnist Ian Mackay referred to him as 'that mercurial moonbeam-chaser'.[20] The BBC's rigorous overlord Lord Reith considered him 'evil, disgusting and loathsome', confiding to his diary, 'To no-one is the vulgar designation shit more appropriately applied.'[21] Both Attlee and his left-wing critic Aneurin Bevan described him as 'evil',[22] while Violet Bonham Carter thought him 'the quintessence of evil'.[23]

There is little doubt that Beaverbrook was racist (though not anti-Semitic). Robert Edwards points to several occasions on which the man of empire cheerfully revealed his prejudice against black 'savages'.[24] Whatever people thought of him, there was an overwhelming consensus that he ran some of the most readable newspapers ever published. His shrewd understanding of people's interests, combined with his love of mischief, ensured that his flagship *Daily Express* sparkled with controversy. Francis Williams believed that the *Express*'s impact on journalism was 'entirely due to his personality'.[25] Some might have argued that his greatest decision was to have appointed Arthur Christiansen, a journalist's journalist, as editor.

Christiansen, always known as Chris, was the stereotypical editor of the period: hard-drinking, hard working, chain-smoking, jacket off, rumpled white shirt, sleeves rolled up, loosened tie, pacing the office, urging his reporters and subs to do his bidding by a mixture of flattery and jovial insults. He could be cruel, but he was popular with his staff and renowned for getting the best from them.[26] His most famous exhortation, that every story must appeal to 'the little man in the back streets of Derby'[27] – his deliberately less metropolitan version of the man on the Clapham omnibus – became the criterion by which most popular editors thereafter were to judge content.[28]

Chris's noticeboard bulletins have been properly described as 'a text book of modern journalism'.[29] They hammered home the pragmatic, and often cynical, realities of popular papers: 'Always, always, tell the news through people' . . . 'One good home story is worth two good foreign stories' . . . 'One good picture is worth 10,000 words' . . . 'You can describe things with the pen of Shakespeare himself, but you cannot beat news in a newspaper.' It is possible to detect from the phraseology that Chris did not write them all. Beaverbrook surely was the author of others, such as: 'Let's make war on adjectives' and 'Good stories flow like honey. Bad stories stick in the craw.' In this, as in so much of his editorship, Chris was merely the front man for his proprietor. Recognised as a great technician, he got involved in every aspect of production by designing pages, writing headlines and even subbing copy whenever he fancied. He worked on instinct and, in pre-TV days, his understanding of how to respond to breaking news was excellent. A big news story had, after all, set him on the path to the top.

The son of a shipwright, Chris was born in Wallasey, Cheshire, and went to the local grammar school. At fourteen, he produced a school magazine virtually alone, reporting events, writing short stories, drawing illustrations and then stitching the pages together on his mother's sewing machine. He joined his local weekly at sixteen, moved to a Liverpool daily, the *Courier*, three years later and was soon running its London office. Like so many ambitious (and underpaid) journalists, he took on an extra Saturday-night job as a *Sunday Express* casual. He soon demonstrated his skills and, aged twenty-two, he became the paper's full-time news editor. He showed amazing dedication by going to night classes for printing apprentices, even winning a diploma, and was thereafter considered to be an expert in typography. Two years later he was promoted to assistant editor and, in October 1930, in charge of the paper late one Saturday night, he had that bit of good fortune young newspaper executives pray for. The airship R101 crashed in flames in France. Chris stopped the presses to publish a special late-morning edition which scooped sleepier Fleet Street rivals, winning the admiration of other journalists and, of course, of Beaverbrook.

The dynamic Chris was then sent to Manchester as the *Daily Express*'s northern editor, where he set about proving his worth by undermining the efforts of the London editor, the sophisticated Beverley Baxter. Chris thought

Baxter's paper 'too soft and too southern for the down-to-earth, hard-done-by northerners'. He finally found a way to prove his point. When the Lancashire cotton-mill workers struck in the face of wage cuts, Chris decided to 'cut out the South of England "flam" . . . and ranged the paper on the side of the strikers'. Beaverbrook, a political maverick, was impressed, especially when he realised that Chris's support for the strikers was not informed by a left-wing agenda.

Chris was just twenty-nine when Beaverbrook made him *Daily Express* editor in 1933, the beginning of one of the greatest of all newspaper partnerships. It worked because Christiansen, who had not the slightest interest in politics, was happy to let Beaverbrook do as he wished in that sphere. As he was later to say: 'I was a journalist, not a political animal; my proprietor was a journalist *and* a political animal. The policies were Lord Beaverbrook's job, the presentation mine.'[30] This candid self-analysis was, according to every witness I have asked, entirely true. But it wasn't anything like as harmonious as its sounds, with each man sticking to his domain. Beaverbrook intervened in every area of the paper, including staffing, features content, deciding which writer should take which assignment, even deconstructing the way stories were worded. He was a hard and relentless taskmaster. His phone calls and streams of critical memos were laced with sarcasm. *FT* editor Gordon Newton reported that 'more than once' he saw Chris 'almost in tears after he had listened to a tape sent by Beaverbrook.'[31]

This 'torture' had the effect of destabilising the paranoiac Christiansen, making him, according to John Junor, 'madly jealous of Beaverbrook's favours.'[32] There is also a lot of anecdotal evidence to show that, in Ian Aitken's phrase, 'Christiansen was a toady.'[33] As Chris once confessed to Junor: 'All I ever want to do is make Lord Beaverbrook happy.'[34] This may appear weak kneed, though it should be seen as a pragmatic acceptance of reality. Christiansen, like all the editors whose jobs depended on the whim of Fleet Street's Lord Coppers, would not have survived without bending the knee to his owner. He recognised, to use one of the industry's clichés, that Beaverbrook owned the train set.

Here, then, comes the second lesson: as privately owned commercial enterprises and, having developed from personal political platforms, most newspapers were not democratic institutions. There was no public service ethic embedded within them, demanding impartiality or neutrality. Owners might pay lipservice to such an ethic in order to assert their own independence from the state or other vested interests. They might even claim that they had a public purpose as part of their sales policy, a pretence to attract readers. For their part, editors might shout loudly about having complete independence from their owners: they, and they alone, made decisions about what went into their papers. But it was all a masquerade. Ownership conferred rights on proprietors which allowed them to do as they wished. There was no separation of powers, formal or informal, between owner and editor. The only brakes on a proprietor's sometimes crazy or impractical demands were subterfuge by his editor, or trades union activity.

Despite the pressures from above there can be little doubt that Chris achieved a great deal with the *Daily Express*. He transformed its look, replacing the former vertical columns by pioneering a new form of jigsaw layout. He introduced a more exciting and versatile Century typeface, using bolder headlines and bigger pictures. He recruited forceful, energetic staff and kept morale high. He preferred to lunch with his senior staff rather than with politicians. Almost every day the doors at El Vino's on Fleet Street would swing open at 1.15 p.m. as the stocky figure of Chris, in his trademark camelhair coat, arrived with his retinue. They would spend more than half an hour drinking 'large ones' before going off elsewhere to eat. Chris's daily soaking up of alcohol and his ferocious addiction to smoking were, in some senses, a reaction to Beaverbrook's pressures. In spite of it all, he maintained a love for his work and a massive sense of optimism which shone through his paper.

The men who made the *Mirror*

Christiansen's main rival, Harry Guy Bartholomew, had the advantage of being his own boss: he was editor-in-chief of the *Daily Mirror* and the *Sunday Pictorial*, and chairman of the companies that owned them. Shares were held by scores of unknown investors, so Bart had no proprietor and therefore thought he could do as he pleased. The 'vulgar, semi-illiterate, cantankerous'[35] Bart treated *Mirror* editor Cecil Thomas as his factotum, though he didn't have everything quite his own way because the *Pictorial*'s ambitious vice-chairman, Cecil King, was always seeking the main chance.

Bart had played a key role in saving the *Mirror* from its pre-war decline and turning it into the favourite paper of Britain's armed forces. A man of 'zest, originality and audacity,' he pioneered the concept of British tabloid journalism.[36] It 'was in some ways more a daily poster than a newspaper', depending 'for its effectiveness on sledge-hammer headlines of a size, blackness and stridency never seen in any British daily newspaper before.'[37] But Bart, despite the 'odd flash of genial charm',[38] grew more and more difficult in the post-war years, gradually losing all sense of proportion as he drowned himself in drink earlier and earlier each day. Like Chris, Bart looked and acted the part of a newspaperman. Unlike Chris, he had had little education and was almost illiterate.[39] Williams thought him 'rough, tough, erratic and ruthless . . . egocentric to a degree notable even in a profession where egomania is an occupational disease'.[40] What Bart did have was a superb grasp of the visual and an uncanny understanding of his readers' wishes: 'his instinct rarely failed him'.[41] He did have blind spots, neglecting sport and surprisingly, given his photographic background, downplaying the use of pictures. But his *Mirror* had 'an almost unerring instinct for the things that move the emotions of millions of ordinary men and women'.[42]

Short, stocky, white-haired, with a smooth, handsome face, he was a fearsome man to almost everyone he met, reserving his greatest insults for any figure he identified as being a member of the establishment. This didn't help his relationship with 'aloof, reserved, quiet-spoken'[43] King, the public-school-educated offspring of the Harmsworth family. They grudgingly respected each other's complementary skills, though King gradually came to realise that Bart was anything but indispensable. 'He was a dreadful man to work with or for,' King later wrote. 'He enjoyed spying on people' and set them at each other's throats.[44] He was also vicious to anyone who appeared likely to challenge his position, and the most notable victim of his paranoia was the greatest of his journalistic disciples, Hugh Cudlipp. Along with Basil Nicholson, it is generally accepted that Bartholomew and Cudlipp formed the triumvirate who transformed the *Mirror* in the late 1930s. Cudlipp, hired at twenty-one as features editor, arrived from the *Sunday Chronicle*, according to King, with 'a galaxy of journalistic gifts . . . a brilliant reporter and sub-editor' with 'a wonderful technique for lay-out'.[45]

When Cudlipp emulated the *Mirror*'s success as the twenty-four-year-old editor of the *Sunday Pictorial*, without any help from Bart, the master set out to destroy his pupil. He also resented King's growing affection for Cudlipp, who regularly referred to him as the world's most outstanding popular paper editor, even managing to laugh off Cudlipp's path-breaking use of a bare-breasted model to illustrate the arrival of spring in 1938.[46] Bart couldn't stand the fact that sales of Cudlipp's *Pictorial* outstripped his *Mirror* by 200,000 and more. He was also irked that the *Pictorial* was proved right in adopting a more robust anti-fascist, anti-appeasement line than the *Mirror*. The arrival of the real war interrupted their hostilities, only for them to resume with greater bitterness from 1945.

After Cudlipp returned from editing the army's paper, the *Union Jack*, to the chair at the *Pictorial*, its sales accelerated once again. Bart finally took his chance to rid himself of Cudlipp in 1948, with the extra advantage of embarrassing King. In Lagos to deal with problems at one of Mirror group's West African stable of papers, King found himself witnessing a riot in which several people were killed. He cabled an exclusive story to the *Sunday Pictorial* late on Saturday night, which Cudlipp not only spiked but failed to pass on to the *Mirror*. The riot was the lead story in papers for the next three days, and the Mirror titles had lost their scoop. Bart fired Cudlipp.[47] He was soon hired by Beaverbrook for the *Sunday Express*, to become editor John Gordon's personal assistant. Bart had, so he thought, won.

It wasn't his only change. He decided to appoint a new *Mirror* editor in place of Cecil Thomas, 'cherubic, courteous and unobtrusive . . . the last man a Hollywood producer would cast in the role of the ruthless tabloid editor.'[48] He chose Sylvester Bolam, bespectacled, moustachioed, grey suited, with the general appearance of a benign bank manager. Bart considered Bolam the most loyal of his troops, if not the most dynamic. He did prove more capable than Thomas in identifying his readers' interests and, given Bart's drinking habits, was left a little more to himself. But he was soon to make a colossal error of judgement. As Francis Williams pointed out, 'the men Bartholomew gathered around him . . . embraced every stunt however contemptible in terms of normal human dignity the public could be got to swallow and set no limits on what was permissible in print.'[49] They also 'invaded privacy shamelessly', which may help to explain why *Mirror* photographer Tommy Lea, under pressure from his picture editor, went to such extraordinary lengths to obtain a mundane wedding picture.

The photographer and the aristocrat

It is surely fitting that, so early in this history, there should occur an example of press intrusion and harassment of the kind that was to be repeated endlessly in the following fifty years. The Tommy Lea libel action was notable for many reasons. It revealed the intense distaste among the middle classes, including the judiciary, for popular newspaper journalism. It illustrated the chasm between social classes at the time: a fading aristocracy was determined to maintain its privacy despite the fascination of the 'idly curious' working class. It showed the folly of journalists suing for libel. Once in the witness box, they face questioning much more intrusive than their original actions and far more likely to bring them into disrepute. It also exemplified the hypocrisy of journalists willing to use a law inimicable to freedom of expression.

Tommy Lea had had a tough war. Initially rejected for military service he joined the RAF, becoming an air gunner-photographer, flying forty-one bomber squadron missions in the Mediterranean. Later, while he was aboard the *Atlantic Castle* in March 1945, the ship was torpedoed and he had to take to a lifeboat. After being invalided out of the service the following October, he was delighted to resume his former job as a *Daily Mirror* photographer. On 18 December that year, he was dispatched to take pictures of a high-society wedding between Miss Mollie Wyndham-Quin and Captain Robert Cecil, heir to the Marquess of Salisbury and son of the opposition leader in the Lords, Viscount Cranborne. As assignments go it wasn't likely to yield a picture demanding a big show, but Tommy was determined to do his best.

Not content with taking shots of the couple outside Westminster Abbey, he decided to attend the reception at Arlington House, which was owned by the Salisburys. On the way he bought himself a red carnation as a buttonhole and, when challenged, announced that he was from 'the paper of the times'. This attempt to pretend that he represented the *Times* rather than the *Mirror* proved futile. Captain Cecil refused Tommy's request to be pictured.

So Tommy, in newspaper jargon, snatched one off. Seconds after being caught in the glare of the flashlight, an infuriated Cecil sprang at Tommy, punched him, stamped on his camera and smashed it.

Cecil, a Grenadier Guardsman and also a victim of war, having suffered paralysis to his right arm, was charged with assault and malicious damage. He was fined £10, ordered to pay £50 costs and an extra £135 towards replacing the camera. Cecil, of good physique, had been 'cowardly' and 'ungentlemanly' to strike 'a little bit of a man', said the magistrate. Justice, thought Tommy and the *Mirror*, had been done. But a writer on an obscure magazine with a tiny circulation, the *Justice of the Peace and Local Government Review*, did not agree. Its issue of 26 January 1946 carried an unsigned article which argued that Cecil was right 'to defend his bride from the insult of having her picture in the gutter Press'. While it may have been wrong 'to strike a social inferior' it was understandable that a 'young man of spirit' had acted as he did (Cecil was thirty years old at the time). The socially inferior Lea was cast as lacking 'elementary breeding' and his paper was castigated too: 'The intrusion (of the baser type of paper in particular) into private life is an unmixed evil.'[50] It was Lea, concluded the article, who deserved the epithets 'cowardly' and 'ungentlemanly', as did his employers.

Unwisely, Lea and the *Mirror* management decided to sue the journal's publishers and printers for libel. The trial, in March 1947, was extraordinary. No one from the magazine appeared to justify the article, leaving it entirely to the Cecils and their retainers to argue their case. Lea proved a poor witness with defending counsel and judge – acting almost like a double act – undermining his original police-court evidence and belittling him. It was obvious that the judge, Mr Justice Hilbery, believed the *Mirror* had no business reporting the Cecil wedding, and he showed his sympathies by asking Lea's counsel with mock incredulity: 'We have no law which protects us from having cameras pushed into our faces and photographs taken when we go somewhere on a public duty?'[51] At one point counsel for the magazine suggested that acceptable behaviour could be gauged by the proverbial man on the Clapham omnibus. Hilbery, in a revealing moment, replied: 'God forbid that the standard of manners should be taken from the man on the Clapham omnibus.'[52]

In his judgement, Hilbery said that Lea was determined to take the picture, with or without permission, because he 'holds the view apparently that he has some high mission as a press photographer to portray to the vulgar, the idly curious and, on some occasion, the morbidly minded people, the private lives of other people ... He does not recognise such a thing as privacy or that people's private lives can be sacred even from the illustrated press.'[53] Lea deserved the criticism in the article, which was not malicious. The judge found for the defendants, with costs.

H. Montgomery Hyde, in a preface to a book giving a verbatim account of the hearings, thought the case 'raised interesting and important points' about the relationship between press and public. There had long been complaints about 'the lengths to which some journalists are prepared to go in the field of news-getting ... victims of accidents and other misfortunes have been rung up in the middle of the night by reporters, pestered for interviews and photographs, their gardens and grounds trespassed upon and every conceivable form of pressure exerted upon them as well as their relatives and servants in order to obtain information on whose "news value" is considered high'.[54]

In a passage which set out the argument which was to flare up time and time again down the years, Hyde contended that the material wasn't of genuine public interest. This was just a front for purveying 'personal gossip and scandal' which was 'designed to satisfy the curious and sometimes morbid appetites of a class of reader which can have no personal connection whatsoever with the incident portrayed'.[55] In other words, it was no business of the common herd to know about their betters. Newspapers were appealing to the prurience of the public. Hyde offered a possible solution to the problem: self-regulatory machinery, a press tribunal, to deal with complaints of intrusion. Failure to do so would, he predicted, lead to legislation which might 'curtail the liberty of the press'.[56]

That thought also occurred to the members of the Royal Commission the following year, but before we come to that it is interesting to note that Tommy Lea went on taking pictures for the *Mirror* into the 1960s, unperturbed by the Cecil affair. In 1950, Cecil was elected Tory MP for Bournemouth West, later becoming the sixth Marquess of Salisbury. He and Lea had fought a war on the same side, but they were as divided from each other as they had been before the war. The battle of the classes had resumed alongside the struggle between people seeking privacy and the popular newspapers seeking to pierce the veil of privilege.

The editor hired and fired by the Viscount's wife

There was no sympathy from other proprietors over the *Daily Mirror*'s libel defeat. They disapproved of any intrusions into the lives of the people with whom they, and especially their wives, mixed. Their papers were altogether different from the *Mirror*, which caused particular embarrassment to the establishment figure of Esmond Harmsworth, the second Viscount Rothermere, who presided over the *Daily Mail*, *Sunday Dispatch* and *London Evening News*, as well as a string of provincial titles. He was shocked to discover, courtesy of one of his persistent critics, Randolph Churchill, that he owned the largest proportion of shares in Mirror group. Disgusted with the *Mirror*'s politics and incensed that one of its guiding hands, Cecil King, was his 'renegade' cousin, he decided to rid himself of his holding. In a secret deal with Bart, which King bitterly opposed when it was too late to halt, Esmond swapped his Mirror shares for the Mail group shares owned by the Mirror. By ending the reciprocal shareholding links, Esmond was able to take total control of his company, Associated Newspapers.

Here was an owner who enjoyed a lifestyle utterly different from that of his papers' readers, different indeed from all but a tiny minority of the population. His father had left vast debts at his death in 1940, yet it appeared not to have affected Esmond's ability to live like a nineteenth-century aristocrat. At his London residence, Warwick House, he and his guests were waited on by a retinue of liveried servants. Dinner was a white-tie event. Women arrived in fur coats and dazzled in sequined evening dresses. It was evidently not quite grand enough to impress his second wife, the vivacious and malicious Ann O'Neill, who nicknamed the house 'Warwick Hut'.[57] She was to have as much, if not more, influence over the *Daily Mail* in the seven years of their marriage as her husband.

In reading the many Harmsworth biographies, it is difficult to conclude that Esmond was anything other than a weak-minded ditherer, the sort of man impressed by the last person he had met. In politics and the newspaper business, he was manipulated by Beaverbrook. In his personal life, he was flagrantly cuckolded by the capricious Ann who, when she married him, was already in love with another man, the dashing and urbane Ian Fleming. The *Sunday Times*'s flamboyant foreign manager, and later the creator of James Bond, became known as 'Lady Rothermere's fan'.

King once remarked that Esmond 'finds it difficult to keep interested in any subject for long, so the papers he manages tend to pursue a rather erratic course'.[58] Despite the family feud between King and most of the other Harmsworths, that assessment seems quite fair. Under his hand, the Mail papers performed very poorly. He allowed Ann too great a hold on the *Mail*'s reins. Her first success was in unseating the editor, Stanley Horniblow, a shrewd Australian who had run the *Mail* in the final year of the war with some panache. According to one smitten staff member, Horniblow dressed well, looked good and was 'as handsome as a matinee idol with golden fair hair and the complexion of a girl'.[59] Another said he 'talked with the most extraordinary upper-class accent . . . terribly plummy'.[60] Popular with staff, he was regarded as an able enough editor by most, though one reporter thought him timid.[61] Ann cared little whether he was good or bad because she favoured Frank Owen, a fiery and dashing Welshman.

Owen was a charismatic figure: tall, good looking, flashy, talkative, an heroic drinker and, according to one of his closest friends, Michael Foot, 'spectacularly heterosexual'.[62] He had been the youngest MP in the Commons in 1929, winning Hereford for the Liberals. When he lost the seat he was hired by Beaverbrook as a *Daily Express* leader writer, often ghosting articles for him. He also formed a close friendship with Christiansen. Despite his 'vehement liberal views',[63] Beaverbrook admired Owen's staccato writing style and made him editor of the London *Evening Standard* in 1938. Owen, then thirty-four, immediately forged an anti-Nazi policy in direct opposition to his owner's appeasement position, but with his tacit consent.[64] Michael Foot became his leader writer, assistant editor and bosom companion.[65] His editorship was interrupted when he was called up, using his skills to good effect to edit an army paper in the Far East.[66]

Owen joined the *Daily Mail* as a columnist in July 1946, a surprising departure for a paper that rarely published a word which knowingly deviated from the owner's viewpoint. The front-page blurb announcing Owen's arrival made a virtue of it: 'His views may not always be those of this newspaper . . .' Even if his appointment didn't reveal Ann's influence, his rapid advancement within the paper certainly did. Some six months after starting, he was asked to stand in for the editor while Horniblow was sent on a visit to the United States, a classic ploy. Owen took his chance and when Horniblow returned in March 1947 he realised 'his authority had been undermined, and he resigned'.[67]

Owen proved to be one of the paper's most popular – if short-lived – editors. His arrival 'brought a great gust of fresh air into the office', said his managing editor Edward Pickering.[68] He inspired George Murray to write leaders, always run on page one, that were 'the political banners of the late Forties'. Owen was considered 'one of the boys . . . perpetually on the editorial floor . . . [and] drank with everyone else in the office pubs like Auntie's and the Mucky Duck'.[69] Tom Pocock, a features writer, described him as 'very macho and tough'.[70]

Early in his editorship Owen, who had struck up a wartime friendship with Lord Mountbatten, published an exclusive story – from Greek sources – that Princess Elizabeth was about to be engaged to Lieutenant Philip Mountbatten.[71] Furious 'official' denials from the Palace press office were gleefully published in the early editions of the next day's three London evenings. Yet, by their last editions, they were reporting the official announcement of the engagement. The *Mail* and Owen were vindicated and the Palace press office was humbled. It was not to be the last case of its kind.[72]

An example of Owen's editing style comes in a Pocock reminiscence. One lunchtime they went first to El Vino's, then to a couple of other bars, before arriving at 'a very grand restaurant, Les Ambassadeurs'. They 'finally ended up with some glamorous women in low-cut dresses in the Milroy nightclub . . . His link with the office was a white telephone among the bottles and every now and then a dispatch rider would come clumping into the club with page proofs. Then the wine waiter would shine his torch so that Owen could read them.'[73] Owen often disappeared from the office for hours, sometimes returning dishevelled and offering limp excuses. He was married to a former Cochran showgirl, whose tours around the building 'always created a sensation'.[74] Just as sensational were Owen's rows with managing director Stewart MacLean, who, he claimed, interfered in editorial hiring and firing.

But his central problem, apart from his sometimes reckless drinking sprees, was Ann Rothermere, who gradually turned against him. Owen complained to Esmond about the way she called his staff to demand that items should go in or be held out. She also introduced a gossip column which she thought contributed more to rising sales than Owen's editorship. The relationship between the Rothermeres at the time was breaking down too. In 1948, Ann gave birth prematurely to a baby which died within twenty-four hours, and which she later admitted had been Fleming's. A distraught Esmond asked her not to see Fleming again, a request she flagrantly disobeyed.

When Owen lost Ann's support, his position was hopeless. His behaviour antagonised MacLean. His politics upset Esmond. He didn't enjoy the 1950 election campaign, trying to accommodate his proprietor's wishes while holding very different opinions. He was fired in May that year after, said Pickering, 'too brief a reign'. He had been 'a brilliant shooting star and, for me, the afterglow still remains'.[75] Perhaps, though, editorship was not his forte. The *Times* observed: 'His talents were more suited to the occasional provocative article than to the daily routine of the editorial chair.'[76] Reginald Cudlipp, *News of the World* editor at the time, agreed: 'Frank never made the grade as we all expected. He continued to write forceful pieces but I don't think he was cut out to be an editor.'[77]

Owen returned to his old mentor, Beaverbrook, firstly as a columnist and roving reporter, and then to write the official biography of Lloyd George. He later sank into obscurity, drinking too much and dying in 1979, aged seventy-four, in Worthing.

Baronial Berrys: creators of two prestige papers

Rothermere's uncertain hold on his papers was echoed to an extent by Lord Kemsley, an owner who immodestly etched his name into every newspaper he owned and every office building his companies inhabited. Kemsley never found a way to make his national daily paper competitive in spite of changing its name (*Sketch* to *Graphic*, and back to *Sketch* again), typefaces, editorial approach and editors: the rather skilful Roland Thornton was replaced in 1947 by Henry Clapp. Kemsley also presided over four big-selling Sunday titles that went to the wall: the *Empire News*, *Sunday Graphic*, *Sunday Chronicle* and *Sunday Dispatch*. But there is no doubt that, by concentrating his attention on the *Sunday Times*, he put that paper on the road to greatness.[78] He ran a vast chain of provincial morning and evening titles that were, under later owners, to prove highly profitable. Every one of his papers carried the slogan 'A Kemsley Newspaper' under the masthead, prompting Herbert Morrison, the deputy prime minister, to call his empire the 'gramophone press'.[79]

Kemsley, born Gomer Berry, was referred to as Lord K or K. He looked like 'an Edwardian grandee mixed with a suspicion of Groucho Marx', wearing a 'carnation . . . pearl tie-pin . . . and homburg hat, of a peculiarly out-of-date style'.[80] One of his closest advisers thought him a dim social climber, but with 'a genius for circulation and advertising'.[81] Many journalists considered K 'too grand by half and on the wrong side of the division between a puritan and a prude'.[82] Denis Hamilton came to regard him as 'benevolently autocratic': although he 'reserved to himself final authority in all matters of policy', this meant 'in practice allowing substantial liberty'.[83]

Like Rothermere, Beaverbrook and his brother Camrose, Kemsley lived in grand style, with a great London house and a thirty-six-bedroomed mansion in Buckinghamshire set in 200 acres. Each weekday, he arrived at his Gray's Inn Road offices, Kemsley House, in a chauffeur-driven Rolls-Royce with black glass windows, to be ushered by a commissionaire to his private lift. At weekends, since the library in his country house was equipped with a teleprinter, the agency tapes would be carried to him on a silver salver by a manservant.

Kemsley's editorial involvement at the *Sunday Times* was moderated by his respect for the editor, the remarkable William Waite Hadley. They had first met when Hadley was editor of the *Merthyr Times* before he went to make a name for himself in London as a parliamentary correspondent for a Liberal paper. In 1930, at the age sixty-four Hadley became assistant editor of the *Sunday Times* and, a year later, editor. 'A tiny man . . . with his high, old-fashioned trilby hat, his spectacles, his little grey clipped moustache, his umbrella, his slightly tottering walk, he might have passed as some official in local government'.[84]

With Hadley in the chair, Lord K 'exacted maximum meaning from the term editor-in-chief'.[85] He formed the policy for Hadley to translate into editorial coherence. Hadley's own politics, influenced by the decline of the Liberal party and his own dislike of socialism, eased his path to the right, and therefore closer to Kemsley's.[86] Despite having 'a curiously incurious mind',[87] Hadley proved to be a great spotter of writing talent. He nurtured valued contributors such as James Agate, Desmond MacCarthy and Robert Ensor. But he was as hopelessly out of touch with the post-war world as Kemsley. In May 1949, Hadley, incited by K, denounced Norman Mailer's novel *The Naked and the Dead* on the front page, calling it 'an obscene book' which was 'too objectionable for review in the *Sunday Times*'. This resulted in 300 letters of complaint from readers, several articles guffawing at the *Sunday Times* in rival papers, and a deluge of orders for the book.

The following year, after prompting from Kemsley's most astute signing, Denis Hamilton, Hadley finally retired, aged eighty-four. Perhaps K's greatest achievement was in appointing Hamilton – 'one of the nicest and shrewdest men in postwar Fleet Street'[88] – as his personal assistant in 1946. A reporter on the *Middlesbrough Evening Gazette* until being called up, Hamilton had a distinguished war record, winning a DSO and becoming an acting brigadier. For the rest of his life he looked every inch the soldier, with his tall, slim, upright, military bearing set off by pressed pinstripe suits and impossibly shiny black shoes. Journalists, not unkindly, often referred to him as 'the brigadier'. By gaining Kemsley's confidence, the diplomatic Hamilton was allowed to take a leading role in developments at the *Sunday Times.* His most notable early success was in persuading Hadley to allow him to search for sales-building material, especially book serialisations. It was a move that was to have far-reaching effects on the paper's fortunes, but his main hopes couldn't be realised until Hadley had gone and he had placed his own man in the chair.

Hamilton took almost no interest in Kemsley's other papers. which he saw as 'a crumbling and preposterous empire'.[89] Foremost among them was the *Daily Sketch*, which attempted to be a right-wing *Daily Mirror*, but without anything like the conviction and technical expertise. The ruse of changing its name to the *Daily Graphic* and utilising a similar bold sans serif typeface to the *Mirror*'s failed to win over the millions of *Mirror* and *Daily Express* readers. Nor did Hamilton show any interest in the *Empire News.* Kemsley's most notable act of kindness towards the editor of that paper, Terence Horsley, ended in tragedy. Knowing of Horsley's love of flying he presented his club with a glider which soon afterwards broke up in mid-air, killing Horsley, a man of forty-five who had been editor only since March the previous year.[90]

These popular papers also failed to impress Kemsley's elder brother, William, Lord Camrose, who 'had a high conception of the professional journalistic function, and disliked vulgar sensationalism'.[91] Once the Berry brothers had split their newspaper empire between them they had moved further and further apart. There was little doubt that Camrose was the better journalist and the better man. Hamilton saw Kemsley as 'a deeply conservative Conservative who had succeeded in life by clinging to his brother's coat-tails and was then saved from real competition . . . by the war'.[92]

Camrose, however, was a more intelligent deeply conservative Conservative. His singular aim had been to ensure that his beloved *Daily Telegraph,* already the best-selling serious newspaper, sold more and more copies without sacrificing its ethos. He was sixty-six in 1945 and the rest of the hierarchy at his paper was ageing too.[93] Camrose was tall and upright, a commanding figure, and much less pompous than his brother. After contracting diabetes in the late 1930s, he required a daily insulin injection. Otherwise, he was a picture of fitness, doubtless helped by his love of walking. He had an 'insatiable appetite for facts'.[94] The political line of the paper was a straightforward, usually unquestioning, adherence to the policies of the Tory party, but Camrose's main passion was for the what-why-where-when-and-how approach to journalism. He demanded that his reporters discover as much as possible about as many stories as possible, making the *Daily Telegraph* a byword for its comprehensive coverage.

Camrose was so concerned about the difference between news and comment that he ran the two areas separately. The editor was responsible for the opinion pages, and the news editor for all other editorial matter.[95] This American-style split of functions worked harmoniously for many years, with the two senior executives reporting directly to Camrose, ensuring that the owner remained in total control of editorial. But the system also tended to create a succession of news editors noted for their dogmatism and ruthlessness, starting with Alex Maclaren, who was regarded as a martinet.[96] The editor, Arthur Watson, was entirely different. He had been in the chair since 1924, before the Berry brothers bought the paper. By 1945, Watson was sixty-five. A tall, upright man with pink cheeks and a large white moustache, he was 'in both appearance and conduct ... a nineteenth century editor'.[97] He was an austere figure – a teetotaller and non-smoker – who remained remote from his staff, though he was respected for his sense of fairness. Politically, he was a natural centrist, a moderate.[98]

Watson had a fine set of writers at his disposal, including J. C. Johnstone, Bill Deedes and, from 1945, Malcolm Muggeridge. Leader writing apart, some writers disliked the paper's atmosphere or, in Harold Nicolson's case, its readers. Nicolson switched to reviewing books for the *Observer* because 'it is quite evident that the *Daily Telegraph* public is not one worth writing literary articles for'.[99] By 1950, it was obvious that the *Telegraph* needed new energy and Watson retired, having spent twenty-six years as editor.

Camrose's single-minded devotion to the *Daily Telegraph* led him to make a disastrous error of commercial judgement. Just before the 1945 election, he sold the profitable, and potentially even more profitable, *Financial Times* to its rival, the *Financial News*. Perhaps it was appropriate that the first major post-war newspaper takeover should have occurred in the financial press as a precursor to the later flurry of mergers and acquisitions. But it was a bad piece of business by Camrose, who later confided that the sale was the greatest mistake he ever made.[100] On the day before the announcement of the election results which brought Labour to power, the *Times* noted, 'It is with mixed feelings that many people will read that the long-standing rivalry between the *FT* and the *FN* is shortly to be ended ... Some will regret the disappearance of the stimulating competition – and often the divergence of view – between the two.'[101]

The origins of the deal are traceable to the blossoming of a wartime friendship between Camrose and Brendan Bracken, former Tory MP, close confidant of Churchill, and a director of the publisher Eyre & Spottiswoode, which owned the *Financial News*. They evidently agreed that, should either wish to sell, the other would have the first chance to make an offer. There was no reason for Camrose to sell. While the negotiations were going on, the *FT* announced bumper profits. It outsold the *FN* and, as its managing director, Garrett Moore, pointed out, although the *FN* had excellent writers it was the *FT* which 'was regarded as the leading City paper for its stock market comment and greater volume of straightforward financial information.'[102] Bracken baulked at the £500,000 asking price, but Moore convinced him it was worth it.[103] Wisely, though, and not without protest from some *FN* staff, the *Financial News* title was dropped in favour of the *Financial Times.* But *FN* staff took over most of the senior posts, including the editor's chair, which went to Hargreaves Parkinson.

Bracken, though a company director rather than an owner, stands well in the pantheon of newspaper proprietors. He was both acquisitive, buying several magazines and a half-share in the *Economist*, and innovative, founding in 1951 the influential magazine *History Today.* He had the kind of bluff, blustering 'outsize personality' so common among press barons (he was later awarded a viscountcy) and which aroused hostility even among those who appreciated his undoubted energy and determination.[104] He was 'inexhaustibly voluble and an overpowering figure'[105] with a 'talent for infuriating and antagonising people.'[106] He was 'a gross Philistine',[107] 'a bully',[108] 'a cad',[109] 'one of the most vivid and contradictory public figures of his day . . . something of an enigma to most of his closest friends,'[110] who was 'loathed and feared . . . in about equal proportions' by the *FT* staff[111] and with 'an orang-outang manner'.[112] The 'moody and incalculable' Bracken was difficult to deal with, swinging 'violently from elation to deep depression or bad temper, from reckless schemes to pusillanimous caution, from meanness to absurd generosity'.[113]

In an anthology of tributes after his death his close friends were kind but some showed their exasperation, such as Geoffrey Crowther: 'No one could be more infuriating about small things.'[114] Bracken was a part-time chairman, devoting most of his time to parliamentary matters, but continued to bully senior executives at weekly lunches, especially the editor. He was also generous, and in a 'wholly characteristic' gesture 'provided the bulk of the funds to set up an excellent pension fund',[115] noting in a letter to Beaverbrook that 'the hard-bitten Tory who runs the *Financial Times* has handed over his nice fat fee arranged by his predecessor, Lord Camrose, to the staff in order that they might have a Pension Fund'.[116] Bracken wrote the *FT*'s Men and Matters column from January 1946, using the 'Observer' byline, but there was 'no evidence . . . that he exercised any tangible influence over . . . leaders'.[117]

During this period, the *FT* campaigned against nationalisation, questioned any number of shibboleths and was harsh on Labour's 1949 devaluation. It gradually became recognised as a 'general business newspaper instead of being largely directed towards investors'[118] and was 'compulsory reading not only for politicians but also for mandarins'.[119] The advertising slogan 'Men who Mean Business read the *Financial Times*' worked well. But Parkinson was already suffering from illness when he had a stroke in the office in October 1950 and, on doctors' advice, he stepped down, dying the following May, aged fifty-four. His successor was destined to turn the *FT* into a first-class paper.

The *Times*: 'an almost perfect newspaper'

John Jacob Astor was a very different kind of owner from the other press barons. Indeed, he doesn't deserve to be called one since his title came more than thirty years after he assumed control of the *Times* and, uniquely, he accepted it only after assuring himself, and his editor, that he took no part in the editorial affairs of the paper. Shy, modest and unassuming, Astor was the antithesis of Beaverbrook.

The only power exercised by him and his co-owner, John Walter the fifth, was the appointment of editors. In 1941, they had chosen Robin Barrington-Ward, a first world war hero whose experiences at the front had turned him against war, a major reason for his support for the paper's appeasement line in the late 1930s. Though Barrington-Ward placed the *Times* unequivocally behind the war effort, Churchill remained suspicious of the man and the paper. The Tory leader was particularly upset by the *Times*'s post-war agenda. He thought he saw the influence of the paper's leftist leader writer, E. H. Carr, in its assaults on his policy on Greece.[120] In retaliation he attacked the paper in the Commons.[121] Nor could he bear the *Times*'s advocacy of pro-welfare social policy.[122] When Churchill lunched with Barrington-Ward in February 1944 he referred scathingly to 'your Christian communism'.[123] Another proprietor thought the *Times* was engaged in a 'flirtation with mild Marxism'.[124] Barrington-Ward was not a socialist but he offered the kind of cautious welcome to the incoming government's social reforms which alarmed Conservatives, and it is a measure of Astor's hands-off policy, given that he was a Unionist MP until 1945, that there was no interference. But the paper was to lose its two main political influences in quick succession. Carr left the paper in 1946 and Barrington-Ward, who had been in poor health, died on board a cruise liner off Dar-es-Salaam. He was fifty-seven.

Doubtless, it was Barrington-Ward's liberalism which prompted Tom Driberg in 1949 to call the *Times* 'an almost perfect newspaper'.[125] Its politics aside, it was far from perfect. The neat, easy-to-follow design did not rescue the paper from a stultifying dullness, beginning with the front-page adverts and unrelieved by the admittedly bright use of pictures on page six. There was no segregation of material, so that parliamentary reports ran next to racing, football and business news. The Commons reports were depressingly pedestrian, invariably beginning: 'The Speaker took the chair at 11 o'clock . . .'

Astor and Walter played safe after Barrington-Ward's death. They gave the job to William Francis Casey, the deputy editor, who had been with the *Times* since 1914 after joining as a sports sub. It was supposed to be an interim choice, since Casey had announced that he would soon retire.[126] He certainly found the strain of editorship heavier than he expected and his relations with staff were not helped by his 'streak of obstinacy'.[127] Even those who admired his skills thought him unsuited to be an editor.[128] The 'indolent and charming' Casey was mostly noted for enjoying 'long and vinous meals at the Garrick Club'.[129]

The other Astor family newspaper was the *Observer*. Owned by Waldorf Astor, John Jacob's brother, it had enjoyed a huge reputation among the nation's policy-makers in the first world war and immediately afterwards due to the editorship of J(ames) L(ouis) Garvin. Garvin's powers waned in the inter-war years as he became more bombastic and arrogant, and he eventually fell out with Astor in the early 1940s. Astor allowed his younger son David to take the leading role in turning the paper into a forum for intelligent writing from a liberal perspective while the paper was edited, somewhat reluctantly, by the drama critic, Ivor Brown, until David returned from his heroic exploits as a marine. His father set up a trust ownership for the *Observer* in 1944, but David was essentially the paper's proprietor because 'he always picked a chairman of trustees who would support him'.[130] In 1948, he formally assumed the editorship, sending Brown back to the stalls.

David Astor was a uniquely interesting man, the product of a privileged, if eccentric, background as the son of multi-millionaire Waldorf and the flamboyant Nancy, the first woman to sit in the Commons. He was born in 1912, the year after his grandfather had purchased the *Observer* from Northcliffe, and his early life was spent at Cliveden, a huge mansion set in 450 acres and served by a staff of eighty. Educated at Eton and Balliol, David inherited enough money at the age of twenty-one to make him independent for the rest of his life. It meant that he was able to escape, to a degree, the stifling grip of his mother and to use his fortune for what he deemed to be the public good: editing the *Observer*, a paper of ideas rather than news. As his biographer rightly argued: 'He was probably the only real idealist to edit or own a major British newspaper this century.'[131]

He had no interest in making money, and remained free from party allegiance, seeing himself as a Liberal–Conservative. That is hardly an adequate description. Influenced by his opposition to any form of totalitarian government, whether fascist or communist, he had an enlightened internationalist outlook and, in domestic affairs, became a champion of the disadvantaged. He gathered together a group of intellectuals, including Isaac Deutscher, Arthur Koestler, George Orwell and Edward Crankshaw, to expound their views for the good of readers 'who wanted to extend their knowledge and were willing to hear new propositions'.[132] For Astor, news would always take second place to ideas, exemplified by his decision to devote most of one issue to a painstaking explanation of the benefits of the Marshall Plan.[133] He was also the first to seize on the awful implications of the National Party's 1948 election victory in South Africa.[134]

Speaking to a press baron beyond the grave

Death struck down one of the barons in 1946. Lord Southwood, the former Julius Elias, who was proprietor of the company, Odhams Press, which owned the *Sunday People* and controlled the *Daily Herald*, died in April. Four months before, he had shown 'schoolboy delight' in being raised from baron to viscount.[135] The *Times*'s obituary was customarily benign: 'a man of unusual perspicacity and managerial ability . . . held in affectionate regard by his staff . . . a good employer . . . quietly engaged in many philanthropic activities on a large scale . . .'.[136] One anecdote said a great deal about him: he bought a magazine at a station which he took back to his executives, telling them it was just the sort of journal they should be producing. An embarrassed director pointed out that they had been publishing it for years.[137]

Odhams didn't own the *Herald* outright. It held 51 per cent of the shares while the Trades Union Congress (TUC) owned 49 per cent, an uneasy partnership which had existed since 1930. To complicate matters, the Labour party, which had played a large role in the *Herald*'s history, was also represented through TUC nominees. Southwood's death didn't make the tensions between the three players any easier. He died childless, and power at Odhams passed into the hand of its board in which the editorial director, John Dunbar, largely oversaw the *Herald*. The board had its bizarre side, containing a number of spiritualists who claimed they continued to receive guidance from Southwood at seances. The *Herald*'s senior columnist, Hannen Swaffer, also took counsel on the paper's plight by talking through a medium to the long-departed Lord Northcliffe.

The *Herald* certainly had problems in the real world. It was the first major title to be exposed by the relaxation of the newsprint restrictions it had been decrying. Once advertisers were allowed to place ads where they wished, they began to turn their backs on the *Herald*. Readers also started to desert. Having climbed to a circulation of 2.1 million in 1947, it fell back as its rivals continued to add sales. By 1950, it was below 2 million once more and on its way down. The *Herald*'s audience was being seduced by the more energetic and less dogmatic *Mirror*.[138]

Looking back, there is much to admire in the *Herald* of the late 1940s: the columns by Michael Foot and Swaffer; the occasional book reviews by John Betjeman; pieces by Arthur Eperon and Marjorie Proops, the latter writing and drawing sketches at the dawn of her prolonged career. Templegate's racing tips were avidly followed in an otherwise lack-lustre sports section. The paper also gained a major talent in 1950 when cartoonist David Low resigned from the *Evening Standard* after more than twenty years and joined, according to Swaffer, 'his Socialist spiritual home'.[139]

In fact, Low didn't prosper as he anticipated in spite of his friendship and admiration for editor Percy Cudlipp, formerly his editor at the *Evening Standard*.[140] Cudlipp was, according to Douglas Jay, 'the oldest and most serious-minded of the three Cudlipp brothers',[141] though some staff considered him 'a trifle snobbish'.[142] He surprised them all by growing into the job after his appointment in 1940. He dealt skilfully with Southwood, but after his death the *Herald*'s internal politics, with the TUC, the Labour party and Odhams Press all holding differing views about the paper, made it increasingly difficult to edit. Cudlipp's major headache was Ernest Bevin, the foreign secretary and former transport union leader, who wished to dominate the paper.[143]

Cudlipp's editorial problem was in trying to satisfy both the unions and the government, a problem he solved by hoisting the anti-communist banner and enthusiastically embracing the language of the cold war.[144] Yet this tended to distance the paper from many of its traditional left-wing readers, as the communist *Daily Worker* regularly pointed out. A typical front-page editorial referred to 'the disastrous experience' of the *Herald*, 'which began like the *Daily Worker* and was then sold to capitalists'.[145]

Offsetting the *Herald*'s decline, the rest of Odhams Press was in good health. *Sporting Life* remained the racing fans' bible, while the vast Odhams magazine empire, with titles such as *Woman*, *Ideal Home*, *Melody Maker* and *Horse and Hound*, was in fine shape too. The *Sunday People* was benefiting from the energy and drive of managing editor Sam Campbell, who had sidelined editor Harry Ainsworth, regarded by many as 'a spiritualist eccentric'.[146] Campbell's *People* won a reputation for populist campaigning journalism. He trained his reporters in the art of detecting, trapping and exposing ration dodgers, bad landlords, petrol thieves and black-marketeers. By 1948, Campbell had redesigned the paper's layout and typography, offering a new newspaper to the post-war generation. He retained Ainsworth's famous confessional series, usually featuring the famous and the notorious, but Campbell extended the genre to ordinary people with remarkable stories to tell, giving rise to headlines such as 'I Took a Lorry Ride to Shame'. His so-called 'magical formula' boosted the sale above 5 million.[147] Campbell sailed close to the wind. According to one of his reporters, and an admirer, Bob Edwards, truth was 'dispensable if he could improve a quote or a story'.[148]

Cocoa king who wanted to be press baron

In January 1946, the *News Chronicle* was delighted to publish fulsome tributes from rival newspapers on reaching its centenary.[149] The *Manchester Guardian* commented: 'It is no mean achievement among so many discouragements to have kept the faith and to have built up in these days of mass circulations the sound property that the *News Chronicle* is today.' The

Times nodded, the *Daily Express* bowed low, the *Daily Herald* swooned. Every paper had a good word to say about the *News Chronicle*'s birthday.

But it was a bogus celebration. The *News Chronicle* was a phoenix which had risen from the ashes of five papers, as prime minister Clem Attlee's subtle message of praise made clear. 'When Charles Dickens started this newspaper in 1846 he intended that it should stand for those ideals of social progress which were dear to his heart,' he wrote, adding: 'The *Daily News* has absorbed during the past century four famous Liberal and Radical papers – the *Morning Star* . . . the *Morning Leader*, the *Westminster Gazette*, and the *Daily Chronicle* . . . My sincere hope is that the *News Chronicle* will long continue to maintain those high traditions . . .'[150]

Sincere hopes do not sell newspapers, and the *News Chronicle*'s celebratory Dorchester Hotel dinner, with Laurence Cadbury presiding, was to be its last hurrah. Cadbury was the son of the man who had bought the *Daily News* at the beginning of the century and one of several Cadbury family trustees in effective ownership of the *News Chronicle*. The family, noted for being Quakers, Liberals and philanthropists, also ran the Bournville chocolate company on which their fortune was founded. Like many Liberal supporters from the middle classes in the 1940s who could see that their party's electoral chances had vanished and who were scared of Labour's brand of socialism, Laurence Cadbury was drawn towards the Conservatives. His 'instincts were Tory' and he 'moved a long way to the right as he grew older.'[151]

On the other hand, Walter Layton, chairman of the newspaper division and effectively editor-in-chief of the *News Chronicle* and its London evening stablemate, the *Star*, was a staunch Liberal.[152] This was far from the only difference between them. Layton was regarded as one of Fleet Street's wise veterans, having served under two ministries in wartime and become the newsprint rationing co-ordinator (see below, pp. 44–6). He was consulted by other proprietors as if he, rather than Cadbury, was the key player. Layton was sixty when he resumed his chairmanship of the Cadbury newspaper company in 1944. Aware of the Cadburys' growing disaffection, he asked if he could buy them out and was dismayed when Cadbury refused to sell the *Chronicle*, offering him only the *Star*, which would not have been viable alone.[153]

Their uneasy relationship worsened when Layton accepted a peerage from the Labour government in 1947. Brendan Bracken told Beaverbrook that Cadbury 'is bitterly jealous of Layton's peerage. Cadbury thinks that the owner of the *News Chronicle* should have gone to the Lords and not the manager.'[154] Nor did Cadbury's annoyance pass. Years later Bracken confided to Beaverbrook: 'Cadbury has never forgiven Walter for extracting a peerage out of Morrison. The cocoa maker says that if there were any peerages knocking around for *News Chronicle* people he, as owner of the business, should have been given one.'[155] Despite the Cadbury family's hostility towards him, Layton maintained firm control of the *News Chronicle*'s editorial policy which also led, in 1947, to the resignation of Gerald Barry as editor. He preferred to run the Festival of Britain rather than cope with the tension between two masters, neither of whose politics he really shared.

During those post-war years the quality of the content was often extremely good. Among the regular highlights were Vicky's cartoons, columns by Arthur Cummings, thoughtful leaders, excellent science articles by Ritchie Calder, Stephen Potter on books and Ian Mackay's delightfully whimsical columns. One related how Mackay, George Thomas of the *Daily Herald* and the Marquess of Donegall formed the levellers, a secret society dedicated to flattening Switzerland.[156] In another, he delivered a superb tribute on the death of union leader Jim Larkin.[157] The *News Chronicle* was a lively and intelligent broadsheet with much to commend it, even if the party it supported was now in the wilderness with only a dozen MPs.

Barry was replaced by Robin Cruikshank, a loyal Layton acolyte, a Liberal supporter and an excellent writer who had previously edited the *Star*.[158] Happier writing than editing, he found Layton's obsession with minutiae exhausting, but both men worked together to ensure that the paper maintained its independent line. In the years up to 1950, however, it is noticeable how keenly the paper tended to back Attlee. Layton finally relinquished the chairmanship in 1950 in favour of Cadbury, but remained on the board.

At the *Star*, the most notable post-war event was a scoop with embarrassing consequences. In November 1947, Chancellor Hugh Dalton was on his way into the Commons chamber to announce his supplementary budget when the paper's lobby correspondent, John Carvel, asked him its main contents. Unaware of the speed of evening-paper publication, Dalton told Carvel about key tax changes. In less than an hour the paper was on sale with the revelation in its 'Stop Press' column before Dalton had even reached that point in his speech. When it was realised what had happened, Dalton felt compelled to resign.[159]

The liberal voice from Manchester

Though the *News Chronicle* remained nominally in the Liberal party camp, another long-term press supporter deserted. The 1945 election 'ended the official link between the editor of the *Manchester Guardian* and the Liberal Party'.[160] It did not end the paper's commitment to small-'l' liberalism, far from it, but it was a recognition of the new realities. The editor from 1944, A. P. Wadsworth, had properly 'sensed the loosening of social class coming out of Hitler's war' and acted accordingly.[161]

Wadsworth admired Churchill but could not face a post-war Tory government, becoming in 1945 a trenchant critic of both the Conservatives and the pro-Tory press, especially Beaverbrook.[162] In fact, his editorship was 'marked by a running duel with the *Evening Standard* and the *Daily Express*.'[163] It prompted Brendan Bracken to call the *Manchester Guardian* 'the greatest viewspaper in the world', a back-handed compliment which ignored the paper's fine reporting record.[164] These polemics aside, most of Wadsworth's leaders were sensible and compassionate, and gradually grew more critical of Attlee's government. By 1950, the paper was praising the Tory leader: 'Mr Churchill attacked the Government on its weakest point, its doctrinaire attachment to nationalisation.' Even so, the leader still managed to be fair, an example of the paper's neutrality throughout that campaign and of Wadsworth's skills.[165] The fact that he had left school at fourteen had not inhibited his rise to editorship. He was regarded rightly as 'one of the intellectually self-made men of the North'[166] and arguably as 'the world's most scholarly newspaperman'.[167]

Wadsworth graduated from his first humble job, as a copy-holder in the reading room of the *Rochdale Observer*, to become a reporter. He was fortunate to find, in his editor William Waite Hadley, a man who enjoyed the role of tutor. Meanwhile, Wadsworth educated himself through night classes tempered by voracious reading of history and economics. By the time he joined the *Manchester Guardian*, aged twenty-six, he was an accomplished reporter and a formidable scholar.[168] Both qualities saw him rise gradually through the ranks. As editor, Wadsworth was vigilant, outspoken and unpretentious, winning the respect of his staff. His output was phenomenal and he wrote most of his paper's leading articles. He also had a dry sense of humour. He once telexed his American correspondent, Alistair Cooke, demanding that he cover a boxing match rather than the launch of a hydro-electric scheme in California: 'Return New York STOP Blood Thicker Than Water.'[169]

That wit was not much in evidence in the paper. With adverts on the front, finance and sport on page two and stage reviews on page three, the great news of the day was carried on page five. Its regional status was underlined by the daily column entitled Our London Correspondence. But deep questions were being asked about the paper as the *Guardian* began to face up to an awful truth. A 1946 survey showed that only a third of its readers lived in and around Manchester.[170] This fact served to reinforce the assessment of the *Guardian* by its new company secretary, Laurence Scott, grandson of its owner–editor C. P. Scott and son of the current chairman, John Scott. After university, Laurence had got a grounding in newspapers, as both journalists and manager, at the *Financial News*, the *News Chronicle* and the *Star*. It was in 1945 that Laurence outlined his three-point programme to his father: to put news on the *Guardian*'s front page; to drop *Manchester* from the masthead; and to print in both London and Manchester. Two years later, he became managing director, which made him heir apparent. To avoid legal problems, he and his father created a new trust just five months before John Scott's death.

Laurence became governing director, assuming ultimate executive power.[171] His determination to print the *Manchester Guardian* in London stemmed from his realisation that the paper would then be able to charge more for publishing national advertising. It was finding it too expensive trying to publish a 'world class paper on an income . . . insufficient to conduct a profitable provincial paper'.[172] He also knew that he couldn't build a bigger audience in Manchester and its suburbs. But the *Manchester Guardian* had a long way to go. In 1950 it was selling 140,000 copies to the *Daily Telegraph*'s 970,000 and the *Times*'s 270,000. Yet Laurence's projections showed that the Guardian required 250,000 sales if it was to be financially secure. For years, it had not seen itself as a genuine political or commercial rival to the *Times*. In 1948, the first step towards competition were evident when it was decided to end the foreign service previously shared with the *Times*.[173] The *Manchester Guardian* was on the threshold of change.

Boardroom intrigue at the *News of the World*

At the other end of the sales league from the *Manchester Guardian* was the hugely successful *News of the World*, aptly nicknamed by Percy Cudlipp 'the Hansard of the sleazy'.[174] Its circulation rose weekly throughout the war and went up even faster afterwards. By 1948 it was selling more than 7 million. But all was far from calm behind the scenes. Its ownership was largely split between two families, the Carrs and the Jacksons, who had fought with each other throughout the 1930s and 1940s. This conflict was exacerbated by disputes between the board and various senior managers.

As the real war neared its end, a new battle erupted at the *News of the World*'s headquarters in Bouverie Street. The paper's editor, Percy Davies, was also the chairman of the company. But he was persuaded to give up the post and concentrate on his editing by Philip Dunn, the ambitious and autocratic representative of the senior member of the Jackson family, Derek Jackson. Dunn had previously frustrated attempts by the senior member of the Carr family, William Carr, to replace his dead brother on the board, and thought he now had total control. His first act was to install his own man as deputy to Davies, choosing a former *Daily Telegraph* managing editor, Robert Skelton, who succeeded to the top job when Davies died in 1946. Dunn 'then embarked on a period of editorial extravagance', encouraging Skelton to hire a corps of foreign correspondents along with several new staff writers in London.[175] None of this disturbed the paper's sales-winning recipe, three parts sensational crime, two parts sport and one part serious comment.

Despite its salacious content, the paper, broadsheet in format, had a sober appearance. Its front page was dominated by reports about domestic politics and foreign events. Page three was probably better read with its court reports under the most intriguing of headlines, such as 'Coffee for soldier: abuse of young wife's kindness' and 'Ride in milk float: mother of nine accuses father of fourteen.'[176] These titillating tales always stopped short of factual detail. In a case involving under-age sex, the paper reported that the girl had taken a young man into a bedroom and skipped straight to the judge's decision after a sentence beginning: 'After describing what transpired . . .'[177] If sex and celebrity could be mixed, so much the better. Society divorce cases were popular: 'Wife's men friends: Decree nisi granted to Lord Rothschild.'[178] Even more popular was murder and celebrity. When a ship's steward was on trial for killing actress Gay Gibson, it was given huge space under the headlines, 'The Mystery of Gay Gibson's Black Pyjamas' and 'What happened in Cabin 126?'[179]

But Dunn's spending, albeit on improving the paper's serious content, did alarm other board members and minor shareholders, while journalists grew increasingly upset by Dunn's dogmatic championing of the Tories. It wasn't surprising that the *News of the World* should back Churchill in 1945. He had been the paper's 'chief contributor' throughout the 1930s, writing long articles and several series. But it was recognised that hundreds of thousands of readers were Labour supporters and it would be wise to leaven the Tory propaganda with some understanding of the demand for a new order.

Dunn then overplayed his hand. While continuing to deny William Carr a seat on the board, he tried to win a place for Derek Jackson. Instead, Carr turned the tables on his rival by promising other directors enhanced roles, and more money, if they forced Dunn's resignation and elected Carr himself on to the board. It worked, and Dunn was ousted with a healthy pay-off as compensation, along with his editor, Skelton. Carr soon assumed control, appointing Arthur Waters as editor, a man who never really wanted the job and who preferred to devote most of his time to running a Covent Garden pub ostensibly owned by his wife Maudie. This was far from the greatest mistake made by Carr, who did nothing to assuage the understandable hostility from Jackson after Dunn's departure. Jackson would have to wait almost thirty years for his revenge.

2. THE PRESS VERSUS THE POLITICIANS

> If for the Bible and *Pilgrim's Progress* are substituted the *News of the World* and the *Sunday Express* it will be evident that popular taste is likely to be in some danger.[1]

Though Labour swept to power in 1945 despite the press's overwhelming support for Churchill and his Tory party, Labour ministers and MPs were eager to constrain newspapers. Press proprietors, smarting from their failure to exert influence on the readers, redoubled their attacks on a party they could not accept in government. Unsurprisingly, Beaverbrook was in the thick of the struggle.

In July 1946, the attorney-general, Hartley Shawcross, delivered a stern attack on 'the gutter press' owned by Beaverbrook and Kemsley, with the latter deciding to sue for libel. Attlee, wishing to prevent Shawcross from resigning to fight the action, demanded that he apologise. Kemsley gleefully emblazoned Shawcross's apology across his papers and encouraged others to do the same. But Beaverbrook's papers remained silent. In accepting Shawcross's grovelling letter of apology, he sent back a note: 'I see no need for bothering you with publication. If nothing further arises, the letter need never be referred to again.' Not only did the cunning Beaverbrook have Shawcross in his debt, ensuring no further criticism from him, they soon became friends.[2]

Shawcross's retreat, though due to political necessity, was humiliating. As he commented years later, even though 'my speeches were brashly and foolishly expressed ... in substance they were correct'.[3] He had told a by-election audience:

> Freedom of the press does not mean the freedom to tell any lies that may happen to suit the particular newspaper proprietor. It does not matter very much how absurd, how malicious, how biased or extreme are the views which newspaper proprietors express, provided they do not cook the news to suit their views. Nobody knows that better than the newspaper proprietors ... They distort the facts, they suppress the news upon which free opinions could be freely formed. A small handful of newspaper proprietors because of their political views, their financial interests, their advertisement revenues and so forth are

terrified of the advent of socialism in this country and are determined that the Labour Government shall not be given a fair run.'[4]

The *Daily Telegraph* report failed to include specific references to Kemsley – brother of the *Telegraph*'s owner – and Beaverbrook. The *Daily Mirror* obliged instead.[5]

The Shawcross argument against 'the Tory stooge press' was blunted by the fact that Labour-supporting papers, particularly the *Daily Herald*, could be accused of socialist bias in their turn. The *Daily Telegraph* was quick to seize the point, calling Shawcross to account in a sarcastic editorial.[6] One other irony seemed to have been missed: a newspaper proprietor, able to exercise unlimited freedom of speech and so reach millions through his papers, was prepared to sue a man for exercising his freedom of speech in front of a couple of hundred people at a political meeting. And the extra twist: both complained that each was denying the other his freedom. To make matters worse for Shawcross, he was then attacked by a paper he had not criticised, the *Daily Mirror*, for his '"cheap, unjustified and offensive" attack on the *News of the World* ... a newspaper which he admitted he had never read'.[7] Shawcross's anger against the press came after more than a year of persistent attacks on Labour, which started from the moment the wartime coalition was dissolved and the 1945 election campaign began.

Despite their dismal track record as political persuaders in the 1930s, the press barons happily used their papers as 'instruments of political warfare' in 1945.[8] Most owners put the full force of their newspapers behind their supposedly unbeatable champion, Winston Churchill, certain that the man who symbolised Britain's military victory would triumph once again. Camrose's *Financial Times* stated confidently: 'The Stock Exchange as a whole has become more and more convinced that Mr Churchill will be put in power again, and takes a cheerful view accordingly.'[9] But, at Camrose's *Daily Telegraph*, an executive had quietly prepared a leader 'on the assumption of a Conservative debacle'.[10] Such prescience was rare. Three days before polling, Beaverbrook's *Daily Express* informed its readers: 'SOCIALISTS DECIDE THEY HAVE LOST'.

Beaverbrook was centre stage. His *Daily Express* tried to foment discord by creating a fake split in Labour's ranks which it dubbed 'the Laski affair'.[11] Beaverbrook censored his London *Evening Standard* cartoonist David Low, though his cartoons appeared untouched in the *Manchester Guardian*. Beaverbrook himself was the subject of more cartoons than any other person. Vicky showed him throwing a spanner in the works apparently for the joy of witnessing the resulting chaos.[12] The *Daily Mirror*'s Zec joined in with a cartoon entitled 'The Brook that's too large for the Beavers', showing the Tory dam of lies and stunts being breached by the flood of Britons trying to build a better country.[13] Michael Foot imperilled his friendship with

Beaverbrook by calling him 'the Old Maid Waiting at the Church Door Again'.[14]

Labour's landslide proved that Beaverbrook and the other Tory barons had overplayed their hand. They could hardly believe the result. So shocked was *Daily Telegraph* owner Lord Camrose that 'an air of stupefaction invaded [his] paper's columns'.[15] Peter Hennessy is probably right when he observes: 'I doubt if newspaper coverage of the 1945 election affected the outcome to any significant degree.'[16] That isn't how it was viewed at the time, a misconception which has haunted the debate about the relationship between press and the political process ever since. As we shall see when looking at elections after 1950, the correlation between direct advice from papers to vote for a certain party and voting patterns is impossible to prove. A much more likely influence is the story-telling and myth-creating in the years leading up to an election.

In the case of 1945, however, that doesn't hold true. Though Churchill was sensitive to any criticism of his handling of the war – shown in his hostility towards the *Daily Mirror* and his banning of the *Daily Worker* at the beginning of hostilities – party political bias in the press during wartime was, if not non-existent, most definitely muted. It is therefore possible to argue that, in terms of press neutrality prior to the campaign, the 1945 election was the fairest poll in the twentieth century.

Hennessy argues persuasively that 'the great shift of opinion owed more to the nation's experience of total war (in terms of both the necessity and effectiveness of state power in achieving results . . .)'.[17] The Churchill-cheerleaders of the press were deluded by their hero's wartime achievements as an individual while the public, without disparaging Churchill, saw greater merit in collective community effort. The state was seen as an effective embodiment of the public will. If it could vanquish Hitler, surely it could conquer economic injustice too?

The Labour party, which offered a practical plan of state intervention along with a vision of society very different from that of the 1930s, therefore embodied the people's post-war desires. The press as a whole appeared not to have understood the groundswell of support for change.

Rather eccentrically, the compilers of a 1945 general election study claimed there was a rough equilibrium in newspaper circulations supporting Churchill and Clement Attlee. There were, they argued, 6.8 million for the Tories and roughly 6 million for Labour.[18] But this was a badly flawed analysis. First, they included the Liberal *News Chronicle* in the Labour camp. It was certainly anti-Tory, but it did not support Attlee. Second, they omitted the Sunday papers, which were disproportionately pro-Tory. Third, they excluded the three London evening papers – two Tory and one Liberal – and the host of regional mornings and evenings, all of which (with the exception of the *Manchester Guardian* and a handful of Liberal titles) were staunch Conservative supporters. The *Times*, it must be said, remained 'peculiarly detached'.[19] Its polling-day leader is best characterised as waffle.[20]

There could not be any doubt about the partiality of certain mass-selling papers on either side of the divide. The *Daily Express* and the *Daily Mail* fought a trenchant battle for the Tories, while the *Daily Mirror* and *Daily Herald* waged a tough campaign for Labour. Both the *Express* and *Herald* were guilty of vicious and inaccurate hyperbole, and probably cancelled each other out. For example, the *Express*'s 'Gestapo in Britain if Socialists win' was countered by the *Herald*'s 'A Vote for Churchill Is a Vote for Franco'.[21] The *Herald*'s headlines 'were more combative than those of the *Daily Mail*'.[22]

If any paper could have been said to have made a difference, even if the degree of difference remains conjecture, it was the *Daily Mirror*. It was suggested at the time that the *Mirror*'s 'Vote For Him' campaign 'may well have won more votes for the Labour party than any other journalistic enterprise'.[23] Most commentators seem to agree.[24] The slogan was cleverly aimed at the wives, girlfriends and mothers of servicemen abroad, many of whom were voting for the first time. They would, naturally, wish to do well by the men yet to return, many of whom were angry that they would have no opportunity to vote. The slogan also gave political expression to the demobbed troops worried about their futures and, with great subtlety, tapped into the sense of comradeship they had experienced. The vote was for others, not just for oneself. It appeared first on 25 June and was repeated every day afterwards. On polling day, the paper repeated Zec's VE day cartoon in which a bandaged veteran held out an olive branch labelled 'Victory and Peace in Europe' and the headline read: 'Don't lose it again'.

As brilliant as this campaign undoubtedly was, even Cecil King conceded that Labour's victory was inevitable. At best, he thought, the *Mirror* 'may have changed a substantial Labour victory into a landslide'.[25] The voting figures indicate that millions of non-*Mirror* buyers, including many hundreds of thousands of *Express* readers, also voted for Attlee, in spite of increasingly hysterical *Express* headlines about the perils of a Labour government. However important the *Mirror* campaign was, it is hard not to conclude that there was a profound desire among the majority of Britons for a different kind of economic and social order from the one personified by Churchill's Tories, who were viewed as privileged, wealthy and stuffy.[26]

Nor should we overlook the *Herald*'s role. Leafing through the passionate, if sometimes clumsy, propaganda carried on all its six pages day after day, the sense that the *Herald* was at one with its readers and the mood of the country shines through. Though the Labour-leaning *Sunday Pictorial*, *Sunday People* and *Reynolds News* sold fewer than the staunchly Tory *News of the World*, *Sunday Express* and *Sunday Dispatch*, the demand for a new order was insistent.

It is easy to detect from coverage in all papers, particularly in the *Express* and *Mirror*, a climate of growing dissatisfaction among people about their living conditions and standards. This is more evident in news and features material which ostensibly had nothing do with election, such as the designs of new houses which stimulated hundreds of letters to each title. At the beginning of 1945, a *Daily Express* panel composed of 'the nation's thinkers and controversialists' discussed the 'vital question': What is the average man fighting for? Among the panel's great and good was a guest, Eighth Army dispatch rider Albert Foxwell, who turned out to be the star performer. When asked why 'the average man' was fighting the war, he replied that he was doing so 'to end all wars, but he is wondering what you have got for him afterwards in the way of housing and education for his children'. This set the tone for the discussion and there was general agreement by all that social conditions had to improve for the returning heroes.[27]

People were certainly angered by rationing, yet there was an intriguing difference of opinion between the *Express*, which called for wholesale removal, and the *Mirror* which claimed that rationing protected the people from profiteers. The *Express*'s line was straightforward, if simplistic, compared to the *Mirror*'s, which demanded continuing sacrifice. Nevertheless, the *Mirror* prevailed – at least, until the election. Afterwards was another story altogether.

Beaverbrook may have made an understandable mistake by equating his paper's sales rise throughout the campaign with political influence.[28] Though downcast at the result, he saw it as a lost battle in a long war and he continued to wage his campaign against Labour.[29] In an echo of Hitler's view that only by constantly repeating a lie can it be imprinted on the memory of a crowd, Beaverbrook was fond of telling his editors: 'Repetition is the key to propaganda.' The result, for the Labour party and several of its members, was painful. First to suffer was the party chairman, Harold Laski. Identified as a communist bogey figure by the *Daily Express*, he was subjected to an almost daily assault in the run-up to the 1945 election, some of which was childish.[30] Other papers joined in and Laski discovered what it was like to be the prey in a press feeding frenzy.[31]

His description of the experience holds true for almost everyone who has faced a similar situation. 'It is a curious sensation,' he wrote. 'Its most singular aspect is the almost complete deprivation of privacy. The Press takes you over as a kind of museum specimen. Journalists ring you up and ask you the most fantastic questions at every hour of the day and night. Views are attributed to you which you never held; habits are ascribed to you which you cannot recognise as your own.' People begin to talk about you as if you had combined 'the less admirable habits of Guy Fawkes with the more pernicious doctrines of Trotsky'.[32]

Laski was not alone. Beaverbrook chose several targets, from backbencher Konni Zilliacos – calling him 'Zilly Boy' at every opportunity – to ministers such as Aneurin Bevan and John Strachey, who endured 'ferocious attacks'.[33] All the Tory papers criticised Labour policy, opposing nationalisation, the formation of the National Health Service, and the use of aid from the United States. Even the massive, and necessary, house-building project attracted a broadside from the *Sunday Times*: 'Stealthily the tide of Socialism creeps up the shore of freedom . . . Millions of small houses are to be built . . . for letting only . . . The Socialist housing policy will assuredly create a race of State tenants, paying rent in perpetuity, with never a hope of owning a brick of their homes.'[34] Papers, especially Rothermere's *Daily Mail*, also sought to exploit differences of opinion within the government, real and imagined, to suggest splits, between Attlee and Laski, between Attlee and Herbert Morrison, and between Bevan and everyone else.[35]

Strachey, as food minister, suffered because of bread rationing. A typical example is a *Daily Sketch* splash, 'REVOLT SWEEPING BRITAIN OVER BREAD', accompanied by a leader which began: 'We can see bread rationing . . . as an unwarranted attack on that hardest-working of all workers, the housewife.'[36] After persistent newspaper criticism of this type Strachey hit back in a Commons speech. He claimed that the 'millionaire press' was 'posing as the housewives' friend' and fomenting a campaign against rationing, which was necessary for the good of the country. He said: 'The Beaverbrook, Rothermere and Kemsley Press is undertaking a raging campaign in this country in favour of agitation to gamble with the bread of the people.'[37]

But none of this appeared in the *Daily Express*'s story on the speech. Instead, it hit back: 'It is an old trick of the demagogue to sneer at the popular press when he cannot answer the argument.'[38] Worse, much worse, was to happen to Strachey later. He was the first genuine post-war victim of a sustained media campaign. His biographer noted how he became 'the butt for criticism, consumer protests and popular jokes'. *ITMA*, the hugely popular radio comedy show, referred to him as 'Mr Streaky'. 'He was the most visible target for press attacks, with writers implying that he was personally and deliberately making the public suffer for doctrinaire reasons.'[39]

Within two years of the election, Attlee was also under assault from his supposed press allies. The *Daily Mirror* was scathing: 'There is no constant, central control of Government. Mr Attlee leaves it to the others. In effect he has contracted out of the country's crisis. His Cabinet should go. So should Mr Attlee.'[40] The *Manchester Guardian*, the *Times* and the *News Chronicle* joined in.[41] The *Mirror* returned to the attack before a crucial by-election at Gravesend in November.[42] Labour still won, a feat the *Daily Telegraph* attributed to socialist propaganda: 'disgruntled though the electorate is with Socialist bungling, it is still susceptible to the gross Socialist misrepresentations of the Conservative record between the wars and of present Conservative policy'.[43]

Sensationalism is good for us, says jailed editor

The popular papers, particularly the Sundays, published more about crime than politics. Their pages were full of gruesome murders, petty assaults, robbery and racketeering. It was an era in which the crime correspondents appeared in their own stories, playing the roles of detectives or father confessors, often both. Senior policemen were lionised and, when they retired, were often signed up to recount their memoirs in lengthy series, such as Fabian of the Yard, former Superintendent Robert Fabian, who dissected old crimes for the *Empire News* among others.

Perhaps the most flamboyant crime reporter in these years was Duncan Webb of the *Sunday People*. One of his classic high-profile exposés concerned a Soho prostitution and extortion racket run by 'four despicable brothers' he dubbed 'the Messina gang'. Under a front-page splash headline: 'ARREST THESE FOUR MEN: They are the emperors of a vice empire in the heart of London', Webb reported in typically colourful style: 'Today I offer Scotland Yard evidence from my dossier that should enable them to arrest four men who are battening on women of the street and profiting from their shameful trade.'[44] The following week Webb was the subject of a front page story after he had been attacked, so he claimed, by two men supposedly linked to the Messinas.

'Tommy' Webb, as he was known to his friends, was working to a formula created by *People* editor Sam Campbell, who put his distinctive stamp on the journalism of the time by investigating and exposing crimes. He gave credibility to the stories by publishing the details of investigations. In the Messina case, he showed how Webb had traced the women to their various addresses and then established the links with the gang exploiting them. Campbell adopted the same pattern in later investigations into slum landlordism, fake religions, football bribery and other social scandals. His rivals soon adopted similar techniques which, many years later, were also taken up by the *Sunday Times*.

Stories about black marketeers were common in post-war papers, though they were occasionally far-fetched.[45] Front and inside pages were dominated by lurid headlines, with reports of gun-toting gangs involved in jewel thefts, kidnappings and strings of burglaries. At the end of 1945, the *Daily Herald* announced: 'WORST MONTH OF CRIME YARD HAS KNOWN'. An unnamed 'official' evidently said: 'We have too many prisoners and too few prisons.'[46] Two years later, the situation was reported to be just as desperate. London seemed like 1920s Chicago with page-one headlines every other day: 'Yard Hunts Armed Bandits', 'Black Market Gang Rob Big Naafi' and '4 Gun Gangs Roam London'.[47] Inner- city street crime was common too. A 'razor gang' was reported to have slashed three people at the Windmill Theatre.[48] A *Daily Mail* front-page leader lamented the crime wave and the 'recession in morality'. It asserted: 'Hardly a day passes without the report of some atrocious act of violence. Murders of children and women after assault, attacks on old people, hold-ups by gunmen, and the shooting of policemen have become almost commonplace.'[49] By 1950, the *Star* leader writer was wringing his hands: 'What is to be done about London's gangs?'[50]

There were also many grim reports about domestic cruelty, such as 'Mother of 61 accused of strangling daughter with silk stockings';[51] foster parents who tethered a four-year-old girl to a bed;[52] and a man who 'held girls before fire until their legs blistered'.[53] The *News of the World*'s pages were full of crime among the penniless and the pathetic. No week passed without mention of murders, though the lesser crimes were tragic too, with stories of paedophilia, parental abuse and sad suicide pacts.

Papers offered differing remedies. In a front-page plea, the *Daily Mirror* urged a 'Ministry for children' and recommended that education rather than prison was necessary so that parents could learn how to run a home and raise children.[54] Other papers were not impressed. The Commons having suspended the use of the death penalty for five years, the *News of the World* called on the Lords to restore it.[55] The *Daily Mail* derided the 'contemporary idea that crime is a disease'. Sending 'sadistic robbers' to hospital rather than jail is no good. 'Society is entitled to ask for retribution.'[56] The *Daily Telegraph* demanded the retention of the birch. In an editorial on the government's reforming Criminal Justice Bill, it argued that although 'humanitarianism . . . is in accordance with modern thought' the 'one main object of punishment is to act as a deterrent to crime. It is, therefore, a strange moment when violent crime is rampant for the abolition of whipping.'[57]

Two of the most high-profile crimes of the era were the Donald Hume 'torso case' and the John George Haigh acid-bath murders. Throughout January 1950, the *News of the World* carried thousands of words on Hume's trial and the *Daily Express*, despite its lack of space, devoted a full page to the judge's summing up.[58] But the coverage of Hume was less sensational than that of Haigh, probably due to what happened to an editor during the Haigh case.

Haigh was accused of murdering a wealthy widow, though it was rumoured that he might be a serial killer responsible for as many as five deaths. Before he was arrested, reporters were tipped off that he might be the killer: one interviewed him, found him out in a lie and passed on the information to police.[59] Once he was charged, papers had to be very careful in writing about the circumstances surrounding any of the murders. The *Daily Express*'s crime reporter Percy Hoskins took the lead: 'ACID BATH MURDER HUNT: Lost widow may be fifth victim.'[60] By keeping Haigh's name out of the story, and therefore not specifically linking him to an acid bath, gory speculation appeared in the next day's splash too. Yet, on an inside page, was a story and picture headlined: 'Haigh waves to hundreds on way to remand jail'.[61] The *Daily Mirror*, keenly aware that it was being trumped by its rival over the acid-bath revelations, could only splash on Haigh leaving court.[62]

This transparent sleight-of-hand just about satisfied the law enabling a person to have a fair trial. But the next day the *Mirror* overstepped the mark. While the *Express* published another splash about 'acid crimes' which didn't mention Haigh's name, the *Mirror*'s front page made an almighty blunder. Under the headline 'The Vampire Confesses', it proclaimed that Haigh was a human vampire who had committed several murders and confessed to two of them.[63] Though there were edition changes to the story during the night after police complaints, the central fact – that Haigh was a murderer – remained.

When this clear-cut contempt of court was pointed out to the Lord Chief Justice, he summoned the *Mirror*'s directors and its relatively new editor, Sylvester Bolam. Lord Goddard did not pull his punches. The *Mirror*'s articles were a disgrace to British journalism. They were prejudicial, violating all sense of justice in which a man is presumed innocent until proved guilty. He described the offence as 'scandalous and wicked' and concluded: 'In the opinion of this court this has been done not as an error of judgment, but as a matter of policy pandering to sensationalism for the purpose of increasing the circulation of this paper.'[64]

The reference to sensationalism bit hard, because Bolam had famously lauded the concept months before in a description of the genre which has never been bettered. In a *Mirror* leader, he wrote: 'We believe in the sensational presentation of news and views, as a necessary and valuable public service . . . Sensationalism does not mean distorting the truth. It means the vivid and dramatic presentation of events so as to give them a forceful impact on the mind of the reader. It means big headlines, vigorous writing, simplification into familiar everyday language, and the wide use of illustration by cartoon and photograph.' In a prophetic last line he trumpeted: 'No doubt we make mistakes, but at least we are alive.'[65] But Bolam's mistake over Haigh was unforgivable. Goddard jailed him for three months and fined the company £10,000.

Bolam went off to Brixton prison in a taxi.[66] He was visited on one occasion by Bart, Cudlipp and cartoonist Philip Zec who arrived in 'a large black Rolls-Royce'. After release, Bolam laughed off his jail term as 'a most valuable experience'.[67] However valuable it might have been, no editor has sought to emulate the experience since. There was no journalistic outcry about Bolam's imprisonment being a threat to press freedom. *Daily Mail* editor Frank Owen later remarked that when Fleet Street editors talked of the case they said with sincerity: 'There, but for the grace of God, go I.'[68] But most journalists had little sympathy for Bolam. Cudlipp later admitted that the *Mirror* had 'asked for trouble' and Charles Wintour thought Bolam had 'displayed a degree of obtuseness which is hard to credit'.[69]

It was odd that it should have happened to Bolam, who was hardly a cavalier editor, and very different from the rambunctious Bart. An economics graduate from Durham University and something of a radical, he was keenly interested in literature, art, music and the countryside. Bolam's standing as an editor suffered from his defence that he had given orders which weren't obeyed. He returned to his desk after serving his time, and was to play a crucial role in the next stage of the *Mirror*'s history.

'The Jews are a plague on Britain'

Despite the suffering of the Jews under the Nazis, there was surprisingly little material about the horrors of the concentration camps until the discovery of Buchenwald. One historian has since noted that it 'received more publicity than any other story in the field of Nazi anti-Semitism, with the possible exception of the "Crystal Night"'.[70] Almost every paper carried compassionate leaders.[71] *Reynolds News* stood out because it dared to recall the years of appeasement 'when most of the British Press was fawning around Hitler's feet' and were willing to overlook German attitudes towards the Jews.[72] That paper also benefited from a dispassionate, and therefore all the more effective, eyewitness report from Tom Driberg which began: 'I had, frankly, like many other people in this country, not quite believed everything that had been printed about it.'[73]

Initially, this discovery did not appear to change the apparently deep-seated resentment towards Jewish people in Britain among every class. A thinly veiled anti-Semitism had long had a hold in the upper echelons of British society, including newspaper proprietors (though, notably, not Beaverbrook, who was on the Nazi black list because he was regarded as 'completely pro-Jewish').[74] During the first world war, the first Lord Rothermere had claimed that production of army uniforms was being delayed because East End Jewish tailors kept running away from Zeppelins.[75] As one of the Harmsworths' biographers pointed out: 'The middle class prejudice against Jews, strong in pre-1914 England, often stirs under the surface of the Harmsworths.'[76]

It stirred again in 1940 when Rothermere's papers fanned hostility to Jewish refugees who had sought asylum from Germany and Austria. His *Sunday Dispatch* continually heaped scorn on 'enemy aliens', describing them variously as fascists, communists and pacifists. A *Sunday Dispatch* report claimed that foreign internees in Holloway jail were living in luxury: 'The alien women, Germans, Austrians, some of them Jewesses ... march round the exercise yard singing German songs.'[77]

The *Daily Mail* and the *Daily Telegraph* made similar allegations, insinuating that all internees and, by implication, all foreigners, including Jews, were likely to be traitors. The *Times* and the *Daily Express* took the opposite view, though it has been suggested – possibly unfairly – that the

Express's unusual liberal stance stemmed from the fact that Beaverbrook was having an affair at the time with a Jewish refugee.[78]

In 1946, there was some evidence of working-class racism towards Jews, though only by a minority. In November that year, a *News Chronicle* poll asked people if they had any ideas about how to solve the problem of Jewish homelessness. Some 47 per cent said they couldn't offer a solution. Eight per cent said Jews deserved little sympathy.[79] Another 1949 poll, in a working-class area of London, showed 8.7 per cent extremely anti-Semitic and 42.7 per cent as 'capable of anti-Semitic statements when pressed'.[80]

By now, with the second Lord Rothermere, Esmond Harmsworth, in charge of the *Daily Mail*, it ran a number of measured articles on the problems facing Jews, a tribute to the influence of its liberal editor Frank Owen.[81] As the debate about the formation of a Jewish state intensified, he also provided space for three writers to air their views, along with half a page for Emanuel Shinwell's passionate speech.[82]

A couple of days after that article appeared, one of Rothermere's friends noted: 'Esmond ... tells me that he had great difficulty in getting his *Daily Mail* people to write an article in support of the Jews ... They say that any such line would harm the paper, because of the strength of anti-semitism in the country.'[83]

If there was such a climate it would not have been relieved by headlines such as 'London watch on Jew terrorists' in the *Daily Telegraph*.[84] Popular papers were just as alarmist: 'Jew terror army admits outrage',[85] '"Happy event" wire from London began Jew terror'[86] and 'Jews disguised as milkmen smuggle explosives into luxury hotel'.[87] These headlines, reporting the bomb blast at Jerusalem's King David Hotel, equated Jew with terrorist, and there was little sympathy for Zionist militants. A rash of racist incidents flared across Britain, but the national press was not only generally restrained in its comment, it eschewed the opportunity to dwell on the British victims by carrying pictures and profiles of the dead. Nor were there any interviews with the bereaved.[88] By the following year a *Daily Express* leader was pleading for an end to the 'hounding' of British Jews. 'No more of this! It disgraces and humiliates the whole nation that even a microscopic minority should seek to penalise innocent citizens for their birth or religion.'[89]

Concerned Labour MPs proposed that anti-Semitism be made illegal, leading to a 1948 government inquiry into the possibility of framing laws against attacks on any racial or religious group. Most of the evidence was about attacks on Jews, but it was decided that there were no special circumstances which could not be covered by the existing laws on seditious libel.[90] This was an odd decision, given the outcome the year before of the most notorious case of press anti-Semitism.

In August 1947, the 17,800-circulation *Morecambe & Heysham Visitor* carried a leading article by its owner–editor James Caunt in which he demanded that the local Jewish community be ostracised until they took practical steps to dissuade Jewry from supporting terrorism. In an intemperate and overtly racist piece, he wrote: 'There is very little about which to rejoice greatly except the present fact that only a handful of Jews despoil the population of our borough. The foregoing sentence may be regarded as an outburst of anti-Semitism. It is intended to be, and we make no apology, neither do we shirk any responsibilities or repercussions.' The article continued:

> It is not sufficient for British Jews, who have proved to be the worst black market offenders, to rush into print with howls of horror and sudden wreaths at cenotaphs. They should disgorge their ill-gotten wealth in trying to dissuade their brothers in the United States from pouring out dollars to facilitate the entrance into Palestine of European Jewish scum, a proportion of whom will swell the ranks of the terrorist organisation and thus carry on the murderous work which British Jewry professes to abhor. There is a growing feeling that Britain is in the grip of the Jews . . . The Jews are a plague on Britain.[91]

Days later Tom Driberg, the Labour MP and journalist, brought parliament's attention to Caunt's words, asking the attorney-general if he had seen the 'seditious libel . . . which was professedly anti-Semitic in character and commended the use of violence against the Jewish community in Britain'.[92] Presciently, Driberg remarked that if the laws 'prove inadequate to deal with this most dangerous disease of anti-Semitism it may be necessary to introduce new legislation'.

The home secretary, Chuter Ede, remarked, 'Expression of opinion was free, but it must not amount to sedition. The preaching of racial and religious hatreds could be sedition.'[93] Soon after, Caunt was charged with seditious libel and appeared first before Morecambe magistrates.[94] Caunt, aged forty-seven, had been editor of the weekly *Morecambe & Heysham Visitor* for nine years. His father had been the editor before him. Caunt told the court he had seen anti-British propaganda in papers and on hoardings in the USA published by Jews. But he was prompted to write his editorial by seeing a *Daily Express* picture of hanged British soldiers in Palestine and the report that a twenty-one-year-old soldier from nearby Blackpool had been shot dead. Caunt was sent for trial.[95]

When he appeared at Liverpool Assizes he denied that his editorial had advocated violence against Jews, and said that he hadn't meant it to do so. His counsel pointed out that there hadn't been a prosecution of an editor under the charge for more than a hundred years. In his summing-up the judge, Mr Justice Birkett, told the jury: 'It is in the highest degree essential – and I cannot over-emphasise its importance – that nothing should be done to destroy or weaken the liberty of the press.' He also pointed out that sedition meant public disorder or insurrection. So the jury retired for just thirteen minutes before acquitting Caunt.[96]

The case was reported in detail in the *Daily Telegraph* – 'Editor acquitted of seditious libel: Judge's warning to jury on weakening liberty of Press' – and the reporter pointed out that the verdict was greeted by 'a burst of applause and a cheer from the public gallery'.[97] Yet the paper didn't comment. The *Daily Mirror* gave it little space. Only the *Manchester Guardian* thought the case important enough to warrant a leader:

> All of us are for the freedom of the press, but we should prefer to be represented by any champion but Mr Caunt. Freedom carries with it responsibilities as well as rights, and like other precious things, it can be used well or ill. Mr Caunt used it to attack the Jews. The jury decided that his leading article ... did not constitute a seditious libel. It was a discreditable piece of work none the less and the last thing we should wish to see held up as a sample of a free press.[98]

It is sobering to recall that Caunt was lionised by his court case. When he died in 1959 he was given 'one of the biggest funerals in Morecambe for years'.[99] He was buried 'with pen in hand' and in his coffin was placed 'an illuminated address bearing the signatures of his 50 employees' and a copy of the transcript of his court case.[100] His funeral was attended by dignitaries from across Lancashire, including the local MP and a representative of the National Union of Journalists.

There was almost no sympathy for the plight of Jews trying to come to terms with the Holocaust. In 1949, in the British sector of West Berlin, a crowd of fifty Polish and other displaced Jews stopped the showing of the British film *Oliver Twist*, claiming that the portrayal of Fagin was an incitement to anti-Semitism. The incident was reported straightforwardly in two papers, but the *Daily Telegraph*'s coverage was noticeably lacking in impartiality: 'Fewer than 100 Polish Jews, many of whom are known as black market operators, again stopped the showing of ... *Oliver Twist*.'[101] Some of the comment was hostile and unpleasant.[102] Perhaps the worst examples were in the provincial press, with references to 'aggressive and cock-a-hoop post-war Jewry'[103] and the need for Jews to acquire 'thicker skins'.[104] The fact that the incident had taken place in Berlin, administrative centre of the extermination programme against Jews, seemed not to concern such papers.[105]

Let us print: the struggle against newsprint rationing

A great deal happened around the world without forensic press coverage. The loss of empire, though an obsession with Beaverbrook and referred to often in his papers' leading articles, didn't generate the kind of news and feature material one might have expected. The communal riots of the Indian sub-continent were ignored by the populars and, though covered by the qualities, were not treated to in-depth reporting. The British government even got off lightly during its retreat from Palestine. Editors may have been reflecting the inward-looking mood of the public coping unhappily with domestic matters. Then again, papers were small and able to argue that there was too little space to do their job properly.

However much the people appeared to appreciate the power of the state, the newspapers feared it. They realised the dangers implicit in its domination and they suspected the Labour government's motives in acquiring greater state control. Their hostility, though manifested in a self-interested way, was cloaked by advancing the principle of press freedom. From 1945 onwards, they ceaselessly attacked the restriction on paper supplies, turning newsprint rationing into a *cause célèbre*. All owners and editors, left and right, regardless of party allegiance, were united in their opposition. Rationing – the term, the concept and the reality – was symbolic of the prevailing austerity which had taken hold of Britain 'like a malignant disease'.[106] A typical tirade by Rothermere was approvingly quoted by the *Times*: 'The light of a free press can be snuffed out just as easily by a lack of paper as by too much censorship. A tyrannical Government which wanted to suppress opinion might hesitate to attack news at its source and yet be bold enough to attack newsprint.' This sort of message was pumped home in every paper, usually on front pages, month after month. There were so many examples I lost count.[107]

However far-fetched, readers were persuaded that the government was responsible for censorship, and the constant references became part of the sombre background music to the general fanfare of anti-rationing propaganda which undermined Attlee's government. They were also effective in upsetting the liberal middle classes for whom the word 'freedom' has a special resonance. The *Financial Times*, soon after Bracken's takeover, joined in the chorus of criticism: 'The effects [of rationing] . . . are insidious and regrettable. If indefinitely prolonged, they could become dangerous and evil. The nation has as much right to be well informed as to be adequately supplied with foreign films and Virginian tobacco.'[108]

No commentator previously has recognised the import of this relentless, almost daily, campaign. Owners working together took every opportunity to publicise their case, taking front-page space to hammer home their views. *News Chronicle* chairman Laurence Cadbury told his company's annual meeting: 'The greater the powers of the State, the more necessary is it to preserve the free play of the critical faculty.'[109] The *Daily Express* argued that the 'dollar crisis is used as a lever to curb the Government's critics. That is the construction the ordinary man will put on this savage blow at the best newspaper Press in the world.'[110] The London *Evening Standard* claimed that a further newsprint cut in July 1947 was a government punishment on newspapers, and rightly pointed out that 'five papers of the Left have condemned the newsprint cut – the *Manchester Guardian, Times, Daily Mirror, News Chronicle, Economist*'.[111]

Backbench MPs, Tory and Labour, were given space to rail against 'the system of paper control'.[112] The print unions were encouraged to protest, and did so. Journalist organisations joined in.[113] Local weekly editors held a protest meeting and described rationing as a form of censorship.[114] Even when restrictions were eased a little, the *Observer* gave front-page space to a Tory party conference resolution which declared that supplies were 'totally inadequate to ensure a well-informed public opinion'.[115] The *Times*'s concern was clear when it devoted three increasingly trenchant leaders in one month to the subject.[116]

When it became clear that the government would accede to requests for a royal commission on the press, owners were outraged that it wasn't dealing instead with 'the newsprint crisis'.[117] This *Daily Express* lead was followed by other papers, including its Labour rival, the *Daily Mirror*.[118] But the government's mind was not changed.

Beaverbrook: 'I run my papers for propaganda'

The idea of a commission sprang from the National Union of Journalists (NUJ). Its general secretary, Clem Bundock, said, 'the freedom of the press must not be choked by the concentration of newspapers into the hands of two or three powerful commercial groups'.[119] He was concerned by closures of regional papers and the consequent loss of political diversity, alarmed at the power of newspaper magnates, and worried about the growth of sensationalism. It is perfectly plausible to view journalistic hostility to the form of individual ownership as self-interest. Frustrated by the demeaning nature of their work as hired hacks, they wished to wrest the powers of editorial control from proprietors in order to provide – in their view – a more impartial service to readers in the public interest. In truth, the union was speaking only for a minority of journalists. Immediately after the NUJ had given evidence to the commission 'a number of branches protested against the nature of the evidence'.[120]

Passionate support for the NUJ view came from several Labour ministers, such as Aneurin Bevan, who referred to 'the most prostituted press in the world, most of it owned by a gang of millionaires . . . The national and provincial papers are pumping a deadly poison into the public mind, week by week.'[121] Labour backbenchers were just as vitriolic, led by the former journalists – and Beaverbrook employees – Tom Driberg and Michael Foot. Foot was later to tell the commission that 'the occupational disease among newspaper proprietors was megalomania'.[122]

There was plenty of opposition, and not just from the obvious sources. The *Daily Mirror*, which had no proprietor, was ambivalent, saying it didn't feel a commission was necessary.[123] The NUJ's right-wing rival, the Institute of Journalists, viewed the commission as an attack on press freedom.[124] Frank

Owen, in his *Daily Mail* column, debunked the idea of an inquiry. 'Mr Morrison and his colleagues, who began by claiming that they came to power in spite of the Press, now complain that the Press is insufferably hostile to them.'[125] He thought there was enough diversity in the market to ensure that readers could shop around for a paper that suited them.

Whether or not there was sufficient plurality was, in essence, the premise of the commission which began its deliberations in April 1947 under the chairmanship of philosophy academic Sir David Ross. The task was taken seriously and, on reflection, the commission didn't perform too badly. It says much for the antipathy towards the press at the time that the commission's inquiries succeeded in making most owners defensive about their operating methods. Rather than assert their right to do as they wished, they tended to deny that they exercised any power. Except, of course, for Beaverbrook. He correctly viewed the commission as a personal attack. It was certainly aimed at him, but not at him alone since there was unease about the collective of 'Tory proprietors'. It was just that Beaverbrook was seen as the owners' mouthpiece and critics hoped that, by proving his guilt, the others would be found guilty by association. But could they show that he ran his papers like a dictator, telling his editors what, and what not, to publish?

Beaverbrook, recalling the previous century's battle between the state and the press, shrewdly built a defence in which his private interest and the public interest were elided (a defence, incidentally, which was to become the norm among owners thereafter). Years before he had written: 'Any newspaper which opposes a Ministry or party machine must be prepared for an indefinite amount of misrepresentation and abuse.'[126] This neatly turned the politicians' argument against press power on its head: in his view it was the press which required guarding from attacks on its freedom by politicians. In a private message from abroad to his general manager requesting information about the progress of the commission, Beaverbrook described it as one of the 'Government Agencies in the persecution of newspapers'. He added: 'Sorrow, sorrow ever more. There is nothing I can say about it except to bow my head in misery. It wouldn't be a bad thing if the Socialists cut off all newsprint entirely.'[127]

When he eventually made his personal appearance before the commission he was anything but bowed. It was, as two of his biographers remarked, 'a triumph of apparent candour and genuine humour'.[128] In a virtuoso performance, he undermined his two main critics, Foot and Driberg, by explaining that his 'directives' to editors were 'really advice' and patronised Foot as 'a very clever fellow, a most excellent boy'. To call his orders 'advice' was an outrageous lie, as many of his best and most loyal editors – including Christiansen, Bob Edwards and Charles Wintour – later revealed.

Much more truthful was Beaverbrook's famous quote to the commission, about running his papers for propaganda. It was not a joke as some have suggested. He also qualified it with a streak of financial realism: 'My purpose originally was to set up a propaganda paper, and I have never departed from that purpose all through the years. But in order to make the propaganda effective the paper had to be successful. No paper is any good at all for propaganda unless it has a thoroughly good financial position. So we worked very hard to build up a commercial position.'[129] Even though Beaverbrook revelled in mischief, this was about as honest a statement as he could have made and one with which many journalists sympathised, including his long-suffering editors. They rejected his 'advice' at their peril. After all, what was the point of ownership if the owner could not guarantee the publication of his own views? In effect, Beaverbrook was throwing down the gauntlet to the critics of private ownership.

Kemsley, on the other hand, diverted the commission from its main concern by taking advice from Denis Hamilton, who suggested that Kemsley put forward an authoritative plan for the training of journalists.[130] This was enthusiastically taken up by the commission and 'the Kemsley Editorial Training Plan . . . laid the foundations of professional training in journalism'.[131]

While Hennessy's view, that the final commission report 'scarcely scratched the paintwork of a Press Lord's Rolls-Royce', is justifiable, there are still nuggets of criticism to appreciate.[132] It made only one substantial recommendation: a General Council of the Press should be set up. This self-regulating body 'would derive its authority from the press itself and not from statute',[133] and 'by censuring undesirable types of journalistic conduct and by all other means, should build up a code of conduct in accordance with the highest professional standards'.[134]

The fact that the commission felt this necessary stemmed from its dislike of the activities of popular papers, highlighted in the *Manchester Guardian*. While the commission admired 'the technical efficiency, alertness and independence of the "popular" papers' it was 'distressed by their partisanship, their triviality, their distortion for the sake of the "human angle", their passion for the dramatic event as against the deeper movements'.[135] The commission registered its abhorrence of sensationalism and was shocked by intrusions into private lives, an indictment 'supported by a large collection of examples'. The commission also pointed out that though 'the Press is virtually a part of the country's political machinery . . . newspapers with few exceptions fail to supply the electorate with adequate materials for sound political judgement'.[136] They were therefore 'not meeting the needs of our society'.[137]

The *Times* agreed. The popular papers' 'defence' of 'giving the public what it wants' – such as stories about crime and sex – was cynical and 'unworthy of a responsible profession'. It added: 'The dilemma of keeping faith with the true values of journalism and appealing at the same time to a simple public remains at the core of this debate.'[138] If we overlook that condescending reference to 'a simple public', this single sentence written in June 1949 sets out the terms of the debate for the following fifty years. The schism between ethical standards and pandering to public taste was to become common to both tabloids and broadsheets.

The *Guardian* was also prescient, if premature, about sales trends. It pointed out that 'the "quality" dailies have over the last decade increased in circulation proportionately more than the "popular" – between 1937 and 1947 by 85.1 per cent against 58.5 per cent . . . The gap in numbers and resources is, of course, immense, but there is this genuine growth of what the Commission calls "a public anxious to learn and to discuss."'[139]

To the dismay of many Labour MPs, the commission had failed to ask many of the right questions about newspapers. There had been no rigorous study of editorial content and its possible effects on readers, for example. Critics of press proprietors had failed to mount a coherent or convincing argument against the mode of ownership and had certainly offered no alternative to it. Owners had seen off the challenge to their positions of power.

Downfall of a minister – and an editor

It is doubtful if the muted press approach to the 1950 election had anything to do with the commission. Among all papers, there was a general air of dissatisfaction with Attlee and little enthusiasm for him to return. Having spent a couple of years criticising the government, the *Daily Mirror* put nothing like its 1945 effort into the campaign. Maurice Edelman's claim that Labour's narrow victory was due entirely to the *Mirror*'s 'final heave' was far-fetched.[140] The Tory press used more subtlety than in 1945, with the *Daily Mail* lampooning Labour rather than demonising it. 'The *Mail*'s line in 1950 was much closer to the public mood, when the electorate was getting fed up with restrictions and shortages, and aspiring to an end to austerity'.[141] Even so, Labour managed to win again.

Years of headlines decrying the need for rationing, along with people's own experiences of its effects, had turned it into a national curse. By then, France and Austria had announced the end to rationing and even Germany was on the verge of ending petrol rations. The *Daily Mail* was probably speaking for the majority when it observed: 'We have spent £200 million on the Germans – and now they can fill their bellies with meat, work 60 hours a week, and beat us hollow in the coming trade war.'[142]

Even so, there was one bit of press misbehaviour in 1950 which should not escape attention. John Strachey, hapless victim of newspapers as food minister, had just become secretary of state for war when the first major spy scandal broke. Klaus Fuchs, a government defence scientist, was accused of passing secrets to the Soviet Union. In a wholly unjustified attempt to link Strachey to the man who came to be known as 'the atom spy', Beaverbrook's

London *Evening Standard* published a front-page story headlined 'FUCHS AND STRACHEY: A GREAT NEW CRISIS: War Minister has never disavowed Communism. Now involved in MI5 efficiency probe'.[143] The rest of Beaverbrook's papers joined in.[144]

This story, 'which represented a kind of nadir in scurrility',[145] originated from John Junor and was passed on to the *Standard* editor, Bert Gunn, by Beaverbrook.[146] Junor, then an occasional stand-in writer of the *Sunday Express*'s Cross-Bencher column, was hardly an unbiased source. He had been selected as Liberal candidate at Dundee West, Strachey's seat, and then stood down in order to give the Conservative a better chance of winning in a straight fight. Strachey's youthful flirtation with communism had long since passed and there was no question of his being anything other than a loyal Briton. In recalling the incident years later Junor offered no apology for the smear on Strachey. Instead he accused Gunn of being 'rather brash with his headlines'.[147] The fall-out was devastating for all concerned. The *Standard* lost its best foreign reporter, James Cameron, who resigned because of the 'shameful slur' on Strachey.[148] Gunn was soon deposed from his editor's chair in a policy dispute with Beaverbrook, famously throwing an ink bottle at the owner's portrait in anger.[149] As for Strachey, he never recovered his political career after the attack.[150]

The year before Strachey had also featured in the political storm over an ill-conceived scheme to grow groundnuts in Tanganyika. Both the *Times* and the *Economist* had called for Strachey's resignation.[151] The Fuchs story, though totally without foundation, was Strachey's third major clash with the press and undermined his confidence.

Finally, we must not overlook 'the biggest newspaper strike since the 1926 General Strike' which occurred at the end of July 1948. Nine titles were not published for twelve days after employers rejected a wage demand by the Typographical Association (TA).*[152]

It is sobering to note a short report from the United States in the *Times* a year later about 'a prototype of photo-composition ... which its sponsors confidently asserted would in time make the present methods of printing obsolete'.[153] At around the same time, the historian of the main craft print union noted the 'possibilities of ... revolutionary changes in the composing room' and commented that 'the development of teletype-setting and photo-composition ... are regarded by the T.A. with not a little trepidation'.[154] This surely ranks as one of the finest combinations of prophecy and understatement.

---

* Later known as the National Graphical Association.

PART TWO: 1951–1955

3. THE BARONIAL RETREAT

> [The] constant yelping about a free press means, with a few honourable exceptions, freedom to peddle scandal, crime, sex, sensationalism, hate, innuendo and the political financial use of propaganda. A newspaper is a business out to make money through advertising revenue. That is predicated on its circulation and you know what circulation depends on.[1]

British newspapers are always at war. They fight battles in their headlines against foreign dictators, against the governments of the day, against a host of enemies, imagined and real. They are perpetually fighting each other, for stories, for sales, for advertising. They are also embroiled, day by day, in a series of internal clashes, between proprietors and editors, between executives and staff, between reporters and subs, between news editors and reporters, between reporters and reporters, and so on down the line. During this era, and for the following thirty years, there was also a continuous trial of strength between management and unions.

Over time, it came to be accepted in Fleet Street that conflict of any kind was both natural and beneficial, and, making virtue of the vice, its practitioners liked to refer to it as 'creative tension'. They pointed to the nature of the job, its immediacy and its subjectivity, arguing that it invited differences of opinion which, in turn, created a climate in which autocrats thrived. This was particularly true of popular papers, where spontaneity and iconoclasm were considered to be the hallmarks of good journalism.

So the history of newspapers, even if it follows a logic dictated by an underlying economic imperative and by changing social developments, is riven with personality disputes. Some of these have been petty, but their outcomes have had a profound effect on the fortunes of individual titles and entire newspaper groups. The early 1950s were marked by a series of disputes with far-reaching consequences: Bartholomew versus King; Rothermere versus his editors, his wife and Randolph Churchill; Beaverbrook versus Tory policies (though not the Tory leader); the Odhams management versus the *Daily Herald* editor; Laurence Cadbury versus Walter Layton at the *News Chronicle*; and Kemsley versus his own demons. As if to prove the point about the need for tension, where there was an absence of dispute, such as at the *Times*, there tended to be lethargy.

The quality papers, both daily and Sunday, looked anything but healthy, though the *Financial Times* and *Daily Telegraph* did buck the trend by increasing sales. Williams argued that growth was inhibited by the small numbers of people who 'benefit from higher education'. Pessimistic about educational improvement, he believed that the qualities had already reached their high point.[2] It was a time when economic realities intruded into the previously ordered lives of proprietors. Profits were harder to come by as costs rose, and some barons began to buckle under the strain. Initially, they were unable to expand their way out of trouble because of continued newsprint rationing, even with their favoured Conservative party in power. So they were paying more for their paper while having to reject the demands of advertisers to increase pagination. Once rationing eased they faced a different problem: now they could add pages and publish more ads, but unions were quick to demand more for the extra work it entailed.

At first, renewed profitability blinded owners because concessions to print workers appeared trivial. The hiring of more staff or a rise of a couple of shillings (10p) here and there mattered less than the chance to publish more copies. This 'bonus' money was then consolidated into regular wage packets, irrespective of input or output. Union leaders within each paper, divided into several different unions and then into different chapels within those unions, gradually came to realise the advantages to be gained by exploiting a set of circumstances specific to the national press. Competition between owners ensured that they rarely adopted a united front; owners were relatively unconcerned about profits; the product had a shelf life of only twenty-four hours. In this climate, in which managements largely acted as the middle men between owners and workers, seeking to placate both, the unions managed to pull off their greatest coup by gaining control of the labour market. They operated closed shops, deciding on manning levels and then supplying the workers.

Proprietors didn't grasp the significance of the month-long national newspaper strike in 1955 because it involved electricians and engineers rather than mainstream print unions and was also related to a wave of union militancy in the docks, in the mines and in transport. So it didn't seem to signal any problem specific to Fleet Street itself. Yet this was the period in which the future pattern of industrial relations 'in the print' was set. Overall, the twenty-six-day stoppage resulted in the loss of 600 million copies and the Newspaper Proprietors Association presented it as a triumph for their policy of standing firm.[3]

Despite some relaxation, newsprint was to be the last commodity subjected to rationing. A frustrated *Times*, couching its argument in the now familiar guise of it being a threat to press freedom, argued: 'The Press should have been at the head of the list for freedom, not at the tail . . . It is time for the Government to show that they no longer rate the service of public opinion so far behind the enjoyment of tobacco, sweets and Hollywood films.'[4] So upset was its owner, Lord Astor, that he circumvented the rationing edict by agreeing to buy paper from a British mill which, due to its better quality, was not classified as newsprint. It cost almost a fifth more than newsprint but the paper took the risk and dropped out of the industry's newsprint pool. It was a disastrous ploy. Soon after terms were agreed, rationing ended and the *Times* was obliged to pay 20 per cent more than the rest of Fleet Street for its paper for the next twenty years.[5] Astor had imperilled his own future.

Lord Kemsley's empire was tottering too. As Bracken gleefully remarked to Beaverbrook: 'Poor Gomer has a lot of trouble on his plate.'[6] First to go was his *Daily Graphic*, sold to Rothermere in 1952. Three years later he merged the *Sunday Chronicle* with the *Empire News*. He also sold off his biggest provincial paper, the Manchester-based *Daily Dispatch*, which had lost its Lancashire preeminence once the *Daily Express* began to print in Manchester. So the *News Chronicle*, trying to stave off its own demise, gratefully swallowed it.[7] Kemsley's right-hand man, Denis Hamilton, did his best to inject some vitality into another ailing title, the *Sunday Graphic*, by elevating its thirty-three-year-old art editor, Mike Randall, to the editor's chair.[8] Sales went up but Randall soon moved on, accepting double the wages to become the number four in the *Daily Mirror* hierarchy.

Kemsley also sold his vast Manchester printing plant at Withy Grove to the *Mirror*, along with his Glasgow titles, the *Daily Record* and *Sunday Mail*. Kemsley told his shareholders that these disposals would 'streamline' the group, enabling it to face the future 'with greater confidence and security'. Bracken, as shrewd as ever, was not fooled: 'The Lord of Withygrove . . . has a noisy mind and is apt to lay down the law on subjects in which he is completely out of his depth . . . which confirmed my view that the greatest mistake he made in his life was to part from his brother Bill [Camrose] who kept him in his proper department, which was the getting of advertising, and never would allow him loose in editorial matters.'[9] Indeed, Camrose remained 'dignified, unostentatious and hard-working', never succumbing to Kemsley's 'delusions of grandeur' as he 'became ever more foolishly plutocratic'.[10]

Whatever their individual characters, even when acting together the press barons could not frustrate the will of parliament. They were forced in 1953 to end their five-year resistance and set up a press council, the central recommendation of the 1948 Royal Commission. Its members, and a vociferous group of MPs, grew impatient with complaints by owners and editors that it would infringe press freedom.[11] After the threat of a Private Member's Bill, a watered-down version of the recommended council arrived in July.[12] Self-regulation had arrived to police the ethics of an industry which liked to cast itself as society's sole moral guardian.

As far as the *Times* was concerned, it had not arrived quickly enough. In 1955, in celebration of the 100 years since the repeal of stamp duty on newspapers, it noted that the 'gargantuan' national press's 'race for mammoth circulations has led . . . to a disgraceful lowering of values. The baser instincts are being pandered to, not only in lasciviousness . . . but in social attitudes and in conduct as well.'[13] Rather than blame journalists it saw the problem in terms of 'the state of newspaper economics' which, by turning the press into 'predominantly a business enterprise' engendered the bad behaviour. It is highly likely that, if it wasn't written by William Haley, it was inspired by him. In different ways the same conundrum – public good versus private profit – was to surface throughout the rest of the century.

Farewell to Bart! Long Live the King!

Arguably the most significant change occurred at the *Mirror*. By the end of 1951, Cecil King decided that the whisky-soaked Bartholomew had to go. The upper-crust Wykehamist could take no more of his belligerent, foul-mouthed boss from the other side of the tracks. Incoherent by 9.30 a.m., King contended that Bart's 'drunkenness reached such proportions that something had to be done'.[14] It was also noticeable that *Daily Mirror* sales slumped dramatically throughout that year, falling by more than 200,000.

So King orchestrated a palace coup, assiduously persuading his fellow directors to vote the 'bullying alcoholic'[15] out of his post as chairman, and electing King himself in his place. The crucial vote in King's favour was that of Bart's friend and protégé, the editor Sylvester Bolam. Philip Zec, the famous wartime cartoonist who was now *Sunday Pictorial* editor and a director, bravely acted as the board's messenger to the drunken Bartholomew. He asked Bart to resign, but Bart refused in the certainty that Bolam would support him. When told that Bolam was voting with the others he cried out: 'Judas!' and then broke down, weeping while drinking copious amounts of whisky, and later sharing a bottle with the bemused hall porter.[16] He also turned up in El Vino's to be met by Cudlipp, Zec and Bill Connor, and there he veered 'tipsily from defiance to remorse'.[17]

Bart was over sixty-five and he had served his paper well. However sad his last days were, and despite the considerable egos of his immediate successors who suffered such poor relationships with him, they gave him his due. King did on one occasion one attempt to airbrush Bart from history, but later made amends.[18] Cudlipp subsequently observed that Bart's had been 'the paramount newspaper' achievement of the twentieth century, and he meant it.[19] Putting the hyperbole in perspective, what Bartholomew did was to edit a paper which appealed directly to working-class readers in the most basic way. Moving on from the Northcliffe formula, which had striven to maintain respectability along with its populism, Bart eschewed the former and embraced the latter. In so doing he was responsible for creating the tabloid form and, to a limited extent, its content. Like Bart, the paper tended to be crude.

King, recognising the problem but lacking the editorial knowledge or expertise to refashion the paper himself, soon called on Bart's young disciple, Hugh Cudlipp. 'Let's get together,' King wrote to him, 'and make a dent in the history of our times.'[20] Cudlipp, deputy to *Sunday Express* editor John Gordon, was delighted. He had 'never really fitted in at the *Express*', being 'outmanoeuvred at every turn' by Gordon.[21] He later referred to his time there as 'two years in the *Express* glasshouse'.[22] So the prodigal son gleefully returned to the *Mirror* family.

The characters and backgrounds of Cecil King and Hugh Cudlipp complemented each other perfectly. King was cold where Cudlipp was hot. King was taciturn where Cudlipp was loquacious. King was intellectual where Cudlipp was instinctual. King was calculating where Cudlipp was spontaneous. As Cudlipp often said of his early years under King: 'He had the knowledge. I had the passion.' What they shared, for very different reasons, was a rebel streak. King was conscious of being his family's black sheep. Cudlipp was a natural enemy of the establishment. Both men cheerfully wrote of their differences, most notably Cudlipp.[23]

King was born in 1901 to Sir Lucas White King, a senior civil servant in India, and Geraldine Harmsworth, a sister of Northcliffe and Harold Rothermere. He enjoyed a typical upper middle-class upbringing, going to Winchester and Oxford, but grew up in awe of his uncle. When he left school, he joined the family firm, starting with the *Daily Record* in Glasgow and then the *Daily Mail* in London for three years, switching from the editorial to the commercial side. Rothermere then moved him to the *Daily Mirror*, which he still controlled, and King became its advertising director in 1929, later combining it with finance director.

King expected to be made chairman and was stung when Bartholomew got the post. King was regarded by an impartial onlooker as 'shy, cold, calculating, with much of his uncle Rothermere's business sense'.[24] Everyone seemed to agree on that point.[25] Cudlipp, even in a friendly assessment, referred to 'the forbidding factor' of King's 'aloofness'.[26] Wintour thought King 'very tall and clumsy' with 'a fastidious mind, artistic tastes and a shyness that made it difficult for him to communicate with others'. He was not alone in considering him 'immensely vain,'[27] as a *Newsweek* description suggested: 'He is a muscular Sidney Greenstreet, a magnanimous John D. Rockefeller, an intellectual Captain Bligh.'[28]

The calculating side of King's nature is illustrated by his concurring with the decision to turn the *Mirror* away from its right-wing agenda in the 1930s. This had nothing to do with his political convictions. It was a commercial initiative aimed at filling a gap in the market by attracting working-class readers who found the Tory papers unacceptable and the *Daily Herald* too worthy. He was also motivated by his own family circumstances: the Rothermeres had little regard for him and he was keen to show them that he, rather than cousin Esmond, was the true inheritor of the Northcliffe mantle as a visionary newspaperman and a political force.

To that end, he was happy to embrace a leftish position in public, once telling a TV interviewer: 'I am interested deep down in the underdog.'[29] It must have been very deep down indeed, though the *Mirror*'s political historian, Maurice Edelman, appears to have been taken in by this remark too, claiming that King had radical instincts. In fact, he didn't have a socialist bone in his body. A product of his class, he happily played the maverick as a means of attaining business success while revelling in the opportunity to thumb his nose at his appalled relations. King's melancholy stemmed in part from his anomalous position: he was a newspaper controller rather than a newspaper proprietor.

Hugh Cudlipp, in spite of his own highly developed sense of self-worth, laboured under no such illusions. He saw himself as a journalist and, if not a socialist, undoubtedly a radical, a propagandist and pamphleteer.[30] Here was a man of genuine star quality, a charismatic Fleet Street titan, a wizard of popular journalism who, enjoying the luxury of King's patronage and the absence of proprietorship, was able to create a newspaper that forged a unique relationship with its readers. The fact that the legend of Cudlipp survived the ignominy of his final years in charge of the *Mirror* organisation, living on through his lengthy retirement, says a great deal about his character and his abilities. He was not without faults, but his virtues immeasurably outdistanced his vices. His rise to eminence was based on precocious journalistic flair. Born in 1913 in Cardiff, the son of a commercial traveller, he left school at fourteen to be a cub reporter on the *Penarth News*. At sixteen, he went to the *Manchester Evening Chronicle* and, the following year, moved on to Blackpool as a reporter. In his nineteenth year, after a spell of sub-editing, he was appointed features editor of the *Sunday Chronicle* in London under the inspirational Jimmy Drawbell.

When the *Daily Mirror* advertised for a features editor, the twenty-one-year-old Cudlipp replied 'for a lark' and got the job.[31] He joined on the same 1935 day as William Connor, who would become famous for his Cassandra column, and Peter Wilson, equally memorable for his sports columns. By twenty-four, he was editing the *Sunday Pictorial*. In spite of his lack of education, his reporting, sub-editing and design skills were superb. Looking at Cudlipp's early work and reading his later books and articles, it is clear where his talent lay. He had a unique way of expressing himself, whether in a headline or a lengthy paragraph. At his best, and his best occurred more often and over a longer period than any other popular journalist of his generation, he struck a chord with readers.

By the time Cudlipp returned as editor of the *Sunday Pictorial* (with the incumbent, Philip Zec, moving gracefully aside) he was thirty-nine, a confident man sure of his skills, aware of Bart's journalistic shortcomings, and anxious to prove that he could carry forward the tabloid revolution. The *Pictorial* was a mixture of highbrow and lowbrow, offering pictures of scantily clad women alongside a column by the populist academic historian

A. J. P. Taylor, who ignored the taunts of friends, such as *New Statesman* editor Kingsley Martin, because it gave him 'the chance of addressing five million people'.[32] That kind of attitude was music to Cudlipp's ears.

Edelman understood that Cudlipp's 'strength as a journalist was, like Bartholomew's, irreverence'.[33] But Cudlipp's was more perceptive and premeditated than Bart's.[34] The *Pictorial* canvas wasn't broad enough for Cudlipp, and King soon elevated him to a more strategic role, promoting him in 1953 to editor-in-chief and editorial director. From this position he would stamp his mark on both of the group's papers, especially the flagship *Daily Mirror*.

Their first decisions were to appoint the able and talented Colin Valdar as editor of the *Pictorial*, and to eject the ineffective and dull Bolam from the *Daily Mirror* chair. King had only kept him in place out of gratitude for his key vote in dislodging Bart. Their choice of replacement, Jack Nener, was very different from Bolam. A former sub, the forthright Welshman, 'sentimental, warm [and] offering the right blend of bounce and emotion for the *Mirror* readership', was anything but dull.[35] He was the personification of a tabloid editor, a better groomed if infinitely more profane version of the editor in Ben Hecht's classic newspaper play *The Front Page*. His volcanic temper, occasionally assumed to provide Cudlipp with entertainment for his guests, and sometimes due to his gout, was legendary. With a cigarette clenched between his teeth, moustache twitching and his bow-tie bobbing as he swore at a sub for some trivial misdemeanour, he set the tone for a generation of tabloid editors.

When I arrived on the *Mirror* subs' desk nine years after he had departed, older staff still spoke of him with awe. Though the junior partner in the triumvirate with King and Cudlipp, Nener played a key role in the *Mirror*'s rise. He certainly understood his audience, knowing what people liked while aware of the need to publish important news, as a recollection by Donald Zec illustrates. He saw Nener hovering over the shoulder of picture editor Simon Clyne, who was on the phone discussing a theological matter with a member of his local synagogue. It was some minutes before Clyne became aware of Nener and, when he did, he cupped the phone and asked: 'You want something, Jack?' 'Yes,' replied Nener. 'I want some tits to go with the rail strike.'[36] Unsurprisingly, Nener generated apocryphal stories and his wife, Audrey Whiting – a long-serving journalist on both the *Daily* and *Sunday Mirror* – disputed one told by Marje Proops. When Cudlipp persuaded Proops to rejoin the *Mirror* as a columnist in 1954, he took her to Nener's office. The dapper, white-haired man in an expensive suit rose, stretched out his hand and said: 'Fucking glad to meet you!'[37]

Nener was a technician. It was Cudlipp who, in Geoffrey Goodman's words, translated 'the feelings, attitudes, beliefs, prejudices, romantic aspirations and illusions, nostalgic dreams and awkward-squad absurdities of the post-war masses into a kind of national common currency'.[38] As a description of Cudlipp's *Mirror* in the 1950s and early 1960s, that has never been bettered. Cudlipp had the art of creating as well as recording news, through such impertinent headlines as 'Should Churchill Retire?',[39] which certainly upset the prime minister.[40] To parody the 'coming-out' balls for debutantes during the London season, Cudlipp instituted a '*Mirror* Debs' ball'. As good as this froth was, Cudlipp's major skill was in bringing alive serious political issues and foreign affairs, making such stories, if not entirely understandable, then certainly interesting enough to read, by 'the politically illiterate'.[41]

His transformation of the *Daily Mirror* was swift and spectacular. Sales did not take off immediately, but the 1951 dip was overcome and for the rest of the decade the paper enjoyed a steady circulation of about 4.6 million, some 500,000 ahead of its nearest competitor, the *Daily Express*. What was different was both the range and presentation of the editorial content. Cudlipp positively revelled in the challenge of making serious topics accessible to everyone. So confident was he of his paper's, and his own, standing that within months of acquiring his job as editorial supremo he wrote a memorable history of the *Mirror*'s first fifty years, ***Publish and Be Damned!*** One of its final lines sums up Cudlipp's underlying philosophy of newspapers, and one of the reasons he was so highly regarded by his peers. 'An immense power for good lies within its grasp,' he wrote of the *Daily Mirror*.[42] Here was a propagandist with a public service credo.

While Cudlipp was improving the *Mirror*, King was beginning to build an international newspaper empire. Bart had already added the popular forces' weekly *Reveille* to the group, achieving a 3 million sale in 1951. Turning to West Africa, where King had bought Nigerian papers in the late 1940s, he then launched a daily paper in Ghana in 1950 and bought another in Sierra Leone. His story of his ventures in the region is offensively patronising and his central editorial aim, 'to keep the political temperature low', was overtly political and vaguely imperialist.[43] A more commercial, and wiser, purchase came in 1955, when King took over Lord Kemsley's debt-ridden, loss-making Glasgow group comprising the *Daily Record*, *Sunday Mail* and *Evening News*.

The ups and downs of two more Cudlipps

The Bartholomew blood-letting at the *Mirror* improved the health of an already healthy patient, but blood-letting at the *Daily Herald* did nothing to cure the paper's sickly state. In 1950, the post of foreign editor was abolished, the Paris and Berlin offices were closed, and the central European stringer was dropped. No correspondent was sent to cover the Korean war. On the plus side, cartoonist David Low joined, but every initiative failed to turn the tide. In 1951, the paper underwent a major redesign, which Allen Hutt claimed was 'the first and only time that a broadsheet has been given the tabloid treatment . . . an object lesson in the error of such an approach'.[44] There were several changes of mind, with new mastheads and remakes of the front page.

The redesign made no difference to sales. The very gradual slippage in the previous couple of years accelerated once the paper fell below the psychologically important 2 million mark. From then on it lost more than 50,000 copies a year. The *Herald*'s historian, pointing to the losses 'running parallel' with the Labour party's 'electoral fortunes', rightly stops short of suggesting a causal link.[45] That would have been too neat an answer.

Then, towards the end of 1953, came 'a thunderclap . . . a totally unforeseen upheaval' when Percy Cudlipp resigned after thirteen years as editor.[46] There wasn't a whisper before his announcement. Hannen Swaffer reported that 'Percy had his afternoon conference as usual . . . without telling anybody he was leaving' and then calmly pinned up his resignation notice in the newsroom.[47]

Cudlipp had had enough of the often conflicting pressure from the trade unions and the Odhams management. The former, in the person of the authoritarian transport union boss Arthur Deakin, demanded the kind of editorial which only Labour party moderates could enjoy, while the latter was pushing for a broader *Mirror*-style agenda. Douglas Jay, both a *Herald* leader writer and a Labour MP, witnessed Cudlipp's frustration. Odhams, he wrote, 'had been constantly pressing him to produce plans for "raising the circulation to four million" and he finally had the bravery to write a memorandum saying bluntly that this could not be done unless very large sums of money were spent'.[48]

As surprising as Cudlipp's departure was his choice of successor: Sydney Elliott, the none-too-successful former *Evening Standard* and *Reynolds News* editor, described as 'a dour but receptive Scotsman'.[49] According to Jay, from the moment of his arrival 'what organisation had previously existed at the *Herald* slid into chaos. Editorial conferences were often incoherent. Responsibilities were blurred.' It became a 'bear garden'.[50] One journalist, Hugh Pilcher, told Jay that 'the situation was now so bad that soon someone would be stabbed in the chest'.[51]

It hardly helped sales when the *Herald*, nominally on the left, launched assaults on Bevanites that were so ferocious they occasionally embarrassed Gaitskell's supporters. Through its privileged position, the paper had an inside track on Labour party events, but its political and journalistic functions often clashed. In 1954, Elliott spiked parliamentary correspondent Leslie Hunter's scoop that Attlee was to retire and name Gaitskell as his chosen successor. He thought it 'premature' and 'unwise' to run the story.[52] Percy Cudlipp was missed: he might well have found a way to have run the story. He went on to write a column for the *News Chronicle* and then to become the successful editor of the *New Scientist*, which were to be the most satisfying years of his career.[53]

While the *Daily Mirror* managed the trick of accentuating the positive aspects of working-class life, cheekily debunking establishment 'enemies' in a way with which people could identify, the *Daily Herald* continued to fight the class war in an unimaginative, if principled, manner. It could be lively, and it did take tentative steps towards populism, but the overall effect was unconvincing. The die was cast for the *Herald*.

Three days before Percy's departure, the third of the remarkable Cudlipp brothers became a Fleet Street editor too. Reg Cudlipp took over from Arthur Waters at the *News of the World*. Waters, almost a part-time editor, 'didn't let the facts interfere with a good story'.[54] According to one of his staff, 'when we couldn't find a picture of the famous white horse at the Wembley Cup Final . . . he had one painted in'.[55] He often wrote the flowery first paragraphs of the *News of the World*'s court reports. Stafford Somerfield provides a superb example: 'He conducted an affair with two wives, one married bigamously, and two other ladies, all on £8 a week, living a life which, as history tells us, has ruined empires, toppled thrones, and brought millionaires to poverty and disgrace.'[56]

Cudlipp's promotion from deputy editor wasn't a surprise. With Waters so often absent, pulling pints at his Covent Garden pub, Cudlipp was the paper's backbone. A 'tall and distinguished-looking man who might easily be mistaken for a diplomat or a judge',[57] he was 'a master of detail' who worked long hours and refused to delegate.[58] Despite his undoubted skill and energy, Cudlipp was aware that he couldn't sustain the paper's sales. The pattern of life was changing, he said. People were beginning to watch TV and going out in cars, and costs were forcing up cover prices.[59] In May 1955 circulation dropped below 8 million for the first time since before the war. The gentle downward sales slide of Britain's and, at the time, the world's highest-selling newspaper had begun.

Beaverbrook: when no news is good news

In 1952, Lord Beaverbrook's portrait appeared on the cover of *Newsweek*. The magazine calculated, by adding together the sales of his *Daily Express* and London *Evening Standard*, that he was then selling more papers per day – 5 million – than anyone else in the world. He was seventy-three, as sprightly, mischievous and meddlesome as ever, even though his political dreams and schemes had come to nothing. He had, said Williams, 'achieved everything except his main purpose': political power.[60] As his biographers pointed out, from 1945 onwards, 'the post-war world order might have been designed to frustrate and annoy Beaverbrook'.[61] Britain was in hock to the United States which was, by now, the dominant power. Britain's empire was being dismantled. His friend Churchill had been defeated and Beaverbrook's access to power, and knowledge, was removed. Beaverbrook could not countenance change. He retained his journalistic nous, but ensured that his papers continued to peddle his imperial ambitions and his scepticism about America.

Renowned for his dislike of the royal family, Beaverbrook was the epitome of a monarch who, convinced he has earned his crown in battle, believes he should be able to exercise superior rights. It's impossible to read the biographies and the reminiscences, and to listen to the anecdotes of those who knew him well, without realising that, in spite of his unworldliness, his lack of grasp of the mechanics of editing a paper, that he was the driving force. Convinced of his own infallibility, he locked all those who worked for him into a psychological straitjacket: I am the boss; I have the power; I know best; you editors are the transient holders of office.

The same could have been said, perhaps, for other proprietors. What set Beaverbrook apart was his awareness of the effect of his daily, sometimes hourly, stream of critical memos on his editors and managers. He knew they dissembled, imitating the way in which staff dealt with the implausible demands of the newspaper owner in Evelyn Waugh's *Scoop*: 'Up to a point, Lord Copper, up to a point.' At times it amused him, at times it appalled him. Power gave him the choice of response: kindness and cruelty were two sides of the same coin.

Though it was never clear to outsiders whether Beaverbrook was fooling himself or not, it is difficult to believe he ever did or said anything without realising its effect. What others would regard as indiscretions were, for Beaverbrook, entertaining diversions, as an illuminating vignette by Robert (Lord) Blake shows. One afternoon in April 1951 Blake was listening to a conversation between Beaverbrook and Brendan Bracken on the terrace at Beaverbrook's country home, Cherkley, in which both men talked of their respect for editorial freedom. 'I have no idea what is going to be in the *Sunday Express* tomorrow,' said Beaverbrook. Bracken nodded: 'I never interfere in the *Financial Times*.' This nonsense was interrupted by a butler bringing the news that Aneurin Bevan and Harold Wilson had resigned from Attlee's cabinet. 'Before I could draw breath,' wrote Blake, 'Beaverbrook was telephoning instructions on the treatment of this startling development to John Junor, the political correspondent of the *Sunday Express*, and Bracken was doing the same to a man . . . who, presumably, had a similar role at the *Financial Times*. When they had finished – and it took quite a long time – they resumed their discussion on editorial freedom as if nothing at all had happened.'[62]

Beaverbrook loved to tease. Asked to explain how his editorials appeared, he replied: 'I just talk into a machine and it comes out in the paper.'[63] His power also allowed him to suppress news. In June 1953 Churchill suffered a stroke while at dinner with the Italian prime minister in Downing Street. After two days, his doctor feared for his life and it was obvious that he couldn't go to the planned summit with Eisenhower in Bermuda. His private secretary, John Colville, called on Bracken, Beaverbrook and Camrose to help in 'silencing Fleet Street'.[64] They paced the lawn at Chartwell, Churchill's home, and composed a bulletin which read: 'The Prime Minister has had no respite for a long time from his arduous duties and is in need of a complete rest. We have therefore advised him to abandon his journey to Bermuda and to lighten his duties for a month'. Colville later wrote of his admiration for the 'success in gagging Fleet Street'.[65] Churchill even recuperated at Beaverbrook's French house in September and it wasn't until he had recovered that 'rumours' of a stroke reported in American papers were 'repeated with blazing publicity by the *Daily Mirror*'.[66]

Churchill's return to power in 1951 had not enthused Beaverbrook to renew his involvement in politics. He had given his friend campaign advice, but the free traders were in the ascendant and his protectionist and imperialist views were scorned. In an act of spite or frustration, or both, Beaverbrook ordered the crusader symbol, which had appeared on the paper's masthead since the 1931 launch of his Empire Crusade, to be chained. Most *Daily Express* readers, if they noticed at all, were probably baffled.

Around the same time he also secretly funded the left-wing weekly *Tribune*, after a plea for money from editor Michael Foot. His motive was never clear. It could have been affection for Foot, his former *Standard* editor. It might have been Machiavellian: to help to ensure the continuing split in the Labour party. He certainly used it as a recruiting ground, eventually hiring three of its leading staff, Bob Edwards, Robert Pitman and Woodrow Wyatt. He rehired Foot too, as chief book reviewer at the *Evening Standard*.

Beaverbrook should have been pleased with the progress of his beloved *Daily Express* in these years, even if piqued at the *Daily Mirror*'s ascendancy. According to his biographers, the paper lost none of its sparkle: 'It was bright all the way through, well subbed, well written, classless, newsy and snappy.'[67] Indeed, other Fleet Street journalists still considered the editor, Arthur Christiansen, to be a master of his craft, evidenced by his front page on the eve of the coronation: 'All This – and Everest Too!'[68] Apart from that headline – written, incidentally, by managing editor Ted Pickering[69] – and another which said 'Be proud of Britain on this day', which caught the growing sense of optimism after years of post-war austerity, that edition doesn't appear now as a classic. The drawing of the Queen's coronation dress looks flat and the good design of the top half is ruined by the use of thick rules and clumsy cut-out picture at the bottom. The copy is merely adequate. But it did capture the mood among a certain section of what we might call the upper working class, the foremen and junior managers. They could just about detect that things were getting better.

Embedded in that affirmative outlook lay the success of the *Express*, as Francis Williams, the shrewdest of commentators, noted at the time. The *Express*, he wrote, 'has brought sophistication to the suburbs, but it also brings romance into thousands of dull lives. It is the paper of escape, but of escape not into an invented world but into the real one miraculously turned brighter than reality, a world in which everything happens at great speed and a higher tension than common experience and all the drab moments are left out.'[70] This echoes Christiansen's rosy view of his own paper: 'When you looked at the front page you said, "Good Heavens", when you looked at the middle page you said, "Holy Smoke", and by the time you got to the back page – well, I'd have to utter a profanity to show how exciting it was.'[71] One of his lieutenants thought that Chris's paper 'persuaded its readers that life was vivid and sparkling when it was . . . quite otherwise, for most people'.[72]

After reading *Express*es from those years my view, admittedly from hindsight, is less positive. The excitement generated by the *Express*, and not to be found in either the *Daily Mail* or *News Chronicle* of the same period, was largely old-fashioned hype. Beaverbrook and Christiansen were Fleet Street's Barnum and Bailey. It worked, of course, as the sales figures prove. In 1955, the *Daily Express* was selling almost 4.1 million copies. Quite apart from Beaverbrook's obsolescent politics, the seeds of the paper's future problems can be detected in the way it ignored reality, failing to make the kind of links with its readers pioneered by the *Daily Mirror*.

Beaverbrook's *Sunday Express* was an altogether different paper from his daily. Editor John Gordon had created a winning formula which consisted of a rigid right-wing editorial line, a patriotic adventure serial, unmalicious gossip about society people, malicious gossip about politicians (in Cross-Bencher), meticulous cartoons of social comment by Carl Giles, and comprehensive sports coverage. From a humble Presbyterian background in Dundee, Gordon was born in 1890 during an age when, he remarked, bringing 'a Sunday newspaper into your home was almost equal to opening the door to the devil'.[73] He began his career in his home city, taking carrier pigeons to football matches to ensure the speedy receipt of results in the office.[74] After serving in the first world war with the Rifle Brigade he joined the London *Evening News* as chief sub-editor. In 1924, he took the same position at the *Daily Express* and just two years later Beaverbrook – recognising 'the burning flame within the granite exterior' – made him editor of the *Sunday Express*.[75]

During his reign, he was responsible for several innovations, including the first crossword puzzle and the first astrology column. The Sunday paper market also gradually outstripped the daily market, a 'tremendous transformation' in which, Gordon noted, 'I played a not inconsiderable part.'[76] As that supreme egotist Hugh Cudlipp later noted, Gordon was 'the supreme egotist'.[77] John Junor, another man not noted for diffidence, regarded Gordon as 'one of the greatest journalists of his time, but it was extraordinarily difficult to like him'.[78] Gordon treated all his staff, of whatever seniority, as his minions. He acted like a grand sub-editor, scrawling hundreds of corrections 'in illegible, microscopic handwriting' on proofs which then 'looked as if a tarantula spider had dipped each foot in blue black ink and crawled over every page'.[79]

Beaverbrook evidently didn't like Gordon too much, nor did he trust his political judgement, designating his son, Max Aitken, to oversee the contents of Cross-Bencher.[80] In 1952, after Gordon had been editor for twenty-four years, Beaverbrook eased him aside, making him editor-in-chief and giving him a column which became hugely popular with its mixture of homespun homilies, gentle political sarcasm and occasional vicious paragraph. Into his chair came Harold Keeble, then an executive on the *Daily Express* and recognised as a brilliant designer. But there is much more to editing than layout, and it proved a disastrous appointment.[81]

Keeble, described with metropolitan snobbery by Princess Margaret's husband Lord Snowdon as having 'a Yorkshire accent but' being 'very grand',[82] was to exercise great influence on several newspapers. During a long career he was responsible for the bold projection of pictures on the *Daily Express* known as Photo News and for the improved design of the *Daily Mail*, and he was mentor both to Mike Molloy years before he became *Daily Mirror* editor and to Deirdre McSharry, who progressed from newspapers to become a fine magazine editor. Though the columnist Anne Scott-James thought Keeble 'a great editor',[83] hardly anyone else did, least of all Beaverbrook, who fired him in 1954.

His next choice proved to be much wiser: John Donald Brown Junor. Here was a man with a similar outlook to Gordon's who was happy to adopt and adapt his editorial formula. He was a much better writer than Gordon and, though he was tough on his staff, nothing like so nasty. Junor got close to Beaverbrook early in his career, sharing his boss's 'enormous disregard of the Establishment and a contempt for privilege'.[84] In 1951, Beaverbrook made him chief leader writer and assistant editor of the *Daily Express*. Just two years later he was deputy editor of the *Evening Standard* and within 12 months rose to be editor of the *Sunday Express* aged thirty-two.

Junor, born in a Glasgow tenement in 1919 and raised in a council house, was the son of a steelworker and an ambitious, upwardly mobile mother. She ensured that he took his schooling seriously and he managed to get into Glasgow University to read English literature, where he also became a prominent Liberal. He joined the Fleet Air Arm at the outbreak of war and in 1944 was made, by chance, editor of its paper, *Flight Deck*. From then on he was determined to be a journalist, and managed to get subbing shifts at the London office of an Australian newspaper group. He also pursued his political career, failing to win Kincardine and West Aberdeenshire for the Liberals in 1945 by just 642 votes. In 1947, he landed a reporting job at the *Daily Express* and soon specialised in covering by-elections. Beaverbrook, ever aware of young talent, chose Junor to act as Beverley Baxter's stand-in for the *Sunday Express* Cross-Bencher column and generously gave him and his wife a rent-free house on his Cherkley estate, which the Junors were to enjoy for ten years.

Junor wanted everyone to believe that he alone was not a toady to Beaverbrook but, like so many employed by the powerful, he often trimmed his sails. He did defy Beaverbrook by refusing to allow a manager into his editorial conferences.[85] But, scared to reveal to Beaverbrook that he was suffering from a stomach ulcer, he accepted champagne from 'the old bugger' as he privately referred to him,[86] consequently suffering appalling pain followed by a haemorrhage.

Beaverbrook took less interest in the *Sunday Express* than he did the London *Evening Standard*. Though outsold by Rothermere's *Evening News*, it carried more political clout and was more sophisticated, if less profitable. It was edited for five years after the war by Bert Gunn, who hired several writers later to become stars, such as Sam White, Paris correspondent for forty years, the film and theatre critic Milton Shulman, who stayed for almost fifty years, and Rebecca West, then a novelist of repute who produced journalism of high quality.[87] One other Gunn signing was a leader writer, Charles Wintour, destined to become the paper's most important figure.

Gunn and Beaverbrook agreed to differ when the editor, eager to compete with the *Evening News* for higher sales, advocated that the *Standard* should be more sensationalist. So Gunn went 'without recrimination or bitterness'[88] in 1950 and a more pliable Beaverbrook man, Percy Elland, took over. As *Daily Express* northern editor, steeped in the Christiansen way of pleasing his proprietor while circumventing his crazier notions, Elland knew how to play the game. Elland, 'a great-hearted, plump, rosy-cheeked man with twinkly eyes and a splendid sense of humour',[89] concentrated on news coverage, granting Beaverbrook complete licence to hire and fire in areas of the paper he cared little about, such as politics, arts and features. In 1952, Beaverbrook sacked the experienced theatre critic Beverley Baxter in favour of the 'unknown' twenty-six-year-old Kenneth Tynan.

Over the next fifteen months, Tynan ensured that he would be known for a long time to come, demolishing some of the most famous actors of the generation. His relationship with the paper was anything but straightforward: he even threatened to sue Elland for libel for publishing letters critical of him. Beaverbrook immediately fired him, appointing Shulman in his stead. Tynan, mistakenly thinking Baxter was to return, explained his departure in his final *Standard* review with the immortal line: 'The older generation is knocking at the door.' It was deleted.[90]

The *Evening News* was a very different kind of paper to the *Standard*. It prided itself on giving working-class boys a chance to become journalists. Youngsters were hired as copy boys, whose duty was to accompany reporters to big events or setpiece stories and then rush their scrawled copy to the nearest phone box to dictate it to the copy-takers at the paper's Carmelite House offices. They were encouraged to go to evening classes and generally graduated to being copy-takers themselves. If they showed promise, they would be given 'little assignments', such as local fires, and often wrote publicity copy for Rothermere's pet Ideal Home Exhibition. Percy Trumble and George Hollingberry, who both later became news editors, were among the many who benefited from that start.[91]

This form of intake set the *News* apart, breeding a clannish loyalty within the office quite different from other Fleet Street papers. There was much less of a turnover in staff with journalists staying for many years. This tended to create a sense of family. Kendall McDonald, another who became a news editor, started in 1950 at about the same time as his father, the former sports editor H. R. McDonald, was retiring. He had joined the *News* in 1902.[92]

Despite many staff coming from outside London, the *News* came to be seen as 'the Cockney paper', revelling in the capital's unique post-war atmosphere. A staid Yorkshireman, Guy Schofield, was editor during the final war years until 1950. He was replaced by John Marshall, who had distinguished himself as a war correspondent. Remembered fondly for his addiction to cricket, Hollingberry recalled: 'You could rush into Marshall's office with a story and find him oiling his bat.' But Marshall, a plump man who enjoyed the good life, had spent his career on the paper and understood its camaraderie. He saw himself as the team captain, picking his bowlers and batsmen with some skill. It allowed the paper's greatest talent, his deputy Reg Willis, to blossom.

In 1954, it was no surprise when Rothermere replaced Marshall with Willis. Every staff member who worked under Willis, a rugged Devonian, was full of admiration for the shirt-sleeved man, invariably in waistcoat or sporting braces, who ran his newsroom with a judicious mixture of severity and kindliness. He was 'very much a journalist's journalist', observed one.[93] Another spoke of him as 'the complete sub'.[94] Willis loved news, wherever it occurred, cheerfully splashing on a jewel robbery whether in west London or New York, ever eager to get a new headline for every one of his eight editions. Topmost of all on the agenda was crime. Reporters cultivated contacts with the police and also depended on contacts who listened in to police radios. On at least one occasion, Sam Jackett arrived at a murder scene before the police.

Dog days at the *Daily Mail*

It is doubtful if Esmond Rothermere noticed or cared about what happened at the *Evening News*. His personal life fell into disarray after his wife Ann left him for her lover Ian Fleming in 1951. She divorced Esmond the following year and immediately married Fleming. Noël Coward was best man. The main effect of the marriage break-up on Esmond was 'to widen the gap between the two sides of his personality'.[95] He grew more silent and aloof in terms of his business, but socially warmer and still more generous than before. As far his newspaper empire was concerned, it might well have been better if it had been the other way round, as the experience of the *Daily Mail* testified.

After Frank Owen's departure as editor in 1950, it was assumed by many, and especially by Ted Pickering, that he would get the job. Instead, Rothermere chose Guy Schofield, editor of the *Evening News*, a man as different from Owen as it was possible to be. Pickering quit and took his American girlfriend off to a nightclub, Les Ambassadeurs in Park Lane. Within the hour a waiter informed him that Lord Beaverbrook was on the phone and, after a brief visit to Arlington House, the tipsy Pick became an *Express* man.[96] Pick was right in thinking that Schofield would 'make it a very straight up and down paper'.[97] Regarded as 'a rather fastidious craftsman',[98] he gave Rothermere what Rothermere thought he wanted: 'a more detailed attention to political and international affairs'[99] and 'a reliable straightforward newspaper in an attractive make-up, coupled with sobriety of treatment'.[100]

The attraction of the make-up is hard to divine from a review of the files. Schofield reduced the headline sizes, introduced more serious content and, fatally, played it safe. The result was a rather stodgy paper which mirrored a description of Schofield as a 'distinguished, solemn and ascetic' character, 'a figure of refinement'.[101] In one respect at least he was like other editors: he was ruthless. Soon after taking over he sacked ten sub-editors, and caused an exodus of reporters.[102] Arthur Wareham, a long-time employee who was appointed assistant editor, thought Schofield was trying to turn the *Daily Mail* into the *Daily Telegraph*. That made the owner happy, at least temporarily, but not the readers. Here was a popular paper, requiring high sales in order to attract mass advertising, trying to go up-market too rapidly. It would certainly not be the last to make this mistake.

Caught between trying to compete with both the *Daily Express* and the *Daily Telegraph*, without identifying a proper market, Schofield's *Mail* was becalmed, selling a steady 2.1 million, some 2 million fewer than the rampant *Daily Express*. But the *Mail* still enjoyed a substantial reputation and was able to attract talent. Perhaps the most memorable of signings was Wally Fawkes, the cartoonist known as Trog who created the strip-cartoon hero Flook, scripted by Humphrey Lyttelton and, from 1956, by George Melly. Cartoonist Leslie Illingworth also joined, as did Peter Black, who later became one of the first, and best, TV critics. Undoubtedly Rothermere's favourite journalist of the period was the fashion editor Iris Ashley, 'a very stylish and slim' woman of forty-four.[103] The vivacious former cabaret singer liked to use herself to model clothes in the paper. After her husband died in 1953, this intelligent and well-connected peer's niece also set her sights on the lonely Esmond.

By 1954, Rothermere had grown disenchanted with Schofield and made Wareham acting editor in his place. The *Daily Mail*, politically challenging under Owen and stultifyingly staid under Schofield, took another sudden policy turn under Wareham. Though a conservative and conscientious man, he encouraged celebrity reporters such as Ralph Izzard and Noel Barber to engage in a journalism of 'scoops and stunts'.[104] Izzard searched for the abominable snowman while Barber got the first report of Vivian Fuchs's South Pole success and later tried, vainly, to cover the Dalai Lama's escape from Tibet.[105]

Rothermere also found his other national titles to be a headache, in spite of their sales success, because, unlike other proprietors, he was exceedingly sensitive to criticism. His *Sunday Dispatch* gained in popularity from the late 1930s onwards, celebrating in 1953 its fifteenth consecutive annual increase in sales, touching 2,750,000. Its appeal, 'skilfully judged by its editor, Charles Eade, was based on salacious fiction often specially written for the newspaper by a leading lady novelist under an assumed name'.[106] Although the 'sex and crime quotient' rose under Eade, it was pretty tame stuff compared to the *News of the World*'s court reports.[107]

When the *Daily Telegraph* attacked the *Dispatch* for sexy journalism, calling it 'the nastiest rag every printed in this country', the *Sunday Express* sportingly rode to the defence of its rival. John Gordon pointed out that the Berrys also owned a women's magazine which was running a serial containing 'a succession of near-rapes, threatened whippings, and proposals to sell the heroine in the White Slave market of Buenos Aires'. This magazine, wrote Gordon, 'pours money into one of Mr Berry's pockets, while the respectable *Daily Telegraph* pours it into the other'.[108]

Rothermere, showing a misplaced confidence in his abilities, was happy to buy one of Kemsley's unwanted titles, the *Daily Graphic*, at the end of 1952. Randolph Churchill commented: 'Eight editors in nearly as many years had failed to achieve even a fifth of the sale of its rival, the *Daily Mirror*, and so poor Lord Kemsley had to sell this paper, which was the only daily London mouthpiece for his not very original views, to Lord Rothermere.'[109] He changed its name to the *Daily Sketch*, telling Bracken he intended to run it as 'a family newspaper'. Bracken was not impressed, thought Kemsley had been lucky to offload the paper and presciently remarked to Beaverbrook: 'I shall be very surprised if the *Sketch* doesn't in the end become as fruity a paper as the *Daily Mirror*.'[110]

Another commentator agreed, arguing that Rothermere 'need never have bought that packet of trouble in the first place'.[111] No real reason, beyond vanity and the wish to spite cousin Cecil, explains why he bothered with it. His justification in the company's annual report was pompous: it was 'felt that this important newspaper could be rebuilt and that it was in the interests of our group to possess a newspaper which would in time compete in the popular picture-newspaper field'.[112]

In sales terms, the *Sketch* didn't do too well under editor Henry Clapp, rising only gently. Its politics remained right wing. Its news content was less eclectic than the *Daily Mirror*'s, relying on easy-to-obtain court reports for most page leads. Clapp may have felt under pressure, but his end came about in a most surprising, and public, way. On 10 September 1953, Randolph Churchill, son of prime minister Winston, personal friend of every proprietor including Rothermere, radio pundit and maverick moralist, rose to speak at the Foyle's luncheon. Employing heavy irony, the 'honest, caddish . . . busybody'[113] announced that he was adjudicating on who deserved the title 'Pornographer Royal and Criminologist Extraordinary'. He suggested that Eade of the *Dispatch* seemed at first to be the strongest candidate but Clapp at the *Sketch* had 'set so fast a pace . . . it was thought to be a dead-heat for Lord Rothermere's two horses'. He claimed that the *Sketch* was 'a paper which wallows in crime to a degree which is fast becoming the envy and despair of other purveyors of sensation. Even the most experienced pornographers are alarmed.'

Then came the charge that hurt Rothermere. It was, said Churchill,

> a little disquieting when you find a man like Lord Rothermere, who inherited three or four million pounds from his father, romping around in the gutter with those whose economic fetters still deny them an escape into a more honourable and salubrious profession . . . I have known Lord Rothermere all my life, but I can only confess myself as utterly baffled that so rich and cultivated a man should hire people to prostitute his papers in this way. It must be a case of pornography for pornography's sake. He has no need to earn a living like some others.[114]

This single speech was to have dramatic consequences for Eade and Clapp. Rothermere, 'the epitome of the newspaper establishment', fired both editors, an outcome of some benefit to Beaverbrook who probably gave Churchill the ammunition to fire.[115]

Within a month of the speech, Rothermere appointed Bert Gunn, the former *Evening Standard* editor who had been sacked for smearing a politician and for wishing to make the paper more sensational. Yet he was supposed to make the *Sketch* more respectable. His arrival spawned a delightful Fleet Street joke about Rothermere: 'When I hear the word culture I reach for my Gunn.'[116]

Gunn, 'who looked like a slightly decayed Roman emperor', according to leader writer Brian Inglis,[117] was considered to be 'brilliant but erratic'.[118] As we have seen, he could also be unscrupulous, though some preferred to give that a better gloss, calling him 'one of the last of the swashbuckler journalists'.[119] He certainly changed the *Sketch*'s fortunes, raising sales from 750,000 to more than 1 million in less than three years. His competitions, in which readers could win a pub, a racehorse, even a Wimpy bar, were very costly, plunging the paper into debt. So bad were finances that it was claimed the final contest would be to 'win the *Sketch*'.

Francis Williams shook his head as the *Sketch* became the country's fastest-growing paper. For him it demonstrated that 'the taste of a large section of the mass public is lower than the most pessimistic had previously suspected'.[120] Even so, in October 1953, Gunn did make one hiring of genuine merit, appointing Kenneth Tynan as theatre critic. When the Society of West End Theatre Managers complained about the savagery of his reviews, Gunn championed his cause but Tynan, unhappy with his platform at the *Sketch*, soon decamped to the paper which gave him the audience and reputation he craved (see below, p. 73)

Gunn had little time for the self-regulatory climate and its ethical judgements. In 1954, he suffered the embarrassment of being censured by the Press Council because of changes to a film review. Guest critic Tom Hopkinson, a former editor of the *Picture Post*, had not been too impressed with the movie *Front Page Story*. He was prevailed on by a features executive to soften his opinions, which he did, but when he read the resulting piece the next day he discovered that there had been a further alteration. A complimentary mention of the film's technical adviser had been inserted. She was Olive Gunn, the editor's wife.[121] A further seven complaints were upheld against the *Sketch* during Gunn's editorship.

Churchill did not stand alone in his fight against what he thought were declining editorial standards. He wrote regularly for the *Recorder Weekly*, founded by William J. Brittain specifically to campaign against press pornography. Within a month of Churchill's Foyle's speech, and noting its success in having prompted Rothermere to sack his editors, Brittain turned his weekly into a daily.

The *Recorder*'s debut leading article proclaimed it as the first daily paper launched in Britain for a generation and promised 'all the news' but 'more background and informed interpretation'.[122] From the start it failed to live up to that pledge, with an absence of proper commentary and no attempt at covering all the news. Every day it carried a statement of its credo: 'The *Recorder* believes in God; has pride in the influence for the good of Britain and the great British empire; takes joy in the happy family; believes in youth and progress; encourages work and a developing industry; seeks opportunity for all to make for themselves a prosperous and fuller life.' It was, in fact, simply a vehicle for Brittain's and Churchill's obsessional dislikes of socialism, homosexuality, indeed any kind of sex (see below, pp. 87–90). The *Recorder* suddenly vanished after publishing its 127th issue in March 1954 with a final leader urging readers to appreciate the glories of the empire, which is 'under attack by Socialists'.[123]

One paper which did please Churchill was the *Observer*. 'Great credit . . . must go to its editor, Mr David Astor. Though slightly muddle-headed on some issues and a little addicted to a priggish approach to some topics and to an exaggerated sympathy for "underdogs", particularly if they are coloured, he has sought to run this . . . paper . . . on the most honourable and progressive lines.'[124] This praise, tinged with racism, came during the period many of the *Observer*'s writers and readers were later to call its golden age. As the files of the period reveal, it was a most eccentric newspaper, featuring lengthy articles on a range of topics which had no especial topicality except for having caught the attention, however briefly, of Astor or one of his writers.

The lack of orthodoxy, a well-meaning amateurism, stimulated unconventional ideas which sometimes worked well. In place of reporting exclusive news stories, the paper developed a form of explanatory article neatly termed, by its respected librarian Willi Guttman, 'a scoop of interpretation'. In other words, writers would seek to explain how and why the week's main event had occurred. It would be many years before the *Sunday Times* caught on to the potency of this form of journalism.

The *Observer*'s main contribution to domestic political thought was to pioneer the middle ground between the two largest parties. Its chief political writer was Hugh Massingham who, though he wrote without a byline, was considered by his successor as 'the founder of the modern political column'.[125] His tolerance pleased Astor but his scepticism and humour probably did not. His columns were marked by their wit and his inside knowledge of Westminster. Many years later his *Sunday Times* rival James Margach discovered how Massingham managed, week after week, to reveal the inner secrets of cabinet meetings. It transpired that Sir Stafford Cripps's wife took tea with Massingham every Friday afternoon and she told him exactly what Attlee and his senior ministers had said across the table.[126]

Astor's greatest achievement was to open people's eyes to the problems of life in sub-Saharan Africa. His paper's unfashionable championing of blacks in South Africa, even to the point of supporting militant resistance, was notable.[127] There was almost no support from other papers, or their owners. Beaverbrook's love of empire did not extend to the indigenous peoples and he held Astor's views in contempt. If you ever want to see Astor, he once advised Bob Edwards, 'put some boot polish on your face'.[128]

There were blind spots in the *Observer*, such as the failure to grasp the importance of both economics and industry.[129] This didn't seem to matter because of the strengths, personified by Astor's most famous signing of the period, Kenneth Tynan. He had already gained a reputation for his controversial views as theatre critic at the *Evening Standard* and the *Daily Sketch*. To take him on meant asking the faithful Ivor Brown to retire, which he did reluctantly, warning Astor that Tynan would prove a disaster. In fact, he became Britain's pre-eminent drama critic over the following nine years. It says much for Astor that he rarely agreed with Tynan, kept his distance from him and disliked much of what he wrote, yet he allowed him complete freedom, restrained only by the wise counsel of the literary editor, Terry Kilmartin.[130] Film critic Penelope Gilliatt also enjoyed a high reputation.[131]

Over at the rival *Sunday Times*, Denis Hamilton's influence was beginning to pay dividends. He had installed the scholarly H(enry) V(incent)

Hodson as editor in 1950, and they set out to improve their paper in spite of Kemsley's interference. They complemented each other: Hamilton was a populist while Hodson, a fellow of All Souls and a former constitutional adviser to the Viceroy of India, was much more serious and thoughtful. The son of a Cambridge anthropology professor, he read economics at Balliol and went on to be a senior civil servant before, on a whim after the war, joining the *Sunday Times*. A man with 'a razor-sharp mind of a scientific bent',[132] he was initially unpopular with staff, rising effortlessly to the editorship without the experience or training of every other journalist. His leaders were lucid, but his leadership was lacklustre. Only occasionally could he evade Kemsley's blue pencil to inject liberal views into the paper. Hodson's enlightened leading article in 1952 calling for a liberalisation of the law on homosexuality was ruined by Kemsley's insertion of the word 'perversion' at every opportunity.[133] Compared to Astor's *Observer*, the Hodson–Hamilton *Sunday Times* of that era, a skimpy ten pages, poorly designed and lacking innovation, was unappealing. Its critics were certainly readable. Otherwise, the most notable successes were the first examples of Hamilton's invention of the 'big read', book serialisations that ran at great length for weeks on end.

Twin challenges to the Paper of Record

While the *Times*, under Astor, was losing sales and trying to divine a way to expand its readership, the *Manchester Guardian*, under Laurence Scott, took the first steps on the road towards his dream of building a new, national audience. His paper's first act had the reverse effect. The increase in the cover price in May 1951 (from 2d to 3d) caused sales to decline, despite it being the first rise for thirty-one years.[134] Soon after, planning started for what became known as the *New Model Guardian*, leading to the paper dispensing with front-page adverts in favour of news.

It didn't happen until 29 September 1952 – when circulation was 130,000 – but it was accomplished with conviction. The response was generally positive and sales began to climb once more. Scott could now look forward to printing in London, which was becoming more and more pressing. The bulk of the copy published by the paper emanated from the capital. London-based staff were increasing. Readership was rising in the south. There was also tension between the two offices with the editor, A. P. Wadsworth, and his London counterpart, John Beavan, finding it difficult to harmonise their responsibilities. Beavan, despite many good qualities, wasn't the equal of Wadsworth and it was he who gave way.

Despite its provincial base the *Guardian* carried political clout and, accordingly, it hurt Labour before the 1951 election by turning its back on the party (see below, p. 83). By 1955, circulation was three times the level at Wadsworth's takeover, and the paper's reputation had never been higher.

Writers such as Victor Zorza, reporting from eastern Europe, and Max Freedman in Washington were respected as correspondents of genuine quality. But, towards the end of the year, the revered conductor of the *Guardian* orchestra became seriously ill. Wadsworth went off to Italy in the hope that sunshine would do him good.[135]

Just as the *Guardian* prospered, so did the *Financial Times* once the City returned to life. One major reason was Brendan Bracken's astute choice of Gordon Newton as editor from 1950. It had been expected that the deputy, A. G. Cole, would be promoted, but Bracken and his managing director, Garrett Moore, opted instead for forty-two-year-old Newton. They had discovered an editor who combined vision with enormous attention to detail. The paper's historian thought him 'one of the most extraordinary editors in post-war Fleet Street and arguably the most successful'.[136] He was probably the most important single person in the *FT*'s first century, deserving of the 'legend in his own lifetime' epithet.

He looked 'not unlike a carved Red Indian, with a glacial, rather hatchet face, tight lips, straight jaw and skin drawn tight over it'.[137] Evidently not an intellectual, as his Pooterish autobiography indicates, he wasn't much interested in the City or the stock exchange but he had one essential journalistic characteristic: he was 'full of practical curiosity'.[138] Leslie Gordon Newton was educated at a Devon public school, Blundell's, and Cambridge, where he excelled at athletics, and became an accomplished violinist. He typically kept quiet about both talents.[139] He wanted to be a doctor, but out of family loyalty joined his father's glass company which soon collapsed. His own business attempts failed too before, at twenty-seven, he was hired by Maurice Green, editor of the *Financial News*, as a filing clerk. He soon moved into editorial, learning the job gradually, leaving once war broke out to become Gunner Newton of the Honourable Artillery Company.[140] He appears to have had an entertaining war as a junior officer and afterwards joined the merged *Financial News/Times* as features editor.

He never expected the editorship, recalling later that it seemed 'ridiculous' when he was appointed by Bracken.[141] He proved to be a hands-on editor, moving from desk to desk, room to room, asking what was happening, commenting on pieces, though writing nothing himself. I didn't write one editorial, he boasted.[142] He rarely smiled, could be abrupt, and was sometimes thought brutal with staff. He seemed to enjoy his reputation as something of an ogre, but he was admired for his decisiveness and honesty. According to David Kynaston, journalists 'came to respect and admire him deeply, even if they were slower to love him'.[143]

As with Camrose and his son at the *Daily Telegraph*, Newton saw journalism as an exercise in relaying factual data. 'We live on facts,' he once wrote. 'They may seem mundane facts. But someone somewhere is relying on us to print just one accurate figure each day. Now multiply that by thousands.'[144] Along with accuracy, he also demanded 'freshness and lucidity' to catch the eye of 'practical people'.[145] He also enhanced the paper's credibility by keeping it 'free from any taint of . . . tipping and puffing'.[146]

Newton's paper was not considered politically partisan, though it usually endorsed the Conservative party at general elections.[147] Many of his star hirings were much more committed, such as William Rees-Mogg, Ronald Butt and Samuel Brittan. Newton also championed the iconoclastic C. Gordon Tether.[148] One of his major decisions was to widen the paper's scope, creating space for arts criticism and taking a tentative step towards sports coverage.

Dealing with his bosses proved one of Newton's greatest difficulties. Bracken, who was given a viscountcy in 1952, largely withdrew from the *FT* in the early 1950s, leaving Moore in charge, but he was still capable of 'uncontrolled bursts of controlled vexation about particular leaders or misprints'.[149] Newton stood up to Bracken more than his predecessor had done, just as he fought off what he deemed to be interference from Moore, who succeeded to an earldom in 1954 and was thereafter known as Lord Drogheda.

The *Times* gives ground to the *Telegraph*

While the *Financial Times* and the *Manchester Guardian* were taking practical steps towards extending their markets, the *Times* merely marked time. A dull caretaker editor, William Casey, was allowed to stay in place for almost four years. The paper survived, however, on the uniqueness of its reputation. When a leading article incorrectly referred to Turkey not having adopted the Roman alphabet (it had done so in 1928) the Turkish government sent for the British ambassador to issue a reprimand. Then the Foreign Office sent for the paper's foreign editor to reprimand him.[150] Similarly, its long-term domestic readers continued to adore the paper. In 1951, the politician and social gadfly Chips Channon noted in his diary: 'How riveting newspapers can be. It is terrible to contemplate that one day one will be dead, and never again be able to read the *Times*.'[151] Such was its cachet among the elite that even the editor of the much more successful *Daily Telegraph*, Colin Coote, always regarded his paper as second-best to the *Times*.[152]

Yet this was far from a glorious period for the *Times*. Casey may have edited 'efficiently and without fuss',[153] but much of the credit should go to his managing editor, Donald Tyerman. Given that Astor's powers as chief proprietor were confined to choosing an editor, he should have given much more thought to his task. It was foolish to have overlooked Tyerman or, indeed, any other young, dynamic personality.[154] Casey, aware of being a stop-gap, didn't treat his job conscientiously and left the office early in the evening. That such an interregnum should have continued for so long reflects badly on Astor, and certainly contributed to his paper's future troubles.

The 1951 issues, with their fifty-six columns of news a day, look rather sad compared to those of the 1930s, with twice as much news space. While Casey plodded on, with the paper's sales remaining static, the search for a replacement assumed a leisurely pace. Eventually, in October 1952, Astor and his fellow proprietor, John Walter, appointed William Haley as *Times* editor. It was hardly a surprise. Bracken had told Beaverbrook of the likelihood six months before.[155] Haley, director-general of the BBC, had also rejected the job previously, out of loyalty to the Corporation.

Haley was fifty-one when he arrived at Printing House Square and his experience, at least on paper, was exemplary. Born in 1901, he had worked his way up from *Times* telephonist and then *Manchester Evening News* sub-editor to become joint managing editor of the *Manchester Guardian* group by the age of thirty-eight. After joining the Reuters board, he built a reputation as a 'high-principled, perceptive and determined' executive by helping to reorganise the news agency's structure.[156] In 1943, he joined the BBC as editor-in-chief, succeeding Lord Reith a year later as director-general and again overseeing considerable reform. Regarded by many of his peers as 'a man of the highest calibre',[157] Haley rose from relatively humble beginnings to become a classic figure in an outmoded establishment. His belief in the media's educational role, and therefore in the public interest ethic, was sincere and he was happy to advance anti-establishment views in order to make his point. Extremely well read and highly literate, he could be pedantic and a trifle pompous.[158] Someone once remarked after his first encounter with the unsmiling and somewhat forbidding Haley: 'I've met a man with one glass eye before – but never a chap with two!'[159]

He had a strong work ethic, urging his staff to do more and leading by example, though some found him 'a rather difficult man of immense rectitude'.[160] He wrote widely, sometimes using a pseudonym, and kept a close watch on every aspect of the paper, issuing daily memos to his executives. He certainly reversed the centre-left drive of Barrington-Ward, which had already begun to wane under Casey, taking the paper back to a safe and rather dull conservatism. His *FT* rival, Newton, thought him 'slow to appreciate that the post-war world was going to be different from anything we had known before'.[161]

But Haley did broaden the paper's scope in an attempt 'to appeal to intelligent readers of all ages and in every walk of life' rather than a small elite.[162] Early in his editorship one of his hunches led to a genuine scoop. Having backed the idea of *Times* writer James Morris joining the expedition to climb Everest, he was rewarded by Morris witnessing the return from the summit by the successful climbers.[163] Despite that exclusive, and Haley's undoubted energy and drive, the Casey years had taken their toll. Sales slipped just a little every year between 1949 and 1955, from an annual average of 235,000 to 220,000. In 1955, Haley also lost the paper's best journalist in Tyerman who, having acted as a loyal deputy to three editors, finally obtained an editorship. He was to prosper at the *Economist* where he proved, as so many had long suspected, that he might well have been a brilliant *Times* editor.

The *Daily Telegraph* began the new decade with a new editor, Colin Coote, who was viewed as a 'charlatan' by some, such as Malcolm Muggeridge, but was highly regarded by his owner, Camrose. He was fifty-six, had been decorated in the first world war and had then spent five years as a Liberal MP before joining the *Times* in 1922 as Italian correspondent. He returned to Britain at the time of the general strike to be parliamentary sketch writer and, later, leader writer. A close friend of Churchill's, he stayed with the *Times* despite his passionate anti-appeasement views, until he was edged out in 1942.

Camrose immediately offered him a chance to write *Telegraph* leaders and he spent the next eight years settling comfortably into the paper. A distinguished-looking man, Coote was well connected, clubbable and certainly clever, turning out readable leading articles in quick order. But he was a languid character, delegating a great deal of work and appearing to lack commitment.[164] Maybe he felt he didn't need to break sweat because 'a new middle class, with a tendency to read the *Daily Telegraph*, was emerging'.[165] There was, it appeared to another commentator of the period, 'a much larger public for a serious journal than was generally believed'.[166]

So, to win sales, all Coote had to do was float with the tide. Similarly, the political tide was also flowing with him and his paper. Delighted with Churchill's return to power in 1951, he denied that the *Telegraph* was the 'mouthpiece' of Tory Central Office. 'The paper has, broadly speaking, a conservative philosophy; but it has never hesitated to attack Conservative Party policy.'[167] However, with the exception of the Eden years, examples are hard to find during Coote's reign, though his *Telegraph* was responsible in 1954 for exposing the Crichel Down land scandal which led to the resignation of the agriculture minister, Sir Thomas Dugdale. Born towards the end of the nineteenth century, Coote found it difficult to accommodate change. Sometimes this was amusing. 'A personal whim of my own is to prefer good handwriting to typewriting.'[168] Sometimes it was reactionary, as with his view that women journalists 'have less initiative' than men, and are more subjective.[169]

None of this mattered to Camrose, who felt sure that Coote would keep the *Telegraph* as he wished it. He was equally confident in the abilities of his sons, Michael and Seymour, gradually handing them responsibility for running the paper, though he continued to go into the office as often as possible. The end came suddenly. In June 1954 he fell ill with a stomach upset and was taken to hospital near his country home in Hampshire. There seemed no reason for alarm but he wrongly assumed that since he was not eating he could do without his insulin injection. It proved fatal and, eight days short of his seventy-fifth birthday, Camrose died. 'He showed', noted his friend Harold Nicolson, 'that one could be a Press Lord and a Gentleman.'[170] This sentiment was echoed in the obituaries.

It had been expected that his elder son, the 'extrovert and gregarious' Seymour, would take control, but 'he chose freedom, rather in the same way as did the Duke of Windsor'.[171] So his younger brother, Michael Berry, assumed the title of editor-in-chief. He was then forty-two, painfully shy – like George VI – and sometimes hard to understand because he spoke indistinctly out of the corner of his mouth. Educated at Eton and Oxford, he went straight into journalism as a trainee reporter on an Aberdeen evening paper followed by a spell on Glasgow's *Daily Record*. He even edited its down-market stablemate, the *Sunday Mail*, then known as the 'Ha'penny Dreadful', when the editor fell sick.

Berry also worked as a sub on the *Daily Dispatch* in Manchester and as a gossip writer in London on the *Daily Sketch* before becoming managing editor of the *Financial Times*. Few newspaper controllers had as much journalistic experience. Like his father, he was serious and hard working. Politically, he was a Conservative and economically 'an unreconstructed Keynesian'.[172] Also like his father, he rarely spoke to staff and adopted a routine based on a meticulous imitation of Camrose's habits. His office was guarded by a butler dressed in black. He dictated a daily memo for display on the noticeboard, listing his likes and dislikes about the previous day's paper. He continued to deal separately with the editors of the news and comment pages. Berry's deep appreciation of his father ensured that the *Daily Telegraph* would remain the most comprehensive of newspapers, admired by journalists across Britain. But his adherence to tradition, alongside his limited business acumen, stifled innovation in both the editorial and commercial arenas.

The *News Chronicle*: a paper on the brink

Walter Layton finally gave up the *News Chronicle* chairmanship in 1950 in favour of Laurence Cadbury, but he remained on the board and kept an eye on what was happening. Cadbury just could not delegate, decision-making was slow, and as the paper entered a new decade it was beginning to fall behind in the highly competitive battle for sales. Circulation continued to fall away.

In 1952 Beaverbrook offered to finance Layton in buying out the *News Chronicle* and *Star*. 'I would be glad to provide money for you . . . The policy of the paper and also the production of news pages would be entirely your responsibility. And I would not interfere. The business side would rest with me . . . We will make a community of interest between the *Express* and the

News Chronicle which will be publicly declared . . .'[173] Layton thought he was too old at 68 for such a venture and, anyway, the Cadburys wouldn't sell. There was also the abyss between Beaverbrook's politics and his own. He turned it down.

The greatest blow to the *Chronicle*'s standing came in 1952 when the celebrated cartoonist Vicky resigned, thought by some to be a sign that the paper was moving to the right. If it was, Cadbury wasn't to blame.[174] The editor, Robin Cruikshank, didn't share most people's admiration for Vicky and he rejected one of his cartoons, harking back to the 1929 crash when American investors were said to have leaped from skyscraper windows, considering it in bad taste. Vicky was welcomed by a grateful *Daily Mirror*.[175] The paper also lost Vernon Bartlett and Ian Mackay, the latter a first-rate industrial correspondent and columnist, but it did gain the wise and talented foreign correspondent James Cameron in 1950.

In 1954, Cruikshank resigned due to poor health. Layton, chairman in all but name once again, decided to take a risk by giving the editorship to thirty-three-year-old Michael Curtis, a former leader writer and occasional deputy. Curtis had written a document setting out the direction the paper should take. He favoured it becoming a Liberal *Daily Telegraph*, and preferably a tabloid, a sort of 'quality tabloid', blending the best elements of the *Evening Standard* and the Paris edition of the *New York Herald Tribune*, an aspiration ahead of its time. Cadbury was keener on the paper becoming more populist.

Layton 'typically went for a compromise'.[176] In a lengthy statement about his hopes for the *News Chronicle* he argued that 'the present generation includes a growing number of people, virile, keenly interested in the dazzling march of science, with unique resources at their disposal for sport, amusement and travel, pitch-forked into the problems of "one world", yet conscious of the many social stresses and unsolved moral problems'. These readers, he said, straddling the fence, want to be 'entertained, but also . . . accurately informed'. Ominously, he added: 'If there is no such public there is no *raison d'être* for the *N.C.*'

Then Layton had a stroke of luck. With profits declining fast in 1955 a looming crisis was averted in November when Kemsley decided to offload the Manchester-based *Daily Dispatch*, then selling about 460,000 copies to a largely elderly working-class audience. So the *News Chronicle* ate yet another title, initially boosting its circulation by 200,000. Curtis's innovative editorship won over a sceptical staff but 1955 ended with another bad omen when A. J. Cummings, the *Chronicle*'s wise political editor of twenty years' standing, went into retirement.

Call me Roy! Enter a new press baron

The *Scotsman*, an Edinburgh-based newspaper with great traditions for fine writing and sensible views, hit bad times in the early 1950s. Its sales, along with those of its evening title, the *Dispatch*, were falling and it was losing money. The owners since the paper's launch in 1817, the Findlay family, were also facing penal death duties. It was obvious that the only solution was a sale but the board, headed by the whisky-loving Sir Edmund Findlay, set one key condition: the buyer must not be English.

One of the *Scotsman* directors recalled that a Canadian newspaper owner of Scottish descent had asked in 1950 about buying the paper. He wrote to him to see if he was still interested. Roy Thomson, 'stout, grey-haired, ruddy-faced, myopic and insulting', arrived in Edinburgh in 1953, aged fifty-nine, and bought the company with the minimum of negotiations.[177] A new, but very different kind of press proprietor had arrived in Britain. Instead of an ideologue who saw journalism as a political weapon, here was an apolitical accountant who viewed journalism as a branch of commerce.

Thomson, born in Toronto in 1894 to a feckless barber and a hotel maid, left school at fourteen, and went to night classes to learn book-keeping. He became a salesman, initially of rope and twine, and later of car spare parts and radios, before opening a radio station in a remote town in Ontario. In a lengthy learning curve, Thomson mastered the art of living on credit, discovering that bankers were susceptible to lending money to debtors as long as they could see a revenue stream of some kind. His candour and his bluff, friendly character played a large part in winning the loyalty of business partners and employees. Always a cent or two away from bankruptcy, for years he operated eight smallish radio stations and a tiny newspaper. In the early days he sold much of the advertising himself, going from door to door, introducing himself, as he was to do throughout his life: 'My name's Thomson. Call me Roy.' He used penny-pinching accounting methods that were simple and effective, for ever pruning costs, paying low wages, and always paying back his banks on time.

He was fifty, in 1944, when he finally turned to building a newspaper empire. He began with four provincial papers and surprised the Canadian newspaper establishment by asserting that he was interested in profit, not propaganda. To make his point, he asked: 'What is editorial content?' and answered: 'The stuff you separate the ads with.'[178] This was endlessly quoted for the rest of Thomson's life, as was his view that his editors had an entirely free hand as long as they didn't come out against God or the monarchy.[179]

Thomson's wife died in 1951 and a man already obsessed by business threw himself still more into his work. He bought more papers in Canada and came to the attention of the world's most famous Canadian newspaper magnate, Lord Beaverbrook. They spent three days together in Nassau in

1952 and though Beaverbrook privately disparaged his upstart compatriot, 'a little guy' who owned 'a lot of little newspapers', Thomson considered him a friend.[180] Thomson also visited Beaverbrook at Cherkley and was taken on a tour of the *Express* plant by Junor, exhibiting a 'goggle-eyed' enthusiasm at the presses.[181] At the time, Beaverbrook didn't see him as a competitor and was amazed at his purchase of the *Scotsman*. It was to be the first of many such surprises. As Thomson's biographer noted, Thomson had an accountant's mind and the flair of a showman.[182] It was to prove a winning combination.

4: ALL THIS – AND CIRCULATION TOO!

The nearer any government approaches to a republic, the less business there is for a king.[1]

Between 1950 and 1955, there was a subtle change, if not in the editorial content, then in its underlying tone. It is possible to note an emergence from the gloom of austerity, marked by the gradual disappearance of stories about rationing, the breathless optimism of the *Daily Express*'s choice of material, the *Daily Mirror*'s muted political coverage, the *Daily Telegraph*'s renewed confidence in Britain. The central reason for this mood swing was the election of a Conservative government in 1951 and the return to power of Winston Churchill. Even the war in Korea didn't dim the Tory euphoria.

Tory papers had been uniformly hostile to Attlee's administration, but the *Manchester Guardian* indicated that the disenchantment with Labour was more widely spread. A significant leading article by editor A. P. Wadsworth, headlined 'Time for Change?', argued: 'The Radically-minded voter . . . would like to be sympathetic to the Labour Government, which, after all, has been the instrument of a mainly beneficent social revolution . . . But the campaign has strengthened the conviction . . . that the Labour Government has come to the end of its usefulness . . .'[2] Three days later another Wadsworth leader concluded: 'For the next few years a Churchill Government is, it seems to us, the lesser evil.'[3]

Since the *Guardian* was viewed as a political force among the opinion-forming liberal middle classes, this advice appeared like treachery to Labour. The party had inured itself to the straightforward attacks from papers such as the *Daily Mail*, which played up the deep splits fragmenting Labour, between Gaitskellites and Bevanites, and pointed to the high cost of living. The *Mail* also improbably seized on the nationalisation of oil in Iran as an example of the danger of Labour's own nationalisations. As for the *Daily Express*, Francis Williams, who understood the relationship between popular papers and readers, knew that overt political propaganda was less effective than the general tenor of its editorial content. 'Although the direct political influence of the *Daily Express* is small,' he wrote, 'its indirect influence over the political – and even more surely the social – attitudes of its many readers may well be profound: it probably, for example, had a great deal to do with creating the mood of irritation against post-war labour shortages and controls that led to the defeat of the Labour Government in 1951.'[4]

Jay's contention that 'the steady swing back of votes' was 'due to the revival of anti-Labour propaganda' missed the point.[5] It was not revived because it had never gone away. (Anyway, Labour polled well in 1951.) But Jay's *Daily Herald* apart, it was possible to detect a 'mood of irritation' in the whole press, including the Labour-supporting *Daily Mirror*. Not even the *Mirror*'s controversial election-day front page, written and designed by Bartholomew, could change that. It said: 'Whose Finger? Today YOUR finger is on the trigger. See you defend peace with security and progress with fair shares. Vote for the party you can really trust. The *Daily Mirror* believes that party is Labour.'[6] With the paper implying that peace was safer in Attlee's hands because Churchill was a warmonger, Edelman reasoned that 'its impetus went ahead of its prudence'.[7] It was a crude and ineffective jibe at Churchill, especially since most Britons regarded him as a war hero, but its greatest failure was in not addressing the people's real concerns. The war which worried them most was economic. Churchill foolishly sued the *Mirror* for libel, though the leader clearly wasn't libellous, and was forced to change tack. He won an apology and a sum of money for a different story published months earlier. The enmity between the *Mirror* and Churchill grew in the following years.

Elsewhere in Fleet Street's baronial halls, there was joy. Rothermere, Camrose, Bracken and Beaverbrook were delighted that their friend Churchill was back in power. Their papers reflected their belief that Downing Street had regained its rightful tenant, though the effervescent spirit was short lived. In February 1952, King George VI died and the papers greeted the news with the kind of solemnity which seems, in hindsight, quite out of proportion to its importance. The *Daily Telegraph* carried the biggest headline it had ever published, with 'hideous' thick black rules between columns.[8] Almost all the editorial space in every paper was given over to the event, along with memorial supplements. Only the *Financial Times* editor, Gordon Newton, appears to have remained unmoved. A young journalist seeking to excite his interest found him reading a detective story.[9] In what turned out to be a lengthy period of mourning, papers seemed to be draped in black too, eventually breaking out of their sombre state by lauding a series of national occasions, most notably the happy coincidence of the coronation of Queen Elizabeth II with the conquest of Everest (by a New Zealander and a Nepalese), followed by a cricket Test match series victory over Australia and, a little later, Roger Bannister's sub-four-minute mile.

Almost every front page in the week leading up to the coronation was dominated by the event, and in the weeks afterwards pictures of the Queen and her sister were scattered throughout most papers. Christiansen's eve-of-coronation page one, 'All This – and Everest Too!', has been granted iconic status by most newspaper historians (as noted above, p. 64), but the *News*

Chronicle's 'The Crowning Glory' was excellent too, and visually more coherent. These triumphalist pages certainly reflected the majority view. But one paper at least dared to take a more sceptical stance. The *Manchester Guardian* ran a cartoon by David Low showing two punch-drunk children in union flag nappies surrounded by the debris of a £100 million spree: empty champagne bottles, military toys and books entitled 'Fairy Princess Tales' and 'Snow White'.[10] The paper received several angry letters about its vulgarity and repulsiveness.[11]

After the popular press's genuflection at the dawn of a new Elizabethan era, it soon betrayed its real intentions towards the royal family. Hollywood stars were a staple diet of news stories, pictures and features, but the home-grown Windsors had yet more sales-winning potential. In June 1953, the *People* became the first British newspaper to publish a story about the romance, reported regularly in papers in the United States and Europe, between Princess Margaret and Group-Captain Peter Townsend. 'It is high time for the British public to made aware of the fact that scandalous rumours about Princess Margaret are racing around the world . . . that the princess is in love with a divorced man.'[12] The *People* demanded an official denial to a story which, it stated with tongue firmly in cheek, 'is, of course, utterly untrue'.

With the story in the public domain at last, the *Daily Mirror* carried out a front-page poll: should the princess be allowed to marry Townsend?[13] Of the 70,142 who returned their forms, only 2,235 said 'No'.[14] This exercise was criticised by the Press Council at its inaugural meeting, strongly deprecating the paper's poll as 'contrary to the best traditions of British journalism'.[15] The *Times* felt moved to protest at the 'scandalmongers' practising 'the cruel business of prying into private lives'.[16]

Cudlipp was not cowed. At the end of 1954, the *Mirror* asked why the royal family were not making more foreign visits. 'It is all the more pity they do not go abroad more often' . . . 'It is ludicrous that the *entire* Royal Family should be condemned to part-time activity in the Mother Country. What can they do here? Twiddle their thumbs? Visit one another? Do the dreary social rounds? Let's have more Royal Tours.'[17] The following day the paper returned to the attack, suggesting that the large numbers of the family turning out to receive guests was a waste of their time. 'Happily,' it argued, 'the remedy . . . is simple . . . FULL EMPLOYMENT for Royalty.'[18] The *Daily Telegraph* called the *Mirror* attack 'boorish' and 'a stupid slander' for suggesting the family should work harder. Then, to the *Mirror*'s delight, Prince Philip waded in with an ironic reference to twiddling his thumbs. Just eighteen months after the coronation, the Windsors and the popular press were at loggerheads, exacerbated by months of speculation about Princess Margaret's intentions.

In March 1955, the *Sunday Pictorial* suggested that the princess was on the verge of deciding whether or not to abdicate her right of succession to the throne in order to marry Townsend.[19] Its daily stablemate kept the pot boiling, culminating in a huge row in the summer after the front page headlined 'Come on Margaret! Please Make Up Your Mind'.[20] Most other papers turned on the *Mirror*, for its 'impertinence' (*News Chronicle*) and 'vulgarity' (*Yorkshire Post*). Once again, the Press Council, chaired by the *Yorkshire Post*'s editor Linton Andrews, was not amused. Princess Margaret's announcement that she would not marry Townsend was issued by the Palace sixteen days after the *Mirror*'s request.

Cudlipp, revelling in his editorial supremacy at the *Daily Mirror*, courted controversy. He published the first account, again culled from American papers, of 'rumours' of Churchill's 1953 stroke.[21] The following year Bracken pointed out that the *Mirror* was 'running a tremendous campaign against Churchill ... a skilful compound of hatred, malice and greasy pity'. He belittled the readers as 'mentally adolescent or natural supporters of the Left' but concluded that the 'bosses of the *Mirror* certainly are a skilful lot'.[22] The *Mirror* was condemned for frequently accusing Churchill of being senile, and therefore in no state to be prime minister,[23] but the memoirs of Churchill's doctor Lord Moran later confirmed that to have been a reasonable point of view.[24]

Anthony Eden succeeded Churchill in April 1955. With newspapers off the streets due to a month-long strike (see above, p. 54), he became prime minister without any press clamour. He immediately announced an election for the following month and his Tory paper supporters accurately gauged the public's support for the new leader. The *Daily Mail* predictably fawned on Eden while being vicious about Labour.[25] The *Daily Telegraph* scorned the very idea of Labour returning to power with the threat of dock and rail strikes looming.[26] The *Daily Express*, with Beaverbrook as maverick as ever, urged Eden to let Churchill make the main TV broadcast.[27] The *Times* considered Labour 'devoid of coherence, vigour, wisdom or vision' while the Tories had not yet had a long enough spell in power 'to exhaust their mandate'.[28]

At the *Daily Mirror*, Cudlipp recognised that Eden was unbeatable and so ran what Beavan believed was his most subtle campaign.[29] His slogan was: vote Labour to 'keep the Tories tame'.[30] This prompted a witty leader of response in the *Daily Telegraph*.[31] As expected, Eden romped home with a sixty-seat majority but, despite his triumph and widespread public approval, his honeymoon with the press proved very short.

Though newspapers kept note of every political twist and turn, they were less adept at tracking social trends. The social diaries, such as the *Mail*'s 'Paul Tanfield', were peopled by Britain's aristocrats doing nothing in particular, exotic foreigners, such as the Maharajahs of Cooch Behar and Baroda, spending money with abandon, and one publicity-seeking *nouveau* couple, Sir Bernard and Lady (Norah) Docker, enjoying an idle life aboard the yacht *Shemara*. Some papers, especially the *Express* and *Mail*, appeared to celebrate the yawning gap between the haves and have-nots, the rich man in his castle, the poor man at his gate. They made little attempt to discover what the latter were up to anyway, unless, of course, it was criminal. Popular music columns were dominated by jazz, with only passing references to 'the rock and roll craze'.[32] Jean Metcalfe, then one of radio's most popular presenters, made no mention of it in her *Daily Mail* record reviews. Even jazz received a poor press, with much finger-wagging tinged with the prevalent racism of the time. 'More and more white teenagers . . . are contorting to the rhythm of the Negro', said the *Daily Mirror*.[33]

It is enlightening too to consider one example of how the press reinforced a prejudice, and – either by genuine misunderstanding or deliberate disingenuousness – managed to exacerbate the problem.

Nudge, nudge: who's that pretty boy in the closet?

In 1952 the *Sunday Pictorial* broke a taboo by referring to homosexuality, a subject previously veiled by the use of baffling euphemisms. It was hardly a sympathetic account: the series was entitled 'Evil Men'.[34] Years later Cudlipp said the articles were recognised even by 'the wretched homosexuals' as 'a sincere attempt to get to the root of a spreading fungus'.[35] That is very doubtful since that series, and many subsequent articles in the mass-market press, made no attempt to separate homosexuality from paedophilia. They were considered to be one and the same. Cudlipp's attitude towards homosexuals can be divined from his admonition to the writer Godfrey Winn when he hired him: 'A lot of people in Fleet Street regard you as a bit of a sissy, but I am going to prove them wrong.'[36] The Cudlippian distaste for homosexuality was widespread in the press and the public, crossing class barriers.

Randolph Churchill complained bitterly about the *Times* reporting 'the unhappy story that the distinguished actor Sir John Gielgud had been fined for importuning'. What offended Churchill was the fact that the paper tried to conceal his identity, referring to the actor as 'a clerk' and omitting any mention of his knighthood.[37] Another typical unsigned article in the *Recorder* alleged that 'the scourge of homosexuality threatens to undermine the moral fibre of the people' and asked: 'Can the disease, if it is a disease, be cured? What makes people behave abnormally?'[38]

According to one of the men who would suffer for it, 'in the British Establishment there was a deep vein of anti-homosexual prejudice'.[39] That might have been true of the owners. But most of the editors of the popular press had not been privately educated, and took the view that the 'establishment' was the problem: it bred homosexuals. The *Sunday Pictorial* argued that the 'vice' flourished in private schools, part of the reason being that they were unregulated. Its 'evil men' series followed an investigation the year before into incidents at the London Choir School involving its owner and principal, a priest. A young teacher told the *Sunday Pictorial* that the man was abusing his pupils and, in spite of any official action, editor Colin Valdar 'pursued the case . . . with remarkable tenacity until the odious cleric stood in the box at Kent Assizes'.[40] It took three years, in which the paper fought off a libel action, before the schoolmaster was convicted of various offences against three former pupils and jailed for ten years.

Over the following years, the *Sunday Pictorial*, equating the man's paedophilia with homosexuality, then launched a campaign to root out any teachers who had been found guilty of homosexual offences. There can be little doubt that 'the climate of the time was violently anti-homosexual'.[41] Homosexuals were therefore prey to blackmailers. The *Sunday Times* theatre critic James Agate was 'blackmailed for decades by a vicious guardsman'.[42]

In 1953, Lord Montagu of Beaulieu was questioned about an incident at his home involving two fourteen-year-old boy scouts who had complained that they had been sexually assaulted by him and a friend. Montagu thought his explanation had convinced the police that nothing had occurred. But he came to believe that the director of public prosecutions was pressured into bringing charges because of 'the threat of exposure from the Beaverbrook press'.[43] When he arrived for his first court hearing some 250 people, alerted by the coded reports in papers, jeered him. Weeks later, once he had given evidence, the jury dismissed the charge.

His ordeal was not over. On 9 January 1954, Montagu was arrested – by Special Branch – along with Michael Pitt-Rivers, a West Country landowner, and Peter Wildeblood, the *Daily Mail*'s diplomatic correspondent, on indecency offences widely regarded as a 'blackmailer's charter'. They were also charged with conspiracy to incite two young airmen to commit what were called 'acts of gross indecency'. Most journalists turned their backs on Wildeblood with the notable exception of Kenneth Tynan, a friend from their days at Oxford, who stood bail for him.

Montagu insisted then that 'nothing happened', a claim he reiterated when breaking his forty-six-year silence on the matter.[44] While admitting that there had been dancing and kissing with the two men, who he said were 'self-confessed homosexuals', Montagu denied any sexual relationship. On the other hand, even if there had been, it wasn't a matter for the court. All three were found guilty and jailed, Montagu for a year and the others for eighteen months. Kathleen Tynan recalled: 'The press embellished the modest incident with stories of orgies and high living, gloating over the fate of these "evil men".'[45] In a further revelation of the growing climate of homophobia, she revealed that the *Evening Standard*'s editor, Percy Elland, sent a note to Beaverbrook to say 'that Scotland Yard was stepping up its action against homosexuals . . . Benjamin Britten had been interviewed and . . . Cecil Beaton was on the list'.[46] Beaverbrook's own attitude towards homosexuals was ambivalent. Though he pursued Montagu, when Tom Driberg pleaded with Beaverbrook to use his influence with the other press barons to suppress reports of a case against him for homosexual offences, he did so. Robert Edwards reveals that Beaverbrook, in a 'sadistic touch', received Driberg while taking a bath.[47]

Despite the outcome, by the end of the Montagu trial it was possible to detect a change of public mood. The *Daily Mirror* reported that it was the two airmen who were heckled by the 300 people outside Winchester Assizes.[48] When Montagu and his friends emerged some time later, after most of the crowd had dispersed, they were surprised by the clapping and backslapping from those who had stayed on. Montagu recalled there were cries of 'good luck' and 'keep smiling'.[49]

The case was in large measure responsible for the setting up of the Wolfenden inquiry a month or so later to consider the laws relating to homosexuality and prostitution. Its subsequent report in 1957 was also influenced by Wildeblood's book, *Against the Law*, written mostly in prison and telling the truth about his homosexuality.[50] Wolfenden's report, described by *Sunday Express* columnist John Gordon as a 'pansies' charter', recommended the decriminalisation of gay sex for men over twenty-one years old and the law was finally reformed in 1967.

One trial and one inquiry cannot erase prejudice. A measure of public sympathy for the treatment meted out to Montagu and his friends did not amount to a tolerance of homosexuality itself. That would have to wait for a generation or more. Popular newspapers would continue to echo the populist view of homosexuals as 'sick' or 'evil', or both. *Sunday Express* editor John Junor was fond of saying, 'only poofs drink rosé'. Alan Watkins recalled: 'Poofs played a disproportionately large role in his [Junor's] demonology.'[51] Yet Junor and Montagu became friends.[52]

The *Daily Mirror*'s columnist Cassandra was altogether less liberal and less forgiving. In 1956, he wrote about the American entertainer Liberace, a TV star who was tremendously, if improbably, popular because of his flashy piano-playing, flamboyant dress, wide smile and camp presentation. Bill Connor had chosen the pen-name because Cassandra was the mythological figure fated to utter true prophecies which would never be believed. Connor, a master of invective, believing himself perfectly cast as Cassandra, was an odd mixture of liberal and reactionary. His column in this period about the hanging of Ruth Ellis, a sustained and heartfelt plea against capital punishment, was a superb example of the former.[53]

His column about Liberace, with its nudge-nudge, wink-wink appeal to the baser views of his readers, illustrated the latter. In what was to become one of the most talked-about journalistic phrases of all time, he described Liberace as 'the summit of sex – the pinnacle of Masculine, Feminine and Neuter. Everything that He, She and It can ever want.' He was a 'deadly, winking, sniggering, snuggling, chromium-plated, scent-impregnated, luminous, quivering, giggling, fruit-flavoured, mincing, ice-covered heap of mother love ... This appalling man ... reeks with emetic language ...

Without doubt he is the biggest, sentimental vomit of all time. Slobbering over his mother, winking at his brother and counting the cash at every second, this superb piece of calculating candy-floss has an answer for every situation.'[54]

It was about as close as Connor could get to calling Liberace a homosexual without using the word, and it was certainly offensive. Liberace sued for libel and the resulting seven-day hearing in June 1959, dubbed 'the case of the year' by the *Guardian*, was covered in minute detail by the *Daily Telegraph*. When Hugh Cudlipp gave evidence it turned briefly into a trial of the *Daily Mirror*'s form of journalism.[55] But the crux of the matter was straightforward: Liberace believed he was being 'accused' of being a homosexual, which he denied. For his part, Connor denied that he had implied that Liberace was homosexual, or that his words imputed such a thing.

The jury agreed with Liberace, who was awarded £8,000 in damages plus £27,000 in legal costs, a tidy sum at the time. Years later, especially after Liberace's death in 1987, much was made of the fact that Liberace had lied: he was, of course, a homosexual. That ignored the opposite fact: Connor also lied. Both he and Cudlipp claimed that there had been no intention to allege Liberace was homosexual, a view Cudlipp maintained ever afterwards. It was a disingenuous defence. The meaning of the words was obvious. Connor knew he was appealing to the anti-homosexual prejudices of his readers, it being the whole point of his piece. Indeed, Cudlipp revealed almost forty years after the event that the paper's in-house lawyer warned before publication of the libel risks because the column 'held Liberace up to ridicule and contempt'. It was malicious. Cudlipp, in typical publish-and-be-damned mood, refused to change a word.[56]

None of this justifies Liberace going to law: he knew he would be lying under oath and it's very doubtful whether that column, even if repeated in kind by other papers, would have affected his career or his standing. Then again, to have admitted the truth in public at the time might well have been harmful. It was also his own business, as it was to remain. He refused to reveal his sexuality throughout his life, even when it would have been legally safe and socially acceptable to do so.[57]

The press portrayal of homosexuality in this period was almost wholly negative. Yet the first seeds of a growing public tolerance can be seen to take root, as the post-trial sympathy towards Montagu and the continuing public affection for Liberace illustrated. Newspapers were to prove slower than the people to change their attitude.

PART THREE: 1956–1960

5. DEATH, DEPARTURE AND DARKNESS

> How is it possible to equate the commercial success that is indispensable to a liberated paper with the business interests that will always encroach upon that liberation?[1]

Despite booming sales for some papers, these were years of darkness in Fleet Street. With television having spread rapidly throughout the land, it seemed to almost everyone in the industry that newspapers were doomed. Several national titles vanished and others looked vulnerable. Many regional dailies and evenings were on their last legs.

The press barons finally started to lose heart, with some realising that their time had passed: Lord Kemsley sold out; Lord Rothermere's empire grew more fragile; Lord Astor's losses on the *Times* were mounting; Lord Bracken died; even the wizard, Lord Beaverbrook, was forced to part company with his most famous of editors though he, like Camrose's son, Michael Berry, continued to prosper. The non-baronial owners suffered too: Odhams gave up on the *Daily Herald*; the Cadburys executed the *News Chronicle* and the *Star*; the Carrs watched the *News of the World*'s sales slip away. It was noticeable that three papers without proprietors – the *Daily Mirror*, and the trust-owned *Guardian* and *Observer* – enjoyed considerable success.

The great crisis came to a head with the closure of the *News Chronicle*, an event regarded then and for years afterwards as cataclysmic. Seen in retrospect after the passage of forty years, the disappearance of a paper with sales of 1.1 million, a liberal political agenda and a reputation for fine journalism appears altogether less catastrophic. What is more remarkable is the fact that, despite the tears and the hand-wringing, not to mention the direct practical effect (the setting up of a second royal commission on the press), there was no attempt to get to grips with the central underlying problem exposed by the closure: rising production costs. Since the loss did not, after all, engender a domino effect, Fleet Street treated the *News Chronicle*'s demise as an aberration, a conclusion to a period of high drama rather than an opening scene.

There was a recognition, at least by some, that fundamental change was taking place, albeit slowly, even stealthily.[2] Between 1940 and 1956, the British population grew by about 7 per cent and newspaper-buying grew even faster. Yet the real story – the story from this point on – was concealed by the numbers involved. While it looked as though popular papers were booming because of their immense sales rises, especially by the *Daily Mirror* and *Daily Express*, the real gains were made by the four daily quality titles: the *Daily Telegraph*, the *Times*, the *Manchester Guardian* and the *Financial Times*.

Francis Williams noted in 1957 that sales of the quality papers 'have risen by 177 per cent since 1930 and by 80 per cent since 1937, compared with a 91 per cent increase in total national paper sales since 1930 and one of 65 per cent since 1937'.[3] Williams's analysis was slightly skewed by his omission of certain titles, such as the *Daily Sketch*, but he had properly identified the underlying trend. The same significant, if small, rises were evident on Sundays, where the *Sunday Times* and the *Observer* were doing relatively better than the mass-circulation titles.

So vast was the gap between the two forms of newspaper that even if owners and editors of the larger-circulation papers were listening, and they probably weren't, they didn't care. They continued to fight each other for sales, and some critics were becoming aware of the unsavoury tactics they used to obtain stories and attract readers. Thomas Matthews, an American who was fascinated and repelled by Britain's popular papers, was sharply critical, deriding 'the commoner practices of tabloid journalism' such as 'the screaming headlines, the "cheesecake", the strip cartoons; even more, the deliberate vulgarism, the more brutal invasions of privacy in the ruthless search for "human interest"'.[4]

This criticism, tempered to an extent by his appreciation of the journalists' technical abilities, was the precursor to many such assaults on the popular press for the rest of the century. Matthews, conflating form and content, also tended to miss the point. The liveliness of the layouts, so alien to a man used to the austere blocks of type common in American papers, was inviting to readers. The 'human interest' component was similarly appealing. The 'vulgarism' was debatable. He was on better ground in condemning the intrusive nature of some reporting.

Support for that argument came from a surprising source: Harry Procter, former *Daily Mirror*, *Daily Mail* and *Sunday Pictorial* reporter who was regarded, if grudgingly, as one of Fleet Street's finest. His memoirs, published in 1958, start out in similar fashion to the usual tales of local-rags-to-street-of-fame-riches recounted tediously by so many retired journalists and editors. As an ill-educated shoe-shop errand boy desperate to be a journalist, he nurtured his ambitions by reading Philip Gibbs's famous novel *The Street of Adventure*. After several false starts, he rose from a Leeds weekly to the *Yorkshire Evening Post*, and on to the *Daily Mirror* under Bartholomew, aged just twenty-two.

'The *Mirror* wanted Sex,' wrote Procter. 'It was not hypocritical about its needs – it was perfectly honest to both its employees, its readers, and its advertisers. Sex . . . sold papers . . . by the million. Hard news was merely the third course.'[5] During the war, told to write an entertaining article about the arrival in Britain of US troops, he took an American soldier on a sight-seeing tour of London. His name happened to be Joe and in his piece Procter called him 'G.I. Joe', a tag which Britons thereafter applied to every American.[6]

Procter upset Bart and decided to move to the *Daily Mail*, where its formidable news editor, Lindon Laing, 'taught me the power of hard facts' and 'the art of exposure', hounding crooks and exposing injustice.[7] He spent eight years at the paper, forming a good working relationship with editor Frank Owen, before Cudlipp persuaded him to join the *Sunday Pictorial* in 1952.

Under the byline 'Harry Procter, Special Investigator' he became famous for exposing criminals of all kinds, from drug peddlers to slum landlords, from white slavers to phoney doctors and headmasters.[8] One of his most controversial stories concerned a brother and sister who were separately adopted as infants and, unaware of their background, had married and had two children. By the time Procter traced them, they had discovered the awful secret and were divorced. The resulting front-page exclusive, 'I MARRIED MY BROTHER',[9] was followed two weeks later with the story of the woman's second marriage to a soldier. But Procter was dismayed by a demand from his editor, Colin Valdar, that the divorced brother attend the wedding reception to be pictured with the happy couple. Procter engineered the event but it left 'a nasty taste in my mouth'.[10]

Devoid of tape-recorders and video cameras, usually working alone, Procter's reporting methods depended on him convincing his targets to make, and sign, confessions. He rarely used subterfuge, depending instead on bluff: he had the gift of the gab and was good at thinking on his feet. But he began to have ethical qualms. He worried about the 'small, very unimportant people' he was 'required by my office' to expose.[11] His concerns grew once he inveigled his way into the affections of the families of two young men accused of murdering a policeman, Christopher Craig and Derek Bentley. He persuaded the father of the former to denounce his son, and the parents of the latter to sell the *Pictorial* their son's final letter from jail before his execution. 'Though I was big-time in Fleet Street, I was unhappy,' Procter wrote. 'I did not like some of the stories I was writing.'[12] Colleagues who detected his disillusion accused him of going 'soft'. Procter, who quit the *Pictorial* in 1957, sadly admitted: 'Perhaps I was.'[13] He spent a brief time in Manchester as a freelance, living on the margins, before returning south, down on his luck and without an income. Procter was seemingly ostracised by Fleet Street. Despite his considerable achievements, his name doesn't appear in any of the books about Mirror group or the *Daily Mail*.

The end of his life was very sad, as I witnessed on one of my first assignments as a teenage reporter on the *Barking & Dagenham Advertiser* in 1962. Procter and his wife Doreen were living in a run-down council house in Dagenham with the two youngest of their six children. I can't recall why I was sent to his front door, but I had no idea of Procter's journalistic eminence (the young care too little about history) and he was both rude and aggressive. Thin, wild-eyed and shoddy, he appeared to be drunk. When I reported back to my editor, who was aware of Procter's past, he commented knowingly that drink had brought about his downfall. In fact, Procter's daughter Val later discovered that her father was almost certainly suffering from an illness which caused him to behave eccentrically. 'He got drunk on one pint,' she said.[14] My second visit to the Procter house was sadder still: it was to confirm his death from cancer. He was just forty-seven. Four of his children – Val, Phyllis, Barry and Jane – went on to become journalists too, though none of them worked on the street of their father's disillusion.

In Fleet Street, editors shrugged aside the criticisms of Procter and Matthews, though they were not too happy about the launch in 1957 of a Granada TV programme, *What the Papers Say*, that took them to task for their content.[15] They excused their methods by pointing to the enthusiastic public response. As far as they were concerned, they were simply giving people what they wanted. In fact, this is an era in which that wasn't entirely true because papers were tending to lag behind their readers' demands. Despite the pressures on them to win sales, editors tended to stick to what they liked to call 'hard news': crime, tragedies, court cases – the juicier the better – and political scandal. Conservative in outlook, they took few risks with content.

Politics aside, they couldn't help but see their audiences in terms of their own preoccupations and prejudices, reflected in their supposedly competing, but very similar, editorial agendas. It is significant that the editors of the five highest-selling papers in 1956 were all men in their fifties, while their owners and controllers – with the exception of the *Daily Mirror*'s forty-three-year-old Cudlipp – were even older. These men understood the public appeal of celebrities, whether they be film stars or singers. Frank Sinatra, Marilyn Monroe and Grace Kelly featured regularly, and papers were also quick to recognise the impact of Brigitte Bardot after the 1956 release of *And God Created Woman*. What baffled all of them was the rise of a youth culture, itself manifested through show business, which was quite unlike anything in their previous experience. It wasn't a newspaper-generated phenomenon and it took editors a long time to realise its implications and, therefore, to exploit it for sales purposes.

Their first reaction was to condemn it.[16] Papers were extremely negative about rock 'n' roll and the young fans who called themselves 'Teddy boys'. Bill Haley's 'Rock around the Clock' spent eight weeks at the top of the US chart from July 1955, and Elvis Presley's 'Heartbreak Hotel' topped it in April 1956. Yet neither received much coverage at the time, and the stories that did appear were anything but sympathetic. A *Daily Sketch* report that 'rhythm-crazed teenagers terrorised a city' was typical of the press's over-reaction to 'delinquent' and 'decadent' music. This lack of appreciation for youth culture even prompted knee-jerk attacks from perceptive music critics, such as Steve Race in *Melody Maker* and the *Daily Herald*'s Mike Nevard.[17] One of the *Herald*'s historians noted that during the Suez crisis, when society's so-called 'enemy within' was 'the malevolent ghost of James Dean' and 'with Hound Dog at number three, and Bill Haley and Lonnie Donegan sharing three other Top 10 places, the paper was preoccupied with Vera Lynn's winter tour and [the band leader] Ted Heath's new line-up'.[18]

Papers were alert to another supposed threat: the influx of black immigrants from the West Indies. In October 1954 the *Empire News* reported race riots in London, reports which prime minister Churchill was assured were exaggerated.[19] Four years later, disturbances referred to by papers as 'race riots' occurred in London's Notting Hill and Nottingham.[20] No one was killed or even maimed, though there was no doubt that several blacks suffered beatings in Notting Hill. Yet the worst struggles were between white youths, usually referred to as Teddy boys, and the police.[21] The *Manchester Guardian* even reported: 'By no stretch of the imagination could the hooliganism that took place be called racial riots.'[22]

Hindsight suggests otherwise: racism, a word not then coined, underlay the disturbances, even if poor whites were expressing a wider dissatisfaction with their place at the bottom of the heap and contempt for the authorities. How else can one explain gangs of youths roaming the streets chanting: 'We want a nigger'?[23] The Notting Hill incidents were due to unscrupulous landlords using black immigrants to force out white tenants protected by rent legislation.[24] In Nottingham, the main disturbance started outside a pub and involved a small group of 'wide boys' who carried knives and organised prostitution. Six whites were stabbed, but the fighting occurred largely between mixed groups, rather than black versus white. Later white Teddy boys, acting as vigilantes, patrolled the area[25] and 'no coloured people were involved'.[26]

Yet the impact created by the press coverage of these 'riots', particularly that in Notting Hill, was so great they became central to a myth about the 'threat' to indigenous white Britons by 'indigent immigrants from the Commonwealth'.[27] The pejorative descriptions of 'foreigners', inaccurate claims about their reliance on National Assistance, and the exaggerated reportage of the incidents themselves imbued the disturbances with a disproportionate significance. Though a *Daily Express* writer properly exposed the myths behind local prejudice against immigrants,[28] the paper's editorial fanned the flames by referring to the 'flood of coloured immigrants'.[29]

The *Daily Mail*, oddly silent in its own leaders, gave Labour MP Maurice Edelman space to urge immigration controls.[30] In the *Daily Mirror*, an admirable front-page cartoon by Vicky equated Teddy boy 'racialist thugs' with Hitler,[31] but next day the paper advocated that immigrants should not be allowed into Britain unless they first had a job and a home.[32] It also urged deporting 'no-goods' such as 'the coloured brothel-keeper'.

The *Daily Herald* condemned the idea of a 'colour bar', but with the higher-selling Labour-supporting *Mirror* adopting such a stance it's no wonder the riots were 'used as examples of the dangers of unrestricted immigration'.[33] The riots, and the way they were reported, can be seen as a defining moment in a growing national debate about the need for immigration controls. In essence, papers seemed to agree that simply by living in Britain black people threatened the rule of law. Lord Salisbury, former secretary of the state for Commonwealth relations and Tory leader in the Lords until 1957, saw the riots as justification for his claim that controls should be imposed on black immigration.[34]

The *Daily Telegraph* argued that 'to panic because a few Teddy-boy thugs pick on coloured men ... would be pitifully short-sighted' but nevertheless called for 'some form' of immigration control.[35] The *Sunday People* ran a splash headlined, 'Coloured crooks to go – Official', claiming, inaccurately, that the government was planning 'to deport coloured undesirables'.[36] The paper partially redeemed itself soon after by publishing a seven-week series based on the disillusion of a Jamaican immigrant who explained how some of his compatriots were pressured by prejudice into crime.[37] Despite its sympathetic gloss, it could be read as a subtle plea for assisted repatriation.

Therefore, not only the events – but the reporting of the events, the representation of them – played a significant role in the introduction of the 1961 Commonwealth Immigrants Bill. One of the foremost academics on the subject pointed to the 'widespread coverage ... of stories relating to race and immigration issues ... a flowering of popular debate about housing and social conditions in areas of black settlement' but also 'a resurgence of extreme right-wing groups'. It was, the 'interplay between these processes [which] produced a wide variety of stereotypes and popular images about black people'.[38] For example, the *Times* reported that in the riot areas 'there are three main charges of resentment against coloured inhabitants'. They were workshy, relying on state benefits; they found houses while whites could not; they indulged in misbehaviour, 'especially sexual'.[39] Though the paper's leading article that day attributed the problem to 'resentments harboured by ignorant [white] folk' and 'youthful ruffianism',[40] other papers were less scrupulous. In the years after the 'riots', blacks – not Teddy boys, who were a passing phenomenon – were identified as the real source of social instability and a continuing challenge to the rule of law.

News Chronicle: murder or euthanasia?

'The death of the *News Chronicle*', wrote James Cameron, 'is the biggest journalistic tragedy for many years ... the most meaningful collapse the newspaper business has seen this generation.'[41] His anguish reverberated along Fleet Street. 'Many papers have died over the years,' Francis Williams lamented. 'None has ever been buried so cynically.'[42] Redundant staff were bitterly upset and lashed out at the way the deed was done, in secret, by rich men. Margaret Stewart wrote of the 'anger that we should be sold like a cake of soap'.[43]

The widespread journalistic view that it had been the fault of the managers and, by extension therefore, of the owners was given credence by Beaverbrook. 'It wanted leadership and they had no leadership,' he said. 'It passed from one weak management to another.' Then, rubbing salt into the wounds, Beaverbrook added: 'If they had placed it in the hands of any good young man he would then have been able to build it up.' He probably believed that but only up to a point: it certainly didn't reflect his genuine view about the reasons for the paper's demise (see below, p. 101). Hugh Cudlipp, writing some years later, blamed the editorial policy, arguing that the paper was 'crucified on the cross of earnest but uninspired journalism and righteous but timid management'.[44] The Cudlipp perception probably comes a little closer to the mark. But a review of the many thousands of words written about the *News Chronicle* before and after its death in October 1960 suggests that the reaction to closure was out of all proportion to the event.

The sale of the *News Chronicle* and its London evening paper, the *Star*, to Rothermere's Associated group so that they could be swallowed whole by the *Daily Mail* and *Evening News* respectively – in other words, obliterated – was certainly sad. Some 3,500 people lost their jobs, though union strength ensured that the print workers soon found employment elsewhere. Most of the journalists moved to the provinces or overseas, went freelance or chose entirely different work.[45] More than a million people were deprived of the chance to buy their paper of choice, though many of them already took other titles as well.

Closure was not as devastating as it was painted, nor did it herald the predicted collapse of Fleet Street. On reflection, it probably had a beneficial outcome. The true picture was obscured because too many commentators confused the secrecy of the sale and the controversial choice of buyer with the act of closure itself. Understandable anger at the sudden announcement, compounded by paltry redundancy terms (the so-called 'cocoa handshake' amounted to just one week's pay for every year of service), should have been separated from the underlying reasons, and necessity, for the sale. Similarly, to blame 'management', even if that meant the owners, did not get to the heart of the matter.

In their haste to shed all blame themselves, too many journalists lost their critical faculties, even one as fine as Francis Williams. In his seminal press history published in 1957, his analysis of the *News Chronicle*'s failings in the mid-1950s was spot on. Asking why the paper had lost circulation despite having distinguished writers, columnists and special correspondents plus the 'priceless journalistic gift of surprise' he answered that it manifested 'a chronic inability to make up its mind what public it is after and communicates its indecision to readers'.[46] In other words, the paper had lost its way editorially. It had also, of course, lost its way politically. Originally identified as the organ of the Liberal party, its transformation into a small – 'l' liberal organ was never convincing.

Yet, once the *Chronicle* was closed, Williams castigated the owner, Laurence Cadbury, not for his paper's editorial failings, but because he had sold it, and the *Star*, to Rothermere, thereby making a commercial rather than a moral or political decision. 'The soul of these great newspapers was not his concern,' wrote Williams. He had sold the *Chronicle* 'to a paper of diametrically opposed interests'.[47] He didn't forget that the *Chronicle* had itself survived only by swallowing rival papers down the years. Nor did he shrink from admitting that the Cadburys had sacrificed considerable sums to keep their papers afloat. He also couldn't deny the falling circulation figures, down from 1.5 million in 1950. But he still regarded the sell-off as an act of murder and the murderer as Laurence Cadbury.

Let's briefly consider what happened in the years leading up to closure, looking at the facts rather than at opinions. After the *News Chronicle* company's profits fell in 1955, it registered a loss the following year, for the first time since 1930. The board was divided over both strategy and tactics, with regular clashes between chairman Laurence Cadbury and the former chairman, Walter Layton. Bracken revealed how deeply divided they were over the appointment of a new managing director and, in 1955, predicted a sale.[48]

At that time Beaverbrook repeated a pledge made three years before to fund Layton in a takeover, which Cadbury opposed.[49] Layton also had exploratory talks with Rothermere and Odhams which was favoured by Layton because a merger with the *Daily Herald* might produce 'a new independent paper of the moderate left'.[50] This plan was backed enthusiastically by the *News Chronicle*'s editor, Michael Curtis, whose other option was to turn the paper into a serious, up-market, news-oriented tabloid.[51] Frank Cousins, general secretary of the Transport Workers' Union, put paid to the merger with the *Herald* by convincing the TUC that it must retain political control over the *Herald* or any successor paper in which the unions had a financial stake. Curtis's tabloid proposal was rejected by the board at an August 1957 meeting which also decided that Layton and Cadbury should resign from the papers' operating boards in favour of John Coope, the new managing director. Curtis, frustrated by the board's failure to adopt either of his ideas, dismayed Layton by also resigning.[52] The *News Chronicle* had lost an excellent young editor.

Coope soon realised himself that the paper's only salvation lay in a merger of some sort and, following Layton's example, opened detailed negotiations with Rothermere in 1958 for a merger with the *Daily Mail*. The result, in March 1959, was a clumsy agreement in which Associated took a three-monthly renewable option to buy the *Chronicle* group for £1,925,000, plus ten shillings (50p) for every reader gained by the *Mail* over 300,000. But this agreement, known as the 1925 Plan, was a long time coming to fruition. By May 1960, the *Chronicle*'s situation had worsened with losses threatening both shareholders and pensioners. Circulation was declining fast: in June 1960 it was selling 1,160,000 copies despite the supposed benefits of absorbing the *Daily Dispatch* in 1955. The *Star* was down to 735,000 from 1,230,000 in 1951. Losses of both papers had increased from £237,000 in 1959 to £300,000 in the first nine months of 1960.

Hopes of avoiding the Rothermere offer, lifted by the interest shown by Australian media magnate Sir Frank Packer, faded. In July, the board faced three options: to soldier on; to put the company into liquidation; to take up the 1925 Plan. Mounting losses ruled out the first; advisers counselled that the second would raise much less money than the third, reducing redundancy payments to staff. So the Rothermere proposal was the only viable option. Layton, now seventy-six, made one last desperate attempt to avoid it, by wooing Roy Thomson. When that failed, Rothermere obtained the titles and, supposedly, the readers' goodwill. For £1.5 million he had bought the titles, the sites, the printing plant and a wharf. Rumours of the sale were still being officially denied when the letters of dismissal were being sent to staff, a nasty manoeuvre but, given the situation, necessary. If Rothermere was to extract the maximum extra circulation for the *Daily Mail* out of the merger, he needed to surprise his rivals. If the news had leaked they would surely have sabotaged his attempts to lure *News Chronicle* readers to the *Daily Mail*.

Amid the storm of protest following the sale, Layton and fellow board member Geoffrey Crowther issued a public statement. 'To our infinite regret we could see no preferable alternative,' they wrote to the *Times*. The sale was 'made in the interests of the staff ... The economics of the newspaper industry are very cruel to a popular paper with a relatively small circulation. It can sell less advertising space than its rivals, and therefore can give its readers less editorial matter to read. Inevitably it appears to offer less for the money. So its circulation ebbs away, and advertisements are still harder to get.' Breaking out of 'this vicious circle' is virtually impossible. Offers were insufficient to give the kinds of guarantees that would have been necessary. They also clarified the reasons for secrecy.[53]

This explanation, which appears entirely truthful, did not placate the critics nor assuage the bitterness. They had brought into the open the key factor which had caused the *Chronicle*'s demise: lack of advertising. Only one contemporaneous commentator acknowledged it – as, eventually, did Beaverbrook.[54] But the shock of the *Chronicle*'s closure was so great that critics tended to overlook the facts.[55] After blaming management for their 'failure to take action earlier', Williams then blamed them for not having negotiated a merger with the *Daily Herald* three years before, a deal he knew the unions had thwarted.[56]

An illuminating *Economist* article (unsigned, but probably written by

Crowther) contended that the *Chronicle*'s problems stemmed from the peculiar economics of the newspaper industry. Popular success had rested on selling at a price well below the cost of production and then depended for profit on 'advertisements got on footing of the inflated mass sales'. Only those with the largest circulations could hope to benefit while, 'for the unsuccessful in the race ... the spiral is remorselessly downwards'.[57] What the article didn't say, though Cadbury later made it clear, was that the abolition of newsprint rationing in 1957 ended the system under which advertising was spread evenly around all titles. Advertisers then turned their backs on the *News Chronicle* in favour of papers with higher sales at a time when commercial television – launched in September 1955 – was also beginning to win a slice of the then relatively small advertising cake.

There is abundant evidence from a study of the files and the views of its staff that the *News Chronicle* was in that most hopeless of situations: it was a mid-market paper selling at a down-market price with the pretensions of appealing to an up-market audience. In advertising terms, it was therefore a basket case. As one of its journalists readily admitted: 'The "Chron" was unsmart, inefficient, non-hip, elderly. It was also kindly, concerned, occasionally courageous and in its own way cultured ... It appeared to believe that teachers and nurses and people who looked after incurables might be as worth knowing as a pubescent ballad singer.'[58] Another staff member, Margaret Stewart, conceded that in 'the last few years, life on the *Chronicle* had become increasingly frustrating and demoralising, with the absence of any clear lead on any issue or any idea what the paper was trying to do'.[59] A third thought it 'increasingly bland'.[60]

It is certainly clear that, from the moment 'the youthful, energetic and misunderstood' Curtis quit as editor in 1957, the *Chronicle* lost direction.[61] Norman Cursley, then fifty-nine and having spent almost thirty years with the company, became acting editor. One of his assistants, Mike Randall, who urged Cadbury to take the paper up-market, was then offered the editorship, but chose to move to a senior position at the *Daily Mail* instead.[62] So Cursley, the plodding climber up the greasy pole, was given the editorship in February 1958. Purser thought him 'indecisive, and far from inspiring', claiming that 'a kind of spiral of demoralisation set in'. There were vague attempts at populism, news lacked direction, the head printer was allowed to assume too much power over production times and, worst of all for a staff which had enjoyed working for a radical paper, it lost its political edge. 'Someone sighed: "If only Dickens were alive"; someone else, "If only Cursley were." '[63]

Indeed, in all the paper's many tear-stained obituaries, it is noticeable that its greatest triumphs were almost all in the distant past: its prescient, principled protests at the handing-over of Manchuria to the Japanese and the Italian rape of Ethiopia; supporting the republicans in Spain; warning its readers of Mussolini's and Hitler's real ambitions. In domestic affairs, the paper had kept the Liberal party honest, helping to detach it from Ramsay MacDonald's coalition. It had been, as its columnist Dogberry pointed out, 'a remarkable paper' with 'vision, imagination, integrity . . . fighting . . . for causes that really mattered'.[64] James Cameron, one of the *Chronicle*'s undoubted stars, also referred to the paper's 'admirable free-thinking radical traditions'. These were eventually 'surrendered because there was nothing at the top but timidity, conventionality and emptiness'.[65]

In such a climate it's unsurprising that Laurence Cadbury took the brunt of the criticism, exacerbated by a shareholder successfully contesting pay-outs to staff because investors had a prior call on the available money for unpaid dividends. When the court eventually ruled in his favour it says much for the vast majority of shareholders that they voluntarily handed back cash to ensure that staff received their redundancy money, with Layton dipping further into his own pocket so that no one would lose out. But it took until the summer of 1963 before it was sorted out. Cadbury's attempt to explain the circumstances to the Royal Commission failed to sway its members too. Its final report stated: 'We cannot escape the conclusion that the failure of the *News Chronicle* was not entirely the result of the inevitable law of newspaper economics: different and more consistent managerial and editorial policy might have saved this newspaper.'[66]

Well, anything is possible, of course, though I doubt whether the paper was saveable from 1940 onwards. It had lost its *raison d'être*. Once the Liberal party became a rump, it no longer had a political point. The *News Chronicle* niche all but disappeared after the war, being eclipsed on the left by the *Daily Mirror* at one end of the market and, gradually, by the *Manchester Guardian* at the other. On the right, the *Daily Express* and *Daily Mail* offered better value than the *Chronicle*. Yes, the Cadburys, for a variety of reasons, did prove poor newspaper proprietors. Laurence Cadbury's heart wasn't in it, and his politics were very different from his father's, shifting perceptibly towards the Conservatives.[67] The paper's opposition to Suez was certainly not his doing (see next chapter). It is highly doubtful if anyone could have saved the *News Chronicle*, not even Beaverbrook's notional 'good young man'.

A great deal of hostility towards Cadbury stemmed from the 'take-over by the true-blue *Daily Mail*, the paper that at one time supported Mosley and Mussolini'.[68] Staff still committed to the paper's liberalism were appalled that the morning after closure the *Mail* appeared with 'a captured banner at its masthead' which read 'incorporating the *News Chronicle*'.[69] Its editor, William Hardcastle, was the *Mail*'s most liberal editor since Frank Owen, but the taint of the former Lord Rothermere's fascist flirtation was not to be forgotten.

Claud Cockburn lampooned the whole episode in a cod conversation between 'Lord Overlord of Ink, owner of the morning *Python* and the evening *Boa*' and his acolyte 'Sir Jiggery Pokery' interrupted by 'an Average Man' who spoke for the bereft readers.[70] It was funny, but it played to old prejudices about press barons. The truth was that the closure presaged the realities of a new economic climate which threatened the existence of family-owned newspapers run for ideological rather than commercial reasons. From this point on, it should be noted that most of Fleet Street's critics would concentrate their fire on managerial incompetence rather than proprietorial privilege.

Williams almost read the runes correctly in asserting that the *Chronicle*'s closure signified 'a greater and greater polarization of the press ... with at one end a few excellent quality papers ... and at the other a greater and greater concentration of a few popular papers'.[71] But he was wrong to add: 'The immediate outlook is dark.' It was not. It was left to Cameron to pose the question that would echo down the years, challenging the nature of capitalist ownership without offering a coherent alternative: 'Here is the most insoluble problem of what we rather fulsomely call the "Free Press": how is it possible to equate the commercial success that is indispensable to a liberated paper with the business interests that will always encroach upon that liberation?'[72]

After the closure, one of the *Star*'s displaced journalists, Edward Martell, showed great initiative in launching his own non-union paper, the *New Daily*. In April 1960, 'the only daily newspaper in Great Britain independent of combines and trade unions' made its first appearance. As the *Economist* noted, 'the interesting thing about this shoestring venture is that it has been launched from the right-wing of politics'.[73] Interesting, and bizarre, it was largely funded by members of Martell's right-wing group, the People's League for the Defence of Freedom. Its policy statement in the first issue announced that it would be loyal to the Crown, assert the independence of Great Britain and the British Commonwealth, and hold firmly to the belief that Britain's right to world leadership had not yet been superseded.[74]

Printed on its own presses in north London, with materials obtained from abroad and a generator to foil possible action by the electricians' union, the sixteen-page tabloid sold few copies. It also found itself quickly on the defensive about its news agenda. For example, it had decided not to write about apartheid, it explained, due to 'saturation' coverage of the topic elsewhere.[75] The *New Daily*, dismissed by Cudlipp as 'a curious, ill-tempered little newspaper',[76] lasted for about five years, but long before its end, in January 1966, it was reduced to a scrappy four-page, A4-sized sheet published twice a week.

Rothermere: hiccups from swallowing the opposition

The *News Chronicle* merger with the *Daily Mail* was generally regarded as a 'well-publicized error of judgement' by Lord Rothermere.[77] It may well have proved a long-term commercial success, in terms of the real estate, but that had not been the point. Hopes that the *Mail* would gain a million new buyers overnight, with *Chronicle* readers switching happily to the *Mail* which arrived through their letter boxes in place of their axed paper of choice, were dashed. But it was far from the disaster even contemporary commentators, with the statistics to hand and the chance to analyse without prejudice, have suggested.[78]

The belief that the *Chronicle*'s whole audience would move *en masse* to the *Mail* was facile. Those kinds of simplistic sums never work out. For a start, it doesn't take account of people who bought another title as well as the *Chronicle.* It's true that many indignant *Chronicle* buyers turned their backs on the *Mail* straightaway. Those who didn't reject it out of their own sense of propriety, aware of its politics and history, were probably influenced by the media frenzy generated by rivals who helpfully reminded them that the *Mail* had an illiberal history, supporting fascism and indulging in dirty tricks against Labour (the Zinoviev letter).

Even so, the *Mail* was selling just over 2 million in the first six months of 1960. By the first six months of 1961, its audited sale was 2,680,000. Given the negative publicity, to have held on to two-thirds of the *Chronicle*'s readership for twelve months was a creditable performance. In that sense at least, the merger initiative can be viewed as a success. As we will see, the difficulty lay in holding on to them beyond the first year, but that doesn't negate the achievement. Esmond Rothermere had pulled off a neat business coup.

This should not blind us to Rothermere's central problem: having secured a new audience for his flagship paper, he had no real idea why they should read it and what he should do with it. He could wheel and deal, but he had no clue why his *Daily Mail* existed, what it was for. From the end of the war it had been left hopelessly in the wake of the *Daily Express* and *Daily Mirror*, floundering around without making waves. A middle-of-the-road conservative, he lacked political passion, and liked his paper to take a centrist route. Rather engagingly, Rothermere thought *Chronicle* readers would flock to the *Mail* because of his self-image as a liberal Conservative.[79]

Though he hardly interfered in day-to-day editorial decision-making, Esmond created a stultifying atmosphere in which editors tended to play it safe. None fitted the bill better than Arthur Wareham, who resembled a bishop,[80] and even styled himself 'The Quiet Man of Fleet Street'.[81] He was the kind of conservative chap who appealed to Rothermere, and they didn't argue, but most of the content was pretty uninspiring. It is hard to know whether Rothermere was really concerned. For reasons he never made clear, he suddenly sacked Wareham in December 1959, and the quiet man went quietly, to be replaced by a huge man, William Hardcastle, who would later become a household name. Hardcastle, the son of a Newcastle doctor, was fifty-one. He had spent most of his career as a reporter, including lengthy spells as a foreign correspondent, before joining the *Daily Mail* as a junior executive in 1952. For six weeks he stood in as editor of the *Sunday Dispatch* before Rothermere chose him to edit the *Mail*. Under him, the paper became much more liberal than in the previous decade, though it was nothing like as radical as in Owen's period, nor was it as exciting.

Hardcastle was a news-man and looked the part. He was overweight and a chain-smoker given to appearing on the news-floor with his shirt-sleeves rolled up. Initially popular, within months of his arrival his journalists came to recognise that he was moody, uninspiring, indecisive and too ready to 'slavishly ape' the *Daily Express*.[82] As editorial morale sagged, so did the mood in the advertising department. Despite the *Chronicle* closure, ad revenue was flat because the *Mail* was unable to charge as much as the *Express* and had difficulty in attracting advertisers. At the same time, union problems worsened.

Rothermere could have taken some heart from the performance of his other morning paper, the *Daily Sketch*, except for his embarrassment at continuing criticism from Randolph Churchill and his ilk. Under Bert Gunn's editorship, sales moved beyond 1.3 million during 1957. That year he was censured because one of his female reporters attempted to smuggle herself, in the boot of a car, into a party at the Duke of Kent's home.[83] Circulation ebbed away by the following year and, with losses reaching an annual £360,000, the *News of the World*'s owner, Sir William Carr, pounced. In the summer of 1959, he offered £1.5 million to buy the *Sketch*, which was printed on his presses, but Rothermere asked for £5 million and Carr walked away.

At the end of 1959, Rothermere moved Gunn to the *Sunday Dispatch*, ousting Walter Hayes (who would later quit journalism for the car industry and end up becoming a senior executive with Ford). In Gunn's place, he installed the *Sunday Pictorial*'s successful, but frustrated, Colin Valdar. Valdar set about proving 'with no cheque book and practically no promotion' that the *Sketch* 'could be viable'.[84] He ditched the contests, cut out fringe overseas sales, ran the paper without deputies or foreign bureaux, and banned the use of hire cars. The *Sketch* was soon producing six issues for less money than one issue of the *Express*.

Despite the cost-cutting, there were odd things to appreciate, such as the work of the chief photographer Stanley Devon, who was renowned for the quality of his pictures.[85] The sports department, according to its long-serving star columnist Laurie Pignon, performed well 'because we were the underdogs and we knew we had to fight, so we tried harder than our rivals'.[86] Pignon viewed his *Sketch* experiences as exhilarating, as did several of his colleagues. This sense of camaraderie would be echoed in future by journalists at other lowly staffed titles such as the London *Evening News*, *Daily Star* and *Today*.

Rothermere's son and heir, Vere Harmsworth, was seconded to the *Sketch* during these years as assistant general manager, and was soon seduced by Gunn's buccaneering style. But the key to Vere's future good fortune lay in the forging of a friendship with the *Sketch*'s ambitious twenty-five-year-old features editor, David English, one of Gunn's favourites. They first met in 1956 when they combined to launch a win-a-pub competition.[87] Vere acknowledged English's talent; English acknowledged Vere's lack of pomposity. Though English went off a couple of years later to become a New York correspondent with the *Sunday Dispatch*, Vere did not forget his good impression of the dynamic young man.

When Gunn moved to the *Sunday Dispatch*, he attracted controversy once again. He ran a story about the divorce of the wealthy tobacco heiress Edwina Wills entitled: 'Who is the mystery man in the Wills divorce?' As the headline implies, although his reporters knew the identity of the man involved, he decided to withhold his name from his first edition in order to foil his rivals. Unknown to Gunn, the *Sunday Express* had similar information and published the name, winning the laurels for its exclusive. Gunn survived the fiasco and even improved sales, but it wouldn't be for long.

Rothermere appeared to show less interest in the London *Evening News* than in his other papers, and certainly didn't use it as a political lever in the way Beaverbrook did the *Evening Standard*. It had some political credibility because of the energy and resourcefulness of parliamentary correspondent John Dickinson, but the key to the *Evening News*'s success – and a pointer to its future failure – was its devotion to news. One of its former senior executives explained its order of priorities: 'news, news, news, with the other bits filling the spaces in between'.[88]

Under editor Reg Willis, though sales slipped away, it managed to end the decade with a respectable 1.2 million circulation, with buyers as far afield as East Anglia and Bristol. The paper also turned a profit. According to literary editor Eddie Campbell, it appealed largely to what he called 'the cloth-cap population'. But he also pointed out that there was something for everyone in the paper over the course of a week because 'there were so many subjects catered for in the bits and pieces'. Every interest – fishing, playing chess, walking or reading short stories – was covered.[89] Indeed, though the *Standard* boasted of its critics, the *News*'s trio – Felix Barker (film), Leslie Ayre (music) and James Green (TV) – had their followings too.

For me, the most memorable column was Courts Day by Day by JAJ. Written by Jimmy Jones, who was happy never to have his full name in print, his daily article was a superbly crafted observation of quirky incidents in various central London courts. His humorous and sometimes poignant vignettes were unique pieces of work, showing compassion for 'the simplest, silliest human soul'.[90] Much less to my liking were the contributions of the Earl of Arran, nicknamed Boofy, who wrote a maverick right-wing column which often provoked controversy. In a typical example, he once outraged the Swiss by dismissing them as having invented nothing but the cuckoo clock. Boofy probably got the job because he was related to Ann, Esmond Rothermere's second wife. The *News*'s other great strength was sport. The first edition was largely produced with racing fans in mind. E. M. Wellings 'was the most controversial cricket writer of his day' and Reg Gutteridge, later famous for his TV commentaries, was an outstanding boxing writer.[91]

When the *News* incorporated the *Star* in 1960, it didn't raise its total sale as much as expected. And the merger was anything but helpful, creating an identity problem at a time when the paper was beginning to face up to the difficulties of TV which, along with the growth of car radios, was squeezing all evening-paper sales.

A press baron bows out

Lord Kemsley's grip on the modern world was anything but firm. He once called Denis Hamilton to announce breathlessly: 'I've achieved it!' Hamilton inquired about the nature of his achievement and Kemsley replied: 'I've succeeded in dialling your number myself! William [the butler] is having the night off.'[92] His grip on his newspaper business was also fragile. The ramshackle edifice of his empire crumbled as, one by one, he sold off his titles to his competitors. Having dispensed with the *Daily Graphic*, *Sunday Chronicle* and *Daily Sketch*, he was left in 1956 with the ailing *Sunday Graphic* and *Empire News*, a string of regionals in desperate need of care and attention, and the moribund *Sunday Times*. Bad as it was, it still amounted to a substantial business, one of the world's biggest newspaper chains.[93]

Kemsley, unlike Rothermere, did have an idea what should be in his main paper and tried to ensure his wishes were met. The difficulty was that his political and social views were reactionary, and his journalistic knowledge was poor. The result was a *Sunday Times* that was respectable, predictable and unchallenging, failing to attract younger readers who preferred the more anarchic *Observer*. As if the barrage of complaints from Kemsley were bad enough, editor Harold Hodson also had to deal with the prejudices of the prudish Lady Kemsley.[94] She, famously, once ordered the reproductive organs of a prizewinning bull to be removed from a picture in one of her husband's papers, leading to a writ for libel being issued by the bull's owner.

It was fortunate for Hodson and the *Sunday Times* that Hamilton was around, diplomatically guiding Kemsley away from some of his sillier acts of censorship while trying to make the paper less dull. Even so, it looked for a while as if the *Sunday Times* would lose its market leadership. In September 1956 it suffered 'the ultimate indignity' when overtaken by the *Observer*.[95] 'There was panic at Gray's Inn Road,' Hamilton reported, 'and Kemsley convened a special Monday conference – "Black Monday" it was called.'[96] Kemsley's salvation came swiftly with the end of newsprint rationing, allowing the paper to breathe and providing space for Hamilton's innovative creation known as 'the big read'. Though Hamilton liked to talk of the educative function of newspapers, offering people who might never have had the opportunity to gain knowledge, he never fell into the trap of condescension. His big read was targeted at aspiring people rather like himself, from grammar school backgrounds perhaps or those from secondary schools, who wanted to better themselves.

Hamilton thought the best way to compete with television was for broadsheets to 'analyse and amplify the news and what lay behind it'.[97] He found that there was an appetite among readers for four- or five-page book serialisations, often over the course of many weeks. It hardly mattered whether it was autobiography, such as Charlie Chaplin's; wartime stories, such as *The Wooden Horse*; or fiction, like Nicholas Monsarrat's *The Cruel Sea*. A grateful audience lapped it up. Perhaps the most successful of all were the memoirs of his friend Field-Marshal Montgomery. The extracts of Monty's story increased circulation by 100,000 copies over fourteen weeks in 1958, and the new readers stayed.

So comprehensive were the serials that when the *Sunday Times* published Arthur Bryant's version of Field-Marshal Lord Alanbrooke's diaries in 1957, Bryant called Hamilton to ask if they were going to serialise the index too.[98] Hamilton didn't entirely corner the market – Lord Camrose's close friendship with Winston Churchill ensured that the *Daily Telegraph* ran the prime minister's memoirs – but the *Sunday Times* got most of what was available. Publishers soon cashed in on the lucrative serial-rights market and Hamilton was forced to pay handsomely for some books: Montgomery's were so expensive he concealed what he paid from Kemsley. This was to be a feature of all similar relationships between editorial spenders and bosses: Harold Evans later hid the truth from Hamilton, as did Kelvin MacKenzie from Rupert Murdoch, and as did I from MacKenzie, and so on.

Anyway, Hamilton's dissembling was justified. The serialisations worked and the *Sunday Times* streaked ahead of the *Observer*. By 1959, the paper's future looked rosy with sales reaching towards 900,000 compared to the *Observer*'s 680,000. It was at this moment of triumph, probably the only genuine example in Kemsley's career, that he dropped a bombshell. He was selling out.

It was, Hamilton said without exaggeration, 'one of the more extraordinary episodes in British newspaper history'.[99] Kemsley's decision stemmed in part from his wife's medical condition. In February 1958, she suffered a trapped nerve in her cheek and was to live for the rest of her life in a darkened room with her face half covered, in continual pain. The pompous social-climber Kemsley, by now seventy-four, was also upset that he didn't get an earldom. He was certainly dismayed by his first major skirmish with print unions and downcast by his shrinking group. He could simply have stepped aside and passed the group on to his four surviving sons, but death duties loomed and they wanted funds to finance their stylish living.

Kemsley organised the sale with meticulous planning and in great secrecy. First, using nominees to conceal his identity, he bought his company's shares at the market price to increase his shareholding from 30 to 42 per cent. Once he had obtained as much stock as possible, on 1 July 1959 he called the Canadian entrepreneur Roy Thomson and asked him to visit his Gray's Inn Road office 'where he would learn something to his great advantage'.[100] At roughly the same time, Kemsley told his directors, including Hamilton, a bare-faced lie. 'Someone is buying our shares,' he confided to them. He was concerned that 'somebody very undesirable' would take control, so he had 'taken steps to sell it into hands I can trust'. Everyone was stunned by the initial news and then angered once it became clear that Kemsley had engineered the takeover himself. Hamilton even threatened to withhold his signature and to urge other shareholders to do the same.

That hint of a rebellion collapsed when Thomson assured Hamilton that he wanted him, and other key directors, to stay on board. Kemsley also insisted that his sons were given jobs and that his wife kept her Rolls, despite her being a recluse. Thomson gave in because the deal was superb for him: for about £3.5 million he secured Britain's biggest regional newspaper group and one of its most important Sunday papers. He didn't have the money but his bankers, Warburg's, made history in the City by engineering a reverse takeover.[101]

A couple of incidents after the takeover reveal a great deal about Hamilton and Kemsley. Hamilton, keen to give Kemsley a good send-off and to mark his place in newspaper history, asked Hadley to write a valedictory tribute in the *Sunday Times*. In return, Kemsley gave Hamilton a *photocopy* of the cheque from Thomson paying the first instalment of £3.5 million. Though Kemsley had just made a fortune, more through Hamilton's efforts than his own, there was no cheque for Hamilton. The pair never met again.[102]

Hadley, who had been such a faithful servant to Kemsley, died the following year. No member of the Berry family attended his funeral. In his turn, Kemsley was ignored 'by cronies, courtiers and politicians alike. From being a Lord of the Press, he became Lord Nobody, dying an old man, forgotten by the greater world.'[103] He died in a Monte Carlo hotel in February 1968 and was reported to have confessed that selling the *Sunday Times* was the greatest mistake of his life.[104] He had taken over a paper selling 263,000 and sold it with a circulation of virtually 900,000. Whatever his faults, that was Kemsley's legacy.

Thomson: a press baron without a title

So Kemsley House in Gray's Inn Road became Thomson House. Thomson had prospered greatly since his purchase of the *Scotsman*. Three years later he had acquired the licence to launch commercial television in Scotland.

Scorning sceptics who thought he would lose money, he funded more than three-quarters of the £400,000 bid and was soon reaping huge rewards as advertisers flocked to the new medium. In another of his famous quotations, he boasted: 'It's just like having a licence to print your own money.' Years later he thought the remark 'injudicious' but correct.[105]

Thomson's Canadian newspaper acquisitions continued throughout the 1950s, and he also began to buy small-town papers in the United States. But his purchase of the Kemsley chain of eighteen papers put him into a different league. It had the potential to make him huge profits as long as he was able to sort out Kemsley's mess. That meant making several difficult decisions, risking antagonism with print unions while trying to cope with experienced press baron rivals who smelled blood. Thomson's first major headache was a ruthless move by Kemsley's nephew, Michael Berry, owner of the *Daily Telegraph.* For more than twenty years the *Sunday Times* had been printed on the *Telegraph* presses. Berry was evidently upset by a meeting with Thomson which began with the Canadian asking whether the presses could be enlarged in order to print more pages (they couldn't) and ended with him asking whether Berry would like to sell him his paper.[106] Four days later Berry gave Thomson six months' notice to quit the *Telegraph* printing hall.[107]

It could have been a savage blow. Thomson's Gray's Inn Road presses, then printing the *Sunday Graphic,* were inadequate to publish the *Sunday Times* even without the *Graphic.* It would take more than a year before the machinery would be ready. By a stroke of good fortune for Thomson, Berry's company secretary had made a mistake: the original 1937 agreement for six months' notice had later been altered to twelve months. When Thomson discovered the error, he played his hand astutely. Instead of contacting Berry straightaway, he waited for a couple of weeks, winning valuable extra time before revealing the truth.[108] Then Berry delayed replying, because he too was playing a clever game, trying to set the date at the optimum time to launch his own *Sunday Telegraph.*[109] Neither man realised what the other was up to. Eventually, it was agreed that the *Sunday Times* would print its last copy at the *Telegraph*'s Fleet Street headquarters on 22 January 1961, the week that the new Gray's Inn Road presses were set to be finished, and, unknown to Thomson, two weeks before Berry's new paper was set to print its first issue.

During 1960 Thomson took advantage of the closure of the *News Chronicle* to deal with other loss-makers. The *News of the World* now needed another northern printing arrangement and Thomson offered them the use of his newly acquired Kemsley presses. As part of the deal, he offered the Carr family his unwanted *Empire News,* which they then merged with the *News of the World.* A month or so later he closed the *Sunday Graphic.* Thomson followed this with another devious move. He convinced the Scott Trust, owners of the successful *Manchester Evening News,* to take his opposition title, the *Evening Chronicle,* under its wing. They would form a joint managership and, in return, he would print both papers. He guessed that, eventually, the logic of running one rather than two titles would lead to closure of the *Chronicle*, for which he would be compensated by loss of earnings from his printing contract, which is exactly what happened in 1963.[110]

By the end of 1960, Thomson had transformed the fortunes of his company, employing the kind of business-oriented strategy which no rival had ever contemplated. He had closed two loss-making titles, introduced better accounting procedures into his slimmer, fitter regional chain and put the *Sunday Times* on course to increased pagination and increased advertising revenue. He also began the incredibly complex and controversial negotiations which would lead to his purchase of the *Belfast Telegraph* from the Baird family, descendants of its founder. In what turned out to be a convoluted process, culminating in an acrimonious trial the following year during which Thomson was falsely accused of deceit, he succeeded in beating off other bids to win the prize.[111] He maintained the paper's Unionist traditions, retaining its liberal editor, Jack Sayers, who tried so hard to pressure the Unionist party into reform.[112] But Thomson, mortified by the court case, never returned to Belfast.[113]

Crisis at the *Daily Herald*

By 1956, the *Daily Herald*'s troubles were becoming more obvious. Once newsprint rationing ended, just as with the *News Chronicle*, the problem of attracting advertising was revealed. The *Herald*'s low ad volume meant it could only provide eight-page issues while the *Daily Express* managed fourteen.[114] It was, asserted James Curran and Jean Seaton, 'progressively squeezed out of the advertising schedules'.[115] The reason? The *Herald* readership was among the poorest and the oldest, and 59 per cent of them were men, the highest male proportion of any paper.[116] They therefore lacked the purchasing-power profile sought by advertisers, who correctly perceived that the *Daily Mirror* was attracting the more prosperous, and younger, elements of the working class.

The *Herald*, with its cloth-cap image, appeared to be a dull relic of pre-war Britain. It also had about it an aura of decline. *Herald* sales fell steadily, finally dipping under 1.5 million in 1960. Readership surveys showed the *Herald* to have a higher level of reader satisfaction than any other paper. But this loyal band was ageing rapidly and, as they died off, they weren't replaced. Naturally, with falling sales, staff turned on the editor, Sydney Elliott: the paper was 'internally in turmoil', recalled leader writer Douglas Jay.[117]

Odhams, in a forlorn attempt to effect a rescue, first explored a merger with the *News Chronicle*, but the TUC scuppered the deal because it wished to retain control. Then Odhams instituted economies, reducing the size of the staff, before turning to market research. The paper needed to be brighter, it concluded. More, in fact, like the *Daily Mirror*, blending the politics and the political commitment with more general-interest material in order to render the paper more commercial. As simple as this might sound, it required an editor, and a staff, more skilled in populist journalism than Elliott to make it work. Their efforts produced instead a paper which looked as though it was suffering from a chronic identity crisis. On some days the paper looked like the *Mirror*, on others the *Express* or *News Chronicle*. It seemed to have lost all sense of direction. One reporter assigned to cover a 1957 royal tour complained that the *Herald* 'may have been the voice of socialism, but when it came to the Royal Family, the symbolic flat cap was doffed in homage ... the Red Flag hauled down and the Royal Standard hoisted'.[118]

In July 1957, the TUC general council ratified a new pact with Odhams which guaranteed the paper's political identity and reminded everyone that it was the unions' mouthpiece. Three months later Odhams's increasingly disillusioned chairman, Surrey Dane, axed Elliott. In an unprecedented show of support for a sacked editor – and concern about his replacement – twelve key senior staff, including the respected parliamentary correspondent Leslie Hunter, immediately quit. Elliott was replaced by Douglas Machray, a forty-six-year-old Scot who had risen through the sub-editorial route to be production editor. Perhaps the dissenters were wrong not to have given Machray a chance. According to Geoffrey Goodman, a lifelong advocate of serious journalism within a populist format, he was a tough operator who understood the commercial necessities while being committed to a liberal agenda.[119] One Fleet Street luminary who joined at the time was cartoonist Philip Zec, who soon after won an award for a cartoon about the crushing of Hungary by the Soviet Union.

Most memories of Machray are marked by his apparently unilateral decision to advocate unilateral disarmament. His front-page leader, headlined 'A policy for staying alive',[120] appeared 'to have fallen like a bombshell among the movement's leaders'.[121] According to Jay, a leader writer who wasn't consulted about Machray's change of direction, the editor 'was genuinely surprised at the outraged protests from Labour leaders'.[122] Jay was out of the loop, because discussions had been going on for days, in bars and in the office, between senior executives, political and industrial writers. The idea sprang from deputy editor Geoff Pinnington who, with assistant editor Andy Ewart, persuaded Machray to make his stand.[123] Political reporter Harold Hutchinson certainly supported the line, as did the vast majority of readers.[124]

The Labour party's left wing – led by Aneurin Beavan, Michael Foot, Barbara Castle and Ian Mikardo – rejoiced, but the shadow cabinet was outraged, as were the TUC, controllers of the *Herald*'s fortunes. Acting in a typically proprietorial manner, the union leaders demanded that Machray ditch the policy. It was an early warning to Machray, as happened to the editors before him, that the *Herald*'s political masters were prepared to stifle journalistic initiative and independence of thought while its commercial master, Odhams, was desperate to have free rein. Richard Crossman guessed where this would lead. 'If the *Daily Herald* ever got loose,' Crossman ventured in 1958, 'Odhams would soon turn it into a Labour rag, like the *People*.'[125]

But that 'rag', with Sam Campbell having formally stepped into the editor's chair in 1958, was selling 5 million copies every Sunday, and increasing in circulation, while the *Herald* was struggling. Within the *Herald*'s Endell Street offices, the split between politics and populism was pronounced, with staff adopting one position or another, failing to forge a workable synthesis. A saddened Douglas Jay finally quit in 1959 after a twenty-two-year association with the paper, believing it had irretrievably lost its way. He lamented: 'The future lay ever more clearly with the *Daily Mirror* and its imitators.'[126] A year later, with Odhams's losses mounting, Dane finally persuaded the TUC to relinquish its hold over editorial policy, promising that the *Herald* would remain 'a newspaper of the Left'.

Machray's reward for having helped to win this freedom was the sack. In 1960, his chair went to John Beavan, who, as his friend Hugh Cudlipp remarked, was 'not by nature an editor, a writer rather than an executive'.[127] Machray's deputy, Pinnington, was disgusted at being passed over and immediately resigned to join the *Daily Mirror*.

Reynolds News, a paper regarded as the '*Daily Herald* on Sundays', was also struggling to survive by this time. Owned by the Co-operative Society, it had 'lost most of its zing' despite boasting of columnists such as J. B. Priestley, Tom Driberg and Woodrow Wyatt.[128] It was overseen by Cyril Hamnett, chairman of the Co-operative Press, who slept on a sofa in the paper's board-room during visits to London. The editor, William Richardson, tended to sleep in the daytime too, leaving his capable managing editor, Eric Wright, to preside over a paper suffering from declining sales in a 'melancholic atmosphere'.[129]

Cudlipp's greatest years as King's consort

The poor *Daily Herald* lived in the shadow of the brilliant *Daily Mirror*. During these years the dominance of Hugh Cudlipp's popular journalism was never in dispute. He was at the height of his powers. Bill Grundy thought the fast-talking, wildly gesticulating man with a large cigar clamped between his teeth 'looked for all the world like an actor–manager of the hammier school'.[130] John Beavan saw him as a film star: 'Spencer Tracy . . . with a touch of Edward G. Robinson'.[131] Both ring true. Cudlipp's stage, or film set, was the editorial floor, where he reigned supreme. When he arrived, everyone deferred to him, from editor to messenger.

Though he often chose martinets as editors, he rarely lost his own temper. According to Mike Molloy, his man-management was impeccable. As he liked to say: 'I don't give orders. I create the atmosphere.'[132] There are many who disagree, and I have been told sufficient anecdotes by witnesses who admired him to suggest that Cudlipp was not only capable of bullying but often relished it. His tantrums, though rare, were mythologised by the staff and people trod carefully around him. He was aware of his power over his executives and occasionally liked to illustrate it. One of the more famous examples involved the then deputy editor of the *Daily Mirror*, Dick Dinsdale. Cudlipp, in a Manchester hotel bedroom, was frustrated by the noise of a television while shouting instructions to his lieutenants in the adjoining suite. So he ordered Dinsdale to throw the TV set through the window, which he did.

A further insight into Cudlipp's working methods – and the fear he generated among underlings – was superbly recalled by a sub-editor who was about to headline and caption pictures of Princess Margaret and Antony Armstrong-Jones on the night they announced their engagement in 1960.[133] Cudlipp, to the surprise, and alarm, of his executives, suddenly appeared at the backbench (the hub of nightly production where senior sub-editors plan the pages) and barked: 'Front and back pages and middle-page spread.' He fanned out a collection of Armstrong-Jones's own pictures and while the distraught night editor fussed over the problem of putting all the material he had planned for four pages elsewhere in the paper, Cudlipp produced a handwritten letter written to him by Armstrong-Jones. He demanded that the words 'Dear Hugh' and 'Yours sincerely, Tony' should be extracted in order to illustrate to readers that cordial relations existed between the *Mirror* and a man who often complained about prying reporters and photographers.

The sub-editor, Perrott Phillips, couldn't help but notice that the letter concerned the *Mirror*'s failure to pay Armstrong-Jones for previous work. No one sought to raise that quibble with Cudlipp, who was now writing headlines for the front, back and all but one of those for the spread.[134] In this single instance, Cudlipp scribbled the obviously cod line 'Another Armstrong-Jones picture here' so that the sub could fill in a proper headline. Phillips dutifully composed one and sent it to the typesetters. Half an hour later the night editor, waving a page proof under his nose, bellowed: 'You have flagrantly disobeyed Hugh's written instructions. Thank God I spotted it and restored what Hugh had written.' There was, Phillips observed, no reasoning with the man: Cudlipp's word was law. By the second edition, he noted, sense had prevailed.

What that episode illustrates is Cudlipp's flair, power and cheek. In varying ways these attributes were constantly on display in the *Daily Mirror* and his enthusiasm for innovation ensured that his paper remained fresh and exciting. 'What newspapers were about, to me,' he explained years later, 'was controversy. Stimulating thought. Destroying the taboos. Taking on the complicated subjects like economics, national health and production, and explaining them in a language all could understand. The paper worthwhile to me was an Open University.'[135]

In the absence of news, Cudlipp sought to make the *Daily Mirror* into the news, an approach his rivals seemed unable to grasp at the time. In one of his most famous front pages he implied that the young Queen and her husband were having marital difficulties. Over pictures showing the Queen at a racecourse in Britain and Prince Philip at a football match in Gibraltar, he wrote the headlines: 'The Palace denies Royal rift. FLY HOME, PHILIP! The way to kill a silly rumour'.[136] His justification for publishing the story was to refute 'ridiculous and baseless ... rumours of discord' reported in American newspapers.

That single issue of the *Mirror* is a good example of its typical fare. On page four, Cassandra launched a devastating attack on the 'idiocy' of a senior naval officer having to resign from the royal household because of his divorce. On page nine, Donald Zec's interview with an Italian actor, Walter Chiari, about his relationship with Ava Gardner began: 'His is the voice that made Ava quaver – and will probably take Walter to the altar.' On page eleven, was an award-winning picture of four Teddy boys singing in church.

This light material was underpinned, and often overshadowed, by articles on substantial subjects. One of its political staff for nine years from 1955, Gerald Kaufman, thought the *Mirror* 'was very, very serious ... setting very high standards, both of political comment and factual accuracy'.[137] Geoffrey Goodman, looking on from the *Herald* during these years, argued that it had 'a special quality of perception about society' which Cudlipp 'translated into journalism'.[138] In this period the *Mirror* 'began to win golden opinions from people in high places accustomed to sniff at popular newspapers'.[139]

Before we get carried away though, we should note that Cudlipp's *Mirror* sometimes failed to recognise the importance of international political events, such as Suez (see below, pp. 132–6). It was also guilty of peddling illiberal views (see race issues above, p. 98). Much of the credit for correcting these mistakes must go to Sydney Jacobson, who had previously worked with Cudlipp at the *Pictorial*. He was hired as political editor and emerged as Cudlipp's most influential lieutenant. Jacobson, who had a liberal journalistic background with the *Statesman of India* and *Picture Post*, was intelligent, witty and wise, often guiding his master away from trouble. He also drew him still closer to the Labour party under Hugh Gaitskell. Both he and Cudlipp contributed to Gaitskell's speeches.[140] They had sided with him in the party's internal dispute, coming out strongly against Aneurin Bevan. Even so, Cudlipp, aware that many readers were sympathetic to Bevan, was happy to have one of his supporters, Richard Crossman, as a *Mirror* columnist. For a time.

Nor did Cudlipp's *Mirror* escape criticism for its human-interest content and its consequent invasions of privacy. Claims that innocent people were hounded by the popular press came to a head in 1958, with a series of increasingly concerned letters in the *Times*, which warned there might be legislation if editors did not desist.[141] Cudlipp was unmoved: 'The *Daily Mirror* has always tried to observe the accepted standards of decent behaviour and to treat all citizens with consideration and respect . . . We believe that news obtained at the cost of personal distress is not worth printing.'[142] Readers were invited by editor Jack Nener to bring any misconduct by his reporters to his notice. Within a fortnight he had received only ten replies, nine of which were 'frivolous'. The other was a case of serious intrusion, but concerned a freelance photographer.[143]

Cudlipp, for all his power and skills, and despite his paper's growing popularity, could not dislodge the Tories from power. The *Mirror* began the critical week before the 1959 election with a page-one message: 'The Time Has Come for the Tories to Go. WHY? – See Tuesday's *Mirror*.' Without ever quite answering the question, he repeated the slogan until the Thursday, polling day, when he removed from the listings all television programmes before 9 p.m. In the resulting blank space was a single line: 'To Hell with the Telly Until We've All Voted'.

Afterwards, with the Tories having romped home, Cudlipp's *Mirror* lampooned the cabinet for its preponderance of Old Etonians. But he was piqued at the outcome. Crossman was sacked. The *Mirror*'s 'Forward with the *People*' slogan was removed. The Jane strip cartoon came to an end. A Cudlipp editorial proclaimed that 'the accent is on YOUTH. The accent is on GAIETY.'[144] Was this evidence, as both the *Evening Standard* and the *Daily Worker* suggested, of 'a major revolution' at the paper?[145] The normally perceptive Francis Williams thought so: 'The Labour party would appear not only to have lost the election. It has also lost the *Daily Mirror*.'[146] Cudlipp later explained these events away as coincidence without any sinister implication.[147] But he was being disingenuous. It is obvious that he wanted the *Mirror* to take a conscious step away from its identification with the Labour party. It was a significant, if short-lived, experiment in depoliticisation, prompted in part by his concern at the paper being bracketed with the losing party once again.

Cudlipp always proudly claimed to be, first and foremost, a journalist. He was an artist in the shaping of a tabloid front page, delighting to say in bold black type what he thought ordinary people would like to hear but other newspapers were too polite to publish. A classic example came in 1960 when the Paris summit conference that spring was wrecked by a Khrushchev walkout: 'Mr K! (If you will pardon an olde English phrase) DON'T BE SO BLOODY RUDE!' Then came the real insult in smaller type below: 'PS: Who do you think you are? Stalin?'[148]

It was an irreverent technique that opened up new frontiers in Fleet Street. His rivals in the popular press might follow his lead, or they might choose to take the righteously opposite line; either way, as Cudlipp saw it, the *Mirror* got talked about. In 1957, he advertised for a strip cartoon for his paper's northern editions. Soon afterwards the legendary Andy Capp cartoon was born and within six months was appearing in the south too. Cudlipp referred to the flat-capped chauvinist as 'a work-shy, beer-swilling, rent-dodging, wife-bashing, pigeon-fancying, soccer-playing uncouth codger, setting an appalling example to the youth of Britain'.[149]

The most important innovation was the 'shock issue' in which page after page was devoted to a single subject, usually exposing some social evil. 'I evolved it,' Cudlipp said, 'as an exercise in brutal mass education.'[150] The first shock issue, in 1960, was a searing account of the suffering of horses shipped from Britain to the butchers of Belgium and France. This was followed by exposures of the scandals of the poorly equipped youth clubs, cruelty to children, pollution, the suicide club of teenagers on ton-up motorbikes, and the neglect of old and lonely people.

Cudlipp, with one foot in management and one in journalism as editorial director, had more power than any editor. That he was allowed such licence was entirely due to chairman Cecil King's conviction that Cudlipp knew best. The king doted on his prince.

Farewell to the best editor the *Express* ever had

It isn't at all far-fetched to suggest that Cudlipp's success played a part in the downfall of Arthur Christiansen, whom Cudlipp considered 'the best editor the *Daily Express* ever had'.[151] Beaverbrook couldn't help but notice that his paper did not have the *Mirror*'s bounce, nor was it able to cement similar cosy links with its readers. Despite that, the *Express*'s circulation was consistent and steadily climbed by 100,000 throughout 1956.

Beaverbrook was also unhappy with Christiansen's growing celebrity. Chris was regularly appearing on television debates, and in one TV interview he inadvisedly referred to the *Express* as 'my newspaper'.[152] There are few remarks more likely to upset a proprietor. Soon after Christiansen's moment of *lèse-majesté*, in August 1956, he suffered a heart attack while staying with Beaverbrook in the South of France. Some months later he appeared to have made a full recovery but early in 1957, without informing Chris (or most of the journalistic staff), Beaverbrook appointed his deputy, Ted Pickering, as editor and gave Pickering's post to Charles Wintour.

So Christiansen, enormously popular with his staff and most of the rest of Fleet Street, had no idea he had been replaced when he was welcomed warmly by colleagues on returning to his office in the spring. He took morning conference as usual and then walked around the editorial floor greeting his drinking mates. Beaverbrook couldn't face telling him he had been fired, ordering a director, Tom Blackburn, to tell him the truth.[153]

Christiansen was stunned and embarrassed. After twenty-four years as editor, recognised by his peers as a superlative technician and an inspiring leader, it was a disrespectful way to fire him. When he finally had a farewell meeting with Beaverbrook they both wept. But Chris told his friends later that Beaverbrook, on seeing him to the lift, remarked: 'Sorry to see you going down.' Wintour was not alone in thinking it 'very cruel'.[154]

Asked why Beaverbrook had been so adamant in refusing to let him go on, Christiansen said that Beaverbrook had told him: 'Forget all about it, Mr Christiansen. I don't want to be shunned at your funeral.'[155] It became Beaverbrook's public excuse: he didn't want to be responsible for hastening his editor's death by putting him under any more pressure. Christiansen brushed aside Beaverbrook's offer of a sinecure, as a consultant, to accept a consultancy at the *London American*, a weekly paper for expat Americans, and acted as editorial adviser to Associated Television. He also memorably played himself in an unmemorable 1962 movie, *The Day the Earth Caught Fire*. 'It wasn't the Chris we all knew and loved,' Derek Jameson remarked. 'He was far too stilted and self-conscious.'[156]

Chris was fifty-nine when he collapsed and died at the Anglia TV studios while waiting to take part in a programme in September 1963. His high standing among journalists guaranteed him handsome tributes and obituaries.[157] He was, observed John Beavan, 'a babe in politics, in literature and the arts – the stock-in-trade of the old school of editor. What he had was a superb gift for knowing what would interest the ordinary man ... He was the first great technician–editor.'[158]

His *Express* successor, forty-four-year-old Ted Pickering, may not have had Christiansen's charisma and public profile, but he was more than able. Slight and rather shy, he was a clever and calculating man, carefully weighing each decision, and noted for his political adroitness. Known universally as Pick, this 'cool individualist from the North Riding of Yorkshire',[159] learned his craft on the *Northern Echo* in Darlington before joining the *Daily Mail*, where he rose through the ranks to become managing editor. In 1951, he was given the same position at the *Express*. Despite his own self-effacing character, Pick was a great admirer of the more flamboyant school of journalists, such as Frank Owen and Hugh Cudlipp. At the *Express* he was not so much the circus master in the big top as the impresario in a nearby caravan, directing events from his office. He owed a great deal to Christiansen's legacy, having one of the best-trained teams of reporters and sub-editors in Fleet Street. Everyone knew how to react to any news situation and precisely how the *Express* should present it.

The quirky regulars, such as Beachcomber and the pocket cartoons of Osbert Lancaster which featured Maudie, Countess of Littlehampton, remained. Beaverbrook was never certain about the point of either, but accepted his editors' views that they had an enthusiastic following. Beaverbrook's favourite was William Barkley, whom he dubbed 'the Prince of Reporters'. Both his output and the speed at which he wrote were phenomenal. One journalist called him 'the most remarkable sketch writer of modern times'.[160] Others thought him a Beaverbrook toady.

Pick managed his paper well and, after a dip in sales in 1958, set new circulation records in the following two years. His first deputy, Wintour, was none too happy in his role, nor about working for the *Daily Express*.[161] He believed the *Evening Standard* was a 'more creative enterprise' and desperately wished to return.[162] His chance came unexpectedly in April 1959 when a sickly Percy Elland resigned the editorship to become chairman and managing director, dying within twelve months. At forty-one, Wintour had achieved his heart's desire.

Tall, austere, more like an academic than a journalist, he looked every inch the product of his class and tended to act like it too. Abrupt and given to speaking his mind, he was so frosty in his dealings with people that he soon earned the nickname 'Chilly Charlie'. Born in 1917, the son of a major-general, he was educated at Oundle and Peterhouse. Towards the end of the war, as a young colonel on the staff of the supreme Allied command, his superb organisational abilities won him several decorations, including the MBE, Croix de Guerre and Bronze Star. He was befriended at SHAEF in Paris by Arthur Granard, a former *Sunday Express* gossip-column writer, who offered Wintour an introduction to Beaverbrook. After just one test article, the twenty-nine-year-old without any background in newspapers joined the *Evening Standard* as a junior leader writer. Within a couple of years he was promoted to political editor.

Wintour was civilised, politically astute, with liberal views and a deep interest in the arts. He appreciated good writing and proved a great talent-spotter. He also benefited from the celebrity of the cartoonist he had persuaded to join the paper some six months before he moved into the editor's chair. After leaving the *Daily Mirror* for the *Standard*, Vicky created one of the most memorable cartoon images of all time, Supermac. By casting Harold Macmillan in the guise of the comic-strip character Superman, he meant to parody the prime minister. Instead, for a long time, the cartoon lionised him and suggested that his government was a success. It may well have played a part in the outcome of the 1959 election. Vicky's 'White Rabbit' (Anthony Eden) and 'Totem Pole' (de Gaulle) were also memorable.

As for Wintour, like Elland and Christiansen, he ceded all control of his paper's political coverage to his boss. In doing so he 'sensibly saved himself much anguish about editorial independence by regarding Beaverbrook not as his proprietor but as his editor-in-chief'.[163] However rational Wintour's strategy may have been, it would have repercussions for his credibility in later years.

At Beaverbrook's *Sunday Express*, John Junor built on the John Gordon formula, creating a unique newspaper, eschewing both the sensationalism of its down-market siblings and the high-mindedness of its up-market cousins.

JJ forged a paper entirely of his own: middle-brow, deliberately sober, quaint, relentlessly right-wing and, most bizarre of all, virtually devoid of genuine news. There was plenty of castigation but no investigation. Though it relied on the war as its main source of content, it was redolent of the pre-war era. Its stock-in-trade were series about acts of valour by unknown seamen, soldiers and pilots who had undergone private ordeals in wartime, illustrated by heavily inked drawings. The leader page was so Tory it was a wonder it wasn't printed in blue. Quirky news stories were really mini-features, starting with lengthy scene-setting descriptions or homilies, known in the business as 'dropped intros', in which the factual point was revealed only after several paragraphs. For reasons never clear to most journalists at the time or since, it worked. Rightly, Bob Edwards compared it to Scotland's *Sunday Post*, another idiosyncratic paper which enjoyed huge sales.

It was Gordon's column which created controversy. At the end of 1955, the novelist Graham Greene selected Nabokov's *Lolita* – then banned in Britain – as one of the year's best books in the *Sunday Times*. Gordon denounced it as 'the filthiest book I have ever read. Sheer unrestrained pornography'.[164] In response, Greene founded the John Gordon Society 'against pornography' in league with the *Spectator*, then edited by Ian Gilmour. It stood for 'family films ... family books ... lectures which will fearlessly attack the social evils of our time' and would 'form a body of competent censors'.[165] Several of Greene's friends, such as Professor Freddie Ayer, Chris Chataway (then of ITN), Christopher Isherwood, Lord Kinross and Angus Wilson, happily joined in with the joke and a meeting attracted sixty people. Greene was elected president and, when home secretary Rab Butler announced that *Lolita* should remain banned, he was elected honorary vice-president. Gordon was eventually lured into a public debate with Greene, during which the noted anti-pornography campaigner Randolph Churchill oddly chose to heckle Gordon.[166]

Beaverbrook enjoyed the fun too. Outwardly, he ran Express Newspapers like an orthodox business. In practice, he 'continued to be a dictator'.[167] Other newspaper proprietors regarded him as a menace. Throughout the 1950s and 1960s, the power of the print unions was growing, marked by extravagant wage demands, spasmodic attempts to censor editorial content, acts of individual sabotage and gross overmanning. The proprietors agreed that the only way to resist the unions was to act together through the Newspaper Publishers' Association. For seven years the NPA chairman was Cecil King. He wrote: 'whatever pledges were made or undertakings signed, when the crunch came it was the *Express* that broke the united front'.[168] Beaverbrook's strategy was to buy industrial peace for himself, sacrificing profits, while leaving the rest of Fleet Street to manage as best it could. It was a dangerous game.

Top people's paper finds it tough at the top

In the twenty-five years up to the mid-1950s, the *Daily Telegraph* attracted readers at a greater rate than any other newspaper in the country, even including the *Daily Mirror.*[169] Its success vindicated the editorial approach of its owner, Michael Berry, the 'matter-of-fact, shy, hard-working, humorous, courteous and conscientious' man who was 'the complete antithesis of the original press baron'.[170] He ran the *Telegraph* with even more attention to detail then his father. Berry was Gradgrind. Facts mattered more to him than ideas. He believed that facts had a magical power all of their own and his obsession helped to make the *Telegraph* the most comprehensive and information-packed of newspapers. It carried more stories on its news pages, even if in a paragraph or two, than any other title.

During my earliest years in journalism I was told by colleagues that, if I read nothing else, I should comb that paper every day. It would provide me, I was told, with a knowledge of all that mattered. Revisiting the *Telegraph* of that era, it doesn't strike me as required reading after all. The main lead was invariably about domestic politics. The second lead, carried on the right-hand side of the page, was usually a foreign report, most often from Washington. Many of the down-page, one-paragraph shorts were utterly inconsequential: 'Senator Medici, the Italian Minister for the Treasury . . . is to see Mr Thorneycroft, Chancellor of the Exchequer, at the Treasury this morning.'[171] Or 'President Eisenhower . . . spent 5½ hours shooting and bagged 10 quail.'[172] Many of them were about royalty: 'The Duke of Cornwall is remaining indoors at Buckingham Palace with a cold.'[173]

Though Berry ensured that the *Telegraph*'s news coverage was as untainted as possible by bias, there was no such reticence on the leader pages. His editorials were conservative in tone, sometimes reactionary, even if the language was moderate. Berry's own views were avowedly anti-socialist but he generally supported centrist Tory policies. Socially awkward, Berry shunned company while his wife, Pamela, sought it out, building a reputation as a society hostess in competition with Ann Rothermere. Berry attended the parties without enthusiasm, preferring life in his Fleet Street tower where he spoke to a select few, and then as rarely as possible.

He doesn't even appear to have revelled in his paper's success, which eclipsed his major rival not only in sales but in profitability too. These were difficult years for the *Times* and frustrating ones for its editor, Sir William Haley. Apart from a significant circulation rise during Suez (see below, pp. 136–7) the paper's sales had dropped 8 per cent since 1949 while rivals were enjoying huge increases: the *Daily Telegraph* was up 12.5 per cent, the *Manchester Guardian* 25.5 per cent and the *Financial Times* 40 per cent. Rising costs had ended the *Times*'s steady record of profit and Lord Astor, contemplating tax exile in France, gradually transferred his shares to his son Gavin, along with the burden of running the company.

Some £200,000 was spent on a national campaign which advertised the *Times* as the paper for the 'top people'. This snobbish and elitist promotion did little for sales, unsurprisingly, but it explains a great deal about the way the paper perceived itself and its function. Haley, who wanted to expand circulation and was therefore no fan of a campaign which was likely to make the paper more exclusive, found his ideas for change blocked. He did manage to amend the promotional slogan to 'Those on their Way to the Top Take the *Times*' but, crucially, he couldn't convince Astor that page one should have news rather than adverts.

After suffering a loss in 1957, the young Astor decided on a thorough financial investigation which was carried out the following winter by the accountants Cooper Brothers, into the *Times*'s organisation, administration and financial position. Their report was damning, citing poor management structure, absence of budgetary control, lack of strategic financial planning, and disappointing advertising revenue and sales compared to rivals. It called for 'simultaneous action on every front: to chase the *Daily Telegraph*'s big circulation, to emulate the *Guardian*'s liveliness, and to recapture the ground lost to the *FT*.'[174] It also proposed that the company protect itself by diversifying and even dared to suggest that adverts on the front page should be replaced by news. Haley found Astor wasn't his only adversary. These kinds of suggestions were heavily criticised by Stanley Morison and managing director Francis Mathew.[175]

Morison saw the *Times* as the organ of the governing class while Haley viewed it in less restricted terms, as a paper 'for intelligent readers of all ages and classes'.[176] But he couldn't see how to satisfy a wider audience unless the paper had more pages. In the event, despite the gravity of the Coopers report, nothing was done. Haley realised the *Times* had fallen behind by failing to develop beyond the political sphere. In an internal memo he pointed out that there was 'a growing interest . . . in science, in technology, in economics, in artistic movements and so on . . .'.[177] The *FT* had beaten the *Times* to the draw in those departments. Haley had more success in moving the night news editor, Colin Watson, to oversee obituaries, which proved a good appointment. In the following twenty-five years Watson broadened the paper's scope considerably.[178]

But Haley's editorial policy was hesitant. The *Times*'s lack of clarity over the doomed Suez invasion, during which the paper changed its mind three times, contrasted poorly with its competitors (see below, pp. 131, 134). On the right, the *Daily Telegraph* was straightforward and lucid in its backing for the government, while the *Manchester Guardian* stood firm in opposition. The *Times*, in sacrificing any claim to being a reliable liberal organ, thereby opened a path to the national stage for its Manchester rival.

The *Guardian*'s editor, A. P. Wadsworth, was ill throughout 1956 and there were at least three serious contestants for his job.[179] Even before

Wadsworth's retirement in October, followed by his death a month later, the senior director, Laurence Scott, had decided on thirty-six-year-old Alastair Hetherington as his replacement.The phrase *un homme sérieux* might have been invented to describe him. He not only survived his Suez baptism of fire, his principled stand enhanced his, and his paper's, reputation.

Hetherington, son of Sir Hector Hetherington, vice-chancellor of Glasgow University, attended Gresham's School and then Oxford, spending vacation time at the *Glasgow Herald* on the subs' desk. He served in the ranks of the Royal Armoured Corps for two years before being commissioned and taking part in the Normandy landings. In a critical battle, for Caen, his regiment suffered such severe losses that it was disbanded. Hetherington, by now a major, became an intelligence officer and was assigned to run *Die Welt*, the paper set up by the British in post-war Berlin. He soon rejoined the *Glasgow Herald* and, in 1950, applied to the *Manchester Guardian*, where he immediately impressed Wadsworth, who found him both serious and exacting. Here was a young man with a liberal heart and a rational head, interested in politics and foreign affairs, able to write lucid polemic. Hetherington shared Laurence Scott's view that the paper could not remain anchored in Manchester. It had a growing national audience and, if it was to expand, it needed the revenue from national advertising.

Both men then decided on a further stage in the paper's transformation – the removal of *Manchester* from the title – though it didn't happen until 24 August 1959. On the day before, readers were told that the change 'acknowledges an accomplished fact. Nearly two-thirds of the paper's circulation now lies outside the Manchester area . . .' But there was to be a frustrating wait for Scott before he could engineer the next part of his plan, to print in London. Even so, the popularity of the *Guardian* rose despite its problems with distribution in the southern counties. By 1960, it had reached a sale of 200,000, within striking distance of the *Times.*

To compound the problems for the *Times*, Gordon Newton's *Financial Times* was supplanting it as the main purveyor of City and financial news. Newton hired well, recruiting two future editors in Fredy Fisher and Geoffrey Crowther, the ambitious Nigel Lawson, Jock Bruce-Gardyne, Patrick Hutber and John Higgins, later arts editor at the *Times.* Perhaps his most significant recruit of the era was Sheila Black, who became the *FT*'s first woman's editor, and 'probably the single most important influence in relaxing the style of the paper during the 1960s'.[180]

Newton accomplished his modernisation at a time when there was considerable boardroom acrimony followed by a change of ownership. Newton, who thought Bracken 'more of a drag than a driving force', was not unhappy when his boss suddenly decided in the summer of 1955 that he no longer wished to write for the paper.[181] Bracken's relationship with the Crosthwaite-Eyre family reached a nadir. He was deposed as an Eyre trustee and then resigned from the chairmanship of the *FT.* Drogheda, the managing director, pleaded with him to stay, pledging to leave with him if he went.

Oliver Crosthwaite-Eyre was told that the City would take a dim view of both men going, so it was decided to put the paper up for sale. A deal was concluded 'with great swiftness and secrecy' in February 1957. Lord Cowdray's Pearson empire acquired just over 50 per cent of FN Ltd, which controlled 51 per cent of the *FT*, for £720,000. Given that the paper was making a yearly profit of some £550,000, it was hardly an exorbitant price.[182] As Bracken pointed out, the changing ownership had put a smile on the face of each successive proprietor. 'Ellerman made a big profit by selling to Camrose. He made a much bigger profit by selling to the Eyres. They made twice as big a profit by selling to Cowdray.'[183]

Now Bracken and Drogheda felt able to stay. Though still a private company under John Cowdray, Pearson was a formidable conglomerate: oil and gas production; banking and finance through Lazards investments; industrial holdings; and regional publishing through Westminster Press. Two Pearson appointees joined the *FT* board: Pat Gibson, editorial director of Westminster Press and therefore a man with newspaper knowledge, and Oliver Poole, who had risen through Lazards, and was deputy chairman of the Tory party. Initial tension between Drogheda, Gibson and Poole soon passed. In announcing the change of ownership, Pearson went to some lengths to assure the City that its ownership of Lazards would not compromise the *FT*'s autonomy. There would not be undue influence on its paper from its banking arm.[184] Bracken was particularly exercised by this, though he soon had reason to celebrate the financial strength of the new concern.

In 1957, Bracken was able to report that the paper had made a profit of £724,410 and was selling 84,000 copies, more than 40 per cent higher than in 1949. Profits were up to more than £1 million by the following year and sales rose to 86,000. But Bracken, suffering from cancer of the throat and growing lonelier by the month, preferred to see the dark cloud rather than the silver lining. He worried unduly over spending by the *FT* on a new building in Cannon Street, sending letters of complaint from his bed in Westminster Hospital.[185] He died on 8 August 1958 at the flat of his friend Patrick Hennessey, chairman of Ford. In a tribute to him, the building was named Bracken House before the paper's staff moved in at Easter 1959. Two *FT* men who were to go on to higher things didn't stay long afterwards: Rees-Mogg departed for the *Sunday Times* as business editor while Nigel Lawson went to the *Sunday Telegraph* as its first City editor.

The paper of the permanent conference

On 10 June 1956, the *Observer* devoted almost the whole of one issue to Khrushchev's so-called 'secret' speech denouncing Stalin. Originally made in

February that year, only scraps had leaked out until Edward Crankshaw obtained the full transcript of 26,000 words in early June. Production editor Ken Obank, one of the few professional journalists on the paper, who designed the pages and ensured the paper was published, suggested to editor David Astor that they run every word.[186]

Risking the wrath of advertisers, Astor threw out seven columns of advertising and gave over the first eight of the paper's fourteen pages to the full speech. A front-page leader explained that it 'should be read as a whole to grasp what has been happening' and to show the perils of single-party rule. It proved to be a huge commercial success, selling out and having to be reprinted. 'Only a bold and imaginative editor could have thrown away a whole issue,' observed John Pringle, rating it as 'one of the most brilliant strokes of journalism in our time'.[187]

Months later, Astor made yet another bold editorial decision by arguing forcefully against the government's Suez policy, again braving objections from advertisers (see below, p. 136). Throughout the 1950s, the *Observer* also campaigned for the abolition of capital punishment. During the run-up to the 1959 election, the paper called for unilateral nuclear disarmament, leading it to support Labour for the first time.

Astor and his *Observer* were still enjoying what liberals were to view ever after as their golden years. It wasn't just the editorial matter that was distinctive either: life in the office wasn't like that of any other newspaper. There are legions of stories about the chaos of the *Observer*, with Astor seemingly unable to curb interminable multilingual debates between writers drawn from a host of middle European countries. When Pringle arrived as deputy editor, he discovered a paper run 'like an experiment in a participating democracy or even a Maoist commune'.[188] Continuing the analogy, he added: 'If Mao Tse-tung invented the permanent revolution, the *Observer* in those days perfected the permanent conference.'[189] Presiding over it, or to be more precise, failing to preside over it, Astor fashioned the paper despite his shyness and indecisiveness. His main skill lay in cultivating talented writers, giving them enough space to flourish, even if it meant indiscipline on a scale unimaginable even in the most lax of Fleet Street regimes. He was, said his biographer, a sort of actor–manager, who drew around him a disparate group of creative artists, writers such as Hugh Massingham, William Clark, John Gale, Patrick O'Donovan and Michael Davie.

Astor's hiring hunches generally paid off. In 1958, acknowledging his paper's lack of economic coverage, he hired a young journalist from the *Financial Times*, Andrew Shonfield, who went on to become one of his generation's most distinguished writers on the subject. Under Anthony Sampson, the Pendennis column prospered with its gossipy but informed coverage of politics. Sampson also became an expert on South African politics. Sports were covered by the philosopher A. J. Ayer, lawyer Louis Blom-Cooper and Clement Freud, while sports editor Clifford Makins also encouraged young talent, such as Hugh McIlvanney, Chris Brasher and Richard Baerlin.

Astor found it impossible to fire people, choosing instead to take those he wished to move on to lunch at the Waldorf Astoria, according to columnist Michael Frayn, 'because it was owned by the family and he always got special rates'.[190] Then, engaging in an elliptical conversation, Astor would convey the message that the person might try another form of work. Asked in 1959 to define the 'ideal' of the *Observer*, he wrote: 'In the character of this paper, ethics matter more than politics. Its particular ethics could be defined as trying to do the opposite to what Hitler would have done. In fact, that may be the historic origin, as the paper's present personality was established in the last war by people being drawn together more by being anti-Fascist than by anything else.'[191] Ethics, however, could not pay the bills. By the end of that year, Astor was writing to Haley at the *Times* about his paper facing 'fairly formidable problems'.[192] Economic realities were about to bite.

All the news fit to pinch

At the other end of the Sunday market, ethics played little part in the battle for readers between the three popular papers. They all regularly fell foul of the Press Council as they fought each other for material. Sam Campbell's *People* – slogan: 'The paper that looks ahead . . . frank, fearless, free' – often railed against the watchdog's strictures in attempting to justify unjustifiable intrusions by his reporters. His paper's articles 'carried black and white moral judgments' because he didn't recognise 'greys'.[193]

It is hard to take seriously the claim that Arthur Helliwell was genuinely 'shocked and staggered' at witnessing afternoon striptease in Soho.[194] Such titillation was the *People*'s stock-in-trade, along with sensationalist series like 'I Was a G.I.'s Slave Bride', which ran for ten weeks in 1958.[195] But there was some fine journalism too, such as the investigation by Duncan Webb which led the paper to campaign against the conviction of Iain Hay Gordon for the murder of a Northern Ireland judge's daughter.[196] Campbell and Webb were posthumously vindicated in 2000 when Hay Gordon was finally cleared.

Campbell's formula worked and throughout 1958 his paper increased its sale. Then the *Sunday Pictorial* raised its game so that, towards the end of 1959, it appeared to have won the neck-and-neck sales race by reaching the figure of 5,250,000. But Campbell's competitive spirit, and an amazing, if tragic, piece of luck, ensured a comeback by the *People*. After a tug-of-war with the newly appointed *Pictorial* editor Lee Howard, Campbell obtained the rights to Errol Flynn's spicy autobiography entitled *My Wicked, Wicked Ways*, which attracted enormous public interest because Flynn had died just a few days after finishing the last chapter. It turned out to be a huge winner, adding 200,000 to the *People*'s sale, overtaking the *Pictorial* and earning the paper a rebuke from the Press Council for its salacious content.

When Reg Payne, previously assistant editor of the *Daily Mirror*, became editor of the *Sunday Pictorial* at the end of 1960, Campbell found himself up against a character in his own mould. They expended great efforts, and large sums of money, trying to buy up the same personalities, stealing stories from each other and perfecting the art of the 'spoiler', the practice of running material designed to fool readers into thinking they had the inside track on an exclusive paid for by a rival.

The *News of the World* was just as competitive, but its steep fall in sales was in marked contrast to the increases at the *People* and *Pictorial*. Editor Reg Cudlipp, answering criticism that the paper was too full of provocative material, reintroduced the *NoW*'s beloved pre-war feature, the short story, and managed to persuade some of the best-known authors, such as Somerset Maugham, H. E. Bates and Ursula Bloom to contribute. His leader pages featured political commentaries by a range of high-profile writers, including Robert Boothby and Aneurin Bevan. This helped the editorial balance, but it didn't make the slightest impact on the downwards sales trend.

By this time the leading figure among the *News of the World*'s warring owners, the Carr and Jackson families, was Sir William Emsley Carr, known as Bill. He had finally succeeded to the chairmanship after a lengthy boardroom squabble with his cousin Derek Jackson. Bill Carr, like so many who inherit businesses, was out of his depth. He knew little about newspapers and still less about the readership. Having a fortune at his disposal, he spent his day gambling, drinking and nursing his gout. He was an heroic drinker, 'a connoisseur of Scotch whisky' who 'maintained his expertise by sampling at least two bottles a day'.[197] This habit was eventually to earn him the memorable nicknames of 'Tipsy Willie' and 'Pissy Billy'.

According to his personal assistant Roger Hall, 'he would have won any competition for the most autocratic chairman in Britain . . . a summons to his office was equivalent to an invitation to take a seat in the electric chair'.[198] The first to suffer the shock was Cudlipp. In 1959, Carr fired him in favour of the man who had made no secret of his lust for the job, the deputy editor Stafford Somerfield.

The paper of sex and scandal had found its ideal editor. The champagne-quaffing, cigar-smoking, gregarious and ribald Somerfield was certain he could stop the sales rot, knew exactly what the readers wanted, and had no misgivings about providing it. The titillating court reports were all very well, but he soon introduced two new forms of provocative content: kiss-and-tell memoirs and saucy investigations, adding spice to the *People*'s formula.

He paid the actress Diana Dors £35,000, a staggering sum in 1960, for a series on her colourful life, revelling in the notoriety it brought him and the paper. Somerfield was the subject of some pretty ripe stories himself. On a visit to the Manchester office he stayed at the Midland Hotel where staff were under instruction not to allow any known prostitutes up to the rooms. When a hall porter spotted Somerfield on his way across the lobby with a girl he recognised he ran to bar the way to the lift, stammering: 'I'm sorry, Mr Somerfield, but I can't let you take this, er, er, woman, er, your wife, upstairs.' Somerfield stared at him for a second, swept past his outstretched arm into the lift, and as he pushed the button shouted to the hapless porter: 'How dare you call this trollop my wife!'

Somerfield exploited the public's hypocrisy, realising that, despite the criticism, the publicity would ensure high sales. The fact that he reversed the circulation slide proved him right, up to a point.

At the end of 1960, the *News of the World* swallowed the Manchester-based *Empire News* from Thomson, then selling almost 2 million. Since many people already bought both titles, it didn't add many copies to the *NoW* sales, but the main benefits were a printing agreement in Manchester and a couple of journalists. Thomson got the northern printing contract from the *NoW* in return and two months later he shut down the loss-making *Sunday Graphic*.

A major casualty of an increasingly competitive climate, with its accent on populism, was the magazine *Picture Post*. Launched in 1938 by Stefan Lorant and Tom Hopkinson, and backed by Edward Hulton, it built a sale of 1.3 million within a year. Its pictorial essays, usually with a social conscience, found a ready audience. A typical example in the early 1940s, written by Sydney Jacobson, told the story of an unemployed man from Peckham: 'Before he lost his job Alfred Smith had ordered artificial teeth and paid 15 shillings towards their cost. He has never been able to get them finished. That is why his cheeks are sunken.'[199]

Hopkinson resigned in 1950 when Hulton killed an article on Korea filed by James Cameron and photographer Bert Hardy. But the audience was already beginning to drop away and Hulton applied pressure for the *Post* to follow the route taken by the more scandalous weekly papers such as *Reveille*, *Weekend* and *Tit-Bits*, which featured 'cheesecake' pictures. It made no difference and, as sales fell away, it lost money. When Hulton closed the magazine in May 1957 he claimed that television was now doing its job better, though larger newspapers were also able to cover *Picture Post* terrain too.

6. SUEZ: THE EXPLOSION OF A MEDIA MYTH

> The daily press and the telegraph, which in a moment spread inventions over the whole earth, fabricate more myths ... in one day than could have formerly been done in a century.[1]

It is ironic, if unsurprising, that the people who work for newspapers should accept the myths they perpetrate as readily as their readers. Generations of journalists after 1956 came to believe that more or less the whole press supported Britain's Suez invasion, and that the newspapers which opposed the venture suffered catastrophic sales losses from which they never recovered. This latter misconception made owners and editors nervous ever after about criticising British military exploits. Yet there is no proof that hostility to Suez cost any paper lasting circulation harm. Indeed, in the *Manchester Guardian*'s case, it helped to build sales. The *Daily Mirror* suffered the merest blip. Neither the *News Chronicle* nor the *Observer*, despite repeated assertions to the contrary, can seriously claim that its principled opposition to the invasion was the sole reason for its decline.

It is possible to view Anthony Eden's premiership entirely in terms of his relationship with the press. Though it would be too far fetched to call him a victim, because he might just have taken a route which avoided the total ignominy he suffered, he would certainly have been lambasted, and possibly hounded out of office, anyway. However he responded to the crisis, it is doubtful if he could have survived. Few newspapers gave him the kind of personal support enjoyed for so long by his party, and his predecessor.

After his years waiting for the press tycoons' favourite leader, Winston Churchill, to die, Eden enjoyed only the briefest of press honeymoons. It was the Tory-supporting papers which treated him most harshly. Within months, as 1956 began, Eden was overwhelmed by hostile criticism. He was characterised as weak and indecisive. 'Few prime ministers,' observed one historian, 'have encountered such a barrage of hostile press criticism as assailed him in January 1956.'[2] The *Times*'s complaint, that his government had lost its grip, was echoed by the *Daily Mail* accusing it of 'delay and indecisiveness'.[3] Most hurtful of all was a broadside from the Tory party's greatest supporter, the *Daily Telegraph*, headlined 'Waiting for the smack of firm government' and written by the deputy editor, Donald McLachlan.[4] The

Daily Mirror and *Daily Herald* joined in, while the *Observer* reported that the 'Eden must go' camp was growing.[5]

This squall appeared to die down for a while, but the *Times* revived anti-Eden sentiments in April by referring to the prime minister's 'unsureness of touch' and 'aberrations under strain'.[6] Press criticism of this kind, much more regularly in evidence in the Labour papers of course, 'had a major impact on subsequent developments'.[7] Eden desperately wanted to prove himself as a resolute leader.[8]

The roots of the Suez conflict went deep into the past, but the immediate reason was the threat to Egypt's Aswan dam project. President Nasser saw its construction as a way of improving his country's prospects, providing water for the Nile valley and electricity for industry. It was to be financed by the British and American governments and the World Bank. But he was devastated in July 1956 to discover that the Americans had pulled out and that the British would follow. The World Bank's offer, contingent on the two governments contributing, would therefore lapse.

Nasser retaliated by nationalising the Suez canal, the waterway through which Europe received its oil, and freezing all the assets of its controlling company. His action was eased by the previous month's agreed withdrawal from Suez by British forces. According to two commentators, Britain's 'press reacted with almost unanimous fury' to Nasser's canal takeover.[9] They certainly did, with almost every daily paper comparing the Egyptian dictator to Hitler and Mussolini, though it must be said that most of them also explicitly rejected gunboat diplomacy. The *Times*, which displayed an initial sense of moderation, was a maverick by travelling in the opposite direction, growing more militant as the rest tempered their advice to Eden, finally performing a last-minute U-turn. Only the *Manchester Guardian* held to a consistent line by opposing any military intervention.

The *Times*'s first sober leader was followed by a trenchant attack on Nasser's 'act of international brigandage' while praising Eden's 'reticent' response.[10] Two days' later it pointed to the threat to the West's interests while cautioning that 'any action' must have the support of both France and the United States.[11] Then, in its fourth leading article within a week, the *Times* compared Nasser's action with Hitler's march into the Rhineland and pushed for an altogether more proactive policy: 'If Nasser is allowed to get away with his coup all the British and other western interests in the Middle East will crumble.' Nasser must be resisted. 'Quibbling over whether or not he was "legally entitled" to make the grab will delight the finicky and comfort the fainthearted, but entirely misses the real issues.' The canal must be in 'friendly and trustworthy hands'. So the government should 'be ready . . . to use force'.[12]

The *Times*'s editor, Sir William Haley, was sailing on his owner's yacht at the time, so it was left to his assistant editor, Iverach McDonald, to write the paper's first editorial.[13] Haley and McDonald were close to Eden and kept in constant touch with him throughout.[14] Incidentally, in the run-up to the invasion, Haley was in the United States for seven 'testing weeks'.[15] It is an oddity of the crisis that Haley's rival editors were also away from their offices, with the *Telegraph*'s Colin Coote in Germany and the *Guardian*'s A. P. Wadsworth gravely ill in bed.

The popular press was swifter to call for action against Nasser. The *Daily Mail*, the great pre-war appeaser, thundered: 'Had we met force with force in the early Nazi days, Hitler would never have had his way . . . Nasser must not get away with this.'[16] The *Mail* demanded immediate reoccupation of the canal zone. The *Daily Express*, with Beaverbrook lamenting Britain's Suez withdrawal and being no fan of Eden's, called it 'an act of brigandage' and asked rhetorically: 'Is Britain going to tolerate this new arrogance?'[17] In subsequent days, the *Express* stepped up its demands for Eden to show 'firmness', while subtly suggesting he might not quite be up to the task. Features about Nasser, as elsewhere, portrayed him as a hate-filled monster.[18] This demonisation of Nasser probably had a greater effect on readers than leading articles urging caution. The *Daily Herald*, rushing to judgement, first said there was 'no room for appeasement' and there must be 'No more Adolf Hitlers!'[19] Yet its tone moderated quickly: 'Talk of military force against Egypt is as empty of sense as Nasser's own speeches.'[20]

The *Daily Mirror*, slow to react after underplaying the story for two days, used belligerent vocabulary to brand Nasser 'a liar, a cheat and a menace' but then warned against the superficially attractive idea of using military force.[21] Two weeks later, in a leading article which ran from page one and across two inside pages, the *Mirror* gave an unequivocal message to Eden: 'NO WAR OVER EGYPT!'[22]

That editorial attacked the *Times*, *Mail* and *Express* for rattling the sabres while taunting them for their previous advocacy of appeasement. From that point on, the *Mirror* kept reminding its readers of the dangers of war though, if Nasser closed the canal, 'it would be Britain's duty to answer aggression by force'.[23] For Eden to occupy Egypt would require full-hearted approval from the British public which the *Mirror* asserted it did not have. To dramatise Eden's warmongering, Cudlipp even published one splash headline in Latin: 'SI SIT PRUDENTIA' (If there be but prudence), the motto on Eden's coat of arms.[24]

The *Daily Telegraph* argued for 'prompt and firm' action.[25] The use of force, it said three days later, would be justified if Nasser closed the canal.[26] The *News Chronicle* said the government was 'fully justified' in retaliating and then, days later, counselled against going it alone.[27]

Of the dailies, the *Manchester Guardian* alone was measured: 'It would be a mistake . . . to lose our heads.'[28] Instead of confronting Nasser, and recognising that the true significance of his move was to threaten oil supplies, it advised a more practical and long-term response: the construction of an oil pipeline and the building of supertankers. To launch an invasion would be immoral. In the following days it maintained a similar calm, consistent line. After a conference at his bedside on 1 August, Wadsworth asked Alastair Hetherington to write the main leader warning the government against the premature use of force.[29] The paper's concern was based on its inside knowledge, through a leak to its Washington correspondent Max Freedman, that Eden was contemplating action.[30] In the same leader, the paper criticised the *Times* for arguing that it was better to strike quickly and that 'quibbling' about legal issues was unimportant. 'Such advice, if adopted, would destroy whatever claim Britain has to be an upholder of international law and morality. It would destroy the United Nations in a day, and it would land Britain in an appalling embroilment with at least three-fifths of the world ranged against her.'

In the following days, Freedman sent a series of private notes to his *Guardian* bosses which alerted them to a growing concern within the US administration that Britain might take action. So, when Eden made a direct comparison between the actions of Hitler and Nasser, the *Guardian* published its most pointed criticism. He 'will be gravely at fault if he tries . . . to create an emotional readiness in this country for war'.[31] This leader particularly upset Eden, who was becoming 'seriously concerned' at the paper's line.[32]

He would not have expected any support from the *Observer*, which adopted a similar stance to the *Guardian*.[33] The following week it said what no one else had dared to say: 'The weakness of our legal position is that the Egyptian Government has a perfect right to nationalise the Suez Canal Company. That our Government and Press have largely given the British public a different impression is no help to us in meeting our difficulties.'[34] Though the *Guardian* had touched on it previously, this is the first specific reference which pointed to the blind acceptance of the government viewpoint, even by newspapers hostile to Eden. The *Observer* was also alone in showing sympathy for Egypt's plight over the Aswan project, and in predicting the rise of nationalist antagonism to colonial powers.[35]

If most early newspaper comments were calculated to spur Eden to use force, by the middle of August it was clear that four dailies – the *Guardian, Mirror, Herald* and *News Chronicle* – were against war. Leon Epstein, who calculated the press division in sales terms said these four together sold 7.7 million while the pro-Eden quartet – *Express, Mail, Sketch* and *Telegraph* – had a combined sale of about 8.3 million.[36] Of the Sunday titles, the anti-war *Observer, People, Reynolds News* and *Pictorial* sold 11.6 million compared to the Eden supporters – *Empire News, Sunday Dispatch, Sunday Express, Sunday Graphic* and *Sunday Times* – which had a joint sale of 10.1 million. Note that Epstein omits the *Times* and the *News of the World*, apparently because he thought them neutral, though both backed Eden up to the point of the invasion. It could be argued that the newspapers' split reflected the split among the population. If so, it suggests that not only was Eden's venture risky in military terms, he was also gambling on his country's political support. Allowing for the obvious disparity between a paper's political views and those of its readers, not to mention considerable apathy, Eden didn't enjoy anything like his nation's full-blown confidence.

There were certainly similar tensions within newspaper offices, especially at the *Times*, where opinion was strongly divided.[37] At the *News Chronicle*, owner Laurence Cadbury opposed his editor, Michael Curtis, for his strong anti-Eden line which was also passionately advocated by the leader writer Richard Moore (father of the later *Daily Telegraph* editor, Charles).[38] At the *Evening Standard*, the chief leader writer, Rudolph Klein, refused to support Eden. Then his deputy, Bob Edwards, also declined to write the Suez leaders. Instead, Beaverbrook allowed him to write a 'personal commentary' in which he opposed war and urged sanctions, illustrating once again both Beaverbrook's ambivalence towards Eden and his journalistic shrewdness.[39] At the *Daily Mirror*, there was a clash between Cecil King and Hugh Cudlipp, with the former urging support for Eden. Cudlipp, his resolution strengthened by political editor Sydney Jacobson, convinced King that to do so would place the *Mirror* on the opposite side to Labour and against all progressive opinion.[40]

In the late summer, there were odd rumours that Eden might use force. W. N. Ewer, the *Daily Herald*'s veteran diplomatic correspondent, told Douglas Jay, the leader writer and Labour MP, that his Foreign Office contacts were saying that Britain was preparing a military expedition: Eden was 'contemplating war'.[41] Jay told Gaitskell, who didn't believe that Ewer was right. So Jay and Denis Healey, with Gaitskell's approval, wrote a letter to the *Times*, warning against any use of force.[42] Cecil King also claimed to have got wind of an intended invasion.[43] Yet neither the *Herald* nor the *Mirror* published the information.

For a substantial period, 'the full flood of hysteria ... subsided'.[44] It revived once the invasion happened, with the press eventually dividing roughly on party lines. The *Express* offered Eden unqualified support, saying the action was 'necessary to safeguard the life of the British Empire.'[45] Beaverbrook then hymned Churchill for endorsing Eden's use of force.[46] His *Evening Standard* argued: 'The time for partisan argument is past. The thoughts of the nation must now be to giving the fullest possible support to the men who are in action on Egyptian soil.'[47] Maverick to the last, Beaverbrook then approved the *Standard* sending Randolph Churchill, a noted Eden critic, to cover the hostilities.[48] The *Mail*, though worried by lack of US support, said 'questions and criticisms' must be put aside because 'we are at war'.[49] Its Harmsworth stablemate, the *Sketch*, thought the government 'entirely right'[50] and added that 'there can be no retreat'.[51] It also took a swipe at the 'low' *Guardian* for encouraging 'righteous conchies' (conscientious objectors), an unsubtle allegation of treachery.

The *Daily Telegraph* had warned at the end of October of the danger of uniting the Arab world against Israel but, with British forces engaged, the paper championed Eden's cause.[52] In his memoirs, *Telegraph* editor Colin Coote explained that his paper's post-Suez view was 'that armed intervention could be justified in principle but had been hopelessly bungled in practice'.[53] The *Sunday Times*, which had been notably moderate in its first comment back in July – 'Armed intervention is neither right nor necessary'[54] – gradually adopted a pro-Eden tone during the late summer and gave him stalwart support after the invasion.[55]

According to one commentator, the *Times* was still acutely conscious of its appeasement in the 1930s and was 'determined not to commit the same error'.[56] Despite that, the paper came out against the government's ultimatum, disappointed Eden by refusing to back the attack on Egypt, and was 'notably balanced and reserved'.[57] After a leader speaking of its 'deep concern', the next day it expressed doubts on 'whether the right course of action has been taken'.[58] The following day it repeated its fears and worried over the morality of possible Israeli collusion.[59] Harold Macmillan, who notoriously changed sides in cabinet, later had the gall to accuse the *Times* of changing sides.[60]

Among those who opposed force, the *Manchester Guardian* was alone in its stand for twenty-four hours. Then the *Mirror* and *News Chronicle* joined in.[61] The *Guardian* thought the ultimatum 'an act of folly without justification ... It pours petrol on a growing fire'.[62] The *News Chronicle*'s first editorial referred to it as 'a gigantic gamble' and next day condemned it as 'folly on the grand scale'.[63] After a day's hesitation, the *Daily Mirror* took a similar stance, calling it 'Eden's war' which was both illegal and immoral. It followed that up by using Labour leader Hugh Gaitskell's words for its headline: 'Disastrous folly'.[64]

The *Observer*, which had to wait four days to comment, devoted the whole of its leader page to Suez, with three separate articles damning the British invasion. In a savage and caustic attack on Eden, it accused his government of 'folly and crookedness'. The government had issued a 'dishonest ultimatum' which it knew Egypt would reject and thus lend a spurious legitimacy to its invasion. Britain and France had behaved 'as gangsters'. It called for Eden's resignation, claiming he had 'deliberately attempted to mislead opinion', and urged Tories to rebel.[65] This editorial 'caused a furore'.[66] It was denounced in the Commons, and three (of the six) *Observer* trustees quit – Lord Portal, Arthur Mann and Sir Keith Murray – a fact which Astor announced on the front page. The paper received a flood of letters, with 866 against the policy (of whom 474 said they were stopping the paper) and 302 in support.[67] Astor dealt with the criticisms head on, reiterating his paper's moral correctness in a leader about patriotism.

But the real revelation came in an unbylined story on page nine headlined 'The Questions of Collusion'. This offered a great deal of evidence in support of what many suspected, that Britain and France had plotted with

Israel to provide a pretence for invasion. As Hugh Massingham, the *Observer*'s political correspondent, wrote the following week: 'The little time bomb – the charge that there was collusion between Britain, France and Israel – ticks quietly on. If it goes off one day, a lot of beliefs and favourite figures will disappear in the ruins.'[68] The charge was gaining momentum. According to Tony Benn's diaries at the time, 'Shirley Catlin (Williams) of the *FT* said the *Times* itself had been secretly briefed of the Israeli attack and the British intervention four days before it took place.'[69] This turned out to be spot on, and years later the collusion was confirmed.[70]

The *Observer*'s denunciation of Eden's Suez adventure 'may well be considered the paper's finest hour'.[71] It couldn't stop the invasion but it did help to create an atmosphere in which Eden was forced to halt the war and later to resign. But did the paper really suffer for its principles? The audited figures prove plainly that the *Observer* didn't take a sudden sales dive. Its sales had been rising before Suez and that rise didn't slow up, increasing from a six-monthly average of 573,000 in the second half of 1955 to 633,000 by the last six months of 1957. Readers who quit were replaced by those drawn to its liberalism.

The problem was that the disappearing readers were those beloved by advertisers while the newcomers, students and Labour voters, were not regarded, in advertising terms, as adequate replacements. For Richard Cockett, 'the Suez episode provided an object lesson in the power of the advertiser over the Western capitalist press'.[72] He claimed that Jewish advertisers and ultra-patriotic British companies, such as English Electric, pulled out their adverts. 'The loss of regular advertisers was the most serious and painful immediate consequence of the paper's stand on Suez.'[73] Nor was advertising the only factor in paper's decline. 'Contrary to popular impression,' asserts Cockett, 'its stance on Suez was only one of a number of factors that began to conspire against the *Observer* after 1956.'[74] It was unable or unwilling to adapt to the industry's changing economic climate which saw its rivals introduce commercial and financial innovations.

That was also true at the *News Chronicle*, where some 25,000 angry readers complained and deserted in protest at the paper's 'vehement denunciation'.[75] Two members of staff, writing after its closure, thought the anti-Eden stance a 'risk' for the paper because of its 'marginal economic position'.[76] A risk perhaps, but it was a minor factor in the *Chronicle*'s demise (see above, pp. 98–104). The *Daily Mirror* suffered a loss of about 80,000 copies, according to Cecil King.[77] Others thought it was a little less.[78] King thought that though 'our readers . . . were against military ventures . . . once troops were involved they must be supported'.[79] Cudlipp agreed, ruefully remarking that once the invasion occurred 'readers were all for bashing the Wogs'.[80] However, despite the circulation dip, the *Mirror* soon won more sales than it had lost.

The *Times*'s erratic line proved beneficial. It was reckoned that the paper increased by 20,000 copies – almost 10 per cent – during the crisis and went on rising afterwards towards a firm 250,000.[81] The *Manchester Guardian* did better still. It was selling 163,000 in June, dipped to 155,000 in August and then rose to more than 180,000 in November. It lost readers in the north but gained many more in the south. The *Manchester Guardian* was winning a national audience, but its former editor, Wadsworth, could not share the good news. He died on 4 November.

On the day of his death, Russian tanks moved into Budapest to suppress the Hungarian uprising. A Low cartoon in the *Guardian* portrayed Khrushchev striding towards a tank and waving to Eden as he prepared to climb into a bomber, captioned 'Me, Too'.[82] The *Mirror* also made the link between Eden's bombing of Egypt and the Soviet attack: 'The twin tragedies of Suez and Budapest mark a turning point in history.'[83] An *Express* cartoon saw it another way: Eden was being pelted with bad fruit for his invasion while Khrushchev was largely ignored.[84]

In subsequent years, in the mythologising of the press response to the Suez crisis, it came to be accepted that there were dangers for British papers opposing a war once British troops were engaged in action. Owners and editors were scared they might be labelled traitors and their sales would plunge. The statistics suggest otherwise even though there was, directly after the invasion, majority support in the country for Eden's policy. Gallup polls published in the *News Chronicle* showed that public approval for Eden increased from 40 per cent to 53 per cent in two weeks at the beginning of November.[85]

There was a sad, and rather silly, postscript to the antagonism between press and parliament. Immediately after the Suez ceasefire, petrol was rationed but certain people, such as doctors and MPs, were allowed extra supplies. In December 1956, a *Sunday Express* editorial referred to people suffering hardship while MPs enjoyed special treatment: 'everywhere the tanks of politicians will be brimming over'.[86] Editor John Junor was called before a House of Commons committee and then summoned to the bar of the Commons to apologise for his supposed breach of privilege.[87] In what one journalistic MP called 'a medieval pantomime', Junor was arraigned before a packed House and managed, with a straight face, to both apologise and defend the freedom of the press.[88] Evidently, Junor 'comported himself with some dignity.'[89] For politicians to demand their pound of flesh from the press over a leading article was a ridiculous conclusion to a shameful episode in British history.

PART FOUR: 1961–1965

7. SEX, SPIES AND AN OVERDOSE OF SOCIOLOGY

> Just one brilliant editor is worth far more than all the eggheads and market research gremlins in the world.[1]

Is the press always society's leader, or does it respond to society's leadership? These were years in which the latter appears to have been the case, because newspapers found themselves at the tail of political and cultural change. The old elite, personified by an establishment rooted in the previous century, was being forced to loosen its grip on British society.

Even if papers did not read the runes, individual journalists recognised the burgeoning of a new world. The *Observer*'s Anthony Sampson wrote his rigorous critique of the old-fashioned institutions, *Anatomy of Britain*, in 1962. The year before, the *Financial Times*'s industrial editor, Michael Shanks, heaped scorn on Britain's industry in *The Stagnant Society*, characterising it as an inward-looking struggle between white-collar management and blue-collar trades unionists which negated all hope of the modernisation necessary to compete in the outside world.

With more nations beginning to outstrip Britain's economic performance, so its international status declined. Running parallel was the disintegration of its imperial past, with the huge swathes of red on the globe diminishing as the winds of change continued to blow across Africa, leading to independence for Sierra Leone, Uganda, Tanganyika and Zanzibar (Tanzania). In Southern Rhodesia, in order to stave off black majority rule, Ian Smith made an illegal declaration of independence. The islands of the West Indies freed themselves from colonial domination too, while violence broke out in Cyprus, Malaya and Aden.

As the Tories struggled to cope with new international realities and an economic reverse after a period of relative affluence, people began to realise the truth behind Vicky's joke portrayal of prime minister Harold Macmillan as Supermac: he had no magic powers after all. Even the Tory papers lost sympathy with his government, while his party seemed to symbolise a past of inherited privilege. By contrast, the Labour party under Harold Wilson was perceived by the working class, and some elements of the middle class, as a vehicle for advance. In the words of one of the party's leading thinkers,

Labour must aim to create 'a society of equals, set free from the twin evils of riches and poverty, mastership and subjection'.[2]

Macmillan bowed to the inevitable in 1963 and resigned. The Conservative party, in an inexplicable misreading of the new egalitarian climate, chose Sir Alec Douglas-Home to succeed him. As the fourteenth Earl of Home, he owned 96,000 acres of land, including a grouse moor or two.[3] A decent enough man, he managed to restrict Wilson's 1964 election victory to just four seats.

Wilson's demand that Britain modernise itself in the crucible of 'the white heat of a second industrial revolution' and embrace new technology sounded go-ahead. But Wilson was no visionary and his call turned out to be a slogan rather than a strategy. While it may have caught the imagination of teenagers – who were then too young to vote – it made little difference to industrial bosses or their workforces. People were somewhat overawed by the prospect of change and there is clear evidence that 'deference . . . was not dead by 1964'.[4] It was one sign that social and cultural change is neither linear nor as swift as newspapers, or market researchers, like to suggest. The past clings on, sometimes for good, sometimes for bad.

Wilson's cause was immeasurably helped by the growth of an anti-establishment mood, evident in the success of BBC TV's satire show, *That Was the Week That Was*, the founding of *Private Eye*, and the rise of a distinct youth culture exemplified by the music of the Beatles and the Rolling Stones. Pop stars came to represent a deeper antipathy towards the rigid class structure and gave rise to a counter-culture. Gradually, newspapers began to tell lurid tales about substances called purple hearts and marijuana, reflecting, or amplifying, society's concern over the use of drugs while deploring outbreaks of violence at seaside resorts as mods fought rockers.

The fact that Penguin Books was prosecuted for publishing *Lady Chatterley's Lover* reinforced the view of the establishment as reactionary, while the fact that the jury found the publishers not guilty and the novel then sold 2 million copies within a year illustrated the new spirit within wider society, brilliantly reflected by Kenneth Tynan's post-trial *Observer* essay.[5] That didn't stop Haley's *Times* from condemning the jury's decision.[6] Nor did the case impress the *Daily Telegraph*'s Colin Welch, who found it 'slightly ridiculous to talk of a *book* corrupting a society in which, if present tendencies are maintained, it may soon be quite usual for a schoolgirl to have an abortion before she can read'.[7] In a foolish adjudication, the Press Council reprimanded the *Guardian, Observer* and *Spectator* for printing the four-letter words in the *Lady Chatterley* case and described their conduct as 'objectionable and unnecessary'.[8]

Middle-class reformers advocating a new liberal agenda often found their hopes dashed. Though the Wolfenden Report recommended reforms to decriminalise homosexual activity, a motion in parliament calling for its early implementation was heavily defeated. While the working-class teenage baby-boomers shouted incoherently for a new order, the old one held on tenaciously. Granada TV's soap opera *Coronation Street* started its run in 1962, portraying a working-class world which appeared ossified in pre-war attitudes, with people complaining about their fate while accepting of it.

The cold war was also heating up, almost boiling over when the Soviet Union attempted to place nuclear missiles in Cuba. America's President Kennedy, who represented to the world an era of youthful change, faced down the Soviets, only to be gunned down himself the following year. With the press playing a leading role, rampant spy mania gripped Britain. Editors, aware of the selling power of sex, quickly grasped that by linking sex to spying – especially in what was still called high society – they had a public-interest figleaf to justify publishing all manner of titillating material which was previously taboo.

While Fleet Street was trying to come to terms with the upheavals within society, it was also coping with a new form of newspaper ownership, personified by Roy Thomson. Even so, it was possible to detect vestiges of individualistic Victorian capitalism mixing incongruously with the remnants of a rural, feudal past. Suddenly, the body that acted collectively for the owners of the national press transformed itself from the Newspaper Proprietors' Association into the Newspaper Publishers' Association. Here was a concrete recognition from the barons, if not of their own mortality, then of the need to appear less authoritarian.

Changing economic circumstances took their toll too. On 27 October 1962, some 300 people in Kent crowded into the village school to say farewell to the lord of their manor. John Jacob Astor V, Baron Astor of Hever, proprietor of the *Times*, chairman of the Press Club for twenty-eight years, first chairman of the Press Council, benefactor, deputy lieutenant for the County of Kent, justice of the peace was leaving Britain because of death duties. The *Daily Worker* scorned his tax exile, contending that he was leaving the country in the interests of his heirs. The *Daily Telegraph* defended his decision as sensible and tax-efficient.

Another baron departed for ever: Lord Beaverbrook died in 1964. By then his empire was minuscule beside that of the International Publishing Company (IPC) run by Cecil King and Hugh Cudlipp. They took over Odhams, bringing the *Daily Herald* and *Sunday People* into the Mirror stable, with unforeseen consequences. The *Sunday Telegraph* was launched while the *Sunday Times* expanded and the *Observer* ran deeper into trouble.

King's Pyrrhic victory over Thomson

Roy Thomson was setting a fast pace in Fleet Street. For all his apparent modesty he genuinely believed that he alone knew how to run newspapers properly and, given that assumption, thought he should own as many as possible. His acquisitiveness made journalists suspicious of his motives and they dismissed him as a profit-seeking Philistine. His unpopularity was undeserved because his critics too easily overlooked the fact that he stuck to his pledge not to interfere in editorial affairs and never demanded that his editors follow a partisan line, even if his 'political neutrality was markedly Tory'.[9]

Other proprietors didn't take to him either, considering him an outsider who was too pushy, too determined and too damned successful. Even his countryman, Beaverbrook, feigned friendship. But Thomson was the grit in Fleet Street's oyster in the 1960s. Almost nothing happened without his being involved in some way. He represented not only new money, but new ideas. Here was a proprietor who saw papers as profit bases rather than political weapons, anathema to every other owner.

Thomson often said, 'I wish I was twenty-five years younger,' and then acted as if he was. His habit, irritating to many he asked, was 'to offer to buy any newspaper which might come into any discussion'.[10] He even flew to Addis Ababa and asked Emperor Haile Selassie for permission to take over the *Ethiopian Herald*.[11] Then he bought a paper in Nigeria, in opposition to titles bought by Cecil King for Mirror group, and later entered into partnership with the Aga Khan in five newspapers in Uganda, Kenya and Tanganyika. Soon he expanded into the West Indies and Australia.

Flush with profits from his Canadian businesses, he was able to buy almost any titles he liked – as long as somebody else didn't want them. In early 1961 he was confident that he would take over Odhams, the owners of a profitable magazine empire, the sales-winning *People* and the ailing *Daily Herald*. Negotiations with Sir Christopher Chancellor, Odhams chairman and general manager of Reuters, had begun when King also made an approach. 'Choosing between King and Thomson is like choosing between prussic acid and arsenic,' noted the *Daily Worker*, unfairly.[12] But both bidders spread poison about each other as they struggled to convince the Odhams board, the unions and the Labour party of the merits of their cases. 'No take-over bid has ever stimulated so much controversy as the Battle of Long Acre,' wrote Cudlipp, years before a spate of more contentious City battles.[13]

Odhams initially favoured Thomson and Labour was split, with leader Hugh Gaitskell none too keen on the *Mirror* bid because of concerns about a further concentration of press ownership. Yet neither Thomson nor King was excited by the newspapers: their main ambition was control of the lucrative magazines, such as *Woman* and *Woman's Own*. Thomson was able to brush aside the monopoly questions raised in the Commons by pointing out that his company had no magazines, no daily paper, and no one could claim that his *Sunday Times* was in competition with the *People*.[14]

That argument put King and Hugh Cudlipp at a disadvantage because the *Herald* and the *People* were competing for the same audience as the *Daily Mirror* and *Sunday Pictorial*. To overcome the problem, Cudlipp made a series of pledges: the print unions were assured that there would be no job losses; the party was placated by a promise that the *Herald* would *never* be merged with the *Mirror*;[15] and, in a final, fateful, commitment, Mirror group agreed to maintain the *Herald* for a minimum of seven years.[16] This proved to be the psychological turning point, swaying the TUC, Odhams and Gaitskell in the *Mirror*'s favour.[17]

Cudlipp also took steps to mollify *People* editor Sam Campbell. During the negotiations, Campbell wrote a pungent editorial decrying the *Mirror*'s 'grab for Odhams Press', arguing that 'this act of piracy should fail ... We hate the idea of this great newspaper being sold over our heads like an old car in a junk yard.'[18] Campbell had previously fallen out with King when editing the *Pictorial*, and wasn't happy at the idea of working under him again. He also thought Cudlipp might cramp his cavalier editorial style. Cudlipp privately assured him he would not.

With Cudlipp and King stressing the *Mirror*'s loyalty to Labour as a pointer to the way they would run the *Herald*, Odhams gave way in March. 'I believe', said Chancellor, 'the *Daily Herald* has a good prospect of becoming a successful and influential newspaper which will play an important part in our national life.'[19] It was a pious hope. Cudlipp, writing with the benefit of hindsight, observed of his magnanimity: 'I know of no other occasion on which the man about to be hanged was given the privilege of selecting his own rope and specifying the time he should spend in the death cell before the definitive act.' He added: 'Nobody sane in publishing would have paid a penny to acquire the *Herald*.'[20] It was, according to one of the *Herald*'s former staff, 'a sad end'. The paper had been sold 'as an appendage'.[21] Many journalists were overjoyed. Cudlipp was viewed as 'a popular press magician' and if he 'could not sort out the *Herald*'s problems then nobody could'.[22]

The *Mirror*'s takeover of Odhams, following so soon after the disappearance of the *News Chronicle*, *Star*, *Sunday Graphic* and *Empire News*, led to calls for another royal commission. Macmillan, bowing to the 'general unease in the industry', appointed Lord Shawcross, the former Labour attorney-general and erstwhile critic of the 'gutter press', as chairman (see above, pp. 32–3). In order to speed up the process, only five people joined the panel to consider three major topics: ownership concentration, union problems and Press Council reform.

Many thousands of words of both written and oral evidence were presented to the Shawcross commission.[23] Owners and editors blamed the unions for all of Fleet Street's ills. The unions and several Labour MPs blamed owners for buying, selling, merging and closing titles while also complaining about concentration threatening diversity. Sir Geoffrey Crowther of the *Economist* spoke of the 'appalling state of affairs': demarcation disputes, working restrictions, overmanning and the evils of the closed shop. Owners, deflecting suggestions that they too ran a closed shop through their National

Proprietors Association, cleverly stressed their competitive, maverick natures instead. Beaverbrook said: 'The trade unions are more powerful than the NPA,' which was 'a pretty ineffective organisation'. King echoed that theme: 'It is very difficult to get a number of proprietors to agree to anything at all.'

The commission, reporting in September 1962, warned that Fleet Street was suffering from an unmistakable malaise. It identified the central problems as overmanning, by as much as a third; excessive, even 'grotesque', demarcation lines; casualisation which was not conducive to good working arrangements; the disgrace of ghost working; and the nightmare caused by managers having to deal with a multiplicity of unions and chapels. It recommended 'better and more authoritative negotiating and consultative machinery'; 'unity on the part of the employers'; and 'a more constructive spirit on both sides together with a genuine will to work the machinery'. None of these measures stood any chance of implementation. The commission did not think that diversity was threatened by concentration or mergers, and couldn't envisage a way of prohibiting acquisitions anyway. Yet it recommended a Press Amalgamations Court to scrutinise newspaper purchases.[24] The government ignored the suggestion, even when five regional evenings were closed down in 1964. When Wilson came to power, rather than set up a separate body, he gave additional powers to the Board of Trade to refer proposed mergers to the Monopolies Commission, a decision which saw out the century.

One area in which Shawcross was influential was in reconstituting the Press Council. The commission was critical of the way in which the industry had starved the council of funds and failed to appoint an independent chairman, as Ross had recommended. If papers failed to improve the council, it said, 'a statutory body should be established'.[25] That threat shocked owners into action: Lord Devlin, a judge, was swiftly appointed as an independent chairman along with four lay members. The council was also empowered to guard against undue concentration of ownership, though how it was supposed to do so was never clear.

A new press baron with new ideas

Thomson laughed off his Odhams failure. 'So I got beaten. Everyone does some time.'[26] For a while, he turned his attentions away from Fleet Street. At the end of 1963, he and Harley Drayton, chairman of the United Newspapers group, took the consolidation of regional papers a significant step further, robbing Edinburgh and Sheffield of a choice of titles.[27] Their swap deal allowed Thomson to merge his *Edinburgh Dispatch* with the *Edinburgh News*, and Drayton to do the same with opposing Sheffield titles.[28]

Thomson didn't view a town or city having a single paper as a threat to democracy nor as the creation of an advertising monopoly. He explained that his plan was to 'put in better management, make them better papers, and they will be more profitable still'.[29] Criticism was muted because, three days later, President Kennedy was assassinated and press commentators were diverted.[30] As a reminder of the sometimes excellent journalism still to be found in the provinces, United's *Sheffield Morning Telegraph*, under the editorship of David Hopkinson, exposed malpractices by the city's police force with the infamous 'rhino whip' revelations.[31] Thomson didn't only close titles. In 1965, he launched the *Reading Evening Post*, the first of an anticipated clutch of evening titles to serve London's outer commuter belt.

Obsessed by his desire for a peerage, Thomson finally got his wishes at the end of 1963, becoming Lord Thomson of Fleet and Northbridge in the City of Edinburgh. For the man who had once said, 'The driving force of my life was poverty,' and who held the royal family in huge respect, it was the ultimate halo.[32] Emboldened by his status and sure of his magic touch, Thomson sounded out the *Times* in 1964 to see if he could buy it. His offer was firmly rejected, but he guessed it would only be a matter of time.

His first major task was to reinvigorate the *Sunday Times*. Some editorial executives thought their new owner 'looked like a Canadian rotarian who very likely owned a small canning factory', but most came to like him.[33] *Sunday Times* editor Harry Hodson was impressed too, but the admiration wasn't mutual. With Thomson and his editorial director, Denis Hamilton, having 'formed an effective partnership', their first concern was Hodson.[34] At fifty-five, he had been editor for twelve years and, according to Hamilton, he was tiring.[35] He couldn't delegate and Ian Fleming, the foreign manager, thought him 'a blinkered Oxbridge don' who never praised his staff.

But who should take his place? Thomson leaned on the 'faintly reluctant' Hamilton and, waving aside his protests, made him editor.[36] Hodson departed – becoming provost of the new centre for Anglo-American studies at Ditchley – but continued to attend Friday leader conferences for the following fourteen years, espousing the conservative cause.[37] So, in October 1961, Hamilton, then forty-three, stepped into his shoes, and the *Sunday Times* was about to enter its own golden age.

Under the Thomson–Hamilton regime, the paper bloomed, with each man feeding off the other's innovative ideas. The pair shared another strength in their ability to delegate. While Hamilton pioneered the intelligent presentation of a forty-eight-page paper, Thomson planned for the birth of his 'own baby, the child of his North American experience': the colour supplement.[38] Thomson's marketing team had worked out that with a million sale the *Sunday Times* would be able to command expensive colour advertising. It would be a first for Britain.

Thomson sorted out the problems of financing and printing the magazine, of which there were many. The print unions insisted the magazine be distributed from Gray's Inn Road rather than its Watford printing plant, adding greatly to the costs, while newsagents demanded money for inserting it into the paper. Hamilton was left to conceive the editorial content to attract the kind of aspiring, new, young home-owners the advertisers wanted to reach. Adopting an optimistic editorial perspective, Hamilton believed 'the British longed to educate themselves in the broadest sense' and set out to provide the kind of editorial to satisfy that longing.[39]

One of Hamilton's first decisions was one of his most controversial: he ousted the original choice of editor, John Anstey, because he considered his designs too staid. He chose instead the iconoclastic thirty-year-old arts director of *Queen* magazine, Mark Boxer, teaming him with a talented deputy, Clive Irving. His other great coup was in securing Lord Snowdon, husband of Princess Margaret, as the magazine's main photographer. With Fleet Street rivals jealous of the appointment, a bogus controversy arose, alleging that the royal family was being compromised.[40] There was a meretricious cross-questioning of Thomson in a TV interview for the alleged 'publicity stunt' hiring.[41] After questions in the Commons, complaints to the NUJ by other photographers and sniping in the rest of the press, Snowdon found himself in the bizarre situation of being pictured while taking pictures.

The omens for the *Sunday Times*'s colour magazine looked anything but good at the beginning. Launched on 8 February 1962, the first issue was a shambles. Critics dismissed it as a flop: only Francis Williams perceived its future potential. Despite its poor showing, sales went up by 150,000 on the first week and about 80 per cent of them stayed on. It suffered terrible losses to start with because advertising agencies were sceptical about the new medium and demanded heavy discounts. Thomson later admitted it cost him $2 million in the first year.[42]

Twelve months later he was feeling confident enough about his baby to celebrate its first birthday by flying a plane-load of Britain's tycoons and senior businessmen to Moscow to meet their Soviet Union equivalents. Thomson may not have been interested in politics but since the meeting with Khrushchev lasted for two and a half hours, far longer than scheduled, the event was seen in the West as the first sign of a thaw in the cold war.[43]

By that time Hamilton had recruited the gifted art editor Mike Rand, who raised the standard of layout and photographic presentation. Although losses on the magazine kept rising, it was soon unable to cope with the rush for colour advertising. Hamilton thought it 'perhaps the most successful single innovation in post-war quality journalism'.[44] He could lay claim to others too: the concept of the 'big read', whether a book serialisation or lengthy articles mixing facts and analysis in the style of *Time* and *Newsweek*; the foundation of Insight, and with it the creation of serious investigative journalism (previously the province of the popular Sunday titles, such as the *People*); and the pioneering of the multi-section newspaper, adding a business section after the magazine.

Hamilton's contemporaries recognised his pre-eminence. Sir William Haley, for instance, considered him 'one of the great journalists of the twentieth century'.[45] He was overshadowed in subsequent years because of the saint-like aura accorded to Harold Evans, his successor, though Evans himself would be the first to acknowledge his debt to him.[46] Hamilton, like many creative people, was not the easiest person to know and was renowned by staff for being 'a mass of contradictions ... one day brisk as a soldier sniffing victory ... the next as languorous and remote as the dreaming poet; or tortured and tortuous and then disarmingly frank and straightforward'.[47] He also suffered from a bad press.

Beaverbrook, scared by the colour magazine's potential impact on his *Sunday Express*, disparaged Hamilton while trying to persuade Thomson to drop the idea.[48] The rest of Fleet Street attacked almost all of Hamilton's ideas, and there were plenty of outside critics for papers to draw on. One female don thought the *Sunday Times* magazine 'evil' because it stimulated the desire for pleasure and possessions.[49] The juxtaposition of the starving and the starry also upset commentators. Boxer's successor as editor, Godfrey Smith, was untroubled, arguing that the middle classes did indeed eat 'soufflés while discussing Biafra'.[50]

Hamilton's other great skill was in spotting and nurturing talent. Acting rather like a commanding officer, he chose his senior staff carefully, explained his battle plans and then let them get on with the fight with the minimum of interference. Moving the dashing Clive Irving from the magazine to run the Insight team was inspired. Promoting William Rees-Mogg, then in his early thirties, from financial editor to political and economics editor, and then to deputy editor, worked well. Together they launched the business section which, like the magazine, suffered from a poor start. It didn't seem to matter. Like so much else that Hamilton did, it eventually came good.

He also had some luck. In December 1962, a gallant attempt to launch Britain's answer to *Newsweek* magazine, *Topic*, came to an end. Hamilton was able to cherry-pick *Topic*'s unemployed stars, such as Nick Tomalin, Alan Brien and Ron Hall, who became the backbone of Insight. In its original incarnation, in February 1963, 'Insight: the news in a new dimension' consisted of thirteen stories across two pages, and these short pieces were soon nicknamed the 'ologies'. Irving quickly realised that these 'scoops of interpretation' required more depth and greater length. If his journalists concentrated on a single subject, they could reconstruct events in detail, using the narrative style favoured by the *New Yorker* magazine. A remarkable breakthrough at the time, this kind of treatment was to become Insight's trademark and leave its mark on British journalism ever after.[51] Undoubtedly the best example was Ron Hall's three-part series on the activities of Peter Rachman, who had fomented racial tension by exploiting tenants. This broke new ground for a serious broadsheet paper, and put the word Rachmanism into the lexicon.

By the autumn of 1963, the energetic Irving decided to expand the Insight technique into politics. Political editor James Margach would provide a file of information while other reporters from the team, including the editors, would try to obtain corroborating evidence for the story. All these files of copy would then be written into a flowing narrative, to give the reader a comprehensive, chronological account of an important political event. When I joined the *Sunday Times* more than twenty years later, that technique had proved so perfect it had not been altered.

The excitement generated by the *Sunday Times* under Hamilton, and resourced by Thomson, saw the paper increase to sixty-four pages. Its sales rose from 885,000 in 1959 to 1,275,000 in 1964, with the marked increase coming after Hodson's departure. During 1965 there were several months when the paper sold more than 1.3 million. Hamilton went on recruiting, often hiring people on a hunch, and sometimes on the strength of stories they brought to the paper. His most famous signing, by far, was the man he appointed as his chief assistant, Harold Evans. The former editor of the *Northern Echo* in Darlington cut his *Sunday Times* teeth on one of the biggest investigative successes of the period, the Fire, Auto and Marine insurance fraud masterminded by Emil Savundra.

Following in Thomson's footsteps

One of the driving forces behind Thomson's desire for a magazine was to ensure that his *Sunday Times* did not lose sale to the market's new title, the *Sunday Telegraph*, launched by Michael Berry at the beginning of 1961. Berry's father, Lord Camrose, had long been keen to launch a Sunday stablemate to the *Daily Telegraph*. Unsurprisingly, his brother, Kemsley, opposed the idea of a paper to compete with his own *Sunday Times* and Camrose backed down.[52] Once Kemsley sold out, Berry decided to go through with the plan, not because he really believed there was a gap in the market for a new title, but as a commercial proposition. Research showed that 60 per cent of *Daily Telegraph* readers bought the *Sunday Express*.[53] Oddly, Berry thought a Sunday title would offer the *Daily Telegraph*'s 'log-jam of able staff . . . a fresh field . . . to exercise their talents'.[54]

Berry's conception of a Sunday title was totally inappropriate – he believed it should be a 'seventh-day edition of the *Daily*'.[55] He chose Donald McLachlan, the *Daily*'s deputy editor, as its first editor. Born in the East End to parents who worked in a hotel and provided him with a good education, McLachlan graduated from Oxford with a first in PPE. After a brief spell as a teacher at Winchester he travelled around Europe and started to dabble in journalism, writing for the *Times* from Germany during Hitler's early years in power. Returning to London, he was bored by *Times* leader writing and went back to Winchester for a couple of years before becoming editor of the *Times Educational Supplement* until joining naval intelligence during the war.

He had been foreign editor of the *Economist* for almost nine years when

Colin Coote appointed him in 1954 as his deputy, but they did not enjoy a good relationship. Neither man respected the other. McLachlan, who thought Coote was idle, did not receive a mention in Coote's memoirs and Coote played no part the launch of the Sunday.[56] McLachlan was disgusted that Coote accepted a knighthood in 1962, and he was also none too happy when he discovered that Coote had, without informing him or having the authority, offered the deputy editorship of the *Sunday* to Peregrine Worsthorne, then a *Daily* leader writer. McLachlan finally agreed with Worsthorne that he should have the title of assistant editor and, his heart's desire, a weekly column.

The same executive split between news and opinion on the *Daily* was repeated on the new title. So the academic McLachlan found himself fighting for space with a bombastic managing director, Brian Roberts. Known to staff as 'Scruffy' because of his poor dress sense, the hot-tempered Welshman had won a demon reputation as night editor of the *Daily*. Sub-editors were in awe of his frequent emotional outbursts, even if they recognised that his good generally outweighed his bad.

It is clear from the *Telegraph* historian's description of the run-up to the launch that too much time was wasted on relatively trivial matters – such as the title of Kenneth Rose's idiosyncratic gossip column – while the grand strategy was ignored.[57] Promoted with the slogan 'Filling the gap', it was supposed to find an audience somewhere between the *Sunday Times* and the *Observer*, but the result was, as Berry admitted, disastrous. 'Alas,' he lamented many years later, 'we couldn't have been more wrong.'[58]

When the first new national Sunday paper in forty years appeared on 5 February 1961, it looked terrible, a jumbled, lacklustre copy of the *Daily*. Its news-filled front page, topped by a pilots' strike threat and the launching of the latest Russian satellite, in no way accomplished the editor's aim of providing 'a newspaper designed for Sunday . . . when the tasks and pleasures of the week are planned'.[59] As the *Guardian* noted witheringly, the only gap it filled 'was between Saturday's *Daily Telegraph* and Monday's'.[60] The *Sunday Express*, concerned enough to have decided to move up-market, relaxed. Its editor, John Junor, shared the general view that the *Sunday Telegraph*'s early issues were a 'dull, drab affair'.[61]

Sales fell away sharply after the first week, though it's hard to be precise about the figures because they were not independently audited until the second half of 1963. It seems fairly certain that Berry's expectation of replicating the *Daily*'s million-plus sale vanished within a month – it was soon falling below the *Observer*'s 715,000 and the *Sunday Times*'s 1 million. Even so, it was a remarkable achievement to obtain a regular 650,000 circulation for such a poor product and proved that it might well have a healthy future. Berry had to steady his nerve because it also ate money, costing some £400,000 to launch and a further loss of more than £450,000 in its first year.[62]

McLachlan and Roberts gradually realised the central problem: a Sunday paper has to be very different from a daily. News doesn't happen and readers generally expect something else anyway. It required more thought to provide features and topical background articles. Worsthorne's column, 'an elegant and paradoxical political commentary',[63] proved an early success, as did the financial pages under City editor Nigel Lawson, then just twenty-nine. Lawson pioneered the reporting of business and industrial matters in simple, easily understood language devoid of jargon. Lawson also showed that, in business, it was possible to find news on a Sunday.[64] One other piece of good fortune was the hiring of the experienced political columnist Hugh Massingham from the *Observer*, who was to enjoy 'an Indian summer' for the following three years.[65] It took time for the *Sunday Telegraph* to build an identity separate from its daily sister. Berry soon learned to compete with his rivals for serialisations, enjoying a publicity success with Chips Channon's revelatory diaries in 1963 and then adding huge sales with the supplement of Lord Denning's Profumo report (see below, pp. 189–90).

By 1964, noting the *Sunday Times*'s success with its magazine, Berry decided to follow suit. Then he changed his mind and placed his magazine in the Friday issue of the *Daily Telegraph*. It gave John Anstey, smarting from his rejection by Hamilton, the chance to prove his worth and there is little doubt that he did so. From its launch in September 1964, for the next twenty-two years under his editorship, Anstey's *Telegraph* magazine carved out a niche quite separate from that of the *Sunday Times*'s more eclectic and lifestyle-oriented product. It won a reputation for its literary and artistic writing, attracting contributions from authors such as Laurie Lee, Edna O'Brien, Anthony Burgess, John Betjeman and John Braine. As a counterweight to the paper's accent on news and politics, it worked superbly by attracting an audience who probably thought the *Telegraph* rather philistine.[66]

In the same month, the paper which had suffered most due to the Thomson–Hamilton revival of the *Sunday Times*, also launched a colour magazine. The *Observer*'s first sixty-four-page issue 'got off to a good start' in contrast to the *Telegraph*'s, which 'misfired', observed Francis Williams.[67] That was somewhat of a surprise because the *Observer*'s magazine decision was made without much enthusiasm by its owner–editor David Astor. He viewed a magazine as a marketing and advertising tool rather than a journalistic enterprise. Astor, and many of his staff, regarded the need to publish a magazine as the end of its golden age.

It came just three years after one of the high points of the *Observer*'s existence, an example of journalism making a real difference. A 1961 article about the plight of people languishing in jail for their political or religious views cast light on a previously unknown, yet widespread, state of affairs. As a direct result of the protests and concern generated by that piece, Amnesty International was formed.[68]

The *Observer* played a crucial role in the future of South Africa too. Early in 1964 the paper advocated sanctions when Astor, concerned that the communists were the only supporters of the black majority, urged the Western liberal democracies to help the black majority.[69] Two of his writers, Anthony Sampson and Mary Benson, also covered the trial of Nelson Mandela, who had been arrested after returning from Britain where he had met Astor several times. It has been forcefully argued that Mandela was sentenced to life imprisonment rather than the death penalty due to publicity in the Western press, especially in the *Observer*.[70]

Good journalism does not always reap the rewards it should. Sales held relatively steady in the early 1960s at about 715,000, while the *Sunday Times* moved ahead. Shaken by the launch of the *Sunday Telegraph*, the *Observer* saw its economic problems mount once it felt the effects of Thomson's investment and Hamilton's innovations at the *Sunday Times*.

The difference between Thomson and Astor became clear to both men when they met at an International Press Institute dinner. Thomson was amazed to discover that Astor had no clue about his paper's finances or even its circulation. Astor then asked him what his policy was on Berlin. 'Thomson was taken aback. "I don't know," he replied. Then, after a few seconds' reflection, "But I am sure I could buy one."'[71] That exchange goes a long way to explaining the 'mystery' about the *Observer*'s decline mooted by Godfrey Hodgson, Washington correspondent with the paper for five years until moving to the *Sunday Times* in 1965 as Insight editor. He questioned why the *Observer* allowed its rival to supplant it, offering the usual answers, about Astor feeling that commercial competition was inimicable to quality journalism or that his commitment after years in the chair began to flag.[72] The truth was that Astor, a rich man without a clue about business, was ignorant of the economic realities.

Only reluctantly did he accept that he must embrace the market. He would have to serialise books, cover a range of lifestyle and consumer topics, deal specifically with women's issues, and even lift his ban on drink advertising. As his biographer noted, this 'desperate search for new readers . . . changed the character of the paper significantly'.[73]

As the paper became more professional, more like other papers, so it lost the quirky distinctiveness which its staff and loyal readers had so enjoyed. Michael Frayn's column was a great addition in 1962, but the *Sunday Times* was now setting the agenda. In 1963 Astor introduced the Daylight column, a rather weak attempt at aping Insight. The magazine not only represented the end of the Astor experiment, it brought home nasty internal economic realities. The *Observer* Trust 'did not allow the paper to earn profits and thus made it almost impossible to borrow money'.[74] There just wasn't enough money in the trust for the necessary expansion, so Astor raised the funds from his own family trust, injecting some £700,000. From this point, the paper depended entirely on his declining wealth to survive. Fortunately, the magazine quickly made enough profits to support the main paper. It also helped boost sales once more, carrying the paper beyond 825,000 by the end of 1965.

Despite Astor's best intentions, and his undoubtedly sincere commitment to liberal campaigning journalism, he always seemed to find himself playing catch-up with the *Sunday Times.* Not only was Hamilton transforming his paper and serious Sunday journalism, it can now be seen that he was laying the foundations for the future of all British newspapers. Aligning himself with President Kennedy in his attempts to create a new political culture and a new world order after the Eisenhower years, Hamilton (rather like Cudlipp, though in a very different style) sought to redefine newspaper practice. He was the first to understand the need for a sort of permanent revolution within a paper: it must innovate or die, it must try constantly to give added value to readers, it must ensure that the editorial is of the highest quality. In his own words: 'It is the *content* of a national newspaper that determines its success, not printing machinery, or distribution, or even budgetary systems.'[75]

The successful launch of colour magazines by the serious Sunday papers appealed to an optimistic middle class enjoying the fruits of the post-war economic revival. It may also have indicated that the middle class was enlarging, though it was possible to misread these signs of social movement, exaggerating their effects, as two of Fleet Street's giants were about to discover.

The paper born of the age market researchers live in

Once the *Mirror* takeover of the *Daily Herald* was complete, Hannen Swaffer, then eighty-two, sent a note to Cudlipp saying he was 'available to do anything you want'. The fervent spiritualist was delighted by Cudlipp's response: he appointed Swaffer the *Herald*'s 'first correspondent on The Other Side'.[76] Cudlipp had less to joke about on This Side. In 1961, the *Herald*'s sales rose by 6,000, the only occasion between 1950 and 1964 when they did, and this was entirely attributable to the closure of the *News Chronicle.* The decline resumed the following year, falling by a further 69,000. Financial losses worsened too, rising from £648,540 in 1960 to £786,000 in the year up to February 1962.[77]

Cudlipp had agreed to keep John Beavan as *Herald* editor. Son of a former mayor of Manchester and one-time London editor of the *Manchester Guardian*, Beavan was considered pompous by most of the *Herald*'s staff. To their consternation, he declared: 'I want to bring the *Daily Herald* into the drawing rooms of Britain.'[78] He also said: 'You can no more have a working class newspaper than you can a working class refrigerator.'[79] Cudlipp, while keen to attract a more prosperous readership, worried that Beavan was alienating the bedrock audience and sent in Dick Dinsdale, then deputy editor of the *Mirror*, as an 'editorial adviser'. It was hardly a recipe for harmony, teaming the middle-class Lancastrian with Dinsdale, a foul-mouthed Yorkshireman, who treated sub-editors with contempt. In a breathless example of euphemism, Cudlipp referred to Dinsdale as 'outspoken' and 'prepared to . . . stamp on any piece of journalistic work he considered less than perfect'.[80] In straightforward parlance, he was a bully and, in Cudlipp's presence, a toady. Perhaps the most famous Dinsdale anecdote concerns one of the many occasions on which he screamed out across the editorial floor: 'What cunt subbed this?' In an ad lib that was to earn the young sub-editor Bob Coole lasting admiration from colleagues, he shouted back: 'What cunt wants to know?'

Beavan, for all his faults, did hire great writers of the left, such as James Cameron and Doris Lessing. His staff also included the excellent Jon Akass and Nancy Banks-Smith, along with one of the best-informed industrial correspondents of the era, Geoffrey Goodman. But Cudlipp was delighted when his friend Sydney Jacobson applied for the editorship. He eased Beavan aside, making him the group's political adviser, where he prospered, and Jacobson set about transforming the paper.

Goodman believed that what Jacobson produced was 'as near to the intelligent left-of-centre daily as the *Herald* got' and might have done better if given more time, and more money.[81] It had a better grip of reporting on youth, though it could still be patronising. There was sensible industrial coverage, with Goodman getting a freer hand on reporting the different strands of thought within the TUC, and an improved political line which returned to support for Gaitskell's nuclear policy. Foreign stories got a show again, along with books, ballet and opera. Jacobson certainly took the *Herald* upmarket, but the slide in sales continued as before, and it was leaking money.

Cudlipp was already confronting his key dilemma. How could he save the *Herald* when his flagship *Daily Mirror* was fighting for the same readership? Dare he let them compete head on, or should the *Herald* find its own audience? If so, what was it?[82] Despite Jacobson's efforts, King and Cudlipp knew they couldn't let the situation at the *Herald* continue when advertisers were deserting by the month. In 1955, its share of sales and advertising revenue were equal at 10.8 per cent but, by 1964, though the paper had 8.1 per cent of the national daily sales, it took only 3.5 per cent of the advertising revenue.[83] Cudlipp, King and Jacobson decided that it was the title itself which needed to change. They convinced the TUC that the *Herald* was no longer viable and bought out their shares, secretly planning to shed the skin of a paper Cudlipp referred to as 'a bloated, listless boa constrictor'.[84]

He and King now put their faith in the academic equivalent of snake charming: a potent mix of sociological theory and market research. In response to what they deemed to be the demands of what they believed to be a newly emergent society, they constructed a new paper with a new title, a new shape, a new typeface and, supposedly, a new editorial agenda. They hired sociologist Mark Abrams, managing director of his own research company, to carry out a deceptively simple task: 'In the light of today's trends', he should 'predict the nature of our society tomorrow'.[85] Abrams's academic credentials were impeccable. His surveys on the condition of the British population, were well regarded.[86] But it is obvious from reading *The Newspaper Reading Public of Tomorrow*, a seventy-six-page report with thirty-nine statistical tables and graphs, that Abrams knew nothing about why people read newspapers.[87] He didn't even consider what kind of paper people wanted to read, or why they were turning their backs on the *Herald*. It was a wholly inadequate snapshot of reading habits. For example, he referred to the sales rises of the 'class' papers and the fall-off of the rest, ascribing this to better education. Yet this entirely overlooked the underlying reasons for the *Daily Mirror*'s success.

One of key faults of market research was illustrated by the interviewees' response to questions in which they tended to tell researchers what they thought they wanted to hear. So, when asked to say which were their main interests from a prescribed list, 58 per cent said it was 'meeting people from overseas' and 54 per cent replied that it was 'learning about new inventions'. Sport got a negligible rating. When it came to detailing their newspaper-reading habits, 45 per cent swore they read the news pages and only 36 per cent the feature pages.[88]

Abrams claimed that the masses, the working class, were on the move, geographically and socially. They were enjoying a more affluent, consumer-oriented lifestyle. Their educational standards were improving. Women were 'rising in status'. According to Abrams, these new Britons were 'secular and critical rather than ideological and undiscriminating'. He added: 'In a post-industrial society consumer politics displace ideological politics.' These conclusions did not pass without criticism at the time,[89] though we might now be more generous in saying that Abrams was ahead of his time. It was heady stuff which went straight to King's head. In accepting the Abrams report at face value, he and Cudlipp made the mistake of using it as a practical guide to action. They decided to refashion the *Daily Herald* into an entirely new paper to appeal to the people they thought Abrams had identified. Though Bill Grundy was later to take a sarcastic sideswipe at sociologists as 'modern astrologers' who made a poor job of casting the *Sun*'s horoscope, he rightly admitted that Abrams was not the real culprit.[90]

King and Cudlipp misunderstood the survey. The changes Abrams indicated, and which read today as a fine piece of forecasting, were happening very slowly and unevenly. Anyway, a change in lifestyle is not necessarily accompanied by an immediate change in culture and in cultural activities, such as newspaper-reading. Abrams, in company with those political soothsayers who made too much of the embourgeoisement thesis, was lured into imagining that change would be rapid.[91] In fact, as the statistical evidence culled from employment classifications in census returns shows, the movement from a working-class mass into what might be termed a middle-class mass has been a long-run phenomenon. ABC1 groups did not outnumber the C2DEs until 1998–9. Social change is altogether more complex. Male readers of the popular papers may not have been wearing flat caps and clogs any longer, but most of them were still manual workers in traditional industries. Nor were they enjoying a vast increase in disposable income. Most of them were unlikely to switch from one newspaper to another. If they did, as we shall see, they certainly didn't make a dramatic leap up market.

Most ironic of all was the failure of proven press wizards like King and Cudlipp to grasp the most obvious fact: the *Herald* was losing the bulk of its readers to their own *Daily Mirror*, not to the 'class' papers. The *Mirror* was eating away at the *Herald*'s audience, not because it represented the aspirations of a newly affluent, well-educated working class, but because it was more entertaining, more independent and more irreverent. *Herald* readers were moving to the tabloid for its brashness, not for its high-mindedness. In mitigation, the commercial pressure on King and Cudlipp to stem the *Herald*'s losses, while attempting to fulfil their pledge to the TUC and Labour party to keep the paper going, was a great burden. Having suspended their critical faculties, the result was a 'new, radical daily', the *Sun*.

Perhaps its best asset was its title, which was chosen on a hunch rather than through meticulous research. According to Cudlipp, he first heard it mentioned by Harry Rochez, an Odhams director, who told him it had been suggested by another director, Basil de Launay.[92] A different version is retailed by Mike Molloy, which Geoffrey Goodman and Cudlipp's widow Jodi have assured me is nearer the truth. Cudlipp and Jacobson were walking along a street near the *Herald* office when they passed a pub called the *Sun*. 'That's it, Sydney,' exclaimed Cudlipp, pointing to the sign.[93]

The *Sun*'s launch was postponed, at Wilson's request, until after the general election.[94] So the *Daily Herald* survived until 14 September 1964 with its successor arising the next day: 'Good Morning! Yes, it's time for a new newspaper . . . The *Sun* is here! The only newspaper born of the age we live in.'[95] That first issue, according to Wintour, prompted laughter at the *Daily Express*.[96] There was little news, the layout was a mess, its shape, halfway between a tabloid and broadsheet, was offputting, while the orange sun on the masthead looked decidedly odd. The *Daily Mail*'s editor, Bill Hardcastle, thought it 'disappointing',[97] as did the independent commentator Francis Williams, who nevertheless counselled against a hasty judgement.[98] Ted Pickering, newly anointed as editorial director, wasn't surprised because, despite the sociological preparation, he discovered that the practical planning was 'horribly skimpy'.[99]

From that first issue, the *Sun* was spurned by a large proportion of its traditional audience and then failed to attract, or even find, Abrams's notional upwardly mobile young go-getters. Sales did improve marginally in the first year, and then resumed their previous decline. There was good writing, from Cameron, Akass, Banks-Smith, Dee Wells, Clement Freud and Auberon Waugh. Cecil King, immodestly contributing a column, was less readable. Innovative features, such as Probe, and the women's pages, under the unisexual title Pacesetters, had their moments, though Probe lost all four of its original team in a dispute.[100] There were some political and industrial scoops, but news took second place to a softer, features-oriented agenda. Pictures tended to be too big and the columns were too wide. It 'flopped', admitted Cudlipp.[101] But the worst was yet to come.

The King is in his castle

For years it had seemed that King and Cudlipp could do no wrong and, outwardly, their empire looked impregnable. In 1961 the *Mirror* papers moved from the now shabby Geraldine House to a new headquarters at Holborn Circus, overlooking Gamages department store. Built for £11 million and designed by Sir Owen Williams, Wembley Stadium's architect, the distinctive glass structure, in red and blue, dominated the junction, just as its titles dominated the newspaper market. On the lobby wall were four medallions bearing the likenesses of Bartholomew, Cassandra, Cudlipp and King. They knew no modesty.

King and Cudlipp took up residence on the ninth floor. King's suite was lavishly furnished in what a *Sunday Express* columnist referred to as a 'potentate setting'.[102] King was now chairman of a company publishing 12 British newspapers, 11 foreign papers, 75 consumer magazines, 132 trade and technical journals and several book imprints. It ran twenty print sites, and had interests in TV, radio, exhibitions and retail shops. After the Odhams takeover, the conglomerate assumed the title of the International Publishing Corporation (IPC) and proclaimed itself the world's largest publishing group with 230 newspaper and magazine titles, employing 30,000 people in Britain, west Africa and the West Indies. At its first annual general meeting, King reported a profit of £6.5 million.[103]

King, who owned only a small number of shares, lived in great style.[104] Wintour thought him 'immensely vain', a view shared by almost everyone who met him.[105] During the 1964 election campaign King surprised staff by putting a red flag on his Rolls-Royce with the slogan 'Vote Labour'.[106] This gesture had a lot to do with his expectation of a cabinet post. Instead, Wilson offered him a junior job at the Board of Trade, which King regarded as an insult. He rejected the offer, just as he turned down a barony, believing he deserved an earldom.

Cudlipp lived well too, eventually in a house in Chelsea's Cheyne Walk. He was shocked by two deaths in 1962: his second wife, Eileen Ascroft, editorial director of Mirror group's Fleetway magazines, took an overdose of sleeping tablets, aged forty-seven. Six months later his brother Percy died aged fifty-seven. The following year Cudlipp married Jodi Hyland, a former editor of *Woman's Mirror*, with whom he was to spend the rest of his life.

For Cudlipp, the *Daily Mirror* remained his greatest journalistic passion. It started life in its new building with a new editor: Lee Howard, aged forty-seven, formerly *Sunday Pictorial* editor and before that editor of *Woman's Sunday Mirror*. Intelligent, a talented writer, he had a great sense of humour but was rather shy. He looked the part: heavily built, he invariably wore red braces stretched across a white shirt with sleeves rolled up. He rarely appeared on the editorial floor, preferring his executives to see him in his office, and he was a good technician. As with his predecessors, he played the engine-room stoker to Commander Cudlipp on the bridge. Howard was apolitical, he just got the paper out to his editorial director's orders. He was still editor when I joined as a news sub in 1971. Introduced to him on my first day, my initial impression was of a gruff, fierce man, but an indulgent smile soon revealed his benevolence. He was nothing like the disciplinarians Nener and Dinsdale.

With Howard in the chair, the *Mirror* achieved a sale of 5 million for the first time on 9 June 1964, claiming a readership of 14 million, more than a third of the adult population. This record, which no other daily paper had achieved before or has emulated since, occurred at the moment when Cudlipp was so enamoured with the Abrams thesis about a changing society. In the light of that research, he began to refashion the *Mirror*, deliberately moving it up market.[107] Serious content appeared in World Spotlight, Inside Page and Mirrorscope. John Pilger's reports from foreign parts were published at great length. There was lightness too, with Donald Zec's showbusiness articles, Felicity Green's fashion features, Christopher Ward's column and the hugely popular Andy Capp cartoon strip. Cudlipp's shock issues gave way to special issues, some of which were excellent, if a little too pedagogic. But editorial life in a company flush with money was beginning to become overly self-indulgent, with every excuse taken for champagne parties, often abroad. A special issue on boom cities was launched on a liner in Liverpool with prime minister Wilson as chief guest. Another, on the Common Market, was edited from Paris where senior journalists severely tested the capacity of a wine cellar. There were executives who did not agree with Cudlipp's new policy, but no one dared to question him. He was fond of saying: 'Other people's opinions don't matter if you know you are right.'[108]

The strange affair of the peer and the gangster

Cudlipp tended not to interfere at the *Sunday People*, where the formidable Sam Campbell continued to hold sway. His brand of investigative journalism came up trumps in 1964 with the exposure of a number of First Division footballers for accepting bribes to fix matches. A successful prosecution followed and a handful of players were banned from playing professional soccer.

Despite this success, Cudlipp was much more interested in the fortunes of the *Sunday Pictorial* and, in 1963, he renamed it the *Sunday Mirror*, which cemented its affinity with the daily while distancing it from the *Sunday People*. It was blurbed as 'the new Sunday paper for The Moderns ... people who not only want to be "with it" but "way out ahead"'.[109] It was soon to prove a little too way out when editor Reg Payne, successor to Lee Howard, embarrassed Cudlipp by publishing a story which illustrated the sharper, more intrusive, post-Profumo trend among the Sunday populars. Payne was a rough diamond, foul-mouthed, irascible, if occasionally funny.[110] King and Cudlipp didn't find anything to laugh about after the *Sunday Mirror* splashed on a story headlined 'Peer and gangster: a Yard inquiry'.[111] Without naming anyone, the report alleged that the Metropolitan Police commissioner Sir Joseph Simpson had ordered an inquiry into a 'homosexual relationship between a prominent peer and a leading thug in the London underworld'. It was said that the peer was 'a household name' and the gangster was running a protection racket.

The following day both the *Daily Mirror* and the *Daily Express* took up the story, again without identifying anyone, but enlarging on allegations of protection racketeering.[112] Simpson issued a statement that day denying that any police investigation was taking place.[113] The officers also arrived at the *Sunday Mirror* to interview Payne and his reporter, Norman Lucas, demanding that they hand over any incriminating material. They refused to do so. Instead, in its next issue, the paper returned to the attack under the teasing headline 'The picture we must not print'.[114] Despite the commissioner's denial, it repeated the central allegations against the two men and claimed it could not publish the photograph of them, sitting together on a sofa, because it would infringe copyright. This time, after more police pressure, Payne agreed to give the Yard its 'evidence'.[115]

Other newspapers, particularly the *Sunday Telegraph* and *Sunday Times*, were fiercely critical of the *Sunday Mirror*. Randolph Churchill called it 'a particularly obnoxious article' and went for King's throat. Was he not the man who had instructed his reporters not to intrude into people's private lives?[116] Bolstered by growing support, Lord Boothby – who had been in France when the story broke, in the company of former *Daily Telegraph* editor Sir Colin Coote – wrote to the *Times*. He claimed that on his return to London he found it 'seething with rumours' that he was the peer concerned and Ronnie Kray was the gangster. He denied he was a homosexual, explained that he had met Kray to discuss a business proposal, which he had rejected, and that he didn't know of Kray's alleged criminal activities. He dared the *Sunday* and *Daily Mirror* to prove otherwise. He later explained that rumours of his name were circulating because he had been identified in the German magazine *Stern*, which had been shown to some Tory MP friends.[117]

On 6 August, in an unprecedented climbdown, the *Daily Mirror* carried a front page statement signed by Cecil King and headlined: 'Lord Boothby: An unqualified apology'. King wrote: 'It is my view, and the policy of this Group, that when a newspaper is wrong it should state so promptly and without equivocation.' Despite not having mentioned Boothby's name in the *Sunday Mirror* or in *Daily Mirror* follow-ups, the paper had been advised that Boothby would undoubtedly win a libel action. The apology was accompanied by a £40,000 payment to Boothby, plus his costs and a £5,000 payment to a hospital.

Within a week, Payne paid for the mistake with his job, though many of his staff thought King had caved in to establishment pressure and that he had been unfairly treated.[118] He was replaced by his thirty-seven-year-old assistant Michael Christiansen, son of Arthur. At the same time, the former *Express* editor Ted Pickering was appointed editorial director of both the *Daily* and *Sunday Mirror*, replacing Cudlipp, who explained that it would give him more time, as chairman, to concentrate on the new *Sun* and the increasing workload of the mushrooming IPC stable.[119]

Francis Williams praised Boothby for dealing so well with what he called a 'smear' and 'a classic example of gutter journalism conducted with almost incomprehensible incompetence'.[120] He was right, of course, and it was a wonder that Lucas survived as crime correspondent for years to come. It transpired, after Boothby's death in 1986, that there may have been some truth in the story when evidence emerged to suggest that he 'was, in fact, bisexual, and it seems possible that his connection with Kray involved some homosexual activity (then still criminal) with youths procured by Kray'.[121] Even so, the paper entirely missed the point: the real story was the Kray brother's genuinely criminal activities, not Boothby's private sexual peccadilloes.

Afterwards, the former *Mail* editor William Hardcastle tried to draw a lesson from the affair, noting Payne's treatment at the hands of his bosses. The image of a strong, free, uncompromised editor, argued Hardcastle, was 'a faded daguerreotype . . . the commercialisation of the press . . . has altered the balance between manager and editor'. An editor was now regarded by 'controlling management as a technician, a fulfiller rather than a creator of policy'.[122] It strikes me that Hardcastle, upset at his own dismissal (see below, p. 170), entirely missed the point. Few editors had been free of proprietorial restraint, and certainly none in the popular press. Cudlipp, who was an editor in all but title, was free because his paper had no owner. Payne was fired, as he should have been, for making a colossal error of judgement, publishing what he could not prove, smearing a man without any evidence.

Another Sunday changed its name and its shape in 1962. *Reynolds News*, acknowledging that it was becoming much more difficult to sell popular broadsheet papers, couldn't hold on to its audience. Despite excellent contributions from J. B. Priestley, fitfully amusing columns by Tom Driberg and seriously good industrial reporting by Charles Timeaus, it failed to appeal. So, in September 1962, the radical paper selling just 300,000 copies a week, underwent a radical overhaul. It changed its size and its title, becoming the tabloid *Sunday Citizen*, and announced the transformation with a suitably quasi-Leninist slogan: 'Praise the past, salute the future'.[123]

It had always been difficult for *Reynolds News* to attract advertising. Once it became the *Sunday Citizen* – soon characterised as 'a poor man's *Sunday Mirror*'[124] – the fall in readership accelerated and the revenue situation worsened considerably. By the end of 1965, with sales down to barely 230,000, Cyril Hamnett, chairman of the Co-op Press and therefore the paper's publisher, made a desperate, and hopelessly naive, plea for help. 'Has the advertising industry no responsibility for helping to maintain variety and independence in the Press?' he said. 'By diversifying a small proportion of its budget it could help to maintain a diminishing number of non-combine independent newspapers.' The response was silence and he was forced to institute economies at a paper already noted for its parsimony. Meanwhile, he and the editor, William Richardson, sought contributions from trade unions and readers in a series of articles which grew increasingly hysterical in the following months. How apt that Hamnett's *Who's Who* entry noted his single recreation as 'the pursuit of the unattainable'.

Battle of the daily broadsheets

Life was very different at the *Daily Telegraph*. Michael Berry was overseeing continued sales rises and improving profits at his paper. He knew he must replace his ageing editor, Colin Coote, though it didn't happen until 1964, by which time he was seventy. After fourteen years in the chair, Coote could point to a rise in sales from 970,000 to 1.3 million. His successor, largely groomed for the role by Berry, was Maurice Green. Educated at Rugby and Oxford, Green was fifty-eight on appointment. He had edited Brendan Bracken's *Financial News* in his twenties before joining the *Times* as financial and industrial editor in 1938, a post he kept – apart from war service with the Royal Artillery – until 1953. He was then promoted to assistant editor, spending eight years in the job until Berry pressed him to become Coote's deputy. Infinitely more popular than Coote, who tried to suggest that he had engineered Green's rise, he was to preside over a period of great success – and significant change – at the paper.[125]

Coote upset Berry by naming Green's number two as Colin Welch. It was to have profound consequences for the paper because Welch's influence on the *Telegraph* for the following twenty years was far greater than that of the men who became editors.[126] A *Telegraph* leader writer from 1949, Welch pioneered the satirical Peter Simple column and wrote wonderfully amusing parliamentary sketches before Coote raised him up. Welch also nurtured other writers, particularly his brilliant successor as Simple, Michael Wharton, and in 1964 was delighted when T. E. (Peter) Utley joined up. There would be others too. Little did Berry realise that the man he disliked for his facetiousness was to lead the paper towards support for the most serious philosophical change in Conservative and British political thinking in a century.

Another senior appointment, of Peter Eastwood as night editor, was also to have far-reaching consequences. Eastwood, product of a Yorkshire grammar school and a local paper, worked his way up the subbing desks of various papers before joining the *Telegraph* in 1948. No one doubted his abilities: he was a masterly sub and a superb organiser. But, in a profession noted for rudeness, he was one of the rudest men ever to work in Fleet Street and his ruthless office politics helped to make life uncomfortable for other executives as well as many reporters and subs. Eastwood's great plus with Berry was his attention to detail. Playing on this strength, he knew he could count on support from his proprietor and dare to confront the dilettantes, as he viewed all those – including the editor – unconnected with the news pages. Eastwood and Berry were both convinced that the *Daily Telegraph*'s success stemmed from its comprehensive news coverage, regarding it as the reason for its sales triumph over the *Times.*

As for the *Times,* it was suffering from chronic financial instability, and with Lord Astor going off to France, a loss of morale. Gavin Astor was now in charge of one the world's most famous, but ailing, newspapers. Yet he had no real clue about how to save it. Having ignored virtually every salient point in the 1958 Coopers inquiry, the paper was in limbo, losing ground not only to the *Telegraph,* but to the *Financial Times,* which had supplanted it as the main purveyor of City and financial news, and to the *Guardian,* with its more coherent, liberal agenda, better writing and sharper analysis.

There were, of course, articles of quality by fine reporters and writers to appreciate in the *Times,* especially once the editor, Sir William Haley, was allocated funds to hire more journalists. By then it was a vain hope to imagine that tinkering with the editorial alone was good enough to carry the *Times* towards an unrealistic sales target. There were structural weaknesses in the company while the paper itself looked old and staid. In desperation, Haley set up a committee towards the end of 1964 to decide how to modernise the paper. To few people's surprise, its major recommendation was to replace ads on the front page with news. There was fierce resistance, and not only from the advertising department. Traditionalists argued that it was the hallmark of the *Times* and that it would be foolhardy to change. Some reasonable ideas, such as the launching of a diary and the introduction of a political cartoon, were rapidly adopted. But the argument over the page-one content rumbled on.

While remaining a national institution, the *Times* had gained the image of a rather eccentric and aged aunt, celebrated for its letters about identifying the year's first cuckoo call and the bizarre adverts in its personal column. Senior journalists had long ago rejected the notion of promoting the *Times* as the top people's paper, but the perception stuck, even within Printing House Square which, in 1963, proudly announced that 70 per cent of the names in *Who's Who* read the *Times*.[127] The financial position was becoming difficult. In 1960 its profits were almost £300,000, a healthy 10.7 per cent of revenues. By 1965, profits had dropped away to £200,000, a mere 3.4 per cent of income. The *Times*'s market share of advertising had fallen and so had circulation, down to 228,000. The £2 million spent on a new building at Printing House Square in Blackfriars was also proving a very expensive investment.

Profits were also hard to come by at the *Guardian*, but its senior director, Laurence Scott, did have a strategy. On 11 September 1961, the first issue of the *Guardian* was printed in London, on Thomson's *Sunday Times* presses at Gray's Inn Road. It was the second stage in Scott's plan to turn the Manchester-based paper into a national, though he had little to celebrate: the company recorded a financial loss in 1962, the first in its history. By the following year he was forced to close the *Manchester Evening Chronicle*, then selling 250,000 copies, by merging it with the *Evening News*.[128] Advertisers, having ignored the paper for years, showed signs of warming after noting that the *Guardian*'s readership profile had a high ratio of ABC1 readers, 25 per cent of whom owned shares.[129] In 1965 Scott reported to staff that the paper had enjoyed the most successful financial year in its history. It wasn't to last, and Scott began laying plans that would outrage editor Alastair Hetherington and his senior staff.

In sales terms, the *Guardian* did not do as well as expected. After it had benefited from the *News Chronicle* closure, which added 30,000 extra buyers,[130] a further 30,000 arrived over the next four years, taking the sale to 275,000 at the end of 1965. The expansion of its southern audience was slow despite improvements. Brian Redhead, features editor for three years from 1959, enhanced the layouts while some of the reporting – especially by Clare Hollingworth in Algeria and Alistair Cooke in the States during the Cuban missile crisis and on Kennedy's assassination – was first rate. With the likes of Philip Hope-Wallace on theatre and Neville Cardus on music, the *Guardian* seemed to be a star-studded vehicle. But all was not as it appeared.

There was criticism from within and without, and the beginnings of what would develop in the broadsheet press, by the 1980s, into the 'dumbing down' debate about the nature of editorial content and the reason for papers existing. Redhead's successor as features editor, John Rosselli, fell out of sympathy with the *Guardian*'s move, as he saw it, towards the *Daily Telegraph*. Rather than widen its appeal, it should ignore the commercial pressures and aim instead to be Britain's answer to *Le Monde*, catering for the intellectual elite.

Arguing from the opposite position, the independent commentator, Clive Irving, thought the paper's relentless diet of lengthy, serious articles was often unpalatable. He launched a broadside in the *Spectator*, lambasting the *Guardian*'s 'political ambiguity ... unctuous moral postures, woolly leaders' and a 'news sense so selective that it amounts to perversity'.[131] This kind of attack hit home, provoking a split between Scott and Hetherington, with the former suggesting that there were problems with the content and the latter even offering his resignation, which was refused.[132] Rosselli did leave, though, for a long and successful career in academe.[133]

By contrast, Gordon Newton's adventurous *Financial Times*, with its better all-round coverage, was finding new friends. Cecil King was moved to remark that the *FT*, 'instead of being a trade paper for stockbrokers ... is becoming a serious paper in its own right'.[134] Its increasing sale, argued its historian, was due to an appreciation of economics as the centre point of public and political life.[135]

In the early 1960s, with unemployment below 2 per cent, rising incomes and a bullish stock market, there was every reason to imagine that the *FT* was catching the prevailing spirit. Whether true or not, it was building a reputation for objectivity, fair-mindedness and accuracy. Even in the contentious area of industrial and labour coverage, its reports were valued by both management and unions. Its pragmatic, rather than intellectual, approach paid dividends in its own balance sheet too: the *FT* made operating profits between £1 million to £1.25 million during these years.

Journalists weep at the death of Lord Propaganda

Rising unsteadily from his chair at the head of the table in the Dorchester, the old maestro acknowledged the applause of his fellow press magnates and a host of executives and editors. It was Lord Beaverbrook's eighty-fifth birthday celebration in May 1964 and he knew, as indeed did most of them, that he was dying from cancer.[136] He gave a virtuoso performance, referring to his life as a series of apprenticeships, in finance, politics and newspapers, without becoming a master of any. Now, he concluded, to a hushed and spellbound audience, 'it is time to become an apprentice once more. I have not settled in which direction. But somewhere, some time soon.'[137]

He went home to Cherkley and died there two weeks later, on 9 June 1964, lying in state for five days, 'a most unusual procedure in England'.[138] Compared in obituaries to Northcliffe and the mythical Citizen Kane, he continued to intrigue and appal. Many journalists hero-worshipped him because he lavished money on journalism. The *Daily Express* had a larger staff than any other paper, with fifty photographers, scores of reporters and numerous foreign correspondents. Planes and boats were hired without a thought. Taxi travel was the norm. Expense accounts were huge.

Virtually everyone who had met him, and several people who had not, imitated Beaverbrook's nasal Canadian growl to repeat his favourite phrases when talking to editors: 'Who is in charge of the clattering train?' . . . 'What's the news?' . . . 'Goodbye to you.' Journalists saw little wrong with Beaverbrook's political control of the paper. He was one of them, a character. Many wept at the news of his death.

Some people never reconciled themselves to Beaverbrook. Cecil King thought him evil. Once asked by *Sunday Pictorial* editor Reg Payne what he thought of Beaverbrook, King replied: 'If I saw him approaching my house I would set my dog on him.'[139] It should not be forgotten that he often encouraged disgraceful misbehaviour by *Express* journalists. One observer claimed that the paper had six reporters following Aneurin Bevan everywhere he went: 'When he took a train they would follow him down the corridor every time he left his carriage to go to the lavatory. Talk about hounding!'[140] (The *Express* was not alone. When Bevan was dying in hospital in 1960, reporters from the *Daily Mail* and *Daily Telegraph* were found in a neighbouring ward.)[141]

Perhaps the best portraits of Beaverbrook in his last years were drawn in their very different ways by the journalist Alan Watkins, who met him first in 1959, and his secretary, Colin Vines, who worked for him from August 1961. Though Watkins had worked for a year in London at the *Sunday Express* he had never seen Beaverbrook. Only when appointed New York correspondent did he realise that he would meet his legendary proprietor. Editor John Junor told him: 'Scrub the nicotine off your fingers, don't light up unless he gives you permission and don't argue with him unless you're very sure of your facts.' He added: 'If you make a bad impression on Beaverbrook it could have a fatal effect on your career. After all, it's his newspaper.'[142]

Beaverbrook regarded *Express* foreign staff as part journalists and part servants, expecting them to smooth his path by organising junkets, buying theatre tickets, generally entertaining him.[143] Watkins, like so many before him, was required to accompany Beaverbrook on aimless walks around Central Park, making small talk. When he discovered tins of Campbell's tomato soup in an office stationery cupboard, a secretary explained that it was Beaverbrook's favourite. They kept a supply because, on a previous occasion, it had once proved impossible to satisfy his request.[144]

Though he was not a journalist, Vines's Pooterish reportage is excellent, a fine example of the virtues of straightforward observation and the (apparent) verbatim record of mundane conversations. He had no illusions about his own skills: 'It was soon obvious . . . that I was the worst secretary Lord Beaverbrook had ever had.'[145] It didn't matter. Having taken a shine to Vines, then in his late twenties, Beaverbrook treated him indulgently, a cross between a grandson and a court jester.[146] In detailing their odd dialogue, Vines reveals Beaverbrook as altogether less worldly than his editors might have suspected. 'Who's Bristow?' Beaverbrook asks one day. Vines replies patiently: 'He's in the *Evening Standard*, a new cartoon strip. He's very good.'[147] Most of the time, though, it was Beaverbrook as master and Vines as pupil.

In one short sentence, Vines also encapsulated his master's combative philosophy: 'The atmosphere of struggle and competition – Lord Beaverbrook approved it.'[148] He also delighted in Beaverbrook's sense of mischief. When Douglas-Home became Tory leader, Beaverbrook sang down the phone to the *Express* editor: 'Sow the seeds of discontent, sow the seeds of discontent' to the tune of 'Polly Put the Kettle On'. Watch where Sir Alec is going, he said, because it's time for us to be going the other way.[149] Beaverbrook continued to fire off memos to his editors, making improbable suggestions and urging writers to attack or praise various politicians, based mainly on whim. Alan Watkins suggests this activity had become ineffectual, but the recipients would not agree.

The greatest clue that Beaverbrook was losing the plot was his sudden changes of *Express* editorship. In four years up to 1961 Ted Pickering had improved the sale from an average 4 million a day to more than 4.3 million, yet Beaverbrook was willing to listen to critics from within, such as the disloyal associate editor Harold Keeble.[150] At the high point of Pickering's success Beaverbrook chose to fire him, on Christmas Eve 1960, kicking him upstairs into a directorship. It was one of the rare occasions on which an editor was sacked while circulation was rising – in the words of a Beaverbrook executive, 'a crass error of judgement'.[151]

Accepting advice from Junor on his successor, Beaverbrook chose Pickering's deputy, Bob Edwards. The handsome thirty-eight-year-old former *Tribune* editor was a strong Labour party supporter who found some of Beaverbrook's attitudes upsetting, such as his prejudice against black people, but he turned a blind eye. He justified taking the job either by being amusingly cynical or by arguing, reasonably enough, that there were large areas of agreement between him and his proprietor over failings within the Tory party. *Express* support for the Conservatives in the 1959 election had been lukewarm. He could also point to Trevor Evans's noticeably even-handed industrial reporting. Edwards also relished Beaverbrook's sense of humour. Edwards once allowed Keeble to design a front page that was disastrous. Next morning Beaverbrook rang: 'Mr Edwards, tell me you were on holiday, tell me you were at home with a cold, tell me you were in a hotel room with a woman, tell me you were drunk, tell me anything, but please don't tell me you were in the office last night.'[152]

Once again, Beaverbrook revealed his faltering grip. Nine months after appointing Edwards, who had maintained Pickering's sale, he suddenly fired him, sending him up to Glasgow to edit his *Sunday Citizen*. Beaverbrook gave the *Express* editorship to Edwards's deputy, Roger Wood, and then, barely a year later, reappointed Edwards. Wood, described by Derek Jameson as 'a whizzkid down from Oxford . . . chubby . . . with a deceptively languid air', had a habit of calling everyone 'dear boy'.[153] He had made his name by building huge sales at the *Daily Express*'s Scottish edition, but was regarded as a 'Max man', a favourite of Beaverbrook's son, and therefore vulnerable to the old man's whims. Years later he became one of Rupert Murdoch's key American executives, editing and rejuvenating the *New York Post*.

It is almost impossible to detect any changes in the *Express* throughout Beaverbrook's four inexplicable switches of editor. The underlying philosophy of the *Express*, according to Cudlipp, remained 'fundamentally materialist . . . appealing to the young man on the way up, encouraging him to accumulate possessions en route . . . preaching that hard work and application can enable every ambitious reader to make his pile like Lord Beaverbrook'.[154] Superficially, this analysis seems fine. The paper did accentuate the positive, glossing over the deeper, darker problems afflicting society. But its greatest failings were in offering a simplistic account of the world, in an unconscious encouragement of xenophobia, and in its cloying predictability. It also lacked a sense of humour. While Cudlipp's *Mirror* appeared to revel in the changes happening in society, with the occasional wag of the finger, the *Express* was altogether more condescending, even world-weary. This solid, narrow agenda was appealing to the older generation, of course, and Beaverbrook could point, in his final months, to his flagship paper's continuing circulation success. Significantly, it was to be downhill ever after.

A couple of years before he died Beaverbrook also enhanced the fortunes of the *Sunday Express* by absorbing the *Sunday Dispatch*, after persuading Rothermere to sell it to him. Its sales had been falling, despite the attentions of the badly behaved veteran editor Herbert Gunn, who retired in ill-health after the takeover and died the following year. Enjoying its new circulation boost, the *Sunday Express* boasted on its front page that it occupied 'the immense chasm' between 'the ponderous, pompous small-circulation "heavy" papers' and those 'which have built up large sales by sensationalism and salaciousness'.[155] Junor, the editor, emerges well from Watkins's recollections, seeming to satisfy Beaverbrook while frustrating his ambitions and cleverly avoiding carrying out his orders.[156] The staff got used to hearing Junor trot out his pet maxims: 'An ounce of emotion is worth a ton of fact' . . . 'Everybody is interested in sex and money' . . . 'When in doubt, turn to the royal family.' For a long time, an editorial formula built around them delighted a huge readership.

One journalist displaced by the closure of the *Dispatch* was its New York correspondent David English. He was considering joining a Manhattan paper until Bob Edwards, having heard (probably from Beaverbrook) that English 'was brilliant but sometimes chanced his arm', hired him.[157] He went initially to Washington for the *Daily Express* and later headed the paper's New York bureau, winning plaudits for his America Column. One of his colleagues, Alan Watkins, thought the dapper, charming English 'had about him something of the Artful Dodger'.[158] The *Daily Mirror*'s American correspondent, Tony Delano, probably thought it a perfect description after witnessing the way in which English managed to cover himself in glory for his coverage of President Kennedy's assassination in November 1963, and the subsequent shooting of his assassin, Lee Harvey Oswald. On the day of Kennedy's death English and Delano were together on a routine job in New York. Although the *Express*'s Washington correspondent, Ross Mark, wrote the story, English caught the first available plane and, on landing in Dallas, called London to insist that the dateline for the final edition be changed to read 'From David English in Dallas', despite not having filed a line of copy. Neither was he a witness to Oswald's murder. Years later Delano was amazed to read an article by English in which he vividly recalled being in Dallas and seeing Kennedy shot.[159]

English returned to the *Express*'s Fleet Street office as foreign editor in 1964, quickly illustrating both his talent and his impetuosity. One afternoon he presented Edwards with a dramatic picture of men chained together in Ghana. It was an exclusive, said English, which they must publish. They did, only to discover the next day that it was a fake. Such was English's boyish enthusiasm, his error was forgiven.

Beaverbrook had his eye on English just before he died. It remains one of the great 'what ifs' of journalism to imagine what would have happened if Beaverbrook had survived long enough to appoint English as *Express* editor. Instead, in the time-honoured fashion of Fleet Street dynasties, Beaverbrook's death put his son, Sir Max Aitken, in charge of his beloved 'clattering train'. The wily Beaverbrook had arranged matters so that he avoided death duties by claiming to have been domiciled in Canada, a lie which ensured that millions stayed within his family's trust. In one of his last interviews he showed that he knew himself better than most of his acolytes and employees. He said: 'On the rockbound coast of New Brunswick, the waves beat incessantly. Every now and then comes a particularly dangerous wave that breaks viciously on the rocks. It is called "Rage". That's me.'[160]

Perhaps the person who knew that best was his son Max, whom Beaverbrook disparagingly referred to as 'the young squire'.[161] During the years Max worked as his father's supposed deputy he was allowed to exercise very little power, and any decisions he did take were usually countermanded or undermined.[162] But Max Aitken's first announcement after his father's death reflected well on him. He disclaimed the title, announcing: 'There can only be one Lord Beaverbrook.' His subsequent decisions about *Express* newspapers were altogether less inspiring.

Rothermere sizes up yet another editor

Beaverbrook's vacillation over editors was an end-of-life quirk. For *Daily Mail* owner Esmond Rothermere it was a life-long habit. As sales continued to slide, editor William Hardcastle came under increasing pressure. His editing was admired by *Express* rival Bob Edwards,[163] and there was some truth in Hardcastle's belief that the *Mail* was 'the popular paper for sensible people'.[164] Its leaders were lucid and, compared to the *Express*, adult. In Vincent Mulchrone, the *Mail* boasted one of the best feature writers of all time, and there were other stars too, such as Anne Scott-James, Olga Franklin, Patrick Sergeant, Barry Norman, Shirley Conran, Bruce Rothwell in Washington and Don Iddon in New York. Bernard Levin's theatre reviews were readable and often controversial. When dealing with a play about premature ejaculation, Levin described it in specific detail. The night editor who ran it uncut was carpeted the next day by Hardcastle on Rothermere's orders. It wasn't long before Hardcastle was fired, after having been sent on a cruise to the States.[165] When circulation fell to 2.5 million in 1963 he was replaced by his assistant, Mike Randall. Rothermere, explaining the switch, delivered one of Fleet Street's most famous quotes: 'I have tried a short fat one, now I'm trying a tall thin one.'[166]

Hardcastle went on to become a household name as the rasping, breathless presenter of radio's *World at One*. Randall, from a *News Chronicle* background, saw himself as something of a crusader and even dared to fly in the face of Rothermere's Conservative allegiance. He gave Bernard Levin a daily column and used Gerald Scarfe as a cartoonist, though neither was sympathetic to the Tories. Levin's invective, with its 'rich satirical flourish', was soon being favourably compared to Cassandra's.[167] When Levin urged readers to vote Labour in 1964, 'Esmond was apoplectic,' initially demanding that everyone involved be fired.[168]

Randall carried out what he thought was a clever redesign, with a fussy use of rules, headlines in boxes and often a split front page without a clear sense of which was the major story. Rothermere gave it a chance to work, defying his fellow owners by holding the *Mail*'s price at 3d rather than 4d (1.25p/1.6p) for three months. This generated extra sales, one of the rare circulation increases in Esmond's time, but it did not last.[169]

Rothermere is credited with pioneering the use of TV promotional adverts in 1964. They were recorded only minutes before transmission, with a broadcaster speaking from the newsroom about stories that would be in the following day's paper. Noting the success of colour magazines, Rothermere even allowed talks to start with Beaverbrook executives about an idea for the *Mail* and *Express* to co-publish a magazine. This plan, which came to nothing, was described as 'the greatest thing since the Stalin–Hitler pact'.[170]

The *Daily Sketch*, despite being 'a bootlace operation',[171] was a great drain on Rothermere's pocket. He suffered two years of losses before achieving the minor triumph, on one week in November 1961, of making a £17 profit. It was not to last and, as so often, the owner decided it was the editor's fault. Colin Valdar is remembered by his staff as an extremely good editor. He is reputed to have walked around with a notebook just in case he came across a story.[172] By the end of his first eighteen months in the chair, sales were edging downwards to 1 million and he was fired in 1962. Valdar later successfully launched the *UK Press Gazette*, the newspaper industry's weekly trade paper. His replacement was Howard French, a none too scrupulous right-winger who managed to bring out a reasonable paper despite dramatic cost-cutting. French, described as 'crusty and colourful' and 'morally stiff',[173] was a former supporter of Oswald Mosley, and later was 'embarrassed' at having been pictured as a Blackshirt.[174]

Rothermere might have expected, with the closure of the *Star*, that his London *Evening News* would have an easy ride. For a while that looked possible. Editor Reg Willis continued to believe in the primacy of news, a philosophy hymned in a magazine feature of that era. One picture of a news conference shows a pugnacious Willis, back to camera, as deputy news editor Percy Trumble reads out his list with other executives squeezed into an airless room.

Trumble was also lauded: 'he knows London better than a cabbie and can "smell" a story before it's happened'.[175] It was Trumble who was woken at 5 a.m. on the fateful morning of 8 August 1963 when a contact called with a tip-off about the story that would be known ever afterwards as the Great Train Robbery. His call was from an 'earwigger', slang for the men who made their living by listening in to police radio calls. There were few details but Trumble, living up to Fairey's praise, had a hunch it was big. Even so, after dispatching two of his best reporters to Buckinghamshire, he couldn't believe that the haul was really £2 million. His swift action, backed by Willis, who gave the story increasing coverage over seven editions, routed the *Standard*. 'It was the greatest moment of my working life,' Trumble recalled, 'and a total triumph for the *Evening News*.'[176]

The other great plus for the *News* was the sub-editing staff, schooled under Willis and priding themselves on their headline-writing abilities. When Muhammad Ali won the world heavyweight boxing title in 1964, the *News* entitled the story 'The Feat of Clay'. It was written by assistant editor Phil Wrack whose other memorable headline came when de Gaulle finally relented on Britain's application to join the Common Market: 'Oui, Oui, All the Way Home'.

The *Evening Standard* was growing, under Wintour, into an entirely different kind of paper from the *News*. He improved and expanded its arts coverage, recruiting and nurturing a new band of writers. Though the *Standard*'s crime reporting never matched that of the *News*, Wintour rose to the occasion on major news events. Of the many front pages reporting Winston Churchill's funeral none was better than the *Standard*'s huge picture of the cortège, photographed a hundred yards from its office, under the headline: 'IN FLEET STREET – THE OLD JOURNALIST'.[177]

When reporters were Public Enemy No. 1

Perhaps the paper which most enjoyed the early 1960s, exploiting the greater degree of sexual licence while apparently condemning it, was Stafford Somerfield's revamped *News of the World*. His owners, the Carr family, hardly intervened and he managed to keep the sale way above 6 million with a judicious mix of sordid court reports, celebrity interviews and pictures, explosive buy-ups, such as that of Christine Keeler (see below, p. 185) and serious feature articles with a 'somewhat Alf Garnett-like Tory bias'.[178] Court stories with enticing headlines such as 'Incident in a watercress bed', 'Hot music at the Silver Slipper Club' and 'Downfall of a model citizen' continued to amuse readers, though from 1962 restrictions in magistrates' courts which precluded preliminary trial reporting robbed the paper of its favourite material. One page would carry a serious report by air correspondent Douglas Bader while another was headlined: 'Why I became a nudist'.

One successful series, by 'Fleet Street's top crime reporter, Norman Rae', was followed soon after by his death. In a front-page tribute to 'the man who never let the paper down' he was described as a 'swashbuckling, shovel-nosed Scot . . . a reporter with the mind of a policeman' who knew murderers personally and 'helped to hang them'.[179] A letter to Rae from a former Scotland Yard commander spoke of past times 'when reporters had to be looked upon as Public Enemy No. 1. By sheer perseverance, a display of perspicacity and persistence they got their stories.'[180]

Sir William Carr's generosity, and flair for publicity, was illustrated by his decision to give American gossip columnist Hedda Hopper a Rolls-Royce because the paper took twelve extracts from her book rather than the agreed six.[181]

This kind of froth could not conceal the *News of the World*'s underlying nastiness, and its willingness to traffic in human misery. Somerfield, realising that Press Council rulings were beginning to inhibit his paper's news agenda, railed against its 'censorship'. Other editors were discovering its power too: the Council reprimanded the *Sunday Express* and *People* for publishing pictures of Princess Margaret water-skiing because the photographers had trespassed to take their shots.[182] After twelve years of the Council's existence, the concept of self-regulation was beginning to take hold.

Another concept was also gaining ground: the strength of trade unionism. On 1 May 1961, there was an odd, but ominous, incident at Fleet Street's smallest newspaper, the *Morning Advertiser*. Founded in the eighteenth century by the Society of Licensed Victuallers, and circulated largely to the liquor industry and bookmakers, it was regarded as a national paper. On that day its journalistic staff walked out in a dispute over pay and conditions. The NUJ's central London branch was delighted if amazed: this was its first stoppage in Fleet Street.[183]

With 100 per cent NUJ membership, and everyone standing firm, the *Morning Advertiser* management announced that the paper could not be published. While the chapel started to organise pickets, the Newspaper Proprietors' Association called an emergency meeting. Under its rules, if industrial action prevented one paper from coming out, then all must stop publication. Late that afternoon, Cecil King therefore announced that the *Daily Mirror* would not be printed.

Union officials, realising that victory was assured, urged the *Morning Advertiser* staff to resume work. They subsequently got their demands and Fleet Street's nationals appeared as usual. The NUJ, which had already seen the value of the print unions having closed shops, could not fail to grasp the lesson. Industrial muscle paid dividends.

8. PROFUMO: THE GREAT NON-STORY THAT RAN AND RAN

> A lie will get three-quarters of the way around the world before truth can put its trousers on.[1]

The Profumo affair was a defining moment in the history of Britain's press. It can now be seen as a classic illustration of press misconduct, a precursor to thirty years of reprehensible behaviour. It was the ultimate example of a media feeding frenzy in which the public interest justification was so flimsy as to be virtually non-existent. People's privacy was invaded. They were pursued and harassed. Much of what was published was inaccurate, misleading and distorted. People convicted of crimes were paid by newspapers. Trial witnesses were promised money, often just before giving evidence. One wretched man also paid the ultimate price.

At a different level, what the affair also revealed was the subtle change that had taken place in the balance of power between owners and editors. As powerful as owners remained, changing ownerships – and especially the arrival of a different form of ownership – meant that the old alliance of barons had collapsed. They could no longer fix matters as they had over Churchill's illness just a few years before. Some wouldn't have wanted to anyway. Even if they were in general sympathy with the government, they were not so enamoured with prime minister Harold Macmillan that they would do anything to help him.

It is significant that early in the affair Macmillan called Beaverbrook to protest at the *Daily Express*'s coverage. Beaverbrook, by now divorced from the Tory party and none too keen on Macmillan anyway, dissembled. Then he privately congratulated his editor, urging him to keep up the good work.[2] Beaverbrook, like other owners, recognised that the key to his newspapers' survival lay in increasing circulation in order to attract advertising revenue. Most wanted editors to do their political bidding, and certainly paid lipservice to the maintenance of ethical standards, but they were more insistent about the need to raise sales. Hired editors were therefore enjoying a greater licence than they had ever known.

With the age of deference in decline, there were also other forces at play among journalists, especially on popular papers. An overly secretive executive and administration encouraged the belief that the 'establishment' (to which most journalists did not belong) had secrets to hide. It was therefore in the public interest to expose them. The establishment was never properly defined, but was taken to mean the civil service, the government, the armed services, the judiciary, indeed the whole legal profession, all other 'professions', and the aristocracy, including, of course, the royal family. In other words, every institution peopled by a recognisable elite, the privately educated and those who had inherited their privileges.

Another important obsession was, unsurprisingly, sex. There was a widespread belief among journalists, and probably their readers, that the upper classes were morally corrupt. It is significant that the notorious divorce case of the Duke and Duchess of Argyll happened in March 1963, with evidence of promiscuity and rumours of high-society orgies. Papers fed prurient appetites with the story of the 'improper photograph' of the Duchess with 'a headless man'.

There was also, in the years leading up to Profumo, something of a spy mania in the press. Early in 1961, five people who formed what was known as the Portland spy ring were tried and sentenced. That year George Blake was arrested and, though his trial was conducted in secret, his sentence of forty-two years was severe enough to attract huge publicity. Barbara Fell, a Whitehall civil servant, was jailed in December 1962 for passing documents to a Yugoslav diplomat. Throughout that November and December, the *Sunday Pictorial* ran a series entitled 'Spies – the facts'. Like other papers, it referred often to the 1951 flight to Moscow of Guy Burgess and Donald Maclean and the continuing hunt for the 'third man'. It was stressed that these men were from the upper reaches of society, underlining the message that the elite were not to be trusted.

A key event was the arrest in September 1962 of Admiralty clerk John Vassall. Blackmailed by compromising pictures of homosexual liaisons while working at the British embassy in Moscow, he was paid to pass secret files to his Soviet contacts over six years. His trial began in January 1963 and it was some ten days after he had been sentenced – in secret – to eighteen years that 'the case blew up in the press' to be 'blazed across the front pages'.[3]

By now newspapers were in a state of hysteria with stories of spies among the elite, and several reporters, and certain editors, became convinced that the establishment was covering up a sordid homosexual scandal involving Vassall. Without any real evidence, they implicated Thomas Galbraith, then the civil lord to the Admiralty, and Lord Carrington, first lord of the Admiralty. Both men eventually emerged with their honour intact and without a stain on their reputations, but it looked nasty for a while.

The other major criticism of the press was the bidding for, and buying of, Vassall's story. When Vassall was arrested his solicitor told him he had been offered £10,000 by the *News of the World* 'for an exclusive and extensive story', and £5,000 by the *Sunday Pictorial* 'for a straightforward account'. He chose the latter 'because it was to the point and would probably pay my costs'.[4] Its series, entitled 'Why I betrayed my country', provoked widespread anger. He had, observed a newspaper lawyer, been paid to 'flaunt' his treachery.[5]

Senior politicians were also outraged. Opposition leader Harold Wilson told the Commons that the press 'should be bound to stop this odious practice of buying for large sums the memoirs of convicted criminals'. No one should make a profit from crime.[6] The government agreed, and set up the Radcliffe Tribunal to inquire into the affair. Its report quite properly excoriated several newspapers, stating that, on investigating more than 250 separate newspaper reports linked to the Vassall affair, it had not found a word of truth in any of them. In conducting his inquiry, Radcliffe did make one grievous error. Five journalists called before his tribunal were asked where they had obtained their information. Following time-honoured press custom they refused to say, 'on the grounds that it would be a betrayal of confidence'.[7]

Two reporters, Brendan Mulholland of the *Daily Mail* and Reg Foster of the *Daily Sketch*, were then found guilty of contempt and sent to jail, for six months and four months respectively, losing their appeal. Lord Denning, who was to hold an inquiry into the Profumo affair, observed: 'There is no privilege known to law by which a journalist can refuse to answer a question which is relevant to the inquiry and is one which, in the opinion of the judge, it is proper for him to be asked.'[8] Twenty years later Denning changed his mind, arguing that 'save in most exceptional circumstances, the newspaper or television company ought not to be ordered to disclose the source of information'.[9] That was far too late to help the duo, dubbed 'The Silent Men', and whose imprisonment united all papers, even those which thought their stories had been trivial and their reporting methods suspect. In Radcliffe's report, Mulholland was accused of carrying out researches around Galbraith's home which were both intrusive and vacuous.[10] Foster refused to say who had informed him of Vassall buying women's clothes.

Mulholland and Foster found themselves as improbable martyrs in the cause of press freedom. On the day they went to jail, the *Daily Mirror* devoted two pages and a sympathetic leader to them. Its columnist Cassandra called them 'honourable men' in contrast to Vassall: 'a base and pervert spy'.[11] The editor of Foster's paper wrote a front-page denunciation of the sentences.[12] Mulholland's paper carried a front-page leader arguing that the jailings struck at the liberty of the press.[13] There was heavyweight support from the *Times* and the *Guardian*.[14] The *Observer* blamed the government for having created a situation in which 'blameless journalists were placed in the impossible position where they must either break a promise or betray one of the basic principles of their craft'.[15]

Despite Fleet Street's unanimous stance, a campaign organised by the National Union of Journalists and a call for an inquiry by MPs, the men served their time. Foster got a shorter sentence because he was fifty-eight to Mulholland's twenty-nine. On the day of Foster's release, his paper said he had been vindicated because his story about Vassall buying women's clothes had been authenticated by the woman who sold them.[16] By the time Mulholland was released, the Profumo affair was taking up so much space in papers that interest in the Silent Men had waned. Even so, there were a hundred journalists at the prison gates to greet him and his own paper did him proud with a front-page picture.[17]

Vassall was a grievous sore for newspapers. Editors were rightly smarting from the jailings and wrongly affronted by Radcliffe's criticisms of their behaviour. 'The Press emerged in a far from favourable light,' noted a newspaper lawyer.[18] 'Its campaign against Lord Carrington had no justification: its attacks on Mr Galbraith were equally baseless,' a Tory politician argued persuasively.[19] Randolph Churchill suggested that the press accept 'a self-denying ordinance' not to purchase 'the life stories of murderers and criminals, pimps and prostitutes, butlers, governesses and nannies'.[20] Turning their backs on Radcliffe, editors were even more convinced that it was an establishment whitewash. The messenger was being shot for the message. Spies existed either because of establishment incompetence or because, being members of the establishment themselves, they were protected by their own kind.

While papers were looking into the Vassall story in the summer of 1962, gossip was just beginning to circulate about the story that would come to be known as the Profumo affair. This was probably due to Stephen Ward's boasting on the cocktail-party circuit.[21] The first published reference appeared in the August 1962 issue of *Queen* magazine, in a column by the magazine's associate editor Robin Douglas-Home. Without naming anyone it noted that while a 'chaffeur-driven Zil drew up at her *front* door, out of the *back* door into a chaffeur-driven Humber slipped . . .'.[22] Despite the oblique clues, it wasn't long before some Fleet Street reporters were able to put names to the people in the cars.

The man in the Humber was believed to have been John Profumo, secretary of state for war, a rising star in the Conservative party. The man in the Zil was Captain Yevgeny (Eugene) Ivanov, assistant naval attaché at the Soviet embassy and a secret service officer. The woman was Christine Keeler, a young model. Some journalists also heard mention of Keeler's 'sponsor' being Stephen Ward, an osteopath and society artist. And that was that. There was no question of them being able to publish. It was gossip without a scintilla of evidence.

Over the following weeks, reporters followed up rumours that Profumo had attended orgies organised by Ward. Gradually, they built up a picture, partly truth, mostly fantasy, about Profumo's relationship with call-girls. Among them was the *News of the World*'s sleuth Peter Earle, who believed that Ward was running 'a high class call-girl ring for top people'.[23] Earle, a flamboyant reporter who manufactured himself into a Fleet Street 'character', was to play a central role in the unfolding of the affair.

He addressed everyone as 'my dear fellow' or 'my old china'.[24] Reputed to drink a bottle of Scotch and smoke sixty cigarettes a day, he had a cigarette dangling from his lip in his regular byline picture. He was renowned for his dry wit and his awareness of his newspaper's notoriety. Once when he was sent to interview a titled woman about her marital problems, she asked him: 'But how do I know you are from the *News of the World*?' Earle, spreading his arms in mock despair, replied: 'Madam, I've already admitted it.'[25] He certainly had a wide range of contacts, which included Ward, 'an acquaintance of mine over the past ten years'.[26]

In mid-December 1962 came the breakthrough journalists were waiting for. One of Keeler's casual lovers, an excitable West Indian called Johnny Edgecombe, was arrested for shooting at Keeler while she was in Ward's West End flat with a friend, Mandy Rice-Davies. Within hours, a reporter from the *Daily Mirror* approached Keeler and told her his paper knew 'the lot'. He was aware that she had received letters from Profumo, he said, and wanted to buy them for £2,000. The next day, 15 December, papers covered the shooting and arrest in as much detail as the law allowed, referring to the central characters and the fact that it had taken place at the home of Ward, a 'society doctor'. This must have been baffling for readers. None of these people were known to the public. Why should a shooting in which no one was hurt be worth so much space?

Keeler was unprepared for 'the nosiness of the press'.[27] She had no money to hire a lawyer and depended on casual friends: Nina Gadd, a freelance writer, and her boyfriend, Paul Mann, who described himself as a racing driver-cum-journalist. They had no experience in dealing with newspaper journalists but they convinced Keeler she could make a small fortune by telling her story.[28] Gadd introduced Keeler to a *Sunday Pictorial* reporter who asked her if she had proof of her relationship with Profumo.[29] Keeler produced a letter, on War Office notepaper, in which Profumo had addressed her as 'darling'. Days later Keeler took more letters to the paper. Executives promised her £1,000 and gave her an advance of £200 when she had allowed them to photograph the letter.[30]

She then told her life story to two *Pictorial* reporters who knew – unlike Keeler – what they wanted from her. They had to find a way of showing a link between Profumo and Ivanov because, although the sexual shenanigans was a great seller, they needed a public interest justification. There must be a spying angle to show that there had been, if not a breach of security, a potential breach. Keeler gradually realised what the reporters were driving at. According to two journalists who reinvestigated the affair in the late 1980s, Keeler then moved from fact into fiction.[31] Eager to please in order to be paid the next instalment of money, she began to embroider details about having asked Profumo sensitive questions at Ward's prompting.

She had no idea of the implications. As far as she was concerned her relationship with Profumo was history. It had ended more than a year before, a lifetime in Keeler's social whirl. Why should a little embellishment hurt anyone? She was nineteen years old when she first met Profumo on 8 July 1961 after Ward had taken her to Cliveden, the Buckinghamshire estate of the third Viscount Astor. With other guests, Keeler and Profumo indulged in swimming-pool frolics and later enjoyed a kiss and a cuddle when he took her on a tour of the house.[32]

Next day Ivanov, whom Keeler had met before in Ward's flat where she was living, joined the party. Ward was amused to see Profumo and Ivanov vying for Keeler's attentions. Later, she drove back with Ivanov to London and, according to both of them in separate accounts, they slept together for the first time that night.[33] Whether either of them told the truth about this crucial matter has been hotly disputed. Did she lie because it was a more saleable and sensational story? Did he lie because it proved his worth to his Soviet masters and to embarrass the British? Ivanov said they slept together the next night too, but apparently that was the last occasion.

What was true? When either sex or spying is at issue, lying is par for the course. Ivanov wrote a book in 1994 which had to be withdrawn and amended after complaints from Profumo's wife, because he also claimed to have had a relationship with her, which she vehemently denied. Even Ivanov's co-author, Gennady Sokolov, conceded that Ivanov may not have been telling the truth, and the book is littered with factual errors.[34] It would appear that the original piece of gossip about cars at the front and back of Ward's flat was invention. What appears to be true is that, within a week of Keeler sleeping with Ivanov, she slept with Profumo at Ward's flat and would do so occasionally for the next four months until Profumo ended the affair. He sent a letter breaking a date which was to be the last communication between them.

The *Pictorial* reporters were delighted with their story, typing it up and getting Keeler to sign every page. But the paper's senior executives, on advice from their lawyers, hesitated. The Edgecombe case was *sub judice.* Despite the letters, the proof of Keeler's sexual dalliances with Profumo and Ivanov was thin, relying on her word alone. It was likely Profumo would sue for libel. Sensing that the paper was getting cold feet, Keeler's friends then urged her to try the *News of the World*, where she met crime reporter Earle. He turned her away, claiming his paper didn't want to get into an auction with the *Pictorial*, and immediately tipped off Ward about Keeler's attempts to sell her story.

Ward and Astor, unaware of the *Pictorial*'s nervousness, then tried to persuade Keeler to withdraw her permission for her story to be published. Ward's lawyer also contacted the solicitor-general, who informed the attorney-general, and they decided to threaten the *Pictorial* with a writ. Profumo was informed of what was happening. He saw MI5 and said he was concerned about accusations of Keeler having affair with him and Ivanov. Profumo then lied to three senior government colleagues one after the other, telling them no impropriety had occurred. All were impressed by his willingness to sue the paper.

Ward called an assistant editor at the *Pictorial* and warned him that the paper would be deluged with writs. Then, having convinced them to renege on Keeler's contract, he cheekily negotiated himself a deal. For £575, he agreed to talk about 'the perils of young girls in London'.[35] The *Pictorial* had allowed 'the scoop of the decade' to pass through its fingers, but it still had the picture of Profumo's 'darling' letter to Keeler in its safe.[36]

Meanwhile, detectives building up a case against Edgecombe followed reporters by interviewing Keeler and Rice-Davies. Again, both told the police what they thought they wanted to hear, accusing Ward of all manner of perversions and sinister activities. By now, the Profumo story was an open secret among journalists, and the *News of the World*'s general manager was alarmed when he heard about it. Mark Chapman-Walker was a former director of research at Conservative Central Office and a close friend of Profumo.[37] He met Macmillan's private secretary, John Wyndham, to tell him what Earle had discovered: Keeler had slept with both Profumo and Ivanov, and the link between them was Ward. Macmillan, who already knew of the rumours and of Profumo's denial, did not react.

On 3 February, the *News of the World* published a picture of Keeler with a story about her being a witness in Edgecombe's coming trial. Bemused readers wouldn't have to wait much longer to discover what it all meant. But Fleet Street was comprehensively scooped in the first week of March 1963 by Andrew Roth, an American who ran a weekly newsletter specialising in political gossip, *Westminster Confidential*, which was sold by subscription to MPs, journalists and diplomats. When Roth first heard the Profumo rumour from a Tass correspondent he dismissed it as malicious gossip. Then a Tory MP gave him a detailed version which he decided to publish. It told how Keeler had tried to sell her story, mentioned the Edgecombe case and a letter to Keeler signed 'Jack . . . on the stationery of the Secretary for War'. The girl had alleged that this man was her client along with Ivanov. Eight months after the *Queen* magazine's first mention, the story was now out in the open.

Profumo was advised that the newsletter's circulation was too small to warrant a writ. Struggling to control events, he and Ward met and, though it isn't known what they agreed, it seems obvious both wanted to ensure that Keeler kept quiet. Did they agree to encourage her to disappear abroad? Profumo denied it in public but soon after, according to Keeler, Ward's solicitor gave her money and told her to leave the country.[38]

The result was disastrous for Profumo and Ward. When Edgecombe appeared at the Old Bailey on 14 March, charged with possessing a firearm with intent to endanger life, the prosecutor announced that Keeler had disappeared. The simmering fuse of the Profumo story suddenly reached the gunpowder and the popular papers exploded next day with headlines about the 'The Vanished Model'. With the Silent Men having just been jailed, editors were delighted at the opportunity to put the government on the back foot.[39]

Of all the front pages, the most sensational was the *Daily Express*'s. Its splash, by political correspondent Ian Aitken, was headlined 'WAR MINISTER SHOCK', claiming that Profumo had offered his resignation 'for personal reasons' following 'speculation about Mr Profumo's future among MPs for several weeks'. Just one column separated it from a picture of Keeler under the headline 'VANISHED: Old Bailey witness'.[40] This juxtaposition of two supposedly unrelated stories, which a naive Lord Denning would later accept as coincidental, was the moment of transformation.[41] It was this which caused Macmillan to call Beaverbrook. Later it would transpire that Aitken's story contained more than a grain of truth: Profumo had seen the chief whip and asked if he ought to resign.

For the following six months, pictures and stories about Keeler and Rice-Davies appeared virtually every day. With the later exception of Princess Diana, they were subjected to greater press harassment than any other individuals over the fifty-five years of this history. Ever afterwards, they would be identified with the incidents, and alleged incidents, during those few months of their late teenage years in 1961. Keeler, having given regular interviews for almost forty years, wrote her second autobiography in 2001, though it was hard to credit some of her claims so long afterwards.[42]

On that first day the *Express* carried four pictures of Keeler in model poses from which, Denning noted bitchily, 'most people could readily infer her calling'.[43] Two days later the *News of the World* published a stunning front-page picture of Keeler, hands on hips, smiling, in a bikini. The camera loved Keeler, a major reason for the iconic status she would achieve. Earle's *News of the World* story, taking its cue from the *Express*'s coded link between Keeler and Profumo, said the Edgecombe shooting had other connotations. It was embarrassing for Christine because her friends were 'rich, powerful, household names'. The case had 'rocked London society'.[44]

One of these friends was Ward, a 'brilliant man, one of London society's best dinner table conversationalists, friend of diplomats, politicians and financiers . . . an artist of near Royal Academician ability'. Ward was quoted as saying that Christine should not have trifled 'with the affections of engaging but primitive people'. Keeler was also quoted: she shouldn't have got involved with a 'coloured boyfriend' because they have 'a completely different set of values from us'. Further down the story, which continued on inside pages, it was said that Ward had guided Keeler in the world of high society. He was able to introduce her to such people because he rented a cottage at Cliveden from Lord Astor. It was there Keeler and Rice-Davies had met lords and ladies and 'diplomats like Captain Eugene Ivanov, a naval attaché of the Soviet Embassy'. Six paragraphs on, without mentioning him again, it stated that Ivanov had returned to Moscow on 17 January.[45]

It was carefully crafted to ensure that it was legally watertight. Now the genie was almost out of the bottle. Surely it would be released if Keeler could be found. While reporters trawled the Mediterranean for her, providing 'mystery' headlines and more innuendo, Macmillan might have expected some sympathy from the serious press. Instead, the *Times*'s editor, Sir William Haley, chose this moment to champion the Silent Men by publishing one of his most vituperative leading articles criticising government heavy-handedness and secrecy.[46] The *Times* conceded that the public resented 'the practices of some newspapers' such as 'intrusion, triviality, distortion, muck-raking, the inversion of values', which were 'real offences'. Newspapers had been warned that they risked 'alienating those very sections of society upon whose good will the freedom and the working conventions of the Press depend', and this had 'now happened'. Yet this was the moment when papers were most needed because we should not believe that 'the encroachments of authority, the corruption of society, and maladministration can safely be left to the powers-that-be to put right . . .'.

In spite of the scathing attack on popular papers, the *Daily Mirror* published the *Times*'s leader on pages one and two the following day, saying it agreed with every word. With the hunt for Keeler continuing, papers finally got another break, courtesy of Labour MPs George Wigg, Barbara Castle and Richard Crossman. They raised the subject of Profumo and Keeler in the Commons as 'a matter of public interest' or, more to the point, as a matter of party political interest. Wigg, then Labour's defence expert, was convinced that Britain's national security had been threatened by Profumo's liaison.

Protected by privilege, papers were now able to link Profumo and Keeler in the same story. On 22 March, every front page mentioned the MPs' speeches and that day Profumo, responding to the pressure, made his famous, and unconvincing, statement to the House in which he said there had been 'no impropriety whatsoever in my acquaintanceship with Miss Keeler'. He added: 'I shall not hesitate to issue writs for libel and slander if scandalous allegations are made or repeated outside this House.' It wasn't a bluff: a couple of weeks later Profumo was awarded £50 damages against the English distributors of an Italian magazine, *Il Tempo*, which had stated that he had had a relationship with Keeler.

Most papers reported Profumo's speech sympathetically, though the *Daily Sketch* did point out that 'the spectacle of a Minister of the Crown having to get up to explain his acquaintance with a 21-year-old girl is, to say the least, unedifying'.[47] The *Guardian* thought Profumo's denials were 'explicit' and concluded: 'Miss Keeler . . . may have an interesting story to tell; but should newspapers seek to buy it from her?'[48]

The *Observer* was even more critical of the rest of the press. Editor David

Astor was the brother of Cliveden's Bill, and it is easy to conclude that his paper's hostility to the invasions of privacy stemmed from his family's embarrassment. But Astor's track record, and the logic of his arguments, suggests that his views were sincerely held. He did not regard Profumo's relationship as a matter of public interest and argued that the affair was 'insignificant when compared, say, with the Government's extravagant blunders over defence ... this country would benefit if people made less fuss about the private lives of Ministers'.[49]

The *News of the World* was the paper that revealed Keeler's hiding place. She had sent a card from Spain to a friend, Paula Hamilton-Marshall, who had spoken to Earle. The opening nineteen words of Earle's story, a tribute to the art of sub-editing, should have warned Profumo and Macmillan that the affair was not going to blow over: 'Christine Keeler, the missing girl witness to whom Mr John Profumo referred in the House of Commons last week ...'.[50] In the same issue, Randolph Churchill railed against the press making 'innuendoes and insinuations' about Profumo. But Churchill had cried wolf too often. No one took him seriously any longer, especially since he was writing about it in a paper which was among the most guilty.

Keeler was finally tracked down to Madrid by 'ten representatives' of the *Daily Express*.[51] Paul Mann negotiated a deal on her behalf. For £2,000, she spoke about being a friend of both Profumo and his wife, denying that she had seen him since 1961. She also obligingly mentioned her friendship with Ivanov. Then she posed for pictures in calf-length boots and a short skirt which appeared on the front page.[52] She excused her disappearance by pretending not to know she had been wanted as a witness in the Edgecombe case. Once the rest of Fleet Street caught up, she said there were 'photographers climbing on the roof opposite trying to snatch pictures, the doorbell and the phone were ringing incessantly'.[53] On arrival at Heathrow she received the kind of press welcome accorded to few film stars. The woman was becoming a kind of press plaything. Even if she said nothing, and she did have a tendency to speak too often, with reporters trawling through her background, interviewing every relative, friend, acquaintance and self-publicising fantasist while turning up the files of scores of photographers, there was endless material.

The *News of the World* led the field. On 31 March its front page was dominated by two headlines illustrating the press's twin obsessions: 'My friends – by Christine' and 'Red for Love', a series about a Czech agent, Lydia Ungrova, found guilty of spying on Western diplomats which was to run for five weeks. Two other spy stories were splashed by papers in subsequent weeks.[54] After Keeler had given evidence in court again, in a case involving another of her West Indian lovers, Lucky Gordon, the *News of the World*'s Earle spun a tale about the 'once-unknown girl' who had 'brought the War Minister of Britain to his feet'.[55] Then he turned his attentions to Rice-Davies. She seemed unable to keep out of the headlines and, jealous of Keeler's growing fame, may well have sought not to do so.[56] Two days later, Rice-Davies picked up another fee, from the *Daily Sketch*, for her story of life with Ward and Keeler. Profumo was not named but was referred to as 'one well-known man'.[57]

Though the Profumo allegations were stalled by his denial, spies and sex remained top of the press agenda, with British businessman Greville Wynne being tried on espionage charges in Moscow and the conclusion of the Argylls' divorce case attracting huge publicity. Sunday papers ran series on the duchess for several weeks, with readers lapping up sordid stories about the upper classes. Meanwhile, the pressure on Profumo built up throughout May, in newspapers and in parliament. On 29 May, Wilson saw Macmillan with a file of information contributed mostly by Wigg, who had received information from MI5 contacts aware of the truth. Though the Labour leadership kept Wigg at arm's length, he had not been restrained from pursuing his quarry. Six days later Profumo confessed to his party's chief whip and resigned on 5 June.

If coverage of the story had been disproportionate previously, then the next few months were beyond compare. The press had achieved their first aim in bringing down a minister, now their target was Macmillan. Better still, the nature of the material, sordid sex in high places, was a guaranteed sales-winner. The day after Profumo's admission that he had lied and was resigning, almost a third of the editorial space available in the popular papers was devoted to the topic.[58] The serious papers also thought it merited a lot of attention, but the *Guardian* commented: 'It would be as well if the Profumo disaster could be allowed to sink as quickly as possible into oblivion.'[59] Some hopes.

The next day Keeler stepped into more press traps, telling the *Daily Express*: 'Our friendship had to end because things became too difficult. It broke up because we were both scared it would ruin his career.' She added: 'Eugene was also a friend of mine at the same time I was going about with Jack. I did see each of them on the same day on two occasions.'[60] These quotes, like many others attributed to Keeler throughout the affair, were plainly suggested to her by a reporter. The former was patently untrue as the 'darling' letter proved: Profumo had broken off their relationship without any discussion. The latter, according to both Keeler's and Ivanov's later autobiographies, was also untrue. The flings had not been simultaneous.

By the standards of what was about to happen the placing of words in a person's mouth was a minor journalistic transgression. It was just one way in which all the leading characters, except for the tight-lipped Profumo and his wife, were manipulated to say whatever was required to provide more titillating headlines. Reading through the popular papers in the early 1960s is a salutary lesson: neither the Cuban missile crisis nor the assassination of President Kennedy received the continuous coverage of the Profumo affair. For instance, the *Daily Mail* carried fourteen Profumo-related splashes between 6 and 29 June, and more than forty pages along with leaders. It relented for one day, 17 June, for a real news story: a Russian woman had rocketed into space.

Despite Rothermere's Tory past, and the fact that Macmillan was on the liberal wing of the party, the paper was clearly gunning for the prime minister.[61] Aside from the politics, the attention focused on Keeler and Rice-Davies was overwhelming. Keeler was the central witness in the trial of Lucky Gordon, who was accused of assaulting her. Court reports ran to thousands of words. In his defence Gordon accused his ex-lover of being a call-girl for Ward, a serious charge which was to have fatal consequences.

One of the papers which delighted in this sideshow was the *Daily Express* which, with breathtaking hypocrisy, decried the scandalous coverage in a leading article that stated what everyone really knew: 'Of course, no one believes that Mr Profumo divulged any secrets.'[62] The *Guardian*, with more justice since it had kept all references to Keeler to a minimum while asking pertinent questions about MI5's part in events, argued that 'a roving investigation into one of the muddier sides of life in the West End is not called for'.[63]

Even if Beaverbrook and the *Guardian* were of one mind, and the former was patently having his cake and eating it, they could do nothing to stem the tide. Ward was arrested on 8 June and charged with living on immoral earnings. The press, seeking a villain, had found their man. The floodgates opened. The *Sunday Pictorial* published on its front page the 'darling' letter from Profumo to Keeler and on its back page the picture that revealed the potent mixture of Keeler's beauty, naivety and shamelessness, a picture that would ever after come to represent the Profumo affair in the public imagination. A challenge to conventional morality, the provocative photograph showed her, obviously naked, straddling a V-shaped chair.[64]

The *News of the World*, having originally rejected her story, now paid her £23,000 – as she observed, 'a whale of a sum in those days'.[65] That picture was used once again to illustrate 'Confessions of Christine', in which she told of her relationships with Profumo, Ward and Ivanov, calling the latter 'a wonderful huggy bear of a man'.[66] The paper added an extra 250,000 sales.[67] By this time criticisms of press behaviour in parliament, and from newspapers such as the *Observer* and the *Guardian*, were insistent enough for the *News of the World*'s editor to justify his purchase. Stafford Somerfield wrote a long front-page leader which disingenuously asserted: 'We do not pry into private lives; we do not retail harmful gossip in our columns . . . but when the nation's security is involved we believe it to be not only our right but our duty to come out into the open.'[68]

The *Daily Express* chose a more subtle pretext for devoting so much space to the story by suggesting that money was the root of the evil. Contrasting its own readers' morality with that of 'a few people of high breeding and grave responsibilities who ought to know better . . . the vast majority of ordinary decent families in Britain have *not* been corrupted by material well-being'.[69] Beaverbrook conveniently overlooked the relationship between his own 'material well-being' and his adulterous promiscuity.

Perhaps the most telling leader came from the *Times* because, in brushing aside the notion that the central concern was security, it offered tacit support to the popular press's line of inquiry. Headlined 'It *is* a Moral Issue' the Haley-inspired leader said: 'Everyone has been so busy in assuring the public that the affair is not one of morals, that it is time to assert that it is.' It was not possible to deny public opinion the right to be a court of morals 'without rot setting in and all standards suffering in the long run'.[70] As historians of the affair properly noted, this line of argument had 'repercussions way beyond the paper's modest circulation'.[71] The *Sunday Times*'s William Rees-Mogg took Haley's argument apart, maintaining in a memorable phrase that it was not a moral issue: 'the life of Britain does not really pass through the loins of one red-headed girl'.[72] Years later Rees-Mogg was convinced he had been correct: 'We didn't think it was right to throw mud at Profumo when he was down. We didn't join in the riding down of the victim and we were more sympathetic to Ward than the rest of the press. The press killed Ward but we had no part in it.'[73]

Stephen Ward's court appearances, which began with a preliminary hearing on 28 June, echoed the trials of Oscar Wilde and, according to the *Guardian*, also resembled the Parnell case.[74] They were exercises in public humiliation. With press encouragement, the authorities had found a scapegoat for the whole sorry mess. Ward was accused of brothel-keeping, procuring, living on the earnings of prostitutes and abortion. He knew he was innocent of them all, but to face a court on such charges was terribly demeaning for the adept social-climber. As an osteopath, Ward had treated a host of famous names, such as Winston Churchill, Anthony Eden, Hugh Gaitskell, Frank Sinatra, Ava Gardner, Douglas Fairbanks Jnr, Lord Rothermere, even Gandhi. As an artist, he had painted members of the royal family (including Prince Philip), Harold Macmillan and Sophia Loren.

One of his patients was the editor of the *Daily Telegraph*, Sir Colin Coote, who had been instrumental in his meeting Ivanov. After he had cured Coote's lumbago, they grew friendly and began playing bridge together regularly.[75] Then Coote invited Ward to draw for the *Telegraph*, sending him to Israel to sketch Adolf Eichmann during his trial. Ward later suggested he do portraits of the Soviet leaders, but he required a visa. By chance Coote had organised a tour of the *Telegraph* for Soviet embassy attachés and the group included Ivanov. Coote introduced Ivanov to Ward, at the Garrick, in order to help him obtain a visa. Though nothing came of the trip to Moscow, Ward and Ivanov became friendly.[76]

Ward also haunted the demi-monde, turning up at nightclubs with the high and the low. He befriended a succession of young women lured to London from the provinces or the suburbs, often allowing them to stay at his flat. Most of these friendships didn't involve sex with Ward, though he did encourage them to sleep with other men, not necessarily for money. A number of them, under pressure from the police and with the promise of payment from newspapers, were prepared to turn on their former mentor. One of the first witnesses, the irrepressible Rice-Davies, told the court she had slept with Bill Astor. That was true, according to Keeler, but she had agreed with the *Daily Express* in advance that, if she mentioned his name, she would receive £500.[77] So the *Express* got their headline, 'Mandy and Astor drama', over a court report which ran to three pages.[78]

While Ward was being tried, three other stories surfaced which added to the public ferment about sex, spies and scandal. On 1 July, Kim Philby was identified in the Commons as the 'third man' and his name was to jostle with Ward's and Keeler's on the front pages for the rest of the month.[79] This was acutely embarrassing for David Astor and the *Observer*. Five years before he had made Philby the paper's Beirut correspondent, sharing him with the *Economist*, after both had accepted the Foreign Office's word that he was not a spy, and that he had been cleared of any wrongdoing in 1955. When he vanished from the Lebanon in January 1963, Astor was left in the dark. The *Observer* finally reported his disappearance straightforwardly in March.[80] When the truth emerged, with Philby breaking cover in Moscow towards the end of July, there was much fun at the *Observer*'s expense. A Giles cartoon in the *Daily Express* showed Castro, Mao and Khrushchev waiting outside the *Observer*'s editor's door as a secretary announced: 'Three more, sir – highly recommended by the Foreign Office.'[81] But Philby's defection was even more embarrassing for the government, adding to the pressures on Macmillan.[82]

The second story concerned Rice-Davies's late lover, Peter Rachman. A *Sunday Times* Insight investigation revealed how Rachman had fomented racial tension by placing West Indian immigrants in empty flats in his properties and encouraging them to misbehave in order to pressure statutory white tenants to leave. Once cleared of all statutory tenants, he would then evict the exploited blacks too in order to sell the empty building at a profit. This technique was dubbed Rachmanism, a word that soon entered the language.[83]

In the following weeks, the Rachman story was taken up by every paper, usually on the front page.[84] The three largest-selling Sundays, the *Pictorial*, *People* and *News of the World*, added a sleazy dimension by claiming that Rachman also ran brothels and organised call-girls. Despite Ward having been committed for trial, papers were able to link him by association with the 'sinister ... slum landlord and vice king' through his friendship with Rice-Davies, 'the whoring pal of Christine Keeler'.[85] Too much can be made of newspapers prejudicing trials, but the fact that the whole press was, day after day, encouraging people to think the worst of Ward made it difficult to imagine that any potential juror would have anything other than a negative image of the man.

The notorious method of juxtaposing stories was used to telling effect by the *Daily Mirror* the day Ward's Old Bailey trial opened. The front page was dominated by a picture of Ward in pyjama trousers, bare-chested, stretching beside his bed. Below it, cut off only by a thin rule, was a striking cross-reference: 'Rachman's widow speaks – See Back Page'.[86]

The next day, just in case no one had got the message, the *Mirror*'s Cassandra spelt it out. Raging against 'the ludicrous archaic laws of libel [which] muffle up the truth', the columnist pointed to 'the Rachman revelations and the ramifications of the Profumo–Ward–Keeler–Rice-Davies chain-reaction affair'.[87] That was in the Sylvester Bolam league of contempt, but passed without court censure.

The third story which muddied the waters at the time concerned a woman known as Mariella Novotny (she had many aliases). Arrested in New York early in 1961 on a charge of prostitution, she fled while on bail to Britain, arriving in June 1961. She immediately offered papers a story about hosting sex parties for famous people. The highest bidder was the *News of the World*, which chose Earle as Novotny's ghost-writer. The central allegation was about a man – rumoured to be a cabinet minister – who dressed as a maid to serve people at an orgy known as 'the feast of the peacocks'.[88] According to Novotny, he was so well known he had to wear a mask to conceal his identity from the other famous participants, who were also not named. There probably wasn't a word of truth in any of Novotny's lurid fantasies but they could not be disproved (and were even believed by two journalists),[89] and they added to the climate of moral turpitude. Ever after, there would be confusion about the Duchess's 'headless man', Novotny's 'man in the mask' and their connection with the Profumo affair. Lord Denning played a key part in that misunderstanding because, having been asked in late June by Macmillan to look into the Profumo affair, he insisted on making all of them a subject for his inquiries.

While it is difficult to calculate the effect of the Philby–Rachman–Novotny stories on Ward's trial, it is easy to see how the evidence played to the public. Throughout early July, with Ward on bail, his name was barely out of the papers. By the time his trial opened, the *Times* thought it important enough to warrant detailed coverage. On some days it received a full page.[90] Every spit and cough of the case was reported in the popular papers, with pictures of the star witnesses arriving and leaving court and changes of dress and demeanour noted, as if attending film premières.

Belatedly, a *Sunday Telegraph* columnist called for restraint: 'Who can doubt that the moral obsession of our own time is sex? ... It is time we regained our sense of proportion.'[91] Yet Denning seemed to be concentrating his attentions on sex by summoning a succession of women for interviews with the maximum of publicity. The fact that his inquiry was running simultaneously meant that several witnesses in the Ward trial, such as Keeler, were called to see Denning soon after stepping from the Old Bailey witness box.[92]

Ward could sense from the first part of the judge's summing-up that he would be found guilty. He swallowed a bottle of Nembutal and dropped into a coma. But the court showed no mercy. The judge concluded his summing-up and the jury returned their verdict: guilty of two charges, not guilty of three. The *Times* carried, separately, full reports of Ward's overdose and of the trial.[93] The popular papers were less inhibited, with the *Daily Mirror* using huge pictures of the comatose Ward being carried on a stretcher into an ambulance which were intrusive and tasteless.[94]

Ward was unconscious for three days before dying. The news report in the *Sunday Times* told of his letter to a friend and carried a headline hinting at the paper's own disgust at the behaviour of the popular press: 'Ward dies: "Sorry to disappoint the vultures"'.[95] But the most revealing story was in the *Sunday Telegraph* by R. Barry O'Brien, who had given evidence on Ward's behalf. As instructed by Ward, half an hour after his death O'Brien delivered a letter to prostitute Vickie Barrett, who had claimed in court that she had regularly had sex with Ward, a damning piece of evidence. According to his story, after reading Ward's letter Barrett 'broke down and confessed to me that she lied to the Old Bailey jury'. While sobbing, she told how police had coerced her into giving false evidence.[96] Later, though, Barrett retracted this confession.

There was little sympathy for Ward. Rebecca West in the *Sunday Telegraph* viewed him as insane, claiming that 'he, almost single-handed, manoeuvred society into an intolerable position'. In a convoluted argument, she suggested that 'we need to examine ourselves'. The 'we' being society as a whole, not the press.[97] Earle wrote a vicious obituary in the *News of the World*, calling Ward an 'utterly depraved man . . . a central figure of evil . . . a coward'.[98] When he retired from journalism in December 1986 he was still claiming Ward to have been a 'diabolical devil' and a 'malevolent manipulator'.[99] The *Guardian* attacked the two *Mirror* titles for competing with each other 'for the privilege of purveying pornography'.[100] This elicited a lengthy letter in defence by Cecil King in which he called the paper 'a querulous maiden-aunt'.[101]

Attention turned to Denning, though five days later the big story was the Great Train Robbery which dominated front pages for weeks afterwards. Ward's inquest received only token coverage.[102] When Denning's report was issued in late September, it was entirely predictable: Ward was the only villain. As Phillip Knightley and Caroline Kennedy pointed out, the judge 'showed more interest in the sex and rumour part of the affair than in security, which was his brief'.[103] The *Sunday Telegraph* took an extraordinary decision, at the owner's suggestion, by publishing the full report, running to more than 50,000 words, in a twenty-four-page tabloid-sized supplement. The paper explained that 'because of the importance of the moral and political issues . . . and because his Report has been called the most readable and absorbing Blue Book ever written, the *Sunday Telegraph* decided to publish it in full as part of its service to readers'.[104] It also boosted the paper's sale by 50 per cent.[105] The *Daily Mirror* granted it eight pages, a quarter of its issue, taking Denning to task for failing to deal with the question of morality. 'Public doubts and worries about morality in high places are left unanswered.' We expect that 'Top *People*' should 'keep out of shady company and behave with some degree of decorum'.[106]

The *Guardian* carried four full pages on the Denning report and a leader called for stricter guidelines on when papers should pay for stories and argued that payments to criminals and prostitutes for their memoirs must be curtailed.[107] The *Daily Telegraph*, while condemning some of the exploitative press coverage, offered a defence that was to become common in subsequent years as an excuse for tabloid content: 'The supply ... depends on the demand.' The 'popular taste of the nation in 1963' dictates what will be read and therefore published.[108]

A *Times* leader agreed with Denning that 'scandalous imputations against public persons are ... a marketable commodity. If the atmosphere is right, traducing reputations and assassinating characters is an easy game to play.'[109] Denning was soft on the press, passing the buck about 'trafficking in scandal' to the Press Council.[110] A month later the Council adjudicated on a variety of complaints against newspapers over the coverage. Some people had criticised the detailed reporting of the court case, some were upset at intrusions into privacy, others were concerned about chequebook journalism. In its four-point 'verdict', the Council admonished papers for publishing 'some intimate details'; bemoaned the glamorising of people concerned in prostitution and vice; deplored 'the publication of personal stories and feature articles of an unsavoury nature where the public interest does not require it'; and singled out for condemnation the *News of the World* for 'exploiting vice and sex for commercial reward ... a disservice both to public welfare and to the press'.[111] In balancing the public interest argument, the Council contended that 'there are few things which discredit the press as a whole more than the memoirs of immoral, criminal people'. But the reporting of trial evidence, though it 'shocked and dismayed many people', was largely justified. Newspapers couldn't take into account the fact that these might be read by young people: they 'must deal with adult questions in an adult manner'.[112]

News of the World editor Somerfield did not accept the Press Council judgement, replying with a pugnacious statement: 'Does anyone suggest that the Christine Keeler story should have been suppressed? A healthy society must surely demand exposure, however sordid . . . In the belief that the public is entitled to know what is going on . . . we have discharged our prime duty . . .' Echoing the *Daily Telegraph* view about supply and demand, he delivered his *coup de grâce*: 'A prodigious and mounting readership tacitly acknowledges the rightness of the course we have followed.'[113] The *Times* dismissed Somerfield's argument: 'To say that as long as this sort of journalism sells papers all influences will be impotent against it is to underestimate both the power of public opinion (which is never a mere counting of heads) and the sensitivity of journalists. If only the broad consensus of disgust is often enough expressed and their own profession will speak out with equal vigour and frequency, the offending editors will learn their lesson in the end.'[114] This was to prove an over optimistic view of both editors and the public.

In a separate, specific adjudication, the Press Council also condemned the *Daily Sketch* for publishing Keeler's home phone number.[115] By this time Keeler was in prison, for committing perjury in the Lucky Gordon trial. On her release from Holloway, in June 1964, she had to be 'smuggled out the back way to avoid the crowd of press photographers'.[116] When she married in 1966, reporters and photographers besieged her house, and several papers published her address. It was, said the editors in a collective statement, a matter of public interest. The Press Council thought otherwise, 'regretting' that her address had been given while making no comment about the harassment.[117] She, like Profumo, was never to escape the notoriety of the affair.

Somerfield was not alone among editors in believing that he was serving the public interest by preventing the establishment from protecting one of their own. Editors believed they had acted as watchdogs on the executive by informing the public about a scandal. Their readers were not 'in the loop' and they were therefore performing their democratic function by drawing attention to facts and events which it was the people's right to know. This kind of argument blithely ignores the press's ability to manipulate the public interest. Readers depend on newspapers to interpret the significance of events, so the weight given to any story – its placing in the paper, the size of the headlines, the amount of copy, the repetition – is suggestive of a story's importance. When every paper gives the same story the same kind of treatment, it underlines its worth. If papers had stuck to a rigid formulation of public interest in the Profumo affair, they would have dealt only with the security danger, which was quickly found to have been bogus. By concentrating on sex, they were appealing to baser appetites among their readers, and they knew it. The public interest was a figleaf for a sales-winning exercise.

It also exposed the dubious claim about competition being good for newspapers. Rivalry among the titles did not result in the emergence of 'the truth', or even an approximation of the truth. The greatest contest was in fostering myths which, of course, proved more saleable. I am not suggesting that papers set out to lie or obtain lies, but there was no genuine attempt to tell the mundane truth either, as some reporters later admitted.[118] Profumo's fling had not compromised national security. Ward was not a spy, not a threat to the nation and not a pimp. Keeler and Rice-Davies were nothing but young girls on the make. Ivanov did not get close to a whisper of a secret. Cliveden was not a centre of depravity. Once the absurd rumours and innuendo are laid aside and we see through to the core, we are left with no real story at all.

Ward has since been viewed as 'a victim of the establishment'.[119] He was just as much, if not more, a victim of the press. It is not in the least far-fetched to suggest that Ward's suicide was the result of newspapers' pressure on the establishment to disown him. Most of his former friends deserted him, including *Daily Telegraph* editor Colin Coote. In his memoirs Coote does his best to distance himself from Ward, minimising the amount of time they spent together playing bridge and referring to his hiring of Ward as an artist as an 'experiment'. In hindsight, he considered Ward an 'ass' whose conversation was 'pretty childish'.[120]

There were honourable exceptions to the chorus of disapproval. *News of the World* features editor Pelham Pound, who had stood bail for Ward and visited him in hospital while he was dying, did not dishonour the man he had befriended.[121] Having refused to condemn Profumo, David Astor thought the vindictive cruelty towards Ward was detestable. Astor's deputy editor at the *Observer*, John Pringle, agreed. He wrote in 1973: 'Looking back now I still feel a sense of shame at the insane glee with which the British press threw itself into that sordid and unimportant story.'[122] It was best summed up by *Daily Express* columnist George Gale, who called the Ward trial 'the most deeply disturbing . . . I have ever had the misfortune to witness'.[123]

PART FIVE: 1966–1970

9. THE KING IS DEAD! LONG LIVE RUPERT!

O what a wond'rous thing
Has mighty Cudlipp done!
He who deposed a King
Has now put out the Sun.[1]

By early 1966 I had been a local weekly paper reporter for more than three years and was nearing the end of an apprenticeship which had required me to attend a day-release college course to obtain a proficiency certificate. We were told that editors would look favourably on those who had 'qualified' by passing tests in shorthand, law, English and practical journalism. Well before the end of the course my fellow students and I realised that the majority of editors, and especially those on the national titles, didn't give a damn about the certificate. All that mattered was whether or not a person could do the job. Employers' statements about the importance of training were pious nonsense.

I regularly took night-time trips to Fleet Street to hang about pubs where the atmosphere, even for an outsider, was intoxicating. The place was still a 'village-size drinks party', a perfect description by the novelist and former *Sunday Pictorial* political editor Frederic Mullally.[2] It was alive with people, whether on the Street itself with its newspaper temples, the *Daily Telegraph*, the *Daily Express* and the Lutyens-designed Reuters buildings, or north up Fetter Lane to the blue and red glass palace of the *Mirror*, or south down Bouverie Street, walking under the *News of the World* clock down to the *Mail*.

My dream of reaching Fleet Street had to wait. But what was this dream about? It had nothing to do with vocation. I had not become a journalist to do good works, to right wrongs, to serve the public interest, and I would be astounded if any of the scores of young journalists I then knew, on rival papers or at college, had done so either. I was in good company: Harold Evans had little idea of 'what journalism was about' at the start of his career.[3] Words like ethics and conscience were not part of our vocabulary. Most of us were seeking personal fame and fortune, and the trouble we took to report on stories or to write well had more to do with building our reputations in order to advance ourselves than with an intense love of the craft itself.

Having convinced myself that the quickest route to a national paper, and quite possibly the most certain route to the top once I got there, was through the sub-editors' desk, I knew I needed experience. Once freed from my apprenticeship obligations, I therefore started out on a familiar journey for aspiring young hacks. First step was to a regional evening, in my case the *Lancashire Evening Telegraph* in Blackburn. After six months on the desk there, I persuaded another sub who earned extra money by doing shifts in the *Daily Mail*'s Manchester office to recommend me for casual work.

In 1967, having performed well enough on my *Mail* shifts, I was given a full-time job as a news sub. I soon discovered that there were scores of novices like me from across Britain using the Manchester springboard to Fleet Street. Competition was fierce in what turned out to be a strange, if wonderfully agreeable, existence. Northern offices were a kind of parallel world to Fleet Street, fully staffed with departments shadowing their southern equivalents, and therefore expensive to maintain. The central task was to produce a paper similar to the main edition, using the same political stories and features telexed from London, along with the main national and international stories of the day. News and sports pages were editionised, ensuring that the various English regions north of the Midlands and up to the Scots border were served with their local stories. At the *Mail*, we also produced editions for north Wales, Scotland and Northern Ireland.

Getting out the first edition was an arduous task, often complicated by the need to prepare front pages without the benefit of the London office's subbed copy. Subs therefore struggled to do their best job with 'raw copy' knowing that, within an hour of going to press, their efforts would be thrown away in favour of the London version for the second and subsequent editions. But some northern editors, eager to prove to owners that they were better than the Fleet Street incumbents, tried to fashion papers sufficiently different from the London editions to prove their worth. It had worked well for Arthur Christiansen, after all.

These hopefuls, sent north to gain experience, were probably in the minority. The majority, for a variety of reasons, had been dispatched to get them out of the way. Their ambitions thwarted, a number of them set a standard for drunken misbehaviour which, even allowing for hyperbole, was extraordinary. Everyone who worked in those offices for any time tells innumerable stories, about the editor who regularly travelled home in a drunken stupor atop the bundles in a newspaper van or another who often crawled on all fours into his office after lunch. The staffs were also split between the largely middle-aged who had made their lives in the Manchester area and the go-getting young using northern offices as a stepping stone to Fleet Street.

My own editor, Larry Lamb, still had Fleet Street ambitions and showed his mettle by 'improving' on the *Mail*'s London edition edited by Arthur Brittenden, using larger headlines and replacing stories or features he considered worthless. It got him into trouble, but Lamb was illustrating qualities that were to make him a memorable editor: he had a mind of his own and wasn't scared to offend even his boss.

While I was learning the skills of headline-writing, rewriting copy and laying out pages, trying to keep from falling off the bottom rung of the national newspaper ladder, the structure of Fleet Street itself was undergoing a seismic change. Two dynasties – the Astors and the Carrs – gave in to the new economic order, succumbing to the pressures of two swashbuckling Commonwealth entrepreneurs, Lord Thomson and Rupert Murdoch. In the most superficial terms, it seemed as though the propagandists were giving way to the profiteers.

In a separate development, another patrician newspaper controller, Cecil Harmsworth King, also vanished from the scene, ousted from the chairmanship of his own creation, the International Publishing Corporation (IPC). Then his successor, Hugh Cudlipp, bowing to financial pressure, was forced to subsume IPC into another company. He also sold the *Sun* to Murdoch with consequences no one could then have predicted. Running against this trend, and harking back to the previous era, the owner of the *Telegraph* titles was ennobled, creating a new press barony. Another national title, the *Sunday Citizen*, disappeared along with a number of regional evenings in Manchester, Birmingham, Bristol, Leeds, Leicester, Nottingham and Edinburgh.

While titles changed hands, and owners came and went, the nightmare of Fleet Street's industrial relations was laid bare by the Economist Intelligence Unit.[4] Prospects for the press, as a business, were hopeless said the EIU. Disaster was around the corner. But its doom-laden report did not take account of the most salient fact of all: even if the new generation of proprietors were more financially calculating than their immediate predecessors they were willing to suspend fiscal logic simply for the joy of newspaper ownership. The EIU study was more detailed than the Royal Commission inquiry which preceded it by four years (see above, pp. 145–6) but it came to the same conclusions: chronic overmanning, poor management and innumerable inefficiencies. It also discovered that costs were rising faster than revenue (while total industry revenue had gone up by 81 per cent, costs increased by 83 per cent). It was, said one commentator, 'a recital of methods of working and managing which resembled a black comedy'.[5]

The report singled out Beaverbrook Newspapers as an especially bad case, which came as no surprise to those who understood that the old man's reason for owning his papers was to make mischief, not money. 'There is a much greater concentration of editorial and non-executive representation on the board than would normally be considered ideal,' said the report, which noted that 'the general standard of middle and senior management with a few notable exceptions was not high . . .'.[6] The *Express* was found to have 60 per cent more reporters than the *Mail*, forty-six staff photographers compared to four on the *Daily Telegraph*, and a library staff 160 per cent greater than that of the *Times*.[7] Michael Berry's *Telegraph* also came in for criticism:

'In our opinion the organisation is not planned and directed as normal commercial business.' Without 'formal systems of budgets or profit planning, it was difficult to see how costs could be controlled at all levels'. Berry, predictably, brushed aside the criticism as 'depressingly superficial'.[8]

The report did take off on a flight of fancy. If there were 'proper production levels' across Fleet Street, it said, there were potential savings of £4,875,000 for the industry, of which more than £1 million alone could be achieved by Beaverbrook. Worse even than this notional guesswork was the prediction that one quality daily, two popular dailies and one quality Sunday were likely to close in five years.[9] As it turned out, one Sunday – the *Citizen*, arguably a popular – did close and the *Daily Sketch*, a popular daily, was forced into a merger (see below, pp. 258–9). Perhaps the doom-mongering was the reason Charles Wintour thought it 'a rather suspect study'.[10] I cannot agree. The EIU report was a wake-up call largely ignored by both proprietors and the unions, its main target.

One detail seized on by owners was the need to improve revenue, and they took the most obvious, but ultimately mistaken, route to correct it. Whenever costs rose they could increase income simply by lifting their cover prices. From 1966 onwards, after years in which newspaper prices had hardly charged, owners began to hike prices every year and, from 1970, every six months. This rising spiral throughout the long economic depression compensated for increases in the costs of labour and newsprint along with erratic advertising revenues, but it was to have dramatic consequences in the 1990s (see Chapter Nineteen).

These were also years of major international and national stories: the Americans put men on the moon; Nigeria was embroiled in a bloody civil war, as was Vietnam; the conflict in Northern Ireland erupted; Britain moved closer to formal ties with Europe; 144 people perished in the Aberfan disaster; Enoch Powell ignited an immigration debate; the Moors murders trial shocked the nation; *Oh! Calcutta!* scandalised the nation; England won the world cup, then lost it. And newspapers made Chi-Chi, a giant panda, famous.

The old lord gives way to the new

On 3 May 1966, four months after the originally agreed date, the *Times* finally replaced adverts with news on its front page. A leader announced: 'The *Times* aims at being a paper for intelligent readers of all ages and classes. The more it can have of them the better.'[11] Within six months its wishes were fulfilled: sales rose by 20 per cent to 300,000. But this notable success proved to be a Pyrrhic victory for the owners, Lord Astor and his son, Gavin, as the brutal effects of newspaper economics took their toll.

The problem was that each copy of the *Times* cost at least three-quarters more to produce and distribute than the 6d (2.5p) cover price. It relied for at least 75 per cent of its income advertising revenue and would, in normal circumstances, have raised its rates once circulation improved. But the swiftness of the sales rise and the fact that ad rates cannot be increased until sales have been audited for at least a six-month period created a crisis for the Astors. The *Times* required an investment of up to £3 million, which wasn't available because it owed the bank almost that much. Gavin Astor's financial advisers also warned him that he, and therefore the paper, were vulnerable to death duties. Knowing his paper was likely to lose more than £320,000 by the end of 1966, he was convinced the only hope of securing its future lay in selling the paper or merging it with a rival.

In City parlance, the *Times* was now in play, and it says much about the lust for newspapers, which defies all normal financial considerations, that there were plenty of players keen to get hold of the loss-maker. They included a syndicate of the Berry family (the *Daily Telegraph* owners), an independent publisher from South Wales, Claud Morris, and even a sort of national trust run in tandem with the BBC.[12] There were other, more serious, possibilities. *Times* editor Sir William Haley initially favoured a merger with the *Observer*, and there was some logic to the idea. Haley admired its journalism. Its editor–proprietor, David Astor, was Gavin Astor's cousin. It was both housed and published in the same building, Printing House Square. But the *Observer* was in trouble itself, with its trust fund barely able to support it, so there was no point in combining the two loss-makers.

There was even a suggestion of a triple merger, *Times–Observer–Guardian*.[13] It was the *Guardian*'s overtures to the *Times* which were to cause the greatest controversy. The *Guardian*'s decision to print in London had been successful in attracting a few more readers, but the extra cost was proving a burden, some £500,000 more than the chairman and managing director, Laurence Scott, had expected.[14] Advertisers still preferred the *Daily Telegraph*. Scott, worried about the failure to improve sales fast enough to attract advertising, was also concerned that if the *Times* was to fall into the hands of, say, Lord Thomson his paper would face two well-heeled rivals and therefore go to the wall. To his mind, a merger between *Times* and *Guardian* was the only answer, a decision he did not reveal to his editor Alastair Hetherington until November 1965, months after his first approaches to the Astors. 'Laurence dropped a small bomb on my head,' Hetherington recalled.[15] Shell-shocked or not, he then met Haley and they soon disagreed over which of them should edit the merged title. In a sense, it was really about which of the papers would end up more unscathed from the union. Neither side could bear the thought of being devoured by the other, and serious talks were discontinued. But the enmity between Scott and Hetherington was far from over (see below, p. 207).

The *Times*'s next suitor was the *Financial Times*, following a chance meeting between its managing director, Lord Drogheda, and Astor's financial adviser.[16] Negotiations started so well and got so far that, for a month or so, they looked as if they might succeed. Drogheda was keen because he believed the 'specialised nature' of the *FT* would always make it 'a second newspaper'.[17] Looking to the future, he could see that it would take enormous resources to carry as much general material as the *Times*, but far fewer resources for the *Times* eventually to carry more business news. So he viewed it more as a love match than as a marriage of convenience, with each complementing the other.

Talks even reached the stage of deciding that the combined paper would be edited by the *FT*'s Gordon Newton, but there were opponents in both camps. Though Haley would have become chairman, with Drogheda as managing director, Haley viewed it as a takeover.[18] On the other side, after giving it some thought Newton disliked the idea. Like his owners, Pearson, he was worried about the *FT*'s identity being submerged.[19] Lord Cowdray, the chairman, sensed that his directors, Pat Gibson and Oliver Poole, were right to be lukewarm, and deliberately authorised a low bid which he knew Astor would reject.[20]

Waiting on the sidelines all along, his original overtures of two years before having been rebuffed, was Lord Thomson. Through his *Sunday Times* editor, Denis Hamilton, he made a series of promises to Astor and Haley. He would keep the paper running for a minimum of twenty-one years, ensure its editorial independence, maintain Astor as president and make Haley the chairman.[21] Thomson offered £1 million at once and a further £1 million in ten years' time, which was cheap even taking into account the need for investment.

At the end of September 1966, the announcement that the seventy-three-year-old Canadian entrepreneur was buying one of the world's most famous newspaper titles was notably untriumphalist because it had to be referred to the Monopolies Commission to ensure that his ownership did not operate against the public interest. Thomson, who was questioned closely, told the commission he had 'made a fortune out of newspapers' and taking over the *Times* was almost an act of philanthropy, a way of giving something back to the industry by saving a great institution. He stood to 'lose a lot of money before the *Times* became viable again'.[22]

It is difficult to understand in retrospect just why Thomson should have been so disliked. At the time, he suffered from widespread hostility. In a House of Lords debate, the Earl of Arran called him a 'rogue elephant'. By contrast, Hamilton saw him as 'the most enlightened newspaper proprietor of modern times, and certainly the most warm-hearted'.[23] He wasn't in the least bit grand, rarely using a secretary and answering his own phone calls, though he did eventually travel by Rolls-Royce.

A new *Times* editor, William Rees-Mogg, was appointed within days of Thomson's takeover. Haley was promoted to chairman, leaving two years later to become editor-in-chief of *Encyclopaedia Britannica*. There was initial concern about Rees-Mogg, the outsider from the *Sunday Times*, though he had the kind of background which reassured the staff. Descended on his father's side from a long line of Somerset squires, his mother was an Irish-American Roman Catholic. Educated at Charterhouse and Balliol, twice defeated as a Conservative parliamentary candidate, the scholarly Rees-Mogg, then aged thirty-eight, couldn't drive or type. Too much can be made of his eccentricities. He was far shrewder, more worldly and more ambitious than those who derided him as a relic of the past usually realised. He also had a fine record as a journalist on the *Financial Times* and as a senior executive on the *Sunday Times*. Writing with a pen, he was a legendarily fluent leader writer.[24]

His first acts were revolutionary: he introduced bylines to the *Times*, reconfigured the running order of the pages, and soon launched a separate business section, finance being one of Rees-Mogg's enduring interests. Within a year he also arranged for a stand-alone Saturday review section. But he had moved too fast. 'Many recruits were unsuitable,' and the business section was regarded as a 'shambles' by staff.[25] One unpopular Rees-Mogg recruit from the *Sunday Times* was Michael Cudlipp, son of Percy, as assistant editor, who ran the news department with an 'excess of zeal'.[26]

There was also much to admire in Rees-Mogg's early period as editor, which showed that he would not be inhibited by his establishment credentials when facing up to a changing world. Politically, though he quit the Tory party, he remained a Conservative. But, having secured complete editorial freedom, he was far from being a backwoodsman, as his recognition of a changing society was to show. In February 1967, he decried the knee-jerk response among other papers to drugs cases.[27] Four months later, when two members of the Rolling Stones were jailed for minor drugs offences, he wrote what probably ranks as his most famous leader: 'Who breaks a butterfly on a wheel?'[28] As the paper's historian John Grigg notes, this single leader, and its far-reaching effects – not least, the swift quashing of the sentences by the court of appeal – helped to establish Rees-Mogg's style of editorship.[29] It did much more. The *Times* set the agenda for other newspapers, transforming their approach to youth culture, and was infinitely more progressive than the *Guardian* at this point.[30]

There were mistakes. After hiring Winston Churchill junior, Winston's grandson, Rees-Mogg relied on his inexperienced correspondent's assessment of the Nigerian civil war to take a pro-Biafran line when persuaded that the rebels' cause was just and that their victory was assured.[31] The hiring of Cecil King, after he had been sacked from IPC, 'was a monumental misjudgement of the politics and mood of the day', thought one commentator.[32] But no journalist can fault Rees-Mogg's support for his news reporters who used subterfuge and secret tape-recordings to expose corrupt policemen, even if he did require some persuasion to run the story.[33]

Thomson backed Rees-Mogg's editorial initiatives with huge investment.

A new advertising campaign cost £300,000; the addition of four extra pages cost £600,000 a year; editorial staff were increased by 40 per cent, with five new overseas posts. The promotion helped to push up sales by a fifth within a year and by more than a third the following year. By March 1969, the *Times* was selling 451,000, a rise of 150,000 over its pre-Thomson circulation. Then came a dose of reality. The paper was still losing money, because the rising revenue was outstripped by rising costs. Hamilton raged: 'It is crazy that our salesmen work very hard to get £10 of new extra revenue and we have to spend £13 more to get the paper out'.[34] It is estimated that Thomson lost £5 million in his first three years of ownership,[35] and probably spent £30 to attract each new reader.[36] Thomson was forced to take the paper into his family company to ease the burden on his shareholders and, in the course of the next fifteen years, the Thomsons were to spend some £70 million on the paper.

It seems bizarre but the decrease in sales was, to an extent, planned. In order to please advertisers, providing them with an overwhelmingly affluent AB readership, the *Times* boasted to the marketing trade about 'trimming the wastage off our profile to give you one certain medium for reaching the true top end of the market'.[37] There is an apocryphal story that Rees-Mogg conveyed this news to the staff by telling them: 'You will have to be much more boring, even more boring than usual.' Despite the problems, Thomson stayed true to his pledge not to interfere with editorial content.

Instead, staff took out their frustrations on the editor. In a direct challenge to Rees-Mogg's editorship in July 1970, twenty-nine journalists, most of them senior executives, with a smattering of young Turks, signed a letter to him expressing their concern over editorial changes which 'diminish the authority, independence, accuracy, discrimination and seriousness of the *Times*'.[38] An angry Rees-Mogg successfully faced down this White Swan revolt (taken from the name of the pub where the conspirators held their meeting), but in retrospect it's possible to see this stand by the 'old guard' as a reaction to the paper's progress, informed by nostalgia for a mythical past. The *Times* had changed and there was no going back.

With the *Times* now yoked to the *Sunday Times*, Hamilton's overall management role enlarged and he handed his editorship to his assistant, the 'human dynamo' Harry Evans.[39] Hamilton went on to act 'as a constitutional monarch, guiding, encouraging, and occasionally warning' his editors,[40] while Evans was to emerge as the most charismatic editor of his generation. Evans, thirty-eight when promoted in 1967, was born in Manchester, the son of a train driver who was the hero of his life.[41] He went straight from school to become, briefly, a local paper reporter before serving in the RAF. He was twenty-one by the time he went to Durham University and, after graduating, joined the *Manchester Evening News* as a leader writer, later becoming assistant editor. A fellowship allowed him to spend two years in the States studying foreign policy. On his return, in 1961, he was appointed editor of the *Northern Echo* in Darlington, and began to build from that unlikely base a reputation for campaigning journalism – exemplified by his call for an official inquiry into the hanging of the innocent Timothy Evans – and for his grasp of newspaper technique, design and typography.

No other editor in the fifty-five years covered by this book has been as hero-worshipped as Evans. In breathless prose, the *Sunday Times*'s official historians described him as 'blazingly blue-eyed, a tiny tornado, with a mind so quick that nobody over fifty can keep up with it . . . he is a paragon of steady temper, even when he is turning things upside down . . . His young staff love him, but whether they really appreciate the greatest of all his qualities, his courage, may be doubted.'[42]

There can be little doubt about Evans's journalistic courage, as we shall see, though his reputation suffered from a degree of revisionism once he had been dethroned. Later still, there was a revision of the revisionism. It is unquestionably true that Evans had the advantage of building on an edifice created with great care and skill by Hamilton, and that fact did become obscured. Before Evans took over it was said that no paper could rival the *Sunday Times* 'in the serious analysis of significant actions'.[43] But Evans's editorial initiatives, his drive and energy, were not of Hamilton's making. For example, the first major investigation Evans ordered, into the Kim Philby affair, revealed the full extent of the damage done to the West, eliciting extravagant praise from the former editor of a rival paper.[44]

Evans also managed to increase sales 'despite the sharpest rises in price in the history of the *Sunday Times*', though the 1.5 million high point he achieved soon after taking over slipped back by almost 100,000 within three years.[45] He recognised the talent of cartoonist Gerald Scarfe, still in his late twenties, who quickly became 'the most significant cartoonist of his generation'.[46] Evans oversaw the development of the colour magazine, which won awards in 1969 for Don McCullin's Vietnam war photographs and in 1970 for a serial, 'One thousand makers of the 20th century'. The magazine benefited from the matched skills of its literate editor Godfrey Smith – even in his younger days 'a Holbein sketch for Henry VIII without the beard'[47] – and the visual sense of Michael Rand. They encouraged young stars, such as fashion writer Meriel McCooey, Philip Norman, Peter Gillman and James Fox.

Evans also avoided falling victim to one of those newspaper hoaxes that can mark an editor for life. Through former Insight editor Clive Irving, the Thomson Organisation got involved with an obscure Polish-born arms dealer who claimed to have discovered the diaries of Benito Mussolini. They were, he said, in the hands of a mother and daughter near Milan. Hamilton, still editor at the time, entered into negotiations to serialise the diaries and a fee of £250,000 was agreed. The saga dragged on for almost two years, by which time Evans had replaced Hamilton. After the documents passed initial examination by so-called experts, an advance of £100,000 was paid by

Thomson's, though not by the *Sunday Times.* Mussolini's son was also paid to renounce his claim on the diaries.[48]

Soon after, Milan's leading paper, *Corriere della Sera*, discovered that the two women had previously been found guilty of forging Mussolini documents. When approached they agreed that they had also forged the diaries. It was the *Sunday Times* which revealed the hoax while omitting to mention its own company's financial embarrassment and how close it had come to publishing a fake.[49] Evans, who had nothing to do with the affair, was unscathed.

The *Observer* could not match the resources of the effervescent *Sunday Times*, and it says a great deal for the quality of its editorial content that it managed to achieve sales of more than 900,000 in 1967–8. This, though, was its peak and thereafter it slumped. Its metropolitan bias played a part in its unpopularity outside the south-east, delightfully illustrated by columnist Katharine Whitehorn in one of her rare pieces from the provinces when she lamented: 'You can't take aubergines for granted outside London.'[50]

Editor-proprietor David Astor was forced in 1967 to engage in a drastic ownership reconstruction, involving a complex issue of two sets of shares. It proved to be only a temporary measure, and the financial situation remained precarious. Rising inflation increased costs and the *Observer* began to lose large sums of money. Within the office, there were changes too as news-gathering assumed greater importance and the old collegiate conferences became noticeably fewer.

Astor's key hiring in 1966 illustrated his willingness to embrace a different kind of journalistic approach. He took on twenty-eight-year-old Donald Trelford, previously editor of Thomson's *Nyasaland Times* in Malawi, as an assistant news editor. Astor was so impressed with Trelford's professionalism that, two years later, he made him his deputy. Trelford had all the management and technical skills Astor, and most of his senior staff, lacked. He wasn't universally popular: some staff thought him shallow and too pliant and, in a cutting reference to his diminutive stature, he was nicknamed 'The Jockey'.[51]

For all that, the *Observer* remained a paper of good writing and challenging ideas, as a 1967 promotional advert illustrated in boasting of its regular stars: Malcolm Muggeridge, Kenneth Harris, Katharine Whitehorn, Michael Frayn, Patrick O'Donovan, Anthony Howard, Robert Stephens and Hugh McIlvanney, undoubtedly Fleet Street's best sportswriter of the fifty-five-year period.[52] Astor also greeted the return, in January 1968, of Kenneth Tynan, who had given up theatre criticism in 1963, to write a weekly arts column.

Astor also had to confront the kind of ideological difficulties facing all liberals on the domestic and international fronts. In the Middle East, for example, the *Observer* was forced to question its support for Israel after the 1967 six-day war, arguing that the annexation of the West Bank was wrong because the Palestinians had rights too.[53] Astor's commitment to freedom of expression was underlined by his central role in setting up Index on Censorship in 1969, but he was obliged to confront an unpalatable truth about freedom in Fleet Street: did proprietors and their journalists have more rights than the printers and manual workers?

In 1970, Astor published a critical article about the state of the industry's printing arrangements. After the first edition had appeared, an official of the National Graphical Association (NGA) complained about an inaccuracy. This was corrected for the next edition, but members of another union, the Society of Graphical and Allied Trades (Sogat), made further complaints, leading to more amendments.[54] The following week, a lengthy letter from the unions was published, which, in turn, elicited a critical response from an anonymous 'Newspaper Worker'.[55] Union leaders again demanded alterations and, when this was rejected, they stopped the presses. Astor caved in, removing the letter. When it came to industrial relations, there was no difference in essence between Astor and Thomson, despite their yawning political differences. They were both newspaper owners and the unions treated them alike.

Thomson's attempts to get to grips with haphazard newspaper economics were evident in his injection of a new, and alien, business sense into his regional papers. When I worked at his company's *Lancashire Evening Telegraph* in Blackburn, there were management moves to stratify pay. We were told that we would be graded in a series of 'bands' based on age, length of service, status of job and so on. To journalists who revelled in the glamour of newspapers as the haunt of the rugged individualist, this notion reeked of Big Brother. It was probably a crude way by which Thomson's financial directors tried to cope with his requirement for editorial budgets in every centre to operate within the same parameters. As Thomson later explained, when originally told by his executives that editorial costs fluctuated wildly, he set out to prove them wrong: accounting procedures could reduce fluctuations.[56] In contrast to his penny-pinching was a willingness to take risks. He launched a new regional evening, in Reading in 1965, projected to be the first of many ringing London.

A new baron, but the same old barony

Michael Berry became a press baron in his own right in 1968, gratefully accepting a life peerage and choosing to title himself Lord Hartwell of Peterborough Court. He was particularly proud of the fact it arrived during a Labour administration. Hartwell could celebrate his *Daily Telegraph*'s excellent circulation, running at a regular 1.4 million by 1970. His fledgling *Sunday Telegraph*, aptly described in 1967 as 'Romantic High Tory',[57] was still learning to fly, but it did record a reasonable 750,000 average and there was no longer any chance of it falling from its nest.

All was not nearly as well as it seemed. Hartwell ran his papers by rote, discussing matters at appointed times with managing editor and editor, later holding an informal conversation with the leader writers. There were occasional lunches at which the nervous, shy, ascetic Hartwell was so ill at ease that it stifled the kind of casual talk from which innovation and ideas spring. *Telegraph* management was hopelessly inadequate, with Hartwell running it 'like a Victorian factory-owner', taking all the major decisions himself.[58] There is no better illustration of the feudal nature of the group than Duff Hart-Davis's reproduction in his official history of a memo from the *Sunday Telegraph* editor posted just before Christmas 1969: 'I have received the following greetings telegram from Lord Hartwell. "Christmas greetings and all good wishes to you and your staff". I have replied: "Staff *Sunday Telegraph* warmly reciprocate all good wishes to you and yours Christmas and after".'[59]

Daily Telegraph editor Maurice Green's room for manoeuvre was slight, but he did preside over one significant change. Hartwell's attention to facts diverted him from the growth of what might be regarded as a clique within the leader-writing and commentary staff. Green's deputy, Colin Welch, a Thatcherite before Thatcher, was a free-market missionary who championed writers such as T. E. (Peter) Utley, Frank Johnson and John O'Sullivan, later adviser to Margaret Thatcher and editor of America's leading journal of the right, the *New Republic*. Without Hartwell realising, 'a non-ideological leader-writing staff' was gradually 'replaced by an intensely ideological one'.[60] These fine writers were often frustrated, however. Perry Worsthorne thought there was 'a dead hand on everything' and the paper's historian saw it as a grey paper in which 'intellectual ideas and fine writing were firmly discouraged'.[61] Hartwell did nothing to curb the malign influence of Peter Eastwood, who was given even more power as managing editor in 1970, which Welch found insufferable.

At the *Sunday Telegraph*, editor Donald McLachlan surprised his staff by resigning in 1966, aged fifty-six, because he wanted to write. Hartwell chose an older man, sixty-year-old Brian Roberts, who had been with the company for twenty-seven years, to replace him. A news man, without much love or understanding for features, his appointment did accomplish one significant change by ending the split editorship between news and comment.

Roberts, a rather cautious journalist, was an unlikely sword-carrier for press freedom, but in 1970 he found himself at the centre of one of the most celebrated newspaper trials of the period. He was charged along with a contributor, Jonathan Aitken, with breaking the Official Secrets Act by publishing a confidential report about the military situation in Nigeria. A growing band of people, including several Tory MPs and the *Sunday Telegraph*, opposed Britain's controversial policy of supplying arms to the Nigerian government during its bloody civil war against the breakaway region of Biafra.

Aitken happened to have dinner with a general who had been an official observer in Nigeria. In confidence, the general showed Aitken a report which appeared to prove that Britain was supplying far more arms to Nigeria than the government was willing to admit. It exposed incompetence and corruption in the Nigerian army, suggesting that aid had been misused and possibly that prime minister Harold Wilson and foreign secretary Michael Stewart had misled the Commons. Aitken photocopied the document, which had been compiled by Colonel Robert Scott, defence adviser to the British High Commission in Lagos. He passed one copy to his friend and mentor, Hugh Fraser MP and, through his literary agent, another arrived at the *Sunday Telegraph.* Hartwell was shown the report and authorised Roberts to pay the agents £750.

Roberts splashed the news under the headline 'Secret British Report on Biafra Leaked' on the same night, by chance, that news broke of the collapse of the Biafran rebellion. The *Daily Telegraph*'s Welch appositely pointed out that it was 'ludicrous' to have made so much of the story since the document was 'designed to prove that what had happened that very day could not happen'.[62] But the government's heavy-handed action in charging Roberts and Aitken under the Act's wide-ranging second section turned the case into a *cause célèbre,* with every newspaper supporting the *Telegraph.* It finally came to trial in June 1971, with both men pleading that they had published in the public interest. The jury cleared them, and Aitken went on to write a book extolling the virtues of press freedom, which was to have an ironic twist for him some thirty years later.[63]

Though the *Telegraph* titles were dull, for the moment at least they had no money troubles. The same wasn't true at the *Guardian,* where Laurence Scott's machinations in failing to bring off a merger with the *Times* widened a rift with editor Alastair Hetherington. Worse was to come when Scott demanded redundancies in which editorial lost 18 per cent of its staff. In announcing the 'cost-pruning', Scott noted in his 1967 annual report that it had been an 'exceptionally gloomy and difficult' year, adding: 'The country cannot remain in the doldrums for ever.'[64]

To quell rumours, Scott felt compelled to write: 'We are not on our deathbed. Let us get over this particular hump.' Then he set out the reasons why he thought the *Guardian* was different from other papers: 'because we have a social purpose and are not in the business just to make profits ... we put the preservation and development of the *Guardian* well before the maximisation of profits.' But reality had intruded, 'to drive home to us that we can no longer afford the comforting luxury of being other than as efficient as we could be'.[65]

In the following year, with Thomson 'pouring money' into the *Times* and increasing sales by 20 per cent to the *Guardian*'s 2.8 per cent fall, Scott concluded that 'we have got to live with a difficult and fiercely competitive situation'.[66] The crisis proved to be Scott's nemesis. After an intervention by his cousin, Richard Scott, chairman of the Scott Trust, he was shunted aside, remaining chairman of the *Guardian* company, while Kenneth Searle became chief executive.[67]

Two more gloomy annual reports followed, but 1970 did seem to mark a turnaround in fortunes, with the *Times* going into reverse and the *Guardian* making 'real headway'.[68] The paper also moved into a bright, new Manchester office. Then another financial crisis hit home and, with the paper losing money, its cover price was increased from 6d to 8d (2.5/3.33p) in February. Scott again pressed for a merger, if not with the *Times*, then with the *Observer*. An irritated Hetherington was having none of it.

His editorship remained a matter of intense internal debate between factions in the office. There were those who applauded his decision in September 1966 to carry six articles by Martha Gellhorn, critical of America's involvement in Vietnam, which she couldn't get published elsewhere. They then deplored Hetherington's change of approach the following year when he urged understanding for the American predicament. Similar differences of opinion raged over the Middle East. As Peter Preston observed, these kinds of dispute 'meant that what the paper said was important. It meant we were serious, there for something.'[69] Through it all Hetherington remained a figure of rigid asceticism, so abstemious he even refused cream with his fruit salad at lunch in order to keep a clear head.[70]

There were welcome innovations. In April 1966, the anachronistic London Letter was replaced by a column entitled Miscellany at Large, written in an idiosyncratic style by Preston for two and a half years before he was promoted to features editor, where Hetherington allowed him to make the biggest change in the paper for years, the creation of a news feature page opposite the leader page. Sports editor John Samuel introduced a full racing service for first time from 1970. Mary Stott, women's editor from 1957, wrestled with the considerable problem of gauging both the form and content of her pages, admitting in 1969 that the *Times* was better at attracting female readers. To redress the balance, the pages were redesigned and Mainly for Woman was renamed *Woman's Guardian*.[71] Indeed, the whole paper was radically, and pleasingly, redesigned in 1969.

King falls, trying to live up to his name

As Thomson took centre stage in Fleet Street, one of its leading actors was escorted from the theatre, shouting incoherently. The autocratic Cecil King, chairman of IPC, suffered from delusions of grandeur and finally overreached himself. His arrogance was well recorded. He once told an interviewer without any hint of irony that he was so far-sighted 'people tend to come round a corner and find me sitting there'.[72] Bill Deedes revealed that King raged at the Tory government in 1963 for its failure to consult him.[73]

As we have seen, King was upset at not being offered a cabinet post after Labour's narrow 1964 election victory, and his enthusiasm for prime minister Harold Wilson had faded well before Labour won in 1966.

Within three months, King was urging Cudlipp to launch an attack on Wilson in the *Daily Mirror*. To placate him, Cudlipp suggested he write privately to Wilson, which he did, on many occasions. He also complained in person to Wilson, and to several ministers. It is undeniable that the *Mirror* began to be more critical of Labour, though Cudlipp claimed he did his best to prevent a split between the party and the paper.[74] At the beginning of 1968, Wilson was suffering from a bad press all round and complained especially about the lukewarm *Daily Mirror*.[75]

King's mood deepened. Convinced that the government could not govern, that the unions were in control while industry was in decline, he could see hyper-inflation around the corner. Recalling his Irish upbringing, he imagined that Britain was on the brink of an Easter Rising. As Louis Heren appositely put it, King 'succumbed to megalomania like his uncles before him'.[76] Seeing himself as the only hope for the country by heading a coalition government, he decided he needed a figurehead to soothe the populace and sought someone connected to royalty. King didn't keep this nonsensical fantasy to himself. Aside from Cudlipp, Frank Rogers, IPC's managing director, also became alarmed, as did one or two other directors.

The first paper to hint that the man responsible for running four national titles and the country's largest magazine empire was planning to overthrow the elected government was the *Guardian*. It revealed that King and Lord Robens, chairman of the Coal Board, wanted to lead a sort of businessmen's government, and further suggested that King was setting himself up as an extra-parliamentary power in the land.[77] King issued a denial but the damage was done. The London *Evening Standard* referred, with its tongue in its cheek, to 'government by the *Daily Mirror*'.[78] Within IPC, there was great embarrassment and strong internal opposition to King from Sydney Jacobson, John Beavan and columnist George Gale, who had taken the Cassandra slot when Bill Connor died in 1967.

At his master's request, Cudlipp arranged a meeting for King with Lord Mountbatten, also attended by the government's former chief scientific adviser Sir Solly Zuckerman. King told them Wilson's government was disintegrating and that, after the military had restored order, Mountbatten should head a national government. 'This is rank treachery,' said Zuckerman. 'I am a public servant and will have nothing to do with it. Nor should you, Dickie.'[79] Mountbatten, a former chief of the defence staff, immediately ended the meeting.

Cudlipp's account of the bizarre conversation at that meeting, held in Mountbatten's London flat, caused some embarrassment when disclosed in 1976.[80] No one realised just how far King had been prepared to go. Undaunted by Mountbatten's rejection, King took the fatal step two days later of demanding Wilson's resignation in a *Daily Mirror* front-page article under his own byline. He also ordered the editors of the *Sun* and the *Daily Record* in Glasgow to carry it. Headlined 'Enough Is Enough', it demanded 'a fresh start under a new leader'.[81] After that political bombshell came financial dynamite. He claimed that 'we are now threatened with the greatest financial crisis in our history ... not to be removed by lies about our reserves'. Since he had been a director of the Bank of England since 1965, and therefore privy to sensitive information about the nation's finances, King's reference to 'lies' had a direct effect on the markets. The pound plunged to its lowest level for three months, and share prices also fell. King resigned that night from the Bank, but the damage was done.

With other papers gleefully stoking the controversy, King's fellow IPC directors reminded each other what King had conveniently forgotten. He was not a proprietor and he had only a tiny shareholding in the company. He was a salaried staff member and therefore, like everyone else, could be removed from his job. Cudlipp had seen King's article in advance and had not attempted to prevent its publication. Explaining his inaction years later, he wrote: 'I could not dissuade a bull from entering a china shop.'[82] He didn't even try to reason with King and must have realised the likely outcome, so it is fair to assume that Cudlipp allowed his old friend and mentor to commit corporate suicide. During the ten days after the editorial appeared directors met in twos and threes at Cudlipp's urging and decided that King must go.

In a replica of the boardroom coup seventeen years before, when King had ousted Bartholomew in his favour, Cudlipp now sought to depose King in *his* own favour. The directors announced their intention to vote him out of office in a letter to King which reached him as he was shaving: 'The feeling is that your increasing preoccupation and intervention in national affairs in a personal sense rather than a more objective publishing sense has created a situation between you and your colleagues which is detrimental to the present and future conduct of IPC.'[83] King refused to resign, and was then dismissed by unanimous board vote in May 1968. After forty-two years with the *Mirror* group, he was bitter at being thrown out. At the subsequent stormy annual meeting, King denounced it as 'a conspiracy of a particularly squalid kind'. Then he turned on Cudlipp. Hugh might be cut out to be a first violin, he remarked, but that didn't necessarily make him into a natural conductor.[84]

There is plenty of evidence to suggest that King wasn't much of a conductor either. He had saddled IPC, and therefore his successor, with a series of problems. Profits were down and the dividend was cut. The expansion had gone wrong in several areas. IPC was now unwieldy, poorly managed and not making anything like the profits it should. It was ripe for takeover, and a number of property companies were also attracted by its ownership of lucrative sites, such as the old Odhams building in Long Acre.

Cudlipp was a journalist, not a businessman. Worrying over the failure of the *Sun*, harried by the problems of a creaking magazine group while still trying to play a leading role in the editorial output of his beloved *Daily Mirror*, he was never at ease wearing King's mantle. Ted Pickering, then editorial director, said Cudlipp was terrific in his first six months as chairman, enthusing the City with his one-man road show, 'but he suddenly lost interest'. He couldn't face a future talking to bankers, brokers and analysts, no matter how good he was at winning their confidence.[85] Cudlipp let the 'suits' take over instead, accepting their advice that the only way to elude the City's predators was to end the company's stand-alone status. So, within two years of King's fall, IPC took shelter within a much larger company, Reed International, which had long supplied newsprint to the *Mirror* papers. It was 'the first time a non-media company had come to dominate a newspaper publishing group in Britain.'[86]

Reed's managing director, Sir Don Ryder, who was soon to become its chairman and chief executive, had been an IPC director since 1963. Politely called a merger, it was a takeover which ensured that Ryder, an erstwhile financial journalist, would now take the principal strategic business decisions. Cudlipp, freed from commercial responsibility, could be a journalist once again, but, to Pickering and many others, the Reed merger was a tragedy. The ruthless corporate world had triumphed.

By this time Cudlipp had also made the business decision that was to haunt him for the rest of his life: the sale of the *Sun* at a knockdown price to the man who would dominate Fleet Street for the next thirty years, Rupert Murdoch.

Enter the great white knight from Australia

Millions of words have been written about Keith Rupert Murdoch, the Australian tycoon who controls a sprawling empire of newspapers and magazines, book publishing, satellite and cable TV broadcasting, movie-making and sports businesses. As he has built his News Corporation into one of the largest and most powerful global media enterprises of the twentieth century, he has attracted continual controversy. For all sorts of reasons, from this point on, he is the major figure in this history. He is of paramount importance because his activities go to the heart of this book: he is the link between the press of the past and the press of the present, maker of propaganda and maker of profits. That he manages to make both simultaneously distinguishes him as much the most significant and interesting of newspaper owners. He is the epitome of the rugged individualist entrepreneur, reckless, restless and ruthless, heedless of regulation. Yet his company is an exemplar of the hydra-headed, profit-driven international corporation, answerable to shareholders.

He maintains that he is a businessman who happens to be in the media business, and has always denied abusing his position by dictating content. As far as most of his British papers are concerned, that has been anything but the truth. But trying to unravel which matters most to him, politics or business, has often been a fruitless task. He has regularly used his political muscle to further his business interests while using his businesses – his newspapers – to espouse his politics. As we shall see, Murdoch would appear to have successfully exploited a synergy between the two.

Despite his vast holdings in the broadcast media, he has never sought to conceal his love of owning newspapers. He was born into them, in 1931, because his family owned papers in Melbourne, Adelaide and Brisbane. His father, Sir Keith Murdoch, was viewed as a journalistic hero for having exposed the slaughter of Australian and New Zealand troops in the 1915 landings at Gallipoli. As a child, Rupert – as he was always known – often visited the *Melbourne Herald* office. He noted how his father thumbed through that morning's pages, marking the good and the bad, a habit he picked up. He enjoyed a privileged childhood on the family's sprawling estates and, by his own admittance, showed early commercial leanings, catching rats and selling their skins. At ten, Murdoch became a boarder at Geelong Grammar, a school for the sons of the wealthy where he soon discovered that newspaper tycoons are rarely liked. The Melbourne middle classes despised his parvenu father and an early dislike of what he would thereafter call the 'establishment' was born. He was regarded as something of a left-winger, but this rebellious attitude proved less of a deep political commitment than another example of his anti-authoritarian convictions.

Still in his rebel phase when he arrived in Britain, to read politics, philosophy and economics at Worcester College, Oxford, he famously kept a bust of Lenin on his mantel-shelf. While standing as a candidate to become secretary of the Labour Club, he was disqualified for campaigning and canvassing, the kind of establishment rules he despised along with middle-class Brits and the English ruling class. He got a third-class degree after cramming by his tutor, Asa Briggs, who befriended him.

In October 1952, his father died, and death duties reduced his estate to just two small Adelaide papers. Soon after, Murdoch got his first real taste of the British national press, as a sub-editor on the *Daily Express*, where assistant editor Ted Pickering took him under his wing, a kindness Murdoch never forgot and repaid handsomely more than twenty-five years later.[87] When Murdoch returned to Adelaide, aged twenty-two, he set about building up his tiny newspaper inheritance and expanded it rapidly. Three traits emerged: he loved gambling; he thrived on confrontation, courting controversy by firing editors and pulling off business coups; and he drove his executives hard, supporting them in public while making their lives miserable in private with his incessant interference. He soon discovered that sleaze equalled sales, especially with his *Sydney Sunday Mirror*. He expanded into TV, bought more papers and, in 1964, launched his country's first genuine national daily, the *Australian*. It lost money, but Murdoch was able to fund it because the rest of his Australian empire returned handsome profits, enough for him to venture abroad, to Britain.

His sights were originally set on the *Daily Mirror*, and, though it wasn't for sale, he had been secretly buying its shares for years. In 1968, he finally got his chance after hearing that the *News of the World*, then selling 6.2 million copies, was facing a takeover battle. As we have seen, there was a long-running feud between the two intertwined families who owned the paper, the Carrs and the Jacksons (see above, pp. 30–1). Fear of death duties prompted the much married eccentric Professor Derek Jackson, scientist, jump jockey and war hero, to put his shares up for sale, about a third of the entire company and quarter of all the voting stock.

Jackson's cousin, the *News of the World* chairman Sir William Carr, didn't have the money to buy him out and he soon discovered that Labour MP Robert Maxwell was preparing to make a full bid for the organisation. The Carr family were horrified and the board unanimously decided to reject the bid. *NoW* editor Stafford Somerfield went public, with a leading article hostile to Maxwell which highlighted his socialist politics and the fact that he was foreign while the paper was 'as British as roast beef and Yorkshire pudding'.[88] Somerfield laughed off widespread criticism of his xenophobia. This was the point at which Murdoch began to take an interest, ordering his merchant bankers, Morgan Grenfell, to buy *NoW* shares. They managed to obtain 3.5 per cent before Maxwell increased his bid, from £26 million to £34 million. Carr, in bed with a debilitating illness, was so desperate to thwart Maxwell that he embraced Murdoch as his 'white knight'.

In a tense shareholders' meeting on 2 January 1969, to decide between Maxwell and Murdoch, the latter emerged as the victor. The 'unknown' thirty-seven-year-old Australian had played his role as saviour perfectly. He pulled if off precisely because the establishment he affected to despise preferred him to Maxwell. The City had doubts about Maxwell's financial dealings, while the Conservative party leadership could not countenance a Labour politician buying a paper that had always supported the Tories. Murdoch was later to say: 'I could smell that the establishment wouldn't let Maxwell in.'[89] It was one of the rare occasions on which he admitted the truth: the establishment had favoured him.

So Murdoch found himself owner of a British institution. Six months later he demanded Carr's resignation as chairman and installed himself in his place. He and Somerfield quickly developed a mutual antipathy, but before that could be resolved Murdoch got embroiled in the kind of controversy that was to become a feature of his ownership. Almost seven years after the Profumo affair, he paid £21,000 to Christine Keeler to publish a reheated version of her memoirs, and 'all hell broke loose'.[90] Murdoch was castigated from all sides. The rest of the press turned on him; the middle classes rose up in horror; Cardinal Heenan withdrew an undertaking to write for the paper.

The Press Council censured the *News of the World* for its unethical exploitation of sex, 'a disservice both to the public welfare and to the press'.[91] Murdoch came off very badly in a TV grilling by David Frost which haunted him for years afterwards. He won still fewer friends by remarking: 'People can sneer all they like, but I'll take the 150,000 extra copies we're going to sell.' Having placed his faith firmly in the market place he wrote a script that was to become his mantra: hostility towards him was orchestrated by the 'establishment'; he was honest and straightforward, a regular bloke; circulation was king; ethics were the province of a narrow elite of bleeding-heart wishy-washy liberals whom he viewed as hypocrites and parasites, reproducing and living off his sensationalism for their own ends.

Murdoch was proved correct about sales. In the last six months of 1969, the *News of the World* sold 6.4 million, its best circulation in six years. But the Murdoch–Somerfield dispute went on. After Heenan's announcement that he wouldn't write for the *NoW*, Somerfield retorted: 'I'm surprised that the Cardinal doesn't want to preach to 18 million sinners.' Murdoch was furious, telling Somerfield that the *News of the World* had only one voice: 'mine'.[92]

Somerfield's end came soon after. In February 1970, he was fired 'in a three-minute noon interview'.[93] Murdoch was laying down the law: he was the boss and editors marched to his tune. He was later, much later, to say of Somerfield: 'I sacked the best editor of the *News of the World*. He was too nasty even for me.'[94] That was a cover-up. It was his lack of obeisance to Murdoch, not his nastiness, which prompted his fall.

In Somerfield's place, Murdoch promoted his deputy, Cyril Lear, who, at six foot five inches tall, accepted the inevitable nickname 'Tiny'. The change of editor made little difference to the content. Soon after Lear's arrival the paper ran an improbable, but true, story about an affair between the wife of a welfare services chief, who happened to be a keen naturist, and a Chinese man working in a bacon factory whose hobby was hypnotism. The fifteen-word headline was quoted endlessly by Fleet Street sub-editors as a classic example of their craft: 'Nudist Welfare Man's Model Wife Fell for the Chinese Hypnotist from the Co-op Bacon Factory'.[95]

Lear was far from Murdoch's ideal as an editor. Undemonstrative, indecisive and well liked by his staff, he kept his job because Murdoch needed a sense of continuity and calm at the *NoW*. Almost from the moment of his takeover, Murdoch had had his sights set on expansion in Britain. Realising that his presses were idle throughout the week, he hinted that he might launch a new daily paper. Cudlipp was to save him the trouble.

One *Sun* sinks and another rises

The *Sun* had never fulfilled the sociologists' dreams. It had neither held its traditional trades union readership nor found a new audience. By 1969,

Cudlipp had realised his pledge to the TUC and Labour party to keep the paper going for seven years. In that time it had lost almost £13 million.[96] IPC was suffering, with profits having slumped from £14 million to £9.4 million. The *Sun*'s sales had fallen 16 per cent over three years and were way below the million, probably less than 800,000. Advertising revenue, never good, was declining fast. Newsprint prices were about to rise.

The civilised Sydney Jacobson had given up the *Sun* editorship towards the end of 1965, with the reins passing to the uncivilised Dick Dinsdale. Dinsdale lacked the kind of vision to take the paper forward, sticking rigidly to the formula set by Cudlipp that was so obviously losing readers. Ernie Burrington, the *Sun*'s night editor, thought Dinsdale was 'a safety-first editor who would prefer to take the teeth out of a daring disclosure or opinion rather than risk writs, complaints to the Press Council and, most of all, the censure of his god in Holborn [Cudlipp]'.[97] Another of Dinsdale's many critics pointed to his dislike for innovation or initiative, declaring that he had 'never been known to be enthusiastic about anything'.[98] Within the office he was notorious for his ill-tempered tirades which often began incongruously: 'Shit on my little yellow boots!' But no one laughed.

Happy to bully his staff, Dinsdale was terrified of upsetting establishment figures. He stayed late in his office to read Nancy Banks-Smith's TV reviews, not to appreciate their consistent brilliance, but because he was scared of her propensity for writing lacerating copy. He spiked a column by another writer, claiming that his scathing attack on Tory leader Ted Heath was libellous. When the writer was told, he said: 'Tell Dinsdale that's my last piece for the paper.' It was journalism's loss: Dennis Potter went on to become Britain's most famous TV playwright and, just before his death, emerged as one of Murdoch's most savage critics.

Neither he nor Dinsdale knew much about Murdoch in 1969. The great bogeyman of the period was a very different would-be newspaper proprietor, Maxwell. Initially, once Cudlipp and the IPC board had decided they could no longer sustain the *Sun*'s losses and announced that the paper would close in January 1970 unless a buyer could be found, it was Maxwell who was their main hope. The unions, as ever calling the shots, objected. They preferred Murdoch. Cudlipp wasn't overly perturbed by the idea of an interloper taking over the *Sun*, believing that if his own editorial magic hadn't worked, there was no hope. Maxwell, who then controlled Pergamon Press and was still smarting from losing out to Murdoch over the *News of the World*, made the first move. Desperate to obtain the paper for nothing, he announced that he would set up a non-profit-making trust. But he couldn't satisfy IPC that he had the funds. Politicians, trade unions and journalists were all sceptical about him – especially because his plans involved cutting the staff by half – and several people he approached to be editor turned him down. Unsurprisingly, Cudlipp then rejected Maxwell's offer.

Murdoch was now able to talk seriously to IPC, and also appeared on TV to say he would publish a 'straightforward, honest newspaper' which would go on supporting Labour. He would be able to print it on the *News of the World* presses which were idle six days a week. When told by his own printers that it was impossible to print a tabloid on presses configured for a broadsheet, he dumbfounded them by showing how it could be done by using crusher bars. Cudlipp and Murdoch rapidly agreed a deal in which Murdoch, for the bargain price of £800,000, and even that payable in instalments, would get the *Sun*. It was virtually a gift.

Murdoch also plundered Cudlipp's staff, hiring two key IPC managers, Bert Hardy and Alick McKay. Hardy, who had been with the Mirror group for twenty years, was frustrated by Cudlipp's failure to let others exercise power – he thought 'his ego overshadowed his talent' – and was delighted to become the *Sun*'s advertising director. 'I could just see that Murdoch was going places,' he said.[99] Murdoch's search for an editor also led him inevitably towards people trained at the *Mirror*. He took counsel from various people, including Cecil King who, by then, wished ill of Cudlipp. He evidently advised Murdoch that the best possibilities were two men who had left the *Mirror* in frustration at not being promoted: Larry Lamb and Bernard Shrimsley. King was certainly not the only one to recommend Lamb, the *Daily Mail*'s northern editor.

At their first clandestine meeting, at Rules restaurant off the Strand, Murdoch and Lamb hit it off. They both regarded the *Mirror* as past its best, believing that it had lost its anti-establishment, radical edge and was failing to reflect the concerns of the younger generation. They thought it was tiptoeing around the new permissiveness of the times. Crucially, both were also critical of Cudlipp's attempt to move the paper up-market by including overtly educative features. They were scathing about a page called Mirrorscope, a sincere attempt at instructive journalism, which was greeted by some commentators and scorned by others as 'a commodity which only some of its target consumers will read some of the time'.[100]

Nor did they expect the October 1969 launch of the *Mirror*'s expensive colour magazine – which was also praised for its quality – to attract many AB readers. They were proved right. The magazine, projected to generate a profit of £12.5 million a year through colour advertising, lost almost £2 million in its first year and, faced with forecasts of losing even more, Reed pulled the plug. The deficit was wholly due to union demands which meant that every member of staff, including those not working on the magazine, was receiving extra payments. In withdrawing it after nine months, the *Mirror* lost a substantial number of readers.[101]

These miscast or at least mistimed *Mirror* initiatives, despite the paper's massive sale, convinced Murdoch and Lamb of its vulnerability. They shared a vision of a tabloid in which entertainment would supersede information, a paper which would adopt the irreverence and iconoclasm of a 1950s-style *Mirror* but within a 1970s agenda, pushing at the barriers of taste and convention. If it was to succeed, it would need to harness, or replicate, the *Mirror*'s rigorous technical expertise. They agreed on hiring Shrimsley, then the editor of the *Liverpool Daily Post,* as Lamb's deputy. For Murdoch, the added advantage of hiring Lamb and Shrimsley was their ambition to prove Cudlipp wrong in having overlooked them.

They were obliged to take on a number of journalists from the paper that would soon be referred to as 'the old *Sun*', and were fortunate in finding several experienced production executives, such as Burrington, Vic Birkin, Jack Paterson, Ray Mills and Jerry Holmberg. Though Murdoch and Lamb were happy when old *Sun* staff preferred to take the redundancy money, they were lucky with some prepared to make the transition: sports editor Frank Nicklin, writers Unity Hall and Liz Prosser, columnist Jon Akass and industrial writer Keith Mason. Even so, there were nowhere near enough people to staff a daily paper in the weeks leading up to the launch of the new *Sun*. Lamb was desperately short of subs and was forced to give inexperienced hopefuls, such as me, a job. With about 125 people signed up, there was still a shortage, so Murdoch drafted in staff on loan from his Australian papers.

Two days before the launch, Murdoch wrote in the old *Sun*: 'The new *Sun* will be a paper that CARES. The paper that cares – passionately – about truth, beauty and justice.'[102] The sad departure of that failed Cudlipp *Sun* was captured in a haunting picture of Dinsdale alone, overcoat on, phone in hand, looking skywards, in the abandoned Endell Street newsroom, its desks empty except for phones and typewriters.[103] Over at Bouverie Street, in an open-plan office on the same floor as the composing room with its chatter of Linotype machines, there was both panic and optimism, followed by a colossal sense of anti-climax.

The paper was three hours late off the presses. Lamb was appalled by what was produced. It was 'so rough at the edges', he wrote later, 'that the word "crude" looked like a wholly objective assessment'.[104] It was in Lamb's nature, at least in that period, to be too self-critical. Then forty, his had not been a conventional journalistic background. Born in the Yorkshire mining village of Fitzwilliam, the son of a colliery worker and miners' union official, he left his grammar school at sixteen and took a clerical job with the council in Brighouse. Following in the footsteps of his socialist father, he became an active trade unionist and, eventually, editor of the union magazine. He was twenty-four before he moved into mainstream journalism, working for a local weekly only briefly before moving on to evening papers in the north-east. He was a good enough sub-editor to get a Fleet Street job, on the *Evening Standard,* soon switching to the *Daily Mail.* It says much for Lamb's skills that he won a coveted place on the *Daily Mirror* subs' desk in 1958, just five years after becoming a journalist. He spent the next ten years working his way up what subs liked to call 'the mouse race'.

It was all too slow for Lamb and, with so much talent above him, he took the risk of moving up to Manchester as northern editor of the *Daily Mail.* He had not long been in the chair when I met him there. He struck me as intimidating and arrogant, with just a hint of the pomposity which would later prove to be his Achilles' heel. He also held his grudges. He asked his former *Mirror* colleague Felicity Green to join the *Sun* and when she turned him down he never spoke to her again.[105] But Green and I agreed that, despite his character defects, he was a brilliant journalist.

Little of Lamb's talent was apparent to outsiders looking at his first issue of the *Sun* on 17 November 1969. The 'exclusive' splash about horse doping was forgettable, though the main front-page picture, featuring a woman 'rumoured' to be Prince Charles's girlfriend, gave a hint of things to come. Sex played a large part: the main book serialisation was Jacqueline Susann's titillating bestseller *The Love Machine*; a fashion feature was headlined 'Undies for Undressing'; and there was a risqué picture showing the Rolling Stones beside a swimming pool as a nude girl walked by. There was serious material too, including an interview with prime minister Wilson attacking the Tories over plans to introduce a new tax called VAT. Despite the technical defects, there was an undeniable sparkle about the paper. It looked a bit like the *Daily Mirror*, but was sufficiently different and fresh to catch the eye, with a sense of immediacy. The *Times*'s view the following day was spot on. After remarking that 'its formula is a simple one . . . sex, sport and sensation', it concluded that the *Sun* might surprise 'tired old Fleet Street'.[106]

Perhaps the analysis in the trade weekly, the *UK Press Gazette*, came closest to the mark. Noting the Cudlippian view, that 'education has advanced so far and so fast that newspapers and television must nourish the new literacy – or perish', it pointed out that *Sunday Posh* might have increased at faster rate than *Sunday Tosh*, but so what? The volume was still far greater for *Tosh.*[107] For his part, Cudlipp dismissed his new rival, shouting to *Daily Mirror* editor Lee Howard at a party on the night of the launch: 'Nothing to worry about here, Lee!'[108] Two weeks later, trying to be sarcastic in the *Mirror*, Cudlipp merely succeeded in drawing attention to his bouncy new rival.[109]

Despite Lamb's misgivings and Cudlipp's scepticism, within three days the *Sun* virtually doubled its sale, reaching 1.6 million. At the end of the *Sun*'s first week, an editorial answered those critics who thought the paper lacked principles. The *Sun*, said the leader, opposed capital punishment, colour discrimination, the Common Market and the Vietnam war, adding significantly: 'We are not going to bow to the Establishment in any of its privileged enclaves.'[110] Was this Lamb or Murdoch talking? This chip-on-the-shoulder anti-establishment message was Murdochian in spirit, complemented by the Lamb's own ethos, manifest initially in his trade union activism and, later, in his political change of heart. Both men saw the *Sun* as the cocky champion of a working class which, though battering at the doors of the white-collar professions and gradually opening them up, was finding it hard going because they were held at bay by the 'establishment'. This was never identified as a single group, but much more loosely, as a concept. In any sphere of life an establishment could be found to attack: a Fleet Street establishment; a trades union establishment; a political establishment; a Whitehall establishment; a City establishment; a royal establishment. This approach was to prove a useful tool in wooing working-class readers.

Murdoch led from the front, getting involved in every aspect of the paper while drawing on his experiences in Australia. He brought in an Australian promotions expert, Graham King, who was full of ideas for reader participation and involvement. Television adverts were used regularly. Murdoch never seemed satisfied, urging Lamb and his senior staff to redouble their efforts in order to win sales. The result, within the paper, was a sense of verve and energy.

To celebrate the paper's first birthday Murdoch hosted a party for staff at a west London hotel. He and Lamb were on good terms with almost every journalist, encouraging their wives to dance with us young subs and joining in the banter. But Murdoch was thinking of other things too. He asked me: 'Where should I expand next?' I was amazed. Wasn't the ownership of Britain's fastest-rising daily and the largest-selling Sunday, along with an Australian stable of papers, quite enough?

That anniversary was also marked by the publication of a naked woman on Page 3, headlined 'Birthday Suit!', probably the most iconic *Sun* innovation of all. (Stephanie Rahn was the first Page 3 girl.)[111] Though the *Times* allowed an advertiser, Fison's chemicals, to use a full-page nude some four months later, a myth has since developed that the *Sun* followed the *Times* in the use of naked models.[112] When the *Sun* started to use nude pictures, which revealed only the girls' breasts, there were few protests. Reader reaction was entirely positive, and it was viewed as a progressive, liberating act in keeping with modern times. It also confirmed sex as an acceptable- and successful – marketing tool. By the end of 1970, the *Sun* was regularly selling more than 1.8 million, and the *Daily Mirror* sale had dived by 600,000 in a year.

In hindsight everyone turned on Cudlipp, blaming him alone for selling to Murdoch. So why did he do it? In the book which comes closest to being his autobiography, *Walking on Water*, he answered his critics convincingly: there had been no alternative.[113] He could not turn the *Sun* into a tabloid without competing with the *Mirror*, nor could he have contemplated launching a down-market version of his flagship paper. Amalgamating the *Mirror* and *Herald* was out of the question because he was bound by a pledge not to do so. There was also the phenomenon of the 'cross-over' readership: it was estimated that more than 40 per cent of *Sun* readers read the *Mirror* as well, so the gain would have been slight. The Monopolies Commission would probably have overruled a merger; there would have been political problems; the redundancy bill would have been colossal, not to mention union opposition to such a plan, which might well have threatened production at the *Mirror*. Closure, putting more than 3,000 people out of work, would have prompted industrial action.

But there is no denying, whatever the insuperable problems he faced, that Cudlipp, who had lovingly nurtured the largest-selling daily in the world, had now undermined it. One further point is important. Even the most fervent of his admirers tell stories about the times when 'Cudlipp went mad', days in which he imposed on the *Mirror* a wholly inappropriate campaign or a lengthy page-one editorial which subs referred to as 'a Cudlipp tablet of stone'. He was far from right all the time.

Old baronies aim for an implausible alliance

With Thomson and Murdoch now setting the pace, the old baronies looked tired and old-fashioned. Sales of Sir Max Aitken's *Daily Express* fell every year after his father's death, and by the end of 1970 it was selling barely 3.5 million, down more than 700,000 from 1964. His *Evening Standard* slipped to 580,000. The company relied on profits from the 'very slightly dated' *Sunday Express*, which was now fading too.[114] It slipped badly in 1970 to below 5 million. Esmond Rothermere's situation was, if anything, worse. His *Daily Mail* fell below the 2 million mark and his *Daily Sketch* dropped below 800,000. His *Evening News* coped better, drifting downwards towards the million, but still way ahead of its rival: its problem was the gradual diminution of advertising revenue. Both Aitken and Rothermere, along with some of their senior managers, even came to the conclusion for a while that the only hope of survival lay in some form of merger.

Aitken, war hero, boating champion and general all-round nice guy, was a hopeless newspaperman, an incompetent businessman and a poor picker of managers. Of all the bad appointments he made, the most influential was that of Jocelyn Stevens. Stevens was described almost correctly as 'the archetypal hero of True Romance fiction: a fun-loving, good-looking, high-living, brilliant millionaire with everything money can buy and much that it can't'.[115] I would certainly omit the adjective 'brilliant', and there was much truth in *Private Eye*'s nickname for him, 'Piranha Teeth'.

Stevens was the grandson of the magazine and newspaper magnate Sir Edward Hulton, and inherited £750,000 as an infant. After Eton and Cambridge, he bought the *Queen* magazine and made himself its editor-in-chief. He did an excellent job, recording the life of his own upper-crust set (his wife was a lady-in-waiting to Princess Margaret), managing to satirise and glamorise them at the same time. Though sales of the fortnightly magazine were small, advertisers were thrilled by the AB readership profile and ad revenue ensured a handsome profit. Stevens became renowned for his spontaneity and ruthlessness, hiring and firing on a whim. Beaverbrook and

King got to hear of the young maverick and both offered him jobs, which he politely refused. Once Beaverbrook died, Aitken renewed the offer and, after selling *Queen* in 1968, Stevens became his personal assistant and, soon, close friend. Months later, Aitken made him managing director of the *Evening Standard* with the single injunction: 'Save it!'[116]

The irony of the appointment wasn't missed by Stevens. Many people believed that in the 1920s Beaverbrook had tricked Stevens's grandfather after he refused to sell his chain of newspaper titles to Rothermere. Beaverbrook, supposedly Hulton's friend, instead acted secretly as a front man for Rothermere. He persuaded the dying man to sell to him and immediately passed all the papers on to Rothermere. Out of gratitude, Rothermere let Beaverbrook keep the *Evening Standard*. Now Stevens was in charge of his ancestor's best-loved former paper.

According to Stevens, he did save the *Standard*, claiming to have improved its advertising revenue by building a strong classified ad section and engineering something of a coup against the rival *Evening News*'s previous domination in that area. According to the *Standard*'s historian, however, the real credit for the expansion in its small ads should go to Owen Rowley, a previous managing director, whose other great claim to fame was introducing crosswords into British newspapers in the 1920s.[117] A later advertising director, Brian Nicholson, also made massive improvements.[118] As for the steadying of sales, that was largely due to editor Charles Wintour, who foresaw that news alone could no longer sell an evening paper. Thomson and Hamilton recognised Wintour's achievements, which was why he was a leading candidate in 1967 for the editorship of either the *Times* or *Sunday Times*, and of ITN.[119] But Aitken accepted the Stevens hype, believing him to be a saviour, and shocked his managing director of the whole group, John Coote, by making Stevens into a joint managing director. A debilitating war between the two was no way to solve the group's deepening problems. Both men recognised that the *Express* editorial staff was 30 per cent larger than that of any other popular paper, but had different ways of solving the problem.

Aitken showed as little skill on the editorial side. *Daily Express* editor Bob Edwards had never got on with 'young Max', and provoked his new boss by deliberately answering his rudeness with rudeness, departing quickly and becoming, a year later, editor of the *Sunday People* (see below, p. 228). Some thirty-five years later, Edwards's loathing for Aitken was undimmed, and he claimed in public that Aitken had destroyed the *Express* papers 'as if he were a saboteur paid by Lord Rothermere'.[120] Pickering disputes this blanket condemnation, arguing that Aitken was far from all bad.[121]

Aitken replaced Edwards with Derek Marks, a hugely respected political correspondent, who was regarded by virtually everyone as an unsuccessful editor.[122] Absorbed by politics and in cultivating the companionship of cabinet ministers, Marks was an editor in the broadsheet rather than tabloid mould. That went for his physical size too, earning him the nickname 'Jumbo'.

Aitken had appointed the wrong man, without the technical or leadership skills, nor the compensation of a good deputy. Aitken, trying to imitate his father, also harried him mercilessly.[123] Jealous, squabbling baronies emerged within the paper, which began to lack the central thrust which had previously made it so coherent. Marks's stultifyingly authoritarian Conservative-party outlook was wrong for the times. Not only did he not have any interest in youth culture or the burgeoning liberation of women, he hadn't the slightest idea how to make a paper bright and confident enough to appeal to them. He did, however, lure Jean Rook away from the *Daily Mail*, successfully promoting her as 'The First Lady of Fleet Street'.[124]

One scoop Marks did run, causing a long-running political controversy, was Chapman Pincher's revelation about the security vetting of Post Office cables.[125] Publishing the story also exposed to the public the use of D-notices, a 'voluntary' system agreed between the media and government to protect state secrets.[126] After prime minister Harold Wilson denounced the *Express*, editors and senior journalists rallied to Marks's side, with the *Mirror*'s Lee Howard resigning from the D-notice committee in sympathy.[127]

Outside the political arena, Marks lacked journalistic vision, showing little insight into changing developments within society. He even failed to note the way in which Wintour's *Evening Standard* was managing to report on and analyse the Swinging Sixties without adopting a tut-tutting tone. Aitken's greatest error was not only in allowing Marks to carry on for too long, but in overlooking the man who should have replaced him: the foreign editor, David English.

Though promoted to associate editor, English desperately wanted the top job and, in pursuit of his ambition, he engineered the kind of high public profile only previously enjoyed by Arthur Christiansen. I recall a 1967 TV documentary about the world's first heart transplant in which English, filmed writing a headline, shouting down the phone and then seeing the page off the stone, stole the show. A colleague predicted that English's name would probably be remembered in Britain longer than that of the surgeon, Christiaan Barnard, and the patient, Louis Washkansky. Another admirer, Louis Kirby, said his first memory of English was his appearance in a *Daily Express* cinema advert screaming down a phone: 'Write it! Write it!'[128]

Aitken's failures in these years set in train the long-term decline of the *Express* titles, and it looked at the time as though another inadequate inheritor, Esmond Rothermere, would do the same to Associated Newspapers. Since his divorce, Esmond's life had assumed a certain regularity for fourteen years: Monte Carlo in winter, West Indies in summer, and the rest of the year in Britain spent between his Gloucestershire stately home, Daylesford, and his London mansion, Warwick House, where he entertained 'in tremendous grandeur'.[129]

He regularly invited twenty people to stay for weekends, entertaining in the grand style, with black-tie dinners, using different rooms for morning and evening drinks, with several maids on hand to serve afternoon tea. In a light-hearted account of what it was like to stay at Daylesford, *Mail* editor Mike Randall told of the intimidating regime.[130] It was so ostentatious that Randall's predecessor, William Hardcastle, often remarked: 'Enough to make you a bloody communist.' Daylesford, built by Warren Hastings in the eighteenth century, also boasted a big indoor swimming pool which Rothermere, who had little grasp of life outside his world, appeared to think a common feature in every home. Another *Mail* editor, Arthur Brittenden, liked to tell of the time he happened to mention to Rothermere during their daily phone call that he had a headache. 'Go home,' advised a sympathetic Rothermere, 'and sit by the pool.' Brittenden replied: 'Thank you, Lord Rothermere, but I don't have a pool.' A perplexed Rothermere exclaimed: 'No pool! No pool! You don't have a pool!'

In 1966, when Esmond was sixty-eight, he married Mrs Mary Ohrstrom, from an oil-rich Texan family, a mother of six sons who was almost half his age. He also changed his mind yet again about the *Mail* editorship. Randall's reputation was high at the time, as he had won the journalist of the year title in the British Press Awards, while *What the Papers Say* named the *Mail* as newspaper of the year.[131] Rothermere gave a lunch in his honour and all seemed set fair for Randall when, a couple of months later, he suffered a back injury which confined him to bed for six months. Rumours reached him that his deputy, Brittenden, was unhappy at remaining 'acting editor'. Randall, who had not been consulted two years before when Rothermere lured Brittenden from the deputy editorship of the *Sunday Express*, could not believe his job was under real threat, so he was shocked when Rothermere sent an emissary to Randall's home just before Christmas 1966 to tell him he must resign. He refused and was fired, a surprise so great that the *Times* splashed the story.[132] Rothermere was condemned by commentators in the *New Statesman*, *Spectator* and *Punch*, and by the *Daily Mirror*'s Cassandra.[133]

That Randall lasted almost three years as editor was surprising. A Labour voter, his liberal politics were not at all to his owner's liking. He annoyed Esmond by sacking one of his former girlfriends, fashion editor Iris Ashley.[134] Overall, he lost about 200,000 in sales. He also championed the designer Leslie Sellers, who achieved brief guru status because of his revolutionary, but controversial, page layouts.[135] It was hardly a surprise that his job went to forty-two-year-old Brittenden, who was thought to have a more populist touch than Randall. He was also more amenable to Rothermere's Tory politics. When columnist Bernard Levin favoured Labour in the run-up to the 1970 election Brittenden pressured him to change his copy. Levin resigned the next day.

I worked in the *Mail*'s northern office during Brittenden's editorship and could see that the paper was on a downhill path. It wasn't as technically proficient as the *Express*, nor as lively as the *Daily Mirror*. Its politics were relentless and predictable, while its features were too often dull. News executives were always looking over their shoulders at the activities of their rivals, especially the *Express*. What the *Mail* really lacked was a sense of purpose. There were good points,and none better than the work of Vincent Mulchrone, a journalist with champagne tastes, able to tell stories in a bar or in the paper with equal facility, and rightly described as 'the Master Reporter'.[136] Sometimes sent on silly assignments, such as fishing for the Loch Ness monster with a bottle of malt whisky as bait, his copy was always entertaining. On the day of the Prince of Wales's investiture in July 1969, I was given the task of subbing his report. Mulchrone's raw copy was a sub-editor's dream, 'a tick-up job', sent to the printers with little more than a type instruction. It was as near a perfect piece of work as I have ever seen. Mulchrone loved deadlines. 'Like fear', he wrote, they 'heighten perception magically'.[137]

Another plus was Patrick Sergeant, the City editor who was told to cut his staff in 1966 and responded by coming up with a wheeze, a weekly section called Money Mail. It not only saved jobs, it attracted readers and advertising and became a fixture. A couple of years later Sergeant suggested that the growing Eurodollar market required coverage and he and Esmond launched the magazine *Euromoney*. It was to make Sergeant a multi-millionaire and become a huge money-earner for Associated.

Brittenden, more of an office politician than a go-getting journalist, exuded charm. Tall, well-dressed, handsome, he had been in newspapers since he was sixteen, on leaving Leeds Grammar School. After cutting his teeth on the *Yorkshire Post* and *News Chronicle*, he spent fifteen years advancing through the Express group. He was a wonderful raconteur and was soon able to dine out on stories about Rothermere. He spoke to his owner at 5.30 p.m. every day and, though he never knew where Rothermere was speaking from, he took it for granted that he almost never came to the *Mail*. Conversation was difficult, but he realised that talking initially about the weather paid dividends. One day he couldn't get a reaction to his lament about the drizzle and, after a long silence, Rothermere barked: 'Why are you telling me that? I'm sitting in the office across the road from you, looking at exactly the same weather as you are.'[138]

Rothermere was delighted when his new wife presented him with a second son and even more pleased when his first son, Vere, finally had a son in December 1967 after two daughters. The heir to the Rothermere title bore the names Harold Jonathan Esmond Vere, but would always be known as Jonathan. There was much less to celebrate about his newspaper empire. Apart from the continuing problems at the *Daily Mail*, where there was too little money for promotion, the *Daily Sketch* looked like a terminal case. Under editor Howard French, it did quite well, adding a couple of thousand sales a year from 1965 until peaking at 915,000 in the summer of 1968. By then it was a mere 150,000 behind the *Sun*, but it suddenly nosedived again and French recognised that his days were numbered. Rothermere delivered the *coup de grâce* in 1969. One key problem for the *Sketch* had long been the constraints placed on it by Rothermere, who thought the *Daily Mirror* guilty of publishing 'soft porn', and viewed the youth-led cultural revolution with distaste. French, also of the old school, took a similar view. His replacement was a very different kind of journalist, a man who understood how to engage with contemporary culture without sacrificing a sense of tradition: David English. Upset by Aitken telling him he must wait to become *Express* editor, the fiercely ambitious English wanted an editorship so badly he was prepared to take the least auspicious chair available by moving to the *Sketch*.

English was thirty-eight, fashionably long-haired and a dapper dresser. One of his greatest admirers, *Sketch* sports writer Laurie Pignon, thought he looked like a spiv.[139] With his sharp suits and his sharp tongue, relieved by a ready wit and a trademark high-pitched giggle, especially when indulging in his favourite pastime, gossiping, he stood out from the crowd. After attending Bournemouth School, he rejected university in favour of a reporting job on the *Christchurch Times*. Pausing only for a brief stop on the *Portsmouth Evening News*, English managed to get on to the *Daily Mirror* by the time he was twenty. Three years later he was features editor of the *Sketch* and one of his traits, his love of stunts, came to the fore. When an American drug company claimed to have invented a pill to coat the lining of the stomach to prevent drunkenness, English organised seven sets of twins to try it out, one taking the pill and the other not. The experiment ended up with virtually everyone, including the journalists, getting hopelessly drunk.[140]

English spent a year with the *Sunday Dispatch* as a foreign correspondent before joining, at the age of thirty, the *Daily Express* as New York correspondent. It was impossible to best English, who fought to win at all costs. He was to bring the same single-minded ruthlessness to his editorships, though his was anything but a one-man show. He set out to build a loyal team of executives, writers and reporters. Despite its hopeless state, English did inject a sense of vitality into the *Sketch*.[141] One of its youngest recruits, Anthea Disney, noted how the 'death-struggle' paper 'was suddenly fun' to work on.[142] She certainly benefited, taking the central role in a typical English stunt which was to make her briefly famous with the public and for ever among fellow journalists. He asked the dark-haired, olive-skinned Disney to pretend to be an Indian, living on a Birmingham estate, to experience the problems of a coloured immigrant. Wearing a sari was easy but, to darken her skin, she risked her health by taking a course of drugs from a doctor in Puerto Rico. It took more than a year for her skin to return to its normal colour.[143]

Similar English initiatives ensured that the *Sketch* was being talked about again, but it made no difference to the slide in sales. He had arrived too late and at the wrong time: his revitalised *Sketch* was soon eclipsed by the

Murdoch–Lamb *Sun*. Fate took a hand. Esmond Rothermere, in failing health, decided to resign the chairmanship in favour of his son, Vere Harmsworth, who had been vice-chairman since 1963. Together, these two men were to set out on a long journey to transform the fortunes of a paper and, eventually, of the Associated empire.

Harmsworth's positive influence on the papers was obvious from the start. When Shirley Conran left the *Observer* magazine in 1969 to become the *Mail* women's editor, Harmsworth decided her pages should be entitled Femail, a clever name that stuck.[144] But his most important strategic decision within weeks of assuming control was to abort his father's reluctant move towards a merger with the Express group.

It has been suggested that, by the late 1960s, all that was keeping Associated going were the profits from the regional papers.[145] But the group also benefited from investments in Southern TV, National Opinion Polls, London taxis, pulp and paper interests in Canada, magazines and property. Esmond's wife had also introduced him to a relative who convinced him to invest in North Sea oil exploration, which was to prove beneficial during Vere's later reconstruction. All this diversification, largely masterminded by a senior executive, Mick Shields, played a crucial part in Associated's later financial stability. It didn't look that way to Esmond in 1970. He authorised his managing director, Marmaduke Hussey, to hold serious, and secret, talks with the Express group for some kind of mutual co-operation. On the Express side, Coote wanted to raise funds by capitalising on his modern print plant to publish a merged *Evening Standard* and *Evening News*. He saw this as a precursor to a 'glittering' *Express–Mail* merger.[146]

With the profitable *Sunday Express* remaining in Express hands, and Aitken's insistence on being chairman in the first year of joint operations, Associated executives were concerned that the *Express* was getting the upper hand. No one was more upset than Harmsworth, who could see his legacy slipping from his fingers at the very moment he was about to take over.[147] Aitken, though initially happy with Coote's initiative, also changed his mind after heeding the outraged pleas of Jocelyn Stevens, who had been excluded from the Coote–Hussey negotiations.

Stevens and Coote were to clash often in the following year. Stevens may have been sensible to oppose the merger with Associated, but there was merit in Coote's plan for the *Standard–News* link-up. With *Evening News* editor Reg Willis retiring at the end of 1966, the new year saw a surprising replacement: John Gold, the paper's successful New York correspondent during the previous eleven years. At forty-one, Gold was considered by Rothermere to be the perfect man to make his paper appeal to a new generation. The staff were not so sure, however high their regard for a reporter who had filed so many exclusive stories, and Gold found Willis an impossible act to follow. Gold was just not cut out to be an editor. Liked by reporters, who appreciated that by mixing in the right circles he was still able to get stories himself, he never really gained their respect. Nor did he have any of his predecessor's production skills. Virtually the whole staff thought he compared poorly to Willis.[148] It would be harsh to blame Gold alone for the sales decline, and it is doubtful if he could have stemmed it. Neither Rothermere nor his son Vere was sure what to do with the *News* as the *Standard* began to win the battle for classified advertising.

Money was also becoming harder to find for every owner. A pay dispute in June 1970, which shut the national titles and both London evenings for three days, ended with a £5 million pay and holidays package for print workers that no group could afford. Aitken spoke for every proprietor in pointing out: 'Conventional financiers and industrialists would suggest we need our heads examining for conducting a business involving such outgoings and risks for so diminutive a profit.'[149]

One paper, the *Sunday Citizen*, found it impossible to soldier on against the financial pressures. Its twenty-eight tabloid pages, an incoherent mixture of pin-up pictures and poorly presented serious material, were unappealing and sales fell to fewer than 250,000. An appeal to the government by the Co-operative Press chairman Cyril Hamnett to divert its advertising to the *Citizen* received 'a dusty answer'.[150] He knew that the once powerful Co-operative Societies were themselves losing the battle to attract customers and could not be expected to fund the paper's mounting losses indefinitely. Editor William Richardson huffed and puffed, writing of the *Citizen*'s non-existent 'fight back from the edge of disaster'. He bemoaned his socialist paper's coming fate in a capitalist world. 'Newspapers once stood for something. They believed in a principle and fought for it. Today most of them are shuffled around like chips in a casino, bought and sold, merged and murdered as the financiers juggle the tokens.'[151]

Five months later the *Citizen*'s front page announced: 'Your Paper Reaches the End!' It had even lost advertising from the Co-op, and costs went on increasing as circulation revenue continued to fall.[152] Hamnett, who was later ennobled, and Richardson, soon to be knighted, did their best to embarrass Labour's prime minister. Two months before, Wilson had made a stupid promise in the Commons, saying that if any newspaper was in danger of closure and 'approached the Government we would then consider whether it was possible to give help while maintaining adequate safeguards'.[153] Naturally, the Co-op Press did just that. Wilson, under pressure from his own MPs to help the *Citizen*, backtracked. It was for the industry to look after its own, he said. As Williamson observed, this made his earlier statement meaningless.[154] In the run-up to closure, it was galling for the *Citizen* to enjoy its greatest advertising volumes in years as rivals – *Observer*, *People*, *News of the World* and *Sunday Mirror* – bought full-page ads in order to lure its readers.

No one even made a serious offer to buy the *Citizen* title, not even Robert Maxwell, who sent a sympathetic letter (and later bought its libraries),[155] nor

Roy Thomson who claimed that reports of him making an offer were a joke. That hurt Richardson who countered: 'He and his kind are sapping the vitality and independence of the Press.'[156] In its final issue in June 1967, the *Sunday Citizen* extolled trade unions and co-operative societies and lambasted Labour for abandoning socialist principles. This paper, it said, 'has never been a traitor to the working class'.[157] But it had undeniably died precisely because it had failed to interest the working class.

Two papers that were still able to command a massive working-class audience were the *Sunday People* and *Sunday Mirror*. Much the more successful of the two was the *People*, with regular sales above 5.5 million. Its great architect, Sam Campbell, died in harness in February 1966, suffering a massive heart attack aged just fifty-eight, having created a paper renowned for its weekly exposures of crime and corruption. Its investigative team, led by Laurie Manifold, was widely admired for its work, by the *News of the World* which couldn't compete with its reporting, by Scotland Yard which benefited from its revelations, and even by the *Sunday Times*'s editor-in-chief Denis Hamilton.[158]

Cudlipp sought out the unemployed former *Daily Express* editor Bob Edwards to take Campbell's place, and Edwards was careful not to change a winning formula. He brought aboard a former *Express* colleague, Terry Lancaster, to write well-informed political commentaries. He also started a book column, initially written by John Braine and then by Tom Driberg. In succeeding years, 1967–8, *People* reporters Ken Gardner and David Farr were named as news reporter of the year in the British Press Awards, the latter for uncovering a slot-machines racket which led to the jailing of a gang. Edwards also presided over the *People*'s highest sale towards the end of 1967 of more than 5.6 million.

Edwards's finest moment came in 1970 when he published details of a massacre by British troops in Malaya. Several of the soldiers confessed to the paper's reporters, telling how they had machine-gunned twenty-five innocent villagers to death in 1949.[159] 'It was a brave piece of editing,' said Alan Hobday, then a senior *People* executive in Manchester and later deputy editor for twenty years. 'Readers didn't like it and many stopped buying the paper.'[160] Sales fell by 200,000 in the course of the year. Edwards was also attacked by senior politicians, including Liberal leader Jeremy Thorpe and Labour's defence minister Denis Healey.[161]

The *People* – Edwards removed the *Sunday* from the title – was lauded by a commentator for its 'reader-pulling Bottomley-John-Bull-at-its-best quality ... while it is like its great rival, the *Sunday Mirror*, in a fondness for all animals, it really prefers the under-dog'.[162] Indeed, compared to the crusading *People*, the *Sunday Mirror* edited by Michael Christiansen was altogether less vibrant, managing to sell 5.1 million until a sudden slump in 1970 wiped 400,000 off the circulation. All the popular Sunday papers were losing sales fast by the end of 1970.

10. SEX, DEATH AND REBELLION

> The only qualities essential for success in journalism are ratlike cunning, a plausible manner, and a little literary ability.[1]

Already in this history there have been several instances of bad behaviour by newspapers in pursuit of stories. This reminds us that, in every era, people have had cause to complain about the press and, consequently, have sincerely believed the contemporaneous situation to be worse than before. Inevitably, therefore, there were regular calls that Something Must Be Done. From 1963 onwards, having noted the treatment meted out to Profumo and those drawn into the case, politicians became particularly exercised by intrusions into privacy. Towards the end of 1969, Labour MP Brian Walden drew up a Right of Privacy Bill, which almost every editor across Britain opposed on the grounds that it would inhibit the press's ability to serve the greater public interest by reporting on matters people in power wished to keep secret. Walden's failed bid would not be the last, especially as the climate changed towards greater sexual permissiveness.

The problem of sex in newspapers grew progressively more problematic for editors in the late 1960s. How far should a paper be prepared to go? For some owners and editors, and the names of Rupert Murdoch and Larry Lamb spring to mind, the answer was straightforward: the market would decide on ethical questions. If the *Sun* and the *News of the World* sold copies in their millions then it was proof that the public found their content acceptable. Other owners, such as Aitken, Rothermere and Hartwell, refused, to use their terms, 'to pander to the public' or even to 'the lowest common denominator'. They believed in 'standards'. Every owner and editor, however, strove to justify themselves by resorting to a Fleet Street cliché about producing 'a family newspaper', a precursor to the later reverence for 'family values'. This acknowledged that there was a boundary between what could and could not be published. In practice, deciding what was acceptable was subjective and liable to change. What papers felt they couldn't publish one year might well be fine the next.

In a general sense, delicate decisions about what readers would find acceptable had long been evident. The fine lines drawn by the *News of the World* over what it should print were calculated not to offend. Court reports titillated, personal memoirs promised much but said little, and journalists knew at just what point they should make their excuses and leave. Elsewhere, the choices of 'cheesecake' pictures in popular papers were designed to tantalise men without upsetting female readers. The *Daily Mirror* had taken the initial steps during the war, with its risqué Jane cartoon strips, and in the years afterwards regularly featured pictures of 'bathing beauties'. But this began to look dated as the cultural revolution of the Sixties, influenced by a growing tolerance towards sex by the iconoclastic baby boomers and the parallel liberation of women, began to take hold. Newspapers were forced to re-evaluate their adherence to former taboos.

Few subjects illustrate so well the difficulty of disentangling the relationship between public and press as that of sex. At what point does nudity become acceptable, for instance, or when is it safe – in terms of sales – to publish details of peoples' intimate bedroom activities? There is a difference between being reactive, by discovering the changing limits of public taste, and being proactive, helping to change those limits. But this is a subtle, reciprocal process in which it becomes virtually impossible to distinguish who did what first. Did 'society' or 'the media' stimulate the sexual liberation of the 1960s? A review of papers in this period suggests that editors were relatively slow to understand the impact of sexual enlightenment and therefore initially uncertain how to exploit it. Senior journalists were at the beginning of a journey, trying to come to terms with their prescriptive tendencies, which had involved drawing a line in the sand while trying to respond to a public demand which was obliterating that line. Regardless of letters to the editor and the views of staff, the only way in which public attitudes could be measured and monitored with any accuracy was through sales. Cudlipp had pushed at the barriers a little. Murdoch was to transform the market place into the final arbiter.

Sunday Mirror editor Michael Christiansen confronted this dilemma in 1966 when he published a picture of a nude woman. A complainant to the Press Council thought it shocking and likely to corrupt the minds of impressionable young readers. In his defence, Christiansen, then aged thirty-nine, cast himself as a progressive: the configuration of the human body was no longer a mystery; sex education was given in many schools; it was difficult to believe any young person would be either shocked or corrupted. Aware of possible controversy, Christiansen had chosen a picture 'by Hatami, the distinguished French photographer'. In other words, it was presented in the guise of 'art'. The Press Council backed the editor, pronouncing that it was a matter of taste within his discretion.[2]

The Council's view contrasts with its statement some twelve years earlier when considering protests about coverage of the Kinsey Report on sexual behaviour. Then it was 'deeply concerned by the unwholesome exploitation of sex by certain newspapers and periodicals' placing 'on record its view that such treatment is calculated to injure public morals'.[3] In the 1950s, any mention of homosexuality, abortion, birth control or venereal disease routinely attracted complaints from readers supposedly concerned lest their children were to read them. In 1955, the Magistrates Association asked the Press Council to instruct papers to suppress the names and addresses of all people under the age of thirty concerned in homosexual cases in order to protect them from the advances of older, and therefore confirmed, homosexuals. The Council refused.[4]

In 1960, the Council denounced articles in three Sunday papers 'dealing with the sexual adventures of persons connected with the stage and screen'. It was to be deplored that the papers 'should have permitted their standards to be debased to a level which was a disgrace to professional journalism'.[5] The central problem, inevitably, was that newspapers which published salacious investigations – into prostitution, for instance, or the availability of pornography – were accused of stimulating interest in the subjects they ostensibly deplored. Information and provocation were two sides of the same coin, a fact which the *News of the World* had long exploited.

The reaction to Kenneth Tynan's nude revue, *Oh! Calcutta!*, illustrated the point well. When it opened first in New York, in June 1969, it was panned by most of the city's critics, but ran for three years, returning in 1976 to run for another ten years, eventually playing in 250 cities across the world.[6] Before it opened at London's Roundhouse in July 1970, the *Times*'s political editor Ronald Butt attacked it as 'the sort of exhibition of sexual voyeurism that used to be available to the frustrated and the mentally warped in the side-turnings of a certain kind of sea-port'. Even a description of the show might damage the minds of the young.[7] The *News of the World* was more appreciative, lauding it as 'the nudest, rudest, most scandalous revue in the world'.[8] Herbert Kretzmer of the *Daily Express* thought it 'a show of our times,[9] while the *Times*'s theatre critic Irving Wardle – at odds with his colleague Butt – wrote that 'there is no reason why the public treatment of sex should not be extended to take in not only lyricism and personal emotion but also the rich harvest of bawdy jokes'.[10] Most critics thought it had 'crashed the sex barrier once and for all'.[11]

But the fascinating reactions came in the two tabloids. The *Daily Mirror*'s review, headlined 'Titty, Tatty, Nude and Crude', set out to show that it wasn't in the least erotic and therefore, by implication, not worth seeing: 'It has more corn than porn.'[12] At the *Sun*, I witnessed a classic example of the way in which writers were cajoled into accepting editorial policy. The paper's regular critic, Fergus Cashin, had filed a piece which took the line the paper wanted to get across, that the revue was voyeuristic muck, but it was thought in the office to be too tame. Deputy editor Bernard Shrimsley phoned Cashin, a renowned drinker, in a noisy bar to suggest some radical alterations, including a new first sentence. The conversation began in some confusion when Shrimsley suggested that the new opening word should read: 'Ye-uck!' Cashin, a liberal user of the Anglo-Saxon expletive, misunderstood and protested that he couldn't start a theatre review 'in a family newspaper' with that word. In the end, without ever really grasping what Shrimsley was saying, he gave in. Shrimsley's rewrite began: 'Ye-uck! That's what I think about *Oh! Calcutta!* It's nude. It's crude. There is no love, no beauty, no happiness.'[13] This appeared on page one next to a picture of one of the female stars.

Aside from the hilarity, the exercise was instructive, not only for the way in which editors on tabloids hold sway over content regardless of individual journalists' views, but for its hypocritical censoriousness. The paper which had been publishing sexy features series for seven months, and would soon present a daily picture of a topless girl, was happy to deplore a nude stage show.

A welcome constraint on press freedom

In 1966, Ian Brady and Myra Hindley were convicted of the horrific murders of two young children and a teenage boy. Evidence against the pair during the 'moors murders' trial at Chester Assizes was so gruesome that some of the supposedly hard-bitten reporters suffered nightmares for years. But that was not the only ghastly aspect of the case as far as the press was concerned. During the cross-examination of the key prosecution witness, David Smith, it emerged that he was under contract to the *News of the World*. He would be paid £1,000 for his story and receive more in syndication rights. He and his wife had already spent a holiday in France courtesy of the paper, which was also paying his hotel expenses throughout the trial.

NoW reporters had been 'minding' the seventeen-year-old Smith and his wife of sixteen, Maureen, for months before the trial, keeping them in a hotel and giving them money as they needed it. In court, it was suggested to Smith by defence counsel that the value of his story would be diminished if the accused were acquitted. He therefore had 'a vested financial interest in their conviction'.[14] A confused Smith agreed, and the judge asked the attorney-general, Sir Elwyn Jones, to investigate what 'seems to be a gross interference with the course of justice'.[15] The *News of the World* immediately announced that Smith was wrong: the amount of the payment would have remained the same whatever the outcome of the case. The paper was not prosecuted for contempt because neither the attorney-general nor the trial judge thought the deal had affected Smith's evidence. But Jones warned that the government would consider outlawing payments to witnesses, a hint to the press to end the practice voluntarily.

Lengthy contemplation by the Press Council, with its chairman Lord Devlin taking political and judicial soundings along with advice from press owners and editors, ended with a three-point declaration of principle. Witnesses should not be paid in advance of appearing in court; they shouldn't be interviewed by papers about their evidence until after the trial;

nobody involved in a crime should be paid 'where the public interest does not warrant it'.[16] This entirely reasonable set of rules upset *News of the World* editor Stafford Somerfield, who wrote: 'The public interest demands that matters which are criminal, vicious and unsavoury should be exposed and not concealed. The greater the evil, the greater the need for exposure.'[17] Fine words, but they missed the point by a mile. Exposure which tainted a witness or rewarded a criminal would no longer be condoned. While agreeing that the 'voluntarily accepted code' placed restraints on press freedom, the *Sun* encapsulated the general view that these were necessary in the interests of justice.[18] It was a landmark decision by the Press Council, a sensible outcome to a sordid episode.

The *Observer* also distinguished itself by carrying a lengthy article by Maurice Richardson, a short-story writer and weekly columnist on crime literature, about the murderers' emotional and psychological make-up. This attempt to explain how they could have committed such crimes stands like a lone beacon amid the hysterical, and sometimes obnoxious, coverage by the popular papers.[19]

The Street of ink and the rivers of blood

Arguably, no single speech in post-war Britain aroused such controversy as that delivered on 20 April 1968 by the Conservative MP for Wolverhampton South-West and shadow cabinet defence spokesman, Enoch Powell. In order to avoid racial conflict, he advocated a cut 'to negligible proportions' of black and Commonwealth immigration, and suggested that immigrants who had already arrived should be encouraged to return. He referred to 'wide-eyed, grinning piccaninnies' and, in a classical allusion to the River Tiber, spoke of it 'foaming with much blood'.[20] This 'rivers of blood' speech, as papers soon referred to it, 'struck a popular chord'.[21] Powell was backed by groups of dockers and meat porters who marched through the East End while letters of support for his views poured in, especially from working-class people living in inner cities. One poll even suggested that three-quarters of the country agreed with him. His party leader, Ted Heath, certainly did not and sacked him.

Since the speech was made on a Saturday, the first reports appeared on the front pages, in every instance, of the Sunday papers. The *People* headlined it as 'a shocker' while the *Sunday Mirror* compared Powell to the lead character in the popular TV show about a racist, lampooning him as 'the Right Hon. Alf Garnett'.[22] The *Sunday Times* ran virtually the whole speech, along with an analysis of Powell's use, or misuse, of statistics and speculation about Heath's likely reaction. It viewed the speech as 'crudely inflammatory . . . By predicting a racial war . . . he does his bit towards bringing it about.'[23] From the other, pro-Powell perspective, the *News of the World* thought 'most people in this country will agree with him' and concluded, in capital letters: 'WE CAN TAKE NO MORE COLOURED PEOPLE. TO DO SO, AS MR POWELL SAYS, IS MADNESS.'[24] *Sunday Telegraph* columnist, and associate editor, Peregrine Worsthorne argued that voluntary repatriation was 'the only honest course'.[25]

Perhaps the most significant reaction came the following day, from the *Times*. An editorial written by editor William Rees-Mogg condemned the speech as 'shameful' and 'evil' because it was 'calculated to inflame hatred between races' and made 'a deliberate appeal to racial prejudice'.[26] The *Guardian* was altogether less critical of Powell. It regarded his speech as inflammatory but did not think his intention was to fan the flames of racialism, while noting tamely that his call for repatriation was 'quite contrary to the official policy of the Conservative party'.[27]

The *Daily Telegraph* and the *Daily Express* were sympathetic to Powell, questioning his language rather than his substantive argument, and grumbling about his dismissal from the cabinet. The *Telegraph* felt that 'whatever the deficiencies of his statistics and the exaggerations of his language ... he was expressing anxieties felt by millions of people ... His congenital disposition to push an argument to its logical and linguistic extremes was not sufficient ground for dismissing him.'[28] The *Express* adopted a similar position: 'However unwise and intemperate Mr Powell's speech may have been ... [he] reflected the feelings of a vast number of people ... Mr Powell may have been impolitic. Mr Heath has been foolish.'[29]

Sunday People editor Bob Edwards, who had called on Powell to be sacked, received 130 letters, all but three opposing his paper's view. He wrote: 'The emotions unleashed by Mr Powell were just a little too unBritish for comfort.' Hostility from his readers didn't stop him from publishing a picture two weeks later which showed fifty hospital workers of varying hues of forty-seven different nationalities under the headline: 'Dear Enoch Powell, if you ever have to go into hospital, you'll be glad of people like these ...'[30]

The journalist faced with the most difficult job was Clem Jones, editor of the paper which covered Powell's West Midlands constituency, the *Wolverhampton Express & Star*. It says much for Jones – and his paper's owners, the Graham family – that they were not swayed by their postbag. The paper received 5,000 letters supporting Powell and 300 against him. In a subsequent poll, in which readers were invited to send in postcards with their views, there were 35,000 in favour of Powell with hardly any against. Yet not only did Jones refuse to sit on the fence, he 'attacked Powell's views in editorial after editorial ... strongly backed by his proprietor ... and with the full support of his editorial staff – though not the rest of the newspaper's staff'.[31] I met Jones in 1998 and he spoke proudly of his part in the affair. In a long and distinguished career, it was his finest moment, though his paper's record on racial matters before he became editor had been less praiseworthy.[32]

Jones was also years ahead of his time in recognising that stories about immigrants required special care. 'Coloured immigration was not a phrase which could be used without bias,' he told a conference of editors in 1968. 'I try to see all stories with a colour angle myself, and to look at them not only in the same way as other stories – that is, at their news value – but also in the light of possible reaction from both coloured and white people, and our special responsibility as communicators to the community.'[33]

Political apathy in Britain and antagonism in Ireland

It was widely expected that Harold Wilson's Labour party would win both the general elections of 1966 and 1970. They did so in the first, gaining a ninety-six-seat majority, and, to their surprise, lost the second, when Ted Heath's Tories secured an overall majority of thirty. Wilson's honeymoon with the press from 1964 lasted well beyond 1966, aided by his deliberate courtship of owners and editors, which no prime minister had previously attempted so blatantly.[34] Newspaper enthusiasm for Wilson had faded by 1970, but he was still considered a winner by most editors.

There were no surprises at either election in terms of press support for the parties, though coverage of the second was noticeably low-key and culminated in the lowest turnout for thirty-five years. Murdoch's *Sun*, just as he had promised, backed Wilson in 1970 with an editorial headlined: 'Why It Must Be Labour'.[35] Murdoch and Lamb were surprised that so many Labour supporters 'voted with their feet'.[36] The defeat was poignantly portrayed in an exclusive *Sun* picture of Wilson and his wife asleep, slumped against each other, as their car sped down the motorway from Liverpool to London.[37]

For a week during the campaign, 9 to 12 June, all papers were off the streets in the south due to a print union strike. This probably had some effect on the outcome, suggesting to the electorate that Labour had failed to reform industrial relations because it was hamstrung by its links to the unions.[38]

It is also likely that the newly enfranchised youth who had been enthusiastic about Wilson's supposed revolutionary message in 1966 tended to abstain in 1970. Though his administration failed to live up to its promises, it coincided with a period of social change which occurred independently of the political process. Working-class baby boomers, such as me, were discovering that it was possible to win through on merit to a life our parents had never imagined possible. Not only that: we could also forge a new world. We were, as one historian has aptly put it, both 'client and patron of the new culture'.[39] Less deferential and less accepting of the status quo, we were anxious to remake society, though most papers didn't seem to reflect this changing reality.

Two very different expressions of hostility to authority became commonplace. Young people took to the streets in somewhat muted copies of the

1968 Paris *événements*, especially in opposition to the Vietnam war. Older people, sensing that they were not getting their full measure of an apparently booming economy, endorsed trade union militancy. Unofficial strikes increased as the level of inflation rose.

These outbreaks of aggression were tame compared to the explosive conflict that erupted in the north of Ireland. In combing the files of every British paper from 1945 until 1968, I came across few references to Northern Ireland. Almost the only mentions for several years were about royal visits, such as the July 1945 tour which started with the King, Queen and Princess Elizabeth flying into Long Kesh aerodrome.[40] One rare example of the underlying conflict came in a short 1946 news report about an IRA hunger-striker who had died in a Dublin prison and was buried in his Belfast birthplace.[41]

By far the most surprising, and fairest, of features appeared in the *Sunday People* in 1950, a full page giving two people the chance to put their opposing views on the possibility of reuniting Ireland. Brigadier-General Dorman O'Gowan, veteran of the North Africa campaign, argued for reunification. St John Ervine, playwright, critic and 'one of the doughtiest champions of Ulster's cause', gave the Unionist view.[42] A *Daily Herald* article by Michael Foot in 1953 proved prescient. He told of religious discrimination which had disfranchised 300,000 people in Northern Ireland and argued that it was time to ask questions 'about this forgotten island where Britain still retains a foothold of responsibility. We should not wait for bomb outrages to shake us from our sloth.'[43]

A very different, and more typical, contribution was a *Daily Mail* interview with Lord Brookeborough, premier of the Stormont government, in 1957. It began: 'Ulster has now received positive proof that Soviet agents are actively aiding IRA raiders operating along the . . . Ulster–Eire border.' The 'proof' amounted to uncheckable assertions by Brookeborough, and the article's soft-focus descriptive style owed more to showbusiness than to a serious political interview: 'after we had drunk our pre-lunch aperitifs, Lord Brookeborough and I walked through the old gardens of his lovely country home'.[44]

Press silence went hand in hand with political silence: there was a Commons convention that Northern Ireland matters were the business exclusively of its own parliament, Stormont, and therefore were not discussed by MPs. So little did Northern Irish affairs concern London-based national papers that few had staff there. Key events went unreported, such as the founding in 1964 of the Campaign for Social Justice, the 1965 founding by Labour MPs of the Campaign for Democracy in Ulster and the launch in 1967 of the Northern Ireland Civil Rights Association.

Riots that lasted for three nights during the 1964 election, prompted by Ian Paisley's demand to the RUC that a tricolour be removed from the Republican headquarters in Belfast, received only cursory coverage. The

Times noted that the 'disturbances' were 'the worst in the city for a quarter of a century', but this wasn't considered of sufficient importance to send a writer to analyse what was happening.[45] Instead, an editorial lamented that the riots 'will disappoint those optimists who thought that religious and nationalist antagonisms were dying away in Ulster' and then reasserted the optimistic view by concluding that it might 'have a sobering effect'.[46] In three days, the *Daily Telegraph* carried two reports totalling five paragraphs.

But the *Telegraph* was under no illusion about the problems of Northern Ireland. In May 1966, it set out the fundamental reasons for Catholic protests against Protestant rule, an article which upset the Belfast *Telegraph*.[47] Almost two months later, Paisley led a protest march against the main Irish Presbyterian Church because of 'Romanizing influences'.[48] The *Guardian* reported the incident a day late.[49] No popular paper mentioned it. It took a visit by the Queen to attract national paper journalists *en masse* to Northern Ireland in July 1966. They were baffled by the virulence of attacks on them by Paisley, who described them 'as an enemy of Protestantism' and accused their papers of 'misrepresentations'.[50] He must have been referring to articles in the *Guardian* and the *Sunday Times* in the previous couple of days.

A young *Guardian* reporter, Brian MacArthur, was the first journalist to write about the huge support for Paisley's views and the first to record concern about gerrymandering.[51] Some thirty-four years after his visit, MacArthur spoke of his bemusement at what he found in Northern Ireland. 'I was trying to phone my copy through from a kiosk surrounded by all these howling people. I didn't know why they were so angry. Like all the other reporters from England, we had no idea about the place.'[52] His second report, about a rally addressed by Paisley, reflected his incredulity: 'It was hard to believe one was living in the twentieth century. If the implications were not so serious for Ulster, the procession would have been comic, even Ruritanian.'[53]

The *Sunday Times*'s Cal McCrystal, an Irishman who did understand the nature of the divisions, also wrote of Paisley's demagogic behaviour fanning 'a campaign of violence against the Roman Catholic minority'.[54] That edition also carried the first really in-depth analysis of the Northern Irish situation, headlined 'John Bull's Political Slum'.[55] It was an intelligent and detailed piece of work which explained why Unionist party reformism was under attack from disgruntled Catholics on one side and Paisleyites on the other. Editor Harold Evans later conceded that the article was written after his paper had, 'like the rest of Britain, forgotten about Ulster for a long time'.[56]

The *Sunday Times*'s investigation made a nonsense of the *Daily Telegraph*'s prediction that the Queen's visit was 'more likely to lessen than increase tension in that troubled Province'.[57] Explaining the reason for the tension, its editorial referred to 'shameless gerrymandering . . . discrimination . . . and various other forms of favouritism . . . designed to preserve Protestant Unionism'. Its own front-page report the next day, headlined 'Concrete slab hits the Queen's car', exposed its over-optimism. Yet this paper which put such store by facts did not seek to tell its readers any more about 'that troubled Province'.

Some papers did not even see it in those terms. In reporting the incident, the *Daily Express* overlooked the existence of nationalists in Northern Ireland by blithely observing that 'Ulstermen [are] regarded as the most loyal subjects in the Commonwealth'.[58] The *Daily Mail* sent its best descriptive writer, Vincent Mulchrone, who did a competent job of reporting the attack on the Queen's Rolls-Royce, but he returned to London straight afterwards.

The *Daily Mirror*, then in the infancy of its Cudlippian mission to inform, carried a very short profile of Paisley the day before the Queen's visit, though its opening sentence, 'There is a new religious bitterness in Northern Ireland,' showed a lamentable grasp of history.[59] There was no explanatory follow-up on 'the inside page', precursor to the educative Mirrorscope, but columnist Cassandra did compare Paisley to Hitler, an article which was scandalously omitted from the paper's Northern Ireland edition.[60]

After that brief flurry of interest, the London press largely turned its back on Northern Ireland. The media showed no interest in civil rights campaigns because 'Ulster was a faraway place that did not sell newspapers or attract viewers'.[61] The single exception was the *Times*, which sent over a team of reporters to discover the extent of discrimination in April 1967. Its survey, headlined 'Ulster's Second-Class Citizens', told of 'overwhelming evidence' of gerrymandering, unfair housing allocation and employment injustice.[62] Unionist leaders were furious and the Stormont prime minister Terence O'Neill immediately denounced the report.[63]

This did not stimulate wider press interest in London. There was no coverage of the occupation of a house in Caledon, Co. Tyrone by Austin Currie in June 1968, a protest at the unfairness of housing allocation designed to attract publicity. Nor was the first civil rights march in August 1968 granted any space, despite violent clashes. But, six weeks later, a Derry march finally did attract huge interest with its television images and newspaper pictures of the RUC baton-charging demonstrators.

Guardian editor Alastair Hetherington admitted that 'like most British papers, the *Guardian* largely ignored Ulster until the Derry disturbances in October 1968'.[64] The long silence meant that, overnight, the British public were presented with a story of a conflict within their own political borders, about which they knew nothing, with obscure origins and a total absence of context. What could it all mean? There was a lot to explain, and with events unfolding fast, popular papers emphasised the violence rather than the politics. Working in the *Daily Mail*'s northern office, I often overheard a news desk executive talking to the Belfast correspondent. One of his most memorable shouted questions during a riot, 'How high are the flames?', summed up the central thrust of the paper's news agenda, dealing with results rather than causes.

The *Observer* tried to make up lost ground. Owner–editor David Astor had been warned in the late 1940s by Lord Longford (Frank Pakenham at the time) that injustice would lead to disaster. 'Moved by a delayed feeling of guilt,' he decided to publish a series of explosive articles by Mary Holland.[65] Her report from the Derry march, headlined 'John Bull's White Ghettos', was a clear-sighted analysis of the reasons for the civil rights demonstrations and a penetrating assault on the legitimacy of Stormont rule.[66]

In the following months, as the British government bolstered O'Neill while pressuring him to introduce democratic reforms, the serious papers did try to make up for lost time. Even so, the commitment was anything but full-hearted. The *Times*'s coverage was 'intermittent and patchy', which isn't surprising given that it was carried out by the paper's north of England correspondent 'as an additional chore'.[67] By contrast, the *Guardian* made amends for its previous oversight, sending reporter Simon Hoggart in 1968. He ended up staying for five years.

One odd coincidence in the policy formulation of the two papers was the backgrounds of two influential figures at each title. The *Guardian*'s early leaders were heavily influenced by the views of John Cole, news editor then deputy editor from 1969, a Northern Ireland Protestant who ensured that his paper didn't adopt Irish unity as its policy. With the *Times*'s Rees-Mogg 'curiously detached', its leaders were written by Owen Hickey, a Catholic with a farm in Co. Tipperary, whose judgement was 'unclouded by his own religious affiliations'.[68] Some thirty years later Rees-Mogg admitted that his paper's policy might have been more radical if he had not deferred to the 'more conservative Hickey'.[69]

In general, there was support for the civil rights protesters after October 1968. The following month five unidentified members of the *Times*'s news team went to Derry to witness a civil rights demonstration specifically to test who might be telling the truth about the violence and its perpetrators. This exercise in self-imposed impartiality resulted in a report which highlighted intimidation of the marchers, and of the journalists, by groups of loyalists.[70] The *Times*'s historian remarked that reporters sent to Northern Ireland by the news desk viewed loyalists 'invariably in a bad light'.[71] This was largely true for other papers, but the realisation that providing civil rights might threaten political stability in Northern Ireland alarmed the *Daily Telegraph*. 'Reform cannot easily be accomplished so long as the powerful minority ... is still fundamentally opposed to the Union.'[72] In other words, discrimination was, though not ideal, understandable, if the population refused to accept the reality of Irish partition and the continuing British link.

Press reaction to the Westminster by-election victory, in April 1969, of Bernadette Devlin, was overwhelmingly favourable. Publishing a picture of her on a swing in an uncle's garden, the *Daily Express* burbled: 'She's Bernadette, she's 21, she's an MP, she's swinging.'[73] The *Mirror* headlined her as 'The Honourable Swinging Member for the marchers'.[74] The *Sun* called her 'a Celtic Joan of Arc' and a 'tiny crusader'.[75] When Devlin spoke two days later of an impending civil war the *Daily Sketch*, which had earlier referred to her as 'Joan of Tyrone', dared to headline her as 'Girl MP'.[76] Even the *Daily Telegraph* thought her 'enthusiastic and honest'.[77]

Her maiden speech was accorded the same kind of reception, with some papers apparently suspending their normal hostility to socialism by overlooking her real message. The headlines were wholly positive: 'Triumph for battling Bernadette' (*Sun*); 'Bernadette MP Blazes into Battle' (*Daily Sketch*); and 'Miss Devlin enthrals packed House with straight-from-the-heart speech' (*Times*).[78] The *Daily Mirror*'s Marje Proops wrote a laudatory profile.[79] But a *Daily Express* editorial was sceptical about Devlin's speech: her 'sneers' at O'Neill were 'totally unjust'.[80] The *Daily Mail*'s lengthy and impartial report was unfairly headlined 'The bitter song of Bernadette', while the *Daily Telegraph* chose not to make any comment at all.

These papers had already made up their minds to support Unionism come what may, while the others, the majority at the time, generally accepted the nationalist calls for civil rights. This implied support even for militant resistance by the Catholic population. All that changed from August 1969, when British troops were sent on to the streets of Belfast and Derry.[81] Suddenly, the tone and content of newspaper coverage altered. Devlin, pictured breaking a stone behind the barricades in Bogside, became a pariah.[82] (By 1972, she was a demon, according to the *Daily Mail*.)[83] Militant nationalists lost all newspaper sympathy. The IRA, hardly mentioned in the previous eighteen months, emerged as the bogeyman enemy. From now on, Britain's press supported its troops and the determination of the Westminster government, whatever its political hue, to maintain the Union.

Reporters began to rely on the army for both information and interpretation. This affected every paper's coverage, whether or not journalists willingly accepted what they were told. The *Guardian*, which gave more attention to the story than any other paper, considered itself balanced by sending out Harold Jackson and Simon Winchester to join Hoggart. Jackson was against partition, while Winchester was regarded as pro-army. Winchester later explained the 'commonality between the ordinary British squaddie . . . and the ordinary British reporter . . . you would understand and sympathise with him . . . like us, he had been sent out from England to do a job'.[84]

It did not mean that Winchester was wholly uncritical. In April 1970, he questioned the use of CS gas to quell a riot in West Belfast.[85] Three months later, after catching the army out in a blatant lie, he wrote that he would be unable in future 'to take the army's explanation about any single incident with less than a pinch of salt'.[86] He appeared to forget his pledge months later when accepting the army's word that soldiers had shot a 'petrol bomber'.[87] The problem for all reporters was their dependence on a source who they encouraged themselves to believe was impartial. For most papers, supporting the troops was a matter not only of patriotism but of commercial logic. Every soldier had a family in Britain and it might have threatened sales to have shown sympathy for the enemy. There were numerous examples of papers treating the soldiers posted to Belfast as if they were fighting a war in a foreign land, therefore requiring food parcels and other home comforts. Indeed, the *Daily Express*, by referring to them as 'Ulster hermits', implied that they were prisoners of war.[88]

Within Northern Ireland, where papers were as segregated as their readers, the title which tended to draw readers from both communities, in spite of its Unionist sympathies, was the *Belfast Telegraph*. Its leading articles had called for reforms throughout the late 1960s, with editor Jack Sayers pressuring O'Neill in private. But Sayers was suffering from poor health by 1969 and the owner, Lord Thomson, persuaded him to retire, appointing Eugene Wason in his place. Thomson argued that, under his ownership, the paper 'became a more liberal and fairer and much better paper' but 'too late to stop the Ulster tragedy'.[89] That is unfair to Sayers, whose commitment to reform is a matter of record.[90] Anyway, could a single paper, and a Unionist one at that, have stopped history in its tracks?

PART SIX: 1971–1975

11. THE SOARAWAY *SUN* AND STRIKEAWAY UNIONS

> In no other industry would lame ducks be allowed to swallow up so many millions of pounds, but then newspapers are unlike any other industry.[1]

About halfway through our history, this is an appropriate moment to take stock. The great post-war boom in newspaper sales had passed. Once newsprint restrictions ended and papers began to increase in size, creating unrestrained competition for advertising and readers, the weakest titles went to the wall. Confronted by new economic realities and the tougher competitive climate, some proprietors walked away. In their place came a new kind of owner – Thomson and Murdoch – more committed to the business of newspapers than to the newspaper business. Old-style dynasties – Aitken, Berry, Astor and Rothermere – lingered on, growing financially weaker, though the latter was more happily placed due to non-newspaper interests. The once ownerless Mirror group was incorporated within a conglomerate, as the *Financial Times* had been for a long time past. The *Guardian*'s trustee ownership looked fragile.

These changes largely reflected, if somewhat belatedly, the changing nature of monopoly capital. But the effect on the tone, design and content of the papers themselves appeared slight. With the arguable exception of the *Sun* from 1969, papers were not dramatically different from those that had gone before. There had been some evolutionary development, with better use of typography, and technological improvements allowing for better picture reproduction, but not much. Most newspapers also published relatively few pages. It wasn't that they couldn't attract advertising, in spite of competition from television, but that the costs of production were so high, and the union-imposed penalties so extreme, that extra pagination didn't make commercial sense. Adverts were often turned away. From the late 1960s onwards, owners and managers were aware of new printing systems that could have reduced manning. Print workers knew about them too, and were determined to retain their jobs by preventing the introduction of cost-saving or, in their terms, job-destroying, technology.

Like all journalists, from the moment I started in newspapers I was introduced to what we called 'the power of the printers'. On my first visit to the print works of my local paper, I was told by a colleague to watch out for myself. The compositors and lino men would want to inculcate the new boy with their ethos: journalists were fussy people who worried about whether this headline fitted with that paragraph, whether rules were straight, whether there were literals (spelling errors) in copy. I would discover that the stone, where pages were made up in metal formes, was a world ruled by members of the National Graphical Association (NGA) where the union leader, known as the father of the chapel, held sway.

In fact, as I got to know the compositors in that small printing outfit in Essex, I was allowed not only to touch the metal type but even to carry it around, a regular sub-editorial ploy to speed up production. They feigned irritation, giving me to understand that I was enjoying a special concession. I was given no such licence at the *Daily Mail* in Manchester, nor at the *Sun* in Fleet Street. Sub-editorial fingertips that strayed too close to type were liable to feel the rap of a pica rule. Friendships between the journalists who worked in the production area, stone subs, and compositors (comps) were very rare indeed.

Even more rare was contact between journalists and members of unions responsible for other parts of the process, such as the National Society of Operative Printers, Graphical and Media Personnel (Natsopa) or Society of Lithographic Artists, Designers and Engravers (Slade). What distinguished all these people, collectively known to journalists by the pejorative term 'inkies', from the reporters, subs and photographers was their disciplined union organisation. For all print workers, virtually every newspaper print factory – local, regional and national – was a closed shop. By comparison, the journalists' union, which I had joined at the urging of colleagues for social rather than industrial reasons, was a weak-kneed imitation of the various printing unions, without influence, authority or credibility. Even where it had signed up every member of staff, it had few closed-shop agreements.

In truth, there was no link between the workers by hand and the workers by brain. Of the many differences between journalists and other print workers, the key distinction lay in their attitude towards their work. Most journalists were committed to the content of their papers, worrying over stories, headlines and pictures, viewing their occupation as a profession and, in some cases, a vocation. They cared. Most print workers, by contrast, treated their work as a job, a repetitive set of mechanical tasks, often carried out in dirty and uncomfortable conditions. Their reward was, by the standards of other manual workers, very good indeed. The reason they were paid so much more than others was their ability to extract the maximum amount of money for the minimum amount of work. Unlike the journalists, they didn't really care whether the paper was published or not.

Since a newspaper, by nature, has a shelf life of only twenty-four hours, printers were able, by threat, by working to rule, by holding meetings at crucial production times, by refusing to break conventional demarcation lines, to bend managers to their will. Union leaders knew that owners could not face the loss of an issue because it wiped out all sales and advertising revenue, the paper's entire income. Antagonism between journalists and printers was common, with the former generally lined up on the side of their editors and owners. During disputes, when print unions refused to cross each other's picket lines, journalists generally did so. But the early 1970s marked a turning point in the activities of the National Union of Journalists (NUJ), which had been a largely ineffective body since its formation in 1907.[2]

Previously regarded by almost everyone in the industry as a bit of a joke, it had gradually built up a considerable membership across Britain (and Ireland). Many of its younger, working-class intake, less deferential, less hidebound by tradition, and conscious of the success enjoyed for so long by printers, decided to adopt similar tactics to the printing unions. The problem for the new militants was in securing 100 per cent membership and then getting members to obey union rules because there were still a significant number of individuals who loathed both the concept and practice of trades unionism. The NUJ finally found a way to overcome this problem by convincing the Labour government to enact legislation enforcing the closed shop.

Owners and editors, rightly fearing that journalists would use their union strength not only for bargaining over wages and conditions but also as leverage to control the editorial content of their papers, were determined not to allow the NUJ to win closed-shop rights. Of all the union battles fought during this period, this can be seen in hindsight as the most significant. The whole nature of the editorial hierarchy would have been thrown into doubt, with individual NUJ chapels nightly contesting the rights of owners and editors to publish certain stories and commentaries. With profits already hard to come by, owners would have lost their chance to make propaganda too. It is therefore plausible to speculate that some owners would have given up altogether. There would have been no point to their ownership. As we shall see, the move to impose journalists' closed shops failed, but increased NUJ militancy was to play an important part in shaping Fleet Street for at least a decade, affecting the fates of some titles.

By the early 1970s it was estimated that, of the eight national dailies, two were making substantial losses, one was breaking even and the other five were making 'inadequate' profits.[3] This financial assessment was, if anything, an understatement of the crisis. It was, however, proof that newspaper ownership was not all about profit. As Larry Lamb was fond of saying about Murdoch's proprietorship of the *Sun*, if Murdoch had wanted to make real money he would have opened a baked-beans factory instead.

Lamb, in maintaining that Murdoch chose to own papers simply because he loved them, endowed his ownership with a philanthropic, even poetic, rationale. However ardent and sincere Murdoch's love, it is difficult to believe it motivated such a hard-headed businessman. Murdoch, unlike so many of his rivals, had such an excellent grasp of the commercial side that he knew, in time, he could make his newspapers profitable, even when overmanned. He was also aware of the realities of power which stemmed from being a national newspaper proprietor, providing continual access to political leaders. Finally, Murdoch knew what Beaverbrook knew, even if he could not afford to be as candid as the late baron: he could make political and economic propaganda with his papers.

Making propaganda in these years was of paramount importance for owners alarmed at the drift of political and industrial events in Britain, and shaken by the impact of the international oil crisis precipitated by the Yom Kippur war of 1973. Inflation took off and strikes became common. Most notably, the miners struck in 1972, causing electricity cuts which restricted most of industry to a three-day week. Railway and dock strikes followed, prompting Ted Heath's Tory government to introduce a pay and prices freeze. Inflation was still a pressing problem, exacerbated by the quadrupling of oil prices, when the miners struck again in February 1974, leading to the imposition of another three-day week (see next chapter). Heath called an election, and lost to Harold Wilson, who led a minority Labour government until a second election in October gave him a working majority. The following year began with a banking crisis and stock prices spiralling downwards, with the *FT* index reaching a low of 146 in January 1975. By the end of 1975 Wilson was obliged to obtain a massive loan from the International Monetary Fund. Newspapers were not disinterested spectators of these events because they were suffering from falling advertising volume and revenue, the virtual doubling in the price of newsprint and continual industrial turmoil. Though few realised it at the time, it was the precursor to a sharp ideological turn, in the Tory party and among senior journalists.

As the *Sun*'s sales rose at a faster rate and volume than those of any paper in the post-war era, rival owners began to panic. Esmond Rothermere and his son Vere decided they could no longer sustain two declining newspapers, closing the *Daily Sketch* and merging it the with *Daily Mail*. Cudlipp shocked everyone by sticking to his pledge to retire at a relatively young age. Aitken, gloomily acknowledging that his company was facing economic disaster and with his flagship paper falling into deep trouble, was forced into making a number of questionable management and editorial decisions.

Editors took the flak too. New ones were appointed at the *Mail* and *Mirror*, while the editorship of the *Express* changed hands three times, the beginning of what was to become known as the paper's revolving-door syndrome. Editors had always been answerable to proprietors for sales, and their fates were largely linked to circulation statistics. Yet those same proprietors often constrained editors from an aggressive pursuit of sales, demanding that editorial material should interest them rather than readers, ordering adherence to a dogmatic political line, monitoring ethical standards, refusing funds for marketing and promotion. Murdoch's attitude to content, while no less prescriptive, elevated sales above any other consideration. Cudlipp, for all his swagger about his papers' circulation success, could not agree. He set his face against adopting the Murdochian approach, as did other owners and editors in these years. Murdoch's impact at this time was largely restricted to the popular papers. In the then separate world of the broadsheets, it was an altogether more complicated story. Thomson may have set the commercial pace, but Hartwell's *Daily Telegraph* was eclipsing his *Times*, which lost sales and money.

Britain's economic plight was reflected in the sudden overall circulation decline of the mid-1970s. Sales of all four of the serious daily broadsheets dived so badly in 1975 that the *Telegraph*, *Guardian* and *Times* were then selling fewer copies than in 1970, while the *FT* sold only 1,000 more. On Sundays, the pattern was similar with all three titles – *Sunday Times*, *Observer* and *Sunday Telegraph* – suffering from the economic malaise. Thomson's *Sunday Times* weathered the storm best of all, enjoying a circulation increase, a period of rising journalistic prestige and reasonable profits. By contrast, Hartwell's *Sunday Telegraph* was stuck on a sales plateau and drained money from its profitable daily title, while the *Observer* continued to suffer a miserable time.

One further, surely obvious, point to have emerged from the study of the preceding years is the paramount importance of owners. Despite their own increasingly fragile grip on the companies which produced their newspapers, they continued to decide the fate of those papers. Editors, no matter how talented they might be, could only perform to the best of their abilities if given enough licence by their masters. They required resources, time, understanding, forbearance and a measure of freedom. In the rare cases where these were available, it was possible to make comparisons. Under Thomson, who provided unlimited electricity, Evans's brilliance at the *Sunday Times* glowed. Rees-Mogg at the *Times*, through drawing current from the same grid as Evans, twinkled much less brightly. David English was about to make sparks with power having passed from the owner, Esmond Rothermere, to his son, Vere Harmsworth. But the editors of the *Express*, despite displaying a range of good qualities, suffered from continual power cuts which never gave them a chance to shine. Murdoch, ever the exception, combined a modern understanding of business with a fierce attachment to the proprietorial rights enjoyed by the old-style barons. His editors had no illusions: he was in charge.

The soaraway *Sun* steals the *Mirror*'s clothes

From the moment they produced their first tabloid *Sun*, Murdoch and Lamb were determined to make it Britain's highest-selling paper. During these years they set new circulation records, building sales at an unprecedented rate. At the beginning of 1970 the *Sun* was selling fewer than 2 million. By the end of 1975, it had risen to 3.5 million. During that time, the *Daily Sketch* closed, probably giving the *Sun* an extra half-million buyers; the *Daily Mirror* lost almost 500,000; and the *Daily Express* lost about 750,000. Murdoch and Lamb, a double act throughout this crucial period, turned the newspaper philosophy of Cudlipp and King on its head. Instead of trying to fashion a paper to appeal to people who were supposedly waving farewell to the working class and all that it stood for, they followed their gut instincts. They believed that the traditional *Sketch*, *Mirror* and *Express* readers, along with the twenty-something baby boomers who had yet to build a newspaper habit, wanted a much more basic diet: sex, scandal, sport, more sex, all leavened with a lively coverage of serious topics.

Reading the files was a trip down memory lane for me, a sub-editor in the cramped Bouverie Street office during the paper's first three years. The most notable feature was the relentless use of sex. Quite apart from the Page 3 girls, who didn't appear every day in the early 1970s, there was a sexy book of some kind serialised every week, such as *The Sensuous Woman*. The women's department, Pacesetters, churned out endless features on the theme of how to have better sex lives. Sport was a key ingredient, despite the *Sun*'s inability to publish reports of evening matches in northern cities. Unlike its rivals, with Manchester and, in most cases, Scottish print runs, every *Sun* was printed in London. This meant that early editions were off the stone and on the trains before a ball was kicked. To compensate, sports editor Frank Nicklin developed features-based content and shrewdly hired George Best, then at the height of his footballing and nightclubbing fame, as a columnist. Such was the *Sun*'s pulling power, the absence of live sport didn't seem to matter.

Cudlipp had shown how it was possible to make the *Daily Mirror* appear to be at the centre of news events, or even to make the news itself. Murdoch's *Sun* adopted the same policy and boosted it by the power of ten. When the paper was banned from a public library in a small Yorkshire town, Lamb splashed the story as 'The Silly Burghers of Sowerby Bridge' and won huge support from people who, just as Lamb desired, viewed such restrictions as a symbol of Victorian prudery.[4] He did the same when TV chiefs censored a *Sun* advert because of a reference to the River Piddle. The *Sun* had stolen the *Mirror*'s clothes, portraying itself as the mischievous champion of a new society which was liberated, tolerant and unstuffy. It made much of its anti-establishment irreverence while seizing on the burgeoning sexual permissiveness, youthful rebellion and social transformation with a certainty its rival failed to match.

The *Mirror*, by contrast, stuck fast to an agenda that seemed rather dated, preferring cuddly pictures of animals to naked women. Turning its back on sexy content, it continued to offer educative features with Mirrorscope replacing the Inside Page. One critic thought Mirrorscope 'spat in the readers' eyes by saying, "This isn't really for you. It's only for the most intellectual among you".'[5] The *Mirror*'s large staff of specialist writers were still able to provide news scoops, such as pop writer Don Short's exclusive about the Beatles' break-up, but the paper had lost its impetus.

In one of the very rare articles in a broadsheet extolling the *Sun*, the *Financial Times*'s Sheila Black referred to it having 'a soaraway, crest of the wave feeling'.[6] Lamb was doubly delighted: not only was Black married to the *Mirror*'s editor, Lee Howard, she had provided him with the slogan that would be used for years afterwards: 'the soaraway *Sun*'.

In spite of the rough-and-ready nature of the *Sun*, Lamb managed to attract three senior production journalists from the *Mirror*, one of whom, Roy Pittila, was to prove the mainstay of the back bench for more than twenty-five years. Although he wouldn't like to admit it, Lamb also relied heavily on Shrimsley, a man of considerable journalistic talent, with a biting wit and ferocious attention to detail. Both Lamb and Shrimsley, whose rivalry was to intensify, were never in any doubt about who called the tune. Murdoch harried them ceaselessly, criticising content, making improbable suggestions for stories or features, demanding ever more sales-winning gimmicks. Fast-paced, breathless and punchy TV commercials reeled off the goodies that could be found the next day. One sales campaign in 1972, which combined TV ads with a leaflet mail-shot into 13 million homes, cost £1.6 million.

Lamb generally handled Murdoch well, heading off his owner's more bizarre editorial ideas, but he could be rough on executives who misunderstood the intentions behind his scrawled sketches on layout pads. His temper, though rarely displayed on the editorial floor, was frightening. Upset by insults from sub-editors on his first visit to the local Fleet Street pub, the Tipperary, Lamb stopped socialising with staff. His shyness was interpreted as aloofness, and he became a remote figure.

This was just one manifestation of the growing distance between staff and bosses as the original climate of camaraderie dissolved. Reporters and sub-editors, sensing that Murdoch was making a fortune from the ever increasing sales, began to demand better pay and conditions, and disruptive NUJ chapel meetings became common. There were several reasons for the new militancy: some former *Herald* and old *Sun* staff had a strong socialist outlook; some newer imports, especially from Australia, held uncompromising views about Murdoch and had experience of union confrontations; some, such as me, were just beginning to realise that there was more to journalism than individual ambition.

Journalists were also reacting to the success, as they saw it, of the print unions, and responding to the wider climate of industrial conflict in which strikes were commonplace. Murdoch, Lamb and Shrimsley – the latter's politics had always been Conservative – began moving in the opposite direction, questioning whether the *Sun* should continue to support a party which was funded by the unions they had come to despise. So the *Sun*'s political line changed, moving gradually to the right. 'We were all Labour-inclined when we started the *Sun*,' Murdoch later said, 'but I think we grew pretty disillusioned along with the rest of the country.'[7] There can be little doubt that many *Mirror* readers were among those who were disillusioned, another reason for a big switch from one paper to the other. The discovery in the late 1960s that many working-class voters were not as loyal to their parties as originally thought was to prove a boon for the *Sun*.[8] Its readership, drawn mainly from the skilled working class in the social group C2, were identified as the nation's most volatile swing voters. Their lack of party allegiance was paralleled by a lack of newspaper allegiance.

From 1970 onwards, the *Sun* was not enamoured with Labour's Harold Wilson but also remained lukewarm towards the Tory prime minister, Edward Heath. Labour's two 1974 victories, during which the *Sun* was broadly agnostic, led to Heath's downfall and by the time Margaret Thatcher replaced him as Conservative leader in February 1975, Murdoch and Lamb had largely made up their minds about taking a radical political step. The *Sun*, bastard heir of the trades union-owned *Daily Herald*, would support the party dedicated to eradicating union power from the land.

In 1972, Shrimsley, then forty-one, was given the editor's chair with Lamb being titled editorial director. Shrimsley, a Northampton grammar school boy who had started at the Press Association aged sixteen, was probably the most intelligent popular paper editor of the era. He had experience as an editor, running the *Daily Mirror* in the north, but left the group in frustration when sidelined by Cudlipp. He had been editing the *Liverpool Daily Post* for a year when he answered Murdoch's call. His intellectual superiority was a strength and a weakness: while most tabloid editors worked on gut instinct and spontaneity, he tended to agonise over decisions and, as he dwelt on them, would have second, third and fourth thoughts. It wasn't a case of indecisiveness; each new thought was usually an improvement. Allied to his inability to delegate, believing that he could and should do everything himself, it didn't make him popular. Senior sub-editors and page designers were often frustrated by Shrimsley's changes of mind and one of them, Jack Paterson, nicknamed him 'the Avon Lady', after the door-to-door cosmetic saleswomen, 'because every time Bernard calls he gives you a new make-up'. But there was no doubting Shrimsley's considerable talent.

Lamb was often abroad on Murdoch's behalf as his restless owner looked to expand his empire. His profits from the *Sun* and the *News of the World* funded his first modest venture into the United States in 1973 when he bought two small papers in San Antonio, Texas. Noting the success of the sensational supermarket tabloid, the *National Enquirer*, Murdoch launched the lookalike *National Star*.

Lamb also oversaw the *News of the World*, soon agreeing with Murdoch that the editor, Tiny Lear, was anything but the right man for the job. The rehash of the Profumo–Keeler revelations showed that, despite the criticism, there was a groundswell of reader interest in scandalous investigations. So Lear hired two key reporters from the *Sunday People*, Mike Gabbert and Trevor Kempson, who were soon masterminding most of the paper's sexy exposés.

Perhaps the most notorious of the period involved a junior minister, Lord Lambton. To obtain its information on Lambton, the paper concealed a camera behind a two-way mirror in the bedroom of a prostitute's flat, along with a tape recorder. He was pictured with two women and was smoking cannabis. But Lear was too nervous to use the material, handing the evidence instead to the prostitute and her partner, who promptly took it to the *Sunday People*. Before anything was published, Lambton heard that the story was circulating and resigned. Lord Jellicoe, leader of the House of Lords, who was involved with another prostitute and feared exposure, also quit.[9] There was yet another public storm about whether the *NoW*'s methods of obtaining material were appropriate. The Press Council censured the paper for giving the film and recordings to 'persons of ill repute', but the *NoW* was exonerated to an extent when Lord Diplock's security commission later adjudged that there had been 'a potential risk to security' in Lambton's behaviour.

It wasn't much of a shock when Lear's editorship came to an end in December 1973 with the paper selling just under 6 million, but his replacement was a surprise. In many respects, Peter Stephens was rather like Lear, mild-mannered, serious and buttoned up. He had been editor of the *Newcastle Journal* for four years until joining the *Sun* in 1970 as an assistant editor, where he was known for his diplomacy. He certainly tried to calm me down on several occasions when, as both a junior executive and a union militant, I managed to anger staff working under me and, for different reasons, the management. Considered to be a safe pair of hands, a notorious inhibition for a popular paper editor, Stephens lasted only a year. Sales began to decline sharply during his regime, though it would be unduly harsh to blame him because the Sunday popular market had begun to collapse. Indeed, as the annual report put it, the *NoW* more than held its market share. In 1975, Stephens was the victim of a set of corporate chessboard moves caused by the deteriorating relationship between Lamb and Shrimsley. There could only be one *Sun* editor, and both thought they should be that one.

To solve the problem, Murdoch gave Lamb back his *Sun* editorship, though he remained editorial director, and moved Shrimsley downstairs to edit the *NoW*. In placating Stephens, who felt he been hard done by in losing his editorship and returning as number three to the *Sun*, Murdoch told him: 'You were too nice a guy to edit the *News of the World*.'[10] Murdoch was not too nice to own it, however.

Cudlipp sails off into the sunset

The early years of the *Sun* were traumatic for the *Daily Mirror* because the paper's executives couldn't grasp what they were doing wrong or what the *Sun* was doing right. There often comes a point at which a successful paper stands for a whole set of values independently of the people who run it. This is both a blessing and a danger. It is the moment when editors and journalists say to themselves: 'What would the *Mirror* say about this?'[11]

For the *Daily Mirror* that point was probably reached by the late 1950s. It had been the case at the *Daily Express* from the 1930s, and would not happen to the *Daily Mail* until the late 1970s. It is not simply a case of a newspaper attaining a personality of its own, though that is one key element. The moment of transformation, from mere newspaper into an institution, occurs when the vast majority of the population – non-readers as well as readers – comes to recognise what a particular paper symbolises. They may not share its values, but they know what they are and can predict fairly accurately what the paper will say, and how it will react, to most situations. There are huge advantages for the paper in achieving such a breakthrough: every journalist on the paper will know how to approach every story, which ones to write, how to 'angle' them, what headline is appropriate, which of them merit follow-ups or features. Similarly, both regular and casual readers become comfortable with the paper: despite the differences, they know what to expect.

The news might surprise. The columnists might shock. The pictures might amaze. The leading articles might inflame. But these essential differences exist within a format of regularity. This is best illustrated by the repetitive nature of the paper's 'furniture', its back-of-paper material, such as crosswords, cartoon strips and entertainment guides. It is the totality of the paper, its politics and its racing-form guide, its crime scoops and its gardening column, which ensure that habitual readers remain loyal. Yet it is this very familiarity for readers, and the constant need for journalists to satisfy it, which can prove disastrous for a paper. After a period of time, the institution finds itself unable to adapt. Editors and journalists tend to become reactive, functioning as the servants of a staid concept. Their paper loses its sense of adventure, failing to move with the times. Trapped by its success by having won the hearts and minds of one generation, it is unable to win over the next. That was the central problem for the *Daily Mirror* from the beginning of the 1970s. When the paper's political historian, Maurice Edelman, asked in 1966, 'Can the *Mirror* retain the impetus of its youth? Can it still blow battle bugles for the young?' it was meant to be a rhetorical question.[12] Neither he, nor Cudlipp, could foresee the *Mirror*'s coming dilemma.

In time-honoured fashion, the first to pay the price of the *Sun*'s success was the *Mirror* editor, Lee Howard. Though he had been planning to retire at sixty, Cudlipp arbitrarily decided he must go a year early. Howard, according to his secretary, was 'surprised'.[13] In fact, he was the single senior *Mirror* executive with a realistic view of the *Sun*'s success. He once told Mike Molloy that he couldn't understand why the *Mirror* didn't sell 7 million: it was failing to appeal to at least 2 million potential readers by being too serious.[14]

Tony Miles, then forty, had been with the *Mirror* since 1954, spending twelve years as one of its best and most prolific feature writers. After grammar school, he had started on a weekly paper at sixteen and made it to the *Mirror* via evening papers in Nottingham and Brighton. Promoted to assistant editor in 1967 and running Inside Page from its inception, his rise to the editor's chair just four years later took rivals by surprise. Though Howard had shown a grudging regard for the *Sun*, Miles refused to be lured in its direction. A tough and prickly character, with a habit of calling everyone 'cock', he wanted the *Mirror* to maintain its distance from a paper he regarded as down-market. One thorn in Miles's side was his northern editor, Derek Jameson, who regarded his London boss as 'the most irascible man I ever met in newspapers'.[15] Jameson wanted to compete head on with the *Sun* and some time in 1974 started to publish Page 3 pictures.[16] When Miles saw what he was doing he ordered him to stop.

For all its difficulties, the *Mirror* was still selling almost 4.4 million and remained a highly professional outfit with, according to one of its former junior executives, 'the best subs' table in the world'.[17] I worked briefly as a *Mirror* sub at the end of Howard's editorship and was amazed at the contrast with the *Sun*: I had come from a racy sports car to a vintage Rolls-Royce. Staffing was much higher, the place worked like clockwork, with greater attention to detail, and it had a glamour the rough-and-ready *Sun* could not match. It was a purring machine, said Ernie Burrington, who worked on the *Mirror* backbench after being fired as night editor of the *Sun* by Lamb.[18] Nonchalance and confidence, however, often breed complacency.

Falling revenue for the *Mirror* also meant that in May 1971 the *Mirror*'s controller – Don Ryder, chairman of Reed International – increased the *Daily Mirror*'s cover price from 2.5p to 4p. 'Prices are too low,' he said. Asked whether Murdoch would see it his way, he replied: 'I'm sure he will. He faces the same economic facts as everyone else.'[19] In fact, Murdoch delayed raising the *Sun*'s price for a good while in order to take advantage of the price differential.

Fleet Street didn't take to Ryder. Renowned as an early riser, reaching the office at 7 a.m. sharp each day, his only known recreation was playing chess with his wife. A sceptical Wintour regarded him in 1972 as a 'somewhat cheerless work-oriented character' who 'has yet to show that he can inspire a newspaper'. Ryder was 'a man with much to learn about newspapers and not too much time to spare for his education'.[20] In fact, Ryder didn't hang around for lessons, leaving to become chairman of the National Enterprise

Board in 1975 when he was ennobled. Before going, he made Alex Jarratt, a former career civil servant, managing director of IPC newspapers, and Jarratt then inherited Ryder's chief executive title.

There was a lack of will at the top. In 1971, when the IRA bombed the Belfast printing plant, virtually destroying the press laid down six years before to experiment with web offset and colour printing, IPC decided not to rebuild it. It wasn't economically viable but it had been a move in the right direction. The *Mirror* therefore withdrew to Manchester to publish its Irish editions.

For Cudlipp, the great days were over. With Murdoch's *Sun* set fair on its upward trajectory and the *Mirror* heading in the opposite direction, he turned his back on Fleet Street. He had told friends years before that he would retire at sixty, a promise he repeated at the Labour party conference in October 1972: 'Our newspapers especially appeal to the younger generations, and I feel it would be an unpardonable vanity for a man of over sixty to have the final word on editorial plans and policies.'[21] Even so, many people didn't really believe it, or want to believe it, when Cudlipp stepped down on his birthday in August 1973 and accepted a knighthood. He was in good health. He was still capable of journalistic flights of fancy. He certainly hadn't groomed a youthful successor at the *Mirror*, although he entertained hopes that the *Sunday Times*'s Harry Evans would succeed him. Evans resisted the temptation.[22] Instead, Cudlipp's friend, Sydney Jacobson, who was sixty-four, initially took his post.

Cudlipp may have been cast down by the *Sun*'s rise, but he had never run from a fight and that played no part in his decision. His widow Jodi stressed: 'He was not, repeat not, daunted by Murdoch's success. He admired Rupert, but despised him for thinking more about money than editorial quality, integrity and ethics.'[23] She believed he truly wanted to do other things, such as writing, making TV programmes, sailing his boat from Chichester harbour, spending time at their Spanish villa, enjoying his relationship with her, and coaching their noisy parrot to squawk: 'Buy the *Daily Mirror*'. In 1974, Sir Hugh became Lord Cudlipp of Aldingbourne and took the Labour whip until 1981 when he switched to the Social Democrats. He was to make a brief, unhappy, return to the *Mirror* building a few years later (see below, p. 398), but the long Cudlipp era had ended.

Jacobson's succession to the top job was fortuitously timed. As the group's political expert, he was in charge in 1974, a year in which there were two general elections, both won by Labour. Jacobson, determined that Labour should succeed, produced poster-style front pages, inspired every leading article and oversaw all political stories. Political editor Terry Lancaster thought Jacobson's contributions significant and prime minister Harold Wilson agreed, rewarding Jacobson, who had previously refused a knighthood, with a life peerage after his retirement in 1975.

Before Cudlipp went, he shuffled the pack at his Sunday titles in March 1972. He relieved Michael Christiansen of his 'increasingly odd' editorship of the *Sunday Mirror* after eight years.[24] An insight into Christiansen's eccentricity was provided by one of his former columnists, Quentin Crewe. After informing him that the paper was going upmarket, he told Crewe he could write about 'butterflies, the habits of elvers, astronomy, aspects of the French Revolution or speculations on the nature of pithecanthropus'.[25] Christiansen should have been sidelined but, out of affection, he was offered a unique choice: the *Daily Mirror* deputy editorship or the sack.[26] Bob Edwards, who had successfully edited the *People* for six years, was translated to the *Sunday Mirror*, his fourth national paper editorship, a record he would hold for years to come. Geoff Pinnington, who had been number two at the *Daily Mirror* and, before that, a highly efficient night editor, was appointed editor of the *People*.

Pinnington was fifty-three by the time he became an editor, and many thought he should have been given the chair at the *Daily Mirror* instead of Miles. Ernie Burrington, Pinnington's deputy at the *People*, believed that Cudlipp 'probably considered Geoff too strong a personality to handle' and, on balance, chose Miles because he appeared more loyal, or perhaps more malleable.[27] Pinnington was, without doubt, his own man. Raised in Cheshire, he won a scholarship to London University's King's College before joining the RAF at the outbreak of war and rising to squadron leader in 38 Bomber Command. He began his journalistic career, aged twenty-seven, at a Middlesex-based group and was rapidly promoted to edit the newly launched *Kensington Post*, which he ran initially from two tables at the local library. Within a year, Pinnington, a lifelong socialist, accepted a drop in salary to take a job at the *Daily Herald*. By 1950 he was northern editor of the *Herald* and wasn't in Manchester too long before becoming deputy editor in London. Ten years later, miffed at losing the editorship to John Beavan, he answered Hugh Cudlipp's call to join the *Daily Mirror* night desk. By the time I worked under him as a sub he was recognised as the *Mirror*'s kingpin, much respected for his production skills and his nurturing of young talent.

It may be argued that Pinnington didn't grasp the *People*'s editorial agenda, pioneered by Sam Campbell, as well as Edwards had done. But his record shows that he wasn't far behind. Under him, the *People* had a string of exposés. One of its most sensational revelations, obtained by a reporter going under cover, was the use of dogs to test the safety of cigarettes: the picture of the 'smoking beagles', as it became known, was one of the most memorable pictures ever published.[28] *People* reporters also revealed a football bribery scandal,[29] disclosed a greyhound betting fraud which led to the arrest of four men,[30] and discovered that the head of Scotland Yard's flying squad had a enjoyed a free foreign holiday courtesy of a pornographer with a crime record. The paper did sail close to the wind in the Lord Lambton scandal, but emerged unscathed.

Pinnington also introduced some softer, *Mirror*-style features, especially once he took the paper from broadsheet to tabloid in September 1974, a management decision prompted by an expectation of increased advertising revenue but unpopular with most of the journalistic staff.[31] On reviewing the files, it is arguable that this was an unfortunate change. Though the *People* was not a serious paper, the broadsheet format gave it a credibility its tabloid offspring never quite managed to capture. Both Pinnington and Bob Edwards at the *Sunday Mirror* were experienced popular-paper journalists, and neither was especially keen to publish material as salacious as that found in the *News of the World*. Both were staunch Labour party supporters, keenly interested in politics, serious men without being in the least stuffy. Yet they had to acknowledge that they had entered more permissive times and, gradually, the content of their papers changed. It marked the beginning of an editorial convergence between two titles which had previously had quite distinct agendas, a move that was to harm both.

Two years later, in 1974, with Cudlipp and Jacobson having gone, Miles was promoted by the Reed board to editorial director. The *Daily Mirror* editorship passed, incongruously, to his deputy, Mike Christiansen, fired just two years before from the *Sunday Mirror* for eccentric behaviour, such as hiring staff based on their cricketing abilities. He had been editor for only a few months when he suffered a stroke while staying with the paper's Paris correspondent, and his deputy, Mike Molloy, took over as caretaker. When it became clear that Christiansen's health was too fragile for him to edit, he was shunted off to investigate the introduction of new technology and Molloy was confirmed as editor in December 1975.

During that period of uncertainty, with the *Sun* continuing to make inroads into its sale, Miles reluctantly relaxed his ban on *Sun*-style tit-and-bum content.[32] To the dismay of some staff and the applause of others, towards the end of 1975 the *Mirror* published a topless picture of the model Jilly Johnson, and nudes appeared occasionally after that, with Jameson's northern editions using them more regularly.

Farewell to the *Daily Sketch*: the night of the long envelopes

Figures released in March 1971 showed that the previous year's annual loss at the *Daily Mail* was £825,000 and at the *Daily Sketch*, £250,000. Costs were rising and the group faced greater losses in future. The second Lord Rothermere, Esmond, was in failing health and wisely allowed his son, Vere Harmsworth, to take the executive decision to deal with a problem which was rapidly turning into a crisis. As deputy chairman of Associated Newspapers, Harmsworth had read a report by management consultants McKinseys, which suggested that the *Mail* – then a broadsheet with sales of 1.8 million and suffering genteel decline – might work better as a tabloid.[33] The circulation manager also favoured the *Mail* becoming 'the first serious, really upmarket tabloid'.[34]

Harmsworth was also aware of the disastrous situation at his current down-market tabloid, the *Sketch*, which was selling barely 800,000 copies. Despite the energy of its editor, David English, and some improvement to its journalism, its prospects had been devastated by the success of Murdoch's *Sun*. English was frustrated, aware that the rest of Fleet Street was counting the days to his paper's closure. His career seemed about to go into reverse and Beaverbrook Newspapers' owner, Max Aitken, chose the right psychological moment to offer him the position he had coveted for so long: the editorship of the *Daily Express*.

English was contemplating the proposal when he was summoned by Harmsworth, a long-time English admirer, and offered a unique challenge. Harmsworth explained the financial imperative of merging the *Mail* and *Sketch*, allowing the group to shed more than 1,700 staff and so make enormous savings on overheads and operating costs. Then he asked English if he would oversee the merger and help to create a new kind of tabloid bearing the *Daily Mail* title. The two men agreed that the *Sketch* had reached the end of its natural life, and rapidly realised that they shared similar views about the *Mail*'s lack of appeal: it was old-fashioned, predictable and unchallenging. In trying to compensate for its shortcomings it had relied on inventive, fussy and ultimately unsuccessful design.

It was also a reactive paper, lacking the kind of journalistic flair exhibited by the *Sun* and the *Mirror*. But these were mass-market papers. Was it possible, in a tabloid format, to avoid looking, sounding and feeling like them, yet incorporate their positive journalistic approach? Could a tabloid *Mail* hold the centre ground, being both serious (and therefore credible) and frivolous (and therefore entertaining)? Could it, in English's phrase at the time, appeal to people who were 'traditional without being reactionary'?[35] Most important of all, was there an audience – middle of the road, middle brow, middle class, politically conservative yet socially aspirant – for such a paper?

To avoid comparisons with the *Mirror* and *Sun* – later known by the generic term 'red-tops' due to their red mastheads and to distinguish them from middle-market tabloids – Harmsworth called his new *Mail* a 'compact'. The name never caught on, but the originality of the editorial concept did, a sober make-up, with a serif typeface and a structure which echoed that of the serious broadsheets. There would still be leader and op-ed pages with lengthy topical features.

The risk they were taking was obvious. Cudlipp and King's attempt to forge a modern paper to reflect changed times and circumstances, the original 1964 *Sun*, had failed dismally. Yet English and Harmsworth were trying to do something very similar just seven years later. They had one important advantage because the profile of the *Mail*'s current readership was far closer in spirit to the new target audience than the old *Sun*'s had been. If they were to stand any chance of success, what they needed was to retain as many *Mail* and *Sketch* readers as possible while gradually wooing the younger generation who would once have chosen the *Daily Express.*

Despite their relative youth – English was thirty-nine, Harmsworth forty-five – they were prepared for a lengthy circulation battle, aware that the *Sun* was attracting a mass audience, that broadsheets were growing and that the centre ground inhabited by the *Mail* and *Express* was being squeezed. By the middle of March, they were convinced enough of their new venture for Harmsworth to announce that the sixty-three-year-old *Daily Sketch* would be closed in sixty-three days' time.[36] Laurie Pignon, a *Sketch* sports columnist, recalled the tense meeting as English addressed his staff. 'We never really knew why the *Sketch* was closed,' he said. 'We believed it subsidised the *Mail* by taking an undue amount of shared costs.'[37] Pignon was one of the *Sketch* staff who prospered by joining the *Mail.*

The merger was Fleet Street's most dramatic episode since the closure of the *News Chronicle.* Managing director Mick Shields exhibited great negotiating skills in getting the print unions to agree to job cuts without industrial action. For journalists, it was particularly traumatic. *Mail* editor Arthur Brittenden was the first to know that his Northcliffe House days were over, but neither he nor his staff foresaw English's intention of engineering a wholesale clear-out of *Mail* journalists in favour of his *Sketch* team. Of the 650 editorial staff on the *Mail* and 180 on the *Sketch,* only 390 were offered jobs, which meant 440 people were to be fired. The method for carrying out this mass cull was by the simple expedient of senior executives handing to their staffs a letter telling them they were not wanted. They were written by editorial director Howard French, the former *Sketch* editor, and were inevitably dubbed 'French letters'.[38] This tear-stained 'night of the long white envelopes' affected some people so badly, such as political editor Walter Terry, that they never forgot or forgave what happened.

Many *Mail* 'stars', including Bernard Levin and Barry Norman, were fired. Levin's response, a vitriolic piece in the *Times,* attracted a libel writ, forcing Levin and the paper to apologise for making unjustified charges against Harmsworth.[39] Norman eventually made a name for himself in a different medium, as television's best-known film reviewer. The *Mail*'s celebrated South African correspondent, Peter Younghusband – famed for once swimming across 'the shark-infested waters of the Indian ocean' to file a scoop[40] – was organising a Rothermere visit when he was fired. Most of the seventy journalists imported into the *Mail* from the *Sketch* were given the senior jobs and English set about developing his own young writers, such as Lynda Lee-Potter, Ian Wooldridge, Ann Leslie and Nigel Dempster.

On 11 May 1971, English's deputy, Lou Kirby, produced the last *Daily Sketch,* composed of just four pages wrapped around the new-look tabloid *Mail,* designed to encourage as many *Sketch* readers as possible to make the switch to the following day's merged title. The ploy failed miserably. Sales dropped so dramatically that within six months they were 100,000 below the total the unmerged *Mail* had enjoyed, a fact gleefully seized on by Charles Wintour, who had no time for English.[41]

The following two years, with sales still sliding, were tough for Harmsworth, who was 'disparaged behind his back'.[42] But Shields ensured that internal opposition to Harmsworth didn't turn into rebellion. A bright grammar school boy, he had joined Associated in 1948, and risen to advertising director before setting up National Opinion Polls, a market-research company under the Associated umbrella. After his secondment to Harmsworth Investments, where he did valuable work by diversifying Associated's interests, Harmsworth's wife pushed for Shields to join the merger project.

So what kind of man was Vere Harold Esmond Harmsworth, son of the second Lord Rothermere? Born in 1925, he was a poor student during his single year at Eton and then at Kent School in Connecticut. He returned to Britain, and briefly Eton, just before D-Day. He failed to get into university and even failed to get a commission, being conscripted in the army as a private, an experience he later told everyone he had thoroughly enjoyed. He impressed the other conscripts, drawn mainly from Glasgow's Gorbals, with his prowess as a boxer. It gave him, he said, an invaluable insight into 'people', his euphemism for the working class.

In 1948 he went to Canada to work in a paper mill producing newsprint before joining the family firm in 1952. He grew disenchanted with the way his father Esmond ran the company and largely fumed on the sidelines until 1971. Harmsworth was a sort of disestablished member of the establishment. He displayed many of the eccentricities of his class, with an apparent disdain for bourgeois notions of respectability. Yet he was to prove a far shrewder proprietor than his father, ensuring that the Harmsworth dynasty would be the only one to own newspapers continuously from the nineteenth into the twenty-first centuries. He seemed uninhibited by the strain of taking over the business while his father was still alive. Tall, rather pudgy even in his forties, he was difficult for outsiders to get to know. The first time I met him, my opening remark was met with silence and, disconcertingly, so was a follow-up question. Yet, when I burbled something about going off to get a drink, he suddenly answered my original question, telling me why, in his opinion, I was wrong. Then he strode off.

In 1957 he married a film actress, Beverley Brooks, who bore him three children, Geraldine, Camilla and Jonathan. She was renowned for her social life, first becoming a salon hostess and later frequenting nightclubs. She earned from *Private Eye*'s – and also the *Mail*'s – gossip columnist Nigel Dempster the unforgettable nickname 'Bubbles'.

Harmsworth and his sisters, alarmed at the possible burden of capital transfer taxes, were to spend most of their lives in tax exile. It meant that Vere lived a nomadic life, staying round the year in Paris, Manhattan and Tokyo, spending only ninety days in Britain at his Eaton Square apartment or his

Sussex house. He and English built up 'an almost telepathic understanding' which was to be the envy of virtually every other Fleet Street editor.[43] By working closely together, sharing a vision of their flagship paper, they overcame the distance, and often froideur, between owner and editor.

In many ways, and as is so often the case with successful editors, the ethos of the *Mail* perfectly mirrored English's own political and social views. He despised socialism and all its works, especially organised labour. He empathised with people, like himself, who were eager to better themselves. He was entrepreneurial, having sold at a good profit a chain of free newspapers launched from his Kent home. Unlike many editors, who paid scant attention to their families, English put his family first and would later transform this into a *Mail* obsession with 'family values'. He and Harmsworth also appreciated the importance of attracting women readers, giving rise to a celebrated campaign slogan: 'Every woman needs her *Daily Mail*'.[44] Harmsworth said they realised 'women were the last emergent group with spending power, and the ability to influence spending'.[45]

In the early years of English's editorship, the *Mail* was rather unsophisticated and very small, often no more than twelve or sixteen pages. It is possible to sense him going through his own learning process, trying out ideas that didn't work, but the formula was clear. His first political target was Harold Wilson, before and after his election in 1974 as prime minister. One *Daily Mail* story of that period sought to show that the brother of Marcia Williams, Wilson's powerful secretary, had benefited from a dubious project to develop coal slag-heaps in Wigan. The smear proved unsuccessful. By the end of 1975, the *Mail* was selling 1.73 million copies, fewer than in its pre-merged state in early 1971. But it had been rising since its deepest trough in 1972 and English could point to the fact that the *Daily Express* had not managed to reverse its faster downward trend, so the gap between the two was narrowing. The *Mail* was on its way.

Harmsworth's London *Evening News*, on the other hand, was going nowhere. John Gold had proved a failure as editor, leading to his replacement in 1972 by his fifty-five-year-old deputy, Don Boddie. Many of the old hands welcomed the decision, but Boddie's skills at production obscured his faults. Two of the most obvious were a lack of vision and a readiness to satisfy Harmsworth's whims which often exceeded his master's wishes. One common complaint of Harmsworth's was that the *Evening News* often spoke above its readers' heads, even publishing words they might not understand. Early in 1973, he happened to mention one multi-syllable example in a book review by the paper's senior critic, Kenneth Allsop. Boddie immediately summoned his literary editor, Eddie Campbell, and ordered him to ensure it didn't happen again. Campbell was eager to keep Allsop, a respected author who was also famous as a BBC TV presenter. So the two men agreed to stick to plainer English. Inevitably, Boddie soon spotted a word he felt too obscure for his readers and shocked both men by firing Allsop on the spot, refusing to change his mind. A sympathetic Campbell urged Allsop to approach Charles Wintour at the *Evening Standard*, which he did, but Wintour told him he had nothing to offer. Allsop, utterly downcast, returned to his Dorset home in May 1973, took an overdose of painkillers, and was found dead the next day. Since there was no suicide note, an inquest returned an open verdict. Campbell, who was eighty-four when we spoke, told me: 'I have never told anyone this, but I know his sacking by Boddie was the trigger that led him to kill himself.'[46]

Boddie, like so many who accede too readily to their owner's demands, discovered that it didn't help. He was fired after less than two years, and the introduction of Lou Kirby into the editor's chair in 1974 led to another radical decision: the broadsheet *News* followed the *Mail* by going tabloid. Kirby, English's deputy, set out to take the *News* into *Mail* territory, a much more difficult task because the *Evening Standard* already had a largely ABC1 readership, the major reason for its grip on the lucrative ad market. Since the *News*'s traditional audience was among the lower social classes it couldn't generate enough advertising revenue.

Kirby, a 45-year-old Liverpudlian who trained on the *Wolverhampton Express & Star*, had spent the rest of his journalistic career from 1953 with Associated, rising through the ranks as a *Mail* reporter and *Sketch* political writer. He was resented by the *Evening News* old guard, as were his imported *Mail* colleagues who took charge of production. 'It was a special newspaper, old-fashioned, and in need of new blood,' recalled Kirby. 'There were a lot of oddballs around but I did come to realise they were a necessary part of the operation.'[47]

Piranha Teeth draws blood in Scotland

While Harmsworth was taking radical action to sort out his family company, Max Aitken was attempting to do the same with his. But he chose a very different way of going about the task. He put his faith in Jocelyn 'Piranha Teeth' Stevens in 1971 by promoting him to the board of Beaverbrook Newspapers and giving him a virtually free hand in sorting out the financial problems besetting the group. A profit of £3.3 million reported in June 1972 shrank to £1.5 million the year after, and an internal report – noting the rise in newsprint prices and in industrial action – projected the likelihood of a loss in 1974. Lloyds Bank was unhappy, threatening to withdraw its line of credit. Managing director John Coote's misguided voluntary redundancy scheme led to 120 journalists leaving, many of them talented individuals who joined the *Daily Mail*.[48] *Sunday Express* editor John Junor thought it 'an almost unbelievable blunder'.[49]

The savings were small, and both Coote and Stevens, along with the rest of the board, knowing that drastic cost-cutting was required, decided on the closure of the Glasgow print works. Before that, Stevens settled accounts with his management rival, Coote. In January 1973, Stevens urged Aitken to place him in total control of the newspapers and kick Coote aside to oversee subsidiary companies and handle newsprint buying. This allowed Stevens to cut corners that Coote found 'distasteful', eventually leading to his resignation early in 1975.[50] For all his bluster, Coote had acted as a wise counsellor to Aitken and he had lost a loyal executive.

Aitken and Stevens knew that the retreat from Glasgow would be unpopular. Just six years before, Aitken had hosted a great banquet in the city to celebrate forty years of the Scottish *Daily Express.*[51] They faced another problem because the group owned the city's *Evening Citizen*, which was also printed on the Albion Street presses. It was then selling 166,000 copies while its rival, the *Evening Times*, sold 181,000. Stevens shrewdly decided to sell the *Citizen* title to the owner of the *Times*, Scottish and Universal Investments (SUITS) chaired by Sir Hugh Fraser. Knowing he would obtain a far higher price if Fraser remained unaware of Beaverbrook's pressing need to dispose of the print works, Stevens kept it secret throughout the negotiations with Fraser, finally persuading SUITS to pay £2.75 million.

Within days, on 19 March 1974, Fraser realised just how clever Stevens had been. It was announced that Beaverbrook was closing Albion Street: printing of the *Scottish Daily Express* and *Scottish Sunday Express* was being transferred to Manchester. The *Evening Citizen* was being merged, well submerged, into the *Evening Times*, meaning that yet another city would be served by a monopoly title.[52] Only 200 of the 2,000 Glasgow staff would be kept on the payroll, and there would be no trouble finding the redundancy money: the sale of the *Citizen*, along with government grants, would cover almost all that was required.

The closure was a bitter affair, far more contentious than Associated's closure of its Edinburgh plant in 1970 which printed the small circulation *Scottish Daily Mail.*[53] Stevens, who was showered with soot by angry printers, said later: 'I hated shutting the Glasgow office . . . but I was completely cold about it because I knew that otherwise we would not survive . . . the Glasgow closure has provided the most immense savings. It has given us a breathing space which will get us into the future.'[54] That was all it was, a breathing space. Beaverbrook's pre-tax profit of £3.2 million announced in June 1975 didn't come anywhere near the total required for urgent investment on new presses at the Fleet Street building. Soon the group's borrowings were in excess of £14 million.

If anything, the editorial situation at the *Daily Express* was worse than the financial. Under Derek Marks's uninspired editorship the paper's decline had steepened, with thousands of readers switching to the *Sun.* In his five-year tenure, Marks lost 600,000 buyers with his rather up-market and decidedly boring recipe, but he seemed astonished when he was fired in April 1971. On hearing the identity of his successor he echoed a comment made almost twenty years before by Kenneth Tynan, commenting acidly: 'I have been persuaded to make way for an older man.'[55] Marks continued to write political commentaries for both Express titles until his premature death in February 1975.

At fifty-six, Marks's replacement, Ian McColl, was six years his senior. A Scot who had spent thirty years in the paper's Glasgow office, he was expected to turn the *Express* into a more aggressive, news-oriented, less highbrow package. Regarded as 'a canny fighter',[56] McColl had been highly praised during his ten years as editor of the Scottish edition, producing a lively paper and running a smooth news operation. An elder of the Church of Scotland, he was famous for campaigning against allowing bishops into the kirk and against a family planning clinic for students at St Andrews University lest it encourage 'unlicensed fornication among the teenagers'.[57] McColl was in awe of his mother and until he was fifty he was a non-smoking teetotaller who remained single. At her death, he took up drink, started smoking and married his secretary who soon bore him a daughter. McColl was remembered by one of his young Scottish recruits as 'the archetypal cinema screen editor, sitting in the middle of the editorial floor attired in a white shirt with the sleeves held up by garters'.[58]

His early editorial changes – 'a sharpening of attitude towards the permissive society, a more than average exposure of the royal family' – suggested that new did not really mean new.[59] McColl, for all his news savvy, failed to understand that features and spin-offs from news stories were of growing importance. In fairness, sales slid only gently during his three years at the helm and it was probably too little time to show his worth. In 1974 he was unceremoniously sent back to Scotland to run the rump of the Albion Street office, having fallen foul of one of Stevens's costly and misguided editorial initiatives: a project launched after extensive market research in March 1973, known as DX 80. This was aimed at taking the paper, a popular broadsheet with pretensions to being part of the serious press, up-market.

Stevens's first choice to pilot the project was the *Sun*'s Larry Lamb, who politely rejected his overtures. *Sunday Express* editor John Junor then suggested to Stevens that he should think about Alastair Burnet, editor of the *Economist* and former ITN political editor. It must have seemed like a good idea. Here was a man with impeccably up-market credentials and the bonus of being widely known through his television newscasting. But Burnet, aged forty-six, didn't have the technical knowledge necessary to change a paper like the *Daily Express.* His newspaper experience was confined to a seven-year stint as a sub and leader writer at the Glasgow *Herald* in the 1950s – he didn't have a clue what to do with a struggling middle-market paper requiring a renewed sense of direction, nor did he have the drive to carry through the necessary root-and-branch reform of its culture.[60] His appointment confirmed what the rest of Fleet Street had been saying for years: Aitken was hopelessly out of his depth and Stevens was no lifeguard.

There was no greater symbol of the group's appeal to generations past than the *Sunday Express* with its unchanging formula. It also dropped 500,000 copies in this period, a loss which apparently occasioned little alarm among executives, nor with its editor, Junor. His predecessor, John Gordon, was still writing his column when he reached the age of eighty in 1970, and received a Rolls-Royce from the company to mark the event. Even when he had a leg amputated, Gordon would struggle into the office. Though his column was considered a major contribution to the paper's success, he wasn't writing much of it any longer. Junor sent him weekly memos as 'suggestions' which were, in effect, items for publication. Junor noted: 'He was able to convince himself that by simply altering a word or two here and there he was still writing his column.'[61]

When he died in December 1974, a commentator pointed out that Gordon had been Beaverbrook's favourite editor and 'certainly the one who shared the largest number of his master's prejudices'.[62] Junor would rank second, handling both Beaverbrook and Aitken with 'a deft mix of subservience and flattery, interspersed with the occasional sharp riposte'.[63] On Gordon's death, Junor took over the column and immediately showed himself a master of the art, coining the memorable catchphrase, 'Pass the sickbag, Alice.' He also turned the wee Scottish town of Auchtermuchty into a byword for traditional values. He chose it, he explained, 'because I wanted a Brigadoon sort of place which had been bypassed by the modern world in which old-fashioned virtues still persisted'.[64]

It was surely ironic that the *Express* titles had just turned their backs on Scotland, losing a huge number of sales because of the negative publicity. Stevens's boast, that the 'bloodstained' closure had been 'executed enormously efficiently', was regarded as unduly callous.[65] In the following thirteen months, some 500 of the sacked printers and journalists fought to set up a workers' co-operative to produce a paper they entitled the *Scottish Daily News*. A sixteen-man action committee representing various unions, led by compositor Allister Mackie, a former 'imperial father' (convenor of shop stewards) and Labour town councillor, set out to turn the dream into reality. They were encouraged by Stevens's agreement that they could have first option on buying the Albion Street works, and by support from Tony Benn, the Labour government's industry secretary, who initially pledged a loan of £1.75 million.

Even though the men pooled their redundancy money, they needed much more and were soon approached by a big man offering 'assistance' and cash: the recently unseated Labour MP Robert Maxwell. Although they were suspicious of his business record, his previous dealings with the NUJ and his persona, they had little alternative but to accept his help. By the end of March 1975, Maxwell decided on a new set of conditions: the *Scottish Daily News* should be a twenty-four-hour newspaper, staff must agree to work unlimited (paid) overtime, and he should be publisher. 'The man's mad,' said

Mackie, before urging his colleagues to 'nod your head dumbly' to get his money and their newspaper.[66] The following month, I was among cheering delegates at the NUJ annual meeting in Cardiff who voted, ill-advisedly and against executive advice, to give money to the project. NUJ officials, showing a wisdom we members lacked, did not trust Maxwell.

In a series of increasingly bitter disputes between Mackie's team and Maxwell, the co-operative revoked his executive authority before they moved back into Albion Street and, on 5 May, published the first issue of their paper. That didn't prevent Maxwell bellowing instructions at staff through a tannoy system. The first issue was seen off stone by a beaming Maxwell accompanied by Benn, who saw himself as 'a watering can' in a garden of blooming co-operatives, none of which was to flourish. The *Scottish Daily News*, a broadsheet, sold all its 260,000 copies the first day and sales increased to 330,000 by the end of the week. Advertising revenue was poor though and sales then vanished quickly. By July, with the paper in crisis, Maxwell had regained his executive hold and he demanded a relaunch, as a tabloid, with a price cut. Editor Fred Sillitto resigned, and the already bad relationship between Mackie and Maxwell worsened: the workers' co-operative had effectively collapsed.[67]

In September, with no sales uplift for the relaunched paper, Maxwell was enraged by a *Sunday Times* Insight investigation headlined 'How Maxwell Sabotaged the Workers' Dream'.[68] He issued a writ, and several members of the works council defended their only source of cash. Despite a vote overwhelmingly in favour of him staying, the peeved Maxwell resigned from the project that week. The 'official' *Scottish Daily News* limped on until 8 November, succeeded by an 'emergency' paper produced by workers who occupied the building. It had been a salutary lesson for all concerned. Surely no printer, journalist or trade union would ever deal with Maxwell again? Surely no group of workers would ever launch a co-operative paper again?

The serious press is seriously stretched

The early 1970s proved a dreadful sales period for the *Times* as it surrendered its 400,000-plus circulation at the beginning of the decade to fall to 310,000 by the end of 1975. Editor William Rees-Mogg failed to capitalise on his early promise, making a number of erratic editorial judgements. His conviction that an international economic disaster could be averted only by returning to the gold standard made for curious leaders and articles. Nor were his readers sympathetic to the paper's support for President Nixon during the Watergate scandal.

It still had its moments, of course, such as persuading every head of government in the European Economic Community to write articles for an issue which marked Britain's EEC entry in 1973. Its comment page was enhanced by the hiring of Bernard Levin as a columnist in January 1971. One analyst who studied the *Times* closely at this time, Martin Walker, thought much of its news coverage excellent, especially from Northern Ireland, the Middle East and Africa.[69]

In truth, the Rees-Mogg *Times* was poorly structured and lacked inspiration. Perhaps he was too consumed by disruptions to the paper's production. In addressing a group of chartered accountants about those difficulties he illustrated a gift for irony too rarely employed in the *Times*: 'We are aiming this year at a new record – that every daily newspaper published in London should operate at a loss.'[70] He knew that, for a shining moment in 1973, there had been a belief that his paper had finally got to grips with its financial plight, having reduced the annual loss to just £187,000. This was the result of cost-cutting measures introduced by the new chief executive and managing director, Marmaduke Hussey. Formerly a senior executive at Associated, he had been hired by Denis Hamilton, chairman and editor-in-chief of both the *Times* and *Sunday Times*, in the conviction that an experienced outsider might have the answers to problems he and the rest of the Thomson organisation could not solve.

It was to prove, in the opinion of many, a disastrous appointment. Hussey, known as Duke, was the son of a colonial civil servant, educated at Rugby and Oxford. Wounded in the battle for Anzio, one of his legs had been amputated after he was captured by the Germans, a disability he overcame with courage and humour. He joined Associated as a trainee and worked his way up to a directorship before answering Hamilton's call. His other claim to fame was his marriage to Lady Susan Waldegrave, daughter of an earl, and a lady-in-waiting to the Queen, a connection which gave Hussey anything but the common touch. He didn't endear himself to journalists either, seeing his task in purely financial terms and personifying the division between editorial and commercial functions. Decisions supposedly made from a strictly business logic inevitably impinged on journalistic sensibilities, of which the most obvious manifestations were a reduction in the size of the *Times* and in the quality of its newsprint, necessitating a change in typeface.[71]

The *Times* cashed in on its ancient Blackfriars site of Printing House Square, selling off the building and the freehold, to move into new offices in Gray's Inn Road alongside the *Sunday Times*. From now on, the fates of the two papers were intertwined, not least because they were being printed on the same presses by the same workers from eight unions organised into sixty-five chapels, a situation which gave union activists enormous power. In the last six weeks of 1975 alone, through a combination of high newsprint costs, inflation and industrial stoppages, the *Times* lost £500,000. The effects of a cover-price increase in April, to 10p, had been wiped out. This kind of financial crisis was not confined to the *Times*, and towards the end of 1974 Hussey conceived a grandiose plan designed to save the broadsheet press from collective doom. He proposed to the *Guardian*, *Financial Times* and

Daily Telegraph that they should form a consortium to produce their titles on a single site, the *Times*'s Gray's Inn Road plant. It would be equipped with the most modern labour-saving technology already in use in the United States. By reducing manning levels and achieving economies of scale, their costs would be decimated. It would also have the advantage of curtailing union power.

Two papers responded enthusiastically, with the *FT*'s managing director, Alan Hare, anticipating that a sale of Bracken House would fund his company's part in the venture. The *Guardian* was sympathetic too, but the *Telegraph* – a key component because of its huge sale, and therefore muscle – was unenthusiastic. Pat Gibson, deputy chairman of Pearson, the *FT*'s owners, tried to coax *Telegraph* owner Lord Hartwell aboard over lunch in January 1975. But Hartwell said he wasn't prepared to enter into the deal unless the *Daily Mail* joined as well. Gibson told *FT* chairman Lord Drogheda the next day that the *Mail* 'is not an appropriate partner'. Anyway, it would never move without the *Daily Express* joining in.[72] The collapse of the consortium project before it was even mooted with the unions, who certainly would have opposed it, showed the depth of distrust between owners. None of them cared to risk the possibility that, in the event of their unions disrupting production, rivals would take advantage of the situation to win sales at their expense. There was a widespread assumption that not being on sale for a period would cause permanent circulation damage. Given this fear, it was hardly likely that they would have shown the united resolve to obtain the necessary redundancies in the face of union hostility.

Instead, with the quiet shelving of the Hussey project, owners first resumed their own internal plans for modernisation and then, in December 1975, they obtained an agreement with the unions to set up a Joint Standing Committee to consider technological changes (see below, pp. 348–9). By this time, owners knew that 'new technology', in the form of computerisation, was the way ahead but they feared the consequences of trying to introduce it. While noting the success of one regional company, T. Bailey Forman, in installing computers at the *Nottingham Evening Post* in 1973, they didn't believe they could withstand similar opposition from their unions. The *Post* survived a six-week strike, marked by a series of clashes with pickets, to make 300 printers redundant. The unions also lost their negotiating rights. National owners were none too impressed with the swaggering of the *Post*'s managing director, Christopher Pole-Carew, who behaved with an air of insufferable superiority. Happy to be known as a union-basher, he later claimed that 'trade unions can actually be a force for evil'.[73]

There were managers at the *FT* who probably agreed with him in private. While the average national income was £3,000 a year, lino operators at the *FT* were earning more than £25,000, while timehands and proof readers were getting more than £15,000.[74] These were the highest manpower costs in Fleet Street, and the effect on the paper's bottom line was significant during these years of rising raw-material costs. A gloomy financial picture had not inhibited the painstaking sales growth of the *FT* throughout the late 1960s and early 1970s, despite rival broadsheets expanding their business and economics coverage. Its prestige also grew, and it was widely seen as an impartial paper, with a Labour government granting editor Gordon Newton, to his surprise, a knighthood for his services to journalism in 1966.[75] A year later he was named journalist of the year in the British Press Awards.

Newton improved the Saturday issue, launched new sections in the daily paper and expanded its profitable surveys supplements. The Lex analysis and C. Gordon Tether's provocative Lombard column remained popular, and a redesign in the late 1960s also improved the paper's look. Then came the beginnings of a trend which was to distinguish the *FT* from every other title, its movement towards creating an international reputation. Lord Drogheda, the chairman who, as managing director, had originally had an 'often turbulent' relationship with Newton,[76] oversaw the introduction of foreign supplements and surveys which had the advantage of improving advertising revenue and bringing the paper to the attention of business people in Europe and the United States.[77]

The industrious, intuitive, anti-intellectual Newton announced in 1970 that he would retire on his sixty-fifth birthday in September 1972 after twenty-three years as editor. He had created a paper respected for its accuracy, its caution and its fair-mindedness, for reflecting rather than shaping opinion. His successor was quickly chosen because Fredy Fisher, the economics editor, was considered to be the only plausible choice. Fisher became deputy editor in 1971 and, in January 1973, moved into the chair. Born in Berlin in 1922, Max Henry Fisher was the son of a lawyer who was forced to flee Germany with his family in 1936. Briefly shipped out to Australia as an enemy alien, he returned to fight in the British army and took part in the Normandy landings. Fredy, as he chose to be known, then read modern history at Oxford before working in the Foreign Office library for seven years.

In 1957, looking for new career, he landed up by chance at the *FT*. For eight years he worked mainly on the foreign side until becoming economics editor and writing many of the leaders. Highly intelligent and ambitious, Fisher 'was not the easiest of people to work for', according to the paper's official historian.[78] Authoritarian and often tactless, he did have vitality and earned the respect of his staff, while adopting roughly the same criteria for the paper as Newton. By the time Newton retired sales had risen to almost 190,000, the highest on record, and went on rising for almost two years until the market plunge towards the end of 1974. Even so, the *FT*'s circulation withstood the economic downturn better than its rivals, and it also reported on its effects fairly and comprehensively. Fisher expanded foreign coverage, placed Lex in the hands of a bright twenty-eight-year-old recruit, Richard Lambert, and boosted home news under the leadership of David Palmer.

In 1975, Drogheda was forcibly retired, 'to his bitter disappointment', on his sixty-fifth birthday.[79] Pat Gibson, who had just been ennobled, assumed the chairman's role but it was the promotion of Alan Hare to vice-chairman that signified the Pearson board's continuing faith in running the company as a family concern. Hare, related by marriage to the Pearsons, was rather shy – 'a nice man with ability', thought Newton[80] – but 'there were some crucial flaws'.[81] He lacked the leadership skills necessary to run a management team confronting intransigent print unions. Then again, he took over at a bad time, with the economic downturn hitting advertising volume. The *FT* was heavily dependent on ad revenue, which accounted for 82 per cent of its income (compared to the *Times*'s 71 per cent and the *Telegraph*'s 61 per cent), and the result was a severely reduced pagination. With the *FT* paying the highest wages, production costs continued to rise and a desperate situation grew worse.

In July 1975, Hare decided on a brave, if naive, way out by announcing that the paper would introduce computer typesetting, with direct input by journalists, resulting in a one-third reduction of the 1,400 workforce.[82] It was a drastic decision but, as the *Sunday Times* remarked, 'time, even for capitalism's own paper, is running out'.[83] Pearson agreed to help redundant staff find new jobs, along with retraining programmes, and even guaranteed bridging salaries to compensate those who had to take a drop in wages. Print union leaders were reasonably sympathetic and by the autumn the TUC's Printing Industries Committee were recommending the plan, viewing it as a possible blueprint for agreements on other titles. But the power of Fleet Street's print workers resided not in their union headquarters but in their own chapels and branches. They had enough muscle to ignore their own leaders and were not prepared to turn their backs voluntarily on their lucrative jobs. Eventually, Hare and the *FT* management came to realise that the big bang just wouldn't work.

While the *FT*'s owners fussed over the idea of a gradual introduction of new technology against mounting concern about falling profits, the Scott Trust had even more to worry about. By mid-1971, the *Guardian* was in trouble again with losses in the previous year of more than £1.1 million. It was saved by the *Manchester Evening News*'s £1.4 million profit, but there was a pressing need to put the flagship paper on a more secure footing. It is a tribute to chairman Laurence Scott that he managed to achieve this before he stood down. His working report for the year up to March 1973 recorded profits for both titles, due to a boom in classified advertising and a price rise for the *MEN*.

Editor Alastair Hetherington would never have been ungracious enough to say that he was delighted at Scott's retirement, but the pair had clashed so often it must have been a relief. Scott's deputy, Peter Gibbings, took over and a period of relative harmony between editorial and management followed. Gibbings questioned the financial logic behind an editorial in December

1973 about a freeze on incomes, but Hetherington considered the call 'no worry' because 'relations with Peter were easy'.[84]

Gibbings oversaw one of the most crucial, and financially beneficial, moves in the *Guardian*'s history. Faced with a potentially crippling rent rise at Gray's Inn Road, the paper found a new building in nearby Farringdon Road with enough space to accommodate journalists and all the pre-press staff. Finished pages could then be sent along the back roads to Gray's Inn for printing as before, Gibbings having renegotiated a reasonable contract with Thomson. That move was to have two important effects: it 'secured the paper's economic wellbeing' and it 'virtually eliminated the influence of the Manchester office'.[85]

Soon after the announcement of the transfer, journalists were confronted in March 1975 by much more surprising news: the resignation of Hetherington, aged fifty-five, after more than eighteen years as editor. 'I was beginning to feel that it was time for a younger editor,' Hetherington wrote in his memoirs. 'The physical strain and mental tension were not lessening . . . I wanted to stop editing while I was still fit.'[86] He also wanted to return to his native Scotland and to enjoy more hill climbing, and had secured the post of controller of BBC Scotland. The strains to which he referred had been compounded by the *Guardian*'s London–Manchester split. As his successor noted, Hetherington 'seemed to edit on the night sleeper to Euston' before the permanent move to London.[87] When he was named journalist of the year in the British Press Awards in 1971, it was a recognition that he had steered the *Guardian* through stormy waters to ensure that it remained secure and independent, certain of its place as a respected national newspaper.

Individual proprietors could simply appoint editors they fancied without debate. The Scott Trust was altogether different, seeing its function in much more democratic terms. But it was initially uncertain how to choose a new editor and decided on a complex consultation process involving trustees, group directors, board members, senior editorial staff and the NUJ chapel.[88] After much discussion an electoral college of ten considered a range of internal candidates – deputy editor John Cole, production editor Peter Preston, news editor Jean Stead, columnist Peter Jenkins and features editor Harry Jackson – and outside nominations such as Labour MP Michael Foot, David Watt of the *FT* and Brian Redhead, editor of the *Manchester Evening News.* Hetherington, like Cudlipp, let it be known that he wanted to be succeeded by the *Sunday Times*'s Harry Evans.

After a series of interviews, much heart-searching and accepting the editorial department's view that it 'admired Cole but favoured Preston',[89] it was Preston who emerged as the winner. Cole was naturally upset but years later graciously admitted that Preston had been the better choice.[90] Preston's 'career had no parallel in journalism'.[91] Born in 1938 in Leicestershire, at ten his father died of polio, which he also contracted. The treatment necessitated him spending periods of nine and six months in an iron lung, and he emerged with severely disabled limbs, including a badly withered arm. It says a great deal about Preston's character that he managed to become a conjuror. At Loughborough Grammar School he also overcame his headmaster's scepticism about his abilities to win a place at St John's College, Oxford. After university he joined the *Liverpool Daily Post* training scheme and then applied to the *Guardian*, quickly finding himself a role as a political reporter and covering major stories in Cyprus and Pakistan. He was regarded as something of a prodigy. During Anthony Howard's brief spell on the paper, news editor Harry Whewell pointed out to him to a new young reporter, saying: 'He's a wonder, that boy.' That boy was Preston.[92]

He picked up experience as education correspondent, writing the Miscellany column and running the features department. Almost everyone who worked with Preston found him difficult to know and impossible to second-guess. He seemed to have honed his shyness into an art form so that the most common single word applied to him was 'enigmatic'. It was difficult to know whether he intended to embarrass people who suffered his silences after asking him questions or sitting through lunches with him, or whether he was embarrassed by their presence. He nevertheless managed to edit the paper effectively. Cole quit soon afterwards to join the *Observer* as assistant editor. Redhead was also miffed, and left to join the BBC, where he prospered as a current affairs presenter.

One of the *Guardian*'s strengths was its women's pages under the leadership of Mary Stott. During her sixteen years in charge she stimulated a debate about the role of women in society and women's journalism, often stoking controversy among readers and within the office. Her greatest find was Jill Tweedie, later described as 'the doyenne of feminist journalists'.[93] Passionate, committed to a wide range of causes, Tweedie's articles blazed from the page. For many, especially non-*Guardian* readers, she came to represent what the paper stood for: an immoderate liberalism. On Stott's retirement in 1973, her baton was passed initially to Linda Christmas, who disliked the idea of the women's-page label and renamed it *Guardian* Miscellany. Preston disagreed and appointed Suzanne Lowry in 1975 to run a page called Guardian Women. It was just one of the many innovations Preston would introduce.

Innovations were non-existent at the *Daily Telegraph*, a vice which a great many of its conservative readers – and a fair number of staff – considered its greatest virtue. Hartwell, who paid no attention to changing social mores, was determined that his editor produce a sober, staid and reliable paper. His senior journalists could carouse for hours every day in the King and Keys gently mocking their unchanged and unchanging paper, and owner, but he remained unaware of the depth of discontent. Nor was he probably aware just how rowdy his staff could be. Rudeness and rough-housing were common in the pub, according to parliamentary sketchwriter

Frank Johnson.[94] I have never forgotten an episode in the Press Club when a well-built, belligerent man I didn't recognise was refused drink by the barman. He suddenly lifted the heavy, antiquated till and pitched it at him, shattering a row of glasses and bottles. 'Who's that?' I asked a colleague, anticipating that it would turn out to be one of the *News of the World*'s better-spoken thugs. 'That's Robert Adam,' he replied, 'the *Daily Telegraph*'s fine arts correspondent.'

Hartwell had to decide in December 1974 on a replacement for editor Maurice Green who retired, aged sixty-eight, after ten years of worthy effort. There were two keen pretenders to his throne – the deputy, Colin Welch, and City editor Kenneth Fleet – but neither impressed Hartwell. Instead, he choose Bill Deedes, then sixty-one, a former *Telegraph* man who had spent a lengthy time away in politics. To recite Deedes's background gives an entirely wrong impression of him. Born in a castle, attended by servants, educated at Harrow, he didn't bother with university and quickly obtained a job as a reporter on the *Morning Post* through family connections. Despite the privilege, wealth and nepotism, the twinkly-eyed Deedes was one of the least haughty, most modest and most likeable of men. Anyway, the wealth vanished before he was an adult in the 1929 crash.

Sent to cover the war in Abyssinia in 1935, one of his supposed rivals was the *Daily Mail* correspondent, Evelyn Waugh, who largely ignored his paper but later wrote the greatest satirical novel about newspapers, *Scoop*. Its hero, William Boot, was modelled in part on Deedes. Two years later the *Morning Post* was merged with the *Daily Telegraph* and Deedes reported for his new paper until he joined the army during the war, winning the Military Cross. He then spent five years on the Peterborough column, until he was elected a Tory MP in 1950. As a backbencher he was able to go on writing for the paper, stopping only when he became a junior minister from 1954. He generally preferred 'the vagrant journalistic life' to the disciplines of Whitehall, and returned to the backbenches in 1957 in order to boost his income by writing once again for the *Telegraph*.[95] He was briefly minister without portfolio in the cabinets of Harold Macmillan and Alex Douglas-Home before Labour assumed power.

He had been an MP for almost twenty-four years, and was preparing to fight the February 1974 election, when he learned about the crisis of succession at the *Telegraph*. Deedes regarded Welch as 'the most influential opinion-former in the office' but he knew that Hartwell thought he 'lacked the gravitas for the editor's chair' and was 'too argumentative'. Like many a genius, Deedes observed, Welch 'was erratic in his personal life and, when he drank too much, was apt to get into scrapes'.[96]

It was characteristic of Welch that he never allowed Hartwell's wounding, and inaccurate, view of him as lacking gravitas to alter his own view of Hartwell as 'one of the straightest men I've ever met'.[97] Under the straight but inflexible Hartwell Welch managed to stamp his mark on the political and economic direction of the *Telegraph*, nurturing writers who shared his beliefs. They were regarded as 'young Turks with Powellite leanings' by one commentator, Bill Grundy, but the undogmatic Deedes was more diplomatic about them, observing only that they 'felt they had a serious political message to deliver'.[98] Such was Deedes's sang-froid that he managed to carry off the role as intermediary between Welch's team and Hartwell without undue tension. Easy-going, charming and utterly without pretension, Deedes always appeared to be smiling but he was a political animal who retained contacts in the highest reaches of government. He lacked that fierce drive and single-mindedness that makes editors truly successful. He refused to do anything to curb the malign influence of the managing editor Peter Eastwood, and he failed to persuade Hartwell to allow him to introduce even the most minor and sensible of changes, such as the inclusion of a page-one index. Knowing the paper required a redesign, he gave way in the face of Hartwell's opposition.

The man who tried Hartwell's patience most was the *Sunday Telegraph*'s deputy editor, Perry Worsthorne. During the Lambton scandal in May 1973, he outraged his proprietor, many BBC viewers and a number of *Telegraph* readers by using the word 'fuck' in a live television interview broadcast early in the evening. It emerged that some of his El Vino friends had dared him to do it, though he later denied having done so for that reason.[99] He was immediately suspended by his editor, Brian Roberts, who recommended to Hartwell that he should be fired or at least banned from appearing on TV for six months. Though Hartwell showed a liberal streak by choosing the latter course, he let it be known that Worsthorne could never expect to rise any further. Worsthorne also lost the valuable friendship and support of Hartwell's wife, Pamela.

With Hartwell's hand so firmly on the tiller, neither Deedes at the *Daily* nor Roberts at the *Sunday* were allowed enough leeway to innovate, and these were barren years in editorial terms for both papers. The really significant moment of the era occurred in June 1974 when *Telegraph* journalists walked out in a wages battle, the first editorial strike in the paper's history.[100] The dispute was quickly settled but it marked a sea change: benevolent dictatorship at Peterborough Court was no longer a guarantee of industrial peace.

Thalidomide: a triumph for responsible journalism?

No single newspaper campaign has enjoyed so much favourable publicity as that run in the *Sunday Times* on behalf of the victims of thalidomide. Some 450 British children were born in 1960 and 1961 with horrific deformities because their mothers had taken thalidomide, a sleeping pill, when they were pregnant. Distillers, the company which marketed the German-made drug in Britain, withdrew it from sale in November 1961, but were soon faced with claims for compensation by parents.

Reports about the effects of thalidomide first appeared in the *Sunday Times* in 1967. Initially, editor Harry Evans showed interest in the scandal because he believed the public had a right to know how the drug came to be produced and marketed, and whether safety procedures were in place to prevent such a mistake reoccurring.[101] The following year the paper began to question whether early settlements agreed with Distillers were fair. Evans was outraged that the sums were relatively small, and that they were made on the basis that parents withdrew their charges that the company had been negligent. By the early 1970s, the *Sunday Times* had amassed documentary evidence (having paid for it) which convinced Evans that the victims' families had been shabbily treated, not least by their lawyers who had accepted Distillers' word about the drug having been properly tested before being sold. Two of his journalists, Phillip Knightley and Bruce Page, were responsible for unearthing most of the proof, though from different angles, at different times. But the difficulty the *Sunday Times* faced in criticising Distillers was that, with many legal cases still outstanding, the paper might well jeopardise future settlements, or be held in contempt of court.

Lawyers acting for Distillers had already silenced the *Daily Mail* when Evans decided, in September 1972, to launch a campaign based around the slogan 'Our Thalidomide Children'. On the first week he devoted three pages to the scandal along with a leader headlined 'Our National Shame'.[102] The paper described proposed settlements as 'grotesquely out of proportion to the injuries suffered', criticised various aspects of English law on the recovery and assessment of damages in personal injury cases, complained of the delay that had elapsed since the births and appealed to Distillers to make a more generous offer. 'The thalidomide children shame Distillers,' it said, and pledged that 'in a future article, the *Sunday Times* will trace how the tragedy occurred'.

No other paper or broadcaster dared to take up the case and Evans ran a second part the following week. He stressed that his articles dealt with morality rather than legality, but the attorney-general obtained a high court injunction banning the *Sunday Times* from publishing its article about the history of thalidomide's invention and production. Evans was unable to publish articles about the children, their problems and the inadequate sums they had been paid in compensation. The result was a public outcry as other papers and television programmes then started to highlight the scandal. MPs staged a parliamentary debate demanding that Distillers face up to its moral responsibilities. Within two months, the Tory government under Edward Heath agreed to set up a trust fund and also launch a royal commission to consider personal injury damages.

Then the *Sunday Times* published a list of the holders of Distillers shares, and scores of them, including insurance companies and merchant banks,

1. The mischief-maker about to meet his maker: Lord Beaverbrook in 1964, the year of his death.

2. Playing at editor: *Daily Express* editor Arthur Christiansen starring as himself in the 1962 film *The Day the Earth Caught Fire.*

3. The overpowering, infuriating and moody Brendan Bracken just after acquiring the *Financial Times.*

4. Deadlines every hour: editors' meeting at the *Evening Standard* in the mid-1970s.

5. The king is dead! Long live the press! People gather at Ludgate Circus to read about the death of George VI in 1952.

6. Brash, pushy and insulting, Lord Thomson owned the *Times* and *Sunday Times* without interfering in their journalism.

7. *Daily Telegraph* owner Lord Camrose: he had an insatiable appetite for facts.

8. The son who lost the *Telegraph*: Lord Hartwell with his socialite wife, Pamela.

9. The cuckolded press baron: Lord Rothermere II and his errant wife, Ann, with actress Anna Neagle in 1947.

10. A couple of swells: Lord Rothermere III and his editorial guru, Sir David English, editor of the *Daily Mail.*

11. Astor's successor, the tenacious Donald Trelford, who edited the *Observer* for eighteen years.

12. Tiny Rowland, the entrepreneur who tarnished the *Observer*'s reputation and lost it thousands of sales.

13. Well they would take pictures, wouldn't they? Mandy Rice-Davies enjoying her newspaper notoriety during the Profumo affair in 1963.

14. Eyeball to eyeball: Hugh Cudlipp and Cecil King confront each other at an IPC shareholders meeting in 1968 after King's dismissal.

15. The *Times* men in 1967: William Rees-Mogg, editor of the *Times*, Harold Evans, editor of the *Sunday Times*, and Denis Hamilton, editor-in-chief of both newspapers.

added to the public pressure. Distillers finally agreed in January 1973 to pay £20 million, to compensate the families, almost ten times the original offer.[103] Evans was not content to leave it there. He pursued the matter of the legal gags which had inhibited press freedom, eventually winning two historic judgements. The injunction was finally lifted in June 1976, and the *Sunday Times* immediately published the article it had prepared four years before. It wasn't until April 1979 that the European Court of Human Rights overturned a House of Lords decision that to publish the original article would have been a contempt of court.

I have necessarily given only a very brief résumé of the affair, and there are at least three books which deal with it in great detail, not to mention Evans's own account.[104] In the following years, the successful outcome of the campaign, along with the legal victories, ensured that the *Sunday Times* and, most especially, Evans himself were crowned with glory. It came to be viewed as a triumph for both investigative reporting and campaigning journalism, as powerful an incentive to would-be reporters as the 1970s Watergate scandal was in the United States.

Yet the *Sunday Times* campaign was not without contemporaneous press critics, including the *Daily Telegraph*'s City editor Kenneth Fleet, the *Sunday Telegraph*'s Perry Worsthorne and the *Economist*.[105] They largely took Distillers' side, accepting that tests had been properly carried out. Many years later, in a classic example of an historical revisionist controversy, a split emerged between two of the journalists involved, Page and Knightley, with a former *Sunday Times* staffer, Peter Wilby, weighing in and Worsthorne taking the opportunity to return to the fray.[106] Knightley asked two salient questions: 'Did we do it right? Would it have been better to have kept out of the whole affair?' He suggested that the campaign might well have been counter-productive: Distillers might have made an earlier, better settlement if there had not been so much publicity, with the *Sunday Times*, as it were, upping the stakes. He revealed that, in some cases, both the method of distributing the trust money and the money itself caused problems for the victims and their families which deepened as the years passed. He also, quite rightly, pointed out that the *Sunday Times* was tardy in reporting on thalidomide.

In a lacerating reply to his former colleague, Page derided Knightley's work in the four years before 1972: 'the basic truth is that the main contribution to getting the story seriously (almost disastrously) wrong, was made by Knightley himself'.[107] He contended that the beneficial effects of the campaign, and the way it was executed – once he got involved – far outweighed the bad. In parallel with Page's argument with Knightley, he entered into a lengthy and acrimonious correspondence with Wilby, who claimed that 'investigative journalism of the sort pursued by Knightley and the old Insight team was never an economic proposition'.[108]

These disputes do not cloud my view of the thalidomide campaign as anything other than a journalistic triumph. Knightley's *mea culpa* was reasoned and sensitive, but it didn't convince me that the *Sunday Times* should have walked away. Page's response to Knightley was disproportionately rude, but his defence of his paper's actions, and of the concept of investigative reporting, was wholly justified. His response to Wilby, however, seemed wide of the mark.

Insight's contribution to journalism has not escaped retrospective criticism, most importantly from another renowned investigative reporter, Paul Foot. He argued that its reputation was 'hideously exaggerated' and that many of its inquiries 'were prompted by London middle-class obsessions' such as antiques trade rip-offs and the siting of London's third airport.[109] A review of the breadth of material covered by Insight over the years suggests that Foot was overstating his case. More pertinently, Wilby has presented a portrait of Evans which helps to explain why Insight, and other sections in the paper, seemed to run themselves. Wilby's description of Evans's haphazard staffing arrangements matches accounts I heard often from staff. Evans's deputy, Frank Giles, agreed, arguing that there were too many 'passengers and parasites' around.[110] Wilby, who joined the *Sunday Times* in 1977, explained: 'Evans recruited promiscuously – at parties, on squash courts, in lifts – bringing ex-antiques dealers, ex-aircraft pilots, ex-vacuum cleaner salesmen and numerous others into the paper because they happened to have some expertise that was useful for a current story ... they hung around, often writing nothing of consequence for months, even years ... some of them ... seemed half-mad ... Yet this eclectic, wasteful mixture made the great *Sunday Times* investigations possible.'[111]

Whatever Evans's faults, he presided over a paper which published in these five years alone ground-breaking material on the conflict in Northern Ireland and the Middle East, began an investigation into the 1974 Turkish Airlines DC-10 air crash in France which eventually uncovered a corporate lie, and defied the government to publish extracts from the diaries of a former Labour minister, Richard Crossman. The *Sunday Times* was revelling in a golden age far more significant and longer-lasting than that previously enjoyed by the *Observer*. No wonder Evans and his staff were so upset by the account of life at the *Sunday Times* written by Arnold Wesker, who was allowed to roam the office in 1971 to obtain material for a play. His essay portrayed even the conscientious reporters as plotters and plodders, spending as much time trying to outsmart each other as getting the story.[112] The Knightley–Page spat illustrates that the existence of internal rivalry need not preclude the production of good journalism.

This was the period in which Evans was lionised. Mike Randall, who ran the news department for ten years, painted a picture of 'Hurricane Harold' as a man who 'curiously combined diffidence with determination and self-doubt with decisiveness'.[113] Evans couldn't sit still, leaving his office during discussions, running from room to room, prevaricating for hours, then indulging in frenzied activity. His staff accepted that he could do everything – initiate, write, sub, design – and he won their affection, despite the frustrations caused by his interruptions and his irritating failure to keep his mind on the subject in hand. 'It was impossible to dislike him,' noted Frank Giles, who admired Evans for 'his ebullience, his humour, his devotion to his profession, his gamin-like charm.'[114]

Evans could not have achieved what he did without either the wise counsel of his editor-in-chief, Sir Denis Hamilton, or the indulgence of his proprietor, Lord Thomson. In a revealing example of Thomson's non-interference, Evans related how, just before one of the 1974 elections, Hamilton told him that Thomson would be 'unhappy' if the *Sunday Times* backed Labour. Evans raised it with Thomson during a phone call. 'He took it is his stride,' wrote Evans, and after making some comments on the relative merits of Wilson and Heath, Thomson said: 'Well, Harold, it's up to you . . . How's the run tonight?'[115] Thomson stuck to what he knew best, investing heavily in North Sea oil and thus ensuring the financial solidity of his empire. Less acquisitive in these years, he was forced to abandon his plan to ring London with new evening titles.[116]

Life at the *Observer* was dismal. Its sales fell to 775,000 by the end of 1973, recovered slightly, and then dived below 700,000 in 1975. It also reported a cash loss of almost £500,000 in 1974, suffering badly from the collapse in classified advertising. Owner–editor David Astor was not only financially drained, lacking the resources to compete at an equal level with his energetic rival, he was also forced to compromise on his editorial purity. The paper boasted many good writers and excellent foreign correspondents, but none of its stories set the pulse alight. Inevitably, its liberal audience gravitated towards the *Sunday Times*.

Astor didn't have Evans's nose for stories and lacked the will for investigative journalism. In 1971, business editor Tony Bambridge thought home secretary Reginald Maudling's involvement in the murky activities of the Real Estate Fund of America should be investigated. But Astor overruled the idea after being convinced by his formidable political correspondent Nora Beloff that Maudling was likely to be the next Tory leader. When Beloff's memo to Astor found its way into *Private Eye* she sued for breach of copyright, backed by Astor, but eventually lost the case.[117] Bambridge was later vindicated when Maudling was forced to resign in 1972 after being implicated in a different corruption scandal.

Astor also confronted a profound and uncomfortable truth within his paper: liberal politics and trades unionism were not compatible. The former emanates from the social theory of individual freedom; the latter rests on the industrial practice of collective discipline. Print union members were not concerned with the editorial content of the paper they worked for, regardless of whether it criticised the workings of monopoly capital, warned of the dangers of dictatorship or defended the rights of workers. Their interests were altogether more straightforward, if short sighted: they wished to extract the greatest possible reward for the least amount of effort. As this sank in, Astor came to view union power as 'no less illiberal than any of the foreign regimes that his paper had fought in the past . . . At the heart of the matter were the very principles of a free society that the *Observer* had always stood for.'[118]

As a proprietor, Astor naturally opposed print union overmanning and continual wage demands. As an editor, he also became intensely worried about growing NUJ militancy, sensing that the journalists' call for a closed shop was not really aimed at increasing their bargaining power, but at securing editorial control. Fearing that a closed shop would inhibit freedom of expression and that the unions would gradually force titles to close, he predicted that Fleet Street would be reduced to 'three or four omnibus papers, produced by feather-bedded printers and written by men of a self-perpetuating guild'.[119]

Astor's hostility to the unions led him to support Heath during his 1974 confrontation with the miners, a move interpreted by many critics as a drift to the right. This upset some of the *Observer*'s staff who were also disillusioned by its support for America's Vietnam intervention, a consequence of Astor's fierce opposition to communism. One 1974 leader in particular, 'The arrival of the militants', caused an open split among *Observer* staff. It argued that a 'free society' was threatened by a few 'fashionable Marxists' and left-wing leaders of the miners' union.[120] Twenty journalists, including columnist Neal Ascherson, feature writer Polly Toynbee and her father Philip, signed a letter of protest to Astor, claiming that the editorial implied readers should vote Tory.

The inescapable truth was that the old *Observer* had vanished and its owner had had enough. According to columnist Katharine Whitehorn, the paper was 'in the doldrums'.[121] Five months into 1975, its losses had reached more than £340,000, with predictions that they would more than double by the year end. Astor's family trust could no longer finance such deficits, and the banks were not prepared to help either. Since the *Observer* had inherited a large print staff with its purchase of Printing House Square from the *Times*, two of its managers conceived the idea of printing the paper outside Fleet Street, but other executives were not prepared to take the risk of challenging the unions. In July 1975, Astor called on one of his trustees, the lawyer Arnold Goodman, to help negotiate a 33 per cent cut in staffing with the unions. Managers opened the company books to union leaders and towards the end of August, Goodman informed Astor that the best they could achieve was a 25 per cent reduction. On 30 September, Astor resigned as editor after twenty-seven continuous years, becoming a trustee. He recommended that his deputy for the past six years, Donald Trelford, should take over, emphasising his 'organising' abilities. Most staff agreed, preferring him to the only other possible candidate, Anthony Sampson.

Trelford, then thirty-eight, had worked first as a journalist in his home city, Coventry, while still a Cambridge undergraduate. He spent a couple of years on the Sheffield *Telegraph* before going to edit the *Times of Malawi*. He returned to Britain to join the *Observer* in 1966. He had several qualities that were to prove useful as editor. He was a clever politician: as an editor in Malawi he had learned to walk the diplomatic tightrope by running a paper under a dictatorial regime. He had a good grasp of production, bags of tenacity and a helping of boyish charm. His early hirings were also shrewd. He took on Alan Watkins as columnist and Adam Raphael from the *Guardian* to cover politics. He also eased Nora Beloff away from domestic politics to cover European affairs.

Journalists lose the battle of the newsroom barricades

After a narrow victory in the February 1974 election, prime minister Harold Wilson pointed to the relatively small number of papers which had supported Labour, the culmination of a consistent anti-Labour, and anti-union, bias. How could he find a way to impose impartiality? Was it possible that some form of economic intervention might stimulate the launching of new papers? Other Labour MPs were also concerned about the implications of the closure of the Express plant in Glasgow, the possible threat to diversity due to further concentration of ownership and supposed invasions of privacy. The result, to the horror of owners, editors and the Conservative party, was the appointment in May of a Royal Commission on the Press, the third since the war.

Chaired initially by Sir Morris Finer, who died at the end of 1974, it was then led by Professor Oliver McGregor, head of a sociology department at London University, a fellow of Wolfson College, Oxford and member of several quangos. The only people on the commission who appeared to have any sympathy at all with Wilson's analysis were Geoffrey Goodman, the *Daily Mirror*'s industrial editor, and David Basnett, general secretary of the General and Municipal Workers' Union. This commission's terms of reference were wider than those of the previous two. It was to consider the economic state of newspapers, how to protect diversity of choice, whether the press was biased, whether anything could be done about it, and where to draw the line between the press exercising its freedom on matters of public interest and the protection of individual privacy. More than three years would pass before it completed its task, by which time owners had come to realise the benefits of telling their tales of industrial woe without censure from the print unions.

The early 1970s were marked by widespread industrial, political and economic conflicts, with strikes, internal Labour party strife and disruption in universities. Provisional IRA bombings in Britain and weekly killings in

Northern Ireland added to the sense of doom, the feeling that the old society was breaking down irretrievably. Much of the industrial friction stemmed from an unprecedented alliance between a frustrated skilled and semi-skilled workforce and a rising group of young, articulate, largely white-collar workers, many of whom believed that, with capitalism in terminal decline, some form of socialism offered a more equable and democratic alternative. Within Fleet Street, where newspapers were reporting the industrial crisis while suffering from its effects, the pressures were especially intense. In the spring of 1971, engineers at the *Express* stopped work in protest against the Heath government's Industrial Relations Bill.[122] To confuse matters, the National Graphical Association (NGA) was relaxed about Tory legislation which appalled almost every other union.

Owners and editors had become used to the difficulties of dealing with print unions, but they were shocked by the gradual rise of militancy among their journalists, and scared of the consequences if they joined forces with the printers. In September 1971, every national paper suffered disruptions during a pay dispute with the NGA, with chapel meetings causing the loss of almost 9 million papers in three nights. Owners then threatened not to pay NGA members.[123] The union reacted by holding even longer meetings, and owners responded by issuing protective notices, announcing that they would not publish from 19 September. That afternoon, a small group of journalists and printers at the *Sun* – including me – tried to defy the shutdown by producing a pirate edition with the provocative front-page headline: 'Fleet Street Bosses Go On Strike'. The eight pages reached the proof stage, but members of another union, Natsopa, refused to print it. We distributed it instead around the streets and, most effectively, to television news reporters.

Next day a group of us, working from the Coach and Horses pub in Whitefriars Street, attempted to publish a renegade *Sun* entitled the *Paper*. Again, we couldn't get it printed, despite an offer of help from the left-wing Workers Press, because of hostility from pre-press union chapels.[124] Papers were shut down for four days until an agreement was reached on 23 September. Those of us who had embarrassed the editor, Larry Lamb, and the management were censured, but not dismissed, one of the very rare occasions on which the print unions showed full-hearted support for the NUJ by threatening to restart industrial action if we were fired.

In July 1972, once the Industrial Relations Bill had been enacted, papers suffered a five-day stoppage when printers struck in sympathy at the jailing of five dockers by the Industrial Court. Print unions showed their strength by organising an efficient rolling strike: as soon as one union went back to work, another stopped. It illustrated the vulnerability of newspapers to a multi-union, multi-chapel workforce.

NUJ members could not help but note the success of collective discipline, and a majority began to see the wisdom of achieving a closed shop. But there were two distinct lines of thought: most viewed a closed shop as a bargaining weapon to extract higher wages while a vociferous minority, especially the younger element (of which I was one), realised it could be a political lever to curb the owners' power over editorial content.

Proprietors rejected the closed shop for both reasons, but cleverly concentrated their propaganda on the political angle, thereby uniting 'editors, writers, publishers, academics, members of other liberal professions and libertarians from all the major parties'.[125] Two of the most influential leaders of opposition to the NUJ's attempt to win closed shop rights were the *Observer*'s David Astor and the *Guardian*'s Alastair Hetherington. Along with Lord Goodman, chairman of the Newspaper Publishers Association, they fought a prolonged, and often bitter, campaign against the Trade Union and Labour Relations (Amendment) Bill, which was piloted through parliament by the employment secretary, and former Fleet Street editor, Michael Foot. In broad terms, the Foot Bill, as it became known, was aimed at restoring trade union rights removed by the Conservative government in 1971, but the additional threat to press owners was a requirement that they allow all their unions to operate a closed shop. Foot argued that proprietors and their managers were more of a threat to freedom than the journalists' union. In a memorable phrase, he remarked that the appointment of editors was like the coronation of the tsars 'in which the newly appointed autocrat would march in procession preceded by his father's murderers and followed by his own'.[126]

Astor was delighted when his political correspondent Nora Beloff eagerly went into battle while Hetherington acted as shop steward for Fleet Street's editors.[127] All three were troubled by the growth of an organised left wing within the NUJ, initially obvious only on provincial papers but, by 1974, evident across Fleet Street too. Their concern about the effects of the new left were bluntly stated by Beloff: 'a conscientious Communist would always put the interests of the party and class war above the bourgeois concept of objective truth'.[128]

As a prelude to forming closed shops, the NUJ removed the special 'associate member' status then enjoyed by editors which allowed them to remain NUJ members without the necessity of abiding by its decisions. The *Sunday Times*'s Harry Evans immediately resigned from the NUJ, but the *Guardian*'s Hetherington accepted full membership. The NUJ stepped up its campaign by demanding that editorial matter provided by non-union writers and artists be blacked. This move convinced editors, quite rightly, that their freedom to hire whom they like and publish what they liked was under threat. *Sunday Mirror* editor Michael Christiansen railed against the loss of his right to buy features from outside contributors.[129]

But the early unity of editors broke down, with Hetherington and the *Evening Standard*'s Charles Wintour preferring compromise. In practical terms, this meant acceding to closed shops and protecting press freedom by appending a charter to the bill. After many more months of wrangling, in which only 'guidelines' for a charter were published with the bill, it was enacted in March 1976. In the process, though the NUJ should have had cause to celebrate, the long debate had widened a deep split between the militants and moderates, with several of the latter quitting the union.

It had been conveniently overlooked that closed shops, in all but name, had existed for years in the editorial departments of Mirror group and Express titles, and the *Sun* was virtually 100 per cent membership too. Apart from using their new leverage to ensure that only union members wrote copy and took pictures, there were no cases in Fleet Street of NUJ closed shops being used to prevent editors publishing what they liked. But the Act undoubtedly reinforced journalists' industrial muscle in the following couple of years. During the February 1974 election campaign, a wave of stoppages by NUJ members fighting for higher wages at Mirror group papers in London, Manchester and Glasgow alarmed every owner.[130] If journalists could halt production over pay, could they do it over content too?

While the Foot Bill was being debated, Fleet Street's industrial relations nightmare grew worse. During 1975, the *Times* lost hundreds of thousands of copies because of so-called 'wildcat' industrial action. In April 1975, the *Daily Mirror* and its stablemates, the *Sunday Mirror*, the *People*, *Sporting Life* and *Reveille*, were not published for ten successive days in the south due to a manning and pay dispute with Sogat. It was the longest break in production since 1955. Mirror group's deputy chairman and chief executive Percy Roberts was outraged when Murdoch's *Sun* took advantage of the closure to offer newsagents an extra farthing per copy, encouraging them to replace the *Mirror* with the *Sun*.

But a rising *Sun* circulation was not as welcome at Murdoch's company, News International, as it might have seemed. Chief executive Bert Hardy grew concerned at the state of the press hall in Bouverie Street, where there was limited space and the condition of the presses was growing worse by the week. He conceived the idea of installing new presses in a purpose-built print centre away from Fleet Street, first selecting land near King's Cross railway station. Unable to agree a deal with Camden council, he then persuaded Murdoch to buy thirteen and a half acres of land in Wapping from Tower Hamlets council.[131] Murdoch, always loath to invest, authorised the purchase of the land because, at a cost of less than £1 million, it was so cheap. He also agreed to the building of the press hall and the purchase of twelve presses. Hardy saw it in terms of efficiency and as a way of reducing staff, maybe by as much as two-thirds, but not as a union-busting exercise. At that time, neither he nor Murdoch, nor anyone in the company, could envisage the idea of operating a new plant without unions.

A huge print hall was constructed but Murdoch, though apparently supportive of Hardy's vision, was too nervous to allow the laying down of the presses and refused permission for the machinery to be removed from its crates. So the Wapping plant became known within the company as 'Hardy's folly'. He didn't share the joke and he was fired by Murdoch four years later.

It was wrongly assumed at the time that he had lost an internal power struggle with *Sun* editor Larry Lamb. In fact, his disagreement was with Murdoch's valued finance guru, Mervyn Rich. Hardy later admitted: 'I did get a bit above myself.'

12. STRIKES, STUNTS AND SCOOPS

Facts may be sacred – but which facts? The media are not a neutral looking glass: we select what we mirror.[1]

The running story of the early 1970s was the sickly state of the British economy and a set of related issues: inflation, unemployment and industrial relations. Trade union leaders, such as Vic Feather, Jack Jones and Hugh Scanlon, became national figures who featured as often in papers as the prime minister, Ted Heath, and the Labour leader he had deposed from Downing Street, Harold Wilson. Unable to win a voluntary deal with unions on curbing pay increases, Heath introduced the Industrial Relations Act in order to stamp out strikes.

In January 1972, Britain's 280,000 coal miners called a national strike for the first time since 1926 after rejecting an 8 per cent pay offer. The popular press, including traditional Tory-supporting papers such as the *Daily Express* and *Daily Mail*, was overwhelmingly sympathetic to the miners. The *Daily Mirror* was wholly supportive of the strikers,[2] while the *Sun*, still in its post-IPC Labour-supporting phase, was also convinced of the miners' case.

Most editors were initially sceptical about the miners getting their way. In reporting the strike vote by the National Union of Mineworkers, a *Mail* news story said they had set out 'on a disastrous, probably suicidal, collision course with the government'.[3] The paper couldn't imagine the strike succeeding or that the men would stay out long enough 'to inconvenience the public'. Similarly, the *Economist* predicted that 'the miners cannot stop the country in its tracks as they once could have done'.[4]

The *Mail* recognised that there was widespread public support for the miners, 'and rightly so', arguing that 'the take-it-or-leave-it attitude of Mr Derek Ezra [Coal Board chairman] . . . is not only insensitive but short-sighted . . . Sympathy for the miners is not only a good cause. It makes sense for Britain.'[5] Heath escaped virtually all press criticism in the early weeks, which was directed instead at employment secretary Robert Carr. A *Daily Express* leader was typical: 'These men do a hard, dirty, dangerous job . . . All they ask is a decent wage. They deserve it. They should have it . . . Make a start, Mr Carr – today!'[6] The *Sun*, day after day, asked: 'Why are we waiting, Mr Carr?' The *Sun* even ran an article by Lawrence Daly, NUM general secretary, as its splash under the headline 'WHY WE ARE GOING ON STRIKE'.[7] Next day, the reply by Ezra was given less space and less prominence, with a fence-sitting leading article which said both sides had convincing cases and should find a way to compromise.[8]

Throughout the strike's first couple of weeks picketing was hardly mentioned on the front pages of the popular papers and was given little space inside. No paper drew special attention to the activities of the flying pickets created by an ambitious young Yorkshire NUM official, Arthur Scargill. A *Sun* story which began 'Strike fury erupted yesterday as miners' pickets clashed with lorrymen breaking their lines' was five paragraphs long on page two, while the paper's major political commentary that day was about Rhodesia's white minority 'police state'.[9] One story about picket violence did make it on to the *Sun*'s front page ten days into the strike, but its leading article, again urging compromise, made no reference to it.[10] After more low-key coverage, the *Sun* finally offered its own 'peace plan' with a front-page leading article: 'STUFF THE NORM! GET THE MINERS BACK TO WORK'. It said the miners were 'a special case . . . because of the exceptional demands of their dirty, dangerous job'. They should get 'an over-the-odds settlement' and it pointed out that 'public opinion is for a fair settlement . . . and won't readily forgive anyone who stands in their way'.[11]

Three weeks into the strike the *Daily Mail* sent its top feature writer Vincent Mulchrone to a Yorkshire pit and he wrote a poignant account of the plight of strikers and their families.[12] Similarly, columnist Lynda Lee-Potter said she was 'biased' in the miners' favour because she came from a mining town and thought it disgraceful that a man had to work seven days a week down a pit to earn a living wage.[13] Five days later the *Mail* published another compassionate feature on the difficulties of a striker's wife managing on a £5 budget.[14] When a young miner was killed by a lorry while picketing at Scunthorpe, the *Daily Mail*'s splash, 'ANGER AS A PICKET DIES', was heavily angled in favour of the strikers. Its editorial comment opened with the phrase, 'A miner is killed on picket duty', and the use of the word 'duty' alone was interesting. It went on to admire the NUM's response to the death as 'restrained and responsible' and urged the setting up of a 'court of inquiry' to deal with 'the just demands of the lower-paid miners'.[15]

One of the great imponderables in such cases is the confidence with which newspapers deliver the message that 'the public' is overwhelmingly for or against anything. Papers asserted from the beginning of the strike that their readers wanted miners to get more money and supported the strike. The *Times* took up that theme in an editorial: 'The impression that the miners are moved by a cruel necessity has maintained public sympathy for them, even where their picketing has overstepped the bounds of both the law and what the British people usually regard as reasonable.'[16] But was the press reflecting genuine public sympathy or did it create it?

Once the strike really bit, drastically reducing the output of electricity, the government declared a state of emergency and industry was compelled to introduce a three-day, sometimes a two-day, week. 'Massive powers cuts are likely to throw tens of thousands out of work next week . . .' announced the *Daily Mail* without a shred of criticism of the miners.[17] Despite their readers suffering daily power cuts, papers didn't change their pro-miners tune. When the beleaguered Heath government appointed a committee of inquiry under Lord Wilberforce, he got some unequivocal press advice. 'Most of us feel – despite the mounting inconvenience of the strike – that miners of all grades are poorly paid for the gruelling and dangerous work they do,' said the *Mail*.[18] 'The public want high-speed justice for the miners,' said the *Sun*.[19]

The following day, both papers attacked Heath. Under the headline 'BLACKED OUT AND FLAMING FURIOUS', the *Sun* ran an editorial as its splash: 'The Prime Minister puts all the blame on the miners. From his speech last night the country would think that he was dealing with a gang of vicious industrial wreckers. The fact is that however awkward the miners are being today it is the Government which has created the mess.'[20] The *Mail*'s leader argued that the chaos would never have happened 'if senior ministers had shown a grain of human understanding. At each stage they have totally misjudged the mood of the miners.'[21]

By the time Wilberforce issued his report, recommending substantial increases for the miners, 1.6 million workers were idle, millions more were on short time and fourteen power stations were closed. The *Sun* urged miners to 'bend a little' by calling off power-station pickets and lifting the ban on maintenance work in the pits.[22] But the NUM executive, after rejecting Wilberforce's compromise, demanded a better deal, which they obtained. The *Daily Express* lauded the final settlement: 'They have been treated as "a special case". And rightly so.'[23] The *Sun* called it 'a triumph for good sense'.[24] Heath emerged from the newspaper coverage as weak and vacillating, the author of the chaos. But could the miners depend on their press allies in a repeat performance?

At the end of 1973, amid an oil crisis, the NUM rejected a pay offer after being convinced that its members deserved much higher wages than other workers, a philosophy trenchantly criticised by the *Financial Times*.[25] With the miners preparing the ground through a series of overtime bans to run down coal stocks, the *FT* praised Heath for having acted 'firmly and sensibly' by declaring a state of emergency and imposing a three-day week from the beginning of January 1974. An NUM ballot showed that 81 per cent of the miners were in favour of a strike from 9 February, so Heath responded by calling a general election for 28 February fighting on a platform of 'Who governs Britain?'[26]

This time, the Tory press rallied to the government's side and the *Sun*, beginning its gradual move towards the right, was more ambivalent. Just before the men walked out, the *Sun* declared that the miners didn't want to strike but they did need more money 'and most people think they deserve it'.[27] But the paper asked the miners to hold their fire, counselling caution as the strike began to bite, and then growing increasingly tetchy with the strikers for 'digging their heels in'.[28] The *Daily Telegraph* was contemptuous of the strike call and ran an article which ingeniously argued that farm workers were more of a special case than miners.[29]

The non-Tory press wasn't too warm about the strike either, with the *Guardian* casting NUM president Joe Gormley, a moderate, as the 'prisoner of a militant Executive'.[30] The *Daily Mirror* claimed that the miners 'are no longer trying to drive a hard bargain. They are demanding unconditional surrender from Mr Heathn.'[31] But when the election date was declared, the *Mirror* produced a poster-style front page with a picture of Heath and a single headline taking up all the rest of the space saying: 'And now he has the nerve to ask for a vote of confidence!'[32] A year after Hugh Cudlipp's departure, the page exhibited his kind of flair and political commitment. The *Mirror* also showed a little more understanding for the striking miners in subsequent weeks.[33]

The *Daily Mail* was decidedly cold towards the miners from the beginning of the dispute, with political editor Anthony Shrimsley – having moved over from the *Sun* – playing a leading role in the paper's anti-strike, pro-Heath policy line. It was widely assumed that the strike would harm the electoral chances of Wilson's Labour party, typified by a *Mail* front page which carried an opinion-poll prediction of a hundred-seat majority for Tories. Its leading article that day said: 'This will be remembered as the Miners' Election. It is the miners whose refusal to heed the will of an elected government has brought us to this situation. It was the miners' victory in the last strike that has been the leading factor in producing the worst inflation in our history.'[34]

The *Mail* pulled out the stops for the Conservatives and the Coal Board, trying to undermine the miners' leadership by telling how NUM general secretary and 'Communist vice-president Mick McGahey' lived it up by staying at 'one of the most expensive hotels in Brussels'.[35] All the *Mail*'s splashes in this period were heavily angled against Wilson and spun positively for Heath, backed by opinion polls which were running clearly in the Tories' favour. One splash began: 'Mr Heath is now totally convinced he will win the General Election. He has just one big anxiety – that his majority might not be big enough.'[36] The next day's splash started: 'Seven days to go – and Mr Edward Heath is steaming strongly back towards 10 Downing Street.'[37]

At the *Daily Express*, political editor Walter Terry led the Tories' charge, heaping praise on Heath.[38] The *Daily Telegraph* warned that Labour offered 'the menace of utter disaster'.[39] The *Financial Times* urged a Conservative victory because, it said, Labour 'could increase the polarisation of society'.[40] More obvious was the polarisation within Westminster, with the Liberals improving their poll rating at the expense of Labour, and within the parties, where Labour was fractured by a left–right split and the Tories were upset by the resignation of Enoch Powell, whose anti-Common Market views led him to urge people to vote Labour.

The *Sun*'s election leaders, most of which were published on page one, were anti-Tory in tone.[41] Other front pages were hardly helpful to the Tories either, such as 'THE DEMON CADGER' about Chancellor Anthony Barber, and a centre-page feature entitled 'What the election is really ALL about' above a picture of the 1930 Jarrow marchers, which was calculated to help Labour by showing tacit support for the striking miners.[42] Yet the *Sun* turned its back on Labour when advising its readers how to vote in a lengthy editorial headlined, 'The Devil and the Deep Blue Sea. In spite of the record, Ted's Tories look the better bet'.[43] It concluded that 'reluctantly, and as a choice of evils, the *Sun* believes that on this occasion . . . it is the Tories who must get its vote'. The *Guardian* sought a third way. After proclaiming that 'class conflict is not the road for Britain' it said it hoped that the Liberals would hold the balance of power.[44]

Despite a definite swing against Heath in the polls, narrowing the gap between the two main parties to just 2 per cent with a couple of days to go, the *Mail*'s splash on election day was headlined 'A HANDSOME WIN FOR HEATH', predicting that he 'will be back in Number 10 tomorrow with a heavily increased Commons majority of 50 to 60 seats'. The *Express* boomed: 'IT'S HEATH BY 5%'. The *Daily Mirror*, as usual, chose to fill its front with a single headline, 'FOR *ALL* OUR TOMORROWS VOTE LABOUR TODAY', and its parliamentary editor Victor Knight correctly predicted, on the basis of Labour's private polling results, that the parties were neck and neck.

Labour won four more seats than the Tories, but the other parties held the balance of power and Heath tried to cling on by seeking a deal with them. Most of the Tory-supporting press thought this a foolish enterprise. The *Sun* advised the Liberals not to 'bail Mr Heath out' because his 'petulant manoeuvring to hold on to power is constitutional, but despicable . . . he should collect his earldom and go'. The *Mail*'s Anthony Shrimsley lamented, 'This is an overall majority for chaos and crisis!' and, when Heath was finally forced to quit Downing Street, a *Mail* editorial castigated him for being 'lured into the tactical blunder of prolonging the agony'.[45]

At the moment when Heath was forced to relinquish power to Wilson, and with the political and economic future of Britain in the balance, it was possible to see where papers were going. They were hostile to Labour and to Wilson, but they were unconvinced that the Tories had a solution and were not enamoured with Heath. The *Sun*, in conceding that it had not backed Wilson, wished him well and urged on him three priorities: to get the miners back to work, to end the three-day week, and to 'borrow big money abroad to meet our massive trading loss'.[46] When the miners' settlement was arranged three days later, the *Sun* was unimpressed: 'It is not a victory to win more and more money that buys less and less.'[47] It also poured scorn on Wilson's decision to give cabinet places to Michael Foot, Tony Benn and Peter Shore, the first two because they were too left-wing, and the latter because of his anti-Common Market views.[48]

Wilson, who pledged to curb excessive wage increases and strikes through a social contract with unions, found it impossible to govern successfully with Britain's first minority government since 1929. So he went back to the country in October to win a bigger mandate. With the polls giving Labour a healthy lead and the result in little doubt, papers considered it a dull campaign. Conservative papers remained unenthusiastic about Heath and didn't put much effort into getting him re-elected. The *Sun* sat on the fence: 'May the Best Men Win – and Heaven Help Us If They Don't'.[49] The most coherent and passionate of pro-Tory stances was adopted by the *Financial Times.* 'We do not believe that the Labour Party has an effective policy to deal with inflation,' it said. 'We also believe that the greatest danger to the economy would arise if a Labour Government with a large majority in the House of Commons but a minority popular vote were to try, either under pressure from its extremists or that of events, to shift the political and economic balance sharply to the left.'[50]

In the event, the Tories got just 35.8 per cent of the popular vote, the lowest since 1935, but Labour managed to secure only an overall three-seat majority. Heath, obliged to stand for election as leader of his party in February 1975, was beaten by Margaret Thatcher. Though the right-wing press was generally pleased to see Heath depart, papers were slow to enthuse about the new Tory leader. She was not yet their champion, but the *FT* pointed the way: 'If Mrs Thatcher can develop a practical and non-doctrinaire programme for reducing State control and enlarging the area of individual choice, she will win considerable support.'[51] While Thatcher was learning the leadership ropes, the main political story of 1975 was about Britain's future links with Europe.

Europe: a choir of editors singing from the same hymn book

'You cannot win a major battle for the minds of the electorate if the whole British press is against you,' lamented Douglas Jay, the Labour MP who was a committed opponent of Britain's membership of the Common Market.[52] Leaving aside the understandable sour grapes at losing the political battle, Jay raised the question that haunts virtually every debate about press influence over its readers.

It was clear by 1971 that most newspapers, with the notable exception of the Beaverbrook-owned *Express* titles, were enthusiastic about Britain becoming a member of the European Economic Community (EEC). The *Financial Times* was a strong advocate of entry from the early 1960s.

The *Daily Mirror* started a campaign in favour of joining in June 1961 after the group's chairman, Cecil King, convinced himself of the Market's merits.[53]

Labour prime minister Harold Wilson dated his pro-Market stance from the 1966 financial crisis, which shook his belief in Britain's economic survival outside the EEC.[54] When his application to join in May 1967 was vetoed by France's General de Gaulle, it was viewed by some papers as a national catastrophe and by many Labour MPs as a blessing. Three years later, with Wilson's Tory successor Ted Heath in power, formal negotiations began and a treaty was finally agreed in January 1972, with Britain joining a year later. Throughout 1971, opinion polls showed that the public was hostile. One Harris poll in May showed a 62–20 majority against entry, so a huge effort was made to change people's minds.[55]

This public relations battle should have been difficult given that the issue split both the main parties, with vocal minorities, led by well-known politicians, speaking out against the idea of entry. Most leading trade unionists were against and Wilson, his hands tied by opposition from within his party, changed his position too. But this substantial grouping against found themselves unable to compete with the overwhelming political and media forces in favour.

It is estimated that the European Commission Information Service spent about £10 million in the ten years from 1960 to persuade 'thousands of opinion-formers' of the EEC's benefits.[56] Heath's government, which also paid for the distribution of propaganda material, produced a White Paper in July 1971 which was 'full of ringing phrases and totally unsubstantiated claims' supported by a spate of ministerial speeches issued to the press which gave 'a glossy interpretation of events'.[57] None of this spending, nor the content of the propaganda, was subjected to press scrutiny or criticism since newspaper owners and editors were so supportive of the government's ambitions. One of the people who did study what happened noted: 'It is indisputable that both bankers and newspaper magnates were disproportionately over-represented among the ranks of those who actively promoted British entry into the EEC.'[58]

At the *Financial Times*, the link was transparent: the *FT*'s owner, Pearson, also controlled Lazard's merchant bank. The first treasurer of the European Movement – which set out to ensure the media didn't fall out of love with the EEC – was Harley Drayton, chairman of the regional paper group United Newspapers, and a former chairman of a conglomerate with interests in commercial television. One of the main pro-Market organisers within the Tory party was George Gardiner, chief political correspondent of Thomson Regional Newspapers (and later a Conservative MP). In the words of one critic, the pro-EEC brigade 'possessed the commanding heights of the British propaganda system . . . The commitment of Fleet Street editors in many cases exceeded that of many pro-Market MPs.'[59] Another observer agreed: 'There is no doubt that the quality press . . . was partisan.'[60] The *Times* under William

Rees-Mogg 'was overtly, massively and sometimes broodingly pro-entry'.[61] The *Guardian*, among the first to urge entry, did question the lack of information, especially about the likely effect on the balance of payments, but its leading articles remained steadfastly in support.[62]

The *Daily Telegraph* was loyal to Heath, though columnist Peregrine Worsthorne worried over the implications of entry. Then he suddenly gave in too. 'It now looks as if the die is cast,' he wrote. 'Let us admit it: the Europeans deserve to win. The sceptics have failed to produce an alternative faith.'[63] By the time of the Commons vote, the *Telegraph*'s editorial reflected its passion for the project. When MPs vote, it said, 'they will be passing a judgment on a civilisation, a culture, an economic union, a nascent defence capability, above all an idea of Europe which cannot be rejected without grievous results for Europe's future and our own'.[64] The *Sunday Times*, the *Observer* and the *Economist* were all unashamed Common Market fans.

There were odd voices against. The *Times*'s economics editor Peter Jay (son of anti-Market Labour MP Douglas) was allowed to air his hostility, as was the cantankerous *FT* columnist Gordon Tether. But they were drowned out by the rest of the material in their newspapers. The *Times* ran five leading articles on the topic, concluding with a leader which warned of threats to industry, jobs, the currency and the nation's standard of living if European negotiations were to fail.[65] Both the *Spectator* and the *New Statesman* were also against (though the former, under editor George Gale, eventually concluded in April 1972 that there was no longer any point in arguing against entry).

As the writer Uwe Kitzinger argued, the readers of the serious broadsheets all received their 'daily news, comment and exhortation predominantly with a pro-entry slant'.[66] Then there were the popular dailies. By far the most important was the *Daily Mirror*, not only because it had the largest sale, but because it was read by more trade unionists and Labour party members than any other. Its propaganda was unrelenting: 'Are a people who for centuries were the makers of history – and who can again help to make history – to become mere lookers-on from an off-shore island of dwindling insignificance? Surely the answer is clear. The terms are known. The prizes are immense. The challenge must be accepted.'[67]

In the following three months there were a series of clarion calls in the *Mirror*, along with lighter, more subtle, encouragement, such as Christopher Ward's 'Guide to the Euro-Dollies' (how do they rate as kissers?). In an attempt at fairness, the *Mirror*'s editorial director, Hugh Cudlipp, invited Douglas Jay to write an article stating his anti-Market case. 'It went in unchanged,' said a surprised Jay.[68] Cudlipp's decision probably had little to do with achieving balance. He sought to placate a growing number of critics from within the trade union movement who felt let down by the *Mirror*. One wrote witheringly in a union quarterly: 'For a paper that boasts of representing the people they show a remarkable hostility towards the leaders of the working class. Towards the representatives of the two largest trade unions (Mr Jack Jones and Mr Hugh Scanlon) they display a show of venom and hatred that all other Tory newspapers combined have little time or room for. Newspaper has always had its uses, for table cloths, and wrapping up fish and chips . . .'[69]

The *Sun* went over the top in its pro-Market leader just before the Commons vote. 'The *Sun* has campaigned for this . . . ever since the *Sun* itself began. No other newspaper can claim as much.'[70] Or as little, given that the *Sun*, in Murdoch's hands for just two years, had existed only since 1964. The *Daily Mail* supported the Tory party's Common Market policy, though it clearly had initial misgivings: far from perfect, it thought, but 'the most hopeful project for uniting Europe in our lifetime'.[71] Once Wilson turned against it, and the unions also confirmed they were against, the *Mail* suddenly warmed to the idea.[72]

From the other side, the *Daily Express* mounted a virulent campaign against entry, making much of the fact that 'it stood alone – with the people'.[73] The treaty was 'a victory won by French diplomacy over British interests'.[74] Once the Commons had voted, the *Express* didn't carry out its threat to become Heath's 'unrelenting enemy'.[75] Instead, owner Sir Max Aitken declared that 'a great mistake has been made. But it has been made by the House of Commons, and the *Daily Express* accepts the verdict . . . So, if Britain has to go into the Market, then the Market must be fashioned to Britain's will . . .'

Papers left nothing to chance, and no critic was too exalted to attack. When Prince Philip claimed that the EEC's Common Agricultural Policy was an example of bad management, the *Mirror* called him a 'chump' and the *Sun* commented: 'It is time our sailor Prime Minister told the sailor Prince which way the wind blows . . .'[76] These comments eclipsed the *Daily Express*'s delight: 'Good for Prince Philip. The people applaud his good sense . . . And wish it were more widely shared by our rulers.'[77]

There were odd quibbles raised by the serious broadsheets, such as the *Times*'s disgust with Geoffrey Rippon, the cabinet minister responsible for negotiating Britain's entry, over his shabby treatment of the Commons. His reports to the House were 'bordering on the contemptuous', said the paper. 'Mr Rippon's approach seems almost as though he has something to hide.' But the *Times* did not break the faith. Though impossible to prove cause and effect, the pro-Market view rang out so loudly from almost every paper's news and feature pages (plus scores of full-page adverts paid for by the European Movement) that a huge number of readers must have been influenced in favour of entry rather than against.[78]

After Britain had joined, Wilson bowed to pressure from the anti-Market forces within his own party. When re-elected, he managed to renegotiate the terms of entry and then agreed to the unprecedented idea of holding a referendum on the issue, a promise included in Labour's October 1974 election manifesto. The build-up to the vote, set for June 1975, was a re-run of the press campaign of four years before, only with a greater intensity, given that it was the people and not MPs who would decide the outcome. 'Virtually the whole press . . . joined in on the pro-Market side,' said Douglas Jay.[79] Even the *Daily Express*, a decade after Beaverbrook's death, changed sides. Only the *Morning Star*, the Scottish titles owned by D. C. Thomson – the *Sunday Post* and *Dundee Courier* – and the trade union-run *Scottish Daily News* campaigned against.

Having had two general elections in 1974, editors recognised that there was little enthusiasm for another visit to the voting booths. They put some effort into the campaign to try to ensure the best possible turnout, but they didn't treat the referendum as seriously as they did general elections. The participants held daily press conferences, which elicited a little less copy than reports of speeches around the country. Inevitably, the greatest press coverage concentrated on the personalities. An exhaustive analysis of daily national newspaper coverage in the period from 9 May until polling day revealed the paucity of splashes devoted to the subject.[80] The *Times*, *Guardian* and *Daily Mirror* carried only five lead stories each about the referendum over that period. The *Sun* carried six, but the *Daily Telegraph* managed just three while the *Daily Express* and *Daily Mail* mustered only two apiece. Excluding the *Morning Star*, the eight mainstream daily titles ran thirty-three splashes on the referendum out of a possible total of 188, about 17.5 per cent. The *Daily Mail* didn't even splash the referendum on polling day, preferring a story about a Saudi export bonanza.[81]

So convinced were most papers of the outcome that four titles which usually commissioned opinion polls in the run-up to elections – the *Daily Mail*, *Times*, *Sunday Times* and *Observer* – didn't bother. When it came to the material that was used, the bias was obvious. A further analysis showed 'grossly unequal treatment of the two sides', with 54 per cent pro, 21 per cent anti and the rest broadly neutral.[82] The *Daily Mirror* was so partisan that 69 per cent of its content – including news and features coverage, leaders, pictures, cartoons and adverts – was pro-EEC and only 15 per cent anti.

Few papers allowed the antis to breathe the oxygen of publicity: the *Guardian* and the *Financial Times* carried signed articles from anti-Marketeers, while the *Daily Express* provided equal space on one occasion for three antis and three Market enthusiasts to state their cases. These were rare moments. 'What did not take place', wrote historian Kenneth Morgan, 'was a proper debate.' In his view, 'the result was a foregone conclusion, with the vast bulk of the press pro-Market and powerful "Britain in Europe" campaigns mounted by finance and industry'.[83] Fellow historian David Childs agreed that the antis faced a 'powerful alliance of the Establishment, most of the press, and big business'.[84]

But right-wing owners and editors had another agenda too, exploiting divisions within the Labour party to attack Wilson's government. The split between the right, who favoured the Market, and the left, who did not, was so deep that Wilson was forced to free his ministers of their usual collective responsibility and allow a free vote. The Tories' newly elected leader Margaret Thatcher adopted the pro-Market position which all but a minority of her party supported. It was widely assumed at the beginning of the campaign by most political editors that Wilson wouldn't be able to pull off a poll victory. Anthony Shrimsley in the *Mail* thought it unlikely,[85] as did Walter Terry of the *Express*: 'The way things are going, the June referendum is in danger of turning into an anti-Europe rout . . .'[86]

The popular papers soon found a way of exploiting their hostility to Labour's left wing while embarrassing Wilson and engendering support for a yes vote. They concentrated almost all their fire on a single figure: energy secretary Tony Benn. He had been a target for press venom for several years because of his enthusiasm for nationalisation and workers' co-operatives, his staunch defences of strikers and his scathing attacks on newspaper owners, all of whom, he said, 'reflect the economic interests which find the Common Market attractive.'[87] By the time the campaign opened, some attacks on Benn had already reached hysterical proportions. In an exclusive interview with the *Daily Mirror* he shrugged off jibes which labelled him 'a Dracula-like bogeyman' but the article was headlined: 'BENNMANIA'.[88] Mirror group's Labour papers sided with Wilson too, and both its Sunday titles decided to make the political differences between Wilson and Benn front-page news, inaccurately forecasting his dismissal in identical headlines: 'BYE, BYE BENN'.[89]

An analysis of papers in the weeks leading up to the vote gives credence to Benn's claim, at a *Tribune* rally in April, that the press was seeking to make it 'a campaign about personalities and about the Labour party'. The other high-profile anti-Market campaigner, Enoch Powell, who had been marginalised by papers since his 'rivers of blood' speech, drew many withering comments, but these were couched in more-in-sorrow-than-anger tones. He was no longer considered a Conservative supporter anyway, after quitting as an MP and urging people to vote Labour over the Market issue. Despite a cluster of anti-Market Tories, the papers didn't perceive a fundamental split within the Tory party.

'The Benn factor', as two analysts of the campaign argued, 'was central to newspapers' treatment of the referendum – to their conceptions of what it was about and to questions of balance and fairness.'[90] Indeed, a *Daily Telegraph* headline, over a story reporting opinion poll findings, stated: 'Benn factor now dominant issue in campaign'.[91] Benn's most significant political strike against entry came when he claimed that almost half a million jobs had been lost since Britain entered the Market, and many more would vanish too. This speech was covered by every paper and elevated to splash status by the *Sun*.[92] A leading article, 'Citizen Benn's wild claim', berated him. The *Mirror* was having none of it either, with headlines such as 'Lies, more lies and those damned statistics' and 'The Minister of Fear'. The pro-Marketeers hit back at Benn in a well-timed series of assaults by cabinet colleagues revelling in the freedom from collective responsibility to attack a fellow minister who was a thorn in their side. Chancellor Denis Healey was first, followed by Wilson and then home secretary Jenkins, all of which were reported on front pages.[93]

The demonisation of Benn was completed by cartoonists and columnists. The *Sun*'s Jon Akass remarked sarcastically, 'Wedgie has decided me – I'm going to vote yes.'[94] The *Daily Telegraph*'s John O'Sullivan adopted a similar tone: 'Mr Benn often complains that the press and television are biased against the anti-marketeers. And he is absolutely right. They keep on reporting him . . .'[95] Peter Jenkins in the *Guardian* said: 'The pros console themselves with the thought that every time the big Benn mouth opens it makes more yesses than noes.'[96]

According to Jenkins, Benn 'dominated the campaign single-handed'.[97] He certainly ensured that employment was the principal issue of the campaign, drawing praise from the *Times* for making his arguments 'the central arguments in the debate'. But the argument over the likely effect on employment and another over the cost of food were shallow. It was virtually impossible for readers to know who was right in their predictions. Would there be more jobs and lower prices? Would the Common Market lead to eternal peace?

Times columnist Bernard Levin, who had earlier called for 'a resounding yes in this fraudulent referendum', summed up the dilemma two days before the poll: 'When all is said and done . . . we shall still have to decide on what grounds we should decide how to vote, before we actually do decide, let alone before we vote.'[98] The *Daily Telegraph* complained about the campaign, which was 'lower, more trivial and at times less honest than the average general election campaign', and was disappointed by the banality of a debate which had been turned into 'a row about jobs, prices and percentages'.[99] A week later the paper thought it detected 'an intellectual, moral and spiritual value' in the EEC.[100]

Two writers who studied all the newspaper output singled out the *Guardian* for providing 'the fullest and most imaginative coverage'.[101] It included a week of full-page 'Europe Extras' which, in pamphlet form, covered forty pages, with contributions from leading campaigners from either side. On the day of the referendum the *FT*'s leader quoted John Donne ('no man is an island') and contended that to pull out 'would be a gratuitous act of irresponsible folly'.[102] The *Guardian*'s leader was headlined: 'A vote for the next century', while the *Times* stressed the peace and goodwill dimension.[103] The *Daily Telegraph* argued that the best use of the referendum would be to give the extreme left 'a massive rebuff'.[104] The *Daily Mail* advocated: 'Vote YES for Britain'.[105] The *Daily Express*, which carried nothing on the referendum on its front page until six days before the vote, told readers: 'The *Express* is for the market.'[106] The *Sun*'s centre pages were unequivocal: 'Yes for a future together, No for a future alone'.[107]

The *Daily Mirror* pulled out all the stops. On polling day, the front page shouted, 'A Vote for the Future' and 'The Most Important Day Since the War', while the centre pages were filled by a picture of nine pupils at an international school in Brussels, one from each EEC country. Eight stood together in a happy, cosy huddle. The ninth stood wistfully alone, arms folded, isolated. 'He's the odd lad out. The boy beyond the fringe. The one whose country still has to make up its mind . . .' The headline said: 'FOR THE LAD OUTSIDE, VOTE YES'.[108] The people answered just one question on 5 June 1975: 'Do you think that the United Kingdom should stay in the European Community (the Common Market)?' The result: 17.3 million voted yes and 8.4 million voted no, amounting to some 64.5 per cent of the total electorate. Mission accomplished then for Britain's newspapers? Perhaps.

It is sobering to reflect that in October 2000, virtually every Danish newspaper urged the Danes to vote in favour of the single currency in a referendum. Yet the popular vote went against. It might be a poor comparison. It might illustrate that the relationship between the Danish people and its press is different from that in Britain. It might suggest that Danish papers are not as good at making propaganda as British ones. It might mean that British papers in 1975 played only a marginal role because the people had, of their own volition, decided that they liked the Common Market. Tony Benn, Enoch Powell and the other anti-Marketeers would not be the only ones who thought that view highly unlikely.

A stunt too far by the king of stunts?

Daily Mail editor David English loved setting the journalistic agenda. For him, it wasn't good enough to report the news; he also wanted to make it, to place his paper at the heart of the action. He saw publicity-generating stunts as a way of forging closer links with current readers and attracting more. Any editor could be reactive, but English preferred to be proactive, to look beyond the news schedule. There can be few better examples of his journalistic enterprise, political opportunism, passionate commitment, questionable ethics, tremendous self-confidence and appetite for self-publicity than his airlift of Vietnamese orphans in 1975. At the beginning of April, with the Vietcong sweeping towards Saigon, many thousands of South Vietnamese were fleeing the country. President Ford pleaded for the rest of the world to help cope with the evacuation of refugees, prompting an international relief operation. In this highly charged atmosphere, with unsubstantiated claims that the people would be vulnerable to violence from the insurgent communists, there was no more emotional topic than the children incarcerated in orphanages.

Ford ordered special airlifts for 2,000 children, a humanitarian act with undeniably propagandistic overtones: in defeat, the US government was attempting to salvage its pride rather than the orphans.[109] The *Mail*'s foreign editor Brian Freemantle suggested that the paper should organise its own airlift and English responded to the idea with characteristic enthusiasm. Freemantle believed that English saw the enterprise 'as putting us on a par with an American president'.[110] He announced his dramatic intervention on the front page, 'The *Mail*'s Mercy Airlift', pledging to bring back 150 orphaned babies from Vietnam.[111] An editorial explained that the paper was offering 'a raft of hope' to those in 'the seas of despair'.

Next day the *Mail* devoted four pages to its 'mercy flight', reporting a 'magnificent' response from readers who were already beginning to send in money. Though the airlift was considered controversial, there was little direct criticism of the *Mail* in other papers. The *Daily Express* reported on Ford's efforts, ignoring the British airlift and carrying a short piece: 'A warning about adopting orphans, "Don't just look for a new pet".'[112] The *Daily Mirror* wrote of 'the growing chorus questioning the wisdom of the babylift organised by the *Daily Mail*', while the *Sunday Times* and the *Guardian* also aired doubts prominently in their news reports.[113]

The *Mirror*'s John Pilger saw the babylift as face-saving propaganda, while Marje Proops warned against adoption as an act of 'impulsive generosity'.[114] By Fleet Street standards though, criticism of the *Mail* was rather oblique, with a tendency not to mention the paper by name. When a *Mirror* editorial did question the airlift – 'Was it right to uproot these children in such an almighty hurry? ... Wouldn't it be better and wiser to channel our goodwill into helping them there?' – there was no mention of the *Mail* or of English.[115] Neither did the *Guardian*, when warning that 'adopting children and transferring them to another country ... is not something to be taken on swiftly', refer to the *Mail* by name.[116]

The *Mail*'s man in Saigon, defence correspondent Angus Macpherson, soon discovered the difficulties of finding the required 150 babies. His first call was to an orphanage run by a small British adoption society, Project Vietnam Orphans (PVO), founded by the Reverend Patrick Ashe. He was caring for sixteen babies but explained to Macpherson that it usually took two years to get official clearance to take such children out of Vietnam. Macpherson, aware that the North Vietnamese army was expected in three weeks, was more worried about his editor arriving within three days.[117] He urged Ashe to contact other orphanages, and one of his first calls was to the Ockendon Venture, another British-run home which had a policy of maintaining orphans within their home countries. Therefore, it hadn't sought official permission to take its children, most of whom were disabled, out of Vietnam. But the Venture's leader, David Tolfree, was also concerned by the widespread rumours of likely Vietcong atrocities and agreed that evacuation, at least for a short time, was justified. To overcome the problem of obtaining exit visas, Macpherson asked for help from the British consul-general in Saigon, Rex Hunt.

By the time the *Mail*'s plane arrived, Macpherson had ninety-nine children under his wing, twenty-two of whom were aged between five and fourteen. Many of the babies were malnourished and very sick, having existed in appalling conditions in some orphanages. Hunt, assured that they were all genuine orphans, expedited the necessary paper work despite many not having birth certificates. 'There was no doubt that I was being used,' he confessed years later. 'I could guess what the *Daily Mail* would say about the Foreign Office if we didn't help. But I thought it was for the good of the children.'[118] Hunt, unused to the Fleet Street relationship between editors and staff, said he was 'surprised' when English spoke 'sharply' to Macpherson because he hadn't been able to round up 'the 150 that English had ordered'.[119]

Once the children were taken on the plane they received medical help from doctors, nurses and other volunteers. One of the cabin crew, George Guy, said most of the children were badly dehydrated (mainly, it should be said, because of sitting for hours in appalling conditions on the coach at the airstrip while awaiting clearance). 'Some of the older kids were traumatised and didn't know what was happening,' recalled Guy.[120] Also on board were several of English's best journalistic troops, including the paper's senior feature writer Vincent Mulchrone and its award-winning photographer Monty Fresco. A couple of reporters, and English, helped to change the babies' nappies. For those who were older, and not suffering from illness, the experience was both baffling and, in at least one case, intensely sad. Though Minh Le, aged twelve, had no parents he had a family headed by an elder sister, and on the way to airport the coach passed his sister's house with him wishing he could say goodbye or, at least, tell her where he was going.

When the plane arrived at Heathrow airport on the night of 6 April it was reported straightforwardly by the *Times*.[121] Thirty of the refugees were said to have pneumonia, and all were alleged to be suffering from dehydration and malnutrition, though some clearly were not. The *Mail* devoted six pages to the airlift. Illness, explained the *Mail*, was the reason it had acted so quickly: 'Left in Vietnam, many would have died ... In Britain, all these 100 [it was 99] orphans will be given a chance to live and a chance to be loved.'[122] The doctors on board confirmed the medical emergency. On page three, next to a picture of editor English carrying one of the children to the plane, was a story which told how he had successfully argued with airport officials who would not allow take-off until they were sure that the children were entitled to leave their home country. The political message was spelled out in the page-four headline: 'Why didn't Cabinet act?'

To help identify the younger babies, some had numbers crayoned on their backs.[123] But in the sweltering heat of the plane, several were rubbed off and a television report showed a nurse cradling a baby without a name and number who said, unofficially, she planned to call the child Raymond after her late husband. The *Guardian* was the first paper to point out the problems of identification.[124]

On the following day, the *Mail* announced that six children had already been placed with adoptive parents, while thirty-four remained in hospital (where three eventually died), and the other fifty-nine were in reception homes. In succeeding days, the paper carried readers' letters saluting its initiative and reports of its readers' fund, which reached £57,000 within a week. The *Mail* milked the story for all it was worth, with headlines such as 'LOVE FLIES IN WITH LITTLE SWAN'.[125]

Before the airlift, a *Daily Telegraph* leader had argued that the best place for the orphans was in Vietnam.[126] Afterwards, without referring specifically to the *Mail*, the *Telegraph* agreed that 'two categories' of children should be flown out of Vietnam: those in need of medical care and 'those of mixed Vietnamese–foreign (American) parentage' because there were 'reports' of communists killing them.[127] In fact, Brian Barron, the BBC foreign correspondent who remained in Saigon after it fell to the Vietcong, said such fears had been unfounded: none of the city's children, including those of mixed race, were harmed. Barron did admit that prior to the arrival of the Vietcong fear was contagious: no one at the time could have been sure of being well treated. But Barron, speaking twenty-six years later, still felt the *Mail* mission had been ethically suspect, talking of English as 'a shabby General Custer galloping over the horizon to save kids in need'.[128] Another TV correspondent, ITN's Geoffrey Archer, filmed a news report while flying back with the children on the *Mail* plane. He told viewers then that, though he had wondered at first if it was right to take the orphans away, having seen their condition he was convinced it was. Looking back after twenty-six years, he said he had later had serious misgivings about the older children being removed from their culture.

The harshest contemporaneous criticism came from the *New Statesman*'s correspondent in Saigon, Richard West, who had once been a reporter for the *Mail* in Vietnam. The arrival of the British plane had been greeted 'with derision', he wrote, because the Vietnamese government 'had already released most of its quota of 1,400 orphans permitted to go abroad' so the *Mail* team had 'worked literally to the point of exhaustion to find babies suitable for evacuation'.[129]

West described English as 'the star of the airport ceremony' in his combat uniform 'inscribed with the words Bao Chi, or "journalist", just in case he happened to meet VC troops on the runway'. West, who thought the mission 'the most disgusting sham I have witnessed in nine years in Vietnam', dismissed one of the recurrent claims about the need to evacuate all the children who were the offspring of American soldiers and Vietnamese women, asserting: 'Few people of intelligence believe the stories that if the Communists arrived they would cut off the heads of children sired by Americans.'

The picture of English carrying the child in Saigon was reproduced, at twice the size, on the front page of the weekly trade magazine, to which he confided: 'The function of a newspaper is not only to report the news, but to help make it.'[130] He said it had been 'a great newspaper enterprise . . . not a stunt'. He added: 'If it was publicity that saved those children's lives, then I am proud to think we engendered that publicity.'

Letters to the *Times* and the *Guardian* expressed concern about the paper's motives and the ethics in removing the children from their home country.[131] Would they really have been at risk? Would they not have been better left in their own culture?[132] Two of the doctors on the flight, Gerald Griffin and Peter Martin Ebel, then defended the airlift in letters to the *Times* and *Daily Telegraph* respectively, claiming that most of the children would have faced certain death if they had been left in an orphanage.[133] Griffin also wrote to the *Guardian* to say that the future for the children if they had stayed was 'continuing medical neglect and almost certain death'. He praised 'the tremendous financial support' from the *Mail*'s readers.[134]

The doctors were backed by the Reverend Ashe,[135] and more letters supporting the *Mail* were published the next day. But an *Observer* report spoke of the 'anxiety' of British adoption agencies about the lack of proper arrangements.[136] Stewart Steven, the *Mail*'s associate editor, weighed in to answer those who believed that funds should have been provided for use within Vietnam: 'If we could be sure that the money given to the Red Cross would go to those most in need, then perhaps there would be a stronger case to call rescue flights like this inappropriate.'[137] This was almost a tacit admission that removing the children was questionable.

News of the orphans quickly vanished from the news agenda. Even some of those involved in settling the orphans believed their removal was only temporary. Morley Fletcher, secretary of the British Council for Aid for Refugees, which was co-ordinating efforts to place the orphans, told the *Sunday Times*: 'We believe that if the situation eventually settles in Saigon it will be in the best interests of the children to go back.'[138] A couple of weeks later journalist Victoria Brittain visited an Ockendon Venture home which was then looking after twenty-three of the children, eighteen of whom were severely handicapped. She wrote that they 'are expected to return to Saigon once the situation is stable'. Indeed, the older children 'look on these days as an interlude. "When are we going back to Saigon?" they ask every morning.'[139] It was not to be: the Venture found it impossible to negotiate the children's return with the Vietnamese authorities.[140]

There were periodic updates in the *Mail* in later years which extolled the virtues of the mission. 'Most are now university students, clever and industrious,' said one example by June Southworth, one of the reporters on the original flight into Saigon.[141] In 1996, she accompanied a group of seventeen orphans who returned, at the *Mail*'s expense, to Saigon (by then, renamed Ho Chi Minh City). She wrote: 'Experts agreed that had the children been left in Vietnam, few would have survived.' She cited one undoubted 'success story', that of Anna Gough, adopted as a wretched thirteenth-month-old baby by PVO volunteer Terry Gough. She had prospered and had nothing to regret about an upbringing which was plainly warm and loving.

But the generally upbeat prose could not disguise the distress of Minh Le at failing to find the sister whose faded photograph he carried with him everywhere. Nor did the updating articles ever mention several other disturbing stories, like that of Long Van La, a young boy crippled by polio, who spent four years at the Ockendon home. He was then fostered out to a family where he was abused, suffered a breakdown at fifteen and spent three years in a home for delinquents. 'All I want is to be loved and be happy,' he told a TV interviewer.[142] Nor did the *Mail* tell its readers that only fifty-one of the orphans were adopted; others were sent to special homes and several never left the Ockendon Venture home to which they were originally consigned. All of this was revealed in a television documentary screened in 2001 which traced many of the ninety-six surviving orphans and discovered that some had suffered terribly in the years following the airlift.[143]

It is, of course, impossible to know what might have happened to the ninety-nine if they had never boarded the *Mail* plane. Many more of them might have died. Several might have led unhappy lives. The disabled children may not have enjoyed the treatment they received in Britain. It was undoubtedly a humanitarian act of sorts, but the removal of children older than five from their homeland and culture was a rash stunt with lifelong consequences. More than a quarter of a century later Brian Freemantle remained convinced that the mission had been worth while, justifying what happened by saying: 'I believe I saved lives.'[144] His sincerity was transparent. What, though, of the lives that were blighted?

Express scoop was a farrago of lies

On 25 November 1972, the *Daily Express* announced a 'world exclusive disclosure' in the size of type usually reserved for the death of a monarch. Under the main headline, 'MARTIN BORMANN ALIVE', there was a helpful reminder to those who might have forgotten, or never known, that he had been 'Hitler's deputy'. Yet another headline announced: 'The *Express* has proof and knows exactly where he is living – until this story reaches him.' The article was unequivocal: at the age of seventy-two Bormann was 'living the life of a prosperous businessman in Latin America'. He had not been killed in 1945 as previously thought, nor had he lived secretly in the Soviet Union as one rumour suggested. He had been under constant surveillance in at least six South American countries.

There were 'secret files' which provided documentary proof of his identity. The whole front page of the Saturday issue was devoted to the story, with promises of more the following week. It was written by foreign editor Stewart Steven, but there was also a picture of a bespectacled, goatee-bearded, balding man identified as sixty-six-year-old Hungarian-born author Ladislas Farago, 'the man who led the *Express* search for Martin Bormann under the threat of death'. Farago was described as 'one of the world's greatest experts on Nazi Germany and a man who in the course of a long and distinguished career has uncovered secret after secret'. He was also said to have 'directed a campaign against Iron Curtain countries at the height of the cold war'.

Steven's piece retailed their amazing journeys 'in the Brazilian heartland ... deep into Paraguay' and along 'the Brazilian–Paraguyan–Argentinian border'. It seemed both romantic and authentic. On Monday the single word 'BORMANN' dominated the front page with a strapline: 'Now the evidence'.[145] Pictures of a man who called himself Ricardo Bauer were, said the paper, really of Bormann. He was talking to an Argentinian special agent 'in charge of the tracking of Nazi fugitives and Communist agents' identified as Jose Juan Velasco. A story inside announced that a West German judge had reopened his file on Bormann.

The world exclusive continued over the following five days with a surprising number of twists and turns. One story revealed that 'sources' within the Argentine intelligence services had admitted sheltering Bormann after the war during the presidency of Juan Perón. It included lots of 'facts', about the day Bormann arrived in Argentina, which boat he sailed on, the exact amount of money he paid out to secure his visa to stay in the country and a photocopy of his 'alien certificate'. New characters entered, such as Adolf Eichmann and Dr Josef Mengele, and one article took a surprising turn by criticising the celebrated Nazi-hunter Simon Wiesenthal. 'Throughout this series,' wrote Steven, 'Mr Farago's information has been of far superior quality to Mr Wiesenthal's.'[146] On the sixth day the mystery deepened when the paper announced that the Argentinian pictured with the man Farago alleged was Bormann, Juan Jose Velasco (not Jose Juan), had been arrested.[147] In the following week, the *Express* referred jubilantly to reports from Germany, New York and Washington about more people coming to believe Farago's claims.

The initial reaction from the rest of the press was muted, given that disproving the story was difficult. The *Times* simply recorded the fact that the *Express* had claimed Bormann was alive,[148] but the older hands were sceptical. Trying to put the *Express*'s story in some perspective, the columnist of the newspaper industry's trade magazine, *UK Press Gazette*, pointed out that 'senior citizens in newspapers have lived through 17 to 25 – the estimates vary – reports of "Bormann Found Alive". All have been, at least, exaggerated.' It added ominously: 'The *Express* story – even to justify its half-page headlines – had better be copper-bottomed.'[149] The *Sunday Times* settled for the *Express*'s Bormann being number 17, and its enterprising

German correspondent Antony Terry handed the Bormann picture to a Munich anthropologist who told him 'with a probability bordering on certainty' that it was not Bormann. He gave his reasons through a convincing picture comparison which was reproduced on the paper's Spectrum pages.[150] Terry also pointed out that the *Express* articles appeared to experts to be 'a masterful conglomeration of every detail, past and present, confirmed and unconfirmed, of the Bormann mystery'.

At the same time as the *Express* ran the Bormann story and picture so did the *New York Daily News*, and it was in that city that the first seeds of disquiet about the story's authenticity, and Farago's credibility, were sown. A *New York Times* report poured scorn on the Bormann pictures. Its Buenos Aires correspondent had interviewed Velasco and shown him the *Daily News* picture. Velasco told him that the man pictured with him was not Bormann but a schoolteacher friend of his called Rodolfo Siri. He said that they had been standing outside a café in Buenos Aires. Velasco also said he was no longer an intelligence agent, that he had never sought Bormann, and that documents used in the *Express* story were forgeries. The *Daily Mail* couldn't conceal its joy, headlining its report: 'That's not Bormann, it's my friend Mr Siri'.[151]

Apparently undaunted, the *Express* carried a series of quotes from Farago denying Velasco's claims and predicting that he would soon reveal 'evidence' that was 'unimpeachably authentic, authoritative and accurate'.[152] The *Mail*, by now convinced that the Bormann story was false, poked fun at its rival. A front-page blurb boasting about a minor scoop of its own, said: 'News – exclusive news – and not fiction. That is the hallmark of the *Daily Mail*.'[153]

The ground crumbled further when Siri's wife said the man in the picture was definitely her husband and not Bormann. But Steven wasn't the only person taken in by Farago's fantasies. He was pursued by publishers and film-makers, and Paramount Pictures announced that it had offered Farago £100,000 for the rights to the Bormann story.[154] Its president, Frank Yablans, even hosted a press conference at which he was forced to defend Farago as journalists cross-questioned him. The *Express* reported the press conference in positive terms, but the *Sunday Times*'s Stephen Aris revealed how Farago had fooled Velasco and Siri.[155] He had obtained the picture by posing as a man who was testing out a new camera. He had falsified the documents and concocted the story of Bormann's movements and other details by mixing together previous stories, just as Aris's colleague, Antony Terry, had suggested two weeks before. It was a pack of lies, a giant hoax perpetrated by a conman.

The innocent Siri, wrongly named as Bormann, was reported to be suffering from threats to his life, and announced that he would sue the *Express* and the *Daily News*. By a remarkable coincidence, the *Times* reported two months later that a skeleton found in a West Berlin railway yard was 'without any doubt' that of Bormann.[156] The following year, on the basis of that evidence, Bormann was declared officially dead by the registrar's office in Berlin.[157] Farago refused to believe it and two years later wrote a book, *Aftermath*, in which he claimed to have met Bormann in a Bolivian hospital run by nuns of the Redemptorist Order. There was no redemption at the *Express* for Steven, who left soon after the fiasco, crossing to the rival *Daily Mail* as assistant editor to David English.

PART SEVEN: 1976–1980

13. SELLING OFF THE FAMILY SILVER

Fleet Street is not an industry noted for its rational behaviour.[1]

On a cold January day in 1979, with strikes seemingly breaking out by the hour across Britain, a sun-tanned prime minister, James Callaghan, returned from a summit meeting in the French West Indies. He was 'in a half-joking, half-tetchy mood' with journalists who asked him questions at the airport, reported the *Daily Telegraph*.[2] He told one reporter: 'Please don't run down your own country by talking of mounting chaos ... I do not feel there is mounting chaos.'[3]

None of the broadsheets considered this a remarkable statement, but the *Sun* insisted that it 'oozed complacency' and, putting words into Callaghan's mouth, ran the headline that was to haunt him ever after: 'CRISIS? WHAT CRISIS?'[4] Though it can reasonably be argued that it was a paraphrase of sorts, its abruptness, apparent nonchalance and hint of paternalism were very different from Callaghan's real words and intention. Anyway, fair or not, the bogus quote stuck. Next day the *Telegraph* referred in its leading article to 'a national crisis', proof of the effectiveness of the *Sun*'s spin.[5] The headline caught the imagination and was taken up by other papers too (see next chapter).

A lorry drivers' strike in the same period depleted newsprint supplies so that most papers were forced to cut their pagination. The *Sun* was reduced to as little as twelve pages, as was the *Guardian*, and the *Sun* often repeated its 'Crisis? What Crisis?' headline, reinforcing the image of a prime minister out of touch with reality.[6] Rupert Murdoch and his fellow owners were certain there was a crisis, and their editors, as both lyricists and composers of the mood music that winter, held sway. Their predictions of a crisis-hit, bankrupt, helpless Britain stretched back to the three-day week under Ted Heath. After Wilson's second election victory in 1974, in an attempt to create some kind of industrial order, he put his faith in the 'social contract', an agreement by which the government offered decent industrial laws in return for the unions' acceptance of voluntary wage restraint. Union leaderships were sympathetic but found it difficult to restrain their rebellious troops.

In March 1976, after Wilson's resignation, he was replaced by Callaghan who was quickly nicknamed 'Sunny Jim' by the press. He was forced to negotiate a large loan from the International Monetary Fund in return for spending cuts of £2 billion. Though this undermined Britain's global status, it seemed to sort out the domestic problem at first, and the country settled into a brief period of prosperity with relative industrial harmony. This state of affairs wasn't reflected in newspapers, as the historian Kenneth O. Morgan noted: 'While the press and media were full of lamentations of woe, the quality of life of large sections of the population seemed to advance steadily.'[7]

By 1977 the social contract began to break down and the TUC voted to return to free collective bargaining that autumn. Firemen went on strike, as did power engineers, water workers and even NHS ambulance drivers. Mass picketing at a little-known photo-processing plant in north London, Grunwick, became a nationally important dispute. Within newspapers, owners and editors were in the forefront of industrial struggles, as both victims and propagandists.

Across Fleet Street there were widespread breaches of pay limits as managements were forced to conspire with their unions in order to ensure continued production. Wage increases were granted far above the government's norm and then covered up by false declarations of productivity or special circumstances. A 1978 survey revealed that in the first six months of that year Fleet Street lost 105 million copies due to industrial action which wasn't restricted to matters of pay and conditions. The *Times* lost an issue in January 1977 when its NGA chapel refused to allow the paper to carry a report about an article in a small-circulation magazine by the former *Observer* owner, David Astor, which criticised the print unions' use of closed shops.[8] The following day a *Times* leader defended its refusal to bow to union pressure.[9]

Pay *was* the motor that drove most disputes. It was relatively easy for unions split into scores of chapels to use a pay agreement reached with one group as the starting point for 'leap-frogging' by others to maintain differentials, particularly when special one-off payments were made. For example, in the very hot summer of 1976, as a self-proclaimed 'convenor' of casual journalists on the *Sunday Mirror*, I was able to extract a £6 per shift 'hot weather allowance' for my NUJ members, all of whom had full-time jobs on other papers. This figure was loosely based on the rumoured extra payment given to men sweating in the machine room.

By this time, another feature of former Fleet Street journalistic life – the instantaneous sacking on the whim of owner or editor – had virtually disappeared. The NUJ had become powerful enough to ensure that no one could be fired, even for incompetence. At the *Sun*, the chapel managed to save the job of a drunken sports writer who had leaped on to a desk, dropped his trousers and exposed himself. At Mirror group, the chapels secured an automatic replacement guarantee 'even of layabouts who were useless'.[10]

Backdoor print deals could hardly remain a secret within the union movement and the newspaper industry was far from the only one in which workers found their way round the pay barriers. With public service workers desperate not to be left behind workers in private industry, who were winning huge awards, there was a rash of strikes across the country. Rubbish piled up in the streets, with London's Leicester Square becoming a dump. Grave-diggers in Liverpool refused to bury bodies. Schools closed because caretakers and cleaners went on strike. In February 1979, when unions reached an agreement which was twice the government's 5 per cent norm, the press revelled in Callaghan's embarrassment.

Callaghan's government was voted out of office in March and Thatcher's Tories won the resulting election with a majority of forty-four seats. Most papers registered intense delight at the outcome, with owners and editors clearly believing that the new Conservative administration, in contrast to Heath's, had the answer to the country's economic and industrial problems. Though the political tide was indeed about to turn, it was too late to keep some press magnates afloat. David Astor and Max Aitken gave up their respective inheritances, the *Observer* and Express Newspapers. One Thomson died and the next one, having painted himself into a corner by keeping the *Times* and *Sunday Times* off the streets for a year, also decided to sell up. One Rothermere died, and the next one closed the London *Evening News* for good. Pearson's *Financial Times* fought vainly to introduce new technology, as did the groups running the Mirror, Telegraph and Express titles. After three years, the Royal Commission reported what everyone already knew: Fleet Street was a basket case staffed by people hell-bent on committing suicide without a Samaritan to offer guidance.

Yet daily newspaper circulations went up between 1976 and 1980. Popular paper sales rose, helped by the launch of a new title, the *Daily Star*, from 11.82 million to 12.51 million, while the four serious broadsheets recorded an overall increase from 2.11 million to 2.28 million. The Sunday figures revealed the underlying divergence of fortunes between the two kinds of newspaper: sales of the four populars dived from 16.75 million to 14.78 million while the three qualities soared from 2.78 million to 3.36 million. With the print unions having gained 'the mastery of Fleet Street',[11] rising sales did not mean rising profits and certainly didn't provide for necessary investment, as Hartwell's Telegraph company was to discover. Improved circulations were reflected in editorial stability, with owners largely switching editors only out of strict necessity. Bucking that trend, however, were the declining *Daily Express*, with another four changes of editor, and the fledgling *Daily Star*, with three editors in its first two years.

By now, the omnipresent figure was Murdoch, who was on his way to becoming a global newspaper tycoon. In 1976, he bought the *New York Post*, *New York* magazine and the *Village Voice*. A couple of years later he acquired his father's old paper, the *Melbourne Herald*. Convinced that he had the magic touch and could turn around even the least hopeful of ailing British papers, he also made bids for the *Observer*, the Express titles and Times Newspapers. Not much happened in the British press without Murdoch being involved.

Sailor Max sells off the Beaverbrook flagship

The sale of the Express titles was anything but straightforward. It was a slow, tortuous battle which ended with the most unlikely of victors, the creation of a monopoly London evening title, the founding of a new daily paper and the confirmation that the era of the individual newspaper-owning entrepreneur, a non-corporate capitalist, was over.

If we ask, what's the point of owning a newspaper?, three reasons spring to mind: to act as a public-spirited purveyor of information, to wield political influence, to make money. The first never did apply to Sir Max Aitken (and, arguably, to no one else but the Scott Trust, the Astors and Lord Hartwell). As for the second, unlike his father, Lord Beaverbrook, Aitken showed no enthusiasm for intervening in the nation's political life, whether directly through the columns of the *Daily* and *Sunday Express*, or indirectly by consorting with the great and the good. He kept his papers faithful to the Tory party, but that was as far as his interest went. By the mid-1970s, the third reason had vanished too as losses piled up, and the bank threatened not to renew its overdraft facility.[12]

Aitken, whose major pleasure was in sailing motorboats rather than navigating Fleet Street's stormy waters, lacked journalistic passion. It would have been entirely understandable if he had repeatedly asked himself in the previous ten years why he bothered to go on bearing the burden. In November 1976, he suffered the first of a series of strokes and soon after authorised his managing director, Jocelyn Stevens, to talk to Rothermere's Associated about a possible merger. To an outsider, the very idea of 'the two dinosaurs' seeking a truce in a battle during which 'forests have been levelled, aeroplanes needlessly hired, expense accounts fudged and marriages smashed' appeared remarkable.[13] But there had been similar talks in 1970 which were aborted partially because of Stevens's hostility (see above, p. 226).

This time Stevens was the prime mover and, it must be said in his favour, he was acting from altruistic motives. The Aitken family was in considerable financial trouble and Stevens was doing his best to rescue them from Max Aitken's incompetence. In the circumstances, cutting a deal with the old enemy made sense. Stevens could understand why Vere Harmsworth at Associated would be receptive: his revamped tabloid *Daily Mail* was doing quite well but his London *Evening News*, selling 536,000 copies, was losing some £4 million a year. Could he save money by merging it with Aitken's *Evening Standard*, also losing money while selling 418,000 but with a growing advertising income? At the same time, was there some way in which he could either eradicate or neutralise the threat from the *Daily Express*?

Associated was better placed than Beaverbrook Newspapers, which was in a sorry state. The company had borrowed £14 million to replace antiquated pressroom machinery. Annual interest payments for the loan had reached £1.9 million by the summer of 1976 and the repayments were becoming an intolerable burden. Losses were running at £1.5 million. Unlike Associated, there had been no diversification into regional papers, no oil and no television. The rise in newsprint prices added to its difficulties. Sales of the *Daily Express* were falling rapidly. Advertisers, noting the ageing profile of the remaining readers, were not keen to spend money. The *Evening Standard* was suffering from an advertising slump. The *Sunday Express* brought in money but that, too, was heading into decline and failing to attract new, younger readers. Its profits were crucial to the group but editor John Junor's formula was terribly outdated. At the end of 1974, sales fell below 4 million and began to drop at an alarming rate thereafter. Junor the columnist had come into his own, but Junor the editor was way past his best.

All of these problems convinced Aitken to sell, and while he was recovering from his stroke in January 1977 he strengthened Stevens's position by appointing him chief executive and joint deputy chairman. This also placed him in charge of Aitken's twenty-six-year-old son, Maxwell, who had been working in a variety of junior executive positions to prepare him for the day he would, so he imagined, inherit the business. It gave Stevens virtually free rein and one of his first decisions was to ape the *Mail* by transforming the *Daily Express* into a tabloid.

At the end of February 1976, the bizarre experiment of moving up-market with Alastair Burnet as editor came to an end. Burnet had become an increasingly isolated figure, having failed to impose his will on the paper by changing its traditional culture. The man who had recommended him, Junor, wrote years later: 'Dear Alastair. He was and is such a lovely man. So gentle, so decent, so compassionate. But he was not cut out to be the editor of a popular national daily.'[14] Arriving at work with a bottle of whisky tucked under his arm, Burnet headed straight for his office and rarely left it all day, famously sending messengers to the local betting office to place his bets. Within weeks, his senior executives realised he had no clue how to run a paper. He also proved to be out of step with Aitken on politics, supporting Ted Heath – a long-time friend – rather than Margaret Thatcher.[15] Aitken instructed another senior executive, Robin Esser, to publish a front-page statement supporting Thatcher, a policy Burnet only discovered the next morning. Though he didn't have the mettle for editing the *Express*, in resuming his broadcasting career he became one of the nation's best-respected television news presenters at ITN.

The *Express* immediately took another editorial lurch: now Stevens expected the paper to attract 'the newly affluent upper working class' plus more women and, of course, the young. The man charged with this task was Roy Wright, aged fifty, promoted from deputy editor of the *Evening Standard*, who was everything that Burnet wasn't. A lifelong newspaperman, he had worked his way up the ladder from local weeklies to Fleet Street and knew a great deal about production. He was, thought Junor, 'an excellent technician and a good handler of news stories. But he lacked the charisma a good editor needs.'[16] Wright, who initially imagined that his central job was to return the *Express* to its traditional news-based formula, was later entrusted with turning it into a tabloid. He had some high-powered help, from his former boss, the *Evening Standard*'s Charles Wintour, who had stood down from the editor's chair. Though Stevens's decision to change its shape was largely carried out for economic reasons, to maximise advertising income, he had noted the *Mail*'s editorial success with the smaller page size.

The first tabloid *Express*, on 23 January 1977, 'was impressive, but less than dazzling'.[17] Its main selling point was the serialisation of a book about the death of Hollywood recluse Howard Hughes. The relaunch, which cost £500,000, delighted Wintour because sales immediately went up by 400,000. But the rivals made a successful counter-attack, with the *Daily Mail* splashing out on two big 'buy-ups' and the *Daily Mirror*, waiting until the first impact had passed, then serialising the engrossing memoirs of Harold Wilson's former press secretary Joe Haines.[18] By the second month, the *Express*'s extra sales began to disappear.

Yet that was also the month in which serious merger talks started between the Express team – Stevens, his joint deputy chairman and finance director Peter Hetherington, and Maxwell Aitken – and Associated, represented by Harmsworth and his managing director Mick Shields. Harmsworth believed he was in the driving seat: his company's latest half-year profits were some £6 million while the Beaverbrook group was facing a loss of more than £1 million. That a bitter sales war between the *Express* and *Mail* should occur during merger negotiations was odd enough. The situation grew more bizarre when Stevens's own management team collapsed: his joint deputies quit, as did two senior managers. With Aitken still recuperating 'Jocelyn ran wild,' said Hetherington.[19] By spring 1977 Hetherington had grown so disenchanted that he supported a coup inspired by Aitken's son, Maxwell, to oust Stevens. When confronted by Hetherington, Stevens refused to accept his notice of dismissal and went to see the ailing Aitken, charming him into submission, urging him to promote Maxwell to his side and to fire the other plotters, including Hetherington.

Having won his internal battle, Stevens forged ahead with the Associated negotiations. He and Harmsworth were conscious that another predator had arrived on the scene: in early January, Sir James Goldsmith revealed that he had bought 35 per cent of Beaverbrook Newspapers' non-voting stock from Rupert Murdoch for £1.6 million. Goldsmith, a wealthy businessman and a controversial figure, had just failed in a bid to buy the *Observer* (see below, pp. 332–3), and was eager to own a national title. Though Stevens was sympathetic, neither Aitken nor Harmsworth wished to accommodate him and Aitken urged Stevens to press ahead with the Associated talks. Both sides soon agreed that merging their two London evenings was the only sensible course. Associated would buy the *Standard* and merge it with the *News*, with both companies sharing the redundancy bill. They would also set up a joint printing company based on a buy-out of Beaverbrook's Fleet Street plant.

To the negotiators it seemed like a dream deal. To Charles Wintour, who had just stood down, aged sixty, after seventeen years as *Standard* editor, it was anything but a good idea. He was now managing director of the *Express* and chairman of the *Standard*, with a powerful voice and a status that Aitken and Stevens could not ignore. He despised the *News* and, by extension, its owners. He argued that if the papers had to be merged, the resulting paper should, in effect, be a reborn *Standard*, retaining the identity he had created and which his successor, Simon Jenkins, was dedicated to continuing. Jenkins, aged thirty-three, was Wintour's protégé, having built a formidable reputation as a polemicist, particularly in his writings about London's architectural environment. Educated at Mill Hill and Oxford, he started his journalistic career at *Country Life* and then became news editor of the *Times Educational Supplement*. From the moment he moved to the *Standard* in 1968, his intelligent writing impressed Wintour, known for his 'ability to spot and encourage nascent talent',[20] and he was advanced rapidly up the executive ladder.

Jenkins and Wintour adopted a similar stance on what they feared to be a takeover by Associated and the likely submerging of the *Standard*'s personality within a down-market *News*. Wintour, who had a high opinion of himself and his paper, considered that the merger would be 'an act contrary to the public interest' because the *Standard* 'does attempt to play some serious role' while 'the *Evening News* does not'.[21] Aitken also got cold feet and urged Wintour to find an alternative buyer.[22] To do so, Jenkins and Wintour then wielded 'every political and social weapon' they could find.[23] While they hunted for a saviour, the project's secrecy was blown in the *Times*.[24] This allowed them to widen their net and throughout April, while talks continued between Stevens and Shields, Wintour kept up pressure to deter the merger, even accepting help from the print union chapels, which organised marches along Fleet Street. Nervous van drivers occupied the Express boardroom.[25]

The rest of the press, alarmed by Associated's growing strength, largely supported Wintour: the *Daily Telegraph* bemoaned a possible loss of diversity.[26] In a conciliatory move, Harmsworth invited Wintour and Jenkins to his Eaton Square home to meet *Daily Mail* editor David English and Lou Kirby, the *Evening News* editor. Harmsworth suggested an advisory committee to select staff but Wintour wrote: 'I was so wound up at any idea that the *Standard*, a paper I loved and whose staff I cherished, might die that I rejected all thoughts of compromise.'[27] Jenkins felt the same way, rejecting

Harmsworth's offer that he become Kirby's deputy. If Jenkins had been offered the editorship instead the deal would have gone through.[28]

For a while, despite Aitken's opposition, Wintour and Jenkins pinned their hopes on Goldsmith, who was the largest shareholder by far and, though he didn't hold the key voting shares, he was aware that Aitken would soon need to raise capital and, under stock exchange rules, would have to issue more voting shares. Then he would pounce by making a full bid. Goldsmith openly expressed his enthusiasm to buy, but the only serious reason he could offer was that the newspaper industry was 'creative, amusing [and] challenging'.[29] He did not mention another pertinent reason: he was anxious to thwart Associated 'as a financial penalty' for having on its staff gossip columnist Nigel Dempster, whom he blamed for allegedly libellous stories about him in *Private Eye*.[30]

Goldsmith's eagerness to become a newspaper tycoon was thwarted by the changed nature of capitalism. Rich as he was, he couldn't afford to buy the paper himself. It would have to be done through his company, Cavenham Foods, and there lay his central problem. In returning that public company to private ownership, he was about to take on a huge loan in France, and his new investors wouldn't take kindly to his buying a loss-making paper which required substantial investment.[31] To try to overcome the problem, Goldsmith pushed his luck by demanding that his stock should be converted to voting shares. While this was being considered, and rejected, the *Standard* celebrated its 150th anniversary, producing its largest-ever issue of sixty-four pages on pink newsprint. Jenkins's leader was pugnacious and optimistic: 'We have been bought and sold many times ... We are determined to play a full and growing role in the future.'[32]

Five days later Wintour – latching on to the *Daily Mail* slush-fund blunder (see below, pp. 345–6) – launched a bitter public attack on Harmsworth in a speech which caused a sensation.[33] He called on Harmsworth 'to put his own house in order before he tries to expand his inheritance any further'.[34] He then pointed to the fundamentally undemocratic nature of inherited wealth. Labour politicians liked the speech, as did the NUJ and other print unions.[35] Aitken certainly didn't, because Wintour seemed to be overlooking the fact that *his* newspaper ownership was also a matter of nepotism. It is extraordinary that Wintour survived this period.

Goldsmith's next manoeuvre was to join forces with another controversial figure, 'Tiny' Rowland, who had recently become a newspaper owner in Scotland, almost by accident. In February 1977, he bought Sir Hugh Fraser's 24 per cent stake in Scottish & Universal Investments (SUITS), a conglomerate which owned a whisky distillery, a book publishers and George Outram's, publishers of the *Glasgow Herald* and the *Glasgow Evening Times*, along with 10 per cent of Britain's biggest stores group, the House of Fraser. The deal caused consternation because both men agreed the purchase without seeking approval from their boards.

What really interested Rowland – who controlled the mining conglomerate Lonrho – was not the papers, but the fact that House of Fraser owned Harrods. Though he did not yet have the funds to launch a full bid for the company, which he viewed as an asset-stripping opportunity, he aimed to use his minority position to good effect. Over the next three years this attempted coup was to develop from a sideshow into a long-running centre-stage saga (see below, pp. 392, 530–1). For now though, Rowland could see benefits in owning the *Express* and formed a joint company with Goldsmith called 'Cavrho'. The alliance collapsed when Goldsmith failed to produce his £7.5 million half-share, despite Rowland offering to loan him the money. Rowland was furious when he later discovered that Goldsmith, who made largely ineffectual statements from the sidelines right up until the papers were sold, made £2 million profit from the sale of his shares.[36]

Rupert Murdoch was next to enter the fray. He met Aitken and offered to provide £10 million in working capital and the introduction of a new management team.[37] He also offered to buy Aitken's 20 per cent holding of voting shares and sent a cheque for £1.4 million 'made out to Sir Max personally'.[38] By now, however, Wintour and Jenkins had found what they believed to be their white knight. In his trawl for buyers, Jenkins had previously approached Nigel Broackes, the chairman of Trafalgar House, a construction and shipping conglomerate. Aitken also sent an emissary to Broackes towards the end of May.[39]

Broackes, an urbane solicitor's son from a public school background, had built up Trafalgar by making a number of lucrative property deals before diversifying into construction. One of his acquisitions was a building firm, Bridge Walker, which had been created by Victor Matthews, a working-class lad who had made his way up from the bottom of the building trade. In 1964, Broackes went into partnership with Matthews, who was fifteen years his senior, each benefiting from the other's different personalities and skills. Broackes, the smooth, financially astute strategist, had vision. Matthews, a shrewd, street-wise, plain-speaking man, was a hard-nosed manager of men and assets. Broackes was an optimist while Matthews was inclined to pessimism, 'doubtful and suspicious of the future'.[40] Their partnership worked so successfully that they acquired two huge construction companies, Cementation and Trollope & Colls, and two of Britain's best-known institutions, the Cunard shipping line and the Ritz Hotel, turning all of them into profitable enterprises. By 1977, Trafalgar had a turnover of almost £600 million.

Having acted as an adviser over the redevelopment of some of its properties, Broackes knew a little about Aitken's problems. He also wanted to solve a problem of his own: Matthews had become 'morbid and morose', he claimed, and was talking of retirement. His wife was also unwell. So, 'at the forefront of my mind', he wrote, 'was the desire to see Victor once again engrossed in a challenge.' He needed 'something to do'.[41]

Both Broackes and Matthews were tempted by Beaverbrook Newspapers' hidden asset – a valuable property portfolio – and they made their decision to buy very quickly. Stevens advised Aitken to return Murdoch's cheque and then warned Associated that it now had a serious competitor. Trafalgar proved it by making a formal bid on 30 June 1977, raising an initial offer of £12.5 million to £13.69 million and finally to a total of £14.59 million. Wintour and Jenkins were relieved when Associated didn't call to offer more, and the next day the *Daily Express* front page extolled the virtues of its new ownership.

In commercial terms, Trafalgar had made a killing. The tangible assets were £21.1 million and the properties were, according to former managing director John Coote, 'grossly undervalued at £26.2 million'.[42] The Beaverbrook Foundation got £3 million of the purchase price, Sir Max Aitken walked away with £1.2 million and his son Maxwell ended up with £99,000. As Aitken stepped for the last time from that famous art-deco Fleet Street building commissioned by his father Lord Beaverbrook, he said: 'I've given up because I got ill . . . I think he [Beaverbrook] would have sold up before long.'[43]

The rest of Fleet Street was distinctly underwhelmed with the new ownership. A *Times* profile of Trafalgar's bosses ended with a barbed comment about Matthews: 'He gives the impression still of being slightly amazed at what has happened to him.'[44] Union leader Owen O'Brien, general secretary of Natsopa, wasn't impressed either, forecasting with an uncanny prescience: 'All we are going to do is to defer the crisis of Beaverbrook Newspapers another couple of years.'[45] Although Trafalgar had bought the papers, Broackes saw Beaverbrook Newspapers as his partner's plaything and took no part in the day-to-day running of the company. Matthews, who immediately cast himself in the role of a pre-war proprietor, explained his home-spun philosophy to the BBC: 'I am just like any other chap that we see walking across the street now who has got to the top and if that can happen in a country in a straightforward way, by hard work, then I am very anxious to maintain that.'[46]

Victor Collin Matthews was fifty-seven. His only experience of newspapers was delivering them as a youngster in Islington. Raised by his mother, his father having fled the family home, he attended a Church of England elementary school in Highbury, leaving to become an office boy in a cigarette factory. At twenty, he joined the Royal Naval Volunteer Reserve as an ordinary seaman and took part in number of dangerous operations during the war. Afterwards, he joined Trollope & Colls as a trainee and worked his way up to contracts manager before being fired, a slight he did not forget when he found himself in charge of the company many years later.[47] Being sacked spurred Matthews to succeed, and the result was his creation in the following years of Bridge Walker, a profitable building enterprise. His chief interests were golf and horse-racing.

Matthews, described by Wintour as 'the most unlikely newspaper publisher of the century',[48] made a number of early errors. First, he maintained Stevens in his chief executive role, thus ensuring that the culture wouldn't change. Given his own lack of knowledge of the industry, it also made him unduly reliant on Stevens, who soon 'had Victor eating out of his hand', noted Junor.[49] Second, Matthews angered Express staff by spending many thousands of the company's pounds refurbishing Beaverbrook's old office for himself.[50] Third, his head was turned by the discovery that newspaper controllers have access to the high and mighty: he was soon accepting invitations to visit the prime minister, the chancellor and Mrs Thatcher.[51] Then he tended to defer too readily to criticisms of his newspapers' contents from such people.[52]

Fourth, Matthews foolishly made a number of public pronouncements about journalism. His most unwise, if truthful, statement was that 'by and large the editors will have complete freedom as long as they agree with the policy I have laid down'.[53] Fifth, just five weeks after moving in, he fired the *Daily Express* editor, Roy Wright, in favour of Derek Jameson. Wright may not have been the best of editors, but it's difficult not to sympathise with him. In his seventeen months as editor he had made some sense of the paper after the Alastair Burnet years while coping with Stevens's erratic managerial style. Ironically, Wright saw Matthews as a breath of fresh air, but he was given no time to savour it. And what convinced Matthews that Jameson was the right man to replace him, apart from their shared heritage as London lads?

Many editors have talked themselves up the promotion ladder, concealing their limited talents by boastfulness, convincing their superiors that they could succeed simply by exercising their formidable personalities. Jameson certainly fell into that bracket, though he did have journalistic skills which, combined with his rough-hewn charm, might have worked well at a red-top. The *Daily Express* was far from being Jameson's perfect arena, though with Matthews making a hash of trying to ape Beaverbrook, and Stevens playing Flashman of *Tom Brown's Schooldays*, perhaps no one could have succeeded.[54]

By the time Jameson arrived at the *Express*, aged forty-seven, his working-class past was widely known since he was given to romanticising his humble origins in pub soliloquies. The first volume of his autobiography revealed that his childhood was grindingly poor.[55] Born and raised in Hackney, east London, he never knew who his father was. He claimed to have learned to read through *Daily Mirror* comic strips Pip, Squeak and Wilfred and Buck Ryan.[56] At fourteen, he got a job as a messenger with Reuters news agency, later wangling some training as a reporter. After national service, he rose through the ranks at Reuters to become chief sub by 1960, when he joined an ill-fated weekly for expat Americans. A year or so later he was hired as a features sub by the *Daily Express* and so began the process of trading on his brash Cockney persona. His reputation for good work, not to mention hyping his occasional contributions to the *Express*'s admired Photonews page, reached the ears of *Sunday Mirror* editor Reg Payne. Jameson was taken on as a features sub on the understanding that he would soon be picture editor.

After Payne's departure, Jameson had a more difficult relationship with his successor, Michael Christiansen, and was 'promoted' to assistant editor of the *Sunday Mirror*'s northern office in 1965. He later ran production in London for four years before returning to Manchester in 1972 as the *Sunday Mirror*'s northern editor. Of his subsequent promotion to the *Daily Mirror* northern editorship, Jameson wrote: 'I was within grasp of my life's ambition to be editor of the world's greatest tabloid paper.'[57]

It was not to be. *Daily Mirror* editor Tony Miles was no fan of Jameson's style nor of his editorial decisions. He exploited the *Sun*'s lack of northern sports coverage, dared to use Page 3 girl pictures and followed a raunchier news agenda than the London-based issue, all of which, conceded *Sun* editor Larry Lamb, 'successfully inhibited the growth of my own newspaper'.[58] But Miles thought Jameson's papers undermined the *Mirror*'s standing, while Jameson thought Miles just didn't like his accent. There were many other Jameson detractors within *Mirror* group, but it has to be said that he was hugely entertaining company. He drank very little but he loved nothing better than regaling people in bars. John Junor thought him 'a real comic' who 'made people fall off their chairs laughing at his jokes'.[59] He also left many gasping with his audacious stretching of the truth, casting himself as the catalyst in scores of incidents and events in which he played, at best, a tangential role.

The man who beat him to the *Mirror* chair, Mike Molloy, made Jameson his managing editor in London, a position which enabled him to advertise his talents, through the grapevine, to other owners. In the summer of 1977 he lunched with Rupert Murdoch soon after he had bid for the *Express.* A month later, he met Matthews, they got on well, and Matthews offered him the *Express* editorship. Jameson's appointment had little initial impact on the circulation decline, but he did introduce a more aggressive style, chasing big stories and competing for buy-ups. He hired an art editor from the *Sun*, Vic Giles, noted for his dazzling page designs. In 1978, he did what no editor since Bob Edwards in 1963 had done by adding substantial sales. He serialised Peter Townsend's autobiography and made a lot of noise with a sexy tale about a woman who kidnapped a Mormon missionary. Considering the *Daily Mail* too 'tidy and feminine' to chase, his agenda was aimed more at winning over *Sun* readers.[60] The sales success has to be understood in those terms too: most of the extra buyers were gained when the *Sun* was off the streets due to a series of industrial disputes.

The *Daily Express*'s most famous columnist of the era, Jean Rook, thought Jameson 'a brilliant, intuitive editor' as well as 'a one-man Palladium show'.[61] But he faced continuous hostility within the organisation from

Stevens, who hadn't been consulted about his appointment, and retaliated by harassing a man he clearly despised. Jameson complained to Matthews that Stevens was 'bullying, arrogant and insulting'.[62] Matthews did nothing about it, allowing himself to be swayed by each man in turn, failing to realise – as Aitken did before him – that Stevens was the company's real problem. Jameson reported that Stevens told him at their first meeting: 'I loathe and detest ALL journalists.'[63]

His detestation, and those whispers in Matthews's ear, were to have an effect. But Matthews had other problems to worry about within a few weeks of becoming a newspaper proprietor. Though he had asked for three months' industrial peace, members of the engineering union demanded pay parity with the highest-paid printers, a 75 per cent rise in wages taking them from £140 to £250 a week. Matthews refused, naturally enough, and the engineers held a disruptive chapel meeting during working hours. When they ignored a request to return to work, Matthews dismissed them.

This fairly typical dispute took an unusual turn when it was discovered that some of the engineers had removed essential equipment from the foundry, making it impossible for page plates to be cast. Matthews talked of industrial sabotage, called in the police, erected barbed wire around the building and threatened to move production to Manchester. He ordered Jameson to carry a front-page leader 'WE SHALL NOT BE MOVED' which suggested that this new owner was going to be tougher than the veteran bosses by confronting his unions. It began: 'Far too many within the industry have cashed in on the vulnerability of newspapers.'[64] Matthews held firm, and the engineers called in their national negotiator, Reg Birch, one of the most experienced, wily and witty of union leaders. He also happened to be founder of a quasi-Maoist offshoot of the Communist party, the Communist party of Britain (Marxist–Leninist), to which I belonged at that time. As he emerged from his first round of talks he was confronted by a TV reporter who thrust a microphone into his face and asked what he thought of the engineers' alleged removal of machine parts. Birch famously replied: 'If I've told my members once I've told them a thousand times not to take their work home with them.'

This outrageous quip was symptomatic of a period in which the unions were so self-confident. After seven days, Matthews reached a settlement with Birch, the significance of which some commentators, notably Charles Wintour, misread.[65] It was assumed that by winning some concessions from the engineers – such as 'the right of the management to manage' and an agreement to consider redundancies – Matthews had won a great victory. In fact, as Simon Jenkins, pointed out, it was a bogus claim: all the sacked engineers were reinstated, the signed agreement did not curb their activities. The real winner was Reg Birch.[66] It also later transpired that the engineers had not taken the foundry parts home with them after all: they had cheekily hidden the equipment in the boot of the managing director's car.[67]

Matthews's singular, but considerable, success was in showing other owners, and possibly even the new Tory government, that unions could be brought to heel in the courts. He won three key actions, against printers and journalists, which prevented them from resorting to disruptive behaviour. These were limited in scope, but a seed had been sown.

As the group showed signs of moving from loss into profit in early 1978, Matthews removed Beaverbrook's name from the company's title, renaming it Express Newspapers. Matthews, like Beaverbrook, took a close interest in the bit of the *Daily Express* probably read by the fewest readers. Nigel Broackes revealed that 'each day's leading articles come in draft to Victor, and sometimes if Eric [Parker, Trafalgar's managing director] or I are there we might say, "Why don't you put in something about . . .?" But beyond that, we do not interfere.'[68] Unlike Beaverbrook, Matthews had no clue about what should happen in the rest of the *Express*, concentrating his mind instead on the bottom line.

A year or so after moving in, Matthews came up with an inventive way to deal with the problem of falling sales, under-capacity and too many workers doing too little. 'Fleet Street is not overmanned,' he liked to say, 'it is underworked'. Eager to utilise greater printing-press capacity in London and Manchester, he called for research into the possibility of launching a new national newspaper. He wondered if it was feasible to challenge the *Sun* and *Daily Mirror* with a new red-top.

The result was the *Daily Star*. It would support Labour, he told a group of sceptical *Express* trade unionists: 'This is your paper, with your politics. It's for you.'[69] The *Star* was originally conceived as a socialist *Sun*, using the same in-your-face techniques and topless pictures. Its editorial content and political line were aimed at attracting both *Sun* and *Mirror* readers. When the Communist party's *Morning Star* went to court to try to prevent the use of its name, the judge ruled that 'only a moron in a hurry' would confuse the two titles.[70]

Matthews made Jameson editor-in-chief of both the *Express* and the *Star*, and accepted his recommendation that the editor should be Peter Grimsditch. Grimsditch was an extraordinary character, part intellectual, part hell-raiser, part nerd. He graduated from Oxford with a double first in classics and joined the *Newcastle Journal* as a reporter in 1966. He switched to subbing and I met him on the subs' desk at the *Daily Mail*'s Manchester, office in 1969 where he displayed journalistic talent, an inclination to be hot-tempered and, on occasion, utterly wayward behaviour. Nothing changed throughout the rest of his career.

He later spent five years with the *Sunday Mirror*, giving me a part-time job when – due to my union activities – no one else would touch me. It was just one example of his willingness to take risks and his total lack of regard for management sensibilities, not to mention his loyalty to friends. Grimsditch believed work should be fun. In the small hours of Friday nights, he encouraged alcohol-fuelled subs to indulge in a variety of childish pranks, such as bizarre races through the office and indoor cricket using a ball composed of rubber bands. He did much the same when he became deputy editor of IPC's doomed weekly, *Reveille*, in 1976. Jameson said of Grimsditch: 'He looked like a manic Steve McQueen and had immense drive and a great capacity for work. Emotional, noisy, reckless – but still superb at his job.'[71] But he had no senior executive Fleet Street experience and neither did most of his staff, the majority of whom were forcibly translated from the northern office of the *Daily Express* to the *Daily Star*.

Billed at its launch on 2 November 1978 as the first new daily for three-quarters of a century, the *Star* was published in Manchester and distributed only in the north at first, selling for 6p, a penny less than the *Sun*. Though Matthews – then the largest individual donor to the Conservative party – had always conceived it as a paper sympathetic to Labour he got cold feet before the launch, telling Jameson: 'Let me make this quite clear. You can support Labour – but we don't want you attacking the Tories.'[72]

Anyway, politics wasn't going to be the *Star*'s selling point, as Jameson made clear. 'Sex sells – that goes for pictures and words. So the *Star* will have its daily quota. Bigger and better than anyone else.'[73] He was also reported saying that the *Star* was 'going to be tits, bums, QPR and roll-your-own fags'.[74] The first edition proved his point. The most innovative feature was the Page 7 'Starbird', a blatant copy of the *Sun*'s Page 3, but printed in colour. On-the-run colour printing was still ten years away for national titles so the *Star* used 'pre-print colour', which involved printing reels of colour 'patches' a day ahead of publication at a specialist plant in Liverpool and trucking the reels to Manchester and London to be mixed with the black-and-white text. The cost was exorbitant.[75]

The first splash, headlined 'Model's Mystery Plunge', was one of those stories that didn't bear too much inquiry since the girl was not a model, the plunge had been no more than three feet and there was precious little mystery.[76] Another page was dominated by a tale of a vicar who painted nudes. Its best read was an extract from the autobiography of former football star Jimmy Greaves. Editorially and technically, it was all rather crude. Both *Sun* editor Larry Lamb and *Mirror* editor Mike Molloy thought the *Star* was 'rubbish'.[77] They underestimated its potential and ignored the fact that it quickly built a large audience. Neither did they spot the significance of a promotion gimmick which was to change the face of all newspapers in the following decade. Starting only in the north-east, the *Daily Star* launched bingo with modest prizes of £5,000 and £10,000. This game ('borrowed' from Plymouth's *Western Morning News*) put up circulation by 35 per cent in the region, so the *Star* then tried it out in its Merseyside edition and sales rose there by 32 per cent. Jameson thought newspaper bingo probably violated the Gaming Act, 'but who's going to sue us for giving money away?'[78]

Despite its surprisingly good beginning, the strain of producing the *Star* with a small and inexperienced staff showed. By the early summer Grimsditch was desperate to take on journalists with a Fleet Street background and gave me another job, as a features sub. Conditions inside the Express building in Great Ancoats, Manchester, were almost Dickensian. A disembodied voice regularly boomed over the tannoy system, 'Flong boy to foundry', and we queued every week in the centre of the office to collect our wage packets. Production of the paper was hand to mouth.

Grimsditch's pronounced maverick tendencies and personality changes, alternating between playful and loud to depressed and silent, induced a lack of respect among staff, even those who initially thought him a refreshing change from the usual editor. He had a bad habit of getting tied down in detail rather than delegating or keeping his mind on the broad canvas. He also suffered from the need to shuttle so often between Manchester and London, where he suffered from the implacable hostility of Jocelyn Stevens. The tall, polished, well-dressed Stevens took a malicious delight in humiliating the slight, shambolic, ill-kempt Grimsditch, patting him on the head and treating him like a schoolboy. With Stevens having the ear of Matthews, it wasn't surprising that he became increasingly sceptical about Jameson's choice of editor.

A breach also gradually opened between Jameson and Grimsditch, and several disputes culminated, in March 1980, in Matthews ordering Jameson to 'play Judas' and fire Grimsditch.[79] Jameson wasn't pleased with Matthews's insistence that he should install himself as *Star* editor instead. Grimsditch was outraged and never spoke to Jameson again. For all his faults, Grimsditch achieved an amazing circulation coup, building a sale of just over 1 million from a standing start and causing the first major blip in the *Sun*'s rising sales since Murdoch's takeover. Doubtless, this lay behind Lamb's decision to hire him as a junior executive at the *Sun*.

Jameson, forced to relinquish his *Express* editorship, was very unhappy at the *Star*. When he appointed me as his features editor, I was close enough to him to realise that, for all his banter, his heart wasn't in it. He discovered a penchant for broadcasting and was soon 'spending less and less time in Manchester and more and more time on radio and television'.[80] He also revealed a surprising vulnerability. Happy to describe himself as the 'the biggest joker of them all',[81] he failed to see the joke when a radio satire show lampooned him. He sued for libel, lost and had to sacrifice his life savings to pay the £75,000 costs.[82]

Matthews never did like the paper he had founded. Rather foolishly he announced that he wouldn't have the *Star* in his own house.[83] He also misunderstood – or was persuaded to misunderstand – the import of a sentiment expressed by Jameson during a TV interview when he said of Matthews: 'He's an Eastender like myself.' According to Junor, Matthews thought Jameson was indicating he was Jewish, which he resented.[84] Though political coverage was sparse, he also grew disenchanted with the *Star*'s left-of-centre line. By the end of 1980, with Matthews urging him to stay more often in Manchester, Jameson pleaded to return to his 'real' job at the *Express*. When Matthews refused, Jameson resigned. The *Daily Star*'s regular sale by then was 1,055,000 and, following dramatic improvements to its content and with its early technical imperfections overcome, it was on the rise.

Jameson had been replaced in the *Daily Express* chair in June 1980 by his deputy, Arthur Firth, the paper's sixth editor in just ten years. Blackpool-born, Firth began his career on the *Lancashire Evening Post* and was thirty-two before he managed to get a place on the subs' desk in the Manchester office of the *Daily Express*. In the following twelve years he rose to become northern editor. Six years later, in 1978, he was called to London as Jameson's number two. Junor's assessment of him was spot on: 'an amiable, placid giant of a man . . . a splendid technical journalist who was liked by everyone'.[85] I worked briefly under Firth as a junior features executive and, along with my colleagues, quickly realised he didn't deserve the job. Tall, ungainly, with hooded eyes and loose, wrinkled skin, he was affectionately nicknamed Lurch after a character in a popular TV series, *The Addams Family*. He was not cut out to be an editor, especially of a paper requiring vision and energy, and I had a feeling he knew it too. That the *Daily Express* should be edited by a man of such limited ability showed how little Matthews and Stevens knew about the role of editor.

In 1980, Matthews became an official press baron, accepting a life peerage from his political heroine, Margaret Thatcher. He took the title Baron Matthews of Southgate, and *Private Eye* responded by dubbing him Lord Whelks. Supposedly jealous of *Sunday Express* editor John Junor getting a knighthood the year before, he didn't show it when hosting a Ritz dinner to celebrate Junor's twenty-five years as editor. It might have been better to have marked the anniversary by easing Junor aside. Instead, the new lord embarked on a very different solution to his problems by completing the merger which had originally led to his takeover. To do so, he found himself negotiating with another relatively new press baron: the third Viscount Rothermere, previously Vere Harmsworth.

Until around 1976, Esmond Rothermere appeared to have been in reasonable health. Alarmed by inflation, he had sold off his great house in London and later sold the magnificent Daylesford house and estate to Baron von Thyssen. He died in July 1978, shortly after his eightieth birthday, suffering from Alzheimer's disease. On the day of his death, the respected Press Association reporter John Shaw made the normal ring-round to relatives and colleagues to request tributes. His call to Esmond's cousin Cecil King produced a surprising response. 'He was a shit,' King started. 'Cold, money-grubbing and completely unsuited to the job he held. When he took over the *Daily Mail* it was the best newspaper in Fleet Street. Look at it now. When he took over the *Evening News* it was the best evening newspaper in the world. Now look at it. Dreadful rags, both of them.'[86]

King did describe Esmond as 'an intelligent man . . . charming when he wanted to be', but his diatribe continued: 'He gave in to the unions. He didn't give a damn about his staff. He was mean. He loved booze and women. He was an absolute disaster . . . the worst newspaper proprietor in the world.' He then questioned Vere Harmsworth's paternity, suggesting that Esmond was not his father, before observing: 'I don't think any of this would go out on PA do you?' Shaw politely agreed, and King concluded: 'I've told you what I think. Try and make the best of it. Please be kind.' How right Cudlipp had been to say of King that he 'deplored sycophantic obituaries'.[87]

Vere Rothermere, as I shall now refer to him, had long been in the driving seat at Associated. With patrician immodesty he told an interviewer: 'I accepted from a very early age that . . . I would become responsible for running a newspaper . . . I regard myself primarily as a newspaper proprietor rather than a publisher or a journalist.'[88] His managing director, Mick Shields, also ensured that his owner wouldn't have to rely on newspapers for his income by ensuring profits from a diversified portfolio.

Rothermere tried hard to buy other papers, bidding for the *Observer* in 1976 and the *Sunday Times* in 1979. By 1980, the continuing problem of losses at the *Evening News* impelled him to reopen talks with Matthews about merging it with the *Evening Standard*. Everyone could see that the market for evening papers was in decline. With television rapidly improving its sports coverage on Saturdays, both the *Standard* and *News* eventually stopped publishing that day. They also began to withdraw from the expensive business of distributing in outlying areas. Matthews, also convinced by the financial logic of combining the papers, entered into talks with Rothermere with an enthusiasm and decisiveness lacking six years before. But the relative financial strengths of the two companies had changed. Express Newspapers was now the weaker of the two. The secret talks between the two companies went on for months before a deal was hammered out.

Rothermere was known for being indecisive. Shields once told John Coote that even on relatively small matters Rothermere disliked making up his mind.[89] He also had a deep family affection for the *News*, which had been his great-uncle Northcliffe's pride and joy. Even so, he had to accept that the future lay with the *Standard*, which attracted advertising, and agreed to fold his own title into it. He also picked up a £6 million redundancy bill, and there was little argument over arrangements for the ownership of the merged paper: each company would hold 50 per cent with an annual rotation of chairmen. Associated also insisted that it would get first option to buy the other 50 per cent if Express Newspapers later decided to sell.

One substantial victory for Rothermere was over the editorship of the new *Standard*. During his two years as editor, Jenkins had not had a happy time. After the turbulence of the takeover battle he was persistently troubled by editorial interventions from Matthews, who was, he said, 'a daily nightmare'.[90] At one point Matthews seriously asked Jenkins to advocate the bombing of Russia in a leading article.[91] Jenkins's resistance to Matthews, and his opposition to his paper's possible submergence by the *Evening News* in the event of a Rothermere takeover, led Stevens to fire him in 1978 and put Wintour back into the editor's chair.[92] Rothermere had never forgiven Wintour for his attack on him years before and insisted he go in favour of the *News* editor, Louis Kirby. Matthews, who couldn't understand the reason for such a wrangle, reportedly told Rothermere: 'I don't care a bugger who the editor is.'[93] This failure to grasp the importance of editorship, which he shared with Stevens, was a giant clue to the reasons for his newspapers' declines.

Evening News journalists, angered when they realised what was happening, staged a one-day strike, forcing Kirby and his deputy, John Leese, to produce the paper alone. When Kirby became the first editor of the merged title, Stevens was far from happy with the choice, claiming: 'It was like the RAF winning the Battle of Britain and finding Goering in charge at the end of the war.'[94] In fact, to amend that analogy, it was like Goering going native and becoming more British than Churchill. In spite of Kirby's claim that the new paper would blend the best of both titles,[95] he virtually eradicated the *News*'s identity in favour of the *Standard*'s. In retrospect, it was a wise decision because the *Standard*'s accent on features was more likely to succeed in the TV age than the *News*'s devotion to hard news. It was also a tribute to Wintour's unceasing lobbying on behalf of the *Standard*'s up-market virtues.

In a hyperbolic feature in praise of the *News* in 1965, it was said that 'to kill it off, you would have to pull down St. Paul's, blow up the Houses of Parliament, knock Nelson off his column, dredge the Thames dry, turn Wembley stadium over to netball and send every last Londoner off to Australia'.[96] It proved altogether much easier than that, creating no shock waves, except in the village of Fleet Street and among its loyal and clannish journalistic staff, 109 of whom lost their jobs. The final issue of 'the Cockney paper' appeared on 31 October 1980, just nine months short of its 100th anniversary, and thereafter known to its journalists as Black Friday. Morning conference was 'as cheerfully meaningful as an entertainment officer's meeting on the *Titanic*'.[97] The last front page was headlined 'After 99 years the News reports its last big story: GOODBYE LONDON'.

Rothermere explained the reason for the closure to a *Daily Mail* reporter: 'We simply could not get our share of what was left once television started taking the bulk of advertising. All other problems stem from that. And when it came down to it, we were losing £4 million for every £1 million lost by the *Standard*. So we had to be the one to go.'[98] His sadness was evident in an article in the final issue: 'My family pioneered modern journalism with the *Evening News* and my own commitment was total ... efforts to sustain the paper were monumental ... millions of pounds have been provided for its support. Fleet Street will be the worse without the *Evening News*.'[99]

It's uncertain whether it was worse. The *New Standard*, as it was retitled, did include some features from the *News*, such as the rock-music gossip column, Ad Lib, run by John Blake. Despite the odd blip, it was hard to discern any sacrifice of quality in a package which included Milton Shulman and Alexander Walker writing about theatre and film, cookery by Delia Smith, sports columns by Patrick Collins, astrology by Patric Walker and cartoons by Jak (Raymond Jackson), whose skills had matured impressively since he started on the *Standard* in 1950. To Wintour's consternation, the *Standard* was to prove safe in Rothermere's hands.

Hold the front page – for a year!

Roy Thomson, Lord Thomson of Fleet, the 'breezy, informal, tubby little guy with bifocals',[100] died in August 1976, aged eighty-two. He left a vast and profitable newspaper and media empire, but his British legacy was anything but secure. Nor was his successor, his son Kenneth, as committed as his father to the *Times*.[101]

The second Lord Thomson, who rarely used his title and didn't take his House of Lords seat, had had a difficult time as his father's heir apparent. Born in 1923, schooled at Upper Canada College, he quickly joined the business after graduating from Cambridge, his father having wangled him a place there.[102] He worked initially on two Canadian papers, in both editorial and advertising departments, before he took charge of the organisation's North American interests. Kenneth was to spend twenty years running that operation before Thomson's death, and along the way was responsible for buying Canada's largest department store chain, the Hudson's Bay Company.

He adulated his father, but often suffered at his hands. On a trip to China with both Thomsons, when Kenneth was forty-nine, Frank Giles was surprised that when introducing his group Thomson would inevitably say: 'This is my son Ken, who doesn't do anything.'[103] Giles found Kenneth 'mild, courteous, likeable', but Denis Hamilton's assessment of him was far sharper. 'I have seen many great fathers succeeded by irresponsible playboys,' he said, clearing Kenneth of that sin by adding that he 'works very hard . . . [and] is a man of high moral character'. Then came the sting in the tail: 'However, either in battle or history, there are no two dynamos in a row.'[104]

Except in his need to wear spectacles, Kenneth was very different from his father. Tall, slim, polished, with a substantial knowledge of art, he preferred to keep a low profile. He bought a palatial London residence, in Kensington Palace Gardens, but spent most of his time in Toronto and ran his empire with the lightest of touches, relying heavily on his right-hand man, John Tory, and allowing senior executives in every division to get on with their jobs. In Britain, it meant that power supposedly resided with Gordon Brunton, who was both the organisation's managing director and its chief executive. It was never entirely clear whether he outranked Sir Denis

Hamilton, chairman and editor-in-chief of Times Newspapers, or Duke Hussey, chairman of the *Times*'s executive board.

Thomson's first priority was to reorganise his empire into a rational structure, creating the International Thomson Organisation. At the British end, it was a much needed overhaul, making sense of such diverse interests as North Sea oil, television, book publishing, travel, holidays, phone directories, regional newspapers and the two *Times* national titles. It was tidy management rather than entrepreneurial risk-taking, and budgetary constraints engendered caution.[105] In Canada though, Thomson did expand wisely, buying the company which owned the country's most prestigious paper, the *Toronto Globe & Mail*. This was the arena in which Thomson was comfortable, but events in London dominated his company's attention from 1978.

The *Times* and *Sunday Times* became the centre of a story they could barely report themselves and, eventually, were unable to report at all. In obedience to the Callaghan government's pay limits, the Thomson Organisation decided not to follow other newspaper companies by getting round the restrictions with under-the-counter deals. This may have been a matter of principle, though it has been suggested that Thomson, with oil and travel interests, was more vulnerable to government retaliation.[106] Whatever the reason, the unions rightly pointed out that they were being paid less than their Fleet Street colleagues. It is also fair to point out that working conditions in the machine room were very poor, especially on Saturday nights when the seventy-two-page *Sunday Times* was being produced, a print run of 1.5 million copies which made it the longest in the world.

Throughout 1977 and the beginning of 1978, the eight unions split into sixty-five chapels found a variety of ways of disrupting production as they sought to coerce Thomson into paying them more money. In April 1978, Hussey wrote to every member of staff to point out that the company had lost £2 million revenue in three months because of industrial anarchy. Brunton decided to set the unions an ultimatum: they must agree a productivity deal by November or the papers would be shut down. No one really believed Thomson was serious, least of all the printers the threat was supposed to cow into submission. As the deadline neared, it became clear that pay was not the only sticking point for the unions. It emerged that the company also wished to agree on the introduction of labour-saving technology. This ensured that the main craft printing union, the National Graphical Association (NGA), would be implacably opposed to any deal which would make their own members redundant because journalists could input copy direct from computers. They were faced with the extinction of their ancient craft and, with it, their future livelihoods.

Meanwhile, disruption of the papers continued as before. In the course of 1978, printing was interrupted seventy-four times, with a loss of 4 million copies, equal to more than two weeks' full production. In the first ten years of owning the *Times*, the Thomson organisation let it be known it had lost £20 million on the paper. But the *Sunday Times* did make money and, even in 1978, the company still managed to make a small profit. The unions scorned Thomson's *Times* loss by arguing that it was peanuts when compared to the 1978 earnings from the company's North Sea oilfields, which amounted to £150 million. Brunton, Hussey and the Thomson organisation had gambled on facing down the unions without having a 'Plan B' if they failed to bring them to heel. So, at 3.55 a.m. on 30 November 1978, the Gray's Inn Road presses stopped and Thomson fulfilled its threat to shut down two of Britain's best-known newspapers indefinitely. *Times* editor William Rees-Mogg, who began his leader, 'It is the first duty of an editor of the *Times* not to be the last one,' condemned the unions for the 'slide into anarchy' which had engulfed the company's 4,300 employees.[107]

Two weeks later staff were served with dismissal notices, though there was little panic by most of the printers because almost all of them were soon working on a casual basis for rival newspapers. Unsurprisingly, with the *Times* and *Sunday Times* off the streets, the *Guardian*, *Daily Telegraph*, *Financial Times*, *Observer* and *Sunday Telegraph* all benefited from higher sales, requiring more staff to run their machines. The NGA had enough money to support its members. For regular readers of the two papers, it was a further example of the winter of discontent, adding to the widely held view that trade unions were too powerful and leading to the government's defeat in May 1979. Talks, or, to be more precise, talks about talks, went on for five months before Thompson management attempted to break the deadlock by publishing the *Times* in Frankfurt. German unions helped to foil that plan, although a few copies of one issue were distributed around Europe.[108]

In his enlightening account of the shutdown, *Sunday Times* writer Eric Jacobs told of the tedium for journalists without papers to produce. Editor Harold Evans helped former US Secretary of State Henry Kissinger write his memoirs. Rees-Mogg held regular conferences. Some staff wrote books, some travelled, some went to the office every day, some stayed away altogether. NUJ chapel leaders called meetings to try to find ways of brokering a peace agreement. Sagging morale took its toll, with many journalists, including Jacobs, turning on the Thomson Organisation and its managers. The journalists 'had no quarrel with anybody . . . They thought of themselves as *Times* men and women, and the experience of being dismissed seemed likely to leave permanent scars. They would never feel the same about their company again.'[109]

In early summer Hamilton intervened, trying to secure a compromise by using his charm. Then Thomson flew to London for a meeting and gradually, as summer moved into autumn, painstaking deals were finally agreed, with each union and every chapel jealously guarding against another gaining an advantage. Finally, after almost a year of closure, the *Times* resumed publication on 13 November 1979, and the *Sunday Times* returned on 18 November.

The stoppage had cost the papers between £35 and £46 million, depending on the accounting. The unions agreed to a steady reduction of manning levels, of some 16 per cent and the NGA kept its grip on typesetting, with only the vaguest of agreements on the introduction of new technology. But a return to work proved to be a return to the pre-closure situation, with production constantly disrupted. The *Sunday Times*, most necessary to the company's income, was hardest hit.[110] When they returned to the streets, to the genuine surprise of almost everyone, the two titles not only regained their circulation, they secured small rises. In the first half of 1980, both the *Times* and *Sunday Times* recorded their highest sales in six years. These were papers with loyal audiences and, despite the best efforts of their rivals to win over new readers, they largely failed to make them stick.

The successful return should have been gratifying for the editors and the Thomson Organisation, but the mood changed suddenly in the summer of 1980 when an entirely unexpected industrial dispute at the *Times* arose. In July, the NUJ put in for a 32 per cent wage increase and management countered with an offer of 18 per cent. An independent arbitrator recommended that 21 per cent would be fairer and the union agreed to accept it. Thomson executives would not and, in a move that shocked virtually everyone, including many of the paper's journalists, the NUJ chapel voted for a strike. Though the vote was anything but unanimous, the journalists knew they would be supported by the NGA refusing to cross their picket lines. The *Times* therefore closed down for yet another week in late August until a compromise, on terms very similar to those originally offered, was reached.[111]

Kenneth Thomson had had enough, and Denis Hamilton realised it too, urging him to sell.[112] Most commentators believe that Thomson immediately put the papers up for public auction because he regarded the journalists' action as a betrayal.[113] But the *Times*'s official historian argued persuasively that Thomson had decided well before to rid his company of the loss-making headache, so the NUJ action 'gratuitously eased his conscience'.[114] Just seven weeks after the strike, on 22 October 1980, Thomson announced that he was dispensing with the papers bought just fourteen years before by his father. Times Newspapers, including the supplements, were up for sale and, if no buyer could be found by March 1981, they would be shut down. By normal business standards, the company looked anything but a good prospect, facing losses of £15 million that year and with continuing industrial relations problems. But, as the Royal Commission properly noted, 'Fleet Street is not an industry noted for its rational behaviour.'[115]

The cachet of national newspaper ownership, especially of two such well-known titles, ensured that non-owners would be interested. Among these hopefuls – numbering almost 50[116] – was Tiny Rowland, creator of the Lonrho mining conglomerate and proprietor of Scottish papers, Robert

Maxwell and Sir James Goldsmith. Both editors also saw a chance to end what the *Times*'s Rees-Mogg called 'an unsatisfactory marriage' by going their separate ways.[117] Rees-Mogg formed a consortium designed to place the *Times* in the hands of its journalists, an idea originally suggested by three members of staff.[118] At the *Sunday Times*, Evans took a similar approach, asking the *Guardian* to buy a 25 per cent stake in a consortium made up of City institutions, unions and the public.[119] Gordon Brunton, the Thomson executive charged with carrying out the sale, dismissed the idea of splitting up the titles and thought neither of the consortia workable, and both collapsed. By the 31 December deadline, the only bidders taken seriously were current press owners Rupert Murdoch and Lord Rothermere, and Rowland, who was then omitted after asking for an extension to the deadline.

Rothermere's Associated Newspapers had tried to buy the papers during the shutdown but, at the time, Thomson told them he had no 'wish' to sell.[120] They put in the highest offer of £25 million, while Murdoch bid just £12 million, but Associated, eager to add the *Sunday Times* to its stable and the Gray's Inn print site, would not give assurances about the future of the *Times*. Murdoch was prepared to give such a guarantee, a crucial factor in both Brunton and Hamilton favouring his bid before they moved into final negotiations at the beginning of 1981.

One outstanding controversy was the role of Harry Evans, who finally gave his consent to a Murdoch takeover after it became clear that his consortium bid had failed. Some of his journalists were upset that he did not try to thwart Murdoch and later accused him of bad faith.[121] Hindsight can be cruel. Evans, who later acknowledged that his judgements made in that period were 'the worst in my professional career', sincerely believed he was choosing the least bad option then available.[122]

Troubles for the last of the owner–editors

David Astor had already given up the *Observer* editorship to Donald Trelford. It was only a matter of time before he relinquished his hold on the paper altogether. By the summer of 1976, less than a year after Trelford's appointment, it was facing the possibility of losing £1 million and sales were falling. Astor couldn't fund the paper any longer and he knew he must sell.

No matter how poor their financial situation, regardless of falling sales, there are always buyers for newspapers. A flood of offers poured in for the *Observer*, from Harmsworth, Sir James Goldsmith, Robert Maxwell, Tiny Rowland, the Hong Kong businesswoman Sally Aw Sian, oil heiress Olga Deterding and unspecified Arab oil sheikhs. Some of these were shrugged aside, but Goldsmith persisted in spite of hostility from *Observer* journalists who disliked the fact that he had launched a series of libel actions against *Private Eye*, and was therefore seen as an enemy of press freedom.[123] He persuaded Trelford to join him with a dozen *Observer* journalists at his house for dinner, and as they sat down each was presented by a butler with a bottle of claret. Goldsmith made a solemn pledge not to interfere if his bid was successful, but no one was convinced that he would honour such assurances. Afterwards, Trelford and his deputy, John Cole, laughed about the preposterous meeting.[124]

For one reason or another, every bidder, except possibly for Harmsworth, was found to be unserious or unsatisfactory. IPC, owner of the *Sunday Mirror* and *Sunday People*, was sounded out but didn't want a third Sunday title. In September, Murdoch was approached and demanded that Trelford be moved sideways, wanting to appoint a right-winger, Bruce Rothwell, as editor-in-chief and the former *Sun* political editor, Anthony Shrimsley, as editor.

If Murdoch really wanted the *Observer*, and all the evidence suggests he did, then this was a tactless piece of negotiating. Setting such a precondition was foolish because Trelford was able to organise an effective opposition both within the office and outside, especially after he leaked the story.[125] Murdoch's ambition provoked controversy in the Commons, fuelled by alarmed *Observer* staff. TV critic Clive James, an Australian, remarked: 'Giving the *Observer* to Rupert Murdoch is like giving your beautiful 17-year-old daughter to a gorilla.'[126]

A defeated Murdoch, who later admitted having underestimated Trelford,[127] lost interest at about the time one of the *Observer*'s veteran journalists, Kenneth Harris, just happened to dine with Douglass Cater, a director of the Aspen Institute, and told him of his paper's problems. On a whim, Cater decided to see if the Institute's wealthy chairman, Robert Anderson, might like to help. Anderson was also chairman of one of the world's largest oil companies, and California's second largest corporation, Atlantic Richfield, known as ARCO. Unusual among Texan tycoons, he was regarded as a political liberal and known as 'the oil man with a conscience'. He agreed to meet David Astor and a senior *Observer* manager, Roger Harrison, and they flew to Los Angeles in November 1976. Within a week, they had agreed a deal. ARCO would buy the paper for just £1, but would immediately provide £1 million to keep the paper going. Anderson pledged a further £3 million in the following three years. He also agreed to be a hands-off proprietor.

Astor and Trelford were delighted with their stroke of good fortune. They had 'saved' the *Observer*. One of the paper's former luminaries, Anthony Sampson, was not so sure. Anderson seemed to him 'too good to be true with his pixie smile under his ten-gallon hat'.[128] Trelford was less pleased when ARCO appointed one of his columnists Conor Cruise O'Brien as his editor-in-chief. Not that it cramped Trelford's style too much, and he set about modernising his paper. One of his innovations, in 1977, was the launching of a column by Sue Arnold, who was simply instructed to make it funny.[129] It became a readers' favourite.

One obvious piece of luck was the dispute which took the *Sunday Times* off the streets for a year from November 1978. It has been argued that the *Observer* went further than other titles in trying to exploit the shutdown by adding sections and expanding its print run.[130] The *Observer* certainly benefited, increasing circulation by a million as advertising rolled in. It did much better than the *Sunday Telegraph*, which had been helped by the switch of the colour magazine from Friday to Sunday in 1976 to give it a better competitive stance. But there were internal tensions when the *Observer* supported Labour in the 1979 election because Anderson favoured Thatcher. Perhaps the most significant moment in the paper's history came in January 1980 when Anderson paid £250,000 to buy the Astor family's 10 per cent stake in the *Observer*. Though David would stay on as a director as a matter of courtesy, his last real link had been severed.

It's doubtful if Lord Hartwell, owner and editor-in-chief of the *Telegraph* titles, imagined at the time that he might suffer Astor's fate. His papers appeared to be doing so well and, to the outsider, there seemed to be no looming financial crisis within that seemingly impregnable Fleet Street landmark of Peterborough Court. In March 1978, Hartwell and his brother, Lord Camrose, set up a trust designed 'to secure the long-term security of the *Daily Telegraph* publications'.[131] This move, the significance of which no one realised, had come far too late. There had been too little profit in the past to fund necessary investment because Hartwell had insisted on keeping the *Daily Telegraph*'s cover price below that of the *Times*. The finances were in a terrible state and paternalism had not stretched to the point of organising a pension fund for employees.

That isn't to say that journalists had suffered from deprivation. When the *Daily Telegraph*'s Africa correspondent, Christopher Munnion, took up his first posting in Rhodesia during Ian Smith's regime he was installed in a huge house in Salisbury set in well-tended acres, with a tennis court and swimming pool, to be looked after by 'a couple of servants'.[132] The Paris bureau, in the 1st arrondissement, was staffed by 'two correspondents, an office manager, a man who made the tea, a woman who cut and filed the newspapers and a ravishing girl who operated the telex machine'.[133]

The *Telegraph*'s London editions were halted for two weeks in October 1978 when the NGA struck, costing the company £1.5 million. During the stoppage, the first since 1955, Hartwell wrote to every employee: 'On the *Telegraph*, Us and Them are the same people.'[134] Despite the naivety, he genuinely believed it was so. More realistically, he wrote: 'Alone in Fleet Street, we are not part of a great conglomerate. Oil, shipping, paper manufacturing, will not come to our aid.'[135]

Hartwell showed a gallantry which was at odds with normal commercial competitive spirit when he refused to take advantage of the *Times*'s shutdown. He ignored a plea to adopt the *Times*'s best features by City editor Andreas Whittam Smith, who was dismayed by his boss's 'pusillanimous approach'.[136] Of course, the paper couldn't help but gain extra readers in the *Times*'s absence, but it made no effort to win them for the long term. In the last six months of 1979, the *Telegraph* enjoyed a sale above 1.5 million and once the *Times* returned it fell back by 100,000, the beginning of an unfamiliar decline in its circulation. The problem for the *Telegraph* was that it had failed to change and had won few if any converts when given a unique chance to market itself to an audience it should have attracted.

Grumblings within the paper about its failure to revitalise its editorial content in order to appeal to new readers were compounded by the frustrations of the writers nursed by deputy editor Colin Welch. They felt the paper was missing the chance to offer full-hearted support to the political and economic radicalism of Margaret Thatcher. These young Turks of the new right, aided and abetted by Peter Utley, 'a monument to High Toryism',[137] discomfited Hartwell. Editor Bill Deedes, ever the diplomat, did what he could to find a compromise between the desires of his proprietor and the desperation of his commentators. Hartwell, even if his influence on leading articles was indirect, did question the content and he was held in such regard that even the Turks tempered 'their monetarist enthusiasm . . . to avoid the frustration of arguing with Lord Hartwell'.[138] They tended to moan to each other instead in lengthy drunken sessions at the King and Keys.

At the *Sunday Telegraph*, when editor Brian Roberts retired aged seventy in 1976 after thirty-seven years with the group, Hartwell played safe. He appointed the 'steady, serious-looking' John Thompson, who had been a political writer and assistant editor with the paper since 1970.[139] It was said that his 'most obvious characteristic is that he is retiring to the point of joining a trappist order'.[140] Previously with the *Yorkshire Evening News* and the London *Evening Standard*, he was fifty-six and regarded as a practical, production-minded journalist. As deputy editor of the *Spectator* under two high-profile editors, Iain Macleod and Nigel Lawson, it was Thompson who actually ensured that the magazine came out every week.[141] Hartwell had deliberately overlooked the claims of deputy editor Perry Worsthorne, who had expected to be promoted, despite saying 'fuck' on television three years before, and made no secret of his disappointment.[142]

Thompson did manage to coax Hartwell into allowing some revision to the design, despite junior managers warning that the unions wouldn't allow it. While stealthily carrying through major changes over a period of time Thompson also brought in a crop of new writers, such as Auberon Waugh, Mary Kenny, Oliver Pritchett, Alex Chancellor and Arthur Marshall. One notable success was an investigation by two reporters into a scandal in which a consultant and several colleagues were found to be stealing National Health Service blood and selling it to Denmark, resulting in the jailing of the consultant four years later.[143]

Thompson got himself into unnecessary trouble in 1978 by attempting to serialise a book by Peter Bessell, a former Liberal MP who was a chief prosecution witness in the trial of Jeremy Thorpe, his party leader. Thorpe, accused of conspiracy to murder a male model who was said to have blackmailed him over their homosexual relationship, was charged in August 1978. Two months later Thompson agreed a contract with Bessell which stated that he would receive £50,000 for up to six extracts from his book if Thorpe was found guilty. In the event of Thorpe being found innocent, however, Bessell would receive only £25,000 for a series of articles. Unsurprisingly, when Bessell was forced under cross-examination to reveal the details of this deal, a huge public row broke out. As the defence pointed out, and the judge agreed, Bessell stood to gain by ensuring that Thorpe was found guilty. By the end of the trial, in which the jury cleared Thorpe, the *Sunday Telegraph* had already pulled out of the contract. Thompson and his paper were fortunate not to be prosecuted for contempt of court. They were severely censured instead by the Press Council for a 'flagrant breach' of guidelines outlawing payments to witnesses.

The paper which undoubtedly profited best from the *Times*'s shutdown was the *Guardian*: its sales jumped from 293,000 to 379,000 over the course of the year, and virtually all the new readers stayed once the *Times* returned. In the first six months of 1980, the *Guardian*'s circulation average was a healthy 375,000. This was a tribute to the silky skills of editor Peter Preston, who carried out a sort of permanent revolution, innovating, introducing new features and sections, but ensuring that his paper maintained its rigour in news coverage and comment. A fine, if cryptic, writer himself, he also favoured intelligent writing. One of his greatest qualities was in spotting talented journalists and then allowing them the freedom to make their way within the paper. Unlike his predecessor, Preston was free to concentrate on editorial matters because concerns about The *Guardian*'s financial health, and its possible sale, had disappeared.

Soon after the *Guardian* finally sounded the retreat from Manchester, in August 1976, its finances began to improve, with income from the *Manchester Evening News*, the launching of free weekly titles, the purchase of a majority stake in the Surrey Advertiser group in 1978, and the Auto-Trader magazine series. Among the various innovations was the 1978 launch of pages dedicated to social services, which had the twin effect of serving the public interest through its editorial matter while proving to be a powerful lure to public authority advertisers. Liz Forgan's appointment as women's editor in 1978 was astute and, though *Guardian* detractors were too ready to denigrate the paper for lacking a sense of humour, the Posy Simmonds cartoons featuring the Weber family turned that notion on its head by mocking the stereotypical *Guardian*-reading family.

The very fact that there was such a stereotype said much about the way in which the *Guardian* and its readers were perceived by the rest of the press and many of its non-readers. Well before the end of Hetherington's editorship, other newspapers reflected a widespread resentment by editors and journalists about what they came to believe was a holier-than-thou attitude by the *Guardian*. They thought Hetherington, and many of his leading articles, sanctimonious. This distaste for the liberal viewpoint, which had also been levelled at Astor's *Observer*, hardened in the early Preston years. The tabloids cultivated the word '*Guardian*' as a term of abuse, casting the paper as the repository of either weak-kneed, bleeding-heart liberals or a fifth column of quasi-communists. Its women staff were derided as feminist harridans and, over time, that phrase became elided in the popular consciousness so that when using the word 'feminists' it was unnecessary to add 'harridans'. It was assumed that they all were.

A similar process happened in the persistent use of the phrase '*Guardian* reader'. The stereotype, brilliantly represented by George Weber in Simmonds's strips, was a bearded school teacher (or social worker) wearing a baggy sweater and open-toed sandals who could always see both sides of every question and whose indecision was therefore final. The underlying assumption was that *Guardian* staff and readers were also hypocrites, members of a supposedly wealthy middle class who could afford the comfort of liberal political views. Broadsheet rivals gradually saw the competitive advantage in reinforcing this largely tabloid innuendo and adopted the insults too, helping them to become common parlance.

Mirror eclipsed by the *Sun* as the *Star* also rises

One paper that certainly had no time for the *Guardian* was the *Sun*. At the beginning of 1978, it became Britain's highest-selling daily paper, overhauling the *Daily Mirror*, which had held the top position since 1949. It was an astonishing achievement: in the space of just nine years, the *Sun* had risen from almost the bottom of the tabloid heap to the top, adding more than 3 million in sales. In so doing, it also irretrievably changed popular newspaper culture.

Accepting that television and radio were far more effective at transmitting 'hard news' in a straightforward fashion, the *Sun* had shown that there was an audience for softer, features-based material and heavily angled news in which comment and reporting were intertwined. It also adopted a more idiosyncratic agenda, presenting offbeat stories that fell outside the more limited remit of broadcast news producers. It cultivated brashness, deliberately appealing to the earthier interests – and, possibly, baser instincts – of a mass working-class audience. In other words, it did not prescribe values, preferring to play to the market and allowing readers to hold sway over matters of taste. The *Sun* unashamedly embraced sex as a selling proposition while the *Daily Mirror* tiptoed around it.

After more than twenty years mulling over the paradoxes which underlay the sales success of the Murdoch–Lamb *Sun*, I eventually wrote a succinct critique of the paper that had 'latched on to the permissiveness of the age' and then 'perverted that ethos of liberalism for its own ends'. I stand by what I wrote in 1995:

> It cultivated sex, yet decried sexual licence in its leading articles. It lured readers to play bingo for huge prizes while lecturing them on the vice of a something-for-nothing society. It encouraged people to sell their sexual secrets while holding them up to ridicule. It cultivated the shallow world of celebrity as a cynical circulation device. It pushed back the boundaries of taste and decency while wringing its hands at the decline of standards. It employed the language of the lager lout while lambasting the growth of youth culture. Its politics were opportunistic, conjoining the radical and the reactionary to extol the virtues of Margaret Thatcher, the supreme mistress of cultural philistinism.[144]

I then overstated my case by saying that the *Sun*'s 'degradation of the newspaper form' had led to the replacement of a public service press by one geared to private profit. That was, as we have seen, historically inaccurate. Murdoch was not responsible for the rise of the commercial press. But it is surely fairer to assert that his *Sun* destroyed the whole notion of popular papers being imbued with any form of public service ethic. It was, I concede, all a matter of degree.

In its first decade, the Murdoch *Sun* transformed the techniques pioneered by the *Mirror* into a less cosy, more hard-edged and undoubtedly more modern formula. There was serious content, but not nearly as much as the *Mirror* offered. By largely dispensing with specialist reporters, the *Sun* narrowed the domestic news agenda. Unlike the *Mirror*, it also had no staff reporters outside Britain, except for the United States, and only rarely sent journalists on foreign assignments. All of this ensured that the editorial costs of the *Sun* were a great deal lower than those of their rivals, though the *Sun* channelled more money into marketing and promotion, a major factor in creating the image of a go-ahead paper that could not be ignored.

Jubilation in Bouverie Street at the moment of sales triumph was offset by a sense of anti-climax, partly because it had appeared inevitable for the past five years, partly because it had become clear that the *Sun* would now never get close to the *Mirror*'s 5 million-plus record, and partly because editor Larry Lamb thought he should have achieved the target far more quickly. This was a view shared by owner Rupert Murdoch, just one of the reasons for tension between the two men. The central dispute underlying their disagreements was over which of them was mainly responsible for the paper's success: Lamb was convinced that his skills were of paramount importance, while Murdoch was just as convinced that he was the dominant force. There could be only one winner of that dispute.

By the mid-1970s, there was one subject about which they were both united, the political necessity of ousting Labour in favour of Margaret Thatcher's Tories. In 1978, Lamb cemented his paper's move to the right by appointing Walter Terry, former political editor of the *Daily Mail* and *Daily Express*, as the *Sun*'s political chief. He also hired a new leader writer, Ronnie Spark, who had been fired from the *Sunday Express* for fiddling his expenses, a fact which didn't inhibit its editor, John Junor, from recommending him to Lamb.[145] Spark's devastating prose was to be among the *Sun*'s most memorable in the following years. Both Lamb and Murdoch were united in joy when Thatcher won the 1979 election, but the difficulties in their relationship surfaced the following year when it became clear that the new *Daily Star* was managing to find an audience by using a *Sun*-style approach.

Quite why Lamb didn't see the *Star* as a serious threat, given that *Sun* circulation sank for the first time during his editorship, remains baffling. The *Sun*, which suffered much worse than the *Mirror* due to the newcomer's entrance, saw sales fall from almost 4 million at the end of 1978 to 3.7 million within two years. Murdoch responded by cutting the *Sun*'s cover price to 10p, making it the same as the *Star*'s. By holding at that price for ten weeks, backed by an expensive TV campaign, he regained 100,000 buyers. Lamb opposed the price cut, but rightly identified bingo as the *Star*'s major plus without showing any enthusiasm for employing the same tactic.[146]

There were other strains too. When Lamb was rewarded by Thatcher with a knighthood in 1980, Murdoch – who had no time for such honours – was unimpressed. He thought Lamb's instruction to his secretary that she must answer the phone by announcing 'Sir Larry Lamb's office' was ostentatious nonsense. Once Murdoch opened negotiations to buy the *Times* and *Sunday Times*, Lamb argued forcefully that he should become *Times* editor. Murdoch laughed at the notion, knowing it would be bitterly opposed by the staff. Lamb's mood darkened in the following weeks when Murdoch took to quoting *Sunday Times* editor Harry Evans continually. Lamb realised that his boss had a new favourite and was upset when Murdoch told him to concentrate his attentions on the interloper in his own market, the *Star*, rather than on events at the *Times*. Lamb then wrote a highly critical memo to Murdoch, who responded by suggesting Lamb take a six-month sabbatical.

Over at the Holborn Circus headquarters of the *Daily Mirror*, there was a very different atmosphere in spite of the paper's eclipse by the *Sun*. Under the chairmanship of Sir Alex Jarratt, Reed showed little enthusiasm for its union-dominated newspapers. Having broken up the old IPC empire, it placed all the national titles into a single division as Mirror Group Newspapers (MGN) and gave chief executive Percy Roberts a single instruction: make a profit. This dispassionate profit-oriented corporate philosophy, so different from the driving individualism of the single proprietor, was to prove the *Daily Mirror*'s Achilles' heel.

The *Mirror* began the period with a new editor, Mike Molloy, who had taken one of the more unconventional routes to the top job by starting his career on the art desk. At thirteen, Molloy went to the Ealing School of Art, but was required to take a year out at fifteen and managed to get a temporary job as a messenger on the *Sunday Pictorial*, working as the 'editor's boy' for Colin Valdar. That gave him a taste for newspapers, and when he finished his art studies aged nineteen he joined the *Daily Sketch* – where Valdar was now the editor – and was given a regular cartoon slot billed as 'the teenage artist'. He also showed a talent for designing pages and two years later, in 1962, was recruited by the *Daily Mirror*'s art bench. He learned his craft well enough to innovate and was responsible for the distinctive style of the Mirrorscope pages as well as drawing a regular pocket cartoon, Virginia.

His big break appeared to have come in 1969 when he was made editor of the *Mirror*'s colour magazine, but Cudlipp was critical of some of its content and it was closed after nine months, having lost £2 million. Though everyone knew that union demands were the major reason for its demise, the aura of failure clung to Molloy. Back on the *Mirror* as an assistant editor, his career took a nosedive – 'nobody would even speak to me', he said – until a lucky turn of events.[147] After prompting from the NUJ, Cudlipp held a series of staff meetings at which it was suggested he should produce a 'shock issue' on pollution. Cudlipp hated the idea but to placate his increasingly fractious journalists he ordered *Mirror* editor Tony Miles to carry it out. Miles wasn't keen either, and handed the task to Molloy. Against all expectations, Molloy's 'shock issue' – the first not to have been personally masterminded by Cudlipp – delighted the sceptical boss. Molloy went from pariah to blue-eyed boy in a day and Cudlipp told him he would soon be an editor.

Molloy was a fresh-faced and fashionably long-haired thirty-five-year-old when he became *Mirror* editor at the end of 1975, surveying what had become a wreckage of a paper. Just before he took over, its sale had fallen below 4 million for the first time since 1948. The *Sun* was rising so rapidly that the gap between the two had narrowed to fewer than 500,000. 'We were facing nightmare problems,' he recalled. 'We were using cheap newsprint from Reed so the *Sun* was better printed. It had more pages, it cost less and it was enjoying a better promotion budget.'[148] Molloy set out to find a way of maintaining a commitment to serious content with an understanding that the *Sun* was supplanting the *Mirror* because it more truly reflected changed popular taste. But turning around a super-tanker takes skill and time, especially if other ships are in the way. It also requires full-hearted effort from the owners and crew, both of whom were somewhat deficient in that respect.

Another difficulty for the *Daily Mirror* was its politics. Imperceptibly, it had moved from being a critical supporter of Labour to being 'a Labour paper'. At a time of growing disenchantment with the Callaghan government and a groundswell of opposition to the unions this identification with Labour was one possible reason for some readers switching to the *Sun*. While the

Mirror found itself trying to report sensibly on the party's internal battles, right and left, unions versus leadership, and so on, the *Sun* exploited these divisions with a simple message: try the Tories instead.

Molloy's recruitment policy owed little to political affiliations. He hired both Harold Wilson's former press secretary Joe Haines as a feature writer (later becoming the leader writer) and one of Wilson's fiercest left-wing critics, Paul Foot, previously with the *Socialist Worker* and then enjoying his second stint on *Private Eye.* Foot said Molloy appeared at his home one summer evening in 1979 and agreed he could have his own 'investigative page'.[149] It was to become hugely popular. Foot and the paper's senior feature writer, John Pilger, gradually came to embody the *Mirror*'s left-of-centre conscience.

Molloy's *Mirror* also benefited from a number of genuine scoops, such as the revelations about England football manager Don Revie having used bribery when running Leeds United, which was masterminded by the 'very talented investigator Richard Stott'.[150] He was also responsible for other exclusives, on the Poulson bribery case and the disappearance of the Labour politician John Stonehouse. A bizarre story about a woman who kidnapped a Mormon missionary and kept him in chains won the *Mirror* the 1978 *What the Papers Say* scoop of the year award and the man who led the team, Frank Palmer, was named reporter of the year in the British Press Awards.

Molloy and Stott were to argue that the *Mirror*'s militant journalists were a prime cause of the paper's failure to take full advantage of its sharper public profile. It is true that the NUJ chapels at *Mirror* group were about the best organised of any in Fleet Street and in Manchester, where the *Mirror* chapel in the late 1960s was the first to negotiate a 'house agreement' separate from the discredited system of nationally agreed rises in the minimum wage. This was a turning point for NUJ chapels in all national papers which quickly demanded similar rights from their managements too. In the *Mirror*'s London office, the chapel's highest-profile leader in the mid-1970s, industrial reporter Bryn Jones, proved to be an articulate champion of the NUJ's cause, pointing continually to the unfairness of manual workers earning more than journalists.

After him came Steve Turner, arguably the most effective NUJ chapel negotiator in Fleet Street history. He was father of the chapel in 1977 when the print unions negotiated a £3,000 'new technology' increase – a payment to allow the tentative introduction of computer typesetting – which was denied to the journalists. Turner argued with MGN's chief executive Percy Roberts that his members should have a comparable increase but, recalled Turner, 'it was obvious that Roberts and his team hadn't taken the journalists' aspirations into their calculations'.[151] Roberts, aware that his deal with the print unions to reduce costs was so catastrophic that it would in fact increase them, rejected the NUJ's demand for a £3,000 rise.[152] Molloy was sympathetic, pointing out that journalists merely wanted 'parity with the men who swept the floors'.[153] But he was less happy about his staff taking industrial action to obtain it.

The chapel held a ballot, which showed a majority in favour of a strike, but Turner pressured MGN by using the print union tactic of holding disruptive chapel meetings. Roberts then made another miscalculation by suspending publication and announcing that the staff were to be dismissed for breaking their contracts. He was convinced that the journalists would give in within a week. Instead, the chapel showed a surprising spirit of defiance, sporting badges with the slogan 'Three Grand in my Hand'.

After the loss of eleven days' papers from 21 November 1977, an uneasy compromise was agreed and, though the journalists got less than £3,000, they had made a point. At an emergency board meeting soon after, it was announced, according to Molloy, that sales of the *Daily Mirror* had fallen to 3.1 million.[154] This myth has persisted ever since,[155] but the official ABC circulation statistics do not bear it out. There was a slump, from which the *Sun* undoubtedly benefited in the short term (even though it also lost a whole issue during the *Mirror* stoppage), but the *Mirror*'s sale in the first half of 1978 was only 127,000 down on the final half of 1977, a drop which was soon reversed.

Anyway, for eleven successive days in July and August 1978 the *Sun* wasn't published because of a dispute with its journalists over a pay deal and a *Daily Mirror* internal circular boasted to its staff that in eight days 8 million copies of the *Mirror* had got into the hands of *Sun* readers.[156] In March 1979, during a *Sun* dispute with its Sogat members, the *Mirror* printed an extra million copies a night.[157] Dogs ate dogs at every opportunity and the sales benefits and reverses tended to even out in the long run.[158]

Journalistic militancy sprang in part from management timidity and from the belief that we were indispensable. How else could one explain the fact that we were in such demand that many of us had several jobs? From 1975, I worked as a casual sub on Fridays and Saturdays at the *Sunday Mirror*. So organised was casualisation that management laid on transport on Friday afternoons to take a group of us who also casualled at the group's weekly *Reveille* magazine, near Waterloo, across the river to the *Mirror* building. In my case, I was able to earn enough from these shifts in just two days to keep a family, leaving me with enough time to take a three-year full-time university degree course. From about 1970 onwards, sub-editors on most daily papers secured four-day week agreements, because of the unsocial hours, and then spent their days off working for Sunday titles or on magazines, such as *Reader's Digest* and *TV Times*. Moonlighting, as it was known, was highly organised and offered the same safeguards to the casual worker as to a full-time employee. Once a person had worked the same shift for thirteen consecutive weeks, he or she changed status from being a 'casual casual' to a 'regular casual'. This allowed the sub or reporter the rights to holidays, sickness benefit and a stake in the staff pension fund.

The *Sunday Mirror* was so dependent on casuals that some of them held key executive positions in the production process. It soon became clear to the union activists among us that we held the whip hand on Saturday evenings as the paper was going to press. We began to exact the maximum advantage by copying the print unions, who regularly held chapel meetings at delicate times, winning extra money and other concessions. This activity was not out of step with the general mood within the building, nor among members of the *Daily Mirror*'s editorial chapel, which was showing increasing signs of militancy.

We did not heed warnings about killing off the golden goose because the company looked invulnerable. Money cascaded from the eleventh-floor cashiers' office known as 'the bank in the sky' where a variety of print workers picking up their nightly shift payments in cash jostled with journalists proffering the yellow chits that provided them with advances on expenses. Paid sabbatical leave was common (as it was at other Fleet Street papers, especially at the *Sunday Times*). Senior Mirror executives of comparatively lowly status had their own drinks cabinets, which were regularly replenished. Mirror group was infected with a hedonistic culture. It wasn't that it was out of kilter with the rest of Fleet Street, it was simply the most extravagant example. But the tide was beginning to turn against such excess.

The *Sunday Mirror*'s editor, Bob Edwards, was no push-over, nor was his tough deputy Joe Grizzard, renowned for his colourful oaths. His favourite, sometimes directed at me, was the incomprehensible: 'The man should be flogged with syphilitic spiders'. But the editors found it difficult to enforce discipline in a company which was ambivalent about owning newspapers and within a corporate structure with layers of separate boards which meant that no single person ever seemed wholly responsible for decision-making. Union strength blossomed in the resulting power vacuum.

As for the *Sunday Mirror*'s content, the balance between serious and light material inevitably tilted towards the light as the down-market trend continued. Edwards's leading articles were models of sensible left-of-centre polemic, informed by his good contacts within the Labour party. Woodrow Wyatt's column provided right-of-centre balance. These, though, were hardly the best-read parts of the paper. To attract readers, the *Sunday Mirror* dipped its toe into the world of kiss-and-tell revelations. One of the first of its kind, the tale of a Nigerian-born model, Mynah Bird, took the paper into *News of the World* territory.

At the in-house rival, the *Sunday People*, editor Geoff Pinnington did his best to maintain the paper's traditions for investigative series. Its most notable success of the period – corruption at Scotland Yard – won investigations editor Laurie Manifold and his team the 1977 *What the Papers Say* award. But the balance between the use of such public interest material and less high-minded stories and series about sex tilted towards the latter. That wasn't a clever option, according to deputy editor Alan Hobday, because the *People*'s main audience was 'the equivalent of America's bible belt, easily offended by sexual matters'.[159]

The same couldn't be said for *News of the World* readers, who bought the paper precisely for its sexual content. Editor Bernard Shrimsley was a man of good taste, tall, slim, well dressed, witty, urbane and refined. Yet the paper he edited, despite his fastidious attention to details of design or choice of pictures, overflowed with thoroughly grubby content. Its leading reporters spent their weeks in the company of prostitutes, and then exposed their activities for what the paper affected to call the public interest. It extended its range to wife-swapping and suburban orgies and, as the paper's historians put it, 'the sleazy world of saunas and massage parlours'.[160] Its most celebrated exposé of the period involved a madam, Cynthia Payne, who ran a brothel in south London in which clients paid their fees with luncheon vouchers.

Shrimsley did his best to balance the sex with serious material too. One notable example was his 1977 revelation of the criminal backgrounds of National Front candidates standing for election, in defiance of the Rehabilitation of Offenders Act which banned mention of convictions more than seven years old. But his major ambition was to transform the *News of the World* from a broadsheet to a tabloid. He did his best to convince Murdoch it was the only way to stop the sales rot. Circulation was dropping swiftly when Shrimsley took over and he was unable to stop the downward spiral. By the time he departed in 1980, after a series of rows with Murdoch, it had reached 4.2 million, a loss of 2 million copies in just ten years. Murdoch, always regarded by outsiders as a man of decision and as having a magic touch with papers, could be as indecisive and as unwise as less successful proprietors. He refused to countenance Shrimsley's tabloid plans and the row led to Shrimsley's departure in 1980.

Shrimsley's job was given to the *Sun*'s veteran news editor Ken Donlan, one of Murdoch's strangest appointments. Donlan, aged fifty-two, raised in Salford, was a devout Roman Catholic, a fervent Manchester City fan and an unquestioning supporter of the Conservative party. He spent fourteen years with the *Daily Mail*, mostly in Manchester, before joining the *Sun* in 1970. He won a reputation for being a tough news desk executive, feared but respected by two generations of reporters. Known by his initials, KD spoke quietly out of the corner of his mouth, sending copy back to reporters with a cryptic demand for 'more top spin, old boy'. No one knew what he meant, but a rewrite seemed to oblige. His news judgement was excellent, but he had neither features skills nor production knowledge. He lacked Sunday-paper experience and I knew that the *News of the World*'s sleazy agenda offended his religious sensibilities. Donlan just wasn't cut out to be an editor and he floundered around unhappily for a few months until Murdoch made his next mistake.

The *Daily Mail*'s unfinest hour

The darkest day in David English's editorship of the *Daily Mail* occurred on 19 May 1977 at a point when his journalistic transformation of the paper was paying dividends. After a bumpy time in the early part of the decade, the *Mail*'s improved quality and energy had resulted in a significant circulation upswing, taking it to more than 1.8 million. English's paper had developed a strong character of its own, punchy, up-beat, with great appeal for women through its Femail pages.[161] But English and his senior team were so hostile to the Labour government that they accepted at face value a totally false story presented to them which appeared to 'prove' the point.

The *Mail*'s splash on that fateful day was headlined 'World-Wide Bribery Web by Leyland: Exposed – the amazing truth about Britain's State-owned car makers'. At the heart of the story was a letter, said to have been sent by Lord Ryder, chairman of the National Enterprise Board and also the cabinet's industrial adviser, to Alex Park, chief executive of British Leyland, then a nationalised car manufacturer. It suggested that Ryder was endorsing a set of illegal activities in order to help Leyland sells cars abroad, including the bribing of agents, the breaking of tax and currency regulations and the use of a 'slush fund'. The implication of the story was that the company couldn't sell cars overseas without breaking the law, that a senior Labour party figure was involved in the illegality, and that the government's industrial strategy of public ownership was therefore a sham. A *Mail* leading article that day was unequivocal: 'No ifs and buts. Lord Ryder must go. His behaviour would be sleazy any time, any place. As the guardian of the millions we are pouring into British Leyland, it is intolerable.'

Despite instantaneous and strong denials from Ryder and Park, the *Mail* played what it thought was its trump card the following day by reproducing a copy of the letter under the headline: 'The documents that prove the case'.[162] What they proved instead was what Ryder, Park and prime minister James Callaghan knew to be the case: the letter was a forgery made up by a disaffected Leyland employee. There was no slush fund and every detail was bogus. The *Mail* had been hoaxed.

Callaghan called the *Mail* 'contemptible' and several Labour MPs recalled the infamous Zinoviev letter, a forgery purporting to show a Russian politician urging Britain's communists to rise up, published by the *Daily Mail* just before the 1924 election, and regarded as a major cause of Labour's defeat. A demand that English should resign was signed by 123 MPs as the *Mail* climbed down on the third day: 'Ryder Forger Confesses'.[163] There was some journalistic sympathy for the *Mail*, not least from the *Sunday Times*, which thought 'the whole issue of the baksheesh economy needs an airing'.[164] The *Times* wasn't harsh on English either: 'The failure of the *Mail* was not in what it tried to do but how it did it . . . By the law of averages some serious mistakes are bound to be made.'[165]

Everyone agreed that, whatever the motives, it was a very bad journalistic error and it couldn't have happened at a worse time for English's proprietor, Vere Rothermere. He was involved in the delicate negotiations over the *Standard–News* merger and it provided Wintour with ammunition in his struggle to avoid a merger (see above, p. 316). The Royal Commission on the Press was also nearing the end of its deliberations and could hardly ignore a mistake of such proportions. English offered his resignation, which Rothermere rejected. It soon emerged that the *Mail* associate editor responsible for overseeing the story was Stewart Steven, architect of the Martin Bormann fiasco at the *Daily Express* (See Chapter Twelve). His offer to resign was also rejected by English and he later denied that the story was motivated by malice because 'everyone knows . . . I am as Socialist'.[166]

English atoned in his paper, but his apology ended with a rant about a mysterious 'ugly bullyboy campaign of intimidation and fear' by people taking part in 'an orchestrated campaign to silence us'.[167] Did he mean Labour party members, the subject of his own campaign, or someone else? More likely, it was a ruse to deflect criticism. With breathtaking chutzpah, English went on to claim that the *Mail* had not intended to smear anyone and tried to excuse the error by pointing out that Ryder hadn't returned his reporter's phone calls, so his silence was taken as proof of his guilt.[168] Few people were convinced by that defence. In an addendum to its final report, the Royal Commission condemned the *Mail*, which it called 'a polemical and politically partisan newspaper', for 'serious misconduct'. It added: 'What is novel is the extreme lengths to which the paper was prepared to go in an attack on the government on inadequately checked information.'[169]

In an expensive legal settlement, the *Mail* had to pay out money to Ryder, a former chairman of the *Daily Mirror*'s owners, Reed International. Sales of the *Mail*, far from being adversely affected, continued to rise. Nor did the *Mail* desist in its attacks on Labour. A couple of days later it accused Callaghan of nepotism for making his son-in-law, Peter Jay, the ambassador to Washington. Incidentally, when news of Jay's appointment reached the *Times* editorial floor, where Jay was economics editor, it was considered so inappropriate that it was greeted with ten seconds of silence, a collective intake of breath.[170]

New technology: the panacea for all ills?

Having set out on a practical, if artless, mission to find ways of injecting political balance into newspapers, the Royal Commission on the Press, chaired by Professor Oliver McGregor, released its report in July 1977 after sitting for three years. Those of us who considered the commission to be either a laughable sideshow or 'an establishment device designed not so much to provide radical critiques as to diffuse controversial situations', were not to be disappointed.[171] We had not expected a recommendation to launch a state-funded title, nor did we imagine the commission urging state intervention to ensure that advertising was spread around in order to support the weaker titles.

Privately, I believed it would find the papers guilty of political bias but, not wanting to clash with the twin concepts of private ownership and press freedom, would offer no realistic solution. The commission didn't want to be caught in that cleft stick. So, despite the facts, it reached the most absurd conclusion of all: 'The evidence we have does not suggest that in either the national or the regional press at present the balance against Labour is a strong one.'[172] How strong did they want it? No wonder one of the modern press's foremost critics, Tom Baistow, called it a 'Panglossian conclusion'.[173] Another commentator regarded it as 'the fudging of an anti-monopoly policy into a preservation policy'.[174]

Most interesting of all though was the conclusion that the introduction of new technology would not affect the inequalities between the stronger and weaker titles. 'Even if all newspapers accomplish the change, competition may still result in some papers closing, since the new technology does little to alter the relative position of competing titles.'[175] It was also noticeable that, in a section on the likelihood of new newspaper launches, there was no mention that the probable reduced productions costs would help such launches.[176]

Two members of the eleven-person commission – Geoffrey Goodman, the *Daily Mirror*'s industrial editor, and David Basnett, leader of the Municipal Workers' Union – refused to sign up to the report's main conclusions and produced a lengthy minority report. They disagreed with a whole range of findings, arguing that 'market pressures ... constitute a serious impediment to existing diversity' and concluding: 'There is nothing inherently virtuous in a massive circulation for its own sake – provided a lesser one can be made economically viable while maintaining professional standards.'[177] They called for a 'third force' which should included 'a paper of the left to help correct the political and cultural imbalance'.[178]

Balance, of course, is a relative term. One frustrated newspaper tycoon believed that the press wasn't right-wing enough. Having failed to buy the Express group or the *Observer*, James Goldsmith decided to use his wealth to publish a journal that would, in his opinion, change the face of British journalism: an equivalent to his French weekly news magazine, *L'Express*, which he entitled *Now!* He hired Tony Shrimsley, former political editor of the *Sun* and the *Daily Mail*, as editor-in-chief. Many journalists were sceptical about joining Goldsmith for two quite separate reasons: some thought him suspect because of his *Private Eye* battle; others didn't believe there was a market for a news magazine in Britain.[179] In the six months it took Shrimsley to recruit a full staff, he did manage to entice some high-fliers such as Patrick Hutber, Frank Johnson and Robin Oakley. Most people who joined did so because of the absurdly high wages on offer.[180]

Now! was viewed as both right-wing and maverick, and its first issue in September 1979 was greeted by a chorus of raspberries. At launch, it claimed a sale of 400,000 which dropped over twelve months 'to barely 125,000 copies'.[181] As its business editor observed, the British public 'showed little wish to buy a weekly news magazine, no matter how colourful its pictures'.[182] Mainstream newspapers quietly applauded *Private Eye*'s relentless campaign which turned *Now!* into a laughing stock among the 'chattering classes' and, according to one of its writers, Frank Johnson, it also coloured the views of advertising agencies.[183] After eighteen months and eighty-four issues the 'unceremonious end' arrived in April 1981.[184] The closure cost 120 people their jobs, including 80 journalists, but there was little weeping because Goldsmith paid everyone a year's salary. Columnist Jon Akass, who left the *Sun* for *Now!* the week before it closed, returned to the *Sun* a week later many thousands richer.

At least Goldsmith's magazine got off the ground. An attempted newspaper launch by the *Daily Telegraph*'s former industrial correspondent, Peter Paterson, never got beyond the planning stage. His idea of starting up a paper provisionally entitled the *Globe* was interesting because he cleverly devised a way of overcoming print union hostility to new technology. Employing his good contacts in Natsopa, he persuaded officials to agree to an exclusive, single-union, closed-shop deal. He also lined up satellite printing using facsimile transmission and a print agreement. A mock-up of his *Le Monde*-style 'serious tabloid' was designed by Dennis Hackett. Paterson's problem was that he couldn't convince anyone in the City to back him.[185] A headline in *World's Press News* summed up the general scepticism: 'Has the *Globe* got an earthly?' So Paterson's project died, but his plan, conceived in 1976, was uncannily prescient.

The underlying assumption of owners throughout these years was that new technology would solve every difficulty, especially the industrial relations nightmare. A major attempt to resolve the stalemate between owners and unions was the establishment of the Joint Standing Committee, with print union general secretaries and Fleet Street chief executives coming together to agree on the introduction of technology and a consequent reduction in jobs.[186] The result was *Programme for Action*, a pamphlet published in November 1976, which set out a raft of proposals for approval by union members. In commending the plan, the general secretaries of the NGA, Sogat, Natsopa and the NUJ and a representative of the electricians' union EETPU, warned that to reject the proposals would be 'extremely grave and have a serious effect on the continued viability of some titles', which, in turn, would threaten 'the maintenance of employment, and the continuation of strong and effective trade union organisation'.[187]

A dispassionate commentator, Roderick Martin, thought the unions had secured a good deal. 'It is difficult to see what union members could have wanted that was not provided in Programme for Action,' he wrote.[188] In fact, the proposals were overwhelmingly rejected by ballots of chapel members in the spring of 1977. The NGA vote against was crushing and, though the Natsopa margin was narrow, the London membership was much more definitely against. The NUJ was the only union to vote in favour. It was clear proof of the gap between the Fleet Street chapels and their national union leaders and, of course, of the differing attitudes between journalists and their printing colleagues.

The vote also killed off a separate attempt to introduce computer typesetting and direct input by journalists at the *Financial Times.* Chief executive Alan Hare was devastated at the failure which tended to undermine his, and the *FT* management's, credibility. Hare was convinced of the long-term benefits of computerisation because 'the basic obstacle to growth' remained 'an unstable cost base'.[189] Despite the loss of its development plan, the *FT* did pull off a signal success in August 1977 by ending a costly deal by which its compositors were allowed extra time off, known as 'blue days'. Management withstood a sixteen-day stoppage to achieve its 'rare and sweet moment of victory'.[190]

A couple of years later the *FT* proved it was in the vanguard of technological change by printing an edition abroad. On 2 January 1979, it used facsimile transmission to publish in Frankfurt, one of the greatest turning points in the paper's history. It had been eager to boost its European sale, then standing at about 14,000, and the German printing was to prove the first step on a long process which was to turn the *FT* into a truly international paper. One less pleasant episode at the *FT* began when the simmering dispute between the editor, Fredy Fisher, and his columnist C. Gordon Tether came to a head. Tether devoted much of his Lombard column to the supposed iniquities of Britain's EEC membership, with a typical example suggesting that Britain was 'prepared to sink its identity and individual freedom in a European super-state'.[191] Fisher acknowledged that Tether was provocative, and therefore valuable, but also found him too often 'windy, overblown and repetitive'.[192]

In July 1976, Fisher decided to terminate the column and Tether took the *FT* to an industrial tribunal for unfair dismissal. During the record forty-five-day hearing, the central debate concerned the fascinating matter of a journalist's rights compared to those of the editor and, by implication, the owner. Fisher asserted that 'no Fleet Street journalist . . . had the right for his articles to be published against the wishes of his editor'. The *FT*'s NUJ chapel didn't support Tether because members thought he was claiming rights that no other journalist enjoyed. Tether lost. It was, observed the *FT*'s historian, 'a sad end to a distinguished career'.[193]

The end to Fisher's editorship in 1980 was much less dramatic. As expected, his deputy Geoffrey Owen took over, with David Palmer becoming deputy editor. Owen, forty-six, was educated at Rugby and Oxford where he read Greats, joining the *Financial Times* straight from university – rather than taking up tennis, at which he excelled – and learning his journalism under Gordon Newton. After a stint as industrial correspondent, he spent most of the 1960s as the US correspondent, returning to London as industrial editor. He left the *FT* in 1967 to join the Industrial Reorganisation Corporation and then had two years with British Leyland as director of personnel and administration. He returned to the *FT* in 1974 as Fisher's loyal deputy.

On Fisher's resignation, Owen inherited a rising sale and, with the gradual economic recovery, an improved advertising climate. During the *Times*'s closure, the *FT* enjoyed its highest circulation on record, slipping back afterwards to about 197,000, just a little less than its best days in 1974. What was significant was the slow but inexorable increase in its overseas circulation. The pink paper was beginning a new decade with a new editor and a new challenge. As with every newspaper, its hopes were pinned on technological advance.

14. DIANA AND MAGGIE, THE MAKING OF PRESS ICONS

The public is not made up of people who get their names in the papers.[1]

On the day of the Queen's coronation in June 1953, *Daily Mirror* reporter Audrey Whiting spotted Princess Margaret with Group Captain Peter Townsend. It confirmed reports in foreign papers that the Queen's sister was enjoying a romance with a divorced man, but her editor refused to publish the story, saying: 'We can't upset the ladies' day . . .' A month later the *Mirror* ran its poll asking readers whether Margaret should be allowed to marry Townsend. (see above, p. 85). It was one of the first matters dealt with by the newly created Press Council after a complaint about the *Mirror*'s 'grossly impertinent and unseemly speculations'. The Council agreed, strongly deprecating the poll 'as contrary to the best traditions of British journalism'.[2] Most popular paper editors thought it a daft adjudication and a poor start for the apparatus of self-regulation. From that moment on, the relationship between the royal family and the press, which had never been harmonious, became one of continual strife.

The Prince of Wales discovered the problem of being a Windsor early in life. In June 1963, fourteen-year-old Charles, while in his second year at Gordonstoun School, took a sailing trip to Stornoway, Isle of Lewis. Fleeing from a crowd he went into a bar and ordered 'the first drink that came into my head', which turned out to be a cherry brandy.[3] This example of under-aged drinking was observed by a freelance journalist who sold the story to Fleet Street. Newspapers reacted hysterically to this minor indiscretion and Charles found himself front-page news.[4] The incident permanently soured his attitude towards newspapers.

A year later the Queen's press officer, Commander (later Sir) Richard Colville, complained to the Press Council about the activities of freelance photographers, such as Ray Bellisario, who were making a living by following members of the royal family and taking 'candid' shots of them. This attention culminated in a picture of Princess Margaret water-skiing on Crown lands in Sunninghill Park watched by the Queen, who was sunbathing. The pictures were published in the *People* and the *Sunday Express*, whose editor, John Junor, defended their use after being assured that the photographer had taken them from a public footpath. A test was carried out and it was discovered that it would have been impossible to take the shots from the footpath, so Junor apologised and the Press Council ruled that the photographs amounted to unreasonable intrusion.[5] Bellisario also suffered, with papers largely obeying a Palace request never to buy his pictures again.[6]

Colville's successor, William Heseltine, argued that the royal family should promote themselves by letting a little light in on the magic, choosing television rather than newspapers. The Queen agreed, and in 1969 allowed a BBC TV team to film her family's daily life. The documentary, running for almost two hours, was watched by 68 per cent of the population.[7] Most royal commentators later believed this peep behind the Palace walls was ill advised, serving only to whet the public appetite for more news and gossip about the Queen's family.

During the 1970s, popular papers vigorously pursued two royal stories: the marital problems of Princess Margaret and the marital possibilities of Prince Charles. One royal historian dates the press's intense competition for royal stories to the period in which Margaret's marriage broke down, viewing it as 'the highway to a new, more raucous kind of press voyeurism, which combined the snobbish, the coy, and the explicitly sexual . . . Rumours became blazoned scandals, and what was left of the old sanctimonious reticence was transformed into competitive ribaldry, couched in the language of homily.'[8] Certainly, once Margaret was officially separated and became involved with a twenty-eight-year-old trainee landscape gardener, Roddy Llewellyn, newspapers cast off any lingering sense of deference. A paparazzi picture in the *News of the World* which showed Margaret lounging on a Caribbean beach with Llewellyn was the precursor to years in which the couple were followed by photographers. Her affair also emboldened papers to question whether she should receive money from the Civil List with headlines such as 'Give up Roddy or Quit Royal Duties'. No one thought to complain to the Press Council, as had previously been the case, about gross impertinence.

Fevered press speculation about Prince Charles's friendships with women meant that every woman he dated (and some he had never met or known) was treated as a potential bride and then subjected to relentless scrutiny, pictured whenever they appeared in public, and endlessly questioned. By the time he left the navy, aged twenty-eight, in 1976 he was routinely described by papers as the world's most eligible bachelor and the question of who, and when, he would marry had become a national preoccupation. Some idea of the intensity of interest in Charles and other members of the royal family is provided by a study of just one Sunday paper's files from July 1980 onwards. Hardly a week passed in which the *Sunday Mirror* didn't carry several royal stories and what follows is only a partial selection. On 6 July, there was a speculative piece, based on the wholly fallacious claims that Charles was enjoying a romance with Princess Marie-

Astrid of Luxembourg, about the problems he would face in marrying a Roman Catholic. The following week, a writer quashed rumours that he was about to marry Marie-Astrid and predicted: 'My own view is that he will marry into the peerage or the landed gentry.'[9] On 20 July, *Sunday Mirror* columnist Woodrow Wyatt, again with a Catholic marriage in mind, urged the abandonment of the Act of Settlement.[10] Elsewhere in the same paper was an article by royal correspondent Audrey Whiting entitled 'Insider's guide to Balmoral'.

On 27 July, the main feature was about 'the latest royal star', Princess Michael of Kent. A week later, the front page was dominated by a picture of Marie-Astrid in bikini with a caption which said she was 'showing off the charms . . . that Charles publicly rejected'. There was also mention of Anna Wallace, who had evidently 'stormed out when Charles ignored her at a Windsor Castle ball'. The front page on 10 August was devoted to an article about Princess Margaret's romance with Llewellyn having cooled. Inside was a story about Prince Charles paying £800,000 for his new home set in 347 acres, Highgrove House, and a leader which complained: 'It is an exorbitant sum in these times of economic thrift with almost two million unemployed.'[11]

What the *Sunday Mirror* didn't know was that in July 1980, while it was concerning itself with Marie-Astrid's religion, Prince Charles had met eighteen-year-old Lady Diana Spencer at a house party in West Sussex. That weekend she went to watch him play polo at Cowdray Park and was pictured by *Sun* photographer Arthur Edwards. Because there was 'no contact' between her and the prince, Edwards filed the print.[12] Two months later, looking down his lens at Balmoral where Charles was fishing, Edwards spotted a girl behind a tree and discovered it was the polo girl, Diana. Out came the filed picture, and the *Sun*'s exclusive, written by Harry Arnold, was headlined: 'HE'S IN LOVE AGAIN: Lady Di is the new girl for Charles'. Arnold's story claimed that 'Prince Charles has found love on the rebound' after his broken romance with Anna Wallace.[13] Inside were pictures of her dodging the camera on the fishing trip headlined: 'Is this the reel thing?' Later editions of the *Daily Star* carried a similar report by its royal reporter, James Whitaker, with pictures by Ken Lennox.

Noticeably, the *Daily Mirror* and *Daily Mail* were unable to publish anything about the new woman in Charles's life because they didn't have any information or pictures. It was nine days before the *Mail*'s Nigel Dempster devoted his column to the subject. Under the headline 'Has Charles found his future bride?' Dempster confidently wrote: 'The two happily married women who influence Prince Charles most on personal matters, Lady Tryon and Camilla Parker Bowles, have both given the Heir to the Throne their approval over his new girlfriend.'[14] The following day every tabloid, having discovered where Diana worked, sent photographers to the London kindergarten. She scooped up two children in her arms, told them they had two minutes and posed with the sun behind her. What the photographers realised, and she did not, was that her skirt was transparent and her legs could be seen in the pictures. But she revealed nothing else, as the *Sun*'s headline made clear: 'CHARLIE'S GIRL. "You know I can't say anything about the Prince or my feelings for him".' The *Daily Star* opted for 'Miss, will you be our Queen?' Next day the *Daily Mirror* offered Diana front-page advice on how to avoid posing for see-through pictures.[15]

It was obvious that the popular papers were already fascinated. Upset by the results of her first brush with them, Diana agreed to pose for *Sunday Mirror* photographer Carl Bruin, who asked her how she would like to be seen. She chose a quilted ski jacket, high-necked blouse and sensible cotton skirt that was anything but transparent. 'I'm learning fast,' she was reported as saying. 'I didn't know what was going on when the photographers came down to photograph me.'[16]

Neither she – nor indeed the editors – could have had a clue as to what was about to happen. Her supposed romance with Charles was hot news and Fleet Street threw all its resources into tracking down her London flat and, having found it, into door-stepping her twenty-four hours a day. Throughout what would become known as the siege of Coleherne Court, she refused to speak to any of the waiting journalists. She was plagued with phone calls. Her flatmates were pursued every time they left home. A reporter tried to talk to Diana through her letterbox. Her employers were outraged when a photographer tried to get into her kindergarten through a lavatory window.

A *Times* reporter described the scene as photographers surrounded the flat, attempted to interrogate her in the street and harassed her as she walked to her car.[17] He spoke to the Queen's press secretary, Michael Shea, who complained: 'We are getting very fed up with inaccurate and invented stories.' He also quoted *Daily Mail* editor David English when he promised to reduce his paper's coverage: 'I think we should leave her alone until there is some significant development.' Paul Hopkins, London editor of the *Daily Star*, faced both ways. After claiming that his paper 'will not be involved in the scrum' he added: 'She is a valid news story. Although we feel sorry for her, it is something that must be done.'

Throughout October and November, the *Sunday Mirror* continued its weekly coverage, even when there was an absence of genuine news. One week it reported: 'Prince Charles dined by candlelight with his favourite new girl last night . . . at the Wiltshire country manor of his friends Andrew and Camilla Parker Bowles.'[18] The following week all it could say was 'Charles dates his Di again', but it got an exclusive of sorts seven days later with a splash headlined 'WHAT THE BUTLER SAW'. Reporter Wensley Clarkson had tracked down a former butler with the Spencer family who told innocuous 'secrets' of Diana's love for swimming and practical jokes.[19]

It was tame stuff which didn't cause a stir, but Clarkson's next venture into print on the following Sunday was anything but tame, provoking one of the biggest controversies of the entire Diana saga. *Sunday Mirror* editor Bob Edwards candidly admitted that he 'often found it a heart-stopping moment' when his news editor enthused about having 'a great world exclusive story'.[20] Experience taught that there was usually a price to pay for a genuine scoop, and it had nothing to do with chequebook journalism. So on the November day his effervescent news editor P. J. Wilson rushed into his office to boast of his latest blockbuster story he was less than enthusiastic.

Wilson told him that a respected freelance journalist based in Wiltshire, Jim Newman, had evidence from what appeared to be an impeccable source that Lady Diana Spencer had spent the night with Prince Charles on the royal train, which was parked in sidings on the outskirts of Chippenham. The cautious Edwards, imagining the furore if his paper incorrectly accused the Prince of Wales of sleeping with his virginal girlfriend, demanded as much proof as possible. Wilson dispatched Clarkson to Wiltshire to test Newman's information.

He soon discovered that Newman's source (who wasn't paid) was a policeman, and that the 'evidence' was a car registration number. It also emerged that the woman had twice 'visited' the train, driving off in the early hours, and a signalman who confirmed seeing a car provided 'a perfect description' of what Clarkson took to be Diana's car.[21] As a final check, Clarkson called the Wiltshire home of Andrew and Camilla Parker Bowles to discover whether Diana had been staying with them. By chance, a maid answered the phone and confirmed that Diana had stayed the previous Wednesday, one of the nights of the supposed train visit. The story, Clarkson later wrote, 'seemed to be signed, sealed and delivered'.[22] What the paper did not do was to contact the Palace press office before publication. The news desk anticipated that the probable response would be 'no comment', which would be fine as far as the *Sunday Mirror* was concerned, but Edwards and Wilson also feared that the Palace might conceivably issue a general statement about the story to the Press Association, thus ruining their story's exclusivity.

So the Palace and the rest of Fleet Street had no inkling until Saturday evening about the *Sunday Mirror*'s world-exclusive splash until they read the first edition which announced: 'Charles and Lady Diana special: ROYAL LOVE TRAIN. Secret meetings in the sidings'.[23] Just as Edwards had anticipated, the balloon went up. The Palace issued an official denial and the Queen's press secretary, Michael Shea, wrote to Edwards to say it was a 'totally false story ... a total fabrication ... Grave exception has been taken to the implications of your story'. He demanded that the paper publish a retraction. The rest of the press ganged up on its rival with the *Daily Mail*'s gossip columnist Nigel Dempster calling it 'drivel'.[24] Diana insisted she had been in her apartment at the Ritz after she and Charles had attended a birthday party.[25] In the following couple of days Edwards and the paper's lawyer, Tom Crone, instructed Clarkson and other reporters to recheck the evidence and to see if there was more. Though the number provided by Newman's police source turned out not to be of Diana's car after all, it evidently belonged to a car owned by her mother, Frances Shand Kydd, which Diana had borrowed at the time. Naturally, this tended to confirm the story. If the policeman had concocted the story, surely he would have given Diana's own car number?

With other details in the jigsaw falling into place, despite the denials from Diana and the Palace, Edwards felt confident. Both Tony Miles, Mirror group chairman, and Sir Alex Jarratt, the Reed International chairman, supported him after listening to his side of the story. So Edwards wrote back to Shea to say he remained 'as convinced about its [the story's] truth as anyone can be who was not there himself . . . I do have strong evidence and . . . I do honestly believe we were right.'[26] Shea replied immediately to say that Charles was on the train but not Lady Diana. There was also an implied threat that the Palace might sue the *Sunday Mirror*. At the end of the week Edwards came up with a clever compromise with which, oddly, the Palace agreed. He would publish the exchange of letters between himself and Shea without any additional comment, which duly appeared.[27] In return, the Palace would not pursue the matter through the courts or by complaining to the Press Council.[28]

The following day, the *Daily Mail* came up with a scoop of its own, the first interview with Diana, in which she denied the train incident. By coincidence, one of her Coleherne Court neighbours was a journalist, Danae Brook. According to Brook's article, when she asked Diana about the royal train story she replied: 'I was soooo shocked! . . . I SIMPLY couldn't believe it. I've never been anywhere near the train, let alone in the middle of the night.' She added: 'Even though they rang me up first and I denied it, they printed it anyway.'[29]

The Brook interview caused controversy too. Unsurprisingly, most of the quotes were about press harassment: 'The whole thing has got out of control,' Diana was reported to have said. 'Everywhere I go there is someone there . . . If I go to a restaurant or just out shopping in the supermarket, they are trying to take photographs.' But it was Diana's emphatic denial of the train incident which fuelled the *Mail*'s renewed criticism of the *Sunday Mirror*. A front-page story falsely suggested that the Queen was considering a complaint to the Press Council and a leading article, headlined 'Distorting *Mirror*', accused Edwards of 'wriggling' with 'nauseating hypocrisy'.[30] The *Guardian* teased Edwards too.[31] Then the *Sunday Times* joined in: 'No, for the umpteenth time, it was not true that Lady Diana had been smuggled aboard the royal train for clandestine meetings with the Prince.'[32] That article, one of the most perceptive of the period, pointed out that 'the present pitch of hysteria' was due to 'a firm belief by Fleet Street that Lady Diana is indeed the girl Prince Charles intends to marry – and the memory that the last time there was a royal romance, the Palace lied'.

Diana's mother, Frances Shand Kydd, wrote to the *Times*, complaining about 'exclusive quotes' being attributed to Diana when she had not spoken to the press, and repeated that her daughter had 'denied, with justifiable indignation, her reported presence on the royal train'. She concluded: 'May I ask the editors of Fleet Street whether, in the execution of their jobs, they consider it necessary or fair to harass my daughter daily, from dawn until well after dusk?'[33]

Edwards's agony was not quite over. The *Sunday Times* sent a reporter to harass him, which he treated good-naturedly.[34] Rightly, it was the conduct of the entire popular press which prompted forty-five MPs to sign a motion deploring the daily harassment and wild speculation. But Fleet Street knew how to head off political pressure: editors attended a Press Council discussion in early December for 'a full . . . and a useful exchange of views' on the ethics of their treatment of Diana. In other words, no action was taken.[35]

The engagement of Charles and Diana was eventually announced in February 1981, but the story of the royal train never really went away for Edwards. Journalists tended to remember it years later. After the royal couple divorced and the disclosures about the true nature of the enduring relationship between Charles and Camilla Parker Bowles, Edwards speculated that the woman his reporters and the original police source had originally believed to be Diana was, in fact, Camilla.[36] There was one outstanding problem with this theory. From the beginning the only real evidence for the story had been the car number plate. Did the policeman get it right? Or did the car that everyone eventually agreed was not Diana's belong to Camilla rather than to Diana's mother? We will probably never know.

Sunny Jim eclipsed by Maggie Thaatchi

The creation of Margaret Thatcher as an iconic media figure did not happen as instantaneously as it did for Diana Spencer. The woman who would become Conservative party leader and Britain's first female prime minister had a poor start to her relationship with the press. The only national morning paper to back her in February 1975 when she stood against Ted Heath for the leadership was the *Daily Mail*.[37] In the first ballot, every other Conservative paper not only predicted a Heath victory but, with the exception of the *Times* which backed Willie Whitelaw, said they preferred him to remain in charge. Newspaper antipathy to Thatcher dated from her years as education minister in Heath's government. In 1971 she was nicknamed 'Mrs Thatcher, Milk Snatcher' when she ended the provision of free school milk in primary schools. Then, after a run of clashes with students and a row over her refusal to hold an inquiry into slum schools, the *Sun* pronounced her 'the most unpopular woman in Britain'.[38]

Most newspaper owners and editors came to view her in a very different light during her years as opposition leader and memories of their previous scepticism were forgotten. Initially, Thatcher was understandably cautious. She had to wrest her party from its continuing belief in the politics of consensus and then cope, from March 1976, with a new and initially popular Labour prime minister in James Callaghan. The economic climate improved, with North Sea oil flowing and inflation falling, and there was a brief period when industrial relations were relatively calm too, but Callaghan could see the economic perils ahead.

While the papers were referring to Callaghan as 'Sunny Jim', Thatcher received relatively little attention, though she did win a new nickname in January 1976 after delivering a broadside against Russian imperialism, drawing from a Soviet critic a comment about her being the 'Iron Lady', a gift to headline-writers. In July 1977, *Daily Mail* writer Russell Lewis applauded one of her Commons performances in a piece headlined: 'The Day that Maggie Won the Next Election'. Even non-Tory journalists began to appreciate her talents too. Writing in March 1978, the *Guardian*'s Ian Aitken cannily noted that 'Mrs Thatcher actually believes what she says and intends to act in a way consistent with her utterances if and when she becomes Prime Minister.'[39]

She was undoubtedly helped by the difficulties which beset Callaghan's government. Despite Labour losing by-elections which forced Callaghan in March 1977 to secure a pact with the Liberals in order to remain in power, press hostility towards the government was muted. Within the Labour party there were widening splits: the left fractured between the Bennites and Trotskyite entrists, such as the Militant Tendency, while some on the right gradually became disillusioned with the need to accommodate the left's socialist agenda. In broad outline, what this right-wing group was beginning to appreciate was a need to reject the party's adherence to Keynesian demand management and embrace monetarist supply-side economics. Yet the Labour left, and the leaderships of virtually all the trade unions, wouldn't countenance what they viewed as a collaboration with capitalism. Unlike Callaghan, Thatcher wasn't weighed down, either by the ideological baggage or by union links.

Callaghan's press star dimmed once the formal agreement with the unions, the social contract, collapsed. In its place the government decided to impose a 5 per cent 'pay norm' at a time when inflation was running at almost 10 per cent and rising. The result was the kind of confrontation with the unions that Ted Heath had previously faced. Callaghan was further hobbled by the Liberals dissolving the Lib–Lab pact in July 1978 in anticipation of a general election in the autumn. Callaghan surprised them, and everyone else, by opting instead to carry on into 1979 by governing with the wavering support of other minority parties while hoping to claw back the Tories' ten-point opinion poll lead.

Both Callaghan's strategy in postponing the election and his government's pay limit failed as one group of workers after another staged strikes to win double-digit rises, at Ford, in the bakeries, on the railways, and then on the roads as petrol-tanker and road-haulage drivers walked out. By January they were joined by more than a million public sector workers (including grave-diggers and hospital porters) and disruption became widespread. The *Sun*, illustrating a surprising knowledge of Shakespeare, called it 'The Winter of Discontent'.[40] Thatcher, unsurprisingly, exploited the situation, as did her newspaper cheerleaders, and the settlement negotiated with the unions in mid-February didn't change the political climate.[41] The public view was that the government was unable to govern and Thatcher's most enthusiastic press champions – the *Daily Mail*, *Daily Express* and the *Sun* – realised that attacking Callaghan and his government was a better way of securing the Tories' re-election than devoting equal attention to Thatcher. The *Sun*'s owner, Rupert Murdoch, and editor, Larry Lamb, had decided many months previously to support Thatcher, but some of the paper's senior executives remained loyal to Labour. Political editor Roger Carroll even took paid leave to become a special adviser to Callaghan in the summer of 1978. The 'irony' of the appointment, according to the *Times*, was 'that many influential Conservatives have come to regard the *Sun*, under Mr Lamb's editorship, as crucial to their electoral success'.[42] Indeed they had.

It was the *Sun* headline 'CRISIS? WHAT CRISIS?' that was to prove important to the growing anti-Labour chorus in January 1979 because it caught the public imagination after most of the other papers and the rest of the media repeated it in one form or another in the following weeks and months.[43] The 'crisis' dominated popular papers throughout January with increasingly gloomy headlines, such as 'The Road to Ruin', 'The Rule of Fear' and, even in the *Mirror*, which ran a regular 'Crisis Briefing' slot, 'This Is Your Strife'.[44] The *Mirror* couldn't overlook the worries of its Labour-voting readers who were just as alarmed at the situation as people who read the *Mail* and the *Express*.

It was clear by this time that most trade unionists were also fed up with strikes just as long as they weren't the ones on strike at the time. Paradoxically, union 'success' and the growth of white-collar union recruitment meant that trades union membership was at a record level, eventually reaching its peak at more than 13 million in 1979. Yet unions were also more despised and distrusted than ever before. The *Financial Times*, worried about what it deemed to be coercion in the workplace through the closed shop and intimidation, argued in June 1977 that workers should have the right not to belong to a union and urged a legal curb on picketing.

It was the *FT*, through its leading articles and the columns of Samuel Brittan, that prefigured many of the economic and industrial policies later enthusiastically adopted by Thatcher. Though mounting industrial unrest convinced Thatcher of the need for a change of economic direction, neither

her philosophy nor her policies were clearly delineated before 1980. Her later championing of monetarism was not spelled out even if she was convinced of the need to abandon state control over incomes. The Tory manifesto pledged to cut taxes, to reform trade unions and to take action against welfare scroungers. There was no mention of denationalisation.

With strikes becoming prevalent and unemployment on the increase, the Conservatives launched a poster campaign created by the inventive advertising agency Saatchi and Saatchi. It showed a queue of people apparently waiting in line for a job at an employment office with the slogan 'Labour isn't working'. At the same time, strikers were feeling the full force of press disapproval. The *Daily Express*'s columnist George Gale called them 'striking jackals', and the *Daily Mail*'s Paul Johnson thundered: 'Why these bully boys must be stopped'.[45] It was noticeable that the growing chorus of concern about trade unions wasn't restricted to right-wing papers. Two days after a *Daily Mail* front page about the lorry drivers' strike, headlined 'Britain under siege', and a thundering *Daily Express* page-one comment entitled 'HAS EVERYONE GONE MAD?', the *Daily Mirror* echoed its Conservative rivals with a front-page comment of its own, headlined 'WANTED. A State of Sanity'.[46] These negative articles were interspersed with occasional pieces praising Thatcher.[47]

In early February 1979, the *Sun* and *Daily Express* enthusiastically reported a 19 per cent poll lead for the Tories.[48] Labour's task looked hopeless and the anti-government press propaganda was relentless, with the *Sun* regularly referring to the prime minister as Jim (What crisis?) Callaghan.[49] By the time Labour was forced to hold an election, after losing a vote of confidence in the Commons on 28 March, it had endured months of unfavourable media coverage. Now it was to fight for votes in the face of a hostile press with – for the first time since the war – only one daily paper, the *Mirror*, in support and every other popular paper firmly committed to the Tories. (The new *Daily Star*, nominally on Labour's side, was hobbled by an injunction from its owner, Lord Matthews, that it must not attack the Tories.) As I cannot say too often, the die was cast well before the election campaign began, but what was fascinating about the coverage was the imbalance between anti-Labour and pro-Thatcher material.

The *Sun* set the tone with an early leader in which it said, as it would continue to say until election day, 'The *Sun* is NOT a Tory newspaper . . . But . . . we WILL be supporting Margaret Thatcher' because of the need to 'SLASH direct taxation . . . REVIVE respect for law and order . . . CURB excessive trade union power'.[50] Three weeks later, in an unbridled assault on Labour, the *Sun* asked: 'How Many Reds in Labour's Bed? Power of the wild men will grow if Uncle Jim is elected again'.[51] It also ran articles by high-profile Labour defectors, such as Lord George-Brown, Sir Richard Marsh, Lord Chalfont and Reg Prentice.

From the outset, the *Daily Mail* was tireless in its support for Thatcher and the Tories but demonstrated it by denigrating Labour, which it cast as 'the most promise-and-bribe-prone Government of modern times'.[52] In April alone, it devoted eight front pages to negative stories about Labour,[53] and only three to positive stories about the Conservatives.[54] By comparison, the Labour-supporting *Daily Mirror* published four negative stories on the Tories,[55] and five positive stories about Labour.[56] One splash, headlined 'Maggie's wild and bitter Britain', could have been construed as positive by the Tories.[57]

Labour's manifesto was rather moderate and middle-of-the-road, which didn't please the party's left-wing. Even so, it was treated by the Tory press as if it was a reworking of the Communist Manifesto. 'Jim's way: even more curbs', said the *Daily Mail*, which warned of 'wild men' who would take over if Labour won. The *Sun* placed Labour's manifesto on page two, the only paper not to grant it front-page space, preferring to splash on a story headlined: 'Sex prisoner locked in a packing case'.[58]

In early April, with the campaign hardly under way, one poll put the Tories 21 per cent ahead of Labour, 'the largest ever recorded for any political party during a General Election campaign since polling began in Britain in 1939'.[59] But the election was not so much a contest between Labour and the Tories, nor even, in a sense, one between Callaghan and Thatcher. It was about the people's desire for a genuine political change that would reflect their altered circumstances and developing sense of individuality. They wanted freedom from the state, and that new spirit was captured by a single Tory policy which offered people the chance to become home-owners. Despite Thatcher's hesitancy and her modest agenda for change, she represented the possibility of a break with the past, almost justifying the hyperbolic declaration of *Daily Express* columnist George Gale: 'This election is about Mrs Thatcher. She is a one-woman revolution.'[60]

In one of the most illuminating articles of the campaign, two *Observer* journalists revealed that there was more to Thatcher's emergence as an electable leader than her politics.[61] She had been carefully groomed on the advice of a former TV producer, Gordon Reece, who ensured that her voice was softened and lowered, encouraged her to adopt a more relaxed manner and advocated a new hairstyle and new clothes. Reece also selected Saatchi and Saatchi to handle the Tories' PR account, a revelation which prompted one of the best headlines of the period, 'The marketing of Margaret Thaatchi', in the *Guardian*.[62]

Anthony Howard, editor of the *Listener* and soon to be the *Observer*'s deputy editor, was full of praise for the way the *Daily Mirror* fought the campaign.[63] He mentioned three successes: the unearthing of an embarrassing letter written on behalf of Mrs Thatcher to a council house tenant; the discovery of another letter soliciting private industrialists to contribute to party funds; and the way in which the paper made capital by trying to shame Thatcher into a TV debate with Callaghan. Howard commended the

Mirror's 'first-class journalistic performance', but good journalism at that stage couldn't stem the political tide. He was right when asserting that 'what appears in newspapers tends to define the issues and topics for consideration in the voter's mind', and right again in pointing out that 'current affairs programmes both in radio and television feed to an alarming degree off what has already appeared in newspapers'. Yet this process had begun long before the campaign. Though the opinion-poll gap between the parties narrowed, most voters' minds were made up and *Mirror* scoops were unable to buck the electoral trend.

The Tories left nothing to chance, using an unsavoury tactic towards the end of the campaign when Mrs Thatcher made a speech extolling the virtues of capital punishment and calling for a referendum. The *Daily Express*, loud in its praise of the Tories throughout,[64] greeted the news with a big front-page headline, 'MAGGIE: I BACK THE ROPE'.[65] Both the *Sun* and the *Mail* splashed on the story too with an unseemly, even savage, glee. Press analyst Tom Baistow, writing in the *Guardian*, found the episode offensive, noting that it occurred when the 'Tory tabloids' had 'exhausted their reserves of Reds under the Callaghan bed'.[66]

By far the most notorious press contribution came in the *Daily Mail* with its front page: 'LABOUR'S DIRTY DOZEN: 12 big lies they hope will save them'.[67] It was a clever and persuasive presentation, listing twelve statements made by Callaghan or his party about what the Tories would, or would not, do if they won the election. The first 'lie', for example, was that a Tory government would increase the price of butter, cheese, bacon and bread; the fourth was a claim that the Tories would double VAT rates; the twelfth was a claim that the Tories would sell off government holdings in national assets. Each one was rebutted by 'the truth', a specific denial of each of the twelve claims. They were, said the *Mail*, 'based on totally false premises'. As we shall see, this article was to have an interesting sequel.

Support for Thatcher was more subdued among other right-wing papers. Peregrine Worsthorne in the *Sunday Telegraph*, for instance, urged Labour voters to 'take a chance on Mrs T', but said that electing her 'is not going to make all that much difference . . . Her proposals amount in effect to very little: a controlled experiment in using market methods to improve the workings of social democracy.'[68] But the *Financial Times*'s election-day leader urged people to vote for a change, arguing that Labour's interventionism in the economy was unproductive and that our 'everyday lives are over-regulated'. It supported Thatcher's pledges 'to reduce direct taxation, to deal with . . . the closed shop' and 'to cut government spending'.[69] The *Sun*'s final election front page was shrewdly aimed at converting people from their, and the paper's, Labour past: 'A message to Labour supporters: VOTE TORY THIS TIME. It's the only way to stop the rot'.[70] Its editorial, written jointly by editor Larry Lamb and the leader writer Ronnie Spark once again started: 'The *Sun* is not a Tory newspaper.'[71]

The Tories duly won the election, securing seventy more seats than Labour, obtaining a forty-four-seat overall majority and achieving one of the biggest swings since the war. Thatcher was initially unpopular with the people: inflation rose to a record high in May 1980; unemployment surged to more than 2 million by autumn; public spending increased; strikes continued to disrupt large industries (and Times Newspapers was shut down); manufacturing industry faced an export problem due to the oil-boosted strength of the pound. IRA bombings were common. There were race riots in Bristol. Nor did Thatcher's opposition to the British team competing in the Moscow Olympics go down well with many people.

Despite a generally favourable press, Thatcher couldn't avoid the consequences of these events and newspaper editors couldn't ignore their readers' growing concerns. While she looked to the long term in dealing with the country's economic plight, guided by the monetarist principles of Milton Friedman, papers grew alarmed at the short-term effects. Editors applauded her early moves to reform the trade unions and were generally supportive of her wish to curb public spending and cut income tax rates, but they grew edgy.

Even so, they rallied to her cause when some members of Thatcher's cabinet – the 'wets' – began to whisper about the need for her to revise her strategy. Her response to these faint-hearts came in a memorable speech at the 1980 Tory party conference when she told delegates: 'The lady's not for turning.' The positive reaction to that declaration emboldened *Daily Mail* editor David English to publish a front page in November 1980 headlined 'Maggie MUST do a U-turn' and calling on her to honour the pledges made in her election manifesto. Far from being a full-blooded attack on the prime minister, it was directed at her 'wet' opponents, urging her to get to grips with the 'weak people' around her.

English's special relationship with Thatcher irked *Sunday Mirror* editor Bob Edwards, a loyal Labour supporter, prompting one of the most vicious dog-eat-dog fights of the era. Referring to English as 'Mrs Thatcher's eager expectant lap-dog', Edwards subjected the *Mail*'s 'Dirty Dozen' election campaign front page about '12 Labour lies' to renewed scrutiny after the Tory government's first nineteen months in office. According to his long *Sunday Mirror* editorial, most of Labour's alleged lies had turned out to be true after all. He took apart every example in order to show that Labour had told the truth: bacon, bread and cheese had gone up by even more than Labour forecast; the Tories hadn't doubled VAT, but they had raised it from 8 per cent to 15 per cent; they had increased National Health Service charges. Edwards concluded: 'The *Daily Mail*'s editor has been proved blazingly wrong in no time at all . . . Either it was the *Daily Mail* that was telling the "12 big lies", or he is a political nincompoop. Take your choice.'[72]

Edwards, generally correct on the substantive details, was writing at a time when the British people appeared to want no part of the Thatcher revolution: Labour was 12.5 per cent ahead of Tories in the polls by the end of 1980. But the owners and editors of Tory press didn't desert Thatcher. Convinced that she held the key to the country's – and their – future prosperity, they put their faith in her economic policies and trade union legislation. They also feared the alternative, with Callaghan stepping down from the Labour party leadership and the dreaded left-winger Michael Foot taking over.

All aboard 'Fleet Street's Petticoat Line'

A woman was leading the Conservative party by 1976, but the main news conferences at almost every national newspaper office were still all-male affairs. There were plenty of women journalists around, including feature writers, columnists, reporters and sub-editors, but very few at executive level. Women's pages, or sections, were edited by women, though heading that ghetto (as most men thought of it) was usually the highest position within the paper's hierarchy they were likely to reach. The exceptions to that rule, such as the *Guardian*'s news editor, Jean Stead, and the *Daily Mirror*'s publicity director, Felicity Green, therefore stood out.

Men took a long time to come to terms with having female colleagues. I recall the shock waves on the *Daily Mail*'s subs desk in its Manchester office in 1968 when the first woman sub-editor arrived. The older subs were particularly upset, wondering how she should be accommodated. One gallant gent complained to the night editor about the threat to the subs' 'traditional badinage', a polite way of asking whether it would upset her if the subs continued swearing. He also pointed out that she couldn't possibly be expected to work on the stone because of the printers' 'rough language' and rudeness. He wasn't really concerned about the woman's welfare or her sensibilities. He was trying to show that she would inhibit 'normal working', that she also wouldn't be able to carry out the full range of subs' work and was therefore likely to obtain special treatment (which would be unfair to men!). Britain was slower to change its habits than elsewhere. In 1972, *Evening Standard* editor Charles Wintour told how in Holland and Canada he found women inputting copy by computer, and commented: 'It is rare enough to see a woman sub-editor. A woman compositor still seems at least a century away.'[73]

While we *Mail* subs in Manchester were getting used to working alongside a woman, the paper's news editor was dealing with the novelty of female reporters, such as Carol Lee and Christine Dunn. Privately, he grumbled that he didn't know what to do with them. In his view, they shouldn't be treated as equals with men because they couldn't do equal work. For instance, how could he expect them to stand on doorsteps or hang out in pubs? An executive who thought he was infinitely more enlightened than the news editor told me that women reporters 'had their uses'. They could empathise with women who were reluctant to speak to men, especially those who were bereaved, and they could also 'use their charms' to persuade men to talk. He gave me a practical example: the hottest rising star of the time was the Manchester United footballer George Best. He usually refused to talk to male journalists – unless they were sports correspondents – but a female reporter from the *Daily Sketch* had managed to secure a long interview with him. How do you think she did that?, he asked, providing the answer with a nod and a wink. It was assumed that women reporters were little short of prostitutes.

Oddly, despite that gross chauvinism, the executive and the news editor agreed about one thing: it was impossible to contemplate women working on night shifts because of the perils that lurked in the shadows after midnight. This attitude was reminiscent of the 1920s on the *Daily News*, precursor to the *News Chronicle*, when two women reporters – Nora Bowes and Gladys Smith – were appointed and, due to an office rule, were not allowed to work late. Bowes was still with *Chronicle* in 1950s when she finally won that right.[74]

The Bowes–Smith experience reminds us also that, despite male prejudice and the lack of women at senior levels, women have a long and honourable history in newspapers. Anne Sebba's excellent book about women reporters charted the important role they played in newspapers going back to the 1850s.[75] She paid tribute to a number of excellent journalists who worked for British newspapers after the second world war, such as Rebecca West, Clare Hollingworth, Hilde Marchant, Anne Sharpley, Olga Franklin and the American who influenced a generation of foreign correspondents, both men and women, Martha Gellhorn. 'There was', as Mary Kenny noted, 'a sort of tradition of the girl star reporter.'[76] Despite that, Sebba found that even in a field in which so many women reporters distinguished themselves, covering wars, they remained in a minority.

That was true also at home, where men were preferred as general news reporters. I could find only one female winner of a domestic reporting award in fifty-five years: Caren Meyer of the London *Evening News* was named campaigning journalist of the year in 1972 for her investigation into a property empire. A National Union of Journalists survey carried out in the summer of 1984 revealed that of the *Daily Mirror*'s thirty-two-strong news reporting team only three were women and that the *Sunday Times* had no woman on its team of nine general reporters. Even at the paper with the best representation of women, the *Guardian*, only nine of its thirty-five reporters were women.

It is possible to reel off the names of several women journalists who achieved success, and some celebrity, during the 1950s, 1960s and early 1970s, but they remained a tiny minority. Marje Proops, whose *Daily Mirror* advice column ran for forty years, wisely observed: 'In the man's world of newspapers ... we just stand out a bit from the crowd because there are comparatively so few of us.'[77] People were misled into thinking there were scores of women in popular papers because, according to Ann Leslie after her four years at the *Daily Express* from 1962, they were more photogenic and enjoyed 'stamp-sized photographs' with their bylines.[78]

But Leslie was under no illusion about the reality: 'The spirit of Fleet Street is still as ineradicably masculine as the old-style men's club' in which women were 'honoured guests in a masculine fortress'.[79] Anne Robinson saw herself as 'the statutory girl' among *Daily Mail* reporters in 1967.[80] Eve Pollard, who was to become one of the first female national paper editors, thought Fleet Street 'was still very much a man's world' when she joined the *Daily Mirror* in 1969. She said: 'Women subs, or lady subs as they used to call them ... were still pretty thin on the ground ... the worst prejudice against women executives in journalism had died down by then, but you still had to fight your corner.'[81] Maybe her memory was playing tricks or she was glossing over the truth, because the worst prejudice had far from passed. Robinson suffered the indignity of being fired from the *Mail* after marrying her deputy news editor Charles Wilson because of a custom that forbade married couples working in the same office. It was Wilson who was ordered by his editor, Arthur Brittenden, to give her the bad news, which he did without protest.[82]

Nor was the bigotry confined to popular papers. When Liz Forgan was women's editor of the *Guardian* in the late 1970s, she thought 'the macho, heavy-drinking, show-off male culture ... very strong ... The daily banter was ... openly and crudely sexist.'[83] Yet it was the *Guardian* which promoted 'the foot-in-the-door news editor', Jean Stead, who was a candidate for the editorship in 1975.[84] It was also the paper that published feminists such as Jill Tweedie, Polly Toynbee, Linda Blandford and Posy Simmonds, who were to play an important part in building a new consciousness about the role of women in society.

Until the 1980s, women were largely excluded from the journalistic male culture which revolved around drink. Women couldn't be members of the Press Clubs in London and Manchester. Notoriously, Fleet Street's most celebrated bar, El Vino, consigned women to its back room, requiring them to sit down and not permitting them to buy a drink. In 1968 a group of women, led by the *Sun*'s Unity Hall and the freelance writer Anna Coote, protested against El Vino's policy by storming the bar, winning publicity but no change in the rules. Other journalists, male and female, were reportedly upset at the escapade, believing it a trivial matter.[85]

The amused reaction to the 'women's lib demo', as it was known at the time, highlighted the fact that Fleet Street's attitudes were little different from those prevalent in the upper reaches of the establishment, where gentlemen's clubs remained barred to women. When she was women's editor at the *Guardian* in the late 1970s, Liz Forgan had a difficult interview with

Times editor William Rees-Mogg and later called him 'a sexist pig' who 'ran the *Times* like a gentlemen's club'.[86]

One traditional way into a national paper for a woman was through what Ann Leslie scathingly referred to as 'the "girlie" ghetto of frocks, gossip and knit-your-own-royals'.[87] Every paper carried features specifically for women from 1945 onwards, such as cooking and fashion, and, though women generally headed the sections, they were still obliged to justify the content to men who showed no reticence, despite their lack of knowledge, in vetoing material. Deirdre McSharry, women's editor of the *Daily Express* for four years from 1962, often found her Paris couture pictures and copy derided by male subs who would say: 'Well, my wife wouldn't wear that sort of stuff.' Their attitude to everything that appeared on women's pages was, she said, 'simply antediluvian'.[88]

The first woman to rise high in the journalistic firmament was Felicity Green, who started her career, as was then common, as a secretary.[89] She quickly impressed the editor of *Woman & Beauty*, and within two years of joining was promoted from her secretary's desk to be fashion editor. She was doing the same job later at *Housewife* when Hugh Cudlipp called to ask her what she thought of the *Woman's Sunday Mirror*. After writing a fierce critique she was hired in 1955 and became Fleet Street's first female associate editor, learning her newspaper craft under editor Lee Howard. She went with him when he was appointed editor of the *Sunday Pictorial* in 1959 and also followed him on to the *Daily Mirror* in 1961, again as associate editor.

After her first six months at the *Mirror*, during which she had proved to everyone that she could do her job well, a senior executive remarked to Green that she was probably finding life better 'now that the hatred has disappeared'. Green was baffled because she had been genuinely unaware of any hatred, though she did realise there was 'a wall of opposition and hostility', especially from 'older men in senior roles who were never going to like the situation' (of her being their boss). But Green, who combined grace with determination, was one of the most skilful office politicians I ever met. She revealed that she took her tactical lead in how to deal with obstreperous men who thought they knew better than her from Lee Howard. 'He once told me, "let them leave the room with their bollocks intact", so that's what I always tried to do.'[90]

Green was eventually promoted to be executive women's editor across the three *Mirror* group titles before being appointed publicity director in 1973. No woman had served on a national newspaper main board before and the trade magazine greeted the news by reporting that Green would be the first IPC director 'to powder her nose before a board meeting', headlining the story: 'All change on Fleet Street's Petticoat Line'.[91] Green's elevation coincided with the appointment as *Daily Mirror* assistant editor of Joyce Hopkirk, editor of *Cosmopolitan* and previously women's editor at the *Sun*. Hopkirk, thirty-six, was remembered by the same magazine, without a shade of irony, 'as Miss Nicholson . . . [who] was both productive and decorative in the 1960 *Daily Sketch* newsroom'.[92]

Despite her directorship, Green always felt that she had been overlooked for the job she most deserved: editorship of the *Daily Mirror*. 'There was no question that, doing the jobs I did as I did, if I had been a man I would have been made editor. But getting a man on the moon was more likely in those days than Fleet Street having a woman editor.' She ran into sexism at board level too. Although the directors knew their papers had many hundreds of thousands of women readers and a growing number of women journalists, their treatment of women was condescending and patronising. Green faced up to boardroom male chauvinism with characteristic humour and pragmatism. 'If I wanted to get agreement for one of my ideas from the other directors I knew I had to disarm them rather than offend them, so I turned up wearing a skirt or a dress, never trousers, and it always worked.'[93]

Green left Mirror group in 1978 after discovering that, as a director, she was paid £14,000 while the *Mirror* editor, Mike Molloy, got £26,000. 'It was because I was a woman,' she said. She gave up newspapers for two years, returning as associate editor of the *Daily Express* under Derek Jameson. From 1986, she enjoyed several very successful years as a consultant in various key roles at the *Daily Telegraph* before a spending a second, frustrating, period at the Express group in the mid-1990s. Talking in 1993, Green was still convinced that the newspaper world was 'totally male-dominated' and that 'all the decisions are made by men'.[94] By the time I interviewed her for this book she said she thought matters had improved a little.

She agreed that the two most popular papers in the 1960s and 1970s, the *Daily Mirror* and the *Sun*, were quicker than others, including the broadsheets, to give women a chance. At the *Sun* under Larry Lamb there was a policy, if not of positive discrimination towards women, then certainly of understanding. Felicity Green had worked closely with Lamb in his *Mirror* days and considered him 'sensitive, intuitive and aware of the force of women'.[95] He was especially proud of his *Sun* women's department, Pacesetters, and of appointing at the beginning of his editorship in 1969 two female features sub-editors – Sue Cook and Deirdre Sanders – whose good sense and journalistic skills dissipated much of the lingering prejudice of male colleagues. Cook, who became the letters editor, disarmed compositors who initially made insulting comments. Sanders went on to run the paper's advice column.

Under Cudlipp, even though he was something of a paternalist,[96] the *Mirror* had a good track record in the recruitment and hiring of women journalists. There were more women reporters in the *Daily Mirror* newsroom than other papers in the late 1960s, and for many years the *Mirror*'s Doreen Spooner was the only female photographer working on a popular paper. The greatest personality of all, of course, was the woman who became the doyenne of advice columnists, Marje Proops. She was constantly asked about the advancement of women in newspapers and was aware of the underlying reasons for the question. In a man's world, men couldn't understand how women could succeed except for the unfair use of feminine wiles. So the knee-jerk reaction to the promotion of a woman was invariably that she had slept her way into the job. Proops had a sensible answer to such nonsense: 'Of course, there are women who use their femininity to further their careers in Fleet Street as elsewhere. There are also women who determinedly outdo men in aggression and toughness ... But my experience of women journalists is that mainly they are no more and no less cunning and manipulative than men.'[97]

Proops's journey to that viewpoint was interesting. She wrote in 1953 that she wasn't in favour of 'this equality business', an opposition she reinforced in her columns for the *Woman's Sunday Mirror*.[98] By the following decade she was advising women to support the Sex Discrimination Act and advocating the virtues of the birth pill while still fighting shy of calling herself a feminist.[99] It was in the 1970s, during her passionate support for abortion reform, that Proops, by now the most famous woman journalist in Britain, openly embraced the feminist cause. Even then, she was, according to Shirley Williams, a *Daily Mirror* journalist who became a senior Labour politician, 'a feminist who likes men'.[100] My own experience of Proops, first as a friend and second as her editor, suggested that Williams was entirely correct. But it has to be said that she was also a feminist who didn't like women to supersede her at the *Mirror*. She was antagonistic to any female who rose to executive status, viewing them as a threat to her position as the first lady of the organisation.[101]

If it took men a long time to accept women as co-workers, it took much longer for them to accept them as bosses. Some men were resistant to the whole idea. During the 1968 controversy I mentioned about the appointment of a female sub-editor at the *Mail*, I was shocked when a sub who wasn't much older than me said with some passion that he would resign the day he was expected to take orders from a woman. Having worked happily under a woman on my first local weekly, I couldn't identify with his animosity. But there were many men who, even if less candid than him, shared his viewpoint. It should also be said that many women found it difficult to accept women as bosses too.

Despite Felicity Green's rise at Mirror group, it was some time before any other woman made her way up the executive ladder. Writing in 1982, Paul Johnson was still talking of Fleet Street as 'a very masculine place'. There were no female proprietors, women were virtually unknown on main boards and no woman had become an editor.[102] Anne Robinson became an assistant editor in 1982 at the *Daily Mirror* and thus one of the duty editors required to stand in for the editor. She was therefore the first woman to edit a national daily on a regular basis. She soon discovered that in the paper's male-dominated culture the last thing required of her was to apply her female intuition to the job. Women were appreciated only if they adopted exactly the same approach as men to the news agenda.[103] In a *Guardian* article which greeted Robinson's rise it was pointed out that the *Mirror*'s London office employed 496 male journalists and just 22 females. Its Manchester office was staffed by 123 people, none of them women.[104] Not that serious papers had much to boast about since their record of promoting women was far worse than the *Mirror*'s. A 1984 survey at the *Financial Times*, which employed 37 women on its journalistic staff of 300, revealed that only one occupied a position which involved her overseeing other people.[105]

At the *Sunday Times*, which was considered to be in the forefront of journalistic innovation throughout the 1960s and 1970s, there were no senior female executives. Perhaps that's the reason that the main writer on the popular Look pages, Jilly Cooper, was encouraged to lampoon sexist attitudes with the lightest of touches. A typical Cooper article in 1972 began: '"What is your bust measurement, Jill?" said the man from Ford's. "Why?" said I, hackles akimbo.'[106] Cooper's column, a precursor to the kind of domestic 'me' columnists that proliferated in the 1990s, was deliberately frivolous, but her approach to writing was copied elsewhere and was a pointer to the way in which women were sidelined into less serious journalism.

The exceptions stood out, such as Frances Cairncross, who was economics correspondent on the *Observer* from 1970 and on the *Guardian* for eight years from 1973. Liz Forgan, who was twenty-seven in 1971 when she was appointed chief leader writer on the *Evening Standard*, loved to observe men's incredulous reactions when she told them what she did. Both later edited the *Guardian*'s women's pages. Two decades later, Veronica Wadley, a senior executive on the *Daily Telegraph* and the *Daily Mail* and later editor of the London *Evening Standard*, was complaining about 'some men' in newspapers being 'so protective and patronising'. She said: 'They simply can't get used to the idea that just because you might be interested in the ideas of Christian Lacroix or Penelope Leach, this doesn't mean that you don't know anything about Major and the money markets.'[107]

Amanda Platell, who rose to a succession of senior jobs, echoed that point when defining the 'institutionalised sexism' of Fleet Street. 'It is not about sex and flirting,' she said, 'it's about pigeonholing women journalists, denying equality of pay and conditions and opportunities, demeaning them and making assumptions about them.'[108] To cope with male antipathy, women came up with a variety of tactics. Platell tended to use charm. Ann Leslie preferred to play men at their own game, writing: 'As a feminist I believed that I should not only be as tough as any man, but make sure that every man knew it.'[109] Wendy Henry, the first female editor of a national, employed a mixture of Platell charm and Leslie toughness. What all three recognised was a need to find a way of piercing the prejudice.

Like Proops, the *Daily Express* columnist Jean Rook disliked female bosses. 'I hated working for women,' she said.[110] Then there was the matter of motherhood. Ann Leslie didn't believe that most women could have a career and raise children.[111] This notion went out of fashion in the 1990s when several of the most senior women managed to combine both.

In some ways, the situation of women changed in the 1990s. Petronella Wyatt, a columnist and interviewer who was deputy editor of the *Spectator* for a while, observed that 'the surest way, these days, of starting a career in journalism is to make sure you are born a woman, particularly a presentable one'. Alluding to the way in which editors, both men and women, set out to hire and promote attractive female columnists, she added: 'There has never been such a demand from the rapacious media maw for women.'[112] But, in essence, this was little different from the situation in the 1960s mentioned above by Ann Leslie, when women were given picture bylines. Male editors in the 1990s saw no contradiction in using women to promote the paper in order to attract readers (especially females) while refusing to advance women within the paper where the power structures were dominated by men. A survey carried out in 1993 by Ginny Dougary looked at who held the seven leading positions on national titles. Out of a possible total of sixty-three places on nine broadsheets (five dailies and four Sundays), only two were held by women. On eleven tabloids (including the London *Evening Standard*) there were eleven women out of a total of seventy-five.[113]

Yvonne Roberts, editor of *Observer*'s Living pages for two years from 1990, found that she was often the only woman at conference. 'I got sick to death of having to remind men that women exist,' she said.[114] Perhaps Veronica Wadley's waspish comment comes closest to the truth: 'We will know that there is equality when there are as many second-rate women in newspapers as there are second-rate men.'[115]

PART EIGHT: 1981–1985

15. NEW TYCOONS FOR OLD

> Seven multinational companies or wealthy families own all the mass circulation newspapers in Britain. Generally speaking, they use their papers to campaign single-mindedly in defence of their commercial interests and the political policies which will protect them.[1]

All change! All change! As Britain's first woman prime minister set the country on a fresh political track while the Labour party ran into the buffers, some of Fleet Street's oldest rolling stock came under new ownership. The Australian-turned-American Rupert Murdoch completed his acquisition of the *Times* and *Sunday Times*, the Canadian Conrad Black took control of the two Telegraph titles, the Czech-turned-Briton Robert Maxwell bought Mirror group and the German-turned-Briton Tiny Rowland bought the *Observer*.

The foreign origin of so many proprietors was an interesting factor. There may well be something in the argument that it takes an outsider unencumbered by the ideological status quo to kick over the traces, but perhaps it was a coincidence and therefore relatively unimportant. These four men couldn't be said to symbolise a turning point in the onward march of global capitalism since our history has already recorded the earlier ownerships of foreigners, such as Beaverbrook, Thomson and ARCO oil. Nor, at first sight, does the new intake suggest that the individual owner was giving way to corporate capital. All four men were prime examples of old-style, rugged, maverick entrepreneurs keen to grind political axes and unembarrassed to use their papers as propaganda weapons.

Second sight offers a slightly different perspective. Though each of them was privately wealthy, none were private owners of their new acquisitions, depending on their companies, all of them international conglomerates, to fund the purchases. In spite of them holding sway over those companies, some were in public ownership and some depended on heavy bank borrowings. None could afford to run their papers at a loss: making profits was now essential. The same was true for the fifth man who assumed control of a national newspaper group in this period: the impeccably British David Stevens, chairman of United Newspapers, one of the country's largest owners of regional papers, which took over the Express group. Unlike his four rivals, he had only a tiny personal stake in his company. Like them, he expected his editors to do his bidding.

These changes of ownership occurred during a period of considerable upheaval and memorable events. Prime minister Margaret Thatcher's growing unpopularity was transformed into adulation by Britain's victory in a war against Argentina to recover the Falkland Islands. Her consequent 1983 election success was followed by victory over the miners' union in a bitter and often violent dispute. Street riots broke out in Brixton. Senior Labour figures – the gang of four – broke away to establish a new social democratic party which attracted thousands of supporters. Prince Charles married Diana Spencer in a fairytale wedding. Fifty-five people died in a fire at Bradford City football club and soon after thirty-eight Italian fans were killed in Brussels during a European final between Liverpool and Juventus. Newspapers played an important role at every turn, with right-wing papers offering sometimes hysterical support to Thatcher during both the Falklands war and the miners' strike, most papers revelling in the Labour party's many splits without offering genuine support to the gang of four, and the tabloids feasting off the sales generated by the royal marriage and its aftermath (see next chapter).

Within newspapers, there were great dramas too. Murdoch took centre stage in several acts, firing Harry Evans from the *Times* and Larry Lamb from the *Sun*, changing the editorship of the *News of the World* four times, and introducing £1 million games of bingo. Lord Rothermere stepped into the spotlight by launching a new title, the *Mail on Sunday*, and almost lost his shirt. Maxwell played the comic and turned the *Daily Mirror* into a laughing stock. But it was the man who made a stunning debut in 1985, Eddy Shah, who held the Fleet Street audience spellbound, at least for a few months.

By far the most significant commercial stroke of luck for the whole national newspaper industry occurred in the wings, and might well have remained concealed but for an article by Geoffrey Robertson and Alexander Chancellor in the *Spectator*.[2] They revealed the bonanza enjoyed by every proprietor and newspaper company in 1984 due to their virtually forgotten holdings in the news agency Reuters.

Since 1941 Reuters had been a trust owned by British, Irish, Australian and New Zealand newspaper groups. By the early 1980s, British proprietors had come to realise that their shares in this increasingly profitable company were worth millions, a 'hidden treasure' which they had 'discovered in the loft'.[3] Given their desperate financial straits, some of them were eager to get their hands on the locked-up money through a public flotation. Lord Matthews, owner of the Express group, was particularly keen while his main rival, Lord Rothermere, owner of Associated, opposed the idea.[4] Alan Hare of the *Financial Times* was a prime mover,[5] but Murdoch was initially hesitant and the *Telegraph*'s owner, Lord Hartwell, also took some time to be persuaded.[6] Journalists, both within the agency and outside, were generally hostile.[7]

Matthews, probably the most cash-strapped of owners and the least committed to the concept of a non-profit-making trust, eventually prevailed in discussions which were often rancorous. It was generally accepted that Sir Denis Hamilton, chief executive of Times Newspapers, a Reuters director since 1967 and its chairman from 1979, played the diplomat to ensure the stock-market sale finally happened, but his role has been disputed.[8] Whoever was responsible, the complex two-tier share issue proved a clever device which allowed owners to realise the agency's value without sacrificing their control. This also allowed for the agency's principles of independence and integrity to be enshrined in the new agreement, assuaging the anger of most critics.[9] Hamilton was able to argue that 'our Fleet Street friends' will get 'something back' from the unions' plunder.[10]

Something back! The resulting windfalls proved beyond the owners' wildest dreams, injecting millions into their coffers. The Express and Mail groups received £56 million. The *Guardian* and the *Daily Telegraph* each got £26 million. One story authoritatively claimed that the sale realised £152 million for national and provincial newspaper groups, but that was an underestimate.[11] The windfall did not pass without harsh criticism,[12] but a more sober account years later argued that 'greed had been scaled down to merely hearty appetite'.[13] Reuters was soon making huge profits, £53 million in 1983 and £90 million in 1985, providing handsome dividends to shareholders. Owners had discovered a gold mine.[14] They were able to plan for a previously unimagined post-Fleet Street future of new buildings and new machinery on greenfield sites. In the *Telegraph*'s case, Hartwell authorised a necessary, though ultimately disastrous, step by borrowing £110 million to build two new printing plants. Murdoch had an even more imaginative scheme in mind, and the Reuters money was just the kind of fillip he needed.

Takeover One: Murdoch buys two more titles

On 22 January 1981, the Thomson Organisation announced that 'conditional agreement' had been reached with Murdoch to acquire the *Times* and the *Sunday Times*. The obvious public interest question was whether, by virtue of his ownership of the *Sun* and *News of the World*, the deal broke the spirit, if not the letter, of anti-monopoly legislation. It would obviously create a greater concentration of national paper ownership than had previously existed, arguably greater than Northcliffe's.

Any impartial reading of the 1973 Fair Trading Act suggested that Murdoch's takeover must be referred to the Monopolies and Mergers Commission (MMC), just as Thomson's had been. But Thomson had set a deadline for completion of the deal, and Murdoch applied pressure on the government by threatening to back out if there was a referral. Exploiting a loophole in the Act, which exempted uneconomic businesses from being referred, trade secretary John Biffen gave his consent. Harry Evans, editor of the *Sunday Times*, who headed up a journalist–management consortium bid for his paper, has written – without refutation – that Biffen distorted the figures to make it seem as though the *Sunday Times* was a loss-maker, when it was not.[15] The speedy clearance was widely viewed as a Thatcher fix, but Biffen always insisted it had not been the case. There hadn't been any pressure from the prime minister one way or the other.

Woodrow Wyatt, a confidant of both Thatcher and Murdoch, later told a different story, boasting that he was responsible for there being no MMC referral. 'I stopped that through Margaret,' he wrote in his diary.[16] Many of the details in Wyatt's diaries have been disputed, and he certainly exaggerated his role in events, but while it is unlikely that Thatcher stayed her minister's hand on Wyatt's word alone, it is entirely plausible that Wyatt lobbied hard on Murdoch's behalf.

One other significant factor was a statement by Evans endorsing the guarantees of editorial independence. Biffen gleefully cited this as a blessing for the deal while ignoring Evans's insistence that he still believed his own consortium was preferable. This partial quotation was also seized on by the *Times*'s official historian John Grigg, one of many errors in his account which make it unreliable on this episode.[17] There were critics from within Evans's own newspaper who were outraged that he did not insist in public on an MMC referral.[18] What Evans knew, for instance, was that the *Sunday Times*, separate from the *Times*, was making a profit and, therefore, its transfer to a new owner should have been automatically referred.[19] In his *mea culpa*, Evans wrote of his mistake in failing to speak out: 'Short of sitting in the stocks in Gray's Inn, I do not know what more I can do to acknowledge the error of my ways.'[20] What must be said in Evans's favour is that, at the time, the only bidder willing to keep both titles going was Murdoch and there was a genuine fear that referral would lead to closure of the *Times*. Hindsight has tended to cloud the issue, with too many people overlooking, or conveniently forgetting, the pressure to secure the papers' futures.

Murdoch, only the fifth proprietor in the 196-year history of the *Times*, addressed the staff the day after his takeover. He told them he would make the paper viable and could point to the tough package he had negotiated with the unions, reducing the workforce by some 20 per cent and winning an agreement from three NGA chapels for the introduction of new technology. There would be a movement from hot metal into cold type.

Journalists were much more interested in whether he would interfere in editorial affairs. Murdoch had agreed to increase the number of independent national directors, from four to six, and to give them sufficient power to guarantee the independence of the editor. The original four were former trade union leader Lord Greene, former Labour politician and Coal Board chairman Lord Robens, economist and merchant bank director Lord Roll and the historian Lord Dacre (better known as Hugh Trevor-Roper). Murdoch's two additions were the former *Daily Express* editor and IPC executive Sir

Edward Pickering and former *Sunday Times* editor Sir Denis Hamilton, Evans's mentor.

On the face of it, this group appeared sympathetic to the editors and, by extension, to the journalists, who remained wary of Murdoch. His takeover reminded deputy editor Louis Heren of a comment by an *Observer* columnist when that paper avoided Murdoch's clutches by choosing an American buyer: 'a well-bred GI's offer of marriage was preferable to the advances of a wild Australian intent on rape'.[21] Was Murdoch going to rape the *Times* and *Sunday Times*? Most of the *Times* journalists who had lived through the Thomson era, and especially those who had worked under the Astors, thought he would. Similarly, the *Sunday Times* staff who had revelled in the Thomson fresh air, prospering under Hamilton and Evans, expected the worst. They had heard stories of Murdoch's interventionist exploits at the *Sun* and in Australia, and they couldn't be other than struck by the way in which his papers uncannily reflected his political and commercial viewpoints. A letter from *Sun* editor Larry Lamb asserting that Murdoch had not dictated his paper's support for the Tories did not allay their fears.[22]

Every journalist was therefore on the lookout for the slightest sign of what might be termed 'Murdochisation' and I believe this suspicion coloured their reaction to their incoming editor. William Rees-Mogg had already let it be known that he would be standing down after fourteen years as *Times* editor, and when Murdoch announced that his successor would be the *Sunday Times*'s celebrated editor, Harry Evans, staff at the *Times* immediately linked the appointment with Murdoch's rapine intentions, undermining Evans's credibility from the outset. Several of the senior staff preferred Charles Douglas-Home, the foreign editor, as did two of the independent directors, Dacre and, more surprisingly, Hamilton, who genuinely thought Evans more suited to the Sunday post.[23] Evans placated those who favoured Douglas-Home by making him his deputy.

It is estimated that more than fifty of the *Times*'s staff departed in the first six months or so after Murdoch's takeover.[24] Some went out of intense dislike for, and distrust of, the new owner. Some could not face working with Evans, and some were persuaded to leave. Though Evans was widely regarded as the most illustrious journalist of his generation, many *Times* staff were less enamoured of him. They were unconvinced by his journalistic philosophy of committed campaigning, viewing it as 'sensational', and they wrongly believed him to be an agent of the dreaded Murdoch. Therefore, they were predisposed to be hostile and it should be remembered that they had been none too welcoming to Rees-Mogg either, as the White Swan revolt had shown (see above, p. 202). Anyway, staff journalists (perhaps all staffs in all kinds of offices) are resistant to any kind of change.[25]

There was also a difference in attitude towards editors between serious and popular papers. On the tabloids, an editor's word was law and an incoming editor – no matter how unwelcome – could expect slavish obedience from staff. Soon after I became editor of the *Daily Mirror*, I gave the sports editor, Keith Fisher, a dressing down for the way he was running his pages. He heard me out, sprang to his feet, saluted and shouted: 'New boss! New ideas!' Such overt sycophancy was not the norm on the quality broadsheets where loyalty was conditional, and Evans was greeted with considerable distrust.

Both Murdoch and Evans felt change was necessary, though they would not have agreed on the form it should take. If Murdoch was seeking energy, then Evans supplied it. If he wanted a greater degree of journalistic professionalism, then Evans was the perfect choice. If he wanted a paper with a more rounded news agenda, then Evans shared that vision. What he did not get – on the evidence of both Evans's supporters and his detractors – was a pliant editor. Murdoch must have known that Evans's changes were bound to offend many of the staff. That factor was hardly likely to frighten Murdoch, whose consistent *modus operandi* when buying new papers was to hire single-minded, sometimes bloody-minded, editors and back them to the hilt if they faced opposition from their journalists. What was so different about Evans and the *Times*? Why did he cave in so readily to what was deemed to be a staff rebellion?

By Evans's own account, he went for revolution rather than reform, sweeping through the office with gusto. It is possible to cast his method of personal involvement in every aspect of the paper in positive terms, as purposeful engagement, or in negative terms, as interference. Whatever it was, a dispassionate comparison of the *Times* under Rees-Mogg and under Evans reveals a marked improvement in the paper's design, with better use of pictures and sharper headlines. More space was given to features, and there was a general improvement of home and foreign news, and of sport.

As staff left, Evans naturally enough turned to trusted former *Sunday Times* colleagues to fill senior roles, although just as many of his signings came from other papers. Among them were the designer Edwin Taylor, features editor Tony Holden, deputy features editor Peter Stothard, business editor Adrian Hamilton, assistant editors Bernard Donoughue and David Hopkinson, parliamentary sketchwriter Frank Johnson, medical correspondent Dr Tom Stuttaford and columnist Miles Kington. According to two of the *Times*'s historians the responsibilities of the new intake 'sometimes seemed to be in conflict with those of ... existing editorial staff'.[26] Again, even if we accept that to be true, and it can be disputed, there was nothing intrinsically strange about an editor trying to introduce a new culture by hiring people already inculcated with his philosophy. On the other hand, the scale of the post-Evans staff turnover was unprecedented, a pointer to the future when the arrival of a new editor would inevitably herald a wholesale change of staff. Even if there was a formation of two camps, old guard and new, it was looser than many have since suggested.[27]

I cannot believe that Murdoch was in the least troubled by matters of personnel. His concerns, as so often, were about the paper's content. His particular worry in 1981 was the ebbing support for Margaret Thatcher, the woman who had been so helpful in smoothing his path for the takeover. So he was not pleased when the *Times* revealed in September that Thatcher's husband, Denis, had used 10 Downing Street notepaper to write to a cabinet minister requesting that he speed up a planning appeal for a housing development on which he was a paid adviser. Murdoch, operating through his managing director Gerald Long, also complained about articles critical of the government's economic policy.[28] Evans's book details his resistance to attempted editorial encroachments by Murdoch over the content of news stories, leading articles and supposedly 'leftist' headlines and pressure to provide more sport at the expense of business news, and to discontinue the parliamentary coverage.[29] They also clashed over budgets because, in his usual fashion, Murdoch failed to provide one.[30]

Though sales of serious papers rarely tell the full story about an editor's worth, they do provide an objective way of measuring success. In Evans's case, the evidence is clear. In Rees-Mogg's last year as editor, 1980, circulation of the *Times* fell very badly indeed from a first-half six-monthly average of 315,000 to a second-half average of 279,000, while the *Guardian* increased slightly and the *Daily Telegraph* decreased only marginally. In Evans's year, sales gradually improved so that, by the time of his departure in March 1982 he could point to a sale of 297,000 and an upward curve that would take the paper way above 300,000 within weeks. It wasn't spectacular but continual union disputes diminished the sale and, looking at the long-term performance of the paper, it can be viewed as a turning point in the *Times*'s fortunes. For his pains, Evans was named *What the Papers Say* editor of the year.

In December 1981, Hamilton was forced to step down as chairman in favour of Murdoch. The departure of a man with a thirty-three-year connection with the *Sunday Times*, who had created Times Newspapers by the 1967 merger of the two papers, and whose personal influence had secured Murdoch's victory, passed without a murmur. Evans was not to go so quietly. One major disagreement between him and Murdoch concerned the transfer of the *Times* and *Sunday Times* titles into the ownership of News International. Evans opposed the move on the grounds that it was done without the approval of the national directors and breached the conditions of the sale agreed with the Department of Trade.[31] Against Murdoch's wishes, Evans carried a detailed story about the matter in the *Times*.

Murdoch's growing disenchantment with Evans towards the end of 1981 coincided with his resentment against the unions for continued over-manning. In February 1982, echoing the ultimatum put to the workers just four years before, Murdoch threatened to close down unless they agreed to 600 redundancies. 'We are bleeding to death,' he said, announcing that the company faced a loss of £15 million that year. In the end, he secured a deal to cut 430 jobs and a further agreement to speed up the introduction of electronic photo-composition. Then he turned his attention to ousting Evans.

There are two distinct views about the situation on the editorial floor in the early months of 1982. The Murdoch version, which he stuck to down the years, was that there was a state of anarchy. 'Harry had to go,' he would say. 'The staff were up in arms. They were demanding that I fire him.'[32] The Evans version, which he never deviated from afterwards, was that there was a plot against him in which some staff were manipulated by his deputy, Douglas-Home, on behalf of Murdoch. A number of the old guard, represented by the group formed in 1979 during the shutdown, Journalists of *The Times* (JoTT), were certainly antipathetic to Evans, and to some of his new executives. There probably was a turf war between the old and new camps, though it's doubtful if this amounted to anarchy. What was not in doubt was Douglas-Home's change of heart: at the close of the summer of 1981 he was still apparently Evans's loyal ally writing him comradely notes; by year's end, he was a disloyal plotter colluding with Murdoch to unseat Evans.[33] According to Stephen Fay, Douglas-Home exploited JoTT 'to create the false impression that a majority of journalists were opposed to Evans'.[34]

In other words, Murdoch either gained the impression from Douglas-Home that there was anarchy or he encouraged Douglas-Home to foment anarchy. Either way, the conditions existed – or, to be more honest, appeared to exist – for Murdoch to fire Evans while suggesting to the national directors that his departure was the only way to placate a rebellious staff. The four original directors were unimpressed by this argument, just as they were by the next bit of pressure, offers of resignation from Douglas-Home and the managing editor John Grant. Murdoch refused to accept them, demanding instead that Evans should resign. He also sanctioned leaks about the increasingly bizarre situation to other newspapers who lapped up the story, turning it into a week-long front-page saga.[35]

For a couple of days, Evans worked on with Murdoch's PR machine portraying his actions in terms of high farce, the equivalent of a student work-in, and suggesting that he had exceeded editorial budgets and hired too many highly paid journalists. It was also falsely suggested that Evans was hanging on to get a better pay-off. It is sobering to reflect that no one spins better than a newspaper proprietor. In spite of continuing support from the majority of the national directors, Evans had no alternative but to resign. The whole edifice of editorial independence erected at the time of the takeover was exposed as a hollow sham. Ultimate power over the *Times* resided with the owner. If the editor didn't do as he wished he could dispense with the editor's services and appoint another.

Finally comes the question that has never been satisfactorily resolved. Right from the start, did Murdoch plan all that happened? Did he remove Evans from his *Sunday Times* power base in order to ensure his eventual control of the editorial content and political line of both of his new papers?

The Machiavellian *Sunday Express* editor Sir John Junor warned Evans in advance what might happen.[36] Most commentators later agreed that Murdoch had acted strategically, realising that he couldn't guide the fortunes of the *Sunday Times* with Evans in charge. By moving him to the *Times* Murdoch then exposed him to its notoriously fractious staff, guessing the likely result. I find this argument too far-fetched. Murdoch's affection for Evans, expressed several times in my company in June and July 1981, was not faked. He regularly began sentences, 'As Harry says . . .' He didn't have a game plan and would, in my view, have been content with Evans as *Times* editor if only he had toed the line. Murdoch has had a lifelong habit of showing great enthusiasms for people and, once he feels they have let him down (which usually means failing to do as he wanted or failing to deliver what he wanted), casting them into outer darkness.

After years of reflection, Evans came to the conclusion that Murdoch had indeed manoeuvred his departure from the *Sunday Times* in order to sack him later, but added a sensible qualification. 'It was not necessarily preordained,' he wrote. 'I got on well with Murdoch as newspaperman rather than power broker. I could probably have survived if I had not insisted on the political independence of the paper, not run the story on Denis Thatcher, not upset Mrs Thatcher, not insisted on defying Murdoch over content, and, perhaps most important of all, if I had not exposed the subsuming of Times Newspapers within News International.'[37] In other words, Evans would have survived if he had been prepared to sacrifice his journalistic principles.

Douglas-Home took his place, realising his long-held ambition to become editor of the *Times* at the age of forty-four after seventeen years with the paper. Charles Cospatrick Douglas-Home, second son of the thirteenth Earl of Home, nephew of former prime minister Alec and cousin of the woman who would soon become Princess Diana, had a very different background to Evans. Educated at Eton, he didn't go to university but, after national service, spent a year as aide-de-camp to the governor of Kenya. He started his journalistic career as a reporter on the *Daily Express* in Scotland, moving to London in 1962 as deputy to the paper's espionage expert, Chapman Pincher, before being promoted to political and diplomatic correspondent.

He joined the *Times* in 1965 as defence correspondent, establishing his reputation with his coverage of the Six Day war in the Middle East, and then winning executive experience as features editor from 1970, home editor from 1973 and foreign editor from 1978. Despite his aristocratic connections, Douglas-Home had made his way to the top in journalism strictly on merit, gaining the respect of colleagues along the way. He wasn't at all stuffy, winning over people with his informal style and a ready sense of humour. Though overweening ambition fuelled his conspiracy against Evans, for ever sullying his reputation with Evans's supporters and with many independent observers, it would appear to be the only blot, admittedly a big one, on his record.

One of Douglas-Home's admirers, literary editor Philip Howard, praised him for taking over a paper 'in a raging storm, with mutiny and panic below decks, and the ship in danger of foundering'.[38] That subscribes, of course, to the Murdoch line about anarchy, and Douglas-Home took little time in ensuring that several senior members of Evans's team would play no part in his paper: eleven were fired, or resigned, within a month. It must be said that a number of Evans's recruits stayed on, including many who were to play important roles in the *Times*'s future, such as night editor David Hopkinson, designer David Driver and features editor Peter Stothard.

Comparing himself to Evans, Douglas-Home told his staff on the day he was appointed: 'My style will be slightly more stable, more mechanical.'[39] So it proved. In many respects he carried on where Evans had left off, largely adopting his blueprint. He proved more amenable to Murdoch than Evans, risking the dismay of staff by overseeing the introduction of Portfolio, a slightly up-market version of bingo. He also acceded to Murdoch's request to hire people from the *Daily Mail*, such as Charles Wilson, whom he promoted to be his deputy, and Anthony Bevins as political correspondent, though Bevins was no tabloid hack.

The biggest change was in the politics of the *Times*, which took a sharp right-wing turn. Douglas-Home was a Tory who appreciated Thatcher's policies, which ensured the minimum of conflict with Murdoch.[40] He revealed to one of Murdoch's biographers that his proprietor was 'one of the main powers behind the Thatcher throne', adding a surprisingly candid insight into their relationship. 'Rupert and Mrs Thatcher consult regularly on every important matter of policy, especially as they relate to his economic and political interests. Around here, he's jokingly referred to as "Mr Prime Minister", except that it's no longer much of a joke. In many respects he is the phantom prime minister of the country.'[41] During the miners' strike, it was not unusual for one of Thatcher's informal advisers and the leader of a right-wing lobby group who organised clandestine operations against the union, David Hart, to appear in the *Times* office. Even some of the conservative-minded members of staff thought his presence sinister. Was he directing the paper's policy on behalf of the prime minister?

Douglas-Home presided over a giant surge in circulation, rising from 300,000 to 480,000 under his editorship during a period in which the *Daily Telegraph* stagnated and the *Guardian* grew at roughly the same rate. One secret Douglas-Home concealed for a long time from his staff was his debilitating and fatal illness. Diagnosed with cancer of the bone marrow, he worked on for months without complaint, dying aged forty-eight in October 1985.

His successor, Charles Wilson, was no surprise to those close to Murdoch because the name was rarely off his lips from 1983 onwards. During his years as Douglas-Home's deputy he was known to *Times* staff as Charlie Two and later nicknamed 'Gorbals Wilson' by *Private Eye*. He had a Glaswegian accent, used colourful language, often lost his temper, enjoyed confrontation and was regarded as tough and uncompromising. But Wilson was also shrewd, he could be subtle, and he wasn't a stereotypical thug.

Born in Glasgow, the son of a miner, he was barely into his teens when his English mother fled the family home and took Wilson and her other two children back to her family in Kingston, Surrey. It didn't help Wilson's education and he left school at sixteen to be a copy boy on the *Sunday People* before training as a reporter in Bristol. It was eight years before he got a reporting job on the *News Chronicle*, moving to the *Daily Mail* when it closed, where he climbed gradually up the ladder to become the kind of autocratic news editor who generates as many stories about his personality as he does stories for the paper. A short, wiry man, who had been a good boxer in his youth, Wilson was able to intimidate much bigger men with his caustic comments on their failings. He was deputy editor of the *Mail*'s northern office for three years from 1971 and then assistant editor of the London *Evening News*. He returned to his native city in 1976 to edit the *Glasgow Evening Times*, then the *Glasgow Herald*, and, in April 1981, launching the ill-fated *Sunday Standard*. Promoted as 'the quality of Scotland', it was an attempt to attract the *Herald*'s daily audience on the sabbath and so depose the growing popularity of the English-based Sunday broadsheets. It was a terrible disappointment. Because it had been launched in a slump, advertising was hard to find and it never came close to achieving its sales target. At its closure in July 1983, the *Economist* summed up the general view: 'It was boring to look at and boring to read, and was losing money at a rate of some £2 million a year.'[42]

Wilson was unscathed by the experience, leaving in 1982 to join the *Times* as Douglas-Home's executive editor. Home news desk staff were the first to feel the heat of Wilson's anger, his warm smile turning in a second to a scowl and then back again without breaking sweat. He was addicted to news, had a passion for horse-racing and believed foremost in the virtue of hard work. He was appointed deputy editor a year later and for three months at the beginning of 1984 Murdoch seconded him to run an American paper he had just bought, the *Chicago Sun-Times*. 'It was one of the most exciting periods of my life, a terrific challenge,' Wilson said. 'People hated me.'[43]

In 1985, Wilson also spent a lot of time away from the *Times* acting as editorial director of a mysterious project to launch a twenty-four-hour newspaper called the *London Post*. He was fifty years old when he was appointed *Times* editor in November 1985, telling staff that he had reached the 'pinnacle' of his journalistic career.[44] There was no doubting his energy, drive, ambition and professional approach to newsgathering. He was, as one of his staff said, 'a superb organiser of journalistic resources'.[45] But he was totally uninterested in politics, in leader-writing, in the intellectual heart of the paper. Was Wilson really the right man to edit the *Times*?

Questions about the editorship of the *Sunday Times* were also raised after Murdoch's takeover. When a tearful Evans told his troops at a staff meeting in February 1981 that he was leaving for the *Times*, he knew that Murdoch had decided to appoint his deputy, Frank Giles, in a caretaker role. Giles was sixty-two and anticipating retirement when Murdoch made him editor in order 'to guarantee continuity . . . for two years or so'.[46] Born in 1919 into a middle-class background, his father died when he was ten, leaving the family financially stretched. He was schooled at Wellington College and went on to Oxford but left before graduating to become aide-de-camp to the governor of Bermuda, his guardian, for three years. From 1942 he worked in the War Office and was briefly attached to the Foreign Office after the war. He joined the *Times* in 1946 as a sub on the foreign desk.

He turned to foreign reporting and from 1953 was chief correspondent in Paris for seven years. Although he was keen to return to Britain, the *Times* had no opening for him so he moved to the *Sunday Times* as foreign editor. He became the paper's deputy editor in 1967, combining it with the foreign editorship for ten years. Giles's relaxed manner, his civility and what his successor called his 'gentlemanly' attitude to editing were the kind of traits that appalled Murdoch.[47] But the appointment ensured that the *Sunday Times* boat didn't rock while the *Times*'s did.

Murdoch was aware that the staff were watching him closely. On his first visit to the *Sunday Times* he made a one-word factual insertion in a leading article, which was of no consequence, but Giles recalled that it 'set the scene . . . on one side, the adventurous, thrusting, impulsive proprietor . . . with a proven record of ruthlessness; on the other, one hundred and seventy or so journalists quivering with nervous expectation, quick to identify or imagine the least sign of impropriety'.[48] Even so, Murdoch wasn't prepared to stand back and let Giles get on with the job. Giles revealed that Murdoch was prone to stab his finger at a proof and ask: 'What do you want to print rubbish like that for?' or 'That man's a Commie.'[49] He thought Hugo Young, the political editor, was left wing. 'Anyone who deviated from Ronald Reagan was left-wing,' noted Giles.[50] Indeed, Murdoch wondered whether Giles and his wife, Lady Kitty, daughter of the ninth Earl De La Warr, were communists.[51]

Giles reluctantly carried out Murdoch's bidding. He was ordered to sack the colour magazine editor, Ron Hall, and replace him with Peter Jackson, editor of the *News of the World* magazine. He was also told to appoint Brian MacArthur, then an executive on the *Times*, as senior deputy editor. From his office Murdoch could see across the bridge into Giles's office, sitting with his back to the window, and made a habit of telling guests: 'There's Frank Giles ruining a great newspaper.' Evans told how Murdoch would sometimes 'stand up with a big grin and with his fingers pointed like a pistol fire bang! bang!' at Giles.[52] The editorial content did lack some sparkle, with Giles largely leaving his executives to run the shop.[53]

Managing director Gerald Long, echoing his master's voice, used budgetary constraints as a weapon to undermine Giles's editorial independence. When Long moved to News International, Giles had to deal with executive vice-chairman Sir Edward Pickering, a Murdoch loyalist who was unimpressed with Giles's editing skills. Then came the giant embarrassment of the Hitler diaries, which made him unpopular with the staff who were appalled at his weakness in agreeing to publication and his insouciance when the paper was under attack (see next chapter).

Murdoch saw his chance and weeks later Giles was told he would be moving aside in the autumn for a new editor and, as compensation, was given the honorific, and hollow, title of editor emeritus. There were two in-house candidates for the editorship, Hugo Young and Brian MacArthur, who many thought 'far more able and better qualified' than the man Murdoch did choose.[54] Instead, Murdoch lighted upon a genuine outsider, Andrew Neil, then working on the *Economist*. He was originally brought to Murdoch's attention by Irwin Steltzer, an American economist who ran an anti-trust consultancy and eventually became one of Murdoch's closest advisers. Neil, who ran a British offshoot of Steltzer's company specifically to promote television deregulation, tried to sign Murdoch, owner of a European-based satellite station Sky Channel, as a client. At that initial meeting in May 1983 Murdoch evidently asked Neil what he thought of the *Sunday Times*.[55] Neil was critical and more meetings followed quickly at which they agreed that the paper was too complacent and too metropolitan. Murdoch then offered him the editorship on the understanding that the paper would be 'strongly for democracy and the market economy'.[56]

Andrew Ferguson Neil had just turned thirty-four, one of the youngest editors ever appointed to a serious broadsheet and the fourth youngest member of the *Sunday Times* editorial staff.[57] Born in Paisley, he went to the town's grammar school and then Glasgow University, majoring in politics and economics. His first job in 1971 was as a research assistant to Conservative environment secretary Peter Walker. In January 1973, he joined the *Economist*, soon impressing the editor Alastair Burnet with his industriousness and his tough intellect. Though Neil always referred to Burnet as his mentor, Burnet left the following year for his disastrous editorship of the *Daily Express* (see above, pp. 265, 313), and Andrew Knight edited throughout the further nine years that Neil stayed with the magazine. After six years as UK correspondent, he spent almost three years in America as the US correspondent and became enthralled by its political and economic culture. He had just been promoted to UK editor when Murdoch met him. Neil had also built a parallel career as a broadcaster, working as a presenter on TV and radio.

Neil was a Thatcherite before Thatcher, an avid free marketeer fervently preaching the cause of deregulation, privatisation and supply-side economics. As a meritocratic Conservative he disliked inherited privilege, finding many of the party's titled and landed elite unacceptable. On social affairs, he tended to be a libertarian. Many *Sunday Times* staff found his political and economic views distasteful but it was Neil's character – what came to be regarded as his chippiness – which coloured most people's views of him. Unafraid of upsetting anyone and revelling in argument, he courted confrontation, believing that the creative juices were stimulated by conflict. But he didn't see debate as a way of resolving matters, rather as a way of enforcing his point of view come what may. It was this autocratic trait which upset many *Sunday Times* journalists used to a more liberal interpretation of internal democracy under Evans and Giles. Neil's style of editorship was similar to that practised on tabloids, with the editor at the apex of a hierarchy (if one omits the owner, of course). Neil accepted that the proprietor was the 'ultimate arbiter of what was in his paper'.[58]

Neil's appointment appalled many of the *Sunday Times* staff, who viewed him as too right wing and too aggressive. Initial hostility towards him was exacerbated by one of his first decisions – to disband the Insight team – and one of his first leading articles which said of the largest ever CND rally against Cruise missiles that it was the 'last gasp of a campaign which has clearly failed'.[59] He also had to deal with the disappointments of his deputy, Brian MacArthur, and his political editor, Hugo Young, at not getting the editor's job. They were among several people who left in the following months, with MacArthur going off to edit a regional paper while Young joined the *Guardian*. Neil then hired Ivan Fallon, *Sunday Telegraph* City editor, as his deputy.

Young had been with the *Sunday Times* since 1973 and was regarded as its most perceptive commentator and he dared in his valedictory column to make a thinly veiled attack on Murdoch.[60] Some months later he was more outspoken, writing: 'The *Sunday Times* used to be a force in the land, a lamp in the darkness. For reasons which are capricious and unnecessary, these it has ceased to be.' It 'makes money, but . . . no longer makes waves'.[61]

Perhaps it was the waves themselves that had changed. Neil's *Sunday Times* supported the government line throughout the miners' strike, often praising the role of Peter Walker, his former employer. Just before the 1984 US presidential election, Neil carried an interview with Ronald Reagan which many of his staff thought too sympathetic.[62] But he also ran a story linking the prime minister's husband to her son's questionable business activities, which was certainly unpopular in Downing Street. (This was, however, merely a follow-up to the *Observer*'s series of stories: see below, p. 392.) Neil's right-wing editorial policy would not necessarily inhibit his decision to publish stories that embarrassed a Tory government.

As for Murdoch, he cemented his global media ambitions by paying $325 million to buy the second half of the Hollywood movie company, Twentieth Century-Fox. He also spent $2 billion to acquire Metromedia, America's largest independent TV network with six major stations, which he transformed into the Fox TV network. This necessitated him becoming an

American citizen in September 1985. Meanwhile, in great secrecy, Murdoch was laying plans that would transform the British newspaper industry.

Takeover Two: Rowland devours the *Observer*

Journalists on the *Observer* who considered Texan oilman Robert Anderson their saviour in 1976 thought him a villain in February 1981. The chairman of Atlantic Richfield had been unhappy with the *Observer*'s opposition to Margaret Thatcher during the 1979 election. He was also less than pleased that the paper had lost more than £8 million since his takeover and, with continuing print union problems, had no hope of turning a profit.

The final straw for Anderson was the rejection by the *Observer*'s directors of his proposal that his friend and biographer Kenneth Harris should become vice-chairman. Immediately after the board meeting there was speculation that Anderson would sell the paper to one of the men declared by the staff as an unacceptable buyer five years before: Tiny Rowland. So it came to pass. Anderson quietly sold 60 per cent of his interest to Rowland's Scottish newspaper subsidiary, Outram's, for some £6 million. He informed *Observer* chairman Lord Goodman only after he had done the deal, explaining that he had kept it secret to avoid the embarrassment which had resulted from the leaking of the Murdoch offer in 1976.[63]

The *Observer*'s former owner–editor David Astor was outraged at both the secrecy and the buyer. He considered Rowland, who represented much that he despised, to be guilty of graft and greed. Leading *Observer* journalists agreed. In a TV interview, one of its former staff, Anthony Sampson, called Rowland unprincipled. Colin Legum, the paper's most respected Africa expert, was appalled. City editor John Davis, who had been critical of some previous Rowland takeovers, was devastated. Editor Donald Trelford was downcast.

Much of the financial success of Rowland's Lonrho group was based on winning exclusive mining rights and other concessions from recently liberated African states by befriending their leaders, regardless of their politics and heedless of their human rights records. Rowland's ruthlessness led to his company being described by Tory prime minister Edward Heath in 1974 as 'an unpleasant and unacceptable face of capitalism'. The tag stuck.

Rowland's logic in acquiring the *Observer* was transparent. The paper was uniquely respected by politicians in black Africa and its leverage might enable him to extend his relationships with governments there, and even mend fences with those he had previously offended. He was involved at that time – in partnership, it should be noted, with Robert Anderson – in trying to secure oil rights in Angola.[64]

The *Times* was not alone in suggesting that there would be a conflict between Rowland's business interests and the ability of his newspaper to report freely.[65] Under pressure, trade secretary John Biffen referred the takeover to the Monopolies and Mergers Commission (MMC) and Trelford sent his staff into action to uncover as much as possible about the mysterious background of their would-be owner. The result was a thirty-page MMC report on Rowland's operations and a strong objection to his purchase. Under the terms of the Fair Trading Act, the MMC had to decide whether Rowland's ownership might adversely affect 'the accurate presentation of news and free expression of opinion'. In June 1981 it delivered its report, clearing Rowland to buy the paper, as long as he accepted a board of five independent directors to protect editorial independence. Trelford condemned the report in a stinging editorial, calling the safeguards 'illiberal, unworkable, unacceptable'.[66] The *Guardian* called the report 'muddle-headed and potentially dangerous'.[67]

Rowland was indeed a man of mystery. Born Roland Walter Fuhrhop of Anglo-German parentage in India in 1917, he changed his name in 1939 after attending an English private school. He was briefly detained in 1942 as a possible war risk because of his parentage. Afterwards, he established an import–export company and then emigrated to Southern Rhodesia where he eventually built up his huge mining conglomerate, Lonrho. Typical of the outsider, he despised the British establishment while seeking to be part of it.

Under Rowland, day-to-day supervision of the *Observer* was put in the hands of Terry Robinson, an 'able, ambitious and ... workaholic' accountant.[68] Most of the senior journalists quickly realised he knew nothing about newspapers. Meanwhile, Trelford devised some form of working arrangement with Rowland, allowing him more or less *carte blanche* on the business pages while protecting the news section. Rowland confided to a journalist: 'I get along well with Donald Trelford. He is very weak.'[69] At Rowland's insistence, City editor John Davis and business editor William Keegan were demoted while columnist Conor Cruise O'Brien was sacked. Rowland insisted that Melvyn Marckus, a former *Sunday Telegraph* journalist, be given the senior business role. Marckus bridled at being known as 'Rowland's man', though he did speak to him regularly.

Rowland was swift to interfere in African coverage, first objecting to pieces by the paper's new African correspondent Richard Hall, and then insisting that a Zimbabwean journalist, Godwin Matatu, should take Hall's job.[70] It was April 1984 before a clash of principle between proprietor and editor led to a genuine crisis. Trelford, accompanied by columnist Neal Ascherson, went to Zimbabwe to interview prime minister Robert Mugabe. Rowland, who had famously backed Mugabe's rival, Joshua Nkomo, during the war against the white minority regime in the 1960s and 1970s, seized on the opportunity to ingratiate himself with Mugabe, telling him: 'I have arranged for my editor to publish an interview in the *Observer*.'[71]

After carrying out the interview, Trelford was offered the chance by Mugabe's opponents to travel to Bulawayo in secrecy to obtain eyewitness accounts of atrocities carried out by the Zimbabwe army's Fifth Brigade in Matabeleland. Rumours about the murders had long circulated but Mugabe had prevented the truth from emerging. When Rowland discovered the nature of Trelford's report, the first independent confirmation of the massacre, he urged him not to publish it, saying that it would ruin his business in Zimbabwe. This was just the kind of prediction the *Times* had made more than three years before: Rowland's commercial concerns were inhibiting the paper's mission to tell the truth.

Trelford refused to be intimidated by his owner's threats of closing down the paper and his story, 'Agony of a Lost People', appeared as written.[72] Rowland's reaction was fierce. He wrote to Mugabe to say his editor's conduct was discourteous, disingenuous and wrong.[73] He then wrote Trelford an open letter, distributed to the rest of Fleet Street, saying Lonrho could not go on supporting a failing editor who showed no concern for its commercial interests. Trelford replied with his own open letter, pointing out that the *Observer*'s circulation had risen by 22 per cent in the eight years of his editorship. The *Daily Mail*, relishing the battle, published both letters.'[74] Trelford and Rowland even exchanged insults on BBC radio, with Rowland accusing Trelford of behaving like an owner–editor.

Trelford's journalists gathered round to support him and, in an extraordinary editorial the following week, Trelford called on the independent directors to protect the newspaper from its proprietor.[75] The directors, despite being browbeaten by Rowland, supported Trelford and condemned Rowland's interference. But Rowland played a shrewd hand, openly having breakfast with Robert Maxwell and enticing him to brag – hardly a difficult trick – that, if the price was right, he would buy the paper. Such was Maxwell's poor standing, almost all the *Observer* staff considered Rowland the lesser of two evils.

Trelford decided to break the deadlock, offering Rowland his resignation. He wrote: 'I could not allow the paper's future and the prospects of its staff to be jeopardised by my personal position, which sadly seems to be all that stands in the way of the paper's development'. Rowland seized the olive branch, insisting Trelford stay, and together they 'concocted a priceless statement' about their shared affection for Africa, the *Observer* and each other.[76] Trelford was required to write an open letter saying that 'the truth about Zimbabwe' was 'more complex than I presented it'. That reconciliation drew the editor and Rowland closer together, confirming the general view of the staff that Trelford was capable of 'dazzling gamesmanship' to hold on to his position and 'marvellously adroit in his handling of Tiny'.[77] Trelford's claim about his sales success also showed how adept editors can be when asked to explain falling circulation. The reason for the *Observer*'s 22 per cent rise was entirely due to the year-long *Sunday Times* shutdown. Its million-plus sale during 1979–80 dwindled month by month in the following five years, accelerating after Rowland bought it. By the end of 1985, it was selling barely 730,000 copies and Lonrho's losses were running at more than £1.5 million a year.

The African drama soon gave way to a Rowland saga that was to do great long-term damage to the *Observer*'s domestic reputation. Rowland spent the early 1980s conducting a guerrilla war to acquire the House of Fraser retail chain which included Harrods. Lonrho made a series of bids which were stymied by Monopolies Commission referrals. At the end of 1984, in a desperate attempt to win his prize, he decided to 'warehouse' his House of Fraser shares, placing them at arm's length with someone unconnected to his direct interests so that he could buy more on the open market. He chose as warehouser an Egyptian-born businessman and owner of the Ritz Hotel in Paris, Mohammed Al Fayed. Far from merely 'looking after' the shares, Fayed decided to build on them to launch a bid of his own. Rowland hit back by using the *Observer* as a propaganda weapon against Fayed and the House of Fraser, demanding that City editor Marckus, who 'felt impotent to refuse the proprietor's request', write as he asked.[78] From this moment on, with Fayed and his brothers finally succeeding in their takeover of House of Fraser, Rowland shamelessly used the *Observer* for his own ends. The paper's credibility was compromised and would go on deteriorating for the following seven years.

Press hostility towards Rowland meant that rival editors didn't take his complaints against the Fayeds seriously enough to launch their own investigations. It was assumed that the brothers were who they said they were and had sufficient funds. One paper that tentatively began to question their claims of vast riches, the *Financial Times*, was swiftly stifled. After a story in May 1985 by *FT* writer Duncan Campbell-Smith the Fayeds' merchant bank threatened a writ and the paper published a retraction. So the *Observer* was the only investigator and Marckus was given funds to deploy two journalists, while Rowland also employed private detectives to pass on information. When some of it proved fake, Marckus's position was compromised.

So synonymous with Rowland did the *Observer* become that stories with which he had no connection were suspected of stemming from him. For example, starting in January 1984, two of the paper's best reporters, David Leigh and Paul Lashmar, wrote a series of articles about the prime minister's son, Mark Thatcher. One claimed that he had exploited his position to earn huge fees in securing a £300 million contract in Oman for his client, Cementation International, a subsidiary of Trafalgar House. The reporters were supervised by assistant editor Magnus Linklater, who had received the original tip. Though it suited Rowland's agenda to destabilise Thatcher, the story had nothing to do with him.

Takeover Three: Maxwell becomes a press tycoon at last

Reed International was desperate to rid itself of Mirror Group Newspapers (MGN). Robert Maxwell had long been desperate to own a national newspaper. The conglomerate without a conscience and the tycoon without an ethical bone in his body were made for each other. Reed had never really been enthusiastic about the most troublesome part of its empire, with its continual union problems, low level of profitability and editorial adherence to the Labour party. By 1984, MGN comprised three London-based national papers, the *Daily Mirror*, *Sunday Mirror* and *Sunday People*, the daily racing paper, the *Sporting Life*, and two of Scotland's best-read titles, the *Daily Record* and *Sunday Mail.* Reed had already carried out an act of corporate vandalism by splitting up IPC, a diversified global publishing company created by Cecil King and Hugh Cudlipp which married the interests of newspapers, books and magazines. Separating the British papers from the rest left them much more vulnerable during the cyclical advertising downturns and erratic rises in costs. As the Express and Telegraph groups had already discovered, it was impossible for a company to rely on national newspaper production to make enough profits for necessary reinvestment let alone provide a dividend.

On a turnover of roughly £250 million, MGN returned poor profits: £2.1 million in 1982 (an 80 per cent reduction from the previous year), £8.1 million in 1983 and £5.7 million in 1984. During its thirteen-year ownership by Reed, the group failed only once to abide by Reed's demand that it turn a profit. To ensure it did so MGN was often so squeezed that it made critical cuts in promotion budget – allowing Murdoch's *Sun* to out-spend the *Mirror* TV advertising budget by four to one – and used sub-standard newsprint. The *Mirror* was also required to have a higher cover price than the *Sun.*[79]

Reed's disenchantment with MGN was party commercial, partly industrial and partly political. Its chairman Sir Alex Jarratt and chief executive Les Carpenter had no stomach to fight the thirteen separate unions whose disputes cost the company £2.8 million in potential profits in 1983–4. There was concern about threats by MGN unions to widen their disputes into other more profitable Reed companies which published books and magazines. Reed shareholders were aghast at discovering that 60 per cent of the Mirror employees earned more than £20,000 a year at a time when the three major titles were all losing circulation.[80] Most of Reed's board were upset at the *Mirror*'s continued support for a Labour party they felt was too far to the left and unreformable.

Reed's favoured solution to cure its headache was to float off MGN as a separate company. In announcing this decision in October 1983 it gave a solemn promise to the MGN board, which included the national paper editors, that it would not sell the group to an individual. Jarratt was adamant.

No single shareholder would be allowed to own more than 15 per cent of the new company, and share capital would be distributed among a large number of ordinary shareholders to keep predators at bay in order to safeguard the papers' 'traditions and character and editorial independence'. Though no predator's name was mentioned, everyone knew of Maxwell's ambitions. Reed rejected a £100 million bid by a consortium of MGN staffs backed by two merchant banks and led by the senior journalists. The reason, explained Reed, was its determination to ensure that the papers should not fall under the control of any one group or faction. This says much about its perception of journalists, not only untrustworthy at commerce but a 'faction' lacking the impartiality to run newspapers.

To expedite the flotation process, Reed told MGN's chairman Tony Miles and chief executive Douglas Long to find a new chairman with a City reputation and, after consultation with the *Daily Mirror*'s City editor Robert Head, they chose Clive Thornton, a former solicitor who had successfully managed the Abbey National building society for several years. He was shocked by what he found at the *Mirror* group, from the strength of the print unions to the extravagance of the senior editorial executives, and especially the alcoholic culture of the whole enterprise. Thornton, who lost a leg in an accident in his teenage years, preferred tea, and a joke was soon circulating: 'In the land of the legless, the one-legged man is king.'

Thornton was ill-suited both to kingship and to dealing with trade unions: he wasn't autocratic enough to cow them nor subtle enough to win them round. They refused to give the no-strike guarantees which he believed were necessary to attract share buyers. He managed to alienate Miles, who had gracefully dropped to deputy chairman, and Long. Then he upset the three main editors by telling them they would lose their board places after the float. After his failure to win concessions from the unions Thornton didn't know what to do. To compound his problems, he announced that *Mirror* staff and readers would receive large blocks of shares which created additional suspicions about the project in the City. He was finally forced to inform Reed that the best he could hope to get from a flotation was a miserable £48 million. As Molloy observed, MGN had 'called in a curate to clean up Dodge City; and what was needed was a fast gun with a heart of stone'.[81]

The gun was on its way. With the City turning up its nose at the prospect of investing in a company that was so obviously an embarrassment to its owners, the Reed board decided that its duty to shareholders to obtain the best possible price gave it no option but to break its word and sell to Maxwell. As rumours circulated, worried union leaders met Thornton, who told them he had advised Reed not to give Maxwell any information. It would be three weeks before Maxwell would be in a position to mount a bid, he assured them, time enough for the journalists and unions to organise a political campaign to prevent it.[82]

Maxwell moved much faster, making an initial offer of £80 million on 4 July 1984, accompanied by a letter pledging the papers' continued allegiance to the Labour party and describing himself as a 'saviour' because flotation would 'expose the group to the law of the jungle'.[83] *Daily Mail* City editor Andrew Alexander immediately predicted the outcome in an open letter to Mirror staff: 'Robert Maxwell will get you in the end.'[84] Two unions, the NUJ and Sogat 82, announced that Maxwell was unacceptable, but Labour party leader Neil Kinnock, advised by his deputy Roy Hattersley, who heeded advice from a Maxwell crony, hedged their bets. When Maxwell increased his offer to £113 million eight days later Reed capitulated. Appropriately, it was Friday the 13th when Maxwell first entered the Mirror group's Holborn Circus headquarters. The journalists' chapel was outraged by Reed's deception, with a majority threatening to walk out on strike, urged on by the angry leader writer Joe Haines, former press secretary to prime minister Harold Wilson and one of the few people on the staff with personal knowledge of Maxwell. 'That man is a liar and a crook and I can prove it,' he said.[85]

There was a bizarre situation in Glasgow on the night of the takeover. Two Scottish union leaders had previously paid for a half-page advert which began, 'The workforce of the *Scottish Daily Record* and *Sunday Mail* do not want to be owned by Robert Maxwell' and concluded that the 'workforce . . . intends to mount the strongest possible campaign to prevent our papers falling into the hands of Mr Maxwell'.[86] By the time the first edition was rolling off the presses Maxwell was already the owner. So the *Record*'s front page in later editions carried the story of his takeover while the unions' call-to-arms advert still appeared on page five. The three London editors – Mike Molloy (*Daily Mirror*), Bob Edwards (*Sunday Mirror*) and Richard Stott (*Sunday People*) – faced a dilemma. Though sympathetic to their journalists and uneasy about Maxwell's takeover, their natural instincts were to ensure that their papers were published. 'We remained the dogs that didn't bark in the night,' Molloy wrote fifteen years later. 'In retrospect, I believe the editors could have stopped Maxwell . . . Had the editors gone over [to the journalists' side] I don't think Reed would have sold.'[87] Edwards agreed that they could have pressured the 'vacillating' Jarratt not to sell.[88] When the editors accepted the situation, so did their staffs.

Maxwell, at last, had the national platform for which he had sought for so long. He had failed to buy the *News of the World* and the *Sun*, his attempt to act as godfather to the *Scottish Daily News* had ended in disaster and vague attempts at acquiring the *Times, Sunday Times, Observer* and Express group had come to nothing. He had a disastrous business track record, had made a fool of himself in the Commons as a Labour MP and had engaged in a bitter battle with print unions and the NUJ at his printing and publishing companies. He was disliked and distrusted by thousands of people who had met him, let alone many more thousands who had not.

Maxwell was born Abraham Lajbi Hoch in 1923, in what was then part of Czechoslovakia, to a poverty-stricken labourer with a sideline in smuggling. When the German army invaded in 1939, the penniless teenager was urged by his family to flee and ended up, aged seventeen, in Britain. He changed his name a couple of times, eventually settling on Robert Maxwell, fought bravely with the British army in Germany, winning the Military Cross, and was promoted from the ranks to captain. During the war he discovered a gift for wheeling and dealing which, once demobbed, he turned to profitable use by selling the rights to German scientific journals. He branched out into scientific publishing, founding a company called Pergamon Press, and got into hot water by buying Britain's wholesale book suppliers and rendering it insolvent.[89]

Pergamon, which became a public company in 1964, made enough money to enable Maxwell to live ostentatiously. In the same year he became a Labour MP, winning the marginal seat of Buckingham. He acquired a number of publishing firms, such as Newnes and Caxton, before entering into talks with an American computer company, Leasco, encouraging its owner to make a takeover bid. After Leasco had spent millions buying up Pergamon shares in 1969, it discovered that almost all the claims made by Maxwell about Pergamon's profitability were false. He had fooled Leasco by switching funds from company to company within his empire. Leasco complained and a subsequent Department of Trade inquiry led its inspectors to deliver a verdict in 1971 which was to haunt Maxwell for the rest of his life. They concluded: 'He is not in our opinion a person who can be relied on to exercise proper stewardship of a publicly quoted company.'

Maxwell, who had also lost his parliamentary seat in 1970 and failed in his bids for the *News of the World* and the *Sun*, looked to be down and out. But he couldn't countenance defeat in business. Despite Leasco's takeover, he had shrewdly maintained a hold on one of the most profitable parts of the company and used this wedge to intrude into Pergamon's affairs, eventually buying it back from Leasco in 1974. During the next six years Maxwell bought up more book companies and printing works, and made vain attempts at buying any national paper that looked vulnerable.

By 1980, in the worlds of business, politics and the media, he was widely considered to be a mixture of buffoon and bandit, an embarrassing self-publicist and, as far as most people were concerned, a lame duck. That all changed when he acquired the British Printing Corporation, a loss-making giant in hock to the National Westminster Bank. Maxwell installed himself as chief executive in 1981 and, to everyone's surprise and the bank's delight, crushed the print unions. After a series of bitter confrontations over three years at the print works in north London and Scotland, punctuated by shut-downs, sit-ins and court injunctions, the NGA and Sogat were forced to accept 2,500 redundancies, some 25 per cent of the total, and the first significant defeat suffered by the print unions. The result was a huge rise in profits for the company that Maxwell renamed the British Printing &

Communication Corporation. NatWest was grateful and Maxwell also won a measure of grudging respect in the City, offset by the fact that his finances were impenetrable because the ultimate ownership of each of his tightly knit inter-linked private companies with their deliberately similar titles resided in Liechtenstein, where secrecy was paramount. Once Maxwell added the Odhams plant at Watford to his empire he became the biggest printer in Europe.

With his reputation partially rebuilt he was able to call on the necessary funds to enable his *Mirror* acquisition. In spite of agreeing a £113 million price for *Mirror* group, Reed returned £23 million which it owed to MGN.[90] At an outlay of £90 million Maxwell had pulled off the best commercial deal of his life because Reed's analysts had done a poor job, dramatically underestimating the value of MGN's assets: the Mirror building was worth almost as much as the total he had paid; the pension fund surplus overflowed; the Scottish property was undervalued; the shares in Reuters were to realise much more than anticipated.[91]

But the money was only one side of the bargain. For a man with a giant ego who had suffered a bad press for more than thirty years, the real pleasure in owning the *Daily Mirror* was the chance to put his own case. He was going to be the star of his own paper despite having announced that 'under my management editors in the group will be free to produce their newspapers without interference with their journalistic skills and judgement'.[92] On its first day under Maxwell, he introduced a new slogan on the *Mirror*'s front page: 'FORWARD WITH BRITAIN'.[93] The New Statesman thought a more apposite line should have been 'FORWARD WITH LIECHTENSTEIN'. It was the first of scores of jokes in the rest of the media about a man who was soon nicknamed 'the bouncing Czech', which he hated, and 'Cap'n Bob', which he accepted, because – as its creator, columnist Keith Waterhouse, lamented – it gave him 'a patina of avuncular geniality'.[94]

The *Mirror* was soon referred to by rivals as the *Daily Maxwell* because pictures of 'The Publisher', as he liked to be known, were rarely out of the paper. Within a month he introduced a £1 million bingo-style game, Who Dares Wins, promoting it himself on television and appearing on the front page (see below, p. 406). He was endlessly pictured meeting East European dignitaries. He intervened and intruded in all sorts of ways, amending assistant editor Geoffrey Goodman's copy on the miners' strike to make it less critical of the Tory government,[95] and then trying foolishly to act as peace-broker between the strikers, whom he did not support, and the Coal Board, who had no time for him. This was followed by his great personal crusade to end famine in Ethiopia, a wholly inglorious venture featured on four successive *Daily Mirror* front pages in which the twenty-two-stone Maxwell was pictured handing out bread to starving people.[96]

Several executives rapidly departed, including the former chairman Tony Miles, and then a slow trickle of people disillusioned by the Maxwell regime began to leave. Inadvisedly, Lord Cudlipp was lured from retirement by Maxwell to act as a consultant. According to his widow Jodi, 'he only joined Maxwell in the hope of limiting damage to the *Mirror*'.[97] He did suggest to Maxwell that he should appear less often in the paper,[98] but he was unable to exert any positive influence and left after no more than a year.

For *Daily Mirror* editor Mike Molloy, it was a dispiriting period. Having suffered the 1978 circulation eclipse by the *Sun* and then watched the gap between the papers widen to more than 200,000, he had been heartened to see it reduced to a mere 39,000 in the month of April 1981 after the *Sun*'s cover price was raised to the same as the *Mirror*'s. But Rupert Murdoch acted ruthlessly to reverse the slide, hiring a new editor, introducing bingo and restoring the old price differential (see below, p. 418).

Mirror group management, hampered by Reed's parsimony, failed to respond and Molloy's hopes of a revival vanished. Within three months the *Sun* was selling 700,000 more than the *Mirror*. The *Mirror* was named as the 1981 newspaper of the year by the *What the Papers Say* judges, largely 'for making fewer concessions to down-marketry'.[99] As sales began to decline slowly Molloy lost heart and, by the time of Maxwell's takeover, to the consternation of his own staff and the unconcealed delight of rivals, he started to write a novel.[100] It was an unprecedented exhibition of sang-froid for a tabloid editor whose paper was under increasing pressure, though he dumbfounded his critics because sales did increase in the first half of 1984, reaching almost 3.5 million at the point of Maxwell's takeover. Molloy despaired at Maxwell's proprietorial style, recalling: 'It wasn't the same any more, like living in an occupied country.'[101] The introduction of the bingo game marginally improved circulation for a couple of months but the Maxwell effect soon wiped out the gains. 'Readers hated him,' said Molloy, who wasn't unhappy to relinquish his ten-year editorship. By the time it came to an end in the autumn of 1985, sales were down to a post-war low of 3 million and soon dipped below that. The situation looked desperate when Molloy stepped aside, to be editor-in-chief of all the Mirror titles, and Richard Stott became editor.

Before we come to the Stott appointment we have to go back a little to prior events on MGN's two Sunday titles. Bob Edwards, *Sunday Mirror* editor since 1972, had an uncomfortable time in the early 1980s, despairing as readers began to desert. His paper's continuous sales slide, keeping pace with that of the *Sunday People*, was in marked contrast to the *News of the World*'s erratic ups and downs which kept it comfortably ahead of its rivals. Edwards had an idea to follow the serious broadsheets by adding a colour magazine but was frustrated by MGN's dithering, itself the result of Reed's tight hold on the company's budget. His mood darkened when the *Sunday Express* and *News of the World* took the initiative and he was still prevented from launching his own magazine.[102] Within the sensationalist red-top tabloid format, Edwards also seemed to find it more difficult to find the right balance of serious and light material that had long been the *Sunday Mirror*'s hallmark. His task became harder still when the *Mail on Sunday* got its act together (see below, p. 416). Upset by the Thatcherite propaganda in Woodrow Wyatt's column, he fired his best-known columnist in 1983.[103] Wyatt, who probably made no impact on sales, immediately joined the *News of the World*. But his going was symbolic of the changed political climate and the difficulties facing the *Mirror* titles which remained faithful to a Labour party then in torment. For a political animal like Edwards it was an unhappy time. And then came Maxwell.

Edwards was regarded as Maxwell's best friend in Fleet Street, even if he sensibly kept the big man at arm's length, and he did act as his informal adviser immediately after the takeover.[104] He stayed on as editor for only five months, accepting a nebulous role as editorial director. From the beginning of 1985, the deputy editor of the *Daily Mirror*, Peter Thompson, took over the *Sunday Mirror* chair. Thompson, a forty-two-year-old Australian, raised in Brisbane and educated at the University of Queensland, spent six years working on papers in his home city and Melbourne before arriving at the *Daily Mirror* as a sub-editor in 1966.

After a couple of years he returned to Melbourne, rejoining the *Mirror* in 1971 as chief sub. I worked under him for a couple of months soon after and was impressed with his unflappability and intelligence. He quickly worked his way up the ladder, becoming Molloy's deputy in 1977. To spend almost eight years as a number two is frustrating for an ambitious person and he was delighted to get his chance at last. But Thompson, who had firm ideas about what he wanted to achieve with the *Sunday Mirror*, took over at the worst possible time. The *News of the World*'s tabloid transformation had bedded in, Maxwell's confrontations with the unions caused countless disruptions to production and Maxwell's own editorial pressures conspired against Thompson. After he had been editor for twelve months, the *Sunday Mirror* was selling 2.8 million, 400,000 fewer than when he started.

The disastrous Maxwell effect also hit the sales of the *Sunday People*, which had celebrated its centenary in October 1981.[105] Geoff Pinnington's ten-year editorship had ended when he retired in 1982, bemoaning the onset of the bingo war. Pinnington is thought to have recommended that his deputy, Ernie Burrington, should succeed him, but chairman Tony Miles chose Nick Lloyd instead, leaving a disappointed Burrington as deputy.

Lloyd wasn't troubled by the implications of publishing newspaper competitions, having masterminded many of them as a senior executive at the *Sun*. He was forty, an Oxford graduate who started as a *Daily Mail* reporter straight from university, moving two years later to the *Sunday Times* as education correspondent and winning promotion to deputy news editor. He was one of the rare people to achieve executive status on a broadsheet and then turn his back on it in favour of a tabloid. He joined the *Sun* after Murdoch bought it, one of three features executives required to fight for prominence in the early days under Larry Lamb. The personable and confident Lloyd emerged the victor, eventually running the news desk. He was soon marked down for higher office and spent four years as assistant editor at the *News of the World* before returning to the *Sun* in the same post in 1976. Lamb liked Lloyd but, anxious about his protégé emerging as a rival for Murdoch's affections, gave him a rough ride. When Lloyd could not realise his hopes of editorship he quit in 1980 to be deputy editor to Bob Edwards at the *Sunday Mirror*. At his *Sun* leaving party he recited a mock version of the Frank Sinatra song 'My Way', changing the main phrase to 'I did it Sir Larry's way', and Lamb's ponderous, ungracious response was hissed by many of the guests.

Miles thought Lloyd had done well enough in his number-two slot at the *Sunday Mirror* to merit an editorship and he was given *carte blanche* to change the whole character of the *Sunday People*.[106] There was some controversy over hiring his wife, Eve Pollard, as an assistant editor which, noted a staff member, 'was certainly a surprising decision'.[107] In his eighteen months as editor he was estimated to have spent up to £1.5 million on buying largely celebrity-based material, kiss-and-tell stories, book serialisations and pictures. By pulling away from the *People*'s investigations tradition he alienated many of the core, long-term readers but attracted a younger element. 'It was slick and bright,' said one observer, 'but it had no real meat on its bones.'[108] Sales remained firm at about 3.4 million while the *News of the World* dipped and Murdoch made Lloyd a generous offer in January 1984 to return to News International as editor of the *NoW*.

Miles again snubbed Burrington, preferring Richard Stott, a hard-nosed *Daily Mirror* executive who had elbowed his way into contention after initial scepticism about his abilities. Stott, born in Oxford and educated at Clifton College, Bristol, started on a weekly paper and then learned a lot in three years with the Ferrari press agency in Kent, where he rubbed shoulders with the man who was to become editor of the *Sun*, Kelvin MacKenzie. From 1968 Stott worked as a reporter at the *Daily Mirror*, winning a reporter of the year award in 1977 for his Don Revie story (see above, p. 341). After more than ten years as the paper's leading reporter Stott applied for an executive position, was turned down by Molloy and resigned. After pressure from above, Molloy relented and Stott was hastily appointed features editor in 1979. He surprised his many critics, doing well enough to earn a series of promotions in the following years, running features and then news and pictures. Here was an editor in the making and when he was given his chance with the *Sunday People* editorship, aged forty.

Stott once more surprised the sceptics. 'He didn't know one end of a layout scheme from another', said a senior executive, 'but he was one fast learner.'[109] He also came to realise that the *People* – always considered the poor man of the *Mirror* group outfit – wasn't staffed by doddering old time-servers. He did clash with his experienced deputy, Ernie Burrington, but they managed to find a sensible way of working together. With his reporting background, he realised the importance of restoring the *People*'s investigative tradition, but changes of direction are not good for sales in the short term. Having inherited a paper selling 3.34 million, it had fallen to 3 million by the time he left. But Stott's swagger, overt ambition and motivational skills made him a prime candidate to become *Daily Mirror* editor in succession to Molloy, and he jumped at the opportunity when Maxwell offered it to him.

Burrington was then rewarded with the *People* editorship he had wanted for years after a recommendation from Bob Edwards, who thought him 'a man of infinite patience and tact'.[110] At sixty, he was the oldest man to be appointed editor of a popular paper. He had started on his local evening, the *Oldham Chronicle*, in the early years of the war before joining the army. He returned to the *Chronicle* after demob and then moved as a sub-editor to Bristol before winning a place on the subs desk at the *Daily Herald*'s Manchester office. Promoted to night editor in 1955 he was recruited by Geoff Pinnington, then the *Herald*'s deputy editor, to move to London as chief sub, rising to night editor. When IPC launched the *Sun* he was made assistant editor and, at Murdoch's takeover, kept that title while running the night desk. He didn't get on with the editor, Larry Lamb, and rejoined *Mirror* group, firstly as a night-desk executive and then as deputy editor to Pinnington at the *People* in 1971.

Burrington immediately set about the task of producing a Pinnington-style *People* with his first objective to stop the decline in circulation. Under Maxwell, though, that was to prove a difficult task. At the *Daily Mirror*, Stott faced a similar problem in trying to stop the sales rot. He injected a much needed sense of urgency to the *Mirror*, which had grown increasingly soporific in the final Molloy years. He also revelled in making tough decisions, symbolised by his firing, on New Year's Eve 1985, of John Pilger. For twenty years Pilger had been the *Mirror*'s most celebrated serious writer, winner of many awards, and widely viewed as the paper's conscience, but Stott considered him a lazy prima donna. Pilger later retaliated by referring to the tubby Stott as 'a bonsai version' of Maxwell,[111] and became one of his former paper's most vitriolic critics.

The power of all Mirror group editors was circumscribed by Maxwell, who was too maverick to be a good manager and made a number of wrong-headed decisions. One of his first was to appoint Patrick Morrissey, a former Beechams marketing executive, as managing director. By referring to papers as 'products', and treating them as such, he upset the editors, who soon ignored him. Despite Maxwell's foolishness he did have two notable successes which should be seen as visionary: winning concessions on overmanning from the print unions and installing presses to print in colour.

After demanding cost-saving reductions in staff in the autumn of 1985, there were incessant stoppages and the loss of several days' newspapers, during faltering negotiations. So Maxwell finally threatened to close the papers, famously declaring in a signed editorial: 'the gravy train has hit the buffers'.[112] The result was a settlement some weeks later in which Maxwell obtained 1,600 job cuts, the largest reduction ever negotiated with the print unions. He then authorised the investment of £68 million to upgrade the *Mirror*'s presses to allow his papers to publish in colour, hopefully from 1988.

Takeover Four: The *Express* train takes another detour

Lord Matthews, chairman of Express Newspapers, savoured the fact that he could get his pro-Thatcherite political views across in his papers. But his enthusiasm for propaganda was tempered by his regard for commerce. Asked by a BBC journalist whether he would close his papers if they were unprofitable he said he would. The interviewer remarked: 'We are talking about newspapers as money, and almost like a commodity . . .' Matthews replied: 'May I say that's how I look at newspapers? As money.'[113] On hearing that remark the former *Daily Herald* and *Sun* editor Lord Jacobson commented: 'Come back, Beaverbrook. All is forgiven.'[114] No wonder Matthews couldn't understand journalists. He once confided to *Daily Telegraph* editor Bill Deedes that his editorial staff seemed interested only in their own work, not even cheering with joy when the company's dividend went up. 'It struck me that he had joined the wrong ship,' wrote Deedes.[115]

I spent an unhappy few months working in the *Daily Express* features room in 1980 before accepting the post of features editor one floor up on the *Daily Star*. In comparing the Express culture with life at News International and Mirror group, what struck me forcibly was that within the Black Lubyanka the management held supremacy over editorial. With the exception of the *Sunday Express*, where Sir John Junor was largely untouched, the other editors were unable to exercise enough power to do their jobs properly. Almost nothing could happen without the imprimatur of managing director Jocelyn Stevens, who gave undue powers to his deputy Andy Cameron and the general manager Tony Bentley. These men, frustrated by their inability to exert their influence over the print unions, preferred to flex their muscles with the editors and their senior executives, leading to endless squabbles over relatively trivial matters. Newspapers cannot work if the managers are more important than the editors.[116]

Arthur Firth was a solid, loveable and wholly inadequate *Daily Express* editor. During a brief sojourn on the *Express* night desk, Kelvin MacKenzie taunted him endlessly. On one famous occasion he adopted the pose of a court official to boom: 'Arthur Percy Firth, you are hereby accused of impersonating an editor, taking this once-great newspaper and reducing it to a daily pile of crap. How do you plead?'[117] Firth laughed it off. It was no surprise when, after barely a year in charge, he was replaced in October 1981 by Christopher Ward, who was, at thirty-nine, some fourteen years younger.

Ward had been recommended to managing director Jocelyn Stevens by another senior executive, Felicity Green, his former mentor from their days on the *Daily Mirror*. Ward's father John had been an *Express* man too. Educated at King's College School in Wimbledon, he started his career on a weekly in the north-east, spent three years on the *Newcastle Evening Chronicle* and, in 1963, was taken on by the *Daily Mirror* as a reporter, soon moving to the subs desk. Green spotted Ward's feature-writing talent and he was given a full-page column in which he charted, as a happy participant, the heady world of pop music and alternative culture in the late 1960s and early 1970s.

Some *Mirror* executives, blinded by Ward's frothy column, were slow to realise that he was a serious and ambitious man with an inner steel core. When they did, he was promoted to assistant editor of the *Sunday Mirror* in 1976 and three years later moved back to the *Daily Mirror* with the same title. He was an interesting choice for the stuffy *Daily Express*: quick-witted and intelligent, with a liberal outlook and a genuine understanding of the effects of the cultural changes wrought by his own generation. Junor was unimpressed with him, though his criticism was silly and superficial, observing only that the well-dressed Ward had 'a penchant for wearing long overcoats of the style much favoured by Chicago gangsters in the 1930s'.[118] More significantly, the *Express* managers didn't like him or rate him.[119]

During his editorship the *Express* had an award-winning scoop about a Buckingham Palace intruder who managed to get into the Queen's bedroom.[120] According to Junor, Ward was away from the office so his deputy, Ted Dickinson, took the bold decision to publish in the face of an official denial from the Palace. In fact, it was Ward who took the responsibility and boasted of the pleasure in public.[121] But Matthews was furious with his editor, telling him: 'You had no business publishing that story if the Queen didn't want anyone to know about it.'[122] It was one of several clashes between the two men and showed that Matthews didn't see the point of newspapers. 'The trouble with you journalists', he told Ward, 'is you're always sticking your noses into other people's business.' He also suspected Ward's politics. When he published a front-page picture of the anti-nuclear protesters ringing Greenham Common under the headline 'Hand in Hand for Peace', Matthews called it 'dangerous Commie stuff'. On similar lines, Cameron thought Ward's coverage of the Falklands war lacked sufficient jingoism.[123]

This carping was bad enough, but Ward's major problem stemmed from the reluctance of management to back his hunches about how to change the paper, and he clashed constantly with the general manager, Tony Bentley.[124] His attempt to introduce a new section on a Saturday, which would have led the field, was thwarted by management timidity. Ward departed after two years (going on to found and run the hugely profitable Redwood magazine publishers) and Matthews appointed the former *Sun* editor, Sir Larry Lamb, in his place, the eighth editor in twelve years. After his downfall at the *Sun* (see below, p. 418), Lamb worked unhappily in Australia for Robert Holmes à Court and then, even more unhappily, rejoined Murdoch to be editor-in-chief of the *Australian*. Once again, the pair clashed, and in February 1983 Lamb wrote to Matthews from Australia 'offering his services' and was appointed editor soon after.[125]

Lamb was looked on with awe by most of Fleet Street's popular-paper journalists and it was anticipated, not least by *Daily Mail* editor David English, that he might be the man to reverse the *Express*'s downward sales trend. By the spring of 1983, the *Mail* was barely 50,000 copies behind its old rival, which was often selling no more than 1.8 million. English's fears were unfounded. Though Lamb was less intimidated by Matthews's managers than Ward, his greatest editing days were behind him. There is much truth in the view of deputy managing director Andy Cameron, who remarked: 'Whatever magic Larry had had on the *Sun* he failed to produce on the *Daily Express*.'[126] He had one big sales benefit within months of his arrival, a bingo-style 'millionaire's club' game launched in September 1983 which added 400,000 sales almost overnight and substantially widened the lead over with the *Mail*, but it gradually dripped away in the following two years as the *Mail* gained ground.

What no one can dispute was Lamb's overweening belief that he was always right and knew more than anyone else. It quickly became evident that he didn't respect Matthews, he managed to upset two *Express* stars, Jean Rook and Kenneth Fleet, and then he foolishly provoked an unnecessary row with the print unions during the miners' strike.[127] Desperate to weaken the miners' leader, Arthur Scargill, Lamb published a front page headlined, 'The truth that Scargill dare not tell: I AM LEADING MY MEN TO DISASTER'. It was a spoof, claiming to be 'the speech that the *Daily Express* believes Arthur Scargill would be making . . . if he cared more about the truth'.[128] In the imaginary speech Scargill confessed to lying and admitted that the strike was political and unwinnable. It might just have passed muster as a feature article inside, appropriately headlined to make clear it was a counterfeit exercise, but promoting it as the paper's lead story gave it a spurious credence. Many readers would not have realised it was a parody.

Print union reaction was predictable. Bill Keys, leader of Sogat 82, demanded equal space for a reply by Scargill's National Union of Mine-workers (NUM).[129] Lamb refused. Keys then appealed to Matthews, who agreed to publish one. At a board meeting that day, Matthews suggested to Lamb that it had been a mistake to run the article as a splash. Lamb bridled, offered his resignation and left the office red-faced, giving the impression he would never return.[130] In the end Matthews and Lamb patched things up.[131] There was a postscript: Sogat 82 prevented the London editions of the *Express* being printed that night after discovering that the NUM statement wasn't to be carried in full.

Despite the rabid anti-Scargill tone of other newspapers (see next chapter), the episode made Lamb look foolish in the rest of Fleet Street, having generated a measure of sympathy for a union leader who was becoming a pariah. *Sunday Express* editor Sir John Junor mused: 'I just wonder whether, rather like Christiansen and Beaverbrook, he [Lamb] had only been any good while he had Rupert Murdoch as a proprietor and that without Murdoch he was lost.'[132]

While Junor sat in judgement on Lamb, he might well have looked to his own laurels. His paper's sale dropped badly in the early 1980s, falling to a poor 2.4 million after the launch of the *Mail on Sunday*. He stuck to the usual round of soft stories, refused to countenance any change to the layout and ignored any hint of turning it from a broadsheet to a tabloid. Junor survived because he was a canny office politician – in Cameron's view, he raised obsequiousness to an art form, treated women with calculated brutality and bullied people who could not answer back.[133] Managing director Jocelyn Stevens thought Junor should be replaced, but nothing was done.

At Matthews's other paper, the *Daily Star*, which he had launched in 1979, he found a new editor to replace Derek Jameson at the beginning of 1981. Lloyd Turner, a forty-two-year-old Australian who had started his career in New South Wales, had emigrated to Britain in 1967 and immediately secured a subbing job on the *Express*. He worked his way up to night editor by 1979, having overcome a lengthy love affair with drink. His machine-gun laugh was a nervous tic rather than an indication of a sense of humour. He had a habit of speaking emphatically in public and then agonising in private, often performing a 180-degree turn. Having reversed his decision he then adopted the same tone of passionate sincerity in announcing his change of mind. Turner had chutzpah. His first address to the staff, extolling the virtues of a purist journalistic ethic 'in defence of the little man' with a 'sword that strikes the mighty' sat oddly with the celebrity-filled paper, featuring topless girls and bingo, which he actually produced.[134]

Turner went on television to pledge that the *Star* would never intrude into the private life of Princess Diana, yet his paper published a sneak picture of her while five months pregnant. He was also given to making grandiose promises to staff about bonuses and office cars which everyone knew he could not fulfil. He was finally exposed as a liar by the Press Council over the Yorkshire Ripper case (see next chapter). He was a reasonable night editor, reacting well to breaking news stories, producing an excellent paper on the day Beatle John Lennon was murdered, for instance. But an editor must have vision and must initiate. In these departments, Turner was sadly lacking. He often wasted money on foolish enterprises such as the hiring of actress Diana Dors, a faded star, as the paper's agony aunt.

Turner started the decade with a huge advantage. His lively paper, with its glossy Page 3 girls and entertaining sports content, rapidly built circulation on the back of bingo before his rivals woke up to the game's sales-winning potential. The *Star* offered relatively modest prizes but the game caught the public imagination and by the early summer of 1981 it was regularly selling more than 1.5 million copies a day. *Sun* bingo was, admitted the paper's official historian, 'a direct steal from the *Daily Star*'.[135] In June 1981 the *Sun* distributed 20 million bingo cards and allocated £850,000 to be spent in prize money over a twenty-week period. Its sales rose by 500,000 in two months and the newspaper bingo craze had taken hold.

The *Daily Express* joined in with its millionaires' club, which upped the stakes by offering a prize of £1 million. The *Daily Mail* launched Casino ('the world's most glamorous game') with a top prize initially of £70,000. The *Daily Mirror*, slow to react at first, introduced in rather half-hearted fashion a £30,000 bingo game. There were powerful voices in Mirror group warning against the trend. The *Sunday Mirror*'s editor Bob Edwards called such games 'the ultimate in newspaper madness' because the money spent – buying TV advertising time for promotion, printing of cards and providing prize money – could only attract readers for a relatively short period.[136] *Sunday People* editor Geoff Pinnington tried to call a halt, comparing the 'bingo trap' to the poverty trap: 'You can't avoid getting into it and then you can't get out.'[137] But no owner or editor was listening. Their experience was that many of the casual readers did stick and they dare not let a rival steal a march. When Maxwell upped the stakes, Murdoch matched him by raising the *Sun*'s bingo prize to £1 million. By the end of 1984, with nearly every paper (including the *Times*) running some kind of game, an estimated £30 million was available from press competitions.

The *Star* wasn't eclipsed at first by all this activity, even though it didn't have the resources to give away £1 million, and it managed to sell more than 1.7 million copies in October 1984, its highest point. It settled down the following year to an average sale of about 1.4 million, still a creditable performance but nowhere near high enough to challenge its main rivals. The *Star* had become an irritant but it wasn't proving to be a genuine competitor. One genuine disappointment for Turner was in failing to convince Matthews to keep the *Star* loyal to Labour in the 1983 election. He was ordered to urge his readers, most of whom were shown by market research to be Labour supporters, to vote for Mrs Thatcher. It is doubtful though if this would made any difference to the circulation figures.

By the time of the election, the newspaper company Matthews was running was very different from the one he had bought. Under pressure from his Trafalgar board colleagues who thought their share price was being dragged down by the poor business image of Express Newspapers, and Fleet Street in general, Matthews decided in 1981 to demerge the paper group. Jocelyn Stevens opposed the flotation, possibly because he was hoping to engineer his own buy-out along with the managing director of the magazine division, Morgan-Grampian.[138] Matthews overcame the opposition in time-honoured fashion: he fired both men. Stevens went off to make a success of magazine publishing and later became rector of the Royal College of Art and after this chairman of English Heritage.

In March 1982, Express Newspapers – which included the hugely profitable Morgan-Grampian, but not the company's half-share in the London *Evening Standard* – was transformed into a public company known as Fleet Holdings. Despite overmanning and production disputes, the company recorded healthy profits, rising from £9.5 million in 1983 to £22.1 million for the year ended June 1984. The share price went up too, but it was still cheap enough to excite the interest of various predators. Its market capitalisation was barely double the value of its stake in Reuters.[139] One of the first to spot Fleet's vulnerability was the Australian media tycoon Robert Holmes à Court, who bought up 10 per cent of the stock.

Matthews tried to thwart a takeover bid through negotiating mergers but these came to nothing and he watched helplessly as a variety of players began to buy Fleet shares. Holmes à Court sold his holding to Robert Maxwell, who added a further 5 per cent from elsewhere and fooled nobody by claiming that it was 'a strategic long-term investment'.[140] A business associate of Tiny Rowland also took an interest. By far the most aggressive buyer was United Newspapers, a profitable regional paper group run by David Stevens. In January 1985, with Maxwell having secured the ownership of Mirror group he had no more use for his 15 per cent Fleet stake and sold it to United for a reputed £30 million. Maxwell had done Stevens a favour for within two months United's holding had reached 20 per cent and it formally announced its intention of launching a bid. Stevens offered £3.75p a share, nearly twenty times their original value, and his £317 million bid was accepted. Matthews pocketed £11 million and retired to Jersey, while the blow was cushioned for those of his nervous executives lucky enough to hold share options, such as deputy managing director Andrew Cameron, who owned 80,000.[141] After an inquiry, the Monopolies Commission cleared the United bid and on 20 October 1985 David Stevens assumed control.

David Robert Stevens had become a newspaper tycoon by accident rather than design. He had enjoyed a comfortable upbringing, his father having made a substantial fortune by inventing the first portable hearing aid. Born in 1936, schooled at Stowe and then Cambridge, graduating with a masters in economics and winning a blue for golf – a lifelong passion – he started out as a management trainee in a merchant bank. His greatest claim to financial fame was in building up a pension fund manager, Montagu Investment Management (MIM), into a sizeable and very profitable company. His financial acumen drew him to the attention of Lord Barnetson, chairman of United Newspapers, which was the first true example in Britain of a regional newspaper chain.[142] When Stevens was invited to join the board in 1974, United owned two morning papers, seven evenings, thirty-two weeklies and eight magazines. Its newspaper flagship was the *Yorkshire Post* and the jewel of its magazine division was *Punch*. Four years before it was described in glowing terms as 'one of the very few newspaper groups in whose managerial talents the Stock Exchange has any confidence'.[143]

Stevens impressed the United board and, on Barnetson's death in 1981, the deputy chairman, Gordon Linacre, stepped aside to let Stevens take the chair. Through more clever acquisitions and tight accounting, Stevens enabled the group to make huge profits. Along the way he picked up more directorships, eventually becoming chairman of half a dozen more companies. A man with a Napoleonic physique and ambitions, it was hard to discern what Stevens was thinking behind his pale grey eyes. He often appeared with a slight, sardonic smile which could change in an instant to rage. He could be unpleasant with staff and occasionally 'extremely nasty', said his deputy managing director Andrew Cameron.[144] A dapper dresser, given to wearing pinstriped suits and highly polished shoes, Stevens looked every inch the City figure he was. It was evident that his acquisition of the Express papers was primarily about money. But that didn't inhibit him from interfering in editorial policy.

As a staunch Conservative Stevens expected all his papers, including the *Star*, to toe the party line. He also influenced what was, and wasn't, published in the business pages. In a candid interview about his role, he said: 'I do interfere, and say enough is enough. I don't ram my views in but I'm quite far out to the right . . . I suppose my papers echo my political views.'[145] He gave examples: he had ordered his editors to stop attacking the royal family and suggested an anti-litter campaign. His first major announcement was about a plan to move the Express titles out of their famous Fleet Street headquarters, the Black Lubyanka, and consequently reduce the 6,500 workforce by more than 20 per cent. Within weeks of the takeover, Stevens also took the fateful decision to sell his company's 50 per cent of the *Evening Standard* to the owner of the other half, Associated Newspapers. Rothermere had triumphed at last.[146]

In the previous April, *Standard* editor Louis Kirby had announced that his paper was changing its name to the *London Standard*. This was necessary, he explained, because 'a metropolitan newspaper' in 'a cosmopolitan city' required 'a wide-angle lens on the world'.[147] It didn't make much sense and the name quietly reverted to the *Evening Standard* eighteen months later.

Meanwhile, during the takeover battle, *Daily Express* editor Larry Lamb suffered a heart attack, necessitating a bypass operation. While recuperating in hospital he was visited by Murdoch who later reported that Lamb belittled both Matthews and Stevens as 'amateurs'. Returning to the office three months' later he quickly surmised that Stevens, as he had guessed, didn't understand national newspapers.

Takeover Five: the Berrys' family silver turns to Black

Lord Hartwell still ran his *Telegraph* titles as if he were feudal baron, a likeable, honest, fair and civilised man, but a baron all the same. In 1982 I became friends with one of Hartwell's nephews who, having been cashiered from the army, appeared to have no visible means of support. Yet he lived in a South Kensington apartment, rose late in the day and spent his evenings in nightclubs. When I asked him how he managed to enjoy such a sybaritic lifestyle he explained that every six months he visited 'Uncle Michael' at his *Telegraph* office, chatted with him for a few minutes and was then handed a cheque for £12,500.

Despite their frustrations at their proprietor's unwillingness to engage with the twentieth century, Hartwell's senior journalists found his paternalism rather engaging. *Sunday Telegraph* columnist Perry Worsthorne, in describing the 'ritual' which greeted Hartwell's daily arrival at the office in Peterborough Court, obviously relished it. Hartwell arrived in 'a modest family car' to be met by commissionaires who 'leap to attention before rushing to hold the lifts for the great man, brushing lesser mortals aside like flies in paroxysms of deference ... He would much prefer to slide in unnoticed.'[148]

Hartwell was seventy in May 1981. He had never varied his routine and had taken little account of the fact that he was surrounded by equally aged figures. His brother, Lord Camrose, was seventy-one. The two key *Daily Telegraph* editorial executives – editor Bill Deedes and managing editor Peter Eastwood – were sixty-seven and sixty-nine respectively. Harbourne M. Stephen, managing director for over twenty years, was sixty-five. Hartwell's contact with the world inside the *Telegraph* was restricted to these elderly men and his links outside were virtually non-existent. He retreated even further into himself when his much more social wife Pamela died in 1982.[149]

Nor was there much hope of a family succession at the top of the company despite both of Hartwell's sons, Adrian and Nicholas Berry, having worked for the *Daily Telegraph*. Adrian started his journalistic career in the provinces, spent three years in New York and, in 1977, joined the *Telegraph* as science correspondent. Neither he nor anyone else thought him cut out for management. Nicholas was more of a businessman, having started in the *Telegraph*'s City office. He moved on to run the educational book publishers Harrap, which he eventually sold for an enormous profit. A friend of mine who was a senior editor at Harrap thought him a clever man but not as clever as he thought he was. His later involvement with the *Telegraph* would prove that point.

Despite Hartwell's paper recording year by year the changing nature of capitalism, in which the private family ownership of a labour-intensive industrial company had become an anachronism, he seemed unable to accept that his own was a classic example. If the company could not generate sufficient profit then it could not hope to invest in essential new plant and machinery. Hartwell did understand that the future lay in photo-composition and web-offset printing, but he initially rejected Stephen's pleas about the need to replace its old presses. He couldn't cope with union opposition either. When one press was removed to save money in November 1982, a strike cost £1.5 million. Five months later more money was lost during a dispute over cuts in manning. Advertising fell away from 1979 onwards and the cost of newsprint rose. Hartwell was forced to increase the cover price four times in two years so that, by autumn 1982, the *Times* and *Daily Telegraph* were selling for the same price for the first time since 1931. With the *Times* under Murdoch's vigorous ownership from 1981 and the *Guardian* adding new sales in a slowly expanding market, the *Telegraph* was losing out. The paper still looked terrible, poorly printed and with a dire, unchanging layout.

By the time Hartwell was convinced of the need to install new presses and to escape the unions, his company was in desperate straits. In the three years up to March 1983, it lost £7.5 million. Three months later he agreed to build on a twelve-acre site on the Isle of Dogs, off West Ferry Road, negotiating a 200-year rent of £100,000 per annum with the London Docklands Development Corporation. The budget for building the plant and installing the presses ran to £74.5 million, and then he discovered he had to quit the Manchester print plant within two years and must spend a further £28 million there as well. He would also require a further £37 million for redundancies and buying out restrictive practices, none of which had been negotiated with the unions anyway.

Hartwell had committed the company to a £140 million regeneration plan without having raised the money. His Reuters shares were worth some £29 million but cashing them in wouldn't solve the problem. When he turned to Rothschild's merchant bank for help its team was amazed at his foolhardiness. But they went about their task as best they could and, in early 1984, a consortium of banks agreed to put up £75 million as long as the *Telegraph* raised £29 million separately. It could only achieve this by a private placing of shares. The placing didn't go well, with institutions worried about the Berry family's continuing control and other investors thinking it too great a risk, so the most they could raise was £19 million. City editor Andreas Whittam Smith suggested to Hartwell that the paper should encourage readers to buy shares, along with an employee share-ownership scheme. When that idea was rejected by Hartwell, Whittam Smith 'felt he had been rebuffed'[150] and was soon preparing to go his own way. Then a potential investor contacted Rothschild to say he was willing to put up all of the necessary £10 million. Hartwell had a saviour who was also to be his nemesis.

Relieved that the caller wasn't the financier Sir James Goldsmith, whom he despised, Hartwell was baffled when told it was someone called Conrad

Black. He had never heard of him, which wasn't so surprising, given that Black's home country, Canada, must rank as one of the most under-reported English-speaking nations in the British press. Hartwell was soon to discover that Black was an influential figure, a substantial north American newspaper proprietor eager to become a truly international media tycoon. Conrad Moffat Black was a big man, six feet tall and bulky, built like a rugby front-row forward, but one who preferred to exercise his brain rather than his limbs. By the time Hartwell first heard his name he had made considerable profits running his newspaper empire. Born in 1944, he grew up in Toronto, the son of a wealthy brewery executive who demonstrated that gambling offers a poorer return than stock-market investment by installing in the family home a slot-machine and a ticker-tape machine.[151]

Black went to one of the best private schools, Upper Canada College, where he showed an early aptitude for turning a fast buck. At fourteen, he and three friends managed to obtain the key to the principal's office and found the final examination papers, selling photocopies to fellow students. They made $1,400 before they were discovered and expelled. The prank didn't prevent him going on to Carleton University, Ottawa, where he graduated with his first degree. He then obtained a law degree at Laval University in Quebec City, where he met Dan Colson who was to play a key role in his *Telegraph* takeover, and finally took a masters degree in history at McGill University. He had by then developed an intense interest in a range of historical heroes, such as Napoleon, Lincoln and de Gaulle, and later wrote a lengthy biography of Maurice Duplessis, the former premier of Quebec. Black was also engrossed by the lives of three press moguls: William Randolph Hearst, and Lords Northcliffe and Beaverbrook.

The self-confident Black was a loquacious, verbose man with a wide vocabulary – revelling in the use, and often misuse, of arcane words – and a terrific memory which enabled him to recite whole speeches from his heroes. His other passion was business. In 1969 he and two friends, Peter White and David Radler, borrowed almost $20,000 to buy a loss-making daily paper in Quebec, the *Sherbrooke Record*. They dispensed with 40 per cent of the staff and gradually made the paper profitable, extending their practice of rationalisation to other papers they acquired. By 1978 they had created a chain of nine dailies and nine weeklies across Canada. Three years later his Sterling chain was making $5 million a year. Black, through his family connections, also took an interest in one of Canada's largest holding companies, Argus Corporation, with some $4 billion in assets. In a series of complex financial manoeuvres, he executed a coup against the old guard within Argus, ultimately gaining control for little more than $30 million and winning media status as Canada's 'boy wonder businessman'. The tag didn't last long.

Within Argus group he shuffled companies, squeezing money from passive investments and selling off businesses, prompting one biographer to question the complexity of his financial engineering.[152] Argus held the largest private stake in the ailing farm equipment manufacturer Massey-Ferguson, which desperately needed government assistance. Black moved in as chairman for two years, found it impossible to sort out the problems and finally withdrew in the most controversial fashion, giving the Argus stake to Massey's pensions funds. This upset some of Canada's financial community and the press turned on him, but Black's defence of his actions appeared entirely reasonable.[153]

Black's passion for making money went hand in hand with his pleasure at exercising political power and influence. To further it he required a national newspaper platform and in 1979 he set his sights on acquiring the *Toronto Globe & Mail*, Canada's leading establishment paper, owned by FP Publications, but he was thwarted when the Thomson group outbid his consortium. In 1985, having also lost out in an attempt to buy another large group of papers, Southam, he created a new flagship company, Hollinger. A magazine writer commented: 'In his fortieth year he finds himself comfortable and rich, but surrounded by a rising chorus of voices questioning his future course and asking why he refuses to fulfil the potential for corporate greatness he once inspired among his peers.'[154]

It wasn't too long before Black took that writer, and almost everyone who knew him, by surprise. In May 1985, Black ran into Andrew Knight, editor of the *Economist*, at the Bilderberg conference outside New York. They had known each other for five years and were on good terms. Knight spoke about the problems being faced by the *Telegraph* group back in London and wondered whether Black might be interested. Though well informed, Knight knew only generally about the group's money difficulties and was not aware of the private placing of shares nor that there was a shortfall. Black was non-committal, but intrigued. When Knight returned to London he discovered the truth about Hartwell's £10 million headache and immediately called Black to tell him he could have 14 per cent of the Telegraph business and would probably be able to negotiate terms to increase that holding. Now Black was very interested and agreed to meet Hartwell at a hotel near New York's Kennedy airport.

Hartwell, accompanied by his managing director Harbourne Stephen, the deputy managing director and a representative from his merchant bank, Rothschild's, swiftly agreed to Black's demand that he should have pre-emptive rights if any new shares were issued. Hartwell miscalculated, imagining that no such call for more funds would be necessary. Black, having read the prospectus carefully, realised that exactly the opposite would be the case. Hartwell, having arrived by Concorde, reboarded the plane just twelve hours after leaving London, unaware that he had just sold his birthright.

Black called on his old friend Dan Colson, godfather to his children, who was then a partner in the London office of a Canadian law firm, to negotiate the deal. Colson, sceptical about the wisdom of the investment, evidently told Black: 'Lie down until the feeling passes.'[155] As he got down to the job of dealing with the legal agreements he then realised the likely outcome: Black was on the verge of owning the *Daily* and *Sunday Telegraphs*. Within six weeks the deal was done.

Black took two places on the board, himself and – at Andrew Knight's suggestion – Frank Rogers, at sixty-five an elder statesman of the newspaper industry, a former Mirror group managing director and current chairman of the regional newspaper and magazine group EMAP. Hartwell was now in a hopeless position and the denouement was to happen much faster than anyone could have anticipated. He discovered that converting to photo-composition would cost much more than budget, as would the manning of the new presses in Manchester. An investigation by the accountants Coopers & Lybrand found that, instead of making £200,000 in the six months up to 30 September 1985, the group had made a loss of £6.5 million, and would go on to lose a total of £8.1 million by March 1986, making a nonsense of a profit forecast of £5 million.

The Berry family suddenly woke up to the danger of losing their precious inheritance. Hartwell's alarmed son Nicholas mounted a woeful attempt to salvage the situation while berating Rothschild's for its handling of matters. Then Hartwell belatedly tried to forge a deal with Fairfax, an Australian newspaper group, to buy out Black's share. But Colson and Black weren't taking that bait. With liquidity problems pressing as the group reached its overdraft limit, Hartwell bailed it out on three occasions with £4 million from his own funds. It couldn't continue and with the banks pressing him news leaked of Hartwell's problems, amid predictions that the Berry family were being forced to cede control.[156] *Telegraph* journalists, asked to accept stringent economies, had no idea that the situation was so critical and their union chapel passed a vote of no confidence in management, absurdly urging the directors to take control. A desperate Hartwell, needing time and funds to tide him over, tried another manoeuvre by asking Andrew Knight to be chief executive. He refused. Hartwell finally announced to the board on 28 November 1985 that he had lost control. His son Nicholas responded by resigning.

The *coup de grâce* came seven days later when the board agreed to a rights issue by which Black's company, Hollinger, would acquire enough shares to give him 50.1 per cent of the total. Hartwell would remain chairman and editor-in-chief, Knight would be chief executive and Black would be in complete control. No referral to the Monopolies and Mergers Commission was required since Black had no other newspaper holdings in Britain. Hartwell's loss of the Telegraph titles for a pittance was 'one of the great financial as well as personal tragedies of the age', wrote Ivan Fallon, City editor of the *Sunday Telegraph*.[157] A deeply disappointed Hartwell tried to explain his downfall by pointing out that the Berrys had no outside financial interests, lamenting: 'Ours was a family situation and we are the last of them.'[158] Later, reflecting on the difference between the old-style proprietors and the new owners, he said: 'I was always terribly shocked when other people ran their newspapers like biscuit factories, just to make money.'[159]

Black's deft handling of the takeover wasn't universally appreciated and he received his first taste of British press resentment. Writing in the *Times*, finance editor Kenneth Fleet referred to him as 'Genghis Khan'. A *Spectator* article by a Canadian author presented Black's activities in his native country in the worst possible light.[160] *Daily Telegraph* editor Bill Deedes didn't join the chorus of disapproval, noting that Black read the *Telegraph* and was a great fan of both its and Mrs Thatcher's political philosophy. He recognised that Black 'represented the new order' for national paper ownership and 'had the effect of putting a more powerful engine behind a very good newspaper'.[161] Deedes was not, it should be noted, trying to save his job.

A new Sunday between the haughties and the naughties

At the end of 1976, Lord Rothermere – having just been unsuccessful in his bid for the *Observer* – announced his intention of launching a Sunday tabloid. It would, he said, be 'aimed at the middle ground' in direct competition with the 'vulnerable' *Sunday Express* and it would be accomplished 'within two years, all things being equal'.[162] Things in Fleet Street were never equal. His lack of printing capacity was a big problem and the financial climate didn't look too healthy either. Five years later, with Mrs Thatcher in Downing Street and a new sense of optimism, Rothermere finally decided to go ahead.

It would have been entirely natural, given their close working relationship, for Rothermere to have consulted his *Daily Mail* editor David English about who should edit a paper he envisioned as a sort of seventh-day *Mail*. The fact that Rothermere reached his own decision about the editorship without reference to English was to make life within Northcliffe House very tough for the man he did choose: Bernard Shrimsley, former editor of the *Sun* and the *News of the World*. Although there was no especial enmity between Shrimsley and English, the *Mail* man viewed him with suspicion, kept him at a distance and politely, but stubbornly, refused to provide him with the resources he sought. No, it would not be possible to use the *Mail*'s New York correspondent, Dermot Purgavie. No, the writer Ann Leslie would not be available. Sorry, but columnist Lynda Lee-Potter was unable to do more interviews. Outwardly, meanwhile, English maintained a perfectly friendly attitude towards Shrimsley as the latter set about finding staff for the paper which was to be titled the *Mail on Sunday*.

By October 1981, Shrimsley had gathered together most of his senior executives, who included his brother Anthony as associate editor, City editor

Christopher Fildes, women's editor Georgina Howell, news editor Iain Walker, fashion editor Kathy Phillips, chief sports writer Patrick Collins, and astrologer Patric Walker.[163] On paper, this looked to be a good team and they had plenty of time to plan what they would do because they were still more than six months away from launch. If English was sceptical about Shrimsley's choice of staff or his ideas about editorial content, he didn't air them. Though he had problems of his own at the *Daily Mail*, which had failed to maintain its upward sales momentum of the late 1970s, the supremely confident English was sure he was driving his paper in the right direction. As for the *Mail on Sunday*, he could afford to bide his time.

In the build-up to launch, the advertising agency Saatchi and Saatchi came up with a slick phrase to define the middle market as somewhere 'between the haughties and the naughties'. Rothermere adopted it as his own. Another S&S slogan asked: 'When will someone produce a Sunday that isn't overwritten or underdressed?' Some of this nonsense appeared in the paper's manifesto, which prompted *Sunday Times* journalist Ian Jack to joke that the authors were more likely to have been Saatchi and Saatchi 'with help from Confucius'.[164] The *Mail on Sunday* certainly wasn't under-resourced, with a £12 million launch budget and a fairly modest sales ambition of 1.4 million.

The first issue on 2 May 1982, during the Falklands war, was a strange beast, restrained to the point of being self-effacing and, in some ways, rather boring. Its sixty-four pages contrived to look both serious and fussy, a bad combination, with headlines that were too small and a run of pages which looked unprepossessingly grey. Most significantly, it didn't resemble the *Daily Mail*. The 'world exclusive' interview with the twenty-two-year-old exiled Shah of Iran was an odd choice of front-page boast, though the serialisation of Billie Jean King's autobiography was a good buy. Willie Donaldson's puckish gossip column probably went over the heads of its audience. Michael Parkinson and Jilly Cooper turned in good work but Arianna Stassinopoulos did not. Among Shrimsley's supposedly brilliant new discoveries was the columnist Alexandra Artley whose artless contribution contained the immortal phrase: 'I hate writing about myself but my cat knows me well . . . take it from the top, kitten . . .' John Osborne reviewed television with the enthusiasm of a teetotaller discussing alcoholic beverages.

One commentator believed Shrimsley had aimed 'too high in the market',[165] while another thought it carried 'a good deal of text, too much in fact'.[166] *Sunday Express* editor Sir John Junor thought the first issues were 'so terrible . . . I felt like dancing'.[167] He was also cock-a-hoop at the rival paper's production problems, which meant that its output was half a million short. Compared to the *Sunday Express*, which had acquired a profitable colour magazine in April 1981, it looked a poor package.[168] Junor shrewdly chose that week to begin serialisation in his magazine of a popular biography of

Princess Diana by Robert Lacey and to run a story in the paper by Frederick Forsyth. Obtusely, Rothermere had decided not to give the *Mail on Sunday* a magazine.

On the eve of the launch, English wrote a fulsome letter to Shrimsley, praising him for having produced 'a beautiful, perfectly formed baby' and forecasting that 'you will be swamped by congratulations on Monday'.[169] A week or so later English was alleged to have told a *Daily Mail* morning conference: 'Gosh, the *Sunday Express* is a bad paper. It's nearly as bad as the *Mail on Sunday*.'

It was a disastrous launch, and, though disappointing first issues are common, the next six or so didn't look too good either, failing to tempt potential readers. The addition of writers such as Shirley Lowe and Taki Theodoracopulos didn't appeal and the fourth issue, with its blurbless front page devoted entirely to the Falklands war, was very odd. What kind of Sunday paper was it that failed to point to its goodies inside? After ten issues, with sales having fallen to 740,000, Rothermere fired Shrimsley.[170] Shrimsley's friends complained of unfairness, blaming production problems for poor circulation, but Rothermere would hear none of it, saying months later: 'The May 2 paper was just not good enough . . . Pretty well everything was wrong.'[171]

English, who had been knighted just the week before for his services to journalism and/or Mrs Thatcher, was overjoyed at the chance to ride to his owner's rescue, styling himself 'interim editor'. He put several of Shrimsley's staff to the sword – including his brother, the features editor and his deputy, and many of the writers – and was briefly nicknamed 'the Knight of the Long Knives'. He shipped in twenty of his own staff, using his trusted executives in key posts, immediately changed the masthead and the typeface to match the *Daily Mail*'s, and set in motion planning for a colour magazine so that the *Mail on Sunday* could compete on level terms with the *Sunday Express*.

In his first issue, English announced: 'Why we are different today . . . It really is the *MAIL on Sunday* . . . it will now have all the drive and flair, the depth of coverage and the crisp lay-out which more than five million *Daily Mail* readers enjoy.'[172] Suddenly, Lee-Potter and Purgavie were temporarily available, as was Leslie, who contributed a piece on the 'feminist myth'. Elkan Allan replaced Osborne as the TV reviewer. Among Shrimsley's signings, Jilly Cooper, Patrick Collins and Christopher Fildes stayed. The following week Harold Wilson's former private secretary, Marcia Falkender, was introduced as a columnist.

Junor said English 'reconstructed the paper virtually overnight' and 'quite miraculously saved it from disaster'.[173] It took just a little longer because English's strategy was to relaunch the paper as soon as the magazine could be published. Entitled You, and edited by John Leese with Dennis Hackett as a consultant, it finally arrived in late September along with a sponsored part-work on cookery and a children's comic. You magazine, with its concentration on entertainment and consumerism, was different in tone and appeal from the equivalent broadsheet glossies and much more professional than its *Sunday Express* rival. Highly praised from its inception, it gave the *Mail on Sunday* a unique appeal at the moment when the main paper was beginning to bed in, having become identifiably a *Mail*-like offshoot. The £3 million publicity for the relaunch, using the slogan 'A newspaper not a snoozepaper', was more than was spent on Shrimsley's original. A grateful Rothermere, who withstood a £24 million loss in the paper's first year, was swift to praise English's 'genius' in turning the *MoS* around.[174]

Within five months, the *MoS* began to make real progress, achieving a sale of 1.3 million, and English's ambitious lieutenant, Stewart Steven, was then appointed editor. Steven, born in Hamburg in 1938, was brought to Britain when his Jewish parents fled Nazi Germany before the war. Educated at Mayfield College, Sussex, he began his career as a political reporter with a features agency before joining the Bristol-based Western Daily Press as its political correspondent. From 1964 he worked for the *Daily Express* successively as political reporter, diplomatic correspondent and foreign editor. It was there that he made his notorious Martin Bormann mistake (see Chapter Twelve). After joining the *Daily Mail* in 1973 he was promoted to associate editor and was responsible for another colossal error, the 1977 Leyland slush-fund affair (see Chapter Thirteen).

Neither of these incidents detracted from English's faith in Steven's journalistic abilities and Steven didn't let his mentor down. The *Mail on Sunday* went from strength to strength in the following two years, rising to a sale of 1.6 million by the end of 1985 and being named newspaper of the year by the *What the Papers Say* judges. They noted that it had 'increased its circulation without lowering its standards' and remarked that its features 'have been consistently original, intelligent and literate'. By then, the *Daily Mail*'s Nigel Dempster was providing a seventh-day version of his gossip column and a previously unknown iconoclast, Julie Burchill, was provoking not only readers but other journalists.

Steven was renowned for dominating conversations, a tendency relieved by a good sense of humour. One evening in a pub off Fleet Street he told a group of drinkers that he was an uncircumcised Jew, explaining that some Jews born in Germany in the late 1930s were given a dispensation by rabbis not to be circumcised. Challenged to prove the fact, he took *Daily Mail* reporter Tim Miles to the lavatory. With a beaming Steven behind him, Miles emerged with raised thumbs to an outburst of cheering.

English, who first told me that anecdote, enhanced his reputation after his *Mail on Sunday* rescue. But he found the going much tougher at the *Daily Mail* because the broadsheets appeared to be poaching on his territory in order to increase sales. He knew he needed to build a new audience among younger readers graduating from parents who had been readers of the red-tops, yet he must continue to produce a paper also appealing to the low-brow members of the settled middle classes. He paid particular attention to ways of attracting more women buyers. Every editor tried to do this, of course, and they all carried women's pages. English kept asking whether there was a way of cornering the market, of creating a slot in the paper, or of adapting even the paper itself, which would fascinate women enough to make it required reading. Cudlipp had previously tried and failed, with both *Woman's Mirror* and the crafting of the old *Sun*'s Pacesetters.

English, intuitively understanding the nature and class of his audience, created what can now be seen as a 'designer paper', a badge or emblem which women could purchase as a daily accessory. He hired and promoted women journalists, such as Lee-Potter and Leslie, who approached topics from a noticeably different angle than men. He also pioneered the use of lengthy features with sharply angled headlines which persuaded readers to stop and read rather than racing through from beginning to end. Over time, English also created a sort of *Mail* journalistic academy, selecting recruits who could be groomed into his way of doing things. After learning the basic ropes the best of them would then go through a sort of executive training, moving from department to department to ensure that they were grounded in every aspect of the job.

Bingo and jingo! Murdoch's new editor for a new Britain

Before Sir Larry Lamb departed for his enforced six-month sabbatical at the beginning of 1981 it was obvious to his senior executives that the rift between him and Rupert Murdoch was not going to heal. Lamb, so important to the *Sun*'s early success, had become a liability in Murdoch's eyes. His hostility towards the idea of running bingo, despite its key role in building sales for the rising *Daily Star*, was considered a bad misjudgement. His ambition to edit the *Times* was an embarrassment. His acquiring of a knighthood, and insistence on its use, was scorned by Murdoch. His certainty that he was always right became unbearable for everyone around him. His expense account was legendary, and News International's managing director Bruce Matthews was fond of telling stories about one Connaught lunch bill in 1980 that totalled £350. He was also famous for asking his lunch guests when choosing wine: 'Would you like this bottle or would you prefer an experience?' The experience sometimes lasted well beyond normal lunch hours.

While Lamb continued to live high on the hog during his sabbatical, there was much speculation about his likely successor. Hardly anyone thought the editorship would go to Lamb's deputy, the former *Daily Mail* editor Arthur Brittenden, who soon let Murdoch know he didn't want the job. Murdoch promoted another possible contender, the kindly, cautious associate editor Peter Stephens, to the post of editorial director, asking him to do the job 'the way Tony Miles does at the *Mirror*'.[175] Stephens, a natural diplomat, was a good choice and rightly interpreted his role as keeping a light hand on the tiller while ensuring that the *Sun* and *News of the World* didn't hit the rocks. Stephens originally expected the *Sun* editorship to go to Nick Lloyd, then deputy editor of the *Sunday Mirror*. Having left the *Sun* in frustration at failing to win promotion Lloyd had many supporters among the staff. He and they were to be disappointed, though, because Murdoch preferred a man thought by many people who knew him to be the wildest of wild cards, a thirty-four-year-old with no public profile and barely known outside two Fleet Street offices. Enter Kelvin Calder MacKenzie.

The bare bones of MacKenzie's background gave little clue to his character. Born in 1946, he was the eldest son of journalist parents, Ian and Mary, whose other two sons, Craig and Drew, also became journalists. Kelvin was sent to a direct-grant grammar school, Alleyn's in Dulwich, south London, which later became a private school. He famously passed only one O level before leaving to work on a south London weekly. He had a spell as a reporter with Ferrari's news agency and then turned to subbing at the *Birmingham Mail*, doing well enough to win a place on the subs desk at the *Daily Express* in Fleet Street. He moved over to the *Sun* as a sub in 1973 and soon stood out from the crowd, not so much for his ability as for his cockiness and total disregard for authority. He was openly critical of some of his superiors, telling them what he thought of their 'pathetic' pages. Abrasive, foul-mouthed and funny, he made remarks about people to their faces that his colleagues only voiced behind their backs.

It didn't take long for editor Larry Lamb to hear about the impertinence of his new recruit and, while recognising that he was a good sub with leadership potential, he didn't appreciate his uncouth style. Nevertheless, MacKenzie was promoted through the ranks and by 1976 was assistant night editor. Lamb never did warm to him and two years later, when asked by Murdoch to suggest recruits for his *New York Post*, he was delighted to recommend his uppity junior executive. It was to prove a crucial step in MacKenzie's career because the *Post*'s editor, Roger Wood, a former *Daily Express* editor (see Chapter Seven), had enough confidence in his new managing editor to give him his head. MacKenzie thrived in the atmosphere of New York's racy tabloid wars.

The main advantage was that Murdoch spent a lot of his time in the *Post*'s shabby downtown office and could observe MacKenzie at close quarters. He was impressed with his attitude, his workaholic philosophy, his confrontational management approach and his broad-brush journalistic skills. MacKenzie often told me that the two years he spent in New York were among the most entertaining of his life. He liked the paper and the city, but his wife Jacqui, also a former reporter, didn't share his enthusiasm and worried over the future schooling of their three young children, pleading to return to Britain.

Much to Lamb's displeasure, Murdoch smoothed MacKenzie's path back to the *Sun* as night editor in 1980. But Lamb had no intention of allowing the troublesome MacKenzie to do as he wished with 'his' paper and the two men often clashed. In February 1981, MacKenzie left to join the *Daily Express* as its night editor and received a stinging letter of rebuke from Murdoch which virtually accused him of treachery. Unknown to MacKenzie it had been a bad moment to leave because Murdoch was already preparing to dispense with Lamb's services.

In spite of Murdoch's anger with MacKenzie he didn't hesitate to call him back from the *Express* by appointing him editor of the *Sun* in April 1981. (Murdoch's request to Nick Lloyd that he become MacKenzie's deputy was politely rebuffed.) Understandably, the *Express* management was appalled at losing MacKenzie after just two months and tried to hold him to contract. With typical swagger, MacKenzie responded by brazenly doing both jobs at once, organising *Express* pages from the night desk while shouting instructions down the phone to *Sun* executives. Full of self-confidence, he treated his *Express* colleagues to character readings laced with his boisterous humour. After losing a public dispute with MacKenzie over the content of a page, one executive tried to ease her embarrassment by saying: 'Well, at least you can give me an A for effort.' MacKenzie replied: 'No, I'll give you an F for fuck off.' *Express* editor Arthur Firth, who had a genuine affection for MacKenzie, laughed off his wayward behaviour, maybe recognising in him the qualities he lacked in himself. A senior executive, Felicity Green, who had experienced Hugh Cudlipp in full flow, was another admirer. She said: 'Kelvin was brilliant, just wonderful, obviously destined for stardom.'[176]

During this period I was working as features editor on the *Daily Star* one floor above the *Express* and I often heard people exclaim: 'Have you heard what MacKenzie said today?' I remember wondering if the man could be as extraordinary as the stories and it wasn't long before I found out. He called me and we met in the corridor outside the art editor's office. Would I rejoin the *Sun*, he asked, as an assistant editor in charge of features? There was one formality. I would need to have dinner with Murdoch and Peter Stephens the following evening. The reason for the meal at the Savoy soon became obvious because, apart from asking about the workings of the *Daily Star*, they were concerned about the likelihood of me leading a National Union of Journalists strike. I let them know it was unlikely and I was appointed.

MacKenzie and I both started at the *Sun* within a week of each other in June 1981 and it didn't take long to appreciate that I was working for a unique individual. Since I was a major source for the detailed portrait of MacKenzie drawn by Peter Chippindale and Chris Horrie in their excellent history of the *Sun*, I can hardly disagree with their reading of him.[177] However, it should be noted that at the time I briefed them I was editor of the *Daily Mirror*, and therefore MacKenzie's direct rival with a vested interest in accentuating his worst features, but I wouldn't take back a word I said to them. They rightly present MacKenzie as a workaholic, manic, abusive, obnoxious, socially gauche bully-cum-comedian with a singular talent for editing a populist tabloid. Many *Sun* journalists who suffered under the lash of his tongue – or were the constant butt of his jokes – would agree. I too endured an edgy and often uncomfortable relationship with him.

But MacKenzie could not have survived as editor and retained the loyalty of the majority of his staff without deploying considerable charm. He was straightforward in his dealings with his journalists because he was unable to hide his feelings. There was a complete absence of office politics during his editorship, with people soon realising it was impossible to suck up to MacKenzie. He believed perspiration was the springboard for inspiration and admired people more for their willingness to work hard than for their creative talents. His temper was offset by a self-deprecating sense of humour. He had many prejudices but he rarely held grudges. He invariably ended one of his legendary bollockings by saying that the matter was now over and would not be referred to again, a promise he always kept. He was far kinder and more understanding in private than in public.

MacKenzie enjoyed the best possible start at the *Sun* because Murdoch cut the cover price and introduced bingo just before his arrival. For reasons which aren't entirely clear, newspaper bingo caught the public imagination and the *Sun*'s circulation took off. News International's genial marketing manager Ron Bacchus was amazed by the response because he had pioneered bingo in the *News of the World* and *Sun* years before without attracting anything like the hysteria which greeted the game in 1981. It meant that without the least editorial initiative from MacKenzie, save the relentless blurbs hyping bingo, *Sun* sales went up from 3.5 million in April to 4.1 million in July. In fairness, MacKenzie never denied the part played by bingo in his early success.

His first tasks were to change the *Sun*'s culture – banning the tradition of regular drinking breaks and imposing a rigorous office discipline – and to appoint executives whom he considered more sympathetic to his way of running a paper, sweeping away people he distrusted. Among the first to go were sports editor Frank Nicklin, women's editor Jo Foley and chief sub David Montgomery. 'I'm not firing you,' Mackenzie told Monty. 'But you've got six weeks to find another job.' Unhappy with Arthur Brittenden as his deputy he replaced him, and Brittenden became the company's corporate relations director. MacKenzie relied heavily on two old hands, night editor Roy Pittila and news editor Tom Petrie, and was pleased that the leader writer, Ronnie Spark, shared his brand of right-wing politics and free-market economics. It wasn't until 1983 that he sacked political editor Walter Terry in favour of the urbane and sensible Trevor Kavanagh.

His most important early recruit was Wendy Henry, who was unhappy as features editor at *Woman* magazine and wrote to ask for a job at the *Sun*. She was initially hired to read books for potential serialisation but was soon running the features department, ostensibly as my deputy. Her portrayal in the Chippindale–Horrie book as a vulgar figure of fun was their only real unfairness because they fed off the prejudices, and hyperbole, of anonymous detractors. She did have a lisp, she did wear an ankle bracelet, she did dress in clothes bought from street markets. So what? Henry had warmth and a good sense of fun and was one of the very few people prepared to stand up to MacKenzie. Fiercely protective of the people who worked for her she often put her own job on the line in defending them, instinctively knowing when to shout back at MacKenzie, when to wheedle and when to walk away. He appreciated her forceful personality and the fact that, like him, she was intensely competitive. Henry was one of the few people who could argue with MacKenzie toe to toe without there being lasting rancour on either side.

It is no exaggeration, nor false modesty, for me to say that Henry's contribution to the MacKenzie *Sun* was far greater than mine. She came up with endless ideas for series, briefed writers carefully, could rewrite at speed and was prepared to work well into the night. Her husband, a *Daily Mail* reporter, understood the Fleet Street tabloid work ethic. She had a huge interest in celebrities and television soaps, immediately latching on to the success of BBC's *EastEnders* at its launch in February 1985. The programme was to figure in scores of *Sun* features and news stories.[178]

The controversy generated by MacKenzie within the Bouverie Street building was mild compared to the controversy triggered by his newspaper's reactionary political propaganda. His coverage of the Falklands war, the miners' strike and the royal family's affairs was considered provocative (see next chapter). He was accused of chauvinism for his response to the January 1984 campaign by French farmers to reduce imports of British lamb with a headline, 'Hop Off You Frogs', which became a slogan on badges sold by the *Sun*. He followed this with a spoof 'raid' on Calais and the publication of anti-French jokes. These kinds of stunts outraged liberal opinion but MacKenzie and Murdoch answered by pointing to the circulation figures, which remained well above 4 million, reaching a peak of 4.27 million in September 1985. Ever increasing bingo prizes, rising to £1 million after Robert Maxwell took over the *Daily Mirror*, helped. But other papers had bingo too, and none prospered as well as the *Sun*. MacKenzie's brand of populist journalism, with its consistent praise of Margaret Thatcher and insistent anti-union message, alongside a diet of celebrity revelations and irreverent humour caught the public imagination.

There was little celebration inside the *Sun* because of continual union disputes, euphemistically known as 'production problems'. Members of the paper's National Union of Journalists (NUJ) chapel, which accounted for 98 per cent of the editorial staff, also showed a militant streak by striking first during the Falklands war (see next chapter) and again in July 1984 after demanding a £3,000 a year rise in line with an increase granted to the print unions. It would be wrong to think Murdoch couldn't afford to give his journalists a healthy rise: the *Sun* made £23 million in 1984, by far the largest profit in Fleet Street.[179] My sympathies were firmly with the NUJ in the second dispute and, after a day's hesitation, I decided to join the strikers. Managing editor Ken Donlan told MacKenzie: 'He has reverted to type. Once a communist always a communist!'

The strike was a failure. Only two issues of the *Sun* were lost, partly because of a bizarre agreement beween the NUJ chapel and the print unions which allowed them to continue working as long as they didn't handle 'scab material'. But they cheerfully did so and angered NUJ pickets by smiling and making irreverent remarks as they crossed the picket lines. A handful of senior executives who worked on with MacKenzie, aided by people 'holed up in the Waldorf Hotel', were therefore able to publish the paper.[180] After just over a week, with NUJ morale crushed and bad blood between pickets and printers, the journalists were forced to return to work. No one at the time could have predicted the awesome consequences of this split. I should also point out that I suffered no recriminations from MacKenzie for my actions.

Although Murdoch was delighted with his *Sun* editor, he had little to celebrate at the *News of the World*. Predictably dismayed by the dull performance of Ken Donlan, who oversaw a sudden sales plunge, he moved him to an unspecified executive role at the *Sun* in April 1981. He then astounded Fleet Street by appointing the editor of a regional evening title without a shred of national paper experience to the *NoW* editorship.[181] The Barry Askew interlude was to prove one of the most entertaining chapters in the paper's colourful history.

Askew had been editor of the *Lancashire Evening Post* in Preston for fourteen years, during which time he had won several awards for his campaigning journalism. It was rumoured that Askew had been drawn to Murdoch's attention by *Sunday Times* editor Harry Evans, but Evans recalled warning Murdoch that Askew was 'a vigorous and tough editor who might be overly aggressive'.[182] Murdoch was not a man to worry about an editor's aggression and, on paper, Askew's record looked impressive. He had entered journalism as a sixteen-year-old, edited a local weekly by the time he was twenty-five, held senior executive posts on the two Sheffield dailies before becoming editor of the *Lancashire Evening Post* at thirty-two. His handling of his paper's more controversial exclusives, such as exposing a chief constable for fiddling his expenses and revealing inadequate conditions at a major hospital, were in the very best traditions of investigative journalism in the public interest.[183]

What happened to Askew on the journey from Preston to Fleet Street has never been explained. From the beginning he behaved in the oddest fashion. Despite spending barely seven months in the job, he managed to win a memorable nickname, 'The Beast of Bouverie Street', for his outrageous misbehaviour. He upset his staff, including one senior executive married to a black woman who struck him after he had made a distasteful racist and sexist remark. He allowed a documentary team to make a fly-on-the-wall TV film about the *NoW* which left the paper looking like a parody of itself: one scene, of a photographer hiding in telephone repair man's tent, was pure Marx Brothers. He also formed too close a friendship with Sonia Sutcliffe, wife of the Yorkshire Ripper, inviting her into the office and promising her secret payments which Murdoch rightly refused to honour. Undoubtedly, some of Askew's problems stemmed from drink, but in journalistic terms he was obviously out of his depth. That he should have been appointed at all illustrates Murdoch's shortcomings in his dealings with the *News of the World*.

Ironically, Askew's sales record looked very good: the paper's decline was reversed for the first time since the era of Stafford Somerfield. But it had nothing to do with Askew. Murdoch had followed the trend set by the Sunday broadsheets by launching a glossy colour magazine in September 1981. He hired Peter Jackson, the experienced *TV Times* editor, to produce the supplement, called Sunday, gave it plenty of resources and promoted it on television. Readers liked the content, which was initially rather up-market, and by the time Askew was fired at the end of 1981 sales were rising by the week. In a pithy comment on his departure, the trade magazine noted that Askew's resignation was 'as expected as his appointment has been unexpected'.[184]

Askew's successor was yet another surprise. When Murdoch called Derek Jameson to ask him to take the *NoW* chair he had been out of papers for almost a year since leaving the *Daily Star* after his disagreement with Lord Matthews. He wasn't really expecting another Fleet Street editorship after his time at the *Star* and the *Daily Express*. His career had been spent in tabloids and Murdoch, by stubbornly refusing to change the format of the broadsheet *NoW*, robbed himself of Jameson's greatest strength, his ability to project tabloid pages. Murdoch was also renowned for disliking editors who enjoyed centre stage, and Jameson was just beginning to emerge as the first Fleet Street character to become a successful TV and radio celebrity.

Jameson's brief from Murdoch was 'more revelation, more investigation, more sensation'.[185] This was hardly a new formula, but it required effort, luck and flair, which were sadly lacking in Jameson's years at the helm. The other big problem for the *News of the World*, and its rivals, was the way in which the *Sun* had usurped their territory. MacKenzie's sensation-packed *Sun*, with its sexy series and no-holds-barred revelations, was just the kind of scandalous journalism which had previously been the preserve of the mass-market Sundays.

The circulation increase generated by the magazine launch turned out to be a momentary blip and *NoW* sales were edging down close to 4 million in 1984 when Murdoch took two key decisions: the paper must, at last, become a tabloid and Jameson, Mr Tabloid, must go. Why he was fired, Jameson wrote years later, 'is still a mystery'.[186] It wasn't much of a secret among senior *NoW* staff, who thought him indecisive despite his braggadocio. Murdoch, who genuinely liked Jameson, laughing along with everyone else at his storytelling, thought him more suited to broadcasting. Junor agreed, claiming that the sacking enabled Jameson to find his true vocation 'as a proper full-time comedian'.[187]

Having snubbed Nick Lloyd so many times in the past, Murdoch finally called on the man who had impressed him many years before at the *Sun*. By now Lloyd was editor of the *Sunday People* but he was delighted to rejoin Murdoch. So, in May 1984, some seven years after a previous editor, Bernard Shrimsley, had pushed for it, the *News of the World* became a red-top tabloid, starting off with a front-page kiss-and-tell story of a model's affair with Prince Andrew.[188] Lloyd maintained a run of similar revelations and sales took off in dramatic fashion, reversing a fifteen-year decline, and Murdoch's regard for Lloyd rose in tandem with the circulation graph.

Murdoch's spontaneous enthusiasms for people often led to sudden promotion. He was so taken with Lloyd's rapid success that a year after giving him the editorship he saw him as a candidate for yet higher management office. He asked him to stand down, supposedly temporarily, to take a course at Harvard Business School. Lloyd, having brought David Montgomery with him from the *People* as his assistant editor, nominated Monty as his stand-in. Montgomery's elevation meant that within the space of five years the *News of the World* had been edited by five different men. Not once had Murdoch considered promoting Phil Wrack, loyal deputy editor to each of his choices. Montgomery was fortunate in taking over a paper that was on an upward sales curve but no one can deny that, of all the editors in that period, he was the most technically proficient, the most confident and the most fearless. The *NoW*'s official historians noted that staff found him 'cold and aloof', but the papers he produced were vibrant and readable.[189] Building on Lloyd's successful formula, he was prepared to take risks in publishing intrusive material about the private lives of celebrities.

A slight, shy Protestant from Northern Ireland, Montgomery was thirty-seven when he became editor. From the moment he left Belfast's Queen's University, he had been dedicated to making it to the top in journalism, ignoring the taunts of colleagues who thought him too overtly ambitious. He joined the Mirror group training scheme for graduates in Plymouth and at the end of his studies won a placement as a sub-editor on the *Daily Mirror* in Manchester. It was considered bad form among the largely cynical subs to show undue enthusiasm for advancement, and Montgomery's willingness to go the extra mile, plus his assiduous courting of the northern editor, Derek Jameson, earned him the nickname of 'the Cabin Boy'.

When he moved to the London office in the mid-1970s, like many daily paper subs he did extra shifts at the *Sunday Mirror*, where I also worked. Although we disagreed over union matters, with him often refusing to attend the disruptive meetings I organised, I found him an engaging and intelligent man. Apparently happy to be an outsider, he was disliked by many *Mirror* subs, especially from 1978 onwards when he gained his first promotion. He joined the *Sun* as chief sub in 1980 and then, as we saw above, fell foul of MacKenzie's purge a year later.

It proved to be the making of Montgomery. His production skills had previously impressed Nick Lloyd when they worked together at the *Sunday Mirror* and he gratefully accepted an assistant editorship from Lloyd at the *Sunday People*. He became the paper's main architect and hoped for advancement when Lloyd quit to edit the *News of the World*. He didn't get it and so followed Lloyd once more to the *NoW*, again as his assistant. When he was made acting editor of the *NoW* all of us at the *Sun* were struck by the irony of Montgomery having an equal status in Bouverie Street with MacKenzie, the man who had treated him so harshly just three years before. MacKenzie, whose brother Craig was a junior executive on the *NoW*, was soon regaling everyone with the story of Montgomery's new nickname. His staff, who thought him overly critical of their efforts, called him 'Rommel', said a gleeful MacKenzie, 'because Monty was on our side'. Personality differences apart, Montgomery was in many ways as ruthlessly efficient at fulfilling his paper's brief as MacKenzie was his.

The *Guardian*'s 'humiliating ordeal'

Successful editors, naturally enough, tend to hold their jobs the longest. The longer they last the greater the number of difficult decisions they are likely to take. The more they take, the greater the chance of making a mistake, regardless of how careful and thoughtful they may be. So it was with the *Guardian*'s Peter Preston in 1983 when he suffered, along with his staff and his paper, a 'most humiliating ordeal'.[190]

The sad saga began when photocopies of two confidential government documents were left anonymously at the *Guardian*'s reception desk. These revealed the date that Cruise missiles, carrying nuclear warheads, would arrive at the US base at Greenham Common, near Newbury in Berkshire, and the Ministry of Defence's plans to handle anticipated protests. By far the most politically sensitive revelation in one of the documents, a memo from defence minister Michael Heseltine to prime minister Margaret Thatcher, was that the government intended to evade parliamentary questions about the arrival of the missiles. Sarah Tisdall, a twenty-three-year-old Foreign Office clerk who thought the evasion 'immoral', photocopied that memo and a further document, placed them in an envelope addressed to the *Guardian*'s political editor and handed it to the commissionaire at the paper's Farringdon Road office on the evening of 21 October 1983.

She later explained that she chose the *Guardian* because there was 'nowhere else to take it' given that the *Times* and the *Daily Telegraph* were 'quite right wing'.[191] Though she wasn't a political activist, she acted partly out of disenchantment with the government in the belief that it was about to engage in a serious deception. She was sure that senior *Guardian* journalists would see the matter in the same light. Tisdall was also aware that a CND demonstration against the siting of the missiles was due the day after she dropped off the documents and later admitted she was aiming to achieve maximum impact with her whistle-blowing.[192] Just as she anticipated, the *Guardian* shared her view about the government's failure to make itself accountable to parliament, so defence correspondent David Fairhall wrote a story based on the documents.[193] The government announced a routine inquiry into the leak but ministers were unaware that the paper had been given a copy of the Heseltine minute until editor Peter Preston decided to publish the full text ten days later.[194] Now it was impossible for the government to ignore the fact that someone in Whitehall had been responsible for a severe breach of ethics, rather than a spot of loose talk, and it demanded that the *Guardian* return the document.

In its first exchange with the Treasury solicitor the paper adopted the customary Fleet Street stance: the source must be protected and there was no question of complying with the demand. The document clearly had markings which might identity the leaker and 'in accordance with time-honoured convention of journalism' it could not hand over the unadulterated document. But, accepting the advice of the paper's lawyers, Preston added a promise that the document would be 'preserved intact'.[195] The government immediately sued for its return, winning the high court case and the appeal, and after 'a paroxysm of regrets' Preston handed over the document in mid-December.[196]

With the document in their hands Whitehall investigators quickly identified the photocopier Tisdall had used and the inquiry was then turned over to the police. Everyone in the Foreign Office with access to the copier was fingerprinted and Tisdall underwent a rigorous interview at Scotland Yard. Though she didn't admit her guilt she turned herself in the next day and was charged with breaching the Official Secrets Act. After pleading guilty she was sentenced to jail for six months.

Many *Guardian* staff were outraged at their paper having been responsible for the imprisonment of a young woman who had acted out of conscience for the public good. Tisdall told the BBC that the paper should have protected her identity, that she didn't think the editor should have handed back the document and that he should have been broken the law by destroying it.[197] Preston did regret hanging on to the document but, having confirmed that he had it 'intact', his lawyers had explained that if he had disobeyed the court the *Guardian* could have been punished with a heavy fine for contempt. The court could then have continued fining the paper until it ran out of money. There was a further problem too, involving the *Guardian*'s stance during the dispute between Eddy Shah and the print unions. The paper had said unequivocally that the unions must uphold the law: it couldn't say one thing and do another.

That explanation didn't prevent Preston suffering from a wave of criticism, including 'voluminous hate-mail', bitter condemnation from the National Union of Journalists and a savage *Granta* article.[198] *Guardian* columnist James Cameron said his paper had 'made a mess of it', but he also blamed the judge and the government. Many *Guardian* staff were much more angry about the affair and a cloud hung over Preston ever after. Fifteen years after Tisdall's jailing another *Guardian* columnist, Paul Foot, referred to his paper's conduct as 'an outrage'.[199] Tisdall served more than three months in prison, where she received many hundreds of letters of support from *Guardian* readers.

Yet, paradoxically, 1980–5 saw the *Guardian*'s sales take off, rising from 375,000 to virtually 500,000, staying ahead of the *Times.* It is difficult to be certain just why the *Guardian* should have done so well, given that there was only a very slight rise in the overall broadsheet market. Some of Preston's editorial initiatives, making the paper more accessible to a wider range of readers, played a part. One notable addition in April 1984 was the launching of a specialist media page under Peter Fiddick, the first of its kind and an acknowledgement of the increasing interest in, and importance of, the expanding media. It should be noted though that editorial were following a path laid by advertising: five years before, the group's innovative advertisement sales director Caroline Marland had sought media classified advertising as part of her development of the job-ads market.[200]

The key to Preston's success stemmed in part from his subtle adoption and adaptation of tabloid techniques. He realised the importance of 'selling' stories, the virtues of brevity and the benefits of being proactive in both news-gathering and features selection. Some of his female staff thought him a little too willing to use illustrations of women, but Preston never allowed his enthusiasm for populist journalism to mar the seriousness of his paper.

Life was altogether more difficult for the owners and managers of the *Financial Times.* Chairman Alan Hare hoped to introduce computerised typesetting to the *FT* by 1984, but the paper was continually hampered by the unions during the complex negotiations. Venting his frustration, Hare said at the end of 1982: 'The Fleet Street work-force is overpaid, over large and protected by restrictive practices. Our outdated technology is the laughing stock of the rest of the world.'[201] In the following summer a dispute between two print unions led to a strike which took the *FT* off the streets for ten weeks. It had long rankled with Sogat 82 machine assistants that they were paid less than NGA machine-minders. When the Hare's managers reached an agreement with the assistants, the 24 NGA minders – only a third of whom were full-time staff – viewed it as a betrayal and demanded to be paid £330 a week. Management, anxious not to start a new round of leapfrogging, refused to bargain, so the minders stopped the presses. Their

NGA composing-room colleagues walked out in sympathy and the union then instructed all its *FT* members to strike.

In a daring bid to crush the NGA, Hare offered Sogat 82 a single-union deal in a new computerised workplace, but its leaders were aware that if they accepted the offer they would face hostility from the other unions. Hare also explored a non-union option, holding talks with T. Bailey Foreman, the Nottingham firm which had faced down the unions in the 1970s and made history by introducing new technology. Managing director Christopher Pole-Carew agreed to print the *FT* but management wouldn't take the risk. Frank Barlow, the *FT* chief executive appointed in 1983, was wisely sceptical about Pole-Carew's capabilities.[202]

Barlow, then fifty-three, was recognised as a tough operator. He had spent most of his career as a newspaper manager, having originally trained as an accountant. He started with IPC in West Africa and the West Indies before joining its London headquarters. He had overall responsibility for setting up the *Irish Daily Mirror* and *Sunday Mirror*, the first national papers to use facsimile transmission and web-offset printing. He left for Westminster Press, the regional paper group owned by Pearson, and became its general manager in 1976. His aggression and determination were key factors in transforming the fortunes of the *FT*. But Barlow was the future, and there was little the *FT*'s management could do in the interim but settle with their strikers as they watched losses rising towards £10 million. The *Daily Telegraph* dared to poke fun at the *FT* for its poor handling of the dispute, claiming that its managers had provoked the NGA, which it referred to as 'the elite of the printing unions'.[203] Given its own acute industrial problems, this attempt to curry favour with its own militant NGA members by criticising another owner's dealings with them was unforgivable. The *FT* finally returned to the streets on 9 August 1983, but it was forced to raise its cover price by 5p to 35p and its profits the following year were way behind those of the *Sun*.

Barlow's hand was strengthened the following year by the retirement of Alan Hare as chairman and his replacement by his son-in-law, Lord Blakenham, who reverted to the former hands-off tradition and let his chief executive run the business. In March 1984, Barlow shrewdly recruited David Palmer, then the paper's deputy editor, as general manager. Barlow played a canny game, avoiding conflict with the unions in order to get the paper back on a profitable path by shelving the introduction of new technology. Screens did arrive, so that journalists in London and Frankfurt could communicate via a system nicknamed Edwin, but there was no question of using them for inputting copy.

Even so, there were clashes. In autumn 1984, the *FT* lost 2.3. million copies and some £3.2 million through what Barlow called 'nihilistic and destructive industrial action'.[204] In October 1985, after the *FT* had lost half its press run one night, it obtained an injunction against a chapel official and issued writs for damages against eighteen machine-minders. Production went relatively smoothly afterwards.[205] Industrial conflict didn't affect the paper's growing sales success, nor its increasing advertising revenue. In 1985, it made a record £12,036,000 profit, a 14 per cent margin, though that achievement needs to put in perspective by comparing it with the fact that the *Wall Street Journal*'s profits were higher than the *FT*'s total revenue. Despite the production difficulties, the editorial department was a haven of relative calm, mainly due to the influence of editor Geoffrey Owen.

He did his best to heal internal wounds with reason and humour, a fact recognised by the paper's historian who noted that Owen 'commanded more than any of the post-war editors the respect and affection of his staff'.[206] After Palmer's move into management, Owen appointed the talented Richard Lambert as his deputy. They then pioneered the introduction in February 1984 of the component that was to make the *FT* synonymous with the stock market, the equities index that was to become known as the Footsie 100. That came just a month after the paper was named as newspaper of the year in the *What the Papers Say* awards, prompting the left-wing TV producer Gus MacDonald to remark that the *FT* represented 'the entirely acceptable face of capitalism'.[207]

Ironically, the left were among the most enthusiastic buyers of the *FT*. I always urged my political friends to read it because it published much more objective reports of industrial disputes than any other title. Ex-Labour MP Philip Whitehead summed it up after the 1984–5 miners' strike:

> I believe the *FT* to be a first-class paper . . . It gives more coverage to both sides of industry and their failings than any other paper, and can be unsparing with the faults of management. Since it is concerned with the health of capitalism this is not surprising. The kind of reader who buys the *FT* needs to know about lousy management. He also needs to know the real picture in industrial relations, not the kind of wild and unrealistic optimism which marks out the Rothermere and Murdoch papers.[208]

A new world around the corner

Fleet Street was being left behind. Reuters and the Stock Exchange were using electronic transmission. Advertisers, who were producing their copy in cold type, were loath to go on supplying hot-metal plates. So-called new technology was being used in hundreds of regional papers and, by 1985, three provincial groups had even secured agreements for direct input by journalists. Important as these factors were, they paled beside the momentous announcement on 25 February 1985 by Eddy Shah that he planned to launch a non-union national newspaper using the latest printing technology.

Shah had sprung to fame just a couple of years before, as a hero to owners, editors and the Tory government, and as a villain to print trade unionists. He was the first newspaper owner to face down the NGA by winning a crucial and bloody industrial dispute. Although he had a somewhat exotic background, being fourth cousin of the Aga Khan, he was very much a self-made man, an entrepreneur who liked to live and work by his own rules. He was born in Cambridge in 1944, his mother English and his father a Persian–Indian who was, in succession, medical student, journalist and lawyer, eventually becoming an expert on international maritime law.

Shah was educated at Gordonstoun and various Sussex schools, running away from home after an argument with his mother to do odd jobs as a stagehand and floor manager at the BBC and Granada studios in Manchester, where he met his actress wife, Jennifer. He then sold advertising for a Manchester freesheet before selling his house to raise money to launch a local free paper of his own. Starting with one title in the Cheshire commuter belt in 1974, he built up a whole string of frees, the Warrington *Messenger* series, and made a great deal of money. He was generally well liked by his employees but when he decided in 1983 to introduce computer typesetting and use non-union labour at his print plant in Warrington, the NGA objected. Shah allowed the union the chance to recruit his non-union staff, but they all rejected the offer to join. The NGA then ordered its eight members at Shah's Stockport works to strike. Six did so, Shah dismissed them, and the situation turned ugly. From the end of October the NGA picketed his plant.

At the time, the only person to understand the significance of the dispute was David Goodhart, the *Financial Times*'s labour reporter.[209] He realised that the NGA was vulnerable for the first time in its post-war history because of two new employment laws enacted by Mrs Thatcher's government. One restricted picketing to a person's place of work while the other outlawed secondary action, such as blacking and sympathy strikes. Employers were allowed to sue unions for damages if they broke those laws. When Shah applied for an injunction against the NGA, Goodhart discerned that here was a man who might just win an historic victory.

The NGA tried to use its industrial muscle at national papers to force owners to persuade Shah to relent. London editions of the nationals were not printed for two days in November as pickets sought to prevent publication of Shah's papers in Stockport. But the union found itself outside the law and was threatened with having its £11 million assets seized. The following week Shah made it clear he would go on printing his papers regardless of pickets blockading his plant and the stage was set for a violent confrontation. Some 2,000 union activists and NGA supporters massed outside his plant, blocking the exit. Shah, buoyed by a sympathetic article and editorial in the *Sunday Times* earlier in the month, called editor Andrew Neil for help. Neil immediately contacted home secretary Leon Brittan, urging him to act, and, when he refused, Neil threatened to publish their tape-recorded conversation in the *Sunday Times.*[210] The police were later reinforced and when they went into action Goodhart reported that 'there were excesses on both sides'.[211] But the battle ended with Shah's vans driving through the pickets, and he later won hundreds of thousands of pounds in compensation from the NGA.

It wasn't until February 1984 that Shah finally met Neil. During their conversation in the Savoy tearoom, Neil asked whether he had thought of pulling off the same trick by launching a national paper.[212] By the following month, Shah was already planning the project, but it took him almost a year to win the necessary financial backing. He raised £18 million from investors who accepted a wildly optimistic forecast of profits, expecting the paper to make £20–30 million in the first year and be floated with a capital value of £200 million within three years.[213]

Once Shah announced his national-paper intentions, the other proprietors made encouraging noises in public. Their support was understandable: they agreed wholeheartedly with his anti-union stance and, at a practical level, they thought it might help them to negotiate new manning levels with their rebellious print unions. But it also put the owners under pressure. Could this provincial interloper be about to beat them at their own game? Shah, lionised until now by proprietors, was about to learn the brutal truth of Fleet Street's jungle: no one gets an even break.

Various owners accelerated important strategic decisions. Associated, fearing a threat to its *Mail* titles, started to build a new printing complex in Surrey Docks four years ahead of schedule. Hartwell's managers pressed forward with the *Telegraph*'s docklands printing plant. Maxwell pushed his colour press manufacturer – which was also making presses for Shah's forthcoming paper *Today* – to supply new machines to Mirror group a year ahead of the original date. It was also in the closing weeks of 1985 that Maxwell negotiated his redundancy programme (see above, p. 402).

Meanwhile, Shah's habit of boasting that he knew better than everyone else, be they owners, editors, journalists or printers, didn't endear him to the wider newspaper community. 'We're going after an industry that's just ripe to be taken,' he said. 'It needs just one guy.'[214] He displayed an entrepreneurial contempt for organised labour; a northerner's loathing of London; an outsider's distrust of journalism, and an amateur's scorn for professionalism. These characteristics, along with his drive, his determination and even his restlessness could have made him a formidable competitor. But it gradually dawned on other owners, especially Murdoch, that though he might be useful he was never going to be a big player.

Shah's vision of a newspaper without print unions also took root in the mind of the disenchanted City editor of the *Daily Telegraph*, Andreas Whittam Smith. As we have seen, he was miffed when Hartwell rejected his idea of raising money for the *Telegraph* by offering shares to readers. In February 1985, a *Business Week* reporter rang Whittam Smith to ask whether he thought Shah's paper would work. 'No,' he replied. But he changed his mind almost as soon as he had said it and next day called Shah to arrange a meeting.[215] Within a month, Whittam Smith was wondering if, without unions and with new technology, he could he do the same as Shah, only better. Over the following months he convinced himself that there was a gap in the market, believing that an audience existed for a paper aimed somewhere between the tabloid and broadsheet agendas which, oddly, might compete with the *Telegraph*. It would also have plenty of colour pictures. This vague concept had similarities to the aspirations of Brian MacArthur, the editor Shah had chosen for *Today*.

Whittam Smith was an unlikely newspaper entrepreneur. He 'looked like an old-fashioned bishop, or possibly archdeacon' and was, in fact, son of a canon.[216] Tall, aloof, quietly spoken, Andreas – named after a village in the Isle of Man – had a thin, enigmatic smile which often gave him the appearance of an indulgent university tutor dealing with a set of dull students. Educated at Birkenhead and Oxford, he spent his first two years after university at Rothschild's merchant bank. He then went into financial journalism and moved upwards on a variety of magazines and papers, becoming the *Telegraph*'s City editor in 1977.

He was forty-eight by the time he set out on his great venture, first enthusing two younger colleagues who had been at Oxford together: Matthew Symonds, thirty-one, the *Telegraph*'s economics leader writer, and Stephen Glover, thirty-two, a writer of leaders and features. Symonds was the son of former *Daily Herald* editor and Mirror group political adviser John Beavan (Lord Ardwick). Schooled at fashionable Holland Park and Oxford, he went through the *Mirror*'s graduate training scheme before joining the *Financial Times*'s syndication department. It was Glover who had helped him on to the *Telegraph* four years before. Glover, the son of a clergyman, was a product of Shrewsbury and Oxford, who stepped straight from university in 1978 on to the *Daily Telegraph*, as a leader writer and then parliamentary sketchwriter. Like many of the writing staff, he had grown frustrated by the stultifying atmosphere at the paper and, after initial scepticism, grew more and more enthusiastic about the paper the trio initially referred to as the *Nation*.

A fourth key player was Douglas Long, the former Mirror group deputy chairman and chief executive, brought on board by Symonds who knew him through his father. He not only helped with the business plan but, once they set out to raise money, lent the team and its project credibility. Over the following months, without a word leaking to their *Telegraph* colleagues, they managed to sort out printing and distribution arrangements, selected a computer system and found an office in City Road, near Moorgate. They also raised £2 million of seed capital, estimating that they would need a further £16 million.

More than seven months after their first meeting, the story finally leaked to the *Financial Times*, 'New Quality Daily Planned'.[217] It named the

Telegraph trio and they immediately resigned, proclaiming a wish to launch their new paper in October 1986. Hardly anyone on Fleet Street really believed this naive group of nonentities stood a chance. All eyes were on Murdoch, the most far-sighted owner of them all. When he announced that he was launching a new evening paper, the *London Post*, most commentators were baffled. Some did see it as a smokescreen. Most believed it was a dream. When the ebullient NUJ general secretary, Harry Conroy, was told that the *Post* would be launched on St Patrick's Day, he asked: 'Who's going to produce it? Leprechauns?'[218] That joke was to ring hollow within a few months.

16. GOTCHA! THE RIPPER, HITLER AND A FAIRYTALE WEDDING

Tabloids are small papers for people with small minds.[1]

For six years from 1975 the press grew ever more excited by a series of murders of young women in various Yorkshire towns and cities. When a pattern emerged the mysterious serial killer was dubbed the Yorkshire Ripper and papers closely monitored a police investigation which was diverted by hoaxes and hampered by some hamfisted detective work. Finally, on 2 January 1981 a man was arrested and, in the words of the attorney-general, Sir Michael Havers, 'the media (with honourable exceptions) lost their heads'.[2]

Four papers named the man, Peter Sutcliffe, before he had been charged. Two even published his picture. Most papers devoted considerable space to details of the thirteen murders and seven attempted murders. 'All newspapers', admitted the *Daily Star*'s deputy editor Ray Mills, 'stretched the strict letter of the law almost to breaking point.'[3] After Sutcliffe was charged and made his first court appearance, papers published quotes by a woman he allegedly attacked and by the woman who was found in his car at the time of his arrest, despite the likelihood of them being witnesses at his trial.

Five days after Sutcliffe's arrest, with questions being asked in the Commons about his trial being prejudiced, the Press Council announced that it would hold an inquiry. At the time, its main concern was the outbreak of 'lynch mob journalism', though this was largely a legal matter since the central point was whether papers were guilty of contempt of court. But in the following months leading up to Sutcliffe's trial which ended in May 1981 two other disturbing ethical issues came to light: the use of chequebook journalism and harassment. Under the chairmanship of Patrick Neill QC, the Press Council did not publish its 198-page, 70,000-word report until February 1983. Its findings didn't receive as much publicity as they should have done, perhaps because it was so long after the event, more likely because it revealed widespread malpractice by so many papers. The report's contents were explosive, exposing several editors as liars and hypocrites.

Criticism of the possible prejudice to Sutcliffe's trial was muted by the attorney-general's decision not to prosecute papers for contempt. What was truly riveting was the section devoted to attempts by editors to pay members of Sutcliffe's family, friends and assorted trial witnesses for exclusive interviews. Some of their activities blatantly contravened the Press Council's declaration of principle in November 1966, which had been agreed with national paper editors, prohibiting offers of payment to witnesses and interviewing them before a trial (see Chapter Ten).

In 1970, following the *Sun*'s publication of the memoirs of train robber Ronnie Biggs, the Council supposedly 'broadened its interpretation' of the declaration. The *Sun* had defended using the chequebook because the money was paid into a trust fund for Biggs's children, not to Biggs himself. The Council didn't like that defence, arguing that payments should not 'enrich' the 'dependents and friends' of criminals. Yet it didn't change the wording of the declaration specifically to exclude payments to members of a convicted person's family or associates. So offers of payments to Sutcliffe's wife, father, brothers and a variety of acquaintances were not, strictly speaking, in breach of the declaration as long as the people concerned were not going to be witnesses. This offered some editors a loophole they couldn't resist. They had made offers of payment, they said, under the mistaken impression that the person was not to be a witness. This was especially true of their dealings with Sutcliffe's wife, Sonia.

In the case of *Daily Star* editor Lloyd Turner's payment of £4,000 to Olivia Reivers this defence was plainly humbug. Ms Reivers was the woman sitting next to Sutcliffe when he was arrested and there was every chance of her being called. The *Star*'s second line of defence – that, even if she did appear, she would not be an 'important witness' – was beside the point. The payment of any witness was prohibited and it wasn't for a newspaper to decide on the person's relative importance. The *Star* also refused to produce its contract with Ms Reivers, claiming it would be a breach of confidence, and earned a rebuke from the Council for concealing evidence. Unsurprisingly, it was censured. A *Daily Mail* reporter offered Ms Reivers £5,000, passing a note to her during a police press conference, and the Press Council duly condemned that approach. The *Sun* was also censured for paying another witness £700 for his diary and photographs.

Most of the controversial approaches were made to Mrs Sutcliffe, and it was she who revealed the editors' duplicity by sending the Press Council the various handwritten notes pushed through her parents' letterbox and the more formal offers sent to her solicitor. The problem for papers was that she didn't release the material until after they had made their initial responses to the Council's inquiries. Several of them had been less than honest in their replies and were caught out by Mrs Sutcliffe's documentary evidence.

Daily Express editor Arthur Firth told the Council in June 1981 that 'no money was offered' to Mrs Sutcliffe by his paper. Ten months later the Council sent Firth copies of four letters: the first was a joint offer by reporters from the *Daily Mail* and *Daily Express* offering Mrs Sutcliffe £50,000; the second was a specific offer of £80,000 by *Express* reporter Alan Rees; the third was a letter from the *Express* deputy news editor pointing out that Rees's note 'does not represent our final offer'; and the fourth was a letter 'dictated by Arthur Firth' which assured Mrs Sutcliffe that his 'highly professional staff' would deal with 'the delicacy' of her interview in a sympathetic fashion. It took Firth five weeks to comment on the dichotomy and he made a classic reply. 'When I wrote to the Press Council . . . I had forgotten that during the first 48 hours after the story broke we had been considering offering money . . .' The Council was not impressed, finding 'such a lapse of memory astonishing', censuring the paper, and deploring 'the attempt it made to mislead the Council'.[4]

The *News of the World*'s on–off relationship with Mrs Sutcliffe was bizarre. The first letter to her by *NoW* editor Ken Donlan said his paper was willing to pay 'a substantial fee' for exclusive rights to her story. Then he wrote later the same day withdrawing from negotiations. A couple of months after that, Donlan having been replaced as editor by Barry Askew, the *News of the World* contacted Mrs Sutcliffe again through one of its principal feature writers, Rosalie Shann. She was described in a follow-up letter from the *NoW*'s northern editor as 'one of the most caring and compassionate writers in journalism'.[5] Askew then visited Mrs Sutcliffe at her home and his assistant editor, Stuart Kuttner, wrote immediately afterwards offering a fee of 'not less than £110,000' for Mrs Sutcliffe's story and promised her 'a seat at the Editor's Desk'.[6] He also offered 'help and support' to Sonia and her parents, including 'private accommodation, travel and other logistics'.

In a remarkable submission to the Council inquiry, the *NoW*'s legal manager, Henry Russell Douglas, attacked Mrs Sutcliffe for releasing letters he considered confidential and therefore refused to enter into any correspondence with the Council about their contents. The Council rapped the *NoW* for its 'lack of candour'.[7] It did not point out that Russell Douglas was a former Press Council member.

The *Daily Mail* was reported in *Private Eye* to be 'leading in the squalid race to "tie up" the Sutcliffe family' and alleged to have made a deal with Sonia Sutcliffe for £250,000.[8] The first part of the story was correct: the *Mail* was trying to sign up members of the Sutcliffe family, including his wife. The second part, about a deal having been agreed, and therefore the amount, was wrong. Neither Sonia nor the *Mail* complained about *Private Eye* at the time, but the story did prompt the parents of Sutcliffe's final victim, Jacqueline Hill, to write to the *Mail*'s editor, David English, to ask whether he was preparing to pay 'blood money'. The *Mail*'s managing editor Alwyn Robinson replied to the Hills that 'not a penny, let alone £250,000, had been or would be paid to Mrs Sutcliffe'. He did concede that another claim in the story, that some members of the Sutcliffe family – his father and two sisters – had been put up in a hotel, was correct.[9] The Hills decided to complain to the Press Council. David English hit back with a two-page denial in his paper under the headline: 'The anatomy of a festering lie!'[10] This blustering article, which made much of the fact that the *Mail* had not agreed to pay any money to Sonia Sutcliffe, concealed more than it revealed. It conceded that Sutcliffe's father and three of his daughters would receive £5,000 for photographs and interviews at the end of the trial. English glossed over the *Mail*'s offers of money to Mrs Sutcliffe by claiming that within four days of Sutcliffe's arrest he had decided that no money should be paid to his wife because *Mail* readers would be 'deeply offended'.[11] Yet, despite the likelihood of causing such offence, in his evidence to the Press Council English claimed that newspapers should be able to talk to Sonia 'in the public interest' and, if necessary, pay her.[12] He was, in other words, having it both ways: denying that he had offered money while justifying such an offer.

English's central problem was over his paper's dealings with Sutcliffe's wife. How could he explain why his assistant editor David Tytler wrote to the Sutcliffes' solicitors nine days after the arrest offering Sonia a large sum of money with the proviso that 'a substantial proportion' of it would have to be used for the benefit of the families of Sutcliffe's victims? English's response was a subtle one: the *Mail* was engaged in a deception because it really had no intention of paying Sonia any money. It was stringing her along in order to prevent rival papers from doing a deal while building a relationship with her in the eventual hope of obtaining an interview without payment.[13] English frustrated the Press Council during its inquiry by refusing to hand over the contract with Sutcliffe's family or any other documents connected with the case. He also refused to attend an oral hearing with the complainant, demanding, against normal procedure, a private hearing. The Council were fortunate that Mrs Sutcliffe wasn't so reticent, providing it with copies of Tytler's offer of money, his second letter offering more and the draft contract.

The Press Council's adjudication was uncompromising. It complained that its inquiry had been impeded by the *Mail*'s failure to disclose material and reproached English for his persistent refusal to appear before it. The Council censured the *Mail* for breaching its declaration by agreeing to pay Sutcliffe's father £5,000 and dismissed its defence of promising money only as a 'negotiating technique'. It concluded that 'a group of senior editorial executives including the editor not only set out to deceive Mrs Sutcliffe but their conduct had the effect of artificially creating and sustaining a chequebook journalism market in her story . . . the explanation offered by the newspaper amounts to a confession that the *Daily Mail* was guilty of gross misconduct.'[14] English had, in effect, been found guilty of evasion, procrastination and hypocrisy. In an extraordinary example of reticence, the Council failed to mention that midway through its inquiries English had been knighted. Nor did it point out that one of the *Mail* executives it criticised, Alwyn Robinson, was a current member of the Press Council.[15]

Jacqueline Hill's parents also objected to the *Sunday People*'s payment to a friend of Sutcliffe's. He was given a £500 lump sum and for three months was paid a further £80 a week. The *People* also agreed to pay the man's girlfriend £2,000 for her story. In a separate deal, the *People* paid £12,500 to a woman Sutcliffe met in Glasgow. In condemning the *People*, the Council found that it had 'violated both the letter and the spirit of the declaration'.[16] It did not point out that *People* editor Geoff Pinnington was a current member of the Press Council.

Almost as a postscript, the Council also found the press as a whole guilty of harassment. Mrs Sutcliffe and Mrs Hill had been 'subjected to wholly unacceptable and unjustifiable pressures by journalists' who 'laid siege to their homes', it said, adding that Mrs Hill had suffered from 'unwarranted intrusion into grief'.[17]

After the report's publication the serious broadsheets laid into the offending papers. The *Guardian* commented: 'Were one quarter of it to be unveiled against (say) some hapless Foreign Office official caught tap dancing before a select committee, then those same editors named here would lustily be calling "resignation".'[18] Indeed they would. Editors had been exposed by an independent panel as liars and one of them had been condemned for gross misconduct. Businessmen and politicians found in breach of rules and similarly censured would never have survived the resulting press onslaught on their reputations. The *Times*'s judgement was also blunt: 'The behaviour of some editors and the money they were prepared to spend is morally contemptible, even if it could have been commercially justifiable.'[19]

But two of the guilty papers were not prepared to apologise for their misbehaviour. The *Daily Mail*'s English called it 'a most unfortunate decision by a body which should be devoting itself to preserving the freedom of the press.'[20] The *Daily Express*, ignoring the fact that it had breached a voluntary code, chose to defend self-regulation by arguing: 'We should beware of attempts to manipulate the public's understandable concern into a campaign for legislative restraints on the press.'[21]

The saga took another twist three days after the publication of the Press Council report when the *Sunday Times* reported that the *Daily Star* had concealed from the inquiry the fact that it had paid four-figure sums to two of Sutcliffe's brothers. The Council launched another inquiry and discovered that the *Star* had indeed paid a total of £26,500 to the men. Editor Lloyd Turner was accused of conduct amounting to hypocrisy and was censured for grossly misleading the Press Council. It noted that the paper paid money 'to precisely the type of recipient that Mr Turner himself suggested should not in future be allowed to benefit – the immediate relatives of a criminal'.[22] Despite this damning indictment, Turner kept his job. Years later it emerged that the *News of the World* had also misled the Press Council by claiming that it hadn't pursued Mrs Sutcliffe's story after April 1981 and that it had not paid her any money.[23] Yet she had spent a week in New York courtesy of the

NoW, accompanied by assistant editor Stuart Kuttner, and the paper had funded trips to see her husband in prison.[24]

In 1984 the story of Mrs Sutcliffe's relationship with newspapers surfaced again when she was introduced to a *Mail on Sunday* reporter, Barbara Jones, who wrote two articles about Sonia. The paper paid money for them to her solicitor. Three years later, with only days to spare before the six-year statute of limitations on libel actions was due to expire, Mrs Sutcliffe suddenly decided to sue *Private Eye* for its January 1981 article, despite never having complained about it in the past. When it came to trial in 1989, *Private Eye* readily admitted that it had made two errors in its story: Mrs Sutcliffe had not agreed a £250,000 deal with the *Mail*, nor had she been entertained at a hotel by the paper.

But Mrs Sutcliffe had refused the *Eye*'s offer of a correction and it was baffled as to why she had waited so long before suing. While giving evidence, Mrs Sutcliffe stated that she had never sold her story to a newspaper, but in admitting that money had been paid by the *Mail on Sunday* to her solicitors she was able to say that she had not received it herself. She was asked how she had managed to find £20,000 in 1987 to avoid bankruptcy and said she had been given a £25,000 loan by 'a private person'. She refused to identify the person, and the jury not only found in Mrs Sutcliffe's favour but set the damages at a record-breaking £600,000, the largest libel award in British legal history, beating the £500,000 awarded to Jeffrey Archer when he sued the *Daily Star* (see below, p. 506).

National newspaper editors who were not normally favourably inclined towards *Private Eye* were astonished by the scale of the damages and concerned about the precedent it might set. It appeared that the *Eye* might collapse into insolvency, but after announcing that it would appeal the magazine had a stroke of luck.[25] A former boyfriend of Barbara Jones came forward to tell the truth about the mysterious £25,000. It had passed through his bank account in a cloak-and-dagger deal agreed between *Mail on Sunday* editor Stewart Steven, Jones and Sonia Sutcliffe. The *Eye* also discovered that Jones had taken a foreign holiday with Sutcliffe, part of which was paid for by another of Jones's boyfriends, none other than the legal manager for Associated Newspapers, owners of the Mail titles. Though none of this new evidence was allowed at the subsequent appeal, the judges ruled that the £600,000 award was unreasonable and should be set aside. Lawyers for both sides then worked out a compromise deal without going to court: Sutcliffe would get £160,000 damages from the *Eye* and her costs would be paid. Other newspapers, such as the *Daily Star* and *Daily Express*, paid Mrs Sutcliffe for libel actions she had launched against them. But one paper, the *News of the World*, decided to fight.

It had published a story which suggested that she had enjoyed a fling with a 'Ripper lookalike' while holidaying with Jones in Greece.[26] Unknown to Mrs Sutcliffe, Jones had written the story and sold it through a picture agency to the *NoW.* In a clever legal manoeuvre, the *NoW*'s lawyers then 'joined' Jones, her photographer, the picture agency and the alleged Greek lover in the action they were facing from Sutcliffe. This had the effect of setting Jones against Sutcliffe, leading to the disclosure of contracts and receipts which revealed that payments had been made by one to the other. Out of the woodwork came details of other payments too, such as the New York trip paid for by the *NoW* and £400 paid in cash to her by assistant editor Kuttner.

During the libel trial in December 1990, Sonia Sutcliffe's credibility as a witness was undermined in a devastating cross-examination by the *NoW*'s barrister, George Carman QC. In his closing speech he accused Sutcliffe of perjuring herself at the *Eye* trial and the jury found for the *NoW.* She was ordered to pay the huge costs of the action which were thought to have all but wiped out her previous damages awards. *Private Eye* had been vindicated. It had got the facts wrong in 1981 but not the substantive truth.

But none of these trials was fought over the main issue of chequebook journalism. Newspapers had fooled their readers by denying that they would ever pay the wife of a mass murderer; they were prepared to go to extraordinary lengths to cover up their duplicity; and they did so while knowingly defying the Press Council's strictures. *Mail on Sunday* editor Stewart Steven authorised his paper's payment of £25,000 in the knowledge that it would go to Mrs Sutcliffe. *Daily Mail* editor David English authorised his executives to negotiate with the woman in spite of a public denial. The episode did have one uncomfortable outcome for English though: following his 'festering lie' headline *Private Eye* always referred to him as Sir David Fester.

Thatcher and the *Sun* versus the Argies

When news broke of the Falklands invasion in early April 1982, I was on holiday and read with amusement a report in the *Times of Malta* that Britain was contemplating sending a task force to do battle for the islands with Argentina. Like the majority of Britons, I had no idea where the Falklands were, let alone what their history was. I only knew of their existence because, as a child, I had collected their stamps. Despite some gung-ho murmurs from an expatriate former naval officer who entertained my wife and me at his villa outside Valetta, it was difficult to imagine Britain going to war over it. I was not the only one: Max Hastings, who was to report from the Falklands so brilliantly for the London *Evening Standard,* thought the idea of sailing across the globe to fight a war 'seemed at first fantastic'.[27]

On my flight back from Malta I overheard people on the plane talking about the invasion and the possibility of sending a task force. There were one or two warlike comments but most people seemed bemused by the idea of

Britain retaking islands with a population of just 1,800 located some 8,000 miles away in the South Atlantic. When I returned to the *Sun* office next morning and told my colleague Wendy Henry how ridiculous it all seemed she laughed too but confided: 'Be careful, pet, that's a very unpopular view to hold round here.' A visit to the newsroom showed me why. News editor Tom Petrie was wearing some sort of naval officer's cap and told me he now wished to be known as Commander Petrie. A map of the South Atlantic was pinned on the board behind him under a picture of Winston Churchill. He was explaining his strategy for 'beating the Argies' when the editor Kelvin MacKenzie burst through the doors and shouted: 'Tom, I want to get those bastards at the Foreign Office today. We're going to give Carrington a ferreting.'

Next day the *Sun* called the Foreign Office a 'safe haven for appeasers since Munich' and carried a cartoon of Foreign Secretary Lord Carrington as a mouse compared to Churchill's bulldog. Carrington was probably more upset by a *Times* leader which told him to 'do his duty'.[28] On the day that the task force set sail he resigned, accepting that he should have foreseen the Falklands invasion because the Foreign Office had been given enough information to make such a deduction. The *Sun* had bagged its first war victim. I soon realised that Bouverie Street was now the unofficial war office with MacKenzie playing chief of staff and Petrie in the role of his aide-de-camp.

Britain's failure to react militarily to the South Georgia incident emboldened Argentina's dictator, General Leopoldo Galtieri, to invade the main Falklands islands two weeks later, quickly overpowering the small garrison of marines. Galtieri, whose military junta was increasingly unpopular in Argentina, had hoped to win his nation's acclaim by acquiring the Malvinas. He reasoned that the United States would make only a token protest; the Soviet Union – which was dependent on Argentinian grain – would back him; much of the Third World would applaud his anti-colonial initiative; and Britain, suffering from an economic crisis, would swallow it. There was only one British navy ship in the area and there was no air base within range. None of these calculations, as the *Economist* pointed out, was accurate.[29]

MacKenzie saw the opportunity not just to support the war against Galtieri, but to open a second front by fighting the war that mattered most to him and to Murdoch, for sales. So he attacked other newspapers, especially the rival *Daily Mirror*. Giving an early notice of its intentions, the *Sun* said: 'Isn't it amazing that there are some people who, in every dispute, believe Britain is wrong and the foreigners right?' It suggested that such people should 'arrange a free subscription to the sinking *Daily Mirror*'.[30]

The *Sun* was far from alone in its sabre-rattling. As the commentator Tom Baistow pointed out: 'four right-wing tabloids switched eagerly from bingo to jingo'.[31] The *Daily Star*, having given up any pretence at maintaining a leftish stance, hired a lawyer to examine a speech by Tony Benn to assess whether he might be guilty of treason. With the task force heading south, the United States tried to avert a war by brokering a deal through the secretary of state, General Alexander Haig, which involved Britain and Argentina holding joint sovereignty of the islands.

The very idea of such a compromise so upset the *Daily Mail* that it even dared to suggest its heroine might not be up to the job, asking: 'Has she got the stomach for it?'[32] The *Daily Express* came closest to revealing the real reason for pursuing the war option: 'nothing but a resounding victory is likely to restore the country's reputation and preserve the Thatcher regime'.[33] Was this the view of editor Christopher Ward or that of the owner, Lord Matthews? His other paper, the *Daily Star,* also demanded action: 'Let's End the War of Politics'.[34] The *Sun*'s response most certainly emanated from its editor with MacKenzie famously splashing on the headline 'STICK IT UP YOUR JUNTA!'[35] Within a week tee-shirts bearing that slogan were being marketed by the paper.

The *Financial Times* had been quick to spot what the tabloids were up to and declared that 'jingoism is not the way'.[36] Calling the seizure of the Falklands 'an outrage', the *FT* nevertheless counselled against reoccupation. 'There is no point in a large expenditure of force to reassert a right which the Prime Minister herself pointed out . . . we have not the means to sustain in the long term.' As the *FT*'s historian noted: 'It was a leader of sufficient detachment that it perhaps already had the *FT* designated as the enemy within.'[37] But MacKenzie didn't choose to attack the pink paper, either out of oversight or because he didn't think a business paper selling so few copies mattered to his readers.

One battle which was fought by every newspaper and broadcaster was the right for its reporters, photographers and cameramen to accompany the task force and the right to report unhindered. Editors were astonished that a force of 100 ships and 27,000 personnel could set sail without journalists aboard. After strong protests, some twenty-nine British media representatives were eventually allowed to travel on the aircraft carriers *Hermes* and *Invincible* and the cruiseliner SS *Canberra.*[38] But the Ministry of Defence (MoD), which sent public relations officers aboard to monitor the activities of the journalists, also insisted on strict rules, forbidding any mentions of the forces' strengths, their intentions, the capability of weapons systems, and even the state of the weather.[39]

The treatment of the journalists varied from ship to ship. The *Daily Mail*'s David Norris was warned to keep a low profile because of mistaken views that his paper had criticised the marines who had surrendered the Falklands.[40] 'There were marines on my ship and I was told to keep out of their way for my own safety,' said Norris. 'It weighed against me when I was trying to file copy.'[41] Some captains refused to meet journalists at all, while others gave them briefings. The battle group commander, Rear Admiral

Sandy Woodward, candidly admitted that he 'had never dealt with this phenomenon before, thus I was unsure how to handle them or what to tell them'.[42] Unlike the army, which had grown used to dealing with journalists during the conflict in Ireland, the navy had virtually no such experience.

Admiral Sir Jeremy Black, the captain of *Invincible*, explained the problem: service people were team players while 'press men were the very antithesis of this. They operate as individuals ... and the only other individual in their firmament is their editor. They will pursue their own ends at any price, having never heard of the word loyalty, and will trample on anyone or anything that stands in their way.'[43] It is hard to fault Black's view, but that doesn't negate the value of journalism: its practice may be upsetting but the principle, that people have a right to know what is done in their name by their armed services, must be upheld.

That principle was hard to divine in the *Sun*'s coverage during the long voyage to the South Atlantic. It applauded the war cabinet's decision on 20 April to repossess the Falklands and heralded the relatively easy retaking of South Georgia five days later with the headline: 'INVASION!'[44] *Sun* reporter Tony Snow, aboard *Invincible*, was prevailed on by news editor Tom Petrie, on the orders of editor MacKenzie, to 'sponsor' a missile and to 'sign' it 'Up Yours Galtieri!' Then, in an echo of its splash eleven days before, the story appeared under the headline: 'STICK THIS UP YOUR JUNTA: A *Sun* missile for Galtieri's gauchos'. The cod picture of the missile was captioned: 'Here it comes, Senors' and the story began: 'The first missile to hit Galtieri's gauchos will come with love from the *Sun*.'[45] Two days later Snow triumphantly reported: 'I saw my missile hit the back of the enemy aircraft. It exploded as advertised. His plane was in flames.'[46] Whether Snow wrote those words, or anything like them, is doubtful: his copy was routinely rewritten.

By chance, the war coincided with entirely unrelated industrial action by the journalists' union chapel, which had voted to strike if Murdoch's management didn't improve an offer over pay and staffing levels. It says a great deal about the difficult relationship between staff and the editor that they decided to go ahead with their strike action just as the task force was closing on the Falklands. On the evening of 2 May, it meant that just a dozen executives, including me, were the only journalists producing the paper when the first genuinely dramatic war news broke: a foreign news agency reported that an Argentinian ship, the *General Belgrano*, had been hit. Features editor Wendy Henry shouted 'Gotcha!', not as a suggested headline but as a spontaneous reaction, the kind of black joke that is common in every newspaper office during tragedies. MacKenzie immediately seized on it and began designing a front page around the headline: 'GOTCHA. Our lads sink gunboat and hole cruiser'.[47] As the first edition was pushed off the stone – with compositors and typesetters working at top speed in sympathy with us strike-breakers rather than their fellow trade unionists on the picket lines – more detailed news of the *Belgrano*'s sinking started to arrive.

We read that the ship had a complement of 1,200 people and had been struck by torpedoes from the submarine *Conqueror*. Gradually it dawned on Petrie that there might have been a huge loss of life and as he read the agency reports aloud the mood among the twelve of us changed, including MacKenzie and Henry. Realising that the 'Gotcha' line might be tasteless and inappropriate, he drew up another front page with a new headline, 'Did 1,200 Argies drown?' Rupert Murdoch was in the building, probably because of the strike, and walked on to the floor as MacKenzie was completing the new layout. He said he liked 'Gotcha' and didn't see the need to replace it. MacKenzie disagreed and subsequent editions carried the less controversial line.

In normal circumstances, without a strike, it's likely that the original page one would have been altered so quickly that few copies would have left the building. But the length of time it took to make the change ensured that hundreds of thousands of the first edition were published and 'Gotcha' came to symbolise ever after the *Sun*'s, and MacKenzie's, cynical, jingoistic, bloodthirsty war coverage. I put the record straight when interviewed by the authors of the unofficial *Sun* history, Stick It Up your Punter, and they gave a very fair account of what happened. But MacKenzie, with his typical swagger and refusal to have anyone clean up his act, happily embraced the legend of 'Gotcha', putting it on the front cover of a book of *Sun* headlines.[48]

MacKenzie never knew that many of the marines and sailors aboard HMS *Fearless* were so disgusted by the 'Gotcha' headline that *Sunday Times* reporter John Shirley witnessed copies of the *Sun* being thrown overboard.[49] The following day's *Sun* didn't go down well either. The front-page headline. 'ALIVE! Hundreds of Argies saved from Atlantic', played down the fact that 368 men were killed.[50] Its leader praised the prime minister in terms that were to become familiar for the next eight years: 'Margaret Thatcher's most dramatic success has come from her handling of the Falklands crisis . . . She has proved herself far more than the Iron Lady. She has been Britannia come to life!'

Next day Britain suffered its own tragedy when the destroyer HMS *Sheffield* was sunk by an Exocet missile with the loss of twenty men. This dramatic news was announced in an interruption to the BBC's Nine O'Clock News by the MoD's official spokesman, Ian MacDonald, who became well known during the war for his extraordinary vocal delivery, earning him nicknames such as 'the I-speak-your-weight-machine' and 'the warm-up man for the Lutine Bell'.[51] There were few jokes though after the *Belgrano* and *Sheffield* sinkings, and the relatively low-key criticisms of both the government and its newspaper supporters grew louder and more insistent.

Samuel Brittan, a fan of Thatcher's economic policy but not of her prosecution of the Falklands war, wrote a piece entitled 'Stop the killing straight away'.[52] The *Guardian* took a similar view to Brittan's, questioning both the wisdom of the war and the wisdom of holding on to the Falklands.

Some six years before, features editor Richard Gott had written a leader suggesting it was time for the Falklands to be ceded to Argentina.[53] The *Daily Mirror*, alone among the tabloids, took an anti-war line, drawing praise from a *Guardian* historian.[54] Warning against the dangers of mounting hysteria and the ultimate cost in British lives, it argued: 'The killing has got to stop . . . if that means both Britain and Argentina need to compromise, then compromise they must . . . It is time to prove that peace through diplomacy is the only policy that pays.'[55] Meanwhile, on BBC TV's *Panorama*, presenter Peter Snow raised the question of the government's truthfulness about the circumstances surrounding the sinking of the *Belgrano*.

All of this was too much for both Thatcher and MacKenzie. Attacking reports which she felt failed to back Britain, she said: 'There are times when it would seem that we and the Argentines are almost being treated as equals and almost on a neutral basis.' That was tame stuff compared to MacKenzie's editorial. That morning I heard his screech of invective down the executive corridor as he called for leader writer Ronald Spark to 'stick it up the traitors'. The result was a *Sun* leader which said of the *Mirror*: 'What is it but treason for this timorous, whining publication to plead day after day for appeasing the Argentinian dictators . . . We are truly sorry for the *Daily Mirror*'s readers. They are buying a newspaper which again and again demonstrates it has no faith in its country and no respect for her people.' MacKenzie was making an overt attempt to win over the *Mirror*'s audience by appealing to their sense of patriotism. Responding to the previous day's *Mirror*, a *Sun* leader alleged: 'There are traitors in our midst . . . newspapers and commentators on radio and TV who are not properly conveying Britain's case . . . The Prime Minister did not speak of treason. The *Sun* does not hesitate to use the word . . .'[56]

The *Guardian*'s supposed offence was publishing a cartoon by Les Gibbard – imitating a controversial wartime cartoon by Philip Zec in the *Daily Mirror* – which showed a British seaman clinging to a raft over the caption: 'The price of sovereignty has been increased – official?' Turning to *Panorama*, the *Sun* asked: 'What is it but treason to talk on TV, as Peter Snow talked, questioning whether the government's version of sea battles was to be believed?'

Next day *Mirror* editor Molloy summoned his leader writer, Joe Haines, to fire back in an editorial headlined 'The Harlot of Fleet Street'. Calling the *Sun* 'coarse and demented', it claimed that it 'has long been a tawdry newspaper. But since the Falklands crisis began it has fallen from the gutter to the sewer . . . The *Sun* today is to journalism what Dr Joseph Goebbels was to truth.'[57] Haines, arguably the best populist polemicist of his generation, concluded: 'A Labour MP yesterday called for the *Sun* to be prosecuted for criminal libel. There is no point in that. It has the perfect defence: Guilty but insane.'

Simon Jenkins, in his *Economist* column, thought the *Sun*'s leader would have made Senator McCarthy blush, prompting the *Sun* to label him

'Curlylocks' who 'typifies those arrogant individuals who know better than anyone else'. It then returned to its previous theme, scorning the 'pacifists, appeasers and elitists . . . who are sabotaging Britain's war against the Argentines . . . It is not jingoism to love one's country.'[58] The National Union of Journalists described the *Sun*'s charges against other media as 'odious and hysterical', but the paper's own chapel, asked to censure MacKenzie, declined to do so. With Tory MPs having taken up the *Sun*'s criticism of the BBC, the *Financial Times* waded in to deride 'the jingoistic bombast which masquerades as patriotism'.[59] These kinds of leader, argued the *FT*'s historian, had 'witnessed a coming of age on the part of the *FT*'.[60]

The *Sun* was unabashed, proclaiming itself 'The Paper That Supports our Boys' and casting reporter Muriel Burden, who passed messages from families to troops and ran a pen pals service, as the 'Darling of the Fleet'. Petrie sincerely believed that the *Sun*'s coverage had earned it a special place in the hearts of the soldiers and sailors, telling the paper's official historian Roslyn Grose: 'We now regard ourselves as the Forces' paper, which the *Mirror* used to be.' But Grose also quoted a wounded officer who recalled, 'Your headlines often made us feel sick,' and revealed that there were 'ritual burnings of the *Sun*'.[61] The *Sun*'s reporter on *Invincible*, Tony Snow also discovered that some of the men he was travelling with were upset by his paper.

Once the task force reached the islands, the MoD demanded that the accompanying correspondents pool their reports, so journalists imbued with the spirit of competition were now expected to help each other. They won an argument to go aboard landing ships in order to witness the action, but they couldn't overcome the fact that the task force controlled all communications, including the transmission of TV footage which reached Britain many days later. Some stories filed by reporters never reached Fleet Street because of MoD censorship.[62]

Even if news was delayed it couldn't be concealed and there was widespread concern at mounting casualties as British ships came under attack. In the light of some public disquiet papers such as the *Guardian*, the *Mirror* and the *FT* continued to question whether it had been right to go to war. It was impossible not to acknowledge, however, that the overwhelming majority of the population backed the task force and its aims, with references to 'the Argies' becoming common.[63] Thatcher evidently considered all speculation from armchair strategists in the media as 'little short of treachery'.[64] But her policy was given support by all Rupert Murdoch's papers, including the *Sunday Times*.[65]

When British troops landed on the East Falklands and set out across the island on foot, a new word was added to the newspapers' lexicon of war: yomping. Reporters went ashore too and were given suitable clothing by the army but got little encouragement from their MoD handlers. Before the hard-fought battle for Goose Green there was a complaint that a broadcast on the

BBC's World Service had given away British positions, increasing the tension between correspondents and army officers. Journalists were informed that some ships had been struck by bombs which had failed to explode, but they were told that if this fact was published it might give the Argentinians a chance to correct their detonator timing devices. In London, confrontations between the official government spokespeople and editors were even more fierce, especially in the light of a belief that papers had been deliberately misled by a briefing about the San Carlos landings. On another occasion, after the government felt it necessary to 'correct' a statement, the *News of the World* editor Derek Jameson exploded: 'I can't make up my mind whether this is a conspiracy or a cock-up.' A BBC editor added: 'Both.'[66]

MacKenzie also grew upset about government news management, complaining to us executives that we were at the mercy of the authorities who were controlling all the information from the theatre of war. It didn't strike me at the time, but it was surely ironic that just weeks before he had criticised *Panorama* for making a similar charge. Despite his anger at government censorship, he maintained his fierce commitment to Thatcher's war. Convinced that he was properly articulating his readers' views he laughed off *Private Eye*'s spoof *Sun* headline, 'KILL AN ARGIE AND WIN A METRO', joking: 'Why didn't we think of that?'

MacKenzie's views on press traitors had some support. Paul Johnson, writing in the *Spectator*, railed against the coverage of the war in the *Mirror* and *Guardian*. The landing had been a success, he wrote, 'but you would not have grasped that from Saturday's *Mirror*'. He then listed its main headlines: 'Many dead in battle for Falklands', 'Tragedy and the Tears: Thatcher fights back her anguish' and '21 die in Sea King plunge'. 'By contrast,' he claimed, 'the rest of the press seized ... on the salient point that the British were ashore in strength.' The *Guardian* 'echoed the gloom', wrote Johnson.[67]

Journalists in the Falklands knew almost nothing of the propaganda war in Britain as they tried vainly to do their job. Michael Seamark of the *Daily Star* was aboard HMS *Galahad* when it was attacked on 8 June and wrote a moving and dramatic eyewitness account of the attempts to rescue men from the burning ship. He sent his copy by helicopter to another ship for onward transmission to London but it mysteriously disappeared.[68] When it was published weeks later the paper tagged it 'the article the Ministry would not let you read'.

Before the final attack on Port Stanley two reporters were overheard by an officer talking on the phone about the forthcoming push which resulted in all journalists being barred from briefings. That didn't deter the most enterprising and experienced of war correspondents from pulling off a great journalistic scoop after the Argentinians hoisted the white flag. Max Hastings, who was covering the conflict for the *Evening Standard*, was at the front line with 2 Para as they prepared to march in triumph into the town when they were suddenly ordered to halt. Hastings wasn't bound by army orders and realised that, as a civilian, he was unlikely to be fired on if he simply walked into the town. So, after giving Chris Keeble, 2 Para's second in command, 'one of his kind of steely-eyed looks ... he walked down the road to Stanley'.[69]

Having assumed the role of civilian to reach the town he then assumed another role, that of a *Times* reporter, to secure an interview with the Argentinian colonel in charge. Other journalists soon arrived at the Upland Goose and quickly wrote their reports, which were handed to Hastings because he alone had secured a ride on a helicopter to a ship and could transmit all the copy via the Marisat satellite system. By chance, he was landed on HMS *Fearless*, which didn't have a Marisat. In his haste to get aboard another ship and file his own dispatch, he is said to have mislaid his colleagues' reports.[70] Hastings's exclusive filled the entire front page of the *Standard* the next day: 'THE FIRST MAN INTO STANLEY'.[71] He won several accolades for his Falklands reporting, achieving a rare double by being named journalist of the year in the British Press Awards and reporter of the year by *What the Papers Say*. Years later he referred to his scoop 'as the happiest moment of my career'.[72] It didn't win him many friends among rival reporters, some believing he had lost their copy on purpose, though most in retrospect gave him grudging respect. According to *Daily Express* photographer Tom Smith, Hastings explained his competitive spirit by exclaiming: 'I'm not here to be a Boy Scout, old boy.'[73]

One unfortunate, for example, was the genuine *Times* correspondent, John Witherow. He and Patrick Bishop of the *Observer* managed to bamboozle their way into a cabin aboard HMS *Fearless* to interview General Menendez after he had agreed the official surrender. But they were discovered and ejected before they could speak to him. Other reporters were outraged by Hastings's actions, most notably Robert McGowan of the *Daily Express* and Jeremy Hands of ITN, who co-wrote a book which claimed that David Norris of the *Daily Mail* beat Hastings into Port Stanley.[74] Norris denied this when I spoke to him around the time of the twentieth anniversary of the war, generously conceding that Hastings reached the Upland Goose before him. 'Max was a brilliant operator,' he said. 'He pulled off some tricks but in the circumstances I say, "good luck to you".'[75] Norris's copy did eventually reach the *Mail* but his editor, David English, felt his reporter had let him down and for some time afterwards refused to speak to him. 'There was no question of me being fired but there was a deathly silence until, eventually, English let me know through an intermediary that he was sorry about things. He had acted wrongly. We got on well in subsequent years.'

The experience of witnessing tragedy at close range had a dramatic effect on several journalists who got very close to the men with whom they marched for days on end. Many of them agreed with John Shirley of the *Sunday Times,* who wrote: 'This has changed my view of military men ... paraded in the press as some sort of macho supermen, they turned out to be thoughtful, reflective human beings.'[76] Shirley was surely referring to tabloid-style depictions of heroism and it was hardly surprising that the *Sun*'s Falklands reporters, David Graves and Tony Snow, were deeply embarrassed by their own paper's coverage. Soon after his return from Argentina, Graves left the paper to join the *Daily Telegraph.*

The war was the making of the *Guardian*'s 'punk cartoonist' Steve Bell, whose savage satires about HMS *Incredible* attracted many letters of appreciation from the paper's audience.[77] The *Guardian* also benefited from the war, adding sales while the *Daily Telegraph* lost them. The *Times* enjoyed a small increase, as did the *Daily Mail.* The pro-war *Daily Express* and anti-war *Daily Mirror* were in a period of decline, but it is reasonable to argue that the rate of the *Mirror*'s fall did increase slightly during the war. Most interesting of all was The *Sun*'s sale. Having risen dramatically with bingo the previous year, it suddenly dipped badly in June 1982, the month the war concluded, climbing back the following month to continue its upward momentum.

Victory appeared to justify the *Sun*'s jingoism and its faith in Thatcher's indomitable spirit, convincing MacKenzie that the troops he had backed so passionately were bound to be grateful to his paper. He was affronted to discover that this was far from the truth: many soldiers and sailors who returned from the Falklands were disgusted by the *Sun*'s war record. Four months after the end of the war, he was even more outraged when he discovered that the widow of Sergeant Ian McKay, who had been posthumously awarded the Victoria Cross for his bravery in the Falklands, had agreed to give an exclusive newspaper interview to the *Daily Mirror*, of all papers, and an exclusive television interview to ITN.

Unable to reach Mrs Marica McKay, MacKenzie ordered an operation, known in the trade as a 'spoiler', to ensure that the treacherous *Mirror* didn't get away with its scoop. One *Sun* reporter managed to speak at length to Sergeant McKay's mother and another evidently picked up a whiff of the contents of Mrs McKay's ITN interview. That was enough for the paper's ingenious and skilled reporter, John Kay, to concoct a story which he and news editor Tom Petrie knew could masquerade as a *Sun* exclusive. But MacKenzie, a competitor who couldn't bear to lose, was so eager to beat the *Mirror* that he overstepped the mark by falsely billing it as a 'world exclusive'. The 'interview' was a fabrication, putting words into Mrs McKay's mouth, devising a fake scenario and even inventing her emotions. It began: 'VC's widow Marica McKay fought back her tears last night and said, "I'm so proud of Ian. His name will remain a legend in the history books forever" . . . Hugging her two children at their home in Rotherham, she said, "I'm proud of Ian's Victoria Cross – but I'd exchange all the medals in the world to have him back".'[78]

Once again the *Daily Mirror* called on leader writer Joe Haines to lead the charge and his editorial, 'The *Sun* Sinks Even Lower', pointed to the lies.[79]

The row might have ended there, as a Fleet Street squabble, but for the intervention of *Observer* diarist Peter Hillmore who viewed it as a serious ethical lapse. His secretary, using her Essex address, made a formal complaint to the Press Council and after Mrs McKay confirmed that she had never spoken to the *Sun* the verdict – which took a disgraceful nine months to deliver – was never in doubt. In upholding the complaint the Council condemned the *Sun* for perpetrating 'a deplorable, insensitive deception on the public'. The *Daily Mirror* jumped at the opportunity to berate its rival once again in another Haines editorial: 'Lies, Damned Lies and *Sun* Exclusives'.[80]

I recall that MacKenzie was hauled over the coals by Murdoch for what was regarded as 'a big mistake'. But the gap between the offence and the Press Council censure was so long that it all seemed like water under a distant bridge by then. A couple of years later, in June 1985, a similar incident occurred when Simon Weston, a former Welsh Guardsman who was severely burned when the *Galahad* was bombed in the Falklands, took part in a BBC documentary. He rejected the idea of being interviewed by the *Sun* and this time a feature writer, under instructions from features editor Wendy Henry, put together an article from old quotes which purported to be an interview with him.[81] The problem was not the accuracy but Henry's rewritten introduction which laboured over distasteful descriptions of his 'hideously scarred' face that 'no one wants to look at'. Weston was mortified and complained in public about the piece, all gratefully reported by the *Daily Mirror*. Aware of Murdoch's wrath, MacKenzie suspended Henry from work, on full pay, for a month. I was sympathetic to Henry at the time and, having re-read the article, I haven't changed my mind. She was a scapegoat, punished because the paper couldn't face the prospect of bad publicity if Weston had pursued his complaint.

Thatcher and Fleet Street versus Foot

The Falklands victory was more of a turning point in the life of Margaret Thatcher than her election victory three years before. As Charles Moore noted in the *Spectator*: 'The pigheadedness of General Galtieri has saved the Conservative Party . . . In the Falklands she [Mrs Thatcher] has found the first really popular issue of her administration.'[82] Throughout the autumn and winter of 1982 her poll ratings were running at a record 80 per cent. Her party was well in the lead too, eclipsing both the Liberal–SDP Alliance, which had lost its initial impetus, and Labour.

Newspapers poured scorn on Labour Leader Michael Foot as he tried, belatedly and unsuccessfully, to purge members of the Trotskyite group, Militant. He was suffering from continual press attacks when Thatcher called a general election for June 1983. From the beginning of the campaign, she seemed set fair for victory, with polls running in her favour, but her press supporters didn't take any chances. The *Sun*, *Daily Mail* and *Daily Express* lauded Thatcher and derided Foot. 'Do You Seriously Want This Old Man to Run Britain?' asked the *Sun*. 'We see a vision of an amiable old buffer, his jacket buttoned too tight, his collar askew, his grey hair falling lankly. His eyes ablaze behind thick lenses . . .'[83] It was a replay of a Worzel Gummidge insult coined by the *Sun* when Foot was adjudged to have been poorly dressed at the 1981 Remembrance Day parade.[84] The personal taunt accompanied the paper's insistent political message about Labour having been 'penetrated at all levels by sinister Marxist forces'.[85] Another article entitled 'The Lefties Who Would Run Britain if Labour Won Power This Week' featured Tony Benn, Arthur Scargill, Paul Boateng and Michael Meacher.[86] The *Sun* also turned its guns on Labour's right by attempting to show that Denis Healey was a hypocrite by owning a house in the country.

Labour's manifesto exacerbated the deep divisions within the party, offering Tory papers endless fodder to show the splits. Leading shadow cabinet members, such as Healey and Roy Hattersley, were unhappy with the pledge of unilateral nuclear disarmament. Others were disturbed by the threat to withdraw from the European market. One senior figure, Gerald Kaufman, openly referred to the manifesto as 'the longest suicide note in history'. The *Daily Mirror* also aired doubts about the manifesto but advised readers to back Labour as the party most likely to cure growing unemployment. Its news page coverage of the 20,000-word manifesto amounted to just 340 words. In contrast, the *Daily Mail* gave it two pages under the headline, 'Britain in Bondage'. Calling it the 'most comprehensive assault on our liberties ever', the writer, Paul Johnson, catalogued eighty supposed 'controls' Labour would impose on everything from the employment of babysitters to prices, without any reference to the main planks of the party's policy.[87]

So one-sided was the paper's coverage that the journalists' union chapel at the *Mail* held a protest meeting at which they agreed to request that editor David English 'give other parties a fair crack of the whip'. English retorted: 'It is unacceptable for anyone to try to influence the editor.' He had not thought it unacceptable, three weeks before polling day, to publish a splash by motoring correspondent Michael Kemp which claimed that the Japanese car manufacturer Nissan would 'scrap plans for a £500 million British plant if Labour wins the election'. According to the *Mail*, up to 35,000 new jobs were at stake 'in areas of high unemployment which are Labour strongholds' and alleged that it was Labour's commitment to withdraw from the Common Market 'that is scaring Nissan'.[88]

This story was based on quotes from two unnamed 'Nissan officials'. It was immediately and emphatically denied by Lord Marsh, a consultant to Nissan, but in the *Mail*'s follow-up the next day, his quote appeared in the fifteenth paragraph of a story headlined 'Car Jobs Rows Boils Over'. A couple of days later Brian Groves, Nissan's marketing manager, told the *Observer*: 'If you ask me, it [the story] came out of Mr Kemp's head.'[89] The Press Council was asked to inquire and, because of the story's political sensitivity during an election campaign, managed to report with unusual speed. Kemp refused to reveal his source but he did hand over shorthand notes of his conversations with the 'officials'. The Council refused to rule that the story had been fabricated but censured the *Mail* for running an insufficiently qualified story under misleading headlines and for the lack of prominence given to the company's denial the following day.[90]

The *Mail* also published an article by the former Mirror group supremo and Labour party propagandist Lord (Hugh) Cudlipp, in which he explained that he had joined the Social Democrats because of Labour's Bennite lurch to left. As much as the *Mail* wished its readers to vote Tory it recognised that many of them normally voted Labour and that it would benefit the Conservatives if they could be converted to the Alliance.

Labour was supported by only the three Mirror titles and the *Observer*, which reached its decision after the oddest of episodes. Owner Tiny Rowland was relatively relaxed when editor Donald Trelford said that he would support Labour, and a leader to that effect was written. Then Rowland changed his mind and another, more circumspect leader was prepared. But deputy editor Anthony Howard reminded Trelford that a BBC TV crew had filmed them during discussions in which they had agreed to support Labour, so Trelford hastily changed tack again.

The *Times* backed Thatcher, as did the *Daily Telegraph*, which politely requested that she change her attitude towards unemployment. The *Financial Times* supported the return of the Tories, but a strike by print unions closed the paper just before the election and the leading article it would have published was carried in the *Guardian* instead. The *Daily Express*, owned by Lord Matthews and edited by Sir Larry Lamb, both of them Thatcher hero-worshippers, ran a leader saying: 'We stand four-square and 100 per cent behind Mrs Thatcher.'[91] Matthews also insisted that the paper he had launched 'for the unions' should not urge its readers to vote Labour, resulting in *Daily Star* editor Lloyd Turner running an editorial headlined: 'Sorry Michael, we can't vote for you'.[92] The *Sun*'s election-day front page was a huge cartoon of Thatcher as Britannia with the headline 'VOTE FOR MAGGIE'.

Rival papers were closely watching the *Guardian* to see if it would stand alone by offering support to the Alliance. Four *Guardian* journalists stood as SDP candidates – leader writers Malcolm Dean, Christopher Huhne and John Torode, and woman's-page writer Polly Toynbee – and Toynbee's husband, Peter Jenkins, wrote a pre-election column which savaged Labour. He lashed 'the self-indulging ideologues and the hypocritical careerists, the guilt-ridden middle class leftists and the cowardly trade union bureaucrats, the sentimentalists, the romantics, and the Don Quixotes who have split and, for the time being, destroyed the party to which millions looked as their instrument of reform and progress'.[93] Given the *Guardian*'s audience, this assault might have been as deadly a blow to Labour as a dozen *Daily Mail* headlines.

But the *Guardian* itself didn't endorse the Alliance. Editor Peter Preston said that 'to avoid trouble' he wrote the really difficult leaders during the run-up to the election 'so that the row, if it happened, was always between whatever faction and the editor, rather than between colleagues'. He recalled that 'it worked okay, if not gloriously ... there was never a huge *Guardian* upheaval because everyone had a say – often in print – and the editor made the final choice'.[94] Preston's main pre-election leader was a masterly example of his recondite style. It was critical of Thatcher for failing to understand that wealth creation and compassion need not be incompatible, but offered no comfort to Labour. Nor was there any clear endorsement of the Alliance, which was seen as 'a volcanic symbol' which 'we would not wish to see ... lost on Thursday at the random whim of the electoral system'.[95] This vague advice to people to vote tactically was neatly summarised by the SDP's historians as urging 'not a Conservative landslide'.[96] In hindsight, Preston was more concerned by his paper's failure to appreciate the positive aspect of Tory policies rather than by its lukewarm response to the SDP: 'we were too slow to see the changes in society that Mrs Thatcher was making, sometimes for the good'.[97] It is fair to point out that one of Preston's central themes in that leader, about political change not occurring as swiftly as people often think (as in the case of the Alliance), later proved entirely correct.

The *Guardian*'s in-house SDP rabble-rouser, Peter Jenkins, had second thoughts about his membership of the new party and resigned from it. 'Peter felt he had made an awful mistake as a journalist,' said his widow, Polly Toynbee.[98] In later years it was still thought, at least among right-wingers, that *Guardian* journalists had been, and remained, the SDP's closest and most loyal supporters. In a witty appraisal of the SDP's factions, *Times* columnist Frank Johnson claimed that they included 'readers of the *Guardian*; and (a much larger group) writers of *Guardian* leaders'.[99]

The Conservative victory was never in doubt, but the size of it was humiliating for Labour, which suffered its worst result since 1935 in terms of seats (209) and its worst since 1918 in terms of vote share (27 per cent). The Tories won 397 seats, despite getting fewer votes than in 1979, and secured 43.5 per cent of the total vote. The Alliance, winning more than 25 per cent of the vote, returned just twenty-three MPs, only six of whom were from the SDP. A closer analysis of voting patterns showed that only 39 per cent of trade unionists voted Labour, and the party polled badly among manual workers, the young and people in the south of England.

Bolstered by her post-Falklands celebrity, bathing in the glow of a largely supportive press, it was a confident Thatcher who set out on her most active phase, privatising public assets while extending both share and home ownership and reforming industrial relations laws. She was also forced to fight another battle, on the domestic front, against the miners' union led by Arthur Scargill. Once again, she received unyielding support from newspapers.

The strike began after it was announced early in 1984 that pits in Scotland and Yorkshire were to be closed. Though strikes in those areas were approved by executive vote, Scargill and his executive opposed calls for a national strike ballot, preferring to convince miners in other coalfield areas by sending pickets. *Sun* editor Kelvin MacKenzie responded by publishing a ballot form in the paper, which the unions initially refused to print, leading to a row between MacKenzie and the National Graphical Association (NGA) chapel leader John Brown. They finally agreed a compromise: the form would be published with an NGA disclaimer next to it stating that its members objected to it, and the following day's paper would include a 'right of reply' written by Scargill.

Although about 40,000 miners, mostly in Nottinghamshire, remained working and set up a breakaway union, the strikers were determined to stop coal supplies reaching power stations and there were many ugly incidents with violent conflicts between pickets and the police. Scargill was arrested at one point and, during another confrontation, while he was addressing a rally of strikers, a news agency photographer pictured him with his hand raised above his head. By deleting the background, and thereby removing the context, it could have been misconstrued as a fascist salute. *Sun* editor Kelvin MacKenzie schemed a front page around it with the headline 'Mine Fuhrer'. Printers refused to work on the page, set the headline or make the block for the picture and, after another bitter row between MacKenzie and Brown, the front page was published with a large typeface statement which said: 'Members of all the *Sun* production chapels refused to handle the Arthur Scargill picture and our major headline on our lead story. The *Sun* decided, reluctantly, to print the paper without either.'[100]

MacKenzie ran into trouble for the third time when violence erupted between pickets and police in south Yorkshire at the end of September 1984. His front-page headline over an editorial critical of union pickets, 'Scum of the Earth', upset printers once more and they refused to publish it unless they had a right of reply which stated that they had produced the page under duress. This time MacKenzie, after speaking to Murdoch, wouldn't agree to a compromise so the paper didn't appear. Management then informed the print unions that they would lose a day's pay, so printers retaliated by ensuring that the *Sun* didn't appear for four days.

This kind of confrontation had a huge impact on Thatcher. One of her newspaper champions was losing money because one group of unions were preventing him from publishing propaganda helpful to her in her struggle with another union. Winning the miners' strike was vital to Thatcher's political and economic strategy and vital to Murdoch's commercial future.

MacKenzie was naturally sympathetic to the Murdochian viewpoint. Like many working-class tabloid journalists born after the war, he was less enamoured of the monarchy than the previous generation and certainly less willing to accept the establishment which it cemented in place. Most of his executives felt the same way even if they were not, like me, committed republicans. Given this situation, in looking at the rows between press and Palace which broke out from 1981 onwards, it appears remarkable that the *Sun* was not even more intrusive and even less careless of the consequences. The reason, clearly, was Murdoch's own sense of what was fair and what wasn't, itself informed by his acute political antennae which detected when threats of legislation turned serious.

One other important feature of the way in which nearly all tabloid editors treated the marriage of Charles and Diana was their favouritism towards Diana. This was motivated by an overlap of personal regard, which grew in some cases into infatuation, and commercial logic. They were captivated by her beauty, glamour and vulnerability, just as their readers were. This gave her a power which, as the years moved on, she was able to exploit. At the beginning though, she endured several difficult lessons about dealing with the press.

The wedding in July 1981 went off like a medieval pageant and almost every paper carried a front-page picture of the couple kissing on Buckingham Palace balcony. The *Sun* borrowed from a 1960s pop song for its main heading, 'Then He Kissed Her', and reporter Harry Arnold managed to obtain a scoop by revealing the secret destination of their honeymoon in a story headlined 'Charles makes Di his Queen of the Nile'.[106] The word 'secret' was to become meaningless in future years to the Prince and Princess of Wales.

Throughout the early months of their marriage Princess Diana was subjected to intense press interest, and she discovered to her apparent surprise that she couldn't walk around in public without being surrounded by photographers. In November 1981, soon after it was officially announced that she was pregnant, she was upset by the attentions of photographers as she went to buy sweets near her Highgrove home. The pictures duly appeared on the front pages of the *Sun* and the *Daily Mirror*, with the latter running one next to a picture of her attending the Remembrance Day ceremony, making a rather asinine comparison between 'the relaxed and the solemn' Diana.[107]

That incident spurred the Queen, on the advice of her press secretary Michael Shea, to use her authority to curb what she regarded as harassment of her daughter-in-law. Every national paper editor, along with the editors of the BBC news and ITN and the editor-in-chief of the Press Association, was invited to Buckingham Palace to meet the monarch. The only editor not to attend was the *Sun*'s Kelvin MacKenzie, who informed Shea that the date and time coincided with a prearranged meeting with Rupert Murdoch. This was both untrue and a calculated snub. MacKenzie was in my office for part of the period when he should have been at the Palace. Shea told the editors that the Queen was concerned about invasions of the royal family's privacy and to illustrate his point about the increasing degree of media interest he lighted upon Murdoch's *Times* rather than his *Sun*. That day's *Times*, said Shea, had published ten separate stories about royalty.[108] He turned then to the specific case of Princess Diana, pointing out that she was twenty years old, pregnant and suffering from morning sickness, yet photographers were laying siege to Highgrove and she felt beleaguered.

In what he probably thought was a subtle way of suggesting that editors were not themselves to blame for the activities of freelance photographers, the paparazzi, he reminded everyone of the Ray Bellisario experience (see above, p. 351). Two editors at the meeting, Bob Edwards of the *Sunday Mirror* and Sir John Junor of the *Sunday Express*, immediately picked up his drift. They were aware that after a Press Council complaint about Bellisario's activities, in which he was found guilty of trespass, he was effectively frozen out of Fleet Street.[109] What Shea was requesting was a repeat performance some twenty years later: would editors please not buy pictures from badly behaved photographers. But times had changed and it didn't strike a chord with editors. Even if those present were to agree on a voluntary embargo, and it's unlikely that any of the tabloid editors would have done anyway, would the absent MacKenzie obey?

There was no agreement either way, though several broadsheet editors murmured their sympathies for the princess's plight, before Shea led the editors into another room to meet the Queen. The only memorable exchange occurred when the short-lived editor of the *News of the World*, Barry Askew, asked the Queen: 'Would it not be better to send a servant to the shop for Princess Diana's wine gums?' His fellow editors froze into silence until the Queen smiled and replied: 'Mr Askew, that was a most pompous remark.' Everyone laughed heartily. Askew, who was living on borrowed time in his job, was pilloried for what some editors thought was a *faux pas* because it was foolishly claimed that he had insulted the Queen. The very notion was an example of deference. Some journalists thought, incorrectly, that Askew's remark played a part in Murdoch's decision to fire him. If so, surely MacKenzie would have gone too, since his not turning up was a far greater insult. Years later, recalling the incident, *Times* editor Harry Evans wrote of Askew pursuing his point with the Queen as an example of his 'characteristic boldness', which puts the matter into proper perspective.[110]

Most tabloid editors published editorials with varying promises about not impinging on the princess's private life in future. 'It is a fair request,' said the *Daily Mirror*, which pledged to respect it.[111] The *Daily Mail*, under the canny David English, promised: 'We shall respect her privacy while at the same time not depriving our readers of the pleasure of sharing her charms.'[112] The *Daily Express*, with an editor of two months' standing, Christopher Ward, and an owner, Lord Matthews, who despised the publication of any story which upset the Queen, said: 'The *Daily Express* will continue ... to record the Princess's public engagements without intruding on her private life.'[113] Matthews's other paper, the *Daily Star*, gave no such promise in the paper.[114] But its editor, Lloyd Turner, interviewed on TV about the Palace meeting, said: 'We will be taking a very hard look at any pictures supplied to us in the future. We must take notice of what the Palace has said.'[115] The *Sun* reported that the meeting had taken place, under the headline, 'Leave our Di alone, says Palace', but MacKenzie wasn't prepared to offer hostages to fortune with an editorial.

The broadsheets were sympathetic to the Queen's point of view, with the *Times* referring to the princess being 'pinned like an errant butterfly to the front pages' in a leading article which anticipated that the press would respond positively 'to the sad sense of beleaguerment'.[116] Murdoch was more exercised by the content of the *Times*'s news story, which reported truthfully that the meeting had been precipitated by the activities of the red-top tabloids and that MacKenzie had failed to attend. Murdoch called editor Harry Evans and asked: 'Why are you always picking on the *Sun*?'[117]

The *Daily Telegraph* described the Queen's request for restraint as 'wholly reasonable' and the leader continued: 'It is never easy to determine where the line between legitimate public interest ... and vulgar, hurtful intrusion is transgressed ...', but the media 'should be under no illusion, however, where public sympathy will lie. For the public will know quite well how tragic it would be were over-zealous intrusions by some sections of our profession come so to prey on the mind that a figure enjoying much public affection felt driven to draw back and shelter from the lights.'[118] These two lines of argument, sensible as they might initially appear, were wholly flawed. First, it would prove impossible to curb tabloid intrusion by relying on 'public sympathy'. Second, the idea that the princess, the royal family's most glamorous figure of all time, would withdraw behind the Palace curtains was utterly implausible. Anyway, the edgy truce between tabloid editors and the Palace lasted for precisely seventy-two days.

In February 1982, the *Sun* and the *Daily Star* published pictures of Diana – who was six months pregnant by then – in a bikini while sunbathing on a remote Caribbean island. She was on holiday with her husband on Eleuthera in the Bahamas. The pictures were taken by the *Sun*'s Arthur Edwards and the *Star*'s Kenny Lennox, while hiding from the princess, and each other, after crawling through undergrowth and concealing themselves behind bushes on a neighbouring island. The *Sun* scooped the *Star* by a single edition.[119]

The *Daily Telegraph* reported the following day that the use of the pictures had prompted a flood of phone protests from the public. A Commons motion protesting at the publication of pictures of a pregnant princess was signed by MPs from all parties. The Press Council immediately ordered an inquiry. The Queen protested about it being an invasion of privacy and 'tasteless behaviour'. MacKenzie responded in characteristic fashion: he ran an apology of sorts but took the opportunity to republish five of the offending pictures under the headline, 'THE SUN, THE QUEEN AND THOSE PICTURES'. The *Sun* was 'deeply sorry' to have caused offence but it was showing 'a legitimate interest in the royal family . . . The pictures were carefree, innocent and delightful. They brought a breath of summer into the lives of millions of our readers . . .'[120]

The *Daily Star*'s Lloyd Turner was ordered by his proprietor Lord Matthews to make a much more sincere apology, though it was couched in similar terms to the *Sun*'s. The paper hadn't meant to offend, but 'we could see nothing wrong in pictures that could have been any young, happy couple on a public beach ... Our interest was out of deep affection for the Royal couple.'[121] Turner, unlike MacKenzie, wasn't allowed to recoup the enormous costs of obtaining the pictures by selling them to the scores of international magazines which sought to buy them.

Daily Mirror editor Mike Molloy, who had resisted enthusiastic requests by his own news and picture desk executives to send a team to the Caribbean, took the opportunity to lambast his red-top rivals. A page-one leader, written by Joe Haines, commented: 'The pictures were squalid in conception, furtive in execution and grubby in publication . . . The *Daily Mirror* decided to respect their privacy. We are not in the business of taking sneak-shots of pregnant women bathing, whether they are princesses or not.'[122]

In a remarkably quick adjudication, the Press Council condemned the *Sun* and the *Star* for 'bringing discredit on the British Press' by 'a gross intrusion' into Princess Diana's personal privacy. The *Sun* was further censured for the form of its apology which was 'made worthless' by republishing the pictures and selling them to foreign publications.[123] It was something of an open-and-shut case since the editors, reporters and photographers declined to attend an oral hearing. Lloyd Turner tried to wriggle off the hook with a letter in which he claimed he had previously informed the Queen's press secretary Michael Shea that he would be sending a photographer and reporter and wasn't asked not to do so. Shea contested the details of that call and the Council as good as called Turner a liar by finding 'as a fact' that the Palace had never withdrawn its request to the press to leave the princess alone and did not give Turner consent to follow her.

In the following months, while she was still pregnant and even during the Falklands war, barely a day went by without an article appearing about Diana along with an obligatory picture, or two, or more. There were several speculative stories about the state of the marriage, Diana's supposed moodiness and her alleged weight losses or gains.[124] Papers ran several gossipy tales about the royal pair, and it was the *Daily Mirror* – apparently forgetting its pledge to respect her private life – which first suggested that Diana might be suffering from an eating disorder.[125]

I was not alone in thinking that much of the stuff I was reading was fantasy. As assistant editor at the *Sun* in charge of the features department, I knew that one of my writers, Judy Wade, was spending a great deal of time with the royal pack of journalists. Without any prompting she became a 'shadow' to the paper's assigned correspondent, Harry Arnold, and was to emerge as the most obsessive Diana reporter of them all. Wade often appeared in my office to tell me that the royal marriage was in trouble, based in part on her own assessment of their body language and on leaks from courtiers about rows between them. Despite having known and liked Wade for many years, I must admit I took most of what she said with a pinch of salt. Other commentators supposedly close to events at the Palace took a similar view to mine. One populist royal biographer who wrote for women's magazines, Douglas Keay, pointed out that rumours about Diana were based on 'fairly flimsy evidence'.[126] But the 'flimsy evidence' piled up week by week and the *Daily Star*, in a classic example of the way in which papers ran with both hare and hounds, illustrated how impossible it was for editors to give up the Diana drug. It published six pages on 'the truth' about Diana's marriage, examining every reported incident and speculation, and then had the effrontery to conclude by demanding an end to intrusive journalism and calling for a 'new understanding between the press and Palace'.[127] Readers were guilty of a similar hypocrisy. Keay put it well: '"Leave the poor girl alone" was the expression used by many well-wishers as, incongruously, they avidly read the latest titbits of news.'[128]

Hitler: 'Serious journalism is a high-risk business'

Rupert Murdoch's commitment to republicanism was a matter of dispute, his commitment to journalism was a matter of debate, but his commitment to making money was never in doubt. Nor was his skill at doing so. He was legendarily good at bringing off profitable business deals because he played his cards shrewdly and was prepared to take risks. But on one notorious occasion his deal-making talents and his risk-taking abilities got him, and the *Sunday Times*, into a lot of trouble.

One day in February 1983, the London representative of Germany's *Stern* magazine, Peter Wickman, called the *Sunday Times*'s deputy editor, Brian MacArthur, to say he had a highly confidential matter to discuss. *Stern* was Germany's biggest-circulation magazine, selling some 1.5 million copies weekly, a hugely profitable glossy production, running up to 300 pages. Owned by Gruner and Jahr, which was three-quarters owned by Europe's largest media company, Bertelsmann, it had to be taken seriously. When they met, Wickman swore MacArthur to secrecy and then revealed that *Stern* had managed to obtain one of the most important finds of modern history: the private diaries of Adolf Hitler. He said *Stern* was preparing to sell the serial rights to these momentous documents, amounting to fifty volumes, around the world. Publication would then be co-ordinated in the United States, Britain and Germany. MacArthur quickly seized on the logistical impossibility of the *Sunday Times* being able to publish simultaneously with *Stern*, which came out on Thursdays. It would have to go to the *Times* instead. He recommended that Wickman meet Sir Edward Pickering who, as executive vice-chairman of Times Newspapers, was Murdoch's most trusted lieutenant in London. He did so, and Pickering then informed Murdoch about the scoop of the century. It didn't take a moment for Murdoch to grasp the worldwide commercial possibilities of such a property.

He and Pickering both realised that there was a giant hurdle to cross before they could think about negotiating: were these diaries that no one had ever heard of before authentic? Meanwhile, a senior *Stern* executive was casting his net for bidders to ensure that the magazine got the highest possible price for the diaries, which had cost *Stern* 5 million marks to obtain. In Britain, Associated Newspapers, owners of the Mail titles, was approached. In the USA, *Time*, *Newsweek* and the *New York Times* were given a chance to make an offer. Pickering told Wickman he wanted Lord Dacre to authenticate. He seemed the perfect choice: as author of *The Last Days of Hitler*, a book hailed as a masterpiece, he was widely regarded as the foremost authority on the Führer. As an independent director of Times Newspapers, he would also have the best interests of the company at heart.

Dacre flew to Zurich, having been asked by *Times* editor Charles Douglas-Home to make a swift decision because of Murdoch's eagerness to open negotiations. Like most of the *Stern* executives, he wasn't able to read the old-fashioned German script and had to rely on translations provided by the magazine. He also had to accept *Stern*'s word that scientific tests had proved satisfactory. Despite the most cursory of examinations he pronounced them genuine, and Murdoch flew to Germany with Douglas-Home and two other senior aides to make an extraordinary offer: $2.5 million for the US rights and $750,000 for British and Commonwealth rights.[129]

That knocked out Associated, which bid just £50,000. But *Newsweek*, owned by the proprietor of the *Washington Post*, Katherine Graham, trebled its first offer of $1 million. After some wrangling, Murdoch then increased his offer to $3.75 million before he and *Newsweek* decided to join forces. At that point *Stern* badly overplayed its hand by demanding yet more and both parties walked out. Murdoch knew he was now in the driving seat and days later, when a desperate *Stern* director contacted him again, he was able to secure both US and British rights for a total of $1.2 million.[130]

It looked to be going very smoothly indeed for the tough deal-maker. What Murdoch didn't know was that *Stern*'s poor negotiating skills were mirrored in its poor handling of the whole diaries escapade. It had taken more than two years to obtain the volumes, bit by bit, through one of its own reporters, Gerd Heidemann, who was both a fantasist and a fraudster.

Obsessed with the Nazis, he had deluded himself into believing that the diaries he was receiving at regular intervals from a man called Konrad Kujau were the genuine article. As the middleman between *Stern* and Kujau he inflated the amounts Kujau demanded for the documents and creamed off thousands of marks for himself. In turn, Kujau was fooling Heidemann because he wasn't obtaining the diaries from a mysterious contact in East Germany as he claimed. He was meticulously forging the diaries day by day in his house near Stuttgart. Kujau had long been a prolific forger of Nazi memorabilia and the diaries, a figment of his fertile imagination, were his *pièce de résistance.*

Stern, due to the need for secrecy and a series of mishaps, had failed to carry out the proper tests on the paper which would have revealed the forgery. So its executives went on planning the publication of their great exclusive for late April 1983 while Murdoch decided how he would handle the matter. His first decision, on 21 April, was to switch the scoop from the *Times* to the *Sunday Times.* He told editor Frank Giles that his paper would be expected to serialise a key section of diaries about the flight to Britain by Hitler's deputy, Rudolph Hess. Giles had been only vaguely aware of the *Stern* negotiations until that point and had been unworried because it seemed like a problem for the *Times* rather than him. Now he found himself embroiled in an internal row with his staff. One of the first complainants was Phillip Knightley who, in recalling the Mussolini diaries fake of 1968, smelled a rat (see above, pp. 203–4). He sent a memo to Giles warning him of his suspicions, but this was ignored. Features editor Magnus Linklater, political editor Hugo Young and Insight leader Paul Eddy were also alarmed.

Linklater was one of the few *Sunday Times* journalists unsurprised by the story, having picked up rumours about the discovery of Hitler diaries from the controversial historian David Irving in December 1982. In January, he had sent Gitta Sereny, recognised as an authority on the Nazi era, to see what she could discover in Hamburg. She interviewed *Stern* reporter Gerd Heidemann, who told her the diaries did exist but without revealing his close involvement. She was about to pursue the matter further by flying to meet a professor who was regarded as an expert in the field when she was recalled by Linklater due to pressure on his expenses budget. If Sereny had met that man, she would have found out that he had recently been embarrassed by buying other Nazi documents forged by Kujau. The hoax might well have been exposed at that point.[131]

Knightley's concerns were assuaged after he had talked to Dacre, who told him he was convinced of the diaries' authenticity.[132] So publication went ahead. The great scoop was heralded on the front page of the *Times*, 'Hitler's secret diaries to be published', and inside was a lengthy article by Dacre explaining why he was certain the diaries were authentic.[133] As that paper was going to press, Dacre was already beginning to have second thoughts and next morning he called *Times* editor Douglas-Home to say he now had doubts about the diaries. It was too late for Douglas-Home to do anything in his paper but, oddly, he failed to pass on Dacre's concerns to his *Sunday Times* opposite number.[134]

The next day's *Sunday Times* front page proclaimed, 'WORLD EXCLUSIVE: The secrets of Hitler's War', and there were five more full pages devoted to extracts and commentary.[135] As the excited journalists who had put the great scoop together surveyed their handiwork once the first edition rolled off the presses on Saturday evening Giles called Dacre. It was their first conversation about the matter and only then did he discover that Dacre had had a change of heart.[136] Before stopping the presses, it was decided that Murdoch must be contacted in the United States, and deputy editor Brian MacArthur finally reached him. After he had explained that Dacre had changed his mind, Murdoch replied: 'Fuck Dacre. Publish.'[137]

As a mighty international storm broke in the following days, with alarm increasing about a possible hoax, *Sunday Times* journalists demanded that Giles speak to a chapel meeting. Giles told them it was not an appropriate matter for the union and announced that he was off to Corfu on holiday.[138] In spite of suspicions and accusations, there was still no confirmation that the diaries were a forgery during the following week, so the *Sunday Times* carried its second instalment of extracts as planned. Finally, five days later, after detailed tests it was incontrovertibly proved that the diaries were a forgery and they were officially denounced by the German government. With Giles away on holiday, it was left to MacArthur to write an apologia to *Sunday Times* readers. Its opening line was priceless: 'Serious journalism is a high-risk enterprise.'[139]

Giles returned from holiday to discover that he was unpopular with staff who were appalled at his weakness in agreeing to publication and at his insouciance when the paper was under attack. Murdoch just wanted rid of him anyway, and he went weeks later. Dacre's reputation didn't seem to suffer, though he did go through agonies.[140] Despite a mutual antipathy between him and Murdoch, he remained a Times Newspapers director until 1988.

Several *Stern* editors and senior executives left the magazine in the following months. The reporter who defrauded *Stern*, Gerd Heidemann, was jailed for four years and eight months. The same sentence was passed on forger Konrad Kujau. And what of the *Sunday Times*'s guilt? According to former editor Harry Evans, the credibility of both the *Times* and the *Sunday Times* was seriously damaged by the episode.[141] Maybe, maybe not. It certainly didn't show in the sales figures: circulation rose substantially during the serialisation of the forgery, subsided a little afterwards, but was otherwise unaffected.

PART NINE: 1986–1990

17. THE WAPPING REVOLUTION

So Will It Be Goodbye to Fleet Street?[1]

Historians who talk of turning points often exaggerate, but 1986 undoubtedly ranks as a revolutionary moment in the history of Britain's national newspaper industry. When Eddy Shah and Brian MacArthur presented the sample edition of their proposed newspaper *Today* to advertisers in the autumn of 1985, they didn't realise just how prophetic their front-page headline – 'So Will It Be Goodbye to Fleet Street?' – would prove. They thought it was they who were breaking new ground by turning their backs on Fleet Street. What they couldn't know was that Fleet Street was preparing to say goodbye to itself. Shah was unaware that he was to be Rupert Murdoch's Trojan horse. While the world was diverted by the activities of the Warrington interloper, and the unions made tentative plans to do battle with the non-union paper he was about to publish, Murdoch was plotting to win a war. It turned out that I, as assistant editor at the *Sun*, was to be one of the infantrymen.

On the afternoon of 21 January 1986, *Sun* editor Kelvin MacKenzie called me to his office and told me to put every important item from my desk and filing cabinets into two black plastic bags. 'You may never get the chance to come back here again,' he said melodramatically. His chauffeur then drove me to the mysterious plant in Wapping we had heard so much, and knew so little, about. In the jargon of those days, I had succumbed to the 'Wapping cough'. As staff began to vanish from Bouverie Street in the final months and weeks of 1985, they were sworn to secrecy about the reason. So they took to explaining away their apparently indefinite disappearance by claiming a minor illness. Having lost some of our most experienced production journalists in previous weeks, we suspected that the great Wapping move was really on after all. After months of rumours about the launch of a London paper, it was now obvious that it had been a blind. Murdoch was seriously going to do what, to be frank, I considered impossible. He was preparing to outmanoeuvre the apparently impregnable print unions.

At Wapping, or Tower Hamlets as Murdoch's managers unsuccessfully wished it to be known, I stepped into a new world. I couldn't believe the press hall. It was at ground level, clean and airy, with shiny blue machines tended by men in spotless overalls. Upstairs, in what was to become the *Sun*'s rough and ready editorial office for the following couple of years, were lines of new desks. On each one sat an Atex computer terminal and keyboard. Several of the screens were live, with a tiny green light – the cursor – blinking away. A posse of electricians scurried around, tugging at wires snaking through open ducts in the floor. A small band of journalists, people I hadn't seen in weeks, even months, were hunched over terminals. So that's what assistant editor Roy Pittilla, assistant chief sub Kelvin Holland and sports editor Peter Pace had been up to.

It had taken Murdoch a long time to reach this point. After years of putting money into the Fleet Street slot machine while flattering the controller of the Westminster casino, the great gambler had finally got four ducks in a row. Duck one was the cash from the Reuters flotation (see above, p. 376). Duck two was the realisation that Fleet Street real estate was worth millions: every press owner's eyes widened when the City of London School had sold its nondescript Blackfriars building to Morgan Guaranty for £96 million. It meant that money spent on new plant in a greenfield site could be recouped, perhaps several times over, from selling the Bouverie Street building. Duck three was Shah's planned launch of a non-union paper, which had the twin effect of opening a second front against the increasingly nervous unions while threatening owners with the kind of cheaply produced competition they had long feared. Duck four, which had also bolstered Shah, was the Conservative government's 1984 Trade Union Act which, among other things, made strike ballots mandatory and outlawed secondary picketing. With this law in place, Murdoch was assured that he could combat inevitable attempts to thwart his newspapers' distribution. His friendly relationship with prime minister Margaret Thatcher had paid off.

Of course, there was much more to Wapping than a line of ducks. As we have seen, Murdoch had originally been persuaded many years before, by his then managing director Bert Hardy, to buy the land and build a press hall (see above, pp. 284–5). For a long time, Murdoch remained sceptical about the idea of printing there and certainly didn't contemplate moving his non-print staff. But his negative experiences with the unions after his takeover of the *Times* and *Sunday Times*, adding to the conflicts he had faced at the *Sun* and *News of the World*, convinced him Hardy had been right. Some time in 1983 intermittent negotiations began with the unions over manning for the new plant, but they looked as if they were going nowhere. In February 1985, Murdoch outlined his Wapping plan to a select group of News International executives in New York.[2] The following month he confirmed a report in the *Sunday Telegraph* that he was to use Wapping to publish a twenty-four-hour paper entitled the *London Post* to compete, supposedly, with the *Evening Standard*.[3]

It cannot be doubted that the *Post* was a ruse to mask activities at Wapping, especially the installation of direct-input technology which Murdoch didn't refer to at the time. Several of the people involved in the

1985 Wapping preparations, journalists and production staff, were still saying with great sincerity years later that the *Post* was not a bogus enterprise. In her meticulous examination of the Wapping events, Linda Melvern did not specifically state that it was a sham, quoting people who held opposing views.[4] But *Sunday Times* editor Andrew Neil was less reticent years later, admitting that it was a 'cover story'.[5] It was certainly a sophisticated bluff because Charlie Wilson, the *Times*'s editor who was nominally the *Post*'s editorial director, even interviewed possible staff.[6] Wilson, according to Neil, also eventually came clean.[7]

Melvern told of a March 1985 meeting – which occurred before the *Sunday Telegraph* leak – between Murdoch's team, including Wilson, and executives of the Atex computer company about the purchase of terminals. It was obvious that the numbers required were far greater than were necessary for a single paper.[8] Murdoch also set in train the creation of a new distribution system, utilising road rather than rail, and again using the *Post* as a cover story when purchasing a fleet of vans and lorries.[9] Of all the problems Murdoch faced, distribution was the most difficult to solve. He had to set up a secure print plant in Glasgow too.

The fact that the *Post* was a front all along illustrates just how calculating the normally spontaneous Murdoch had to be. He had to plan at least a year in advance and events do suggest that he had previously decided to shift his editorial staff too, a fact denied afterwards and used as an excuse for the inadequate working conditions Wapping staff initially encountered. There had never been any secret about the building of the printing plant itself: during its long construction there were several references in the trade press, including an artist's impression in 1982 and details of the presses being installed.[10] But no one could conceive of leaving Fleet Street.

From the summer of 1985 onwards, Wapping was the unsecret secret. Everyone was aware that the plant existed. Everyone knew Murdoch was, at some stage, going to print his papers there. Everyone suspected that Big Things were going on, and none of us at the *Sun* was convinced about the likelihood of the Post ever being published, despite the disappearance of two middle-ranking production executives. David Banks said he was going to New York to study print technology. Graham Courtenay, a backbench fixture for fifteen years, organiser of election coverage and the weekly rota, claimed to have left to become a county cricket club press officer. Neither held a leaving party, so no one believed them. Nor were we convinced when we discovered that another of our former staff, Michael Hoy, was leaving Murdoch's *New York Post* for Wapping.

At Gray's Inn Road, there was similar bafflement at the absences of Richard Williams, the *Times*'s deputy sports editor, and James Adams, an assistant editor of the *Sunday Times*. In the late autumn, I was told that my experienced features editor, Jerry Holmberg, wouldn't be around for a while 'and maybe never', added MacKenzie. Whenever I called Holmberg in the following weeks, he appeared to be in high spirits but wouldn't be drawn on exactly what he was doing. All he would say was: 'You won't believe it!' Rumours swept the building. There were stories of a covert workforce of non-union men, tales of dummy runs on new presses and gossip about new-fangled computer systems that could do 'everything'. We were still unsure. Fleet Street history and normal journalistic scepticism suggested that Murdoch couldn't really produce papers without skilled press men and he certainly wouldn't be able to distribute them without bypassing the unions.

Most of us also thought Murdoch's intransigence in negotiations with the unions must, at best, be an attempt to get the optimum reduction in manning. The very idea of a wholesale sacking was impossible to imagine. On the other hand, there was MacKenzie, more ebullient than ever, desperate to share more than he should with his senior executives, muttering gleefully about 'showing the bastards' while punching the air. I often heard him say: 'Just you wait. I tell you, the boss [Murdoch] is a fucking genius.' Sometimes he would walk through the composing room, taunting the men making up pages: 'You lot haven't got much fucking longer ... You're history.' The printers were baffled: was he just being his usual obnoxious self, or did he know something they didn't? Asked to explain, he would simply hold a finger to his lips and give an exaggerated wink.

By that time, MacKenzie certainly knew that there was a fresh staff of printers at Wapping, though he might not have known exactly who they were. It would appear that Woodrow Wyatt, a columnist with the *Times* and the *News of the World* since 1983, and a former Labour MP who had become a Thatcherite convert, was party to the secret because he played a key role in the clandestine recruitment process. According to his diaries, he was responsible for putting together Eric Hammond, general secretary of the electricians' union, the EETPU, and Bruce Matthews, managing director of Murdoch's newspapers, 'having sounded Eric out first if he'd be willing to let electricians run the works at Tower Hamlets'.[11] Hammond, disliked by other trade union leaders who regarded him as an opportunist right-winger, had no time for the print unions and jumped at the chance to provide staff for Wapping, thus securing a single-union deal for the plant.

His agreement had to remain secret if Hammond was to avoid intense hostility from the rest of the movement and maybe from some of his own members. To cover Hammond's tracks, Murdoch later lied to a *Guardian* journalist about the EETPU's involvement.[12] On the same day, Wyatt noted in his diary: 'The secrecy has been kept perfectly.'[13] In fact, soon after Hammond's meeting with Matthews, he authorised his well-organised Southampton branch to provide recruits for a special job in London. By August, some 400 electricians' union members from Southampton had been hired for the *London Post*.[14] A further 100 were taken on in the following months. They travelled to and from Wapping by special coaches and few of them ever operated as electricians. Most were retrained to run the presses while several of the younger women, some of them relatives of union leaders without work experience of any kind, became compositors, learning how to 'paste up' pages. Murdoch was to remain grateful ever after to Wyatt for his help in securing Hammond's compliance.

While all this was happening, talks between senior News International executives and leaders of the print unions about staffing the *London Post* went ahead with varying degrees of seriousness. In the autumn of 1985 Murdoch gave the unions a three-month ultimatum to reach an agreement over substantial cuts in staff. Their response was to organise a ballot giving them the right to call a strike if Murdoch tried to impose compulsory redundancies. But the die was cast. Murdoch knew exactly what he was going to do, daring on 18 January to print a special section of the *Sunday Times* at Wapping without a union agreement. One article even boasted of how computers had been secretly installed at Wapping. At an edgy meeting with all the print unions five days later Murdoch told them that 'the horse has bolted at Tower Hamlets'.[15] He was no longer prepared to listen to a compromise. Having provoked the unions into a strike, a legal necessity, he knew he was about to pull off the most remarkable 'midnight flit' in history, transferring production of all four of his newspapers overnight and locking out the entire non-journalistic workforces of his two huge printing works at Bouverie Street and Gray's Inn Road. What was crucial, therefore, was convincing as many journalists as possible to make the switch to Wapping with the very minimum of discussion.

Those of us who were already at Wapping did not attend the *Sun*'s lengthy NUJ chapel meeting on 24 January which agonised over whether to make the move. Some of us listened to part of the debate over the phone. It was clear that the chapel father, Malcolm Withers, was against the plan, reminding members that the union's policy was to stand fast with their printing colleagues. In the early evening, MacKenzie suddenly appeared on the floor and asked to speak. Lacing his words with only the minimum of humour, he made an impassioned plea for his journalists to go, saying that those who didn't would be deemed to have dismissed themselves. He answered questions and then left to speak to Murdoch. On his return, he said every journalist would receive £2,000 for 'retraining' on the new technology. This time barely able to hold his temper he sensibly left the room quickly.

I was on the phone to a colleague in the features room, asking about the mood of the meeting, when MacKenzie returned for a third time. I couldn't make out what he was saying but there was a great deal of laughter and my friend promised to call back. When he did, it was to say that there had been a vote: 100 to 8 in favour of going to Wapping. They had rejected a plea from the NUJ's general secretary Harry Conroy. 'No one wanted to listen,' he later wrote. 'They kept referring to their own dispute two years previously when production workers had walked through their picket lines – so why should they support the print unions now?'[16] That wasn't an excuse: it had, as we have seen, severely demoralised us journalists. It had changed my mind so greatly that I didn't go through the kind of soul-searching about Wapping suffered by many of my colleagues, most of whom didn't even share my background as a communist and union activist. I also realised that the division between the NUJ and the other print unions, especially the NGA, had hardened over the years, with added fears about which of them would monopolise the new technology.[17]

The other undeniable fact was the lack of trade union discipline among journalists. As Conroy has argued, what gave compositors their industrial muscle was not 'the hands on the keys' but 'the ability to take their hands off the keys all at the same time'.[18] Journalists, independent, individualistic, fiercely ambitious, depending on the patronage of editors and senior executives for advancement, all enjoying differing rates of pay, never came to terms with the concept of collective action, let alone its practice. Chapel meetings tended to be exercises in anarchy rather than democracy, during which the officials were often treated to as much abuse as the management. There were odd moments of wit. On one occasion when the *Sun* chapel was in broad agreement about the filthy state of the newsroom, a sub, Chris Harrigan, intervened to protest that a clean-up would drive away the flies, 'and they're the only friends I've got here'.

There was no laughter after that fateful Wapping vote as the journalists, having been told they would never have the chance to return, began to strip their desks and filing cabinets. Downstairs, *News of the World* journalists were quick to follow the *Sun* chapel's lead and voted overwhelmingly to go, swiftly packing up.[19] The breach between those who were going and those who would not struck me when my secretary, who had become a good friend, called to say she was quitting. Her father, a member of Sogat, was a union official at the *Daily Mail* and she could not contemplate upsetting him by crossing a picket line.

Over at the *Times*, editor Charlie Wilson followed MacKenzie's lead by addressing his journalists. He told them about the *Sun* vote and how important it was for them to go to Wapping too. There would be £2,000 for retraining plus free membership of a private health scheme. He explained that they would work a direct-input system and concluded: 'I implore you to come with us.'[20] The journalists, refusing to be railroaded, decided to get together the next day and held an emotional ten-hour meeting in a hotel ballroom. Though a vote to go to Wapping was passed it was put to one side by a second decision to reconvene the following evening. About fifty staff went to Wapping regardless. After a further seven-hour meeting, during which some journalists 'became so distraught they could hardly speak',[21] The *Times* chapel voted by a three-to-one majority in favour of going. By that time many were in tears.

A similar, prolonged struggle to 'do the right thing' happened at the *Sunday Times*. Editor Andrew Neil, who had known about Wapping from the spring of 1985, was excluded from the early planning, evidently because Murdoch considered him a security risk.[22] Yet he was to emerge as the project's most articulate ideologue in the following months. Many of his journalists were unsympathetic to him, to Murdoch and to the Wapping venture, so he faced some stiff questions when he addressed 130 'sullen and apprehensive' staff at the Mount Pleasant hotel.[23] After telling them that Wapping would be 'a liberating experience, free from the tyranny of print unions', Neil urged them to seize the time.[24] His most forceful opponent was one of the *Sunday Times*'s most respected executives, features editor Don Berry, who had spent eighteen years with the paper and was genuinely admired by Neil. He accused the company of having 'insulted and betrayed' the paper's journalists.[25] Berry's contribution, anti-Murdoch in tone rather than anti-Neil, had a considerable impact on staff who looked up to him. In the end, after a meeting which had lasted almost seven hours, the chapel voted sixty-eight to sixty to go to Wapping.

Almost half of the sixty 'no' voters refused to go. These 'refuseniks' included some of the *Sunday Times*'s most illustrious figures, such as Berry, the Middle East correspondent David Blundy, foreign correspondent Isabel Hilton and literary editor Claire Tomalin. Murdoch and Neil authorised attempts to lure them with a special deal but it fell through. Some refuseniks tearfully gave in a week later after personal appeals by senior executives. Others eventually sought jobs elsewhere, along with the refuseniks of the *Times* and the *Sun*. A few who went to Wapping left soon after, unhappy at having to cross picket lines which were anything but peaceful.

Murdoch had expected trouble. 'Fortress Wapping', as it became known, was a newspaper factory fenced by twelve-foot-high spiked steel railings topped by coils of razor wire and monitored by closed-circuit TV cameras. Uniformed security guards patrolled the perimeter and guarded the entrance. Everyone was issued with colour-coded, numbered passes. During the first week, journalists on all four titles came face to face with the anger of the 5,500 strikers whose jobs and, in many cases, crafts and skills had been eliminated for ever. To avoid contact, staff were urged to arrive by car or travel in special coaches with wire-covered windows. People who dared to walk in were abused, spat at and threatened. Neil, relishing his role as the public face of Wapping, was given special protection along with senior managers.[26] Violence was common, particularly on Saturdays, as a couple of thousand pickets, augmented by supporters from other unions and assorted anarchists and left-wingers, tried to prevent the delivery trucks from leaving the plant. Setpiece fights between pickets and police, in which many people were injured, often featured on TV news bulletins.

Inside the plant, even computer illiterates rapidly learned how to work the new machines under the watchful eye of David Banks and his Atex mentor from Chicago, Marlene Rae, nicknamed the fastest typesetter in the West. MacKenzie was cock-a-hoop, for once ignoring his rule that readers aren't interested in a paper's internal affairs, his first Wapping-produced front page was headlined: 'A New *Sun* Is Rising Today'.[27] After the *Sun* and the *Times* were published that night Murdoch telephoned his former managing director, Bert Hardy. 'Thank you, Bert,' he said. 'You were right and I was wrong.' Hardy was delighted at the sentiments and amazed that Murdoch had found the time to bother.[28]

During the first weeks, we were soon revelling in the joys of direct input. On the stone, as we still insisted on calling the paste-up boards, we could do virtually as we pleased. We could not only touch the finished typeset material, known as bromides, we could carry them around and cut them to fit. Many of the people hired to paste up the pages were young women, prompting one sub to joke that he must be in need of psychiatric help: he had fallen in love with a compositor! In the early days there were frustrations as we struggled to make edition times and I spotted a figure in a grey sweater stooped over a board, seemingly taking ages to stick down a piece of copy. 'For fuck's sake,' I shouted. 'Are you going to take all night with that?' The man turned slowly and I was about to add another epithet when I realised it was Rupert Murdoch, mucking in *pour encourager les autres.* He just smiled. It wasn't the kind of incident to disconcert him nor cause him to hold a grudge.

The picketing lasted for almost thirteen months before the unions agreed to settle, accepting severance terms which were, on the whole, generous. For once, the word redundancy meant what it said. Most of the men were never to enter a printing works again. Their skills had become obsolete. Though it has since been fashionable to decry them as dinosaurs and Luddites (which I have never viewed as a term of abuse), their actions were entirely logical and, for them, beneficial. They made a lot of money in the dozen or so years they sustained their highly paid jobs and staved off the introduction of a technology which rendered them redundant.

In the space of one night Murdoch transformed the British newspaper industry, heralding a new industrial revolution which was to lead directly to the electronic super-highway. As the *Sunday Times*'s personal finance editor, Diana Wright, remarked: 'How many other industries have gone from the equivalent of steam to microchip in a week, without interrupting production?'[29] Wapping marked the beginning of the end of Fleet Street. If it had not happened, Lord Rothermere observed, there would have been bankruptcies and closures.[30] Murdoch's breakthrough was all that rival groups needed to dust off their long-held plans to dispense with the expensive services of print unions, take their computers from the packing cases and move away to pastures new.

Robert Maxwell's train at Mirror group, was already moving, after he had secured an agreement for a substantial cut in staff. The week after Wapping, the *Guardian* announced that it would adopt computer typesetting and move its printing operation to a £23 million plant in London's Docklands.

Staffing would be reduced by 200 from a total of 1,000. A week or so later, Associated announced that it was setting up a print centre at Surrey Docks for its Mail titles (which was eventually opened in June 1987 at a cost of some £100 million, enabling severe staff cuts). In May, United Newspapers said it was planning to leave the *Express*'s famous Fleet Street landmark, the Black Lubyanka. In July, the *Financial Times* proclaimed its intention to embrace the new technology and build a new printing plant. In September, Conrad Black's group announced that it would print the two *Telegraphs* in Docklands, so cutting 2,000 from a staff of 3,300. Finally, the *Observer* revealed plans to move to Battersea by March 1987, with its paper being printed in regional centres across Britain.

The print unions didn't give in without a struggle. In the summer of 1986, the Guardian and Telegraph groups dropped their demands for legally binding collective agreements. In September, the Telegraph then reached a deal with the unions – including a no-disputes undertaking – which it trumpeted as a 'benchmark' for the industry. Some commentators misread the signs, concluding that the unions would regain the ascendancy. The basic structure of chapel power was still intact in most groups, wrote Simon Jenkins, who forecast that, Murdoch aside, unions would 'win back negotiating leverage over new composing technology'.[31] I tended to share this view at the time, but the predictions were wrong: the owners had won a significant and long-lasting victory.

A rival executive estimated that Murdoch's costs were instantly reduced by £80 million a year after Wapping.[32] His papers quickly became immensely profitable: News International's profits in the year up to June 1986, just six months after the move, were up on the previous year by 74.2 per cent to £83.3 million. The *Sun* alone made 40 per cent more than in the previous twelve months.[33] The following year, up to June 1987, NI's profits rose to £111.5 million. Even allowing for the Wapping move and start-up costs of more than £60 million, the improvement to Murdoch's coffers was immense. At that time, the *Sun* alone was thought by analysts to be making £1 million a week. Murdoch, by now a Hollywood mogul and American TV magnate, also continued his global media shopping spree, buying the *South China Morning Post* in Hong Kong, more key papers in Australia and the American book publishers, Harper & Row. At the same time he was investing heavily in plans to launch his satellite television network, Sky TV. None of the other newspaper owners were now in the same league.

Even more significant than the changes at the old titles was the promise of new newspapers. It became fashionable for right-wing ideologues of the Wapping revolution to seize on Mao Tse-tung's quote about 'letting a hundred flowers blossom'. They argued that breaking the unions, and thus reducing the cost of production, would enable many more papers to be launched. Eddy Shah was well down the road with *Today*, as was Andreas Whittam Smith with his *Independent*, seeing the period as a new 'golden age'.[34] In something of a frenzy over the following three years various titles were launched. There were four dailies: *Today*, the *Independent*, the *North West Times* and the *Post*; eight Sundays: *Sunday Today*, the *News on Sunday*, the *Independent on Sunday*, the *Sunday Correspondent*, *Sunday Sport*, *Sunday Life*, *Scotland on Sunday* and *Wales on Sunday*; and a twenty-four-hour title, the *London Daily News*. They enjoyed mixed fortunes, reminding me of another horticultural quotation from Chairman Mao about the need to distinguish between 'fragrant flowers and poisonous weeds'. The first tender shoot to appear was Shah's *Today*.

Eddy wasn't ready, but Andreas was

Eddy Shah was a folk hero among Thatcherites, but business is business, red in tooth and claw. His greatest ideological supporters, Murdoch and Neil, also flabbergasted him by pulling off the Wapping coup before he could launch. He therefore lost two key promotional assets for his new paper: publishing outside Fleet Street and eliminating print unions. Murdoch had now achieved both. But Shah still had the singular advantage of colour pictures, at least for a few months until Maxwell's machines came on stream at the *Daily Mirror*.

What though, apart from its non-union lineage and use of colour, was the point of *Today*? Before launch, I attended a magazine editors' luncheon addressed by editor Brian MacArthur, who spoke grandly of his paper, a tabloid, appealing to Middle England. Asked to elucidate, MacArthur struggled to be more explicit, talking airily of creating a serious–populist hybrid, a 'quali-pop', for the burgeoning middle classes. 'I came to curse the phrase,' he wrote later. 'To me it meant ordinary, decent families with children at school, occasionally going to church, driving Fords or Volvos, shopping at Sainsburys or Tescos, sometimes holidaying in Britain, still believing in some of the old-fashioned virtues and hoping to instil them in their children – families, I suppose, like my own and my neighbours who might vote Tory or SDP but who also worried about schools and hospitals and dirty cities.[35]

Most people at that lunch were doubtful about the project, aware that *Today* was aiming for territory already staked out by the *Daily Mail*, but their scepticism was tempered by a respect for MacArthur's journalistic pedigree. He was forty-six, having started his career at the *Yorkshire Post* after graduating from Leeds University. Spells as a reporter with the *Daily Mail* and the *Guardian* were followed by three years as education correspondent with the *Times*, and a year as deputy features editor, before becoming the founding editor of the *Times Higher Educational Supplement*. Five years later he returned to the *Times* as home news editor, leaving to join the *Evening Standard* as deputy editor to Charles Wintour. In 1979, he accepted Harry

Evans's invitation to be his chief assistant at the *Sunday Times* for a couple of years, leaving with Evans to take a similar position at the *Times*. After Evans's sacking, he returned to be joint deputy editor of the *Sunday Times*. He was piqued at not being made editor when Frank Giles was replaced by Andrew Neil and, in 1984, surprised many staff by leaving Fleet Street to take the editorship of the *Western Morning News* in Plymouth. When Shah was looking for an editor, several of the people he consulted, including both Murdoch and Neil, recommended MacArthur. It is true that he had no populist tabloid experience, and some commentators believed he was the wrong man for the job.[36] Yet the whole point of *Today*, at least in MacArthur's mind, was to find a way of popularising serious journalism, mixing the tabloid form with a broadsheet agenda.

Shah appeared altogether less sure of what his newspaper should be, in spite of a rather guileless set of aims. All that was missing from his biblical-style list was a Thou Shalt before each commandment: 'To support true democracy and not the false democracy of collectivism . . . To support freedom from all coercive monopolies . . . To protect those who suffer from an irresponsible invasion of privacy . . .'. MacArthur overlooked Shah's naivety and ignored his antipathy to staff drawn from Fleet Street. Among his key hirings were Jonathan Holborow from the *Mail on Sunday* and IPC Magazines executive Jane Reed. Three other subsequently well-known recruits were Alastair Campbell, as news editor, Amanda Platell and Colin Myler. Other important matters were outside MacArthur's remit, such as Shah's wildly optimistic circulation predictions, advertising expectations and financial projections. Some £2 million was spent on a television ad campaign featuring personalities in sunglasses, supposedly dazzled by the colour, and shouting in unison: 'We're ready, Eddy!' *Today*'s journalists were telling former colleagues that they were anything but ready.

It wasn't a great surprise that the first issue on 4 March 1986 was disastrous, with production delays making it late off the presses. Poor distribution meant it reached hundreds of shops far too late, or not at all. The colour registration was hopelessly blurred, quickly giving rise to jokes about 'Shah-vision'. Though corrected in following weeks, the tag stuck. A BBC TV fly-on-the-wall documentary also portrayed the tension, showing footage of Holborow and Shah shouting at each other. As for the content, the main front-page picture was of the Queen (with Princess Diana inside) and the splash was an impenetrable spy story. The main article announcing *Today*'s arrival was by Simon Jenkins, then political editor of the *Economist*, followed by a modest leader. What was striking was the dissonance of the serious leader pages with the jazzy presentation of news. On the second day, Diana was on the front and the Queen was inside. It may be unfair to single out this fact, but scanning the first month there were an awful lot of royal pictures and stories. In other words, it was little different from its rivals.

Shah also discovered an uncomfortable truth about newspaper competition: however willing rival owners had been to applaud his initiative, they were not prepared to give him a free ride. There was no room for sentiment, so the *Daily Mail* and *Daily Express* spent heavily on TV promotional advertising to prevent him securing a circulation toehold. *Today* sold an average of more than 300,000 in its first six months, better than many expected but not enough to make it viable. It did have an effect on its rivals – after three months, the *Mail* lost 61,000 and the *Express* more than 100,000, year on year[37] – but it proved no more than an entertaining novelty, and was widely considered to be a disaster.[38] It may have proved that publishing a non-union national paper with colour pictures was feasible, but these were not selling points with the public. *Today* had failed both to carve out a distinctive editorial agenda and to find a new audience: Middle England turned out to be a mirage.[39]

It had its moments, getting an exclusive interview with Libya's Colonel Gadaffi a week after a failed attempt to blow up an El Al plane at Heathrow. It also splashed on a story which claimed that the Queen had urged the prime minister to impose sanctions against South Africa.[40] When the *Sunday Times* published a similar story a couple of weeks later the balloon went up, plausible evidence that *Today* was not being taken seriously. A false story about Princess Diana being pregnant was unfortunate. One unusual deal that was to have a critical outcome for the paper involved the serialisation of a book by Jeffrey Archer, the former Tory MP who was then the party's deputy chairman. Instead of accepting a fee he took a tiny shareholding in the company of just 0.01 per cent.[41]

MacArthur, unlike most editors, was noted for his geniality. He even appeared to take an act of treachery by Holborow (he asked Shah for MacArthur's job) with an equanimity which amazed other journalists. A disaffected Holborow soon returned to the *Mail* as deputy editor, aware that MacArthur was taking counsel from Dennis Hackett, the vastly experienced former editor of both *Queen* and *Nova* magazines, *Daily Express* associate editor and the influential consultant who oversaw the launch of the *Mail on Sunday*'s magazine, You.

It was commercial rather than editorial problems which beset Shah. Within three months he realised he was in deep financial trouble because the editorial budget was higher than planned, the advertising revenue was lower than anticipated, and sales revenue was not being collected efficiently. He desperately sought new investors or a partner, flirting with Mohammed Al Fayed, Australia's media magnate Kerry Packer, Robert Maxwell and even Rothermere before sealing a deal with the *Observer*'s owner, Tiny Rowland. Rowland's Lonrho invested £14 million, paying £10 million to buy out other shareholders, thus giving Lonrho 35 per cent with Shah retaining 51 per cent and staying on as chairman. 'I did not believe in Father Christmas until today,' he said. MacArthur came under pressure once Terry Cassidy, the managing director Rowland imported from his Scottish newspaper operation, discovered that *Today* was losing £3 million a month.

In an attempt to turn the paper around, a relaunch was agreed, new staff were hired and *Today* became the Football League's official sponsor. Shah grew unhappy with his editor and, in early 1987, less than a year after launch, MacArthur accepted an offer from Murdoch and Neil to return to the *Sunday Times* as executive editor. His place was taken by Hackett, who obtained his biggest sales surge during the general election by taking up the cause of the Social Democratic party (SDP), urging people to vote for the Alliance and calling for tactical voting. Sales went up by 30,000 to 340,000. This political stance caused a rift between Rowland, who had pledged his support to SDP leader David Owen, and the Thatcherite Shah, who wrote to the *Times* to dissociate himself from *Today*'s line.

Today's financial difficulties were compounded by the cost of producing *Sunday Today*, which had been crafted by its editor, Tony Holden, into a 'stylish and witty quality'.[42] Finding an audience after a disastrous launch in a market dominated by the *Sunday Times* and the *Mail on Sunday* proved impossible, so Shah demanded it go down-market and agreed with Holden that he wasn't the man for that job.[43] By firing him on the week of the Rowland takeover Shah ensured that Holden, whom he liked, got a decent pay-off. His successor, Peter McKay, didn't get on with Hackett and departed swiftly. Towards the end of 1986, the former *Daily Mirror* assistant editor Bill Hagerty became its third editor within a year but, with sales below 250,000, the paper was losing money and, midway through the election, *Sunday Today* was closed. 'Lonrho probably saved fourpence,' Hagerty said.[44] In fairness, it saved a great deal more than that.

By early summer 1987, Rowland was facing a £6 million loss at the *Observer* and a projected £28 million loss at *Today*, despite securing deals with Murdoch and Maxwell to use spare capacity on its presses. He let it be known that *Today* was up for sale. *News of the World* editor David Montgomery, who had tried and failed to raise £20 million to buy the paper himself, urged Murdoch to buy it instead. On 13 June 1987, the day after Thatcher's third election victory, Murdoch met Rowland to agree a tentative deal in which he agreed to pay £40 million in instalments over a number of years. But Rowland, still locked into a feud with Fayed, suddenly pulled out because of a *Sunday Times* article which he thought too sympathetic to Fayed.

The story of the Murdoch deal was leaked to the *Independent*, presumably by Rowland, flushing out another bidder. Maxwell, upset at the failure of his London paper (see below, p. 493), wanted to make life difficult for Rothermere and to give his *Daily Mirror* the competitive edge over the *Daily Mail*. He had two ideas: he could either close *Today* and use its colour presses for the *Mirror*, or he could redefine *Today*, rename his *London Daily News* as *Tonight* and create a double-titled twenty-four-hour paper. Rowland set 30 June as a deadline: if there was no sale by then he would shut *Today*. It looked as though Maxwell's offer of £10 million cash and £30 million in loan stock was bound to succeed. But Shah, who still owned 10 per cent of the shares after gradually disposing of his stake, wasn't keen on Maxwell and, under takeover rules, Maxwell couldn't coerce him to accept the deal unless he controlled a full 90 per cent. He was short by just 0.01 per cent, the stake held by Jeffrey Archer.

Shah, still preferring Murdoch, initially held out against Maxwell's blandishments and an offer of £100,000. When it was upped to £250,000 with *Mirror* share options he gave his agreement. Maxwell then made a stupid error by boasting on the phone to Murdoch that he had won. In the course of the conversation, Murdoch, astute as ever, realised Maxwell had not yet got his hands on Shah's shares.[45] He contacted Rowland and offered £38 million in cash. Rowland agreed, but he set one final hurdle: the deal would have to go through without a referral to the Monopolies and Mergers Commission. How could Murdoch, owner of four papers, justify buying a fifth? Lord Young, the secretary of state, was told by both sides that if the agreement wasn't immediately approved the title would be closed. Young caved in, later facing harsh questions from Labour MPs in the Commons about handing another paper on a plate to his party's greatest press cheerleader.

The Press Council found the non-referral difficult to stomach. Chairman Sir Zelman Cowen and director Kenneth Morgan, a former NUJ general secretary, issued a statement: 'There could hardly be a more obvious increase in concentration than the acquisition of a fifth national newspaper by a group that already owns four.' The *Daily Telegraph* and the *Guardian* took a similar stance. Maxwell, angered at losing out yet again to Murdoch, was the only alternative bidder and he owned three papers which together had an even larger sale than Murdoch's. What could the government do in such circumstances but concede?

So *Today*, the first flowering of a post-Wapping era envisioned as a golden age of greater newspaper diversity, ended up in the hands of the world's leading press tycoon. Shah had failed to beat Fleet Street, lacking the know-how and the money. However, the men who planted the next seed enjoyed an altogether different experience.

As we have seen, the three former *Telegraph* journalists – Andreas Whittam Smith, Matthew Symonds and Stephen Glover – were well into their planning for the launch of a new broadsheet paper, initially entitled the *Nation*, before the end of 1985 (see above, p. 433). In January, they agreed that its title should be the *Independent*.[46] Like Shah, they were shocked by Wapping because it wiped out their paper's competitive cost advantage.[47] But Wapping was to prove one of the *Independent*'s greatest assets, helping it to attract both staff and readers. Many journalists from the *Times* and *Sunday Times*, worried by the ethics of union-busting, and conveniently overlooking the fact that they were about to work on a non-union paper made possible by Murdoch's move, wanted to cleanse themselves of Wapping.

The founders, as they became known, had raised considerable finances before their plans leaked, having set October 1986 as the target for the first issue of the first quality national paper launched for 131 years (since the *Daily Telegraph*). The original conception of a populist broadsheet gradually turned into a much more serious enterprise as they decided to fill a different gap, aiming deliberately up-market for territory they felt the *Times* had vacated, and for a younger audience which they felt the *Daily Telegraph* (under Hartwell or its new owner, Conrad Black) unable or unlikely to attract.

A stream of journalists applied to join, including many of the Wapping Diaspora and disaffected staff from the two Telegraph titles. From the *Times* and *Sunday Times* came political editor Tony Bevins, economic editor Sarah Hogg, columnists Peter Jenkins and Miles Kington, writers James Fenton, Isabel Hilton and Tim McGirk. The two *Telegraphs* provided literary editor Sebastian Faulks, Washington correspondent Alexander Chancellor (former editor of the *Spectator*), South Africa correspondent Tony Allen-Mills and cartoonist Nick Garland. Two key people also joined from the *Guardian*: writer John Torode and sports editor Charlie Burgess. From elsewhere came the bustling home editor Jonathan Fenby, lifestyle editor Audrey Slaughter and cartoonists Michael Heath and Colin Wheeler, while former *Times* editor William Rees-Mogg was persuaded by Whittam Smith to contribute a regular column.

It was an impressive and experienced line-up, and many of them were fired by a desire to prove to their former owners, Murdoch and Black, that there was a market for an avowedly serious broadsheet. They also had a financial stake in their new paper's success, most of them having agreed to take share options. The three founders had already granted themselves substantial shareholdings in the company, Newspaper Publishing. With start-up costs of £18 million, less than a third of the money lavished on the *Mail on Sunday* launch four years before, some £2 million was spent on a TV and poster promotion campaign with a slogan that turned out to be a real winner: 'The *Independent*. It is. Are you?' That simple phrase was particularly effective at a time when the more liberal *Times* readers were questioning the ethics of Murdoch's press ownership and the ruthlessness of his move to Wapping and its resulting violence. The *Independent* sought to appeal to people who felt uncomfortable about papers run by high-handed proprietors and who were also growing disenchanted with the Thatcherite philosophy espoused by the *Times* and *Sunday Times*. These were the people pejoratively labelled 'the chattering classes' by Andrew Neil during his many TV and radio broadcasts in defence of Wapping.

The first issue of the *Independent* on 7 October 1986 pulled off that most difficult of tricks, looking for all the world as if it had been around for ever. It was novel, yet somehow comfortable, with a front page that managed to appear both 'clean' and 'busy', a neat combination. It also announced itself as a solid, reliable, serious newspaper. Sales in the first week of about 500,000 a day fell swiftly to a less than spectacular average in the first month of 332,000. Was the *Independent* taking the same downward path as *Today*? With its three rivals promoting heavily and adding circulation too, there was more concern at City Road when sales fell in the following two months, slipping even further in January 1987, while the other three recovered from the seasonal dip. Was the new *Independent* too worthy, as critics, including some board members, suggested?

A boardroom row in December, which ended with chief executive Douglas Long being ousted and Whittam Smith adding Long's job to his editorship, created little confidence inside or outside the building. Nor was morale improved when Whittam Smith and Symonds fell out.[48] Then it was discovered that Robert Maxwell had secretly bought 4 per cent of the shares and was buying more. But the *Independent*'s technical expertise improved, its journalistic standards remained high, and its audience was beginning to grow throughout the spring when it got the kind of scoop which lifted its public profile still higher.[49] It obtained a copy of the then unpublished book *Spycatcher* by a former member of MI5, Peter Wright, which revealed all kinds of questionable behaviour by Britain's secret services.

It was one of those stories that set the news agenda for several days, placing the *Independent* at the heart of events when it was sued by the government for contempt of court. Whittam Smith and his new paper were cast as defenders of press freedom, proclaiming that they had acted in the public interest. That story reinforced the idea that the *Independent* was a high-minded enterprise and, by implication, indicated that those who bought it were similarly elevated. The *Independent* became a badge. It also found itself quite by accident and regardless of the *Telegraph* background of the founders and many of the staff, regarded as the new paper of the liberal establishment.[50] Named newspaper of the year in the *What the Papers Say* awards before it was even a year old, it won a reputation for doing things differently, sometimes by design – as in Whittam Smith's championing of stylish photography – and sometimes by accident, as in the case of not reporting royal stories.[51] It also stood above the fray in the 1987 election, refusing to support any party, and was the first to establish well-written, informative, signed obituaries as the norm under James Fergusson.

The *Independent* also got the credit for leading a revolt against the lobby system, marshalled by the combative and fiercely independent Tony Bevins. He informed Thatcher's press secretary Bernard Ingham that he would not abide by the lobby rules which demanded that briefings be unattributable. Ingham said it was unacceptable and Bevins then invited the *Guardian* and the *Observer* to join his rebellion. The *Observer* rejected the idea but the *Guardian*'s editor, Peter Preston, went part of the way. Though the revolt didn't last long, there were later concessions and it certainly played a part in opening up the system to scrutiny in the long run. Andrew Marr, then a political correspondent with the paper, later paid tribute to Bevins after his untimely early death as 'one of the real creators' of the *Independent*.[52] It was one example among many of the way in which *Independent* staff often took the initiative themselves, with Whittam Smith giving them the space to do so.

After *Spycatcher*, sales took off throughout the rest of the year and the next. By October 1988, two years after its launch, the *Independent* was selling 400,000 and had dramatically expanded the broadsheet market. Yet its main victim was not the *Daily Telegraph*, as it originally imagined, but the *Guardian*, which had lost 80,000 buyers. The *Times* was down by 40,000 copies and the *Telegraph* by just 25,000. Now that it had attracted a youthful and prosperous readership, advertisers gave it more and more support, though the company made a terrible mistake by appointing too few classified-sales staff and building no substantial base in this most lucrative of markets.[53]

Despite its claim to a right-wing economic stance and support for the free market, the *Independent* was perceived as a largely liberal anti-Thatcherite paper. Thatcher herself certainly saw it that way too, complaining to Woodrow Wyatt: 'The *Independent* is a misnomer – it is not independent at all. It is dedicated to trying to destroy me.'[54] It was viewed as a fresher, less hair-shirt paper of the centre left than the *Guardian*: middle class in tone, cultured, fair, non-partisan, and living up to its excellent title. This could be overstated. A *Sunday Telegraph* profile of the *Independent*, headlined 'How *Guardian* Man lost his soul and was reincarnated', identified a traditional *Guardian* reader in stereotypical terms as 'the high-minded, the Fabian, the Wet, the liberal with both a small and big "l"'. These people had flown to the *Independent*, it said, and predicted 'the death of *Guardian* Man and the birth of *Independent* Man'.[55] Instead, it suggested, its rival had embraced *Guardian* women, feminists and Marxists. Good knockabout stuff, but poor analysis. More appositely, Michael Leapman argued that many *Guardian* and *Times* readers might well have preferred the *Independent* just because it pioneered a comprehensive arts and leisure listings service.[56]

Throughout these years, Whittam Smith was gaining a public image of saintliness which he deserved only up to a point. At a meeting of owners I attended I noted how deeply he had thought about any number of issues. For example, when the thorny question was raised about how editors should deal with orders from the police to hand over pictures taken at riots, he said he had solved that problem quite simply. Once he had selected the shots for publication all other negatives and prints were destroyed. Then there could be no argument: his paper and his photographers could not be accused of doing the police's work.

But the Whittam Smith halo subsequently slipped. The comprehensive account of the *Independent*'s early years by Stephen Glover had a sad ending, with friends and colleagues falling out as the dreamers became schemers. For a good while, as Glover pointed out, 'almost everyone seemed to love us'.[57] Another innovation, the launching in September 1988 of a deliberately unglossy and classy Saturday magazine under the editorship of Alexander Chancellor was well received by readers. Augmented by a separate Weekend section inside the main paper, the Saturday package was soon selling 30,000 more than the weekday issues. The magazine was also the precursor to thoughts about the launch of a Sunday stablemate, though Whittam Smith and the board blew hot and cold in the following months. Newspaper Publishing reduced a first-year loss of £9.46 million to £1.56 million by the end of its second year and looked on course to make a profit. A Sunday launch would threaten its profitable hopes.

There was relatively little alarm when news broke that a group of people were hoping to launch a Sunday broadsheet. In a half-hearted defensive action, an attempt was made to forge a link with the *Observer*, but its owner Tiny Rowland, ignored the overture. It didn't seem to matter because the *Independent* was doing so well during the summer of 1989, selling above 400,000 with ease and getting to within striking distance of both the *Guardian* and the *Times*. From this point on the *Independent*'s story is inextricably bound up with the fortunes of the enterprise which eventually became the *Sunday Correspondent*, the catalyst for the launching of its own *Independent on Sunday*. The *Correspondent*'s genesis was much like the *Independent*'s, with a couple of journalists – David Blake, a former news editor on the *Times*, and David Lipsey, editor of *New Society* and a former writer on social affairs for the *Sunday Times* – getting together with Gavyn Davies, an economist with Goldman Sachs, and Douglas Long, the chief executive ousted by the *Independent* the year before, to dream an improbable dream. If there was a daily market for a tycoon-free radical paper, then there must be a Sunday market too, especially since the *Observer* had lost much of its liberal cachet under Rowland.

Like the *Independent*'s founders they set out to raise £18 million. Unlike them, Blake and Lipsey saw themselves as equals and couldn't, or wouldn't, decide who should take the leading Whittam Smith role. Instead they agreed to be joint deputy editors and sought a high-profile editor. Long tried to enthuse David Dimbleby, the TV presenter and chairman of his family's firm which owned local papers in Surrey, with the idea. For a couple of months it appeared as if he might take the job and when he didn't Davies approached the *Guardian*'s deputy editor, Peter Cole.[58] Then forty-two, Cole had a good journalistic pedigree, reporting for the *Evening News*, running the *Evening Standard*'s diary and spending ten years as an executive on the *Guardian*. Along with chief executive Nick Shott, hired from the regional group United Newspapers, Cole's initial task was to raise money. This proved much more difficult than eighteen months before, due to the October 1987 stock market crash and with the first signs of a recession alarming potential investors.

They struggled until the *Chicago Tribune* group stepped in at the last minute after the *Guardian* reneged on its original offer. The launch date was set for September 1989 but, once again, timing was against the *Correspondent*. The growing success of Saturday issues of the dailies was putting pressure on Sunday circulations. Advertisers were retreating as the recession bit more fiercely than anticipated, and agencies were notably cool towards the new title.

Journalists were much more enthusiastic and, as with the *Independent*, Wapping supplied the largest number of recruits. From the *Sunday Times* came foreign editor Jon Connell, foreign correspondent Angus Roxburgh, picture editor Mike Cranmer, health services specialist Jeremy Laurence, second section editor Mick Brown and sports writer Dudley Doust. From the *Times* came business editor Margareta Pagano and arts editor Chris Peachment. Other major signings were foreign correspondent David Blundy from the *Sunday Telegraph*, chief reporter Simon Freeman, a former *Sunday Times* investigative journalist, magazine editor Henry Porter, also an ex-*Sunday Times* diarist, and the *FT*'s gifted labour correspondent Phil Bassett. These heavyweight signings underlined Cole's promise to produce a paper 'with good writing by journalists freed from proprietorial control'.[59] So convinced were he, Blake and Lipsey of their venture's future that they hired two graduate trainees straight from Oxford university, Ian Katz and Jonathan Freedland, who were to prove among the brightest journalists of the coming generation.

Whittam Smith and his colleagues watched with increasing alarm as the *Correspondent* solved its problems and hired staff. How dare this upstart steal its thunder? Despite internal tensions, the founders were feeling supremely confident, having narrowed the circulation gap with both the *Times* and the *Guardian* to just a couple of thousand. Advertising, though, was falling away due to the recession and the profit forecast was running at just £4 million. In early September 1989, with the *Correspondent* weeks away from launch, they decided to risk launching a Sunday title in January 1990 with Glover as editor.

The *Correspondent* team were devastated, realising that it would severely undermine their chances of success. Another man who thought such a contest ridiculous was the Virgin entrepreneur Richard Branson. Through his friend, and biographer Mick Brown he arranged a pow-wow between the *Correspondent* and *Independent* at his house to see if there might be a last-minute merger. It failed in the face of Whittam Smith's insistence on a 'full takeover' rather than a part-share. That was out of the question for the *Correspondent*'s investors.[60] Suddenly Whittam Smith, the newspaper saint, became a sinner in the eyes of many of his media supporters, who claimed he was acting like any other press baron by trying to strangle a newcomer at birth. 'The *Independent*'s image has been irrevocably changed by its Sunday action,' wrote one commentator. 'It has not been a clean fight, this will we/won't we titillation riding on the back of an honourable title which did so much to change the industry.'[61] Lipsey was outraged. The *Independent on Sunday*, or *Sindy* as it became known in the trade, was launched 'deliberately to destroy us', he wrote later.[62]

While Glover set about creating dummies and hiring staff for the *Independent on Sunday*, the *Correspondent* set in train its £5 million launch programme. In the face of concerted advertising campaigns from rivals, who made considerable improvements to their own papers, the *Correspondent* deliberately concentrated in its promotional slogans on its independence: 'Great, but not Wapping' and 'Concise, but not Tiny'. *Sunday Times* editor Andrew Neil, senior horticulturalist in the garden of a hundred flowers, was one of the few to welcome the rival, seeing it as 'a child of Wapping', adding optimistically: 'I want to see as many newspapers as the market will bear and a diversity of ownership.'[63] That didn't stop him from doing all he could to ensure that his paper offered fierce competition to the newcomer.

The first issue of the *Sunday Correspondent* on 17 September 1989 was, in every sense of the word, a worthy attempt. The front page was dominated by a picture of an injured Cambodian baby with a routine domestic political story at the top. The rest was taken up by an index. It was uninspiring, grey and rather bland. There were two broadsheet sections and a magazine, and the paper had the feel of the *Observer* without its urgency and its well-known columnists. It did improve, winning some critical acclaim but, with the exception of the first month, it never came close to achieving its 362,000 break-even sales target. By January 1990, even before the *Independent on Sunday*'s launch, it was selling only 260,000.

That was nothing like the kind of circulation that could ensure its future, and its chances of growth were scuppered once the *Sindy* arrived. Glover's was an innovative package, with its main broadsheet section, a tabloid business news section and a much praised Review supplement. He had attracted high-quality staff too, such as literary editor Blake Morrison, associate editor Stephen Fay, home editor Peter Wilby, economics editor Christopher Huhne, the former *Times* theatre critic Irving Wardle and writers like Lynn Barber and the *Observer*'s award-winning columnist Neal Ascherson. His best signing, initially as a consultant, was undoubtedly Ian Jack, who had spent sixteen years at the *Sunday Times* as chief sub, editor of the Look section and foreign correspondent, winning two awards in 1985 as both journalist and magazine writer of the year. He left soon after the Wapping move and wrote for the *Observer* and *Vanity Fair*. Jack, a forty-one-year-old softly spoken Scotsman, was influential in creating the stylish appeal of the Review, which he looked back on years later as 'the best thing I did in terms of creating and shaping a newspaper section'.[64]

Jack's talent was well illustrated on the front page of the first issue, which carried a large picture of a woman cuddling her baby daughter moments after she had been rescued from a kidnapper. Jack wrote the excellent headline: 'Enter young mother, with a smile saying what words can't'.[65] The splash, on the terms of Nelson Mandela's release, was fine but the bottom of the page looked dull. The *Independent* brand was good enough to draw a larger audience than the *Correspondent* could command. Within two months of launch the *Sindy* settled down to a regular sale of 340,000, fewer than its aim for a regular 500,000 sale. It had to withstand promotions from the three established titles, which boasted of substantial additions. The *Sunday Times* increased to an eight-section paper, offering new arts, books and sports supplements. The *Observer* relaunched its magazine and returned its business news to a separate section. The *Sunday Telegraph* abandoned its traditional selling point – that it offered readers everything in one newspaper – by introducing a new Review section and an entertainment magazine called 7 Days.

Murdoch and Neil looked on with some amusement as the *Correspondent* and the *Sindy* tore strips off each other, stealing some sales away from the *Observer* and the *Sunday Telegraph*, but hardly denting the *Sunday Times*'s regular sale of more than 1.1 million. Five titles were chasing what many considered to be a finite audience which, even if it was to grow, would do so slowly. To make matters worse, the recession was worse than expected. The *Correspondent*'s sales collapsed, down below 200,000 by April and under 150,000 by August.

Desperate for money, the *Correspondent* board sought backers for a refinancing and the *Guardian* relented, putting in £2 million, while the *Chicago Tribune* provided still more. Robert Maxwell also made a substantial investment. It just wasn't enough and a second bid for refinancing brought Sir John Nott, chairman of Lazards merchant bank and former Tory defence minister, on to the board. Maxwell again increased his holding. Cole accepted advice to turn his broadsheet into what was optimistically referred to as Britain's first quality tabloid and he had prepared several dummies when Nott informed him that investors, as a condition of giving new funds, required a new editor.[66] Cole ruefully remarked: 'Whether it is a single proprietor or a group of major investors, it is the money men who call the tune.'[67]

John Bryant, managing editor of the *Times* and a former senior executive at the *Daily Mail* for fifteen years before that, was deemed to have the necessary combination of experience on broadsheets and tabloids to edit a relaunched *Correspondent*. His tabloid was interesting, but it was a hybrid which failed to catch the public imagination and lasted just nine issues before the board decided that the losses, running at £250,000 a week, were unsustainable. The *Correspondent* closed in November 1990 and, in a brutal final memo, staff were given an hour to leave the building.[68] The failure had cost some £35 million.

Over at the *Sindy*, the *Correspondent*'s closure made some difference to the fragile sales figures, which eased up smoothly towards 380,000, but advertising revenue was down substantially on the previous year. With the *Independent* also suffering from falling revenue, the founders' company desperately needed more funds, which were eventually secured from newspapers in Italy, *La Repubblica*, and Spain, *El Pais*. They contributed £21.5 million, each taking a stake of more than 12 per cent in Newspaper Publishing. Even so, by the end of 1990, hopes of the papers moving into profit looked very slim indeed.

Flowers refuse to blossom while a weed prospers

Just before the launch of the *Independent* a very different sort of paper arrived on the newsstands: the *Sunday Sport*. It was a calculated debasement of the coinage of the tabloid form by eschewing a news agenda, offering instead a diet of sex, sport and simple-minded stunts. Its publisher, David Sullivan, conceived it as a cheap and effective way of advertising his sex products, but he soon saw himself as a budding press tycoon.[69]

Born in Glamorgan in 1949, Sullivan was raised in Essex and Watford and graduated from London University with a degree in economics. After a spell in advertising, he set up in the pornography business, first selling pictures of nude women by mail order and then publishing a magazine, *Private*. He followed this in 1975 by launching a soft-porn magazine entitled *Whitehouse*, poking fun at Mrs Mary Whitehouse, the self-appointed guardian of the nation's morals. A year later his attempt to launch *Private National News*, a US-style 'sex-scandal newspaper in magazine format', flopped.[70] He moved on to produce sex films and also created a chain of Private sex shops before he was convicted in 1982 of living off immoral earnings for running two brothels masquerading as saunas, a case gleefully reported by the *News of the World*.[71] His nine-month prison sentence was reduced to three months on appeal and he served just seventy-one days. It didn't prevent him becoming a millionaire through his various pornographic activities, living in considerable style and owning several racehorses.

Many of his enterprises were joint operations with brothers David and Ralph Gold, who also owned sex shops. The pair each held 25 per cent of *Sunday Sport* to Sullivan's 50 per cent when it was launched on 14 September 1986, circulating initially in London and the south-east. The first front page set a trend, combining a picture of a busty blonde model with a splash which had a wholly misleading headline: 'Charles sex romp shock'. It transpired that the romper had only the most tangential of relationships with the Prince of Wales. Sullivan laughed off a chorus of hostility from the rest of press, the NUJ and the Campaign for Press and Broadcasting Freedom by pointing to his circulation figures: despite its restricted sales area, its first four issues sold an average of 280,000 copies.

It was an astonishing achievement for a paper financed on a shoestring and all the more surprising given that the Independent Broadcasting Authority banned Sullivan from advertising *Sunday Sport* on TV. The founding editor, Austin Mitchelson, made one high-profile signing – taking on former England football captain Bobby Moore as sports editor – before he was fired after the fifth issue. Sullivan relied on executive editor Mike Gabbert, a former *News of the World* and *People* journalist, to find a replacement and he chose an old colleague, John Bull. His major contribution was to feature women on the front page with improbably large breasts.

By March 1987, once able to publish across Britain and allowed to advertise on radio, the regular sale rose to 500,000. Bull left six months later and Drew Robertson, a former *Sun* sports journalist, gave the *Sport* a surreal twist with front-page headlines that were to become famous, such as 'World War Two bomber found on moon', 'Martians to invade Wimbledon' and 'Space Aliens turned my son into an olive'. He also cropped pictures so that girls appeared to be projecting from the page in 3D. For just a moment, this nonsense was considered post-modern and it was therefore fashionable to read the *Sport*.[72]

The *Sport* had illustrated that there was some kind of male-only audience for a paper even sleazier than the *News of the World* and the other Sunday tabloids. Although some cynics believed the *Sport* proved the old adage that no matter how far down-market a paper might go there would still be a sizeable readership, most believed it was a maverick joke which would have only short-term success. Spurned by advertising agencies, its only ad content came from Sullivan's own companies. It was a marginal publication existing on the fringes. No one in Fleet Street could possibly take it seriously, could they? Before we come to the twist in that tale, let's look at the other less enduring post-Wapping start-ups.

After the *Sport* and *Independent* launches, Robert Maxwell tried his hand. Murdoch's great feint, about publishing a *London Post* to compete with the *Evening Standard*, set Maxwell thinking. Since the *Evening News* title had vanished in 1980, many journalists – and proprietors – believed that the *Standard* would be vulnerable if faced with some decent competition. But the problem in challenging its metropolitan monopoly was difficult to overcome because the gap in the market, once filled by the *News*, was below the *Standard*'s. A *Sun*-style tabloid, for instance, might appeal to a large working-class audience. In advertising terms, though, such a paper would be unlikely, especially in the short term, to attract customers. With the *Standard*'s excellent readership profile and its grip on classified advertising, a down-market competitor would struggle for ad revenue.

Maxwell hired Charles Wintour, still bristling from his loss of the *Standard* six years before, to help set up a rival to compete with the *Standard* on its own middle-class territory. They eventually settled on a title, the *London Daily News* (*LDN*), and Maxwell eagerly accepted Wintour's recommendation of an editor. Magnus Linklater had worked under Wintour for five years in the 1960s as editor of Londoner's Diary. He then spent fifteen years in a variety of senior executive positions at the *Sunday Times*, leaving in 1983 to become managing editor (news) at the *Observer*. Linklater, aware of his lack of tabloid background, asked *Sunday Mirror* editor Mike Molloy to suggest a possible deputy editor who might compensate for his inexperience. One of the names he put forward was mine and Linklater duly lunched me. I was so enthusiastic at that meeting that I gave the false impression I would definitely accept the job. Struck by Linklater's sense of purpose, I was taken with the challenge of creating a serious paper within a popular format and thought it might just work. But the lunchtime excitement wore off the longer I thought about Maxwell, and Linklater was miffed when I declined the offer.

Linklater knew Maxwell was a monster, of course, but he accepted his word that the *LDN* would be a separate company with its own chairman, former News International manager Bill Gillespie. In the event, Maxwell fired Gillespie and interfered in every way possible, freezing hirings and freezing budgets, prevaricating and then complaining when it became clear his own hopelessly unrealistic launch date could not be achieved. Taking Linklater completely by surprise, he announced at a press conference that the *LDN* would be a twenty-four-hour newspaper, publishing new editions from morning to night. Linklater blinked in public and protested in private, but accepted the situation. It was only one of many crucial mistakes Maxwell made.

Rothermere, owner of the *Standard*, was not prepared to give Maxwell even half a chance of getting a competitor off the ground and pulled off a masterstroke. On the *LDN*'s launch day, 24 February 1987, the London public were surprised to find that they now had a choice of three evening papers: the *Standard*, the *LDN* and the *Evening News*, raised from its grave by Rothermere as a way of confusing the market place. With 'News' in two titles, it negated Maxwell's promotion material. Then Rothermere halved the cover price of the *Evening News* to 10p. Maxwell responded by cutting his to 10p, a crass error because cheapness tarnished the concept of the *LDN* being a quality product competing on equal terms with the up-market *Standard*. Rothermere cut his *News* again, to 5p.

Years later the Irish media tycoon Tony O'Reilly, having been previously told by Rothermere what led him to think of relaunching the *News*, mischievously invited Rothermere to explain to his dinner guests – who included a couple of Catholic bishops – how he had come up with the idea. Rothermere replied: 'Well, I was in me bath with me mistress when . . .' I was disappointed when Rothermere wrote to the *Guardian* to deny this anecdote, which I have since been assured was entirely true. Rothermere also ensured that Maxwell's inadequate distribution system was further debilitated by bribing the close-knit groups who control much of the London network of paper sellers not to promote the *LDN*. Without a trace of embarrassment the

Standard's former managing director Bert Hardy smiled as he told me: 'We took steps to buy the loyalty of street vendors.'[73] The *LDN* printing arrangements were also poor, so the result was inevitable: Maxwell's paper never achieved a sale that came close to the *Standard*'s 522,000. At best, it probably sold no more than 200,000.

In spite of all this, Linklater and his journalists produced a reasonably competent paper, though the marriage of *Guardian*-style features and *Daily Mail*-style news never quite worked. A typical example of the resulting incongruity was a front page dominated by a picture of a star, such as Joan Collins, arriving at Heathrow airport while the inside pages were devoted to a detailed analysis of the *Spycatcher* scandal or the future of the Official Secrets Act. Nor was the all-important sports coverage up to the mark. Then there was the overarching problem that no one really understood what a twenty-four-hour paper should be, or how it should operate.[74]

The relationship between Maxwell and his editor, never close, deteriorated further before the June 1987 election when Linklater refused to publish a pro-Labour editorial which had already appeared in the *Mirror*. Maxwell was also displeased with a column by Ken Livingstone which supported allegations that British troops had been involved in dirty tricks and assassinations in Northern Ireland.[75] In July, five months after launch, Maxwell closed the *LDN*. Soon after, Rothermere then shut down the *Evening News*, its spoiling task accomplished, and the *Standard* retained its monopoly.

It had gained a new editor in October 1986 when John Leese succeeded Lou Kirby, who took on a senior editorial role at Associated. Leese, born in Warwickshire in 1930, was editor of the *Coventry Evening Telegraph* by the age of thirty-two and six years later became deputy editor of the London *Evening News*. He stayed within the Rothermere empire, winning plaudits for his editing of the *Mail on Sunday*'s award-winning magazine You. He was an excellent technician with a good news sense but he set out to reinforce the *Standard*'s up-market image by concentrating on sophisticated features material. Leese played a crucial role in the defeat of Maxwell, overseeing the relaunch of the *News*, and he smiled indulgently when Maxwell later threatened to publish a free London evening, entitled the *Londoner*. The idea came to nothing, but Maxwell had far from satisfied his appetite for wasting money on new titles (see below, p. 516).

Next out of the starting gate was the *News on Sunday*, a paper conceived as a workers' co-operative, with a left-wing editorial agenda. It was doomed from the start, hopelessly idealistic, riven by internal disagreements and faction-fighting and drastically under-capitalised. A comprehensive account of its tortuous life, by Peter Chippindale and Chris Horrie, was aptly subtitled *Anatomy of a Business Failure*.[76] No self-consciously left-wing popular paper, such as the *Daily Herald* and *Reynolds News*, had managed to succeed in post-war Britain, including those which had substantial audiences and, in the

Herald's case, well-heeled ownership. A central problem in both cases was the failure to attract enough advertising revenue, a factor the *News on Sunday* collective did not grasp.

The idea for the paper was conceived before Wapping by a disparate group of Marxist-minded activists, who thought there was a large audience for a mass-market left-leaning title. This group, collectively known as the founders, enthused *Daily Mirror* writer John Pilger and the ex-Mirror group chief executive Clive Thornton with their idea. They were also encouraged by some wildly optimistic market research showing a huge gap in the market for a populist alternative Sunday tabloid. Thornton was an early casualty of the ramshackle committees, leaving in frustration, but two heavyweights – Nick Horsley of Northern Foods and Gerry Taylor, the former *Guardian* managing director – played key roles as chairman and consultant respectively. Brian Whitaker, one-time editor of the *Sunday Times* Insight team, also joined in a senior editorial post.

During the lengthy process of raising £6.5 million start-up money, mostly from trade unions and leftish London councils, Pilger recommended that Keith Sutton, then editing a pro-picket paper, the *Wapping Post*, should be editor. Sutton, forty, had been a sub-editor on many Fleet Street titles, working his way through university by subbing on the *Sunday Mirror* where he was one of the most militant, yet sensible, members of the casuals' chapel which I chaired. He was certainly a radical but he was to discover that under the umbrella of radicalism shelter an infinite variety of people with divergent ideas. Pilger, the editor-in-chief, soon found himself at odds with the founders. He first took issue with their decision to locate the paper's headquarters in Manchester. Then he railed against the structure of committees which resolved, or often failed to resolve, policy matters. As the staff of the *Scottish Daily News* had previously discovered, running a paper without a hierarchy is a hopeless proposition. 'Committees have failed the *News on Sunday*,' Pilger later wrote. 'Committees too often draw comfort from their own procedures and mediocrity; at worst they become cabals . . .'[77]

Pilger and Sutton also fell out. Pilger the purist couldn't countenance Sutton's ambition to create a radical *Sun*, arguing that it was a contradiction in terms. He preferred a paper which reflected in its look and content a departure from anything that had gone before, restoring the unspecified 'lost arts of tabloid journalism' exemplified by 'the old *Daily Mirror*'.[78] Reading his manifesto, it is uncertain whether it would ever have attracted a large audience, but his central point – that producing a left-wing *Sun* was specious – should have been debated more seriously. Pilger was outraged at one of Sutton's early dummies, arguing that it was banal, unserious and unworthy. He and Sutton then began producing entirely separate dummies.[79]

Pilger quit when the founders and their various committees backed Sutton, though they were very critical of his dummy too. He ignored their complaints, convinced that his approach would pay off. Before publication a row broke out over their advertising agency's promotional slogan for *News on Sunday*: 'No tits, but a lot of balls'. The founders thought it sexist and vulgar. It was overruled but not before it had appeared in the trade press, provoking yet more anger. One irony apparently overlooked by almost everyone was that the paper's production costs were relatively low because journalists could directly input copy. The NGA were given the paste-up jobs, but it was the despised Wapping revolution that had made *News on Sunday* financially feasible.[80]

Under the slogan 'Britain's bravest and brightest', some 1.5 million copies were printed of *News on Sunday*'s first issue on 26 April 1987. Its forty-eight poorly designed monochrome pages were uninviting, with a splash about a Brazilian man offering his kidney for sale and no news story of any consequence. It was an amateur production from beginning to end. The stirring editorial, headlined 'We Have a Dream', boasted about being a paper 'committed to equality, justice and freedom' and pointed proudly to the fact that 'we're not owned by a Murdoch or a Maxwell . . . We're a small outfit with a fraction of the budget of our competitors . . .'[81] It sold 518,000 copies and over the course of the following three weeks, with much improved design but patchy content, the sale fell to 230,000. Panic set in. It was estimated that each copy was costing £5 to produce and selling for 35p. When news of the company's financial crisis leaked to the *Financial Times*, creditors demanded to be paid.[82] Charles Wintour was called in to investigate and his report was damning.[83]

One of the original investors, Owen Oyston, the Blackpool-based estate agency millionaire, attempted a rescue. Sutton was fired after the sixth issue and Oyston gave his job to David Jones, an independent television producer with little newspaper experience, to turn it into a *Daily Mail* lookalike. He went after six weeks and Whitaker ran it jointly with a former *Mail* and London *Evening News* executive, Bill Nutting, for a while. Nutting was still in charge in October 1986 when sales had fallen to 130,000 and the paper was losing £85,000 a week.[84] Oyston couldn't sustain such losses and closed it the following month. Another post-Wapping flower had failed to bloom.

Manchester also played host to the next couple of failed launches. The first, in September 1988, was the *North West Times*, billed as the first new paid-for regional morning newspaper in Britain since 1873. It was further proof that even experienced newspaper executives can lose their senses when the dizzying prospect of newspaper ownership beckons. Roger Bowes, an ex-director of Express Newspapers, Peter Coulton, former northern ad sales director at the *Daily Telegraph*, and Robert Waterhouse, an experienced journalist, launched their title on start-up capital of just £1.5 million. Expecting to sell 60,000 copies of their *Guardian*-style paper across the north-west region, the shoestring budget meant there was little marketing. Content was unappealing and sales, which never reached anywhere near their projection, were down to 15,000 when they closed it seven weeks later. Fifty journalists and thirty-five commercial staff lost their jobs.

The day after the collapse of the *North West Times*, on 10 November 1988, Eddy Shah made his second attempt at becoming a national press tycoon by launching the *Post*. Once again seduced by the powers of technological innovation, he was convinced that he could produce a paper cheaply using 'new' desk-top publishing and publishing in 'full colour'. But what kind of paper? And why? What was the point? Where was the market niche for yet another red-top daily tabloid? Making much of the paper's Manchester location, he hired a Fleet Street veteran – former *Daily Star* editor Lloyd Turner – to edit. The pair announced that their new tabloid would be 'clean': no nudes, no invasions of privacy, no sleaze. Turner's senior staff were drawn largely from Fleet Street and, apart from the novelty of the computer system, they couldn't understand the point of the exercise. Once again, Shah seemed to believe that simply by reducing unit costs, he could beat his rivals, claiming he could break even with a circulation of just 350,000.

Advertisers, having seen his failure at *Today*, were sceptical. Readers were completely apathetic. Shah had shown misplaced faith in market research which 'found' that some 12 per cent of tabloid readers were dissatisfied with their papers. If they were, they weren't any better satisfied with the *Post*, a paper created without a reason and without a market. 'Hello Britain! It's great to see you,' said the first day's front page but Britain was looking elsewhere.[85] It was a lacklustre paper and, after just thirty-three issues, the *Post* was closed on 17 December. It died as it had been born, in obscurity, costing Shah £3.5 million – not that he worried much, having sold his *Messenger* papers in Warrington for £32 million.[86] He went off to reinvent himself as a novelist, but his *Post* did have one intriguing legacy. A clever and ambitious young woman managed to transmute her role as features secretary into one of go-getting, go-anywhere journalistic dogsbody. By the turn of the century, Rebekah Wade was to become the youngest female to edit a national paper.

Three successful launches, in 1988 and 1989, were *Sunday Life* in Belfast, *Scotland on Sunday* in Edinburgh and *Wales on Sunday* in Cardiff. This trio had the advantage of being set up by Thomson Regional Newspapers (TRN) in areas where their dailies – the Belfast *Telegraph*, the *Scotsman* and the *Western Mail* respectively – already had substantial readerships. They were carefully targeted, heavily researched, sensibly staffed and, most importantly, had the resources which enabled them to build sales gradually. All were still prospering in 2003.

TRN's experience apart, Shah's double failure and the other collapses showed that the new climate for papers was nothing like as favourable as the Wapping propagandists had argued. Cheaper pre-press production costs were illusory: distribution costs had increased, newsprint prices were rising, competition for advertising was cut-throat, finding print capacity at a reasonable rate was getting more difficult and the requirement to publish in colour was a heavy additional expense. A start-up still required huge funds. A newspaper also requires a purpose, or a unique selling proposition, if it is to have any chance of building an audience. Gaps in the market often turned out to be mirages. Reflecting on the failed launches in 1990, the former *Daily Mail* industrial correspondent Monty Meth asked rhetorically: 'Whatever happened to those claims . . . that if we broke the print workers' resistance to new technology it would lead to a proliferation of new newspapers?'[87]

Wapping, Hollywood and outer space: Murdoch rules the planet

Murdoch was elated by Wapping. If he wished, he could have squeezed his rivals by reducing ad rates and cover prices while increasing his promotional spend. But Wapping was widely unpopular for a while and all four titles suffered a sudden fall in sales. The *Sunday Times* lost 120,000 copies in three months; by mid-summer the *Sun* had fallen below 4 million for the first time in four years; the *News of the World*, which had begun selling more than 5 million in the second half of 1985, fell back; the *Times* did rather better initially, but it resumed a downward trend by the end of 1986. The *Sun*'s advertising agency, used to creating quickfire ads which plugged the paper's contents, devised a light-hearted generic advert designed to divert people's attention from the Wapping violence. At the meeting to decide whether it should be broadcast, Murdoch asked us one by one what we thought of it and we all murmured approval until he reached his managing director, Bruce Matthews, who said simply: 'It's rat shit.' Murdoch concurred and the ad was never shown.

That kind of candid, down-to-earth advice from the loyal, if wayward, Matthews didn't save his job. He was one of the first senior management casualties at Wapping, a psychological blow from which he never recovered.[88] Murdoch refused to give his former favourite, Nick Lloyd, any power either, so he sought a position elsewhere, becoming editor of the *Daily Express*. 'I'd had enough of ordering paper clips,' Lloyd remarked without a smile. Running News International at Wapping was to be a poisoned chalice in the coming years.

During this period, Murdoch took full control of the book publisher Collins, where he had held a 41 per cent stake for some years. He also paid a huge sum, $3 billion, for Triangle, the US publishers of *TV Guide*, the world's largest-selling weekly magazine. He was upset at being forced to sell off the *New York Post*, because of his purchase of a TV channel in the city, but he was on the verge of making television history in Britain by launching satellite TV.

Though the *Sunday Times*'s editor, Andrew Neil, clearly enjoyed

Murdoch's confidence at this point, it was *Sun* editor Kelvin MacKenzie who remained his favourite son. Soon after we arrived at Wapping MacKenzie had a sign put up announcing: 'You are now entering *Sun* country.' I then dug up a quote from Arthur MacEwen, first editor of William Randolph Hearst's *San Francisco Examiner*, which was also emblazoned on a wall: 'News is anything that makes a reader say, "Gee Whizz!"' This customising of the office was partly an animal-like marking of territory and partly symbolic of the euphoric post-Fleet Street sense of self-confidence.

To MacKenzie, Murdoch was king-emperor and the power which radiated from his throne invested in the *Sun* editor a potent sense of invulnerability. Having worked under him for a little over five years I had often witnessed him saying and doing extraordinary things, but he rapidly became yet more manic than before, willing to take greater and greater risks.[89] Not only could I no longer find any satisfaction in the job, I was finding it more and more difficult to excuse MacKenzie's behaviour. He was out of control and I decided to quit. There were moments of fun such as the harmless, if untrue, front-page splash, 'Freddie Starr Ate My Hamster', an iconic headline which became synonymous with the *Sun* ever after.[90] A ridiculous battle between the *Sun* and *Daily Star* to save a Spanish donkey, Blackie, from supposed death was also innocuous.[91] Less amusing for the amiable deputy news editor, Stuart Higgins, was an episode in which he was delegated to act as a lightning rod for readers' complaints. The *Sun* announced: 'Want someone to yell at? Scream at? Fume at? Ring Higgy the human sponge. He'll soak it up.'[92] The human-sponge epithet was to follow Higgins down the years.

But there was a darker side to MacKenzie's activities which none of his normal confidants could restrain. In 1987 the *Sun* topped the Press Council's complaints league with twenty-two complaints, of which fifteen led to censure, amounting to almost 40 per cent of that year's complaints upheld against national papers. The following year, six were upheld. MacKenzie scorned the Press Council's adjudications. One case involved a lorry driver who had refused to cross the Wapping picket line. According to the *Sun*, he was motivated by revenge against the *News of the World* for a story about him, and the *Sun* also revealed a previous conviction for a petty crime. When the Press Council backed the man, the *Sun* carried the judgement but repeated the allegations, accusing him of 'scuttling to the Press Council'. Chairman Sir Zelman Cowen then issued a statement saying the *Sun* should not have attacked a man exercising his right to complain. MacKenzie responded yet again with its 'lying trucker' accusation. It was one of the disputes which helped to bring about the Press Council's demise (see next chapter).

By now, kiss-and-tell stories were as prevalent in the *Sun* as they were in the Sunday tabloids, and it was one of these that caused the first of MacKenzie's several colossal errors of judgement and helped to undermine

Murdoch's faith in him. The first was a series of articles accusing singer Elton John of unlawful sexual practices, all based on the uncorroborated word of a homosexual prostitute and drug addict. In February 1987, MacKenzie published a three-page exclusive with a front-page headline, 'Elton in Vice Boys Scandal'.[93] John's lawyers served a writ for libel the next day, but the *Sun* published a second instalment, 'Elton's Kinky Kicks', which attracted a second writ. Still convinced his stories were correct, MacKenzie hit back with a front-page leading article: 'You're a Liar, Elton'.

The first story was speedily knocked down by the *Daily Mirror*, where former *Sun* man John Blake revealed that Elton has been out of the country on the date named in the story by the *Sun*'s source. Undeterred, MacKenzie followed up a couple of months later with unrelated pictures headlined 'Elton Porno Photo Shame'.[94] Finally, he published an absurd story about John's guard dogs having had operations to remove their ability to bark, 'Mystery of Elton's silent dogs'.[95] This was easily disproved, and another writ arrived. What MacKenzie failed to acknowledge was that *Sun* readers genuinely liked Elton John, were relatively untroubled about his self-confessed homosexuality, and didn't think the paper's bullying of the star was justified.

Though the source for the original articles was initially kept away from rival journalists, spending a month in Spain at the *Sun*'s expense, the *Mirror* eventually tracked him down and obtained his confession that he had made up the story: 'My sex lies over Elton'.[96] On the December 1988 morning that John's libel case was due to be heard at the High Court, lawyers for both sides reached an unprecedented deal which resulted in John being paid £1 million in an out-of-court settlement, and the *Sun* publishing a front-page apology: 'SORRY ELTON. *Sun* pays rock star record sum'.[97] 'I felt a great sense of shame that Elton John had to suffer in that way,' MacKenzie told the *Sun*'s official historian. 'The truth about the whole sorry business is that the *Sun* was taken in . . . by a very plausible young man who turned out to be an expert liar . . . we deserved to suffer. If you pay people like rent boys or prostitutes, who live by deceit and criminality, you should be wary about believing them.'[98]

At about the same time, the *Sun* was also compelled to pay damages to Mrs Carmen Proetta, the key witness to the Gibraltar shootings of three IRA members, whose testimony in a TV documentary called into question the government's version of events. The *Sun* falsely alleged that she was a prostitute, calling her 'the tart of Gib'. With readers' complaints against the *Sun* running at an all-time high, News International prevailed on MacKenzie to create an in-house ombudsman, and former managing editor Ken Donlan took on the task at the beginning of 1989.

Then came the most inexplicable mistake of all. In April 1989, ninety-five Liverpool football fans were crushed to death at Hillsborough stadium. Four days later the *Sun*'s front page was headlined in giant letters: 'THE TRUTH', and alleged that the fans had urinated on police, stolen from victims and beaten up a policeman who was trying to give the kiss of life. The story began: 'Drunken Liverpool fans viciously attacked rescue workers . . . it was revealed last night . . .'[99] The reaction on Merseyside was immediate and devastating. Newsagents led a boycott, some hid the paper, others refused to sell it. A petition protesting against the article was signed by 7,000 people. Hundreds of thousands stopped reading the *Sun*, losing it more than 200,000 sales within a week, and most didn't return. The *Daily Mirror*, itself criticised for its use of pictures of the crush, picked up more than 70,000 extra sales for a while. Even the *Daily Express*, then on a downhill slide, became popular on Merseyside for six weeks. Unsold copies of the *Sun* piled up. No one expected the boycott to last. It was one of the most dramatic sales falls in British newspaper history.

Confronted by 349 written complaints about the Hillsborough coverage affecting some thirty-five newspapers, the Press Council held a swift inquiry. It exonerated papers for publishing the distressing pictures because, even if upsetting and possibly intrusive, the Council considered there was a public interest reason for running them. It took a very different attitude towards the *Sun*'s 'Truth' front page, condemning the headline as 'insensitive, provocative and unwarranted' and finding that the article was 'unbalanced and . . . misleading'.[100]

Sun ombudsman Donlan had already ruled that the headline was wrong, and MacKenzie made one of his rare appearances on radio to issue a public apology. He told BBC 4's *The World This Weekend*: 'It was my decision, and my decision alone, to do that page one in that way, and I made a rather serious error.' Murdoch also felt it politic to issue a statement: 'Our coverage that day was uncaring and deeply offensive to relatives of the victims.'[101] In a television interview earlier that year he had agreed that the *Sun* sometimes went too far, 'and if it does I stamp on it'.[102]

The *Sun* also managed to offend journalists within Wapping by carrying a picture of the body of ex-*Sunday Times* foreign correspondent David Blundy in the morgue after he had been shot dead in the El Salvador civil war.[103] Blundy's former colleagues on the *Sunday Times* and his new ones at the *Sunday Correspondent* were outraged at the tastelessness of using the picture. The Press Council agreed, ruling that publication was 'insensitive and an error of judgement'.

Within this same five-year period, MacKenzie also upset the French, with headlines such as 'Up Yours, Delors',[104] the Japanese with 'Nips Are Drips',[105] homosexuals with 'PULPIT POOFS CAN STAY',[106] and the Queen (publishing her private Christmas card before she had even sent it out).[107] That cost £100,000, paid to charities of the Queen's choice, when she successfully sued for breach of copyright once it was proved that the *Sun* had bought the picture from a man who had stolen it from a processing lab. In a re-run of the Elton John case, the *Sun* headline was 'Sorry!'[108]

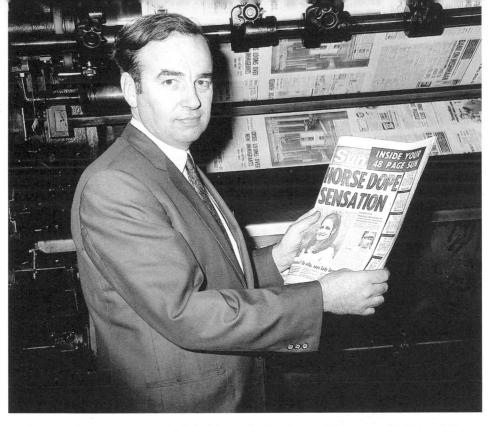

16. *Sun* king Rupert Murdoch holds up the first issue of his new tabloid in 1969 when it was selling 800,000 copies.

17. Thank you, my son: Murdoch and *Sun* editor Kelvin MacKenzie with the first *Sun* produced at Wapping in 1986.

18. A rare picture of a happy Lord Matthews after launching the *Daily Star* in 1978.

19. 'I suppose my papers echo my political views': Lord Stevens, chairman of Express Newspapers, with his late wife, Meriza.

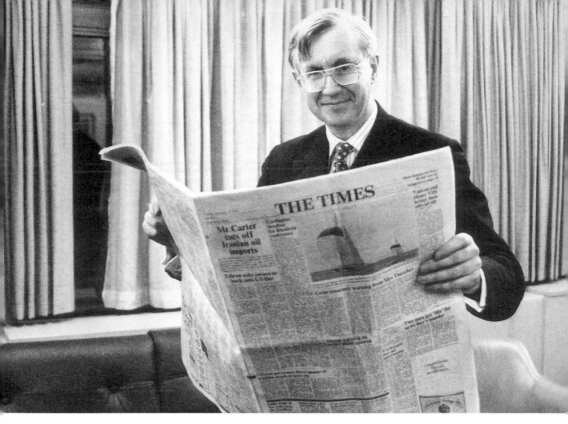

20. After surviving an office coup William Rees-Mogg edited the *Times* for a turbulent fourteen years.

21. How it was in the 1960s: *Daily Mail* sub-editors, with baskets and spikes, cut and paste copy to be set by Linotype men.

22. How it still was in the 1980s: a compositor at the *Times* makes up a page in hot metal ready to be moulded into a flong.

23. A heated end to hot metal: violence broke out regularly during more than a year of picketing after Murdoch's 1986 move to Wapping.

24. Not really ready, eh, Eddy? Murdoch's Trojan horse, Eddy Shah, with the first edition of *Today* in 1986.

25. An editor for a record-breaking thirty-two years, Sir John Junor.

26. A rogue celebrates his own life story: Robert Maxwell at the 1988 launch of the Joe Haines biography.

27. A lord-in-waiting: Conrad Black with his journalist wife, Barbara Amiel.

28. Beans baron turned press baron: Tony O'Reilly, owner of the *Independent*, outside at one of his Irish houses.

29. The *Mail* dynasty continues: Lord Rothermere IV took over the Associated Newspapers empire in 1998.

30. *Guardian* editorial succession: Alastair Hetherington says farewell after nineteen years in favour of Peter Preston who edited for twenty years.

31. From pornographer to press tycoon: Richard Desmond bought Express Newspapers in 2000.

Another MacKenzie trick was to steal material from the *News of the World* – itself known for stealing – encouraging executives to hack into the *NoW*'s computer system. It was so obvious that stories were disappearing to the *Sun* that *NoW* editor David Montgomery complained bitterly to Murdoch. In finally confessing his sin some fifteen years later, MacKenzie told of Murdoch's subtle way of dealing with the dispute. During a routine phone call Murdoch asked him as usual if there was much news about. 'I said it was very quiet,' MacKenzie recalled, 'and Murdoch replied: "Hmm, it must be quiet on the *News of the World* then".'[109]

As with all his executives and editors, Murdoch could give MacKenzie a bad time. After a telling-off, it was common for MacKenzie to emerge from his office rubbing his bottom and half jokingly talk of having had 'a good kicking from Gorilla Biscuits'. In public, Murdoch always spoke well of the man he occasionally referred to in private as 'the young Hitler'. He told one interviewer: 'MacKenzie is what he is. He's out there screaming, and he's good. Somehow it works.'[110]

What would happen, though, if it didn't work? In 1988, at its sales peak, 4,305,162 people registered for the first *Sun* lotto game, acknowledged as a record entry for a newspaper competition.[111] By the end of 1990 the *Sun* had lost the best part of 500,000 buyers in two years and was recording its lowest regular sale since 1981. The recession played a part, but the *Daily Mirror* didn't suffer anywhere near as badly. People were obviously turning their backs on the *Sun* because of its misbehaviour.

Andrew Neil: spies, sighs and the launch of Sky

In January 1987 I joined the *Sunday Times* in an undefined position 'to help' on the Focus pages. As may have been obvious from this history so far, there was virtually no staff cross-over between tabloids and broadsheets. They existed in separate worlds, which didn't change with Murdoch's takeover. Among the rare examples was John Bryant, who left the *Daily Mail* for the *Times*, but to go from a red-top to a broadsheet was a very rare step. It was a measure of Andrew Neil's willingness to take risks that he hired me, albeit after a recommendation from Murdoch.

The previous year had been anything but easy for Neil. In March 1986, the NUJ chapel came close to passing a motion of no confidence in him.[112] I soon discovered that he was unpopular but also grudgingly respected. In spite of his lack of newspaper experience, he combined a breadth of vision with an acute eye for detail. He was immensely knowledgeable about politics and economics, had an excellent grasp of international affairs and was clever enough most of the time to cover up in those areas – such as arts and literature – where he was weakest. He could be savage at news conferences, humbling those executives whom he suspected were not 'up to speed' on matters. He had a range of favoured phrases. The editors of the home and foreign desks were used to hearing that they must 'hit the ground running' on a story, and if they failed they were guilty of taking part in 'amateur night out'. Correspondents who got too close to their sources were 'fans with typewriters'. He had an intuition about who was pulling their weight and who was sympathetic to him, but he didn't seek approbation, revelling in conflict and confrontation. Most importantly, Neil could never be accused of sycophancy. He was cowed by no one, whether it was the prime minister, the Queen or his owner, Murdoch.

Sales were well down on five years previously, when the *Sunday Times* had been regularly selling more than 1.4 million, but they ran at a respectable 1.2 million throughout 1987 and rose substantially the following year as memories of the violent picketing receded, with the paper making a virtue of its growing range of supplements. Not until the recession bit in 1990 did they tail off, ending up below 1.2 million. Anecdotal evidence, backed up by market research, suggested that the public found big Sunday papers too intimidating because there was too much to read. As so often, there was a difference between what they said and what they did. The *Sunday Times*'s size proved one of its greatest assets. Apart from its basic value-for-money appeal to consumers, its comprehensive multi-section format meant that it was able to appeal to specific sectional interests within families. Neil, an admirer of the *New York Times*, was always pushing Murdoch to let him add yet more supplements.

Neil soon moved me to run the Review section, a position for which most of the staff considered me entirely unsuited, a major plus in Neil's eyes. It was there that I discovered some of the intellectual depth and artistic integrity of the *Sunday Times* which had survived the various defections since Murdoch's takeover, the appointment of Neil and the Wapping move. The arts editor, John Whitley, was a man of substance who overcame his initial suspicions of the man from the *Sun* to be a helpful and resourceful colleague. In turn, I had to protect him from Neil's (entirely correct) suspicion that he was not 'on side' and (entirely incorrect) view that he wasn't good at his job.[113]

There was much to admire about the *Sunday Times*, such as columns by Simon Jenkins and Robert Harris, the tireless work of political editor Michael Jones and his number two, David Hughes, the contributions of Professor Norman Stone, the book serialisations in the Review, a stream of well-written articles, especially those by Russell Miller, in the glossy magazine. Though I was unsympathetic to the paper's political line, just as I had been at the *Sun*, I could appreciate the professionalism. Even Neil's detractors, such as the *Observer*'s John Sweeney, admired his paper, writing: 'Like it or hate it, the *Sunday Times* each week runs articles that repay reading. It has captured the flavour of our times.'[114] Neil's self-absorption and self-confidence meant that he loved to be at the centre of events, revelling in the controversies which his paper provoked. One of the most sensational was a story about the differences of opinion between the Queen and prime minister Margaret Thatcher.[115] He stood up to a fierce assault, sure that his reporter, Simon Freeman, had faithfully reported a story given to him by the Queen's press secretary, Michael Shea.[116]

Later the same year he withstood internal office scepticism to run an exclusive Insight story about Israel's secret nuclear-arms programme.[117] Photographs and other documentary evidence were given to the paper by a disillusioned Israeli nuclear technician, Mordechai Vanunu, but Neil insisted on a rigorous check in case of a hoax. During that period, Vanunu was lured to Italy by an Israeli secret agent, kidnapped and smuggled out to Israel. He was tried for treason and sentenced to eighteen years' jail. Subsequent criticism of the *Sunday Times*, and of Neil in particular, for dithering over the story and failing to protect Vanunu was unfair. No one could have predicted that Mossad would go to such lengths to snatch the courageous whistle-blower.[118]

Seven weeks after the Vanunu story, the *Sunday Times* splashed on allegations made by a former MI5 agent, Peter Wright, that the secret service had attempted to bring down the former prime minister Harold Wilson.[119] The following April, just before his book, *Spycatcher*, was to be published in Australia and the United States, the *Independent* obtained a copy (see above, p. 484). Injunctions were issued against the *Guardian* and the *Observer* preventing them from publishing any material, but Neil negotiated the serialisation rights with the Australian publishers and, in great secrecy, published extracts in July 1987.[120] A four-year court battle followed which culminated, in November 1991, in a European Court ruling that the British government had breached Article 10 of the European Convention on Human Rights by banning publication of *Spycatcher*.[121] Neil was vindicated.

It is sobering to reflect that Neil attracted much more publicity for a court case about an entirely trivial matter: his relationship with a young woman called Pamella Bordes, a former Miss India. They were introduced at Tramp nightclub by Lord Rothermere's estranged wife, Bubbles, in March 1988. Their affair began the following month and, as I can testify, it was anything but peaceful. She was clearly infatuated with him, often hysterical, and there were several splits and reunions. After one row she famously slashed his shirts and jackets.[122] Their tempestuous affair eventually ended in November and she contacted Neil only once after that, to inform him that she had become a parliamentary researcher. In March 1989, Murdoch called Neil during the *Sunday Times*'s busiest period, a Friday evening, and said: 'It seems that one of your former girlfriends is a call-girl.' He told him that a story on Bordes would be the splash in that weekend's *News of the World*.[123]

Neil later spoke to *NoW* editor Patsy Chapman, who gave him a copy of the story she was preparing to publish which alleged that Bordes was willing to go to bed with a reporter for £500. It was the result of a classic sting operation, later described in detail by one of the team, Gerry Brown.[124] It left no doubt in Neil's mind about Bordes's misbehaviour. The thin public-interest justification for exposing Bordes was her part-time role as a House of Commons researcher, working for a Tory MP. The story might well have died because Bordes vanished abroad and it was blindingly obvious that she had never been a threat to the nation's security. In another twist, *Observer* editor Donald Trelford – who had been casually introduced to Bordes by Neil – accused News International of implicating him in the affair. Suddenly the tabloids, with the *Sun* taking the lead, had a new angle to pursue: two broadsheet editors involved with the same girl. Neil was very upset by the *Sun*'s front page, 'Dirty Don tried to pull my Pam says randy Andy', noting years later: 'Rupert gave Kelvin the green light to go to town in the *Sun*.'[125]

A third broadsheet editor gave the story renewed legs the following weekend. Peregrine Worsthorne of the *Sunday Telegraph* ran an editorial which pompously argued that Neil was unfit to edit a serious newspaper because of consorting with Bordes.[126] Neil thought it implied he had dated Bordes knowing she was a prostitute, which I knew to be completely untrue. Neil regarded Worsthorne's editorial 'as a serious attack on my personal integrity and professional reputation' and asked for the paper to publish 'a clarification ... making it clear that I had known nothing of Bordes's nocturnal activities'.[127] When that plea was rejected he sued for libel. The following month, the *Daily Mail* paid Bordes to tell her life story, though the writer, Lynda Lee-Potter, was so incredulous at her account she allowed her scepticism to show through. Even so, some details proved embarrassing for Neil, who wasn't placated by an oily call from *Mail* editor David English trying to excuse the inexcusable by publishing her nonsense in the first place.

For more than six months, Bordes retreated from public attention, but Neil refused to shelve his libel action. Worsthorne's offending leader had not been written off the cuff. As one of his friends pointed out, Worsthorne pined for the return of the nineteenth century 'when distinguished gentlemen edited important newspapers from booklined studies'.[128] He lamented what he considered were falling standards in Fleet Street where 'oiks became editors because proprietors think oiks can make more money than educated, cultured people with high intellectual standards'.[129]

Worsthorne's proprietor, Conrad Black, didn't think his editor should have written about Neil's private life, but he backed him in the court action, principally because he didn't think the piece libellous. Neil's proprietor, Murdoch, agreed. Woodrow Wyatt reported that Murdoch was 'very cross', especially because his company stood to pay out £200,000 in legal costs if Neil lost, yet he had sued without consulting Murdoch. He thought Neil had 'made a fool of himself by reviving the whole bloody thing'.[130] The resulting week-long trial in January 1990 certainly confirmed Murdoch's fears about the case attracting bad publicity. It offered papers a chance to rehearse the whole Bordes episode and to report on the titillating evidence about Neil thrown up by the *Sunday Telegraph*'s defence lawyers. The jury found in Neil's favour but awarded him £1,000 damages and his co-defendants, News International, just 60p, the price of a copy of the *Sunday Times*. He had won, as he wrote later, by the skin of his teeth.[131]

That case played a part in Murdoch distancing himself from Neil. While agreeing that Neil was a brilliant editor running a 'magnificent' paper, Murdoch was often irritated with him.[132] Yet they appeared to have been so close the year before when Neil took on the extra role of executive chairman of Sky Television in the months ahead of its successful launch, leaving his senior executives to run the *Sunday Times*. Murdoch and Neil, both beaming, stood together at the Sky launch party in February 1989.

Sky gradually won an audience, with enthusiastic cross-promotion in the *Sun* and *News of the World*, though the *Times* and *Sunday Times* were more muted in their support. Murdoch faced down considerable pressure from politicians concerned by the way in which his satellite-TV venture had evaded regulations restricting newspaper proprietors from owning more than a 20 per cent stake in terrestrial TV. In its first full year, up to June 1990, Sky cost Murdoch about £10 million a week. But he devoured his only competition in November that year, merging with the ailing British Satellite Broadcasting and reducing his losses to set the stage for later profitability.

The downward spiral as sleaze moves mainstream

Some *News of the World* staff expected their former editor, Nick Lloyd, to return to the paper once he completed his course at Harvard Business School. Instead, while Lloyd was being groomed, rather unhappily, for a management role, David Montgomery kept the editorship. Already regarded as a risk-taker and aware that the *Sun* was encroaching on his kiss-and-tell territory, he decided to be more outrageous in order to counteract his paper's post-Wapping sales drop. Revelling in the climate of misbehaviour, he unleashed the *News of the World*'s hounds, happy for them to amass evidence of supposed wrongdoing by using the increasingly sophisticated listening devices that were becoming available at the time. His most sensational exclusive by far, in October 1986, was about Jeffrey Archer, deputy chairman of the Conservative party and best-selling novelist, who was accused of sending an emissary to pay money to a prostitute, Monica Coghlan.

NoW reporters witnessed and pictured Coghlan being offered, and then refusing, an envelope containing £50 notes which were thought to total £2,000. They also tape-recorded phone calls between Archer and Coghlan in which he urged her to go abroad. The five-page story, headlined 'Tory Boss Archer Pays Vice Girl', implied that Archer had had a sexual relationship with the woman but it took care not to state that as a fact.[133] Archer denied ever meeting the woman, maintaining that he had paid her for research connected with his latest book. The following Saturday, the *Daily Star* was not as reticent as the *NoW*. In a story headlined 'POOR JEFFREY: Vice girl Monica talks about Archer – the man she knew', it alleged that he had met Coghlan after all.[134] Although it appeared from the headline that Coghlan had spoken to the paper, the quotes had come from a nephew. Archer then issued libel writs against the *Star* and the *NoW*.

In the resulting High Court case in July 1987, during which the newspapers co-operated with each other, Archer painted himself as a man above sexual reproach, a pillar of the community devoted to his family. His wife, Mary, proved to be a superb witness. *Star* editor Lloyd Turner was expected to give evidence for the paper, but was troubled that he would be compelled to reveal the source of transcripts he had obtained of the Coghlan–Archer phone calls. The *Star*'s counsel and its chairman, Lord Stevens, decided he shouldn't go into the witness box.[135] In the event, it probably didn't make any difference to the outcome. The judge, Mr Justice Caulfield, made a celebrated, eccentric summing-up which amounted to a eulogy to Archer's wife. 'Remember Mary Archer in the witness box,' he said. 'Has she elegance? Has she fragrance? Would she have, without the strain of this trial, radiance?' Caulfield then asked of Archer: 'Is he in need of cold, unloving, rubber-insulated sex in a seedy hotel?'

The jury awarded Archer a record £500,000 and the *Star*'s owners, Express Newspapers, paid out £700,000 in costs. The *News of the World* settled out of court, paying Archer £50,000 in damages and £30,000 in costs. When the result was announced, Turner was stunned.[136] He knew his days as editor were numbered, though he would never have guessed the circumstances which would lead to his swift departure (see below, p. 509).

Montgomery's position at the *News of the World* wasn't in the least threatened by the Archer episode so his paper carried on as before, uncovering the secrets of the famous. In March 1987, the *NoW* ran a salacious story about TV presenter Russell Harty's homosexual dalliances based on the word of a young male escort.[137] Eighteen months later Harty died and his friend, the playwright Alan Bennett, used his funeral oration to berate the *NoW* for exposing his homosexuality after 'trawling public life for sexual indiscretions'.[138] He even accused the paper of being responsible for Harty's death, claiming that by panicking him to work harder he was too exhausted to fight off an attack of hepatitis. Reporters had delved into every aspect of Harty's life and, when he was fighting for his life in hospital, photographers had trained their cameras into his room from a flat opposite.

None of this criticism appeared to ruffle Murdoch, who promoted Montgomery by translating him from the *News of the World* to *Today* in August 1987 (see below, p. 517). If Montgomery's editorship had been controversial, it was nothing to the ructions caused by his successor, Wendy Henry, the first woman editor of a national paper since 1903. I worked for five years with her at the *Sun* and believed her to be Murdoch's most inspired choice of *NoW* editor since buying the paper.

I had misgivings about her taste, evidenced by some freakish features while at the *NoW*'s magazine and an unfortunate rewriting of an article about Simon Weston (see Chapter Sixteen). Despite that, I thought she had all the attributes required by an *NoW* editor: a love of sexy scandals; a kaleidoscopic knowledge of celebrities and their peccadilloes; an intense interest in life's frivolities, from astrology to the latest storyline on the nation's TV soaps; and a facility to create a story, and a headline, out of apparently innocuous copy. Her *NoW* deputy, Phil Wrack, agreed. 'She's always had an unerring instinct for spotting a story that will interest *News of the World* readers,' he said.[139] True, these strengths were offset by weaknesses. In bending stories to her whim, she could be guilty of distorting the truth; she was bored by politics and anything remotely serious, though in this she probably mirrored the feelings of her readers; and her management skills were imperfect. She tended to love – and protect – staff who loved her, but she had no time for those she felt opposed her. Then again, most tabloid editors were hardly noted for a caring attitude towards people they didn't believe to be 'on side'.

Henry, born in Manchester and schooled at Lytham St Annes, was the daughter of a market trader. She started her journalistic career as a freelance in her home city, managing to obtain an exclusive story about the daughter of the last woman hanged in Britain, Ruth Ellis. She joined the *Daily Mail*'s northern office in 1975, leaving within twelve months to spend three years reporting for the *News of the World* in London. After a couple of years as features editor at *Woman* magazine, in 1981 she was appointed features editor of the *Sun*, and, as we have seen, played a key role on the paper (see Chapter Fifteen). She also impressed Murdoch with her editorship from 1986 of the *News of the World*'s Sunday magazine. If Murdoch wanted, as he once demanded of Derek Jameson 'more revelation, more investigation, more sensation', then Henry was an ideal choice as *News of the World* editor. Of course, even the *NoW* requires balance, and the failure to achieve that was her undoing. In my experience, Henry was much less ruthless than her reputation suggested and certainly less cavalier. She took chances, but only having weighed up the risks. When she bought the diaries of a model, Fiona Wright, who claimed to have had an affair with Sir Ralph Halpern, head of Burtons, she called me at the *Sunday Times* to ask if I would read part of the copy. 'What do you think?' she kept asking. 'Should we do it? It's not quite there, is it?'

A lot was unprintable, even in the *News of the World*. In the end, in trying to enhance one incident, she got into trouble with Murdoch.[140] Nor did he take kindly to the issue in which she published a picture of septuplets. The genuine photograph showed only six, because one was too weak to be pictured, so Henry decided to add a seventh by reproducing one of the babies twice.[141] Her most notorious exposé was of the well-liked TV presenter Frank Bough, who – after realising the paper had obtained detailed evidence during a three-month investigation – negotiated a deal in which he 'confessed' to have attended orgies and taken drugs.[142] Bough's initiative enabled him to cover up certain details he didn't want people to know in return for allowing the story to be published. Doing such deals later became a regular habit for the paper. It would approach its celebrity victims with its reporters' evidence and see if they would be agreeable to confessing their sins. One bonus was that the paper wouldn't face legal action.

With the *NoW* attracting odium, Murdoch tried to curb Henry's excesses in phone conversations she later described to me as terrifying. She pointed to the rise in circulation as justification. In August 1988, a year after she took over, the *NoW* sale reached 5,454,441, its highest circulation in thirteen years (which it was never to attain afterwards). Surely she was giving the people what they wanted. Wasn't that Murdoch's central credo? But Murdoch, warned by cautious executives about the build-up of political hostility and the outrage of other editors, considered Henry too loose a cannon. 'Sales aren't everything, Wendy,' he is reported to have told her.[143]

By December 1988, with growing concern about tabloid misbehaviour among politicians and broadsheet editors who feared the advent of a privacy law, Murdoch asked Henry once again to tone things down and change direction. She was said by her friend Eve Pollard to have 'exploded with Rupert', an outburst of anger she later regretted.[144] It ended with her resignation, having served sixteen months as editor. 'The repercussions' of her reign 'continued to be felt well after her departure in the form of writs', commented the paper's official historians.[145] Her replacement as editor – another woman and another former senior *Sun* executive, Patsy Chapman – was so distressed at the need to publish so many apologies and announcements of legal actions being settled that she insisted on distancing herself from them by adding the phrase: 'This story was published under a previous editor.'

While Henry's career seemed to be over, Chapman's appeared to have taken off. She had spent her eighteen years largely as a technician, a sub-editor with a flair for writing witty copy and headlines on the *Daily Mirror* and the *Sun*. Her Page 3 girl captions were particularly admired for their flippancy. She rose through the ranks under MacKenzie, eventually running the night desk until he chose her to be his deputy. She shared Henry's view of the paper's essential diet – 'a bit of froth and showbiz, something sexy'[146] – but she was not as hard-nosed.

Chapman was imbued with a natural caution which her detractors pejoratively described as indecisiveness. Under her, the paper substituted sauciness for sleaziness, a slight, but significant, degree of difference. From the moment she took over, sales went back into decline. As proof of the public's hypocrisy, a Mori opinion poll commissioned in November 1989 by the *News of the World* revealed that 73 per cent of people surveyed thought the paper intruded too much in the lives of public figures.[147] Yet sales went down immediately the paper began to be less intrusive.

Could a paper alienate readers by going too far down market? The experience of the misguided experiment by the chairman of United Newspapers, David Stevens, suggested that it could. By the early summer of 1987, the newly ennobled Baron Stevens of Ludgate was growing increasingly worried about the state of the *Daily Star*, despite its reasonable sales performance, managing a creditable average of almost 1.3 million in the first half of 1987 when the *Sun* and the *Mirror* were struggling. To most people inside and outside the *Star*, its major need was extra resources, and maybe a new vision and/or a new editor, but it wasn't in need of major heart surgery. According to the Express group's managing director, Andy Cameron, the board thought the problem was editor Lloyd Turner's 'worthy and caring' agenda which wasn't 'a good formula for a down-market tabloid'.[148] Nor was Stevens impressed with the *Star* losing the Archer libel action.

While Stevens and Cameron were mulling over what to do, deputy chairman Sir Gordon Linacre picked up a rumour that the owner of *Sunday Sport*, David Sullivan, was negotiating with Rothermere's Associated Newspapers to launch a *Daily Sport*. Stevens believed such a paper would injure the *Star* and, therefore, the group.[149] Cameron was delegated to contact Sullivan and they came up with an astonishing plan to give Sullivan editorial and marketing control over the *Star*. In other words, the *Star* would become, in all but name, the *Daily Sport*. United, owner of the staid *Yorkshire Post*, *Punch* magazine and a host of well-respected regional titles, would also invest in Sullivan's company. It was a win–win deal for the owner of a chain of sex shops and a string of pornographic magazines.

So, in August 1987, United signed a five-year agreement with Sullivan's company, Apollo, paying £2 million for 24.8 per cent of Apollo's stock. Cameron was also appointed to Apollo's board. Turner was sacked and Sullivan's editorial adviser, Mike Gabbert, replaced him as editor. What Cameron, who initially found Gabbert 'bright, bouncy and full of ideas', only later discovered was that 'he was a raging sex maniac and gutter rat', an 'archetypal sleaze journalist . . . low-life . . . utterly amoral'.[150] He didn't know that Gabbert had been sacked from the *News of the World* in 1972 for sexual and financial misbehaviour.

After the *NoW* disgrace, Gabbert ran a golf club for ten years before returning to journalism in 1982 as editor of a regional paper, the *Sunday Independent* in Plymouth. He left there under a cloud as well for an elaborate expenses fiddle before joining up with Sullivan. At fifty-one, Gabbert had never expected to return to Fleet Street, let alone as a national paper editor. 'My aim', he bragged, 'is to punch a big hole in Mr Rupert Murdoch's newspapers.'[151] Forecasting a rapid rise in sales to 2 million, he proudly expounded his editorial philosophy: there must be 'the biggest boobs possible' in every edition.[152] His first, and most notorious, example was a set of titillating pictures of a fifteen-year-old girl who was vowing to go topless when she turned sixteen. The exploitative nature of the exercise, and the use of scores of nude pictures and salacious stories, appalled many of the staff, especially women's editor Alix Palmer, who dared to say so in her column. She soon resigned, as did her supposed replacement, Moira Petty, and features editor Ian Mayhew. Leader writer David Buchan was fired for calling the Gabbert *Star* 'a soft-porn rag'.

People protested in their hundreds by telephone and letter. MPs from all parties complained. Circulation plummeted by half a million copies.[153] Advertisers threatened a boycott, with Tesco cancelling a £400,000 contract and others, including the Co-op, letting it be known that they were on the verge of pulling out. Gabbert responded by saying he would reconsider the direction in which he was taking the paper, which amounted to cutting down just a little on the nudes. After eight weeks of the *Daily Star/Sport*, Stevens and Cameron realised they had made a disastrous mistake. Gabbert was fired. United compensated Sullivan by returning the Apollo stock for free and making a further payment of £1 million. It had been a ruinous exercise for Express Newspapers. The *Star*'s already tenuous claim to be a credible alternative to the *Sun* and the *Daily Mirror* was shattered.

Stevens appointed a new editor, Brian Hitchen, a former *Mirror* and *Daily Express* executive who was then *Sunday Express* deputy editor. His brief was to make it a 'proper' tabloid again.[154] But the damage to the paper's reputation was so severe that Hitchen could do nothing to stem the tide as readers drifted away. By the end of 1990, it was selling barely 850,000 copies. Under Hitchen, the once left-of-centre *Star* became hysterically right wing and some of his ideas to clean up the paper, such as banning all sex-related adverts and dropping the daily use of topless model pictures, were vetoed by Stevens.[155]

Sullivan used his windfall from Express Newspapers to do as he originally planned, launching the *Daily Sport* in August 1988, beginning with a Wednesday-only issue, later expanding to Fridays and Saturdays, then going daily late in 1990. He more than covered the extra production costs because much of the advertising was for his own company's lucrative telephone sex lines. His first editor, Gabbert having died soon after the Stevens fiasco, was none other than the launch editor of the *Daily Star*, Peter Grimsditch (see above, p. 332). He thought Sullivan 'much more honest' than other newspaper controllers, even if he did bombard him with faxes telling what he wanted.[156] Unlike the *Sunday Sport* edited by Drew Robertson, Grimsditch's paper didn't go in for fantastical tales. Not that it was much of a paper either, relying on a diet of sexy pictures and stories. Indeed, it was Robertson's title which caused one of the greatest rows of the period, an intrusion into privacy so indefensible that it was to remain the most quoted example of journalistic misbehaviour for the following decade (see next chapter).

Sullivan was not content with his *Sport* titles, and decided to buy into an established group, purchasing 5 per cent of Portsmouth & Sunderland, a company with three evenings and several weeklies. Within eight days, after hostility from the P&S board, he sold them to Associated Newspapers and made a £500,000 profit. In January 1990, he bought 7.4 per cent of the *Bristol Evening Post* and announced that he was considering a bid. The Department of Trade and Industry immediately asked the Monopolies and Mergers Commission to investigate.

The panel found conclusively against Sullivan, arguing that he 'could be expected to influence editorial policy and the character and content' of the Bristol papers. Basing its view largely on what had happened at the *Daily Star*, it therefore rejected his takeover on public-interest grounds.[157] Both the *Independent* and the *Times* thought the decision unfair: the character of an owner was irrelevant, his money was as good as anyone else's. The market should be as free for pornographers as it was for anyone else.

Maxwell: a man running newspapers the British way

Soon after Murdoch's move to Wapping, a chauffeur-driven Rolls-Royce pulled up on the Highway, the main road where pickets gathered daily to roar at the people going into the plant. Out stepped Robert Maxwell to a mixture of cheers and jeers from a group of printers. A van with a TV news team arrived seconds later, and the big man was filmed walking along the steel fence talking to camera about Mirror group having 'done things the British way, by negotiation, not confrontation'. Unlike Murdoch, he had treated the unions properly, 'like Englishmen'.[158]

This was a truly wonderful Maxwellian moment. Here was a Czech-born naturalised Briton who owned companies across the world criticising an Australian with vast global interests who had just taken American citizenship for treating the print unions just as he had five years before at the British Printing Corporation. Maxwell had a selective memory and he wasn't going to miss an opportunity to extract the maximum advantage from a rival's difficulties while winning himself publicity. It was true that he had managed to negotiate redundancies, but he had not secured direct input by journalists and the NGA still ruled the paste-up boards, while the other print unions held sway on the presses. He did, however, have one important ace up his sleeve having had the foresight to install presses and expensive pre-press machinery capable of publishing his *Mirror* titles in colour. Murdoch, in his haste to set up Wapping, had not prepared for colour.

The Wapping effect, along with the sharper edge of Richard Stott's editorship, gave the *Daily Mirror* a sales uplift during 1986. From June 1988, with the *Mirror* being published in colour in London and the south-east, sales rose by 70,000 and the paper achieved a consistent 3.1 million sale up to 1990. Stott, though a long-time friend and ex-colleague of Kelvin MacKenzie's, capitalised as often as possible on the *Sun*'s reckless behaviour. There were losses along the way as the old *Mirror* guard departed, such as assistant editor Geoffrey Goodman, political editor Terry Lancaster and columnist Keith Waterhouse, who joked that his column was a sort of music-hall act which could move from theatre to theatre. He chose to take his curtain calls at the *Daily Mail* instead, after sixteen years with the *Mirror* during which time he had written the paper's style book, a witty debunking of tabloid journalese.[159]

The most significant act by the pugnacious Stott was the way in which he gradually convinced Maxwell to stop promoting himself so often in the paper, though he was disheartened by Maxwell's insistence that the *Mirror* serialise his official biography in 1988.[160] Generally, he managed to restrict Maxwell's appearances so successfully that Maxwell grew increasingly unhappy with his editor, despite the paper's strong showing, and turned for advice to his managing director, Ernie Burrington, and his editor-in-chief, Mike Molloy. The completely unexpected result – to me and to virtually everyone in newspapers – was that Maxwell asked me to become *Daily Mirror* editor.

I had previously turned down two Maxwell posts, as deputy editor of his *London Daily News*, and the editorship of the *Sunday People*. The *Mirror* was a different proposition. It was the paper I had read as a young boy. I venerated Hugh Cudlipp. Of all the papers I had yet worked for, its politics were closest to mine. My wife, Noreen Taylor, was a highly valued feature writer on the paper. There was Maxwell, of course, but I had worked for Murdoch, MacKenzie and Neil and survived. Surely he couldn't be tougher than them? At the end of 1989, I accepted the offer and left the *Sunday Times* a month later.

Stott, who was shunted back to the *People*, was understandably upset by the decision, consoling himself with the belief that he had been ousted because he had been strong enough to resist his proprietor: he was fond of saying that he had to go so that Maxwell 'could have his train set back'. I think there was a lot of truth in that. Certainly, right from the start of my tenure, Maxwell attempted to play engine driver, signalman and station-master. Coming from Wapping, I noted that his compromise with the unions inhibited the freedom of journalists to do as they wished. I also realised that, whatever talents Maxwell might have as an entrepreneur, he lacked any managerial skills and had hired too many executives without newspaper experience. I was glad that my appointment virtually coincided with the departure of the most senior, Patrick Morrissey, who didn't grasp my frosty response when he referred at our first and only meeting to the *Mirror* as 'the product'. But the newspaper career of the former Beechams marketing executive wasn't over (see Chapter Nineteen).

Once I moved in as editor in February 1990 Maxwell tried to interfere as often as he could. I wasn't unduly concerned that the leading articles were his province, written by Joe Haines and then blessed by Maxwell. But he also wanted to write the copy announcing the new bingo contest, attempted to change the headline when Nelson Mandela was freed from jail, and even tried to tinker with the layout on the day of a mass protest in Moscow against the Communist party. There were scores more examples in my biography of Maxwell written soon after his death.[161] One of his most annoying habits was to wait until I had left for the night, appear on the editorial floor and force the duty editor to publish pictures of him. Yet Maxwell chose this period to give an interview to the *Guardian*'s Hugo Young in which he said he now banned stories about himself unless they had 'genuine news value'.[162] This was genuine news to me. Both Maxwell's size – he was over twenty stone – and his ego were enormous. His self-deception was so great that he believed that by using the *Mirror* as a personal bulletin board he helped his newspaper and his business, not to mention exercising immense political influence.

In fact, by the time I became editor his business was in deep trouble. He had paid far too much to buy the American publisher Macmillan in 1988 and, despite mounting, unserviceable debts, he went on buying or investing in all sorts of unprofitable enterprises, such as Oxford United football club, two soccer clubs in Israel, the Panini football sticker firm and newspapers in Croatia and Turkey. He continually forecast the imminent demise of Murdoch's empire while his own was imploding. As for the *Daily Mirror*, it maintained a reasonable sales record throughout 1990. While the *Sun* dropped more than 150,000 copies, the *Mirror* held fast with a 3.1 million average. The sales gap between the two, running at a million for the previous two years, was reduced to 790,000. I should have known better than to imagine that Maxwell cared, though the fact that MacKenzie did gave me some pleasure.

Maxwell's interference at the *Mirror* was far greater than at his other two national titles, but he faced problems with those as well. The *News of the World* was so far ahead, leaving the *Sunday Mirror* and *Sunday People* to scrap it out for second place in a market that had been transformed by the *Mail on Sunday*. The red-top trio were fighting to appeal to a declining audience, yet couldn't find a way of moving up-market, the direction being taken by the next generation of their traditional readerships. Peter Thompson, a thoughtful man, became frustrated by his inability to turn his idea of what the *Sunday Mirror* should be into reality. 'It was in his head but he couldn't make it work,' said Mike Molloy, who was drafted in by Maxwell to replace him in 1986.[163] Less kindly, another colleague said: 'Peter lost his nerve and blew up.' Molloy, who had no wish for another editorship, did a reasonable job, with his deputy, John Parker, playing a key role. They put a brake on a sales slide that was threatening to become an avalanche, even achieving a modest rise. Again, Maxwell seemed uninterested in this success because he had developed a fixation about appointing a woman editor. In 1988, he got his woman, Eve Pollard, who had spent the previous eighteen months editing the *Mail on Sunday*'s You magazine.

Pollard, who was forty, knew many of the older *Sunday Mirror* staff well, having spent ten years there as women's editor until 1981. She had also been assistant editor at the *People* during the time when her husband, Nick Lloyd, was its editor, so she understood the Sunday agenda. Pollard's first job was as an assistant to the fashion editor of *Honey* magazine in 1967, moving on to *Petticoat* and later the *Mirror* magazine. In 1970, she became women's editor of the *Observer* magazine for a year, before her long stint at the *Sunday Mirror*. She later oversaw the launch of *Elle* in New York, and then returned to London to edit the *News of the World*'s colour magazine.

Pollard's stewardship of the *Sunday Mirror* had its controversial moments, not so much for the stories she published as the high-handed way she dealt with her staff. Unafraid of confrontation, she was prone to lose her temper. But gender played a part in the criticisms. I discovered in the thirteen months that we worked in neighbouring offices that she exhibited qualities which won men reputations as great editors. She was driven, often changed her mind, was capable of giant mood swings from laughter to temper tantrums, could be ruthless and relied on a close-knit coterie of advisers. In other words, she resembled many male Fleet Street editors who were regarded as legends. Though it became common for me to hear she had 'gone off her head' there was a sexist tinge to most opinions, including those expressed by women. Her experienced deputy, Colin Myler, diplomatically calmed staff while acting as reliable consultant on decisions about news stories. During her editorship, virtually everyone agreed that Pollard launched an excellent colour magazine. She also had Maxwell to deal with, and the frustrations of trying to squeeze resources from him, even those within her agreed budget, added to the tension. Little could happen in Mirror group without his signature and he obliged every editor and executive to bend the knee in order to obtain it.

Pollard's other frustration – shared by her rival at the *People* – was the problem of the company owning two Sunday titles whose agendas had converged and were now competing in the same market. Expensive television promotions by the *Mirror* tended to have their greatest impact on the *People*, and vice versa, leaving the *News of the World* virtually untouched. In company terms, this was a huge waste of money, paying out more than £250,000 a shot to lure readers from one of its titles to another and then a further £250,000 to swap them back. The *People*, once the stronger of the two, was never really cherished by Mirror group. Its investigative component, its original *raison d'être*, became just another part of the package, and the nature of its investigations changed as it moved into the field of exposing prostitution, the dubious territory already inhabited by the *News of the*

World, and celebrity kiss-and-tell stories.[164] This was largely the province of the *Sunday Mirror*, which was seen, naturally enough, as the genuine 'sister' to the *Daily Mirror*.

Ernie Burrington was *People* editor until 1988, having maintained a 2.9 million sale for a couple of years while getting his fair share of exclusives. His paper suffered a bad circulation reverse in 1988 when Maxwell's managers struggled to fulfil instructions to build colour presses as soon as possible. The *People*'s printing and distribution arrangements in the south were severely disrupted, causing shortfalls and late deliveries, compounded by the use of ancient machines in Manchester which repeatedly broke down and hit the northern sale. By the end of 1988 the *People* was selling almost 300,000 fewer copies than at the beginning of 1986. It confirmed the view of old hands at the *People*, such as deputy editor Alan Hobday, that it was the Cinderella paper at the *Mirror*'s ball. It came last in order of priority within Mirror group, with the least office space, a lower staff budget and less promotion money.

Maxwell then surprised Burrington by offering him the title of deputy chairman and assistant publisher. Another surprise was his replacement as editor, John Blake. He had been assistant editor of the *Daily Mirror* for a couple of years after helping to invent and then run the *Sun*'s Bizarre gossip column. Blake, forty, but with the demeanour of someone much younger, had worked his way up from a local newspaper in east London to the *Evening News*, transferring to the *Standard* in the 1980 merger. He was a well-liked figure with a gentle disposition, concealing an ambitious streak. He wasn't tough or rigorous enough to run the *People* and his well-meant attempt to reposition it as a paper for young people was ill conceived. He attempted to win new readers by nicknaming it 'the *Sunday Peeps*' and introducing a page called Brunch. One executive asked sarcastically: 'How do we think that will go down on Barnsley market?' The experiment didn't work, sales slipped further, and Blake was relieved of his editorship in March 1989. Maxwell then appointed Wendy Henry, who had been kicking her famous high heels for three months after her departure from the *News of the World*. Henry had powerful enemies within the *Mirror* camp who were not only upset by her being another example of the growing number of people they regarded as Murdoch imports, such as Pollard and Blake, but alarmed by her *NoW* reputation. She gave her detractors, only too pleased to whisper to Maxwell, plenty of ammunition.

There was a false story about Major Ron Ferguson, necessitating a humble apology the following week, followed by murmurs about a lack of taste in publishing a front-page picture of the half-naked body of Ayatollah Khomeini being manhandled in his coffin.[165] A couple of weeks later Henry was inundated with complaints from readers for using pictures of dismembered bodies after an air crash in which 109 people died, headlined 'KILLING FIELDS: The pictures television could not show'.[166] The Press

Council condemned publication and Maxwell told her: Do it once more and you're dead.

For several months there was no public controversy but plenty of internal sniping about her paper's vulgarity. Then, in November, came a *Sunday People* which upset the public and the Palace. Two front-page pictures showed seven-year-old Prince William in his school uniform urinating against a wall with a clever headline, written by Alan Hobday, Henry's deputy: 'THE ROYAL WEE!' Prince Charles was reportedly appalled. But more readers complained about the picture on page three which revealed the operation scar on entertainer Sammy Davis Jnr's neck due to radiation therapy for throat cancer. This also had a clever, if tasteless, headline, 'Sad Scar Sammy!'[167]

Maxwell fired Henry immediately, explaining to a trade magazine that both pictures exemplified unacceptable intrusions into privacy, later telling the *Guardian* that he had been horrified by the picture of Davis's 'raw. racked, cancerous throat'.[168] It was likely that Maxwell also bowed to pressure from some senior executives, but he kept Henry on as editor of the *People*'s magazine, which she had launched in September. The timing was also significant because Maxwell was already planning to remove Stott as *Mirror* editor in my favour.

He therefore persuaded Stott to retake the *People* editorship by promising to let him lead a buy-out and run it as a private company. Stott agreed on condition that Henry departed, and Maxwell reluctantly let her go. Whether Maxwell would have eventually honoured his promise to Stott is difficult to know, but in the following year Stott laid his plans on the assumption that it would happen. In the context of the nonsensical vicious circle of internal competition between the Sunday titles within Mirror group, the idea certainly made sense.

During my *Mirror* editorship I had a front-row seat during another of Maxwell's calamitous enterprises, the launch of the *European*, a weekly English-language paper to be sold across Europe. Initial research looked good because potential readers appeared enthusiastic, but advertising – which would be crucial to the paper's revenue – was another matter. Few companies had pan-European advertising budgets and ad agencies were highly sceptical. I uncovered evidence when writing my Maxwell biography which pointed to Maxwell having stolen the whole concept of the *European* from plans prepared originally by Helmut Schmidt, the former West German chancellor and publisher of the Hamburg-based *Die Zeit*.[169] Regardless of its conception, Maxwell made the birth as painful as possible. Having installed Ian Watson, the former number two at the *Sunday Telegraph*, as editor, he announced that he, Maxwell, was editor-in-chief and set out to make life intolerable for everyone involved.

The launch of the *European* on 11 May 1990 was estimated to have cost £50 million and was anything but a success. Watson's professionalism ensured that the editorial content, though gathered quickly, looked reasonable and read well. There were intelligent articles, particularly from Watson's deputy Peter Millar, and an entertaining column by the actor Peter Ustinov. Its general philosophy was supportive of European integration. But who was the paper for? Was there a real audience? Distribution was hopeless, with copies turning up at newsagents across Britain, and remaining unsold, while many major European airports had no supplies. Maxwell's claim that the first issue had sold a million copies was so blatant a lie that staff were embarrassed. In the following months, with the paper's editorial gradually improving, no one inside the company or out could discover genuine sales figures. What was obvious was that it was costing a fortune, as much as £1 million a week during its first six months.

With immense and pressing financial problems throughout his empire and an inability to exert as much control as he wished at his newspapers, Maxwell decided to seek out an editorial supremo. At the end of October 1990, he met the *Sunday Times*'s Andrew Neil at the Savoy to discuss the possibility of him becoming chief executive. Neil strung Maxwell along for a time, enjoying the fun, but wisely rejected the offer.[170] To those of us who saw, or heard, him every day it was plain that Maxwell was losing his grip.

Murdoch's £20 million post-Wapping headache

When Murdoch bought *Today* it was unclear what he hoped to achieve. Had he spent £38 million merely to deny Maxwell its presses? His first act was to relieve Dennis Hackett of the editorship and put in the man who had first urged him to buy it, David Montgomery, then editor of the *News of the World*. Monty was a fine and confident production journalist. Arriving late in the afternoon after being appointed, he impressed his new staff by immediately redrawing the paper's first thirteen pages and writing all the headlines himself.[171] The following day he changed *Today*'s appearance, replacing the *Mail*-style serif typeface with a bold sans, and then set about targeting a wider audience than the previous regime.

The relaunch was everything that the launch had not been: a coordinated professional operation, with editorial and promotion meshing, backed by the proper resources. Big-money games were introduced, free insurance was offered in a leaflet delivered to more than 5 million homes and hundreds of thousands were spent on TV advertising. 'We are going to appeal to greedy people,' Monty explained, 'the children of the Thatcherite social and industrial revolutions.' This mixture of right-wing populism and celebration of consumerism certainly gave the paper a point of view, one very different from its previous social democratic stance. *Today* now had pace and a superficial gloss that had been missing, but there was obsessive coverage of TV commercials, with stories of the actors involved.

So remarkable was his transformation that *Today* was named by *What the Papers Say* judges as the 1987 newspaper of the year. The citation noted that it was now a paper 'supremely sure of itself, its readership and what it stands for', adding that it 'unreservedly reflects the Thatcher philosophy'. Monty's aim was to attract the young upwardly mobile group known as yuppies, or those people aspiring to be yuppies, and it appeared to work. By the summer of 1988, *Today* was selling more than 500,000 copies, rising to 614,000 by September 1989, prompting Murdoch to boast that *Today*'s finances would soon be reaching break-even point.[172] Unlike most tabloid journalists, Montgomery developed an excellent grasp of the commercial aspects of newspapers and Murdoch made him managing director, giving him a status enjoyed by no other News International editor.

Though he lacked the passion and extrovert personality of Kelvin MacKenzie, he was just as prepared to take risks as his *Sun* rival, both in his paper and with his owner. Murdoch was relaxed about Monty's penchant for plundering material from other titles, a common tabloid trait. Monty took this to a new level, shamelessly stealing ideas and articles from the *Daily Mail* and *Daily Express*, earning him the nickname of Jackdaw. In response, Montgomery displayed a stuffed bird in his office and brazenly used the byline Jack Daw when writing about his rivals. But Murdoch was outraged by Monty's spending. He exploded when he discovered that Monty had defied him by paying the highest-recorded book serialisation fee, £750,000, for the autobiography of singer Michael Jackson. Murdoch also took particular objection to the amount Monty spent in buying the serial rights to Donald Trump's autobiography. The series flopped, failing to win any new readers, and a rift had opened between Murdoch and Montgomery that widened in the following months.

A notable aspect of Monty's *Today* regime was his positive discrimination in favour of women journalists. Though a deeply awkward and shy man, he enjoyed the company of women, promoting more females to executive positions than any editor before him. Working sixteen-hour days six days a week, he did without a deputy for many months until he eventually appointed Amanda Platell, a sub-editor with excellent visual flair who learned quickly. He briefly turned his paper 'green' in the hope of attracting readers interested in environmental issues.

One measure of Monty's success was to compare his sales achievement with that of his main rivals, the *Daily Mail* and *Daily Express*. The *Mail* was still being skilfully edited by Sir David English but his efforts weren't reflected in the circulation figures, which were anything but buoyant in the late 1980s. Having pushed the sale above 2 million in 1978, he watched it slide by almost 300,000 over the following eight years. At the *Daily Express*, where editor Larry Lamb was replaced by Nick Lloyd in April 1986, the decline was even more dramatic, falling from 2.5 million in 1978 to 1.8 million by the spring of 1986. So the *Express* was just 70,000 copies ahead of the *Mail* when Lloyd moved into the chair.

It was Lloyd's third editorship, but this was his first chance with a daily paper and much was expected of him. He immediately ran into two major problems: David Stevens and Eddy Shah. Used to dealing with Murdoch, and with a natural charm, Lloyd initially handled the spiky Stevens quite well. Stevens wasn't a proprietor and, as chairman of United Newspapers, he had only a tiny personal stake in the company. But he was able to assume the role of owner by virtue of his considerable influence over his board. He demanded a strongly pro-Conservative-party line in his papers and didn't confine his interference to politics. When *Express* columnist Jean Rook attacked Prince Philip as a sponger the Queen Mother complained to Woodrow Wyatt. He passed on the complaint to Stevens, who promised to talk to Rook.[173]

But Lloyd was more exercised by Stevens's commercial attitude. He was the first example of a national press controller who rigorously applied the rules of accountancy to his newspapers, preferring cost-cutting to investment. This parsimony didn't extend to himself. When the *Express* left its famous Fleet Street building, the Black Lubyanka, for a new headquarters on southern side of Blackfriars Bridge, Stevens established himself in a vast ninth-floor office with a butler dancing attendance and installed a bust of himself in the foyer, just as Beaverbrook had done.[174]

Adding to Lloyd's internal problems was Shah's launch of *Today* directly into the market the *Mail* and *Express* were already fighting for. The *Express* suffered most, despite *Today*'s poor start, and the situation worsened once Murdoch bought it and put Montgomery in charge. But Murdoch wasn't a spendthrift and finally ordered Montgomery to cut costs by making staff redundant. By November 1989 Murdoch was privately referring to Montgomery as a 'bastard'.[175] MacKenzie, picking up the new climate, confided to friends that Monty's days were numbered. With fewer resources, *Today*'s circulation declined to 540,000 in the last half of 1990. More significantly, it was also losing £10 million a year.[176]

The *Times* was losing about £10 million too. Sales had risen in the first period of Charlie Wilson's editorship, reaching more than 500,000 in May 1986, as he sought to broaden the paper's agenda and cover the news more aggressively, seeing the potential in attracting readers from the *Daily Mail* and *Daily Express*. The *Times* 'is moving towards the middle market', *Mail* editor Sir David English pointed out in 1987. 'It is no longer an up-market paper.'[177] Wilson also intruded on the *Mail*'s territory by trying to woo female readers.[178]

The post-Wapping malaise and the *Independent*'s success hit the *Times* hard. Wilson, previously Murdoch's blue-eyed boy, suffered from that most sinister and ominous of Murdochian punishments: silence. The calls from proprietor to editor became rarer and when they did occur Murdoch always seemed to be in a bad temper. Again, it was MacKenzie who read the signs when Wilson requested advice on how to cope with Murdoch. Wilson also suggested to Woodrow Wyatt, who told him he liked the *Times*'s leaders, that he should commend them to Murdoch.[179] Wyatt, party to Murdoch's private thoughts, knew that it was a hopeless task. Wilson is 'very nice', Murdoch confided to him, 'but he has no intellectual authority and the leaders don't give you that feeling'.[180] To the outside world, the leading articles which were the most contentious were those Murdoch most liked, the ones published in the period of picketing outside Wapping. Without hard evidence, relying on rumour and anecdote, several editorials referred to instances of bad behaviour by the print unions outside the gates, such as arson at a Dockland warehouse.[181] Several old *Times* hands found this departure from truth into propaganda unacceptable. Surely it was a case of the once-principled *Times* covertly supporting the commercial interests of its proprietor?

Having agreed that Wilson lacked authority,[182] Murdoch searched for a replacement, eventually accepting the advice of his newly appointed chief executive at Wapping, Andrew Knight, who favoured his former *Economist* colleague Simon Jenkins. The announcement that Jenkins was replacing Wilson came in March 1990. Wilson, who was given a non-job in charge of European development, received the news of his sacking, according to Murdoch, 'like a gentleman who had just been hit in the stomach'.[183] He was soon recruited by Maxwell to run the *Sporting Life*.

Jenkins, then forty-six, the former editor of the *Evening Standard*, was thoughtful, cultured, articulate, literate and a very readable columnist, having won the 1988 *What the Papers Say* award for his articles in the *Sunday Times*. Conservative but not dogmatic, Jenkins was a 'more traditional and clubbable editor for the *Times*' than Wilson.[184] Indeed, Jenkins was identifiably one of the great and the good: a member of the boards of British Railways, London Regional Transport and the South Bank, he had also served on two royal commissions and had been influential in the movement to save Britain's heritage. Married to the American actress Gayle Hunnicutt, he had a deep interest in the theatre and the arts. He was also the author of nine books, including two on the newspaper industry.[185] Most commentators read the change of editors as the end to a vulgar period and a return to intellectual rigour, evidenced in the *Independent*'s headline: 'Exit a rough man, enter a smooth one'.[186]

Jenkins, who admired what Whittam Smith had achieved, had just agreed to join the *Independent* to write a column when Murdoch called him and persuaded him, against his better judgement, to become *Times* editor. His agreed remit with Murdoch was specific: to compete head on with the *Independent*, which was just 24,000 copies behind. He must restore the *Times*'s authority, guiding it away from its quasi-*Daily Mail* stance. Jenkins thought it might be too late, believing the *Independent* would soon overtake the *Times*. He also knew that he and Murdoch were birds of a different feather. But turning down an editorship, even when the owner is unacceptable, is surprisingly difficult. In the final discussions over his appointment, Jenkins is reported to have said: 'Rupert, leave me alone for two years to do the job.' He went on to make it clear he couldn't imagine staying any longer than three years.

In his inaugural address to staff, Jenkins named the *Independent* as 'our prime target'.[187] Murdoch's prime target, however, was the *Daily Telegraph* (and, quite possibly, the *Daily Mail*) but that agenda would have to wait. The immediate struggle was to prevent the *Times* from falling to last place in the daily broadsheet market. Jenkins was chosen specifically as the personification of the kind of reader who was thought to have gravitated to the *Independent*.

One of Jenkins's first decisions was to fire the *Times*'s home affairs specialist, David Walker, for daring to write about the paper's internal affairs in the *Listener*. Walker mused on whether Jenkins would reverse the trend which had given rise to editorials serving Murdoch's commercial interests.[188] There were, he said, two kinds of leader-writers on the *Times*: the 'true believers' who shared Murdoch's beliefs and the 'lost souls whose hearts are no longer in it'. Jenkins regarded the article as a foolish act of bravado.[189] But Walker felt he had reached the point where he must 'level with the world' by illustrating that the paper 'which had once cleaved to the norms of objectivity and impartiality had become a Thatcherite organ captive to the commercial interests of Rupert Murdoch'.[190]

Black and Knight: from mutual appreciation to mutual loathing

Murdoch's desire for the *Times* to supplant the *Daily Telegraph* as the highest-selling broadsheet was matched by the determination of its new owner, Conrad Black, not to let it happen. When he became the majority shareholder in February 1986 it looked anything but an easy task. The *Telegraph* had lost 300,000 sales in five years and was shedding buyers at the rate of 10,000 a month – half of them to the graveyard – while the *Times* had risen by 55 per cent and the *Guardian* by 40 per cent. The rivals were doing better in attracting display advertising too. Even classified, traditionally the *Telegraph*'s strong point, was down by ten pages a week. Financial losses were estimated at £1 million a month.[191] Yet Black remained in Canada, relying on his chief executive, Andrew Knight, to sort out the mess. One continuing embarrassment was Lord Hartwell's insistence on attending the office every day despite having lost control. Knight issued an order that no manager was to talk to Hartwell about company business, a harsh but understandable instruction. Knight got wind of Murdoch's Wapping move before it happened and held back in staffing negotiations for the company's new West Ferry print plant, realising he would secure a better deal in a climate where the unions were on the defensive.

Knight was to prove an able manager. Having resigned the editorship of the *Economist* after an eleven-year stint to become Black's senior British executive, he showed enormous aptitude in transforming a loss-making business into a profitable enterprise. But he later made two errors of judgement which clouded his initial success. Neat, dapper, cool rather than cold, self-contained, with a disconcerting habit of smiling even when under pressure, Knight had spent years networking at the highest levels. A New Zealander, the son of an air force officer, he hadn't the least trace of an accent. After Oxford, he worked as a financial and investment analyst with a merchant bank before switching to journalism, first joining the *Investors Chronicle* and then the *Economist*, where he rose after eight years to be editor. Garland, the *Telegraph*'s cartoonist, thought Knight 'a Martian' because of his 'guarded manner' and 'emotional stillness'.[192] He was one of many detractors in the editorial department, but Knight's greatest triumphs were on the business side. Initially, he also made at least one wise journalistic decision, recommending that Max Hastings succeed Bill Deedes as editor of the *Daily Telegraph* as soon as possible.

Deedes was seventy-two and in his twelve years in the chair it had become clear, even to those who liked him, that he was far too amiable a character to be an editor. Immortalised in *Private Eye*'s Dear Bill correspondence as the golfing partner of the prime minister's husband, he was the antithesis of a hard-headed, hard-working dynamo. Garland saw him as 'an actor and a fantasist' whose 'favourite part is the flannelled fool, the Bertie Wooster sidekick'.[193] He was one of the few who dared to tell the truth about Deedes's habit of wishing to be loved by everyone. Another was *Telegraph* writer Frank Johnson who thought Deedes 'too affable to upset anyone'.[194]

After moving gracefully aside in favour of Hastings, Deedes was ennobled as Baron Deedes of Aldington and then defied convention, and the passing of the years, to continue working for the paper, becoming a valued columnist and feature writer. He accepted the wholesale changes engineered by his successor without a murmur. Other veteran staff were much more critical. To assuage their fears Knight held a staff meeting to talk about the paper's tough financial situation, pointing to the dark force who had caused their crisis. 'Murdoch has changed everything,' he told them. 'He has said he is going to double the circulation of the *Times* and when Murdoch says he'll do something he usually does it.'[195]

Hastings, who was forty, had made his journalistic name through his war reporting, especially in the Falklands (see Chapter Sixteen). The son of two journalists, Macdonald Hastings and Anne Scott-James (Lady Lancaster), he was educated at Charterhouse and Oxford. He went first to the BBC as a documentary researcher, combining that work from 1965 with reporting when he joined the *Evening Standard* where he soon won a reputation for pushiness. He pleaded with editor Charles Wintour to appoint him to cover the 1967 Six Day war and received a memo which said: 'You are the fifth (and least qualified) person who has today asked to go to the Middle East.'[196]

A tall, lean figure, bombastic yet often genial and politically broad-minded, Hastings subsequently carved out a role for himself as a roving correspondent, reporting conflicts in Ireland, Nigeria and Cambodia. Fellow reporters learned that Hastings was a formidable rival, willing to take risks, cut corners and use any amount of ingenuity to ensure he could file exclusives. He left the *Standard* for a couple of years to report for BBC current affairs programmes, returning to the paper in 1973. He briefly edited the *Standard*'s Londoner's Diary, but continued to travel the world, returning to the Middle East and reporting on the fall of Saigon. His exploits in the 1982 Falklands war were the stuff of journalistic legend, but his reporting talents in the field did not necessarily qualify him to become an editor. He had precious little experience of working in an office, let alone editing, and his appointment as *Daily Telegraph* editor was a risky one. He turned out to be the man for the hour, a tough but inspiring editor who took strategic decisions which were to prove invaluable.

Hastings set about modernising the *Telegraph*, to make it more appealing to a younger audience, and recognised that its greatest blind spot was its lack of features material. He hired Veronica Wadley, a *Mail on Sunday* executive, as an assistant editor to cure the problem. She was pregnant at the time, so he called on the former *Daily Mirror* queen bee, Felicity Green – by then a consultant on a women's magazine – to oversee an immediate change. She had never worked on a broadsheet, the *Telegraph* had no features editor, no art desk and no picture researcher. But she managed to introduce the paper to the mysterious world of features, receiving sympathetic help from Hastings's key signing, Don Berry, one of the *Sunday Times*'s Wapping refuseniks.[197]

Berry helped Hastings to reconfigure and redesign the paper, making it much neater, introducing a more logical run of pages and expanding the features allocation. Three other early hirings who were to prove influential were military historian John Keegan to write about defence; Hugh Montgomery-Massingberd, from *Burke's Peerage*, who transformed the obituaries into delightful reads, an eclectic mixture of 'long lineages, powerful actresses and bizarre country-house eccentrics';[198] and fashion editor Kathryn Samuel whose straightforward brief from Hastings was to 'bring the fashion pages into the eighties'.[199]

None of this, in the end, was to prove as controversial as Hastings's political views. He understood that the *Telegraph* must remain Conservative but he was determined that it shouldn't be a house magazine for the Tory party. Nor did he accept many of the *Telegraph*'s political assumptions, such as its opposition to sanctions against South Africa's apartheid government, believing they were a justifiable pressure to enfranchise the black majority. A leading article to that effect, moving the paper into the pro-sanctions camp, didn't enrage *Telegraph* readers, but it alarmed Conrad Black. As early as June

1986, Hastings was known to be taking stick from both Black and Knight.[200] Black was horrified by Hastings's opposition to the bombing of Libya, making what he called 'one of my rare interventions ... in editorial policy'.[201] He criticised Hastings's 'seriously fallacious analyses' of Britain's role. Bowing to supposed proprietorial rights of interference, Hastings defended Black. 'I've never really believed in the notion of editorial independence,' he said. 'I would never imagine saying to Conrad, "You have no right to ask me to do this" ... because Conrad is ... richly entitled to take a view when he owns the newspaper.'[202]

To his credit, Hastings continued to step out of line. His was one of the few papers to question the decision which had led the SAS to gun down three IRA members in Gibraltar. A memorable *Telegraph* leader stated: 'The Government ... should explain why it was necessary to shoot dead all three terrorists on the street rather than apprehend them.'[203] This was a slap in the face for Thatcher, and an argument unlikely ever to have been advanced by Peter Utley, the strongly pro-Unionist writer whose departure for the *Times* at the beginning of 1987 was viewed by many veterans as the end of an era.

He was just one of the ageing staff Hastings was happy to let go, along with a younger recruit, the prime minister's daughter, Carol Thatcher.[204] A furious Margaret Thatcher never spoke to Hastings throughout the rest of her premiership. Another major resignation around the same time was John Anstey after twenty-two years as editor of the colour magazine. He had avoided casting the magazine in the image of its glossy Sunday counterparts, preferring it to be a forum for good writing, deliberately making it more literary and more committed to the arts with a great deal less lifestyle material. Its new editor, Felicity Lawrence, saw things differently and benefited from the assistance of Felicity Green.

Knight's other change of editor, at the *Sunday Telegraph*, proved less felicitous. John Thompson, who was sixty-five, let it be known he wanted to retire and Knight proposed that the sixty-two-year-old Perry Worsthorne should take over.[205] It was a giant gamble: Worsthorne had the affectations of a journalist from a long-past era, a writer with narrow interests, quite unlike the more modern kind of editor who was expected to have a thorough grasp of every aspect of the job, including production, design and marketing. Peregrine Gerard Worsthorne, a dandified dilettante with an aristocratic disdain for bourgeois values, seemed a most unlikely choice. His father was a Belgian Catholic who changed his name from Koch de Gooreynd to Worsthorne two years before Perry's birth. After his parents divorced, when he was five, he spent most of his early years being looked after by the family butler. Educated at Stowe, Cambridge and then Oxford, he joined the *Glasgow Herald* as a sub-editor in 1946 and a couple of years later moved to the *Times* to sub on the foreign desk before being sent to the paper's Washington bureau.

He stayed there until 1953, falling out with the *Times* by championing the cause of Senator Joe McCarthy, and switched to the *Daily Telegraph*. He moved over to the *Sunday Telegraph* as deputy editor in 1961, becoming the paper's star columnist renowned for his idiosyncratic and maverick views expressed in colourful prose. Michael Leapman believed he became famous for 'stretching High Tory philosophy to the very edges of logic and for contesting the liberal assumptions that dominated political debate in the 1960s and 1970s'.[206] Yet even those who disagreed with his politics, such as Geoffrey Goodman, often liked him. 'Behind all his arrogant snobbery, his lavish vanity, the rodomontade and dilettante posturings,' wrote Goodman, 'there beats the heart of a generous, endearing, courteous and warm fellow.'[207] The elegant, white-haired gent in his well-tailored suits and Garrick bow-tie doubtless agreed.

One who certainly did not was Lord Hartwell who had never forgiven Worsthorne for saying 'fuck' on TV thirteen years before (see above, p. 275). When Hartwell heard the names of the two new editors of his beloved *Telegraph* titles he resolved to oppose them. He launched a protest at the board meeting, falling silent when a director passed him a pad with '80 per cent' written on it, indicating that Black now controlled that much stock.[208] As the board voted in the new editors Hartwell finally realised he had lost all his influence.

In the summer of 1987, the *Telegraphs* left Fleet Street's Peterborough Court for South Quay on the Isle of Dogs, then a wasteland served by unpunctual river taxis, the inefficient Docklands Light Railway, and minibuses or cars which were often stuck in heavy traffic. Hastings's mother said memorably of her son's trek to the paper's new home: 'He's got to go practically to the sea every day to do his work.'[209] A thoroughly disheartened Hartwell never did go to the new building. His legacy, the new presses at West Ferry, produced much improved papers and enabled many more pages to be printed. This extra value helped Hastings in his editorial revolution, and he was able to point to good circulation figures.

Worsthorne's experiences on the *Sunday Telegraph* were not so happy. Given the chance he had always wanted, he belied his age by throwing himself into the editor's role with relish, writing his column and signed leading articles. His paper had a quirky style all its own, but it was professionally put together by his deputy Ian Watson. Sales did well in the first two years, rising above 750,000 by the end of 1987, but the *Sunday Times*'s multi-section formula stopped its growth. A lengthy promotion campaign extolling the virtues of the *Sunday Telegraph*'s single section didn't work and then, in September 1988, Knight made a bad error by switching the colour magazine from the Sunday title to the *Daily*'s Saturday issue. Worsthorne wasn't even at the meeting which took this momentous decision. There was a sort of logic. By switching to the *Daily*, with its much higher sale, it could substantially increase the magazine's advertising rates.

But it crippled any hope of advance for the Sunday title and its replacement, a colour section called 7 Days, was no compensation.

With circulation back down at 650,000, Black grew concerned that Worsthorne's 'splendid efforts' in producing 'a high Tory, Little England eccentric, and reactionary newspaper' had failed to attract readers.[210] Knight then compounded his magazine mistake in May 1989 with a far worse blunder. He decided that the two *Telegraphs* should be merged into a seven-day operation under the single editorship of Hastings. Worsthorne was sacked over a Claridge's breakfast – 'two perfectly poached eggs on buttered toast' – and told he would be responsible in future only for overseeing the *Sunday Telegraph*'s three comment pages.[211] Worsthorne's previous dislike for Knight turned to loathing, and he was not alone. Most of the senior journalists across both titles were convinced that Knight's merger plan wouldn't work and morale suffered. Daily and Sunday papers are so distinct in Britain, unlike in the United States, that the practice of reporters and feature writers working for two titles can rarely be harmoniously accomplished. In the event, the merger was never fully realised before it was scrapped.

Knight also lost Black's confidence. Black rarely visited Britain in the three years after his takeover and remained a largely mysterious figure. He gained some journalistic attention after an April 1986 visit to Chequers when he appeared to know more than Mrs Thatcher about the Conservative party's history.[212] His view of Hartwell's *Telegraph* – 'a nickel and dime store in Parry Sound [a small town in Ontario] is run better than this place' – was also widely quoted. He was doubtless delighted that, having paid $67 million for the company in 1986, it was generating almost the same amount in profits two years later. By autumn 1989, however, Black had decided to assume day-to-day control, taking Knight's chief executive title and making him joint deputy chairman with Sir Frank Rogers. In public, Knight put a good face on the decision: 'We have created a kingdom,' he said. 'Now it's time the king took over.'[213] Privately, Knight was upset, believing Black didn't appreciate all he had done for him.

Knight's merger was disentangled. In October 1989, a separate editor was appointed to the Sunday title. Hastings chose Trevor Grove, his assistant editor, a former *Evening Standard* colleague he had lured from the *Observer*, where he was editing the magazine. Grove, forty-four, faced a tough job because sales had fallen to 612,000, the lowest point in the *Sunday Telegraph*'s history, and he could see that turning the situation around was going to take time. By 1990, circulation was bumping along at 590,000, an indictment of Knight's misguided policy which he later conceded had not worked.

Criticism of Knight has to be offset against his undoubted success in turning a company that was basically bust when he was appointed into one that was soon making a healthy profit. He effected a remarkable transition in the company's fortunes, negotiating a reduction of the workforce from 3,900 to virtually 1,000 with, it should be said, considerable assistance from Joe Cooke, a senior manager. A deal between Black and Lord Stevens of United Newspapers to increase the size of the West Ferry plant to sixteen presses eventually enabled the printing of 2.5 million papers a night. Their joint-ownership deal, which allowed each side pre-emptive rights should either one be sold off, would have interesting repercussions some thirteen years later (see Chapter Twenty-one).

Knight, having sold 2.1 million shares to realise £14.5 million, quit suddenly in December to become executive chairman of News International. When he informed Black, the Canadian was outraged, smelling betrayal.[214] The Black–Knight disagreement soon went public. The first salvo was fired by Worsthorne and Frank Johnson who wrote a vicious profile of Knight in the *Sunday Telegraph*.[215] Ivan Fallon, in later editions of the *Sunday Times*, called it 'one of the most poisonous, score-settling pen profiles seen in journalism in recent years'. Worsthorne was getting back at Knight for his sacking as editor. The next shot was revealed in a letter from Black to Knight which was leaked to the *Times*. Black accused Knight of a 'prolonged ... courtship with our principal competitor while continuing as the ostensible chief executive of the *Daily Telegraph*'. By selling shares and receiving *Telegraph* board papers when he knew he was to join Murdoch 'raises substantial ethical questions'.[216]

Knight, described by Woodrow Wyatt as 'a strange fish ... a real Vicar of Bray',[217] wrote back to contest his former friend's viewpoint, observing that Black's letter 'says more about you than about me'. Indeed it did. In one way, it showed that Black was going to be a proprietor in the old mould: self-willed, combative and maverick. In another way, the episode illustrated just how changed the newspapers and their owners had become. Now their once-private relationships with executives were regarded as news for the rest of the media to consume. Black appeared to eschew the tradition by which owners dealt discreetly with their editors, occasionally writing letters of protest for publication. These letters were something of a ploy, suggesting that all disagreements between owner and editor occurred in public, concealing the fact that Black was just as liable to harangue his editor in private.

Black's publishing empire expanded dramatically in these years. In May 1986 his company, Hollinger, bought thirty-four small-town papers in the US for $106 million.[218] Over the following six years the group acquired 288 small-circulation titles. In 1989 he outbid Robert Maxwell to buy the *Jerusalem Post* and then acquired the *Spectator* magazine, appointing Dominic Lawson as editor to replace Charles Moore, whom he installed as Hastings's deputy. Black was now playing the role of newspaper tycoon to the hilt.

The Scribe of Auchtermuchty joins the enemy

Sir John Junor, the self-styled Scribe of Auchtermuchty and by far the longest-serving editor of the post-war period, was finally prevailed on to resign the *Sunday Express* chair in July 1986. He was sixty-seven and had spent thirty-two years as editor. But there was life in the old dog yet. He asked to carry on writing his JJ column, a request his owner, David Stevens, was only too delighted to grant because of its undoubted success. Junor approved of his successor, Robin Esser, who had worked impressively in his brief reign as *Daily Express* executive editor under Larry Lamb. Esser knew he was facing a difficult, if not impossible, task at the *Sunday Express.* Junor had inherited a paper selling 3.2 million, helped it rise by a further million, and then watched from 1970 onwards as sales dwindled away to virtually 2.1 million. While Junor refused to countenance any change, either to the broadsheet shape or to his tired editorial formula, the effervescent tabloid *Mail on Sunday*, edited with dynamism by Stewart Steven, began to supplant its middle-market rival.

Esser was selected as a safe pair of hands, never a good reason to appoint an editor. Though Express group managing director Andy Cameron later criticised him for being 'too safe', if that was the case then he and Stevens were at fault for failing to make a more adventurous choice.[219] A Yorkshire grammar schoolboy who went up to Oxford, where he edited *Cherwell*, Esser started his career in 1957 as a freelance reporter. Three years later he joined the *Daily Express* and in 1963 was promoted to edit the William Hickey column. Within two years he was features editor, spending a brief spell running the New York bureau, before being recalled in 1970 to edit the *Express*'s northern editions. After three years in Manchester he returned to London as associate editor. In 1977, he doubled his salary by moving to Associated and becoming consultant editor at the London *Evening News*, losing his job when the paper closed. Following a freelance stint he rejoined the *Daily Express* to run its Saturday magazine section and, in 1985, graduated to the role of executive editor.

Esser therefore had the right kind of experience for editorship, but even the most senior executives are often shielded from the reality of dealing with owners. He soon discovered the insurmountable problem at Express group: Stevens stifled editorial initiative by refusing to allocate decent resources for editorial innovation. Esser's editorial dilemma was also obvious: how could he move the paper forward while retaining the quirky charm which appealed to the bulk of its ageing audience? He made cosmetic changes, amending the layout and introducing new columns, but he was hamstrung by the inflexible pagination, with the paper pegged at thirty-two broadsheet pages.

To try to combat the *Mail on Sunday*'s success with part-works – long-run weekly serials which could be collected as books – Esser was forced to turn himself into a commercial promotions manager by persuading the motor industry to sponsor a part-work. It prompted the only sales uplift during his editorship, but Stevens refused to allow more, making matters worse by raising the cover price.[220] Esser had his moments of journalistic pleasure, such as the excellent front page on the day the ferry, the *Herald of Free Enterprise*, sank.[221] Otherwise, he had little to celebrate and oversaw a poor sales record. The *Sunday Express* was more than 500,000 ahead of the *Mail on Sunday* when he took over but, in April 1989, to his acute embarrassment, his rival overtook him. His circulation had fallen to 1.9 million and, in time-honoured fashion, his days were numbered.

Stevens and Cameron began the search for a new editor and the result, in August 1989, was the firing of Esser in August 1989 (he was made group editorial consultant) and the astounding appointment of Robin Morgan, a thirty-five-year-old middle-ranking executive on the *Sunday Times*. Cameron was withering about Esser, observing that he had started as caretaker editor and finished in the same role.[222] He was to be just as cutting about his replacement. Even Morgan, known for his immodesty and chutzpah, couldn't believe his luck. He had been under a cloud for his inept handling of an investigation into the Gibraltar IRA shootings and, to escape the bad atmosphere, had applied for the editorship of the *Yorkshire Post*. Those of us who knew of his application didn't expect him to land the top job at United Newspapers' regional flagship and we were proved right, but in an entirely unexpected way. Morgan performed so well at the interview with United's deputy chairman, Sir Gordon Linacre, that Linacre recommended him to Stevens for the *Sunday Express* editorship instead.[223] It made sense only to Stevens, who had an absurd notion about transforming the *Sunday Express* into a slightly more populist *Sunday Times*.

To that end, Morgan's record appeared perfect. He had started on a local weekly straight from his West Midlands grammar school, spent six years at an evening in Hemel Hempstead and joined the *Sunday Times* in 1979, learning his craft at the feet of Harry Evans's finest executives. He was eager and energetic but also erratic and frequently eccentric. Having worked closely with him for a couple of months when I first joined the *Sunday Times*, I recognised his journalistic qualities. He had the ability to visualise a page, could pull together very readable 4,000-word Focus articles and often championed and protected inexperienced staff. These pluses were offset by occasional indiscipline, lapses of concentration and a cavalier attitude. He tended to produce his best work only when put under pressure from above. He also talked too much. Morgan hired several former *Sunday Times* colleagues and made a fist of moving the paper as far away from the Junor era as possible, speeding up a modernisation process begun under Esser. But taking the paper into direct competition with the Sunday broadsheets was a poor strategic decision. Anyway, like Esser, he was starved of resources and couldn't hope to realise Stevens's vague ambitions on a restricted budget. Sales went on declining.

According to Cameron, Morgan was hopelessly miscast in the role of editor. He was 'a disaster . . . a mistake and a bad one . . . a prime example of someone being promoted not one notch above their ability but half a dozen'.[224] His standing wasn't improved by his disappearance on the Saturday night that news broke of a major tragedy: the Thames cruiser, the *Marchioness*, was struck by a bulk carrier and sank within sight of the *Express* offices.[225] All attempts to locate Morgan failed, so deputy editor Charles Garside stopped the presses and produced a new edition with just four members of staff.[226] For an editor to be out of contact with his paper was considered wholly unprofessional and many *Sunday Express* journalists held him in contempt thereafter, not least because he informed Garside a week later that he no longer wanted him to continue as his deputy.

One great loss to Morgan's paper was the JJ column. The wily Junor had worked away happily under Esser but he had a big-money offer to join the *Mail on Sunday* and latched on to the change of editorship to make his move. Though Junor later wrote that he 'did not care for' Morgan, he had no intention of staying.[227] He complained about not being consulted about Morgan's appointment – and why should he have been? – and then supposedly took offence at an interview by Morgan.

Luring Junor from the *Sunday Express* was a great coup for the *Mail on Sunday*, guaranteeing that some readers would switch with him. It was a further example of the very different philosophy at Associated, which was prepared to spend large sums of money on editorial content in the belief that it paid dividends. Lord Rothermere was particularly delighted with the *Mail on Sunday*'s performance after its poor start. To overtake the *Sunday Express* just seven years after launch was a notable feat. The strategy of creating a middle-market paper in the image of the *Daily Mail*, but with a personality of its own, had worked. After winning the *What the Papers Say* editor of the year award in 1985, Stewart Steven was then named editor of the year in the 1990 British Press Awards. He had truly put his previous errors behind him.

There were few accolades for another Sunday title. Throughout the late 1980s, *Observer* owner Tiny Rowland used his paper's business pages to attack his commercial enemy, Mohammed Al Fayed. City editor Melvyn Marckus wrote almost every week about some financial matter involving Fayed, the owner of Harrods.[228] Senior staff, such as deputy editor Tony Howard and managing editor Magnus Linklater, raised their concerns with editor Donald Trelford. Other journalists treated any story provided by Rowland with extreme caution, including David Leigh who protested that a scurrilous tale about Mark Thatcher was 'journalistically unacceptable'.[229] Unlike the journalists, who saw themselves as inheritors of the Astor tradition for independence and fair-mindedness, Rowland did not care about the paper's loss of kudos among its liberal audience. He saw it only as a propaganda vehicle to further his business interests. He was careless how he obtained material, sometimes paying for forged documents, and in one instance the *Observer* was compelled to apologise for falsely claiming that Fayed was anti-Semitic. There were, in fairness, other occasions when the stories were correct and revelatory.[230] But who really cared?

In 1989, one of Rowland's investigators obtained a leaked copy of the Department of Trade and Industry report into the Fayed brothers. Trelford immediately put together an unprecedented sixteen-page Thursday issue of the *Observer*, devoted solely to extracts from and comments from the DTI report.[231] Trelford maintained ever after that it was his own idea. It was a scoop that wouldn't hold until the Sunday and he felt the contents helped to clear his paper's name. Whether it was Trelford's or Rowland's idea, and whatever Trelford's motives, the inevitable result was to tarnish the paper's reputation for years to come, and it probably ruined Trelford's for all time.

In fact, some of the report was an absorbing read, especially the accusations of bad conduct levelled at senior politicians, civil servants, City figures and leading lawyers. But Fleet Street dogs prefer to eat Fleet Street dogs. Instead of taking up the substantive charges in the report, most papers turned on the *Observer* and Trelford. The effect of the widespread criticism on the paper's circulation was catastrophic. Sales had been going down in the previous couple of years but from April 1989 they fell rapidly from just over 700,000 to 650,000 and then, with the launches of the *Sunday Correspondent* and *Independent on Sunday*, collapsed to barely 550,000. In the five years from 1986, the *Observer* lost 28 per cent of its regular buyers. It also lost many of its best staff including Linklater, Leigh and Paul Lashmar. Deputy editor Howard departed in 1988 after a failed coup against Trelford.

The owner even decided to depart as well. After the special issue, Rowland had no further use for the paper whose reputation he had destroyed. Despite a claim in March 1988 at the annual meeting of his company, Lonrho, that the *Observer* was 'highly profitable', it was widely known that its losses were mounting. As we have seen, the first unacceptable bidder was the *Independent*'s Andreas Whittam Smith. Then Rowland surprised everyone by hanging on, having staunched some of his company's losses by disposing of *Today*. Trelford also weathered the storm, reflecting on the truth of a comment by his sacked columnist Conor Cruise O'Brien: 'The editor of a newspaper, ultimately, has no more freedom than the owner chooses to accord.'[232]

The *Observer*'s fate was already on the minds of some senior *Guardian* executives, especially that of editor Peter Preston. He recognised that in terms of their liberal editorial approach the two titles made an ideal fit. The fact that the Scott Trust, the *Guardian*'s owners, could even contemplate expansion was due to the healthy state of the group's finances. It had benefited from a £70 million Reuters windfall in 1984 and by the spring of 1990 it had 'paid off all its debts and mortgages'.[233]

But the circulation story was very different: the birth of the *Independent* had a dramatic effect on the *Guardian*'s sales. In May 1986, the *Guardian* achieved its highest recorded monthly sale – 538,000 copies – and its rise looked unstoppable. By May the following year it was selling 480,000 and began dropping sales regularly, losing a further 50,000 copies by the end of 1990. It's difficult to divine exactly why this happened. Perhaps it was due to the *Independent* being less identified with increasingly unpopular left-wing causes. While the *Guardian* appeared to represent pre-Thatcherite liberalism, the *Independent* accepted Thatcher's economic values – free market, anti-collectivist and meritocratic – without buying into her social and cultural philistinism, her espousal of Victorian values. Maybe the *Guardian*'s relatively new audience didn't appreciate the stereotype of male *Guardian* readers as brown-rice-eating, bearded wearers of open-toed sandals and hair-shirts or, just as pejoratively, the image of women readers as militant lesbians.

Preston wondered how to cure this problem and in a 1989 memo, following market research, he speculated about the paper having fallen into an anti-Thatcherite rut in which every ill in society was blamed on her. He also questioned the slanting of headlines and stories, upsetting staff who were already on the verge of a revolt over pay. They were also unhappy with Preston appointing Jonathan Fenby as his deputy after Peter Cole left for the *Sunday Correspondent*. In fact, Fenby's running of news was later considered positive.

The enigmatic Preston managed to calm his journalists' fears, restoring morale despite his other-worldly attitude. A short description by the paper's official historian captures him perfectly: 'he would wonder aloud, sometimes leaving strange linguistic vapour-trails for readers (and staff) to gaze upon'.[234] He also took a risky step in February 1988 by introducing a revolutionary redesign by David Hillman which mixed serif and sans typefaces. Generally regarded as unpopular, there were many protests by readers for a while, but it was modified and people soon got used to it.

Preston also showed a pragmatic side, incorporating those *Independent* innovations he regarded as sensible. When the *Times* ran a sixty-four-page, four-section Saturday paper, with a colour supplement, the *Guardian* responded with a weekend section in tabloid format. The result was a huge boost for Saturday sales. But there was no question of the *Guardian* abandoning its commitment to the kind of anti-establishment journalism that marked it out from the rest of the press. One notable achievement in the period was the work of reporter David Beresford, who published a chronicle of the 1981 Irish hunger strikes which served as a model to all journalists for its unparalleled combination of exclusive material and dispassionate analysis.[235]

At the *Financial Times*, it wasn't so much the incursion of the *Independent* as the stock market crash of 1987 which halted its steady rise.

Some 10 per cent of its 300,000 sales were wiped off within a couple of months, taking the gloss off its notable success of two years earlier in taking a further step towards internationalisation by printing an edition in New Jersey. The *FT* wasn't able to recover quickly, finding itself in the slipstream of the post-Wapping changes rather than the vanguard.[236] Chief executive Frank Barlow managed to negotiate a deal with the unions to introduce computer technology in March 1986, but it wasn't until almost two years later that journalists were allowed to have direct input. He stressed, unconvincingly, that the outcome was 'the very opposite of a Wapping'.[237] A couple of months later, in July 1988, the *FT* moved to a new £33 million Docklands printing plant. The new plant, on the corner of the busy intersection of the East India Dock Road and the Blackwall Tunnel, soon became a landmark feature with its glass walls allowing people to glimpse the huge new offset presses. It looked like a vision of the future. In fact, it was to prove more symbolic of the past.

The *FT*'s editorial line consistently supported the Thatcher government's supply-side measures, praising anti-union legislation, tax reforms and the movement towards the privatisation of utilities. But there remained a strong Keynesian theme in its call for initiatives to cure unemployment. Editor Geoffrey Owen was knighted in 1989 and began to make preparations for his retirement in favour of his deputy Richard Lambert. Despite the oncoming recession, the *FT* was looking to the future with renewed hope.

18. PUBLIC INTEREST AND THE FREEDOM TO BE PRIVATE

> Journalists say a thing that they know isn't true, in the hope that if they keep on saying it long enough it will be true.[1]

For a while in the late 1980s some tabloid papers went through a sort of Wild West stage. Their editors shot first and asked questions later. They made up the rules as they went along, treating their own sheriff with disdain. They thought they could do as they pleased, and their lawlessness worsened once the unions were kicked out of town. They ignored the murmurs of dissent from the good folk who preferred to read the broadsheets and spurned the warnings from the upright citizens who threatened them with retribution.

As the chorus of disapproval grew louder, an old-timer decided to break his self-imposed silence. On the last day of October 1988, the seventy-five-year-old tabloid pioneer Lord Cudlipp walked slowly to the lectern at Fleet Street's St Bride's church to address the memorial service for his old friend and colleague Lord Jacobson. He then delivered a damning assault on the tabloid press he had left behind fifteen years before. He raged against the papers' prurience, their love for trivia and their cavalier intrusions into privacy, contrasting it all with his belief in the educative role of tabloids. He maintained that the current owners and editors had 'decided that playing a continuing role in public was no longer any business of the popular press'. Cudlipp argued that 'investigative journalism in the public interest' had given way to 'intrusive journalism for the prurient' in which 'nothing, however personal, was any longer secret or sacred and the basic human right to privacy was banished in the interest of public profit'. He derided bingo, 'the daily nipple count' and the pandering to 'voyeurs'. With a satirical flourish, he suggested that owners and editors 'apparently live in fear of instant bankruptcy if they dare to mention ... the activities of the human race when not in bed'.

Cudlipp was right. Stories about the sexual peccadilloes of the famous – actors, businessmen, cricketers, politicians, royals – had become common currency. But few editors took any notice of Cudlipp's speech and the situation grew worse with innumerable complaints about exaggerated or untrue stories, intrusions into privacy and a general air of cynical, commercial exploitation fired by intense competition. Some instances, especially those involving the *Sun*, appear in the previous chapter. A few more examples further illustrate the point.

Many royal stories were wholly incorrect. In November 1988, the actress Koo Stark was awarded £300,000 damages against the *Sunday People* for wrongly suggesting that she had continued a relationship with Prince Andrew after she had married. In March 1989, Viscount Linley, Princess Margaret's son, sued *Today* for falsely claiming that he had thrown beer in a pub, winning £35,000 when the case went to court a year later.[2] In April 1989, the *Sun* ran a story about the theft of private letters to Princess Anne which someone had tried to sell to the paper. They were handed to Scotland Yard and during a subsequent police investigation a maid was questioned. *Today*, assuming she was the culprit, ran a splash which didn't name the woman but gave clues to her identity under the headline: 'Royal Maid Stole Letters'.[3] Later, Linda Joyce, the maid who was entirely innocent, became one of the tabloid press's most persistent critics, helping to found an organisation called PressWise to help victims of press abuse. In August 1988, the *Sunday Mirror* ran a story about a British man whose wife and two daughters were killed in a fire in Greece which suggested, incorrectly, that he had dug his wife's grave because of 'greedy Greek undertakers'.[4] It was a year before the Press Council upheld his complaint.

Against this background it's little wonder that both the Press Council and the concept of self-regulation fell into disrepute. Complaining often led to the complainant suffering from more bad publicity because newspaper editors on the wrong end of adjudications often repeated the offending material when attacking the Council, thus undermining it in the eyes of politicians and the public.[5] Broadsheet editors also thought it ineffective in its policing of the tabloids. Most owners generally disliked what they considered to be a brake on their freedom, with Rupert Murdoch characteristically referring to it as 'a pussy-footing arm of the establishment'.[6] Many complainants who won their cases, let alone those who didn't, were disenchanted. Virtually all the victors felt they didn't receive the recompense they deserved.

Down the years from its inception in 1953 the Press Council was continually reformed, usually in response to an upsurge of political pressure. This inevitably led to tinkering, such as increasing the number of lay members, accompanied by rhetoric about enhancing its impartiality and restoring its authority in spite of being funded by the industry it served and being unable to administer any penalty beyond compelling a guilty paper to publish its adjudication. By choosing a succession of retired judges or senior lawyers as chairmen, the Press Council appeared to have quasi-legal status. Yet it was nowhere near as scrupulous and fair as a law court, with oral hearings that were rarely helpful in obtaining reasonable adjudications. In only one respect was it similar to the judicial process: it took an interminable time to reach its decisions. That is not to criticise the lay members who served on it nor the paid officials, all of whom tried to act with good sense and objectivity. They were locked into a system with two seemingly irreconcilable contradictions at its heart: self-regulation was incompatible with independence; and regulation without punishment lacked public confidence.

It was obvious from its inception that newspaper owners, editors and journalists resented its existence. They were reluctant to set up the council in the first place and thereafter treated it with disdain, maintaining that it inhibited their freedom. One objection by editors was its lack of consistency in adjudications, a problem which sprang largely from the Council's – and the editors' – resistance to the drawing up of a code of practice for journalists. The lack of a code was one factor that convinced the NUJ, which had continually revised its own code of ethics since 1936, to withdraw from Council membership in 1980 after deciding it was incapable of reform.

By the end of the 1980s, it's fair to say that no one on either side – press or public – trusted the Press Council. Owners came to view its brief as being far too wide and ill defined, encouraging it to make pronouncements on a range of issues, such as the changing pattern and structure of ownership and even disputes between owners and editors, which were bound to bring it into conflict with the very people who were paying for it. Proprietorial dissatisfaction led inevitably to editorial cynicism. Most editors believed that the Council's adjudications lacked rigour, while tabloid editors were particularly upset by the Council straying into matters of taste, and therefore making too many subjective decisions. As far as they were concerned, the proper arbiter of right and wrong should be the market place.

In spite of the fact that the Council's only sanction was to censure a paper and then require it to publish its adjudication, editors were fiercely critical whenever a ruling went against them. They couldn't accept even this tame punishment for their misdeeds, often expressing their feelings in critical commentaries published alongside adjudications. A number of MPs, Tory, Labour and Liberal, thought the self-regulatory apparatus to be a charade, but the most coherent opposition came from lawyers, led by the thrusting Australian barrister Geoffrey Robertson, who wrote a book in 1983 which damned the Press Council as a sham.[7] He argued that the Council's decision-making weighed heavily in favour of journalists and against the interests of those who complained. It had no machinery for dealing with genuine grievances about matters of accuracy, one of the most common complaints. It was terribly slow, with some complainants waiting years for redress. It had failed to lay down authoritative principles to ensure that all journalists were aware of the ethical lines they must not cross.

There was also a political dimension to the hostility against the Press Council. With Labour out of political power for so long many of the party's members were convinced their election failures were largely due to the propaganda of the right-wing press and they viewed any move to curb editors' freedom favourably. Many supported Labour MP Frank Allaun in 1982 when he drafted a Right of Reply Bill which would have obliged papers to publish statements correcting factual inaccuracies or distortions at equal length to the original report and within three days of it. If they failed to do so, they would face fines of up to £40,000.[8] While the *Sun* thundered, 'Kill this evil bill', the broadsheets argued that it was a wholly impractical scheme.[9] Most MPs agreed, despite applauding its sentiments, so the bill failed to get a second reading.

This failure didn't signify any diminishing of political hostility to the Press Council, and later that year the Labour party produced a policy document which announced that it would replace the Council and introduce a statutory right of reply.[10] There was trenchant support for these moves from the Campaign for Press and Broadcasting Freedom, an energetic pressure group set up by media unions in 1979. The Press Council's report into the disgraceful newspaper dealings with the family of the Yorkshire Ripper in 1983 (see Chapter Sixteen) provoked the *Times, Financial Times* and the *Guardian* to call for a stricter regulatory regime. A *Guardian* editorial concluded: 'If the Lords and tycoons and conglomerates who own so much of our press would agree to follow the Press Council to the letter, then it might just hold up. But it is the final fix of free medicine in the Last Chance Saloon.'[11] It was not the last we would hear of that mythical drinking establishment.

A new Press Council chairman took over in 1983, Sir Zelman Cowen QC, who looked, on paper at least, to be a good choice. An Australian barrister and academic, he had just spent five years as governor-general of his country, winning praise for the tactful way he dealt with affairs during a period of bitter political acrimony. It turned out to be an easier job than chairing the Press Council in what was regarded as 'the Dark Ages of British journalism . . . invasion of privacy, fabrication, chequebook buy-ups, identification of rape victims, use of subterfuge, racism . . . Not to mention the irrepressible march of bonk journalism'.[12]

Cowen maintained a consistent line in defending self-regulation, often pointing to the perils – such as another right of reply bill proposed by Labour MP Ann Clwyd – if papers didn't behave.[13] But Cowen and the Council were treated with contempt by almost every tabloid editor and he was unable to impose his authority over them. He finally went public with his frustrations, complaining to the *Guardian* about 'serving on a body which is structured in such a way that you can't be sure of full compliance and full obedience. I could wish . . . for more willingness to co-operate on the part of the press . . . It is idiotic of the press when it fails to comply.'[14] The industry's representatives eventually withdrew their support for Cowen, yet he was to have the last laugh by recommending a successor who was to prove even less welcome to most editors and, eventually, to owners as well. Louis

Blom-Cooper QC assumed the Council's chairmanship in 1989 at a time when the tabloid press was, as we have seen, running amok. He set about his task of cleaning up the press with the kind of energy and enthusiasm tabloids feared, initiating investigations and planning reforms of the Press Council's operation.

Blom-Cooper's enterprise was rapidly undermined by a government worried about the successful progress of two private members' bills through the Commons, one on right of reply (sponsored by Labour MP Tony Worthington) and another protecting privacy (drawn up by Tory MP John Browne). Supporting Browne, Tory MP Jonathan Aitken told the House of Commons: 'The reporter's profession has been infiltrated by a seedy stream of rent boys, pimps, bimbos, spurned lovers, smear artists with grudges, prostitutes and perjurers.'[15] But prime minister Margaret Thatcher couldn't afford to upset her supportive press owners by allowing either proposal to pass into law and devised a way of stifling MPs' wishes. Home secretary Douglas Hurd announced in July 1989 that Sir David Calcutt QC, master of Magdalene College, Cambridge, would head a special committee of inquiry into privacy.

The Press Council had been effectively bypassed, but a disappointed Blom-Cooper carried on with his own review. One of his key decisions was to draw up a code of ethics, a concept editors had resisted for twenty years. Meanwhile, with Calcutt under orders to report by the summer of 1990, there was continuing concern among broadsheet editors that press freedom was about to be compromised by tabloid misbehaviour. *Guardian* columnist Hugo Young even backed the idea of a privacy law, observing in his usual magisterial style: 'It is time to end the professional blackmail by which it is pretended that the interests of the *Sun* have anything in common with the interests of the *Guardian*.'[16]

Sun editor Kelvin MacKenzie had previously made his viewpoint clear in a *Sun* editorial which Murdoch later admitted he 'fiddled with . . . a bit'.[17] It attacked the 'Establishment' with a capital E as 'a growing band of people in positions of influence and privilege who want OUR newspaper to suit THEIR private convenience. They wish to conceal from the readers' eyes anything they find annoying or embarrassing.'[18] The leader warned: 'When politicians supposedly serving the public are on the private make, we shall tell our readers.' Given Murdoch's involvement in its composition this leader would hardly have dampened MacKenzie's natural enthusiasm for making mischief.

Throughout the Calcutt crisis Murdoch remained more ambivalent than any other proprietor about the need to clamp down. When Woodrow Wyatt referred to female editors Eve Pollard (*Sunday Mirror*), Wendy Henry (*Sunday People*) and Pat Chapman (*News of the World*) as 'three bordello lady keepers' Murdoch expressed his annoyance.[19] His public stance as a supporter of reform was always tempered by his private and sincere belief that the market was the best mechanism to settle matters of press conduct.

The names of Murdoch and MacKenzie were often on the lips of broadsheet editors who were keen to defend press freedom while bringing the tabloids to heel. To that end, it was decided – under the auspices of the Newspaper Publishers Association (NPA) – to set up a committee of editors chaired by the *Independent*'s Andreas Whittam Smith. I attended one of these NPA meetings in 1990 (as Robert Maxwell's representative) and was struck by the lack of cohesion and coherence among a group of powerful individuals who were used to getting their own way. Whittam Smith, Conrad Black and the chairman, Sir Frank Rogers, made by far the most sensible contributions. Lord Rothermere amazed everyone by saying that a privacy law seemed like a rather good idea after all, a bizarre intervention given that he was among the owners who had previously agreed to oppose it. He was ignored. Within months, with tabloid editors alarmed by the likelihood of an anti-tabloid agenda emerging unless they played an active role, Whittam Smith's committee of five was expanded to include every editor. Even so, the broadsheets won the day by insisting that the only guarantee of avoiding legislation lay in drawing up their own code of practice. This seemed like a better prospect to tabloid editors than having one imposed by Blom-Cooper.

The pressure for reform was exacerbated by the success of a weekly TV programme on Channel 4 which highlighted the sins of the tabloids. Launched in April 1989, *Hard News* was presented by the *Financial Times*'s media correspondent Ray Snoddy and turned the tables on papers by investigating the backgrounds to their stories, exposing distortions, inaccuracies and unethical behaviour. It later emerged that members of the Calcutt Committee were influenced by its revelations.[20] But its most memorable interview, in December 1989, was with Home Office Minister David Mellor, who made an impassioned attack on tabloids for their intrusiveness and for their 'morbid' coverage of the Hillsborough football disaster. In an echo of that *Guardian* leader of six years before, he concluded: 'I do believe the press – the popular press – is drinking in the Last Chance Saloon.'[21] This time around the phrase caught the public, and journalistic, imagination, concentrating everyone's mind on the need to act swiftly and decisively.

For some six months Calcutt's committee – an MP, two lawyers, a former lay member of the Press Council, *Times* editor Simon Jenkins and former *Financial Times* journalist Sheila Black – went about their task with diligence. Apart from accepting written submissions, they were treated to one of *Sun* editor Kelvin MacKenzie's virtuoso performances at an oral hearing in which he claimed that his paper had already cleaned up its act. By stressing that his decision had been prompted by complaints from readers he implied that he was responding to market pressure rather than the concerns of broadsheet editors or politicians. But he did admit that Murdoch – prevailed on by his principal advisers Sir Edward Pickering and Andrew Knight – had played a part.[22]

Then came an incident which was to colour the committee's final report. Gorden Kaye, a popular actor on the TV series *'Allo 'Allo*, was gravely injured when a piece of wood speared his car during a violent storm in January 1990. Tabloid reporters besieged London's Charing Cross Hospital for news of the actor, who was in a critical condition on a life support machine. A reporter and photographer from the *Sunday Sport* defied medical staff by entering Kaye's room to take pictures and even attempted to interview him. Kaye's agent tried to obtain an injunction to prevent the *Sport* publishing its scoop but the judge, Lord Justice Glidewell, concluded reluctantly: 'It is well known in English law that there is no right of privacy, and accordingly there is no right of action for breach of a person's privacy.'[23] His sympathies were obvious, hinting that parliament might like to consider passing such a law. The *Sport* then boasted of its 'victory over censorship' by publishing its pictures, offering the spurious justification that it was doing so to reassure the actor's fans that he was recovering and, when censured, replied with the headline: 'Bollocks to the Press Council'.[24]

It didn't matter to Calcutt's team or to MPs that the *Sport* was a marginal and a maverick paper. The incident had proved the point that no one's privacy was sacrosanct and the resulting 124-page report by Calcutt, in May 1990, reflected the committee's concern about invasion of privacy and the ineffectiveness of the Press Council to deal with the problem. Though they recommended that self-regulation should be given 'one final chance', they suggested that the Press Council should be replaced by a Press Complaints Commission (PCC).[25] Calcutt believed the Press Council's twin functions – campaigning for press freedom and adjudicating on complaints – were incompatible. Blom-Cooper disagreed, but the industry accepted Calcutt and he departed unhappily.[26]

Calcutt, who had favoured a privacy law from the start, saw the PCC as a stop-gap measure before the inevitable setting up of a statutory tribunal which would have the power to fine papers and compensate their victims.[27] But he provided the government with a breathing space before it dared to take that step by offering newspapers a probationary period of eighteen months to see if they could make the PCC operate properly. There were other important recommendations too. Three new criminal offences should be created to prevent intrusion by journalists, basically an extension to the laws of trespass. The PCC should run a twenty-four-hour hotline. People who complained should not have to sign a legal waiver.

One key sentence in Calcutt's report should not go unnoticed. 'We have found no reliable evidence to show whether unwarranted intrusion into individual privacy has or has not risen over the last 20 years.' As this history has shown, there were countless examples from 1945 onwards and the committee's wise reflection was too often overlooked in the following years.

The first reaction to Calcutt from within newspapers was shock. The second was to get organised. Proprietors accepted the Advertising Standards

Authority's machinery for funding and overseeing self-regulation and, by October, they had created the Press Standards Board of Finance (Pressbof), a committee of eleven representatives of owners chaired by Guardian group chairman Harry Roche. It was also charged with the delicate task of selecting a PCC chairman and quickly chose Lord McGregor of Durris. Pressbof and its paymasters thought Oliver McGregor an excellent choice. Aged sixty-nine, he had enjoyed a distinguished academic career as an economic historian, had chaired the 1977 Royal Commission on the Press, had chaired the Advertising Standards Authority and was a fervent believer in self-regulation. Politically, having started out as a Labour peer and become a cross-bencher, he was considered neutral.

McGregor's first major decree, demanding that editors draw up their own code rather than accept one imposed by the PCC, was his wisest decision. Having become editor of the *Daily Mirror* in February 1990, I found myself at the centre of subsequent events. I ignored a stricture by my owner, Robert Maxwell, not to get involved and joined in with other national and regional editors to construct a code. As the only editor at those meetings with experience at senior level in both broadsheets and tabloids, I understood the central contradiction: the former liked to feel their stories served the public interest, the latter wished to publish material that interested the public.

In what turned out to be a shrewd move, though I admit being motivated by mischief, I proposed that *News of the World* editor Pat Chapman should chair the code committee. Her paper was widely considered to be second only to the *Sun* as the greatest sinner, and it was obvious that if she approved some kind of ethical code it would stand a good chance of being accepted by everyone. That is just how it turned out. With great tact, Chapman oversaw a series of meetings which drew up a sensible and workable code, flexible enough to satisfy tabloid editors yet rigid enough to ensure that it inhibited the worst forms of misbehaviour. Our thorniest problem, given that intrusion was Calcutt's paramount concern, was trying to define the boundary between privacy and press freedom. This was solved, with the cautious appreciation of broadsheet editors, by creating a relatively simple public interest test.

The code wisely decided that the famous could enjoy their privacy only when in a private place. While the code details were being hammered out and with every editor aware that Calcutt and parliament were watching, most papers were careful not to take risks during 1990. Wendy Henry, fired six months earlier from the *Sunday People*, declared that what she called 'the clean-up campaign' had caused sales to fall. Unemployed at the time, she was freer to speak her mind than *Sun* editor Kelvin MacKenzie, who privately agreed with her. But he realised the rip-roaring days were over and signed up to the code with Murdoch's blessing, and probably at his urging.[28]

Not that it made much difference to MacKenzie's brand of journalistic recklessness. In August 1990, the *Sun* made another horrendous mistake by publishing a picture of the Prince of Wales with a friend, Lady Romsey, under the headline, 'Charles hugs his old flame: Prince shares tender moments with lovely Penny beside the pool'.[29] The implication of a romance between the couple was obvious, but it emerged the next day that the prince had been consoling Lady Romsey after she had learned that her four-year-old daughter had been diagnosed with cancer. In reporting this, an unrepentant *Sun* reused the same intimate picture, snapped while they were in a private place. The paper did apologise two days later, but the Press Council thought it too little too late and censured the *Sun* for intruding into the couple's privacy and for making a false innuendo.

It was surely apt that the *Sun* should be the subject of the Press Council's final adjudication in December 1990. From 1 January 1991 it would be the Press Complaints Commission's task to deal with MacKenzie and his ilk. But a change of regulator wouldn't eradicate a deeper malaise within the press, the political distortion which was so prevalent that the victims rarely, if ever, bothered to complain.

Baa baa green sheep: legends of the loony left

Media myths have much in common with urban myths: the stories are apocryphal, endlessly retold, inevitably embellished and extraordinarily difficult to quash. Throughout the 1980s, many Labour-run local authorities were dominated by left-wing groups and personalities who took every opportunity to thwart the policies of the Tory government, often against the wishes of the Labour party leadership. They opposed the imposition of the poll tax and rate-capping, struggling to prevent central government from imposing its will over local government and arguing that more money, rather than less, was required to provide adequate services.

In the course of this defiance, some also attempted to promote a political agenda which was the antithesis of the prevailing Tory doctrine, championing the causes of people they identified as underdogs, such as ethnic minorities, homosexuals, Aids sufferers and nuclear disarmers. This alternative political viewpoint engendered policies and initiatives which attracted hostility from both the government and the press, giving rise to the invention of a phrase which entered the national vocabulary: 'loony-left councils'. One fairly typical *Sun* diatribe against these councils began: 'They hoist red flags, insult the Royal Family, refuse people their legal rights to buy their own homes and add anti-bomb messages to street signs.'[30]

Though loony leftism was considered by newspapers to be a national phenomenon – with Liverpool and Sheffield often cited as examples – most press interest was concentrated on certain London boroughs, such as Islington, Camden, Brent, Haringey and Lambeth, along with the Inner London Education Authority (ILEA) and the Greater London Council (GLC).

Two Labour politicians in particular, GLC leader 'Red Ken' Livingstone and Brent council leader 'Barmy' Bernie Grant, became favourite targets.[31] They were the metropolitan versions of 'loony' Labour MP Tony Benn who, while he was standing in the Chesterfield by-election in 1984, was treated to one of the *Sun*'s more questionable stunts. To prove him mad, the paper sent a dossier about Benn to an American psychiatrist. Unaware of his subject's identity, Dr David Hubbard cabled back a report which stated that the person was 'a Messiah figure . . . greedy for power . . . driven by his own self-interest and thinks of himself as God'. This was published under the headline, 'Benn on the couch'. *World in Action* later contacted Hubbard, who told its interviewer he hadn't realised that people would take his material seriously, that it wasn't objective and, anyway, he hadn't exerted much effort in gauging Benn's personality.[32] The important point of the exercise was to marginalise Benn and all who were thought to share his views, such as Livingstone and Grant.

By 1985 newspapers, including those which supported Labour, became obsessed with publishing ever more outlandish claims about the activities of loony-left councils. In so doing, they were responsible for purveying a number of 'bizarre reports . . . which have either been conjured out of thin air or have contained more artificial additives than true ingredients'.[33] The scale of the myth-making was so pervasive that many people believed the tales even after they were later proved to be false. Councils often pursued papers to publish retractions, but they were rarely obtained and, when they were, it was customary for the retraction to be tucked away, unseen by the majority of people who had read the lie days, weeks and sometimes months earlier. Some carefully worded retractions occasionally reinforced the idea that the paper had been largely correct, and their grudging nature often suggested to readers that there could not have been smoke without a fire.

Just before the 1987 election a detailed report by the media research group at London University's Goldsmiths' College revealed many of the loony-left stories to be either wholly inaccurate or 'grotesque distortions of what actually happened'.[34] One of the most enduring fictional stories was about the banning of black bin liners by Haringey council because they were considered racially offensive. Instead, people would be expected to use grey bags.[35] The *Mail on Sunday* employed a technique that was common to all such stories, relying for its substantive allegation on anonymous, unidentified, unverifiable sources: 'staff' in the parks department were said to have been given the instruction by 'a storeman' at Haringey's central depot. After protests, the paper ran a disingenuous paragraph the following week which began: 'Black dustbin liners at the centre of a council race storm are not to be banned after all.' Note the sleight of hand. Though admitting that the central point of its previous story was untrue, it reinforced the feeling that something had happened by falsely maintaining that there had been a 'storm'. The use of 'after all' hinted that it might well have happened but for publicity in the paper.

In the following years I often heard people relate the bin-liner story. The myth had taken hold, just as it did with the *Sun*'s February 1986 story of the 'Loony Left-wing councillors [who] have banned children from reciting the nursery rhyme Baa Baa Black Sheep – because they claim it is racist'.[36] This was a reworking of a story which appeared five days before in the *Daily Star*.[37] Both papers claimed that a playgroup in Hackney had suppressed the rhyme, quoting an unnamed council spokesman as saying that nurseries should be 'discouraged' from using it because 'it reinforces a derogatory and subservient use of the word "black" among our youngsters'. According to the *Sun* version, a nursery had even reacted to the instruction by writing new words which began, 'Baa Baa White Sheep'.

Eight months later this false story resurfaced in a different form in the *Daily Mail*, switching boroughs and colours. This time 'the ban [was] ordered during a racism awareness course run by Bernie Grant's Haringey Council' where playgroup leaders, who were 'instructed to attend', were ordered to replace the word black with green.[38] A playgroup leader helpfully explained that 'it's wrong to sing the rhyme because it's derogatory towards black people'. Almost every 'fact' in this story was untrue: there was no ban on the rhyme, no one had been told to replace black with green, attendance at the course was voluntary, and most people who were there couldn't recall the rhyme even being discussed. Yet a *Mail* leading article that day boomed: 'Is there no escape from the long arm of the Loony Left? . . . The first reaction may be to laugh. But such fanaticism is not funny . . . Town hall tyrants . . . persecute . . . and humiliate . . . They should be disowned by the Labour Party, to which they belong and so driven from public office. And if the Labour Party won't do it, then the voters should.'[39] Next day, obviously believing in the report's veracity, *Mail* columnist Keith Waterhouse referred to Haringey's playgroup leaders as 'one more manifestation of a long line of meddlers, bluenoses and Lady Bountifuls with nothing else to do with their time'.[40] Haringey council denied the story and threatened to sue for libel. *Mail* reporters later contacted some twenty playgroup workers in a vain attempt to stand up the report.

But the sheep story had taken such a hold that it had a predictable, if ironic, outcome. A year after its original manifestation the *Daily Mail* told a heartrending, and true, tale about a retarded boy who hummed the tune of 'Baa Baa Black Sheep' while at his Islington playgroup. His parents then received a letter from one of the group's volunteer teachers, on Islington council notepaper, which said: 'We do not encourage the rhyme Baa Baa Black Sheep as it has been identified as racially derogatory and is actively discouraged by Islington Council.'[41] There was no such instruction, as an Islington council spokesman explained, calling the letter 'an over-zealous interpretation of our equal opportunities policy'. The volunteer had believed the previous press stories and acted accordingly. This story was also published by the *Daily Express*, the *Daily Telegraph*, the *Sun* and the *Daily Mirror*.

By chance, the humming story broke during a closely fought by-election campaign in another London constituency, so the Labour party took pains to counter the negative publicity. The following day's *Mail* carried a picture of Labour leader Neil Kinnock's wife, Glenys, and the party's candidate enjoying a sing-song with children at a Greenwich playgroup. The song? 'Baa Baa *Black* Sheep'.[42]

It is likely that some stories designed to embarrass left-wing councils started out as jokes which journalists got to hear about and believed to be true or, more cynically, knew were false and decided to transform into fact anyway. So the litany of falsehoods continued. Several papers claimed that Ealing council had decreed that children's Wendy houses be renamed 'home corners' to avoid sexism. It was untrue. The *Sun* claimed that Camden council wanted to build its own £55 million coal-fired electricity station because it was opposed to the Central Electricity Generating Board's use of nuclear power. It would also withhold payment of the council's electricity bill. Both matters were evidently raised at Labour group meetings but neither was close to being implemented. Haringey council was alleged to have instructed its workers to drink only Nicaraguan coffee, reported by the *Sun* under the headline: 'Barmy Bernie is going coffee-potty. Staff must drink Marxist brew'.[43] It was no truer than a recurring apocryphal tale about the GLC demanding that black coffee be renamed coffee without milk. One of the difficulties in teasing out the accurate from the inaccurate was that many of the stories did have some basis in fact, a kernel of truth which was over-simplified or embroidered.

Perhaps the most enlightening moment in the saga arrived with the *Sun*'s attempt to lampoon loony leftism by devoting a full page to a spoof Monopoly-style board game entitled LOONYOPOLY.[44] Every square contained references to policies by Labour councils. At Islington, for example, the player could ban heterosexuals from using libraries and bus stops; Lambeth's 'joke' was about replacing council labourers with lesbian body-builders; at Haringey, there was a choice of appointing Zulu tribesmen to supervise comedians at local workingmen's clubs or renaming the high street Colonel Gadaffi Drive. Explaining that these were purely fictitious – 'potty policies ... exaggerated for a laugh' – the paper claimed they were 'based on the daft decisions that really have been taken in these topsy-turvy Labour-controlled boroughs!' It would have been closer to the truth to have pointed out that the game was based on the potty policies fabricated by journalists. But its real significance lay in the fact that it was published at all, proof that by the end of 1986 the concept of loony leftism was so established that Britain's largest-selling daily paper could assume that its 12 million readers would understand the parody.

Even Thatcher's paper tigers couldn't save their heroine

No modern prime minister enjoyed such a long love affair with the majority of the British press as Margaret Thatcher. Before she stood for her third term the *Daily Mail* published a cartoon which suggested she would easily outstrip her rivals.[45] Owners and editors of Tory papers were utterly convinced of her merits and of the Labour opposition's unfitness for office, and the idea that she might be cast out of Downing Street was anathema. She received unstinting support from her newspaper fan club despite a noticeably rocky start to her campaign. During the first hesitant week, with the *Times* noting that Neil Kinnock's Labour opposition was doing 'astonishingly well', both the *Daily Express* and *Daily Mail* registered concern about the Tory machine.[46]

Thatcher's press support was somewhat muted in the second week too until the papers began to reinforce the message that Kinnock could not be trusted in Downing Street. Though acknowledging that Labour's campaign was proving better than expected, editors decided that a negative message, creating a climate of fear about a possible Labour administration, was their most effective propaganda weapon. A *Daily Express* story claimed that a million jobs would vanish if Labour came to power.[47]

Then came a rather odd row between Thatcher and the *Times* which, according to tradition, had always carried an interview with the prime minister at election time. Due to an oversight one had not been arranged with Thatcher and she was persuaded with some reluctance to fit it into her schedule. The night before the interview she suddenly pulled out because she was upset by the paper's front-page headlines, such as 'Labour piles on pressure in marginals', and the use of a picture of Kinnock and his wife rather than one of her.[48] She evidently felt she had done a lot to help Murdoch at Wapping, yet his paper was encouraging a late swing to Labour.[49] *Times* editor Charles Wilson ordered his political editor Robin Oakley to sort out the mess and, after a series of late-night phone calls, Thatcher agreed to the interview two days before the election. What was so significant about this tiff were the differing expectations on each side: Thatcher expected the *Times* to put a positive spin on her campaign while the *Times* considered that it had a right to interview her. In its pre-election editorial the paper made it clear where its sympathies lay by urging the return of the Conservative administration.

In the end the fears of Thatcher and her adoring editors proved groundless. She made history by winning a third successive victory, achieving a majority of 102 (down from 144), while Labour's vote increased by only 3 per cent, gaining it an extra twenty Parliamentary seats. Both major parties were relieved by the poor showing of the third force: the Alliance, hamstrung by its dual leadership – the SDP's David Owen and the Liberals' David Steel –

ran a hopeless campaign. By comparison it was later adjudged that Kinnock had 'fought, personally, a highly effective and energetic campaign', and there was no question of him losing his leadership.[50] Yet he was persistently portrayed by the Tory-supporting papers either as a weak leader unable to deal with the militants (a.k.a. left-wing 'loonies') within his party or as a fellow-traveller of the left. It reinforced the message which had been hammered home in right-wing papers for four years: Labour was a poorly-led, divided and suspect party. The *Sun*'s official historian conceded that her paper was vicious about Kinnock.[51] *Sun* cartoonist Franklin routinely depicted Kinnock as small, ineffective and incompetent.

For Thatcher, who regularly featured in cartoons as a heroine, the sweetness of victory turned sour surprisingly quickly. Her win was more an acclamation of what she had achieved in the past rather than what she promised for the future. In essence, the Tories had been returned to power by virtue of telling voters that the country's problems had been solved. Council houses were being sold; tax reforms had been introduced; unions had been reformed into obscurity; most of the big privatisations had occurred, or were in the pipeline, while the next – water and electricity – were less popular. What more could Thatcher do?

Thatcher's announcement in April 1988 that her government would replace local rates by introducing a community charge – poll tax – was widely ridiculed well before it was introduced. It also caused alarm within her own ranks, as did her negative attitude towards the European Union. By contrast, Kinnock was seen to be leading a pro-European party and to have established a new realism within Labour. By 1989, Labour's poll ratings had revived, and it was winning by-elections (after the disastrous loss of Glasgow Govan) and then did well in the European elections.

Senior journalists were the first to realise the depth of the rift within the Tory party. As early as April 1989, *Daily Mail* editor Sir David English and *Times* deputy editor Peter Stothard spoke privately of their concern at Thatcher's prospects.[52] The central internal party problem was a growing split over Europe, specifically whether Britain should sign up to the Exchange Rate Mechanism (ERM). When that row led in October to Chancellor Nigel Lawson's resignation Murdoch also grew concerned about Thatcher's future.[53] Then came the embarrassing episode of Thatcher facing a leadership contest against the 'stalking horse' Sir Anthony Meyer. Even this political pipsqueak, who everyone conceded had no chance of winning, didn't escape a press smear. A *Daily Express* front page, 'Sir Nobody in KGB Sex Plot', raked over an incident which had happened in 1958 when Meyer was the victim of a clumsy blackmail attempt in Moscow.[54] The story, such as it was, had already been reported in the *Sun* in 1970.[55]

By the beginning of 1990 there was widespread hostility to the poll tax. Though newspapers raged against the violence which broke out following a peaceful demonstration in March, editors were struck by the fact that 40,000 people took part. Both Simon Jenkins at the *Times* and Andrew Neil at the *Sunday Times*, reflecting a sizeable weight of opinion within the Tory party, were opposed to the poll tax. One *Times* editorial concluded bluntly: 'The poll tax must go.'[56] Murdoch confided to Woodrow Wyatt that the *Sun*'s Kelvin MacKenzie, despite trying to portray it sympathetically,[57] was also worried about the unfairness of poll tax and the political implications.[58]

Thatcher wasn't prepared to listen to compromises urged by party members or the press. But in early October 1990 she did reluctantly give in to pressure from senior ministers who threatened to resign unless sterling joined the ERM. The *Sun*, aware of public disquiet, straddled the fence, urging people to keep the faith ('Maggie is the Tories' only hope'), and then urging her to sack Geoffrey Howe, her deputy and the leader of the House.[59] He went the following day, prompting the *Sun* to ask: 'MAGGIE: IS THIS THE END?' Four days later the paper also criticised the Queen's speech as 'a big yawn'.[60] Meanwhile, Woodrow Wyatt was telling Andrew Neil that his leading articles were anything but supportive of the prime minister. Neil replied that he was 'a hundred per cent for Mrs Thatcher'.[61] But Neil was clearly moving away from the prime minister, soon afterwards suggesting in an editorial that she ought to go because she was a liability to the Tories.[62] After a similar broadside Thatcher complained about the *Sunday Times* to Wyatt, who told her that Murdoch was also upset at his paper's stance.[63]

Neil's *Sunday Times* was ahead of the game. On 13 November, Howe delivered one of the most devastating parliamentary speeches of all time. Next day Michael Heseltine challenged Thatcher for the leadership, forcing her to face a ballot, and newspaper offices were suddenly alive with a mixture of excitement and panic. At the Labour-supporting *Daily Mirror*, which I was editing at the time, there was a heady sense of exhilaration fuelled by first-hand reports of Tory disarray delivered by the ever smiling political editor Alastair Campbell. Despite his known Labour sympathies and closeness to Neil Kinnock, he had many good contacts among Conservatives and forecast that she would not survive. At the Tory-supporting, avidly pro-Thatcherite *Sun*, there was apprehension bordering on hysteria. How could they save their champion? MacKenzie went straight on to the attack to support 'Maggie the Lionheart'.[64] In an open letter to Tory MPs his paper warned against voting for Heseltine, daring to add: 'Remember, it was OUR readers who put YOU in office.'[65]

Murdoch clearly agreed with the *Sun*'s sentiments, but two of his other editors – Neil at the *Sunday Times* and David Montgomery at *Today* – thought it was time for Heseltine. We are indebted to Woodrow Wyatt for revelations about Murdoch's feelings during this period and the pressure he applied. He told Wyatt that Montgomery 'is being a pain in the arse'.[66] Monty came into line by backing Thatcher, but Neil wasn't for turning. Murdoch asked his chief executive, Andrew Knight, to convince Neil not to back Heseltine and to soften his attacks on Thatcher. Neil, who had resisted

Murdoch's own blandishments earlier in the year to stick with Thatcher, wouldn't budge.[67] Wyatt revealed that Murdoch wanted to sack Neil, 'for other reasons too', but didn't feel the timing was appropriate.[68] Murdoch was also diverted by the pressing need to sort out his immense debt burden. Neil's *Sunday Times* continued to campaign for Heseltine while the *Times*, edited by Simon Jenkins, went the other way. It had been one of the first papers to urge Heseltine to stand, and later leaders could be read as sympathetic to his cause, but on the day there was a long editorial supporting Thatcher.[69]

The *Daily Express* had been heavily committed to Thatcher for years, but there was a wobble. Chairman Lord Stevens is said to have overruled a plan by the editor, Nick Lloyd, to run a front page headlined 'It must be Heseltine', instructing him to go on supporting Thatcher.[70] From then on, the *Express* backed her stoutly, with headlines boosting her case and undermining Heseltine's. Stevens even went into print himself, writing a long opinion piece which began on page one headlined 'You Can't Let Maggie Go!'[71] The link between profits and propaganda could not have been clearer. Stevens's belief was that a Tory government under Thatcher provided the best climate for United Newspapers to make profits which, as chairman of a public company, was his primary duty to shareholders. To help her remain in power he was using his paper as a propaganda weapon. From his perspective it was a rational business decision to support her. Murdoch said as much to Andrew Neil: 'It may just be my cheque book talking but this country cannot afford a Labour government.'[72]

The press majority in Thatcher's favour appeared to make little difference to the outcome. In the first ballot on 20 November, Thatcher won by a 204–152 margin, four votes short of the required majority for an outright victory, and she was initially inclined to fight on. The *Sun* urged her to do so, and Murdoch telephoned her with a similar message.[73] Conrad Black later revealed that he and David English joined a 'last-ditch Thatcher defence meeting'. Still believing she wouldn't quit, Black and Hastings 'worked out' an editorial which offered her continuing support.[74] She resigned before most *Telegraph* readers had a chance to see it.

Members of Thatcher's own cabinet were nothing like as steadfast as the press barons and their editors. She realised she had lost their confidence and went off to the Palace to tender her resignation to the Queen, shedding a tear as she left, a moment captured in an historic newspaper picture by *Daily Mirror* photographer Ken Lennox.[75] The *Sun* mourned her passing by devoting twenty-four of its forty-eight pages to her.

Does this episode prove the press to be powerless? It isn't as simple as that. Bellow as they might, the papers were not able to influence the narrow constituency – just 373 Tory MPs – who decided their leader's fate. Persuading MPs how to vote was infinitely more difficult for papers than persuading the electorate. MPs, most of whom had made up their minds how they would vote, were unlikely to have cared about the pro-Thatcher propaganda during the week leading up to the ballot and they weren't about to be swayed by journalists. The MPs were aware that there had been a public mood swing against Thatcher. Some interpreted this antagonism as stemming from policies, such as the poll tax and ERM. Many also knew from first-hand experience that the Prime Minister could be dictatorial – the underlying theme of Howe's resignation speech – and believed the public had grown disenchanted with her style and the very fact that she had been around for so long. What is undeniable is that news reports and commentaries in every paper in previous months – about the poll tax, the European debate, the resignation of Nigel Lawson and the subsequent rift in the Tory party climaxed by Howe's resignation – contributed to the growing public disillusion. The accumulation of negative headlines and stories about the government must have made an impact on readers.

However much owners and editors lamented their inability to stop Tory MPs from doing their bidding, they quickly set about trying to influence their choice of successor. Black and Hastings, aware that research suggested some 90 per cent of all Conservative constituency association officials read the *Telegraph* titles, came up with a strategy to halt Heseltine's bandwagon by promoting both Chancellor John Major and Home Secretary Douglas Hurd.[76] The *Daily Telegraph* endorsed Hurd while the *Sunday Telegraph* plumped for Major. Murdoch was equally determined that Heseltine should fail.[77] From the moment of Thatcher's resignation the *Sun* came out strongly for Major.[78] In a rare swipe at another Murdoch paper, it referred to 'opportunists of the *Sunday Times*' for supporting Heseltine, who in various *Sun* articles was treated as if he was a closet socialist. The *Daily Express* backed Major too while mourning Thatcher's departure: 'The electorate may not always have loved her but they respected her strength of character and her remarkable intellectual abilities . . . While Margaret Thatcher may have gone, Thatcherism must not be allowed to die.'[79]

In the second ballot on 27 November, Major was two votes short of a complete victory but his rivals stepped aside and acknowledged him as the new leader. 'The torch of Thatcherism' has passed 'into safe hands' with Major, said the *Express*.[80] The *Sun* called him 'the best man' and looked forward to 'the Age of Major'.[81] It was the *Daily Star* editor, Brian Hitchen, who signalled the clearest indication of trouble to come when writing: 'Britain's greatest ever Prime Minister has been forced out by pygmy politicians who put their own job security before the good of their country . . .'[82] Editors and owners would never forgive the Conservative party for its treatment of their leader. They had supported Major to avoid Kinnock's Labour party, but for how long could he command their loyalty?

Smears as a journalist is executed for doing his job

It would be unforgivable to conclude this section without mentioning the execution of *Observer* journalist Farzad Bazoft, who was hanged in March 1990 in Iraq after being convicted of spying. He had travelled to the country on assignment for the *Observer* after pleading for the chance to investigate the mystery of a huge explosion at a rocket-testing site near Baghdad in August 1989 in which hundreds of people died. He suspected, as did other journalists and various Western intelligence agencies, that it was the result of secret nuclear research. Even for the most experienced foreign correspondent it would have been a risky venture. For Bazoft, a thirty-one-year-old relative newcomer to reporting, it was foolhardy. Worse, he was from Iran, a country which had just fought Iraq to a standstill in a bitter and bloody eight-year war. But he had been to Iraq before, liked the Iraqi people and had previously made good contacts in Iraq's London embassy.

In carrying out his mission he made many naive mistakes. He persuaded an English nurse, Daphne Parish, to drive him to the site in an ambulance, with Bazoft posing as a doctor. He made two visits in this guise, during which he collected a shoe, pieces of clothing and some ash samples. He tried to convince the British embassy to send the items for analysis to London by diplomatic pouch. Officials refused to do so and warned him to leave Iraq as quickly as possible. Instead, that night he bragged in a hotel bar to another journalist about having a big story. Next day his bid to get a Swiss tourist to act as courier also failed.

He was then arrested with his 'evidence' at the airport as he prepared to fly out. Parish was also picked up and the pair were held in solitary confinement for six months while they were relentlessly interrogated. Bazoft was tortured and eventually made a drug-induced confession. Throughout their imprisonment there was a low-profile campaign to get them released, headed by *Observer* deputy editor Adrian Hamilton. The Foreign Office showed little inclination to help. Two senior *Observer* journalists who regarded Bazoft as a friend as well as a colleague, defence correspondent Ian Mather and Helga Graham, organised nightly vigils outside the Iraqi embassy. But there was scant coverage of Bazoft's plight in most of the British press.

In early March, after a travesty of a trial on a spurious charge of 'undermining' Iraq's security and conducted entirely in Arabic, which neither defendant understood, Bazoft and Parish were found guilty. He was sentenced to death and she was given a fifteen-year jail term. Prime minister Margaret Thatcher appealed for clemency, but seven days later Bazoft was hanged and his body was dumped in front of the British embassy in Baghdad. An Iraqi minister is said to have remarked: 'Mrs Thatcher wanted Bazoft alive. We gave her the body.'

Most of the journalists working at the *Observer* that weekend were in tears. Helga Graham said years later that it was madness for the paper to let him go. Ian Mather thought him 'a nice fellow, ambitious and always eager to get ahead' but concluded that 'as a journalist, he was somewhat of a loose cannon . . . an accident waiting to happen'.[83] Adrian Hamilton was kinder about Bazoft's abilities: 'He was a journalist in search of a story. Naive? Yes, but naive in a way that all the best young reporters are, eager at the sniff of a good story. That was Farzad. Eager. And determined, determined to be a journalist and a good one, whatever it took.'[84] In a tribute on the tenth anniversary of Bazoft's death, Hamilton reiterated his viewpoint, wondering 'if over-enthusiasm can ever be thought a failing in a reporter'.[85]

Even though many colleagues thought him impulsive and immature, it doesn't explain why other newspapers didn't campaign more strongly on Bazoft's behalf. I recall that soon after his arrest, when I was running the *Sunday Times*'s newsroom, our correspondents were given hints by Foreign Office and secret service contacts that there might be more to the affair than first appeared. Even some of the more experienced staff read this as a guidance that Bazoft might be a spy.

Given that Britain was then cosying up to Iraq's dictator, Saddam Hussein, it is entirely plausible that the security services thought it necessary to blacken Bazoft's name for what they deemed to be the greater good. An Iraqi claim that Bazoft was spying for Israel was given credence when Tory MP Rupert Allason – who wrote spy books under the pseudonym Nigel West – said Bazoft was 'quite likely' to have been an Israeli agent. *Observer* editor Donald Trelford called it a 'despicable' allegation.[86] Allason adduced as proof the fact that Bazoft's address book contained the name of an Israeli businessman, but it transpired that the name had been given to him by Trelford.[87]

Immediately after Bazoft's death it emerged that he had been sentenced to eighteen months' jail in June 1981 for robbing a bank in the Midlands. The leak raised questions about the motive and identity of the leakers, but inevitably cast more suspicion over Bazoft's role.[88] Most press reports tended to concentrate their fire on the inhumanity of Bazoft's captors. A *Sunday Telegraph* article by Geoffrey Wheatcroft was typical, describing Iraq as 'a tract of land inhabited for the most part by primitive tribesmen' led by Hussein who 'morally . . . lives in the stone age. Even to speak of Bazoft's death as judicial murder is to miss the point; it was human sacrifice, as practised by tribes just emerging from the other higher mammals.'[89] This was the kind of anti-Iraqi propaganda and demonisation of Hussein which would reach a crescendo in future months. It prompted at least one writer to adopt a controversial stance by questioning the concept of investigative reporting when journalists from the West travelled to Third World countries.

Accepting that Bazoft was not a spy in the formal sense – acting specifically for a country's secret service – Hugh Roberts argued that he could still be defined as a spy by applying a broader interpretation. Seen from the perspective of the Iraqis, 'the distinction between spy and investigative journalist is a distinction without a difference'. Both seek out secrets. In Bazoft's case, he 'was behaving as a spy . . . because he intended to . . . reveal an Iraqi state secret which was bound to be of interest to states hostile to Iraq . . . This sort of journalistic caper can be got away with in America and Britain and probably most Western democracies these days. It is suicidal in the Middle East.'[90]

PART TEN: 1991–1995

19. A MEDIA MAGNATE GOES TO WAR

> If I have learned anything in my thirty-seven years in journalism, it is that nothing fails like success ... bright young journalists are always being promoted beyond their true capacities.[1]

Five years on from the Wapping revolution there had been a dramatic change in national papers: in size, extra sections, design, use of colour, range of content and editorial approach. No longer was it feasible to make comparisons with the press that existed in the 1970s, let alone 1945. By 1991 every title, broadsheet and tabloid, had enlarged far beyond the imaginations of the proprietors and journalists of earlier generations. Now it was possible to publish huge numbers of pages on the run, to insert pre-printed sections, and to have other supplements and magazines collated at the point of sale. Newspapers had become packages: the old corner shop of eight poorly printed, monochrome pages with its restricted editorial diet had been transformed into a new supermarket, offering scores of well-illustrated pages and a seemingly limitless range of content. But competition ensured that no idea, good or bad, remained the province of one paper for long. Every supermarket felt it necessary to stock the same goods while claiming they were qualitatively better than those of their rivals.

All the tabloids created large Saturday editions, turning a previously poor day into the week's bestselling issue. They were helped by the deregulation of television programme details, which freed the copyright from the TV companies and allowed papers to publish seven-day guides, thereby prompting the launch of entertainment-based Saturday magazines. Having significantly reduced the cost of production by ousting the print unions, owners could offer added value to potential buyers. Newspapers had always been advertising vehicles. Now they often resembled marketing agencies, offering readers opportunities to take low-cost holidays, enjoy cut-price restaurant meals and spend cheap evenings at the opera. The *Sunday Times* launched its own credit card. A relaxation of commercial television rules allowed tabloids to sponsor ITV shows linked to big-money games. High-minded papers, such as the *Independent*, offered cash prizes. Despite these lures, overall circulation dipped as the effects of a worldwide recession in 1991 began to bite. Every group therefore found it necessary to increase their marketing and promotion budgets to sell fewer papers which, because of their dramatic growth in size and a downturn in advertising revenue, were costing ever more to produce.

A threat by the government to remove newspapers' zero rating for Value Added Tax receded in the face of a united onslaught by owners and editors against a so-called 'tax on knowledge'. Given some of the editorial content, it was debatable whether readers could genuinely gain any knowledge. It certainly appeared as though many more of them were happy to do without papers. Between the first half of 1990 and the first half of 1993, ten of the eleven national daily titles lost sales, with the *Sun* registering the worst drop and the *Times* coming perilously close to falling below the *Independent*. The *Daily Mail* was the only paper to add sales, but these amounted to a mere 10,000. A global recession, in which 'virtually every newspaper in the English-speaking world . . . found its advertising revenue down by a third or more', added to the air of despondency.[2]

One man believed he had the solution to this circulation crisis: Rupert Murdoch. He decided to cut the cover prices of his two main daily titles and thereby started a full-scale price war. Before we consider what happened it's important to understand more about Murdoch, whose domination of the British newspaper industry throughout the 1980s and 1990s was being matched by his interests across the globe.

By this time Murdoch was on the path to becoming the world's greatest media tycoon and, even if his global corporate strategy had been hard to divine in the past, one was starting to emerge. Though his ownership of newspapers still gave him personal pleasure, his main aim was to build a company to distribute TV programmes to the entire planet. He had turned Fox TV into the fourth US network and improved the prospects of his Hollywood film studio, 20th Century-Fox. In Europe, he had developed European satellite TV and had realised both the limitations of competing cable TV delivery and the potential of satellite technological advances. He also came to understand the value of vertical integration. By owning the content (programmes and films), operating the distribution system (satellite transponders) and controlling the gateway (encryption), he could dominate television everywhere. With BSkyB, which began making money in 1992 after its first three years of giant operating losses, he dominated Britain and much of Europe. His Star TV satellite enterprise was aimed at monopolising Asia, with its untapped markets in China and India. JSkyB was a similar operation in Japan. He was involved in an Australian cable partnership and in satellite ventures in Mexico and Brazil. But the richest market remained the United States and he was to spend the following years trying to attain that goal.[3]

It is a measure of Murdoch's extraordinary appetite for his business that he had reached this strong position after coming within a whisker of losing his empire. In the final months of 1990, his umbrella company, News Corporation, was in financial trouble because of its colossal debt and falling profitability. Murdoch faced meltdown when one of the 150 banks to which News Corp owed money threatened to foreclose. But he owed too much for the big banks to allow him to go under and, after a series of cliffhanging decisions, the bankers agreed to refinance his debt. He had to agree to a restructuring and to having the banks look over his shoulder when making key appointments. For a man who thrived on acquisition, the price was painful. He had to sell off his American magazine division and the *Star*, the supermarket check-out tabloid he had launched in 1974. He closed down the *Melbourne Sunday Herald*, sold his stake in Pearson and was forced to dilute his family's holding in News Corp.

Murdoch knuckled down and won back the confidence of the banks by turning all his loans into long-term debt and managing to raise capital as well. Within twenty-eight months he extricated himself from the banking constraints and was free to go on acquiring and building. He had, in the words of his media tycoon rival Conrad Black, bet the company and won. Murdoch liked the description, with its bravado overtones of risk-taking, and would later use it himself. He was also lucky, even regaining his beloved, loss-making *New York Post* in 1993.[4]

Luck played little part in one of his first decisions after his debt crisis: the launching of Britain's newspaper price war. Far from being a gung-ho general, he showed initial reluctance in the face of his Wapping executives' enthusiasm. Tests carried out in one area suggested that the *Sun*'s circulation would improve if its 25p cover price were cut by a fifth, so Murdoch gave the go-ahead. On 12 July 1993, the *Sun*'s front page was dominated by the announcement: 'ONLY 20p. BIGGEST PRICE CUT IN HISTORY OF NEWSPAPERS'. Tabloid rivals were taken by surprise, with the ailing *Daily Mirror*, then suffering a financial crisis, only able to make a token response by reducing its price for one day to 10p. *Daily Star* editor Brian Hitchen, who wasn't allowed to follow suit, tried to laugh it off, describing it as a desperate measure by desperate men.[5]

Most commentators expected it to be a short-term phenomenon, but in late August the paper announced it would stay at 20p until the following year at least.[6] By then *Sun* sales, which had fallen below 3.5 million in June, showed every sign of heading back towards 4 million. Meanwhile, the decline of the *Mirror*, *Star* and *Daily Express* had accelerated, the *Daily Mail*'s growth had gone into reverse and Murdoch's other Wapping tabloid, *Today*, was badly weakened.[7] By October, the *Sun* was the only tabloid which could boast both month-on-month and year-on-year sales rises.

Serious commentary on the tabloid price war was relatively muted until Murdoch shocked the industry by opening a new front: at the end of September 1993 he cut the price of the *Times* from 45 to 30p. This was viewed as an outrage by rivals, particularly the *Independent*, which was facing a liquidity problem. Editor Andreas Whittam Smith was convinced Murdoch was trying to put his paper out of business, complaining that he was using a cross-subsidy which would be illegal in many countries because the *Times* was losing money.[8] Despite the *Sun*'s success, most observers and City analysts thought that cutting the cover price of the *Times* would make only a marginal difference to its circulation.[9] It might get an initial sales burst, then people would return to their usual paper. The *Independent* was taking no chances and, along with members of the Labour party's front bench, complained to the Office of Fair Trading that Murdoch was guilty of predatory pricing. After an informal and rapid investigation, the OFT decided to take no action, declaring that there was a fine line between aggressive pricing and predation.[10]

The trade magazine thought the possible demise of the *Independent*, which suffered an immediate and continuing sales downturn as the *Times*'s circulation soared, would be unjust.[11] It soon emerged that the paper was an innocent casualty of the war. Murdoch's main target was the *Daily Telegraph*, as he confided to both Woodrow Wyatt and *Daily Mail* editor Sir David English.[12] According to English, when he told Murdoch that he now saw the *Telegraph* as the *Mail*'s main rival rather than the *Daily Express*, Murdoch replied: 'Don't worry about the *Telegraph*. Leave them to me. I'll put them out of business for you.' He aimed to claw away at the *Telegraph*'s audience in order to make the *Times* into the largest-selling daily broadsheet. In so doing he hoped to eat into its lucrative classified advertising and turn the loss-making *Times* into profit.

Stung by hostility to his initiative, Murdoch offered an economic rationale for his decision: newspapers had increased in price at twice the rate of inflation. For example, the price of the *Times* had risen 80 per cent since 1987 while inflation had increased by only 40.7 per cent. Therefore, he was acting as the consumer's friend by cutting prices. Conrad Black was unimpressed by the argument, pointing out that prices had gone up because papers were offering added value, with more pages, more supplements and more colour.

Then the *Independent*'s controllers launched the most bizarre counter-attack of the entire war. Just one month after the *Times*'s price cut they *increased* their cover price from 45 to 50p. Having shot themselves in the foot, they would limp ever after. *Telegraph* owner Conrad Black, who tried to walk tall in the early months as his paper gradually lost sales to the *Times*, perpetrated his own form of self-mutilation. He had originally belittled the *Times* as 'a schlocky Murdoch tout-sheet' which would never attract the 'very sophisticated, intelligent, literate' broadsheet readers who 'know crap when they see it'.[13] By May 1994, he had changed his mind about his readers' sophistication. It was impossible to ignore the debilitating effects of the price war and he knew that the *Telegraph*'s circulation was on the verge of slipping below the psychologically important and commercially vital 1 million mark for the first time since February 1953.[14] He chose that month, on behalf of his main company, Hollinger, to sell 12.5 million *Telegraph* shares – about

9 per cent of the total – for £73 million. The trade, through one of the City's most blue-blooded of stockbrokers, Cazenove, seemed unremarkable. Black would still control the company and it was assumed he was merely raising capital, possibly for an acquisition.

I interviewed Black in his office a month later. By then the official audited circulation figures for May had been released, revealing that the *Telegraph* sale had fallen to 993,000 while the *Times* had risen to 517,000. Naturally enough, we talked about the problems he was facing and, in typically florid language, he spoke of 'Rupert opening his arteries' while 'trying to kill us' and calling the price war 'a Darwinian crusade'. He gave no clue about his intentions, but a day or so later he announced that the *Daily Telegraph* – 'to protect its market dominance' – would reduce its price from 48 to 30p. Anticipating that the cut would slice £40 million off the paper's sales revenue in a full year, it was fund managers who opened their arteries the next day as the market marked down the *Telegraph* stock to almost half the price Black had obtained for his shares five weeks before, and he was cast in the City in the role of chief villain.[15] The stock exchange cleared the *Telegraph* group of any wrongdoing after an unprecedented one-day inquiry, but Cazenove resigned as its broker after a nine-year association with Black.[16]

I didn't share the City's animus against Black, reflected in several reports in rival papers.[17] He had certainly done nothing illegal and I didn't see it as immoral either. Murdoch had him cornered. Black, who had spent £8 million in promotion trying to stave off a price cut, said his company was facing its 'biggest challenge since the move out of Fleet Street eight years ago'.[18] The *Telegraph* had made only £53 million profit the previous year. Hollinger, having taken over a Canadian group in 1992, wasn't flush with funds. He needed a war chest to prepare for his price cut. He further inflamed City opinion by threatening to take the *Telegraph* back into his own hands if the share price continued to fall.[19]

Black had come to realise what many of us were also coming to accept: the price war may have started out as a temporary aberration but it was on its way to becoming a fundamental part of the newspaper market. The trouble for Murdoch's rivals was that he was entering the poker game with more chips than anyone else and considerably more daring. When Black cut the *Telegraph* price he discovered just how much of a gambler he was confronting. Murdoch immediately slashed the *Times*'s midweek price by a further third, to 20p, and the Saturday issue to 30p, making it 40p cheaper than the Saturday *Telegraph*.

The crazy economics of this initiative were laid bare. About 15p of the *Times*'s price went to the news trade to cover distribution and the production cost amounted to 16p a copy. So every *Times* sold at 20p represented an 11p loss to News International, a deficit calculated at £1.2 million a month.[20] Offsetting this loss was the fact that the *Times* was yoked to the hugely profitable *Sunday Times*, which made more than enough to sustain its stablemate. Soon the two papers were on offer to readers for just £1. Though News Corp's results bore the scars of the price war, with the first nine months costing the company some £45 million, it didn't imperil its existence.[21]

The same couldn't be said for the crisis-hit *Independent*, and it responded to the new turn of events with the fiercest criticism. Deputy editor Matthew Symonds pointed out that Murdoch was giving the *Times* away for free and called on 'politicians of all parties' to curb 'the overweening power of a man who is contemptuous of most of the institutions and values which give society its worth'.[22] Two senior Labour figures needed little prompting. Robin Cook, the shadow industry secretary, called again for an Office of Fair Trading investigation into predatory pricing while Mo Mowlam, shadow heritage secretary, argued that the price war would result in 'fewer newspapers ... less choice for readers ... less diversity of political opinion'. She claimed the government was sitting on its hands because it feared alienating Murdoch.[23]

A couple of days later the OFT announced that it would make new inquiries into the price war as its effects began to spread. With papers desperate to boost sales, owners made huge efforts to sell in places they had served poorly for years, such as Scotland and then Ireland, offering cut-price deals at the start of regional circulation campaigns. Hardly a week passed without one paper or another reducing its price for a day, causing headaches for the owners of provincial morning papers who couldn't afford to match the cuts of their national rivals.[24] Competition to attract casual readers – the newspaper equivalent of floating voters – was fierce.

Then the *Independent*, having suffered a potentially catastrophic sales reverse, felt compelled to join the war. It first compromised its purist line against price-cutting in early July 1994 by reducing its cover price in the Midlands from 50 to 35p. Weeks later it announced a nationwide cut to 30p.[25] Only the *Guardian* stood aloof, losing some sales but not enough to cause a panic. It was therefore spared the financial reverses which News International, the Telegraph group and the *Independent*'s owners suffered. Share prices began to slip as stockbrokers warned of red figures to come, with one analyst's report entitled 'Rupert Murdoch Ate My Profits' and another, 'More blood to spill'.[26]

To ease matters at Wapping, where *Sun* sales had sailed beyond 4 million, that paper's price was raised to 22p in August. Meanwhile, in bullish submissions to the OFT, Murdoch's executives put a benign spin on what they termed 'competitive pricing'. Their arguments prevailed when the OFT, after a three-month inquiry, cleared both the *Times* and the *Daily Telegraph* of predatory pricing by announcing that the price war was healthy for consumers.[27] Years later an economist contended that the OFT had been wrong to see the cut in terms of the whole market because one paper, the *Independent*, had suffered worse than any other, which amounted to predation.[28]

At the Davos world economic forum in January 1995, Murdoch and Black jested about the price war in a sort of double act. These were fake smiles because both knew that escalating newsprint costs were making their low cover prices unsustainable and, after a reduction in pagination and a pruning of copies for distribution, there was a lull in the war.[29] The *Sun* added another penny to its price in February and a further 2p in June, selling at 25p to the *Daily Mirror*'s 27p. In July, the *Times* raised its price from 20 to 25p, the *Daily Telegraph* went from 30 to 35p, and the *Independent* from 30 to 35p. But the impact of the war was far from over. Some broadsheets were now trying to lure readers through direct-mail voucher offers and cut-rate subscription schemes. Profits remained depressed and in November, with both the *Times* and the *Daily Telegraph* adding another 5p to their prices, came the war's first major casualty: Murdoch closed *Today*.

His executives denied that the price war had played a part in the decision, arguing that the paper showed no sign of turning a profit in any imaginable circumstances. On the other hand, it had recently shown every sign of making a journalistic impact after a difficult couple of years. Well before the end of 1990, Murdoch had had enough of *Today*'s headstrong editor and managing director, David Montgomery, as Liberal Democrat leader Paddy Ashdown witnessed.[30] Murdoch didn't take kindly to Monty's attempt to form a consortium to engineer a management buyout of the paper, while Monty didn't agree with Murdoch's demand in January 1991 that he make forty-five journalists redundant and move *Today* from its Vauxhall Bridge office into Wapping. Two months later Monty was removed from the editor's chair and moved to an office without a role.

Murdoch gave the editorship to the *Sun*'s deputy editor Martin Dunn. He was thirty-six, clever, hardworking and affable, qualities which had enabled him to work well alongside *Sun* editor Kelvin MacKenzie. He had also made a good fist of acting as the *Sun*'s public face on radio and TV. A product of the grammar school in Dudley, Worcestershire, he started out on his local weekly and then the *Birmingham Evening Mail*. His first Fleet Street job was as a reporter on the *Daily Mail* for two years before freelancing in New York and becoming the *Sun*'s US correspondent. He shone in that role and, on returning to Britain in 1984, ran the *Sun*'s pop gossip column. He was briefly deputy editor of the *News of the World* until MacKenzie made him his deputy in 1989.

The *Today* editorship was regarded within Wapping as a poisoned chalice because of falling sales and poor staff morale. The paper had lost its way after several changes of direction under Montgomery and no longer had a clear *raison d'être*. It was wrongly assumed that Dunn would take *Today* down-market.[31] In fact, Dunn struggled with poor resources and without detectable management enthusiasm to give the paper a middle-market appeal. He had commitment and flair, but circulation went down to 430,000.

Dunn and Murdoch agreed in January 1992 to reposition *Today*, changing the typeface to sans serif and aggressively targeting the audiences of the *Daily Mirror*, *Daily Express* and, more controversially, the *Sun*. By sticking more rigidly to the mainstream news agenda, eschewing off-beat splashes and *Hello!*-style features, and remaining fairly apolitical, Dunn succeeded in changing *Today*'s fortunes. Within two months sales were back over 500,000 and by February 1993 were a commendable 540,000. At this point Dunn accepted an offer from Murdoch to edit one of his American papers, the *Boston Herald*. In a valedictory interview Dunn explained: 'Readers are won by sheer hard work, not trying to bribe them anymore. It's a guerrilla war to win readers . . . not an all-out assault.'[32] His successor was Richard Stott, who had been out of work since being deposed from the *Daily Mirror* three months before (see below, p. 569).

Stott thought Dunn's paper was good but 'lacked the vital ingredients of heart and vision'.[33] He set out to give it more edge through campaigns and investigations while hiring several high-profile ex-*Mirror* colleagues, such as columnist Anne Robinson, women's editor Mary Riddell – who later became his deputy – and Alastair Campbell, who wrote a political column. Stott's record at *Today* was impressive, especially since he was tripped up by the price war. He persuaded News International's managers to grant him the occasional price cut but relied mostly on some gutsy popular journalism to win new readers. *Today* campaigned against 'fat cat' business executives, exposed delays by London's ambulance service that led to the death of a young boy and revealed a Ministry of Agriculture cover-up over mad cow disease. Its series of exclusives on the singer Michael Jackson's relationship with young boys won an award.

On three days in August 1994, when its price was reduced to 10p, it sold over a million copies an issue and recorded its highest-ever monthly sale of 656,000. That artificially inflated figure eventually came back to a more realistic, but creditable, average of 560,000. When Alastair Campbell left in the autumn of 1994 to become press secretary to the new Labour party leader, Tony Blair, he hailed *Today* as 'the journalistic success story of the decade'.[34] It was not, however, a business success story and its future was widely rumoured in March 1995 to be under review. News International tried to dampen speculation with a statement: 'We are delighted with the success of *Today* under the editorship of Richard Stott. We have no intention of closing it.'[35] Two months later Murdoch announced 'a multi-million pound investment programme' for *Today*.[36]

In fact, Murdoch couldn't stomach the losses. *Today* had eaten up £149 million and he didn't see any prospect of it ever making money.[37] Ominously, it emerged in August that the owner of Harrods, Mohammed Al Fayed, had been in talks with News International about buying the paper.[38] His offer was said to be too low to be taken seriously and Murdoch decided instead on closure in mid-November. His chief executive, Les Hinton, gave the reasoning: 'With a modest circulation, insufficient growth and rapidly rising costs we have no alternative.' He didn't mention one benefit for Wapping: it would allow the presses to print additional copies of the *Sun*. So Stott sadly drew up a final front page: 'GOODBYE. It's been great to know you'.[39] Murdoch was quoted in that last issue: 'I have never closed a newspaper in this country and I hope I never do so again.'

There were two immediate scrambles. The shocked staff, totalling 180, lobbied for the eighty jobs on offer on Murdoch's other Wapping titles while delighted rival tabloid editors lobbied to attract *Today*'s bereft readers. The desperate *Daily Mirror* offered their readers £5 if they signed up a former *Today* reader, while the *Daily Mail* and *Daily Express* carried front-page banners welcoming *Today*'s buyers. The final issue of *Today* loyally urged its readers to switch to the *Sun* and it was widely predicted that Wapping would retain 40 per cent of the total. In fact, the *Daily Mail* proved to be the outright winner of the spoils (see below, p. 595).

Football manager editors aim for sales goal

Only one national newspaper editor in place on 1 January 1991 was still editing the same paper on 31 December 1995. This five-year period witnessed the greatest turnover of editors in this history: the *Daily Mirror* had five; the *Sunday Express* and *Sunday Mirror* both had four; while the *Independent, Observer, Independent on Sunday, Sunday Telegraph, News of the World* and *Sunday People* had three apiece. Several commentators likened editors to soccer managers who were fired when their team suffered poor results regardless of their previous track record or, more usually, despite their being given far too little time to build their team and find a measure of success.[40] Too many newspaper controllers were either unwilling to give editors the necessary time, or belatedly realised they had made poor choices in the first place. Some went on repeating their mistakes.

The position of editor had also become much more complex. Editors' responsibilities had always been diverse, demanding of one person atop a hierarchy that he or she possess an unlikely combination of abilities. An editor was required to initiate editorial ideas, lead a team, be capable of writing headlines and designing pages, manage staff, function as senior marketeer and public relations officer, grasp the subtleties of national politics, assume legal responsibility, act as the paper's public face and, usually the most difficult of all, deal personally with the owner and/or senior managers. By the early 1990s it was also expected that editors should understand the commercial aspects of their paper.

It's no wonder that these pressures began to tell, despite the financial rewards. Editors' salaries increased dramatically from 1990 onwards. Before that, most had enjoyed perks, such as chauffeur-driven cars and generous expense allowances, but their wages hadn't tended to keep pace with the growth in pay for top-level business managers. Many newly appointed editors began to negotiate lucrative contracts, with benefits such as share options and golden handshakes.

Another pressure on editors came from the rest of the media, including rival newspapers. As we saw in the previous chapter, television had turned the spotlight on tabloid misbehaviour. Two BBC radio programmes were soon broadcasting weekly shows about the media.[41] By this time, in recognition of the continuing expansion of media, most broadsheets had followed the *Guardian* by appointing media correspondents. They wrote about developments in TV and radio, and also looked closely at what the tabloids were doing, questioning their motives and investigating the stories behind their stories. It wasn't long before broadsheet editors realised that their media reporters could do the same to other broadsheets as well. The dogs were soon eating the dogs, the beginning of a phenomenon dubbed 'media narcissim' by the *Guardian*'s political editor Michael White.

The *Times* held out against this initially because editor Peter Stothard thought readers weren't interested. 'I was wrong about that,' he later admitted.[42] His wife, the novelist Sally Emerson, was less sanguine about 'the new breed of media commentators', perceiving them as ex-editors 'peddling alcohol-free gossip, sniffing . . . over circulation figures, scissoring the reputations of the editors [they] would like to be', and telling readers 'what was once known only to the writers'.[43] She was upset because of nagging criticism of her husband, but editors were rapidly becoming public figures, and the result of them being called to account for their actions was that some emerged as personalities by appearing on TV and radio news and current affairs programmes to defend their activities. Others maintained the tradition of letting their papers talk for them, but most, even if they avoided the cameras themselves, recognised that someone on their paper would have to represent their arguments in the broadcast media when they were under attack. Editors were now being scrutinised with the same intensity as they themselves scrutinised political leaders and business people.

Maxwell drowns and the *Daily Mirror* sinks

By the beginning of 1991 my brief period as editor of the *Daily Mirror* was reaching its unhappy end. In the face of interference from my owner, Robert Maxwell, I had become increasingly stubborn. I wouldn't agree to his demand that I fire one of my columnists, John Diamond. I did all I could to thwart his plans to use an outside editor to launch a TV listings guide. I refused to publish a readers' offer of pills purporting to improve children's IQ levels (made by a firm with which Maxwell was financially involved). I also stymied his attempt to coerce a *Mirror* reporter and photographer sent to cover the Gulf war to act as salesmen for his company's outdated encyclopaedias: he expected the journalists to hawk books to troops in their foxholes.[44] We both knew it was over and we agreed that I would leave at the conclusion of the war against Iraq, which happened to occur only six days later. The morning after I departed with one year's pay-off, having agreed not to work for a rival paper for six months, Murdoch called and asked if I would like to return to Wapping. I thanked him and said I hoped to do so once I had served my time in purdah. Meanwhile, Maxwell gave the *Daily Mirror* back into the safe hands of *Sunday People* editor Richard Stott.

Stott handled Maxwell better than most – the key reason Maxwell had removed him in my favour at the end of 1989 – and the paper's editorial side prospered. The commercial side was a very different matter. Rumours about Maxwell facing a grave financial crisis were sweeping the building when he set about raising money by turning Mirror Group Newspapers (MGN) into a public company by separating it from his main company, the Maxwell Communications Corporation (MCC). The flotation, the fulfilment of a pledge made when he bought the papers in 1984, was determined by Maxwell's liquidity problems.

In the build-up to flotation he made some unwise moves, causing confusion about whether the famous Holborn building was to be included (it wasn't) and provoking cynicism by deciding to release only 49 per cent of the shares to the market.[45] Much more shrewd was his use of the *Mirror*'s celebrated strip cartoon character Andy Capp as a lure to persuade *Mirror* readers to invest. It proved tough to attract institutional investors but he managed it and MGN became a public entity in May 1991. It gave Maxwell little pleasure because he was now in deep trouble, having overstretched himself through hugely expensive acquisitions, such as the *New York Daily News* and several other companies. He was also perceived by many people, in the City and among other media owners, as a dodgy prospect. *Telegraph* owner Conrad Black confided to Woodrow Wyatt that he wouldn't deal with Maxwell because he was so dishonest.[46] Murdoch also regarded him as a crook.

In the following months, with Maxwell's empire facing meltdown, he confirmed Black's and Murdoch's assessment by engaging in a series of desperate and illegal manoeuvres, the most controversial of which involved using his employees' pension funds to settle loans and to buy up his own shares in secret. That wasn't enough to get him out of trouble and at the end of October 1991 he was aware that he was about to be exposed in public. Then he disappeared abroad to spend a couple of days taking an aimless cruise on his yacht around the Atlantic islands of the Azores and Canaries. One evening he ordered his captain to put to sea off Tenerife and when the yacht returned next morning the crew discovered that Maxwell was missing. Hours later his body was hauled from the sea.

Was it an accident? Had he been murdered? Did he commit suicide? The mystery has never been solved but I was convinced – for reasons outlined in my book *Maxwell's Fall* – that he had taken his own life to avoid facing the public ignominy over his pensions plunder, which would almost certainly have led him to prison. My inquiries into the specific circumstances of his disappearance overboard convinced me that I was correct.[47] Of course, no one knew about him stealing the pensions at the time and *Daily Mirror* editor Richard Stott loyally began his eleven-page coverage of his death with a front-page headline, 'THE MAN WHO SAVED THE MIRROR', observing that Maxwell had left the paper 'strong financially'.[48]

Hindsight made a nonsense of that affectionate tribute, but Stott was as unaware as the rest of us of the enormity of Maxwell's crime. He wasn't mourned by everyone. On the night of his death pubs in Glasgow near the *Daily Record* office ran out of champagne.[49] The *Independent on Sunday* broke with tradition and spoke ill of the dead by declaring that Maxwell was 'a liar, a cheat and a bully' whose untruthfulness 'was an instinct, a habit, and above all, a weapon'.[50] It was a bold statement weeks in advance of that truth being confirmed.

Maxwell's sons, Kevin and Ian, took the reins immediately after their father's death, assisted by MGN managing director Ernie Burrington. They spent most of their time helping accountants with their inquiries until the fateful moment on 1 December when it became clear to everyone involved that more than £500 million was missing, including £300 million from pension funds. Suddenly the *Daily Mirror*, to protect its credibility with its readers, quite apart from its editor's journalistic desire to tell the truth, was forced to change tack.[51] It became open season in the press on Maxwell and on everybody linked to him, especially his family. Ian and Kevin, who severed all connection with *Mirror* group, were eventually prosecuted for various fraud offences. Years later they were both cleared of all charges after a lengthy trial. In the immediate months after the pensions revelation the *Mirror* titles were in limbo, with control exercised by the administrators and ownership residing in a consortium of banks headed by NatWest. There were tentative approaches from possible buyers, such as Pearson and Lonrho, but most companies were scared off by the pensions black hole.

Stott failed to stitch together a management buyout, having engaged former British Rail chairman Sir Peter Parker to head his bid. I favoured Dr Tony O'Reilly, chairman and chief executive of Heinz who owned the Irish *Independent* newspaper group. He was keen to become a British press tycoon, had experience running papers successfully and could raise the cash. He was rebuffed because the banks were wary of selling to an individual entrepreneur or company. They also rejected a bid from a consortium which included Lord (Clive) Hollick, a director of Hambros bank and chairman of Meridian Television.[52]

Instead, they were to spend weeks quietly negotiating with the former editor and managing director of *Today*, David Montgomery, who led a team which also included Hollick. Rather than attempting a takeover,

Montgomery's plan was to act on behalf of the banks, installing himself as chief executive, cutting costs and maximising profits in order that the shares held by the banks could be sold for as much as possible. The advantage of having Hollick on board, quite apart from his financial acumen and his status in the City, was his political commitment to the Labour party. When the announcement came in October 1992 it was one of Fleet Street's greatest shocks.

What the banks didn't realise was that Montgomery's standing within journalism, especially at *Mirror* group, was dreadful. Monty had won few friends in his younger days working on the Holborn titles, and his controversial editorships of the *News of the World* and *Today* had lowered his reputation still further. Both Stott and Hagerty were known to dislike him intensely, as did Joe Haines, Maxwell's biographer and an MGN director. *Daily Mirror* staff voted 278–4 not to co-operate with Monty until he gave assurances there would be no sackings and that he wouldn't interfere in editorial affairs. He also survived a narrow vote by the board to elect him chief executive, a task made easier by the fact that Haines had already walked out.

Monty calmed staff by saying: 'I have definitely no plans for job cuts in editorial departments. The editors of all titles remain in their positions.' Meanwhile, Hollick privately assured the *Mirror*'s political editor, Alastair Campbell, that the papers would remain solid for Labour, and Stott was told by Monty that his job was safe. So Stott placated his worried staff and the planned industrial action was called off. Montgomery, his team and the banks sighed with relief: if the paper had not been published it is likely their coup would have collapsed. It didn't take long for everyone to realise their mistake. Stott and Hagerty were dismissed within a month in a synchronised *Godfather*-style purge. When Stott protested that he had been given a false assurance, Monty told him: 'Ah well, I had to do a bit of tap-dancing then.' Challenged later about having told a lie, Monty cynically replied that his statement was 'accurate at that time'.[53]

Staff culling soon began in earnest. Scores of journalists were made redundant in the first couple of months of the new regime as Montgomery sought to introduce a more Spartan culture to a company he had long despised for its excesses, real and imagined. Several of the best-known writers, such as Anne Robinson, Alastair Campbell and Paul Foot, departed. It all proved a little too rich for Hollick. He protested against some of the staff cuts and against the failure to widen the share ownership to employees while complaining about Monty's secrecy. Finding himself isolated on the board he resigned in March 1993, citing 'governance and policy matters' as his reason.[54] By that time he had served Monty's purpose.[55]

Montgomery's ruthless cost-cutting efficiency was matched by his determination to ensure that no *Mirror* employee would lose his or her pension. Six months before his death Maxwell had hired former *Times* editor

Charlie Wilson to run his popular racing daily, the *Sporting Life*, and he became editor-in-chief of all the *Mirror* titles. Wilson gave Monty support while he was preparing his coup and backed him at the crucial board vote when he arrived. Monty put him in charge of sorting out the pensions mess, a task which he carried out with undeniable energy and eventual success.

Montgomery was less sure-footed in his choice of editors. In November 1992, he gave the *Daily Mirror* to David Banks, who was then editing one of Murdoch's Australian papers, the *Sydney Telegraph-Mirror*. Banks was forty-four, a huge, loveable bear of a man with a gift for telling funny stories, who had been universally popular in his years as a sub-editor and junior executive. He hadn't set the world alight in more senior roles and proved a disaster as an editor in a situation where he had to justify to old friends a string of unpopular redundancies. A Warrington grammar schoolboy, he had started on his local paper and spent several years with the *Daily Mirror* in the 1970s. A lengthy stint on the *Sun* as night editor in the 1980s was followed by jobs on the *New York Daily News* and in Australia.

He spent an ignominious couple of years as *Mirror* editor, arriving when it was selling 2.87 million and being fired in April 1994 when it was 2.50 million, though the price war caused most of the grief. In later years, in an ironic self-assessment, he admitted editing the *Mirror* 'with a refreshing lack of distinction'.[56] Montgomery moved his *Sunday Mirror* editor, Colin Myler, to replace Banks. Again, it wasn't an inspired choice. Myler had been editing the *Sunday Mirror* for a couple of years without any notable success but with one memorable moment of controversy.

It came in November 1993 when he published pictures of Princess Diana exercising at a private gym.[57] Myler and his chief executive, David Montgomery, had agreed to pay £100,000 to the gym's owner, who had taken the pictures months earlier with a hidden camera.[58] Unknown to Myler two other Sunday papers had rejected them because they thought them intrusive. The princess was cast as a victim by other newspapers and a public row erupted after an injudicious public statement by the Press Complaints Commission's hapless chairman Lord McGregor, who urged advertisers to boycott *Mirror* titles. A furious Montgomery immediately withdrew his papers from the PCC and it took a deal of behind-the-scenes diplomacy, involving Murdoch and the *Daily Mail*'s editor-in-chief Sir David English, to persuade Monty to return, thus saving the self-regulatory system from collapse. Myler's own embarrassment, when protesters turned the tables on him by trying to get telephoto pictures of his wife through their bedroom window, was overlooked.[59] The princess started legal action against *Mirror* group which was later resolved before reaching court.

Myler was a dapper Liverpudlian who started his career at a Southport news agency and as a freelance in Manchester. From 1974 he reported for the *Sun* and then the *Daily Mail*. Later he did well as the *Sunday People*'s northern news editor and was called to its London office. He also impressed as news editor at the launch of *Today* and as the *Sunday Mirror*'s deputy editor. There was no doubting his competence but he just didn't have what it takes to edit a daily tabloid. In fairness, his circulation record at the *Daily Mirror* was remarkably consistent, maintaining a 2.5 million average throughout his eighteen months in charge.

Myler's downfall was due to one of the most astonishing executive appointments in the Mirror group's history, but we need to travel across to Wapping once again, to the offices of the *Sun*, before we continue with the *Mirror*'s story. The *Sun*'s circulation nose-dived from 1990 onwards, a state of affairs unknown to Kelvin MacKenzie in his previous nine years as editor. His paper remained as controversial as it had ever been, regularly upsetting the establishment, particularly the royal family. The *Sun* made a laughing stock of England football manager Graham Taylor in June 1992 by portraying him as a turnip and calling for his resignation.[60] Six months later MacKenzie provoked a storm by publishing the Queen's Christmas message two days before it was broadcast.[61] He explained that a BBC employee had provided a transcript of the tape.[62] The Queen, who was said to be 'very distressed', sued the *Sun* for breach of copyright and the paper responded by offering £200,000 to two charities in a front-page apology which, according to Woodrow Wyatt, was drafted by Murdoch.[63]

In January 1993, MacKenzie appeared in front of the Commons select committee on privacy and told MPs they would be 'nuts' to introduce privacy laws. That month, proving that he wasn't guilty of double standards, he laughed off a *Mail on Sunday* story entitled 'Gotcha Kelvin' which revealed that he was having an extramarital affair. Pictured with a woman in a Barbados hotel, he sportingly invited the photographer for a drink. In April, he plundered an exclusive interview from the *Times*'s magazine – with a rock star revealing that he had Aids – before it was published. The freelance writer sued the *Sun* for breach of copyright while the *Times* wrote of its 'regret' at its Wapping stablemate's action. These were normal examples of MacKenzie's irreverence, but for those in the know there was a clue that he was losing his way: his loyal news editor, Tom Petrie, rowed with deputy editor Neil Wallis and MacKenzie let Petrie leave.

He had little choice but to side with Wallis since he was allowing him to take more decisions than any of his previous deputies. He also gave Petrie's replacement, Stuart Higgins, more leeway. It was a sign that MacKenzie was becoming unhappy with his job and the reason was obvious. He and Murdoch were no longer getting along and he was particularly irked by Murdoch's quizzical refrain: 'Are you losing your touch?' For once, MacKenzie couldn't cite good sales – the figures were at their lowest point since he had become editor in 1981. After one telephone argument in March 1993, he told colleagues that 'old Gorilla Biscuits' had gone too far. He faxed a letter of resignation and walked out. But Murdoch urged his Wapping chief, Gus Fischer, to track him down and Murdoch duly apologised.[64] The *Sun*'s circulation problem was saved by cutting its price, and it would be easy – but incorrect – to imagine that *Sun* readers had deserted because of MacKenzie's bad behaviour. In fact, there was a much more fundamental reason for its decline which had been ignored after being identified years before and which the price war would conceal for years afterwards.

In 1985 the *Sun*'s advertising agency produced a report into the paper's future prospects which warned of the 'disturbing' trends of an ageing and increasingly down-market readership. It urged Murdoch and MacKenzie 'to actively attract a more upmarket reader ... to move the profile of the *Sun* reader a notch or two upmarket'.[65] This was a prescient piece of forecasting which seemed largely irrelevant at the time, given the *Sun*'s success.

Anyway, that report was hardly on MacKenzie's mind as he worked through the final months of 1993 without his usual enthusiasm. Murdoch had promised to find him a new post elsewhere in News Corp's empire and, in January 1994, it was announced that he would take a senior role at BSkyB. On one point, everyone agreed: after thirteen years, MacKenzie was going to be a hard act, if not an impossible one, to follow. Murdoch chose Stuart Higgins, who had been editing the *News of the World* for a couple of months since its editor, Patsy Chapman, had fallen ill.

Higgins seemed to outsiders an unlikely choice, mainly because of the human sponge episode (see Chapter Seventeen). He was very different from MacKenzie in the more courteous way he treated people and was to do rather better than critics expected. At thirty-seven, he was both an experienced on-the-road operator and an experienced desk editor. He started in journalism aged sixteen at the news agency in his home city, Bristol, and six years later was appointed the *Sun*'s west of England district reporter, cultivating a friendship with a country lady, Camilla Parker Bowles, that was to prove invaluable in later years. He did well enough to win the New York correspondent's post and wasn't too pleased when MacKenzie became editor and pulled him back to London as a general reporter. The demotion rankled. But his reporting work was competent and he enjoyed a spell as the royal correspondent before moving up the news-desk ranks.

His *Sun* was no less controversial than MacKenzie's. His most sensational scoop alleged that footballer Bruce Grobbelaar had taken bribes to fix matches.[66] Higgins thought his video evidence would prove conclusive when Grobbelaar was tried on conspiracy charges in January 1997. The jury was deadlocked so he was retried months later and cleared of all charges. Grobbelaar followed up by suing the *Sun* for libel, winning an award of £85,000 plus his £500,000 legal bill.[67] But the *Sun* didn't have to pay because the court of appeal quashed the jury's libel verdict in January 2001.

Higgins upset Prince Charles when the *Sun* asked for girls to contact the paper if they had kissed his thirteen-year-old son, Prince William.[68] But he landed a genuine royal scoop a couple of months later in revealing that the Queen had urged Prince Charles to divorce Princess Diana.[69] While Higgins was judged to have stepped out of his former editor's shadow, MacKenzie's story as BSkyB's managing director was very different. He soon clashed with the tough chief executive Sam Chisholm and head of news Ian Frykberg.[70] Murdoch backed Chisholm, and MacKenzie quit after eight months, refusing a pay-off despite all attempts to give him one.[71] Then, in October 1994, MacKenzie shocked everyone – especially Murdoch – by accepting a senior post with his former enemy, David Montgomery, at Mirror group.

As *Sun* editor he had been implacably opposed not just to the *Daily Mirror* as a commercial rival but to its political and journalistic ethos. Though he was appointed to run Mirror Television, no one imagined he would be able to resist getting involved in the newspaper side. In an attempt to diversify from papers into TV, and believing cable companies' forecasts that their industry was on the brink of becoming hugely successful, Montgomery had hired the flamboyant former BBC executive Janet Street-Porter to launch a cable channel called L!ve TV. By appointing MacKenzie as managing director of the TV division, and giving him a seat on the board, he ensured that he out-rank the more experienced Street-Porter and the pair soon came into conflict.

In the months leading up to L!ve TV's launch in June 1995, MacKenzie reached the conclusion that Street-Porter's concept was wrong headed and he was often overheard calling her 'a nightmare'.[72] Once it went on air, L!ve TV was plagued with production and technical difficulties and was panned by every critic. Street-Porter departed within three months and MacKenzie took over, revamping the output and dreaming up a succession of controversial publicity stunts such as the news bunny, topless darts and the weather read by women in bikinis. It succeeded in winning the channel a public profile but few viewers and Montgomery was criticised for spending £30 million on his 'mad pursuit of a new electronic future'.[73]

As expected, MacKenzie did eventually persuade Monty to let him take an interest in the papers and he soon played a central role in deciding the *Daily Mirror*'s future direction. At the *Sun* he had been so impressed by the energy and passion of his young gossip-column editor, Piers Morgan, that he had recommended him to Murdoch as the next *News of the World* editor (see below, p. 602). In the late summer of 1995 MacKenzie – who recognised in his protégé many of his own brash, irreverent and sometimes vulgar qualities – tempted Morgan, then just thirty, with the idea of becoming *Daily Mirror* editor. He took the bait and in September 1995 Morgan replaced Colin Myler, who was forced to accept the post of the paper's managing director. Morgan was to have a profound influence on the *Mirror* in the coming years.

Mirror group's two Sunday titles had been in circulation decline for years before Maxwell's era and he refused to invest at the levels which might have helped. His *Sunday Mirror* editor, Eve Pollard, resigned in May 1991 to go to the *Sunday Express* after failing to get the *Daily Mirror*'s editor's chair she felt she deserved. Maxwell gave her job to Bridget Rowe, editor of *TV Times* magazine. At forty-one, Rowe had spent most of her career in women's magazines with only a few months' experience as assistant editor of the *Sun*. Forceful and verbose, she took no prisoners in arguments. But she didn't halt the *Sunday Mirror*'s decline during her eighteen months there, being transferred to the *Sunday People* once Montgomery took control. As we have seen, Colin Myler replaced her until swapping to the *Daily Mirror*. The fourth editor within three years was Tessa Hilton, a forty-three-year-old product of the Mirror group's Plymouth training scheme who had impressed Montgomery as his assistant editor at *Today*. She had subsequently succeeded in one of the toughest of posts, running the *Daily Mail*'s Femail section for three years. In her first eighteen months as *Sunday Mirror* editor she managed to achieve a sales plateau with a paper which caused few waves.

After I had gone from the *Daily Mirror*, Maxwell called my deputy, Bill Hagerty, and said he should come to his office to meet the new editor. When he arrived Maxwell told him Stott would edit the *Mirror* again and added: 'You're the editor of *People*'. Hagerty was so flabbergasted he fell backwards and Maxwell hoisted him off the floor by the shoulders.[74] Hagerty was fifty-one, and had thought his brief stint editing the short-lived *Sunday Today* had been his last opportunity as an editor. Born in Ilford, Essex, he started in local papers in east London and moved into Fleet Street with the *Sunday Citizen* and *Daily Sketch*. He then spent fourteen years with the *Daily Mirror* as writer and executive and four more years on the Sunday titles, leaving briefly for *Today*, and returning to Holborn as the *Sunday Mirror*'s deputy editor. He was a sound, sure-footed manager with a sergeant-major's bark offset by a keen sense of humour. Like all *Sunday People* editors, he faced the problem of running the group's worst-resourced paper.

Sales drifted downwards despite the *People*'s public profile being raised by landing one of the most talked-about stories of the era. Hagerty's news editor Phil Hall returned briefly to the role of reporter to reveal that a married cabinet minister, the heritage secretary David Mellor, was having an affair with an actress.[75] The paper was accused of obtaining the story through illegal phone-tapping but it transpired that the phone was bugged by the man who owned it, which wasn't an offence. The case caused a furore because Mellor's government responsibilities covered the press and he had recently ordered a review of the workings of the Press Complaints Commission. He also provoked more criticism when he attempted to counter the *People*'s allegations by posing for photographers with his smiling wife, children and parents-in-law. The Mellor story made little if any impact on the *People*'s sales. One of the reasons Hagerty's paper didn't get full recognition for its scoop was that, unbeknown to Hagerty and his team until years later, the *News of the World* were paying a woman member of staff to leak material to one of their executives.[76] Even in a dog-eat-dog world, this was considered bad form.

As for Mellor, he remained in his job for a further two months until an odd coincidence. A friend of Mellor's, Mona Bauwens, had previously sued the *Sunday People* for a story published two years before about the holiday she had spent with Mellor and his family in Marbella.[77] The *People*, then edited by Stott, considered it inappropriate that he had taken the holiday at the start of the Gulf crisis with Bauwens, who was the daughter of the Palestine Liberation Organisation's finance minister. Mellor wasn't called to give evidence but his wife did and it emerged that Bauwens had paid for the holiday, a gift Mellor had not declared to parliament. In a famous attack on Mellor, the *People*'s barrister, George Carman QC, said in court that if a politician 'behaves like an ostrich and puts his head in the sand, thereby exposing his thinking parts, it may be a newspaper is entitled to say so'.[78] The jury was split over whether Bauwens had been libelled and she didn't ask for a retrial. There was no split in the press about the need for Mellor to resign, with the *Daily Telegraph* accusing him of arrogance, misjudgement and immaturity.[79] He quit that day and made a speech in which he condemned newspapers.

The *Independent* loses its independence

The *Independent* dream was over. It's difficult to know who said it first because it was said so often from 1990 onwards, once the dreamer-in-chief, Andreas Whittam Smith, faced up to the reality of his company's financial crisis.[80] Everything had appeared to go well for the first couple of years. Now the opposite was happening against the backdrop of a deepening recession. The upward sales trajectory went into reverse. The launch of the *Independent on Sunday* proved more of a burden than expected. Whittam Smith had also been forced to accommodate the Italian and Spanish investors – *La Repubblica* and *El Pais* – with seats on his Newspaper Publishing board. In the year up to September 1991, NP lost £10.3 million and the southern Europeans, as Whittam Smith disdainfully called his saviours, provided yet more money. The situation eased just a little in the following two years. Though *Independent* sales continued to slide, the *Times* fell faster and by 1992 they were neck and neck. Advertising revenue was flat, but NP made a tiny profit of £28,000 and looked on course for a larger profit in 1993. Within the papers, however, there was turmoil. The first major falling-out occurred between Whittam Smith and his fellow founder Stephen Glover, editor of the *Independent on Sunday*, which was losing £150,000 a week.[81]

The *Sindy*'s sale improved a little after the *Sunday Correspondent* closure but Whittam Smith, desperate to curb costs, wanted to integrate the two titles and exert control over the paper. Glover resisted and his relationship with Whittam Smith and their other co-founder, Matthew Symonds, deteriorated so badly that he resigned in May 1991. He went off to write a bitter account of the *Independent* saga, prompting former *Correspondent* editor Peter Cole to remark with justice: 'Hell hath no fury like a sidelined founding father.'[82] Whittam Smith, who was still editing the daily paper, chose Ian Jack to replace Glover at the *Sindy*, originally as executive editor on the understanding that the titles would be integrated. Jack skilfully avoided a full merger and was crowned editor in September 1992. Despite finding it 'strange to edit without much of a budget' he created a forum for excellent writing, ensured that the Review magazine maintained its high quality and gave the paper a clear political philosophy which, broadly, was 'sort of oppositional left-wing'.[83]

Jack promoted the fledgling talents of writers such as Allison Pearson, Zoë Heller, Helen Fielding and Nick Hornby. Sales rose briefly above 400,000 towards the end of 1992, doing particularly well during the election campaign, and then falling back in the following three years. Jack believed that if the *Sindy* had been 'niche marketed' it could have established a firm identity. In fact, because of a lack of money and belief, it was hardly promoted at all. His paper begged several questions about the nature of modern newspapers and the reading public. Was it too intelligent? Was its Review section too austere? Was its news agenda too narrow? Was there a big enough market to support a consciously highbrow paper? Was the audience for a liberal, leftish Sunday too small to sustain two titles?

These questions were just as relevant to the *Independent*. From 1992, the editorial cracks showed as many of the original staff, having lost their missionary zeal, drifted away. Among the disillusioned were columnist William Rees-Mogg, who left for the *Times*, political editor Tony Bevins and foreign editor Godfrey Hodgson, one of the paper's most experienced practitioners. Hodgson said that Whittam Smith's entrepreneurial energy, vision and willingness 'to invest in quality' had been undone by his autocratic insistence on both commercial and editorial control, becoming, in effect, 'a press baron without a coronet'.[84] On the other hand, it was Whittam Smith's gradual withdrawal from day-to-day journalism which upset several members of staff because his deputy, Symonds, was considered to be too acerbic. Morale wasn't improved by a March 1993 redesign which many thought unnecessary.[85] By then Whittam Smith was engaged in tortuous negotiations with Tiny Rowland, owner of the *Observer*, in the hope of securing his company's future.

Rowland had signalled his intention of selling his paper in February 1992 after several previous false alarms. His main company, Lonrho, was facing problems with debts of more than £1 billion and the *Observer* was adding to the red ink, losing £14 million in 1990 and a further £14.9 million in 1991. Rowland's editorial interventions had robbed the paper of its status and sales were falling fast, down by 100,000 in the eighteen months to June 1992. Veteran staff were leaving and morale at the Marco Polo building, its grandiose Battersea headquarters, was very low. Yet Rowland seemed in no hurry to sell. Negotiations started and stopped twice in 1992, though it was obvious at the end of the year, despite denials, that the *Observer* was for sale.[86]

From this moment on the fate of four papers – the *Independent* titles, the *Observer* and the *Guardian* – were intertwined. The *Guardian*'s editor Peter Preston was eager for his owner, the Scott Trust, to buy the *Observer*. Whittam Smith was just as eager, indeed desperate, for his company, Newspaper Publishing, to buy it. When Preston realised early in 1993 that NP had raised a £26 million borrowing facility, he went into action, offering to buy 60 per cent of the *Observer* immediately and the rest in three years. Rowland went on negotiating with NP and, on 1 April, Whittam Smith thought he had secured a deal to buy the *Observer*, which he planned to merge with the *Independent on Sunday*. Under the deal, Lonrho would get 15 per cent of NP and a seat on the board, and a deferred payment of £11 million would be made in 1996. Lonrho preferred a cash deal and that proved one of the *Guardian*'s trump cards. The other was the public alarm generated by *Observer* journalists who believed their 201-year-old title selling more than 500,000 copies was about to be subsumed into the three-year-old *Independent on Sunday* selling 380,000. They were, of course, also worried about losing their jobs.

When the story broke of Whittam Smith's supposedly done deal he was cast as the villain and the *Guardian* – which pledged to maintain the *Observer* as a separate entity – as the white knight.[87] On the next evening, Whittam Smith's team overplayed their hand: three *Independent* executives toured the *Financial Times* press hall where the *Observer* was being printed as if they already owned the paper. No deal had been signed and though Rowland was upset by the visit it probably played no part in his later decision. What it certainly did generate was extra political pressure, with eighty Labour MPs signing a motion opposing the *Observer*'s closure.

Observer editor Donald Trelford wrote a leader playing down reports of his paper's demise as 'mischievous and irresponsible', but his staff were taking no chances and wrote to Rowland pleading for him to sell to the *Guardian*.[88] Over the next couple of days, the *Guardian*'s chairman Harry Roche and managing director Jim Markwick met Rowland and his deputy to hammer out a deal. Whittam Smith, locked out of negotiations and given no room for manoeuvre, finally knew the truth at the end of the week when the *Guardian*, in a modest report at the bottom of the front page, announced its victory for a 'rumoured' £27 million.[89] The '*Guardian* angel', as some papers headlined the takeover, had won its prize.

The deal was generally welcomed by commentators who saw the logic of amalgamating two left-wing titles. It made 'great intellectual and spiritual sense', wrote one. Another, while agreeing, did wonder if there was a market for four Sunday broadsheets.[90] Doubtless, Whittam Smith agreed since that was the reasoning behind his attempt to merge the titles. *Sindy* editor Ian

Jack also stressed that it had never been intended to kill off the *Observer*.[91] That defence didn't prevent Whittam Smith being derided by rivals for acting like other press tycoon predators. It was unfair because he was trying to secure his papers' futures, though I never believed it would have saved his company from its inevitable takeover. Whittam Smith was the most obvious victim of the battle, soon losing control of his papers and watching the *Independent on Sunday* go into a long sales decline. There were victims on the other side too: Trelford lost his job, as did many *Observer* staff, and Preston's triumph was short-lived once the harsh commercial realities and editorial shortcomings of the *Observer* were revealed.

Whittam Smith's fall was swift, painful and controversial. In May, NP's distinguished chairman, Sir Ralf Dahrendorf, resigned. He had opposed the *Observer* bid and had grown disenchanted with Whittam Smith's authoritarian management style. His place was taken by one of the board's non-executive directors, Ian Hay Davison, chairman of Storehouse. Whittam Smith was then pressured to give up his chief executive role in July 1993 and it took three months to replace him with Patrick Morrissey, the unexceptional ex-Mirror group managing director (see above, p. 512). By that time the *Independent* had been struck by the devastating effects of the price war, just as Murdoch had forecast privately to *Daily Mail* editor Sir David English. When talking to Murdoch in the late summer of 1993 about the *Independent*'s prospects, English had ventured that the cost of making the *Independent* viable would be 'vast'. According to English, Murdoch replied, 'Much more than vast,' and proceeded to reveal his plans to cut the *Times*'s price.[92]

What Murdoch couldn't predict was the *Independent*'s catastrophic response. Morrissey's decision to increase the cover price of the *Independent* from 45 to 50p (20p more than the *Times*) and that of the *Independent on Sunday* to £1 when the much bulkier *Sunday Times* was selling for 90p.[93] Rarely has there ever been such a disastrous mistake, as Whittam Smith was later to concede.[94] Within six months the *Independent* had lost 60,000 copies, almost a fifth of its total, while the *Independent on Sunday* shed 15 per cent of its sales. Much-needed circulation revenue vanished at the same time as advertising revenue slumped. Bank lines were due to expire in March 1994 and the Italian and Spanish investors, holding 38 per cent of Newspaper Publishing, were scrambling for cover. The drama had turned into a crisis and there was only one answer: to take shelter inside a larger group.

Despite the *Independent*'s problems there was no shortage of interest. Carlton Communications, Associated, Pearson and the *New York Times* thought about it.[95] The *Telegraph*'s Conrad Black and the *Express*'s Lord Stevens held preliminary talks. Irish newspaper entrepreneur Tony O'Reilly let it be known that he was considering a bid.[96] TV tycoon Lord Hollick was identified as a late entrant in the race.[97] But it was Mirror group's acquisitive chief executive David Montgomery who emerged as the strong front-runner.

Whittam Smith favoured Montgomery, as did his co-founder Matthew Symonds, an old friend of Monty's. The three of them also convinced the Italians and Spanish that Mirror group had the answer to the *Independent*'s troubles. Whittam Smith produced projections to show that some £10 million could be saved by merging the two companies' back-office activities and through joint printing arrangements. As takeover rumours heightened, it all got rather messy. Almost all the journalists opposed Montgomery, with the National Union of Journalists chapel voting heavily against him while being heavily critical of chief executive Patrick Morrissey.[98] The Newspaper Publishing board split, with Whittam Smith, Symonds, the advertising director and the Italian and Spanish members all supporting the *Mirror* group bid. The other directors, led by chairman Ian Hay Davison, stood out against it.[99]

Newspapers are never genuinely neutral when analysing their rivals' difficulties, but there was a degree of unanimity about Montgomery's unsuitability to run broadsheet titles. Where was the fit with Mirror group's tabloids? asked the *Guardian*.[100] One man certainly agreed with that sentiment: Tony O'Reilly, owner of two broadsheet papers in Ireland which were coincidentally also entitled *Independent*. Having lost out to Montgomery at Mirror group, he was keen not to miss another chance to become a British press tycoon. I lent my support to O'Reilly, joining his team in Paris in January 1994 as he prepared his bid. His first hope was to break apart the pro-Monty camp, but even his legendary charm couldn't persuade the Italian and Spanish shareholders to change their minds. His next major move weeks later was altogether more dramatic: in a dawn raid on the market O'Reilly scooped up 24.9 per cent of NP stock for something over £20 million. This scuppered the careful stock-holding arrangements worked out between Mirror group and the consortium. Amid our celebrations at Charterhouse merchant bank that afternoon O'Reilly's wise chief executive, Liam Healy, counselled against too much champagne. It was, at best, half a coup. It wasn't nearly enough for victory and probably wouldn't deter Montgomery or Whittam Smith from their chosen path.

Healy was correct but it gave O'Reilly an edge, especially when he picked up more stock in late February, making him the largest single shareholder with 29.9 per cent. It was the maximum he could own without making a full bid which, to my disappointment, he seemed reluctant to do. By then, Mirror group and the Whittam Smith consortium had stitched together a new £74.7 million deal. On O'Reilly's behalf, I met the leaders of the *Independent*'s NUJ chapel, who were clearly against Montgomery but also uncertain about O'Reilly. Short of industrial action, which they feared would threaten the existence of the papers and for which there was no likely majority, there was nothing they could do except register their concern. At least 100 MPs, worrying about the competition implications, signed a motion urging restrictions on Mirror group's power to interfere in *Independent* editorial affairs. The deal was nodded through without comment by the government.

O'Reilly lobbied for board seats, which were denied him until it was realised that he had considerable negative power because of his one-third shareholding. He could block any changes to NP which required the support of 75 per cent or more of shareholders. Montgomery bowed to the inevitable and reached an accommodation with O'Reilly. Throughout the months there were lame attempts to depict the struggle between Montgomery, an Ulster Protestant Unionist, and O'Reilly, a Dublin Catholic nationalist, as an extension of the Northern Irish conflict. It was hopelessly wide of the mark. O'Reilly had no animosity towards Unionists, many of whom he counted as friends, and ran Irish papers which were implacably hostile to republicanism and all its works. He owned businesses within Northern Ireland and, like most global entrepreneurs, was a political pragmatist.

Anthony John Francis O'Reilly was born in 1936, the son of a Dublin civil servant, and educated at the Jesuit-run Belvedere College. After obtaining a law degree, he qualified as a solicitor and famously played rugby for Ireland and the British Lions. He joined the state-owned Irish dairy board and made a marketing hit with Kerrygold butter which brought him to the attention of the giant US food corporation, Heinz. In 1969, at just twenty-seven, he became Heinz's managing director and three years later its chief operating officer. He wasn't content with being a hired hand and from the early 1970s, while continuing to steer Heinz, he ran his own food-retailing company, Fitzwilton. In 1973, he paid just £1 million to acquire the majority interest in Ireland's Independent Newspapers, eventually controlling some 75 per cent of the entire Irish newspaper market. He also found time to obtain a doctorate and diversified his business empire into cable TV, outdoor advertising, mining and, later, Waterford Wedgwood china and glass. By the time he made his British bid his newspaper company was worth £400 million and his personal wealth – boosted by a multi-million salary from Heinz, where he became chairman in 1989 – was estimated at $1 billion.

In so many ways the charismatic O'Reilly was quite unlike the dour Montgomery, but they initially agreed what needed to be done with the *Independent* titles, so the uncomfortable partnership had a relatively smooth beginning. After the takeover, *Independent on Sunday* editor Ian Jack laid down his marker in a candid leading article: 'Mr Montgomery is not popular among journalists, having fired a good editor of the *Daily Mirror* and many others of its staff . . . Mr Montgomery has nothing to do with the editorial content of the *Independent on Sunday*. We are as free from interference as we have always been.'[101] There are, however, many forms of interference which stop short of a newspaper boss telling an editor what to put in his paper. Most importantly, the owner controls the money. Not that there was much money around at Newspaper Publishing. It was discovered that Whittam Smith's board had locked the company into onerous printing contracts and that during the battle for the *Independent*'s future its advertising revenue had fallen.[102] Montgomery's answer was the same as it had been at Mirror group: to cut staff numbers.

He also decided that the axe should fall on the man who had helped him into power. Within weeks there were rumours of Whittam Smith being deposed as *Independent* editor, and by early summer open discussion about his successor began appearing in rival papers. In July, the *Financial Times*'s deputy editor, Ian Hargreaves, was chosen and Whittam Smith agreed to continue as chairman.[103] Hargreaves agonised for two weeks over whether to take the job because there was a lot to concern him, such as Whittam Smith's role, Montgomery's influence and restricted budgets.[104] He was a good choice, an intelligent and industrious man of forty-three with a fine journalistic pedigree. After Burnley grammar school and Cambridge, he began at the *Keighley News* and then spent two years with the *Bradford Telegraph & Argus*. He joined the *Financial Times* in 1976 as an industrial reporter, worked for a spell as New York correspondent and returned to London as an assistant editor. He was recruited in 1987 by BBC director-general John Birt to run news and current affairs, where he implemented far-reaching changes. An undogmatic leftist who acknowledged the strength of free-market capitalism, he argued that BBC could become an effective global multi-media player only by transferring to the private sector.[105] In 1990, he returned to the *FT* as deputy editor.

Hargreaves's experiences at the *FT* and the BBC had not prepared him for the difficulties facing the *Independent*, which required perpetual crisis management from the moment he was appointed. Before he arrived, deputy editor Matthew Symonds quit and several staff were made redundant.[106] Those left had to cope with technological changes as the papers were moved from their City Road offices to join Mirror group in Canary Wharf tower. With sales down by 19 per cent in a year, the *Independent* was drawn reluctantly, and supposedly temporarily, into the price war, selling for 30p from August 1994.[107] That stopped the circulation fall, giving Hargreaves a little breathing space, but rapid staff turnover proved debilitating.

After he hired Martin Jacques, former editor of the magazine *Marxism Today*, as his deputy, a couple of senior executives left and there were more redundancies before Hargreaves produced a redesigned paper in October.[108] Meanwhile, liquidity problems worsened. When more capital was required, the group's Italian backer pulled out, selling its stake to the Mirror group and O'Reilly, and, though the Spanish partner stayed put, its holding was diluted. Losses mounted throughout 1995 due to poor sales and the effects of the price war. Whittam Smith was required to step down as chairman in March 1995 in favour of O'Reilly's trusted lieutenant, Liam Healy.[109] The dreamer would remain as a director and a weekly columnist. It was an especially sad week for Whittam Smith, who had previously made so much of his paper's freedom from proprietorship: the Advertising Standards Authority ruled that the paper could no longer use its promotional slogan about being independent because it was no longer true.[110] Hargreaves soon discovered what a lack of independence meant. He and *Sindy* editor Ian Jack were alarmed at demands from Mirror group that they reduce their staffs still further, and their resistance to cutting their budgets angered chief executive David Montgomery.[111]

Ian Jack decided he had had enough and quit to edit the literary magazine *Granta*, almost a year to the day after he had issued his warning to Montgomery to stay off his turf. 'It's a bad business,' he told staff in a tearful farewell speech. 'There are people in Mirror Group who think they can run a newspaper with some middle-ranking executives whose job is to fill in the gaps between the adverts, with a good marketing department – and I don't want to be any part of that.'[112] The *Sindy* chair passed to Jack's deputy, Peter Wilby. He was fifty, with a lengthy track record as an education correspondent. After grammar school in Leicester he graduated from Sussex University and worked for the *Observer* for seven years from 1968, rising from researcher to education reporter. He then specialised in education for the *New Statesman* and the *Times Higher Educational Supplement* and spent nine years at the *Sunday Times*. He joined the *Independent* at its launch as education editor and was promoted to deputy editor of the *Independent on Sunday* in 1991. A sensible and principled man, he had witnessed Jack's difficulties at first hand and was just as unsympathetic about firing staff.

Hargreaves was also upset by Jack's departure. Considered by the majority of his staff to be a good, if austere, editor, he was destabilised by whispers that his job was being offered elsewhere and sought assurances about his position, which were given by O'Reilly.[113] I later discovered that the rumours were true: both Montgomery and his managing director, Charles Wilson, spoke to Andrew Jaspan – then serving his notice at the *Scotsman* after being appointed editor of the *Observer* – about taking the *Independent* editorship. Hargreaves soldiered on, often working fourteen-hour days six days a week, without seeing any positive sales results and with the paper losing £1 million a month.[114] After fourteen months, much of it spent in acrimonious dispute with Montgomery's Mirror group managers over cost-cutting demands, Hargreaves was sacked in November 1995. O'Reilly, who had championed Hargreaves originally, thought him stubborn. His departure was 'as brutal as an Iraqi execution', said one commentator.[115] Another, believing it to be the final nail in the *Independent*'s coffin, saw the paper's demise as 'a story of courage dissipated, idealism crushed, power usurped, enthusiasm smothered'.[116] Most of the demoralised staff agreed and were none too happy when Montgomery and O'Reilly decided to replace Hargreaves with an acting editor: Charles Wilson, Mirror group's managing director and the former editor of the *Times*. What an irony! Here was the man who had lost his *Times* post partly because of the *Independent*'s rise now becoming its editor.

If life at the *Independent* was harsh, then it was far from easy going at the

Guardian and its new Sunday stablemate. Within days of buying the *Observer*, *Guardian* editor Peter Preston explained the facts of life to staff: there must be redundancies and cost savings.[117] He named his own deputy, Jonathan Fenby, as editor which seemed a sensible appointment. Fenby was experienced, energetic and eager for a real challenge. He was fifty, educated at King Edward VI School in Birmingham, Westminster School and New College, Oxford. He joined Reuters in 1963 and remained with the agency until 1977, serving as the Paris bureau chief for five years. He worked for the *Economist* as correspondent in both Paris and Bonn before joining the *Independent*'s 1986 launch to run the home desk. Two years later he became the *Guardian*'s deputy editor.

Fenby's qualities as a prolific writer, a good analyst and a well-liked executive should have prepared him well for the *Observer* chair. In fact, according to reports from within, he was a rabbit caught in headlights. It must be conceded that he faced a lot of problems, having to produce a paper in considerable disarray, with journalists leaving and arriving with bewildering rapidity in the early months as he tried to impose a new culture and sense of discipline. Some of the *Observer*'s most famous bylined writers – such as Alan Watkins, Neal Ascherson and Adam Raphael – departed. The paper's deputy editor, Adrian Hamilton, was asked to move aside, as leader page editor, in favour of John Price. Tony Bevins was hired as political editor and Rebecca Nicolson became magazine editor. Preston also loaned Fenby one of his most talented executives, features editor Alan Rusbridger.

Fenby benefited from an expanded paper, with extra sections and two magazines, and carried out a redesign. His paper also won publicity for its scoop which revealed the government's secret contacts with the IRA. But the years of decline and the *Observer*'s loss of credibility were always going to be hard to overcome and by August 1994, with sales down to 460,000, there were vague rumours about the paper's future being in doubt as losses continued at £1 million a month.[118] Four months later, Tiny Rowland offered to buy the *Observer* back for £3 million, a bid which wasn't taken seriously and was dismissed out of hand.[119]

There was, however, serious contemplation by the Scott Trust about the future of Fenby and the man who championed him, Peter Preston. Preston, at fifty-six, had been editor of the *Guardian* for twenty years and was a towering figure in the paper, viewed by many as both irreproachable and irreplaceable. Months before, he had told the Trust's chairman, Hugo Young, that he had edited for long enough.[120] Yet he was also enjoying unrivalled editorial success, having just been voted the editors' editor by a poll of thirty-four editors for the second successive year.[121] That accolade was hardly surprising since Preston had played a leading role in one of the most important newspaper scoops of the twentieth century.

In October 1994, the *Guardian* splashed on a story which claimed that two junior members of the Conservative government had been paid – when they were backbenchers – to ask Commons questions on behalf of Harrods owner Mohammed Al Fayed.[122] One of them, Tim Smith, immediately admitted it was true, apologised and resigned. The other, Neil Hamilton, denied the claim and sued the paper. Six days later, the *Guardian* revealed that Hamilton had enjoyed a free six-day stay at the Paris Ritz, owned by Fayed, and he was forced to resign too. The original tip had come from Fayed to Preston in the spring of 1993 and *Guardian* journalists had worked for fifteen months to verify the details.[123] The initial government response was positive: prime minister John Major set up a committee under Lord Nolan to look into the conduct and interests of MPs.

Within days came another sensational story involving the Paris Ritz. The *Guardian* revealed that Jonathan Aitken, the chief secretary to the Treasury, had stayed at the hotel in September 1993. The *Guardian* suggested that his bill had been paid by a Saudi Arabian arms dealer, Said Ayas. Since Aitken was at that time minister of defence procurement, the implication of impropriety was obvious. Aitken denied the charge, explaining that his wife had paid part of the bill and that, due to an error, Ayas's nephew had paid the rest. What followed was a classic example of the messengers turning on one of their own. Within days, the *Sunday Telegraph* revealed how the *Guardian* had obtained confirmation of its Aitken story, by sending what it called a 'forged letter' on House of Commons notepaper.[124] Other papers, especially the *Daily Telegraph*, criticised Preston.[125] Several high-profile columnists, such as Woodrow Wyatt, Paul Johnson and John Junor, attacked his use of subterfuge.[126] Even William Rees-Mogg, who as *Times* editor had once authorised the use of secret tape-recording by his reporters, turned on Preston. Tory MPs, ignoring the substance of the allegations against Aitken, accused Preston of a lack of ethics, with one calling him a 'whore from hell'.

Preston patiently explained that he and the Ritz's owner, Fayed, had devised a minor act of subterfuge in order to protect Fayed as the story's source. (He had later dropped his insistence on anonymity.) *Guardian* reporters already knew the story but needed documentary evidence. So, by agreement with Fayed, Preston sent the Ritz a faxed letter on House of Commons paper purportedly from Aitken requesting a copy of his hotel bill. There had been no deception because both parties knew what was happening. Preston, employing one of his many apt phrases, described it as a 'cod fax'.[127]

But the explanation failed to stem the tide of abuse as MPs voted to call Preston before the Committee of Privileges because of his alleged misuse of Commons notepaper. Now most papers did rally to his side. The *Daily Telegraph*, while still deploring the subterfuge, argued that the MPs' decision was disproportionate to the offence. The *Daily Mirror* thought the Commons was 'at its most pompous, self-centred worst', the *Independent* called it an 'exaggerated and silly response' while the *Daily Mail* observed that MPs 'do protest too much.'[128] Next day a *Mail* leader, headlined 'A Parliament that deserves contempt', savaged Tory MPs for calling Preston to account. Preston remarked: 'They're out to barbecue somebody and I'm the piece of pork.' He was burned enough to resign from the Press Complaints Commission and was further scorched by a poll of news editors which came down narrowly against his use of subterfuge.[129] The London Press Club chose that month to give the *Guardian* an award for its 'exemplary' journalism.

The Aitken story went quiet for six months until March 1995 when the *Independent* revealed that he had been a director of an armaments company at a time when it was covertly exporting guns to Iran. The following month ITV's *World in Action*, which had worked in collaboration with the *Guardian*, devoted a programme to Aitken's links with the Middle East and the arms trade.[130] Aitken issued writs for libel against the TV producers, Granada, and the *Guardian*, making a flamboyant speech in which he pledged 'to cut out the cancer of bent and twisted journalism in our country with the simple sword of truth and the trusty shield of traditional British fair play'. He later resigned from the cabinet to devote himself to fighting his case. It was two years before his libel action reached court, and its sensational conclusion is discussed in the next chapter.

Preston also had to deal with another headache towards the end of 1994 when the *Spectator* alleged that the *Guardian*'s literary editor, Richard Gott, had worked for the Soviet secret service.[131] Gott, a veteran staff member, denied that he had been a KGB agent and denied taking money. But he admitted flying at Soviet expense on four occasions to various places in Europe to talk to a KGB man and failing to inform the paper about these clandestine meetings. Preston accepted Gott's resignation, and he published their switch of letters.[132]

Adding to the pressure on Preston throughout 1994 were the continuing problems at the *Observer*. He had fought hard to bring it into the *Guardian* camp and felt a tremendous sense of responsibility to the Scott Trust when it didn't work out. He was also alarmed by the possible consequences for the *Guardian* if it went on failing. So Preston, in agreement with his fellow Trust members, decided to leave the editor's chair at the *Guardian* to become editor-in-chief, giving him time to get more involved at the *Observer*. His first tasks would be to replace Jonathan Fenby as *Observer* editor and to oversee the appointment of his own successor. The Trust's first thought for the *Observer* was Ian Jack, the *Independent on Sunday*'s disenchanted editor, but he rebuffed their overtures.[133] Preston then enthusiastically recommended that the *Scotsman* editor Andrew Jaspan should take over, which was to prove a calamitous decision.

Jaspan, forty-one, had a reputation as a circulation-builder and disciplinarian with creative skills, all of which were exaggerated beyond his capabilities. He had enjoyed success, but only in a limited arena. Manchester-born and educated at Beverley Grammar School, Marlborough College and

Manchester University, he started in journalism in 1976 by founding a listings magazine in his home city. He then worked in Manchester for the *Daily Telegraph* and the *Daily Mail* before moving to the *Times* in London in 1983. Two years later he joined the *Sunday Times*, where he spent three undistinguished years as its assistant news editor. When the *Sunday Times* launched a separate Scottish section in 1988 he was sent to Glasgow as launch editor. He certainly made a good fist of that job and was recruited the following year by Thomson Regional Newspapers to edit their Edinburgh-based *Scotland on Sunday*, where he improved sales from 58,000 to 90,000. His bosses were delighted enough to promote him to their flagship title, the *Scotsman*, which he edited from August 1994 until the Scott Trust called in February 1995.

In trying to explain his 'talent', a colleague referred to him as a 'bastard' who 'can rant, rave and swear' with a 'legendary capacity for work'.[134] Not only were these qualities not designed to endear him to *Observer* staff, they were largely untrue. Jaspan just wasn't the man the Scott Trust thought he was. From the moment he started many of his journalists didn't respect him and senior *Guardian* and *Observer* executives were soon questioning Preston's wisdom in having pushed for Jaspan's appointment. They derided his September relaunch – with its odd headline typeface and coloured masthead – as a waste of time and money. Sales rose, but only back to the level Jaspan had inherited six months before.

One of the first people to recognise that Jaspan's appointment had been an horrendous mistake was the new editor of the *Guardian*, Alan Rusbridger. He had been *Guardian* deputy editor for only eight months when Preston stood down and his succession to the top job was anything but straightforward. Unlike papers owned by proprietors, the *Guardian* set about choosing its editor in democratic fashion, by the vote of its journalists. There were four candidates, all of them internal: Rusbridger, chief leader writer Vic Keegan, City editor Alex Brummer and foreign correspondent Martin Walker. A selection panel interviewed staff, hustings were organised by the union chapel, candidates produced manifestos. The quartet were quizzed about their politics. Rusbridger was seen as the most likely winner, but Walker exhibited supreme confidence. Brummer was thought a little too mercurial while Keegan was viewed as the safe compromise. After the gruelling round of electioneering and much soul-searching by staff, the poll was held, giving Rusbridger 138 votes out of a possible 251, streets ahead of the others. The Scott Trust was relieved: its members favoured Rusbridger too.

Rusbridger was forty-one, educated at Cranleigh and Cambridge, and started out as a reporter on the *Cambridge Evening News*. He joined the *Guardian* in 1979 and in the following seven years worked as reporter, columnist and feature writer. He was briefly TV critic at the *Observer* and, just as briefly, Washington correspondent of the ill-fated *London Daily News*, in 1987. He returned to the *Guardian* in 1988 to edit the Weekend section and a year later was promoted to features editor, becoming deputy editor four years later. In some ways Rusbridger's manner resembled Preston's: he rarely gave away what he was thinking, listening to what people had to say and then privately making his decision.

Since he was widely reckoned to be uninterested in politics or economics, his critics initially labelled him a lightweight concerned only with froth. It was a fundamental misconception: Rusbridger would prove himself a serious and thoughtful editor. His first major appointment was Georgina Henry, the media editor, as his deputy. He reconfigured the pages, and set about ensuring that the *Guardian* didn't fall into the trap of becoming a niche paper. He hired several high-profile staff, such as diarist Matthew Norman, columnist Mark Lawson and Liz Jobey, to launch and edit a review section. But Rusbridger also realised that the *Guardian* couldn't escape from the continuing pall of gloom which hung over the *Observer*. In their years working together he and Preston had admired each other. Now they found themselves at odds. Their disagreement would prove to be, in the words of one executive who respected both men, a bitter and depressing episode.

Murdoch starts hire-and-fire merry-go-round

It was significant that Rupert Murdoch could attract hostility from people who had never met him and from those who had been very close to him. When Dennis Potter, the greatest British television playwright of his generation, was dying he revealed in a TV interview that he had named his cancer Rupert. He explained: 'No man is more responsible for polluting the press and, in turn, polluting political life.'[135] He accused Murdoch of putting 'a commercial value on everything' so that people were transformed from citizens into consumers. It wasn't a sudden rant. In a considered article the year before Potter had called Murdoch a 'drivel-merchant, global huckster and so-to-speak media psychopath, a Hannibal the Cannibal'.[136] Murdoch even considered launching a libel action after Potter's TV accusations.[137]

Unlike Potter, *Sunday Times* editor Andrew Neil knew Murdoch well, agreed with him on most political and economic issues and certainly didn't see him as a devil. But they fell out all the same. In his memoirs, Neil referred scathingly to Murdoch as the 'Sun King', an egotist who wanted to make every decision and hog whatever limelight radiated from his businesses.[138] Neil had similar characteristics, so their falling out was a clash of egos in which, of course, the employer was bound to triumph over the employee. At the lavish party to celebrate Neil's tenth anniversary as editor in September 1993 it was possible to detect the tension between Murdoch and his most effective propagandist. I noted clear signs of Murdoch's distaste. As much as he appreciated Neil's journalistic qualities he disliked his penchant for attracting personal publicity, whether through his broadcasting activities or his oft-reported bachelor-about-town private life. It infuriated Murdoch that Neil managed so successfully to host current affairs radio programmes and be on call as a TV pundit while editing the paper.

Neil's *Sunday Times* never seemed to be out of the headlines. His 1992 serialisation of Andrew Morton's semi-authorised biography of Princess Diana attracted huge publicity and extra readers.[139] Four weeks later the paper was embroiled in a controversy over the Goebbels diaries.[140] Then the *Sunday Times* suffered one of its blackest episodes, being compelled to apologise to some of Britain's most senior executives for a series of blunders about their pay, requiring a lengthy apology across the front and back of the business section. Two journalists were forced to leave and a third was suspended.[141]

Neil's swift remedial action saved the paper from protracted legal action and it is inconceivable that his job was imperilled by the error. Less than eighteen months later the situation was very different. The key incident was the *Sunday Times*'s investigation of Britain's £234 million aid donation to Malaysia to build a dam over the Pergau river. The National Audit Office regarded the project as a mistake: it would push up electricity prices and ruin an area of rainforest. Neil's reporters discovered that the dam's construction was linked to a £1 billion arms deal, a potentially illegal use of aid money.[142] His paper followed up by claiming that a British company building an aluminium smelter in Malaysia had been prepared to make 'special payments' to the country's prime minister, Mahatir Mohamed, and members of his government.[143]

In subsequent weeks, the paper asked more questions about the use of aid as bribes, a campaign which, naturally enough, upset both the British and Malaysian governments. Murdoch had reason to worry too because of a possible threat to his loss-making Asian satellite business, Star TV. He had already accommodated the Chinese by dropping BBC World from his package. Now he might lose the lucrative Malaysian market. The opening words of his protest call to Neil were laced with sarcasm: 'It's the great Andrew Neil. Not content with taking on one fucking prime minister, you have to take on two.'[144] But Murdoch wasn't troubled by Neil offending John Major. His demands that Neil drop 'this Malaysian business' showed how worried he was about offending Mahatir. A month later, News International's chief executive Gus Fischer hinted to Neil over lunch that he might like 'to make big money' by working elsewhere in the empire.[145] Weeks later, in May 1994, Neil announced that he was off to New York to front a new news programme for Murdoch's Fox TV. It was suggested that this might be a temporary posting, though none of us believed it.

John Witherow, head of news, was appointed acting editor, leapfrogging the deputy, Ivan Fallon, who quit, and executive editor Sue Douglas, who stayed on as acting deputy. Unlike Neil, Witherow preferred a low profile and would rarely stick his head over the Wapping parapet. Aged forty-two, he was born in Johannesburg and moved to Britain aged four, going to a minor public school and York University. He also spent two years doing voluntary service in South-West Africa (now Namibia), which led him to broadcast for the BBC World Service. He was a Reuters trainee before becoming a reporter on the *Times*, where he covered the Falklands war. After a brief spell at Murdoch's Boston paper, he joined the *Sunday Times* in 1984, and worked up from home news reporter through a succession of jobs to head the news department. He was perfect for Murdoch, combining writing and production skills along with trenchantly right-of-centre political and economic views. In one important respect, Witherow showed that he was a worthy successor to Neil by happily risking establishment wrath.

He oversaw the publication of the cash-for-questions investigation and serialised Jonathan Dimbleby's biography of the Prince of Wales.[146] Largely seen as the reply to Morton's Diana book, it boosted sales to 1,630,000 in its first week, helped by a price cut. The following month, November 1994, Witherow was confirmed as editor when Neil, realising that his American TV project was going nowhere, shook hands with Murdoch on a pay-off package. Four months later, Murdoch ditched his loyal Wapping chief, Gus Fischer, who confided to Woodrow Wyatt that 'Rupert really wants to be an old-fashioned newspaper proprietor and have everybody running about doing exactly what he tells them, right or wrong.'[147] Fischer's second-in-command, John Dux, also departed. The closer to the Sun King, the more likely one was to get burned.

Times editor Simon Jenkins knew that too. To his intense embarrassment, it was revealed in July 1992 that Murdoch was romancing *Evening Standard* editor Paul Dacre behind his back. Jenkins had never intended to remain as editor beyond three years, a limit he had previously agreed with Murdoch. Under their arrangement he still had eight months to go and was justifiably furious when news that Dacre had been offered his chair leaked.

When Jenkins complained to News International chairman Andrew Knight, he was told that Murdoch had 'fallen in love' with Dacre. Knight had once been Jenkins's supporter but he had lost faith in him, complaining to Woodrow Wyatt that the *Times* was dull and Jenkins had failed to improve it.[148] In fact, Jenkins had followed the brief he had agreed with Murdoch and Knight, taking the paper up-market and investing it with more authority. Labouring against a cut in budget and rise in cover price, he had achieved a considerable amount by bringing in new critics as well as hiring political editor Peter Riddell and economics writer Anatole Kaletsky. He also created a new *Times* typeface and changed its internal culture, but this didn't interest Murdoch. He was obsessed with beating the *Daily Telegraph* and, though sales of the *Times* did gently decline under Jenkins's watch, both the *Telegraph* and *Independent* lost more copies. Murdoch wanted a new editor regardless of the facts. Jenkins accepted the situation and, delighted with Murdoch's failure to hire Dacre, stepped gracefully aside when the paper's United States editor, Peter Stothard, was appointed his successor.

It was ironic that the classics scholar Stothard was more attuned to Jenkins's journalistic ethos than to Dacre's. He was forty-one, a product of Brentwood School and Trinity College, Oxford, where he co-edited *Cherwell.* After a spell in advertising, he joined the BBC in 1974 and spent five years there before being appointed by Harry Evans as a business and political correspondent at the *Sunday Times*, moving with his mentor to the *Times* in 1981. He survived the Evans putsch, becoming chief leader writer until 1985 when he accepted the deputy editor slot under Charlie Wilson. Four years later he moved to the States as the paper's US editor. He relished politics, in both theory and practice, and combined this with a hard-headed approach to journalistic decision-making.

A month after his arrival in September 1992, some twenty staff were fired while the paper expanded its news, sport and arts coverage and increased its use of colour. These changes were said to be 'aimed at making the authority of the *Times* more accessible'.[149] Accessibility was to become Stothard's watchword in the coming years as he sought to widen the readership, but no editorial initiative was as effective as the price war. The *Times* was at a ten-year circulation low of 354,000 in August 1993 just before Murdoch slashed its price. By the end of 1995 it was 670,000 and still rising. Critics argued that the extra sales were entirely due to its cheapness but the new readers stayed, suggesting that they enjoyed Stothard's content. The following year there was greater controversy when one day's issue of the *Times* was 'sponsored' by Microsoft and 1.5 million copies were distributed free, rightly described by Stothard as 'a landmark in newspaper publishing'.[150]

The *Times*'s rise badly injured its old rival, the *Daily Telegraph*, owned by Conrad Black. His papers had entered 1991 with a degree of optimism despite the recession, soon moving into the Canary Wharf tower which was to become – when Mirror group and the Independent titles arrived – a sort of Fleet Street in the sky. In these years Black expanded his global newspaper holdings, buying a chunk of the Fairfax group in Australia, several more papers in Canada and the *Chicago Sun-Times*, making his company, American Publishing, the second-largest by number of titles. He also installed his old friend Dan Colson as *Telegraph* deputy chairman, a wise lawyer with a cool head who seemed to enjoy taking tough decisions.

Black entered into both British society and his role as newspaper tycoon with relish. His estranged wife Joanna returned to Toronto with their three children, and after divorce Black married Barbara Amiel, a columnist with the *Sunday Times*, in July 1992. She and Black shared right-wing political views, a passionate support for Israel and, most notably, a distaste for journalism. Amiel wrote of journalists: 'I think we are all made of merde and the craft is merde.' The only reason to go on with the job was to prevent 'an even worse sewer, that of star chambers and secret power-holders in high places' from flourishing.[151] Black liked journalism enough to engage in it himself occasionally, once commanding space in his *Daily Telegraph* to rant against women wearing long skirts.

Under editor Max Hastings, the *Telegraph* had been transformed from its pre-Black era. It was better designed, carried more features and was much more appealing to both younger and female readers than in Hartwell's day. Yet it couldn't attract as many new buyers as it was losing, so the circulation graph showed a gentle decline. The price war exacerbated problems for Hastings and his team. Hastings won a reputation for ruthlessness by firing a number of high-profile executives, such as magazine editor Felicity Lawrence. He had evidently made up his mind, without much hard evidence, that she was a Labour party subversive.[152] Another of his victims, Alexander Chancellor, said after his sacking: 'I think it's an itch with Max, like someone having to drink blood once in a while, or they die.'[153]

The real headache for Hastings was over politics. His brand of Conservatism, more Whiggish than Tory, was very different from Black's unyielding free-market standpoint. There were, however, journalists within the group who shared Black's views and foremost among them was Hastings's own deputy, Charles Moore. He was expecting to go to Washington as the paper's US editor when he received the call in October 1992 that was to change his life. Hastings was editor-in-chief of both Telegraph titles, having deposed Perry Worsthorne in favour of his friend Trevor Grove. For a while Worsthorne ran the comment pages as a private fiefdom while Grove looked after the rest of the paper. Hastings ended this arrangement by prevailing on Worsthorne to retire in September 1991 while allowing him to continue writing his weekly column. Worsthorne, knighted at Margaret Thatcher's recommendation earlier in the year, accepted with good grace and Grove looked to be making a reasonable fist of editing when Hastings informed him that 'they want you out'.[154] They, meaning Black, had decided that the right-wing propagandist Moore should edit the *Sunday Telegraph* and that Grove should return to the *Daily Telegraph* as deputy to Hastings.

Charles Hilary Moore was on the eve of his thirty-sixth birthday when he was given his editorship. His father Richard had been the senior leader writer on the *News Chronicle* and a member of the Liberal party, and his mother a Sussex county councillor. Schooled at Eton, where he declared himself a Liberal, his political views moved to the right in his final year at Trinity College, Cambridge, and by the time he joined the *Daily Telegraph*'s Peterborough column his sympathies were Tory. A leader writer by the age of twenty-four, he was recruited by Alexander Chancellor to join him at the *Spectator*, succeeding Chancellor as editor in 1984. In these years he became known as the leader of 'the young fogeys' and earned the *Private Eye* sobriquet Lord Snooty. By the time he was appointed *Daily Telegraph* deputy editor in 1990 he happily accepted himself as 'upper-middle class – a member of the highly educated, upper professional classes'.[155] Considered High Church as well as High Tory, he was upset by the Church of England's decision to ordain women priests and converted to Roman Catholicism in 1994.[156] His wife Caroline, whom he met at university, was a Cambridge don, the first female fellow in the history of Peterhouse, who gave up her post to look after their twins.

Moore's *Sunday Telegraph* carried leaders and commentaries which were much more to Black's liking. Aside from politics, Moore also showed an aptitude for running the paper, maintaining its quirky appeal without losing its sense of authority. His sales were steady and then rose by 100,000 after the price war because of the cut-price subscriptions offered in tandem with the *Daily Telegraph*. Throughout this period Black, though appreciative of Hastings's talents, remained unhappy with what he perceived as a centrist political stance and applied pressure on his editor. In June 1994, Hastings was ordered to fire Trevor Grove, then co-deputy editor alongside Veronica Wadley, in favour of the right-wing polemicist and *Spectator* deputy editor, Simon Heffer. One commentator noted that the *Telegraph*'s political complexion had lurched to the right.[157]

The following year, when prime minister John Major resigned the Tory party leadership (see next chapter), there was a split between Hastings and Heffer. Hastings approved a leading article which stopped short of advocating Major's removal. Heffer, who wanted to see Major ousted, protested to Black, who took Heffer's side and a new editorial calling for Major's head appeared. Headlined 'Time for a change of leadership' it applied to both Major and Hastings as far as Heffer was concerned. Hastings was fed up with the political pressure from above. Having reluctantly accommodated Heffer as his deputy he was soon being leaned on to make *Spectator* editor Dominic Lawson a co-deputy, which would have meant dismissing or demoting Veronica Wadley. It was while he was resisting this manoeuvre that he met Sir David English, editor-in-chief of the Associated titles.

English asked him to consider taking over the *Evening Standard* editorship, pointing out that his salary would improve from the *Telegraph*'s £185,000 to £400,000. On 29 September 1995, Hastings resigned, taking Black by surprise. Whom should he appoint in Hastings's place? Who was sufficiently right-wing and journalistically competent to edit his flagship paper? He talked first to former *Sunday Times* editor Andrew Neil, but they couldn't reach a deal. He then spent ten days pursuing *Daily Mail* editor Paul Dacre without success. Eventually he went no further than his own group, translating Charles Moore from the *Sunday* to the *Daily Telegraph* chair. Wadley quit, as did Heffer, who was disappointed at not being to chosen to edit any of the group's titles. Despite being third choice, Moore was delighted, confident that his views and those of his owner would never clash.

The *Sunday Telegraph* editorship went to Dominic Lawson whose five-year spell as *Spectator* editor had secured the magazine a high profile. He exposed *Guardian* literary editor Richard Gott's KGB meetings and his interview with cabinet minister Nicholas Ridley, in which he unfavourably compared modern Germany to Hitler's state, led to Ridley's resignation. He ignored tradition by publishing an article giving a verbatim account of a lunch attended by the Queen Mother and ran an interview with a Palace courtier – written by my wife – during which he described the Duchess of York as 'vulgar, vulgar, vulgar'. These articles were examples of Lawson's journalistic philosophy about making mischief. He was thirty-eight, educated at Westminster School after a brief unhappy spell at Eton, and Christ Church, Oxford. He began as a BBC researcher in 1979 and two years later joined the *Financial Times*, the paper where his father, the former Chancellor Nigel Lawson, had started his journalistic career. He was deputy editor of the *Spectator* from 1987. Like Moore, Lawson largely shared Conrad Black's political outlook. Sir David English's poaching of Hastings had worked out rather well for Black.

English could reflect that he had finally stopped a hire-and-fire merry-go-round that was started by Rupert Murdoch almost four years before when he tried to lure Paul Dacre to be editor of the *Times*. English had prevented that happening by giving up his own editorship. In May 1992, he celebrated his twenty-first anniversary as *Daily Mail* editor with a Grosvenor House party. He was in his usual ebullient form, but his old friend and colleague, *Mail on Sunday* editor Stewart Steven, was less than happy. Though his paper was coincidentally celebrating its tenth anniversary, English refused to share the party.

It was a sign that the men had grown apart, with Steven having made no secret of his desire to succeed English. There was good reason for Steven to feel he had a right to the senior position: he had steered the *Mail on Sunday* to a dominant position in the market, having managed to get sales above 2 million on several months. In an interview to mark the moment, Steven claimed its strong points were its nose for a big story, an innovative colour magazine and his decision to edge up-market, adding pointedly that he had done this 'against the inclination of senior colleagues'.[158] Steven also risked the wrath of his owner, Lord Rothermere, by refusing to fire his controversial columnist Julie Burchill when she offended Rothermere by praising the Soviet spy Kim Philby.

By contrast, English's *Daily Mail* circulation story did not read as well. He had ended the 1980s selling 250,000 fewer than at the beginning and sales had slipped still further in the 1990s. No one doubted that English was running a paper that journalists admired, but did the public admire it? English's relationship with Rothermere remained as sound as it had been at the start of their twenty-one-year joint reign, but English had groomed several executives over the past decade and he knew it was time to let the next generation have a go. Murdoch, by trying to poach Dacre, made up his mind for him. He had moved Dacre to edit the *Evening Standard* in March

1991 when its editor, John Leese, resigned due to ill health (dying six months later). Leese had done a fine job, not so much in adding sales volume as in improving the readership profile by attracting a more affluent audience. Dacre had a run of unparalleled sales success at the *Standard* soon after he arrived, a factor noted by Murdoch, who also liked Dacre's approach to the job – hard-working, disciplined, confrontational – and his brand of uncompromising right-wing politics.

The only way English could prevent Dacre from accepting Murdoch's offer was to step aside himself. Rothermere agreed, making English both chairman of Associated and editor-in-chief, the most powerful journalist in British newspapers since Hugh Cudlipp at Mirror group. English immediately took the opportunity to move Steven to the *Evening Standard* and promote another senior *Daily Mail* executive, Jonathan Holborow, to the *Mail on Sunday*.

The clear winner from this reshuffle was Dacre, the product of a journalistic family. His father, Peter, was a *Sunday Express* journalist and a younger brother, Nigel, was on his way to becoming editor of ITN television news. Raised in north London, Dacre won a state scholarship to University College School, Hampstead, and then went to Leeds University, where he met his wife Kathleen, and won an award for editing the best student newspaper. The *Guardian* once took the trouble to hunt down some of his work on issues such as drug taking, homosexuality and race, which supposedly showed a liberal streak.[159] In 1971, after a six-month trial on the *Daily Express* in Manchester – fixed up by his father's boss, John Junor – he was given a full-time job, spending time in Belfast and later, in London, as reporter, feature writer and features executive. From 1976, Dacre was the *Express*'s American-based correspondent until he was recruited in 1980 by English as the *Daily Mail*'s New York bureau chief. He returned to London three years later as *Mail* news editor, working his way through various assistant editor posts until his 1991 elevation to the *Evening Standard*.

He was renowned for his desire, and ability, to do everything: conceive an idea, commission the writer, lay out the page, compose the headline, rewrite the copy, and keep on tinkering with it until deadline. This won him a nickname as 'the grim tweaker'.[160] He was quick to stamp his authority on the *Daily Mail*, ensuring that everyone understood that he was the editor and that his strings were not being pulled by English. If anything, Dacre's *Mail* was more stern and unbending in its criticism of 'progress' and more shrill in its championing of family values. Few critics missed the opportunity to point out that these values were often expressed by articles attacking adultery. Yet the *Mail*'s owner, Rothermere, lived openly with his Korean mistress, Maiko, while his wife, Patricia, always maintained that she and her husband were still living 'together but apart'. After her death, Rothermere married Maiko in December 1993. The *Mail*'s patriotic stance was also considered hypocritical when Rothermere was a tax exile. Journalists enjoyed these sallies but the public didn't seem to notice. Dacre's sales held up so well that the *Mail* defied the price war by raising its price, but his great circulation breakthrough came with the closure of *Today*.

Dacre's rivalry with Jonathan Holborow, spurred by English's sense of mischief and belief in creative tension, was legendary within Associated. Now they were to be enemies in different camps. Holborow was fortunate because the *Mail on Sunday* was in the ascendant. His career path had been anything but straightforward since leaving his public school, Charterhouse. At eighteen, he joined the *Maidenhead Advertiser* and spent four years there followed by a couple of years on papers in Lincoln. Our paths crossed on the *Daily Mail* in Manchester in the late 1960s and he went on to a variety of junior *Mail* posts until he became news editor in the London office for five years from 1975. Deciding that he wasn't seeing enough of his children, Holborow then took the unfashionable and, in career terms, usually unwise step of turning his back on national papers. He bought a house in west Wales and took on the editorship of the *Cambrian News* in Aberystwyth for two years. English asked him to return to Fleet Street in 1982 to help him at the *Mail on Sunday* during its critical post-launch period. He left to be deputy editor at *Today*'s launch in 1986, returning yet again to the *Daily Mail*, becoming English's deputy in 1988. His *Mail on Sunday* rarely sparkled, benefiting from the addition of Night & Day magazine, which pioneered lengthy reportage, the glossy revamping of You magazine under Dee Nolan, and a financial section from September 1994.

Steven had to watch this value added to his beloved old paper from his unhappy vantage point at the *Evening Standard*. The manner of his removal from the *Mail on Sunday* always rankled. He was about to board a flight to Dundee to attend the funeral of one of his executives killed in a climbing accident when he was summoned by English.[161] He settled down to accept his well-remunerated fate, approaching the task with his typical brio, provoking controversy and winning much praise for his campaign to save Bart's Hospital. His sales record at the *Standard* wasn't brilliant but it wasn't disastrous either.

Then, in August 1995, came a remarkable gaffe. The *Standard* published an article headlined 'Tony Blair's fatal lack of vision' under the byline of former Labour shadow cabinet member Bryan Gould who was, by then, vice-chancellor of a New Zealand university.[162] The problem with this assault on Blair was that Gould hadn't written it. Before the mistake was discovered, great damage had been done, with comments from MPs and journalistic follow-ups in other papers, many of which reflected badly on Gould. It transpired that there had been a mix-up of faxes: the offending article had been written by the nineteen-year-old son of Tory home secretary Michael Howard, prompting a front-page apology from Steven.[163] Gould sued, accepting damages and costs. Six weeks later Steven was replaced by Hastings.

We have far from finished yet with departing editors. To no one's surprise, after a loss of 200,000 copies in two years, Robin Morgan's reign at the *Sunday Express* came to an end in February 1991.[164] So eager was the United Newspapers chairman, Lord Stevens, to dismiss him that he had no replacement ready. Morgan complained that he hadn't received management support or resources – such as extra pagination or TV promotion – to compete with his rival, the *Mail on Sunday*. Managing director Andrew Cameron replied tartly that, before spending money on marketing, it was necessary to have a product worthy of promotion. That attitude merely confirmed that Stevens had appointed the wrong man. For the good of the paper, he should either have backed Morgan properly or sacked him much earlier. Either way, Stevens was at fault. It is undeniable that Morgan's complaints about lack of resources were echoed by almost every editor who worked for Stevens, and he had identified a crucial weakness, not only within the United regime but in papers owned by public companies.

The need to satisfy investors seeking short-term profits inhibited a public company from competing with private owners able and willing to take risks. Perhaps this was the reason Woodrow Wyatt considered Stevens a 'nonentity' compared to other press magnates.[165] He was cautious while they tended to gamble. Stevens recognised that the Express titles required enormous investment to give them any hope of being revitalised and it made greater financial sense to extract as much profit as possible while managing their decline. His was the impeccable logic of the market. Entrepreneurs preferred to defy logic.

It didn't take long for *Daily Express* editor Nick Lloyd to grasp that Stevens was no Rupert Murdoch, but he knew what should be done editorially despite the lack of resources. He must appeal to younger readers and to women, as the *Daily Mail* had done for years, and he therefore concentrated on imitating the *Mail*. He created a Nigel Dempster-style gossip column, for example, and introduced more features. These efforts tended to be too mechanistic, lacking both the gloss and the technical proficiency of the *Mail*, not to mention the behind-the-scenes sweat expended on detail. His political allegiance to the Conservative party, contrasting with the *Mail*'s more maverick relationship with John Major's government, also suffered from a similar lack of subtlety. But Lloyd achieved a measure of circulation success by halting the previous decline and then maintaining sales above 1.5 million for three years until the middle of 1993, when the *Express* was hit by Murdoch's price war.

Knighted in February 1991 after Margaret Thatcher's downfall, Sir Nicholas Lloyd was renowned for his political networking, whether on the golf course, as a regular visitor to Downing Street or hosting soirées at his north London home along with his wife, Eve Pollard. The couple also achieved an historical first, not only by becoming the first husband-and-wife team to edit national papers but by doing so within the same organisation. After Morgan was fired, Lloyd lobbied hard for Pollard to get the *Sunday*

Express chair. She was editing the *Sunday Mirror* at the time and was cheesed off that, on my departure from the *Daily Mirror*, she wasn't promoted in my place, quite apart from her continuing frustrations in dealing with Robert Maxwell. So, in May 1991, Stevens gave Pollard the job, making her the third editor in three years of a paper that had previously had three in fifty-eight years.

Pollard's major achievement was in persuading Stevens to turn the *Sunday Express* from broadsheet to tabloid, a change long overdue. It emerged in its new guise on 5 July 1992 with ninety-six pages and a glossy magazine which was described by one critic as *Hello! on Sunday.*[166] It was glitzy, with bags of royal articles and a gushing feature on Norma Major, the prime minister's wife. Pollard said she wanted the paper to be 'less Colonel Blimp-like', which it certainly was, but it was also hollow.[167] It proved to be a sales flop too. With too little promotion, the initial fillip provided by its novelty soon disappeared and circulation resumed its steady decline. As a trade magazine pointed out, the *Sunday Express* had a new magazine, a second section, a new review and a London supplement, yet 'still had zip to show for it'.[168] There were other problems too. Pollard became infamous for her short temper at work, prompting managing director Andy Cameron to call her 'an appalling manager of staff'.[169] Her many TV appearances rankled with Stevens and Cameron too.

Pollard, more confrontational than her husband, clashed often with Stevens, arguing that her paper's budget was inadequate. This belief led to the dismissal of her deputy, Charles Golding, and another of her staff for their clumsy attempts to embarrass United by exposing the company's investment policy.[170] A month later, in what was seen as the final straw, Pollard and Stevens fell out over a story involving Princess Diana, with whom Stevens's wife was friendly. He had prevented the *Daily Express* from running allegations about Diana obsessively phoning a man, but a similar story appeared in the first edition of the *News of the World* and Pollard insisted that she should be able to use the spiked *Daily Express* copy for later editions of the *Sunday Express.*[171] Stevens reluctantly agreed but next day it was revealed that at the time one of the calls was supposed to have been made Diana was lunching with Lady Stevens.[172]

Pollard was fired ten days later and Stevens moved Brian Hitchen from the *Daily Star* to take over. The bald, stocky, swaggering Hitchen's interests and those of his paper were indistinguishable: a mixture of right-wing politics, sensational crime stories and vulgar features. As a Press Complaints Commission member, he had shown no embarrassment at being censured for an article describing homosexuals as 'poofters' and 'pansies'. He virtually adopted the Parachute Regiment and displayed a large Union flag next to his desk.

Hitchen, who was fifty-eight and had survived a quadruple heart bypass operation in his early forties, had stopped the *Star*'s sales rot but couldn't turn its fortunes around. He had hired a good deputy in Phil Walker, previously deputy editor at the *Daily Mirror* for five years, so the act of succession at the *Star* was no problem and Hitchen could concentrate on the *Sunday Express*. The problem was that he saw the paper in terms of its past, looking back to the Junor era and beyond. Doubtless its older readers agreed with him that the paper 'is as British as roast beef and so am I'.[173] These were sentiments unlikely to appeal to a youthful audience. He also broke with the convention that an incoming editor doesn't speak ill of his predecessor, contemptuously dismissing Pollard's paper as 'a daft magazine . . . a rotten product' which had 'no authority, no cutting edge, no opinion'.[174] Hitchen had opinions all right and he was only too delighted to pass them on in a column so conspicuously politically incorrect that it won admiration from other right-wing columnists.[175]

Towards the end of 1995, with Lloyd disaffected and Hitchen's *Sunday Express* apparently going nowhere, Stevens decided to bring in two much younger and untried editors. There were many reasons for Lloyd's unhappiness, quite apart from the sacking of his wife. He had to witness some 15 per cent of his workforce – including forty journalists – being made redundant in the summer of 1995.[176] He was downcast by a rise in cover price without promotion. Then he discovered, as did many others, that Stevens and Cameron had made approaches to at least two people about the *Daily Express* editorship: Martin Dunn, editor of the *New York Daily News* and former editor of *Today*, and Veronica Wadley, deputy editor at the *Daily Telegraph*. Lloyd resigned in November 1995 after almost ten years as editor. He didn't know until later that former *Sun* editor Kelvin MacKenzie had also been sounded out. He, like the other two, wisely rejected the idea of working for Stevens. But there are always people hungry to edit and he found one eager candidate in the *Sunday Times*'s deputy editor, Sue Douglas, who had been passed over when Andrew Neil departed.

Douglas, who was thirty-eight, had had a somewhat colourful career. After school in Kingston, Surrey and graduating from Southampton University with a degree in biochemistry she worked briefly for a management consultants, for a medical magazine and then as a feature writer on the *News of the World*. She spent two years working on papers in South Africa, returning to London in 1982 to join the *Mail on Sunday* as medical correspondent. Editor Stewart Steven took a shine to the clever young woman who quickly showed she could handle even the most difficult of staff and promoted her up through the ranks to be his associate editor. It was she who famously launched Julie Burchill as a columnist. She was switched to the *Daily Mail* as an assistant editor in 1987 because Sir David English was sceptical about her talents. While trying to prove herself she was subjected to his special brand of discipline, a relentless sequence of praise and rebuke. Douglas candidly admitted that men assumed she had slept her way to the top. In 1989, that gossip was given new impetus when Burchill wrote a novel which chronicled the rise of a journalist named Susan Street who did just that. Though shown the manuscript in advance, Douglas didn't take it seriously.[177] Neither did *Sunday Times* editor Andrew Neil, who hired her as executive editor in 1991.

As far as Stevens was concerned she was perfect for the *Daily Express* and after an interview for the job Douglas presumed that she would be appointed. Then Stevens's wife happened to sit next to the personable Richard Addis, associate editor of the *Daily Mail*, at dinner one evening. She told her husband about his charm and intelligence and Addis suddenly found himself being interviewed. He too had had an interesting past, having been a novice monk for two years in between leaving Rugby and going on to Cambridge. He first edited a small trade magazine and for two years wrote a diary for *Marketing Week* before joining the *Evening Standard*'s Londoner's Diary. His rise to executive status was fast, working for the *Mail on Sunday, Sunday Telegraph* and *Daily Mail*. Well educated, soft-spoken, almost diffident, he resembled a prep-school master and was quite unlike the usual rumbustious tabloid editor, describing himself as 'an Anglo-Catholic, a royalist ... a Christian Tory'.[178] Stevens, like his wife, thought the amiable thirty-nine-year-old dreamer ideal and gave him the *Daily Express* editorship and forced Douglas, to her annoyance, to accept the *Sunday Express* post. Both Addis and Douglas would have been apoplectic if they had known what else Stevens was up to, despite his persistent denials that his company was for sale.

Intruding into the grief of self-regulation

The Press Complaints Commission came into being on 1 January 1991 and had a difficult birth and infancy. The first major complaint was made by Labour MP Clare Short against the *News of the World*, whose editor Patsy Chapman was on the commission. She took no part in the meeting which found her paper guilty of inaccuracy and intrusion, obliging her to publish a 2,300-word adjudication. Politicians on one side felt the paper escaped lightly; tabloid editors on the other were concerned that the ruling gave too much protection to MPs. The next ruling condemned the *Sunday People* for invading the privacy of the baby daughter of the Duke and Duchess of York by twice publishing naked pictures of her inside a walled garden.[179] *People* editor Bill Hagerty and his owner, Robert Maxwell, attacked the PCC and its chairman, Lord McGregor, in much the way that papers had routinely criticised the previous Press Council and its chairman. They hadn't realised the change of political mood and the very real threat of legislation. Though the *Sun* had cleaned up its act to an extent, in the PCC's first year it headed the list of shame with five complaints upheld. Many MPs were unimpressed with the PCC and one of them, Labour's Clive Soley, had wide support for his private member's bill on Press Freedom and Responsibility which was designed to make the press behave, laying stress on the need for accuracy, apologies and the right to reply.

Several incidents in 1992 undermined the PCC. When the *Sunday Times* published extracts from Andrew Morton's book about Princess Diana, McGregor made a fool of himself by issuing a public condemnation of papers. He ignored warnings that both the Princess and the Prince of Wales were leaking stories themselves by speaking of the 'odious exhibition of journalists dabbling their fingers in the stuff of other people's souls'. Newspapers rounded on him and he was quickly informed that the princess was the source of the Morton book. Months later he admitted that the princess had made a mockery of his attempt to protect her, but the damage to his credibility, and therefore to the PCC's, was done.[180]

The atmosphere grew worse when the *Daily Mirror* carried compromising pictures of the Duchess of York, prompting the *Sun* to reveal secret tape-recordings of calls by Princess Diana to a friend. In the Commons, heritage secretary David Mellor made what sounded like veiled threats about the possibility of legislation to protect privacy because Sir David Calcutt, the man responsible for the creation of the PCC, was conducting a review of its operation.[181] Then the *Sunday People* ran its exposure of Mellor's affair with an actress (see above, p. 574), which had all the hallmarks of a challenge to MPs to do their worst. Soley's bill got an easy ride for its second reading and, in January 1993, Calcutt pushed for a statutory tribunal to replace the PCC with the power to restrain publication, impose fines and force corrections.[182]

Almost every editor and senior journalist – from the *Sun*'s Kelvin MacKenzie to the former *Times* editor Lord Rees-Mogg – rose up against Calcutt's plan, arguing that it was an unacceptable form of censorship. Even Soley thought Calcutt wrong-headed, as did the government, which shied away from criminalising journalism and shelved Calcutt's second report. Press owners amended the PCC rules to ensure lay members were in the majority on the commission and agreed to set up a PCC telephone helpline, while editors tightened their code of practice to outlaw bugging and eavesdropping. Even the *Sun* agreed to make the code part of their journalists' contracts of employment. Accepting that papers were trying, the government then effectively killed off Soley's bill.

The next crisis was the publication by the *Daily* and *Sunday Mirror* of pictures of Princess Diana exercising in a gym in November 1993 (see above, p. 570). Once again, Lord McGregor overstepped the mark by appearing on television to urge advertisers to boycott the Mirror titles. Mirror group's chief executive David Montgomery responded by withdrawing his company from the PCC. By this time, the *Mail*'s editor-in-chief, Sir David English, was chairman of the editors' code committee and the PCC's highest-ranked member. A natural diplomat, it took all his skills – plus vocal support from

Rupert Murdoch – to encourage Montgomery back into the self-regulation process.[183] It was now obvious to owners and editors that Lord McGregor should not continue as chairman beyond his contract. Meanwhile, to ward off political criticism the PCC appointed a so-called privacy commissioner, Professor Robert Pinker, to investigate cases of intrusion. To compound problems, McGregor got into trouble again in August 1994 during a radio interview in which he said a *News of the World* story had not breached the code, only to admit afterwards that he hadn't read the paper. Surely, I wrote at the time, he had put his foot in it for the last time.[184]

A demoralised PCC needed a new figurehead and I was not alone in thinking that the man selected was entirely wrong for the job: Lord Wakeham of Maldon, a former Conservative minister regarded as Margaret Thatcher's arch-fixer. Since leaving government he had secured many directorships and it was feared that such interests would compromise his impartiality.[185] Immediately after taking over at the beginning of 1995 he seemed to confirm his critics' concerns by trying to draft Thatcher's former press secretary, Sir Bernard Ingham, on to the commission. He was forced to drop that idea and was soon engaged in the kind of behind-the-scenes diplomacy with owners, editors, politicians and royal courtiers that would be the hallmark of his chairmanship.

Gradually, if somewhat erratically, the editors' code did put a brake on tabloid editors' more reckless misbehaviour, though the *News of the World*, rather than its Wapping stablemate, the *Sun*, emerged as the PCC's greatest challenge. The era began with Patsy Chapman as *NoW* editor, who was described by her columnist Woodrow Wyatt as 'a jolly little girl' and 'a pretty little thing'.[186] Though these were condescending and sexist remarks they say a lot about the way Chapman was perceived. In spite of her paper's occasional venality, she was a light-hearted woman who disarmed everyone who met her. This was a façade, however, because she suffered terribly from stress and her key PCC role added to her difficulties. She was under constant pressure because she had inherited a paper selling more than 5.3 million which, some five years later, was down to 4.6 million. She felt betrayed by her deputy editor, who was dismissed for leaking unflattering stories about her to *Private Eye*. She was devastated by the death of a photographer, Ed Henty, who was killed in April 1993 by an IRA bomb planted at Bishopsgate in the City of London.[187] He was a freelance on assignment for the *NoW* and video film showed that he had ignored police warnings to enter a cordoned-off area.[188] Despite that, Chapman took his death personally.

Chapman hosted a lavish party in October 1993 to celebrate the *News of the World*'s 150th anniversary, making a speech in which she said she was 'proud to carry on a tradition as British as the Sunday lunch', but two months later she felt unable to continue as editor and took sick leave, which led to her leaving permanently.[189] The *Sun*'s assistant editor, Stuart Higgins, stood in as editor for a couple of months until he succeeded Kelvin MacKenzie as

Sun editor. Murdoch, on the strong recommendation of MacKenzie, then elevated the *Sun*'s high-profile pop gossip columnist, Piers Morgan, to the editorship of the *News of the World*. At twenty-eight, Morgan became the youngest person to edit a national paper since Hugh Cudlipp edited the *Sunday Pictorial* in 1952. Woodrow Wyatt lunched with the 'boy' and described him as 'tall and slight, a pleasant-looking fellow with a strange accent' who was 'a trifle too pleased with himself'.[190] Most people would have agreed with the latter view: Morgan was loud, cocky and irreverent, characteristics offset by a good sense of humour. In that sense he was like his mentor, but, unlike MacKenzie, he wasn't a bully.

His Irish father having died when Morgan was a year old, his mother married Glynne Pughe-Morgan. The couple ran a pub and later his stepfather – whom Morgan always regarded as his father – ran a meat-trading business. Morgan was sent to a private prep school in Sussex until, at thirteen, with his family undergoing a money crisis, he went to a comprehensive. This switch in schooling not only provided Morgan with an insight into both middle- and working-class life, it later enabled him, perhaps unconsciously, to alternate between the two in his manner and speech. After school and a temporary job in the City he took a course at Harlow Journalism College and fetched up on a south London weekly, the *Wimbledon News*. He dropped the Pughe from his name (to enable his byline to fit more easily) and was soon working on casual reporting shifts at the *Sun*. Spotted as a good prospect, he was taken on as a full-time showbusiness reporter in 1989 and, soon became editor of the paper's Bizarre column. With more and more pop stars refusing to talk to the *Sun* because of its hard-edged agenda, MacKenzie encouraged Morgan to use his mixture of charm and chutzpah to persuade stars to have their pictures taken with him. This soft approach worked and Morgan's face became as famous in the *Sun* as the people he posed with.

Morgan wasn't content with being a gossip columnist though, showing the kind of flair and determination which marked him out as a future tabloid high-flier. But he was also inexperienced, with a maverick spirit, and Murdoch was taking a risk by making him editor of a paper which depended for its sales success on a diet of sensational stories at a time when self-regulation was looking shaky. A catalogue of controversial exposures followed. Questions were asked about the methods used to obtain a story about Princess Diana's phone calls to a male friend.[191] There was doubt about the relevance of revealing that a bishop had been convicted twenty-six years before on a charge of gross indecency. Several Tory MPs fell foul of his reporters too (see next chapter). After a salacious story about an MP, one of Morgan's columnists, Woodrow Wyatt, wrote in the *Times*: 'That anyone is entitled to their privacy in their homes, in their cups or in their beds, is a concept wholly alien to the *News of the World*.'[192] Murdoch conceded in a fax to Wyatt that the *NoW* had gone 'over the top' but remonstrated with him for demanding a privacy law.

Murdoch's patience with Morgan eventually snapped when the paper was found to have intruded into the privacy of Countess Spencer by publishing pictures of her in the grounds of a clinic.[193] In his complaint to the PCC her husband claimed that Morgan's paper had breached three clauses of the editors' code of practice. It was such a blatant case that the PCC swiftly ruled in Lord Spencer's favour, but PCC chairman Lord Wakeham wasn't content to leave the matter there, realising he had a chance to show self-regulation in a positive light. In an unprecedented move, Wakeham wrote to Morgan's owner, Murdoch, enclosing the PCC adjudication. Murdoch responded by admonishing Morgan in public, referring to him as a 'young editor who went over the top' and reminding him of his 'responsibility to the code'. It was hardly noticed at the time that the PCC also censured *Sunday People* editor Bridget Rowe for a similar offence.

The episode reflected well on Wakeham because he had illustrated that the most powerful press owner supported the code. Morgan stayed at the *NoW* for only four months more, leaving to edit the *Daily Mirror*. He was succeeded in September 1995 by his deputy, Phil Hall, the man who had previously been responsible for exposing David Mellor's affair. Hall, aged forty, was an Ilford grammar schoolboy who excelled at athletics, becoming Essex county 400-metre champion. Like Morgan, he trained at the Harlow Journalism College. He spent ten years from 1974 at weeklies in east London before joining the *Daily Mail*'s Weekend magazine as a sub-editor. He switched to reporting a year later with the *Sunday People* and rose rapidly to news editor, moving briefly to the same position at the *Sunday Express*. He joined the *News of the World* in 1993 and was promoted by Morgan after five months to deputy editor. More cautious than Morgan and less arrogant, he was equally determined and his paper continued its tradition of exposing sexy secrets.

At the other end of the spectrum, the *Financial Times* caused no alarums for the PCC. Richard Lambert succeeded Sir Geoffrey Owen as editor at the beginning of 1991 at what was to prove a difficult moment, with the Gulf war causing an advertising downturn and the recession reversing the previous upward sales momentum. He also had to deal with a group of staff who suffered from repetitive strain injury (RSI) due to using computers, leading to a protracted legal battle. Lambert, forty-six, had been on the *FT* throughout his career, after Fettes College and Balliol, doing a variety of jobs, running the Lex column, financial editor and New York correspondent, before his appointment as Owen's deputy in 1983. A wise and cautious journalist, Lambert oversaw a dramatic shift in the *FT*'s news coverage with investigations pioneered by the dynamic head of news, Alain Cass.

Cass ran a special team which scored two powerful hits with its inquiry into the collapse of the Bank of Credit and Commerce International and a ten-month investigation into the affairs of Robert Maxwell. On the day Maxwell died, the *FT*'s Bronwen Maddox had built up an almost complete picture of the complex Maxwell web which proved that his companies' debt was crippling. This was to be the basis of an award-winning six-part series which began on the day the Maxwell brothers were arrested.[194] These hard-edged investigations caused concern in the financial establishment, which saw the *FT* as its paper of record. 'The City did get stroppy with us,' said Lambert, 'but it didn't harm us because we got things right.'[195] After Cass departed, those kinds of investigation ceased but the *FT* got better at breaking stories about acquisitions and mergers. It was helped by its continuing internationalisation, moving into Asia and strengthening its American base, which meant it had correspondents with their ears to the ground around the globe.

The *FT*'s owner, Pearson, made the mistake of building its own printing press hall in east London which, given the paper's short print run and its inability to secure other contracts, wasted money. Papers no longer needed to own their own presses and it was found to be cheaper to close it and print at the Telegraph–Express plant at West Ferry. Pearson also adopted a corporate strategy to transform itself into a multi-media company, spinning off some of its non-media interests such as Royal Doulton and selling its stake in Camco oil. In a shopping spree, it paid large sums for Thames Television, Grundy Worldwide and Extel Financial. Its acquisitive managing director Frank Barlow also paid £313 million for a Californian software company, Mindscape, which was to prove disastrous. More positively, it sold off its stake in BSkyB, which enabled Pearson to clear its debts. At the *FT*, Lambert's watchword was shareholder value and it was obvious that his owner, Pearson, was following that philosophy.

One man who didn't understand such a concept was, of course, Robert Maxwell. He had spent millions on the *European* by the time he died and it was assumed that his dream weekly would die with him.[196] Long before his death he had replaced his first editor, Ian Watson, with John Bryant who, ominously, had just administered the last rites to the *Sunday Correspondent*. After Maxwell's death, Bryant saw no future for the *European* and quit to be deputy editor of the *Times*. But his deputy, Charlie Garside, decided to save the paper and managed to keep it going until, in January 1992, it was bought from the administrator for something less than £3 million by David and Frederick Barclay. The fifty-seven-year-old publicity-shy identical twins lived in Monte Carlo and ran a conglomerate which controlled hotels and shipping and were reputed to be worth £450 million. In a rare quote from David, he said: 'Privacy is a valuable commodity.'[197]

They promised to fund the paper for at least five years and put David's thirty-six-year-old son, Aidan, in charge of the management, naming Garside as editor. He had a background in tabloid journalism, had been deputy editor of the *Sunday Express* and an assistant editor, overseeing pictures, at the *Times*. He did his best with the *European* but it didn't sell many copies, given its huge distribution area, and lost many millions more. The next couple of years were messy with Garside leaving and returning months later. There were signs of a professional approach at the beginning of 1995 when the newspaper veteran Bert Hardy was tempted out of retirement to become chief executive, but the *European* went on losing money. Hardy's role became clearer at the end of the year when the Barclay Brothers paid £95 million to purchase the *Scotsman* and *Scotland on Sunday* from the Thomson organisation. Were the secretive millionaires on their way to being media tycoons?

Another would-be press tycoon, David Sullivan, publisher of the salacious *Sunday Sport*, found it difficult to build an audience with his daily paper, and his editor Peter Grimsditch objected to the phone-sex ads. After several rows, Grimsditch departed, explaining, 'I was trying to take the paper from the gutter to the kerb.'[198] In September 1992, Sullivan also started a northern weekly, the *News & Echo*, but it collapsed because Westminster Press stole his thunder by launching *Yorkshire on Sunday* weeks before.

Grimsditch's British editing career wasn't quite over and it should be noted that he departed after first taking part in a truly visionary venture. He was chosen to edit *Tonight*, a paper to be given away free five evenings a week outside London tube stations from July 1994.[199] It was funded by Derek Clee, who had made a fortune as a tumble-drier manufacturer based in Halifax. Clee's research had shown that London could sustain a free newspaper alongside the *Evening Standard*. Produced on a shoestring, it was an unappealing sixteen-page tabloid which made little if any impact. It couldn't attract advertising and the distribution of its notional 100,000 print run was patchy.[200] Well before the end of the year it was appearing only once a week and in January 1995 Grimsditch was fired.[201] This under-funded, amateur enterprise limped on for a couple of months, but it wasn't as foolish a notion as it seemed at the time. It gave the *Standard*'s owners, Associated, something to think about. Could a paper given away to London commuters really work?

20. WAS IT REALLY THE *SUN* WOT WON IT?

> If Neil Kinnock wins today will the last person to leave Britain please turn out the lights.[1]

No post-war election spawned as much disputed analysis of press coverage and its possible impact as the one in 1992. After a hard-fought campaign between Margaret Thatcher's successor, John Major, and Labour's Neil Kinnock the result was in the balance up to polling day. When Labour lost, *Sun* editor Kelvin MacKenzie couldn't contain his delight, running a piece which suggested his paper had been the key factor in deciding the outcome with the headline: 'IT'S THE SUN WOT WON IT!'[2] Major didn't agree.[3] But Kinnock appeared to give the boast credence by claiming he had been treated to one of the crudest, most vulgar and most disingenuous barrages of biased propaganda of any election campaign since 1945.[4] That was a revealing comparison because Labour triumphed in spite of the 1945 press onslaught. Indeed, as the *Independent* pointed out, the popular press's bias against Labour 'is a truth with which Labour has lived – and won famous election victories'.[5] So why was there a different result this time? Had the papers become more influential? Were the 1992 readers more open to persuasion than those in 1945?

Labour's director of communications, David Hill, spoke of 'the extraordinarily warped public perception of Neil Kinnock' being 'the product of the day-to-day vilification of him in tabloid newspapers', but he didn't necessarily mean only during the campaign.[6] *Guardian* journalist Martin Linton, a former Labour party worker who later became a Labour MP, was convinced that the campaign journalism alone had been responsible for the defeat and set out to prove it.[7] His thesis, based on an interpretation of poll data, suggested that the *Sun*'s coverage was responsible for an 8 per cent swing to the Conservatives by its readers who previously claimed to be Labour voters. This may have accounted for as many as half a million extra votes for the Tories. By contrast, there was no discernible swing among *Daily Mirror* readers.

Linton's argument was fiercely contested by two psephologists who countered that there was no provable correlation between the votes cast and newspaper readership.[8] Linton was supported to an extent by Ivor Crewe, who claimed that the swing to the Conservatives of about 9 per cent among

Sun readers, along with below-average swings among *Mail* and *Express* readers, may have delivered some six marginal seats to the Tories.[9] Crewe's claims were thought unconvincing by a group of academics led by Peter Golding who argued that 'what really counts is the longer term forging of beliefs in a culture that may well have become inexorably conservative'.[10]

The intensity of the debate echoed down the years to the dawn of newspapers, back to Fleet Street's beginnings with the launching of the *Daily Courant* in 1702, a paper sustained by political bribes in the belief that what a paper printed could make a difference. For 300 years, therefore, the same question has been asked without anyone being able to provide a definitive answer: can a paper exert enough power over its audience to affect the outcome of an election? One central problem with almost every attempt to answer it has been analysts' dependence on press coverage in the immediate run-up to general elections. This approach provides only a snapshot, stopping time, rather than showing a continuous development. It doesn't allow for the evolving of opinions among the public in the years leading up to an election, let alone the much more dramatic and complex long-term formulation of views within society. That's why Golding's argument, about the significance of beliefs being built up over time, is so compelling.

The importance of the *Sun*'s final blitz on Kinnock has to be seen in the context of the bombs that rained down on him in the years before. Linton approvingly quoted a *UK Press Gazette* editorial which correctly pointed out that for editors 'to claim they have no influence over the decisions, opinions and attitudes of readers would be a suicide note sent to all advertisers'.[11] But advertising depends for its success on repetition, with short-term major marketing campaigns taking place against a background in which people already have some notion of the company or product they are being asked to buy. That's why branding is of paramount importance. As the *Daily Telegraph* has pointed out, though the British press 'wields less power than is sometimes supposed . . . in influencing public opinion and especially votes . . . it can be formidably effective in setting the nation's agenda for good or ill'.[12]

Kinnock understood this process too. Despite his understandable outburst immediately after his election loss he didn't really think the *Sun* alone had cost him victory with its campaign coverage. He realised that what happened in those final weeks was the *culmination* of a much longer process in which he had been vilified by the media.[13] While it is impossible to state with any certainty that the *Sun* swung the election single-handedly in the four weeks leading up to 9 April 1992, it is highly probable that Kinnock's press coverage as a whole in the previous *years* did make a crucial difference. Alastair Campbell, then political editor of the *Daily Mirror* who may well have been appointed Kinnock's press secretary if he had become prime minister, agreed: 'The chances of ever winning were greatly diminished by the fact that, day in and day out, newspapers attacked the Labour Party – and

Neil Kinnock in particular – virulently; and that was bound to have had an effect on the way politics was perceived during those years in which people are actually making up their minds.'[14] Having sifted the evidence, largely by researching the *Sun*'s files from 1983 until 1992, it's hard not to agree with Campbell's assessment of the potency of the drip-drip effect. What follows is necessarily random, but it reflects a true picture of the way in which Kinnock was depicted for eight years in Britain's highest-selling paper.

The knocking began on the day of his election as party leader in 1983. The *Sun* called him 'The Nowhere Man' because 'he has been nowhere. He has never proved himself in any government office. He has no intellectual depth, no coherent philosophy.'[15] Kinnock also suffered the embarrassment of falling over on Brighton beach while posing for photographers, an incident seized on by the *Sun* and *Daily Mail* which ran pictures on their front pages.[16] Footage of the waves lapping at Kinnock's feet was used endlessly on TV, in the popular satire show *Spitting Image*, reinforcing for years afterwards the image of a clumsy and/or unlucky politician.

Kinnock couldn't win with the right-wing press. If he adopted the habitual Labour stance in support of trade unions he was attacked, especially by the *Sun* after Wapping, which perceived any intention to amend strike laws as a personal affront. One such example, under the headline, 'Labour chief's threat to the *Sun*', contended: 'If the country wants to turn the clock back and make Britain once more ungovernable, it will vote Labour.'[17] Yet, when Kinnock appeared to take initiatives which had been continually urged on him by the right-wing press, such as sidelining Labour's militant elements, his efforts were derided as window-dressing. Papers belittled his inexperience and taunted him at every opportunity. A visit to the United States in 1987 was considered disastrous because he met President Reagan for just nineteen minutes. As we saw in Chapter Eighteen, he was denigrated as a weak leader before and during Labour's 1987 election defeat. That abuse continued over the next five years. As early as 1988, the *Sun* was predicting that he would lose the next election, asking what job would 'suit a 46-year-old politician with the gift of the gab'.[18] Despite this character assassination, by spring 1989 Labour had inched ahead in the polls for the first time in a year and a concerned *Sun* asked: 'Can Kinnock Cash In on Tories' Slide?'[19]

Six months later the *Sun* greeted Labour's annual conference with a feature poking fun at Labour's leadership: 'Opening Today: A nearly new show starring Kinnochio. GONE WITH THE WINDBAG'.[20] Two days later it claimed MPs were 'bored to sleep by Neil's big speech' and a week after that it ran a picture of Kinnock with his mouth open, offering readers £10 if they could snap a photograph of him with his mouth closed.[21] The *Daily Mail*, sensing a growing hostility to Thatcher, was eager to punch home the political message that Kinnock's internal party reforms were 'only skin-deep'.[22] The ousting of the Trotskyists and the marginalising of the Bennite left wasn't real, just as Kinnock's own conversion to multilateralism wasn't genuine. *Mail* columnists Paul Johnson and George Gale asserted that Labour's reforms were a tribute to Thatcher rather than to Kinnock, a theme echoed in a *Mail* splash some days later, 'Kinnock's Con-Trick'.[23]

With Thatcher under pressure throughout 1990 and her newspaper supporters anxious to maintain her in office, they ensured that Kinnock should remain a bogeyman figure. To that end, the *Sun*, the *Daily Mail* and the *Daily Express* often ran articles accusing Labour of policy initiatives which were far from true. One claimed that Labour was planning to tax video rentals, prompting the *Sun* to comment: 'Isn't it amazing. Mr Kinnock hasn't even arrived at No 10, but already his cold breath can be felt in your front room.'[24] When South Africa's recently released political prisoner Nelson Mandela attended a Wembley concert, the *Sun* transformed Kinnock's relatively mild gesture, raising an index finger, into a 'black power salute'.[25] Less than a week later a *Sun* article before the local elections warned that voting Labour would cause sterling to collapse, drive companies to the wall and necessitate heavy borrowing because of high public service spending. The *Sun* did the borrowing by repeating the headline from the *Mail* six months before, 'Kinnock's Con-Trick'.[26]

Popular newspaper hostility had become so common by the time Kinnock visited America to meet President George Bush Snr in July 1990 that the *Sunday Times* was moved to sympathy by reporting on the tabloids' 'game of hunt-the-gaffe'. On the eve of his visit to the White House several papers carried a story about Kinnock attacking Bush, variously described as a clanger, a major error or an own goal.[27] But a tabloid journalist confessed to the *Sunday Times* correspondent that it was 'pure invention'. Another reporter explained that Kinnock's speeches were ignored by his paper while gaffes were always published.[28] Kinnock also fell foul of the *Sun*'s fiercely anti-European philosophy. While Thatcher was the 'champion' for fighting off a European super-state, Kinnock would be 'shaking the clenched fist of Euro-power . . . warbling, "Deutschland über Alles"'.[29]

A common theme was that Kinnock was unduly influenced by his wife who, the *Sun* presumed, was far to his left: 'Is Glenys a Red in Neil's Bed?'[30] He was also the butt of continual criticism for his supposedly 'lacklustre Commons performances' which allegedly induced opposition within the party, leading to claims that John Smith would prove a better leader.[31] After a Labour by-election victory, with a much reduced majority in April 1991, the *Sun* said of Kinnock: 'The cruel truth is that, for all his energy and his long tongue, the nation simply does not rate him as a possible prime minister.'[32]

His credibility was further undermined by a story about a silly fracas when a group of youngsters threw an empty beer can at him while he was talking to his daughter in his front garden: 'Kinnock scuffles in street'.[33] This incident emboldened the *Sun* to publish a totally false story which claimed that Kinnock had thrown an ashtray at an MP headlined 'Is Kinnock too hot-headed to handle power?'[34] Six days later, after much pressure, an apology appeared: 'We accept that no such incident took place and the meeting bore no resemblance to our account of it.'[35] The following month, just before a parliamentary by-election and a round of local elections, the *Sun* broke a story claiming that Kinnock was linked to a fugitive Cypriot tycoon who was under police investigation because of £10 million allegedly missing from his company.[36] The man was a friend of the Kinnocks who had donated money to the Labour party but, said the paper, there was no question of impropriety on Kinnock's part. In that case, what was the point of giving it such prominence? Kinnock rightly dismissed it as a smear.

As opinion polls turned against Major in early summer 1991, the *Sun* reiterated its 'complete faith' in the prime minister, warning that the alternative was Kinnock.[37] By the autumn conference, the paper told its readers Kinnock was a 'dud' who was 'out to mug us all' with high taxes.[38] With the possibility of a November election, the *Sun*'s assaults on Kinnock and Labour were relentless. Sterling was 'on the ropes because opinion polls suggested Labour might win'.[39] On a day when the front-page headline announced, 'OFFICIAL: Don't vote for us if you want tax cut, say Labour' page three was devoted to a piece claiming that 'Kinnock family tree is a load of cobblers.'[40] Two days later, having hunted down Kinnock's former school rugby teammates from thirty-one years before, the *Sun* asked them what they thought of Kinnock's chances of being prime minister and, according to the paper's account, most gave him the thumbs-down.[41] Kinnock was later contacted by several of those men to say the feature was a travesty.[42]

Before we consider the election coverage itself it's important to note that the *Sun* was not alone in demeaning Kinnock, nor were the negative stories confined to tabloids. In early February, the *Sunday Times* ran a story which maintained that Kinnock had had contacts with the Kremlin at the height of the cold war.[43] David Hill, Labour's director of communications, tried to spoil the story in advance of publication by informing several daily papers that Kinnock was about to be smeared. Indeed, the story didn't amount to much, reiterating what everyone knew: Kinnock had once been a unilateralist. Editor Andrew Neil was forced to concede that contents bills boasting of 'Kinnock's Kremlin connection' were inaccurate, and the *Daily Mail* – one of Labour's most persistent critics and usually willing to fire any bullet in its direction – turned its guns instead on the *Sunday Times*, calling its revelations 'excessively hyped'.[44] This criticism had more to do with dog-eat-dog Fleet Street rivalry than concern for Kinnock. The only daily tabloid to present Kinnock in a positive light throughout the period was the *Daily Mirror*. It was then selling about 3 million while the other five which backed Major – *Sun, Mail, Express, Star* and *Today* – had a joint sale of 8 million. Overall, taking account of broadsheets and all the Sunday titles, papers supporting the Tories accounted for 67 per cent of the total readership.

While Major was making up his mind about the date of the election he received a call from Lady Rothermere, the wife of the *Daily Mail*'s proprietor, to say it would be wrong for him to choose April.[45] What is so significant about that incident, apart from her poor advice, which he ignored, was the fact that he took her call. Why should a prime minister accept a phone call from a newspaper owner's estranged wife?

When, on 11 March, he did announce the election, the polls put Labour marginally in the lead and the Tory papers, alarmed at the weakness of the Conservative campaign, set out to make theirs much more effective by heaping scorn on Kinnock. Their initial sallies were directed at Labour's tax plans, distorting the details to make them appear far more swingeing than they were. A sample of the many headlines from just three papers gives some idea of the ferocity of the attacks: 'Road to ruin with Kinnock' and 'Who Do You Think You Are Kidding Mr Kinnock?' (*Express*); 'Companies "afraid to invest under Kinnock",' 'Labour votes to tax poor' and 'If you make it – they'll take it' (*Mail*); 'Labour to squeeze backbone of Britain' and 'Labour Squeeze on Triers' (*Sun*).

Towards the end of the campaign, with the result still in doubt, came an ugly twist. Home secretary Kenneth Baker made a speech critical of both the Labour and the Liberal Democrat immigration policies. The *Daily Express* played the race card by headlining the story 'Baker's Migrant Flood Warning' and claiming that 'Labour would open the floodgates to a wave of immigration'.[46] A *Sun* editorial talked about the 'threat of massive immigration' under a Labour government. Some weeks earlier the *Daily Mail* had alleged that 'Kinnock "won't curb flood of bogus refugees"'.[47] Then the *Sun* pulled out its big guns. The day before polling its front page was headlined 'A Question of Trust' and compared 'solid, dependable' Major with the 'novice' Kinnock, 'a man with a short fuse . . . no great intellectual'.[48] There followed nine pages bearing the slogan 'Nightmare on Kinnock Street', including a page in which a 'leading psychic' asked dead world leaders to name the man they would vote for. Kinnock got Stalin's vote; Major picked up Queen Victoria.

There were other matters which may have had an impact on voters, such as Labour's triumphalist rally at Sheffield when the polls were running 8 per cent against the Tories. Major thought it did make a difference, along with concerns about devolution and the belief that the Tories could best handle the recession.[49] I doubt if the rally – which received more coverage after the election than at the time – or devolution were significant factors, but he was surely right about public scepticism of Labour's economic capabilities. This was a long-held viewpoint throughout the post-war years, exacerbated by Harold Wilson's sterling devaluation and Jim Callaghan's union problems. It was reinforced by the attacks on Kinnock which continually suggested he was an economic incompetent.

Major had two surprises on election day: the *Financial Times* backed

Labour and the *Daily Express* correctly reported a late Tory surge in the polls.[50] The *Sun* ran its most memorable piece of political propaganda to keep readers focused on the awful consequences of a Labour victory with a front page depicting Kinnock's head in a light bulb and the headline 'If Neil Kinnock wins today will the last person to leave Britain please turn out the lights'.[51] Major may have been the beneficiary but he later reflected that the pages were 'cruel'.[52]

Despite the sudden poll movement, most commentators had predicted a narrow Labour win or a hung parliament, as did BBC's exit poll. In fact, Labour suffered a bad defeat, winning only 34 per cent of the vote to the Tories' 42 per cent. 'Less than half the working-class had voted Labour,' noted historian Kenneth Morgan, who argued that the party had 'allowed itself to be placed repeatedly on the defensive by Tory tabloid newspapers ... [The *Sun*'s] personal attacks on Neil Kinnock undermined his and his party's morale.'[53] According to Mori, 45 per cent of *Sun* readers voted Tory while 50 per cent voted for Labour or the Liberal Democrats. It was noticeable that in certain key marginals which were narrow Tory victories the *Sun* did have high penetration.[54] But did they switch because of what they had read?

The *Sun* initially thought they had, immediately laying exclusive claim to having engineered victory with that 'IT'S THE SUN WOT WON IT!' headline. Former prime minister Thatcher confided to colleagues that 'Tory journalists ... like Mr Paul Johnson and Mr Kelvin MacKenzie' had been responsible for Major winning. She also told *Daily Express* editor Sir Nicholas Lloyd: 'You won it, Sir Nicholas, you won it.'[55] That view was reinforced by the former Tory treasurer Lord McAlpine who said: 'The heroes of this campaign were Sir David English, Sir Nicholas Lloyd, Kelvin MacKenzie and the other editors of the grander Tory press. Never in the past nine elections have they come out so strongly in favour of the Conservatives. Never has the attack on the Labour party been so comprehensive.'[56]

It was significant that Kinnock quoted McAlpine in full when announcing his resignation, but he also managed to imply that it was the sustained nature of the anti-Labour and personal barrage which had been the real problem.[57] Editors were quick to deny any responsibility for Labour's defeat. MacKenzie tried to brush off his *Sun*-wot-won-it boast as a joke, while English preferred sarcasm: it was 'very flattering' of Kinnock to suggest the *Mail* had won the election for the Conservatives but it 'ascribes far more influence to us than we would give ourselves'.[58] Other editors, including those of a non-Tory persuasion, agreed with MacKenzie and English. An *Observer* editorial thought it 'facile to blame the Tory tabloids ... the reasons for Labour's defeat go much deeper'.[59] The *Guardian*, employing a perceptibly Prestonian phrase, thought the idea of Tory papers having swung the election 'drifts toward the higher shores of implausibility'.[60]

So the editors who had set out to achieve a Conservative victory were cleared of all charges. In spite of doing all they could to influence voters they ended up suggesting it was an insult to the British people to think they could be swayed by the press.

Time for Major to get the Kinnock treatment

Were newspapers drunk with power after the 1992 election? Did owners and editors imagine that they could make or break prime ministers? These are fair questions when we consider what happened within six months of the Tories being returned to office. That was how long it took for press delight – or, more properly, relief – at John Major's victory to turn into outright hostility. As a Labour party official observed: 'The knife sharpened by the *Sun* on Neil Kinnock is now being deployed against John Major.'[61] Major soon realised that the papers which had supported him had done so out of continuing loyalty to Margaret Thatcher rather than a genuine belief in his own leadership, and an understanding that he represented, when compared to Kinnock, the lesser of two evils. The turning point came on 16 September 1992, known as Black Wednesday.

The economy was already in poor shape due to the recession when a speculative run on a weakened pound turned into a torrent. Major raised interest rates to 12 per cent, then 15 per cent, but sterling continued to fall. Some £30 billion in reserves were spent by Chancellor Norman Lamont in failing to shore up the currency and he and Major were forced to pull out of the European exchange rate mechanism (ERM). It amounted, in effect, to a devaluation of the pound, confirmed sceptics in their hostility to the European Union and unleashed the most savage press criticism of a government since James Callaghan's final months in office some fourteen months before. For Major, the unremitting hostility would last for the best part of five years. Underlying the newspapers' stance was the antagonism of several owners to further European integration. Rupert Murdoch, Conrad Black and Lord Rothermere were bitterly opposed to the Maastricht Treaty negotiated in December 1991, a key stage in the process of creating a closer union of European nations.

The *Sun*'s vitriolic campaign against the single currency had predated Thatcher's downfall and its response to the ERM fiasco was vicious. *Sun* editor Kelvin MacKenzie claimed that Major called to ask him how his paper would be playing the story, and he said: 'Prime Minister, I have on my desk in front of me a very large bucket of shit which I am just about to pour all over you.' Major evidently replied: 'Oh Kelvin, you are a wag.'[62] Next morning the manure duly arrived with a front-page headline alluding to heritage secretary David Mellor's dalliance with an actress: 'Now we've ALL been screwed by the Cabinet'.[63] *Sun* columnist Richard Littlejohn followed up with a series of hostile articles, the start of what would become a relentless personal campaign against Major's government.[64]

The *Daily Mail* lashed 'devalued Chancellor' Lamont and railed against 'flip-flop government'.[65] The High-Tory *Daily Telegraph* adopted a similar stance, even if its tone was more moderate, calling for Lamont's resignation and pointing to Major's loss of credibility.[66] A commentary by deputy editor Charles Moore castigated Major for his flawed European policy and unsound economic strategy.[67] The *Sunday Telegraph* weighed in by calling into question Major's leadership abilities.[68] At the *Times*, Peter Stothard had assumed the editorship on the week of the ERM crisis. Soon after, he published a surrealist portrait of Major living in a flat above Admiralty Arch dining on junk food with only the cares of state for company. The *Times* columnist, and its former editor, William Rees-Mogg called Major the most over-promoted of Conservative prime ministers.

Within a week of the ERM embarrassment, Major sampled his first experience of a press feeding frenzy. Two months before, he had shrugged aside Fleet Street's calls to fire David Mellor after the *Sunday People* exposed his affair with an actress. When it emerged that Mellor had taken a holiday at the expense of the daughter of the Palestinian Liberation Organisation's finance minister without informing parliament, Major wasn't able to resist the press pressure (see above, pp. 574–5). Later, Major rightly saw Mellor's departure – memorably headlined in the *Sun* as 'Toe Job to No Job' – as the 'first scalp'.[69]

The *Sun* was looking for Major's scalp virtually every day. A week after Mellor's resignation, it claimed the Tories hadn't a clue how to deal with the slump and the next day's front page asked: 'Is It Time for Mrs T?', inciting what it hyped as 'Bring Back Maggie' fever.[70] This was followed by a front-page 'open letter' to the prime minister – 'Dear Mr Major, do you have a plan to get us out of this bloody mess?' – and two days later yet another splash headline which asked: 'Is Major a Goner?'[71] The *Daily Mail* was a little more circumspect, trying to bolster Major while letting it be known that it sympathised with his anti-European critics, such as Thatcher and Norman Tebbit.[72] In his *Spectator* column the *Daily Telegraph*'s deputy editor Charles Moore made one of the many assaults he would launch against a prime minister for whom he had no respect. 'Mr Major may come from Brixton,' he wrote, 'but he is treating his own people as if he were a Bourbon.'[73] The feeling was mutual: Major thought Moore 'a clever but foppish figure who . . . adored Margaret Thatcher and was heavily influenced by her', remarking that he and Moore were 'oil and water'.[74]

Within days came conclusive evidence that the Tory press would never be Major's press. In a complete reversal of their 1984 attitudes towards the coal miners, right-wing papers suddenly took up their cause. Michael Heseltine, president of the Board of Trade, felt that his announcement about the need to shut down thirty-one of Britain's remaining fifty pits, though unfortunate, was hardly surprising and therefore relatively uncontroversial. Instead, he and Major were hit by a tidal wave of newspaper opposition to 30,000 miners losing their jobs during a period of rising unemployment.

The *Sun*, scourge of the miners eight years before, published a remarkable front page. It was empty except for a box in the centre of the white space with a picture of Heseltine and the headline: 'This page contains ALL that Michael Heseltine understands about the worries and fears of ordinary working people in depression-hit Britain.'[75] An editorial reminded the people of the Mellor affair, devaluation and the 'unseemly' way Lamont was clinging to office. The *Daily Mail* showed sympathy for miners too, asking why, in a recession, Major should close the pits 'in one fell swoop' instead of phasing them out.[76] *Today* and the *Daily Star* were also hostile. The *Daily Telegraph* noted the 'extraordinary unanimity, even among newspapers which traditionally support the Conservative Party, about the Government's lamentable showing, above all since "Black Wednesday"'.[77] The *Times* gave away the press's real agenda by taking Major to task for his lack of political strategy and his 'futile fixation on Maastricht'.[78] The *Financial Times* also lamented the government's failure to provide a strategy: 'A pall of gloom has descended over Britain.' It accepted that the deepening global slump wasn't the government's fault but questioned the wisdom of closing pits 'at the bottom of a recession'.[79]

Even the *News of the World* lambasted Major over his failure to save miners' jobs, contrasting his reluctance with his attempt to save the job of 'his adulterous cabinet crony David Mellor'.[80] Both the *NoW* and the *Sunday Times* put black borders on their front pages to signal what the latter called 'Depression Britain'. The *Mail on Sunday* said affection for the prime minister had drifted into anger. The *Sunday Telegraph* was savage: Major had sullied his honour and exposed his incompetence. Naturally, the Labour-supporting *Daily Mirror* lashed Major too, calling his government a 'hard-faced killer', but it was the Conservative papers' opposition to the pit closures which shocked Major. The *Daily Mail* – rock solid for the Tories throughout its history – ran a series of biting leaders demanding Lamont's head.[81]

Major's single press supporter at the time, and for years to come, was the *Daily Express*. Its chairman, Lord Stevens, and its editor, Sir Nicholas Lloyd, refused to join the Fleet Street chorus though one line in their finger-wagging post-ERM leader probably made Major wince: 'As Margaret Thatcher said, you can't buck the markets.'[82] Lloyd showed his real feelings at the October 1992 conference when he rounded on *Mail* editor Paul Dacre to ask: 'Are you trying to put John Smith into Downing Street?'[83] The *FT*'s wise commentator Joe Rogaly had astutely predicted when Dacre replaced Sir David English in July 1992 that the new *Mail* editor would give Major a rougher ride than his predecessor because of his more right-wing economic inclinations.[84] English remained editor-in-chief and still had the ear of Lord Rothermere, but they let Dacre – who thought Major lacked both conviction and courage – have his head.[85]

There was some sympathy for Major's plight. Political commentator Bruce Anderson thought the relationship between the Tory leadership and

Tory press was the worst since Baldwin versus Beaverbrook and Rothermere in the 1930s. He concluded: 'In the whole history of modern British politics no important political figure has been portrayed so inaccurately as Major.'[86] Major rightly identified Europe as the problem. When Liberal leader Paddy Ashdown met Major in November 1992 he sensed his 'fear' of the press, especially of Murdoch and Black. Major told Ashdown they and other members of their 'cabal' – Simon Jenkins, Charles Moore and Peregrine Worsthorne – 'wanted to destroy the treaty by any means possible'.[87]

Perhaps Major was naive about the press too. Having dined at the home of *Sunday Times* editor Andrew Neil, along with his paper's senior executives, he was upset when the paper reported what he considered were his off-the-record views.[88] Nor was it clever of Major to institute a second inquiry into the operation of press self-regulation when most of the disputed stories were about politicians. He also suffered from one media blow that was definitely below the belt. Alastair Campbell, then a *Sunday Mirror* columnist, claimed to have observed on a plane journey with Major that the prime minister tucked his shirt into his underpants, thereby making them visible. *Guardian* cartoonist Steve Bell picked up on this sartorial *faux pas* and depicted Major ever after wearing Y-fronts *over* his trousers.

Newspaper coverage didn't get much better for Major in 1993. Owners and editors remained unhappy, and *Mail* editor Paul Dacre showed the depth of that disillusion, and the continuing nostalgia for the Thatcher era, in a significant interview. While lauding the fact that 'hard work and making profit are no longer stigmatized,' he claimed that 'the present prime minister has undermined those [Thatcherite] values'.[89] After Lamont's resignation, the *Sun* turned its guns on his replacement as chancellor, Kenneth Clarke. Columnist Richard Littlejohn's anxieties about the state of the government and the nation were captured in a catchphrase, 'You couldn't make it up', which became famous and helped to win him a special *What the Papers Say* award as irritant of the year in 1993. A *Sun* poll before the October 1993 conference, headlined 'Quit now Major and bring back Maggie', summed up the thoughts of its owner, Murdoch.[90] It was noticeable that his *Times* was also questioning every aspect of Major's programme – his economic policy, his energy policy, his failure to allow a referendum on Maastricht – and asking whether he was fit to govern. *Daily Express* editor Sir Nicholas Lloyd thought *Times* editor Peter Stothard was simply trying to make a name for himself.[91] Meanwhile, Major complained to the generally supportive *Times* and *News of the World* columnist Woodrow Wyatt about papers 'doing this drip, drip, drip thing saying I'm no good and the party's no good'.[92]

Major's standing with the press was at an all-time low when he made a speech that October which eventually made his premiership a misery. He made a rallying call for the party to go 'back to basics' and to uphold 'family values' which was wrongly, but effectively, misinterpreted by the press as a sort of moral crusade. It provided a public interest excuse for papers to publish a series of stories about the private lives of Tory ministers and MPs. Where David Mellor had gone, it appeared many of his colleagues had gone too. So began what Major would later describe as 'one of the silliest sagas in modern British politics: the hunt, using fair means or foul, by the tabloid press for gossip about the private lives of Tory MPs'.[93] It was more than that, though. Amid the sex revelations were stories of genuine concern, about corruption at the heart of government and greed. The press lumped all these stories together under the single word, sleaze, with the tabloids failing to distinguish between vice and villainy.

One of the most serious stories emerged in October 1992 during the prosecution of three men for exporting arms-related equipment to Iraq. During the court case the former defence procurement minister Alan Clark admitted that the government had given the nod to the sale despite knowing that the materials could be used for weaponry. A subsequent inquiry headed by Lord Justice Scott took more than three years to report, mounting a stinging attack on the government's powers to control exports. By that time, Major had suffered at least thirty-four separate instances of so-called sleaze. The term itself, and the catalogue of stories which were designated as sleazy, became so much part of the period that the *Independent on Sunday* devoted a special supplement to them.[94] Some were simply about sexual misdemeanours, but these became the best known because they were revealed in the popular papers, particularly the *Sun* and *News of the World*, and often with memorable headlines. After Mellor, the roll-call continued with environment minister Tim Yeo, who was exposed on Boxing Day 1993 by the *News of the World* as having a 'secret love child' with an unmarried Conservative councillor.

His case was interesting for two reasons: first, there wasn't the least public interest reason for the story, and, second, it showed how the Prime Minister's initial defence crumbled after unrelenting pressure, setting a pattern for the future. When Major refused to fire him, the *Sun* ran a daily attack which was followed up by the *News of the World* and every other Sunday tabloid, all demanding that Yeo resign. Reluctantly, he did so and the *Sun* headlined his going: 'Off Yeo Go, You Dirty So and So'.[95] Major thought the treatment an act of cruelty.[96] Yeo's ordeal didn't end with his resignation. After a *Mail on Sunday* investigation, he was forced to confess to having fathered a second illegitimate child many years before.[97]

Realising the danger of the back-to-basics crusade being misused, a *Times* leader called on Major to clarify its meaning, so he tried to explain that it wasn't about 'personal morality'.[98] It was too late: the muckrakers were going about their business and discovered a lot of muck to rake. There were echoes of the Profumo affair in these months. Standards of government came to the fore, with accusations of sleaze. A *Sunday Mirror* story of adultery led to the resignation from his junior government post of Hartley Booth MP. Former minister Alan Clark, a serial philanderer, betrayed little embarrassment when the *News of the World* revealed that he had had affairs with a judge's wife and their two daughters. But it added to the aura of a government mired in immorality, as did the enforced resignation in March 1994 of the chief of the defence staff, Sir Peter Harding, exposed by the *News of the World* for having an affair with Lady (Bienvenida) Buck, the wife of a Tory MP.[99] A year later, another *News of the World* story which told of an unmarried Tory MP, Richard Spring, being involved in 'three-in-a-bed romp', aroused ethical concerns.[100] It emerged that the woman involved had hidden a tape-recorder under her bed to provide evidence to the paper on the understanding that she would receive £25,000 for her tale.[101] Morgan escaped PCC censure because Spring, who resigned his junior government post, refused to make a complaint. It was intrusive, without any public interest defence, but Major realised that 'our blood was in the water and the media sharks circled'.[102]

Some of the cases depended on innuendo about homosexuality. One Tory MP was revealed to have shared a bed with another man on a visit to France. A second MP was outed by the *NoW* when it wrote of his 'three-in-a-bed sex romp' with two other men. A couple of other cases were tragic. Stephen Milligan, a Tory MP who had previously been the *Sunday Times*'s foreign editor (and an excellent colleague of mine), was found dead in bizarre circumstances, having accidentally suffocated while performing an act known as autoerotic asphyxiation. The tabloids had a field day with the sordid details. Lord Caithness, minister for shipping and aviation, had to resign when his wife shot herself after discovering his infidelity.[103]

All of these stories were featured in the tabloids for weeks, prompting uncompromising comments on Major's government. The *Sun*'s Richard Littlejohn called it 'a sleazy, dishonest administration led by a political pygmy', and his paper's leader writer later delivered a similar verdict. The *Guardian* showed sympathy for the victims, observing that the tabloids were now too powerful for errant ministers to survive exposure of their private lives. Broadsheets were accused of being hypocritical by tabloid editors for recycling the revelations, but it was impossible for serious papers not to report the effects of such stories. They had to explain why ministers had resigned. They were also able to point to the fact that they were engaged in exposing altogether more grave matters of genuine public interest.

For example, the *Sunday Times* exposed Tory MPs for taking money to ask parliamentary questions. An Insight reporter, posing as a businessman, offered ten MPs of each of the main parties £1,000 to ask a question. Two Tories, Graham Riddick and David Tredinnick, both of them very junior members of the government, accepted the deal. Riddick had second thoughts and returned his cheque; Tredinnick said he was planning to give his to charity. When the story appeared in the *Sunday Times*, the pair complained they had been set up.[104] Both resigned their posts, but the fact that MPs chose to debate journalistic ethics rather than the conduct of their own members further sullied relations between press and government.

The controversy over that cash-for-questions scandal was minor compared to the series of revelations later in 1994 when the *Guardian* ran stories about two Tory MPs accepting cash from Harrods owner Mohammed Al Fayed to ask parliamentary questions on his behalf[105] (see above, pp. 583–4). The information Fayed gave to the *Guardian* also resulted in an accusation against Jonathan Aitken, then chief secretary to the Treasury, that a Saudi Arabian arms trader had paid for his stay at the Paris Ritz (see above, pp. 584–5).

Meanwhile, most papers had been asking searching questions about the share dealings of Lord Archer, former deputy Tory party chairman. By an odd coincidence, he had bought 50,000 shares in Anglia Television the day after his wife, one of the company's non-executive directors, had attended a board meeting at which a bid was discussed. When the bid was duly made four days later, boosting the price of Anglia stock, Archer sold his shares, making a profit of almost £80,000. Though he was cleared of any wrongdoing by a Department of Trade and Industry inquiry, it didn't stop him attracting opprobrium from newspapers.

The anti-Tory propaganda in papers which were the party's traditional allies had its anticipated effect. In May 1995, a Mori poll revealed that the largest drop in Tory support had occurred among readers of the *Daily Telegraph*, *Times* and *Financial Times*. There was also a noticeable peeling away of support among *Sun*, *Daily Mail* and *Daily Express* readers.[106] Given those results, it might seem strange that Major chose the following month to make the most dramatic gesture of his premiership by resigning as Tory leader and challenging his critics to oppose him. However, Major knew it wasn't the public who had the vote but a constituency of 329 Tory MPs voting in secret. Would they be as influenced by the headlines as *Telegraph* readers? His resignation was greeted with howls of derision from a press which had been undermining him for almost three years. The *Sunday Times* said baldly: 'Major is a loser and he must go.'[107] When the Welsh secretary John Redwood stood against Major, the *Daily Telegraph* referred to his 'courage' in competing with the prime minister.[108] But Redwood wasn't the papers' favoured replacement, with the *Times*, *Sun* and *Mail* among those hoping that Michael Portillo would come forward. That didn't stop the *Sun* from sticking the knife into Major with its headline, 'Redwood versus Deadwood'.[109]

Regardless of who was standing, the press of all political persuasions was overwhelmingly against the idea of Major being re-elected. In the run-up to the vote, the *Daily Mail* printed a front-page headline 'Time to Ditch the Captain' over a cartoon of the 'Toryanic' ship going down. After a litany of criticisms of Major the paper called on Tory MPs to deny him their votes so that a 'real' leadership battle could be fought between Michael Heseltine and Portillo.[110] The *Times* called for a new leader. The *Guardian*, the *Independent* and *Today* said Major's time was up. The *Daily Telegraph*, despite editor Max Hastings's misgivings, said it was 'time for a change of leadership' (see above, p. 592). The *Sun* was predictable: 'If John Major is the answer to the country's problems, then heaven knows what the question was.'[111] The Sunday titles took a similar line. Only the *Daily Express* and *Daily Star* gave Major full-hearted support.[112]

Major won with a large majority and the press never forgave him for it. The *Sun*, which Major called 'the house magazine of England-against-the-world' edited by 'an oddball and a bully with a streak of populist genius', went on attacking him.[113] Major's press champion, Lloyd, laid into the 'right-wing ideologues of the North London cocktail circuit high on champagne and zealotry' who had a fetish about Europe.[114]

After his victory, Major was reported to have said: 'We're going to get the millionaire press.'[115] The millionaire press had other ideas, and – more importantly – a glamorous alternative. As early as March 1993, *Sun* editor Kelvin MacKenzie was entertaining Labour's 'youthful rising stars' – Tony Blair, Gordon Brown and Mo Mowlam – at the Savoy.[116] Labour leader John Smith generally enjoyed a good press in the two years before May 1994, when he died of a heart attack. He left his party some 20 per cent ahead in the opinion polls and the press commentator Stephen Glover noted that, even before Smith's funeral, newspapers had 'fallen head over heels in love with Mr Blair'.[117] Blair was elected leader in July and immediately set about reforming his party's constitution and attitudes. He hired the former *Daily Mirror* political editor, Alastair Campbell, as his personal press officer, a choice which drew some praise.[118] Blair, Campbell and Peter Mandelson had noted how badly their previous leader, Neil Kinnock, had been treated by the press and were determined to ensure it didn't happen again. To that end, they set out to woo as many owners as possible. They found themselves knocking at an open door with Rupert Murdoch.

Within a month of Blair's election, Murdoch told Germany's *Der Spiegel* magazine that he 'could even imagine' supporting Blair.[119] What this quote showed – regardless of denials to the contrary – was that Murdoch understood the value of his support. Campbell knew it too, realising that there wasn't too high a price to pay for the *Sun*'s endorsement. So Blair, risking criticism from his own party for consorting with Murdoch, agreed to fly to Australia to address Murdoch's News Corporation conference. His trip upset the traditional Labour-supporting papers, such as the *Guardian* and the *Observer*, which asked: 'Does Blair need the Murdoch press *that* badly to win?'[120] Mirror group editors were angry too, having suffered so badly from Murdoch's price war. Blair's speech was considered controversial because he pledged to open up the media market. He did say he would ensure that no single company would enjoy excessive dominance, but it was feared he might be doing a deal which would relax cross-media ownership rules and give Murdoch the chance to increase his television holdings in Britain. In the following eighteen months, there were at least three more unpublicised meetings between Blair and Murdoch.

Murdoch wasn't Blair's only press suitor. In October 1995, the *Mail* group's owner Lord Rothermere and editor-in-chief Sir David English let it be known they were thinking of changing sides. English revealed that he had asked Rothermere whether it would be possible to visualise the *Mail* supporting Labour in the next election. His lordship evidently replied: 'It certainly would not be impossible.'[121] Columnist Paul Johnson, a fervent Thatcherite who wrote regularly for the *Mail*, *Standard* and *Spectator*, became a Blair convert.[122] The election was almost two years away but the press already knew who it did and didn't want.

PART ELEVEN: 1996–2003

21. IS IT DUMB TO CHASE READERS?

Nobody ever lost money underestimating the intelligence of the public.[1]

The newspaper price war exposed the underlying drama of declining British newspaper circulation. Sales statistics were not as they seemed. People were buying fewer papers than they had done at any time since the 1950s and distribution departments were forced to devise a variety of schemes to prevent their overall sales figures from plunging and thus threatening their advertising revenue.

Cutting cover prices was only one way in which owners stimulated people to read their papers. In order to compete and to maintain respectable circulation figures, owners also initiated a variety of covert ways of providing cheap papers to an audience with an apparently diminishing interest in buying full-price copies across the counter, or having them delivered, every day. Conrad Black's Telegraph group pioneered the use of cut-price subscription copies on a large scale, winning many thousands of subscribers after sending out vouchers by direct mail. Rupert Murdoch's *Times* and *Sunday Times* followed the initiative to a limited extent. The Guardian group, and later the Independent titles, widened their market by publishing and selling outside Britain. With the *Sunday Times* leading the way, most titles moved into the Irish market and also marketed more aggressively in Scotland.

None of these initiatives was as controversial, or – in their original form – as murky, as the use of multiple-selling, known as bulk sales. This involved the selling of thousands of copies at a fraction of their cover price to airlines, hotel chains, rail companies, fast-food outlets, betting shops and a host of leisure-event organisers so that they could be given away free to their customers and clients. When these schemes first started it was a nightmare for the official auditors of the Audit Bureau of Circulations (ABC). Could they trust the figures of publishers who claimed to have sold many quires of papers at a penny a copy to a betting shop chain? How could they be certain that bundles of papers at airports were really distributed to passengers? Was there any proof about the commercial deals between papers and these new bulk-buyers?

Rival groups accused each other of cheating, claiming that copies were being dumped in order to boost flagging sales figures. Advertisers were concerned and demanded clarity. The ABC council, composed of newspaper and magazine representatives along with media buyers, were pressured to clean up the system and, from January 1995, multiple sales were listed separately, the beginning of a process which led to the identification of all discounted and foreign sales. Rules were also drawn up to prevent the misuse of bulk sales and to provide greater transparency. But the smell of bad business practice tended to linger. At best, carefully targeted bulk-selling was used as a sampling exercise to attract people who had never read that particular title before. It was also true that some copies given out for free, on planes for example, were usually read from cover to cover and therefore justified their inclusion in circulation figures. But it was much more difficult to believe that copies stacked in a betting shop or at the counter of a roadside restaurant received much attention.

There was another problem with the promiscuous use of bulks: the stimulation of a belief among people that it wasn't necessary to pay for a newspaper. This phenomenon would be exacerbated with the launch of free daily morning newspapers and the growth of free weekly advertising papers (see below, p. 631). The need to maximise sales didn't only affect the methods of distribution. Sales figures, backed up by research, showed that fewer people were buying more than one title every day and that many were happy to buy papers only three or four days a week. Therefore, editors became acutely aware of the need to make their papers more comprehensive and to create specialist sections.

Perhaps the most controversial, and misunderstood, changes occurred among the daily broadsheets. Their key ingredients throughout the century had been news, analysis and comment. All gradually broadened their scope to incorporate features, but this trend accelerated during the early 1990s with every title using colourful front-page blurbs to sell material that would never have been previously published in what was regarded as the 'serious' or 'quality' press. Though this approach had long been the province of their Sunday stablemates, its adoption by the dailies was widely criticised. It was argued that broadsheets were copying tabloids and therefore 'dumbing down' in order to maximise sales. Among several sins, they were accused of abandoning their public service remit by reducing the space given to foreign news, cutting back on the coverage of parliament and increasing the numbers of columnists and commentators. Some critics, especially from the United States, scoffed at the use of big colour pictures, bold headlines and the alleged brevity of articles.[2] Others contended that the former impartiality in domestic news coverage had been compromised by heavily angled headlines and biased reporting, an accusation previously levelled only at tabloids.

Anthony Sampson, a modern historian and former *Observer* journalist, articulated the concerns of many commentators when he argued that 'in the last twenty years most people accept that there has been a fundamental change in broadsheet newspapers' away from 'consistent coverage of serious events towards short-term entertainment, speculation and gossip'. In his lengthy assault, he maintained that the media could no longer lay claim to provide the first draft of history and were guilty of presenting to readers a 'sense of a discontinuous, disconnected world'.[3] Sampson rightly conceded that journalists were prey to recalling a 'golden age of brilliant drunks and layabouts in Fleet Street pubs' because much of the knee-jerk criticism, especially from older journalists and politicians, tended to be informed by a misguided nostalgia about a non-existent golden age of journalism. But Sampson's substantive point was badly flawed too. Having closely read the broadsheets over a fifty-eight-year period I have reached the conclusion that they have always presented a 'sense of a discontinuous, disconnected world' which, viewed in retrospect, does approximate to a very rough first draft of history.

Sampson's analysis, and that of similar detractors, also overlooked the economic realities facing British (as distinct from foreign) newspapers: there were several titles competing with each other for an audience. To complicate matters, the audience also continually proved itself fickle. In a full-hearted response to those who accused papers of dumbing down, *Times* editor Peter Stothard claimed that broadsheets shared a determination 'to reach out to new constituencies of readers and reverse the decades of decline'. Papers had to be relevant to peoples' lives, had to appeal to casual readers and, therefore, had to broaden their coverage.[4] Stothard was supported by *Guardian* editor Alan Rusbridger.[5] They illustrated how increased pagination allowed them to devote more space to foreign stories than twenty years before. Extra pages of comment and analysis provided a larger platform for debates, allowing papers to offer a range of opinions about issues compared to the previous era when there was room only for a single point of view. Domestic news coverage was infinitely more comprehensive. Features content – whether about health, divorce, sex, relationships, pop music, parenthood, childhood, whatever – broadened a paper's scope.

Much more space was allocated to sport, providing room for writers to breathe and also permitting the coverage of minority-interest sports. Pages of listings offered readers a service they had never enjoyed before. Editors were delighted with their expanded papers and asked, not without irony, whether critics who were complaining so loudly about substantive differences were being unduly influenced by changes in style rather than substance. Indeed, broadsheet editors discovered that they could incorporate the tabloid agenda without unduly compromising their authority and their central mission to inform and explain. Overall, their circulations were to increase or, at least, remain static while the tabloids continued to decline. Red-top tabloids woke up to this problem far too late and found it impossible to cast off their vulgar past and win back lost credibility. It is truly ironic that Hugh Cudlipp had understood this trend in the middle 1960s when launching the

Sun and changing the *Daily Mirror*: he had simply been too far ahead of his time (see Chapter Seven).

One consistent complaint levelled by politicians was about the supposed failure of papers to report MPs' speeches in the Commons. There was a measure of truth to this charge, but it failed to take account of the changed political environment. Parliamentary debating was less important because of the evolution of a presidential style of government and because the Commons worked differently, with MPs spending more time in committees. The broadcasting of parliament, which began at the end of 1989, also eroded interest in old-style gallery coverage. Again, memory played tricks. Lengthy parliamentary reports in the past were often wildly over-written, repetitive and, for the modern reader, far too formal and pompous.

The dumbing-down debate was also underpinned by snobbery. Many critics harked back to a time when broadsheets sold only to an elite of which they were part. They were ignoring the demographic, sociological and cultural changes wrought as a result of growing affluence and greater educational attainments. These had made a nonsense of society's former divisions in which broadsheets had served a relatively small, serious elite while the tabloids sold to the unserious masses. This split, which had long been debatable, was certainly not relevant by this time. The notion that there were serious people who wanted to read only serious news was untenable. A rounded human being of the 1990s could appreciate reading about domestic political in-fighting, developments in rock music, the state of British football and the problem of Third World debt. Nor was it fair to assume that the so-called masses, now benefiting from tertiary education and then earning their living from intellectual rather than manual work, formed an homogeneous market. We were on our way to becoming, as prime minister Tony Blair declared, a more inclusive society.

Perhaps the most visible difference between the papers of the past and those of the 1990s was the proliferation of columnists. Both broadsheets and tabloids published scores of writers every day, usually offering their opinions on the news. Gradually editors and writers became more innovative, pushing the column genre into new areas. The most famous was Bridget Jones's Diary, written by Helen Fielding in the *Independent*. Personal or domestic columns – pejoratively called 'me' columns – also became common, especially in supplements and magazines. It was John Diamond in the *Times* who elevated this form above its typically trite introspection by charting the progress of his terminal cancer.[6]

There was another profoundly important element affecting newspaper readership: the liberation of women from the constricting housebound roles of wife and mother. In the post-war years it had been assumed that men – the so-called heads of the household – decided which paper to buy, though tabloids, such as Cudlipp's *Daily Mirror*, the Lamb *Sun* and the English *Daily Mail*, went out of their way to appeal to women. By contrast, broadsheets tended to speak mostly to men. With the exception of the *Guardian*, serious papers were noticeably slower than the populars in providing material specifically aimed at women. Every paper had a token women's editor (often a grand title for fashion editor) but there was very little space for female-oriented features. As we have seen (Chapter Fourteen), men dominated the newspaper hierarchies, ensuring that a male news agenda was paramount.

With the growing independence and affluence of women, it was obvious they now chose which papers they read rather than accepting the title chosen for them by husbands or partners. There was, incidentally, a great deal of truth in the sarcastic observation by the *Sunday Times* columnist India Knight that the phrase 'dumbing down' was 'increasingly and disdainfully used to mean "stuff that women might like"'.[7] Why should a woman's choice of editorial content be of less intellectual value than a man's? Why should it be less relevant for women to read about relationships than for men to read about a football match?

The rise of Middle England's champion

No paper was better placed to take sales advantage of the increase in female newspaper-buyers, the blurring of class divisions and the unashamed growth of free-market individualism than the *Daily Mail*. It had spent years honing its philosophy of an embattled middle-class Middle England pulling up its drawbridge to protect itself from the ravages of a modern multi-cultural, politically correct and morally relativist society. For years, while it remained in a lengthy circulation trough, the only people who appreciated the cleverness of the *Mail*'s approach were other journalists.

It had long been assumed that the *Mail*'s problem was being stuck in the middle, squeezed between the broadsheets above and the red-tops below. In fact, from 1996 onwards, the middle was the place to be. Census returns showed that Britain's social-class pattern had changed, with the so-called upper categories, ABC1, becoming more numerous than the C2DEs: the working-class were no longer 'the masses'. The *Mail* was perfectly positioned to appeal to those people who were unwilling to graduate to the broadsheets and yet could no longer stomach the red-tops. It was a fascinating paper, full of contradictions which excited conflicting passions. Praised by many journalists for its technical proficiency, it also disgusted just as many who considered it hypocritical, pretending to be better than other tabloids while employing many of their methods. Despised for its right-wing political stance, it was self-confident enough to attack the Conservative party. Admired by hundreds of thousands of women for its female editorial content, many other women were disgusted by its anti-feminist agenda.

The first major coup for editor Paul Dacre was in winning over the vast majority of *Today*'s audience after its closure in November 1995. Two months later, for the first time since 1980, the *Mail* zoomed past 2 million sales and went right on climbing month by month. It celebrated its 100th anniversary in May 1996 in a mood of jubilation. It was now 800,000 ahead of its old rival, the *Daily Express*, with its sights set on overtaking the *Daily Mirror*. Dacre showed his journalistic bravery, and a loathing for racism, with a famous front page accusing five men of killing black teenager Stephen Lawrence under the headline, 'MURDERERS'.[8] He saw it as a failure of British justice and campaigned for months while shrugging aside complaints that he was conducting a 'trial by tabloid'.[9] Criticism a couple of years later, that the *Mail* was guilty of racism for publishing so many articles attacking the arrival of asylum seekers, carried more weight.[10]

Dacre's sales and editorial success enabled him to withstand internal political pressure during the 1997 election which saw Tony Blair's New Labour sweep John Major's beleaguered Tory administration from power. The *Mail*'s owner, Lord Rothermere, clearly favoured Labour, as did Sir David English, the Associated chairman and editor-in-chief. Dacre, though no supporter of Major, was more sceptical about Blair. The difference of opinion emerged in public when Rothermere gave a radio interview after taking his seat on the Labour benches in the Lords. He said that he and Dacre 'don't agree on many things . . . He is a great editor and therefore he is entitled to his views in the paper, but if they start to affect the circulation, that will be different.'[11] Sales, it would appear, were more important than propaganda for Rothermere at that point.

In June 1998, English – who had always appeared to be in robust health – died of a heart attack, aged sixty-seven. The *Mail* ran five pages under the slogan 'The making of a legend', with friends and rivals contributing heartfelt eulogies.[12] A profoundly sad Rothermere resumed the chairmanship of Associated and made his son, Jonathan Harmsworth, his deputy. A couple of months later he criticised Dacre once again in public, suggesting that the *Mail* had gone down-market – with salacious 'tabloidy reporting' – in its attempts to generate sales.[13] Three weeks later seventy-three-year-old Rothermere died, like his friend English, of a heart attack. In a family business the succession was straightforward: Jonathan, aged thirty, became the fourth Lord Rothermere and chairman of Associated Newspapers. There was a brief flurry in rival papers about alleged City concern at the old-fashioned nature of dynastic ownership but the Harmsworth family owned 80 per cent of the voting shares in the holding company and was unassailable.

The new press lord had been educated at Gordonstoun and Duke University in North Carolina. His father had been determined that he should learn the business from the ground up and his first job in 1993 was as a trainee reporter on Mirror group's Glasgow-based *Sunday Mail*, knocking on doors in some of the city's roughest areas. His progress was overseen by the kindly and wise managing director, Murdoch MacLennan. After a brief period on the *International Herald Tribune* in Paris and three years on the *Kent Courier* in Tunbridge Wells as a senior manager, he became managing director of Associated's *Evening Standard*. A colleague remarked: 'Jonathan is very good at making people underestimate him.'[14] Affable, unassuming and not in the least grand, he wisely rested on the experienced triumvirate who ran the company: Dacre, raised up to editor-in-chief after English's death, the chief executive Charles Sinclair, and his first journalistic mentor, Murdoch MacLennan, who was now Associated's managing director.

There was much for the new Rothermere to appreciate about his inheritance. In October 1998, the *Daily Mail* overtook the *Daily Mirror*'s circulation, making it the second-highest-selling daily. In February 1999, the Daily Mail & General Trust (DMGT) became one of Britain's top 100 companies. It also fell to him to approve one of Associated's riskiest newspaper ventures: the launch of a free paper, the *Metro*, to be given away at London train stations every morning.

A Swedish newspaper group had enjoyed success with free papers in various European capitals and was known to be planning to repeat the exercise in Britain. News International looked at the idea but rejected it as too costly and left the field open to Associated. After it had agreed a deal with London Underground for exclusive use of its stations, *Metro* was launched in March 1999 and two months later some 300,000 *Metros* were being given away in London. It was common to see scores of copies being read on Tube trains. This rattled *Evening Standard* editor Max Hastings, who expressed mixed feelings about his own company putting a rival in the field.[15] *Metro* extended to other cities later in the year, though there was spirited resistance from the owners of regional companies defending their territory, such as the Guardian Media Group in Manchester and Trinity-Mirror in Newcastle. Wars ended with partnership agreements and by the beginning of 2002 *Metro* was being given away in eight cities with a total circulation of 900,000, making it the fifth-largest national title. *Metro* was slow to make money and initially ate into profits. Associated, with its variety of profitable businesses including regional papers, the two Mail titles and the *Evening Standard*, could afford to wait, and by 2002 it was in the black.

Dacre didn't wait long after the deaths of English and Rothermere to dispense with the services of *Mail on Sunday* editor Jonathan Holborow. His paper's sales had risen for six years but there had been embarrassing mistakes. The most recent was a false claim that actress Brooke Shields had been arrested on a drugs charge. Holborow's humbling personal apology took up almost half a front page and Associated was required to pay £100,000 to charity. The *Mail on Sunday* had also wrongly accused a member of Sinn Fein of having an affair with an American peace negotiator and wrongly claimed that Prince William used a royal aide to vet girlfriends. In 1994, the *MoS* was censured for breaching the code of practice when a reporter used subterfuge to enter Germaine Greer's house.

Holborow was fired while he was on holiday in September 1998 and replaced by Peter Wright, deputy to Dacre and his close friend. Wright, forty-five, educated at Marlborough College and Cambridge, had worked on the *Daily Mail* since 1979 after three years on an evening paper in Hemel Hempstead. He had worked his way up the career ladder at the paper, always just a rung or so below Dacre, becoming his deputy in 1995. He was inculcated with the *Mail* work ethic, combining an attention to detail with a broad grasp of his paper. His revamp six months after taking over was rather conventional: when the magazine Night & Day was turned into a glossy it lost its previous unique approach. He was caught up in controversy too, running a story about the schooling of the prime minister's daughter which was adjudged by the Press Complaints Commission to be in breach of the editors' code. But Wright would never give Dacre the kind of headaches he might have had if Holborow had stayed.

It was wrongly imagined that Dacre would also swiftly remove Max Hastings from the editorship of the *Evening Standard*, given that its sale was anything but healthy. Instead, he kept him in place for almost four years. Hastings had had his problems, apologising to Labour deputy leader John Prescott for doctoring a picture which made it look as though he had been drinking champagne rather than beer. In January 1997, he was hauled before a judge to explain why the *Standard* had published a two-page feature about Belmarsh prison which broke a court order by mentioning the criminal histories of IRA men. It led to their trial, for an escape attempt, being abandoned. The *Standard* was fined £40,000 for contempt of court.[16] The paper advised readers to vote Labour in 1997 but Hastings, well known for his love of country pursuits, said he would not do so himself because he couldn't support a party that wanted to ban fox-hunting. A man of stern principle, Hastings also took a defiant stand against the Tory party's nominee for London mayor, Lord Archer. At one point Archer accused Hastings of running a 'vicious, personal vendetta'.[17] But Hastings was to be vindicated in the most spectacular fashion (see below, p. 653).

He eventually departed in January 2002 to be replaced by Veronica Wadley, his former *Telegraph* deputy editor. Wadley, forty-nine, an ex-debutante schooled at Benenden, started as a junior at Condé Nast magazines. She learned fast. At twenty-two, she launched a magazine in South Africa. Back in Britain in 1978, she joined the *Telegraph* magazine, moving to the *Mail on Sunday* in 1981. She spent five years there before joining Hastings at the *Telegraph*. When Hastings left to edit the *Standard*, she joined the *Daily Mail* as head of features, later becoming Dacre's joint deputy editor. Wadley has her work cut out if she is to staunch the *Standard*'s circulation loss.

The rise of the Mail group was in stark contrast to the continuous crisis at its old adversary, Express Newspapers. Throughout the 1990s, as managing director Andy Cameron admitted, the company was simply managing its titles' decline.[18] Towards the end of 1995, the *Express* owner, United News, was so obviously for sale that denials by its chairman, Lord Stevens, were ignored.[19] There was speculation about a variety of suitors but no one got a whisper about the winner, who had been talking to Stevens in secret for six months, Lord Hollick's media and financial services company MAI. Both men referred to the deal as a merger, with Stevens remaining as chairman and Hollick assuming the chief executive role.

For all sorts of reasons this was a bizarre and controversial deal. Firstly, it bust open the cross-media ownership rules because MAI owned two ITV companies and was therefore barred from buying national newspapers. To overcome the problem Hollick 'warehoused' the Express titles, meaning that neither of the merged companies had voting control over them but would be able to derive the full 'economic interest' from them. It was, said one government minister, 'an inherently unsatisfactory way of getting round the spirit of the law by relying on the letter'.[20] Secondly, the merger wasn't really about the *Express*. It just happened to be part of a larger company which wanted to protect itself from a hostile bid and therefore merged with another company which wished to do the same. By forming a £3 billion conglomerate they made their new joint company, called United News & Media, too large a prey for a predator. Hollick also saw it as a necessary stage to achieve his ultimate ambition to control if not the whole ITV network then a substantial slice of it. In other words, the once proud Beaverbrook empire had become a pawn in a larger game.

Thirdly, Lord Stevens of Ludgate and Lord Hollick of Notting Hill were truly an odd couple to form a press-owning partnership.[21] Stevens was a Conservative; Hollick had been a member of the Labour party since he was fifteen. Under Stevens, the two *Expresses* and the *Daily Star* had been fervent Tory supporters. Could Hollick stomach that true-blue allegiance while exercising daily control over them, especially with a general election on the horizon?

Clive Hollick, then fifty, was highly regarded for his business acumen, and his Labour sensitivities had not inhibited him from making ruthless decisions on occasion. After Southampton Grammar School and Nottingham University, he learned his financial trade at Hambros merchant bank, becoming its youngest director at twenty-eight. By the following year he was running his own company after putting forward a plan to rescue a failed fringe bank, Vavasseur. He used the initials of one if its subsidiaries, the Mills & Allen International poster site group, as the name for his reformed company. He expanded MAI into financial services, building it into one of Britain's top 100 companies. Then he branched out into television with Meridian and Anglia. He also helped to found a left-leaning think-tank, the Institute for Public Policy Research, a service to the Labour party which led to its leader Neil Kinnock nominating him for a peerage in 1991. Hollick, however, preferred people not to use his title. He attracted a hostile press just before the 1992 election when it was revealed that he had paid members of his senior staff in gold bars in Jersey to avoid tax.

Directly after the merger announcement Hollick said it wouldn't make commercial sense for the *Express*es to become Labour papers. 'I'm a professional businessman, not a newspaper proprietor. I'm not looking to wield illusory power.'[22] Then again, there wasn't much profit in owning Express Newspapers, which made £18 million in 1995, a 42 per cent drop on the previous year. The division formed a tiny fraction of the main company, but media narcissism ensured that its fate would attract far greater publicity than any of Hollick's other businesses.

It was soon obvious that, despite the talk of merger and the continuing presence of Stevens, Hollick was in charge. He ordered Stevens's bust to be removed from the front hall of Ludgate House, fired Stevens's senior executive Andy Cameron and appointed Stephen Grabiner, managing director of the Telegraph group, as executive director.[23] For the editors of the *Daily* and *Sunday Express*, Richard Addis and Sue Douglas, the situation was tricky. They had been in their jobs for less than a month when they found themselves with a boss they had never met. Worse, they now had two lordly bosses.

Before Hollick's arrival Addis had made sweeping changes to the daily title with new columnists, a celebrity-led letters page and the exhumation, yet again, of the William Hickey column. In a rapid revamp, he made the paper appear more like the *Daily Mail* but picked up no readers from *Today*'s closure and watched his sales dive due to the imposition of a January price rise without effective promotional support. Both Addis and Douglas soon became aware of the difficulty of working under two men with opposing political views. Addis had been appointed by Stevens on the understanding that he would support John Major and the Conservative party. A wettish sort of Tory himself, he was happy to agree. But Addis told me of cases in which a leading article would draw criticism from each of them: Stevens would call to say it was not Tory enough; Hollick would call to argue that it was too pro-Tory.[24]

It was a political story that won Douglas notoriety when she headlined a remark made privately by prime minister John Major about other European leaders, 'A Bunch of Shits'.[25] Newsagents reported protests from shoppers and the majority of calls to the paper were hostile. Significantly, it was Lord Stevens she called before publishing, winning his support.[26] Douglas was to lose her job for an entirely different reason. In August 1996, Hollick decided to merge the *Daily* and *Sunday Express* in a seven-day operation, an initiative which had failed elsewhere. His move was based on financial expediency rather than editorial efficiency. It would enable a 15 per cent cut in the £45 million editorial budget, losing 85 of 480 jobs.[27] Hollick chose Addis as editor-in-chief and expected Douglas to work under him. She found this unacceptable and discovered she had lost her job by mobile phone while on holiday on a remote Scottish island. She had edited just thirty-three issues.

Two months later came a wholly irrelevant decision to rename the *Daily Express* the *Express*, and the *Sunday Express* the *Express on Sunday*. No wonder the *Mail on Sunday*'s editor, Stewart Steven, wrote of the *Express* controllers: 'Neither ... know anything about newspapers. The result is catastrophic ... Lord Stevens made mistake after mistake ... Lord Hollick, by his recent actions, is compounding them.'[28] Felicity Green, the vastly experienced newspaper executive, agreed. She was working at the *Express* as a consultant and witnessed the problems caused by the seven-day decree. Addis was overwhelmed, she said. Like many others she thought Hollick listened more to his accountants than to his journalists.[29]

Hollick was also keen to stamp his political imprint on papers which had been traditionally Tory, but, as part of his merger agreement with Stevens, it was Stevens who called the political tune. Simon Walters, deputy editor of the *Express on Sunday*, contended that 'one of first things' Hollick did after taking over the *Express* 'was to ditch its slavish pro-Tory line'.[30] In fact, it took him a while to bring it off, as the 1997 election endorsement for the Tories proved. The *Daily Star*, which had been hysterically anti-Labour in the three previous elections, backed Tony Blair but Stevens wouldn't countenance the *Daily Express* doing the same. The eve-of-election leader just about plumped for Major, and Addis received two phone calls. Stevens rang to complain that it wasn't enthusiastic enough. Hollick called in what Addis described as 'a rage' to say he wasn't prepared to support a Tory government and threatened to issue a press release dissociating himself from the editorial. Addis advised him to speak to Stevens. Both calls to Addis were witnessed by one of his staff, Jasper Gerrard.[31]

Addis believed that Hollick never came to terms with losing that battle and that both his and Stevens's days were numbered from that point. If so, Hollick had to wait a long time to eject Stevens, who didn't retire until July 1999. Addis was more vulnerable, however, despite his paper's support for Blair after the election. But we must leave the extraordinary *Express* story for a while to divert to another drama whose story crosses paths with that of the *Express*.

The *Independent* dreamers dream on

The air of gloom at Express Newspapers was mirrored by the sagging morale at the Independent titles. The joint owners, Mirror group and Tony O'Reilly's Irish Independent Newspapers, stumped up a further £23 million in April 1996 after a round of staff cuts the month before.[32] They also appointed a new editor to the *Independent* after several months of Charlie Wilson's caretaker administration. To few people's surprise, Andrew Marr, the paper's associate editor and political columnist, was elevated to the chair.

Marr, thirty-six, was the brightest star on the paper, an intellectual with a populist streak and an offbeat sense of humour. After Dundee High School, Cambridge and three years as a trainee he joined the parliamentary staff of the *Scotsman*. He was on the political team of the *Independent* from its launch until 1988, returning briefly to the *Scotsman* as political editor before a three-year spell on the *Economist*. From 1992, he was the *Independent*'s chief political commentator, winning a couple of awards. He impressed O'Reilly's camp but Mirror group's chief executive David Montgomery wasn't happy with him from the start. There was no political interference, as Marr ecstatically wrote when celebrating the paper's tenth anniversary: the *Independent* editor 'remains that rare and happy soul – a journalist without a proprietor whispering political demands in his ear'.[33] That didn't mean that there wasn't management criticism of his choice of content, which Montgomery largely disliked, along with incessant demands about the need to cut budgets.

Nor did Monty have much time for the *Independent on Sunday*'s editor Peter Wilby, who had won considerable publicity for his republican campaign. Monty thought the paper too serious and too mainstream, and demanded more lifestyle features, pressure which Wilby resisted. His eighteen-month editorship came to an end in October 1996. Monty then named Rosie Boycott as editor of the *Sindy*, the first woman editor of a broadsheet since Rachel Beer at the end of the nineteenth century. Again, there was a split: Monty, who had recruited Boycott, favoured her much more than O'Reilly did. Here was a woman who had spent her forty-five years living at full pelt, most of it in defiance of her middle-class background. She attended Cheltenham Ladies College and Kent University, co-founded the feminist magazine *Spare Rib*, and went travelling to the Far East, briefly landing in jail in Thailand. She was a liberal user of drugs, soft and hard, and an alcoholic. On her return to Britain in 1971 she became deputy editor of *Honey* magazine and, after a lengthy spell in a drying-out clinic, she wrote a candid account of her adventures.[34] She worked briefly for the *Daily Mail* and *Sunday Telegraph* before returning to magazine journalism, first at *Harpers & Queen*, and then at *Esquire*, which she edited with distinction, doubling its sale and winning magazine editor of the year awards two years running.

Boycott was an interesting choice for the *Sindy* and won a great deal of publicity by launching a campaign for the legalisation of cannabis, which earned her the unwanted nickname 'Rizla Rosie', though she stressed that she was no longer a user herself. She designed a five-section *Sindy* and a new Review, but one commentator thought it remained an insubstantial paper.[35] Marr also revamped the *Independent*, going for broke with a challenge to journalistic convention by largely ignoring the daily news agenda. He ran analytical essays or pieces of inspired writing as splashes, often illustrated with striking pictures or cartoons. It was a stimulating experiment but too quirky and too unpredictable to engage readers and failed to halt the decline, which was unsurprising since it was accompanied by a cover-price rise. Marr was also disappointed with the failure to spend more on an otherwise good promotional campaign which used the slogan 'It's changed. Have you?'

Montgomery was openly hostile to Marr's unconventional approach while O'Reilly, at least initially, was warmer. Despite denials to the contrary, the split between the owners was widening. After a loss of £15 million in 1995 came one of £20 million the following year, and Monty demanded a £4 million cut in the editorial budget. O'Reilly, keen to run his own ship, made a £60 million bid to buy out Mirror group at the end of 1997, which was rejected.[36] In a desperate bid to cut costs O'Reilly and Montgomery agreed to merge the two *Independent* titles into a seven-day operation. They also agreed that Boycott, rather than Marr, should become overall editor. Marr refused to work under Boycott, claiming that she 'had mingled her blood with Monty's', and was ordered not to return to the Canary Wharf office.[37] With readers turning their backs on both papers, which were losing some £500,000 a month, the relationship between O'Reilly and Montgomery became fraught and in March 1998 Monty sold Mirror group's 46.4 per cent stake to O'Reilly for £30 million, but with a five-year printing and distribution contract. O'Reilly also bought out all the smaller shareholders, including the founder Andreas Whittam Smith.[38] Monty attributed the papers' failure to Murdoch's price war and to 'poor editorial appointments . . . because of divided ownership'.[39]

It had been a long road to total ownership for O'Reilly, who formally retired from his executive role at Heinz in April 1998. He had now become a global media player on a grand scale with papers in South Africa, Australia and New Zealand as well as his Irish home base. He was also preparing for dynastic succession, with three of his sons working in senior positions. Unlike most newspaper owners in Britain he received a generally positive press, though he wasn't without his critics, especially in Ireland.[40]

But the real question about his *Independent* takeover is whether he had achieved his ambition too late to turn the papers around. He pledged to invest £50 million over five years and then, in a bizarre twist, he lured Marr back to work in harness with Boycott. Marr would be editor-in-chief and oversee the opinion pages of both titles while she, the editor, dealt with the rest.[41] This so-called 'dream team' nonsense lasted less than seven weeks as Boycott and Marr worked to different agendas. Boycott realised that she didn't have O'Reilly's confidence, complained that she hadn't been given promised investment and quit in April to become editor of the two *Express*es.[42] Marr left a week later to write columns and later became a household name as the BBC's political editor.

O'Reilly selected his next *Independent* editor-in-chief with care and made an excellent choice in Simon Kelner, an intelligent, down-to-earth journalist with a wide range of editing experience. Kelner, forty, understood the

Independent ethos, having been a member of the original launch team. After Bury Grammar School and a traineeship at a South Wales weekly, he specialised in sport at a Kent evening paper and the *Observer*, becoming the *Independent*'s deputy sports editor for two years. He was sports editor at the ill-fated *Sunday Correspondent* and the *Observer*, where he switched to running the magazine in 1991. He was sports editor of the *Independent on Sunday* for a couple of years, moving on to run its features department and the news operation. For two years from 1996 he won accolades for his editing of the *Mail on Sunday*'s Night & Day magazine, impressing Sir David English with his flair as he had done other hard-to-please veterans, such as Charlie Wilson.

Kelner hired the *Sunday Telegraph*'s able deputy editor Kim Fletcher to edit the *Independent on Sunday* and they both set about producing sensible papers while planning for redesigns. Kelner also maintained the *Independent*'s anti-establishment editorial agenda by opposing the war in Kosovo. When Kelner's relaunch came in June 1998 – the seventh revamp by the sixth editor in seven years – it was a clear attempt to return the paper to its original look and reintroduce an orthodox approach. He managed to achieve a sales plateau but couldn't attract new readers, despite hiring some high-profile columnists, and relied on judicious price-cutting initiatives at the end of the year to increase his sale only slightly.

Kelner was dissatisfied with the *Sindy*'s performance and sent his executive editor, Tristan Davies, to 'assist' Kim Fletcher at the beginning of 1999. He remained unhappy and dismissed Fletcher in June, naming a replacement that made most journalists' eyes pop: Janet Street-Porter. A *Guardian* writer called it 'a frivolous appointment' while the *Daily Telegraph* thought it 'bizarre' and carried a damning leader headlined, 'Send in the clowns'.[43] Fletcher's deputy, Rebecca Nicolson, walked out, explaining that there had been 'no moral support' for the paper's editorial stance and 'little promotional support'.[44]

Most criticism of Street-Porter was dog-eat-dog stuff, of course, but it was a measure of Fleet Street's amazement. She had the highest public profile of any editor appointed throughout these fifty-eight years, but it wasn't one likely to appeal to a sober, middle-class broadsheet audience. She was a self-obsessed, publicity-seeking iconoclast who tended to annoy rather than engage, and there were question marks over her limited journalistic background. Aged fifty-three, she had started as an editorial assistant at a magazine after Putney Grammar School and a brief period studying architecture. In 1969, she joined the *Daily Mail* and wrote a banal 'youth' column. Her distinctive voice, a strangled estuarial whine through a portcullis of gleaming teeth, won her a job as a radio host and, later, as a presenter on a couple of TV magazine shows where she was unfairly cast, she thought, as a 'hideous cockney character'.[45] She went behind the camera to work as a producer and famously invented 'yoof TV' at Channel 4 and the

BBC, where she built an empire until being eased aside in December 1993. She then created L!ve TV for Mirror group, with disastrous results (see above, p. 573).

After the *Sindy* appointment, she defended herself against 'snobbish and sexist abuse' by explaining what she hoped to achieve as editor: 'A multicultural society needs a polymorphous journal, and that is what we shall be.'[46] She also asked an interviewer: 'Do you think Tony O'Reilly, a multi-millionaire businessman, would appoint an editor who doesn't know what she's doing?'[47] The answer, I'm afraid, was yes. But the oddity was that her failure stemmed more from the fact that she was too conventional an editor rather than, as predicted, too outrageous. She waited seven months before delivering a redesign which was rather flat and included a magazine entitled Reality which was oddly sized and too unfocused in its content. One excellent hiring, however, was political columnist Steve Richards. Kelner and O'Reilly persevered with Street-Porter longer than expected, replacing her in May 2001 with Kelner's most trusted lieutenant, Tristan Davies, who carried out yet another redesign.

Kelner and Davies were recognised by other journalists for their skills, but they were unable to staunch the sales slides. Both *Independents* were disproportionately reliant on multiple sales to maintain any semblance of a reasonable circulation figure. Early in 2002, Kelner tried another relaunch which proved a conspicuous failure. It wasn't his fault: the *Independent* dream had died long before he took over and no one doubted that he had done his best.

Broadsheets resist the sales decline

The other broadsheets didn't face anything like the problems of the *Independent* titles. Though they were forced to top up their circulations with bulk sales and discounting, they performed much better than most of the tabloids. It was possible to determine from an analysis of the sales figures stretching back to the war that there had been not only a growth of broadsheet sales but a very gradual switch from tabloids to broadsheets.

The *Guardian* had a brand loyalty that the *Independent* could never match and was able to point to its continuing independence due to its ownership by the Scott Trust. Under Alan Rusbridger's editorship the paper prospered journalistically and financially. Rusbridger shared some of the reticent traits of his predecessor Peter Preston but he exercised firm control over all that mattered and had a strong strategic sense. David Walker, a journalist who joined in 1998, thought the office 'paradisiacal', having previously worked at the *Times* and the *Independent*.

Rusbridger's major headache was in assuming responsibility for the *Observer*, where he had to make hard decisions. By the beginning of 1996 the majority of the Scott Trust and most *Observer* staff had lost faith in editor Andrew Jaspan. He was out of his depth and was routinely described as 'hapless'.[48] There was no question of the *Observer* being sold, but Harrods owner Mohammed Al Fayed did make a bid in March 1996 which was bluntly rejected.[49] Within a week, Jaspan was fired and the man who had supported him, former *Guardian* editor and Scott Trust member Peter Preston, lost his role as editor-in-chief. Jaspan, believing he was the victim of a brutal putsch, claimed to have suffered from acrimonious squabbles with veteran staffers, recurring tensions with management and hostility from Rusbridger. He went on to write several articles and letters complaining about his dismissal.[50] Scott Trust chairman Hugo Young answered back at first but gave up when Jaspan refused to relent.[51]

The Scott Trust, with Young in the vanguard, chose Will Hutton to succeed Jaspan and gave Rusbridger the additional task of being the *Observer*'s executive editor. Hutton, described by Young as 'a brilliant journalist and a significant thinker', was the celebrated author of a surprise bestseller about Britain's economic problems, a polemic against monetarism which offered a blueprint for revival.[52] He had also been named political journalist of the year in 1993 for his coverage of the ERM crisis. Hutton, aged forty-five, attended Chislehurst Grammar and Bristol University before beginning a career as a stockbroker. He gave that up to work briefly for a satellite TV business channel and then spent ten years with the BBC on *Newsnight* and *The Money Programme*. He joined the *Guardian* in 1990 as economics editor, adding an assistant editor title to his name five years later. He had a formidable knowledge of politics and economics, but it was recognised that he required help in other areas where he had no experience. He was given two deputies, Paul Webster, the *Guardian*'s home news editor, and Jocelyn Targett, who was tempted away from his editorship of the *Mail on Sunday*'s magazine Night & Day. Formerly the *Guardian*'s arts editor, thirty-year-old Targett was seen as Rusbridger's protégé and a likely successor to Hutton.

Hutton followed the pattern which had been fashionable for several years whenever there was a change of editor: first, senior staff were fired in favour of new imports; second, a root-and-branch redesign was carried out. Hutton's revamp arrived six months after he took control but it achieved only a temporary halt to the downward sales slide which accelerated throughout 1997. By the spring of 1998, Hutton's paper was coming under consistent criticism from both inside and outside the Farringdon Road building where *Guardian* journalists were alarmed at its potential for ruining their own paper. With the *Observer*'s sales edging towards 400,000, many staff found themselves agreeing with critiques from an ex-editors' club, which included Donald Trelford, Jonathan Fenby and Peter Cole.[53]

Long before this point Hutton and his overly ambitious deputy, Jocelyn Targett, had fallen out. Hutton had once talked excitedly of the 'two-way flow' at his editorial meetings, but I attended one in which it was obvious that Targett had no respect for Hutton and was openly disloyal.[54] Though Hutton lost the confidence of his staff, there was little support either for Targett, who privately devised plans to create a sort of 'no news' newspaper which majored on lifestyle. It was ironic that while Rusbridger was given the backing of the Scott Trust to do something about the crisis Hutton's *Observer* scored its first major success with a news investigation, the so-called cash-for-access scandal.[55] Reporters discovered that lobbyists were taking money to introduce business people to ministers. Later that month, July 1998, Hutton gracefully, maybe even gratefully, moved aside in favour of the *Guardian*'s assistant editor, Roger Alton. Hutton retained his column and was, albeit briefly, editor-in-chief, while Targett was required to leave. He may once have been Rusbridger's favoured son but he had pushed his luck too far.

Alton, the fourth editor of the *Observer* in five years, seemed to be facing an impossible task. As Hugo Young admitted, the Scott Trust had made mistakes.[56] The month after Alton's arrival the sale fell to its lowest since 1949 and the situation looked hopeless, even to Alton. He was that rarest of senior executives, genuinely popular, with a way of getting the best from staff without resorting to verbal violence. Aged fifty, he was educated at Clifton College and Oxford. A graduate trainee on the *Observer* for a year in the mid-1960s, he spent four years as a reporter on the *Liverpool Daily Post* and then joined the *Guardian* in 1973. He worked his way up from the subbing desk through a variety of jobs: deputy sports editor, arts editor, magazine editor and features editor.

Alton steered a commonsense journalistic course in order to stop the rot, trying to make the paper more professional and winning more resources to provide added value. Three tabloid sections appeared at the beginning of 1999, and eighteen months later the launch of a glossy monthly magazine dedicated to sport made a huge impact, spawning another on food. By January 2000, the *Observer*'s renaissance was showing on the sales graph and circulation had improved well enough for Alton and Rusbridger to dream of taking the paper back over 500,000.

In news terms, the *Observer*'s greatest coup under Alton came with its scoop in January 2001 which revealed that government minister Peter Mandelson had helped a controversial Indian tycoon, Srichand Hinduja, to obtain British citizenship after he and his brother had agreed to donate £1 million to bail out the Millennium Dome.[57] The revelation led to Mandelson's resignation from government two days later, for the second time, and caused one of the biggest rows ever to engulf Tony Blair's administration.[58]

Before Alton went to the *Observer* he had played a major part in the *Guardian*'s modernisation by helping to forge its tabloid second section, G2, which became the template for the paper's rivals. Rusbridger was determined to ensure that the *Guardian* was seen as a mainstream rather than a niche paper without sacrificing its liberal agenda. To that end, he boosted both sports and business coverage. In partnership with advertising, he also oversaw the development of what were colloquially known as the G3 sections, the supplements for media, society and education, which attracted both advertisers and readers.

Arguably, Rusbridger's greatest journalistic moment came in October 1996 when the disgraced ex-Tory minister Neil Hamilton abandoned his £10 million libel action against the *Guardian*. A headline across the top of the paper's front page, 'A liar and a cheat', was generously called 'a classic of British journalism' by the *Times*'s press commentator.[59] It was one of the main reasons for Rusbridger being named editor of the year in 1996 and the editors' editor by the *Press Gazette* the following year. Rusbridger's potentially worst moment occurred in February 1996 when the IRA bombed Canary Wharf, causing irreparable damage to the *Guardian*'s nearby printing plant. After the explosion, *Telegraph* owner Conrad Black called Rusbridger with an offer to produce that night's *Guardian* on his West Ferry machines. Rusbridger was grateful, and the *Guardian*'s southern editions have been printed there ever since.

A run of healthy profits from 1998 enabled Rusbridger to innovate – creating extra sections such as the Editor and the pocket-sized listings magazine – and to invest in new media. The *Guardian*'s commitment to on-line journalism, pioneered by Ian Katz and Simon Waldman, was rewarded with a website which rivals acknowledged as the best of its kind. The *Guardian* also led the way in trying to make itself more accountable to its readers. It appointed one of its most experienced journalists, Ian Mayes, as readers' editor to deal with complaints about editorial content. He wrote a daily corrections and clarifications column which achieved a notable popularity.[60] As a practical example of journalistic freedom within the paper it was hard to beat the case of Guardian Media Group chairman Bob Gavron when it was revealed that he had given £500,000 to the Labour party a couple of months after learning that he was to be ennobled. In her *Guardian* column Polly Toynbee took him to task, arguing that he should have refused the honour.[61] He stepped down from his chairmanship six months later.

Unlike Rusbridger, *Times* editor Peter Stothard had great difficulty in convincing people that he was free from the demands of his owner, Rupert Murdoch. When Murdoch's publisher HarperCollins refused to publish a book by former Hong Kong governor Chris Patten which offended the Chinese government, it made headlines in most papers. The *Daily Telegraph*, like the rest, suggested that Murdoch was appeasing the Chinese in order to persuade them to accept his Star TV satellite system.[62] The story ran for a week without the *Times* carrying a word until a short piece appeared giving Murdoch's point of view.[63] Stothard, who conceded that he might have underplayed the Patten row, was immediately embroiled in another controversy when his paper's former East Asia editor, Jonathan Mirsky, claimed that the *Times* had not covered China 'in a serious way . . . because of Murdoch's interests'.[64] Stothard, who was no fan of Mirsky's journalistic skills, was incensed, claiming that coverage of China was 'wholly and solely in the hands of the editor'. He added: 'I have never taken an editorial decision to suit Mr Murdoch's interests, nor have I ever been asked to.'[65] Three years later Stothard was again forced to assert his autonomy after the *Times*'s former Middle East correspondent, Sam Kiley, claimed his reports were regularly censored by editors who lived 'in terror' of upsetting Murdoch. The paper followed a pro-Israeli line dictated by Murdoch.[66] Stothard dismissed the charge as 'a farrago of nonsense'.[67]

Stothard's honesty cannot be doubted but he found himself continually facing allegations about bias in his paper's coverage of any topic which touched on Murdoch's business interests. He might have been carrying out a normal journalistic job or making impartial editorial decisions, but his rivals were quick to spot Murdoch's agenda. For example, was the *Times*'s attack on Greg Dyke's suitability to be BBC director-general because of his £55,000 donation to the Labour party really untainted by the fact that Murdoch's BSkyB competed with the BBC?[68]

By far the most contentious episode of Stothard's editorship was the Ashcroft saga. In a series of articles in June 1999, the *Times* raised concerns about the huge contributions to the Tory party by its own treasurer, Michael Ashcroft, revealing that he was a US resident, with substantial business and political interests in Belize, owning its biggest bank. He was also Belize's representative to the United Nations.[69] The following month the *Times* took the story into a new area, suggesting that leaked Foreign Office memos raised suspicions about Ashcroft's integrity.[70] Then the paper received a long letter from Britain's former high commissioner in Belize which, among other things, detailed how Ashcroft had advised the Belize government how to regulate offshore financial services while himself being the owner of such offshore services.[71] Five days later, another *Times* story made allegations about Ashcroft being linked to money-laundering and drug-trafficking because he was named in America's Drugs Enforcement Administration files.[72] Ashcroft declared 'enough is enough' and issued a writ. Other papers turned on the *Times*, accusing it of 'attack journalism' or 'target journalism'.[73]

After sporadic warfare in the following months as a court case neared it was unexpectedly announced that Ashcroft and the *Times* had reached what amounted to a deal: the libel action had been dropped.[74] Murdoch had been involved in brokering the agreement, with Jeff Randall, editor of *Sunday Business*, playing a walk-on role. The *Times* published a front-page statement in which it made clear that it had no evidence of Ashcroft ever being involved in money-laundering or drug-related crimes. As the *Daily Mail* noted, the *Times* hadn't apologised.[75]

Neither Ashcroft or Stothard was adversely affected by the affair. The following year Ashcroft was ennobled as Lord Ashcroft of Belize. Stothard was accepted as a member of the Garrick Club and the *Times* was named by *What the Papers Say* as the newspaper of 1999. Its sales were still running at well over 700,000 and Stothard's future looked rosy. But in March 2000 he was forced to take leave of absence while undergoing debilitating treatment for a cancerous kidney tumour. His deputy of a mere eight weeks' standing, Ben Preston – the thirty-six-year-old son of The *Guardian*'s ex-editor, Peter – took control until Stothard was fit enough to return.

Stothard was just five months away from reaching his tenth anniversary as editor in 2002 when Murdoch announced that he was being replaced as *Times* editor by Robert Thomson, the US editor of the *Financial Times*. Thomson, a forty-year-old Australian who started out on a Melbourne paper at eighteen, had spent most of his career with the *FT*, learning Mandarin to work in China and Japanese to work in Tokyo. He had impressed his *FT* editor, Richard Lambert, while running, in succession, the foreign desk, the weekend edition and the New York office. Considered as a successor to Lambert, he was still consoling himself at not getting the job when Murdoch called. So what did he plan to do with the *Times*? He told me: 'There is – and Rupert perceived this before I did – a greater opening for what you might call a fact-based newspaper at the quality end of the market, a paper which is not at all ideological in its news pages and being as objective as any journalism can be objective.'[76] In other words, the paper of record that the *Times* of the pre-Murdoch era had always claimed to be.

Stothard, meanwhile, became editor of the *Times Literary Supplement* and assured everyone that he had previously agreed with Murdoch that he would move on after ten years. He wasn't at all unhappy that Murdoch had moved the goal post just a little forward. It wasn't clear if a similar deal had been agreed between Murdoch and *Sunday Times* editor John Witherow, who had begun his editorship in 1994. He maintained a much lower profile than almost every national paper editor, quietly adding sales month by month, reaching a regular average of 1.4 million by summer 2002.

There was some truth in the contention by one of its former executives that the *Sunday Times* became 'a mid-market package in broadsheet clothing'.[77] With its multi-section format, which included three magazines and a classified jobs supplement, it is unlikely that any reader got through the lot, but its comprehensive approach paid dividends. Witherow's decision to move the comment back into the main section was a big improvement, providing a heart to an otherwise often lifeless run of news pages. It remained a resolutely right-wing paper – giving Murdoch no reason to be overly critical – but its politics too often intruded into its news agenda. In March 1998, Labour's deputy leader, John Prescott, claimed that a *Sunday Times* reporter was acting as an *agent provocateur* in his Hull constituency party.[78] The following year I criticised the paper for setting out to rubbish ecological activists, anti-genetic engineering demonstrators and global capitalism protestors.[79]

It also had to apologise for a series of mistakes involving the royal family. It wrongly claimed that Prince Charles was buzzed by a helicopter piloted by the Earl of Suffolk.[80] It claimed the Queen would 'never' meet the Prince of Wales's mistress, Camilla Parker Bowles, but reported six months later that she had.[81] It then falsely alleged that the prince was 'exploring' the possibility of marrying Camilla in the Church of Scotland.[82] Eyebrows were raised by a payment of £65,000 to serialise a book by Jonathan Aitken after he was jailed for perjury. This appeared to break the editors' code which forbade giving money to people convicted of crimes, and the Press Complaints Commission – of which Witherow was a member – investigated. The PCC cleared the paper because money had gone not to Aitken, who was bankrupt, but to his creditors.[83]

The *Sunday Times*'s reputation survived these mishaps largely unscathed, partly because Witherow refused to be lured into the limelight. Charles Moore, the *Daily Telegraph* editor, took the opposite path, appearing on public platforms in Northern Ireland to support the Unionist cause and making regular TV and radio appearances to defend his paper's political viewpoints, such as opposition to the single European currency. He enjoyed attacking the rest of the press for its flawed ethics and campaigned fiercely against the supposed imperfections in the process of self-regulation. Moore tended to draw as much fire himself. The *Times*'s press commentator, Brian MacArthur, detected that reports on certain issues – Europe, Ulster and the House of Lords – were 'slanted to suit the editor's political line'.[84] The *Guardian*'s Hugo Young inveighed against the *Telegraph*'s 'conversion of journalism into propaganda'.[85] Former *Telegraph* editor Max Hastings joined the chorus of disapproval, saddened that having 'spent ten years trying to stop the *Telegraph* being the *Torygraph* . . . we are now back with the *Torygraph*'.[86]

These complaints were not so much about the pages of comment as about the selection of news stories and the heavily angled way in which they were written and headlined. Moore regarded this propagandist approach as a sign of his paper's passion. It stood for something and wore its heart on its sleeve. This approach was unlikely to upset his proprietor, Conrad Black, because he and Moore were of one mind on most major policy matters. They both disliked the idea of the euro. They both wanted the Tory party to return to its days of Thatcherite glory. They both loathed Bill Clinton's administration in the United States, applauding the victory of George W. Bush and extolling the virtues of his post-11 September policy. They also agreed about the need to offer full-hearted support to Israel.

Nor did Black think it necessary to keep his views to himself. He launched a stinging public attack in March 2001 against a columnist in his *Spectator* magazine for expressing what he called 'hatred for Israel' and uttering 'a blood libel on the Jewish people'. He widened his argument to lambast 'large sections of the British media which habitually apply a double standard when judging the Israelis and Palestinians'. Journalists were guilty, he claimed, of anti-Semitism.[87] This rebuke prompted four journalists – A. N. Wilson, Piers Paul Read, William Dalrymple and Charles Glass, all of whom had written in the past for Black's publications – to respond in kind. They complained that Black was abusing his proprietorial position by interfering in editorial policy and argued that there was no longer balanced reporting on the Israeli–Palestinian conflict.[88]

Black's determination to control his own papers' fate led him, through his holding company, Hollinger, to buy up the outstanding minority shares in the Telegraph group and thus return it into his private hands.[89] But his entrance into the price war, and his use of cut-price subscription sales, severely dented his profits. In January 1997, the *Daily Telegraph* achieved a sale of 1,142,094, its highest in six years and its sixth consecutive monthly improvement. But it had meant a sacrifice of millions of pounds, necessitating budget cuts, and sales trickled away after that. Following a decision to end its over-reliance on bulk sales in the autumn of 2002, it was selling 920,000 by the spring of 2003.

By that time Black had become a *bona fide* press lord. Baron Black of Crossharbour finally took his seat in the House of Lords, supported by his political heroine, Baroness Thatcher, in October 2001. It was the end of a tortuous route to the ermine he had previously denied wishing to wear. Asked in 1998 if he wanted a peerage, he had said: 'It is not an ambition of mine.'[90] That fitted with his previous statement that he didn't want to be 'another Commonwealth social climber rushing across the Atlantic with my coat tails trailing behind me in search of a peerage'.[91] When he changed his mind, after being nominated for the honour by Tory party leader William Hague in 1999, Canada's prime minister Jean Chretien invoked a rarely used ordinance that bars Canadians from receiving foreign titles. Black sued him for 'abuse of power', lost and was forced to renounce his Canadian citizenship to become a lord. Black seemed to be turning his back on his homeland. Having launched the *National Post* in Toronto in 1998 to compete with the *Globe & Mail*, he disposed of it in 2001, after losing many millions of Canadian dollars on the venture. He also sold the majority of his Canadian newspapers and many of his American titles, but he kept the *Chicago Sun-Times* and the *Jerusalem Post*.

Black had few complaints about the content of his *Sunday Telegraph* under editor Dominic Lawson. For a brief moment in the early autumn of 1997 it achieved a sale of more than 930,000 and looked as though it might soar above a million. It settled back down to a regular 800,000-plus for the next five years, with its quirky mixture of mainstream political coverage, offbeat news and features and readable right-wing commentators, such as deputy editor Matthew d'Ancona and the Irish polemicist Kevin Myers. Lawson, arguing that his column had run its 'natural lifespan', levered out seventy-three-year-old Sir Peregrine Worsthorne in 1997 after thirty-five years as a *Sunday Telegraph* columnist. He took infinite care with every bit of copy, persistently tweaking up until deadline. According to Worsthorne he combined tabloid values 'with up-market metropolitan sophistication', which, on reflection, was a rather clever combination.[92] Lawson was involved in a bizarre episode at the end of 1999 when two Labour MPs named him, under the cloak of parliamentary privilege, as a paid agent of MI6. It transpired that during his editorship of the *Spectator*, Lawson had run three articles under a pseudonym by a man who was said to be a member of the intelligence services. Lawson managed that most difficult of tricks, denying it strenuously while appearing amused.[93]

There was little to amuse staff at the *Financial Times* in 1996. Its owner, the Pearson conglomerate, demanded thirty redundancies from the journalistic total of 339 and, for the first time, some would be compulsory.[94] The journalists' chapel unanimously declared that they had no confidence in editor Richard Lambert and his deputy, Andrew Gowers, and rival City commentators gleefully pointed out that the *FT*, which lectured other companies on best business practice, was late in sorting out its own mess.[95] In the end, there was no strike, but morale was badly hit.

It seemed to count for little that the *FT* was now being printed in Hong Kong to serve the Asia–Pacific region, the seventh country outside Britain to publish copies of the pink paper.[96] *FT* journalists wondered whether they were paying for mistakes by Pearson, which was mid-way through a whirlwind of buying and selling. Questions were being asked about the wisdom of managing director Frank Barlow's purchase of software company Mindscape. Had he gone one acquisition too far? One sad disposal was of the sixty Westminster Press regional titles – such as the *Brighton Evening Argus*, *Bath Chronicle* and *Northern Echo* – which had been with the group since 1917. They were bought for £305 million by Newsquest, which already owned 120 titles and would later be swallowed by the giant US chain Gannett. Pearson moved into television, buying a stake in Channel 5, and increased its educational- and reference-book holdings while selling off interests such as Madame Tussaud's.

During this restructuring Barlow retired and Pearson surprised the City by appointing Marjorie Scardino as its chief executive, making her the first woman to head one of Britain's top 100 companies. The forty-nine-year-old American had made a success as chief executive of the *Economist*, the influential global-selling business magazine part-owned by Pearson. *FT* staff were pleased to hear she had a journalistic background, having been a reporter, and was married to a journalist. Together the couple had founded an award-winning paper, the *Georgia Gazette*. She started in January 1997 and proved to be a breath of fresh air, announcing a £100 million investment in the *FT* over five years to increase its international sale. This strategy was deemed so important that from July 1997 editor Richard Lambert decamped to New York to run the US edition while deputy Andrew Gowers took over in London. The *FT* then relaunched in the States, where it was heavily outgunned by the *Wall Street Journal* (*WSJ*), but its aim was to find a niche as a less insular paper. Gowers also gave the *FT* a new look with a more logical configuration. On Lambert's return a year later it was Gowers who carried the *FT* torch abroad, this time in Hamburg where the *FT* joined with Gruner & Jahr to produce a German edition, *Financial Times Deutschland*. Gowers found himself in an old-fashioned newspaper war when Germany's publishers formed an alliance with the *WSJ* to provide robust competition, but he survived and the paper sold reasonably well. The *WSJ* also revamped its European issues in order to compete with the *FT*, which had built up a significant sales lead in continental Europe.

Lambert retired from the *FT* in September 2001 and Gowers was promoted to editor, though there was strong competition from Lambert's protégé, the *FT*'s US editor, Robert Thomson. He had previously been responsible for revamping of the *FT*'s Saturday issue, which had grown in popularity. But Gowers had far superior experience. At forty-three, he was the youngest editor since Sir Gordon Newton and had spent eighteen years with the paper in a variety of posts since starting in the foreign department. Educated at Trinity School Croydon and Cambridge, he started out as a Reuters trainee 1980 before joining the *FT* in 1983. He saw the *FT*'s priority as expanding its foreign sales by imitating what he had achieved in Germany, launching editions in other languages.

Tabloids bid farewell to the Princess of Sales

By the mid-1990s, it was accepted that media coverage of the royal family had turned their often dysfunctional relationships into a real-life soap opera. Over the course of more than fifteen years, the lead actors in many hundreds of stories were Prince Charles and Princess Diana, the Duke and Duchess of York, Prince Edward (and later his wife, the Countess of Wessex) and Princess Michael of Kent, with a host of friends, casual acquaintances and cronies playing walk-on roles. It was the fragile marriage of Charles and Diana which received the most intense attention from tabloids, magazines and, not infrequently, the broadsheets.

Editors knew that they could increase sales by publishing any picture of the glamorous Diana or by running any story, good or bad, true or false, serious or trivial. She was a marketable commodity, a guaranteed circulation winner. She wasn't *a* celebrity, she was *the* celebrity, the most-recognised woman on the planet. Photographers followed her every move, with a growing band of freelancers, aware of the high value of almost any picture, willing to stalk her around the clock. Though she often showed signs of distress at the attention, with occasional flashes of temper at intrusions into her privacy, she eagerly colluded with journalists to publicise what she saw as her cause. During her marriage, editors defended their obsessive coverage by pointing out that she would one day become queen and what she did or said, or even thought, was a matter of legitimate public interest. Once the marriage broke down, they relied for a public interest defence on the fact that she was the mother of the boy standing second in line to the throne. There was little doubt that the public were interested, of course, as sales figures proved.

Newspapers, helped by judicious leaks from the princess and a variety of courtiers, police and servants, registered every nuance of the disintegrating marriage. After the revelation in 1987 that the couple had stayed in separate suites during an official visit to Portugal, scores of stories were published in the following five years which suggested that the couple spent almost no time together. Many of the tales were leaked by Diana to her favoured conduits, the royal correspondents of the *Daily Mail* and the *Daily Star*. Rivals, particularly at the *Daily Mirror* and the *Sun*, found good sources for exclusives too.

By 1991, with speculation about the state of the marriage having reached fever pitch, Diana took a decisive step: she made contact with Andrew Morton, the former *Daily Star* correspondent who was then freelancing. Keeping him at one remove, to provide later deniability, she tape-recorded her story and Morton put questions to her through an intermediary. The result was the explosive book by Morton, *Diana, Her True Story*, which, as we saw in Chapter Nineteen, caused such controversy when serialised by the *Sunday Times*.[97] The key claim was that Prince Charles had been involved in an adulterous relationship with his former girlfriend, Camilla Parker Bowles. In the following weeks and months, Charles's friends leaked his side of the story, painting Diana as a mentally ill, obsessive, immature hysteric. However true this might have been, it didn't shake the tabloid editors' favouritism towards Diana. They readily cast their Princess of Sales as the victim and Charles as the villain.

A series of negative stories, such as the *Sun*'s Squidgygate revelation of an intimate phone conversation between her and a friend, James Gilbey, didn't change the tabloid – or public – perception of her as a saint.[98] Nor did the *Sun*'s claim eight days later that Diana had had a relationship with James Hewitt. On 3 November 1992, every tabloid ran a front-page story about Diana and Charles being openly at war with each other. The Queen's press secretary, Michael Shea, referred to the tabloids as 'a cancer in the soft underbelly of the nation'.[99] But the couple's official separation was soon announced by prime minister John Major, and the *Daily Mail* sprang to defend the press, denying that the media had played any part in the marriage breakdown, declaring that papers, in exposing the truth of their unhappiness, had been vindicated.[100]

Throughout 1993 Diana evidently felt that she was losing the public relations war with her estranged husband.[101] This led her to announce her withdrawal from public life in December that year, unleashing another round of tabloid hand-wringing and accusations against Charles.[102] Six months later Charles admitted in a TV interview with Jonathan Dimbleby that he had been unfaithful after his marriage had irretrievably broken down. Much of the press reaction to the programme was untypically positive about the prince.[103]

Worried about subsequent signs of the papers turning on her, such as a *Sun* article calling her a Jekyll and Hyde character, she found it much more difficult to control her press image.[104] By this time she was being routinely hounded by photographers whenever she appeared in public, and editors seemed to delight in running unflattering pictures of her along with stories that suggested her halo had slipped.[105]

Diana then took a most reckless step by secretly recording a long interview with the BBC's *Panorama* in which she spoke of her husband's adultery and admitted her own infidelity with Hewitt.[106] She spoke of the damage the media had inflicted on her and of her fear that the public were being misled about her. The Queen had clearly had enough and instructed the couple to divorce. It said much about the penetration of the royal household's secrets that even this delicate matter was revealed exclusively by the *Sun* after the 'discovery' of certain letters.[107] Divorce in August 1996 made no difference to the relationship between Diana and the press: she remained the tabloids' first and last resort in cranking up sales, and competition for stories about her was, if anything, heightened. Tabloid editors argued that by giving the Panorama interview she had, in effect, intruded into her own privacy. *Daily Mirror* editor Piers Morgan was fond of saying that 'you can't dance with the devil and not expect to be pricked by the horns'.

The devil could prick himself too, as *Sun* editor Stuart Higgins soon found out. He was generally admired for his divorce scoop and for his subtle handling of Camilla Parker Bowles, whom he had befriended as a youthful district reporter, but his desire for Diana scoops led him to make the worst mistake of his career. Presented with a videotape purporting to show Princess Diana and James Hewitt making love, he ran several stills across five pages with the headline 'Di Spy Video: She's Filmed in Bra and Pants Romp with Hewitt'.[108] But the film's producer confessed the next day that it was a fake. Higgins was forced to make what the *Times* called a grovelling apology.

The unhappy princess was pursued by papers for months until, in July 1997, she accepted the hospitality of Harrods owner Mohammed Al Fayed to stay at his St Tropez house. Fayed's son, Dodi, joined the house party, and a friendship between him and Diana developed over the next couple of weeks until they were pictured together in early August on a yacht in the Mediterranean by an Italian paparazzo who had received a tip-off, probably from Diana. *Sunday Mirror* editor Bridget Rowe paid £300,000 for the set of pictures which she ran across ten pages. But when they were passed on to

Mirror editor Piers Morgan he was unhappy that the couple were not pictured kissing, so he had one grainy shot electronically manipulated to make it look as if they were, a deception which he cynically defended.[109]

For the next three weeks the tabloids carried pages about Diana and Dodi every day, digging up stories about Dodi's past and buying up former girlfriends. Meanwhile, the paparazzi chased the couple wherever they went. At the end of August they arrived in Paris and were shadowed around the city by photographers for two days. On the night they arrived for dinner at the Ritz, owned by Dodi's father, they were irritated by the attention and after their meal they agreed to be driven back to Dodi's apartment by the security chief, Henri Paul, rather than their chauffeur. Paul, who had consumed far too much alcohol to be driving, took off at high speed, followed by several photographers on motorbikes. The car crashed, killing Princess Diana, Dodi and Paul.

Initially, the paparazzi were blamed for causing the death of the woman dubbed by prime minister Tony Blair as 'the people's princess'. Her brother, Earl Spencer, said the tabloids had ruined her life and that the press 'had a direct hand' in the tragedy. Editors and proprietors had 'blood on their hands' after hounding the princess.[110] In the extraordinary national wake that followed, the tabloids reeled under an onslaught of public criticism, with renewed calls by MPs for privacy laws. A war broke out between the *Daily Mail* and *Daily Telegraph* after the *Mail* promised to ban paparazzi pictures. *Telegraph* editor Charles Moore denounced the pledge as gross hypocrisy because the *Mail* had been one of the most intrusive papers. Perhaps the public were hypocritical too: calls to boycott papers collapsed when it became obvious that people were buying many thousands of extra copies. Even in death, Diana remained Fleet Street's most potent sales weapon.

The Press Complaints Commission (PCC), responding to public disquiet, decided that Something Must Be Done, but wasn't certain what it should be. Tabloid editors were relieved to discover that the driver was drunk, seizing on the fact to protest their innocence. It wasn't wholly convincing proof since the only reason he drove at all was because photographers were milling around outside the Ritz. Then again, why did Diana – the most photographed woman in the world – want to avoid them? After all, she had colluded with journalists in the past and what was so awful about being pictured with her new friend?

Earl Spencer reiterated his disgust for the tabloid press during his sister's funeral oration, redoubling calls for action. Yet the PCC's chairman, Lord Wakeham, was one of several level heads who realised that there was no easy answer. It was extremely doubtful whether any law would have prevented the crash and, given that it had happened outside Britain, no domestic law would have made a difference. In the end, editors agreed that the minimum they could do was to protect Diana's sons from suffering intrusion during their years of education. There was a lengthy and sometimes bitter battle among editors at various PCC-organised meetings called to tighten the editors' code of practice.[111] As a result there were amendments to seven clauses, including the outlawing of 'persistent pursuit' by photographers, extra protection for children and a tightening of the definition of privacy. Broadsheet editors didn't feel the reforms went far enough in curbing tabloid misbehaviour. In one important respect, they were correct because pledges by various editors not to use paparazzi pictures were quickly forgotten. But it was also true that one of Wakeham's main aims, to protect Diana's sons, was achieved. The episode also helped to ensure that the code of practice would remain central to editors' thinking when publishing any story or picture.

The *News of the World* continued to sail close to the wind. A story about a nineteen-year-old daughter of a Tory MP working as a prostitute was hardly defensible.[112] I also took issue with the exposure of two Newcastle United directors who were tape-recorded boasting of sexual flings, mocking the club's fans, gloating over making money on football merchandise and exulting over the sale of a star player who had an injury. They were deceived by the *News of the World*'s senior investigative journalist, Mazher Mahmood, who dressed up as an Arab sheikh.[113] They were led to believe that he wanted to negotiate a business deal with them and later argued that they were telling him what they thought he wanted to hear. Forced to resign, they complained they had been the victims of an elaborate scam.[114] Mahmood's fake sheikh also caught out a TV actor who was encouraged to sell him drugs which landed him in prison.[115] In a later sting, with another reporter playing the sheikh, the Countess of Wessex was taped boasting of how her royal connections helped in her public relations business, raising questions anew about the relevance of subterfuge and the use of entrapment.[116]

Judges began to baulk at convicting people caught in *News of the World* stings. A BBC radio presenter who was filmed snorting cocaine was fined for possession but a charge of supplying the drug was dropped because of the *NoW*'s undercover methods.[117] When the son of Camilla Parker Bowles was secretly tape-recorded admitting to buying and taking cocaine, the broadsheets regarded it as an unacceptable 'tabloid sting'.[118] Similar criticism was levelled at the paper's exposure of taped boasts by England rugby captain Lawrence Dallaglio that he took drugs. *NoW* reporters posed as representatives of the razor company Gillette, who approached Dallaglio about a sponsorship deal.[119] The *Daily Telegraph* could see no public interest in the story and attacked *NoW* editor Phil Hall for entrapping the player.[120]

The *News of the World* managed to overstep the mark with one of its stock-in-trade kiss-and-tell stories when a *Coronation Street* actress complained to the PCC that a former fiancé's tale was intrusive.[121] The PCC agreed, ruling in a landmark adjudication that there were boundaries to be drawn even if a person was telling the truth about another. Nor was it necessarily a defence if the subject had previously spoken about her relationship. Hall accepted, on reflection, that the story was in poor taste and had invaded the woman's privacy.

But Hall and his paper were widely applauded for breaking one of the most outstanding exclusives at the end of 1999 by revealing that Lord (Jeffrey) Archer had concocted a false alibi for the court case twelve years before when he had sued the *News of the World* and the *Daily Star* for libel over his payment to a prostitute, Monica Coghlan (see above, pp. 505–6). Archer's former friend Ted Francis told the *NoW* that Archer had persuaded him to lie about them having they dined together on the night he was supposed to have met Coghlan. Francis wrote to Archer's solicitors with his bogus story but, in a bizarre twist, the *Star* changed its evidence to a different night and Francis's alibi wasn't required.[122]

Archer, who was the Conservative party candidate for London mayor, stood down from the election immediately he realised what the paper was about to publish. Francis had made contact with the *NoW* through the celebrity PR Max Clifford and was paid a fee of £15,000. The paper's reporters then checked Francis's claims by monitoring phone calls between Francis and Archer. During one of the calls Archer revealed that he had changed his diary to take account of their bogus meeting.[123] Archer's downfall was celebrated by several papers but none more so than the *Evening Standard* whose editor, Max Hastings, had long believed him unacceptable. In a superb piece of controlled invective, the *Standard* described Archer as 'incapable of shame . . . a man who has lied, bamboozled and battered a path to public office . . . bereft of truth, honour or regret'.[124] Both the *Daily Star* and the *News of the World* demanded that Archer pay back the money, £500,000 and £50,000 respectively, they had paid him in libel damages.[125]

The *Star*'s editor at the time, Lloyd Turner, had not lived to see himself vindicated, having died aged fifty-eight in September 1996. His widow commented: 'I shall always wonder whether the stress precipitated his premature death.'[126] Another tragedy occurred before Archer came to trial for perjury: the prostitute, Monica Coghlan, was killed in a car accident in April 2001. Three months later Archer was jailed for four years for perjury and perverting the course of justice.[127] In July 2002, Archer paid the *NoW* £300,000 to cover its damages and legal fees, and six months later paid the *Star*'s owners £1.8 million.[128]

Phil Hall's jubilation at exposing Archer's duplicity wasn't long lived: he was fired in May 2000. There appeared to be no rational reason, even though sales had just dipped below 4 million, because he had apparently fulfilled his brief. Months later Hall was still puzzling over why he had lost his job. Was he removed simply to promote the ambitious deputy editor of the *Sun*, Rebekah Wade?

That seemed hard to credit, but there was no other rational explanation. Wade, appointed a couple of days before her thirty-second birthday, was educated in her native Cheshire and at the Sorbonne, becoming fluent in

French. She worked briefly in Paris on an architecture magazine and then in Cheshire for Eddy Shah's Messenger group. She showed her mettle at Shah's ill-fated *Post* where she was hired as a secretary but inveigled her way into reporting. After its closure she joined the *News of the World*'s Sunday magazine, aged just 20, as a feature writer while training at the London College of Printing. Editor Piers Morgan spotted a rising talent and took a gamble by promoting her to features editor. Many of the more experienced staff, far from being envious, were soon singing her praises. She rose up the ladder under Phil Hall to become his deputy and was translated, to the disappointment of *Sun* editor Stuart Higgins, to be his deputy in February 1998. Nor did she hit it off with Higgins's successor, David Yelland, who said her greatest skill was in 'schmoozing show-business people'.[129] A consummate networker, Wade also had a celebrity boyfriend, a former TV soap star, Ross Kemp, whom she married in July 2002.

Wade soon gained widespread notoriety among broadsheet journalists, lawyers, police and social workers for running one of the most controversial campaigns of all time. After the murder of eight-year-old Sarah Payne, she pledged to name and shame 100,000 convicted paedophiles as a public service to parents.[130] The *News of the World* demanded that everyone should have the right to know the identity of child sex offenders within their area, calling it 'Sarah's Law'. In two weeks the paper pictured and named eighty alleged paedophiles. As predicted by Wade's many critics, vigilante activity broke out in various places across Britain, with threats to innocent people and a bizarre incident in which a paediatrician's home was daubed with graffiti.[131]

Several papers were appalled. The *Daily Telegraph* called it 'a rabble-rousing witch-hunt'.[132] *Independent* editor Simon Kelner attacked Wade personally.[133] The *Observer* pointed out that paedophile murders were very rare.[134] The *Daily Mail* initially reproached Wade for a lack of judgement, but later called it 'a brave campaign if somewhat over-zealous and ill-thought through'.[135] After a crisis meeting and a promise by the Home Office to consider the whole matter, Wade agreed to drop the name-and-shame part of its campaign. But the Home Office stood firm in its refusal to allow public access to the sex offenders' register. Wade returned to the *News of the World*'s more familiar diet of kiss-and-tell exposures before her next promotion (see below, p. 663).

Wade's paper sold better than her Sunday red-top rivals. The *Sunday Mirror* suffered from a series of preposterous changes of mind by its owners after a dispirited Tessa Hilton quit as editor in July 1996 the day after Bridget Rowe was promoted to be managing director of both the *Sunday Mirror* and *Sunday People*. Following Hilton's departure, by my count there were five acting editors before Brendan Parsons was given the job in January 1998, only for him to take compassionate leave within three months. The chair then passed to Colin Myler, who at least had a decent track record with the paper as a deputy editor even if his *Daily Mirror* editorship had been less than effective. He faced a tough task after three years of neglect during which sales had fallen by 200,000. With the aid of direct-mail marketing, he appeared to weather the storm for a while, but a further 200,000 had vanished by the time he made the greatest mistake of his career. He published an interview with the father of an Asian student who was the main prosecution witness in the trial of two Leeds United footballers charged with affray and assaulting him.[136]

The jury were considering their verdict at the time and the judge decided that the article, which claimed the assault was motivated by racism, might influence them and halted the trial. He recommended that the paper and the editor be charged with contempt of court. Myler resigned four days later. His decision to publish was puzzling, but the fact that the office lawyer he consulted gave him the go-ahead was stranger still. The players, Lee Bowyer and Jonathan Woodgate, were retried at the end of the year. Bowyer was cleared of causing grievous bodily harm and affray; Woodgate was found guilty of affray and ordered to do 100 hours' community service. Four months later, the *Sunday Mirror* was fined £50,000 and ordered to pay £54,160 towards the attorney-general's costs for its contempt. The paper's counsel explained that the contempt was the result of bad legal advice.

It had been an odd episode and the only beneficiary was the woman chosen to replace Myler as *Sunday Mirror* editor: Tina Weaver. Aged thirty-six, she had been deputy to *Daily Mirror* editor Piers Morgan for three years and had enjoyed a rapid rise to the top flight. She started at a Bristol news agency, joined the *Sunday People* as a reporter, then did stints at the *Daily Mirror* and *Today* where she won the 1994 British Press Awards accolade as reporter of the year for revelations about the singer Michael Jackson. She returned to the *Mirror* in 1995 and obtained a scoop about the prime minister's wife being pregnant. But reporting and editing are different skills and she found it impossible to stem the sales slide.[137]

Weaver's in-house competitor, the *Sunday People*, had an even greater circulation headache. Bridget Rowe, editor until August 1996, couldn't reverse the downward trend. Her successor, Len Gould, an excellent production veteran who had been an executive on *Today* and the *Daily Mail*, had an even worse time of it by presiding over the loss of 300,000 copies in little more than two years. He was replaced in January 1998 by Neil Wallis, an entertaining character with a wealth of experience as a reporter and executive, who had been *Sun* deputy editor for several years. Raised in a council house in Skegness, from the age of eight he attended a special school for asthmatics. He worked his way up from local weeklies and regional evenings to the *Sunday People* before joining the *Daily Star*. He sailed close to the wind as a reporter, attracting so many writs they were known as the Wallis Collection. He picked up a nickname, the Wolfman, because of his story which suggested, without much evidence, that the Yorkshire Ripper struck only at full moon.

Despite his colourful reputation, Wallis had been too shrewd an operator to get into real trouble. He had risen at the *Sun* precisely because he was good at walking the tightrope without falling off. He also found life heavy-going at the *People*, losing sales steadily as people moved inexorably away from the Sunday red-tops towards the *Mail on Sunday* and the broadsheets. Selected to represent Mirror group on the PCC, he campaigned vigorously behind the scenes for tabloids against what he perceived to be broadsheet hypocrisy.

His crusading zeal took a substantial knock in October 2001 when he ran a series of naked pictures of radio and TV presenter Sara Cox, and her husband on their honeymoon.[138] The couple were outraged at the intrusion into their privacy – they were pictured on a private beach – and scandalised by suggestions that they might have colluded in such a tasteless exercise. Cox took legal steps to prevent the pictures from being resold and contacted the PCC. Wallis, realising he had breached the editors' code, which as a PCC member he was especially on his honour to uphold, let it be known he had been misled about the pictures' provenance when buying them. He then made an agreed apology in his paper the following week. It didn't satisfy Cox, however, and she pursued the *People* through the courts, winning with her husband a £50,000 settlement in June 2003. Wallis had, in the words of a fellow *Mirror* group executive, driven a coach and horses through self-regulation. Later, he was to deliver an entirely different surprise.

Red-tops struggle to find a black-top audience

Few battles were as fascinating as that between the *Daily Mirror* and the *Sun* as they tried to woo a more middle-market audience without losing the majority of their traditional readers. The fight was slow in starting because both owners and senior journalists took a long time to grasp the reality of their predicament. The price war had concealed the fact that the downturn in sales wasn't cyclical. It was a long-term trend exacerbated in the case of the red-tops by the changing demographic pattern in which the working-class of fifty years before – blue collar with a single breadwinner – no longer formed the majority of the population. Red-tops were not simply out of fashion or favour, their future was imperilled by the disappearance of their traditional audience. With the *Sun* selling almost 4 million throughout 1996 and the *Daily Mirror* 2.3 million – plus the *Daily Star*'s 700,000 – there didn't seem any reason for concern. Seven million daily red-top sales equated to a readership of virtually 20 million. Crisis? What crisis?

At the *Daily Mirror*, editor Piers Morgan was convinced that the way to beat the *Sun* was to copy it, relying on his paper's continuing attachment to

Labour to provide the only real difference. He was supported in this approach by his mentor, Kelvin MacKenzie, who was promoted to deputy managing director at the beginning of 1997. Still in charge of Mirror L!ve cable TV, he now took a leading role in running the newspapers. Morgan's desire to out-*Sun* the *Sun* led him to produce tasteless and sometimes juvenile papers. The most obvious example was his notorious front page during the 1996 European football championship before Germany played England in the semi-finals. Over a picture of English players wearing second world war helmets Morgan ran the headline: 'Achtung! Surrender! For You Fritz Ze Euro 96 Championship Is Over'.[139] The war analogy continued across inside pages too.

The *Sun*, with 'Let's Blitz Fritz' and the *Star* with 'Herr We Go – Bring on the Krauts,' were also guilty of xenophobic language. But it was the *Mirror* which attracted opprobrium from rival papers ('England deserves better than this orgy of jingoism,' said the *Daily Mail*), from MPs and from the public. The PCC was inundated with complaints but didn't issue an adjudication, viewing it as a matter of taste and therefore not covered by the editors' code. Morgan tried to brazen it out by claiming it was all a joke, but in later years he admitted the error, one of several occasions in which he disowned his past misdeeds.[140] His editorship soon attracted fire from former *Mirror* luminaries, such as Joe Haines and John Pilger.[141] He shrugged aside the criticism, making his paper more like the *Sun* by dropping the *Daily* from its title in February 1997 as part of a £16 million relaunch, involving an editorial revamp and a direct marketing initiative. The *Mirror* under Morgan was no more successful than the *Daily Mirror*, though ructions among the senior management hardly helped his cause.

In five years under chief executive David Montgomery, Mirror group had done much to cure the post-Maxwell malaise. The banks responsible for handing his team the company were delighted that he had turned it round so swiftly. Monty had reason to smile too, enjoying a huge salary and cashing in share options at a profit. But the City remained sceptical about the direction he was taking: analysts were unimpressed by the L!ve TV fiasco and baffled by the expensive acquisition of the Birmingham-based regional group Midland Independent Newspapers for £297 million. The purchase of a 90 per cent stake in the staunchly Unionist and loss-making *Belfast News Letter* made little sense. Was it a vanity buy by Montgomery, the Protestant lad from Bangor?

Shareholders showed increasing concern too, blocking Monty's attempt to become chairman in the autumn of 1997. He lost two senior executives: managing director Charlie Wilson quit in February 1998, followed in June by MacKenzie who, in another of his surprise moves, took over Talk Radio with financial backing from his former boss, Rupert Murdoch. Mirror group's share price hit a fifty-two-week low and a stockbroking analyst predicted Montgomery wouldn't last six months.[142] The acquisition of more northern

Irish titles, the *Derry Journal* group, was seen as irrelevant and more evidence of a possible private agenda. An outsider, Victor Blank, who had a good City reputation as managing director of Charterhouse merchant bank and deputy chairman of Great Universal Stores, was voted in as chairman. He quickly grasped Mirror group's central problems: it was unable to expand into terrestrial TV because of cross-ownership regulations, was becoming a tempting takeover target and was suffering because Montgomery was viewed negatively by several institutional investors.

Journalists were also hostile to Monty, a resentment fuelled by his handling of the group's once predominant racing paper, *Sporting Life*. It lost a third of its sales in 1996 and was overtaken by its rival, *Racing Post*, a title launched ten years before by Sheikh Mohammed. The competition ended in April 1998 when Mohammed turned his back on British racing and sold his paper for a nominal sum to Mirror group. The company chose to close *Sporting Life* and continue with *Racing Post*, announcing that *Sporting Life* would be resurrected in future as a daily sports paper. *Guardian* media editor John Mulholland was hired to edit the new paper, given a budget of £20 million and told to recruit 120 staff. But Mulholland became disillusioned with Montgomery, believing that he had no real intention of launching the paper, and departed in August 1998. *Sporting Life* was not printed again, living on as a website which passed through several hands.

When Blank and his board realised at the beginning of 1999 that bidders for the group did not want Montgomery to stay they paid him off, handsomely. Trinity, a regional chain run by chief executive Philip Graf, emerged as the winners by agreeing to pay £1.2 billion. Graf, who was born in Northern Ireland, developed a passion for newspapers as a schoolboy reader of the *Belfast Telegraph*, and that passion survived through his student years at Cambridge. Initially unable to find a press job he joined an oil company until he got his break with the *Belfast Telegraph*'s owners, Thomson Regional Newspapers. He worked in the marketing, advertising and research departments of the London headquarters until he was transferred to the *Telegraph*, becoming group circulation and marketing controller.

He left in 1983 and crossed the Irish Sea to be assistant managing director of the *Liverpool Daily Post and Echo*, emerging as its most dynamic manager during the company's expansion and change of name in 1985 to Trinity. Graf became chief executive and in the following years the group acquired local and regional titles in Scotland, Wales, Yorkshire, Surrey, Sussex and south London. It was the 1996 acquisition of a large chunk of the Thomson group for £330 million which carried Trinity into the big league, making it Britain's largest regional publisher. Sadly for Graf, a Monopolies and Mergers Commission inquiry into his Mirror takeover decided that, as a condition of the merger, Trinity must dispose of the *Belfast Telegraph*.[143] Graf disputed the logic but reluctantly accepted the decision and the creation of Trinity-Mirror was formally sealed on 6 September 1999.

The Mirror board had previously been in the process of rationalising the group by selling off the old Holborn building, disposing of a stake in Scottish TV and putting L!ve TV up for sale. Graf concurred, killing off the laughable L!ve TV a month later. But what had driven him, beyond the profit motive, to buy the Mirror titles? Graf, like his late hero and boss, Lord Thomson, loved papers without having any interest in trying to dictate their content. 'I enjoy being around journalists and being involved with them,' he said, but because he thought enjoyment 'an indulgence' avoided seeing his editors too often. He concluded: 'As long as the papers are in line with what we've all agreed is the editorial philosophy and editorial thrust of the papers, I want to let them get on and edit.'[144]

As far as the *Mirror* was concerned he was therefore happy to let editor Piers Morgan have his head. Morgan also had the confidence of his chairman, Blank, giving him enormous power over the paper. While agreeing that the *Mirror* should remain loyal to Labour, he showed a maverick streak when being critical of the government, keenly aware that the *Sun*'s switch to support Labour had denuded him of the paper's traditional special relationship. He also had to face up to the fact that by 1999 the *Daily Mail* was regularly selling more than the *Mirror*. Morgan went through a phase of what he would later concede was rather irresponsible behaviour, attracting yet more fire from former senior staff.[145] He embraced his arrogance, proudly telling one interviewer that Tony Blair's press secretary 'always jokes that whenever I go in to see Blair, I have to remember that I'm not the prime minister'.[146]

There were lasting innovations, such as the addition of M magazine for women, the creation of a celebrity gossip team called the 3am girls and the launch of a second gossip column, Scurra. But Morgan's reputation was mired by his involvement in the 'City Slickers' affair. He had created the Slickers column in 1998 to make City news as palatable for readers as showbiz news, promoting the two writers – James Hipwell and Anil Bhoyrul – as personalities. Their share-tipping was couched in the argot of City traders, exhorting readers to 'fill your boots' by 'piling into' a variety of stocks, many of them in the new technology sector. One day in January 2000 a Slickers story announced that Viglen, a computer hardware company, was about to launch a separate internet division.[147] Its shares immediately doubled in price. A couple of weeks later a short *Daily Telegraph* news report revealed that, the day before the Slickers' revelation, Morgan had bought £20,000 worth of Viglen shares.[148]

Morgan denied knowing in advance about his writers' story. 'I never see the City column before the market shuts,' he told the *Telegraph*. He viewed his purchase as a long-term investment and had not profited by selling the shares. It was also pointed out that Viglen's chairman, Sir Alan Sugar, was a regular *Mirror* columnist. Other editors and many MPs were appalled by Morgan's actions, complaining that he had indulged in a form of insider trading. The *Sun* took the opportunity to embarrass its rival, dubbing the affair 'Mirrorgate'. Three inquiries, by Trinity-Mirror, the Press Complaints Commission and the Department of Trade and Industry were announced. Trinity's investigation swiftly cleared Morgan but the two City Slickers were fired for gross misconduct, for writing about shares in which they traded. The PCC inquiry took three months and acquitted Morgan of breaching the editors' code of practice but decided he had 'fallen short of the high professional standards' demanded by the code. It was, said the *Times*'s press commentator, the harshest adjudication against an editor since Morgan's admonishment when editing the *News of the World*[149] (see above, p. 603).

It is hard not to believe that Morgan would have been fired had he not been considered by his bosses, Graf and Blank, to be indispensable. In an interview a year later Morgan admitted: 'It was bloody stupid of me to ever think that I could actively trade in the stock market and not at some stage come into conflict with the paper.'[150] *Mirror* readers appeared much less concerned than other journalists, making only a handful of complaints. But the City Slickers episode haunted Morgan, with headlines generated by occasional leaks from the DTI inquiry (which had not been completed at the time of writing).[151]

If Morgan was chastened by the affair, as he often remarked, it was difficult to tell. Promoted to editor-in-chief of both *Mirror* titles in April 2001, he was soon back to his swaggering old self despite a continued decline in sales. Then came the 11 September atrocity at New York's World Trade Center and a dramatic conversion. Morgan suddenly announced with typical immodesty that he had seen the light and it was time to resurrect the old *Mirror* news agenda.[152]

He began to put serious news on the front page, highlighting foreign tragedies and challenging the Labour government's policies in the boldest of fashions. This change of direction culminated in an official relaunch in the spring of 2002 in which the paper reverted to its old *Daily Mirror* title, gave up using a red masthead (removing the blight of being called a red-top) and announced that it would adopt a campaigning approach. 'The changes are not about going up-market,' Morgan said. 'They are about becoming a serious paper with serious news, serious sport, serious gossip and serious entertainment.'[153] He reintroduced the Cassandra column and agreed to publish occasional pieces from writers such as the *Guardian*'s Jonathan Freedland and, most controversial of all, John Pilger. He obliged by attacking Tony Blair and America's foreign policy, with one trenchant article even prompting an unprecedented protest from a New York-based Trinity-Mirror investor.[154] Morgan had taken six years to find his way back to the *Mirror*'s Cudlippian traditions, eliciting praise from his widow.[155]

But Morgan could have done with some advice from Cudlipp before launching his trenchant criticism of prime minister Tony Blair for going to war against Iraq in March 2003. As Cudlipp discovered over Suez (see Chapter Six), *Mirror* readers do not revel in criticism of the government at times of conflict. Morgan was forced to tone down his attacks on Blair as readers turned away – he had misread his audience. He was in good company because it appeared that Murdoch was also prepared to race ahead of the public.

The period began with Stuart Higgins still in the *Sun* editor's chair and benefiting from extra sales picked up by publishing in Ireland and Spain. Higgins's legendary success as the breaker of royal scoops suffered a tremendous blow when he was hoaxed over the Princess Diana video (see above, p. 650). The mistake angered Murdoch and put a cloud over the Higgins editorship. The following March the *Sun* made a great political U-turn, turning its back on the Conservatives in favour of Tony Blair's New Labour. Its front-page announcement, 'The *Sun* Backs Blair', was considered to be the vindication of a strategy by Blair's press secretary, Alastair Campbell, to win over the paper which had done so much to destroy Neil Kinnock.[156] From Murdoch's point of view, it was simply a case of supporting a man he expected to win and a man with whom he felt comfortable. There was another bonus for the *Sun*. It robbed their traditional rival, the *Mirror*, of being Labour's only tabloid supporter. In future months the two papers would vie to win Labour-friendly political exclusives, with the *Sun* – which Campbell wished to keep sweet – generally obtaining more.

Higgins was not a political animal, preferring the safer ground of old-style *Sun* sensationalism, symbolised by his front page which reporting the arrest of singer George Michael on a sex-related charge, 'Zip Me Up Before You Go Go'.[157] He was displeased when News International's chairman, Les Hinton, ignored his protests and forced him to accept Rebekah Wade as his deputy editor. Higgins and Hinton had clashed over other matters too and, with sales having fallen by more than 5 per cent in six months, it wasn't long before he was asked to resign.

His replacement in June 1998 was so surprising that the trade magazine greeted his appointment with the headline 'Who the HELL is David Yelland?'[158] It transpired that Yelland, thirty-five, was the deputy editor of Murdoch's *New York Post,* and wasn't considered by his British contemporaries to be editor material. He had been eager to be a journalist from the age of eleven before arriving at his Humberside grammar school. After gaining a degree in economics at Lancashire Polytechnic he went into local journalism with the *Buckinghamshire Advertiser*, the *Northern Echo* and the short-lived *North West Times* before freelancing for the *Sunday Times*'s business section. Appointed as a business reporter on the *Sun* in 1990 by Kelvin MacKenzie, he was swiftly promoted to City editor. 'He was brilliant,' said a colleague, who told how he translated arcane City jargon into easy-to-grasp *Sun*-style copy.[159] He didn't shine at all when posted to New York and resigned from the *Sun*. He was rescued by Murdoch to work as business editor on the *New York Post* and did well enough to be promoted to deputy editor. Yelland, who suffered from tasteless jokes about his baldness – caused by alopecia – was shy and rather staid. Totally unlike the brash Mackenzie and Morgan, he proved to be just as determined and combative as them.

Like them, he was also given to changes of mind and direction. Generally supportive of Blair, he shared Murdoch's distaste for the single currency as one of his earliest front pages illustrated. Next to a picture of Blair he ran the headline, 'Is THIS the most dangerous man in Britain?' because of his supposed desire to 'scrap the Pound'.[160] Four months later he debunked Tory leader William Hague by borrowing from a Monty Python sketch to produce a front page with Hague's head superimposed on a dead parrot hanging upside down from a perch, headlined, 'This party is no more . . . it has ceased to be . . . this is an EX-party.'[161]

Within weeks Yelland provoked controversy after four cabinet ministers had been revealed as homosexuals: 'Tell Us the Truth Tony: Are we being run by a gay mafia?'[162] The leading article argued that 'the public has a right to know how many homosexuals occupy positions of high power'. But Yelland realised he had gone too far and spent the rest of the week trying to row back from that position, eventually performing a U-turn, pledging that it wouldn't reveal the sexual preferences of people unless there was an 'overwhelming public interest'.[163]

His greatest humiliation came in May 1999 with the misguided publication of a topless picture of Sophie Rhys-Jones, the woman who was about to marry Prince Edward (and become the Countess of Wessex).[164] The snap, taken eleven years before, showed her bikini top being playfully lifted by radio and TV presenter Chris Tarrant. Palace officials said the Queen considered it 'premeditated cruelty'. Most papers condemned the *Sun*. The *Guardian* called it 'soft-core porn, not journalism'.[165] The *Daily Telegraph* saw Murdoch as the villain: next to a picture of him with his new partner Wendi Deng it ran the headline: 'How would you like to see *your* lover nude on Page 3, Mr Murdoch?'[166] It pointed to Murdoch's double standards: 'when his own marriage broke up recently, he expressed an understandable desire to avoid intrusive publicity . . . yet his papers offer no such mercy to other members of the human race'.[167] Murdoch left Yelland in no doubt that he disapproved and Yelland apologised the next day.[168]

The episode seemed out of character given that Yelland had admitted he would prefer to drop Page 3 pictures and appeared at his happiest publishing political stories.[169] Even then, he showed a lack of instinct. Robbed of Princess Diana as a sales gimmick, he joined other tabloid editors in trying to replace the dramas of the royal couple with the mundane activities of footballer David Beckham and Spice Girl Victoria Adams.[170]

Most of Yelland's problems stemmed from trying to make his paper more serious without losing its sense of fun and frivolity. In other words, his agenda and Morgan's were entirely similar. Sadly, their competitiveness was anything but good-natured. Once firm friends in their novice years at the *Sun*, they fell out badly, using their papers to lampoon each other in increasingly childish ways. When they drew back from that nonsense, they reopened a new front in their war by making rude remarks about each other in memos to staff which were judiciously leaked.[171] But it was Yelland who was, eventually, to lose out.

Even with the help of price cuts Yelland found it difficult to maintain sales, and in January 2003 Murdoch persuaded him to take a management course in the United States and replaced him with *News of the World* editor Rebekah Wade. She immediately let it be known that she would adopt a more sceptical view of the Labour governent and soon launched a campaign demanding tighter laws to prevent 'bogus' asylum-seekers staying in Britain. Her place was taken at the *NoW* by her thirty-four-year-old deputy, Andy Coulson. He had previously been something of a self-publicist when editing the *Sun*'s Bizarre column but happily knuckled down to a lower profile role once he started to rise up the executive ranks. One of his mentors at the *Sun* had been Neil Wallis, editor of the *Sunday People*, and knowing of his friend's growing sense of frustration with his Trinity-Mirror managers he asked him to become his deputy editor at the *NoW*. Wallis accepted, becoming the first national editor to give up an editorship of his own volition in order to to take a lesser post.

Wallis resigned at a sensitive time for Trinity-Mirror because its chief executive, Philip Graf, was serving out his final weeks after also having resigned. Graf's decision to quit, announced in September 2002, was widely viewed as an admisison that the coupling of the regional Trinity with the national Mirror group had been unsuccessful, for the company's market value had been virtually halved since the merger. Graf smilingly dismissed such criticism, just as he did similar attacks on another controversial decision to accompany the *Daily Mirror*'s serious revamp with a price cut. This provoked the *Sun* to retaliate and, after a short war, in which both companies sacrificed profits, the *Sun* emerged the sales winner.

With Trinity-Mirror suffering from falling profits and sales, media analysts argued that Graf should, at best, sell off the *People* or, at worst, demerge the company and sell all the national titles. He resisted both ideas and it was left to his successor, Sly (Sylvia) Bailey, to sort out the group's problems. Bailey, forty, was lured away from being chief executive of IPC, the giant publisher of magazines which reached about half the British population. She found the task awaiting her at the Mirror papers far harder than any she had tackled previously, as one of her first chores – appointing a new *People* editor – proved. Several people turned the job down until Mark Thomas, deputy editor of the *Sunday Mirror*, was finally persuaded in late March 2003 to take it. Bailey was under no illusions that devising a strategy to turn around the whole company was going to be far from straightforward.

Express crusader bows the knee to a pornographer

We left the *Express* story with Richard Addis as an unhappy editor-in-chief coping with a Tory chairman, Lord Stevens, and a Labour chief executive, Lord Hollick. Eventually, Hollick managed to turn the blue papers red, offering support to New Labour. But politics weren't the central problem the two *Express* titles faced. For partisan popular newspapers, politics are really a starting point which informs the direction and tone of the content. What the *Express*es lacked was a sense of mission, a purpose. They were also unable to compete at a journalistic level with their rivals, especially the *Daily Mail*. They didn't break many, if any, important stories and they couldn't compete when it came to bidding for book serialisations, a core feature of sales-building for any paper.

Hollick, who didn't seem to understand any of this, did realise his papers were going nowhere fast. Circulation didn't plunge, but it did dwindle away and he lost faith in Addis, replacing him with *Independent* editor Rosie Boycott in April 1998. Former *Daily Express* editor Chris Ward, having scented that Hollick was as clueless as the two previous owners, greeted her appointment by declaring that all Express editors were 'united by a common bond: an absolute contempt for successive Express managements who ran the place into the ground'.[172] Boycott shrugged aside such warnings because she believed Hollick to be different. He promised her access to the vast resources of the main company, United News & Media (UNM), to help her turn round the paper's fortunes. They agreed she should make it appeal to a younger and more progressive audience, and to that end she set about transforming the *Express* into a sort of broadsheet in tabloid clothes, making it more serious and more campaigning. Beaverbrook had adorned the *Daily Express* masthead with the figure of a crusader and Boycott used it as a metaphor, seeing her role as a propagandist against injustice. In broad terms, she accepted Tony Blair's reforming zeal and was an uninhibited supporter, in her first two years at least, of the Labour government. It was proof that Hollick now held sway over Stevens.

Boycott's political agenda attracted like-minded souls, such as Tony Bevins who quit the *Observer* to become political editor, her former *Independent* partner and rival, Andrew Marr, who wrote a column, and the reporter Ros Wynne-Jones who wrote most of the main features. All four members of the *Observer*'s investigative unit later quit to join Boycott too. Bevins believed it possible to lure away a significant number of Labour voters who bought the *Daily Mail*, which were estimated to account for 38 per cent of its audience. The problem, however, was that just as many, if not more, traditional Tory-voting *Express* readers were leaking away to the *Mail*. In order to prevent this happening too quickly, Boycott maintained in place the brilliant right-wing columnist Peter Hitchens. He was luckier than many colleagues whom Boycott identified as either too old or too obtuse. Their departures upset some staff, especially the senior production executives, who muttered darkly about Boycott's naivety. It meant the office was divided between an unhappy old guard and the newer Boycott brigade. That split personality was evident in the paper too, with one media academic speaking for many people when she argued that it was 'hard to make out what the *Express*'s tone is likely to be – or the nature of its new persona'.[173]

Boycott also had to face the eternal problem of what to do with the *Express on Sunday*. Her initial move was to draft in Amanda Platell, the former *Today* deputy editor and Mirror group manager, with the title of executive editor to run the Sunday operation. Given the direction Boycott was planning for the daily, it was an odd choice. Platell was a good technician and a superb handler of staff, but she had two strikes against her: she wasn't a natural left-winger, and she had the kind of tabloid background Boycott didn't respect. Platell was soon complaining, with some justice, that she had to produce a paper on a shoestring: it was claimed that only twenty-six staff worked on the *Express on Sunday* compared to 200 on the *Mail on Sunday*. Boycott understood that problem, but thought Platell too resistant to the seven-day operation. The stage was set for a major fall-out which came in November 1998 over the delicate matter of cabinet minister Peter Mandelson's sexual preference. The story of his gayness had become front-page news that month and he was extremely angry when the *Express on Sunday* published a picture of his Brazilian partner and even more incensed that it had been doctored to hide the fact that it had been taken against his will.

Six weeks later Platell was fired and three other senior staff left at the same time amid claims that Boycott was acceding to Mandelson's demand that heads should roll. Boycott insisted that her reasons had nothing to do with Mandelson: Platell was off message, running a paper that was too down-market and too right wing. Confirmation of Platell's political leanings came in March 1999 when she was appointed the Conservative party's head of news and media. Boycott gave Platell's job to Michael Pilgrim, a former *Observer* magazine editor and *Independent* managing editor, and the following month, sensibly, the *Express*es reverted to their former titles.

Hollick had had problems of his own early in 1998, having lost two directors in quick succession – including the much heralded executive director Stephen Grabiner – causing shares to dip and prompting questions about his management style.[174] By 1999, he was growing more irritated at the media's interest in the ailing performance of the *Express*, striving to make it clear that Express Newspapers represented only 4 per cent of UNM's profit.[175]

Everyone nodded in agreement, but he was missing the point: it is impossible to own national papers and not be under the spotlight.

Uncertain what to do with Express Newspapers, Hollick called in a consultancy group which reported that the papers required a level of investment which might be difficult to justify to shareholders.[176] According to Boycott and her loyal deputy, Chris Blackhurst, it was possible to date Hollick's withdrawal of interest in the papers from May 1999 when it was announced that *Sunday Express* circulation would be allowed to 'find its own level'.[177] A former Express executive, Bernard Shrimsley, rightly saw it as 'the final act of surrender'.[178] From that month onward, Boycott was continually frustrated by the absence of resources and aggravated by the plethora of rumours about the papers being for sale. The Barclay brothers, owners of the *Scotsman* and the *European*, let it be known through their publisher, Andrew Neil, that they were interested.[179] When I wrote in July that the Express group was on the block I received a letter of denial from UNM's communications director.[180] Neil called me to say I was correct, providing details which confirmed that he was telling the truth.

Hollick, it transpired, had other plans. In November 1999, it was announced that UNM would merge with Carlton Television to create the largest ITV broadcaster. Carlton's chief, Michael Green, was evidently eager to keep the Express papers within the enlarged company. But the deal unravelled because Carlton's biggest rival, Granada, demanded referral and the subsequent Competition Commission report agreed to the merger only if UNM disposed of the lucrative Meridian licence, thus undermining the merger's financial rationale.[181] The Labour government could do little but accept the report, despite Hollick's belief that it should ignore the recommendation.

Hollick's grand plan was foiled and he soon sold off his TV holdings to Granada. From this point the *Daily Express* began to be more critical of the government, but I believe that that was Boycott's decision rather than Hollick's.[182] It was only a matter of time before Express Newspapers was sold and rumours suggested plenty of interested parties, some of them wide of the mark. One that was true was a £75 million bid by the Barclay brothers which Hollick rejected as far too low. Then news leaked of a bid, supposedly close to £100 million, by another set of brothers, Srichand and Gopichand Hinduja. They ran a global oil-trading, banking and manufacturing conglomerate, with interests in film, cable TV and telecommunications. But there were question marks about bribery allegations in their native India, which they strenuously denied, and concern about their eagerness to cosy up to British political leaders.[183] UNM finally admitted receiving 'unsolicited offers' which it was 'obliged to consider'.[184]

What no one seemed to notice was a hint in the *Daily Mail*'s gossip column that a company called Northern & Shell, owned by Richard Desmond, was keen to buy the Express titles.[185] People were diverted instead by Conrad Black's Telegraph group showing an interest, which made some sense given its fifty–fifty partnership with the Express group in West Ferry printers.[186] Associated, owners of the Mail titles, joined the fray with an offer of £125 million and a pledge to invest £50 million a year for five years.[187] Hollick's unpalatable response was to demand that bidders make a £60 million non-refundable deposit to enter the final round.

In mid-November it was confirmed that Desmond was the front-runner in a *Sunday Times* article which pointed out that his company's fortune had been made from selling pornographic magazines and from the celebrity weekly *OK!*[188] Three days later Desmond was declared as the new owner of Express Newspapers, leaving rival bidders 'gasping with anger and fury'.[189] He paid £125 million cash, some £97 million of which came from Commerzbank of Germany, following six weeks of secret negotiations after Desmond sent a note to Hollick in October stating: 'If you want a quick and quiet deal, I'm your man.'[190]

There had been many maverick newspaper owners down the years but Richard Clive Desmond was in a league of his own. Described in the *Times* as a 'misogynist, bully and vulgarian', his personal dealings with people and the nature of his pornographic empire made the rest of the industry blink.[191] He was born in Edgware in 1951, the son of a former *Express* circulation rep who was managing director of the screen advertising company Pearl & Dean. His parents split when he was eleven and he and his mother lived in a flat above a garage. He went to Christ's College, a Finchley grammar school, and became obsessed with drumming, leaving school at fourteen without any qualifications. Desmond's first jobs were selling classified ads which he combined with drumming at night. By twenty-one, he had his own house, a couple of record shops and some property. He successfully launched *International Musician* magazine and, in 1982, he forged a deal with Bob Guccione, the US owner of *Penthouse*, to produce a British edition which he sold off many years later. In the mid-1980s, he made a killing from running premium-rate sex phone lines which were later suspended by BT for being 'too explicit'.[192]

In 1992 Desmond moved into top-shelf titles and negotiated a distribution contract with Lord Stevens's United News which turned out to be disastrous for United. As part of the settlement to escape the contract, Stevens bought Desmond's non-adult magazines for £17 million, a cash mountain Desmond used to launch *OK!* magazine as a challenge to the market-leader, *Hello!*[193] Desmond's Northern & Shell offices in Docklands were opened in 1993 by the Duke of Edinburgh and Desmond – a noted supporter of charities – presented him with a cheque for the London Federation of Boys' Clubs. A group of women picketed the event because of his pornographic magazines with titles such as *Big Ones, Women on Top, Black & Blue, Electric Blue, Asian Babes, Nude Wives, 40 Plus* and *Readers' Wives.* Desmond launched an adult TV channel in 1995 which made losses initially but with the growth of satellite television became very profitable. He also set up pornographic websites. In 2000, *OK!* magazine started to outsell *Hello!* partly because Desmond was willing to pay huge sums for exclusives, such as £1.8 million for pictures of Michael Jackson's baby and £1 million for the wedding of David Beckham and Posh Spice Victoria Adams.

But why did Desmond buy the *Express*? The *Independent* saw it as a 'crusade for respectability'.[194] Desmond said he did it for the money, proclaiming, 'I expect the *Express* to make me a billionaire,' and adding: 'I want to emulate Beaverbrook in making the *Express* No. 1 in the middle market.'[195] He reiterated this boast in a circular to staff, promising to 'spend whatever it takes' to surpass the *Daily Mail*. Respectability arrived early with an invitation to Downing Street to meet Tony Blair and weeks later Desmond, previously regarded as a Tory, donated £100,000 to the Labour party, a controversial gift that remained secret until May 2002.[196] At the time Desmond was still wondering whether the government would refer his bid to the Competition Commission on the grounds of his being an unsuitable owner of a newspaper, a sanction used to prevent pornographer David Sullivan from buying a title in Bristol (see above, p. 511).

There were mixed feelings about Desmond at the *Express*. Editor Rosie Boycott and many senior staff were appalled, while some were delighted with the prospect of Boycott being unseated and the possibility of Desmond pumping in much-needed funds. An exodus of senior journalists, managers and ad executives started within days. Columnist Peter Hitchens resigned after twenty-four years with the paper and moved to the *Mail on Sunday*, one of six to make that switch, including the famous Gambols strip cartoon. Political editor Tony Bevins resigned on principle without a job to go to (dying suddenly of pneumonia three months later). Columnist Mary Kenny walked away. Leader writer Stephen Pollard wrote a final editorial with the acrostic FuckyouDesmond and was immediately fired from his new job with the *Times* before he could start it.

Boycott found herself in a difficult position. She couldn't walk out and become an editor elsewhere, so she wanted her severance pay, and she didn't want to save Desmond money by quitting. Desmond didn't want to fire her in case it triggered a Competition Commission inquiry into his fitness to own the paper. So there was a lengthy standoff with occasional rows. As for Hollick, he was booed out of the building and then upset the majority of staff by giving twenty-five selected people cheques for £40,000. Heavily criticised for having sold out to Desmond, and for doing so in secrecy, he and his chairman, Sir Ronald Hampel, explained that it made financial sense for the company's shareholders.[197]

Boycott finally departed along with deputy editor Chris Blackhurst at the end of January 2001, having secured their pay-offs, and the assistant editor, Chris Williams, became editor. Most of the staff were delighted with Williams's promotion. He didn't rate Boycott as an editor but loyally produced the paper asked for. Regarded as a top-flight production man, forty-nine-year-old Williams started on a weekly in his native Liverpool, subbed at the Press Association for six years, joined the *Daily Express* in 1977 and rose to features editor. He left for the *Daily Mail* where his skills were appreciated but his languid style was disparaged, so he rejoined the *Express* in 1995 as number three.

Determined to prove his worth, especially to his former *Mail* bosses, he overlooked Desmond's other activities to get on with the job. The *Mail*, however, couldn't help but take advantage of Desmond's Achilles' heel, believing that his pornography empire offered a first-class opportunity to lure *Express* readers. Its first sally was a long article entitled 'Desmond the Degrader'.[198] A *Guardian* investigation into the extent of Desmond's empire provided more ammunition, revealing that one of his websites carried 'repellent' content, such as pregnant women posing naked.[199] *Guardian* columnist Francis Wheen dug deeper still to discover the exploitation of women in the slums of Bombay and Rio.[200] The *Mail* group then made a direct-mail shot to *Express* buyers pointing out that the *Express*es had been bought by a pornographer, listing some of the titles, and asking, 'Do you really want an X-rated paper in your home?' It invited recipients to try the *Daily Mail* and *Mail on Sunday* at a £20 discount while offering newsagents a £5 bonus if they persuaded *Express* buyers to switch to the *Mail*.

Desmond countered with a *Daily Express* series attacking the previous generations of the Rothermere family, owners of the *Mail* titles. In the final episode he fired his nuclear weapon by revealing that the current Lord Rothermere (Jonathan Harmsworth) had an illegitimate thirteen-year-old son, the result of a liaison with a woman who worked for his mother. She was living with the child in her native New Zealand. So much, sneered the *Express*, for the *Mail*'s 'crusade against single mothers'.[201] The story of Rothermere's son had first emerged in *Punch* magazine but no mainstream paper had reported the fact before. The *Mail* hierarchy's reaction was astonishing. Managing director Murdoch MacLennan met Desmond and agreed the terms of a truce: Associated would withdraw its direct-mail initiative and its titles would no longer refer to Desmond as a pornographer in return for Desmond never mentioning Rothermere's illegitimate son. Desmond had secured a significant victory in which freedom of the press was the loser.

Controversy dogged Desmond's first year of ownership. He sold off the four *Express* internet sites to his stockbroker for £1, making forty-six journalists redundant without compensation. He announced that 145 *Express* jobs would be cut, a quarter of the papers' workforce. He also fired *Sunday Express* editor Michael Pilgrim, who claimed he had been obliged to suppress stories for commercial reasons and to publish others.[202] Pilgrim was replaced by the engaging forty-one-year-old editor of *OK!* magazine, Martin Townsend, who had been a pop music journalist with *Today* and had worked on the *Mail on Sunday*'s You magazine. Meanwhile, Williams tried to produce a *Daily Express* that was more mainstream than Boycott's paper, though he soon discovered that Desmond liked to make decisions about the front-page content. Bad publicity quickened the sales decline: when Desmond bought the *Daily Express* it was selling 1,033,000; a year later it was struggling to sell 950,000, and by the spring of 2002, its sales were below 900,000. The *Sunday Express* lost 100,000 sales in eighteen months, and the main beneficiaries of both falls were the two *Mail* titles. But Desmond reversed both declines by the end of 2002 by price-cutting and selling more copies abroad.

He also saw his *Daily Star* prosper, though its surprising sales turnaround predated his arrival. Under editor Phil Walker it was known for its sexy pictures, usually of *Baywatch* TV star Pamela Anderson, and outrageous punning headlines, such as 'Vasectomy dad has sniplets' and 'We tikka more care of phew'. By 1997, sales were falling at more than 10 per cent a year and Hollick demanded a cut in the *Star*'s 190-strong staff. Despite Walker's opposition, forty were culled in the summer. Walker, editor from September 1994, was a former *Daily Mirror* deputy editor who had also been an associate editor of the *Daily Express*. He was intelligent, earnest and likeable, yet his paper was raucous and he would have preferred to adopt a different tone. So he took to heart focus-group research which showed that young people tended to consume news in 'nuggets' and redesigned his paper in June 1998 accordingly. But he was given too little promotion and the circulation kept on declining. Four months later Hollick ordered that forty-six journalists should go, virtually a third of the remaining complement. This time Walker, who wasn't in the best of health having undergone several unsuccessful operations for a collapsed windpipe, wasn't prepared to oversee the cuts and quit.

With sales down to 650,000 and falling his deputy, Peter Hill, took over. Hill had joined the *Star* at its launch some nineteen years before, but there has rarely been so clear a case of the man and his product being totally dissimilar. The quiet-spoken Hill subbed at the *Daily Telegraph* for seven years and was studying philosophy as a mature university student when asked to work for the *Star*. His favourite reading was Thomas Hobbes's *Leviathan*, and he insisted that Hobbes helped him as a popular paper editor because 'he was brilliant in his analysis of the way people behave'.[203] Hill believed that people liked television and fun. 'We like bottoms', he once remarked, 'because bottoms are fun'.[204] He also said that if his paper entertained people and made their day brighter 'then haven't I done a bit of good in the world? I'm a benefactor of mankind.'[205] Hill, using endless pictures of Page 3 model Jordan, went on producing a paper which was sexy but rarely tacky, light-hearted and full of celebrity, with a staff totalling just 106.[206] The formula eventually worked, and circulation gradually picked up throughout 2000, with extra sales being added month after month in the following two years. 'It's a mystery', confessed Hill with a broad smile when the turnaround was in its seventh month.[207] It was even more so three years later when sales were well over 800,000. By this time Desmond had taken over and boosted the *Star*'s resources. Thrilled at the *Star*'s rising sale, he tried to buy the *People* to repeat the formula with a Sunday title but was rebuffed by its owners, Trinity-Mirror. So, in a bold step in September 2002, he launched the *Daily Star on Sunday*, which settled into a regular 450,000 sale by the following year.

Desmond's success with the *Daily Star*, which eschewed virtually all serious news and comment, played a part in a change of mind and directioin at other red-tops. It was a factor in the replacement of Yelland by Wade at the *Sun*. It also had an impact on the *Daily Mirror* where Morgan, as we have seen, in pursuing the logic of his serious news agenda and scepticism of the Labour government, came out fiercely against the invasion of Iraq by the United States and Britain in March 2003. While Wade's *Sun* maintained its customary jingoistic stance, offering Tony Blair full-hearted support, Morgan's *Mirror* ran a series of anti-war front pages.[208] *Sun* sales increased while the *Mirror*'s dropped below 2 million for the first time in seventy years. Morgan's immediate response, at the behest of his new boss, Sly Bailey, was to water down his serious news content, returning to celebrity-based stories on page one.[209] Would the red-tops ever be able to escape from trivia?

Hail and farewell

With mainstream national-newspaper buying in decline and the growth of magazines devoted to specific interests and age-groups, there was a theory that papers aimed at niche markets would prosper. They would attract advertising based on their small but well-defined target audience. Too often, experiments tended to show a gap between theory and practice.

Robert Maxwell's dream paper for a united Europe, the *European*, fell because its niche was never properly identified and, even if it had been, its publishing costs were far too high for it to return a profit. The Barclay brothers poured money into the project after buying the paper in 1992, without any reward, and the *European* lost £13.5 million in 1995 alone.[210] The brothers hired Andrew Neil as publisher, making him responsible for all the titles within their Press Holdings group, which included the *European*, *Sunday Business*, the *Scotsman* and *Scotland on Sunday*. The once-successful *Sunday Times* editor attacked the job with his customary enthusiasm and self-confidence. He dismissed the *European*'s editor Charlie Garside, put himself in his place and carried out a complete revamp, turning it into a tabloid. He saw this as the first stage of a larger transition into a colour magazine, a quasi-*Economist*.

The central problem with Neil's *European* was its tactless editorial agenda which reflected his own hostility to the European Union and opposition to the single European currency. This was an unpopular line to promote in a paper previously dedicated to furthering European integration. Deputy editor Peter Millar resigned because of the paper's Europhobia – which he considered even more overt once Neil appointed former Tory MP Gerry Malone as editor – and claimed that several opinion-formers thought the paper anti-European.[211] The *European* was closed down in December 1998 when sales fell from 150,000 to a reputed 70,000, and maybe 35,000.[212] The Barclays can't be faulted for their generosity, having pumped some £74 million into the venture.[213]

Neil also played a key role in the topsy-turvy existence of *Sunday Business*. Launched in April 1996 by Tom Rubython, owner of *Business Age* magazine, it ran into trouble even before the first issue was published because of the failure to pay its printers in advance and anger from certain companies at the content of the dummy issue. Rubython got into more hot water, failing to sell enough copies or to attract advertising.[214] He sold out in September 1996 to a consortium headed by a Yorkshire construction millionaire, Gordon Brown, who kept Rubython in charge until they fell out. Deputy editor Anil Bhoyrul took over as acting editor, but he was fired early in 1997 as sales fell to 50,000 and writs arrived over contentious stories.[215]

By the time the Barclay brothers bought the title for £100,000 in August that year, sales were down to barely 20,000. Neil oversaw a relaunch in February 1998 under the editorship of his former *Sunday Times* business editor Jeff Randall. Their two-section pink paper was a truly professional product, winning praise from rivals and commentators.[216] Priced at 50p, it was hoped to build a regular 80,000 circulation, an ambition which proved unattainable. With *Sunday Business* haemorrhaging cash, Neil argued that the paper had been an editorial success but a commercial flop. To staunch the losses he doubled the cover price. Sales fell away and an aghast Randall resigned in February 2001, later becoming the BBC's first business correspondent.

Nils Pratley succeeded Randall to head up another re-launch, which also failed. In a desperate attempt to save the paper from extinction, Neil struck a deal with the Press Association in December 2001 under which they would run the paper together, after renaming it the *Business*. Almost fifty journalists were made redundant, Pratley departed and this time Neil halved the cover price, back to its original 50p. Circulation improved dramatically, running at more than 85,000 throughout the first half of 2002. But the cost to its benevolent owners was revealed to be £32 million in three years.[217]

Sport proved as difficult a niche market as business. An ambitious attempt to win a large audience with a sports-only Sunday paper, *Sport First*, was launched in March 1998 by Keith Young, owner of a modest enterprise called Parliamentary Publications which produced Westminster's magazine, the *House*, and the Church of England's official paper. *Sport First* started as a forty-eight-page broadsheet, priced at 50p, edited by former *Daily Express* sports editor David Emery. It soon switched to a tabloid format and within six months was selling a respectable 67,000 copies a week. By the following year he achieved an 83,000 sale, though Emery moved on. Young, who found it hard to sustain the paper, continually looked for a partner with deeper pockets but kept going in spite of difficulties. By the end of the soccer season in spring 2003, sales were down to a mere 40,000.

Young did considerably better than Birmingham travel agent Clifford Hards, who launched what was billed as Britain's first 'green' newspaper, *Planet on Sunday*. It arrived in shops on 16 June 1996, sold a respectable 110,000 copies and never appeared again. Editor Adrian Mitchelson was stunned by the decision but Hards said he didn't like the content and that no one would buy a second edition because it was so terrible.[218]

Many other would-be publishing tycoons and hundreds of journalists saw no future in print, setting out to make their fortunes and their names with electronic publishing. They were heavily influenced by a combination of dot-com fever and the predictions of super-highway missionaries. 'Newspapers are going to be delivered electronically, and quite soon,' said one visionary, Patrick Maines, director of the Media Institute in Washington in 1994. 'In a few years, the news will come out of your television – or what we now call television.' He predicted 'interactive journalism: reporters linked up to film, archive material, all on the one screen'.[219]

This dream of convergence still seemed a long way off in 2003. Meanwhile, the best electronic publishing was carried out by established newspaper groups, notably the *Guardian* and the *Financial Times*. Both groups invested heavily in their website ventures, though the *FT* suffered substantial financial losses until it began charging for access, picking up 53,000 subscribers by spring 2003. Both Andrew Gowers, editor of the *FT*, and Alan Rusbridger, editor of the *Guardian*, saw the virtue in breaking down the distinction between print and cyberspace journalists and eventually integrated their staffs. Popular papers were less enthusiastic about finding audiences for their websites: though the *Sun* and the *Daily Star* attracted male surfers by promoting their Page 3 girls, the *Daily Mail* and *Daily Express* ignored the web.

There is no end to this newspaper story, of course. Owners and controllers of newspapers go on trying to make profits and propaganda. Some are better at the former, some better at the latter. Some do neither very well. For more than half of this history the man who has most successfully accomplished both has been Rupert Murdoch.

Therefore, it is fitting to conclude by referring to an exclusive story which revealed that Murdoch's companies routinely paid virtually no tax. In 1997, for example, News Corporation paid just 7.8 per cent tax on operating profits of £800 million while, between 1985 and 1995 News International recorded profits of almost £1 billion, yet had paid only £11.74 million in tax, some 1.2 per cent.[220] This tax avoidance was totally legal, but it said a great deal about the difficulties national governments were facing in dealing with global capital. What was so fascinating was that the revelation was published in the *Independent*. No word appeared in the *Times*, the paper of record. The power of the propagandist in deciding what should, and should not, be published reminds us all how precious diversity of ownership remains.

NOTES

ABBREVIATIONS

BJR	*British Journalism Review*	*NS*	*New Statesman*
Cit	*Sunday Citizen*	*Obs*	*Observer*
DH	*Daily Herald*	*PG*	*Press Gazette*
DMir	*Daily Mirror*	*Pic*	*Sunday Pictorial*
DNB	*Dictionary of National Biography*	*RN*	*Reynolds News*
DS	*Daily Sketch*	*SCorr*	*Sunday Correspondent*
DTel	*Daily Telegraph*	*SExp*	*Sunday Express*
EN	London *Evening News*	*Sindy*	*Independent on Sunday*
ES	London *Evening Standard*	*SMir*	*Sunday Mirror*
Exp	*Daily Express*	*SP*	*Sunday People*
FT	*Financial Times*	*Spec*	*Spectator*
Guard	*Guardian*	*SSport*	*Sunday Sport*
Indy	*Independent*	*Star*	*Daily Star*
JH	*Journalist's Handbook*	*STel*	*Sunday Telegraph*
LDN	*London Daily News*	*SunBus*	*Sunday Business*
Mail	*Daily Mail*	*SunD*	*Sunday Dispatch*
MG	*Manchester Guardian*	*SunT*	*Sunday Times*
MoS	*Mail on Sunday*	*TES*	*Times Educational Supplement*
NC	*News Chronicle*	*UKPG*	*UK Press Gazette*
NoS	*News on Sunday*	*Worker*	*Daily Worker*
NoW	*News of the World*	*WPN*	*World's Press News*
NPD	*Newspaper Press Directory*	*WSJ*	*Wall Street Journal*

1. PRINTING FOR VICTORY

1 Morgan (1999), p. 28
2. *DMir*, 8.1.45:1
3. Williams (1957), p. 228
4. *NPD*, 1946/7:48
5. No audited figures available. In April 1945, it sold 895,939, according to the *Leader* 7.7.45. Name change from *Sketch* to *Graphic* 5 July 1946 and back from *Graphic* to *Sketch*, 1952
6. In June 1945, the *Daily Telegraph* sold 813,332 and the *Times* 204,000; see the *Leader* 7.7.45
7. No ABC audit until 1955

8. Cudlipp (1962), p. 55. Sales reputedly rose by 700,000
9. *DH*, 'The British buy most newspapers', 19.7.50:2. Cf. *World Communications*, Unesco report, HMSO, 1950
10. Whitcomb (1990)
11. *Report of the Royal Commission on the Press, 1947–1949* (1949), Cmd 7700, pp. 15–16
12. Taylor (1972), p. 574
13. Chisholm and Davie (1992), p. 455
14. Morgan (1999), p. 48
15. Taylor (1972), p. 585, message dated 1.1.48
16. Edwards (1998), p. 3
17. Cited Chisholm and Davie (1992), p. 492
18. Taylor (1972), pp. 163, 345
19. Foot (1980), pp. 79–80
20. Mackay (1953), p. 105. Cf. *NC*, 9.11.50
21. Chester (1979), p. 15
22. Harris (1982), p. 194; Taylor (1972), p. 574
23. Anne Chisholm, *DTel*, 30.7.00
24. Edwards (1988), pp. 79–81
25. Williams (1957), p. 218
26. Junor (1990), p. 56
27. Christiansen (1961), p. 163
28. Cecil King preferred 'the bus driver's wife in Sheffield', King (1969), p. 101
29. Williams (1957), p. 220
30. Christiansen (1961), p. 144
31. Newton (1997), p. 147
32. Junor (1990), p. 56
33. Ian Aitken conversation with author, 27.03.01
34. Junor (1990), p. 56
35. Williams (1957), p. 226
36. Cudlipp (1953), p. 49
37. Williams (1957), p. 227
38. Ibid., p. 226
39. King (1969), p. 103; Edelman (1966), p. 38
40. Williams (1957), p. 224
41. Cudlipp (1953), p. 53
42. Williams (1957), p. 229
43. Ibid., p. 230
44. King (1969), p. 104
45. Ibid., p. 108
46. Cudlipp, 'Exclusive: the first nude in Fleet Street', *BJR*, vol. 5/3, 1994
47. Cudlipp (1976), pp. 182–3
48. Cudlipp (1953), p. 66
49. Williams (1957), p. 227
50. Hyde (1947), p. 2
51. Ibid., p. 29
52. Ibid., p. 156
53. Ibid., p. 226
54. Ibid., pp. 3, 8

55. Ibid., p. 9
56. Ibid., p. 12
57. Bourne (1990), p. 157
58. Letter to Lady Cripps, 18.4.42, King (1970), p. 311. Cited in Bourne (1990), p. 154
59. Cited in Taylor (1998), p. 57
60. Ibid.
61. Procter (1958), p. 113
62. Foot (1980), p. 86
63. Williams (1993), p. 116
64. Griffiths (1996), pp. 280–1
65. Foot (1980), p. 86
66. Williams (1993), pp. 83–110
67. Taylor (1998), p. 58
68. Williams (1993), p. 115
69. Ibid., p. 116
70. Taylor (1998), p. 58
71. *Mail*, 9.7.47
72. *UKPG*, 1.12.80
73. Taylor (1998), p. 59
74. Arthur Wareham, quoted by Taylor (1998), p. 59
75. Williams (1993), p. 119
76. 'Lively Fleet Street character,' *Times*, 23.11.79:VI
77. Williams (1993), p. 119
78. Hobson et al. (1972), p. xix
79. Hamilton (1989), p. 67
80. Hobson et al. (1972), p. xx; King (1969), p. 122
81. Hamilton (1989), p. 55
82. Hobson et al. (1972), p. xix
83. *DNB*
84. Hobson et al. (1972), p. 190
85. Ibid., p. 279
86. *DNB*
87. Hobson et al. (1972), p. 192
88. Hennessy (1992), p. 329
89. Hamilton (1989), p. 71
90. *Times*, 25.4.49:4
91. *DNB*
92. Hamilton (1989), p. 71
93. Hart-Davis (1990), p. 148
94. Ibid., pp. 28, 82
95. Ibid., pp. 154–5
96. Ibid., p. 157
97. Ibid., p. 59
98. Ibid., p. 76
99. Nicolson (1968), p. 163
100. Hart-Davis (1990), p. 149; Kynaston (1998), p. 142
101. *Times*, 26.7.45:7
102. Drogheda (1978), p. 114
103. Lysaght (1979), p. 257

104. Robin Bruce Lockhart, 'Brendan Bracken – Founding Father', *History Today*, April 1991, p. 12
105. *DNB*
106. Einzig (1960), p. 100
107. Lysaght (1979), p. 83
108. Drogheda (1978), p. 84
109. Colville (1985), 18.5.40
110. Boyle (1974), p. 7
111. Kynaston (1988), p. 162
112. Foot (1980), p. 78
113. Lysaght (1979), pp. 123–4
114. Bracken (1958), p. 64
115. Lysaght (1979), p. 259
116. Cockett (1990), p. 90
117. Kynaston (1988), p. 173
118. Lockhart, op. cit., p. 14
119. Kynaston (1988), p. 184
120. Hennessy (1992), p. 327; Haslam (1999), p. 114; Coote (1965), p. 170
121. Koss (1984), p. 625
122. Hennessy (1992), p. 328
123. Koss (1984), p. 617
124. Hartwell (1992), p. 325
125. Driberg (1949), p. 8
126. Woods and Bishop (1985), p. 329
127. *DNB*
128. Pringle (1973), pp. 53, 183
129. Giles (1986), p. 68
130. Cockett (1991), p. 174
131. Ibid., p. 135
132. Ibid., p. 136
133. *Obs*, 22.6.47
134. 'The meaning of Malan', Obs, 30.5.48:4. Cf. 'City under siege', 17.9.50
135. Minney (1954), p. 352
136. *Times*, 11.4.46:7
137. Arthur Greenwood, *SunT*, 14.4.46:6
138. Richards (1981), p. 161
139. *SP*, 29.1.50
140. Richards (1981), p. 159; Low (1956), pp. 287, 379
141. Jay (1980), p. 82
142. Draper (1988), p. 24
143. *DNB*
144. Richards (1981), p. 163
145. *Worker*, 1.11.48:1
146. Edwards (1988), p. 40
147. Cudlipp (1962), p. 292
148. Edwards (1988), p. 41
149. 'One Hundreds Years Today', *NC*, 21.1.46:1
150. Ibid.
151. Hubback (1985), p. 131

152. Ibid., p. 133
153. Ibid., p. 197
154. Cockett (1990), p. 85
155. Ibid., p. 175
156. Mackay (1953), pp. 78–80
157. Ibid., pp. 89–91
158. Hubback (1985), p. 199
159. Ibid., p. 200
160. Ayerst (1971), p. 564
161. Ibid., p. 554
162. *MG*, 12.6.45
163. *MG*, 7.6.45; Ayerst (1971), p. 561
164. Ibid., p. 560
165. *MG*, 21.2.50:6
166. Ayerst (1971), p. 415
167. Ibid., p. 624
168. Pringle (1973), p. 31
169. Ayerst (1971), p. 579
170. Ibid., p. 596
171. Ibid., p. 590
172. Ibid., p. 592
173. Ibid., p. 573
174. Bainbridge and Stockdill (1993), p. 115
175. Ibid., p. 123
176. *NoW*, 7.1.45:3
177. *NoW*, 11.1.48:3
178. *NoW*, 8.7.45
179. *NoW*, 21.3.48:1, 3

2. THE PRESS VERSUS THE POLITICIANS

1. Q. D. Leavis, *Fiction and the Reading Public* (Chatto & Windus, 1932), p. 271
2. Shawcross (1995), p. 149
3. Ibid., p. 147
4. 'Attack on Press by Sir H. Shawcross', *DTel*, 20.7.46:4
5. *DMir*, 22.7.46
6. *DTel*, 31.7.46:4
7. *DMir*, 1.8.46:2
8. Hennessy (1992), p. 327
9. *FT*, 5.7.45
10. Coote (1965), p. 230
11. *Exp*, 16.6.45; McCallum and Readman (1947), p. 209
12. 'Getting things out of control', *NC*, 8.6.45
13. *DMir*, 22.6.45
14. *DH*, 15.6.45
15. Hart-Davis (1990), p. 150
16. Hennessy (1992), p. 327

17. Ibid.
18. McCallum and Readman (1947), p. 181
19. Ibid., pp. 181–2
20. 'Time To Vote', *Times*, 5.7.45
21. *Exp*, 5.6.45; *DH*, 18.6.45
22. McCallum and Readman (1947), p. 190
23. Ibid., p. 205
24. Ibid., p. 213; King (1969), p. 119
25. King (1970), p. 295
26. Childs (1997), p. 4
27. *Exp*, 3.1.45
28. *Exp*, 5.7.45: 1, 'How inscrutable are the thoughts of the people!', *Exp*, 27.7.45: 4.
29. 'Millions of pounds wiped off share values', *Exp*, 27.7.45:1
30. Cf. William Barkley, 'Goody goody, but Mr Attlee will have to ask Mr Laskee', *Exp*, 19.6.45
31. Martin (1953), pp. 168–79
32. 'On Being Suddenly Famous', *NS*, 14.7.45
33. Morgan (1999), p. 64
34. *SunT*, 28.4.46:4
35. Cf. *Mail*, 20.6.45; Bourne (1990), p. 163
36. *DS*, 29.6.46:1
37. 'Press Lords Accused', *DMir*, 4.7.46:1
38. *Exp*, 47.46:4
39. Newman (1989), p. 109
40. *DMir*, 28.7.47
41. *NC*, 29.7.47:2
42. *DMir*, 28.11.47:2
43. *DTel*, 28.11.47:4
44. *SP*, 3.9.50:1 and 2
45. 'Black market men now sell jeeps', *DMir*, 20.1.45
46. *DH*, 11.12.45:1
47. *EN*, 27.3.47:1, 1.4.47:1; 30.4.47:1
48. *DH*, 16.7.48:1
49. *Mail*, 8.7.49:1
50. *Star*, 28.2.50:4
51. *DMir*, 20.1.45
52. *NoW*, 30.7.50
53. *DMir*, 20.2.45
54. *DMir*, 28.2.45:1
55. *NoW*, 16.5.48:2
56. *Mail*, 8.7.49:1
57. *DTel*, 5.11.47:4
58. *Exp*, 27.1.50:7
59. Procter (1958), p. 111
60. *Exp*, 2.3.49:1
61. *Exp*, 3.3.49:1, 5
62. 'He winces as the police put handcuffs on him', *DMir*, 3.3.49:1, 5
63. *Exp*, 4.3.49:1; *DMir*, 4.3.49:1
64. *DMir*, 26.3.49:1, 7; *Exp*, 26.3.49:3; Wintour (1972), p. 131

65. Cudlipp (1953), pp. 250–1
66. *DMir*, 26.3.49:1
67. Cudlipp (1953), p. 254
68. Ibid., p. 253
69. Cudlipp (1962), p. 333; Wintour (1972), p. 131
70. Sharf (1964), p. 143
71. Cf. *DTel* and *MG*, 28.4.45
72. *RN*, 22.4.45:2
73. 'Buchenwald by Tom Driberg: I saw it myself', *RN*, 29.4.45:4
74. Schellenberg (2000), pp. 164, 266
75. Bourne (1990), p. 87
76. Ferris (1971), p. 213
77. 'Alien Women in Luxury', *SunD*, 7.1.40
78. Gillman and Gillman (1980) p. 79; one Beaverbrook paper was certainly unsympathetic to Jewish immigration: *ES*, 16.1.39. Cf. Griffiths (1996), p. 281
79. *NC*, 28.11.46; Sharf (1964), p. 201
80. Robb (1954), pp. 69–72
81. Cf. *Mail*, 1.5.46:2; 23.7.46:1
82. *Mail*, 15.5.48:6
83. Nicolson (1968), p. 140
84. *DTel*, 12.11.46
85. *DMir*, 24.7.46:1
86. *DMir*, 25.7.46:1
87. *Exp*, 23.7.46:1
88. Cf. *DMir*, 23.7.46; 24.7.46
89. *Exp*, 5.8.47:2
90. Report of the Porter Committee, cited by Sharf (1964), p. 203
91. *Morecambe & Heysham Visitor*, 6.8.47
92. *Times*, 14.7.47:2
93. *Times*, 19.9.47:4
94. *Times*, 24.9.47:2
95. *Times*, 14.10.47:2; *MG*,14.10.47:2
96. *Times*, 18.11.47:3
97. *DTel*, 18.11.47:5
98. *MG*, 18.11.47
99. 'Mr J. Caunt buried with notebook and pencil', *Morecambe Guardian*, 30.1.59
100. *An Editor on Trial: Rex versus Caunt, Alleged Seditious Libel* (Morecambe Press, 1948)
101. *DTel*, 22.2.49. Cf. *MG*, 21.2.49; *Times*, 21/22.2.49
102. Sharf (1964), p. 153
103. *Edinburgh Evening Dispatch*, 1.3.49
104. *Dundee Courier*, 23.2.49
105. Sharf (1964), p. 154
106. Morgan (1999), p. 76
107. Cf. *DS*, 15.7.47:1; *Obs*, 3.8.47:1; *Mail*, 19.7.46:2; *Exp*, 22.8.46:2
108. *FT*, 27.12.45:2
109. *Times*, 23.5.46:9
110. *Exp*, 21.7.47:2
111. *ES*, 14.7.47:1, 2

112. *NC*, 17.7.47:1; *DS*, 17.7.47:1, 2
113. *Times*, 27.9.47:2
114. *Times*, 30.9.47:3
115. 'Newsprint "totally inadequate"', *Obs*, 15.10.50:1
116. *Times*, 6.5.48:5, 25.5.48:5 and 26.5.48:5
117. 'Why an inquiry?', William Barkley, *Exp*, 22.8.46:2
118. *DMir*, 23.7.46:2
119. *Exp*, 23.7.46:3
120. *NPD*, 1948, p. 55
121. May 1958, cited in Herd (1952), p. 313
122. Foot (1980), p. 111
123. *DMir*, 23.7.46:2
124. *Times*, 27.9.47:2
125. 'Let's take a look at Fleet Street', *Mail*, 19.7.46:2
126. Beaverbrook (1925), p. 27
127. E. J. Robertson papers in *Daily Express* archives. Cf. Taylor (1972), p. 584
128. Chisholm and Davie (1992), p. 458
129. *Report of the Royal Commission on the Press, 1947–9* (1949) Cmd 7700, paras 87–8
130. Hamilton (1989), p. 67. Cf. Kemsley (1950)
131. Hennessy (1992), p. 329
132. Ibid.
133. Cmd 7700, op. cit., para. 656
134. Ibid., para 663
135. *MG*, 30.6.49:4
136. Cmd 7700, op. cit., para 657
137. *MG*, 29.6.49:4
138. *Times*, 30.6.49:5
139. *MG*, 30.6.49:4
140. Edelman (1966), pp. 176–7
141. Bourne (1990), p. 164
142. *Mail*, 21.1.50
143. *ES*, 2.3.50:1
144. Newman (1989), pp. 119–20
145. Wintour (1972), p. 60
146. Junor (1990), pp. 47–8
147. Ibid., p. 48
148. Chisholm and Davie (1992), p. 470; Cameron (1967), pp. 87–90. Cf. M. Foot on Cameron, *DNB*
149. Griffiths (1996), p. 323; Edwards (1988), p. 54
150. Thomas (1973), p. 268
151. Newman (1989), p. 116
152. *NPD*, 1949, p. 51
153. 'Type-composing by photograph', *Times*, 17.9.49:4
154. Musson (1954), p. 522

3. THE BARONIAL RETREAT

1. Raymond Chandler, *The Long Good-Bye* (1953), Chapter 32
2. Williams (1957) pp. 232–3
3. 'It should not have happened', *Mail*, 21.4.55:1
4. *Times*, 24.3.54
5. Woods and Bishop (1985), p. 339
6. Cockett (1990), p. 132
7. Koss (1984), p. 652
8. Randall (1988), p. 31
9. Cockett (1990), p. 164
10. Hart-Davis (1990), p. 179
11. Wintour (1972), p. 57
12. Robertson (1983), pp. 9–10
13. *Times*, 29.6.55:11
14. King (1969), p. 105
15. Wintour (1972), p. 186
16. King (1969), p. 105
17. Frederic Mullally, *BJR*, vol. 10/2, 1999
18. Edelman (1966), p. 154; Cudlipp (1976), p. 65
19. Cudlipp (1976), pp. 67–8
20. King (1969), p. 123
21. Junor (1990), p. 56
22. Cudlipp (1962), p. 164
23. Cudlipp (1976), pp. 260–71
24. Matthews (1957), p. 50
25. Williams (1957), p. 230
26. Cudlipp (1953), p. 279
27. Wintour (1972), p. 186
28. Brodzky (1996), p. 50
29. BBC interview, 27.8.64, cited in Edelman (1966), pp. 46, 156
30. Cudlipp (1976), p.p. 174, 213, 405–6
31. King (1969), p. 108
32. Sisman (1994), p. 203
33. Edelman (1966), p. 43
34. Williams (1957), p. 231
35. Edelman (1966), p. 158
36. Donald Zec, 'Fiddlin' my way to Fleet Street', *BJR*, vol. 11/1, p. 18
37. Patmore (1993), p. 114; Gray (1990), p. 269
38. Geoffrey Goodman, Cudlipp obit, *Guard*, 18.5.98
39. *DMir*, 26.1.54:1
40. Moran (1966), pp. 455, 522. Cf. *DMir*, 17.8.53:1
41. Williams (1957), p. 231
42. Cudlipp (1953), p. 285
43. King (1969), p. 158
44. Richards (1997), p. 164; Hutt (1960), p. 47
45. Richards (1997), p. 164
46. Jay (1980), p. 228

47. *WPN*, 4.12.53
48. Jay (1980), p. 229
49. Richard Clements, 'A salute to the two-headed horse', *BJR*, vol. 8/4. p. 74
50. Jay (1980), p. 229
51. Ibid.
52. Richards (1997), p. 165
53. Sir Harold Hartley, *Times*, 9.11.62:17
54. Bainbridge and Stockdill (1993), p. 178
55. Somerfield (1979), p. 103
56. Ibid., p. 105
57. Bainbridge and Stockdill (1993), p. 177
58. Somerfield (1979), p. 108
59. Bainbridge and Stockdill (1993), p. 182
60. Williams (1957), pp. 214–15
61. Chisholm and Davie (1992), p. 455
62. Gourlay (1984), p. 31
63. Bob Edwards, Hugh Cudlipp memorial lecture, 24.10.00
64. Chisholm and Davie (1992), p. 477
65. Colville (1985), p. 669; Hartwell (1992), p. 338
66. Hartwell (1992), p. 338
67. Chisholm and Davie (1992), p. 469
68. *Exp*, 2.6.53:1
69. Pickering interview with author, 19.2.01
70. Williams (1957), p. 219
71. Christiansen (1961), p. 147
72. Wiggin (1972), p. 110
73. 'Scoops on Sunday', Brodzky (1966), p. 62
74. *DNB*
75. Beverley Baxter, cited in *DNB*
76. Brodzky (1966), p. 63
77. Cudlipp (1962), p. 101
78. Junor (1990), p. 97
79. Cudlipp (1962), p. 101
80. Junor (1990), p. 31
81. Edwards (1988), p. 100
82. Gray (1990), p. 181
83. Ibid., p. 186
84. Junor (1990), p. 60
85. Ibid., pp. 85–6
86. Watkins (1982), p. 90; Junor (2002), p. 66
87. Griffiths (1996), p. 318
88. Ibid., p. 323
89. Junor (1990), p. 80
90. Tynan (1987), p. 105
91. Hollingberry conversation with author, 7.11.00
92. McDonald conversation with author, 7.11.00
93. Bob Trevor, 'Day of Infamy', *PG*, 3.11.00:17
94. McDonald conversation with author, 7.11.00
95. Taylor (1998), p. 68

96. Pickering interview with author, 19.2.01
97. Taylor (1998), p. 70
98. Wintour (1972), p. 208
99. Associated Newspapers, annual report, 1952
100. Associated Newspapers, annual report, 1953
101. Taylor (1998), p. 71
102. Procter (1958), pp. 133–4
103. Taylor (1998), p. 90
104. Wintour (1972), p. 208
105. Taylor (1998), pp. 87–9
106. Wintour (1972), p. 211
107. Bourne (1990), p. 167
108. Cudlipp (1962), p. 303
109. Hobson et al. (1972), p. 285
110. Crockett (1990), p. 137
111. Wintour (1972), p. 210
112. Associated Newspapers, annual report, 1953
113. Hobson et al. (1972), p. 338
114. Bourne (1990), p. 168
115. Wintour (1972), p. 211; Taylor (1998), p. 97
116. Bourne (1990), p. 169
117. Inglis (1990), p. 193
118. Wintour (1972), p. 210
119. Kenneth Brown, 'The paper only a journalist could love for long', *UKPG*, 15.3.71:10
120. Williams (1957), p. 242
121. Levy (1967), pp. 123–4
122. *Recorder*, 27.10.53:1
123. *Recorder*, 25.3.54:1
124. *Recorder*, 1.12.53:4
125. Watkins (1982), p. 112
126. Margach (1979), p. 146
127. Trevor Huddleston, 'For God's Sake, Wake Up!', *Obs*, 30.8.53:3
128. Edwards (1988), p. 83
129. Cockett (1991), p. 138
130. Tynan (1987), p. 135
131. Pringle (1973), pp. 146–7
132. Hobson et al. (1972), p. xxiii
133. Obit, *Times*, 15.4.99
134. Ayerst (1971), p. 603
135. Ibid., p. 618
136. Kynaston (1988), p. 200
137. Ibid.
138. Ibid.
139. Newton (1997), p. vii
140. Ibid, p. 38
141. Ibid., p. 63
142. Ibid., p. 65
143. Kynaston (1988), p. 205

144. *Punch*, 13.1.65
145. Kynaston (1988), p. 206
146. Ibid., p. 207
147. Ibid.
148. Newton (1997), p. 86
149. Kynaston (1988), p. 215
150. Pringle (1973), p. 61
151. Channon (1967), p. 460, 4.6.51
152. Hart-Davis (1990), pp. 167–8, 170
153. Woods and Bishop (1985), p. 329
154. Giles (1986), p. 68
155. Cockett (1990), p. 130
156. Read (1992), p. 180
157. Hamilton (1989), p. 132
158. Cf. 'The Formation of Public Opinion', Haldane memorial lecture, 1958
159. Hamilton (1989), p. 132
160. Leon Pilpel in Gray (1990), p. 150
161. Newton (1997), p. 98
162. Woods and Bishop (1985), p. 332
163. Ibid., p. 333
164. Hart-Davis (1990), p. 170
165. Coote (1965), p. 246
166. Herd (1952), p. 270
167. Coote (1965), p. 227
168. Ibid., p. 221
169. Ibid., pp. 254–5
170. Nicolson (1968), 15.6.54
171. Worsthorne, *Times*, 9.5.83:9
172. Hart-Davis (1990), p. 193
173. Hubback (1985), p. 232
174. Ibid., p. 231
175. Cudlipp (1976), p. 207
176. Hubback (1985), p. 234
177. Braddon (1965), pp. 166–8
178. Ibid., pp. 110, 114
179. Ibid., p. 120
180. Ibid., p. 321
181. Junor (1990), p. 67
182. Braddon (1965), p. 127

4. ALL THIS – AND CIRCULATION TOO!

1. Thomas Paine, *Common Sense* (New York: Barnes & Noble, 1995), p. 20
2. *MG*, 22.10.51
3. *MG*, 25.10.51
4. Williams (1957), p. 216
5. Jay (1980), p. 210

6. *DMir*, 25.10.51:1; King (1969), p. 119
7. Edelman (1966), p. 177
8. Hart-Davis (1990), p. 178
9. Kynaston (1988), p. 218
10. *Guard*, 3.6.53:8
11. Ayerst (1971), p. 610
12. *SP*, 14.6.53:1
13. *DMir*, 13.7.53:1
14. *DMir*, 17.7.53:1
15. *Times*, 22.7.53:8
16. *Times*, 24.7.53:9
17. *DMir*, 16.11. 54
18. *DMir*, 17.11.54
19. *Pic*, 6.3.55
20. *DMir*, 15.8.55:1
21. Hartwell (1992), p. 338
22. Cockett (1990), p. 158
23. *DMir*, 29.6.53; 26.1.54; 1.4.54
24. Moran (1966). Cf. Young (1966), pp. 297–8
25. *Mail*, 22.4.55:1; 30.4.55:1; 12.5.55:1; 18.5.55:1
26. *DTel*, 23.5.55:6
27. *Exp*, 3.5.55:6
28. *Times*, 25.5.55:11
29. Cudlipp obit, *Indy*, 18.5.98
30. *DMir*, 24.5.55:1
31. *DTel*, 25.5.55:6
32. Max Jones, 'The Spinning Disc', *DH*, 9.2.55
33. Patrick Doncaster and Tony Miles, 'Where the Hoo-ray Henrys step out', *DMir*, 17.1.55:7
34. *Pic*, 25.5.52:1, 6, 15; 1.6.52:12; 8.6.52:12
35. Cudlipp (1962), p. 317
36. Winn (1967), p. 322
37. *Recorder*, 27.10.53
38. *Recorder*, 13.11.53:4
39. Montagu (2000), p. 98
40. Cudlipp (1962), p. 319
41. 'I've waited a long time for this', *STel*, 10.9.00
42. Tynan (1987), p. 110
43. Montagu (2000), p. 100
44. Ibid., p. 107
45. Tynan (1987), p. 110
46. Percy Elland to Beaverbrook, 15.1.54
47. Edwards (1988), p. 95
48. *DMir*, 25.3.54
49. Montagu (2000), p. 115
50. Peter Wildeblood obit, *Guard*, 16.11.99; Montagu (2000), p. 107
51. Watkins (1982), p. 87; Junor (2002), pp. 117, 210, 212, 270–1
52. Montagu (2000), p. 204
53. Cassandra, 'The woman who hangs today', *DMir*, 13.7.55

54. Cassandra, *DMir*, 26.9.56
55. Cudlipp (1976), pp. 233–8
56. 'Laughter in court', *BJR*, vol. 3/2, 1992
57. Liberace obit, *Times*, 6.2.87

5. DEATH, DEPARTURE AND DARKNESS

1. James Cameron, *West London Press*, 21.10.60
2. Williams (1957), p. 207
3. Ibid., p 209
4. Matthews (1957), pp. 47–8
5. Procter (1958), p. 58
6. Ibid., p. 84
7. Ibid., p. 91
8. Ibid., p. 137
9. *Pic*, 20.2.55:1
10. Procter (1958), p. 156
11. Ibid., p. 199
12. Ibid., p. 211
13. Ibid., p. 219
14. Val Lewis conversation with author, 8.11.00
15. Inglis (1990), p. 211
16. Barker and Petley (2001), p. 174
17. Chambers (1985), pp. 19, 30; Richards (1997), p. 169
18. Adrian Smith, 'The Fall and Fall of the Third *Daily Herald*, 1930–64', paper delivered at Institute for Contemporary British History conference, 10.9.96, p. 14
19. Lamb (1987), p. 17
20. *Exp*, *DMir*, *Mail*, *DH*, 1.9.58:1, 2.9.58:1
21. Frank Owen, 'Bring back the cat?', *DS*, 4.9.58:8
22. *MG*, 2.9.58:1
23. *MG*, 3.9.58:1
24. Jephcott (1964)
25. Banton (1959), p. 171
26. *Exp*, 1.9.58:2
27. *Times*, 1.9.58:9
28. Merrick Wynn, *Exp*, 3.9.58:6
29. *Exp*, 1.9.58:4
30. 'Should we let them keep pouring in?', *Mail*, 2.9.58:4
31. *DMir*, 2.9.58:1
32. *DMir*, 3.9.58:1, 20
33. Solomos (1989), p. 48
34. Letter to *Times*, 2.9.58:11
35. 'Our colour problem', *DTel*, 2.9.58:8
36. *SP*, 12.10.58:1
37. 'Britain? I call it Black Men's Hell', *SP*, 16.11.58:2, 3
38. Solomos (1989), p. 49
39. *Times*, 3.9.58:7

40. *Times*, 3.9.58:11
41. James Cameron, *West London Press*, op. cit. Cf. Cameron (1967), pp. 276ff
42. Francis Williams, 'The Murder of the *News Chronicle*: A Failure of Management', *NS*, 22.10.60, p. 593
43. Margaret Stewart, 'The Night the Blow Fell', *NS*, 22.10.60:593–4
44. Cudlipp (1962), p. 371
45. Peter Lawrence, 'Death in the afternoon', *PG*, 13.10.00
46. Williams (1957), pp. 211–12
47. Williams, *NS*, op. cit.
48. Cockett (1990), pp. 171, 175
49. Ibid., p. 172
50. Hubback (1985), p. 236
51. Michael Curtis, 'Death of a Newspaper', *NS*, 6.11.64
52. Hubback (1985), p. 237
53. *Times*, 20.10.6
54. Grundy (1976), p. 112
55. Cf. Glenton and Pattinson (1963); *Spec*, 21.10.60
56. Francis Williams, *NS*, 22.10.60:593; 29.10.60:636–7
57. *Economist*, 22.10.60, p. 320
58. Philip Purser, *Spec*, 21.10.60, pp. 588–9
59. Stewart, *NS*, op. cit.
60. Lawrence, *PG*, op. cit.
61. Purser, *Spec*, op. cit.
62. Randall (1988), p. 62
63. Purser, *Spec*, op. cit.
64. Hubert Phillips, *Spec*, 21.10.60:590–1
65. Cameron, *West London Press*, op. cit.
66. *Report of the Royal Commission on the Press, 1947–9*, (1962), Cmnd 1811, para. 254
67. Bourne (1990), p. 174
68. Margaret Stewart, *Spec*, 21.10.60
69. *Economist*, 22.10.60, p. 320
70. Claud Cockburn, *NS*, 29.10.60, pp. 642–4
71. *NS*, 22.10.60
72. Cameron, *West London Press*, 21.10.60
73. *Economist*, 29.4.60
74. 'An experiment in independence', *New Daily*, 25.4.60:8
75. 'News values', *New Daily*, 6.5.60:8
76. Cudlipp (1962), p. 238
77. Taylor (1998), p. 135
78. Bourne (1990), p. 174
79. Ibid.
80. Randall (1988), p. 63
81. Title of Wareham's unpublished memoir, Taylor (1998), p. 108
82. Randall (1988), p. 66
83. 'Press intrusion at Duke of Kent birthday party', *DTel*, 17.1.57:9
84. Kenneth Brown, 'The paper only a journalist could love for long', *UKPG*, 15.3.71:10
85. Devon (1957)

86. Pignon conversation with author, 3.11.00
87. Bourne (1990), p. 202
88. Kendal McDonald conversation with author, 7.11.00
89. Eddie Campbell conversation with author, 4.11.00
90. David Wainwright, 'The man who brought justice day by day', *EN*, 29.10.80:15
91. Bob Trevor, 'Day of Infamy', *PG*. 3.11.00
92. Hamilton (1989), p. 92
93. Thomson (1975), p. 60
94. Hamilton (1989), p. 84
95. Ibid., p. 82
96. Ibid., p. 84
97. Ibid., p. 85
98. Ibid., p. 88
99. Ibid., p. 91
100. Hobson et al. (1972), p. 317; Hamilton (1989), p. 92; Thomson (1975), p. 59
101. Braddon (1965), pp. 219–23; Hobson (1972), p. 319
102. Hamilton (1989), p. 97
103. Ibid., p. 98
104. Hobson et al. (1972), p. 322
105. Thomson (1975), p. 56
106. Ibid., p. 78
107. Ibid.
108. Ibid., p. 80
109. Hart-Davis (1990), p. 228
110. Braddon (1965), p. 242
111. Brodie (1995), pp. 270–88
112. Cf. Gailey (1995)
113. Braddon (1965), p. 253
114. Richards (1997), p. 167
115. Curran and Seaton (1991), p. 118
116. Hulton Readership Surveys, 1956–60
117. Jay (1980), p. 252
118. Draper (1988), p. 79
119. Richards (1997), pp. 171–2
120. *DH*, 26.2.58
121. Richards (1997), p. 172
122. Jay (1980), p. 252
123. Ernie Burrington email to author, 25.4.01
124. *DH*, 27.2.58
125. Crossman (1981), p. 668
126. Jay (1980), p. 252
127. Cudlipp (1976), p. 248
128. Anthony Howard, 'The Accidental Journalist', *JH*, no. 58, July 1999
129. Ibid.
130. Grundy (1976), p. 21
131. Cudlipp obit, *Indy*, 18.5.98
132. Mike Molloy, Cudlipp obit, *DMir*, 18.5.98
133. Perrott Phillips, 'Cudlipp – a man who could do anyone's job better', *PG*, 10.7.98
134. 'The announcement that surprised the world', *DMir*, 27.2.60

135. Cudlipp (1976), p. 174
136. *DMir*, 11.2.57:1
137. Patmore (1993), p. 115
138. Geoffrey Goodman, Cudlipp obit, *Guard*, 18.5.98
139. Cudlipp obit, *Indy*, 18.5.98
140. Cudlipp (1976), pp. 212–13
141. *Times*, 1.2.58:7
142. *DMir*, 29.1.58:1
143. Andrews (1962), p. 155
144. *DMir*, 13.10.59
145. *ES*, 14.10.59
146. 'Shattered *Mirror*', *NS*, 17.10.59
147. Cudlipp (1962), p. 123
148. *DMir*, 17.5.60:1
149. Cudlipp (1976), p. 403
150. Ibid., p. 242
151. Ibid., pp. 174, 289
152. Vines (1968), p. 92
153. Wintour (1989), p. 96
154. Chisholm and Davie (1992), p. 473
155. Jameson (1988), p. 158
156. Jameson (1990), p. 43
157. Cf. London Letter, *Guard*, 28.9.63:6
158. John Beavan, *DMir*, 28.9.63:2
159. Cudlipp (1976), p. 289
160. Geoffrey Wakeford in Brodzky (1966), p. 150
161. Wintour (1989), p. 96
162. Chisholm and Davie (1992), p. 83
163. Ibid., p. 512
164. *SExp*, 29.1.56
165. Greene (1989), pp. 76–88
166. *Exp*, 26.7.56
167. Chisholm and Davie (1992), p. 511
168. Gourlay (1984), p. 41
169. Williams (1957), p. 209
170. Wintour (1972), pp. 184–5
171. *DTel*, 21.2.57:1
172. *DTel*, 11.2.57:1
173. *DTel*, 9.2.57:1
174. Grigg (1993), p. 25
175. Woods and Bishop (1985), pp. 344–5
176. Haley memo, 5.2.59, cited in Woods and Bishop (1985), p. 345
177. McDonald (1984), p. 321
178. Obit, *Times*, 9.1.01:23
179. Taylor (1993), pp. 11–12
180. Kynaston (1988), p. 280
181. Newton (1997), p. 75
182. Kynaston (1988), p.253
183. Ibid.

184. *FT*, 5.2.57:1
185. Kynaston (1988), p. 267
186. 'Observer's Lost World', *STel*, 25.4.93
187. Pringle (1973), pp. 143–4
188. Ibid., p. 135
189. Ibid., p. 142
190. Frayn in Gray (1990), p. 168
191. Cockett (1991), p. 68
192. Ibid., p. 235
193. Nat Rothman, *DNB*
194. *SP*, 27.4.58:6
195. *SP*, 19.1.58:2, 3
196. *SP*, 9.2.58:1
197. Bainbridge and Stockdill (1993), p. 166
198. Ibid., p. 170
199. Cited in William Hardcastle, 'Pictures of the War', *Listener*, 29.10.70

6. SUEZ: THE EXPLOSION OF A MEDIA MYTH

1. Karl Marx, letter to Ludwig Kugelmann, 27.7.1871, *Collected Works of Karl Marx and Frederick Engels* (Lawrence & Wishart, 1989), vol. 44, p. 177
2. Lamb (1987), p. 13
3. *Times*, 2.1.56; *Mail*, 3.1.56
4. *DTel*, 3.1.56; Coote (1965), p. 278; Hudson and Stanier (1997), p. 125
5. *Obs*, 8.1.56:1
6. 'Running in', *Times*, 5.4.56
7. Hudson and Stanier (1997), p. 125
8. McDonald (1984), p. 259
9. Hudson and Stanier (1997), p. 130
10. *Times*, 27.7.56:11; 28.7.56:7
11. *Times*, 30.7.56:9
12. *Times*, 1.8.56:9
13. Woods and Bishop (1985), p. 335; Hudson and Stanier (1997), p. 131; McDonald (1984), p. 260
14. McDonald (1984), p. 262
15. Ibid., p. 265
16. 'Hitler of the Nile', *Mail*, 27.7.56:1
17. *Exp*, 27.7.56:4
18. 'This man Nasser', *Exp*, 31.7.56:4
19. *DH*, 28.7.56:1
20. *DH*, 30.7.56:4; 3.8.56:4
21. *DMir*, 30.7.56:1, 2
22. *DMir*, 14.8.56:1, 8, 9; cf. Edelman (1966), p. 158 for Cudlipp's role
23. *DMir*, 15.8.56:1
24. *DMir*, 12.9.56:1
25. *DTel*, 27.7.56:6
26. *DTel*, 30.7.56:6

27. *NC*, 28.7.56:4; 2.8.56:4
28. *MG*, 28.7.56:4
29. 'Military action', *MG*, 2.8.56:6
30. Hetherington (1981), p. 4
31. *MG*, 10.8.56:4
32. Hetherington (1981), p. 7
33. *Obs*, 5.8.56:4
34. *Obs*, 12.8.56:6
35. *Obs*, 19.8.56:6
36. Epstein (1964), esp. pp. 154–63
37. Woods and Bishop (1985), p. 336; McDonald (1981), p. 263
38. Glenton and Pattinson (1963), p. 105; Hubback (1985), p. 235; Michael Curtis, 'Death of a Newspaper', *NS*, 6.11.64
39. Edwards (1988), p. 71
40. Cudlipp (1976), pp. 226–7; obit, *Indy*, 18.5.98
41. Jay (1980), p. 254
42. *Times*, 7.8.56
43. King (1969), p. 130
44. Francis Williams, *NS*, 25.8.56:211
45. *Exp*, 1.11.56:6
46. *Exp*, 5.11.56:6
47. *ES*, 5.11.56
48. Griffiths (1996), p. 331
49. *Mail*, 1.11.56:1
50. *DS*, 1.11.56:2
51. *DS*, 2.11.56:2
52. *DTel*, 1.11.56:6; 2.11.56:8
53. Coote (1965), p. 283
54. *SunT*, 29.7.56:6
55. 'Doing UNO's business', *SunT*, 4.11.56:10
56. Hudson and Stanier (1997), p. 131
57. Francis Williams, *NS*, 10.11.56:582
58. *Times*, 31.10.56; 1.11.56:11
59. *Times*, 'A Lack of Candour', 2.11.56
60. Macmillan (1971), pp. 112–13
61. Ayerst (1971), p. 624
62. *MG*, 31.10.56
63. *NC*, 31.10.56:4; 1.11.56:4
64. *DMir*, 1.11.56:1; 2.11.56:1
65. *Obs*, 4.11.56:8
66. Cockett (1990), p. 223
67. *Obs*, 11.11.56:2
68. *Obs*, 18.11.56:9
69. Benn (1994), p. 212; McDonald (1984), p. 268
70. Cockett (1990), p. 231
71. Donald Trelford letter to *Times*, 3.5.93
72. Cockett (1990), p. 232
73. Ibid., p. 233
74. Ibid., p. 208

75. Philip Purser, Spec, 21.10.60:588–9
76. Glenton and Pattinson (1963), p. 105
77. King (1969), p. 131
78. Cudlipp (1962), p. 112; Edelman (1966), p. 159; obit *Indy*, 18.5.98
79. King (1969), p. 131
80. Cudlipp (1976), p. 230
81. Woods and Bishop (1985), p. 337
82. Ayerst (1971), p. 625
83. *DMir*, 4.11.56
84. *Exp*, 4.11.56
85. *Economist*, 17.11.56:577
86. *SExp*, 16.12.56
87. Junor (1990), pp. 106–11
88. Beverley Baxter, *DTel*, 24.1.57:13
89. Watkins (1982), p. 90; Junor (2002), pp. 85–7

7. SEX, SPIES AND AN OVERDOSE OF SOCIOLOGY

1. Hugh Cudlipp, cited in Hobson et al. (1972), p. xxviii
2. Cole (1956), p. 5
3. *Obs*, 20.10.63
4. Childs (1997), p. 112
5. *Obs*, 6.11.60
6. McDonald (1984), pp. 359–61, 226
7. *Encounter*, February 1961
8. Taylor (1961), p. 55; Cudlipp (1962), p. 366
9. Edelman (1966), p. 186
10. Thomson (1975), p. 94
11. Braddon (1965), p. 247
12. Edelman (1966), p. 186
13. Cudlipp (1962), p. 242
14. Braddon (1965), p. 259
15. Edelman (1966), p. 189
16. Cudlipp (1962), p. 229
17. Edelman (1966), p. 190
18. 'Plain speaking about the grab for Odhams Press', *SP*, 12.2.61:12
19. Edelman (1976), p. 190
20. Cudlipp (1962), pp. 247–8
21. Jay (1980), p. 280
22. Richards (1997), p. 176
23. *Report of the Royal Commission on the Press, 1961–2* (1962), Cmnd 1811
24. Ibid., para. 337
25. Ibid., para. 325
26. Braddon (1965), p. 263
27. Schofield (1975), pp. 44–5
28. Thomson (1965), p. 38
29. Jackson (1971), p. 25

30. Braddon (1965), p. 308
31. Geoffrey Baylis, 'The Sheffield Affair', in Brodzky (1966), pp. 87–90
32. Braddon (1965), p. 314
33. Hobson et al. (1972), p. xxvii
34. Grigg (1993), p. 8
35. Hamilton (1989), p. 103
36. Braddon (1965), p. 266
37. Hobson obit, *DTel*, 14.4.99
38. Hobson et al. (1972), p. xxvii
39. Mark Boxer, cited in Hamilton (1989), p. 112
40. Hobson et al. (1972), p. 357
41. John Freeman's *Face to Face* on BBC TV. Cf. Thomson (1975), pp. 123–4
42. Braddon (1965), p. 283
43. Ibid., p. 290; Harry Henry in Gray (1990), p. 296
44. Hamilton (1989), p. 111
45. Hobson et al. (1972), p. xxxi
46. Evans (1983), pp. 13–15
47. Hobson et al. (1972), p. xxx
48. Braddon (1965), p. 272
49. Hobson et al. (1972), p. 372
50. Ibid., p. 373
51. Ibid., pp. 381–4
52. Cockett (1990), pp. 137–8
53. Junor (1990), p. 223
54. Hart-Davis (1990), p. 229
55. Hartwell (1992), p. 329
56. Coote (1965), p. 294; Hart-Davis (1990), p. 197
57. Hart-Davis (1990), pp. 233–7
58. Hartwell (1992), p. 330; Hamilton (1989), p. 104
59. 'Letter from The Editor', *STel*, 5.2.61:8
60. *Guard*, 6.2.61
61. Junor (1990), p. 223
62. Hart-Davis (1990), p. 239
63. Silvester (1997), p. 481; Watkins (1982), p. 203
64. Hobson et al. (1972), p. 396
65. Watkins (1982), p. 119
66. Anstey (1989)
67. Williams, *NS*, 11.9.64
68. 'The Forgotten Prisoners', *Obs*, 28.5.61
69. *Obs*, 19.4.64
70. Cockett (1991), p. 197
71. Ibid., p. 141
72. Hodgson, *BJR*, vol. 3/2, 1992
73. Cockett (1991), p. 243
74. Pringle (1973), p. 152
75. Hamilton (1989), pp. 118–19
76. Cudlipp (1962), p. 282
77. Richards (1997), p. 175
78. Ernie Burrington conversation with author

79. *NPD*, 1961, p. 16
80. Cudlipp (1976), p. 248
81. Richards (1997), p. 177
82. Richards, *History Today*, December 1981, p. 16
83. Curran and Seaton (1997), p. 91
84. Cudlipp (1976), p. 249
85. Grundy (1976), pp. 93–4
86. Abrams (1945); Abrams and Rose (1960); Granada Viewership Survey, 1959
87. Abrams (1964)
88. 'Market research showed us what we wanted', *WPN*, 18.9.64:28
89. 'Mediator', 'The world on which the Sun will rise', *WPN*, 17.7.64:13
90. Grundy (1976), pp. 23, 94
91. Abrams and Rose (1960). Cf. Goldthorpe and Lockwood (1963) and Goldthorpe et al. (1967)
92. Cudlipp (1976), p. 249
93. Mike Molloy, Cudlipp obit, *DMir*, 18.5.98
94. *DMir*, 4.9.63:24
95. *Sun*, 15.9.64:1
96. Wintour (1972), p. 214
97. *WPN*, 18.9.64
98. 'Light on the Sun', *NS*, 25.9.64
99. Pickering interview with author, 19.2.01
100. Foot in Glover (2000), p. 81
101. Cudlipp (1976), p. 250
102. John Gordon in ibid., p. 273
103. *DMir*, 16.7.63:5
104. Cudlipp (1976), p. 278
105. Wintour (1972), p. 186
106. Edelman (1966), p. 156
107. Mike Molloy, Cudlipp obit, *DMir*, 18.5.98
108. Ibid.
109. *Pic*, 31.3.63:1
110. Jameson (1988), pp. 175–6
111. *SMir*, 12.7.64:1
112. *DMir*, 13.7.64:1, 5; *Exp*, 13.7.64:1
113. *Times*, 14.7.64:10
114. *SMir*, 19.7.64:1 (NB This single page is inexplicably missing from the filed copy in the British Museum Newspaper Library)
115. 'Newspaper to hand over photograph', *Times*, 23.7.64:10
116. *Spec*, 24.7.64
117. *Times*, 5.8.64:5
118. Jameson (1988), p. 180
119. *WPN*, 14.8.64:1
120. *NS*, 14.8.64
121. John Grigg, *DNB* 1986–90, p. 41
122. *NS*, 18.9.64
123. *RN*, 19.9.62:1
124. Roy Shaw in Hoggart (1967), p. 128
125. Coote (1965), p. 95

126. Worsthorne in Welch (1997), p. 15
127. Sampson (1965), p. 152
128. *Manchester Evening Chronicle* closed 27.7.63
129. Survey by Institute of Practitioners in Advertising, 1964
130. Working report, 1959–60, p. 15
131. *Spec*, 20.9.63
132. Taylor (1993), p. 67
133. John Rosselli obit, *Guard*, 19.1.01
134. Cited in Sampson (1965), p. 144
135. Kynaston (1988), p. 302
136. Beaverbrook's cancer was diagnosed in July 1962, Vines (1968), p. 125
137. Chisholm and Davie (1992), p. 524; Cudlipp (1980), p. 296
138. Chisholm and Davie (1992), p. 523
139. Cudlipp (1976), p. 290
140. Ernie Burrington conversation with author
141. Levy (1967), pp. 338–9
142. Watkins (1982), p. 13
143. Chisholm and Davie (1992), p. 516
144. Watkins (1982), p. 14
145. Vines (1968), p. 66
146. Ibid., p. 124
147. Ibid., p. 215
148. Ibid., p. 131
149. Ibid., p. 235
150. Edwards (1988), p. 102
151. Coote (1992), p. 89
152. Edwards, Hugh Cudlipp memorial lecture, 24.10.00
153. Jameson (1988), p. 174
154. Cudlipp (1962), p. 371
155. *SExp*, 18.6.61
156. Watkins (1982), pp. 11–12
157. Terry Lancaster, *Indy*, 12.6.98
158. Alan Watkins, *DTel*, 12.6.98
159. Delano, *Sindy* Review, 21.11.93:23
160. Cudlipp (1980), p. 231
161. Vines (1968), p. 216
162. Taylor (1972), p. 654
163. Edwards (1988), p. 123
164. Bourne (1990), p. 206
165. Ibid., p. 192
166. Taylor (1998), p. 138
167. Linton Edwards, 'Levin: Cassandra's first real rival', *WPN*, 28.8.64:10
168. Randall (1988), pp. 8–10; Bourne (1990), p. 175
169. Randall (1988), p. 107
170. *WPN*, 14.8.64:ii
171. Laurie Pignon conversation with author, 3.11.00
172. Ibid.
173. Taylor (1998), p. 176; Rook (1989), p. 55
174. Bourne (1990), p. 181

175. Douglas Fairey, 'London Pride', *Weekend*, 7–13.4.65
176. Percy Trumble, 'I woke up to the story of a lifetime', *EN*, 28.11.73
177. *ES*, 27.1.65:1
178. George Melly in Hoggart (1967), p. 143
179. *NoW*, 2.9.62:1
180. Letter from H. Young, *NoW*, 9.9.62:2
181. *NoW*, 19.5.63:10
182. Francis Williams, *NS*, 25.12.64; Levy (1967), pp. 236–9; Bellisario (1972), pp. 92–9
183. Terry Cockerell, 'Fleet Street's first ever strike action!', *Bylines*, no. 4, September 2000

8. PROFUMO: THE GREAT NON-STORY THAT RAN AND RAN

1. Cordell Hull, cited in Hobson et al. (1972), p. 492. Also attributed to James Callaghan, 1.11.76
2. Beaverbrook's grandson Tim Aitken, quoted by Chisholm and Davie (1992), p. 519
3. Vassall (1975), p. 150
4. Ibid., p. 145
5. Levy (1967), p. 385
6. Ibid., pp. 385–6
7. William Redpath, 'Top Secret: Source of Information', in Brodzky (1966), p. 210
8. Cited in Heward (1997), p. 118
9. Denning (1982), p. 251
10. *Report of the Tribunal Appointed to Inquire into the Vassall Case and Related Matters* (1963), Cmnd 2009
11. *DMir*, 7.3.63:2, 5, 6
12. *DS*, 7.3.63:1, 2, 10, 11
13. *Mail*, 7.3.63:1, 8
14. *Times*, 7.3.63; 'A journalist's duty', *MG*, 7.3.63:8
15. *Obs*, 10.3.63:10
16. *DS*, 8.5.63:20
17. *Mail*, 6.7.63:1
18. Levy (1967), p. 385
19. Norman St John Stevas, *STel*, 28.7.63:4
20. *NoW*, 28.4.63:10
21. Keeler and Fawkes (1983), p. 72
22. Knightley and Kennedy (1987), p. 4
23. Bainbridge and Stockdill (1993), p. 192
24. Ibid., p. 189
25. Earle obit, *Times*, 26.4.97:25
26. *NoW*, 7.4.63:6
27. Keeler and Fawkes (1983), p. 73
28. Knightley and Kennedy (1987), p. 130
29. Keeler and Fawkes (1983), p. 106
30. Ibid., p. 107

31. Knightley and Kennedy (1987), p. 131
32. Keeler and Fawkes (1983), p. 64
33. Ibid., p. 66; Ivanov (1994), p. 100
34. Ivanov (1994), p. 13
35. Keeler and Fawkes (1983), p. 115; 'The model, MI5, the Russian diplomat and me by Stephen Ward', *Pic*, 17.3.63:1, 16, 17
36. Knightley and Kennedy (1987), p. 137
37. Bainbridge and Stockdill (1993), p. 193
38. Keeler and Fawkes (1983), p. 114
39. 'Vassall "new evidence" sensation' and 'Silent Men storm grows', *DMir*, 15.3.63:1
40. *Exp*, 15.3.63:1
41. Denning Report, Chapter XI, para. 163
42. Keeler and Thompson (2001)
43. Denning Report, Chapter XI, para. 161
44. 'The two worlds of Christine Keeler', *NoW*, 17.3.63:1
45. Ivanov, for what it's worth, says it was 29 January, Ivanov (1994), p. 210
46. 'It IS happening here', *Times*, 18.3.63
47. *DS*, 23.3.63
48. *Guard*, 23.3.63
49. *Obs*, 24.3.63:10
50. *NoW*, 24.3.63:1
51. Keeler and Fawkes (1983), p. 119
52. *Exp*, 26.3.63:1
53. Keeler and Fawkes (1983), p. 120
54. 'All Out Spy Alert', *NoW*, 28.4.63:1; 'A-Scientist on Secrets Charge', *DMir*, 29.4.63:1
55. *NoW*, 7.4.63:6
56. 'Christine's friend attacked', *NoW*, 14.4.63:1
57. *DS*, 16.3.63
58. *Exp*, 6.6.63:1, 2, 4, 5, 7; *Mail*, 6.6.632:1, 2, 9
59. *Guard*, 6.6.63:1, 7, 10
60. *Exp*, 7.6.63:1
61. 'Mac under fire', *Mail*, 7.6.63:1; 'Mac: the end', *Mail*, 18.6.63:1, 6, 7
62. *Exp*, 7.6.63:8
63. *Guard*, 7.6.63:10
64. *Pic*, 9.6.63
65. Keeler and Fawkes (1983), p. 134
66. *NoW*, 23.6.63:1
67. Bainbridge and Stockdill (1993), p. 194
68. *NoW*, 23.6.63:1, 10
69. *Exp*, 13.6.63:10
70. *Times*, 11.6.63
71. Knightley and Kennedy (1987), p. 193
72. 'A time for justice', *SunT*, 16.6.63
73. Cited in Hobson et al. (1972), p. 389
74. *Guard*, 29.6.63:8
75. Knightley and Kennedy (1987), p. 68
76. Ivanov (1994), pp. 29–32
77. Keeler and Fawkes (1983), p. 35

78. *Exp*, 29.6.63
79. *Exp*, 3.7.63:1; *Exp*, 17.7.63:1; Malcolm Muggeridge, *STel*, 7.7.63:5; *Times*, 31.7.63:10
80. 'Journalist missing in Middle East', *Obs*, 3.3.63:1
81. *Exp*, 4.7.63:8
82. Cockett (1991), pp. 155–6
83. 'The life and times of Peter Rachman', *SunT*, 7.7.63:6
84. *Exp*, 9.7.63:1; *DMir*, 9.7.63:1; *Exp*, 11.7.63:7; *SunT*, 14.7.63:5; *DMir*, 17.7.63:1; *DMir*, 18.6.63:1; *DMir*, 19.7.63:1; *DMir*, 20.7.63:1; *SunT*, 21.7.63:5; *Exp*, 22.7.63:1; *Exp* 23.7.63:1
85. *DMir*, 15.7.63:1
86. *DMir*, 22.7.63:1
87. *DMir*, 23.7.63:6
88. *DMir*, 30.6.63:5
89. Summers and Dorril (1987), pp. 63–71, 116–17
90. *Times*, 26.7.63:8; 27.7.63:5
91. 'In Our View', *STel*, 28.7.63:12
92. *Times*, 31.7.63:10
93. *Times*, 1.8.63:10, 24
94. *DMir*, 1.8.63:1, 10, 11
95. *SunT*, 4.8.63:1
96. 'Ward is dead: Miss Barrett says she lied', *STel*, 4.8.63:1
97. *STel*, 4.8.63:10
98. *NoW*, 11.8.63
99. Knightley and Kennedy (1987), p. 260
100. *Guard*, 5.8.63
101. Cf. William Rees-Mogg, *SunT*, 11.8.63:8
102. *DMir*, 10.8.63:5
103. Knightley and Kennedy (1987), p. 250
104. *STel*, 29.9.63
105. Hart-Davis (1990), p. 245
106. *DMir*, 26.9.63:1, 2, 14, 15, 16, 17, 18, 32
107. *Guard*, 26.9.63:10
108. *DTel*, 27.9.63:16
109. *Times*, 26.9.63:13
110. Denning Report, Chapter XXII, paras 341–2
111. Press Council report, 1964, pp. 17–19
112. Levy (1967), pp. 387–8
113. *NoW*, 6.10.63:1 and 11
114. *Times*, 7.10.63:11
115. Levy (1967), p. 257
116. Keeler and Fawkes (1983), p. 158
117. Levy (1967), pp. 257–8
118. Draper (1988), pp. 279–88
119. Knightley and Kennedy (1987), p. 260
120. Coote (1965), pp. 286–8
121. Summers and Dorril (1987), pp. 214, 232
122. Pringle (1973), p. 151
123. *Exp*, 5.8.63

9. THE KING IS DEAD! LONG LIVE RUPERT!

1. Entry by George van Schaick in *Spectator* contest, Cudlipp (1976), p. 253
2. Frederic Mullally, 'Fleet Street in the Forties', *BJR*, vol. 10/1, 1999, p. 51
3. Harold Evans, *Prometheus Unbound*, Iain Walker memorial lecture, May 1997 (Reuter Foundation), p. 3
4. EIU report 1966. Cleverly (1976), p. 17
5. Clive Irving, 'The Last Days of Fleet Street', *Listener*, 16.7.70
6. Cited in Griffiths (1996), p. 343
7. Irving, *Listener*, op. cit.
8. Hart-Davis (1990), p. 219
9. Grundy (1976), p. 51
10. Wintour (1972), p. 198
11. 'Modern Times', *Times*, 3.5.66
12. Monopolies Commission report. Cf. *Times*, 1.9.65
13. Hetherington (1981), p. 168
14. Taylor (1993), p. 64
15. Hetherington (1981), p. 152
16. Kynaston (1988), p. 336
17. Drogheda (1978), pp. 189–90
18. Woods and Bishop (1985), p. 355
19. Newton (1997), pp. 99–100
20. Drogheda (1978), p. 193
21. Braddon (1965), p. 324
22. Thomson (1975), p. 173; Woods and Bishop (1985), pp. 357–8
23. Hamilton (1989), p. 150
24. Evans (1983), pp. 222–3
25. Heren (1985), p. 168; Grigg (1993), p. 39
26. Grigg (1993), p. 31
27. 'A dangerous press campaign', *Times*, 28.2.67
28. *Times*, 1.7.67
29. Grigg (1993), p. 64
30. Taylor (1993), p. 206
31. Grigg (1993), pp. 104–6
32. Walker (1982), p. 49
33. Grigg (1993), pp. 118–19; Leapman (1992), pp. 50–1
34. Denis Hamilton, 'The problems at the Times', *UKPG*, 22.12.69:7
35. Woods and Bishop (1985), p. 360
36. Lord Thomson, *Commonwealth Press Union Quarterly*, December 1969
37. *Campaign*, 21.9.70
38. Grigg (1993), p. 143
39. Maurice Wiggins, cited in Hobson et al. (1972), p. xxix
40. *DNB*, 1986–90, p. 180
41. Evans (1983), p. 368
42. Hobson et al. (1972), p. xxxii
43. Benedict Nightingale in Hoggart (1967), p. 88
44. Donald McLachlan, *Spec*, 1.3.68
45. Hobson et al. (1972), p. xxxiii

46. Brodzky (1966), p. 217
47. Hobson et al. (1972), p. 242
48. Knightley (1997), pp. 133–8
49. *SunT*, 13.2.68
50. Roy Shaw in Hoggart (1967), p. 134
51. Hall (1987), p. 159
52. *Cit*, 14.5.67
53. David Astor, 'Israel: the real challenge', *Obs*, 11.6.67
54. *Obs*, 17.5.70; Melvern (1986), p. 38
55. *Obs*, 31.5.70
56. Thomson (1975), p. 118
57. George Melly in Hoggart (1967), p. 148
58. Hart-Davis (1990), p. 218
59. Ibid., p. 285
60. Worsthorne in Welch (1997), p. 17
61. Hart-Davis (1990), p. 221
62. Ibid., p. 229
63. Aitken (1971)
64. Working Report, 1966–67
65. Working Report, Special *Guardian* issue, 5.1.67
66. Working Report, 1967–68
67. Taylor (1993), pp. 91–5
68. Working Report, 1970–71
69. Roy (1998), p. 74
70. Taylor (1993), p. 124
71. Ibid., pp. 211–13
72. Jocelyn Stevens, *Queen*, 15.3.61
73. Deedes (1997), p. 189
74. Cudlipp (1976), p. 296
75. Wilson, *The Labour Government, 1964–70* (Penguin, 1974), entry dated 24.1.68
76. Heren (1985), p. 160
77. *Guard*, 19.2.68:1
78. *ES*, 20.2.68
79. Zuckerman (1988), pp. 464–5
80. Cudlipp (1976), p. 326
81. *DMir*, 10.5.68
82. Cudlipp (1976), p. 330
83. Ibid., p. 351
84. Ibid., p. 365
85. Pickering interview with author, 19.2.01
86. Wintour (1972), p. 190
87. Ibid. According to Ernie Burrington, Murdoch's subbing tutor was Jack Paterson, who later worked for him at the *Sun*
88. *NoW*, 20.10.68
89. Shawcross (1992), p. 137
90. Somerfield (1979), p. 141
91. *UKPG*, 20.10.769:11
92. Bainbridge and Stockdill (1993), p. 229
93. *ES*, 26.2.70:1

94. Tina Brown, diary entry 17.1.81, in Evans (1983), p. 124
95. Bainbridge and Stockdill (1993), p. 233
96. Cudlipp (1976), p. 250
97. Burrington email to author, 25.4.01
98. Ken Smiley in Gray (1990), p. 156
99. Hardy interview with author, 26.10.00
100. *UKPG*, 17.11.69:3
101. Molloy interview with author, 9.5.01
102. *Sun*, 15.11.69
103. *UKPG*, 24.11.69
104. Grose (1989), p. 16
105. Green interview with author, 14.9.01
106. *Times*, 18.11.69
107. 'The Sun – touch-paper to a myth', *UKPG*, 24.11.69. Cf. *UKPG*, 1.12.69:11
108. Molloy interview with author, 9.5.01
109. *DMir*, 2.12.69
110. *Sun*, 22.11.69
111. *Sun*, 17.11.70
112. *Times*, 17.3.71
113. Cudlipp (1976), pp. 251–2
114. Paul Barker in Hoggart (1967), p. 61
115. Chester and Fenby (1979), p. 44
116. Coote (1992), p. 72, suggests it was already trading profitably
117. Griffiths (1996), p. 333
118. Coote (1992), p. 57
119. Ibid., p. 60
120. Edwards, Hugh Cudlipp memorial lecture, 24.10.00
121. Pickering interview with author, 19.2.01
122. Chester and Fenby (1979), p. 42; Griffiths (1996), p. 340
123. Coote (1992), p. 90
124. Rook (1989), pp. 58–60
125. 'CABLE VETTING SENSATION', *Exp*, 21.2.67:1
126. Pincher in Gray (1990), p. 290
127. Hedley and Aynsley (1967), p. 56
128. *Indy*, 12.6.98
129. Wyatt (2000), p. 308
130. Randall (1988), pp. 1–5
131. Ibid., p. 116
132. 'Daily Mail dismisses its editor', *Times*, 16.12.66
133. *DMir*, 19.12.66
134. Taylor (1998), pp. 161–2
135. Randall (1988), p. 102. Cf. Sellers (1968) and Sellers (1975)
136. John Marshall, 'What characters we are', in Brodzky (1966), p. 190
137. Ibid., p. 94
138. Bourne (1990), p. 178
139. Pignon conversation with author, 3.11.00
140. Geoffrey Levy, *Mail*, 11.6.98:9
141. Bourne (1990), p. 202
142. Taylor (1998), p. 178

143. Ibid., p. 180
144. Ibid., p. 211
145. Bourne (1990), p. 179
146. Coote (1992), p. 73
147. Bourne (1990), pp. 180–1; Griffiths (1996), p. 352
148. Bob Trevor conversation with author, 3.11.00
149. 'In danger – the job we all love', *ES*, 9.6.70
150. *Cit*, 27.11.66:1
151. Ibid.
152. *Cit*, 14.5.67:1
153. *Cit*, 21.5.67:2
154. 'Words without meaning by Mr Wilson', *Cit*, 11.6.67:2
155. Haines (1988), pp. 346–7
156. *Cit*, 21.5.67:2
157. *Cit*, 18.6.67:2
158. Edwards (1988), p. 159. Cf. Stott (2002), p. 204
159. 'Horror in a nameless village', *SP*, 1.2.70. Cf. *Times*, 2.2.70:1; 5.2.70:1, 5
160. Hobday conversation with author, 22.4.01
161. Edwards (1988), pp. 164–5
162. Whitefriar, *Smith's Trade News*, 20.5.67

10. SEX, DEATH AND REBELLION

1. Nicholas Tomalin, 'Stop the Press, I want to get on', *SunT* magazine, 26.10.69
2. Press Council report, 1966. p. 87; Levy (1967), p. 225
3. Press Council report, 1954. p. 21; Levy (1967), p. 322
4. Press Council report, 1956. p. 26
5. Levy (1967), p. 323
6. Tynan (1987), p. 285
7. *Times*, 23.7.1970
8. *NoW*, 23.8.70:3
9. *Exp*, 28.7.70
10. *Times*, 28.7.70
11. Tynan (1987), p. 294
12. *DMir*, 28.7.70:3
13. *Sun*, 28.7.70:1
14. Levy (1967), p. 439
15. Ibid., p. 438
16. Ibid., pp. 487–8
17. Ibid., p. 446; Somerfield (1979), p. 117
18. *Sun*, 28.7.66
19. Cockett (1991), p. 168
20. *Times*, 22.4.68
21. Childs (1997), p. 150
22. *SMir*, 21.4.68:3; *SP*, 21.4.68:1
23. *SunT*, 21.4.68:1, 2, 12
24. *NoW*, 21.4.68:12

25. *STel*, 21.4.68:16
26. 'An evil speech', *Times*, 22.4.68:11
27. *Guard*, 22.4.68:8
28. *DTel*, 22.4.68
29. *Exp*, 22.4.68
30. Edwards (1988), p. 162
31. John Dodge, 'The British Press and Race Relations', Strasbourg lecture, January 1969
32. Foot (1969), p. 36
33. Jones (1996), p. 34
34. Glover (2000), p. 268
35. *Sun*, 17.6.70
36. Morgan (1999), p. 313
37. Grose (1989), p. 70
38. Grigg (1993), p. 142
39. Morgan (1999), p. 258
40. 'The Royal visit to Ulster', *Times*, 18.7.45:4
41. 'IRA plant tricolour in Ulster church', *Mail*, 13.5.46:1
42. *SP*, 24.9.50:4
43. Michael Foot, 'Ulster, the bomb on our doorstep', *DH*, 3.6.53
44. Noel Barber, 'This is "Hungary in Ireland"', *Mail*, 4.1.57:4
45. *Times*, 1.10.64:12; 2.10.64:12; 3.10.64:5
46. *Times*, 3.10.64:9
47. 'Ghostly no-man's land of past conflicts', *DTel*, 17.5.66; 'Shadow and substance', *Belfast Telegraph*, 17.5.66:1
48. *Times*, 7.6.66:1
49. *Guard*, 8.6.66:6
50. *Times*, 4.7.66:10
51. '200,000 potential supporters for Mr Paisley in Ulster', *Guard*, 1.4.66:4
52. MacArthur conversation with author
53. 'Mr Paisley carries the banner', *Guard*, 2.7.66:4
54. *SunT*, 3.7.66:1
55. *SunT*, 3.7.66:11
56. Harold Evans in Sunday Times Insight Team (1972), p. 8
57. *DTel*, 4.7.66:12
58. *Exp*, 5.7.66:1
59. 'Man behind vicious crusade', *DMir*, 4.7.66:7
60. *Belfast Telegraph*, 13.7.66
61. Rose (1999), p. 174
62. *Times*, 24.4.67
63. *Times*, 25.4.67
64. Hetherington (1981), p. 294
65. Rose (1999), p. 94
66. *Obs*, 6.10.68
67. Grigg (1993), p. 108
68. Hickey obit, *Times*, 5.12.00:27
69. Rose (1999), p. 81
70. 'Londonderry, Saturday, November 16', *Times*, 18.11.68:8
71. Grigg (1993), p. 109

72. 'Defending the Union', *DTel*, 5.11.68:16
73. *Exp*, 19.4.69:1
74. *DMir*, 19.4.69:1
75. *Sun*, 19.4.68:1, 7
76. *DS*, 19.4.69:6; 21.4.69:1
77. *DTel*, 19.4.69:14
78. Front pages, 23.4.69
79. *DMir*, 24.4.69:13
80. *Exp*, 24.4.69
81. Curtis (1984), pp. 24–8
82. 'Madness in Ulster', *Mail*, 14.8.69:1
83. 'Bernadette – Out of control' and 'The fall and fall of Bernadette', *Mail*, 1.2.72:1, 6
84. Winchester (1974), p. 124
85. Ibid., pp. 32, 69
86. Ibid., p. 71
87. Curtis (1984), p. 27
88. Ibid., p. 28
89. Thomson (1975), p. 94
90. Gailey (1995)

11. THE SOARAWAY *SUN* AND STRIKEAWAY UNIONS

1. Adam Raphael, *Guard*, 28.8.74
2. Mansfield (1943); Bundock (1957)
3. Wintour (1972), p. 201
4. *Sun*, 8.1.70. Cf. Grose (1989), p. 25; Chippindale and Horrie (1990), pp. 39–40
5. Harry Henry in Gray (1990), p. 293
6. Chippindale and Horrie (1999), p. 45
7. Grose (1989), p. 36
8. Chippindale and Horrie (1999), pp. 55–75
9. *UKPG*, 11.6.73:4–6
10. Stephens conversation with author, 28.3.01
11. Edelman (1966), p. 157
12. Ibid., p. 197
13. Annie Miles conversation with author, 24.10.00
14. Molloy interview with author, 9.5.01
15. Jameson (1988), p. 206
16. Jameson, 'Page Three girls: Yes, I am to blame', *Exp*, 16.1100:13
17. Ken Smiley in Gray (1990), p. 156
18. Burrington interview with author
19. 'A fourpenny Mirror', *UKPG*, 31.5.71
20. Wintour (1972), p. 190
21. Cudlipp (1976), p. 413
22. Evans (1982), p. 160
23. Lady Cudlipp email to author, 24.8.00
24. Edwards (1988), p. 167; Jameson (1988), p. 196
25. Crewe (1991), p. 177

26. Edwards (1988), p. 205
27. Burrington email to author, 25.4.01
28. Mary Beith, 'Misery of the captive chain smoker', *SP*, 26.1.75:1, 24–5
29. *SP*, 18.9.72
30. *Times*, 23.9.75
31. Hobday interview with author, 22.4.01
32. Molloy, *BJR*, vol. 10/4, 1999
33. Bourne (1990), p. 205
34. Taylor (1998), p. 208
35. Ibid., p. 209
36. *UKPG*, 15.3.71
37. Pignon interview with author, 3.11.00
38. Wintour (1989), p. 183
39. Bourne (1990), p. 212
40. Glover (2000), p. 68
41. Wintour (1972), p. 201
42. Bourne (1990), p. 206
43. Ibid., p. 208
44. *UKPG*, 12.3.73
45. Vere Harmsworth in Gray (1990), p. 133
46. Eddie Campbell conversation with author, 4.11.00
47. Kirby interview with author, December 2000
48. Coote (1992), p. 106
49. Junor (1990), p. 160
50. Coote (1992), p. 110
51. *Exp*, 8.11.68:11
52. Last issue of the *Glasgow Evening Citizen* published 28.3.74
53. Coote (1990), p. 104
54. Russell Miller, *SunT*, cited in Chester (1979), p. 56
55. Coote (1992), p. 92
56. *UKPG*, 3.5.71:17
57. Coote (1992), p. 104
58. Conroy (1997), pp. 17–18
59. *UKPG*, 3.5.71:17
60. Chester and Fenby (1979), p. 58
61. Junor (1990), p. 280
62. George Gale, *Spec*, 4.1.75
63. Coote (1992), p. 88
64. Junor (1990), p. 280
65. McKay and Barr (1976), pp. 22–3
66. Ibid., p. 11
67. Ibid., p. 95
68. *SunT*, 28.9.75
69. Walker (1982), p. 50
70. *Accountant*, 27.2.75
71. Woods and Bishop (1985), p. 362
72. Kynaston (1988), p. 408
73. 'War of words in Nottingham press battle', *Guard*, 8.2.79
74. Kynaston (1988), p. 410

75. Newton (1997), p. 103
76. Ibid., p. 91
77. Kynaston (1988), pp. 374–5
78. Ibid., p. 393
79. Newton (1997), p. 106
80. Ibid.
81. Kynaston (1988), p. 409
82. Ibid., p. 411
83. *SunT*, 13.7.75
84. Hetherington (1981), p. 334
85. Taylor (1993), p. 191
86. Hetherington (1981), p. 362
87. Peter Preston, 'The Rise and Rise of a Qualipop', *100 Years of Fleet Street* (London Press Club, 1982)
88. Taylor (1993), p. 194
89. Ibid., p. 196
90. Cole (1995), p. 108
91. Taylor (1993), p. 129
92. Howard, interviewed by Kenneth Roy, 'The Accidental Journalist', *JH*, no. 58, July 1999. Cf. Stott (1973), pp. 80–1
93. *SunT*, 17.2.91
94. *BJR*, vol. 1/3, 1990
95. Deedes (1997), p. 117
96. Ibid., pp. 254, 258
97. Ronald Stevens, *BJR*, vol. 8/3, 1997
98. Deedes (1997), pp. 258–9
99. Worsthorne (1993), p. 223
100. Hart-Davis (1990), p. 259
101. Evans (1983), pp. 59–60
102. *SunT*, 24.9.72
103. Evans (1983), p. 71
104. Ibid., pp. 58–79. Cf. Murray Rosen, *The Sunday Times Thalidomide Case: Contempt of Court and the Freedom of the Press* (Writers & Scholars Educational Trust, 1979); Sunday Times Insight Team, *The Thalidomide Children and the Law* (André Deutsch, 1974); Sunday Times Insight Team, *Suffer the Children: The Story of Thalidomide* (André Deutsch, 1975)
105. Evans (1983), p. 72
106. Knightley (1997), pp. 155–78; Page, *BJR*, vol. 9/1, 1998; Peter Wilby, *Sindy*, 7.9.97; Peregrine Worsthorne, *NS*, 29.8.97
107. Page, *BJR*, op. cit., p. 52
108. Wilby conversation with author, 20.4.01
109. Glover (2000), p. 80
110. Giles (1986), p. 201
111. Wilby, *Sindy*, op. cit.
112. Wesker (1977)
113. Randall (1988), pp. 128–44
114. Giles (1986), p. 157
115. Evans (1983), p. 6
116. Thomson (1975), p. 191

117. Ingrams in Glover (2000), p. 136
118. Cockett (1991), p. 256
119. Astor, 'How the British Press Censors Itself', *Index on Censorship*, January 1977, p. 8
120. *Obs*, 12.2.74
121. Whitehorn in Gray (1990), p. 197
122. Max Aitken, *SExp*, 28.2.71
123. 'Downfall in the dailies', *UKPG*, 20.9.71:5
124. '4 Lost Days: £3 million', *UKPG*, 27.9.71:5–6
125. Beloff (1976), p. 9
126. House of Commons, 5.11.74, quoted in Hetherington (1981), p. 350
127. Taylor (1993), p. 314
128. Beloff (1976), p. 50
129. Ibid., p. 61
130. 'Fleet Street in trouble', *Guard*, 21.2.74: 'New move to end press crisis', *DMir*, 22.2.74:2
131. Hardy interview with author, 26.10.00

12. STRIKES, STUNTS AND SCOOPS

1. Harold Evans, *Listener*, 16.7.70:75
2. *DMir*, 7.1.72:2, 9; 17.1.72:1; 25.1.72:2
3. *Mail*, 6.1.72:1
4. *Economist*, 8.1.72
5. 'How bleak is their valley now', *Mail*, 7.1.72:6
6. *Exp*, 7.2.72
7. *Sun*, 7.1.72:1, 2
8. 'Why we can't offer more to the miners', *Sun*, 8.1.72:1, 2
9. Anthony Shrimsley, *Sun*, 13.1.72:6
10. *Sun*, 19.1.72
11. *Sun*, 27.1.72
12. 'All muck and no money', *Mail*, 27.1.72:6
13. *Mail*, 2.2.72
14. Celia Haddon, *Mail*, 7.2.72
15. 'End this strike', *Mail*, 4.2.72:6
16. *Times*, 9.2.72:13
17. *Mail*, 11.2.72
18. *Mail*, 11.2.72:6
19. 'Let's see some action', *Sun*, 11.2.72
20. *Sun*, 12.2.72
21. 'Why your lights are going out', *Mail*, 12.2.72
22. *Sun*, 15.2.72
23. *Exp*, 19.2.72
24. *Sun*, 19.2.72
25. *FT*, 29.11.73
26. Ian Aitken, *Guard*, 6.2.74:1
27. 'What Ted can do today', *Sun*, 6.2.74

28. *Sun*, 18.2.74
29. Robin Page, 'An even more special case', *DTel*, 6.2.74:16
30. *Guard*, 8.2.74
31. *DMir*, 6.2.74:1
32. *DMir*, 8.2.74
33. *DMir*, 12.2.74:1, 3
34. 'What this election is really about', *Mail*, 8.2.74:6
35. 'How McGahey lived it up in Brussels', *Mail*, 11.2.74:1
36. *Mail*, 20.2.74
37. *Mail*, 21.2.74
38. 'The Heath's on fire', 12.2.74:10; Derek Marks, 'Why Ted Heath is the one man to pull Britain through', *Exp*, 27.2.74
39. *DTel*, 27.2.74:8
40. Kynaston (1988), p. 401
41. 'The prices nightmare', *Sun*, 16.2.74; 'What a botch-up', *Sun*, 22.2.74
42. *Sun*, 26.2.74
43. *Sun*, 27.2.74
44. *Guard*, 27.2.74
45. *Mail*, 2.3.74; 5.2.74
46. *Sun*, 5.3.74
47. *Sun*, 8.3.74
48. *Sun*, 6.3.74
49. *Sun*, 8.10.74
50. *FT*, 10.10.74
51. *FT*, 12.2.75
52. Jay (1980), p. 490
53. Edelman (1966), p. 165
54. Evans (1975), p. 65
55. Ibid., p. 45
56. Ibid., p. 101
57. Ibid., pp. 102–3
58. Ibid., p. 104
59. Ibid., p. 110
60. Kitzinger (1973), p. 337
61. Ibid., p. 338
62. Mark Arnold-Foster, *Guard*, 14.7.69
63. *DTel*, 16.8.71
64. 'The Last Opportunity', *DTel*, 21.10.71
65. 'Dead Failure of New Start', *Times*, 4.5.71
66. Kitzinger (1973), p. 342
67. *DMir*, 8.7.71
68. Jay (1980), p. 456
69. Brother A. Jones, *The Way*, September 1971
70. *Sun*, 29.10.71
71. *Mail*, 20.5.71
72. Cf. *Mail*, 4.6.71
73. Cf. *Exp* leaders 4.5.71; 'Europe: It's a dead duck', *Exp*, 7.5.71; 'The Great Betrayal', *Exp*, 14.5.71
74. *Exp*, 22.5.71

75. *SExp*, 23.5.71
76. *DMir*, 22.7.71; *Sun*, 23.7.71
77. *Exp*, 22.7.71
78. Kitzinger (1973), p. 332
79. Jay (1980), p. 489; Cf. Butler and Kitzinger (1976), p. 217
80. Butler and Kitzinger (1976), pp. 218–23
81. *Mail*, 5.6.75:1
82. Butler and Kitzinger (1976), p. 224
83. Morgan (1999), p. 365
84. Childs (1997), p. 191
85. 'Has Harold the master magician pulled one trick too many?', *Mail*, 24.3.75
86. 'Who speaks for Europe?' *Exp*, 24.3.75
87. Butler and Kitzinger (1976), p. 217
88. *DMir*, 9.5.75
89. *SMir/SP*, 11.5.75
90. Butler and Kitzinger (1976), p. 236
91. *DTel*, 20.5.75
92. 'Benn's jobs scare storm', *Sun*, 19.5.75:1
93. *Times*, 26.5.75:1; *DTel*, 26.5.75:1; *Mail*, 26.5.75:1; *FT*, 26.5.75:1; *Times*, 28.5.75:1; *Morning Star*, 28.5.75:1
94. *Sun*, 4.6.75
95. *DTel*, 5.6.75
96. *Guard*, 5.6.75
97. *Guard*, 2.6.75
98. *Times*, 29.5.75; 3.6.75
99. *DTel*, 22.5.75
100. *DTel*, 29.5.75
101. Butler and Kitzinger (1976), p. 230
102. *FT*, 5.6.75
103. *Guard*, *Times*, 5.6.75
104. *DTel*, 27.5.75
105. *Mail*, 4.6.75
106. *Exp*, 27.5.75
107. *Sun*, 4.6.75
108. *DMir*, 5.6.75
109. Cf. *Guard*, 4.4.75:1
110. 'Orphans of the Airlift', *Secret History*, Channel 4, 9.8.01
111. *Mail*, 4.4.75
112. *Exp*, 5.4.75:5
113. 'Row grows over babylift', *SunT*, 6.4.75:1; *Guard*, 7.4.75:1
114. *DMir*, 5.4.75
115. *DMir*, 8.4.75:2
116. *Guard*, 8.4.75:12
117. 'Orphans', *Secret History*, op. cit.
118. Ibid.
119. Ibid.
120. George Guy conversation with author, 8.8.01
121. 'First Vietnam orphans land at Heathrow', *Times*, 7.4.75:1
122. *Mail*, 7.4.75:1

123. Barry Wigmore, 'No names, just numbers scrawled on their backs', *EN*, 7.4.75
124. *Guard*, 8.4.75:1
125. *Mail*, 8.4.75
126. 'Suffer little children', *DTel*, 5.4.75:14
127. 'Mercy not strained', *DTel*, 8.4.75:16
128. 'Orphans', *Secret History*, op. cit.
129. 'The Babies That Weren't for Burning', *NS*, 11.4.75
130. *UKPG*, 14.4.75
131. *Times*, 8.4.75:15
132. 'The orphans of Vietnam', *Guard*, 9.4.75:15
133. *Times*, 10.4.75:17; *DTel*, 10.4.75:18
134. 'No options for the mercy flight', *Guard*, 14.4.75:12
135. *Times*, 11.4.75:15
136. Polly Toynbee, 'Adoption doubts', *Obs*, 6.4.75:1
137. *Guard*, 7.4.75:20
138. *SunT*, 6.4.75:1
139. *TES*, 18.4.75:6
140. 'Orphans', *Secret History*, op. cit.
141. *Mail*, 6.4.96:40–2
142. 'Orphans', *Secret History*, op. cit.
143. Ibid.
144. Ibid.
145. *Exp*, 27.11.72
146. *Exp*, 2.12.72
147. 'Bormann-hunter arrested', *Exp*, 2.12.72
148. *Times*, 25.11.25:1
149. 'Dog Watches Dog', *UKPG*, 4.12.72
150. 'The seventeenth Martin Bormann', *SunT*, 3.12.72
151. *Mail*, 11.12.72:4
152. 'Bormann: I've got even more proof, says Farago, *Exp*, 11.12.72:2
153. *Mail*, 11.12.72
154. 'Bormann story goes on film', *Exp*, 13.12.72
155. *Exp*, 14.12.72:2; *SunT*, 17.12.72
156. 'Berlin skull "is Bormann's"', *Times*, 9.2.73
157. *SunT*, 3.2.74:6

13. SELLING OFF THE FAMILY SILVER

1. *Royal Commission on the Press, 1974–7* (1977), Cmnd 6810, para. 6.18
2. *DTel*, 11.1.79:24
3. 'Cool Callaghan plays down cries of chaos', *Guard*, 11.1.79:1
4. *Sun*, 11.1.79:1, 2
5. *DTel*, 'Mr Callaghan's Duty', 12.1.79:8
6. *Sun*, 16.1.79; 19.1.79
7. Morgan (1999), p. 395
8. 'How the British Press Censors Itself', *Index on Censorship*, January 1977
9. 'Conditions of Freedom', *Times*, 15.1.77

10. Edwards (1988), p. 210
11. Deedes in Gray (1990), p. 138
12. Jenkins (1979), p. 46
13. Michael Davie of *Observer*, cited in Chester and Fenby (1979), p. 62
14. Junor (1990), p. 220
15. Rook (1989), pp. 86, 160
16. Junor (1990), p. 221
17. Chester and Fenby (1979), p. 94
18. Haines (1977); *DMir* serialisation from 7.2.77
19. Chester and Fenby (1979), p. 107
20. Coote (1992), p. 51
21. Cited in Chester and Fenby (1979), p. 109; Griffiths (1996), p. 354
22. Wintour (1989), p. 155
23. Jenkins in Griffiths (1996), p. 355
24. Sheila Black, *Times*, 6.4.77
25. Chester and Fenby (1979), p. 146
26. *DTel*, 29.4.77
27. Wintour (1989), pp. 182–3
28. Ibid., p. 183
29. 'Goldsmith's Eye View', *STel*, 15.5.77.21
30. Wansell (1987), p. 246
31. Ibid., p. 252
32. *ES*, 20/5/77:1
33. Wintour (1989), p. 170
34. Chester and Fenby (1979), p. 205
35. Griffiths (1996), pp. 358–9
36. Coote (1992), p. 117
37. Atticus, *SunT*, 5.6.77
38. Chester and Fenby (1979), 227
39. Ibid., p. 228
40. Broackes (1979), p. 177
41. Ibid., p. 246
42. Coote (1992), p. 119
43. Griffiths (1996), p. 359
44. *Times*, 1.7.77:6
45. Chester and Fenby (1979), p. 239
46. Griffiths (1996), p. 359
47. Cameron (2000), p. 33
48. Wintour (1989), p. 151
49. Junor (1990), p. 250
50. Cameron (2000), p. 34
51. Broackes (1979), p. 249
52. Jenkins (1979), p. 101
53. Ibid.
54. Cameron (2000), p. 20
55. Jameson (1988), pp. 37–83
56. Ibid., p. 62
57. Ibid., p. 205
58. Ibid., p. 208

59. Junor (1990), p. 252
60. Jameson (1990), p. 25
61. Rook (1989), p. 87
62. Jameson (1990), pp. 22, 33
63. Ibid., p. 24
64. *Exp*, 10.9.77. Cf. *Times*, 9.9.77:1; 12.9.77:2
65. Wintour (1989), p. 159
66. Jenkins (1979), p. 103
67. Cameron (2000), p. 37
68. Broackes (1979), p. 250
69. Author present at meeting, October 1978
70. *Times*, 19.10.78:12
71. Jameson (1988), p. 7
72. Jameson (1990), p. 71
73. Jameson memo, Chippindale and Horrie (1990), p. 83
74. Porter (1984), p. 194
75. Cameron (2000), p. 61
76. Ibid., p. 45
77. Jameson (1990), p. 75
78. Ibid., p. 77
79. Ibid., p. 80
80. Wintour (1989), p. 161
81. Jameson (1990), p. 11
82. *Week Ending*, BBC Radio 4, 21.3.80
83. Jameson (1988), p. 12
84. Junor (1990), p. 241
85. Ibid., p. 252
86. Verbatim transcript of conversation, provided by former PA editor-in-chief David Chipp
87. Cudlipp (1976), p. 260
88. Gray (1990), p. 131
89. Coote (1992), p. 118
90. Jenkins conversation with author, 26.6.01
91. Jenkins (1986), p. 129
92. 'Return of the wizard', *Guard*, 16.1.79:9
93. Wintour (1989), p. 163
94. Griffiths (1996), p. 363
95. Ibid., p. 364
96. Douglas Fairey, 'London Pride', *Weekend*, 7–13.4.65
97. Brian James, *Mail*, 1.11.80
98. Griffiths (1996), p. 362
99. 'My sadness, by the Chairman', 31.10.80; cf. Bob Trevor, 'Day of Infamy', *PG*, 3.11.00:17
100. Godfrey Smith in Gray (1990), p. 299
101. Leapman (1992), p. 70
102. Goldenberg (1985), p. 52
103. Giles (1986), p. 185
104. Goldenberg (1985), p. 57
105. Ibid., p. 70

106. Woods and Bishop (1985), p. 366; Jacobs (1980), p. 5
107. *Times*, 30.11.78
108. Jacobs (1980), pp. 86–103
109. Ibid., p. 148
110. Grigg (1993), p. 534
111. 'Pay formula ends NUJ strike', *Times*, 30.8.80
112. Hamilton (1989), p. 177
113. Woods and Bishop (1985), p. 374; Gray (1990), p. 89
114. Grigg (1993), p. 538
115. Cmnd 6810, op. cit., para. 6.18
116. Grigg (1993), p. 556
117. *Times*, 23.10.80
118. Hugh Stephenson, Edward Mortimer and Geraldine Norman formed JoTT, Journalists of *The Times*, in June 1979
119. Taylor (1993), p. 294
120. Jacobs (1980), p. 120
121. 'Questions Harold Evans doesn't answer', Magnus Linklater, *Journalist*, November–December 1983
122. Evans (1994), p. xxiv
123. Wansell (1987), p. 244; Ingrams in Glover (2000), p. 137. Cf. Ingrams (1979)
124. Hutchins (1998), p. 99
125. *Mail*, 21.10.76
126. Bower (1993), p. 393
127. Porter (1984), p. 186
128. Sampson (1982), p. 434
129. Gray (1990), p. 240
130. Jacobs (1980), p. 111
131. Hart-Davis (1990), p. 263
132. Munnion in Glover (2000), p. 65
133. Glover (1994), p. 10
134. Hartwell obit, *DTel*, 4.4.01
135. *Mail*, 17.10.78:2
136. Hart-Davis (1990), p. 330
137. Glover (1994), p. 14
138. Peregrine Worsthorne, *Times*, 9.5.83:9
139. Hart-Davis (1990), p. 317
140. Porter (1984), p. 194
141. Garland (1990), p. 10
142. Watkins (1982), p. 204
143. *STel*, 26.10.80; *UKPG*, 16.7.84
144. *Literary Review*, December 1995
145. Chippindale and Horrie (1990), p. 68; Watkins (1982), p. 87; Junor (2002), p. 130
146. Chippindale and Horrie (1990), p. 84
147. Molloy interview with author, 9.5.01
148. Ibid.
149. Foot in Glover (2000), p. 83
150. Porter (1984), p. 166; *DMir*, 5.9.77. Cf. Stott (2002), pp. 173–81
151. Steve Turner interview with author, 7.7.01
152. Edwards (1988), p. 211

153. Molloy, *BJR*, vol. 10/4, 1999
154. Ibid.
155. Haines (1988), p. 340
156. *Times*, 4.8.78:2; *UKPG*, 21.8.78:5
157. *Sun*, 9.3.79:1
158. In the first eleven months of 1977, the *Daily Mirror* failed to publish 36 million copies because of union disputes and the *Sun* 30 million. *UKPG*, 5.12.77:1
159. Hobday conversation with author, 22.4.01
160. Bainbridge and Stockdill (1993), p. 251
161. Chester and Fenby (1979), p. 75
162. 'Slush Money: The Secret Bank Deals', *Mail*, 20.5.77
163. *Mail*, 21.5.77
164. 'Bribes: the next step', *SunT*, 22.5.77:1
165. *Times*, 25.5.77
166. *UKPG*, 30.5.77
167. David English, 'A message from the Editor to YOU the reader', *Mail*, 21.5.77:6
168. 'Two reasons why editor could not check his story', *UKPG*, 30.5.77
169. Cmnd 6810, op. cit., addendum 7, p. 107
170. Brian MacArthur conversation with author
171. Baistow (1985), p. 60
172. Cmnd 6810, op. cit., para. 10.126
173. Baistow (1985), p. 59
174. Tunstall (1996), p. 385
175. Cmnd 6810, op. cit., para. 5.43
176. Ibid., para. 6.26–8
177. Ibid., p. 242
178. Ibid., p. 243
179. Wansell (1987), p. 268
180. Nicholas Owen 'The Goldsmith kitchen', *JH*, no. 51, October 1997
181. Wansell (1987), p. 288
182. Owen, *JH*, op. cit
183. Glover (1994), p. 50
184. Wansell (1987), p. 294
185. Paterson conversation with author, 4.6.01
186. Cmnd 6810, op. cit., para. 1.13
187. Foreword to *Programme for Action*, November 1976
188. Martin (1981), pp. 198–9
189. Kynaston (1988), p. 415
190. Ibid., p. 429
191. *FT*, 2.6.75
192. Kynaston (1988), p. 419
193. Ibid., p. 420

14. DIANA AND MAGGIE, THE MAKING OF PRESS ICONS

1. Woodrow Wilson
2. Press Council report, 1954, pp. 21–2

3. Holden (1988), p. 95
4. 'Prince on the carpet over a cherry brandy', *Mail*, 20.6.63:1
5. Press Council report, 1965, pp. 3–8
6. Bellisario (1972), pp. 62, 120–3
7. *Royal Family*, screened 21.6.69
8. Pimlott (1996), p. 438
9. *SMir*, 13.7.80
10. 'Set Prince Charles free!', *SMir*, 20.7.80
11. 'All right for some!', *SMir*, 10.8.80
12. Grose (1989), p. 58
13. *Sun*, 8.9.80
14. *Mail*, 17.9.80
15. 'Lady Diana's slip', *DMir*, 19.9.80
16. 'The Real Me by Lady Diana', *SMir*, 21.9.80
17. John Witherow, 'Harassed Lady Diana remains calm and polite', *Times*, 26.11.80:3
18. *SMir*, 26.10.80
19. *SMir*, 9.11.80
20. Edwards (1988), p. 171
21. Clarkson (1990), p. 12
22. Ibid., p. 25
23. *SMir*, 16.11.80
24. *Mail*, 18.11.80:19
25. Edwards (1988), pp. 176–7; Porter (1984), p. 166
26. Edwards (1988), p. 179
27. *SMir*, 23.11.80
28. 'Palace ends clash with newspaper over prince', *Times*, 24.11.80:3
29. *Mail*, 24.11.80
30. 'The Queen may complain over "love train" story', *Mail*, 25.11.80
31. *Guard*, 26.4.80:15
32. Elizabeth Grice, 'Diana and the newshounds', *SunT*, 30.11.80:13
33. *Times*, 2.12.80:13
34. Atticus, 'Hounding the hounder', *SunT*, 7.12.80:32
35. *UKPG*, 8.12.80
36. Edwards conversation with author
37. *Mail*, 23.1.75; 1.2.75
38. *Sun*, 25.11.71
39. *Guard*, 3.3.78
40. *Sun*, 3.5.79. Cf. *Sun*, 30.4.79; Shawcross (1992), p. 211
41. 'Maggie's key to victory', *Mail*, 14.10.78:1
42. *Times*, 22.6.78:2
43. Cf. *Exp*. 19.1.79:3; 23.1.79:2
44. *DMir*, 12.1.79
45. *Exp*, 22.1.79; *Mail*, 8.1.79:6
46. *Mail*, 6.1.79; *Exp* 6.1.79; *DMir*, 8.1.79
47. *Mail* and *Exp*, 17.1.79
48. 'A Smack in the Eye for Jim', *Sun*, 6.2.79; 'Maggie leaps ahead', *Exp*, 6.2.79
49. *Sun*, 15.2.79
50. 'Where we stand', *Sun*, 30.3.79:2

51. *Sun*, 24.4.79
52. *Mail*, 4.4.79:6
53. *Mail*, 3.4.79; 4.4.79; 7.4.79; 9.4.79; 10.4.79; 19.4.79; 23.4.79; 26.4.79
54. *Mail*, 6.4.79; 12.4.79; 20.4.79
55. *DMir*, 4.4.79; 9.4.79; 26.4.79; 30.4.79
56. *DMir*, 7.4.79; 10.4.79; 19.4.79; 23.4.79; 28.4.79
57. *DMir*, 17.4.79
58. *Sun*, 7.4.79
59. Anthony King, *Obs*, 8.4.79:1
60. *Exp*, 23.4.79
61. Adam Raphael and Geoffrey Wansell, 'The selling of Maggie', *Obs*, 22.4.79:9
62. *Guard*, 30.4.79:12
63. *Obs*, 15.4.79:12
64. Griffiths (1996), p. 366
65. *Exp*, 26.4.79
66. 'The marketing of Margaret Thaatchi', *Guard*, 30.4.79:12
67. *Mail*, 26.4.79
68. *STel*, 29.4.79:16
69. 'A change of direction', *FT*, 3.5.79
70. *Sun*, 3.5.79:1
71. Grose (1989), p. 37
72. 'Who were the fibbers?', *SMir*, 28.12.80
73. Wintour (1972), p. 199
74. Taylor (1961), p. 45
75. Sebba (1994)
76. Gray (1990), p. 228
77. 'A question of gender', *100 Years of Fleet Street* (London Press Club, 1982)
78. Ibid., p. 82
79. Ibid., p. 81
80. Robinson (2001), p. 76
81. Pollard in Gray (1990), p. 128
82. Robinson (2001), p. 86
83. Dougary (1994), p. 68
84. Taylor (1993), pp. 192, 196
85. Gray (1990), p. 229; Robinson (2001), p. 106
86. Dougary (1994), p. 70
87. Glover (2000), p. 227
88. Gray (1990), p. 208
89. Ibid., p. 209
90. Green conversation with author, 14.9.01. *Woman's Sunday Mirror* launched 13.2.55, later became *Woman's Mirror* and was eventually absorbed into *Woman* magazine
91. *UKPG*, 19.3.73
92. Dog Watches Dog, *UKPG*, 19.3.73
93. Green conversation with author, 14.9.01
94. Patmore (1993), p. 130
95. Green conversation with author, 14.9.01
96. Ibid.
97. 'A question of gender', op. cit.

98. Patmore (1993), pp. 77, 129
99. Ibid., p. 188
100. Ibid., pp. 77, 247
101. Robinson (2001), p. 184
102. 'Give a girl a break', *Spec*, 17.7.82
103. Robinson (2001), pp. 195–200
104. 'She who must be obeyed', *Guard*. 13.3.82
105. NUJ survey, 1984
106. 'Rally ho!' *SunT*, 10.12.72:42
107. Dougary (1994), pp. 97–8
108. Glover (2000), p. 144
109. Ibid., p. 227
110. Rook in Gray (1990), p. 213
111. Leapman (1992), p. 37
112. Wyatt in Glover (2000), pp. 71–2
113. Dougary (1994), pp. 116–20
114. Ibid., p. 101
115. Ibid., p. 95

15. NEW TYCOONS FOR OLD

1. Tony Benn: *Arguments for Democracy* (Jonathan Cape, 1981), p. 103
2. 'Reuters: the price of greed', *Spec*, 22.10.83:11–14. Cf. *Spectator* for following three weeks
3. Taylor (1993), p. 292
4. Read (1992), pp. 353–4
5. Jenkins (1986), p. 158
6. *Guard*, 10.6.82
7. Robertson and Chancellor, op. cit.
8. Read (1992), p. 345; Hamilton (1989), pp. 188–9
9. Alexander Chancellor, 'Notebook', *Spec*, 3.3.84:5
10. Read (1992), p. 365
11. *UKPG*, 11.6.84
12. Lawrenson and Barber (1985)
13. Read (1992), p. 369
14. Gray (1990), pp. 92–4
15. Evans (1983), pp. 141–53
16. Wyatt (2000), p.147
17. As an example of Grigg's unreliability note his absurd claim that Evans's 'merits as an editor had not, perhaps, been fully tested', p. 577
18. 'Questions Harold Evans doesn't answer', Magnus Linklater, *Journalist*, November–December 1983
19. Evans (1983), p. 150
20. Evans (1994), p. xxv
21. Heren (1985), p. 168
22. *Times*, 29.1.81
23. Hamilton (1989), p. 181

24. Leapman (1983), p. 221. This is borne out by the leaving dates of staff listed in Appendix B, Grigg, pp. 582–92
25. 'Why I wrote this book, by ex-*Times* editor Evans', *UKPG*, 31.10. 83
26. Woods and Bishop (1985), p. 378
27. Leapman (1983), p. 224. Cf. Donoughue (2003), pp. 285–7
28. Evans (1983), p. 287
29. Ibid., pp. 313, 320, 321
30. Ibid., pp. 304–9
31. Ibid., pp. 357–67
32. Murdoch in author's presence (more than once)
33. Evans (1983), pp. 291, 373; Donoughue (2003), p. 289
34. Glover (2000), p. 243; Fay conversation with author, 30.5.01
35. 'Dirty tricks at The Times', *Mail*, 15.3.82; '*Times* directors meet in row over editor', *Exp*, 12.3.82; 'Warfare as Evans hangs on', *Guard*, 13.3.83
36. Evans (1983), pp. 177–8
37. Evans email to author, 27.6.01
38. *UKPG*, 4.11.85
39. Woods and Bishop (1985), p. 379
40. Heren (1985), p. 170
41. Kiernan (1989), p. 311
42. 'One down, more to go?', *Economist*, 9.7.83
43. Shawcross (1992), p. 286
44. Melvern (1986), p. 79
45. Walker conversation with author, 26.6.01
46. Giles (1986), pp. 198–9
47. Neil (1996), p. 12
48. Giles (1986), p. 202; Evans (1983), p. 140
49. Giles (1986), pp. 202–3
50. Ibid., p. 216
51. Evans (1983), p. 289
52. Ibid., p. 215
53. Knightley (1997), p. 249
54. Foot in Glover (2000), p. 85
55. 'The View from the Goldfish Bowl', *Guard*, 22.10.83; Neil (1996), p. 22
56. Neil (1996), p. 27
57. Melvern (1986), p. 96
58. Neil (1996), p. 38
59. 'Sunset for CND', *SunT*, 23.10.83:16
60. 'The Press we don't deserve', *SunT*, 4.3.84
61. 'Rupert Murdoch and the *Sunday Times*: A Lamp Goes Out', *Political Quarterly*, vol. 35/4, October–December 1984
62. 'The Nouveau-Right *Sunday Times*', *Literary Review*, January 1985
63. Harris (1987), p. 151
64. Sampson (1982), p. 435
65. *Times*, 27.2.81
66. *Obs*, 5.7.81
67. *Guard*, 30.6.81. Cf. *Guard*. 6.7.81
68. Bower (1993), p. 279
69. Hall (1987), pp. 176–7

70. Ibid., pp. 161–6
71. Donald Trelford, 'The patter of Tiny's feet', *Obs*, 12.3.00
72. *Obs*, 15.4.84
73. *Guard*, 18.4.84
74. *Mail*, 19.4.84:15
75. *Obs*, 22.4.84
76. Trelford, *Obs*, op. cit.
77. Hall (1987), pp. 181, 188
78. Bower (1993), pp. 478, 488; 'The Bloody Harrods Battle', *Obs*, 10.3.85
79. 'We could have stopped Maxwell', Mike Molloy, *BJR*, vol. 10/4, 1999
80. Les Carpenter to Robert Head, *Daily Mirror*, City editor, unpublished interview January 1988. Cited in Haines (1988), p. 387
81. Molloy, *BJR*, op. cit.
82. Conroy (1997), pp. 135–6
83. Haines (1988), p. 389
84. *Mail*, 5.7.84
85. Pilger (1986), p. 516
86. Conroy (1997), pp. 136–7
87. Molloy, *BJR*, op. cit.
88. Edwards (1988), pp. 219–20
89. For a comprehensive account of Maxwell's career, Bower (1995)
90. Thompson and Delano (1991), p. 204
91. Haines (1988), p. 417
92. Maxwell press statement, 13.7.84
93. *DMir*, 14.7.84:1
94. Waterhouse, *Mail*, 2.4.01:14
95. Haines suggests it was 'to make it read better'. Haines (1988), p. 394
96. For a different view, ibid., p. 399
97. Lady Cudlipp email to author, 25.8.00
98. Edwards (1988), p. 247
99. *UKPG*, 22.2.82
100. *Black Dwarf* was published in 1985
101. Molloy conversation with author, 9.5.01
102. Edwards (1988), p. 213
103. Edwards, Hugh Cudlipp memorial lecture, 24.10.00
104. Edwards (1988), pp. 219, 224, 229
105. *SP*, 16.10.81
106. Burrington email to author, 25.4.01
107. Porter (1984), p. 173
108. Burrington email to author, 25.4.01
109. Hobday conversation with author, 22.4.01
110. Edwards (1988), p. 237
111. Pilger (1986), p. 528
112. *DMir*, 25.11.85
113. Interview by Richard Kershaw, 1979, quoted by Porter (1984), p. 153
114. 'Fleet Street: a down market era', *Listener*, 3.1.80
115. Deedes (1997), p. 267
116. Robin Esser conversation with author, 21.6.01
117. Chippindale and Horrie (1990), p. 82

118. Junor (1990), p. 252
119. Cameron (2000), pp. 136–8
120. 'Intruder at Queen's bedside', *Exp*, 10.7.82
121. *SunT*, 18.7.82:4
122. Christopher Ward, 'The sacked editors' club wishes you well', *Indy*, 18.4.00
123. Cameron (2000), p. 137
124. Ibid., pp. 137–8
125. Ibid., p. 138
126. Ibid., p. 142
127. Rook (1989), pp. 62, 82–6
128. *Exp*, 9.5.84
129. Sogat 82 was formed, in 1982, by the merger of the National Society of Operative Printers and Assistants (Natsopa) and the Society of Graphical and Allied Trades (Sogat 75). In 1991, Sogat 82 merged with the National Graphical Association (NGA) to form the Graphical, Paper and Media Union. Cf. J. Moran/ *NATSOPA: Seventy-Five Years* (Heinemann, 1964); <www.warwick.ac.uk/services/library/mrc/ead/039nat.htm>
130. Junor (1990), p. 253
131. 'Sir Larry's crisis week', *UKPG*, 14.5.85
132. Junor (1990), pp. 254–5
133. Cameron (2000), p. 108. Cf. Junor (2002), pp. 159, 163–76
134. Cameron (2000), p. 48
135. Grose (1989), p. 92
136. Edwards (1988), p. 233
137. Heren (1985), p. 179
138. Wintour (1989), p. 164
139. Ibid., p. 168
140. Haines (1988), p. 388
141. Cameron (2000), p. 52
142. Schofield (1975)
143. Press Council survey, 1970
144. Cameron (2000), p. 54
145. *Indy*, 8.3.89
146. *ES*, 18.12.85:1
147. Louis Kirby, *ES*, 29.4.85:2
148. Peregrine Worsthorne, 'The voice of the silent majority', *Times*, 9.5.83:9
149. Hart-Davis (1990), p. 269
150. Deedes (1997), p. 321
151. Monte Black obit, *DTel*, 14.1.02
152. Siklos (1995), pp. 78–9
153. Ibid., p. 74; Black (1993), pp. 255–63
154. Peter Newman, *Maclean's*, 25.2.85
155. Siklos (1995), p. 127
156. *Times*, 9.11.85
157. Hart-Davis (1990), p. 423
158. *DTel*, 14.12.85
159. Hart-Davis (1990), p. 423
160. John Ralston Saul, *Spec*, 23.11.85
161. Deedes (1997), p. 334

162. *Times*, 23.12.76:1
163. 'Shrimsley picks his team for the Mail on Sunday', *UKPG*, 26.10.81
164. Ian Jack, 'Fleet Street war – with Knight of the Long Knives', *SunT*, 18.7.82:4
165. Leapman (1992), p. 181
166. Paul Johnson, 'Action stations', *Spec*, 8.5.82
167. Junor (1990), p. 223
168. *UKPG*, 29.3.82
169. Bourne (1990), p. 225
170. 'Mail on Sunday editor quits', *Times*, 6.7.82:2
171. *UKPG*, 13.9.82
172. *MoS*, 11.7.82
173. Junor (1990), p. 223
174. *UKPG*, 13.9.82
175. Stephens conversation with author, 28.3.01
176. Green conversation with author, 14.9.01
177. Chippindale and Horrie (1990)
178. 'Great, mate!' *Sun*, 20.2.85:7
179. Goodhart (1986), p. 188
180. *Socialist Worker*, August 1984
181. *Times*, 15.4.81:4
182. Evans email to author, 27.6.01
183. Schofield (1975), p. 123
184. 'Askew out after nine months', *UKPG*, 4.1.82
185. Jameson (1990), p. 85
186. Ibid., p. 91
187. Junor (1990), p. 252
188. 'Andrew and the playgirl!' *NoW*, 20.5.84; *UKPG*, 28.5.84
189. Bainbridge and Stockdill (1993), p. 277
190. Taylor (1993), p. 249
191. Tisdall interview with BBC <news.bbc.co.uk/01media/500000/audio/_503665_tisdall.ram>
192. *World in Action*, 26.3.84
193. *Guard*, 22.10.83
194. 'Heseltine's briefing to Thatcher on Cruise timing', *Guard*, 1.11.83
195. Taylor (1993), p. 250
196. Ibid., p. 251
197. Tisdall interview, BBC audio, op. cit.
198. Taylor (1993), p. 252; 'The Guardian and Sarah Tisdall', *Granta*, no. 12, summer 1984
199. Foot in Glover (2000), p. 85
200. Peter Fiddick, *BJR*, vol. 4/2, 1993
201. *Times*, 13.12.82
202. Kynaston (1988), p. 481
203. *DTel*, 10.8.83
204. Kynaston (1988), p. 497
205. Ibid., p. 449
206. Ibid., p. 502
207. Cited in *FT*, 24.1.84
208. *NS*, 8.3.85

209. *FT*, 17.11.84:11. Cf. 22.11.83:11; 23.11.83:1; 24.11.83:10
210. 'A battle for Britain', *SunT*, 4.11.83
211. *FT*, 25.11.83
212. Neil (1996), p. 78; Shah in Gray (1990), p. 308; MacArthur (1988), p. 35
213. MacArthur (1988), pp. 40, 65
214. Ibid., p. 205
215. Ibid., p. 41
216. Glover (1994), p. 8
217. *FT*, 27.12.85
218. Conroy (1997), pp. 180–1

16. GOTCHA! THE RIPPER, HITLER AND A FAIRYTALE WEDDING

1. John Junor in Gray (1990), p. 124
2. *Press Conduct in the Sutcliffe Case: A Report by the Press Council* (1983), Chapter 6, para. 3
3. Ibid., 7.16
4. Ibid., 16.44, 47, 49
5. Ibid., 16.69
6. Ibid., 16.67
7. Ibid., 16.71
8. *Private Eye*, 30.1.81
9. Press Council report, op. cit. 17.44
10. *Mail*, 7.5.81
11. Press Council report, op. cit. 17.60
12. Ibid., 17.59
13. Ibid., 17.81
14. Ibid., 17.112
15. Ibid., 17.76
16. Ibid., 17.38
17. Ibid., 18.29, 32
18. *Guard*, 4.2.83
19. 'Let Dog Eat Dog', *Times*, 4.2.83:13
20. *Mail*, 4.2.83
21. *Exp*, 4.2.83
22. *Times*, 26.9.83
23. Press Council report, op. cit., 16.61, 77, 78
24. *Ripping Yarns: A Private Eye* Report (1991), p. 6
25. Ibid., p. 11
26. *NoW*, 4.12.88
27. Hastings (2000), p. 270
28. *Times*, 5.4.82
29. *Economist*, 24.4.82
30. 'Paper warriors', *Sun*, 2.4.82
31. Baistow (1985), p. 62. Cf. Morgan (1999), p. 460
32. *Mail*, 5.4.82:6
33. *Exp*, 6.4.82:2

34. *Star*, 20.4.82
35. *Sun*, 20.4.82
36. *FT*, 5.4.82
37. Kynaston (1988), p. 465
38. Brian Hitchen, Brighton *Evening Argus*, 1.9.01
39. Hudson and Stanier (1997), p. 169
40. 'SHAMED', *Mail*, 3.4.82. Cf. 'Bravery of marines outnumbered 10 to 1', *Mail*, 6.4.82
41. Norris conversation with author, 17.1.02
42. Woodward (1984), p. 109
43. Cited in Hudson and Stanier (1997), pp. 170–1
44. *Sun*, 26.4.82
45. *Sun*, 1.5.82:2
46. 'The Sun's Sidewinder downs bomber', *Sun*, 3.5.82
47. *Sun*, 4.5.82
48. John Essery, ed., *Gotcha: Classic Headlines from The Sun* (Signet, circa 1993)
49. Shirley conversation with author, 26.2.02
50. *Sun*, 5.5.82:1
51. Hudson and Stanier (1997), p. 181
52. *FT*, 6.5.82
53. *Guard*, 15.1.76
54. Taylor (1993), p. 234
55. 'Might isn't right', *DMir*, 6.5.82
56. 'Dare call it treason', *Sun*, 7.5.82
57. *DMir*, 8.5.82
58. 'The Men of Blood', *Sun*, 12.5.82
59. *FT*, 12.5.82
60. Kynaston (1988), p. 467
61. Grose (1989), p. 61
62. Morgan (1999), p. 460; Childs (1997), p. 230; Knightley (2000), p. 480
63. Morgan (1999), p. 459
64. Hudson and Stanier (1997), p. 175
65. 'The war that had to be', *SunT*, 23.5.82:14
66. Hudson and Stanier (1997), p. 182
67. 'Battle honours', *Spec*, 29.5.82
68. Mercer (1987), p. 164
69. Blakeway (1992), p. 158
70. McGowan and Hands (1983), p. 277
71. *ES*, 15.6.82
72. Hastings (2000), p. 379
73. Smith conversation with author, 18.1.02
74. McGowan and Hands (1983)
75. Norris conversation with author, 17.1.02. Cf. Letter to Daily *Mail*, 17.1.02:63
76. *SunT*, 18.7.82:12
77. Taylor (1993), p. 236
78. 'Pride and Heartbreak of two VCs' Widows', *Sun*, 21.10.82
79. *DMir*, 22.10.82
80. *DMir*, 8.8.83:2
81. 'Falklands hero Simon fights for new life', *Sun*, 11.6.85

82. *Spec*, 29.5.82
83. Profile by Ronnie Spark, *Sun*, 2.6.83:16
84. *Sun*, 10.11.81:2
85. *Sun*, 10.5.83
86. *Sun*, 7.6.83:16
87. *Mail*, 17.5.83:16
88. '35,000 jobs lost if Foot wins', *Mail*, 16.5.83
89. *Obs*, 22.5.83. Cf. *SunT*, 22.5.83:57
90. *Guard*, 4.6.83; *Times*, 4.6.83:4
91. *Exp*, 9.6.83
92. *Star*, 7.6.83
93. *Guard*, 6.6.83
94. Preston email to author, 4.9.01
95. 'A last look at the election', *Guard*, 8.6.83; Taylor (1993), p. 319
96. Crewe (1995), p. 260
97. Preston email to author, 4.9.01
98. Toynbee conversation with author, 6.9.01
99. *Times*, 16.9.86
100. *Sun*, 16.5.84
101. 'Royal Family's fury at the siege of Sandringham', *Obs*, 2.1.81
102. *Times*, 3.1.81:1
103. 'Shotgun Prince and a *Sun* girl', *Sun*, 3.1.81
104. 'Royal fences', *Sun*, 5.1.81:2
105. *DMir*, 5.1.81
106. *Sun*, 30.7.81
107. *Sun* and *DMir*, 9.11.81:1
108. *Times*, 8.12.81
109. Bellisario (1972), pp. 21, 101
110. Evans (1983), p. 363
111. 'Peace and goodwill', *DMir*, 9.12.81
112. 'Diana's private life', *Mail*, 9.12.81
113. 'A Princess's private life', *Exp*, 9.12.81
114. 'Diana: "Cool it" plea to the press', *Star*, 9.12.81:3
115. 'Princess Pursued', Douglas Keay, *Woman's Own*, 1.10.83
116. 'The captive Princess', *Times*, 9.12.81
117. Evans (1983), p. 364
118. 'That fierce light', *DTel*, 9.12.81:14
119. 'Di-Land in the Sun' and 'Bahama Mama', *Sun*, 18.2.82; 'Bikini Girl Diana', *Star*, 18.2.82
120. *Sun*, 19.2.82
121. 'Enough is Enough', *Star*, 19.2.82
122. 'The Princess and the Press', *DMir*, 19.2.82
123. *Times*, 4.3.82:2; *UKPG*, 8.3.82:6
124. 'Why Di Keeps Throwing a Wobbly', *Sun*, 2.4.82
125. 'Is it all getting too much for Diana?' *DMir*, 15.11.82
126. Keay, *Woman's Own*, op. cit.
127. *Star*, 3.2.83
128. Keay, *Woman's Own*, op. cit.
129. Harris (1986), p. 265

130. Ibid., p. 287
131. Ibid., pp. 234–6
132. Knightley (1997), p. 145
133. 'Secrets that survived the bunker', *Times*, 23.4.83
134. Harris (1986), p. 311
135. *SunT*, 24.4.83
136. Harris (1986), pp. 314–15
137. Ibid., p. 315; Knightley (1997), p. 147
138. Harris (1986), p. 343
139. *SunT*, 8.5.83
140. *DTel*, 28.1.03:16–17
141. Evans (1994), p. 463

17. THE WAPPING REVOLUTION

1. Front-page headline pre-launch issue, *Today*, September 1985; MacArthur (1988), p. 71
2. Melvern (1986), p. 80
3. *STel*, 10.3.85
4. Melvern (1986), pp. 22, 106, 149–51, 181
5. Neil (1996), p. 97
6. Melvern (1986), p. 88
7. Neil (1996), p. 98
8. Melvern (1986), p. 131
9. Ibid., pp. 158–9
10. 'Our Wapping dream is going up', *UKPG*, 22.282
11. Wyatt (1998), p. 69; Wyatt (2000), p. 147
12. Melvern (1986), p. 21
13. Wyatt (1998), p. 69
14. Melvern (1986), pp. 194–5
15. Ibid., p. 16
16. Conroy (1997), p. 189
17. Baistow (1985), pp. 87–90. Cf. Goodhart and Wintour (1986), pp. 172–83
18. Conroy (1997), p. 188
19. Bainbridge and Stockdill (1993), pp. 293–4
20. Melvern (1986), p. 82
21. Ibid., p. 85
22. Melvern letter to author, 2.5.00
23. Neil (1996), p. 126
24. Melvern (1986), p. 95
25. Ibid., p. 100; Neil (1996), p. 128
26. Neil (1996), pp. 133–4
27. *Sun*, 27.1.86
28. Hardy conversation with author, 26.10.00
29. *JH*, no. 40, January 1995
30. Gray (1990), p. 135
31. Jenkins (1986), p. 220

32. Frank Barlow in Kynaston (1988), p. 503
33. Chippindale and Horrie (1999), p. 274
34. Whittam Smith, *BJR*, vol. 1/1, 1989
35. MacArthur (1988), p. 89
36. Leapman (1992), p. 87
37. MacArthur (1988), p. 157
38. Garland (1990), pp. 75, 123
39. MacArthur (1988), p. 105
40. Stephen Lynas, 'The Queen warns Thatcher', *Today*, 7.6.86
41. MacArthur (1988), p. 155
42. Ibid., p. 128
43. Holden email to author, 12.6.01
44. Hagerty conversation with author, 25.6.01
45. Shawcross (1992), pp. 187ff
46. Garland (1990), p. 6
47. Glover (1994), p. 53
48. Ibid., pp. 122–31
49. *Indy*, 27.4.87
50. Frank Johnson, *BJR*, vol. 1/3, 1990
51. Glover (1994), p. 144
52. Obit, Andrew Marr, *Indy*, 26.3.01
53. Georgina Henry and Nigel Wilmott, 'The battle for Sunday', *Guard*, 11.9.89:21
54. Wyatt (1999), p. 197
55. *STel*, 18.9.88:13
56. Leapman (1992), p. 171
57. Glover (1994), p. 159
58. Cole conversation with author, 6.6.01
59. Leapman (1992), p. 103
60. 'Sundays "merger move"', *Guard*, 11.9.89:2; Peter Cole, 'Title Fight', *SunT*, 25.4.93
61. Georgina Henry, 'The Independent's seven-day juggling act', *Guard*, 11.9.89:23
62. David Lipsey, 'It was – but not any more', *JH*, no. 42, summer 1995
63. Henry and Willmott, *Guard*, op. cit.
64. Jack conversation with author, 7.6.01
65. *Sindy*, 28.1.90
66. Peter Cole, 'Son of Corrie: the incredible shrinking new quality', *Guard*, 24.9.90:21
67. Peter Cole, 'The Ageing of an Editor', *BJR*, vol. 2/1, 1990
68. 'Tabloid relaunch fails to save *Sunday Correspondent*', *Guard*, 28.11.90:8
69. Killick (1994), p. 72
70. *Guard*, 16.6.76
71. 'King Porn is caged at last', *NoW*, 16.5.82
72. Andy Medhurst, 'Is That All There Is?' *Listener*, 22.3.90
73. Hardy conversation with author, 26.10.00
74. Haines (1988), pp. 427–8
75. Nick Davies email to author, 10.6.01
76. Chippindale and Horrie (1988)
77. Pilger, 'The birth of a new *Sun*?', *NS*, 2.1.87
78. Ibid.

79. Chippindale and Horrie (1988), p. 88
80. Ibid., pp. 84, 128
81. *NoS*, 26.4.87:10
82. Ray Snoddy, '*News on Sunday* faces cash crisis', *FT*, 6.5.87
83. Chippindale and Horrie (1988), p. 188
84. Ibid., p. 231
85. *Post*, 10.11.88
86. Shah in Gray (1990), p. 309
87. *BJR*, vol. 2/2, 1990
88. Wyatt (2000), p. 172. Cf. 'Pillar of the Murdoch empire', *Campaign*, 17.8.84:31
89. Chippindale and Horrie (1999), p. 232
90. *Sun*, 13.3.86
91. Chippindale and Horrie (1999), pp. 253–4
92. Ibid., pp. 247–8
93. *Sun*, 25.2.87
94. *Sun*, 16.4.87
95. *Sun*, 28.9.87
96. *DMir*, 6.11.87
97. *Sun*, 12.12.88:1
98. Grose (1989), p. 112
99. *Sun*, 19.4.89
100. Press Council report, July 1989
101. Chippindale and Horrie (1999), p. 407
102. Terry Wogan interview, BBC1, 8.2.89
103. 'British news ace killed', *Sun*, 18.11.89
104. *Sun*, 1.11.90; 'Frog Off . . . Kick them in the Gauls'. Cf. 'FILTHY FRENCH SINK OUR HOLS', *Sun*, 13.4.90:1
105. *Sun*, 1.8.89
106. *Sun*, 12.11.87
107. *Sun*, 13.10.88
108. *Sun*, 16.11.88
109. MacKenzie speech to Broadcasting Press Guild, March 2001, *Indy*, 20.3.01
110. Charles Wintour, *SCorr*, 5.11.89:54
111. Grose (1989), p. 89
112. Garland (1990), p. 69
113. Neil (1996), p. 63
114. *Listener*, 15.12.88
115. 'Queen dismayed by "uncaring" Thatcher' and 'The African Queen', *SunT*, 20.7.86
116. Neil (1996), pp. 195–207
117. 'Revealed: the secrets of Israel's nuclear arsenal' and 'Inside Dimona', *SunT*, 5.10.86
118. Foot in Glover (2000), p. 85
119. 'How MI5 "plotted to topple Wilson"', *SunT*, 23.11.86
120. 'My MI5 memoirs, by Peter Wright', *SunT*, 12.7.87
121. Neil (1996), p. 319
122. Ibid., p. 261
123. *NoW*, 'Call Girl Works at Commons', 12.3.89
124. Brown (1995), pp. 270–88

125. *Sun*, 25.1.90; Neil (1996), p. 179. Cf. *Sun* 15.3.89
126. 'Playboys as editors', *STel*, 19.3.89
127. Neil (1996), p. 278
128. Garland (1990), p. 43
129. Ibid.; *Spec*, 1.3.86
130. Wyatt (1999), p. 229
131. Neil (1996), p. 282
132. Wyatt (1999), p. 247
133. *NoW*, 26.10.86
134. *Star*, 1.11.86. Cf. *Star*, 20.7.01
135. Cameron (2000), pp. 152–3
136. David Mertens, *PG*, 27.7.01
137. *NoW*, 1.3.87
138. Chippindale and Horrie (1990), p. 297
139. Gray (1990), p. 164
140. Bainbridge and Stockdill (1993), p. 279
141. Ibid.
142. Ibid., p. 319; Brown (1995), pp. 245–69
143. Chippindale and Horrie (1990), p. 333
144. Wyatt (1999), p. 23
145. Bainbridge and Stockdill (1993), p. 280
146. Ibid., p. 281
147. Phil Goff, *BJR*, vol. 4/1, 1993
148. Cameron (2000), p. 69
149. Killick (1994), p. 91
150. Cameron (2000), p. 72
151. *FT*, 4.9.87
152. *UKPG*, 7.9.87
153. Cameron (2000), p. 78
154. Ibid., p. 79
155. 'Star man', Brighton *Evening Argus*, 1.9.01
156. Killick (1994), p. 103
157. *Report of the Monopolies and Mergers Commission on Mr David Sullivan and the Bristol Evening Post plc*, May 1990
158. His papers carried leaders making the same point, *SP*, 6.4.86:6
159. *The Daily Mirror Style Book* (1980), *Newspaper Style* (1989)
160. Haines (1988)
161. Greenslade (1992)
162. 'Maxwell the megaphone', *Guard*, 5.3.90:25
163. Molloy conversation with author, 9.5.01
164. 'Scandal of the £250–a-day council house call-girls', *SP*, 23.2.86
165. *SP*, 30.4.89:1; 16.6.89:1
166. *SP*, 23.7.89:1, 12–13
167. *SP*, 19.11.89
168. *UKPG*, 27.11.89; 'Megaphone', *Guard*, op. cit.
169. Greenslade (1992), pp. 123–6
170. Ibid., p. 251
171. Platell conversation with author, 16.1.02
172. Wyatt (1999), p. 158

173. Ibid., p. 285
174. Cameron (2000), p. 64
175. Wyatt (1999), p. 197
176. Ibid., p. 382
177. Leapman (1992), p. 181
178. Garland (1990), p. 106
179. Wyatt (1999), pp. 68–9
180. Ibid., p. 12
181. Walker conversation with author, 26.6.01
182. Wyatt (1999), p. 206
183. Ibid., p. 254
184. *Indy*, 14.3.90:13. Cf. 'Tory wets detect "one of us" in new man at the *Times*', *Guard*, 14.3.90:6
185. Unhappy with his first effort, Jenkins (1979), he wrote a much better follow-up, Jenkins (1986)
186. *Indy*, 14.3.90:13
187. Leapman (1992), p. 169
188. David Walker, 'Follow my leader', *Listener*, 29.3.90
189. Jenkins conversation with author, 26.6.01
190. Walker conversation with author, 26.6.01
191. Black (1993), p. 368
192. Garland (1990), p. 208
193. Ibid., p. 47
194. *BJR*, vol. 1/3, 1990
195. Garland (1990), p. 40
196. Hastings (2000), p. 127
197. Green conversation with author, 14.9.01
198. Glover (2000), p. 155
199. *JH*, no. 37, 1994
200. Garland (1990), pp. 157, 181; Hastings (2002), pp. 128–9, 132–3
201. *DTel*, 16.4.86; 17.4.86; 18.4.86. Cf. Garland (1990), pp. 108–9; Black (1993), pp. 365–6; Hastings (2002), p. 67
202. Interview on Channel 4, *Three of a Kind*, July 1989, quoted by Anthony Bevins, *BJR*, vol. 1/2, 1990
203. 'Explanation needed', *DTel*, 8.3.88:16; Hastings (2002), pp. 133–6
204. Black (1993), p. 469; Hastings (2002), pp. 76–7
205. Garland (1990), p. 66
206. Leapman (1992), p. 164
207. Goodman, *BJR*, vol. 4/4, 1993
208. Garland (1990), p. 93; Hastings (2002), p. 27
209. Gray (1990), p. 188
210. Black (1993), p. 403
211. *Spec* diary, 8.7.89:6
212. Black (1993), p. 366
213. *FT*, 18.11.89
214. Wyatt (1999), p. 220
215. 'The constant smiler with the knife', *STel*, 7.1.90
216. Exchange of letters in *Times*, 18.1.90
217. Wyatt (1999), p. 382

218. Siklos (1995), p. 165
219. Cameron (2000), p. 126
220. Esser conversation with author, 21.6.01
221. 'Doors of death', *SExp*, 8.3.87
222. Cameron (2000), p. 127
223. Ibid., p. 131
224. Ibid., pp. 129–32
225. '125 in Thames cruiser sinking', *SunT*, 20.8.89
226. Cameron (2000), pp. 133–4
227. Junor (1990), p. 330. His final *Sunday Express* column appeared 5.8.89
228. Bower (1993), p. 530
229. Ibid., p. 504
230. Peter Wickman, 'In search of the fabulous Pharaohs', *Obs*, 15.6.86
231. 'Exposed – the Phony Pharaoh', *Obs*, 30.3.89
232. *Times*, 12.4.89
233. Taylor (1993), p. 298
234. Ibid., p. 313
235. *Ten Dead Men: The Story of the 1981 Hunger Strike* (Grafton Books, 1987)
236. Kynaston (1988), p. 501
237. Ibid., p. 504

18. PUBLIC INTEREST AND THE FREEDOM TO BE PRIVATE

1. Arnold Bennett, *The Title* (Chatto & Windus, 1918), p. 61
2. *Today*, 28.3.89; *Guard*, 27/28/29.3.90
3. *Today*, 25.4.89:1
4. Snoddy (1992), pp. 1, 9–10
5. 'Paper they can't gag', *Sun*, 8.10.82; 'This vital case – by The Editor', *Mail*, 8.12.76; John Junor, *SExp*, 3.9.78
6. Evans (1983), p. 164
7. Robertson (1983)
8. *Times*, 18.2.82:4
9. *Sun*, 8.3.83
10. *Labour's Plan* (Labour Party, 1983), p. 26
11. *Guard*, 4.2.83
12. Alan Rusbridger, 'Grey days for a Dark Ages lamp-bearer', *Guard*, 16.11.87
13. Zelman Cowen, *Difficulty, Damage, Danger – but Hope*, Press Council report, 1988
14. Rusbridger, *Guard*, op. cit.
15. *Guard*, 22.4.89
16. 'Private lives in the news of the world', *Guard*, 24.1.89
17. Grose (1989), p. 40
18. *Sun*, 6.2.89
19. Wyatt (1999), p. 159
20. Snoddy (1992), pp. 100–1
21. *Hard News*, 21.12.89; *Times*, 22.12.89:5
22. Snoddy (1992), p. 102

23. *Times*, 17.3.90:4; 21.3.90:51
24. *SSport*, 4.3.90:1, 16. 17
25. *Report of the Committee on Privacy and Related Matters* (1990) Cmnd 1102, p. 77
26. Louis Blom-Cooper, 'The Last Days of the Press Council', *BJR*, vol. 2/3, 1991
27. Shannon (2001), pp. 28–9
28. Wyatt (1999), p. 224
29. *Sun*, 16.8.90
30. 'Loony Lefties', *Sun*, 5.5.83:9
31. 'Red Ken clowned King of London', *Sun*, 8.5.81; 'Comrade Bernie', *Exp*, 11.10.85
32. *Sun*, 1.3.84:9; *World in Action*, 5.3.84; letter to Press Council from Tony Banks, Michael Foot, Merlyn Rees and Eric Heffer, 20.3.84
33. 'The Press and the Loony Left', *Guard*, 4.5.87
34. 'Media Coverage of Local Government in London', unpublished (1987), p. 3; Cf. Jolyon Jenkins, 'The green sheep in Colonel Gadaffi Drive', *NS*, 9.1.87
35. *MoS*, 2.3.86
36. 'Lefties baa black sheep', *Sun*, 20.2.86:3
37. 'Now it's Baa Baa Blank Sheep! "Racist" rhyme banned', *Star*, 15.2.86
38. 'Baa, baa, green (yes, green) sheep', *Mail*, 9.10.86:3
39. 'The new insanity', *Mail*, 9.10.86
40. 'Rhyme and reason', *Mail*, 13.10.86:8
41. 'The little boy who made the mistake of humming Baa Baa Black Sheep', *Mail*, 20.2.87:3
42. 'But just look who's singing Baa Baa Black Sheep now', *Mail*, 21.2.87
43. *Sun*, 5.12.86
44. 'Roll up for the *Sun*'s barmy board game', *Sun*, 17.11.86:9
45. *Mail*, 27.4.87:9
46. *Times*, 23.5.87; *Exp*, 22.5.87; *Mail*, 23.5.87
47. *Exp*, 2.6.87
48. *Times*, 8.6.87
49. Tyler (1987), p. 232
50. Morgan (1999), p. 490
51. Grose (1989), p. 44
52. Wyatt (1999), p. 74
53. Ibid., p. 182
54. *Exp*, 24.11.89
55. Leapman (1992), p. 186
56. *Times*, 5.5.89
57. '10 Ways Maggie can help us like poll tax', *Sun*, 28.4.90
58. Wyatt (1999), p. 271
59. *Sun*, 29.10.90; 30.10.90
60. *Sun*, 8.11.90
61. Wyatt (1999), p. 371
62. *SunT*, 4.11.90
63. Wyatt (1999), p. 384
64. *Sun*, 20.11.90:6
65. *Sun*, 19.11.90:1, 6
66. Wyatt (1999), p. 388
67. Neil (1996), pp. 244, 248
68. Wyatt (1999), p. 389

69. *Times*, 5.11.90:17; 15.11.90:17; 17.11.90:11; 20.11.90:13
70. Cameron (2000), pp. 156–7
71. *Exp*, 20.11.90:1, 8
72. Neil (1996), p. 244
73. *Sun*, 21.11.90; Neil (1996), p. 251
74. Black (1993), p. 426
75. *DMir*, 23.11.90
76. Black (1993), p. 427
77. Neil (1996), p. 252
78. 'MAJOR BY A MILE' and 'Why we say it must be Major', *Sun*, 26.11.90:1, 6
79. *Exp*, 23.11.90:8
80. *Exp*, 28.11.90:8
81. *Sun*, 28.11.90
82. 'TRUE BRIT', *Star*, 23.11.90:1
83. *British–Iranian Business News*, March 2000
84. Ibid.
85. Adrian Hamilton, 'Lessons yet to be learnt', *Obs*, 12.3.00
86. *Times*, 17.3.90:2
87. Richard Ingrams, 'The things I could tell you about Rupert Allason', *Obs*, 21.10.01
88. 'Who Was This Man?' *SunT*, 18.3.90:14, 15
89. *STel*, 18.3.90
90. 'Murder in Mesopotamia', Hugh Roberts, *Labour & Trade Union Review*, Ernest Bevin Society, 1990

19. A MEDIA MAGNATE GOES TO WAR

1. Wiggin (1972), p. 82
2. Godfrey Hodgson, *BJR*, vol. 5/3, 1994
3. Chenoweth (2001)
4. Murdoch was forced to sell it in 1988 to comply with Federal Communication Commission rules barring the ownership of a TV station and a daily newspaper within the same city. He was given an FCC waiver in 1993 when the paper looked likely to close
5. *Guard*, 13.7.93
6. '20p Until Next Year', *Sun*, 22.8.92
7. *Indy*, 18.7.93
8. *Indy*, 2.9.93
9. *Indy*, 3.9.93
10. *FT*, 5.9.93; *Indy*, 12.10.93; OFT press release no. 65/93, 14.10.93
11. *UKPG*, 13.9.93
12. Wyatt (2000), pp. 273, 358; *Spec*, 23.10.93
13. Siklos (1995), p. 375
14. Hart-Davis (1990), p. 162
15. 'Blood on the Street', *SunT*, 26.6.94. Cf. Hastings (2002), pp. 362–3
16. *FT*, 1.7.94

17. 'Is Black facing his Waterloo?' *Obs*, 26.6.94; 'Black's financial own-goal', *SunT*, 26.6.94
18. *Guard*, 25.8.94
19. *SunT*, 26.6.94
20. *FT*, 30.6.94
21. *Guard*, 11.11.93; 6.5.94
22. *Indy*, 29.6.94
23. 'A Black day for the free Press', *DMir*, 25.6.94; *Guard*, 29.6.94
24. *UKPG*, 4.7.94; 18.7.94; *Guard*, 1.8.94
25. *FT*. 1.8.94
26. Smith New Court, July 1994; NatWest Securities, August 1994
27. OFT press release no. 42/94, 21.10.94; *UKPG*, 31.10.94
28. Claire Morris, 'The *Times* price cut: predatory pricing or canny competition', Royal Economic Society conference paper, October 1998
29. *DTel*, 8.6.95
30. Ashdown (2000), p. 95. Entry for 30.10.90
31. *Marketing*, 11.4.91
32. *UKPG*, 8.2.93
33. *Today*, 17.11.95. Cf. Stott (2002), p. 341
34. *Today*, 13.10.94
35. *Indy*, 25.3.95
36. *Times*, 27.5.95
37. *DTel*, 17.11.95
38. *SunT*, 20.8.95
39. *Today*, 17.11.95
40. *PG*, 6.9.96
41. *Mediumwave*, Radio 4 and *Stop Press* (later *Paper Talk*), Radio 5 Live
42. *Times*, 23.4.99
43. *Guard*, 28.6.99
44. Greenslade (1992), pp. 205–6, 223–4, 249–50, 265–7
45. *SunT*, 31.3.91; *FT*, 18.4.91
46. Wyatt (1999), p. 475
47. Greenslade (1992), pp. 360–7
48. *DMir*, 6.11.91
49. Conroy (1997), p. 150
50. *Sindy*, 10.11.91
51. 'Millions Missing From Mirror' and 'Maxwell: £526 Million Is Missing', *DMir*, 4–5.12.91
52. 'Red Baron captures true blue papers', *SunT*, 11.2.96
53. Hagerty conversation with author, 25.6.01. Cf. Stott (2002), pp. 325–6
54. Horrie and Nathan (1999), p. 161
55. Wyatt (2000), p. 172
56. See website <http://www.bigboysbreakfast.cwc.net/about.htm>
57. 'Di Spy Sensation', *SMir*, 7.11.93
58. *Times*, 9.11.93; *PG*, 15.11.93
59. *Indy*, 10.4.01
60. 'Go Now', *Sun*, 19.6.92
61. *Sun*, 23.12.92
62. *Times*, 24.12.92

63. Wyatt (2000), p. 178; *Sun*, 15.3.93
64. Neil (1996), p. 175
65. 'Seeing the *Sun* into the 1990s', ARC/Everett, May 1985, unpublished
66. *Sun*, 9.11.94
67. 'How Grobbelaar saved his name', *Guard*, 29.7.99
68. *Sun*, 25.10.95
69. 'Queen Orders Divorce', *Sun*, 21.12.95
70. Horrie and Nathan (1999), pp. 130–1
71. Gus Fischer conversation with author
72. Horrie and Nathan (1999), p. 243
73. *Guard*, 20.11.95
74. Hagerty conversation with author, 25.6.01 and email, 26.11.02
75. *SP*, 19.7.92
76. *Obs*, 26.11.95
77. 'Top Tory and his pal from the PLO', *SP*, 2.9.90:1, 5, 6
78. *DTel*, 23.9.92:2
79. *DTel*, 25.9.92:16
80. Peter Cole, 'Free spirit that lost its way', *SunT*, 6.2.94; Godfrey Hodgson, 'Quality v. executive cars', *BJR*, vol. 5/3, 1994; Alex Renton, 'The day the dream died', *ES*, 3.3.94; Cal McCrystal, 'The Dream That Died', *Obs*, 19.11.95; Bill Hagerty, 'The incredible shrinking Indy', *NS*, 29.1.01
81. Glover (1994), p. 258
82. Peter Cole, *BJR*, vol. 4/2, 1993
83. Jack conversation with author, 7.6.01
84. *BJR*, vol. 5/3, 1994
85. David Lipsey, 'It was – but not any more', *JH*, no. 42, summer 1995
86. *ES*, 16.12.92
87. '*Observer* on its deathbed: 201-year-old paper to go in deal with *Independent*, *ES*, 23.4.93
88. 'About ourselves', *Obs*, 25.4.93
89. 'Guardian bid wins battle for Observer', *Guard*, 30.4.93
90. Peter Cole, *SunT*, 2.5.93; Peter Fiddick, *DTel*, 30.4.93
91. 'How silence led to an own-goal', *Sindy*, 2.5.93
92. *Spec*, 23.10.93
93. *FT*, 9.10.93
94. *SunT*, 6.2.94
95. *Guard*, 11.10.93
96. Ivan Fallon, *SunT*, 19.12.93
97. *Obs*, 23.1.94
98. *UKPG*, 3.1.94
99. *FT*, 25.1.94
100. 'Paper chase: The battle for a newspaper', *Guard*, 12.1.94
101. 'We guard our freedom', *Sindy*, 20.3.94
102. *Guard*, 21.5.94; *UKPG*, 23.5.94
103. *Guard*, 2.7.94
104. *SunT*, 24.7.94
105. *Guard*, 11.7.94
106. *UKPG*, 4.7.94
107. *FT*, 1.8.94

108. *UKPG*, 19.9.94; 'Hargreaves clears out more *Indy* staff', *UKPG*, 3.10.94; 'Hargreaves revamp', *UKPG*, 10.10.94; 31.10.94
109. *Obs*, 19.3.95
110. *Guard*, 18.3.95
111. *ES*, 15.3.95:64
112. *SunT*, 26.3.95:5; *Guard*, 27.3.95
113. *Times*, 18.3.95; *UKPG*, 3.4.95
114. *UKPG*, 21.8.95:13; *Guard*, 27.10.95
115. *Guard*, 20.11.95
116. *Obs*, 19.11.95
117. *UKPG*, 24.5.93
118. *ES*, 14.9.94
119. *Guard*, 30.1.95
120. Leigh and Vulliamy (1997), p. 187
121. *Guard*, 13.1.95
122. 'Tory MPs were paid to plant questions, says Harrods chief', *Guard*, 20.10.94
123. Leigh and Vulliamy (1997), pp. 155–78
124. 'Caught in the Net', *STel*, 30.10.94
125. *DTel*, 1.11.94
126. Wyatt (2000), p. 430; Johnson, *Times*, 2.11.94; *Spec*, 5.11.94; Junor, *MoS*, 6.11.94
127. *Guard*, 1.11.94
128. All 3.11.94
129. *UKPG*, 7.11.94. The result was 49 per cent against and 47 per cent in favour
130. *Guard*, 10.4.95
131. Alasdair Palmer, 'Who Guards the *Guardian*', *Spec*, 10.11.94
132. *Guard*, 9.12.95
133. Jack conversation with author, 7.6.01
134. *Guard*, 1.8.94
135. *Without Walls*, Channel 4, 5.4.94; *Obs*, 27.3.94
136. *BJR*, vol. 4/2, 1993
137. Wyatt (2000), p. 196
138. Neil (1996), pp. 160ff
139. Morton (1992); *SunT*, 7.6.92
140. *SunT*, 5/12.7.92
141. *SunT*, 18.10.92
142. *SunT*, 23.1.94
143. *SunT*, 20.2.94
144. Neil (1996), p. 424
145. Ibid., p. 428
146. Dimbleby (1994); *SunT*, 16.10.94
147. Wyatt (2000), p. 488
148. Wyatt (1999), p. 631
149. 'The Start of New Times', *Times*, 12.10.92
150. *Times* press release, 21.8.95
151. *SunT*, 17.10.93
152. Felicity Green conversation with author, 14.9.01
153. Glover (2000), p. 244
154. Grove conversation with author, 4.7.02
155. *Sindy* mag, 31.1.93

156. 'Why I shall become a Catholic', *STel*, 13.3.94
157. Stephen Glover, *ES*, 22.6.94; Hastings (2002), p. 288. Cf. pp. 351, 366
158. *Indy*, 22.4.92
159. *Guard*, 23.9.96
160. *Spec*, 18.7.92
161. *Indy*, 11.7.92
162. *ES*, 14.8.95
163. *ES*, 17.8.95
164. Cameron (2000), p. 134
165. Wyatt, *Times*, 24.6.93
166. *Guard*, 6.7.92
167. *Media Week*, 30.10.92
168. *Campaign*, 15.7.94
169. Cameron (2000), p. 158
170. Ibid., pp. 161–2
171. 'Di's Cranky Phone Calls to Married Tycoon', *NoW*, 21.8.94; *PG*, 29.8.94
172. *Sindy*, 28.8.94:5
173. *UKPG*, 5.8.94:1
174. 'News sells, not "rich-white-trash" stories', *UKPG*, 27.3.95:13
175. *SExp*, 11.9.94:31; *DTel*, 8.8.94:15
176. *FT*, 19.7.95
177. Dougary (1994), p. 134
178. *Guard*, 27.11.95
179. *SP*, 14.7.91; 4.8.91
180. *Times*, 13.1.93. Cf. Hastings (2002), pp. 326–49
181. Shannon (2001), pp. 92, 96
182. *Review of Press Self-Regulation* (1993), Cmnd 2135
183. Shannon (2001), p. 143
184. *Times*, 24.8.94
185. *Guard*, 13.3.95; 'A job too many for Wakeham', *BJR*, vol. 6/2, 1995
186. Wyatt (1999), pp. 529, 598
187. 'Huge IRA blast rocks City', *Obs*, 25.4.93
188. *Guard*, 8.7.93
189. Wyatt (2000), p. 339
190. Ibid., pp. 326, 341, 447
191. 'Di's Cranky Phone Calls', *NoW*, op. cit.
192. *Times*, 11.4.95
193. 'Di's sister-in-law in booze and bulimia clinic', *NoW*, 2.4.95
194. 'Sins of the father', *FT*, 15.6.92. Cf. Award, *FT*, 20.5.93
195. Lambert conversation with author, 3.7.01
196. *Indy*, 5.12.91
197. 'The twins in the shadows', *DTel*, 8.1.92; 'The party poopers', *STel*, 11.10.92
198. Killick (1994), p. 129
199. '*Tonight* takes on *Standard* in new London newspaper war', *Guard*, 22.7.94
200. *Indy*, 12.6.94; *Guard*, 22.7.94; *Marketing*, 28.7.94
201. *FT*, 20.12.95

20. WAS IT REALLY THE *SUN* WOT WON IT?

1. *Sun* page-one headline, 9.4.92
2. *Sun*, 11.4.92
3. Major (2000), p. 708
4. 'Defenders of the faith', *BJR*, vol. 3/2, 1992
5. *Indy*, 14.4.92:18
6. 'Did the tabloids destroy Kinnock?', *Indy*, 15.4.92:15. Cf. David Hill, 'Watching and hoping for the worms to turn', *Indy*, 28.4.93
7. Martin Linton, 'Was It the *Sun* Wot Won It?', 7th Guardian lecture, 30.10.95
8. John Curtice and H. Semetko, 'Does it matter what the papers say?' in Heath et al. (1994)
9. Peter Golding, Michael Billig, David Deacon and Sue Middleton, 'Two shows for the price of one', *BJR*, vol. 3/2, 1992. Cf. Ivor Crewe and A. King, 'Did Major win? Did Kinnock lose? Leadership effects in the 1992 election', in Heath et al. (1994)
10. Golding et al., *BJR*, op. cit.
11. Martin Linton, 'Maybe the *Sun* won it after all', *BJR*, vol. 7/2, 1996. Cf. David McKie, in Gareth Smyth, ed., *Turning Japanese*? (Lawrence & Wishart, 1993)
12. *DTel*, 28.10.94
13. Kinnock letter to author, 19.3.97
14. Anthony Howard, 'Dealing with Mr Murdoch', in Glover (2000), p. 261
15. *Sun*, 3.10.83:6
16. 'SPLASH HIT!' and 'Still All At Sea', *Sun*, 3.10.83:1, 4–5; 'CANUTE KINNOCK', *Mail*, 3.10.83
17. *Sun*, 24.2.86:2
18. *Sun*, 6.10.88
19. *Sun*, 13.4.89
20. *Sun*, 2.10.89
21. 'Snap this trap', *Sun*, 9.10.89
22. *Mail*, 4.10.89
23. *Mail*, 14.10.89
24. *Sun*, 14.4.90
25. 'Short-fuse Kinnock puts his foot in it', *Sun*, 18.4.90:6
26. *Sun*, 24.4.90:6
27. Cf. 'Kinnock's Outburst Rocks U.S.', *Exp*, 20.7.90
28. *SunT*, 22.7.90:4
29. *Sun*, 30.4.90:6
30. *Sun*, 26.10.90:6
31. *Sun*, 3.12.90; 4.12.90
32. *Sun*, 6.4.91:6
33. *Sun*, 2.4.91
34. *Sun*, 3.4.91:6
35. *Sun*, 9.4.91:4
36. *Sun*, 8.5.91:1
37. *Sun*, 3.6.91:6
38. *Sun*, 1.10.91; 5.10.91
39. *Sun*, 11.10.91
40. *Sun*, 21.10.91

41. 'Scrum Down', *Sun*, 23.10.91
42. Kinnock email to author, 23.4.02
43. 'Dialogue with the Kremlin', *SunT*, 2.2.92:1, 12–13
44. 'Editor Climbs Down on Kinnock "Kremlin Link"', *Mail*, 3.2.92:2, 6
45. Major (2000), p. 288
46. *Exp*, 7.4.92
47. *Mail*, 16.3.92:2
48. *Sun*, 8.4.92
49. Major (2000), p. 303
50. 'TORY SURGE: Polls show late boost for Major', *Exp*, 9.4.92:1; Major (2000), p. 304
51. *Sun*, 9.4.92
52. Major (2000), p. 304
53. Morgan (1999), pp. 511–12
54. *Times*, 14.4.92
55. Mandrake, *STel*, 19.4.92:19
56. *STel*, 12.4.92
57. Labour party press release, 13.4.92
58. *Mail*, 13.4.92
59. *Obs*, 19.4.92:20
60. *Guard*, 18.4.92
61. *Sindy*, 26.9.93:19
62. Chippindale and Horrie (1999), p. 442
63. *Sun*, 17.9.92
64. Cf. *Sun*, 18.9.92; 21.9.92; 24.9.92; 5.10.93
65. *Mail*, 17/18.9.92
66. *DTel*, 17.9.92:18
67. *DTel*, 18.9.92:18
68. *STel*, 20.9.92:20
69. *Sun*, 25.9.92; Major (2000), p. 553
70. *Sun*, 1.10.92; 2.10.92; 3.10.92
71. *Sun*, 15.10.92; 17.10.92
72. *Mail*, 7.10.92:6
73. *Spec*, 10.10.92
74. Major (2000), pp. 194, 359
75. *Sun*, 14.10.92. The wording in a subsequent edition was amended to read: 'This page is dedicated to Michael Heseltine. It represents all that he understands about the worries and fears of ordinary working people in depression-hit Britain. Nothing. Absolutely nothing.'
76. 'Just another 31,000 jobs lost', *Mail*, 14.10.92:6
77. *DTel*, 16.10.92
78. *Times*, 16.10.92
79. *FT*, 17.10.92
80. *NoW*, 18.10.92
81. *Mail*, 2.10.92
82. *Exp*, 17.9.92:8
83. *NS*, 16.10.92:23
84. *FT*, 14.7.92
85. *Esquire*, October 1993:75

86. *Guard*, 12.10.92
87. Ashdown (2000), p. 202
88. Major (2000), p. 317
89. *Campaign*, 20.8.93
90. *Sun*, 4.10.93
91. *Campaign*, 29.10.93
92. Wyatt (2000), p. 439
93. Major (2000), p. 551
94. 'Sleaze: a guide to the scandals of the Major years', *Sindy*, 23.7.95
95. *Sun*, 6.1.94
96. Major (2000), p. 556; 'Basic Instinct', *SunT*, 9.1.94
97. *MoS*, 9.1.94
98. *Times*, 10.1.94; Joe Rogaly, *FT*, 11.1.94
99. 'Chief of Defence in Sex and Security Scandal', *NoW*, 13.3.94
100. 'Tory MP, the Tycoon and the Sunday School Teacher', *NoW*, 9.4.95
101. *Indy*, 16.4.95
102. Major (2000), p. 552
103. *Times*, 10.1.94
104. *SunT*, 10.7.94
105. *Guard*, 20.10.94
106. *Times*, 3.5.95
107. *SunT*, 25.6.95
108. *DTel*, 27.6.95
109. *Sun*, 9.5.95
110. *Mail*, 4.7.95
111. 'Vote Major and you let Labour in', *Sun*, 3.7.95
112. 'Major remains the best leader', *Exp*, 27.6.95; 'We're PROUD to say we are right behind him', *Star*, 27.6.95
113. Major (2000), p. 359
114. 'It was the *Express* wot won it for Major', *Sindy*, 9.7.95
115. *Sindy*, 9.7.95
116. *FT*, 3.3.93
117. *ES*, 19.5.94
118. Nicholas Jones, *Guard*, 12.9.94
119. *Indy*, 10.8.94
120. 'Flying too close to the *Sun*', *Obs*, 16.7.95; Hugo Young, *Guard*, 11.7.95
121. *Spec*, 7.10.95
122. 'Why I believe in Tony Blair', *ES*, 29.3.95

21. IS IT DUMB TO CHASE READERS?

1. H. L. Mencken, *Chicago Tribune*, 19.9.26 (one of many variations on a theme he regularly used)
2. These criticisms were aired at three conferences: at Ditchley, in February 1997, attended by editors from Britain, the US, France and Germany, organised by the Ditchley Foundation; at the *Financial Times* in February 1999, 'The Media and

Public Confidence', organised by the International Communications Forum; and at Hammersmith in March 1999, 'Culture Wars: Dumbing Down, Wising Up?', organised by *LM* magazine.

3. 'Journalism and history: whatever happened to the first draft?', 4th Goodman lecture, Royal Society of Arts, 7.12.99
4. *Guard*, 16.6.97; 'Looking up from the coalface', *BJR*, vol. 8/2, 1997
5. 'Versions of seriousness', *Guard*, 4.11.00
6. John Diamond, *C: Because Cowards Get Cancer Too* (Vermilion, 1999); John Diamond, *Snake Oil and Other Preoccupations* (Vintage, 2001)
7. *SunT*, 24.9.00
8. *Mail*, 14.2.97
9. *DTel*, 18.2.97; 'Two Wrongs', *Times*, 15.2.97
10. *Indy*, 9.2.99
11. *DTel*, 24.5.97:14
12. *Mail*, 11.6.98
13. *Indy*, 8.9.98
14. *Obs*, 6.9.98
15. *Times*, 10.3.00; *Indy*, 7.11.00
16. 'Alcatraz-on-Thames . . . no way out', *ES*, 22.1.97; *DTel*, 1.11.97
17. *ES*, 3.4.98
18. Cameron (2000), p. 12
19. *Guard*, 2.11.95
20. *Guard*, 9.2.96:2
21. 'Red Baron captures true blue papers', *SunT*, 11.2.96
22. *DTel*, 9.2.96:30
23. *FT*, 4.5.96; *Indy*, 7.5.96
24. Addis conversation with author, 11.7.02
25. *SExp*, 21.4.96
26. *Times*, 24.4.96
27. *FT*, 4.9.96
28. *MoS*, 15.9.96
29. Green conversation with author, 14.9.01
30. *Spec*, 30.5.98
31. Addis conversation with author, 11.7.02; Jasper Gerrard, *Times*, 14.4.00:15
32. *FT*, 13.4.96
33. *Indy*, 7.10.96
34. Boycott (1984)
35. John Diamond, *ES*, 22.1.97
36. *Guard*, 19.12.97
37. *Guard*, 31.1.98
38. *FT*, 6.3.98
39. *FT*, 10.3.98
40. Fintan O'Toole, 'A baron of beanz', *Obs*, 8.3.98:20. Cf. Walsh (1992)
41. *Times*, 12.3.98
42. *Times*, 24.4.98
43. Isabel Hilton, *Guard*, 7.7.99; *DTel*, 1.7.99
44. 'Fear and loathing at the *Sindie*', *DTel*, 9.7.99
45. Horrie and Nathan (1999), p. 40
46. *Sindy*, 4.7.99

47. *Times*, 30.7.99
48. *Indy*, 12.3.96
49. *FT*, 16.3.96; *Times*, 18.3.96
50. *Times*, 10.7.96; *NS*, 12.7.96; *PG*, 12.7.96; *PG*, 26.7.96; *Indy*, 14.4.97
51. *Times*, 19.7.96; *PG*, 19.7.96
52. Will Hutton, *The State We're In* (Jonathan Cape, 1995)
53. Trelford, *Indy*, 16.6.98; Fenby, *Times*, 17.4.98; Cole, *Indy*, 9.6.98
54. *PG*, 20.9.96
55. *Obs*, 5/12.7.98
56. *BJR*, vol. 10/3, 2000, p. 14
57. 'Mandelson helped Dome backer's bid for passport', *Obs*, 21.1.01
58. 'Mandelson and Blair go to war over "lies"', *Obs*. 28.1.01
59. *Guard*. 1.10.96; Brian MacArthur, *Times*, 2.10.96
60. 'Cleaning the *Guardian*'s dirty laundry', *PG*. 29.5.98
61. *Guard*, 10.9.99
62. *DTel*, 27.2.98
63. *Times*, 28.2.98
64. 'Murdoch's Chinese wall', *DTel*, 3.3.98
65. *DTel*, 4.3.98
66. *ES*, 5.9.01
67. *Guardian* website, 7.9.01
68. *Times*, 10/11/12/14.6.99
69. 'The man who bankrolls the Tories', *Times*, 5.6.99; 'Financier's role is unhealthy, say Tory MPs', 7.6.99; 'Tories silent on level of funding from Ashcroft', 8.6.99; 'Ashcroft in £1.6m move to Westminster', 9.6.99
70. '"Shadow" over Tory Treasurer', *Times*, 13.7.99
71. *Times*, 16.7.99
72. *Times*, 21.7.99
73. *Guard*, 29.3.00:9. Cf. Bruce Anderson, *Spec*, 17.7.99; 24.7.99; *STel*, 18.7.99; *DTel*, 23.7.99; *SunBus*, 19.9.99
74. 'Dramatic end', *Guard*, 9.12.99
75. *Mail*, 10.12.99
76. *Guard*, 20.5.02
77. Peter Cole, *Indy*, 15.9.98
78. *Obs*, 14.3.98; *Indy*, 15.3.98
79. *SunT*, 27.6.99; 25.7.99; 17.10.99
80. *SunT*, 16.1.00; 20.2.00
81. *SunT*, 4.6.00
82. *SunT*, 22.10.00:2
83. *Times*, 13.5.00
84. *Times*, 3.12.99
85. *Guard*, 2.12.99
86. *Times*, 10.3.00
87. *Spec*, 3.3.01
88. *Spec*, 10/17.3.01; William Dalrymple, *Guard*, 16.3.01; Charles Glass, *Obs*, 18.3.01
89. *Indy*, 27.5.96:17
90. 'The view from Canary wharf', *BJR*, vol. 9/2, 1998
91. Hart-Davis (1990), p. 333
92. 'Language, truth and Dominic', *Sindy*, 20.12.98

93. 'The spy and the *Spectator*', *Guard*, 17.12.98; '*Spectator* sport', *Guard*, 18.12.98
94. *FT*, 18.4.96
95. *DTel*, 20.4.96; *WSJ*, 21.5.96
96. *FT*, 19.3.96
97. Morton (1992 and 1997)
98. *Sun*, 24.8.92. The *Sun* later printed the entire transcript, 2.3.93
99. *Times*, 1.12.92
100. *Mail*, 10.12.92
101. *DMir*, 11.10.93; *Sun*, 12.10.93
102. *Sun*, 4.12.93
103. Dimbleby (1994); 'Charles: I've never loved Diana', *NoW*, 16.10.94
104. 'Two faces of tormented Di', *Sun*, 4.3.94
105. 'Di's cranky phone calls to married tycoon', *NoW*, 21.8.9; *NoW*. 6.8.95; 24.9.95; *Sun*, 30.9.95; *Exp*, 30.9.95
106. Screened on 20.11.95
107. 'Queen Orders Divorce', *Sun*, 21.12.95
108. *Sun*, 8.10.96
109. *PG*, 8.8.97; Shannon (2001), p. 267
110. *Times*, 1.9.97
111. Shannon (2001), pp. 272–85
112 'Tory MP's daughter is £500 vice girl', *NoW*, 1.2.98
113. *NoW*, 15.3.98
114. *Guard*, 25.3.98
115. 'London's Burning Star is Cocaine Dealer', *NoW*, 24.8.97
116. *NoW*, 1/8.4.01
117. 'We film top BBC radio star as he snorts coke', *NoW*, 25.4.99; *Mail*, 14.10.99
118. 'This is Camilla's son high on coke', *NoW*, 16.5.99; *DTel*, 17.5.99; *Indy*, 18.5.99
119. 'England rugby captain exposed as drug dealer', *NoW*, 23.5.99
120. 'The downfall of Dallaglio', *DTel*, 25.5.99; 'What's Mr Hall got to hide?', *DTel*, 26.5.99; 'Hall of infamy', *DTel*, 31.5.99
121. 'Street star's 8-month marathon of lust', *NoW*, 23.1.00
122. 'Archer Quits As We Expose False Alibi', *NoW*, 21.11.99
123. 'The editor who broke Archer', *Indy*, 23.11.99
124. 'The Way We Live Now', *ES*, 22.11.99; *DTel*, 26.11.99
125. 'Give Us Our Cash Back', *Star*, 22.11.99
126. 'It cost Lloyd his life', *Star*, 20.7.01; *PG*, 27.7.01
127. 'How a false alibi lit a 14-year fuse', *Guard*. 20.7.01
128. *NoW*, 14.7.02; *DTel*, 2.10.02
129. *PG*, 19.11.99
130. 'NAMED, SHAMED', *NoW*. 23.7.00
131. *Indy*, 5.8.00; *STel*, 3.9.00
132. *DTel*, 24.7.00; 'Why it's time to name and shame Rebekah Wade', *DTel*, 2.8.00
133. 'Shame on you, *News of the World*', *Indy*, 15.8.00
134. *Obs*, 23.7.00
135. *Mail*, 24.7.00; 5.8.00
136. *SMir*, 8.4.01
137. 'Can Weaver polish the *Mirror*?', *DTel*, 5.7.01
138. *SP*, 18.10.01
139. *DMir*, 24.6.96

140. *STel*, 26.9.99
141. Haines: *Punch*, 21–27.9.96; Pilger: ITV documentary, *Breaking the Mirror – the Murdoch Effect*, 18.2.97; *Guard* Weekend, 15.2.97
142. *SunBus*, 1.3.98
143. The *Belfast Telegraph* and four sister titles were acquired for £300 million by Tony O'Reilly's Independent News & Media in August 2000
144. 'Amiable Ulsterman at Trinity Mirror', *BJR*, vol. 12/1, 2001
145. *PG*, 6.8.99; 13.8.99; 20.8.99
146. Helena de Bertodano, *STel*, 26.9.99
147. 'Sugar to join net goldrush', *DMir*, 18.1.00
148. '*Mirror* editor saw his shares soar after paper tipped company', *DTel*, 2.2.00
149. *Times*, 15.5.00
150. *Guard*, 23.4.01
151. '*Mirror* staff quizzed over share scandal', *Guard*, 27.10.00; *Times*, 14.11.00, 10.3.01, 20.4.01, 10.5.01
152. Speech to Society of Editors conference, Belfast, 22.10.01
153. Trinity-Mirror press release, 28.5.02
154. 'Mourn on the Fourth of July', *DMir*, 4.7.02; *MoS*, 7.7.02
155. Lady Cudlipp conversation with author
156. *Sun*, 18.3.97
157. *Sun*, 9.4.98
158. *PG*, 12.6.98
159. Patrick Hennessy, *Indy*, 7.6.98
160. *Sun*, 24.6.98
161. *Sun*, 6.10.98
162. *Sun*, 9.11.98
163. 'Private lives', *Sun*, 12.11.98
164. 'SOPHIE TOPLESS', *Sun*, 26.5.99
165. *Guard*, 27.5.99
166. *DTel*, 27.5.99. Murdoch and Deng were married the following month, 25.6.99
167. *DTel*, 27.5.99
168. 'SORRY, SOPHIE', 27.5.99; 'KRM didn't like it', *PG*, 19.11.99:17
169. *PG*, 19.11.99
170. 'Our Love', *Sun*, 26.1.98; 'Posh Baby', *Sun*, 21.7.98; 'Mr & Mrs Becks', *Sun*, 6.7.99
171. Cf. 'Morgan thanks Murdoch for keeping Yelland in work', and '*Sun* "closing in" on *Mirror* as price war hots up', *Guardian* website, 22.7.02
172. 'The sacked editors' club wishes you well', *Exp*, 18.4.00
173. Jean Seaton, *Prospect*, October 1998
174. 'Hollick's Revolving Door', *SunT*, 15.2.98; 'United in Conflict', *STel*, 15.2.98
175. *SunT*, 13.12.98; *SunBus*, 8.3.99
176. Chris Blackhurst, *Management Today*, February 2001; 'Bad days at Blackfriars', *Guard*, 29.1.01
177. *PG*, 7.5.99
178. *PG*, 21.5.99
179. *STel*, 23.5.99
180. *Guard*, 12.7.99; letter to author from Ricardo Tejada, 15.7.99
181. *ES*, 21.7.00
182. *Spec*, 30.9.00:30, *Indy*; 3.10.00
183. *SunT*, 15.10.00; *SunBus*, 14/21.1.01

184. *FT*, 17.10.00
185. Ephraim Hardcastle, *Mail*, 18.10.00
186. *FT*, 23.10.00
187. *SunT*, 29.10.00; *FT*, 31.10.00
188. 'Porn king enters Express race', *SunT*, 19.11.00
189. *Times*, 24.11.00
190. *SunT*, 26.11.00; *Times*, 20.7.01
191. *Times*, 24.11.00
192. *Today*, 22.3.88
193. 'Man on top', *Indy*, 26.6.93
194. *Indy*, 23.11.00
195. *SunT*, 26.11.00
196. 'Riddle of the porn baron's cheque', *NS*, 20.5.02
197. *FT*, 23.11.00
198. *Mail*, 9.12.00
199. *Guard*, 22.12.00
200. *Guard*, 17.1.01
201. *Exp*, 22.2.01. Cf. *Punch*, 4–17.12.99
202. *Obs*, 20.5.01
203. *Indy*, 20.3.01
204. *Times*, 26.4.02
205. 'Shit stirrer extraordinaire', *Varsity*, Cambridge student newspaper, 5.10.01
206. *PG*, 26.11.99
207. *Times*, 4.8.00
208 'Target Baghdad . . . a war based on lies', *DMir*, 27.8.02; 'UNlawful, UNethical, UNstoppable', *DMir*, 18.3.03; 'SHOCKING AND AWFUL', *DMir*, 22.3.03; 'SICKENING', *DMir*, 25.3.03
209. 'Free DVDs of Absolutely Fabulous', *DMir*, 28.4.03; 'POSH OFF', *DMir*, 30.4.03; 'DIANA'S GHOULS', *DMir*, 2.5.03
210. *SunT*, 15.12.96
211. *FT*, 10.10.98; *Guard*, 7.12.98
212. John Parry, *PG*, 4.12.98; Peter Taylor, *Times*, 11.12.98
213. 'It'll cost you . . .', *Guard*, 19.2.01
214. *Indy*, 14.5.96
215. *ES*, 19.2.97
216. *SunBus*, 1.3.98
217. 'Paper's relaunch proves to be a costly business', *Guardian* website, 8.4.02
218. *NS*, 7.6.96; *FT*, 20.6.96; *Indy*, 21.6.96
219. *Guard*, 25.6.94
220. 'A tangled tax web', *Indy*, 4.2.98

BIBLIOGRAPHY

GENERAL

Adams, Valerie, *The Media and the Falklands Campaign* (Macmillan, 1986)

Andrews, Linton, *Problems of an Editor: A Study in Newspaper Trends* (Oxford University Press, 1962)

Ashdown, Paddy, *The Ashdown Diaries: 1988–1997* (Allen Lane, 2000)

Baistow, Tom, *Fourth-rate Estate* (Comedia, 1985)

Banton, Michael, *White and Coloured* (Jonathan Cape, 1959)

Barker, Martin and Petley, Julian, eds, *Ill Effects: The Media Violence Debate* (Routledge, 2001)

Bellisario, Ray, *To Tread on Royal Toes* (Aberdeen: Impulse, 1972)

Beloff, Nora, *Freedom under Foot: The Battle over the Closed Shop in British Journalism* (Temple Smith, 1976)

Benn, Tony, *Years of Hope: Diaries, Papers and Letters, 1940–62*, ed. Ruth Winstone (Hutchinson, 1994)

Blakeway, Denys, *The Falklands War* (Sidgwick & Jackson, 1992)

Boyce, George, Curran, James and Wingate, Pauline, eds, *Newspaper History* (Constable, 1978)

Boycott, Rosie, *Take a Nice Girl Like Me* (Chatto & Windus, 1984)

Brendon, Piers, *The Life and Death of the Press Barons* (Secker & Warburg, 1982)

Brodie, Malcolm, *The Tele: A History of the Belfast Telegraph* (Belfast: Blackstaff Press, 1995)

Brodzky, Vivian, ed., *Fleet Street: The Inside Story of Journalism* (Macdonald, 1966)

Bundock, Clement, J., *The National Union of Journalists: A Jubilee History, 1907–57* (NUJ, 1957)

Butler, David and Kitzinger, Uwe, *The 1975 Referendum* (Macmillan, 1976)

Cameron, James, *Point of Departure* (Arthur Barker, 1967)

Camrose, Viscount, *British Newspapers and their Controllers* (Cassell, 1947)

Chambers, I., *Urban Rhythms: Pop Music and Popular Culture* (Macmillan, 1985)

Channon, Henry, *Chips: The Diaries of Sir Henry Channon,* ed. Robert Rhodes James (Weidenfeld & Nicolson, 1967)

Childs, David, *Britain Since 1945* (Routledge, 1997)

Chippindale, Peter and Horrie, Chris, *Disaster! The Rise and Fall of News on Sunday* (Sphere, 1988)

Clark, Alan, *Diaries,* ed. Ion Trewin (Weidenfeld & Nicolson, 1993)

Cleverly, Graham, *The Fleet Street Disaster* (Constable, 1976)

Cockett, Richard, ed., *My Dear Max: The Letters of Brendan Bracken to Lord Beaverbrook, 1925–1958* (Historians' Press, 1990)

Cole, G. D. H., *World Socialism Restated* (*New Statesman* pamphlet, 1956)

Coleridge, Nicholas, *Paper Tigers* (Heinemann, 1983)

Colville, John, *The Fringes of Power: Downing Street Diaries, 1939–1955* (Hodder & Stoughton, 1985)
Conroy, Harry, *Off the Record: A Life in Journalism* (Argyll Publishing, 1997)
Coward, Noël, *The Noël Coward Diaries*, ed. Graham Payn and Sheridan Morley (Weidenfeld & Nicolson, 1982)
Crewe, Ivor and King, Anthony, *SDP: The Birth, Life and Death of the Social Democratic Party* (Oxford University Press, 1995)
Crossman, Richard, *The Backbench Diaries of Richard Crossman*, ed. Janet Morgan (Hamish Hamilton, 1981)
Curran, James and Seaton, Jean, *Power without Responsibility* (4th edn, Routledge, 1991; 5th edn, Routledge, 1997)
Curtis, Liz, *Ireland and the Propaganda War* (Pluto, 1984)
de Burgh, Hugo, ed., *Investigative Journalism: Context and Practice* (Routledge, 2000)
Delano, Anthony, *Slip-Up* (André Deutsch, 1977)
Denning, Lord, *Lord Denning's Report* (Cmnd 2152)
Denning, A. T., *What Next in the Law* (Butterworths, 1982)
Dimbleby, Jonathan, *The Prince of Wales: A Biography* (HarperCollins, 1994)
Dougary, Linda, *The Executive Tart and Other Myths* (Virago, 1994)
Downing, Taylor, ed., *The Troubles* (Thames Macdonald/Futura, 1980)
Draper, Alfred, *Scoops and Swindles* (Buchan & Enright, 1988)
Driberg, Tom, *Colonnade* (Pilot Press, 1949)
Economist Intelligence Unit, *The National Newspaper Industry: A Survey* (EIU, 1966)
Edwards, Robert, *Goodbye Fleet Street* (Jonathan Cape, 1988)
Engel, Matthew, *Tickle the Public* (Gollancz, 1996)
Epstein, Leon D., *British Politics in the Suez Crisis* (Pall Mall Press, 1964)
Evans, Douglas, *While Britain Slept: The Selling of the Common Market* (Gollancz, 1975)
Foot, Michael, *Debts of Honour* (Davis Poynter, 1980)
Foot, Paul, *Immigration and Race in British Politics* (Penguin, 1965)
——, *The Rise of Enoch Powell* (Cornmarket Press, 1969)
Fyfe, Hamilton, *Sixty Years of Fleet Street* (W. H. Allen, 1949)
Gailey, Andrew, *Crying in the Wilderness* (Institute of Irish Studies, Queen's University, 1995)
Gibb, Mildred A. and Beckwith, Frank, *The Yorkshire Post: Two Centuries* (Leeds: The Yorkshire Conservative Newspaper Co., 1954)
Gillman, Peter and Leni, *Collar the Lot* (Quartet, 1980)
Glover, Stephen, ed., *The Penguin Book of Journalism: Secrets of the Press* (Penguin, 2000)
Gray, Tony, *Fleet Street Remembered* (Heinemann, 1990)
Greene, Graham, *Yours etc: Letters to the Press, 1945–89*, ed. Christopher Hawtree (Reinhardt Books, 1989)
Griffiths, Dennis, *Plant Here the Standard* (Macmillan, 1996)
Grundy, Bill, *Press Inside Out* (W. H. Allen, 1976)
Haines, Joe, *The Politics of Power* (Jonathan Cape, 1977)
Harris, Kenneth, *Attlee* (Weidenfeld & Nicolson, 1982)
Harris, Robert, *Selling Hitler* (Faber, 1986)
——, *Gotcha! The Media, the Government and the Falklands Crisis* (Faber, 1990)
Hastings, Max, *Going to the Wars* (Macmillan, 2000)

Heath, A., Jowell, R. and Curtice J., eds, *Labour's Last Chance? The 1992 Election and Beyond* (Aldershot: Dartmouth, 1994)
Hedley, Peter and Aynsley, Cyril, *The D-Notice Affair* (Michael Joseph, for Beaverbrook Newspapers, 1967)
Hennessy, Peter, *Never Again* (Jonathan Cape, 1992)
Henry, Harry, *Behind the Headlines – The Business of the British Press* (Associated British Press, 1978)
Herd, Harold, *The March of Journalism* (Allen & Unwin, 1952)
Heren, Louis, *The Power of the Press?* (Orbis, 1985)
Heward, Edmund, *Lord Denning: A Biography* (Chichester: Barry Rose Law Publishers, 1997)
Hewison, Robert, *Culture & Consensus* (Methuen, 1995)
Hobson, J. W. and Henry, H., *The Hulton Readership Survey* (Hulton Press, 1947)
Hoggart, Richard, ed., *Your Sunday Paper* (University of London Press, 1967)
Holden, Anthony, *Charles: A Biography* (Weidenfeld & Nicolson, 1988)
Hudson, Miles and Stanier, John, *War and the Media* (Sutton Publishing, 1997)
Hutchins, Chris and Midgley, Dominic, *Goldsmith: Money, Women and Power* (Mainstream, 1998)
Hutt, Allen, *Newspaper Design* (Oxford University Press, 1960)
Inglis, Brian, *Downstart* (Chatto & Windus, 1990)
Ingrams, Richard, *Goldenballs* (André Deutsch, 1979)
Ivanov, Yevgeny, *The Naked Spy* (Blake, 1994)
Jackson, Ian, *The Provincial Press and the Community* (Manchester University Press, 1971)
Jay, Douglas, *Change and Fortune* (Hutchinson, 1980)
Jenkins, Simon, *Newspapers: The Power and the Money* (Faber, 1979)
—— *The Market for Glory: Fleet Street Ownership in the Twentieth Century* (Faber, 1986)
Jephcott, A. Pearl, *A Troubled Area: Notes on Notting Hill* (Faber, 1964)
Jones, Clement, *A History of the Guild, 1946–1995* (Guild of Editors, 1996)
Keeler, Christine and Fawkes, Sandy, *Nothing But . . .* (New English Library, 1983)
—— and Thompson, Douglas, *The Truth at Last: My Story* (Sidgwick & Jackson, 2001)
Kemsley, Viscount, *The Kemsley Manual of Journalism* (Cassell, 1950)
Killick, Mark, *The Sultan of Sleaze: The Inside Story of David Sullivan's Sex and Media Empire* (Penguin, 1994)
King, Cecil Harmsworth, *The Cecil King Diary, 1965–1970* (Jonathan Cape, 1972)
Kitzinger, Uwe, *Diplomacy and Persuasion: How Britain Joined the Common Market* (Thames & Hudson, 1973)
Knightley, Phillip, *The First Casualty* (Prion Books, 2000)
—— and Kennedy, Caroline, *An Affair of State* (Jonathan Cape, 1987)
Koss, Stephen, *The Rise and Fall of the Political Press in Britain,* vol. 2: *The Twentieth Century* (Hamish Hamilton, 1984)
Lamb, Richard, *The Failure of the Eden Government* (Sidgwick & Jackson, 1987)
Lawrenson, John and Barber, Lionel, *The Price of Truth: The Story of the Reuters Millions* (Edinburgh: Mainstream, 1985)
Leapman, Michael, *Treacherous Estate* (Hodder & Stoughton, 1992)
Levy, H. Phillip, *The Press Council: History, Procedure and Cases* (Macmillan, 1967)
Low, David, *Low's Autobiography* (Michael Joseph, 1956)

McCallum, R. B. and Readman, Alison, *The British General Election of 1945* (Oxford University Press, 1947)
McGowan, Robert and Hands, Jeremy, *Don't Cry for Me Sergeant Major* (Futura, 1983)
Mackay, Ian, *The Real Mackay* (News Chronicle Publications, 1953)
McKay, Ron and Barr, Brian, *The Story of the Scottish Daily News* (Edinburgh: Canongate, 1976)
Madge, C. and Harrisson, T., *Mass Observation: The Press and its Readers* (Art & Technics, 1949)
Major, John, *John Major: The Autobiography* (HarperCollins, 2000)
Mansfield, F. G., *Gentlemen, The Press! Chronicles of a Crusade: The Official History of the National Union of Journalists* (W. H. Allen, 1943)
Margach, James, *The Anatomy of Power* (W. H. Allen, 1979)
Martin, Kingsley, *Harold Laski* (Victor Gollancz, 1953)
Martin, Roderick, *New Technology and Industrial Relations in Fleet Street* (Oxford University Press, 1981)
Matthews, Thomas, *The Sugar Pill* (Victor Gollancz, 1957)
Melvern, Linda, *The End of the Street* (Methuen, 1986)
Mercer, Derrik, *The Fog of War* (Heinemann, 1987)
Montagu of Beaulieu, Lord, *Wheels within Wheels: An Unconventional Life* (Weidenfeld & Nicolson, 2000)
Morgan, Kenneth, O., *The People's Peace* (Oxford University Press, 2nd edn, 1999)
Morton, Andrew, *Diana, Her True Story* (Michael O'Mara, 1992)
——, *Diana, Her True Story – In Her Own Words* (Michael O'Mara, 1997)
Musson, A. E., *The Typographical Association* (Oxford University Press, 1954)
Newman, Michael, *John Strachey* (Manchester University Press, 1989)
Nicolson, Harold, *Diaries and Letters, 1945–1962*, ed. Nigel Nicolson (Collins, 1968)
Pimlott, Ben, *The Queen: A Biography of Elizabeth II* (HarperCollins, 1996)
Porter, Henry, *Lies, Damned Lies and Some Exclusives* (Chatto & Windus, 1984)
Procter, Harry, *The Street of Disillusion* (Allan Wingate, 1958)
Randall, Michael, *The Funny Side of the Street* (Bloomsbury, 1988)
Read, Donald, *The Power of News: The History of Reuters, 1849–1989* (Oxford University Press, 1992)
Rice-Davies, Mandy and Flack, Shirley, *Mandy* (Michael Joseph, 1980)
Robb, J. H., *Working Class Anti-Semite* (Tavistock Publications, 1954)
Robertson, Geoffrey, *People Against the Press* (Quartet, 1983)
Robinson, Anne, *Memoirs of an Unfit Mother* (Little, Brown, 2001)
Rook, Jean, *The Cowardly Lioness* (Sidgwick & Jackson, 1989)
Rose, Peter, *How the Troubles Came to Northern Ireland* (Macmillan Press, 1999)
Royal Commission on the Press, 1947–1949, Cmd 7700
Royal Commission on the Press, 1961–1962, Cmnd 1811
Royal Commission on the Press, 1974–1979, Cmnd 6810
Rust, William, *The Story of the Daily Worker* (People's Press Printing Society, 1949)
Sampson, Anthony, *Anatomy of Britain* (Hodder & Stoughton, 1965)
——, *The Changing Anatomy of Britain Today* (Hodder & Stoughton, 1982)
Schellenberg, Walter, *Invasion 1940* (St Ermin's Press, 2000)
Schofield, Guy, *The Men That Carry the News: A History of United Newspapers* (Cranford Press, 1975)
Sebba, Anne, *Battling for News* (Hodder & Stoughton, 1994)
Sellers, Leslie, *The Simple Subs' Book* (Oxford: Pergamon, 1968)

Sellers, Leslie, *Keeping Up the Style* (Pitman, 1975)
Shannon, Richard, *A Press Free and Responsible* (John Murray, 2001)
Sharf, Andrew, *The British Press and Jews under Nazi Rule* (Oxford University Press, 1964)
Shawcross, Hartley, *Life Sentence* (Constable, 1995)
Silvester, Christopher, *The Penguin Book of Columnists* (Viking, 1997)
Sisman, Adam, *A. J. P. Taylor: A Biography* (Sinclair-Stevenson, 1994)
Smith, Anthony, *The British Press since the War* (David & Charles, 1974)
Snoddy, Raymond, *The Good, the Bad and the Unacceptable* (Faber, 1992)
Solomos, John, *Race and Racism in Contemporary Britain* (Macmillan, 1989)
Stephenson, Hugh, *Claret and Chips: The Rise of the SDP* (Michael Joseph, 1982)
Summers, Anthony and Dorril, Stephen, *Honeytrap: The Secret Worlds of Stephen Ward* (Weidenfeld & Nicolson, 1987)
Sunday Times Insight Team, *Ulster* (Penguin, 1972)
Tatchell, Peter, *The Battle for Bermondsey* (Heretic Books, 1983)
Taylor, A. J. P., *English History, 1914–1945* (Oxford University Press, 1965)
Taylor, H. A., *The British Press: A Critical Survey* (Arthur Barker, 1961)
Taylor, S. J., *Shock! Horror! The Tabloids in Action* (Bantam Press, 1991)
Thomas, Denis John Roy, *Challenge in Fleet Street: A Candid Commentary on today's National Newspapers* (Truth Publishing Co., 1957)
Thomas, Hugh, *John Strachey* (Eyre Methuen, 1973)
Tunstall, Jeremy, *Newspaper Power* (Oxford University Press, 1996)
Tyler, Rodney, *Campaign! The Selling of the Prime Minister* (Grafton, 1987)
Vassall, John, *Vassall: The Autobiography of a Spy* (Sidgwick & Jackson, 1975)
Wansell, Geoffrey, *Tycoon: The Life of James Goldsmith* (Grafton, 1987)
Watkins, Alan, *Brief Lives* (Hamish Hamilton, 1982)
——, *A Short Walk down Fleet Street* (Duckworth, 2000)
Williams, Francis, *Dangerous Estate* (Longmans, Green & Co., 1957)
Winchester, Simon, *In Holy Terror* (Faber, 1974)
Wintour, Charles, *Pressures on the Press* (André Deutsch, 1972)
——, *The Rise and Fall of Fleet Street* (Hutchinson, 1989)
Woodward, Sandy, *One Hundred Days* (Collins, 1984)
Wright, Peter, *Spycatcher* (New York: Viking, 1987)
Wyatt, Woodrow, *The Journals of Woodrow Wyatt*, vols. 1–3, ed. Sarah Curtis (Macmillan, 1998, 1999, 2000)

DAILY HERALD

Abrams, Mark, *Condition of the British People, 1911–45* (Gollancz, 1945)
——, *Social Surveys and Social Action* (Heinemann, 1951)
——, *The Newspaper-Reading Public of Tomorrow* (Odhams, 1964)
—— and Rose, Richard, *Must Labour Lose?* (Penguin, 1960)
Fienburgh, Wilfred, *25 Momentous Years* (Odhams Press, 1955)
Goldthorpe, John H. and Lockwood, David, 'Affluence and the British class structure', *Sociological Review*, July 1963
——, Lockwood, David, Bechhofer, Frank and Platt, Jennifer, 'The Affluent Worker and the Thesis of Embourgeoisement: Some Preliminary Research Findings', *Sociology*, vol. 1, January 1967

Minney, R. J., *Viscount Southwood* (Odhams Press, 1954)
Richards, Huw, 'The Daily Herald: 1912–64' *History Today*, December 1981, pp. 12–16
——, *The Bloody Circus: The Daily Herald and the Left* (Pluto Press, 1997)

EXPRESS GROUP

Beaverbrook, Max, *Politicians and the Press* (Hutchinson, 1925)
Broackes, Nigel, *A Growing Concern* (Weidenfeld & Nicholson, 1979)
Cameron, Andrew, *Express Newspapers: The Inside Story of a Turbulent Decade* (London House, 2000)
Chester, Lewis and Fenby, Jonathan, *The Fall of the House of Beaverbrook* (André Deutsch, 1979)
Chisholm, Anne and Davie, Michael, *Beaverbrook: A Life* (Hutchinson, 1992)
Christiansen, Arthur, *Headlines All My Life* (Heinemann, 1961)
Coote, John, *Altering Course: A Submariner in Fleet Street* (Leo Cooper, 1992)
Driberg, Tom, *Beaverbrook* (Weidenfeld & Nicholson, 1956)
Gourlay, Logan, ed., *The Beaverbrook I Knew* (Quartet, 1984)
Howard, Peter, *Beaverbrook* (Hutchinson, 1964)
Jameson, Derek, *Touched by Angels* (Ebury Press, 1988)
——, *Last of the Hot Metal Men* (Ebury Press, 1990)
Junor, John, *Listening for a Midnight Tram* (Chapmans, 1990)
Junor, Penny, *Home Truths: Life around My Father* (HarperCollins, 2002)
Taylor, A. J. P., *Beaverbrook* (Hamish Hamilton, 1972)
Vines, Colin, *A Little Nut-Brown Man* (Leslie Frewin, 1968)
Wiggin, Maurice, *Faces at the Window* (Nelson, 1972)
Wignall, Trevor, *I Knew Them All* (Hutchinson, 1938)
Young, Kenneth, *Churchill and Beaverbrook* (Eyre & Spottiswoode, 1966)

FINANCIAL TIMES

Boyle, Andrew, *Poor, Dear Brendan* (Hutchinson, 1974)
Bracken, Brendan, *1901–1958: Portraits and Appreciations* (Eyre & Spottiswoode, 1958)
Drogheda, Lord, *Double Harness* (Weidenfeld & Nicolson, 1978)
Einzig, Paul, *In the Centre of Things: The Autobiography of Paul Einzig* (Hutchinson, 1960)
Kynaston, David, *The Financial Times: A Centenary History* (Viking, 1988)
Lockhart, Robin Bruce, 'Brendan Bracken – Founding Father', *History Today*, April 1991
Lysaght, Charles Edward, *Brendan Bracken* (Allen Lane, 1979)
Newton, Gordon, *A Peer without Equal: Memoirs of an Editor,* ed. Malcolm Rutherford (privately printed by Intype London, Wimbledon, 1997)

MAIL GROUP

Bourne, Richard, *Lords of Fleet Street: The Harmsworth Dynasty* (Unwin Hyman, 1990)
Devon, Stanley, *Glorious: The Life-Story of Stanley Devon* (Harrap, 1957)
Ferris, Paul, *The House of Northcliffe* (Weidenfeld & Nicolson, 1971)
Pound, Reginald and Harmsworth, Geoffrey, *Northcliffe* (Cassell, 1959)
Taylor, S. J., *The Great Outsiders* (Weidenfeld & Nicolson, 1996)
——, *The Reluctant Press Lord* (Weidenfeld & Nicolson, 1998)
——, *An Unlikely Hero* (Weidenfeld & Nicolson, 2002)
Thompson, J. Lee, *Northcliffe: Press Baron in Politics, 1865–1922* (John Murray, 2000)
Williams, Gron, *Firebrand: The Frank Owen Story* (Worcester: Square One, 1993)

MIRROR GROUP

Bower, Tom, *Maxwell: The Final Verdict* (HarperCollins, 1995)
Clarkson, Wensley, *Dog Eat Dog: Confessions of a Tabloid Journalist* (Fourth Estate, 1990)
Crewe, Quentin, *Well, I Forget the Rest* (Hutchinson, 1991)
Cudlipp, Hugh, *Publish and Be Damned!* (Andrew Dakers, 1953)
——, *At Your Peril* (Weidenfeld & Nicolson, 1962)
——, *Walking on Water* (Bodley Head, 1976)
——, *The Prerogative of the Harlot* (Bodley Head, 1980)
Edelman, Maurice, *The Mirror: A Political History* (Hamish Hamilton, 1966)
Greenslade, Roy, *Maxwell's Fall* (Simon & Schuster, 1992)
Haines, Joe, *Maxwell* (Macdonald, 1988)
Hyde, H. Montgomery, *Privacy and the Press* (Butterworth, 1947)
Kersh, Cyril, *A Few Gross Words* (Simon & Schuster, 1990)
King, Cecil Harmsworth, *Strictly Personal: Some Memoirs of Cecil H. King* (Weidenfeld & Nicolson, 1969)
——, *With Malice toward None: A War Diary*, ed. William Armstrong (Sidgwick & Jackson, 1970)
Moran, Lord, *Winston Churchill: The Struggle for Survival, 1940–65* (Constable, 1966)
Patmore, Angela, *Marje: The Guilt and the Gingerbread* (Little, Brown, 1993)
Pilger, John, *Heroes* (Jonathan Cape, 1986)
Stott, Richard, *Dogs and Lampposts* (Metro, 2002)
Thompson, Peter and Delano, Anthony, *Maxwell: A Portrait of Power* (Corgi, 1991)
Whitcomb, Noel, *A Particular Kind of Fool: Autobiography of a Newspaper Man* (Anthony Blond, 1990)
Winn, Godfrey, *The Infirm Glory* (Michael Joseph, 1967)
Zuckerman, Solly, *Monkeys, Men and Missiles* (Collins, 1988)

MURDOCH

Chenoweth, Neil, *Virtual Murdoch* (Secker & Warburg, 2001)
Kiernan, Thomas, *Citizen Murdoch* (Robert Hale, 1989)

Leapman, Michael, *Barefaced Cheek: The Apotheosis of Rupert Murdoch* (Hodder & Stoughton, 1983)
Munster, George, *Rupert Murdoch: A Paper Prince* (Melbourne: Viking, 1985)
Regan, Simon, *Rupert Murdoch: A Business Biography* (Angus & Robertson, 1976)
Shawcross, William, *Murdoch* (Chatto & Windus, 1992)
Tuccille, Jerome, *Murdoch: A Biography* (Piatkus, 1989)

NEWS CHRONICLE

Crosfield, John, *A History of the Cadbury Family* (J. Crosfield, 1985)
Gardiner, A. G., *Life of George Cadbury* (Cassell, 1923)
Glenton, George and Pattinson, William, *The Last Chronicle of Bouverie Street* (Allen & Unwin, 1963)
Hubback, David, *No Ordinary Press Baron: A Life of Walter Layton* (Weidenfeld & Nicolson, 1985)
Mackay, Ian, *The Real Mackay* (News Chronicle Publications, 1953)
Martell, Edward and Butler, Ewan, *The Murder of the News Chronicle and the Star* (Christopher Johnson, 1960)
Wagner, Gillian, *The Chocolate Conscience* (Chatto & Windus, 1987)
Waitman, R., *News Chronicle* article in *World's Press News*, 17 January, 1946
Williams, Francis, 'The murder of the News Chronicle', *New Statesman*, 22 October, 1960

NEWS OF THE WORLD

Bainbridge, Cyril and Stockdill, Roy, *The News of the World Story* (HarperCollins, 1993)
Brown, Gerry, *Exposed!* (Virgin, 1995)
Somerfield, Stafford, *Banner Headlines* (Shoreham, West Sussex: Scan, 1979)

TELEGRAPH GROUP

Aitken, Jonathan, *Officially Secret* (Weidenfeld & Nicolson, 1971)
Anstey, Joanna, ed., *Echoes: Twenty-five Years of the Telegraph Magazine* (W. H. Allen, 1989)
Black, Conrad, *A Life in Progress* (Toronto: Key Porter Books, 1993)
Coote, Colin, *Editorial* (Eyre & Spottiswoode, 1965)
Deedes, W. F., *Dear Bill* (Macmillan, 1997)
Hart-Davis, Duff, *The House the Berrys Built: Inside Story of the Daily Telegraph, 1928–1986* (Hodder & Stoughton, 1990)
Hartwell, Lord, *William Camrose: Giant of Fleet Street* (Weidenfeld & Nicolson, 1992)
Hastings, Max, *Editor* (Macmillan, 2002)
Siklos, Richard, *Shades of Black* (Heinemann, 1995)
Welch, Colin, *The Odd Thing about the Colonel & Other Pieces* (Bellew/Daily Telegraph, 1997)
Worsthorne, Peregrine, *Tricks of Memory* (Weidenfeld & Nicolson, 1993)

THE *GUARDIAN*

Ayerst, David, *Biography of a Newspaper* (Collins, 1971)
Cole, John, *As It Seemed to Me* (Weidenfeld & Nicolson, 1995)
Hetherington, Alastair, *Guardian Years* (Chatto & Windus, 1981)
Leigh, David and Vulliamy, Ed, *Sleaze* (Fourth Estate, 1997)
Roy, Kenneth, ed., *Alastair Hetherington: A Man of his Word* (Irvine: Carrick Publishing, 1998)
Stott, Mary, *Forgetting's No Excuse* (Faber, 1973)
Taylor, Geoffrey, *Changing Faces: A History of the Guardian, 1956–88* (Fourth Estate, 1993)

THE *INDEPENDENT*

Crozier, Michael, *The Making of the Independent* (Gordon Fraser, 1988)
Fallon, Ivan, *The Player: The Life of Tony O'Reilly* (Hodder & Stoughton, 1994)
Garland, Nick, *Not Many Dead* (Hutchinson, 1990)
Glover, Stephen, *Paper Dreams* (Penguin, 1994)
Horrie, Chris and Nathan, Adam, *L!ve TV: Tellybrats and Topless Darts* (Simon & Schuster, 1999)
Walsh, C. H., *Oh, Really O'Reilly* (Dublin: Bentos, 1992)

THE *OBSERVER*

Anstey, Joanna and Silverlight, John, eds, *The Observer Observed* (Barrie & Jenkins, 1991)
Bower, Tom, *Tiny Rowland: A Rebel Tycoon* (Heinemann, 1993)
Brown, Ivor, *Old and Young: A Personal Summing Up* (Bodley Head, 1971)
Cockett, Richard, *David Astor and the Observer* (André Deutsch, 1991)
Hall, Richard, *My Life with Tiny* (Faber, 1987)
Harris, Kenneth, *The Wildcatter* (Weidenfeld & Nicolson, 1987)
Pringle, John Douglas, *Have Pen: Will Travel* (Chatto & Windus, 1973)
Trelford, Donald, *Observer at 200* (Quartet, 1992)
Tynan, Kathleen, *The Life of Kenneth Tynan* (Weidenfeld & Nicolson, 1987)

THE *SUN*

Chippindale, Peter and Horrie, Chris, *Stick It Up your Punter* (Heinemann, 1990; revised edn. Pocket Books, 1999)
Grose, Roslyn, *The Sun-sation: The Inside Story of Britain's Best-selling Daily Newspaper* (Angus & Robertson, 1989)
Lamb, Larry, *Sunrise* (Macmillan Papermac, 1989)

THE *SUNDAY TIMES*

Evans, Harold, *Good Times, Bad Times* (Weidenfeld & Nicolson, 1983; 3rd edn, Phoenix, 1994)
Giles, Frank, *Sundry Times* (John Murray, 1986)
Hamilton, Denis, *Editor-in-Chief: Fleet Street Memoirs* (Hamish Hamilton, 1989)
Hobson, Harold, Knightley, Phillip and Russell, Leonard, *The Pearl of Days: An Intimate Memoir of the Sunday Times, 1822–1972* (Hamish Hamilton, 1972)
Jacobs, Eric, *Stop Press* (André Deutsche, 1980)
Knightley, Phillip. *A Hack's Progress* (Jonathan Cape, 1997)
Neil, Andrew, *Full Disclosure* (Macmillan, 1996)
Wesker, Arnold, *Journey into Journalism* (Writers and Readers Co-operative, 1977)

THE *TIMES*

Braddon, Russell, *Roy Thomson of Fleet Street* (Collins, 1965)
Donoughue, Bernard, *The Heat of the Kitchen* (Politico's, 2003)
Goldenberg, Susan, *The Thomson Empire* (Sidgwick & Jackson, 1985)
Grigg, John, *The History of the Times, 1966–1981* (Times Books, 1993)
Haslam, Jonathan, *The Vices of Integrity* (Verso, 1999)
McDonald, Iverach, *The History of the Times*, vol. 5: *Struggles in War and Peace, 1939–1966* (Times Books, 1984)
Macmillan, Harold, *Riding the Storm* (Macmillan, 1971)
Sinclair, David, *Dynasty: The Astors and their Times* (Dent, 1983)
Thomson, Roy, *After I Was Sixty* (Nelson, 1975)
Walker, Martin, *Powers of the Press: The World's Great Newspaper* (Quartet, 1982)
Wilson, Derek, *The Astors: Landscape with Millionaires* (Weidenfeld & Nicolson, 1993)
Woods, Oliver and Bishop, James, *The Story of the Times* (revised edn, Michael Joseph, 1985)

TODAY

Goodhart, David and Wintour, Patrick, *Eddie Shah and the Newspaper Revolution* (Coronet, 1986)
MacArthur, Brian, *Eddy Shah, Today, and the Newspaper Revolution* (David & Charles, 1988)

INDEX

Edge Hill University
WITHDRAWN